The Oxford Handbook of
Psycholinguistics

Edited by

M. Gareth Gaskell

Consulting editors

Gerry Altmann, Paul Bloom, Alfonso Caramazza, and Pim Levelt

OXFORD
UNIVERSITY PRESS

OXFORD
UNIVERSITY PRESS

Great Clarendon Street, Oxford OX2 6DP

Oxford University Press is a department of the University of Oxford.
It furthers the University's objective of excellence in research, scholarship,
and education by publishing worldwide in

Oxford New York

Auckland Cape Town Dar es Salaam Hong Kong Karachi
Kuala Lumpur Madrid Melbourne Mexico City Nairobi
New Delhi Shanghai Taipei Toronto

With offices in

Argentina Austria Brazil Chile Czech Republic France Greece
Guatemala Hungary Italy Japan Poland Portugal Singapore
South Korea Switzerland Thailand Turkey Ukraine Vietnam

Published in the United States
by Oxford University Press Inc., New York

First published in paperback 2009

British Library Cataloguing in Publication Data

Data available

Library of Congress Cataloging-in-Publication Data

The oxford handbook of psycholinguistics / edited by M. Gareth Gaskell; consulting
editors, Gerry Altmann . . . [et al.].
P. ; cm.
Includes bibliographical references and index.
ISBN 978-0-19-856897-1 (alk. paper)
1. Psycholinguistics -- Handbooks, manuals, etc. I. Gaskell, M. Gareth. II. Title
Handbook of psycholinguistics.
[DNLM: 1. Psycholinguistics -- Handbooks. 2. Language Development -- Handbooks. BI
455.A3 098 2007]
BF455.094 2007
401′. 9 -- dc22

2007012019

Typeset in Minion
by Cepha Imaging Pvt Ltd, Bangalore, India
Printed in Great Britain
on acid-free paper by
Ashford Colour Press Ltd, Gosport, Hampshire

ISBN 978-0-19-856897-1 (Hbk.)
978-0-19-956179-7 (Pbk.)

10 9 8 7 6 5 4 3 2 1

Preface

Why put together a handbook of psycholinguistics? I have asked myself this question on many occasions over the last eighteen months, with a printable answer not always readily available. But of course there are many good reasons: psycholinguistics is a young and fast-changing science, and a handbook provides a simple means of collecting together a representative and authoritative range of views on the current state of the art. Psycholinguistics is also multidisciplinary, meaning that researchers in one sub-discipline can easily lose track of current progress in adjoining areas. A good illustration of this problem is provided by the rapid growth of neuroimaging research in psycholinguistics. In many cases, neuroimaging and behavioral studies relating to the same theoretical issue are artificially separated by publication in different specialist journals, making it more difficult for a researcher to remain fully versed in the latest developments in both areas.

Perhaps most crucially, psycholinguistics is expanding at a rate that is both exciting and daunting. This is partly a consequence of the youth of the research field, but recently it is perhaps more a reflection of the expansion of science on a global scale. This means that a researcher in 1991 looking for articles matching the key words "discourse processing" published in the preceding five years would have only 16 articles to read, whereas the same search for the five years preceding 2006 produces 276 returns. Similar ratios are found for "lexical access" (60 vs. 1023) and "language comprehension" (113 vs. 2,021). Very roughly speaking, the overall size of the literature in these and other similar areas has doubled in the last six years or so. This is an extraordinary pace of development; it is great news in terms of the progress of the science, but makes collections such as this one all the more crucial.

The Oxford Handbook of Psycholinguistics has been compiled in an attempt to produce a collection of reviews that reflect all of the above properties of psycholinguistics: its youth, its rate of change, its diversity, its multidisciplinarity, and its growth as a science. When I began to draw up a list of topics and authors it seemed like my original brief of "about forty chapters" would be luxurious—easily enough to cover all aspects of psycholinguistics, with a few assorted extras. As time went on, though, the feeling of extravagance wore off, and the number of absolute "must have" chapters grew, resulting in a final line-up just under fifty.

The six sections of the *Handbook* cover the basic divisions within psycholinguistics, with the first four providing a broad sweep from perception to production. Section I covers the processes leading up to word recognition, both for speech and for written language, while Section II deals more with structure, organization, and meaning within the mental lexicon—partly from a perception perspective, but also with some insights from production. Section III moves on beyond the word to higher-level aspects of comprehension, and Section IV covers the major research areas in language production. In all these sections, the majority of the chapters focus on research relating to one subcomponent of the system, but there are also separate chapters, where applicable, dealing with modeling issues (statistical and/or connectionist), neuroimaging research, bilingual and multilingual processing, cross-linguistic research, and insights from disorders of language. Section V then provides a smaller-scale sweep through the language system focusing on issues relating to language development and language learning. Finally, Section VI contains a more diverse set of reviews, providing perspectives either across psycholinguistics as a whole (e.g. from the study of sign language or language evolution), or from the point of view of a neighboring research field (e.g. working memory or artificial language processing). Presumably, it is bad form for an editor to single out one section as a favorite, but I have to confess that mine is (narrowly) this last section, because it was the one that was the most enjoyable to set up, and because I learned so much from it. Perhaps a worthwhile project in the near future would be to assemble a full volume of perspectives of this type—certainly it would have been easy to find many more for this volume.

All the chapters have a focus on recent developments in the field. This does not in any way mean that they ignore theory or data published before the turn of the century; but this focus does allow the reader to get to grips with the latest developments without trawling through extended discussions of dated issues. This focus on new developments also allows the chapters to remain reasonably brief and accessible to both undergraduate and graduate students, while still satisfying current researchers in the field.

Drawing up the list of authors was a major challenge, and for their help in this regard I sought the advice of the consulting editors: Gerry Altmann, Paul Bloom, Alfonso Caramazza, and Pim Levelt. Their ideas and support made an enormous difference to the final product, and I am immensely grateful to them. Nonetheless, the ultimate responsibility for the selection of authors was mine. Beyond this point, responsibility for the material lies with the authors of the individual chapters, who were given guidelines as to the type of chapter requested, but were also allowed substantial freedom to structure their chapters as they preferred. The resultant diversity in style is a positive aspect of the *Handbook*, making for a more readable and engaging volume. All chapters were reviewed, mostly by a fellow contributor, and authors were extremely accommodating in responding to these reviews and to my own comments. The review process for me was a wonderful educational experience: I would like to say that I soaked up every single word of the volume, but, having read through Chapter 19, I am forced to concede that I may have missed the odd function word.

My primary thanks go to the authors of the chapters, who without exception contributed authoritative and elegant reviews, and responded with generosity to all my requests. They also should be thanked separately for acting as reviewers on their fellow authors' chapters, alongside Matt Davis, Yuki Kamide, Jelena Mirković, and Sharon Thomas. At Oxford University Press, the help of both Martin Baum, who provided the initial idea for the *Handbook*, and Carol Maxwell, who dealt with the chapters and authors, was invaluable. As mentioned, the consulting editors provided a great deal of help with the development of the structure of the handbook, and I should also like to thank Sandie Cleland, Nicolas Dumay, Simon Garrod, William Marslen-Wilson, and Antje Meyer for providing feedback on the author list. Finally, a personal thank you to Catherine and Philip Gaskell, for their nature and nurture, and to Lou, Stan and Frank Gaskell for their continuing encouragement, support, and stimulation.

Gareth Gaskell
York, September 2008

M. Gareth Gaskell is Professor of Psychology at the University of York, UK. His research in psycholinguistics has largely focused on speech perception, spoken word recognition, connectionist modelling and vocabulary acquisition.

Contents

Contributors

Alario, F.-Xavier GRNC, Parc Científic Universitat de Barcelona and Hospital Sant Joan de Déu and Departament de Psicología Bàsica, Universitat de Barcelona, Spain; CNRS and Université de Provence, France

Aznar-Besé, Noemí Department of Psychology, University of Houston, USA

Belke, Eva Department of Linguistics, University of Bielefeld, Germany

Berndt, Rita Sloan University of Maryland School of Medicine, USA

Blumstein, Sheila E. Department of Cognitive and Linguistic Sciences, Brown University, USA

Bornkessel-Schlesewsky, Ina D. Junior Research Group, Neurotypology, Max Planck Institute for Human Cognitive and Brain Sciences, Leipzig, Germany

Caravolas, Markéta Department of Psychology, University of Liverpool, UK

Costa, Albert GRNC, Parc Científic Universitat de Barcelona and Hospital Sant Joan de Déu and Departament de Psicología Bàsica, Universitat de Barcelona, Spain

Craighero, Laila Department of Biomedical Sciences and Advanced Therapies, Section of Human Physiology, University of Ferrara, Italy

Crowther, Jason E. Department of Psychology, Rice University, USA

Curtin, Suzanne Departments of Linguistics and Psychology, University of Calgary, Canada

Dijkstra, Ton Nijmegen Institute for Cognition and Information, University of Nijmegen, The Netherlands

Emmorey, Karen Laboratory for Language and Cognitive Neuroscience, San Diego State University, USA

Federmeier, Kara D. Department of Psychology, Neuroscience Program, and the Beckman Institute for Advanced Science and Technology, University of Illinois, Urbana-Champaign, USA

Fernández, Eva M. Queens College and Graduate Center, City University of New York, USA

Ferreira, Victor S. Department of Psychology, University of California, San Diego, USA

Fitch, W. Tecumseh Department of Psychology, University of St Andrews, UK

Fowler, Carol A. Haskins Laboratories and Department of Psychology, University of Connecticut, and Department of Linguistics, Yale University, USA

Friederici, Angela D. Max Planck Institute for Human Cognitive and Brain Sciences, Leipzig, Germany

Frost, Ram Department of Psychology, The Hebrew University, Israel

Garrett, Merrill Department of Psychology, University of Arizona, USA

Garrod, Simon Department of Psychology, University of Glasgow, UK

Gaskell, M. Gareth Department of Psychology, University of York, UK

Gathercole, Susan E. Department of Psychology, University of York, UK

Gleitman, Lila R. Department of Psychology, University of Pennsylvania, USA

Glenberg, Arthur M. Department of Psychology, University of Wisconsin–Madison, USA

Goldrick, Matthew Department of Linguistics, Northwestern University, USA

Gómez, Rebecca Department of Psychology, University of Arizona, USA

Hernández, Arturo E. Department of Psychology, University of Houston, USA

Indefrey, Peter Max Planck Institute for Psycholinguistics and F. C. Donders Center for Cognitive Neuroimaging, Nijmegen, The Netherlands

Jesse, Alexandra Department of Psychology, University of California, Santa Cruz, USA

Kessler, Brett Department of Psychology, Washington University in St. Louis, USA

Koenig, Melissa A. Institute of Child Development, University of Minnesota, USA

Kutas, Marta Departments of Cognitive Science and Neurosciences and Center for Research in Language, University of California, San Diego, USA

Levi, Susannah V. Department of Speech-Language Pathology and Audiology New York University, USA

Lupker, Stephen J. Department of Psychology, University of Western Ontario, Canada

Marslen-Wilson, William D. Medical Research Council Cognition and Brain Sciences Unit, University of Cambridge, UK

Martin, Randi C. Department of Psychology, Rice University, USA

Massaro, Dominic W. Department of Psychology, University of California, Santa Cruz, USA

McQueen, James M. Max Planck Institute for Psycholinguistics, Nijmegen, The Netherlands

Meyer, Antje S. School of Psychology, University of Birmingham, UK

Moore, Roger K. Department of Computer Science, University of Sheffield, UK

Moss, Helen E. Center for Speech, Language, and the Brain, Department of Experimental Psychology, University of Cambridge, UK

Phillips, Colin Department of Linguistics, University of Maryland, USA

Pickering, Martin J. School of Philosophy, Psychology, and Language, University of Edinburgh, UK

Pisoni, David B. Speech Research Laboratory, Department of Psychological and Brain Sciences, Indiana University, USA

Port, Robert F. Department of Linguistics, Department of Cognitive Science, Indiana University, USA

Pulvermüller, Friedemann Medical Research Council Cognition and Brain Sciences Unit, University of Cambridge, UK

Rastle, Kathleen Department of Psychology, Royal Holloway, University of London, UK

Rayner, Keith Department of Psychology, University of Massachusetts, Amherst, USA

Rice, Mabel L. Department of Speech–Language–Hearing: Sciences and Disorders, University of Kansas, USA

Rizzolatti, Giacomo Department of Neurosciences, Section of Physiology, University of Parma, Italy

Sebastián-Gallés, Núria GRNC, Parc Científic Universitat de Barcelona and Hospital Sant Joan de Déu and Departament de Psicología Bàsica, Universitat de Barcelona, Spain

Seidenberg, Mark S. Department of Psychology, University of Wisconsin–Madison, USA

Shillcock, Richard School of Philosophy, Psychology, and Language Sciences, University of Edinburgh, UK

Singer, Murray Department of Psychology, University of Manitoba, Canada

Slevc, L. Robert Department of Psychology, University of California, San Diego, USA

Smolík, Filip Department of Speech–Language–Hearing: Sciences and Disorders, University of Kansas, USA

Snowling, Margaret J. Department of Psychology, University of York, UK

Staub, Adrian Department of Psychology, University of Massachusetts, Amherst, USA

Tanenhaus, Michael K. Department of Brain and Cognitive Sciences, University of Rochester, USA

Taylor, Kirsten I. Center for Speech, Language, and the Brain, Department of Experimental Psychology, University of Cambridge, UK

Treiman, Rebecca Department of Psychology, Washington University in St. Louis, USA

Trueswell, John C. Department of Psychology, University of Pennsylvania, USA

Tyler, Lorraine K. Center for Speech, Language, and the Brain, Department of Experimental Psychology, University of Cambridge, UK

Ullman, Michael T. Departments of Neuroscience, Linguistics, Psychology and Neurology, Georgetown University, USA

Van Gompel, Roger P. G. School of Psychology, University of Dundee, UK

Vigliocco, Gabriella Deafness, Cognition, and Language Center, Department of Human Communication Science and Department of Psychology, University of London, UK

Vuong, Loan C. Department of Psychology, Rice University, USA

Vinson, David P. Deafness, Cognition, and Language Center, Department of Human Communication Science and Department of Psychology, University of London, UK

Wagers, Matthew Department of Linguistics, University of Maryland, USA

Werker, Janet F. Department of Psychology, University of British Columbia, Canada

Woodward, Amanda Department of Psychology, University of Maryland, USA

Xu, Fei Department of Psychology, University of British Columbia, Canada

Ziegler, Johannes C. Centre National de la Recherche Scientifique and University of Provence, France

SECTION I

Word Recognition

CHAPTER 1

Representations and representational specificity in speech perception and spoken word recognition

David B. Pisoni and Susannah V. Levi

1.1 Introduction

Approaches to the study of speech perception and spoken word recognition have undergone rapid change over the last few years due to theoretical and methodological developments in various subfields of cognitive science. In contrast to the traditional view that speakers only represent abstractions of linguistic structure from the speech signal, several exemplar-based approaches (e.g. Goldinger, 1998; Goldinger and Azuma, 2003; Johnson, 1997) to the study of speech perception and spoken word recognition have emerged from independent developments in categorization (Kruschke, 1992; Nosofsky, 1986) and frequency-based phonology (Bybee, 2001; Pierrehumbert, 2001). These alternatives offer fresh ideas and new insights relating to old problems and questions related to variability and invariance (Pardo and Remez, forthcoming). In this chapter, we will discuss how these new approaches—coupled with previous insights—provide a new framework for questions which deal with the nature of phonological and lexical knowledge and representation, processing of stimulus variability, and perceptual learning and adaptation (see papers in Pisoni and Remez, 2005).

The fundamental issue in speech perception and spoken language processing research is to describe the cognitive processes involved in a listener's recovery of her interlocutor's intended message. This complex problem has been typically broken down into several more specific research questions. First, what stages of perceptual analysis intervene between the presentation of the speech signal and recognition of the intended message? Second, what types of processing computations occur at each stage? Third, what are the primary perceptual processing units and what is the nature and content of representations of speech in memory? We provide an overview of some recent developments in the field that bear directly on the third question (for overviews of work pertaining to the first two questions, see McQueen, Chapter 3 this volume; Gaskell, Chapter 4 this volume). In this chapter, we will present evidence and provide arguments indicating that speakers encode and represent both individual instances (or exemplars) they have encountered and abstractions over those instances.

The chapter is structured as follows. Section 1.2 outlines the traditional view of speech perception and identifies some problems with assuming such a view in which only abstract representations exist. Section 1.3 discusses some new approaches to speech perception which retain detailed information in the representations.

In section 1.4 we discuss a view which rejects abstraction altogether, but then show that such a view has difficulty dealing with a range of linguistic phenomena. Section 1.5 provides a brief discussion of some new directions in linguistics that encode both detailed information and abstraction. Finally, in section 1.6 we discuss the coupling of speech perception and spoken word recognition.

1.2 **The traditional view of speech perception**

1.2.1 **Overview**

The traditional approach to speech perception has relied on the assumptions of generative linguistics, which adopts a formalist view and focuses on two related problems: describing the linguistic knowledge that native speakers have about their language (their so-called "linguistic competence") and explaining the systematic regularities and patterns displayed by natural languages. Within the domain of speech perception, linguists have made several foundational assumptions about speech, assuming that speech is structured in systematic ways and that the linguistically significant information in the speech signal can be represented effectively and economically as a linear sequence of abstract, discrete units using an alphabet of conventional phonetic symbols (e.g. *speech* is represented with the segments /s/, /p/, /i/, /tʃ/). Segmental representations are designed to code only the linguistically significant differences in meaning between minimal pairs of words in the language (Twaddell, 1952), and segments therefore encode idealized abstractions of speech sounds. The strong view from generative linguistics is that a speaker's representation of the sounds in her language excludes redundant or accidental information that is present in the speech signal but not linguistically contrastive. Two examples of this traditional view are given below.

> . . . there is so much evidence that speech is basically a sequence of discrete elements that it seems reasonable to limit consideration to mechanisms that break the stream of speech down into elements and identify each element as a member, or as probably a member, of one or another of a finite number of sets. (Licklider, 1952: 590)

> The basic problem of interest to the linguist might be formulated as follows: What are the rules that would make it possible to go from the continuous acoustic signal that impinges on the ear to the symbolization of the utterance in terms of discrete units, e.g., phonemes or the letters of our alphabet? There can be no doubt that speech is a sequence of discrete entities, since in writing we perform the kind of symbolization just mentioned, while in reading aloud we execute the inverse of this operation; that is, we go from a discrete symbolization to a continuous acoustic signal. (Halle, 1956: 510)

This traditional view that speech is encoded by speakers as a linear sequence of abstract symbols has been adopted across a wide range of related scientific disciplines that study speech processing, such as speech and hearing sciences, psycholinguistics, cognitive and neural sciences, and engineering (Peterson, 1952). The theoretical underpinnings of this view date back to the early Paninian grammarians, who first noted that words have an internal structure and differ from each other in systematic ways reflecting the phonological (and morphological) contrasts of a particular language. Although not often made explicit, this view relies on several important theoretical assumptions that are worth mentioning because they bear directly on theoretical issues related to the nature and content of lexical representations.

First, the traditional view of the representation of speech assumes that a set of discrete and linear symbols can be used to represent what is essentially continuous, parametric, and gradient information in the speech signal (Pierrehumbert and Pierrehumbert, 1990). Second, in this view, the symbols representing phonetic segments or phonemes in speech are abstract, static, invariant, and context-free, having combinatory properties like the individual letters used in alphabetic writing systems. Although speech can be considered as a good example of a "particulate system" (Abler, 1989; see section 1.4 below), some degree of uncertainty still remains about the precise elemental primitives of speech, even after many years of basic and applied research. For example, what is the size of the basic building blocks of speech? Are they features, phonemes, syllables, or gestures? Are they perceptual or articulatory in nature, or are they both?

Third, the traditional view of speech perception relies heavily on a set of psychological processes that function to "normalize" acoustically different speech signals and make them functionally equivalent in perception (Joos, 1948). In this view, it is generally assumed that perceptual normalization is needed in speech perception in order to reduce acoustic-phonetic variability in the speech signal, making physically different signals (e.g. from different speakers) perceptually equivalent by bringing them into conformity with some common standard or referent (see Pisoni, 1997).

1.2.2 **Problems with the traditional view of speech perception**

Several aspects of the traditional view of speech as a linear string of discrete symbols are difficult to reconcile with the continuous nature of the acoustic waveform produced by a speaker. Importantly, the acoustic consequences of coarticulation, as well as other sources of contextually conditioned variability, result in the failure of the acoustic signal to meet two formal conditions: linearity and invariance. This failure in turn gives rise to a third related problem: the absence of segmentation of the physical, acoustic speech signal into discrete units (first discussed by Chomsky and Miller, 1963). This section provides an overview of these issues faced by the traditional view of speech, leading to the suggestion that speakers must represent detailed information about the speech signal in addition to the abstracted representations discussed above.

1.2.2.1 Non-linearity of the speech signal

One fundamental problem facing the traditional view is the lack of linearity. The linearity condition states that for each phoneme in the message there must be a corresponding stretch of sound in the utterance (Chomsky and Miller, 1963). Furthermore, if phoneme X is followed by phoneme Y in the phonemic representation, the stretch of sound corresponding to phoneme X must precede the stretch of sound corresponding to phoneme Y in the physical signal. The linearity condition is clearly not met in the acoustic signal because of coarticulation and other contextual effects which "smear" acoustic features for adjacent phonemes. For example, perceptual cues regarding the place of articulation for onset stop consonants (e.g. /b/ vs. /d/ vs. /g/) are located in the formant transitions into the following segment which follows the release of the consonant. This smearing, or "parallel transmission" of acoustic features, results in stretches of the speech waveform in which acoustic features of more than one phoneme are present (Liberman et al., 1967).

1.2.2.2 Lack of acoustic-phonetic invariance

Another important property of the speech signal which is problematic for the traditional view is the fact that speech lacks acoustic-phonetic invariance (Chomsky and Miller, 1963). Acoustic-phonetic invariance entails that every phoneme must have a specific set of acoustic attributes in all contexts (Estes, 1994; Murphy, 2002; Smith and Medin, 1981). Because of coarticulatory effects in speech production, the acoustic properties of a particular speech sound vary as a function of the phonetic environment. For example, the formant transitions for syllable-initial stop consonants which provide cues to place of articulation vary considerably depending on properties of the following vowel (Liberman et al., 1954).

In addition to within-speaker variation, acoustic-phonetic invariance is also absent when we look across speakers of a language producing a particular segment in a particular context. For example, men, women, and children with different vocal tract lengths exhibit large differences in their absolute formant values in the production of vowels (Peterson and Barney, 1952). In each case, the absence of acoustic-phonetic invariance is inconsistant with the notion that speech is represented only as an idealized string of discrete segments.

1.2.2.3 Difficulties with speech segmentation

The non-linearity of the speech signal coupled with the context-conditioned variability leads to a third problem with the traditional view of speech perception: how do we segment the speech waveform into higher-order units of linguistic analysis such as syllables and words? The previous sections highlighted that the speech signal cannot be reliably segmented into discrete acoustically defined units that are independent of adjacent segments; in fluent speech, it is typically not possible to identify where one word ends and another begins using simple acoustic criteria. Precisely how the continuous speech signal is mapped onto discrete symbolic representations by the listener continues to be one of the most important and challenging problems for speech perception research, and critically suggests the existence of additional representations that encode the gradient, continuous aspects of the speech signal.

The description of the problem of speech segmentation was first characterized by Charles Hockett in his well-known Easter egg analogy.

> Imagine a row of Easter eggs carried along a moving belt; the eggs are of various sizes, and variously colored, but not boiled. At a certain point the belt carries the row of eggs between the two rollers of a wringer, which quite effectively smash them and rub them more or less into each other. The flow of eggs before the wringer represents the series of impulses from the phoneme source; the mess that

> emerges from the wringer represents the output of the speech transmitter. At a subsequent point, we have an inspector whose task it is to examine the passing mess and decide, on the basis of the broken and unbroken yolks, the variously spread out albumen, and the variously colored bits of shell, the nature of the flow of eggs which previously arrived at the wringer. (Hockett, 1955: 210)

A major stumbling block for the traditional view is that it has routinely assumed a bottom-up approach to speech perception and spoken word recognition where phonemes are first recognized from the speech signal and then parsed into words (Lindgren, 1965; Gaskell, Chapter 4 this volume; McQueen, Chapter 3 this volume). An alternative view of speech perception that we will discuss in section 1.6 does not suffer from this problem because it allows for a top-down approach where words are recognized as whole units first, and then segmentation into phonemes follows as a natural consequence as required by the specific behavioral task and processing demands on the listener. We believe that this latter view is critical for providing an account of speech perception which incorporates both detailed instance-based representations and abstractions over those instances.

In sum, the traditional view of speech perception which asserts that only abstract representations exist faces several problems in light of the fact that the speech signal is continuous. The next section will discuss new methods of approaching speech perception and spoken word recognition that take into account the continuous nature of speech and that represent in memory highly detailed information about the signal.

1.3 New approaches to speech perception and spoken word recognition

While traditional theories of word recognition and lexical access assumed that the mental lexicon consisted of a single canonical entry for each word (Marslen-Wilson, 1984; Morton, 1979; Oldfield, 1966), recent episodic approaches to the lexicon have adopted ideas from "multiple-trace" theories of human memory which propose that multiple entries for each word are encoded and stored in lexical memory in the form of detailed perceptual traces that preserve fine phonetic detail of the original articulatory event (Elman, 2004; Goldinger, 1996; 1998; Goldinger and Azuma, 2003; Johnson, 1997). In contrast to the traditional views of the lexicon as containing linear strings of idealized sound segments, current episodic approaches to spoken word recognition and lexical access emphasize the coupling between the neural encoding of prior perceptual experiences and the representations of sound structure active in speech processing (see Goldinger, 1998 for a full exposition of this idea). In this section, we provide arguments that speech exhibits non-analytic properties (section 1.3.1), which favors an account in which individual episodes (or exemplars) are stored in memory (section 1.3.2). Section 1.3.2 further contains a synopsis of previous experiments revealing that particular components of the speech signal—unnecessary for identification of the linguistic target—are stored in memory and affect behavior across several language processing tasks (section 1.3.3).

1.3.1 Non-analytic cognition

Over the last twenty years, a large number of studies in cognitive psychology on categorization and memory have suggested that we encode and retain "instance-specific" information across a wide variety of cognitive domains (Brooks, 1978; Jacoby and Brooks, 1984; Schacter, 1990; 1992; Tulving and Schacter, 1990). According to a non-analytic approach to cognition, the stimulus variability which is present in these instances is viewed as "lawful" and informative in perceptual analysis (Elman and McClelland, 1986). Specific perceptual episodes are encoded in memory and active in the cognitive processes involved in recognition (Kolers, 1973; 1976). Given the emphasis on the details of individual percepts, the problem of variability raised in section 1.2.2.2 can be approached in fundamentally different ways by non-analytic accounts of perception and memory. Other examples of stimuli that encourage a non-analytic approach to perception are visual object recognition (Gautier and Tarr, 2002) and faces (Rhodes et al., 2004).

When the criteria used for postulating episodic or non-analytic representations (discussed in Brooks, 1978) are examined with respect to speech, it is apparent that a number of distinctive properties of speech make it amenable to this approach (Jacoby and Brooks, 1984). This section focuses on several properties that encourage a non-analytic processing strategy, including: high stimulus variability; complex stimulus–category relations; classification of inputs under incomplete information; and classification of structures with high analytic difficulty. These criteria—and their relationship to the speech signal—are summarized briefly below.

1.3.1.1 High stimulus variability

Stimuli with a high degree of acoustic-phonetic variability are compatible with non-analytic representations. Speech signals display a great deal of physical variability due to factors associated with the production of spoken language. Among these factors are within- and between-talker variability, such as changes in speaking rate and dialect, differences in social contexts, syntactic, semantic and pragmatic effects, and emotional state, as well as a wide variety of context effects due to the ambient environment such as background noise, reverberation, and transmission media (Klatt, 1986). These diverse sources of variability produce large changes in the acoustic-phonetic properties of speech. Variability must be taken seriously and approached directly because it is an integral property of natural speech, as well as all biological systems.

1.3.1.2 Complex stimulus–category relations

Speech also displays a complex relation between the stimulus and its category membership, another property of non-analytic systems. Despite the large amount of variability in the speech signal, categorization is reliable and robust (Twaddell, 1952). The conventional use of phonemes as perceptual units in speech perception entails a set of complex assumptions about category membership. These assumptions are based on linguistic criteria involving principles such as complementary distribution, free variation, and phonetic similarity. In traditional linguistics, for example, the concept of a phoneme as a basic primitive of speech is used in a number of quite different ways. Gleason (1961), for example, characterizes the phoneme as a minimal unit of contrast, the set of allophones of a phoneme, and a non-acoustic abstract unit of a language. Thus, like other category domains studied by cognitive psychologists, speech sounds display complex stimulus–category relations which place strong constraints on the class of categorization models that can account for these operating principles.

1.3.1.3 Classifying stimuli with incomplete information

Classifying incomplete or degraded stimuli is also consistent with non-analytic analysis. Speech is a system that allows classification under highly degraded or incomplete information, such as silent-center vowels (Jenkins et al., 1999), speech processed through a cochlear implant simulator (Shannon et al., 1995), speech mixed with noise (Miller et al., 1951), and sinewave speech (Remez et al., 1981). Correct classification of speech under these impoverished conditions is possible because speech is a highly redundant system which has evolved to maximize the transmission of linguistic information. In the case of speech perception, numerous studies have demonstrated the existence of multiple speech cues for almost every phonetic contrast (Raphael, 2005). While these speech cues are for the most part highly context-dependent, they also provide reliable information that can facilitate recognition of the intended message even when the signal is presented under poor listening conditions. This feature of speech perception permits very high rates of information transmission using sparsely coded and broadly specified categories (Pollack, 1952; 1953).

1.3.1.4 Classification of stimuli with high analytic difficulty

Stimuli with high analytic difficulty are those which differ along one or more dimensions that are difficult to quantify or describe. Because of the complexity of speech and its high acoustic-phonetic variability, the category structure of speech is not amenable to simple hypothesis testing. As a result, it has been extremely difficult to construct a set of explicit formal rules that can successfully map multiple speech cues onto discrete phoneme categories. Moreover, the perceptual units of speech are also highly automatized; the underlying category structure of a language is learned in a tacit and incidental way by young children.

1.3.2 **Evidence favoring episodic approaches to speech perception**

The recent episodic approaches to the lexicon considered here (e.g. Goldinger, 1998; Johnson, 1997) assume that spoken words are represented in lexical memory as a collection of individual perceptual tokens rather than as abstract word types. Evidence supporting episodic exemplar-based approaches to representation in the mental lexicon has accumulated over the last few years.

According to episodic views of perception and memory, listeners encode "particulars," that is, specific instances or perceptual episodes, rather than generalities or abstractions (Kruschke, 1992; Nosofsky, 1986). Abstraction "emerges" from computational processes at the time of retrieval (Estes, 1994; Nosofsky, 1986). A series of studies carried out in our lab has shown that "indexical" properties of a speech token (e.g. information about a talker's voice and detailed information about speaking rate) are encoded into memory and become part of the long-term memory representation that a listener has about the words of her language (Pisoni, 1997). Rather than discarding talker-specific details of speech in favor of only highly abstract representations, these studies have shown that human listeners encode and retain very fine episodic details of the perceptual event (Pisoni, 1997). This evidence further supports the claim that assuming the existence of only abstract symbolic representations of speech cannot account for basic phenomena in speech and language processing.

1.3.2.1 Encoding and storage of variability in speech perception

A number of studies from our research group have explored the effects of different sources of variability on speech perception and spoken word recognition. In a series of studies, we specifically introduced variability in our stimulus materials using tokens from different talkers and different speaking rates to directly study the effects of these variables on perception (Pisoni, 1993). For example, Mullennix et al. (1989) observed that the intelligibility of isolated spoken words presented in noise was affected by the number of talkers used to generate the test words in the stimulus ensemble. In one condition, all the words in a test list were produced by a single talker; in another condition, the words were produced by fifteen different talkers. Across three different signal-to-noise ratios, identification performance was always better when subjects were presented with stimuli produced by a single talker than for subjects presented with stimuli produced by multiple talkers. Thus, variability in the speaker's voice led to a decline in spoken word recognition performance. These findings replicated results originally reported by Peters (1955) and Creelman (1957), and suggest that the perceptual system is highly sensitive to talker variability, and therefore must engage in some form of "recalibration" each time a novel voice is encountered.

In a second set of experiments, Mullennix et al. (1989) measured repetition latencies to the same set of words presented under single- and multiple-talker test conditions. They found that subjects were slower and less accurate in repeating words presented in multiple-talker lists compared to single-talker lists. As all the test words used in the experiment were highly intelligible when presented in the quiet, these results are difficult to reconcile with a view in which spoken word recognition requires that the speech signal be "normalized," leading the perceiver to discard information regarding talker identity. Thus, the data from these studies raised a number of additional questions about how different perceptual dimensions of the speech signal are processed and encoded by the human listener.

One important issue raised by these results is whether linguistic information (e.g. identity of speech sounds) is processed separately from indexical (or extralinguistic) information such as the identity of the speaker. To address this issue, Mullennix and Pisoni (1990) used a speeded classification task to assess whether attributes of a talker's voice are perceived independently of the phonetic form of words. Subjects were required to attend selectively to one stimulus dimension (e.g. either talker voice or phoneme identity) while simultaneously ignoring the other dimension. Across all conditions, Mullennix and Pisoni found that when subjects were required to attend selectively to one dimension, the other dimension interfered with their performance. If these perceptual dimensions were processed separately, as was originally assumed, interference from the non-attended dimension should not have been observed. However, the observed pattern of results suggested that words and voices were not processed separately; that is, the perception of one dimension (e.g. phoneme) affected classification of the other dimension (e.g. voice). Not only did we find mutual interference between the two dimensions, but we also found that the pattern of interference was asymmetrical. It was easier for subjects to ignore irrelevant variation in the phoneme dimension when their task was to classify the voice than it was for them to ignore the voice dimension when they had to classify the phonemes.

To further study the effects of indexical properties on speech perception, we carried out a series of memory experiments to assess the mental representation of speech in long-term memory. Experiments on serial recall of lists of spoken words by Martin et al. (1989) and Goldinger et al. (1991) demonstrated that specific details of a talker's voice are not lost or discarded during early perceptual analysis but are perceived and encoded in long-term memory. Using a continuous recognition memory procedure, Palmeri et al. (1993) found that detailed episodic information about a talker's voice is also encoded in memory and is available for explicit judgments even when a great deal of competition from other voices is present in the test sequence.

In another series of recognition memory experiments, Goldinger (1998) found strong evidence of implicit memory for attributes of a talker's voice which persists for a relatively long period of time (up to a week) after perceptual analysis has been completed. Moreover, he also found that the degree of perceptual similarity between voices affects the magnitude of repetition priming effects, suggesting that fine phonetic details are not lost and the perceptual system encodes detailed talker-specific information about spoken words in episodic memory representations (see Goldinger, 1997).

Another set of experiments was carried out to examine the effects of speaking rate on perception and memory. These studies, designed to parallel the earlier experiments on talker variability, also found that the perceptual details associated with differences in speaking rate are not lost as a result of perceptual analysis. In one experiment, Sommers et al. (1992) found that identification of words was affected by variation in speaking rate (i.e. fast, medium, and slow) compared to a condition in which the same words were produced at a single speaking rate. However, when differences in amplitude were varied randomly from trial to trial, identification performance was not affected by variability in overall signal level.

Effects of speaking rate variability have also been observed in experiments involving a serial recall task. Nygaard et al. (1992) found that subjects recalled words from lists produced at a single speaking rate better than the same words produced at several different speaking rates. Interestingly, the differences appeared in the primacy portion of the serial position curve, suggesting greater difficulty in the transfer of items into long-term memory. The effects of differences in speaking rate, like those observed for talker variability in our earlier experiments, suggest that perceptual encoding and rehearsal processes are influenced by low-level perceptual sources of variability. If these sources of variability were automatically filtered out or normalized by the perceptual system at early stages of analysis, differences in recall performance would not be expected in memory tasks like the ones used in these experiments.

Taken together, the findings on variability and speaking rate suggest that details of the early perceptual analysis of spoken words are not lost as a result of early perceptual analysis. Rather, detailed perceptual information of spoken words is represented in memory. In fact, in some cases increased stimulus variability in an experiment may actually help listeners encode items in long-term memory because variability helps keep individual items more distinct and discriminable, thereby reducing confusability and increasing the probability of correct recall (Goldinger et al., 1991; Nygaard et al., 1992). Listeners encode speech signals along many perceptual dimensions, and the memory system apparently preserves these details much more reliably than researchers believed in the past.

1.3.2.2 Talker-specific speech perception and spoken word recognition

Our findings on the effects of talker variability and speaking rate on perception encouraged us to examine perceptual learning in speech more carefully. Specifically, we investigated the rapid tuning or perceptual adaptation that occurs when a listener becomes familiar with the voice of a particular talker (Nygaard et al., 1994). This problem has not received very much attention in the field of human speech perception despite its obvious relevance to problems of speaker normalization, acoustic-phonetic invariance, and the potential application to automatic speech recognition and speaker identification (Bricker and Pruzansky, 1976; Fowler, 1990; Kakehi, 1992).

To determine how familiarity with a talker's voice affects the perception of spoken words, Nygaard et al. (1994) trained two groups of listeners to explicitly identify a set of ten unfamiliar voices over a nine-day period. After this initial learning period, subjects participated in a word recognition experiment designed to measure speech intelligibility. Subjects were presented with a set of novel words at several signal-to-noise ratios. One group of listeners heard the words produced by talkers that they were previously trained on, and the other group heard the same words produced by a new set of unfamiliar talkers. In the word recognition task, subjects were required to identify the words rather than recognize the voices. The results revealed that subjects who heard novel words produced by familiar voices were able to recognize the novel words more accurately than subjects who received the same novel words produced by unfamiliar voices. An additional study with two new sets of untrained listeners confirmed that both sets of voices were equally intelligible, indicating that the difference in performance found in the original study was due to training, not inherent intelligibility between the two sets of words.

These findings demonstrate that exposure to a talker's voice facilitates subsequent perceptual processing of novel words produced by that talker. Thus, speech perception and spoken word recognition incorporate highly specific perceptual knowledge about a talker's voice.

More recently, Allen and Miller (2004) have also shown the effects of talker-specific knowledge in a task which examined listeners' sensitivity to sub-phonemic acoustic differences. Listeners were trained on the voices of two talkers, one with long voice onset times (VOTs) and one with short VOTs. During the test phase, listeners were able to generalize talker-specific VOT differences to novel words, indicating that listeners' sensitivity to sub-phonemic acoustic-phonetic differences was retained and used in subsequent language processing tasks.

Similarly, Eisner and McQueen (2005) and Kraljic and Samuel (2005) also observed talker-specific sub-phonemic attunement for fricatives. Eisner and McQueen trained listeners with an ambiguous fricative in either an [f]- or [s]-biasing lexical context. During the testing phase, listeners categorized more stimuli on the f/s continuum depending on their previous training, but only when the same voice was used during both training and testing. Thus, listeners attended to talker-specific knowledge when categorizing ambiguous stimuli. In a similar experiment with ambiguous [s] and [ʃ] stimuli, Kraljic and Samuel showed that perceptual learning of talker-specific characteristics is retained up to at least 25 minutes.

What kind of perceptual knowledge do listeners acquire when they learn to identify a speaker's voice? One possibility is that the perceptual operations (Kolers, 1973) used to recognize voices become part of "procedural memory" and are activated when the same voice is encountered again in a subsequent intelligibility test. This kind of procedural knowledge might increase the efficiency of the perceptual analysis of novel words produced by familiar talkers because detailed analysis of the speaker's voice would not have to be carried out over and over again as each new word was encountered. Another possibility is that specific instances—perceptual episodes or exemplars of each talker's voice—are encoded and stored in memory and then later retrieved during the process of word recognition when new tokens from a familiar talker are encountered (Jacoby and Brooks, 1984).

Whatever the exact nature of this perceptual knowledge turns out to be, the important point to emphasize here is that prior exposure to a talker's voice facilitates subsequent recognition of novel words produced by the same talkers. Such findings demonstrate a form of source memory for a talker's voice that is distinct from the individual items and the specific task that was employed to familiarize the listeners with the voices (Glanzer et al., 2004; Johnson et al., 1993; Mitchell and Johnson, 2000; Roediger, 1990; Schacter, 1992). These findings provide additional support for the view that the internal representation of spoken words encompasses a phonological description of the utterance as well as information about the source characteristics of the specific talker. The results of these studies suggest that normal speech perception is carried out in a "talker-contingent" manner; the indexical and linguistic properties of the speech signal are closely coupled in perceptual analysis.

Differences in the processing of detailed voice information and more abstract lexical information can be dissociated by familiarizing listeners with voices speaking in a foreign language. Inspired by previous work which showed that listeners were better able to identify voices speaking in a language familiar to the listeners (e.g. Goggin et al., 1991; Sullivan and Schlichting, 2000; Thompson, 1987), Winters et al. (2006) trained two groups of monolingual English listeners to identify the same ten voices speaking either in English or German. Following four days of training, listeners carried out a generalization task, in which they were asked to identify the same ten voices but in the untrained language (either German or English). Listeners from each group were able to generalize to the untrained language, indicating that the listeners' detailed knowledge of each speaker's voice characteristics is (at least) partially independent of the particular language being spoken. Further, voice information must be at least partially separate from lexical information, since listeners were able to generalize both to and from German, a language for which they had no lexical entries. However, the two groups differed in the degree to which they were able to generalize to the untrained language. Listeners trained in German were able to generalize to English with no loss in voice identification performance, whereas listeners trained in English exhibited a marked decline in their voice identification performance when presented with the same voices in German. This difference in generalization suggests that the listener's encoding of the indexical properties of the speech signal are not entirely dissociated from the listener's linguistic knowledge, and thus that knowledge of the training and testing languages can mediate performance in a voice-identification task.

1.3.3 Summary

The evidence presented in this section is consistent with a view of speech perception and spoken word recognition in which all information in the speech signal is processed and represented. This approach contrasts with the traditional view of speech perception in which a listener is assumed to analyze the speech signal for its linguistic content, and discard extralinguistic information. This traditional view in which the speech signal is "normalized," and only abstract, symbolic representations are stored, is clearly not sufficient to account for the data presented above. In the next section, we will discuss the extreme position which states that abstract, symbolic representations are not necessary at all for language processing, a possibility which we ultimately reject in favor of a hybrid view in which listeners store the instances they encounter as well as abstractions over those instances.

1.4 **The end of abstract representations?**

A more radical approach to cognition in which there are no internal representations of the external world has been proposed recently by a group of artificial intelligence (AI) researchers working on behavior-based autonomous robotics and biological intelligence (Beer, 2000; Brooks, 1991a; 1991b; Clark, 1999). According to this perspective, called "embodied cognition," mind, body, and world are linked together as a "coupled" dynamical system (Beer, 2000; Clark, 1999); internal mental representations and information processing are not needed to link perception and action directly in real-world tasks, such as navigating novel, unpredictable environments. Modest degrees of intelligent behavior have been achieved in robots without computation and without complex knowledge structures representing models of the world (Brooks, 1991a; 1991b). Intelligent adaptive behavior reflects the operation of the whole system working in synchrony, without a central executive guiding behavior based on internal models of the world.

Although most research on embodied cognition has come from AI and is related to constructing autonomous robots and establishing links between perception and action in simple sensory-motor systems, the arguments against the necessity of abstract, symbolic representations and the mainstream symbol-processing views of cognition and intelligence have raised a number of issues that are directly relevant to current theoretical debates throughout cognitive science. With regard to representations in speech perception and spoken word recognition, these issues are concerned directly with questions about "representational specificity" and the necessity of lexical representations typically assumed to be active in spoken word recognition and comprehension. A strong non-representational view of spoken language has been proposed recently by Port and Leary (2005), who argued that discrete representations are not needed for real-time human speech perception.

Although the non-representational theorists have argued that it is not necessary to posit mediating states corresponding to internal representations of the external world, there are several reasons to believe that their global criticisms of the traditional symbol-processing approach to cognition may not generalize gracefully to more complex knowledge-based cognitive domains (Markman and Dietrich, 2000). Compared to the simple sensory-motor systems and navigational behaviors studied by researchers working on autonomous robotics, there is good consensus that speech perception and spoken language processing are "informationally-rich" and "representationally-hungry" knowledge-based domains (Clark, 1997) that share computational properties with a small number of other complex self-diversifying systems. These are systems like language, genetics, and chemistry that have a number of highly distinctive powerful combinatorial properties that set them apart and make them uniquely different from other natural complex systems that have been studied in the past.

William Abler (1989) examined the properties of self-diversifying systems and drew several important parallels with speech and spoken language. He argued that human language displays structural properties that are consistent with other "particulate systems" such as genetics and chemical interaction. All of these systems have a small number of basic "particles," such as genes or atoms, that can be combined and recombined to create infinite variety and unbounded diversity without blending of the individual components or loss of perceptual distinctiveness of the new patterns created by the system.

It is hard to imagine that any of the non-representationalists would seriously argue that speech and spoken language is non-representational or non-symbolic in nature. Looking at several selected aspects of speech and the way spoken languages work, it is obvious that spoken language can be offered as the prototypical example of a symbol-processing system. Indeed, this is one of the major "design features" of human language (Hockett, 1960). Evidence for symbolic representations comes from myriad sources of language data. Here, we briefly discuss two types of evidence that reveal the existence of discrete representations of sound structure in language.

The first general line of evidence we offer in favor of discrete representations of sound structure comes from linguistics. Indeed, one of the fundamental assumptions within the generative linguistics tradition (e.g. Chomsky and Halle, 1968; Prince and Smolensky, 1993/2004) is that the continuous acoustic wave form is represented by speakers at various "grain" sizes, such as phonological features (subsegmental structure), phonemes (segmental structure), and syllabic and metrical structure (suprasegmental structure). These assumptions have proven quite useful in accounting for language-internal and cross-linguistic phonological patterns. For example, segments are composed of bundles of features, and these features are used to define natural classes of segments (fricatives, stops, etc.). It has been argued that sound change—both synchronic and diachronic—occurs at the level of natural classes. Additionally, although we discussed some criticisms of the traditional view in section 1.2.2 in which the only sound structure representations are discrete idealized symbols, there are certain phonological phenomena in human languages in which it appears that segments are discrete and psychologically real entities (or symbols) which may be individually manipulated in language use. One phonological phenomenon which reveals the psychological reality of the segmental level of representation is metathesis, in which adjacent segments are transposed to create a new sound structure sequence, as in the dialectal example *ask* → [æks]. This resequencing of the /s/ and /k/ critically requires that these sound structure elements are represented—at some point in the processing system—as abstract symbols in a string which can be reordered. The reader is referred to Elizabeth Hume's metathesis database (Hume, 2000) for a wide variety of metathesis examples across the world's languages.

An additional source of evidence suggesting that there is a level of discrete sound structure representation comes from studies of speech errors. For example, Nooteboom (1969) analyzed a corpus of speech errors in Dutch, and found that 89 percent of the errors involved a single segment (also see Jaeger, 1992; 2005 for similar data in children). An additional piece of evidence comes from the "repeated phoneme effect" (Dell, 1984; MacKay, 1970; Nooteboom, 1969), in which errors are more likely in sequences containing a repeated phoneme (e.g. the vowel in *time line*) than sequences without repeated phonemes (e.g. *heat pad*), indicating that the language processing system represents sublexical units. This result has been observed in both spontaneous speech errors and experimentally induced errors (Dell, 1984; 1986). Additionally, Stemberger (1990) reported that while repetition of identical segments increases the rate of speech errors, repetition of featurally similar segments does not. In addition to these speech production errors, it has been reported that a large number of misperceptions in fluent speech involve segments rather than syllables or words (Bond, 2005; Bond and Garnes, 1980; Bond and Robey, 1983).

It is worth noting that most speech error studies have analyzed speech transcribed into strings of phonemes, which leaves open the possibility that the segmental errors reported in these studies are an artifact of the methodology. In addition, there are several articulatory and acoustic studies which have provided evidence that certain speech errors typically thought to involve discrete insertions or substitutions actually result from gradient errors in production (e.g. overlapping gestures; see Pouplier, 2003). However, a recent articulatory study with an aphasic speaker indicates that discrete vowel segments can be inserted to "repair" problematic sound structure sequences. Buchwald (2005) reported on an aphasic English speaker (VBR) whose deficit leads her to insert a vowel in word-initial consonant clusters (e.g. *bleed* → [bəlid]). VBR's articulations were recorded with ultrasound imaging while she produced consonant cluster words (e.g. *bleed*) and words with schwa between the same two consonants (e.g. *believe*). The articulatory and acoustic data indicated that her productions of words with inserted schwa were identical to her productions of words with lexical schwa, and thus inconsistent with several gradient accounts of vowel insertion based on changes along the temporal dimension. This result indicates the existence of discrete, manipulable vowel units which may be inserted in the case of aphasic speech errors.

In our view, the current debate that emerges from the criticisms of traditional, symbolic representations is not about whether spoken language processing is strictly a symbol processing system. In the case of sound structure, the evidence is clear: we encode the instances we encounter, and form abstractions such as segmental representations. The principal theoretical issue revolves around a precise description of the exact nature of the phonetic, phonological, and lexical representations used in spoken language processing and the interaction among the abstractions and the encoded exemplars.

In our view, two major questions have emerged. First, how much perceptual detail of the original speech signal is encoded in order to support language processing. Second, how much detail can be later discarded as a consequence of phonological and lexical analysis? The evidence described in the last two sections suggests that it is unlikely that there is only one basic unit of perception or only one common representational format active in speech perception and spoken word recognition. Rather, there is strong evidence for the existence of multiple units and representations—with different degrees of abstraction—that are used in parallel (see Pisoni and Luce, 1987).

The next section discusses some new directions in linguistic research that may be viewed as attempts to account simultaneously for the encoding of detailed information of perceptual experiences and for abstractions over those experiences.

1.5 **Integrating abstractions and exemplars: new views from linguistics**

In natural language contexts, one type of evidence that we encode the particular exemplars comes from certain phonological processes that affect words differently depending on their frequency of occurrence. Pierrehumbert (2001), citing Hooper (1976), noted a three-way distinction in the application of schwa lenition (or weakening) among words with word-medial obstruent-liquid clusters based on their relative frequency. For high frequency words, no schwa is present in the acoustic record (e.g. between the [v] and [r] of *every*); for words of low frequency, there is a schwa (e.g. mamm[ə]ry); and for mid-frequency words, there is a syllabic [r] (e.g. *memory*). This example is critical, as it contains a process targeting an abstract phonemic category (words with medial obstruent-liquid clusters), but applying differentially to particular members of that category depending on the number of times they have been encountered. Pierrehumbert proposes a framework in which individual exemplars of each word are stored and form part of the representation of a given lexical item. This framework permits a treatment of these frequency-based lenition effects if we assume that the representation of forms targeted by the lenition process changes at a rate commensurate with the absolute number of times we encounter that form.

Bybee (2005) has also recently suggested that fine phonetic details of specific instances of speech are retained in lexical representations. In Bybee's model, individual tokens/exemplars are stored in memory and the frequency of these tokens accounts for resistance to morphological leveling (e.g. *keep/kept~*keeped* versus *weep/wept~weeped*), phonetic reduction (e.g. the frequent *I don't know*), and grammaticalization (e.g. *gonna* < "going to" from the general motion verb construction *journeying to*, *returning to*, *going to*, etc.; Bybee, 1998; 1999; 2005). The notion that acoustic-phonetic variability in speech needs to be captured and represented in some fashion in linguistic representations to reflect actual experience has been taken up by several other proposals in generative linguistics (see Steriade, 2001a; 2001b; papers in Hume and Johnson, 2001).

At this point, most of the proposals incorporating the strengths of exemplar-based accounts and accounts using abstract representations are in the speech production domain. Johnson (1997; 2005) has also proposed a model of speech perception that stores exemplars and therefore does not lose any token-specific details such as information about a talker's voice. While this proposal is consistent with the large body of results discussed in section 1.3.2, it is not at present integrated with a view in which sublexical information—abstracted over the stored exemplars—is represented separately by the language processing system. In short, while there are several exciting and promising new research directions, a full account of the wide body of data discussed in this chapter remains an active area of inquiry.

1.6 **Representations and mechanisms in spoken word recognition**

The discussion has so far focused on lexical and sublexical representations of speech without addressing the specific processing mechanisms involved in spoken word recognition. This section discusses several mechanisms of spoken word recognition proposed in the literature, and the types of representations associated with these mechanisms.

As discussed earlier, the traditional symbol-processing approach to spoken word recognition has a long history dating back to the early days of telephone communications (Allen, 1994; 2005; Fletcher, 1953). The principal assumption of this bottom-up approach to spoken language processing is that spoken words are recognized by recovering and identifying sequences of phonemes from the acoustic-phonetic information present in the speech waveform. If a listener could recognize and recover the phonemes from the speech waveform, she would be successful in perceiving the component words and understanding the talker's intended message (Allen, 2005). As foreshadowed in section 1.2.2, the primary problem of this bottom-up approach is its inability to deal with the enormous amount of acoustic-phonetic variability that exists in the speech waveform.

The bottom-up, "segmental view" of spoken word recognition was fundamentally transformed by Marslen-Wilson and his colleagues (Marslen-Wilson and Welsh, 1978), who argued convincingly that the primary objective of the human language comprehension system is the recognition of spoken words rather than the identification of individual phonemes in the speech waveform (see also Blesser, 1972). Marslen-Wilson proposed that the level at which lexical processing and word recognition are carried out in language comprehension should be viewed as the functional locus of the interaction between the initial bottom-up sensory input in the speech signal and the listener's contextual-linguistic knowledge of the structure of language. Thus, spoken word recognition was elevated to a special and privileged status within the conceptual framework of the Cohort Theory of spoken language processing developed by Marslen-Wilson and his colleagues (Marslen-Wilson, 1984). Speech perception is thus no longer simply phoneme perception, but the process of recognizing spoken words and understanding sentences. In Cohort Theory, segments and phonemes "emerge" from the process of lexical recognition and selection. Lexical segmentation, then, may actually be viewed as a natural by-product of the primary lexical recognition process itself (Reddy, 1975).

Closely related to Cohort Theory is the Neighborhood Activation Model (NAM) developed by Luce and Pisoni (1998). NAM confronts the acoustic-phonetic invariance problem more directly by assuming that a listener recognizes a word "relationally" in terms of oppositions and contrasts with phonologically similar words. Like the Cohort Model, the focus on spoken word recognition in NAM avoids the long-standing problem of recognizing individual phonemes and features of words directly by locating and identifying invariant acoustic-phonetic properties. A key methodological tool of NAM has been the use of a simple similarity metric for estimating phonological distances of words using a one-phoneme substitution rule (Greenberg and Jenkins, 1964; Pisoni et al., 1985). This computational method has provided an efficient way of quantifying the "perceptual similarity" between words in terms of phonological contrasts among minimal pairs.

As Luce and McLennan (2005) have recently noted in their discussion of the challenges of variation in speech perception and language processing, all contemporary models of spoken word recognition assume that speech signals are represented in memory using traditional abstract representational formats consisting of discrete features, allophones, or phonemes. Current models of spoken word recognition also routinely assume that individual words are represented discretely. All of the current models also assume that the mental lexicon contains abstract idealized word "types" that have been normalized and made equivalent to some standard representation. None of the current models encode or store specific instances of individual word "tokens" or detailed perceptual episodes of speech (but see Goldinger, 1998; Kapatsinski, 2006 for an alternative). Not only are the segments and features of individual words abstract, but the lexical representations of words and possible nonwords are assumed to consist of abstract types, not specific experienced tokens.

An exception to this general pattern of thinking about speech as a sequence of abstract symbols was the LAFS model proposed by Klatt (1979). The LAFS model assumed that words were represented in the mental lexicon as sequences of power spectra in a large multidimensional acoustic space without postulating intermediate phonetic representations or abstract symbols (also see Treisman 1978a; 1978b). The recognition process in LAFS is carried out directly by mapping the power spectra of sound patterns onto words without traditional linguistic features or an intermediate level of analysis corresponding to discrete segments or features. While this approach successfully incorporates the details of perceptual experiences in the representations and mechanisms of spoken word recognition, it misses the critical generalizations available to the proposals that include abstract lexical and sublexical representations.

1.7 **Conclusions**

Evidence from a wide variety of studies suggests that highly detailed perceptual traces representing both the "medium" (detailed source information) and the "message" (linguistic content of the utterance) of the speech signal are encoded and stored in memory for later retrieval in the service of word recognition, lexical access, and spoken language comprehension. A record of the processing operations and procedures used in perceptual analysis and recognition remains after the primary recognition process has been completed, and this residual information is used again when the same source information is encountered in another utterance. The fine phonetic details of the individual talker's articulation in production of speech are not lost or discarded as a result of early perceptual processing; instead, human listeners retain dynamic information about the sensory-motor procedures and the perceptual operations. This information becomes an integral part of the neural and cognitive representation of speech in long-term lexical memory. The representation of speech is not an either/or phenomenon where abstraction and detailed instance-specific exemplars are mutually exclusive; evidence exists for both detailed episodic traces and abstract representations of sound structure, and both must be represented in memory.

The most important and distinctive property of speech perception is its perceptual robustness in the face of diverse physical stimuli over a wide range of environmental conditions. Listeners adapt very quickly and effortlessly to changes in speaker, dialect, and speaking rate, and are able to adjust rapidly to acoustic degradations that introduce significant physical perturbations to the speech signal without apparent loss of performance. Investigating these remarkable perceptual, cognitive, and linguistic abilities, and understanding how the human listener recognizes spoken words so quickly and efficiently despite enormous variability in the physical signal and in listening conditions, is the major challenge for future research in speech perception and spoken word recognition.

Acknowledgments

Preparation of this chapter was supported by grants from the National Institutes of Health to Indiana University (NIH-NIDCD T32 Training Grant DC-00012 and NIH-NIDCD Research Grant R01 DC-00111). We wish to thank Cynthia Clopper, Daniel Dinnsen, Robert Goldstone, Vsevolod Kapatsinski, Conor McLennan, Robert Port, Steve Winters and especially Adam Buchwald for invaluable discussions and comments on this chapter.

References

Abler, W. L. (1989) On the particulate principle of self-diversifying systems. *Journal of Social Biological Structure*, 12: 113.

Allen, J. B. (1994) How do humans process and recognizer speech? *IEEE Trans. Speech Audio*, 2: 567–77.

Allen, J. B. (2005) *Articulation and intelligibility*. Morgan & Claypool, San Rafael.

Allen, J. S., and Miller, J. L. (2004) Listener sensitivity to individual talker differences in voice-onset-time. *Journal of the Acoustical Society of America*, 115: 3171–83.

Beer, R. D. (2000) Dynamical approaches to cognitive science. *Trends in Cognitive Sciences*, 4: 91–9.

Blesser, B. (1972) Speech perception under conditions of spectral transformations, I: Phonetic characteristics. *Journal of Speech and Hearing Research*, 15: 5–41.

Bond, Z. S. (2005) Slips of the ear. In D. B. Pisoni and R. E. Remez (eds), *The Handbook of Speech Perception*, pp. 290–310. Blackwell, Oxford, UK.

Bond, Z. S., and Garnes, S. (1980) Misperceptions of fluent speech. In R. A. Cole (ed.), *Perception and Production of Fluent Speech*. pp. 115–32. Erlbaum, Hillsdale, NJ.

Bond, Z. S., and Robey, R. R. (1983) The phonetic structure of errors in the perception of fluent speech. In N. J. U. Lass (ed.), *Speech and Language: Advances in Basic Research and Practice* (vol. 9), pp. 249–83. Academic Press, New York.

Bricker, P. D., and Pruzansky, S. (1976) Speaker recognition. In N. J. Lass (ed.), *Contemporary Issues in Experimental Phonetics*, pp. 295–326. Academic Press, New York.

Brooks, L. (1978) Non-analytic concept formation and memory for instances. In E. Rosch and B. Lloyd (eds), *Cognition and Categorization*, 169–211. Erlbaum, Hillsdale, NJ.

Brooks, R. A. (1991a) New approaches to robotics. *Science*, 253(5025): 1227–32.

Brooks, R. A. (1991b) Intelligence without representation. *Artificial Intelligence*, 47: 139–59.

Buchwald, A. B. (2005) Sound structure representation, repair, and well-formedness: Grammar in spoken language production. Ph.D. dissertation, Johns Hopkins University.

Bybee, J. L. (1998) The emergent lexicon. *Chicago Linguistic Society*, 34: 421–35.

Bybee, J. L. (1999) Usage-based phonology. In M. Darnell, E. Moravcsik, F. Newmeyer, M. Noonan, and K. Wheatley (eds), *Functionalism and Formalism in Linguistics*, vol. II: *Case Studies*, pp. 211–42. Benjamins, Amsterdam, Netherlands.

Bybee, J. (2001) *Phonology and Language Use*. Cambridge University Press, Cambridge.

Bybee, J. L. (2005) The impact of use on representation: grammar is usage and usage is grammar. Presidential address, Annual Meeting of the Linguistic Society of America, Oakland, CA.

Chomsky, N. and Halle, M. (1968) *The Sound Pattern of English*. Harper & Row, New York.

Chomsky, N. and Miller, G. A. (1963) Introduction to the formal analysis of natural languages. In R. D. Luce, R. Bush, and E. Galanter (eds), *Handbook of Mathematical Psychology*, vol. 2, pp. 269–321. Wiley, New York.

Clark, A. (1997) *Being There: Putting Brain, Body, and World Together Again*. MIT Press, Cambridge, MA.

Clark, A. (1999) An embodied cognitive science? *Trends in Cognitive Sciences*, 3: 345–51.

Creelman, C. D. (1957) Case of the unknown talker. *Journal of the Acoustical Society of America*, 29: 655.

Dell, G. (1984) Representation of serial order in speech: Evidence from the repeated phoneme effect in speech errors. *Journal of Experimental Psychology: Learning, Memory and Cognition*, 10: 222–33.

Dell, G. (1986) A spreading activation theory of retrieval in sentence processing. *Psychological Review*, 93: 283–321.

Eisner, F., and McQueen, J. M. (2005) The specificity of perceptual learning in speech processing. *Perception and Psychophysics*, 67: 224–38.

Elman, J. L. (2004) An alternative view of the mental lexicon. *TRENDS in Cognitive Sciences*, 8: 301–6.

Elman, J. L., and McClelland, J. L. (1986) Exploiting lawful variability in the speech waveform. In J. S. Perkell and D. H. Klatt (eds), *Invariance and Variability in Speech Processing*, pp. 360–85. Erlbaum, Hillsdale, NJ.

Estes, W. K. (1994) *Classification and Cognition*. Oxford University Press, New York.

Fletcher, H. (1953) *Speech and Hearing in Communication*. Krieger, Huntington, NY.

Fowler, C. A. (1990) Listener–talker attunements in speech. *Haskins Laboratories Status Report on Speech Research*, 101:–2, 110–29.

Gautier, I., and Tarr, M. J. (2002) Unraveling mechanisms for expert object recognition: bridging brain activity and behavior. *Journal of Experimental Psychology: Human Perception and Performance*, 28: 431–46.

Glanzer, M., Hilford, A., and Kim, K. (2004) Six regularities of source recognition. *Journal of Experimental Psychology: Learning, Memory, and Cognition*, 30: 1176–95.

Gleason, H. A. (1961) *An Introduction to Descriptive Linguistics*. Holt, Rinehart, & Winston, New York.

Goggin, J. P., Thompson, C. P., Strube, G., and Simental, L. R. (1991) The role of language familiarity in voice identification. *Memory and Cognition*, 19: 448–58.

Goldinger, S. D. (1996) Words and voices: episodic traces in spoken word identification and recognition memory. *Journal of Experimental Psychology: Learning, Memory, and Cognition*, 22: 1166–83.

Goldinger, S. D. (1997) Talker variability in speech processing. In K. Johnson and J. W. Mullennix (eds), *Talker Variability in Speech Processing*, pp. 33–66. Academic Press, San Diego.

Goldinger, S. D. (1998) Echoes of echoes? An episodic theory of lexical access. *Psychological Review*, 105: 251–79.

Goldinger, S. D., and Azuma, T. (2003). Puzzle-solving science: the quixotic quest for units in speech perception. *Journal of Phonetics*, 31: 305–20.

Goldinger, S. D., Pisoni, D. B., and Logan, J. S. (1991) On the locus of talker variability effects in recall of spoken word lists. *Journal of Experimental Psychology: Learning, Memory, and Cognition*, 17: 152–62.

Greenberg, J. H., and Jenkins, J. J. (1964) Studies in the psychological correlates of the sound system of American English. *Word*, 20: 157–77.

Halle, M. (1956) Review of *Manual of Phonology* by C. D. Hockett. *Journal of the Acoustical Society of America*, 28: 509–10.

Hockett, C. D. (1960) The origin of speech. *Scientific American*, 203: 88–96.

Hockett, C. F. (1955) *Manual of Phonology*. Indiana University, Bloomington.

Hooper, J. D. (1976) Word frequency in lexical diffusion and the source of morphophonological change. In W. Christie (ed.), *Current Progress in Historical Linguistics*, pp. 96–105. North-Holland, Amsterdam.

Hume, E. (2000) http://www.ling.ohio-state.edu/~ehume/metathesis/index.html)

Hume, E., and Johnson, K. (eds) (2001) *The Role of Speech Perception in Phonology*. Academic Press, San Diego.

Jacoby, L. L., and Brooks, L. R. (1984) Non-analytic cognition: memory, perception, and concept learning. In G. Bower (ed.), *The Psychology of Learning and Motivation*, pp. 1–47. Academic Press, New York.

Jaeger, J. (1992) Phonetic features in young children's slips of the tongue. *Language and Speech*, 35: 189–205.

Jaeger, J. J. (2005) *Kids' Slips: What Young Children's Slips of the Tongue Reveal about Language Development*. Erlbaum, Mahwah, NJ.

Jenkins, J. J., Strange, W., and Trent, S. A. (1999) Context-independent dynamic information for the perception of coarticulated vowels. *Journal of the Acoustical Society of America*, 106: 438–448.

Johnson, K. (1997) Speech perception without speaker normalization: an exemplar model. In K. Johnson and J. W. Mullennix (eds), *Talker Variability in Speech Processing*, pp. 145–66. Academic Press, San Diego, CA.

Johnson, K. (2005) Resonance in an exemplar-based lexicon: the emergence of social identity and phonology. *UC Berkeley Phonology Lab Annual Report*, 95–128.

Johnson, M. K., Hashtroudi, S., and Lindsay, D. S. (1993) Source monitoring. *Psychological Bulletin*, 114: 3–28.

Joos, M. A. (1948) Acoustic phonetics. *Language*, 24: 1–136.

Kakehi, K. (1992) Adaptability to differences between talkers in Japanese monosyllabic perception. In Y. Tohkura, E. Vatikiotis-Bateson, and Y. Sagisaka (eds), *Speech Perception, Production, and Linguistic Structure*, pp. 135–42. Ohmsha, Tokyo.

Kapatsinski, V. M. (2006) Towards a single-mechanism account of frequency effects. *Proceedings of LACUS 32: Networks*, pp. 325–35. Hanover, NH.

Klatt, D. H. (1979). Speech perception: a model of acoustic-phonetic analysis and lexical access. *Journal of Phonetics*, 7: 279–312.

Klatt, D. H. (1986) The problem of variability in speech recognition and in models of speech perception. In J. S. Perkell and D. H. Klatt (eds), *Invariance and Variability in Speech Processing*, pp. 300–19. Erlbaum, Hillsdale, NJ.

Kolers, P. A. (1973) Remembering operations. *Memory and Cognition*, 1: 347–55.

Kolers, P. A. (1976) Pattern-analyzing memory. *Science*, 191: 1280–81.

Krajlic, T., and Samuel, A. G. (2005) Perceptual learning for speech: is there a return to normal? *Cognitive Psychology*, 51: 141–78.

Kruschke, J. K. (1992) ALCOVE: an exemplar-based connectionist model of category learning. *Psychological Review*, 99: 22–44.

Liberman, A. M., Cooper, F. S., Shankweiler, D. P., and Studdert-Kennedy, M. (1967) Perception of the speech code. *Psychological Review*, 74: 431–61.

Liberman, A. M., Delattre, P. C., Cooper, F. S., and Gerstman, L. J. (1954) The role of consonant–vowel transitions in the perception of the stop and nasal consonants. *Psychological Monographs*, 68: 1–13.

Licklider, J. C. R. (1952) On the process of speech perception. *Journal of the Acoustical Society of America*, 24: 590–94.

Lindgren, N. (1965) Machine recognition of human language. *IEEE Spectrum*, Mar. and Apr.

Luce, P. A., and McLennan, C. T. (2005) Spoken word recognition: the challenge of variation. In D. B. Pisoni and R. E. Remez (eds), *The Handbook of Speech Perception*, pp. 591–609. Blackwell, Oxford.

Luce, P. A., and Pisoni, D. B. (1998) Recognizing spoken words: the Neighborhood Activation Model. *Ear and Hearing*, 19: 1–36.

MacKay, D. G. (1970) Spoonerisms: the structure of errors in the serial order of speech. *Neuropsychologia*, 8: 323–50.

Markman, A. B., and Dietrich, E. (2000). Extending the classical view of representation. *Trends in Cognitive Sciences* 4: 470–75.

Marslen-Wilson, W. D. (1984) Function and process in spoken word recognition: a tutorial review. In H. Bouma and D. G. Bouwhis (eds), *Attention and Performance X: Control of Language Processes*, pp. 125–50. Erlbaum, Hillsdale, NJ.

Marslen-Wilson, W. D., and Welsh, A. (1978) Processing interactions and lexical access during word recognition in continuous speech. *Cognitive Psychology*, 10: 29–63.

Martin, C. S., Mullennix, J. W., Pisoni, D. B., and Summers, W. V. (1989) Effects of talker variability on recall of spoken word lists. *Journal of Experimental Psychology: Learning, Memory and Cognition*, 15: 676–84.

Miller, G. A., Heise, G. A., and Lichten, W. (1951) The intelligibility of speech as a function of the context of the test material. *Journal of Experimental Psychology*, 41: 329–35.

Mitchell, K. J., and Johnson, M. K. (2000) Source monitoring: attributing mental experiences. In E. Tulving and F. I. M. Craik (eds), *The Oxford Handbook of Memory*, pp. 179–85. Oxford University Press, New York.

Morton, J. (1979) Word recognition. In J. Morton and J. C. Marshall (eds), *Structures and Processes*, pp. 108–56. MIT Press, Cambridge, MA.

Mullennix, J. W., and Pisoni, D. B. (1990) Stimulus variability and processing dependencies in speech perception. *Perception and Psychophysics*, 47: 379–90.

Mullennix J. W., Pisoni, D. B., and Martin, C. S. (1989) Some effects of talker variability on spoken word recognition. *Journal of the Acoustical Society of America*, 85: 365–78.

Murphy, G. L. (2002) *The Big Book of Concepts*. MIT Press, Cambridge, MA.

Nooteboom, S. G. (1969) The tongue slips into patterns. In A. A. van Raad (ed.), *Leyden Studies in Linguistics and Phonetics*, pp. 114–32. Mouton, The Hague.

Nosofsky, R. M. (1986). Attention, similarity, and the identification-categorization relationship. *Journal of Experimental Psychology: General*, 115: 39–57.

Nygaard, L. C., Sommers, M. S., and Pisoni, D. B. (1992) Effects of speaking rate and talker variability on the representation of spoken words in memory. *Proceedings 1992 International Conference on Spoken Language Processing*, Banff, Canada, Oct. 12–16, pp. 209–12.

Nygaard, L. C., Sommers, M. S., and Pisoni, D. B. (1994) Speech perception as a talker-contingent process. *Psychological Science*, 5: 42–6.

Oldfield, R. C. (1966) Things, words and the brain. *Quarterly Journal of Experimental Psychology*, 18: 340–53.

Palmeri, T. J., Goldinger, S. D., and Pisoni, D. B. (1993) Episodic encoding of voice attributes and recognition memory for spoken words. *Journal of Experimental Psychology: Learning, Memory, and Cognition*, 19: 309–28.

Pardo, J. S., and Remez, R. E. (2006) The perception of speech. In M. Traxler and M. A. Gernsbacher (eds), *The Handbook of Psycholinguistics*, Elsevier, New York.

Peters, R. W. (1955) The relative intelligibility of single-voice and multiple-voice messages under various conditions of noise (Joint Project Report No. 56, pp. 1–9). US Naval School of Aviation Medicine, Pensacola, FL.

Peterson, G. (1952) The information-bearing elements of speech. *Journal of the Acoustical Society of America*, 24, 629–37.

Peterson, G. E., and Barney, H. L. (1952) Control methods used in a study of the vowels. *Journal of the Acoustical Society of America*, 24: 175–84.

Pierrehumbert, J. B. (2001) Exemplar dynamics: word frequency, lenition and contrast. In J. Bybee and P. Hopper (eds), *Frequency and the Emergence of Linguistic Structure*, pp. 137–58. Benjamins, Amsterdam.

Pierrehumbert, J. B., and Pierrehumbert, R. T. (1990) On attributing grammars to dynamical systems. *Journal of Phonetics*, 18: 465–77.

Pisoni, D. B. (1993) Long-term memory in speech perception: some new findings on talker variability, speaking rate and perceptual learning. *Speech Communication*, 13: 109–25.

Pisoni, D. B. (1997) Some thoughts on "normalization" in speech perception. In K. Johnson and J. W. Mullennix (eds), *Talker Variability in Speech Processing*, pp. 9–32. Academic Press, San Diego.

Pisoni, D. B., and Luce, P. A. (1987) Acoustic-phonetic representations in word recognition. *Cognition*, 25: 21–52.

Pisoni, D. B., Nusbaum, H. C., Luce, P. A., and Slowiaczek, L. M. (1985) Speech perception, word recognition and the structure of the lexicon. *Speech Communication*, 4: 75–95.

Pisoni, D. B., and Remez, R. E. (eds) (2005) *The Handbook of Speech Perception*. Blackwell, Malden, MA.

Pollack, I. (1952) The information of elementary auditory displays. *Journal of the Acoustical Society of America*, 24: 745–9.

Pollack, I. (1953) The information of elementary auditory displays II. *Journal of the Acoustical Society of America*, 25: 765–9.

Port, R., and Leary, A. (2005) Against formal phonology. *Language*, 81: 927–64.

Pouplier, M. (2003. Units of phonological encoding: empirical evidence. Ph.D. dissertation, Yale University.

Prince, A., and Smolensky, P. (1993/2004) Optimality Theory: constraint interaction in generative grammar (technical report). Rutgers University, New Brunswick and University of Colorado, Boulder.

Raphael, L. J. (2005) Acoustic cues to the perception of segmental phonemes. In D. B. Pisoni and R. E. Remez (eds), *The Handbook of Speech Perception*, pp. 182–206. Blackwell, Oxford.

Reddy, R. D. (1975) *Speech Recognition*. Academic Press, New York.

Remez, R. E., Rubin, P. E., Pisoni, D. B., and Carrell, T. D. (1981) Speech perception without traditional speech cues. *Science*, 212(4497): 947–50.

Rhodes, G., Byatt, G., Michie, P. T., and Puce, A. (2004) Is the fusiform face area specialized for faces, individuation, or expert individuation? *Journal of Cognitive Neuroscience*, 16: 189–203.

Roediger, H. L. (1990) Implicit memory: retention without remembering. *American Psychologist*, 45: 1043–56.

Schacter, D. L. (1990) Perceptual representation systems and implicit memory: toward a resolution of the multiple memory systems debate. *Annals of the New York Academy of Sciences*, 608, 543–71.

Schacter, D. L. (1992) Understanding implicit memory: a cognitive neuroscience approach. *American Psychologist*, 47: 559–69.

Shannon, R. V., Zeng, F. G., Kamath, V., Wygonski, J., and Ekelid, M. (1995) Speech recognition with primarily temporal cues. *Science*, 270(5234): 303–4.

Smith, E. E., and Medin, D. (1981) *Categories and Concepts*. Harvard University Press, Cambridge, MA.

Sommers, M. S., Nygaard, L. C., and Pisoni, D. B. (1992) Stimulus variability and the perception of spoken words: effects of variations in speaking rate and overall amplitude. *Proceedings 1992 International Conference on Spoken Language Processing*, Banff, Canada, Oct. 12–16, pp. 217–20.

Stemberger, J. P. (1990). Wordshape errors in language production. *Cognition*, 35: 123–57.

Steriade, D. (2001a) Directional asymmetries in place assimilation: a perceptual account. In E. Hume and K. Johnson (eds), *The Role of Speech Perception in Phonology*, pp. 219–50, Academic Press, San Diego.

Steriade, D. (2001b) The phonology of Perceptibility Effects: the P-map and its consequences for constraint organization. MS, UCLA.

Sullivan, K. P. H., and Schlichting, F. (2000) Speaker discrimination in a foreign language: first language environment, second language learners. *Forensic Linguistics*, 7, 95–111.

Thompson, C. P. (1987) A language effect in voice identification. *Applied Cognitive Psychology*, 1: 121–31.

Treisman, M. (1978a) A theory of the identification of complex stimuli with an application to word recognition. *Psychological Review*, 78, 420–25.

Treisman, M. (1978b) Space or lexicon? The word frequency effect and the error response frequency effect. *Journal of Verbal Learning and Verbal Behavior*, 17, 37–59.

Tulving, E., and Schacter, D. L. (1990). Priming and human memory systems. *Science*, 247, 301–6.

Twaddell, W. F. (1952) Phonemes and allophones in speech analysis. *Journal of the Acoustical Society of America*, 24: 607–11.

Winters, S. J., Levi, S. V., and Pisoni, D. B. (2006). The role of linguistic competence in cross-linguistic speaker identification. Talk presented at the 80th annual meeting of the Linguistics Society of America, Albuquerque, NM.

CHAPTER 2

Audiovisual speech perception and word recognition

Dominic W. Massaro and Alexandra Jesse[1]

2.1 Introduction

The goal of this chapter is to describe how our understanding of speech benefits from having the speaker's face present, and how this benefit makes transparent the nature of speech perception and word recognition. When observing modern life with the omnipresence of mobile phones, voice messaging, and streaming over the internet using VOIP, one might erroneously think of speech communication as becoming a purely auditory phenomenon. Although speaker and listener still often face each other in situations in which communication is not aided by technology, modern technology freed us from the need to talk to each other in person. Certainly, these modern communication methods find a wide acceptance, but people are reluctant to forfeit face-to-face communication.

The preference for face-to-face communication might have little to do with language understanding but could simply reflect a preference for direct human contact. However, there is evidence that our preference for talking to each other face-to-face is not only for this social norm but actually serves the purpose of providing information that aids understanding the communicated message. The face in communication is valuable for several reasons: emotion is better understood with the face presented along with the voice (Ellison and Massaro, 1997; de Gelder and Vroomen 2000; Massaro and Egan, 1996; Vroomen et al., 2001); many back-channeling and turn-taking cues essential for effective and efficient dialog are apparent in the face, gestures, and body; and of course the face adds to the intelligibility of the conversation (see Massaro, 1998 for an overview). Thus, face-to-face communication is the ideal venue for seamless exchanges among interlocutors.

If visual speech in communication is available, then an important question is if and when it is used as source of information for audiovisual speech recognition. Proponents of so-called auditory dominance (Sekiyama and Tohkura, 1991; 1993) have argued that visual speech merely is a back-up source when the auditory signal is not sufficient for recognition. However, this notion has been falsified by research showing that information from the face is used whenever available, even when the auditory signal itself is not ambiguous (McGurk and MacDonald, 1976) and when participants are instructed to ignore all visual information in their judgment (Massaro, 1987) or are instructed to simply report what they heard (McGurk and MacDonald, 1976). Furthermore, the information provided by the visual signal is not completely redundant, because the addition of visual information improves spoken word recognition above and beyond the

[1] Alexandra Jesse is now at the Max Planck Institute for Psycholinguistics, 6500 AH Nijmegen, The Netherlands.

level of performance predicted by pure redundancy (Massaro, 1998: ch. 14). People generally benefit from having visual speech available (Jesse et al., 2000/2001; MacLeod and Summerfield, 1987; Massaro and Bosseler, 2003; Sumby and Pollack, 1954), not just those with hearing loss. And as noted by Summerfield (1987: 3), bimodal speech perception "provides an opportunity to study the perception and memory of speech through a novel modality, and audio-visual speech perception provides the opportunity to study two perceptual systems working in collaboration to analyze the phonetic events." Therefore, an account of spoken word recognition needs to consider the role of visual information in speech communication.

This chapter will give an overview of the main research questions and findings unique to audiovisual speech perception research as well as discussing what general questions about speech perception and cognition the research in this field can answer. The influence of a second perceptual source in audiovisual speech perception compared to auditory speech perception immediately necessitates the question of how the information from the different perceptual sources is used to reach the best overall decision. This need to process multiple sources of information also exists in auditory speech perception, however. For example, as described in the chapter by McQueen (Chapter 3, this volume), acoustic cues and context information are naturally combined to determine the overall percept. Audiovisual speech simply shifts the focus from intramodal to intermodal sources. As we will see in section 2.3, these two forms of processing are not necessarily qualitatively different from each other. It is essential, however, that a model of speech perception operationalizes the concept of processing multiple sources of information so that quantitative predictions can be made. The main theoretical approaches to explain integration and audiovisual speech perception are introduced and critically discussed. Furthermore, this chapter provides an overview of the role of visual speech as a language learning tool in multimodal training.

2.2 **Information and information processing in audiovisual speech perception**

The most basic finding in research on audiovisual speech perception is that adding visual speech to auditory speech improves performance substantially. The audiovisual benefit, for example for bisyllabic words, is comparable to a 15 dB change in signal-to-noise ratio (Sumby and Pollack, 1954; as reported in Grant and Seitz, 2000). Some researchers (Grant and Seitz, 2000) hypothesize that this benefit could be even larger for continuous speech material, since visual speech could be informative about word boundaries, prosody, and stress patterns. Indeed, the correlation between visual-only recognition and audiovisual recognition scores is higher for sentences than for single consonants (Grant et al., 1998). The audiovisual benefit has been shown for speech items ranging from single syllables (e.g. Massaro et al., 1993a) to words (e.g. de la Vaux and Massaro, 2004; Sumby and Pollack, 1954), sentences (Jesse et al., 2000/2001; MacLeod and Summerfield, 1987), and even paragraphs (Reisberg et al., 1987). Although this benefit can be most easily observed when auditory speech recognition is impaired by noise, even intact auditory speech benefits from additional visual speech information (Arnold and Hill, 2001; Reisberg et al., 1987).

There is no doubt that, in general, auditory speech is more informative than visible speech. But the audiovisual recognition benefit emerges from both the complementary and redundant nature of visual and auditory speech information (see e.g. Walden et al., 1974). Auditory-visual speech complementarity means that one modality is more informative on those dimensions on which the other modality is less informative. For example, information about the manner of articulation (e.g. /ba/ vs. /ma/) and about voicing (e.g. /pa/ vs. /ba/) is easier to distinguish acoustically than visually (Massaro, 1987; 1998; Summerfield, 1987). Voicing information is fairly robust in the auditory signal even if noise is added, whereas little voicing information can be found in the visual signal. On the other hand, information about the place of articulation is highly confusable in auditory speech (e.g. /ma/ vs. /na/; Miller and Nicely, 1955), but not very confusable in visual speech. In addition, auditory place information is particularly vulnerable to the addition of auditory noise (Miller and Nicely, 1955). As a consequence of this complementarity, we would expect a lower audiovisual benefit if the response alternatives in a study share the same place of articulation than if they are relatively distinguishable on the basis of the place of articulation. This audiovisual benefit should be especially easier to show with noise added to the auditory speech signal.

There is also evidence that the two perceptual sources of information even provide complementary information about different subsets of a linguistic feature: The auditory signal seems to provide mostly information about the place of articulation for middle or back consonants, whereas the visual signal is mostly informative about the place of articulation of labial consonants (Jesse, 2005). Psychoacoustically, an alveolar segment like /d/ is highly discriminable because there may be less upward masking of the second formant by the first (Tillmann, 1985, pers. comm.), whereas a labial segment like /b/ is similar to /v/ and /ð/. Visually, the open mouth for /d/ is less prominent than the labial closure for /b/; furthermore, there is less uncertainty for /b/ because there are many more segments articulated with an open mouth than with a labial closure.

In addition to the complementarity of auditory and visual speech, the audiovisual benefit also arises from the redundancy of visual and auditory speech (Walden et al., 1974). Two redundant observations are always beneficial relative to just one if they are analyzed in the appropriate way. For example, although place information is available through visual information about mouth closure, place information is also provided by the formant structure in the auditory signal. Summerfield (1987) observes the existence of unique multimodal cues as a third reason for the existence of an audiovisual benefit. For example, in order to detect if a plosive is voiced or voiceless, the time between seeing the release of the plosive and hearing the onset of the vocal cord vibration is informative about perceiving voicing onset. On the other hand, either of these properties independently is insufficient to make a reliable voicing categorization. This audiovisual benefit arises from the time between the onset of the auditory information about the vocal cord vibration and the visual information of seeing the release of the stop consonant. Breeuwer and Plomp (1986) showed that for plosives in a vowel–consonant–vowel context the voicing feature is more accurately recognized when bimodal rather than unimodal information is provided. The presented auditory information was a sequence of glottal pulses that can be assumed to provide no information by itself about the identity of the presented consonant. The visual condition alone showed only poor performance levels that were near chance. However, adding the pulses to the visual presentation of the speaker significantly improved recognition.

The size of the audiovisual benefit therefore depends on the distribution of information within and between these two modalities, or, more specifically, on the degree of redundancy, complementarity, and audiovisual uniqueness. However, the audiovisual benefit depends not only on the available *information*, i.e. the decrease in ambiguity through the signal presentation about the nature of the percept (Shannon, 1948), but also on the *processing* of the information (Massaro and Cohen, 1999). Perceivers differ in their ability to recognize unimodal auditory and unimodal visual speech, so that these performance levels have to be taken into account when assessing if they also differ in their skill in integrating both sources of information in audiovisual speech. The question of whether or not all the information available to the perceiver is integrated can only be answered if we also know the information that is available to the perceiver. In addition, we would need to know if a poor result is due to poor integration or to other processing factors, such as limited working memory capacity or difficulties in application of linguistic knowledge, or if it is due to less auditory and/or visual information (Grant et al., 1998).

Generally, perceivers are fairly good at extracting and using information from the face. This is a robust phenomenon that can be found even when visual information is degraded, as is the case when the perceiver is not directly facing the speaker, the facial image is blurred, or is viewed from a large distance (Campbell and Massaro, 1997; Erber 1971; 1974; Jordan and Sergeant, 2000; MacDonald et al., 2000; Massaro, 1998; Munhall et al., 2004; Vitkovich and Barber, 1994). The pervasiveness and obligatory nature of the integration of visual and auditory speech was revealed by studies that showed that integration occurs even when the perceiver is instructed to ignore either the auditory or the visual information (Massaro, 1987); or if the visual and auditory information is temporally misaligned (Campbell and Dodd, 1980; Massaro and Cohen, 1993a; Massaro et al., 1996; Munhall et al., 1996; van Wassenhove, 2004).

The perceiver also integrates auditory and visual speech that is phonetically mismatched (McGurk and MacDonald, 1976). This phenomenon has been widely studied, mostly with the aid of the McGurk effect. In the McGurk illusion, an auditory /ba/ is presented together with a mismatching visual /ga/. The perceiver, however, will often have the illusion of perceiving a /da/, /va/, or /ða/ (Massaro, 1998). People are not always consciously aware of the mismatch, and will fall victim to this illusion even when instructed to ignore the lips (Summerfield and McGrath, 1984), when the gender of voice and face mismatch (Green et al., 1991), or even when silently producing one sound segment while listening to someone else's mismatching voice over headphones (Sams et al., 2005). A simplified explanation of the McGurk fusion is that the alveolar /d/ is a compromise of the contradicting place information from the bilabial /b/ and the velar /g/ (however, see Massaro, 1998).

The McGurk effect has been extensively studied (see e.g. Green and Gerdman, 1995; Green et al., 1991; MacDonald and McGurk, 1978; Mills and Thiem, 1980; Rosenblum et al., 1997; Sams et al., 1997; Sekiyama and Tohkura, 1991; 1993). The McGurk illusion gives also insight concerning the distribution of information over time. Other than fusion responses (e.g. /da/), the combination response /bda/ is also common when an auditory /da/ is presented with a visual /ba/. However, the mismatching information of a visual /ba/ and an auditory /da/ is not usually perceived as the combination /dba/. This might be because place information about /ba/ is available earlier in the visual than in the auditory signal (Massaro and Cohen, 1993a; Smeele, 1994). However, it is important to note that data obtained from the McGurk effect is not usually in an informative range to evaluate models of integration (Massaro, 2003; Schwartz, 2003). A more informative paradigm to evaluate the validity of quantitative models of integration is provided by experiments that create ambiguity by creating a continuum between two endpoint speech segments *within* a modality which are then presented as orthogonal audiovisual combinations. An expanded factorial design (Massaro, 1998) includes unimodal conditions in addition to these audiovisual combinations.

Other questions regarding integration are *when* the visual and auditory speech information is integrated and what the window of integration is. A late integration process would first categorize the information provided by each perceptual source before integration occurs. In comparison, an early integration process would integrate the support provided by the two sources of information before recognition occurs. This mechanism would integrate continuous values rather than categorical labels. Behavioral and neuropsychological research provides direct evidence for early integration (Besle et al., 2004; Colin et al., 2002; Schwartz et al., 2004) and also shows that processing models with an early integration mechanism, like the Fuzzy Logical Model of Perception (Massaro, 1998; see section 2.3 below) and the Pre-labeling Model (Braida, 1991), give a better description of audiovisual consonant recognition data than a Post-labeling Model, where only discrete labels are integrated (Braida, 1991).

One of the major challenges in speech recognition is that perceptual information about a single segment unfolds over time rather than being presented instantaneously. Not only are cues for the identity of the speech segment distributed over time, but also there are some dynamic cues in the speech signal (Kewley-Port, 1983; Rosenblum et al., 1996). Information is not packed and aligned like beads on a string. It might be believed that the challenge for the system is to determine what information belongs to which segment in time, and to integrate these pieces of information to recognize speech. In this case, the system has to keep track of all this information for a short period of time and integrate the information belonging to the same percept. This would not be a trivial task, because information given at a certain point in time can be informative about different parts of the utterance. To complicate this issue further, information belonging to the same segment is not always exactly co-occurring in time in the two modalities in audiovisual speech (Munhall and Tohkura, 1998). Often visual information is available earlier than auditory information for a certain segment (Massaro and Cohen, 1993a; Smeele, 1994). For example, if the initial phoneme of an utterance is a bilabial plosive, then the production of a bilabial closure is needed to build up air pressure for the sudden release of the plosive sound. During the production of this bilabial closure, the available visual information (i.e. closing of the lips) is accompanied by silence. Visual information about the place of articulation is available before auditory place of articulation information. Place of articulation is not the only information that is available earlier in the visual signal. Information for the identification of vowels is available earlier in the visual than in the auditory signal (Cathiard et al., 1995).

However, a less intelligent system might be equally successful in combining multiple sources of information in speech perception. Rather than having to keep track of which cues belong to which segments, the system could simply integrate the simultaneously arriving cues to obtain degrees of support for the various segments. A segment that receives successive support across time would emerge as a percept. This interpretation appears to be consistent with the observations that bimodal speech perception is relatively robust with respect to temporal asynchrony between the presentation of information from the two modalities, especially when the visual information leads (Campbell and Dodd, 1980; Massaro and Cohen, 1993a; Massaro et al., 1996; Munhall et al., 1996; van Wassenhove, 2004). Accurate recognition performance persists across small asynchronies and actually improves compared to the aligned condition when visual information leads by about 80 to 120ms (Grant and Greenberg, 2001; Greenberg and Arai, 2004). This might be due to a constraint of the earlier arriving information on the processing of later arriving information. For example, early arriving visual place of articulation information might "prime" (Greenberg and Arai, 2004: 1068) speech representations that share this place of articulation. Visual information would constrain the set of possible word alternatives before auditory information becomes available. For example, if a word like /pin/ is presented with leading visual information, then information about the labial closure is already available before the onset of auditory speech. Visually, labial closure provides information about place and manner of articulation. Therefore, early in processing the candidate set can be restricted to words starting with /b/, /m/, or /p/. Candidates like SIN, FIN, THIN, SHIN, GIN, WIN, TIN, DIN, or KIN could be excluded. As we will see in the next section on word recognition, visual speech information is indeed influencing the set of competing lexical candidates in audiovisual word recognition. By definition, this would have to occur if people successfully lipread the given visual information. The recognition advantage found for leading visual speech (80–120ms) could also be due to increased processing time required by the visual signal relative to that required by the auditory signal. For example, optimal auditory-visual localization occurs when the visual speech is presented 80–120ms before the auditory speech signal (Lewald and Guski, 2003).

2.2.1 The lexicon and word recognition

As we have seen in the previous sections, visual information is not only used whenever available in order to understand spoken language, but also contributes substantially to our understanding. It is therefore self-evident that a full account of spoken word recognition should also consider the role of visual speech information.

While the speech signal unfolds, the incoming information is evaluated in terms of its support for lexical representations (see e.g. Connine et al., 1993; Marslen-Wilson and Zwitserlood, 1989; Shillcock, 1990; Tabossi et al., 1995; Zwitserlood, 1989). The support, and therefore the recognition, of a word is dependent on the degree to which the perceptual input matches the lexical representation of the word and mismatches alternative word candidates (see Gaskell, Chapter 4 this volume; McQueen, Chapter 3 this volume). The contribution of visual speech to audiovisual word recognition should be substantial, since visual speech primarily provides information on the place of articulation of consonants, which is a critical feature in spoken word recognition (Greenberg, 2005). Many words are only distinguishable by the place of articulation of one of their constituent consonants (e.g. met vs. net; Greenberg, 2005). Visual speech should therefore be an important source for lexical recognition.

While the importance of lexical similarity has been widely studied for the recognition of auditory spoken words (see Gaskell, Chapter 4 this volume; McQueen, Chapter 3 this volume; Pisoni and Levi, Chapter 1 this volume), it has only been recently addressed in the recognition of visual spoken words. As in auditory speech, Auer and colleagues (2002; Mattys et al., 2002) found that in a speech-reading task, words with more visually highly confusable competitors are recognized less accurately than words with fewer visual highly confusable competitors. Auer's results were obtained for both deaf and normally hearing adults when presented only with visual speech. This generalizability across participants suggests that the experiment taps into a general process of speech perception. Auditorily based confusability of the target words with competitors could not account for these results. There was no significant correlation between this measure and accuracy for either participant group. This seems to be evidence that the evaluation of the auditory and visual signal are independent processes. It is also in accordance with recent results that the similarity among visual and auditory words is primarily determined by different features (e.g. Jesse, 2005). Therefore, we expect that visual and auditory competitor measures would not strongly correlate.

Auer (2002) failed, however, to find an effect of intelligibility of the segments of a target word. Keeping competitor structure and word frequency constant, a difference in segmental intelligibility of the target word produced only weak effects. Auer argued that this might be due to a restriction of variability in visual confusability. Mattys et al. (2002), on the other hand, presented evidence for the influence of intelligibility of a target word's segments on the word's correct identification by varying the target's lexical equivalence class as a measure of competitor similarity influence (Mattys et al. 2002). A lexical equivalence class (LEC) is a set of words that are visually highly confusable, if not indistinguishable. The LECs are formed on the basis of phoneme equivalence classes (PECs; Auer and Bernstein, 1997). All visual phonemes that are highly confusable with each other are defined as belonging to the same phoneme equivalence class. Or in other words, all highly confusable visual phonemes are members of the same *viseme* class (Fisher, 1968: 800). The cut-off point here is arbitrarily chosen so that 75 percent of all confusion responses to a phoneme fall within its PEC. The LEC of a word has less uncertainty than can be estimated from the PECs of a word. This is the case because not all members of one PEC are permissible in a word context. For example, if a word has a phoneme from a PEC of three phonemes, but only two out of the three phonemes form words, the lexical constraints reduce the uncertainty about this phoneme. More specifically, if for example, /m/, /b/, and /p/ are the only members of the same PEC, then given the word context /_ɪn/, /p/ and /b/ form words (*pin*, *bin*), but not /m/ (*min*). Therefore, *pin* and *bin* would still be in the same LEC, but not *min* Given that there might be a reduction in uncertainty for other phonemes of the same word as well, lexical permissibility constraints might greatly reduce the difficulty in identifying a word. Evidence for this distinction also comes from studies in auditory word recognition (Ganong, 1980; Marslen-Wilson et al., 1996) where the lexical competitor space influenced the interpretation of an ambiguous phoneme. An ambiguous sound was treated as being an example of the target word, if there was no competitor. For example, if the rhyme /_ɪn/ is preceded by a phoneme that is ambiguous between /b/ and /m/, then it will be interpreted as /b/, since only /b/ forms a word in this context. If there was a competitor that was equally supported by the auditory signal, then both competitor and target were maintained as possible candidates (Marslen-Wilson et al., 1996).

Mattys and colleagues (2002) showed for visual speech that the size of a LEC predicts identification accuracy. Words in larger LECs are less accurately recognized than words in smaller LECs. In addition, it was found that the frequency of the target word facilitated its correct identification. This was true for all LEC sizes and despite equating of the mean frequency of all LECs. Further, the effect of LEC size and frequency separately accounted for variance above and beyond the variance explained by differences in PECs.

This research on lexical similarity effects in visual speech shows that similar if not the same processes are involved in visual and auditory word recognition. For both, word recognition is determined by competition in the lexicon. This competition is influenced not only by the similarity of the input with the candidate words, but also by what phonemes are lexically permissible in a certain context. This has also been shown to be the case for audiovisual spoken word recognition. The work of Brancazio (1999; 2004) showed that the lexical status of unimodal items influences the identification of audiovisually mismatching McGurk stimuli. Visual information had the strongest influence on the percept (i.e. was most likely to lead to a fusion response) when the auditory stimulus was a non-word but the audiovisual fusion was a word. When both auditory stimulus and audiovisual fusion percept were words or non-words, the visual influence was weaker. However, the visual influence was the weakest when only the auditory stimulus was a word. This can be explained in terms of overall goodness of support (e.g. as predicted by the Fuzzy Logical Model of Perception; Massaro, 1998). For example, an auditory non-word only yields perceptual support, and not much lexical support. The visual information supports the visual target word but also words and non-words that are similar. The fusion response is the candidate that is most supported by the information integrated from both perceptual sources. Candidates that are also words are further supported by lexical information. Therefore, the visual target will benefit not only from being the best candidate given the mismatching perceptual sources but also from the lexical support.

2.2.2 Facial information for speech perception

Visual speech contributes to successful speech recognition; however, the question arises as to what parts of the face are responsible for this phenomenon. Obviously the movements of the lips are one of the main contributors (see e.g. Ijsseldijk, 1992; Marassa and Lansing, 1995; Ouni et al., 2005; Thomas and Jordan, 2004), and are sufficient to provide an audiovisual speech advantage. In comparison, lines shaped like a mouth are not able to improve speech recognition (Summerfield, 1979). The characteristic position and movement of the lips contribute to a general audiovisual recognition benefit probably because they mainly convey visual place of articulation information. Place of articulation information can also easily be observed by position and movement of teeth and tongue (MacLeod and Summerfield, 1987; Summerfield, 1987). Information about a front place of articulation is readily apparent in visual speech (see e.g. Jesse, 2005). Labial closure, for example, indicates the production of bilabial consonants. A tuck of the lower lip underneath the upper front teeth reveals the production of labiodental fricatives. In addition to information from the lips, the visibility of teeth and tongue positions and movements during production also contribute to speech reading (Preminger et al., 1998). Consonants with a mid place of articulation (dental to postalveolar) can be distinguished by their characteristic tongue tip movement during their production. Dental consonants can further be distinguished from other consonants with a mid place of articulation by dental adduction—i.e. whether or not teeth are seen and move vertically closer during their production. Back place of articulation is less easily transmitted visually. But for example, the time-course of lip protrusion that is distinctive for /w/ helps its recognition (Summerfield, 1987). Voicing and nasality are produced by the vocal cords and the soft palate respectively, which is difficult to observe directly (however, see discussion of multimodal voicing cues above; Breeuwer and Plomp, 1986).

Vowels are discriminated visually most successfully based on the lip rounding (i.e. protrusion and opening of the lips) and the height of the tongue (Breeuwer and Plomp, 1986; Jackson et al., 1976; Montgomery and Jackson, 1983). The visual signal seems to contain more information on lip rounding than on tongue height (Benguerel and Pichora-Fuller, 1982). Diphthongs are generally more identifiable visually than monophthong vowels (Wozniak and Jackson, 1979).

Other areas in the face besides the lips are informative about visual speech, such as the movements of the jaw (Benoît et al., 1996) and the cheek (Preminger et al., 1998). There is information on the chin and sides of the cheek, and some information might be at the upper cheeks and the sides of the nose (Preminger et al., 1998). Campbell (2001) applied an independent component analysis to speaker video data and showed that lips and teeth are functional cues for lip-reading, but so are jaw, skin wrinkling, neck, and chin movement. The importance of these cues was then validated in a perception experiment. It should not be surprising that facial areas outside the mouth region are informative about the speech signal, since the muscles connected to the lips also consequently move other regions. For example, Munhall and Vatikiotis-Bateson (1998; see also Yehia et al., 1998) investigated the correlation of movements of different regions of the face. They found almost perfect positive correlation ($r \geq .95$) between the movement of the mouth and other regions in and outside the face (e.g. cheeks). However, areas outside the mouth contain information independent from the mouth (Vatikiotis-Bateson and Yehia, 1996; reported in Munhall and Vatikiotis-Bateson, 2004). This is in agreement with studies showing that only about 40–60 percent of all eye fixations during visual and audiovisual speech perceptions are on the mouth region (Vatikiotis-Bateson et al., 1998). How often a listener fixates on the mouth region seems to depend on the quality of the auditory signal (i.e. increasing mouth fixations with decreasing signal-to-noise ratio; Vatikiotis-Bateson et al., 1998) and the task (i.e. more fixations on the eye level for prosodic categorization than for segmental identification tasks; Lansing and McConkie, 1999). However, fixation at a certain region cannot be interpreted as a measure of where the information in the face is located. Even parafoveal vision provides sufficient visual information, for example, to produce McGurk responses. Fixations on regions outside the mouth do not impact the influence of visual speech information on incongruent audiovisual speech perception (Paré et al., 2003).

But what information is transmitted by these regions other than the mouth? Smeele (1994) examined the importance of jaw, lips, and oral cavity in producing a McGurk effect. She showed that the presentation of either the oral cavity or the lips is sufficient to obtain McGurk combination responses, but almost no fusion responses. In order to obtain fusion responses, both lip and oral cavity information was necessary. McGurk illusions rarely occurred if only information from the jaw was presented with the auditory signal. It seems that jaw movement alone does not provide sufficient place of articulation information in order for visual speech to have a noticeable impact on the overall percept. On the other hand, the movement of other non-oral areas of the face seems to carry enough information to impact audiovisual speech perception (Preminger et al., 1998; Thomas and Jordan, 2004). For example, when participants were presented with a video-manipulated speaker who only moved the areas outside the mouth but not the mouth region itself, a substantial influence of visual speech information on audiovisual speech recognition (as measured by McGurk responses) was found (Thomas and Jordan, 2004). It seems therefore that, while the addition of seeing the jaw of a speaker is not sufficient to contribute place of articulation information, the movement of the head as a whole is. However, information from the mouth region alone transmits usually sufficient visual information. Seeing the face moving in addition to the mouth does not add to the influence of visual speech on the audiovisual percept, nor does it further improve the recognition of visual-only speech (Thomas and Jordan, 2004; see also Ijsseldijk, 1992; Marassa and Lansing, 1995). Furthermore, seeing a static mouth in combination with the moving face precludes the influence of visual speech on audiovisual speech perception compared to seeing a moving face alone (Thomas and Jordan, 2004).

Two basic questions related to this research need to be addressed. One question is whether visual speech contributes to perception through featural cues (e.g. through the correlation between movements of the lips and other facial regions) or through configurational cues (i.e. the relative spatial distance between two or more features in the face, e.g. the chin and the nose during articulation). The second question is whether static information (i.e. fixed configurations of the face during speech) or dynamic information plays a role in speech reading and audiovisual speech perception. Degrading featural information, for example by blurring the video image, decreases accuracy in visual speech perception as well as the influence of visual speech on the perception of congruent and incongruent audiovisual speech in noise and in quiet (Thomas and Jordan, 2002). Similarly, degrading configurational information by rotating or completely inverting the whole face reduces the influence of visual speech information (Jordan and Bevan, 1997; Massaro and Cohen, 1996; Rosenblum et al., 2000; but see Thomas and Jordan, 2002). However, the influence of inversion on speech perception might be stimulus-dependent (Massaro and Cohen, 1996; Rosenblum et al., 2000). Future research is necessary to investigate this issue more thoroughly, but it appears that the configurational change through rotation only impacts the information transmitted, not the processing of information (Massaro and Cohen, 1996). Overall, it is also to be noted that while speech perception seems to be impacted by changes in featural and configurational information, such as through blurring and rotation, audiovisual speech perception is generally quite robust against the impact of these variables.

With regard to the second basic question—whether seeing the speaker contributes static or dynamic information to visual and audiovisual speech perception—it can be said that while static information can be sufficient for speech recognition (Campbell, 1986; Campbell et al., 1986), the dynamics of the face and lips are also informative about the visual percept. Brooke and Summerfield (1983) showed that vowels are produced with characteristic lip and jaw trajectories. These trajectories are distinguishable on account of their difference in movement, velocity, and acceleration. Analogous to classic studies of motion perception (Johansson, 1973), Rosenblum et al. (1996) tested the influence of time-varying information by replacing the face with point-lights that were positioned strategically on the face. The configurations that were tested had point-lights only at the lips, or at the lips and at the teeth and tongue. A third configuration had point-lights at lips, teeth, tongue, and on the face. An audiovisual recognition benefit was found for the presentation with lights only on the lips. However, performance in presentation conditions with lights on lips, teeth, and tongue was substantially better than in conditions with lights only on the lips. The points on the face did not add to the audiovisual benefit above and beyond the benefit found for the condition with point-lights on lips, teeth, and tongue (Rosenblum et al., 1996). Time-varying information was also sufficient to produce the McGurk illusion (Rosenblum and Saldaña, 1996). However, performance with point light displays is significantly poorer than it is with the full face displays (Cohen et al., 1996).

In summary, audiovisual speech perception is quite robust vis-à-vis different forms of image distortions (e.g. blurring, viewing angle, or inversion). This might be due to the fact that although the lips are the main contributors to visual information, other non-oral areas of the face also transmit information. This information is partially redundant with the information from the lips, but also partially unique. Furthermore, the type of information provided by visual speech can be robust against visual distortions.

2.3 Theories of audiovisual speech perception

A theory of audiovisual speech perception needs to describe the visual psychophysics of visual speech as well as how visual speech is evaluated and integrated with auditory speech. Furthermore, it needs to explain to what extent this additional source of information is considered when making a decision about what was perceived. It thereby needs to explain how these processes account for the audiovisual benefit, the McGurk effect, and the other phenomena described in the previous section. The theory can either postulate processes that are unique to speech recognition or try to explain audiovisual speech recognition as part of a general approach to pattern recognition. Although most of the influential theories of auditory spoken word recognition (see Gaskell, Chapter 4 this volume), such as TRACE (McClelland and Elman, 1986), Cohort theory (Marslen-Wilson, 1987), Merge (Norris et al., 2000), or the Neighborhood Activation Model (Luce and Pisoni, 1998), do not deal with visible speech, this neglect seems to be a restriction in research focus rather than reflecting the assumption that visual speech has no influence in face-to-face communication.

2.3.1 Psychoacoustic accounts

Psychoacoustic theories discount the influence of visual speech. This class of theories assumes that speech processing is nothing else than the processing of complex sounds. More recent versions of psychoacoustic theories now acknowledge the influence of visual speech (e.g. Diehl and Kluender, 1987), but lack an account of how and to what degree visible speech is influential. Not surprisingly, psychoacoustic theorists could only give a secondary role to visual speech in order to preserve the very nature of psychoacoustic theories: that acoustics are central in understanding spoken language. As we have seen in the examples described above, however, visible speech cannot be relegated to a secondary role in a satisfactory account of audiovisual speech perception.

2.3.2 Motor theory

The basic assumption of the motor theory is that speech is perceived in terms of gestures (Liberman and Mattingly, 1985; Mattingly and Studdert-Kennedy, 1991). The perceiver attempts to recover the articulatory gestures that produced the speech in order to understand what was said. This assumption was motivated by solving the "invariance problem" that there is no identifiable one-to-one correspondence between the acoustic signal and phonemes that could contribute to speech recognition. It is argued by the motor theory, however, that there is a lawful relationship between specific phonemes and the articulatory gestures used to produce them. Supposedly, due to coarticulation with the subsequent vowel, the same consonant can be acoustically different, but will be articulatorily somewhat similar.

As a consequence of this gestural mediation assumption, speech perception is postulated by motor theorists to be special and different from auditory perception in its processes and information sources (Liberman, 1996). This phonetic module is specific to auditory as well as visual speech. Both sources are integrated through the common gestural representation of both visual and auditory speech signals. However, research has shown that the same processes involved in other pattern recognition domains can also account for the integration of multiple sources of information in speech perception (Massaro, 1998). There is no need to postulate a special processing module for speech. There is little empirical evidence that directly support the mediation of speech perception by gestures.

2.3.3 Direct perception

Direct perception theory also claims that gestures are the primary objects of speech perception, but does not assume that speech is special (Fowler 1986; 1996). Rather, the direct perception theory for speech perception is placed within Gibson's (1966) framework of direct perception, which postulates that persons directly perceive the causes of sensory input. In spoken language, the cause of an audible-visible speech percept is the vocal-tract activity of the talker. Accordingly, it is reasoned that visible speech should influence speech perception because it also reveals the vocal-tract activity of the talker. Speech perceivers therefore obtain direct information from integrated perceptual systems from the flow of stimulation provided by the talker (Best, 1995). The observed influence of visible speech is easily predicted by this theory because visible speech represents another source of stimulation, providing direct information about the gestural actions of the talker. However, we know of no convincing evidence for the gesture as the primary object of speech perception (see Massaro, 1998; Ohala, 1996). For now, it seems most parsimonious to assume that the objects of speech perception are relatively abstract symbols (Nearey, 1992; but see Pisoni and Levi, Chapter 1 this volume, for a discussion).

2.3.4 Pattern recognition accounts

Speech perception can also be described as a case of pattern recognition that involves the evaluation of all available sources of information as well as the integration of this information in order to reach a decision on what was perceived. The underlying processes of pattern recognition would be domain-general; however, the sources of information involved in recognition would most likely be domain-specific. Visual speech is therefore simply another source of information that is considered to understand what was said. The information provided from watching the speaker will be integrated with all other available information. Integration is a general algorithm that applies to all available sources of information. In speech, these other sources could involve, among others, lexical or context knowledge, or knowledge about phonology, syntax, semantics, or pragmatics. The same algorithm operates on the integration of multiple cues independently of whether these cues were all obtained from the same modality or from different modalities.

The Fuzzy Logical Model of Perception (FLMP, Massaro, 1998) gives such a pattern recognition account of speech perception. According to the FLMP, all sources of information are evaluated independently of each other and integrated. The output of the evaluation process is knowledge about the degree to which each source of information matches the prototypes for each possible alternative as stored in long-term memory. Prototypes are summary descriptions of the best exemplars of a category. Fuzzy truth values are the common metric in which the degree of support from all sources is expressed. Support values are expressed as fuzzy truth values ranging between zero and one. Values at the .5 level represent complete ambiguity. In other words, if one were to create a stimulus that is completely ambiguous on a continuum between /ba/ and /da/, then the support value would be .5. With an increase or decrease of this value away from .5, ambiguity decreases. Integration of information follows a multiplicative combination of these support values. When combined in a relative decision rule, this allows accounting for better performance based on two imperfect sources than on considering only either one. For example, given a two-alternative forced-choice task between /da/ and /ba/, the degree of support provided by the auditory information for /da/ can be noted as a_i and the support for /ba/ as $(1- a_i)$. Similarly, the support provided by the visual information for /da/ is written as v_j, and the support for /ba/ as $(1-v_j)$. The overall support for /da/ from visual and auditory speech information is the product of the support value v_j and a_i. All available information is used to form a decision. There is no information loss due to integration.

Perceptual identification is, however, based on the degree of overall support for one alternative relative to the summed overall support for all other alternatives. For example, the relative degree of support for /da/ is equal to the overall support for /da/ divided by the sum of the overall support for all alternatives, namely here for /da/ and /ba/.

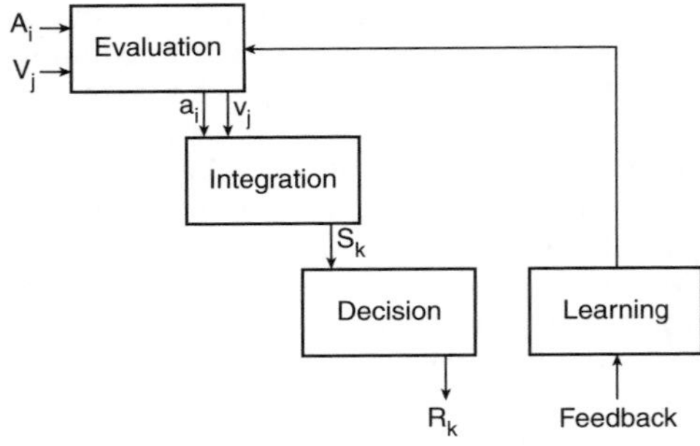

Figure 2.1 Schematic representation of the three processes involved in perceptual recognition. The three processes are shown to precede left to right in time to illustrate their necessarily successive but overlapping processing. These processes make use of prototypes stored in long-term memory. The sources of information are represented by uppercase letters. Auditory information is represented by A_i and visual information by V_j. The evaluation process transforms these sources of information into psychological values (indicated by lowercase letters a_i and v_j) These sources are then integrated to give an overall degree of support, S_k, for each speech alternative k. The decision operation maps the outputs of integration into some response alternative, R_k. The response can take the form of a discrete decision or a rating of the degree to which the alternative is likely. The feedback is assumed to tune the prototypical values of the features used by the evaluation process.

$$P(/da/ \mid A_i V_j) = \frac{a_i v_j}{a_i v_j + (1-a_i)(1-v_j)} \qquad (1)$$

The FLMP predicts that the influence of a source of information on the decision increases to the degree that other sources are ambiguous. Cognitive sources of information (e.g. context knowledge) are treated exactly the same way by this information-processing model. Their independently evaluated support for each alternative is combined multiplicatively with the degree of support from all other sources. Therefore, the FLMP does not assume that cognitive sources of information modify the perceptual input, but rather that all information is solely passed on and integrated to determine the overall relative support for each alternative. This central assumption stands in marked contrast to interactive activation models and anticipated the Merge model (Norris et al., 2000; see Massaro, 2000 for a commentary).

Given the quantitative nature of the FLMP, it provides better testing conditions than verbal models like the motor theory. The FLMP has been broadly evaluated in different areas, tasks, materials, and participant populations (see Massaro, 1998 for an overview). This provides evidence that although the amount and type of information between studies differs, the processing of this information adheres to the same principles of pattern recognition as outlined by the FLMP. The integration algorithm of the FLMP has been evaluated by comparing the ability of the model to fit behavioral data against model implementations with alternative integration rules (see Massaro, 1998 for an overview). For example, in contrast to the FLMP, an averaging integration model would predict that the overall degree of support can never exceed the degree of support provided by the most informative source of information. Therefore, audiovisual speech can never be more informative than unimodal speech. An additive model (see e.g. Cutting et al., 1992; Cutting and Bruno, 1988) would make the same predictions as an averaging model when combined with the relative goodness rule for decision. The FLMP provides a better account of pattern recognition than competitor models that had an averaging or an additive rule of integration (e.g. Massaro and Cohen, 1993b; Massaro, 1998).

Given this success of the FLMP's integration algorithm, a natural question is: what is the postulated underlying neural mechanism? Generally, there are at least three different neurologically plausible solutions for how integration of visible speech with auditory speech might occur. Auditory and visual neurons transmit modality-specific information to other neurons. The three solutions differ with respect to how the auditory and visual information is shared during the chain of processing from input to output. In the first case, the processing of the visual modality activates the location that receives activation from the other modality. We call this "sensory penetration" because information from the visual modality impacts on the neurons processing the auditory modality. As illustrated in Figure 2.2a, the activation from the visible speech is sent to a location whose primary function is to receive activation from the auditory modality. This neurological instantiation represents a so-called non-independence model of integration in which one modality is never represented independently of the other modality.

A second type of brain integration involves simple feed-forward convergence. As illustrated in Figure 2.2b, the neural activation from the auditory and visible speech activates a third location that is sensitive to the inputs from both modalities. An important set of observations from single-cell recordings in cats could be interpreted in terms of convergent integration (Stein and Meredith, 1992).

Non-convergent temporal integration, illustrated in Figure 2.2c, involves integration-like behavior, but there is no location at which the separate modality-specific information is integrated. This type of integration involves the combination of information from two or more

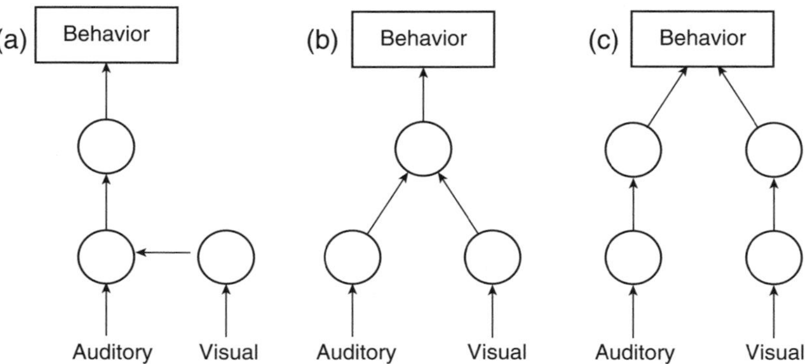

Figure 2.2 Schematic representation of the neural processing involved in sensory penetration (2a), simple feedforward convergence (2b), and nonconvergent temporal integration (2c).

remote regions of the brain. Corticocortical pathways (pathways that connect regions of the cortex) synchronize the outputs of these regions and enable them to feed forward, independently but synchronously, to other areas. This type of integration would influence some output process rather than producing some higher-order integrated representation for storage or further processing by other parts of the brain.

The FLMP is consistent with the latter two models, but not the first one, by predicting the simultaneous but independent influence of both audible and visible speech. What is sufficient for an implementation of the FLMP is neural activity along two independent channels that simultaneously influence behavior.

2.4 Visual speech as a language learning tool

As the previous sections outlined, visual speech contributes to the robust and successful recognition of speech. Therefore, it holds promise for educational applications such as language tutoring for second-language learners, for children and adults with hearing impairment, and for autistic children. Language tutoring that includes presentations of visual speech is not only critical for speech-reading acquisition, and the production training of new and old vocabulary, but also for the general acquisition of new vocabulary (Bosseler and Massaro, 2003; Hardison, 2003).

It has been shown that speech-reading can be improved by training (Massaro et al., 1993b; Walden et al., 1977). When trained to recognize consonant-vowel syllables presented auditory-only, visual-only, or audiovisually, participants improved in all three presentation conditions (Massaro et al., 1993b). Results of two recent experiments show that participants seem to learn the same amount during visual-only presentations with auditory speech feedback and audiovisual speech-reading training (Geraci and Massaro, 2002). From the research presented throughout this chapter, we can conclude that humans naturally can speech-read, but also can improve when trained. It follows that speech-reading is a valuable skill for robust speech recognition and can be enhanced when needed, for example, to compensate for hearing difficulties. When trained with supplementary visual speech, hard of hearing children between the ages of 8 and 13 improved their speech perception and production skills (Massaro and Light, 2004). Their acquired production skills generalized to a new set of words that had not been included in the training sessions. The speech production skills deteriorated somewhat after six weeks without training. These results are evidence that the training method, rather than some other experiences, was responsible for the learning.

Multimodal speech training has also been shown to be effective for vocabulary acquisition of children with autism. This is despite the evidence showing that autistic children are impaired in face processing (Dawson et al., 2002; Rogers 1999; Williams et al., 2001) and tend to avoid face-to-face contact with others (Happe, 1998). However, de Gelder and colleagues (1996) reported evidence that children with autism are less influenced by visual speech in audiovisual speech recognition paradigms than normally developing children matched for mental age. But the smaller visual effect for children with autism does not necessarily reflect non-optimal integration, but rather could be due to less information from the face. The latter explanation is supported by reanalysis of the data of de Gelder et al. within the framework of the FLMP (Massaro and Bosseler, 2003), which showed that the children with autism seem to apply the same optimal integration algorithm as their comparison group. Furthermore, the behavioral data showed that audiovisual speech training can be effective in teaching new vocabulary and speech-reading to autistic children (Massaro and Bosseler, 2003). A more recent investigation provided evidence that indeed the face facilitated this learning (Massaro and Bosseler, 2006).

Information provided by the face is also helpful for the acquisition of a foreign language. Second-language learners would benefit from audiovisual presentations not only for the purpose of learning new vocabulary but also for accent reduction training. For example, native Japanese speakers benefited from facial information when learning the perception and production of the American English /r/ and /l/ (Massaro and Light, 2003). The successful training also led to generalization of the skill to new words.

2.5 Conclusion

Although we often talk at a hidden distance, the absence of the face reduces information support for understanding. Multimodal conversation in face-to-face situations reveals the complexity and richness of language and the challenge of uncovering the processes that allow us to communicate so seamlessly. This chapter is unique in this handbook because it specifically addresses the multimodal nature of perception (see also

Frost and Ziegler, Chapter 7 this volume) and word recognition in speech. We encourage the reader to apply some of the concepts developed in this chapter in their reading of other related chapters. What challenges do other approaches provide, and how might they be tested within our framework? Analogously, are there concepts and findings that can enrich the other descriptions of language processing found within this volume?

References

Arnold, P., and Hill, F. (2001) Bisensory augmentation: a speechreading advantage when speech is clearly audible and intact. *British Journal of Psychology*, 92: 339–55.

Auer, E. T. Jr (2002) The influence of the lexicon on speech read word recognition: contrasting segmental and lexical distinctiveness. *Psychonomic Bulletin and Review*, 9: 341–7.

Auer, E. T. Jr, and Bernstein, L. E. (1997) Speechreading and the structure of the lexicon: computationally modeling the effects of reduced phonetic distinctiveness on lexical uniqueness. *Journal of the Acoustical Society of America*, 102: 3704–10.

Benguerel, A. P., and Pichora-Fuller, M. K. (1982) Coarticulation effects in lipreading. *Journal of Speech and Hearing Research*, 25: 600–607.

Benoît, C., Guiard-Marigny, T., Le Goff, B., and Adjoudani, A. (1996) Which components of the face do humans and machines best speechread? In D. G. Stork and M. E. Hennecke (eds), *Speechreading by Humans and Machines: Models, Systems, and Applications*, pp. 315–25. Springer, Berlin.

Besle, J., Fort, A., Delpuech, C., and Giard, M.-H. (2004) Bimodal speech: early suppressive visual effects in human auditory cortex. *European Journal of Neuroscience*, 20: 2225–34.

Best, C. T. (1995) A direct realist perspective on cross-language speech perception. In W. Strange (ed.), *Speech Perception and Linguistic Experience: Theoretical and Methodological Issues in Cross-Language Speech Research*, pp. 167–200. York Press, Timonium, MD.

Bosseler, A., and Massaro, D. W. (2003) Development and evaluation of a computer- animated tutor for vocabulary and language learning for children with autism. *Journal of Autism and Developmental Disorders*, 33: 654–73.

Braida, L. D. (1991) Crossmodal integration in the identification of consonant segments. *Quarterly Journal of Experimental Psychology: Human Experimental Psychology*. Special Issue: *Hearing and Speech*, 43: 647–77.

Brancazio, L. (1999) Contributions of the lexicon to audiovisual speech perception. *Dissertation Abstracts International*, 59: 5591B. (UMI No. 9909779).

Brancazio, L. (2004) Lexical influences in audiovisual speech perception. *Journal of Experimental Psychology: Human Perception and Performance*, 30: 445–63.

Breeuwer, M., and Plomp, R. (1986) Speechreading supplemented with auditorily presented speech parameters. *Journal of the Acoustical Society of America*, 79: 481–99.

Brooke, N. M., and Summerfield, A. Q. (1983) Analysis, synthesis and perception of visible articulatory movements. *Journal of Phonetics*, 11: 63–76.

Campbell, C. S. (2001) Patterns of evidence: investigating information in visible speech perception. *Dissertation Abstracts International*, 61: 3869B (UMI No. 9979917).

Campbell, C. S., and Massaro, D. W. (1997) Perception of visible speech: Influence of spatial quantization. *Perception*, 26: 627–44.

Campbell, R. (1986) The lateralization of lipread sounds: a first look. *Brain and Cognition*, 5: 1-21.

Campbell, R. and Dodd, B. (1980) Hearing by eye. *Quarterly Journal of Experimental Psychology*, 32: 85–99.

Campbell, R., Landis, R., and Regard, M. (1986) Face recognition and lipreading: a neurological dissociation. *Brain*, 109: 509–21.

Cathiard, M.-A., Lallouache, M. T., Mohamadi, T., and Abry, C. (1995) Configurational vs. temporal coherence in audio-visual speech perception. *Proceedings of the 13th International Congress of Phonetic Sciences*, 3: 218–21.

Cohen, M. M., Walker, R. L., and Massaro, D. W. (1996) Perception of synthetic visual speech. In D. G. Stork and M. E. Hennecke (eds), *Speechreading by Humans and Machines: Models, Systems, and Applications*, pp. 153–68. Springer, Berlin.

Colin, C., Radeau, M., Soquet, A., Demolin, D., Colin, F., and Deltenre, P. (2002) Mismatch negativity evoked by the McGurk-MacDonald effect: a phonetic representation within short-term memory. *Clinical Neurophysiology*, 113: 495–506.

Connine, C. M., Blasko, D. G., and Titone, D. (1993) Do the beginnings of spoken words have a special status in auditory word recognition? *Journal of Memory and Language*, 32: 193–210.

Cutting, J. E., and Bruno, N. (1988) Additivity, subadditivity, and the use of visual information: a reply to Massaro (1988). *Journal of Experimental Psychology: General*, 117: 422–4.

Cutting, J. E., Bruno, N., Brady, N. P., and Moore, C. (1992) Selectivity, scope, and simplicity of models: a lesson from fitting judgments of perceived depth. *Journal of Experimental Psychology: General*, 121: 364–81.

Dawson, G., Carver, L., Meltzoff, A. N., Panagiotides, H., McPartland, J., and Webb, S. J. (2002) Neural correlates of face and object recognition in young children with autism spectrum disorder, developmental delay, and typical development. *Child Development*, 73: 700–717.

de Gelder, B., and Vroomen, J. (2000) The perception of emotion by ear and by eye. *Cognition and Emotion*, 14: 289–311.

de Gelder, B., Vroomen, J., and van der Heide, L. (1996) Face recognition and lip-reading in autism. *European Journal of Cognitive Psychology*, 3: 69–86.

de la Vaux, S. K., and Massaro, D. W. (2004) Audiovisual speech gating: examining information and information processing. *Cognitive Processing*, 5: 106–12.

Diehl, R. L., and Kluender, K. R. (1987) On the categorization of speech sounds. In S. Harnad (ed.), *Categorical perception*, pp. 226–53. Cambridge University Press, Cambridge.

Ellison, J. W., and Massaro, D. W. (1997) Featural evaluation, integration, and judgment of facial affect. *Journal of Experimental Psychology: Human Perception and Performance,* 23: 213–26.

Erber, N. P. (1971) Effects of distance on the visual reception of speech. *Journal of Speech and Hearing Research,* 14: 848–57.

Erber, N. P. (1974) Effects of angle, distance, and illumination on visual reception of speech by profoundly deaf children. *Journal of Speech and Hearing Research,* 17: 99–112.

Fisher, C. G. (1968) Confusions among visually perceived consonants. *Journal of Speech and Hearing Research,* 15: 474–82.

Fowler, C. A. (1986) An event approach to the study of speech perception from a direct realist perspective. *Journal of Phonetics,* 14: 3–28.

Fowler, C. A. (1996) Listeners do hear sounds, not tongues. *Journal of the Acoustical Society of America,* 99: 1730–41.

Ganong, W. F. (1980) Phonetic categorization in auditory word perception. *Journal of Experimental Psychology: Human Perception and Performance,* 6: 110–25.

Geraci, K., and Massaro, D. W. (2002) Teaching speechreading: is unimodal or bimodal training more effective? MS.

Gibson, J. J. (1966) *The Senses Considered as Perceptual Systems.* Houghton Mifflin, Boston.

Grant, K. W., and Greenberg, S. (2001) Speech intelligibility derived from asynchronous processing of auditory-visual information. In D. W. Massaro, J. Light, and K. Geraci (eds), *Proceedings of the AVSP 2001,* pp. 132–7. Aalborg, Denmark.

Grant, K. W., and Seitz, P. F. (2000) The use of visible speech cues for improving auditory detection of spoken sentences. *Journal of the Acoustical Society of America,* 108: 1197–1208.

Grant, K. W., Walden, B. E., and Seitz, P. F. (1998) Auditory-visual speech recognition by hearing-impaired subjects: consonant recognition, sentence recognition, and auditory-visual integration. *Journal of the Acoustical Society of America,* 103: 2677–90.

Green, K. P., and Gerdman, A. (1995) Cross-modal discrepancies in coarticulation and the integration of speech information: the McGurk effect with mismatched vowels. *Journal of Experimental Psychology: Human Perception and Performance,* 21: 1409–26.

Green, K. P., Kuhl, P. K., Meltzoff, A. N., and Stevens, E. B. (1991) Integrating speech information across talkers, gender and sensory modality: female faces and male voices in the McGurk effect. *Perception and Psychophysics,* 50: 524–36.

Greenberg, S. (2005) A multi-tier framework for understanding spoken language. In S. Greenberg and W. Ainsworth (eds), *Listening to Speech: An Auditory Perspective.* Erlbaum, Hillsdale, NJ.

Greenberg, S., and Arai, T. (2004) What are the essential cues for understanding spoken language? *IEICE Transactions on Information and Systems,* E87-D(5): 1059–70.

Happe, F. (1998) *Autism: An Introduction to Psychological Theory*. Harvard University Press, Cambridge, MA.

Hardison, D. M. (2003) Acquisition of second-language speech: effects of visual cues, context, and talker variability. *Applied Psycholinguistics,* 2: 495–522.

Ijsseldijk, F. J. (1992) Speechreading performance under different conditions of video image, repetition, and speech rate. *Journal of Speech and Hearing Research,* 35: 46–71.

Jackson, P., Montgomery, A. A., and Binnie, C. A. (1976) Perceptual dimensions underlying vowel lipreading performance. *Journal of Speech and Hearing,* 19: 796–812.

Jesse, A. (2005) Towards a lexical fuzzy logical model of perception: the time-course of information in lexical identification of face-to-face speech. Doctoral dissertation, University of California, Santa Cruz.

Jesse, A., Vrignaud, N., Cohen, M. M., and Massaro, D. W. (2000/2001) The processing of information from multiple sources in simultaneous interpreting. *Interpreting,* 5: 95–115.

Johansson, G. (1973) Visual perception of biological motion and a model for its analysis. *Perception and Psychophysics,* 14: 201–11.

Jordan, T. R., and Bevan, K. M. (1997) Seeing and hearing rotated faces: influences of facial orientation on visual and audiovisual speech recognition. *Journal of Experimental Psychology: Human Perception and Performance,* 23: 388–403.

Jordan, T., and Sergeant, P. (2000) Effects of distance on visual and audiovisual speech recognition. *Language and Speech,* 43: 107–24.

Kewley-Port, D. (1983) Time varying features as correlates of place of articulation in stop consonants. *Journal of the Acoustical Society of America,* 73: 322–35.

Lansing, C. R., and McConkie, G. W. (1999) Attention to facial regions in the segmental and prosodic visual speech perception tasks. *Journal of Speech, Language, and Hearing Research,* 42: 526–39.

Lewald, J., and Guski, R. (2003) Cross-modal perceptual integration of spatially and temporally disparate auditory and visual stimuli. *Cognitive Brain Research,* 16: 468–78.

Liberman, A. M. (1996) *Speech: A Special Code.* MIT Press, Cambridge, MA.

Liberman, A. M., and Mattingly, I. (1985) *The* motor theory of speech perception revised. *Cognition,* 21: 1–36.

Luce, P. A., and Pisoni, D. B. (1998) Recognizing spoken words: the neighborhood activation model. *Ear and Hearing,* 19: 1–36.

MacDonald, J., Andersen, S., and Bachmann, T. (2000) Hearing by eye: how much spatial degradation can be tolerated? *Perception,* 29: 1155–68.

MacDonald, J., and McGurk, H. (1978) Visual influences on speech perception processes. *Perception and Psychophysics,* 24: 253–7.

MacLeod, A., and Summerfield, Q.(1987) Quantifying the contribution of vision to speech perception in noise. *British Journal of Audiology,* 21: 131–41.

Marassa, L. K., and Lansing, C. R. (1995) Visual word recognition in 2 facial motion conditions: full face versus lips-plus-mandible. *Journal of Speech and Hearing Research,* 38: 1387–94.

Marslen-Wilson, W. D. (1987) Functional parallelism in spoken word-recognition. *Cognition*, Special Issue: *Spoken Word Recognition*, 25: 71–102.

Marslen-Wilson, W. D., Moss, H. E., and van Halen, S. (1996) Perceptual distance and competition in lexical access. *Journal of Experimental Psychology: Human Perception and Performance,* 22: 1376–92.

Marslen-Wilson, W., and Zwitserlood, P. (1989) Accessing spoken words: the importance of word onsets. *Journal of Experimental Psychology: Human Perception and Performance,* 15: 576–85.

Massaro, D. W. (1987) *Speech Perception by Ear and Eye: A Paradigm for Psychological Inquiry*. Erlbaum, Hillsdale, NJ.

Massaro, D. W. (1998) *Perceiving Talking Faces: From Speech Perception to a Behavioral Principle.* MIT Press, Cambridge, MA.

Massaro, D. W. (2000) The horse race to language understanding: FLMP was first out of the gate, and has yet to be overtaken. *Behavioral and Brain Sciences,* 23: 338–9.

Massaro, D. W. (2003) Model selection in AVSP: some old and not so old news. In J. L. Schwartz, F. Berthommier, M. A. Cathiard, and D. Sodoyer (eds), *Proceedings of Auditory-Visual Speech Processing Conference*, pp. 83–8. St Jorioz, France.

Massaro, D. W., and Bosseler, A. (2003) Perceiving speech by ear and eye: multimodal integration by children with autism. *Journal of Developmental and Learning Disorders,* 7: 111–44.

Massaro, D. W., and Bosseler, A. (2006) Read my lips: the importance of the face in a computer-animated tutor for autistic children learning language. *Autism: The International Journal of Research and Practice.*

Massaro, D. W., and Cohen, M. M. (1993a) Perceiving asynchronous bimodal speech in consonant-vowel and vowel syllables. *Speech Communication,* 13: 127–34.

Massaro, D. W., and Cohen, M. M. (1993b) The *paradigm* and the fuzzy logical model of perception are alive and well. *Journal of Experimental Psychology: General,* 122: 115–24.

Massaro, D. W., and Cohen, M. M. (1996) Perceiving speech from inverted faces. *Perception and Psychophysics,* 58: 1047–65.

Massaro, D. W., and Cohen, M. M. (1999) Speech perception in hearing-impaired perceivers: synergy of multiple modalities. *Journal of Speech, Language, and Hearing Science,* 42: 21–41.

Massaro, D. W., Cohen, M. M., and Gesi, A. T. (1993b). Long-term training, transfer, and retention in learning to lipread. *Perception and Psychophysics,* 53: 549–62.

Massaro, D. W., Cohen, M. M., and Smeele, P. M. T. (1996) Perception of asynchronous and conflicting visual and auditory speech. *Journal of the Acoustical Society of America,* 100: 1777–86.

Massaro, D. W., Cohen, M. M., Gesi, A. T., and Heredia, R. (1993a) Bimodal speech perception: an examination across languages. *Journal of Phonetics,* 21: 445–78.

Massaro, D. W., and Egan, P. B. (1996) Perceiving affect from the voice and the face. *Psychonomic Bulletin and Review,* 3: 215–21.

Massaro, D. W., and Light, J. (2003) Read my tongue movements: bimodal learning to perceive and produce non-native speech /r/ and /l/. In *Proceedings of the 8th European Conference on Speech Communication and Technology* (*Eurospeech'03/ Interspeech'03*)(CD-ROM, 4 pp.). Geneva.

Massaro, D. W., and Light, J. (2004) Using visible speech for training perception and production of speech for hard of hearing individuals. *Journal of Speech, Language, and Hearing Research,* 47: 304–20.

Mattingly, I. G., and Studdert-Kennedy, M. (eds) (1991) *Modularity and the Motor Theory of Speech Perception.* Erlbaum, Hillsdale, NJ.

Mattys, S. L., Bernstein, L. E., and Auer, E. T. Jr (2002) Stimulus-based lexical distinctiveness as a general word-recognition mechanism. *Perception and Psychophysics,* 64, 667–79.

McClelland, J. L., and Elman, J. L. (1986) The TRACE model of speech perception. *Cognitive Psychology,* 18: 1–86.

McGurk, H., and MacDonald, J. (1976) Hearing lips and seeing voices. *Nature,* 264: 746–8.

Miller, G. A., and Nicely, P. A. (1955) An analysis of perceptual confusions among some English consonants. *Journal of the Acoustical Society of America,* 27: 338–52.

Mills, A. E., and Thiem, R. (1980) Auditory-visual fusions and illusions in speech perception. *Linguistische Berichte,* 68/80: 85–108.

Montgomery, A. A., and Jackson, P. L. (1983) Physical characteristics of the lips underlying vowel lipreading performance. *Journal of the Acoustical Society of America,* 73: 2134–44.

Munhall, K. G., Gribble, P., Sacco, L., and Ward, M. (1996) Temporal constraints on the McGurk effect. *Perception and Psychophysics,* 58: 351–62.

Munhall, K. G., Kroos, C., Jozan, G., and Vatikiotis-Bateson, E. (2004) Spatial frequency requirements for audiovisual speech perception. *Perception and Psychophysics,* 66: 574–83.

Munhall, K. G., and Tohkura, Y. (1998) Audiovisual gating and the time course of speech perception. *Journal of the Acoustical Society of America,* 104: 530–9.

Munhall, K. G., and Vatikiotis-Bateson, E. (1998) The moving face during speech communication. In B. Dodd, R. Campbell, and D. Burnham (eds), *Hearing by Eye, part 2: The Psychology of Speechreading and Audiovisual Speech,* pp. 123–39. Taylor & Francis, London.

Munhall, K. G., and Vatikiotis-Bateson, E. (2004) Spatial and temporal constraints on audiovisual speech perception. In G. A. Calvert, C. Spence, and B. E. Stein (eds), *The Handbook of Multisensory Processes,* pp. 117–88. MIT Press, Cambridge, MA.

Nearey, T. M. (1992) Context effects in a double-weak theory of speech perception. *Language and Speech,* 35: 153–71.

Norris, D., McQueen, J. M., and Cutler, A. (2000) Merging information in speech recognition: feedback is never necessary. *Behavioral and Brain Sciences,* 23: 299–370.

Ohala, J. J. (1996) Speech perception is hearing sounds, not tongues. *Journal of the Acoustical Society of America,* 99: 1718–25.

Ouni, S., Cohen, M. M., Ishak, H., and Massaro, D. W. (2005) Visual contribution to speech perception: measuring the intelligibility of talking heads. *Proceedings of the Auditory-Visual Speech Processing Conference,* pp. 45–46. British Columbia, Canada.

Paré, M., Richler, R., ten Hove, M., and Munhall, K. G. (2003) Gaze behavior in audiovisual speech perception: the influence of ocular fixations on the McGurk effect. *Perception and Psychophysics,* 65: 553–67.

Preminger, J. E., Lin, H. B., Payen, M., and Levitt, H. (1998) Selective visual masking in speechreading. *Journal of Speech, Language and Hearing Research,* 41: 564–75.

Reisberg, D., McLean, J., and Goldfield, A. (1987) Easy to hear but hard to understand: a lip-reading advantage with intact auditory stimuli. In B. Dodd and R. Campbell (eds), *Hearing by Eye: The Psychology of Lip-Reading,* pp. 97–113. Erlbaum, Hillsdale, NJ.

Rogers, S. J. (1999) Intervention for young children with autism: from research to practice. *Infants and Young Children,* 12: 1–16.

Rosenblum, L. D., Johnson, J. A., and Saldaña, H. M. (1996) Visual kinematic information for embellishing speech in noise. *Journal of Speech and Hearing Research,* 39: 1159–70.

Rosenblum, L. D., and Saldaña, H. M. (1996) An audio-visual test of kinematic primitives for visual speech perception. *Journal of Experimental Psychology: Human Perception and Performance,* 22: 318–31.

Rosenblum, L. D., Schmuckler, M. A., and Johnson, J. A. (1997) The McGurk effect in infants. *Perception and Psychophysics,* 59: 347–57.

Rosenblum, L. D., Yakel, D. A., and Green, K. P. (2000) Face and mouth inversion effects on visual and audiovisual speech perception. *Journal of Experimental Psychology: Human Perception and Performance,* 26: 806–19.

Sams, M., Mötönen, R., and Sihvonen, T. (2005) Seeing and hearing others and oneself talk. *Cognitive Brain Research,* 23: 429–35.

Sams, M., Surakka, V., Helin, P., and Kättö, R. (1997) Audiovisual fusion in Finnish syllables and words. *Proceedings of the Auditory-Visual Speech Processing Conference,* pp. 101–4. Rhodes, Greece.

Schwartz, J.-L. (2003) Why the FLMP should not be applied to McGurk data … or how to better compare models in the Bayesian framework. *Proceedings of the Audiovisual Speech Perception Conference,* pp. 77–82. St Jorioz, France.

Schwartz, J.-L., Berthommier, F., and Savariaux, C. (2004) Seeing to hear better: evidence for early audio-visual interactions in speech identification. *Cognition,* 93: B69–B78.

Sekiyama, K., and Tohkura, Y. (1991) McGurk effect in non-English listeners: few visual effects for Japanese subjects hearing Japanese syllables of high auditory intelligibility. *Journal of the Acoustical Society of America,* 90: 1797–1805.

Sekiyama, K., and Tohkura, Y. (1993) Inter-language differences in the influence of visual cues in speech perception. *Journal of Phonetics,* 21: 427–44.

Shannon, C. E. (1948) A mathematical theory of communications. *Bell Systems Technical Journal,* 27: 379–423.

Shillcock, R. (1990) Lexical hypotheses in continuous speech. In G. T. M. Altmann (ed.), *Cognitive Models of Speech Processing: Psycholinguistic and Computational Perspectives,* pp. 24–49. MIT Press, Cambridge, MA.

Smeele, P. M. T. (1994) Perceiving speech: integrating auditory and visual speech. Doctoral dissertation, Delft University of Technology.

Stein, B. E., and Meredith, M. A. (1992) *The Merging of the Senses.* MIT Press, Cambridge, MA.

Sumby, W. H., and Pollack, I. (1954) Visual contribution to speech intelligibility in noise. *Journal of the Acoustical Society of America,* 26: 212–15.

Summerfield, A. Q. (1979) Use of visual information in phonetic perception. *Phonetica,* 36: 314–31.

Summerfield, A. Q. (1987) Some preliminaries to a comprehensive account of audio-visual speech perception. In B. Dodd and R. Campbell (eds), *Hearing by Eye: The Psychology of Lip-Reading,* pp. 3–51. Erlbaum, London.

Summerfield, A. Q., and McGrath, M. (1984) Detection and resolution of audio-visual incompatibility in the perception of vowels. *Quarterly Journal of Experimental Psychology,* 36A: 51–74.

Tabossi, P., Burani, C., and Scott, D. (1995) Word identification in fluent speech. *Journal of Memory and Language,* 34: 440–67.

Thomas, S. M., and Jordan, T. R. (2002) Determining the influence of Gaussian blurring on inversion effects with talking faces. *Perception and Psychophysics,* 64: 932–44.

Thomas, S. M., and Jordan, T. R. (2004) Contributions of oral and extraoral facial movement to visual and audiovisual speech perception. *Journal of Experimental Psychology: Human Perception and Performance,* 30: 873–88.

van Wassenhove, V. (2004) Cortical dynamics of auditory-visual speech: a forward model of multisensory integration. Doctoral dissertation, University of Maryland.

Vatikiotis-Bateson, E., Eigsti, I.-M., Yano, S., and Munhall, K. G. (1998) Eye movement of perceivers during audiovisual speech perception. *Perception and Psychophysics,* 60: 926–40.

Vitkovich, M., and Barber, P. (1994) Effects of video frame rate on subjects' ability to shadow one of two competing verbal passages. *Journal of Speech and Hearing Research,* 37: 1204–10.

Vroomen, J., Driver, J., and de Gelder, B. (2001) Is cross-modal integration of emotional expressions independent of attentional resources? *Cognitive and Affective Neurosciences,* 1: 382–7.

Walden, B. E., Prosek, R. A., Montgomery, A. A., Scherr, C. K., and Jones, C. J. (1977) Effects of training on the visual recognition of consonants. *Journal of Speech and Hearing Research,* 20: 130–45.

Walden, B. E., Prosek, R. A., and Worthington, D. W. (1974) Predicting audiovisual consonant recognition performance of hearing-impaired adults. *Journal of Speech and Hearing Research,* 17: 270–78.

Williams, J. H., Whiten, A., Suddendorf, T., and Perrett, D. I. (2001) Imitation, mirror neurons and autism. *Neuroscience and Biobehavior Review,* 25: 287–95.

Wozniak, V. D., and Jackson. P. L. (1979) Visual vowel and diphthong perception from two horizontal viewing angles. *Journal of Speech and Hearing Research,* 22: 354–65.

Yehia, H. C., Rubin, P. E., and Vatikiotis-Bateson, E. (1998) Quantitative association of vocal-tract and facial behavior. *Speech Communication,* 26: 23–44.

Zwitserlood, P. (1989) The locus of the effects of sentential-semantic context in spoken-word processing. *Cognition,* 32: 25–64.

CHAPTER 3

Eight questions about spoken word recognition

James M. McQueen

3.1 Why?

Why are psycholinguists interested in spoken word recognition? Imagine a typical listening situation. The phone rings, and you find yourself being addressed by an unknown speaker. How do you come to realize that this person wants to sell you a carriage clock? There may be aspects of the situation and of the speaker's ingratiating conversational style that might help you deduce that this is a cold call, but it is only by recognizing the words you hear that you can recover the speaker's full intentions (i.e. that they are selling carriage clocks and not car insurance). Because each sentence that you hear comes from an unlimited set of potential sentences, it would be impossible to derive what speakers mean by trying to recognize their utterances as wholes. But utterances are made from a limited set of words that, for fluent speakers of a language, will usually already be stored in long-term memory. So speakers' messages must be decoded via recognition of their parts.

Successful communication thus depends on word recognition. Since word recognition is at the heart of the language comprehension process, it has also always been a central topic in psycholinguistics. This chapter reviews current evidence on spoken word recognition, focusing on what I take to be the key aspect of the process: the way in which the listener derives from a spoken utterance a satisfactory lexical parse (i.e. an estimate of what word forms the speaker intended, in a plausible order). My assumption will be that this process entails abstraction, that is, a type of decoding in which the specific acoustic realization of any given utterance is mapped onto stored knowledge about the phonological form of individual words. I make this assumption because it is only via recognition of specific tokens in the speech signal as instances of particular lexical types that semantic and grammatical knowledge about those words can be retrieved and used in comprehension.

I also assume that, in normal comprehension, the listener does not necessarily make explicit and categorical decisions about the identity of each and every word form in every utterance that they hear. The process is likely to be more stochastic. Thus, while certain psycholinguistic tasks may require listeners to make absolute decisions about the words they are hearing, word recognition in normal listening is more continuous; that is, there need be no definitive "magic moment" (cf. Balota, 1990) at which each word form is absolutely identified. Word recognition instead seems to involve the derivation of a number of different possible (sequences of) word forms, weighted by their likelihood of being correct. As we will see, as plausible hypotheses about the word forms in an utterance become available, their grammatical and semantic properties are retrieved, so that possible interpretations of the meaning of that utterance can be built.

3.2 What?

So, to begin, what information in the speech signal is used in word recognition? There are, broadly speaking, two classes of information that are extracted from the signal and used in lexical access: segmental information (i.e. that which distinguishes among speech sounds) and suprasegmental information (i.e. that which specifies the prosodic characteristics of words). I discuss each of these information sources in turn below.

Note that the ensuing discussion assumes a prelexical level of processing which acts as the interface between auditory and lexical processing. Scharenborg et al. (2005) argue that the prelexical level is required to solve the "invariance problem"—the problem that the highly variable speech signal must be mapped onto discrete lexical representations. I further motivate the assumption of a speech-specific prelexical level in McQueen (2005); to summarize, "word recognition would benefit if at least part of the speech code could be cracked prelexically" (p. 264). I should mention here, however, that this assumption is controversial in many ways—about the nature of the representations at the prelexical level, about whether the processes operating there are speech-specific, about the role of visual cues in speech processing, and even about whether there is a prelexical level (see Pisoni and Levi, Chapter 1 this volume; Massaro and Jesse, Chapter 2 this volume; Stevens, 2002; and Diehl et al., 2004, for further discussion).

Segmental information specifies which sounds are in an utterance, and hence must be the primary determinant of successful word recognition. It is thus not surprising that computationally implemented models of spoken word recognition (TRACE, McClelland and Elman, 1986; Shortlist, Norris, 1994; the Distributed Cohort Model, DCM, Gaskell and Marslen-Wilson, 1997; ARTWORD, Grossberg and Myers, 2000; PARSYN, Luce et al., 2000) all assume a prelexical stage of processing in which a representation of the segmental content in the input speech signal is constructed for use in subsequent lexical access. See Gaskell (Chapter 4 this volume) for further discussion of models.

Given the indisputable role of segmental information in word recognition, many experiments on this issue have focused on a more specific aspect of segmental processing: the effect of mismatch between the input and stored lexical knowledge. Marslen-Wilson and Zwitserlood (1989), for example, showed that mismatch on an initial phoneme (e.g. the Dutch word *honing* 'honey', changed into *woning* 'dwelling') appeared to be enough to block lexical access. In a cross-modal priming task, presentation of a prime such as *honing* facilitated responses to the target *bij* 'bee', but the prime *woning* had no such effect. (See Grosjean and Frauenfelder, 1996, for a review of tasks used in spoken word recognition.) Marslen-Wilson and Zwitserlood's result confirms that segmental match is critical for lexical access, but also suggests that the word recognition process is rather intolerant of any segmental mismatch.

Although this conclusion has, in its essence, stood the test of time, subsequent research has suggested a number of refinements. First, segmental mismatch is more disruptive of lexical access in word-initial than in word-final position (Allopenna et al., 1998). This is because of the temporal nature of speech: a word with a final mispronunciation is, prior to the arrival of that mispronunciation, perfectly consistent with the intended word, but a word with an initial mispronunciation is immediately put at a disadvantage. Second, in spite of the initial perfect match of a word with a late mispronunciation, the mismatching sound, when it arrives, still interferes effectively with the word recognition process, even in long words (Frauenfelder et al., 2001; Soto-Faraco et al., 2001). Such results suggest that mismatching evidence tends to weigh more heavily against a word than matching evidence weighs in its favour (Norris, 1994). Third, mismatching segments appear to be more disruptive in short than in long words. Thus, for example, there is stronger evidence that words with an initial mismatching phoneme can be accessed when they are polysyllabic (Connine et al., 1993a) than when they are monosyllabic (Gow, 2001). Fourth, lexical neighbourhood plays a role. If the mismatch creates another word (e.g. *buns* becoming *guns*) no evidence that the source word has been accessed is found (Gow, 2001), but when the mismatch creates a non-word (e.g. *cat* becoming *gat*), there is evidence of access of the source word (Milberg et al., 1988). Marslen-Wilson et al. (1996) also demonstrate that the presence/absence of similar-sounding words influences the effect of segmental mismatch.

Finally, phonetic distance (the similarity between the intended and mispronounced sounds) plays a critical role in determining the effect of segmental mismatch. The more dissimilar the mismatching sound is to the sound in the word's correct pronunciation, the more disruptive that sound is in lexical access (Connine, Blasko, and Hall, 1993; 1997; Marslen-Wilson et al., 1996, but see also Soto-Faraco et al., 2001, for results contradicting this view, and Ernestus and Mak, 2004, for evidence that these effects further depend on the informational value of the mispronunciation). These studies all examined mismatches which involved discrete substitutions of one phoneme by another. More subtle effects of phonetic similarity have also been observed, when changes involving less than one phoneme are created. One way to achieve this is to cross-splice stimuli (Dahan, Magnuson, Tanenhaus and Hogan, 2001; Marslen-Wilson and Warren, 1994; McQueen et al., 1999; Streeter and Nigro, 1979; Whalen, 1984; 1991). Cross-splicing the initial consonant and vowel of *shop* with the final consonant of *shock*, for example, produces a stimulus which sounds like *shock*, but which contains (in the vocalic portion) acoustic evidence consistent with a final /p/. The interfering effects of these cross-splicings on lexical access depend on lexical factors (whether the entire sequence is a word or non-word and whether its components derive from words or non-words). This suggests that the phonetic mismatch created by the cross-splicing influences not only prelexical but also lexical processing.

Disruptions of phonetic detail can also be created without cross-splicing. Andruski et al. (1994), for example, artificially reduced the Voice Onset Time (VOT) of the initial stop consonants of words such as *pear*. VOT is a major phonetic cue in English to the distinction between voiceless stops (e.g. /p/, with long VOTs) and voiced stops (e.g. /b/, with short VOTs). In a cross-modal priming task, responses to targets (e.g. *fruit*) were faster after *pear* than after an unrelated word. But this priming effect became smaller as VOT was reduced (see also McMurray et al., 2002; Utman et al., 2000). These results suggest again that detailed information about segmental distinctions influences lexical processing, especially since these effects depend on lexical factors (whether the critical sequence with a voiceless or voiced stop is a word or not; van Alphen and McQueen, 2006). The influence of this kind of phonetic detail on lexical access also depends on the usefulness of that detail in the making of lexical distinctions (van Alphen and McQueen, 2006): the stronger the phonetic cue (e.g. to whether a stop is voiced or voiceless), the greater the influence of that cue on lexical processing.

Segmental information thus strongly constrains lexical access. The presence of even a small amount of mismatching information (i.e. of even less than one whole phoneme) is enough to disrupt word recognition. But mismatch effects do not depend solely on phonetic similarity; they also depend on variables such as word length, position of the mismatch, lexical factors, and informational value, and on the interaction of all of these variables.

Suprasegmental information also constrains lexical access. This type of information goes beyond the segmental make-up of the speech signal, and specifies instead the prosodic structure of words (e.g. their syllabification and lexical-stress pattern) and the position of a word in the intonational structure of an utterance. The role of lexical-stress information in word recognition has received considerable attention (see Cutler, 2005 for review). The stress pattern of a word is the way in which its syllables differ in accentuation (compare e.g. *trusty*, with stress on the first syllable, and *trustee*, with stress on the second syllable), and may be signalled by differences in pitch, duration, and amplitude. As in studies on uptake of segmental information, experiments on lexical stress have focused on the effects of mismatch. Experiments on the recognition of English minimal pairs such as *trusty/trustee* (Cutler, 1986) suggested that the acoustic differences between the members of such pairs did not influence lexical access: cross-modal priming effects on targets which were associates of both members of the pair were found irrespective of which member of the pair was the preceding prime. Such minimal pairs are very rare, however. More recent experiments have used larger sets of materials consisting of words which begin with the same segments but have different stress patterns (e.g. *admiral/admiration*), and fragment priming (e.g. the prime *admi-* with either primary or secondary stress on the first syllable). These priming experiments, and related studies using word fragments with other tasks, suggest that the incorrect stress pattern in a word fragment disrupts lexical access in Dutch (Cutler and Donselaar, 2001; Donselaar et al., 2005) and Spanish (Soto-Faraco et al., 2001), but also in English (Cooper et al., 2002). Yet other studies, using a variety of techniques (e.g., Connine et al., 1987; Cutler and Clifton, 1984) also suggest that listeners use lexical-stress information in lexical access.

There are, however, cross-linguistic differences in the role of lexical stress. Not all languages make lexical-stress distinctions. Clearly speakers of such languages cannot use stress information. But they may use other types of suprasegmental information instead. Japanese speakers, for example, appear to use the pitch-accent patterns of Japanese words in lexical access (Cutler and Otake, 1999), and Mandarin speakers use tone information (Fox and Unkefer, 1985). Furthermore, within languages that do have stress distinctions, some have free stress, where stress can be placed in different syllabic positions (e.g. English), and others have fixed stress (e.g. French). Listeners of fixed-stress languages are likely to use stress information less in lexical access, since it is predictable and therefore does not enhance lexical distinctions.

Indeed, French listeners, for example, appear not to be sensitive to lexical-stress information (Dupoux et al., 1997). Finally, even within free-stress languages, there is variability in how much value stress information appears to play. Cutler (2005) summarizes evidence that Dutch listeners tend to be more sensitive to stress information than English listeners. This may be because stress information per se has greater informational value in Dutch than in English. Change of lexical-stress pattern may be more often accompanied by a segmental change (e.g. reduction of the unstressed vowel to schwa—compare the first syllables of the noun *conduct* and the verb *conduct*) in English than in Dutch. The conclusion on the uptake of lexical-stress information thus resonates with that on the uptake of segmental information: stress information is used in lexical access when it is available, but its usage appears to depend on its informational value.

Suprasegmental information that specifies the position of segments in the prosodic hierarchy is also used in word recognition. This type of information includes word-internal properties (the syllabification of segments within words), and properties referring to increasingly larger domains—the prosodic word, the phonological phrase, and the intonational phrase (see e.g. Shattuck-Hufnagel and Turk, 1996 for review). Information about all these different levels of prosodic structure appears to constrain the lexical access process. In each case, experiments have involved the manipulation of fine-grained phonetic signatures of prosodic structure.

At the syllable level, fragment priming from spoken Italian sequences on responses to visual target words is stronger when the syllabification of the sequence (e.g. *si.l* or *sil.*, where a period indicates a syllable boundary) matches the syllabification of the target (e.g. *si.lenzio* 'silence' or *sil.vestre* 'sylvan'; Tabossi et al., 2000). These syllabification differences appear to have been signalled by durational differences in the fragments. At the prosodic-word level, differences in the acoustic duration of consonants as a function of whether they are word-initial or word-internal (Gow and Gordon, 1995) or as a function of whether they are word-initial or word-final (Shatzman and McQueen, 2006a) modulate word recognition. Once again, it appears that acoustic cues to suprasegmental structure differ in their importance. Thus, although Shatzman and McQueen (2006a) found that the signal contained several acoustic signatures that could potentially be used by listeners in lexical disambiguation of Dutch sequences such as *een staart / eens taart* ('a tail' / 'once tart'), duration of the critical consonant (the /s/) appeared to be the most important cue.

There are also durational differences between monosyllabic words (e.g. *cap*) and the same sequence appearing as the initial syllable of a polysyllabic word (e.g. in *captain*). Such differences are used to determine the goodness of fit of the lexical representations of the shorter and longer words (Davis et al., 2002; Salverda et al., 2003). Salverda et al. interpret this as evidence for uptake of information about a prosodic-word boundary (there is such a boundary after e.g. *cap* in *cap tucked*, but not after the first syllable of *captain*). At the next level up, Christophe et al. (2004) found that lexical access in French was faster for the first word in a two-word sequence (e.g. *chat grincheux*, lit. 'cat grumpy') when there was a phonological phrase boundary between the two words than when the sequence fell within a phonological phrase. Finally, Cho et al. (2007) have shown that the phonetic detail associated with intonational phrase boundaries (specifically, the acoustic correlates of the articulatory strengthening of segments in domain-initial position) is used to modulate word recognition.

The answer to the "what?" question therefore appears to be this: the signal contains information specifying the segmental and suprasegmental content of an utterance, and listeners appear to extract that information and use it in word recognition, to the extent that it is useful for lexical disambiguation. Stated this way, this conclusion may seem unsurprising. But it is worth bearing in mind for at least two reasons. First, as we will see below, although other constraints are also involved, the primary determinant of word recognition is the information in the signal itself. Second, the notion that the weight assigned to acoustic evidence in word recognition depends on its informational value may be critical in understanding why there can be differences in the apparent effects of different types of evidence (e.g. in comparisons across languages). Thus, while the speech signal is rich in information, some aspects of the signal are more important in word recognition than other aspects.

3.3 **Where?**

Where are the words in the continuous speech stream? The recognition process, at least when confronted with a multi-word utterance, must determine not only which words are in that input but also where they begin and end. This is because there are no fully reliable cues to the location of word boundaries in continuous speech (Lehiste, 1972; Nakatani and Dukes, 1977). Spoken word recognition in normal listening therefore entails segmentation of a quasi-continuous signal into a discrete lexical parse.

The primary source of evidence that is used for solving this segmentation problem is the speech signal itself. Although there is no fully reliable word-boundary cue in speech—no auditory equivalent of the white spaces between words in a written English text like this—there are many less reliable cues, and listeners appear to use them when they are available. We have already seen one such set of cues: Suprasegmental information signalling prosodic structure helps to solve the segmentation problem. Thus, for example, durational evidence favouring *captain* over *cap* (Davis et al., 2002; Salverda et al., 2003) signals that there is no word boundary after the /p/. Likewise, phonological-phrase boundary information can help French listeners segment *chat grincheux* and reject a parse with no word boundary between the first two syllables (*chagrin* ...; Christophe et al., 2004). The same kind of segmentation-based story can also be told for the other studies on prosodic structure reviewed above.

The speech signal contains other suprasegmental information that is used in segmentation. In particular, metrical structure provides evidence on where word boundaries might be. English listeners appear to be sensitive to the rhythmic distinction between strong syllables (those with full vowels) and weak syllables (those with reduced vowels such as schwa). They appear to have picked up on the fact that (content) words in English tend to begin with strong syllables (Cutler and Carter, 1987; Cutler and McQueen, 1995). Thus, when asked to spot real words in nonsense bisyllabic sequences, English listeners find it more difficult to do so in sequences with two strong syllables (e.g. *mintayve*) than in strong–weak sequences (e.g. *mintesh*; Cutler and Norris, 1988; Norris et al., 1995; see also Cutler and Butterfield, 1992).

There are important crosslinguistic differences to consider here, however. Thus, Dutch listeners also show sensitivity to the metrical strong–weak difference (Vroomen and de Gelder, 1995; Vroomen et al., 1996), but listeners of French and Japanese obviously cannot, because these languages do not make this metrical distinction. What appears to be true across languages, however, is the use of rhythmic information in segmentation. Thus, because Romance languages such as French, Catalan, Spanish, and Italian have syllable-based rhythm, speakers of these languages appear to use syllabic information in segmentation (Cutler et al., 1986; Pallier et al., 1993; Sebastián-Gallés et al., 1992; Tabossi et al., 2000; but see also Content et al., 2001). Similarly, because the rhythm of Japanese is based on the mora (a subsyllabic structure), Japanese listeners use moraic information in segmentation (Cutler and Otake, 1994; Otake et al., 1993; McQueen et al., 2001).

Listeners also use phonological knowledge in segmentation. Knowledge about the phonotactic restrictions on syllable structure in a language (e.g. that the sequence /mr/ in English cannot occur within a syllable) could be used to indicate the location of likely word boundaries (e.g. between the /m/ and the /r/). Listeners appear to use this kind of absolute phonotactic knowledge in segmentation (Dumay et al., 2002; McQueen, 1998; Warner et al., 2005; Weber and Cutler, 2006). Probabilistic phonotactic knowledge (i.e. knowledge that sequences of sounds vary in how likely they are to occur at a word boundary) is also used (van der Lugt, 2001). Vowel harmony (e.g. in Finnish; Suomi et al., 1997) provides another source of word-boundary information. In Finnish, there are restrictions on which vowels can co-occur within a word; there are effectively two distinct sets of vowels that never both occur within the same word. Listeners appear to have learned to use the knowledge that, if a sequence of speech contains vowels from these two sets, there must be a word boundary between those vowels (see also Vroomen et al., 1998).

There is, however, a very different way in which the segmentation problem is solved. It appears that the manner in which the word-recognition process works provides a means of finding where the words are. As we have already seen in the discussion of the effects of mismatching information, multiple lexical hypotheses appear to be considered simultaneously as speech is heard. Thus, to take just one previous example, words which differ in their onsets or their offsets from the word in the input (e.g. *speaker* and *beetle* given *beaker*; Allopenna et al., 1998) are considered in parallel with what ultimately proves to be the correct hypothesis. A common way of thinking about this process is in terms of activation—a concept derived in large part from Morton's (1969) logogen model. Representations of word forms that are consistent with the information in the current input are said to be activated, with their activation level reflecting their goodness of fit.

The concept of multiple lexical activation is supported by a large body of other evidence. Words beginning in the same way as other words are jointly considered (e.g. in Dutch, *kapitaal* 'capital', when the onset of *kapitein* 'captain' is heard; Zwitserlood, 1989; see also Moss et al., 1997; Zwitserlood and Schriefers, 1995), as are onset-embedded words such as *cap* in *captain*, as discussed previously. Words ending in the same way as other words are also activated when the longer word is heard (e.g. offset-embedded words such as *bone* in *trombone*; Isel and Bacri, 1999; Luce and Cluff, 1998; Shillcock, 1990; Vroomen and de Gelder, 1997), though the evidence is weaker than for onset embeddings (see e.g. Luce and Lyons, 1999; Shatzman, 2006). Furthermore, words straddling word boundaries in the signal (e.g. *tulips*, given the input *two lips*) also appear to be activated (Gow and Gordon, 1995; Tabossi et al., 1995).

In addition to this evidence on multiple activation, there is also evidence for a form of competition among the activated candidate words. Thus, as the number and frequency of similar-sounding words increases, word recognition becomes harder (Cluff and Luce, 1990; Luce and Large, 2001; Luce and Pisoni, 1998; Vitevitch, 2002; Vitevitch and Luce, 1998; 1999). It appears that, as the number of words in the lexical neighborhood increases, competition gets fiercer, and recognition is delayed. Gaskell and Marslen-Wilson (2002) show that the size and nature of priming effects arising from word or word-fragment primes depends on the number of words beginning in the same way as those primes. They interpret this as evidence for competition between the prime words and the co-activated words beginning in the same way. Words starting at different points in time also appear to compete. For example, listeners find it harder to spot the real word *mess* in a nonsense sequence which is the onset of a real word (e.g. *domes*) than in one which is not (e.g. *nemess*; McQueen et al., 1994). The increased difficulty in the former case suggests competition between the two words (*mess* and *domestic*). The number of words beginning at a different point in the signal from the target word also influences target recognition (Norris et al., 1995; Vroomen and de Gelder, 1995), again suggesting a competition process. Blumstein (Chapter 9 this volume) discusses evidence that the activation and competition process is disrupted in aphasia. Further evidence for competition comes from the research on mismatch reviewed earlier. With respect to segmental mismatch, the evidence that the influence of mismatching information depends on lexical factors suggests competition among activated lexical alternatives. With respect to suprasegmental mismatch, it appears that mismatching lexical-stress information produces inhibitory priming effects when the mismatch is consistent with another word (Donselaar et al., 2005) but not when it is not consistent with another word (Cutler and Donselaar, 2001). This is presumably because the competition process is stronger in the former case.

We can now return to the segmentation problem. The process of multiple activation of lexical hypotheses, and in particular their relative evaluation through competition, provides a means to solve the segmentation problem. If word hypotheses have to fight for control of their parts of the input, then the result will tend to be a lexical parse with each part of the input accounted for by only one strongly activated hypothesis, and no parts left over. Competition thus finds word boundaries even when there are no cues to those boundaries in the speech signal (McClelland and Elman, 1986 and Norris, 1994 provide computational simulations confirming this behavior in TRACE and Shortlist, respectively, both models instantiating lexical competition).

Listeners therefore appear to work out where the words are in spoken utterances in three ways: they use information in the speech signal which specifies the location of likely word boundaries, they use phonological knowledge to assist in this process, and they rely on a process of competitive evaluation of multiple lexical hypotheses. There are two open issues. The first concerns the relative importance of these different sources of information. A start has been made to address this. Mattys et al. (2005) have recently argued, on the basis of experiments directly contrasting knowledge-driven and signal-driven cues for segmentation in English, that lexical cues (e.g. whether the context of a target word was a word or a non-word) tend to outweigh signal-based segmental cues (e.g. whether segments were coarticulated with their contexts), which in turn tend to outweigh signal-based suprasegmental cues (e.g. whether the stimuli began with strong or weak syllables; see also Mattys, 2004).

The second issue concerns how these different sources of information are integrated. Norris et al. (1997) have proposed an algorithm by which signal- and knowledge-based cues to likely word boundaries influence lexical competition. The idea is that activated candidate words are evaluated with respect to whether they are aligned with the boundaries signalled by, for example, metrical structure. If those words are found to be misaligned with those boundaries, their activation is penalized. A word counts as being misaligned if there is no vocalic portion between the edge of the word (its beginning or its end) and the signalled likely word boundary location. The reason for this definition of misalignment is that a sequence without a vowel cannot be a possible word. A parse involving, for example, a candidate word followed by a vowel-less residue and then a likely word boundary is very improbable. Evidence for this simple vowel-based Possible Word Constraint (PWC) has now been found in a range of languages including English (Norris et al., 1997; 2001), Dutch (McQueen, 1998), Japanese (McQueen et al., 2001) and Sesotho (Cutler et al., 2002). As has been argued in greater detail elsewhere (Cho et al., 2007), it is however unlikely that the PWC penalty is the only mechanism by which word boundary cues modulate the competition process. Embedded words such as *cap* in *captain* are not misaligned with any likely word boundary, and yet their strength as competitors does appear to vary as a function of signal-based information (i.e. their duration; Davis et al., 2002; Salverda et al., 2003). Competition may therefore be modulated by boosts for aligned candidates as well as by penalties for misaligned candidates (see also Norris et al., 1995).

3.4 **Which?**

Which words did the speaker intend? This question lies at the heart of the spoken word recognition problem; it is the question the listener must answer. We already have a partial picture about how the listener does just that. Words that are consistent with the current input are activated, as a function of how good a match there is between the input and stored phonological knowledge about those words, and they compete with each other for recognition. Segmental and suprasegmental information in the signal modulates this competition, by indicating which words are in the input and where they begin and end.

But there is more to it than that. Phonological knowledge, beyond that concerning the words themselves, also plays an important role. We have already seen that word recognition is influenced by language-specific segment sequence constraints (e.g. those due to phonotactic and vowel-harmony restrictions). Knowledge about the alterations to the signal that are the result of phonological processes is also brought to bear. One such process is place assimilation. In English, for example, a coronal consonant such as /t/ at the end of a word such as *night* can sound like a bilabial /p/ when the following consonant has a bilabial place of articulation (e.g. in *night bus*). The evidence reviewed above suggests that *nipe* would be a poor match to *night*, and indeed, when presented in isolation, such assimilated forms do not strongly activate their source words (Marslen-Wilson et al., 1995). Furthermore, when the assimilation process creates another word (e.g. *right* becoming *ripe*) but the following context that caused that assimilation is not presented, the altered input activates both words (*ripe* and *right*; Gow, 2002). A number of studies, however, have shown that when following context is present, and that context licenses the assimilation, the altered word is recognized correctly (Coenen et al., 2001; Gaskell and Marslen-Wilson, 1996; 1998; 2001; Gow, 2001; 2002; Mitterer and Blomert, 2003).

These results suggest that language-specific phonological knowledge about place assimilation is being used in word recognition, as it were, to undo the effects that the assimilation process had during speech production. Two comments on this conclusion need to be made, however. First, the assimilation process tends to be phonetically incomplete (e.g. the final consonant of the first word in *night bus* is not identical to a natural word-final /p/; it has phonetic features consistent with both a /p/ and a /t/; Gow, 2002). Listeners are sensitive to this fine-grained information, as they are to many other types of acoustic detail (as discussed earlier), and they use it in word recognition (Gow, 2002). Second, this kind of fine detail may be processed by low-level perceptual mechanisms, and so recovery from at least some kinds of assimilatory processes may not depend on language-specific knowledge. Thus, listeners who do not speak Hungarian nonetheless show similar sensitivity to native Hungarians to the effects of Hungarian liquid assimilation (Mitterer et al., 2006) and Hungarian voicing assimilation (Gow and Im, 2004). Other studies comparing native and non-native listeners on their sensitivity to assimilation phenomena, however, have found effects of language-specific knowledge (Otake et al., 1996; Weber, 2001). It is therefore probably the case that recovery from the effects of assimilation in word recognition will depend in some cases on language-universal perceptual mechanisms and in others on language-specific phonological knowledge.

Other types of phonological process which alter the realization of words in the speech signal and which have been examined for their effects on word recognition include resyllabification (Gaskell et al., 2002; Vroomen and de Gelder, 1999), liaison (the combination of resyllabification and surfacing of latent consonants in e.g. French; Gaskell et al., 2002; Spinelli et al., 2003), neutralization (e.g. the realization of intervocalic stops in American English as flaps;

Connine, 2004; McLennan et al., 2003), reduction (the deletion of single or multiple segments from words; Ernestus et al., 2002; LoCasto and Connine, 2002; Mitterer and Ernestus, 2006; Utman et al., 2000), and epenthesis (e.g. the insertion of the vowel schwa into the canonical form of a Dutch word; Donselaar et al., 1999). Space restrictions prevent detailed discussion of these phenomena. It is worth noting, however, that, as with assimilation, word recognition in the context of such processes entails a combination of phonological knowledge (e.g. knowledge about where epenthesis is legal; Donselaar et al., 1999), and the use of fine-grained phonetic detail to help recover the speaker's intentions (e.g. in the resolution of ambiguities between *dernier oignon* 'last onion' (with liaison) and *dernier rognon* 'last kidney' (without liaison); Spinelli et al., 2003).

A key issue concerning all these phonological processes, including assimilation, is the nature of the form-based lexical representations involved. Are citation forms as well as their variants (e.g. *pretty* with a [t] and *pretty* with a medial flap) stored in the mental lexicon? If so, then variant pronunciations could of course be recognized via retrieval of those forms. If not, they would have to be recognized through some kind of phonological inference that would map them onto their citation forms. The jury is still out on this issue. It may be that its conclusions will vary for different types of phonological process. Thus, for example, while the evidence suggests that assimilated forms are not stored in the mental lexicon (if they were, then, counterfactually, their recognition would not depend on following context), the evidence on neutralization suggests that both flapped and unflapped forms are stored (Connine, 2004; McLennan et al., 2003). Frequency of occurrence of pronunciation variants may determine which forms are stored (Connine, 2004). For example, words such as *pretty* occurred in their flapped variants in 96 percent of tokens in a corpus of American conversation (Patterson and Connine, 2001).

Frequency of occurrence is certainly another constraint used by listeners during word recognition. The work by Luce and colleagues discussed earlier on the effects of lexical neighborhood has shown that it is not just the number of similar-sounding words that determines ease of recognition, but also their frequency of occurrence. Other research with a variety of experimental paradigms also suggests that word frequency influences lexical activation (Connine et al., 1990; Connine, Titone and Wang 1993; Dahan et al., 2001a).

Listeners also use contextual information to determine which words speakers intend. Swinney (1979), in a cross-modal associative-priming study, showed that both meanings of an ambiguous word (e.g. the insect and spying meanings of *bug*) were activated at the offset of that word, irrespective of whether the preceding context biased interpretation of the word in one or other direction, but that shortly thereafter only the contextually appropriate meaning was still active. Similarly, Zwitserlood (1989) showed that while the speech signal was consistent with two Dutch words (e.g. *kapitein* and *kapitaal*, at the /p/ in *kapitein*), meanings associated with both words were activated, even in a strongly biasing context, but that as the speech signal unfolded, context influenced lexical activation. In strongly biasing contexts, priming effects were stronger for the appropriate meaning even before the signal provided disambiguating information (e.g. at the /t/ in *kapitein*), but in more weakly biasing contexts, both meanings remained active until after the signal provided disambiguation. These classic studies suggest that contextual information is not used to determine which words are considered for recognition, but is used rapidly thereafter to select among the set of activated candidates.

Many other studies support this conclusion. Thus, results from a wide range of experimental paradigms suggest that multiple senses of ambiguous words are simultaneously active, even in contexts where semantic or syntactic constraints could bias interpretation in favour of one sense (Blutner and Sommer, 1988; Conrad, 1974; Lackner and Garrett, 1972; Lucas, 1987; Oden and Spira, 1983; Onifer and Swinney, 1981; Seidenberg et al., 1982; Tanenhaus and Donenwerth-Nolan, 1984; Tanenhaus et al., 1979; Whitney et al., 1985; see Lupker, Chapter 10 this volume, for further discussion). But several semantic-priming studies have indicated that context can bias meaning activation (most strongly when an ambiguous word has a dominant and a subordinate meaning, and the context favours the dominant meaning; e.g. Moss & Marslen-Wilson, 1993; Simpson, 1981; Tabossi, 1988a; 1988b; Tabossi and Zardon, 1993).

A critical distinction that needs to be made here, however, is that between representations of word form (phonological representations) and representations of word meaning (conceptual representations). Differences in identity (i.e. form-based) priming and associative (i.e. meaning-based) priming on the same sets of materials (Gaskell and Marslen-Wilson, 2002; Norris et al., 2006) or between identity priming and eye-tracking data (Shatzman, 2006) support this distinction. Indeed, some type of form/meaning distinction must be made: Conceptual (and grammatical) knowledge must be stored so that interpretations of the meaning of utterances can be built, but that knowledge can only be accessed on the basis of phonological information. If one accepts this distinction, then the evidence from semantic priming on contextual biases in meaning activation does not necessarily speak to whether form-based representations were activated, because it is then possible that activation of phonological representations could occur without activation of conceptual representations. The data showing activation of multiple meanings in spite of contextual biases, however, do necessarily imply activation of form-based representations. The data on ambiguous words are thus consistent with the view that context does not determine which word forms are considered in the recognition process, but does influence selection, certainly among conceptual representations.

Research on the influence of sentential context on phonetic decision-making (van Alphen and McQueen, 2001; Borsky et al., 1998; Connine, 1987; Connine et al., 1991; Miller et al., 1984; Samuel, 1981) suggests that context can act as a bias on decision-making but does not influence prelexical processing. In the gating task (Grosjean, 1980), where listeners are asked to identify words on the basis of incremental fragments of those words ("gates"), listeners produce contextually inappropriate responses, primarily at earlier gates (Tyler, 1984; Tyler and Wessels, 1983). Both these sets of data once again suggest that spoken word recognition is based on what has been termed the principle of bottom-up priority (Marslen-Wilson, 1987; Marslen-Wilson and Tyler, 1980): the signal is the primary means by which listeners recover speakers' intentions, and context plays a secondary (but nonetheless strong and rapid) role. Data from a recent eye-tracking study are consistent with this view. Dahan and Tanenhaus (2004) show that verb-based thematic constraints have a powerful influence on sentence interpretation. Thus, when Dutch listeners heard a sentence onset such as *Nog nooit klom een bok* ... ('Never before climbed a goat ...'), they looked at pictures in a concurrent visual display of a goat, but not of a bone (*bot*), presumably because bones are inanimate and thus cannot climb. But when phonetic information favouring *bot* was inserted (by splicing the initial consonant and vowel from *bot* into *bok*), listeners did look at the bone. Phonetic evidence thus, at least temporarily, overrode the contextual bias.

3.5 **When?**

The speech signal is temporal in nature, and thus it is important to ask when, as that signals unfolds over time, the phonological forms of words are recognized. Marslen-Wilson (1987) estimates, on the basis of data from a variety of tasks, that word recognition occurs about 200 ms after word onset. This is of course an estimate of average recognition time: some words can be recognized very early, but others are recognized only after their acoustic offset (Bard et al., 1988; Grosjean, 1985). The temporal structure of speech certainly imposes strong constraints on recognition. Several lines of evidence discussed earlier support this conclusion. We saw that mismatching information in word-initial position tends to have a stronger inhibitory effect on word-form activation than word-final mismatch, because words with initial mispronunciations have to recover from a poor start, while words with final mispronunciations can be highly activated before the mismatching material arrives. A similar argument can be made to explain why the phonological representations of onset-embedded words (e.g. *cap* in *captain*) appear to be more strongly activated than those of offset-embedded words (e.g. *bone* in *trombone*): the longer words have a greater advantage over offset- than over onset-embeddings (Luce and Lyons, 1999; Shatzman, 2006). It was also suggested earlier that the recognition process is rather intolerant of mismatching information. The idea that evidence inconsistent with a lexical hypothesis may weigh more heavily than evidence supporting that word is consistent with the view that the process of word recognition entails a continuous form of optimization. As material inconsistent with a given lexical hypothesis appears, it is rapidly used to disfavor that word in the form-based competition process.

A critical factor determining when a word can be recognized is its Uniqueness Point (UP)—the point as one moves left to right through a word at which the information in the signal uniquely specifies that word. Many short words do not become unique before they end (Luce, 1986). It is these words that tend not to be recognized until after their offset. But the UP in longer words is often before offset. For such words strong relationships have been found between UPs and various measures of recognition time. These measures include phoneme-monitoring latency to phonemes varying in serial position (Marslen-Wilson, 1984), recognition point in gating (Marslen-Wilson, 1987; Tyler and Wessels, 1983; note that recognition point is an operational definition of when subjects can identify a target word in the gating task correctly and confidently; Grosjean, 1980), shadowing latency (i.e. speed to repeat spoken words; Radeau and Morais, 1990) and gender decision times (e.g. deciding whether

French nouns are masculine or feminine; Radeau et al., 1989). The UP effect, at least in the latter two tasks, may however depend on speaking rate: the effect in both shadowing and gender decision tends to be larger at slower speaking rates (Radeau et al., 2000). Furthermore, we have already seen that sentential context can influence the recognition process prior to a word's UP (e.g. Zwitserlood, 1989). Confirming evidence comes from electrophysiological studies (van Berkum et al., 2003; van den Brink et al., 2001; Van Petten et al., 1999) which have shown that, before a word's UP has been reached, event-related brain potentials vary depending on the contextual appropriateness of that word.

It is thus not the case that timing of word recognition is determined completely by when words become unique. Nevertheless, it is clear that word recognition is strongly influenced by the two factors underlying the UP concept: the information in the speech signal, and when that information is taken up. Analysis of how the pattern of responses in the gating task changes as more of the speech signal is heard also suggests that acoustic detail is taken up rapidly and continuously (Lahiri and Marslen-Wilson, 1991; Marslen-Wilson and Warren, 1994; McQueen et al., 1999; Smits et al., 2003; Warner et al., 2005; Warren and Marslen-Wilson, 1987; 1988). Analyses of how the lexical activation pattern changes over time, using priming paradigms (e.g. Davis et al., 2002; Gaskell and Marslen-Wilson, 2002; Zwitserlood, 1989), eye-tracking paradigms (e.g. Allopenna et al., 1998; Dahan, Magnuson and Tanenhaus 2001; Dahan, Magnuson, Tanenhaus and Hogan 2001; Salverda et al., 2003), and, most recently, the tracking of hand movements directing a computer mouse towards a display on a computer screen as spoken words are heard (Spivey et al., 2005), all confirm that there is continuous modulation of the lexical competition process as the speech signal unfolds.

These kinds of data suggest that word recognition tends to be as early as available constraints allow. As I argued at the outset, however, there may be no magic moment at which a word's phonological form is definitively recognized. Psycholinguistic tasks which require explicit judgements about what words have just been said provide discrete estimates of recognition time. While it is critical to consider the extent to which these measures reflect task-specific processing, it is perhaps just as critical to bear in mind that there may be no equivalent of these explicit judgements, and thus no instantaneous "recognition time", in normal speech comprehension.

There are two reasons why it appears to be wrong to think of the recognition of phonological word forms as a serial and categorical process. The first is the evidence already reviewed on activation of lexical conceptual representations. Much of the evidence on the activation of multiple lexical candidates used the cross-modal associative priming task (e.g. Tabossi et al., 1995; Shillcock, 1990; Zwitserlood, 1989) or measures of eye movements to pictures of objects mentioned in spoken instructions, or pictures of their phonological competitors (e.g. Allopenna et al., 1998; Salverda et al., 2003). The effects measured with both these paradigms indicate that there is rapid spread of information to the conceptual level of processing, and, critically, that this information spreads before a unique lexical form has been identified. Secondly, there are cases of form-based ambiguities which the signal might never be able to resolve (e.g. in oronyms such as *tulips/two lips*; Gow and Gordon, 1995). Although we have seen that there are subtle acoustic cues which help solve these ambiguities, it appears that at least in some cases (see e.g. Spinelli et al., 2003) these cues are not powerful enough to resolve them fully. In these cases, alternative form-based parses must be passed forward for resolution (using contextual information) at higher levels of processing. These arguments thus suggest that word-form recognition is probabilistic and incremental. The recognition system tends to settle on one most likely lexical parse of the phonological word forms in an utterance, but does not always do so. It tends to settle fast, but information is passed continuously to processes responsible for deriving an utterance interpretation.

3.6 How?

How, then, are words recognized? I will answer this question, and summarize the previous review, by discussing the representations and the processes that appear to be involved in word recognition. I have described three representational types: prelexical, word-form and word-meaning representations. Though this three-way distinction is not uncontroversial, it does tend to be made (albeit in different ways) in models of spoken word recognition (Gaskell, Chapter 4 this volume). More detailed discussion about the nature of prelexical and lexical-conceptual representations, and about the way in which morphologically complex words might be represented at the form and meaning levels, can be found in other chapters in this volume.

The focus has instead been on the recognition of the phonological form of words. But I have said little about the nature of form-based representations. This is largely because this issue is far from resolved. Perhaps words are represented only in their canonical pronunciations, or perhaps multiple pronunciation variants are stored. As already noted, the answer to this question is likely to depend on the frequency of occurrence of different pronunciations. The content of form representations (however many there are for each word) is also not yet resolved. Content may be very restricted (to the minimal abstract phonological specifications required to derive the word's pronunciation; Lahiri and Marslen-Wilson, 1991). Alternatively, it may be more fully specified but still phonologically abstract (e.g. strings of phonemes in TRACE, McClelland & Elman, 1986, and Shortlist, Norris, 1994), or richly specified, including speaker- and situation-specific detail (e.g. in a model where particular episodes of words that the individual listener has heard are stored, Goldinger, 1998). Furthermore, phonological knowledge might be stored in localist representations (e.g. as in TRACE and Shortlist) or in a distributed fashion (e.g. as in the DCM, Gaskell and Marslen-Wilson, 1997; 2002).

The picture is much clearer about the processes involved in word recognition. We have seen data showing that form-based recognition entails the parallel evaluation of multiple lexical hypotheses and a process of competition among those hypotheses. It appears that processing is cascaded (McClelland, 1979), both from the prelexical level to the word-form level and from word forms to word meanings. Processing is cascaded with respect to information flow and with respect to time. Thus, the evidence that fine phonetic detail influences lexical processing shows that there is a continuous flow of information from the prelexical level to the word-form level (e.g. McQueen et al., 1999); likewise, the evidence of activation of lexical meaning before the speech signal can uniquely specify a word's identity (e.g. Zwitserlood, 1989) shows that there is graded flow of information from form to meaning representations. This means that, in the temporal dimension, processing is incremental: as the speech signal unfolds, lexical hypotheses are continually updated, leading usually, but not always, to only one very probable lexical parse of the input utterance.

We have also seen that word recognition involves the evaluation of multiple information sources: segmental and suprasegmental information in the speech signal (modulated by its usefulness), frequency of occurrence biases, phonological knowledge, and contextual constraints. Particular algorithms have been proposed for how these sources of information are integrated. Lexical competition is the primary algorithm, but the PWC (Norris et al., 1997) has been proposed as a means by which cues to likely word boundaries can modulate the competition process. It is possible that the competition process is influenced only by positive information in the input (i.e. through bottom-up facilitation), but an additional algorithm of bottom-up inhibition (Norris, 1994) may be the means by which mismatching information has a stronger effect on lexical activation than matching information. Finally, the bottom-up priority restriction imposes strong constraints on the recognition process: only information in the signal can determine which word-form representations are considered.

One final "how?" question that has not yet been touched on is that concerning feedback. In addition to bottom-up flow of information from the prelexical level to the word-form level, is there also top-down information flow back to the prelexical level? Norris et al. (2000) review the large literature on lexical involvement in phonetic decision-making. They argue that all of these effects can be explained without feedback, and that data from Pitt and McQueen (1998) suggest that there is no feedback. The debate has continued since then, however, with arguments for feedback (Magnuson, McMurray, Tanenhaus and Aslin, 2003; Mirman et al., 2005; Samuel, 2001; Samuel and Pitt, 2003) and against it (McQueen, 2003). A factor that undoubtedly will be involved in resolving this debate is the plasticity of the speech-recognition system. Norris et al. (2000) argued that feedback could be of no benefit to on-line word recognition (passing lexical decisions back to the prelexical level will not improve those lexical decisions). But feedback could be of benefit in perceptual learning. Norris et al. (2003) show that listeners can use lexical knowledge to adjust their interpretation of a speech sound that is spoken in an unusual way. Since it thus appears that there is feedback for learning, the question for future research will be whether apparent demonstrations of feedback in on-line processing (i.e. feedback as a word is being heard) are in fact the result of longer-term learning effects, or are indeed true on-line effects that might arise epiphenomenally, that is, as a consequence of the need for feedback for perceptual learning.

3.7 Whither?

Whither spoken word recognition? I end with a few more remarks on future directions in word recognition. The flexibility of the recognition system will need to be considered more fully, both with respect to prelexical processing, as we have just seen, and with respect to lexical processing. Researchers have recently been asking how new words are learned and integrated into the word-recognition system (Gaskell and Dumay, 2003; Magnuson, Tanenhaus, Aslin and Dahan et al., 2003), and how prior phonological knowledge constrains the recognition of novel words (Shatzman and McQueen, 2006b). A special case of word learning is in second-language acquisition (Dijkstra, Chapter 15 this volume): how do listeners learn the words of a new language, and what consequences does this have for lexical representation and process? One direction research will therefore undoubtedly take in the next few years will be the development of more dynamic accounts of spoken word recognition.

Current investigations using the Norris et al. (2003) perceptual learning paradigm suggest that, at least under some circumstances, detail about how a specific speaker makes a phonetic contrast is stored by listeners (Eisner and McQueen, 2005; Kraljic and Samuel, 2005). These findings are consistent with other results showing talker-specific effects in memory for words and in speech processing (reviewed in Goldinger, 1998, and Eisner and McQueen, 2005; see also Pisoni and Levi, Chapter 1 this volume). It is not yet clear, however, where or how talker-specific detail (and other episodic detail) is stored; most models of spoken word recognition have been silent on this issue (see McLennan and Luce, 2005 for recent discussion). Spoken word recognition research will therefore need to address how specificity effects can be reconciled with the need for phonological abstraction (i.e. recognition of specific tokens in the signal as instances of particular lexical types).

The review of uptake of fine-grained segmental and suprasegmental information made clear that the speech signal is not just a sequence of phonemes. Prelexical processing involves the extraction of a segmental representation of an utterance, but this representation is not sufficient for word recognition. Prelexical processing also entails the extraction of rich sources of information specifying suprasegmental structure. Current models of spoken word recognition do not fully specify how this might be done. It is to be hoped that this situation will change.

Pause for thought should you ever be pestered by a carriage clock telesales person. A complex process of continuous competitive evaluation of candidate word forms will ensue, the inner workings of which you, as a listener, will largely be unaware. Nevertheless, you will probably settle rather quickly on a unique lexical parse of the word forms in the sales spiel. That is why, in spite of the fact that you have never heard the speaker before and never previously been bothered in this way, you will be able to slam the phone down rapidly and confidently. Unless of course your cold-call or time-keeper predilections are different from mine.

3.8 Who?

Allopenna, P. D., Magnuson, J. S., and Tanenhaus, M. K. (1998) Tracking the time course of spoken word recognition using eye movements: evidence for continuous mapping models. *Journal of Memory and Language*, 38: 419–39.

Alphen, P., van., and McQueen, J. M. (2001) The time-limited influence of sentential context on function word identification. *Journal of Experimental Psychology: Human Perception and Performance*, 27: 1057–71.

Alphen, P., van., and McQueen, J. M. (2006) The effect of Voice Onset Time differences on lexical access in Dutch. *Journal of Experimental Psychology: Human Perception and Performance*, 32, 178–96.

Andruski, J. E., Blumstein, S. E., and Burton, M. (1994) The effect of subphonetic differences on lexical access. *Cognition*, 52: 163–87.

Balota, D. A. (1990) The role of meaning in word recognition. In D. A. Balota, G. B., Flores, d'Arcais, and K. Rayner, (eds), *Comprehension Processes in Reading*, pp. 9–32. Erlbaum, Hillsdale, NJ.

Bard, E. G., Shillcock, R. C., and Altmann, G. T. M. (1988) The recognition of words after their acoustic offsets in spontaneous speech. *Perception and Psychophysics*, 44: 395–408.

Berkum, J. J. A., van, Zwitserlood, P., Brown, C. M., and Hagoort, P. (2003) When and how do listeners relate a sentence to the wider discourse? Evidence from the N400 effect. *Cognitive Brain Research*, 17: 701–18.

Blutner, R., and Sommer, R. (1988) Sentence processing and lexical access: the influence of the focus-identifying task. *Journal of Memory and Language*, 27: 359–67.

Borsky, S. Tuller, B., and Shapiro, L. P. (1998) "How to milk a coat": the effects of semantic and acoustic information on phoneme categorization. *Journal of the Acoustical Society of America*, 103: 2670–6.

Brink, D., van den, Brown, C. M., and Hagoort, P. (2001) Electrophysiological evidence for early contextual influences during spoken word recognition: N200 versus N400 effects. *Journal of Cognitive Neuroscience*, 13: 967–85.

Cho, T., McQueen, J. M., and Cox, E. A. (2007) Prosodically driven phonetic detail in speech processing: the case of domain-initial strengthening in English. *Journal of Phonetics*, 35: 210–430.

Christophe, A. Peperkamp, S. Pallier, C. Block, E., and Mehler, J. (2004) Phonological phrase boundaries constrain lexical access: I. Adult data. *Journal of Memory and Language*, 51: 523–47.

Cluff, M. S., and Luce, P. A. (1990) Similarity neighborhoods of spoken two-syllable words: Retroactive effects on multiple activation. *Journal of Experimental Psychology: Human Perception and Performance*, 16: 551–63.

Coenen, E. Zwitserlood, P., and Boelte, J. (2001) Variation and assimilation in German: consequences for lexical access and representation. *Language and Cognitive Processes*, 16: 535–64.

Connine, C. M. (1987) Constraints on interactive processes in auditory word recognition: the role of sentence context. *Journal of Memory and Language*, 26: 527–38.

Connine, C. M. (2004) It's not what you hear but how often you hear it: on the neglected role of phonological variant frequency in auditory word recognition. *Psychonomic Bulletin and Review*, 11, 1084–9.

Connine, C. M., Blasko, D., and Hall, M. (1991) Effects of subsequent sentence context in auditory word recognition: Temporal and linguistic constraints. *Journal of Memory and Language*, 30: 234–50.

Connine, C. M., Blasko, D. G., and Titone, D. (1993) Do the beginnings of spoken words have a special status in auditory word recognition? *Journal of Memory and Language*, 32: 193–210.

Connine, C. M., Clifton, C. E., and Cutler, A. (1987) Effects of lexical stress on phonetic categorization. *Phonetica*, 44: 133–46.

Connine, C. M., Mullennix, J., Shernoff, E., and Yelen, J. (1990) Word familiarity and frequency in visual and auditory word recognition. *Journal of Experimental Psychology: Learning, Memory, and Cognition*, 16: 1084–96.

Connine, C. M., Titone, D., Deelman, T., and Blasko, D. (1997) Similarity mapping in spoken word recognition. *Journal of Memory and Language*, 37: 463–80.

Connine, C. M., Titone, D., and Wang, J. (1993) Auditory word recognition: extrinsic and intrinsic effects of word frequency. *Journal of Experimental Psychology: Learning, Memory, and Cognition*, 19: 81–94.

Conrad, C. (1974) Context effects in sentence comprehension: a study of the subjective lexicon. *Memory and Cognition*, 2: 130–8.

Content, A. Meunier, C. Kearns, R. K., and Frauenfelder, U. H. (2001) Sequence detection in pseudowords in French: where is the syllable effect? *Language and Cognitive Processes*, 16: 609–36.

Cooper, N., Cutler, A., and Wales, R. (2002) Constraints of lexical stress on lexical access in English: evidence from native and nonnative listeners. *Language and Speech*, 45: 207–28.

Cutler, A. (1986) *Forbear* is a homophone: lexical prosody does not constrain lexical access. *Language and Speech*, 29: 201–20.

Cutler, A. (2005) Lexical stress. In D. B. Pisoni, and R. E. Remez, (eds), *The Handbook of Speech Perception*, pp. 264–89. Blackwell, Oxford.

Cutler, A., and Butterfield, S. (1992) Rhythmic cues to speech segmentation: evidence from juncture misperception. *Journal of Memory and Language*, 31: 218–36.

Cutler, A., and Carter, D. (1987) The predominance of strong initial syllables in the English vocabulary. *Computer Speech and Language*, 2: 133–42.

Cutler, A., and Clifton, C. E. (1984) The use of prosodic information in word recognition. In H. Bouma, and D. G. Bouwhuis (eds), *Attention and Performance X: Control of Language Processes*, pp. 183–96. Erlbaum, Hillsdale, NJ.

Cutler, A., Demuth, K., and McQueen, J. M. (2002) Universality versus language-specificity in listening to running speech. *Psychological Science*, 13: 258–62.

Cutler, A., and Donselaar, W. van (2001) *Voornaam* is not a homophone: lexical prosody and lexical access in Dutch. *Language and Speech*, 44: 171–95.

Cutler, A., and McQueen, J. M. (1995) The recognition of lexical units in speech. In B. de Gelder and J. Morais (eds), *Speech and Reading: A Comparative Approach*, pp. 33–47. Erlbaum, Hove.

Cutler, A., Mehler, J., Norris, D., and Seguí, J. (1986) The syllable's differing role in the segmentation of French and English. *Journal of Memory and Language*, 25: 385–400.

Cutler, A., and Norris, D. (1988) The role of strong syllables in segmentation for lexical access. *Journal of Experimental Psychology: Human Perception and Performance*, 14: 113–21.

Cutler, A., and Otake, T. (1994) Mora or phoneme? Further evidence for language-specific listening. *Journal of Memory and Language*, 33: 824–44.

Cutler, A., and Otake, T. (1999) Pitch accent in spoken word recognition in Japanese. *Journal of the Acoustical Society of America*, 105: 1877–88.

Dahan, D., Magnuson, J. S., and Tanenhaus, M. K. (2001) Time course of frequency effects in spoken word recognition: evidence from eye movements. *Cognitive Psychology*, 42: 317–67.

Dahan, D., Magnuson, J. S., Tanenhaus, M. K., and Hogan, E. M. (2001) Subcategorical mismatches and the time course of lexical access: evidence for lexical competition. *Language and Cognitive Processes*, 16: 507–34.

Dahan, D., and Tanenhaus, M. K. (2004) Continuous mapping from sound to meaning in spoken-language comprehension: immediate effects of verb-based thematic constraints. *Journal of Experimental Psychology: Learning, Memory, and Cognition*, 30: 498–513.

Davis, M. H., Marslen-Wilson, W. D., and Gaskell, M. G. (2002) Leading up the lexical garden-path: Segmentation and ambiguity in spoken word recognition. *Journal of Experimental Psychology: Human Perception and Performance*, 28: 218–44.

Diehl, R. L., Lotto, A. J., and Holt, L. L. (2004) Speech perception. *Annual Review of Psychology*, 55: 149–79.

Donselaar, W., van, Koster, M., and Cutler, A. (2005) Exploring the role of lexical stress in lexical recognition. *Quarterly Journal of Experimental Psychology*, 58A: 251–73.

Donselaar, W., van, Kuijpers, C., and Cutler, A. (1999) Facilitatory effects of vowel epenthesis on word processing in Dutch. *Journal of Memory and Language*, 41: 59–77.

Dumay, N., Frauenfelder, U. H., and Content, A. (2002) The role of the syllable in lexical segmentation in French: Word-spotting data. *Brain and Language*, 81: 144–61.

Dupoux, E., Pallier, C., Sebastián-Gallés, N., and Mehler, J. (1997) A destressing deafness in French. *Journal of Memory and Language*, 36: 399–421.

Eisner, F., and McQueen, J. M. (2005) The specificity of perceptual learning in speech processing. *Perception and Psychophysics*, 67: 224–38.

Ernestus, M., Baayen, H., and Schreuder, R. (2002) The recognition of reduced word forms. *Brain and Language*, 81: 162–73.

Ernestus, M., and Mak, W. M. (2004) Distinctive phonological features differ in relevance for both spoken and written word recognition. *Brain and Language*, 90: 378–92.

Fox, R. A., and Unkefer, J. (1985) The effect of lexical status on the perception of tone. *Journal of Chinese Linguistics*, 13: 69–90.

Frauenfelder, U. H., Scholten, M., and Content, A. (2001) Bottom-up inhibition in lexical selection: phonological mismatch effects in spoken word recognition. *Language and Cognitive Processes*, 16: 583–607.

Gaskell, M. G., and Dumay, N. (2003) Lexical competition and the acquisition of novel words. *Cognition*, 89: 105–32.

Gaskell, M. G., and Marslen-Wilson, W. D. (1996) Phonological variation and inference in lexical access. *Journal of Experimental Psychology: Human Perception and Performance*, 22: 144–58.

Gaskell, M. G., and Marslen-Wilson, W. D. (1997) Integrating form and meaning: a distributed model of speech perception. *Language and Cognitive Processes*, 12: 613–56.

Gaskell, M. G., and Marslen-Wilson, W. D. (1998) Mechanisms of phonological inference in speech perception. *Journal of Experimental Psychology: Human Perception and Performance*, 24: 380–96.

Gaskell, M. G., and Marslen-Wilson, W. D. (2001) Lexical ambiguity resolution and spoken word recognition: bridging the gap. *Journal of Memory and Language*, 44: 325–49.

Gaskell, M. G., and Marslen-Wilson, W. D. (2002) Representation and competition in the perception of spoken words. *Cognitive Psychology*, 45: 220–66.

Gaskell, G., Spinelli, E., and Meunier, F. (2002) Perception of resyllabification in French. *Memory and Cognition*, 30: 798–810.

Goldinger, S. D. (1998) Echoes of echoes? An episodic theory of lexical access. *Psychological Review*, 105: 251–79.

Gow, D. W. (2001) Assimilation and anticipation in continuous spoken word recognition. *Journal of Memory and Language*, 45: 133–59.

Gow, D. W. (2002) Does English coronal place assimilation create lexical ambiguity? *Journal of Experimental Psychology: Human Perception and Performance*, 28: 163–79.

Gow, D. W., and Gordon, P. C. (1995) Lexical and prelexical influences on word segmentation: evidence from priming. *Journal of Experimental Psychology: Human Perception and Performance*, 21: 344–59.

Gow, D. W., and Im, A. M. (2004) A cross-linguistic examination of assimilation context effects. *Journal of Memory and Language*, 51: 279–96.

Grosjean, F. (1980) Spoken word recognition processes and the gating paradigm. *Perception and Psychophysics*, 28: 267–83.

Grosjean, F. (1985) The recognition of words after their acoustic offset: evidence and implications. *Perception and Psychophysics*, 38: 299–310.

Grosjean, F., and Frauenfelder, U. H. (eds) (1996) *A Guide to Spoken Word Recognition Paradigms*. Psychology Press, Hove, UK.

Grossberg, S., and Myers, C. W. (2000) The resonant dynamics of speech perception: interword integration and duration-dependent backward effects. *Psychological Review*, 107: 735–67.

Isel, F. and Bacri, N. (1999) Spoken word recognition: the access to embedded words. *Brain and Language*, 68: 61–7.

Kraljic, T., and Samuel, A. G. (2005) Perceptual learning for speech: is there a return to normal? *Cognitive Psychology*, 51: 141–78.

Lackner, J. R., and Garrett, M. F. (1972) Resolving ambiguity: effects of biasing context in the unattended ear. *Cognition*, 1: 359–72.

Lahiri, A., and Marslen-Wilson, W. (1991) The mental representation of lexical form: a phonological approach to the recognition lexicon. *Cognition*, 38: 245–94.

Lehiste, I. (1972) The timing of utterances and linguistic boundaries. *Journal of the Acoustical Society of America*, 51: 2018–24.

LoCasto, P. C., and Connine, C. M. (2002) Rule-governed missing information in spoken word recognition: schwa vowel deletion. *Perception and Psychophysics*, 64: 208–19.

Lucas, M. M. (1987) Frequency effects on the processing of ambiguous words in sentence contexts. *Language and Speech*, 30: 25–46.

Luce, P. A. (1986) A computational analysis of uniqueness points in auditory word recognition. *Perception & Psychophysics*, 39, 155–8.

Luce, P. A., and Cluff, M. S. (1998) Delayed commitment in spoken word recognition: evidence from cross-modal priming. *Perception and Psychophysics*, 60: 484–90.

Luce, P. A., Goldinger, S. D., Auer, E. T., and Vitevitch, M. S. (2000) Phonetic priming, neighborhood activation, and PARSYN. *Perception and Psychophysics*, 62: 615–25.

Luce, P. A., and Large, N. R. (2001) Phonotactics, density, and entropy in spoken word recognition. *Language and Cognitive Processes*, 16: 565–81.

Luce, P. A., and Lyons, E. A. (1999) Processing lexically embedded spoken words. *Journal of Experimental Psychology: Human Perception and Performance*, 25: 174–83.

Luce, P. A., and Pisoni, D. B. (1998) Recognizing spoken words: the Neighborhood Activation Model. *Ear and Hearing,* 19: 1–36.

Lugt, A. H., van der (2001) The use of sequential probabilities in the segmentation of speech. *Perception and Psychophysics,* 63: 811–23.

Magnuson, J. S., McMurray, B., Tanenhaus, M. K., and Aslin, R. N. (2003) Lexical effects on compensation for coarticulation: the ghost of Christmash past. *Cognitive Science,* 27: 285–98.

Magnuson, J. S., Tanenhaus, M. K., Aslin, R. N., and Dahan, D. (2003) The time course of spoken word learning and recognition: studies with artificial lexicons. *Journal of Experimental Psychology: General,* 132: 202–27.

Marslen-Wilson, W. D. (1984) Function and process in spoken word-recognition. In H. Bouma and D. G. Bouwhuis (eds), *Attention and Performance X: Control of Language Processes,* pp. 125–50. Erlbaum, Hillsdale, NJ.

Marslen-Wilson, W. D. (1987) Functional parallelism in spoken word-recognition. *Cognition,* 25: 71–102.

Marslen-Wilson, W., Moss, H. E., and Halen, S., van (1996) Perceptual distance and competition in lexical access. *Journal of Experimental Psychology: Human Perception and Performance,* 22: 1376–92.

Marslen-Wilson, W. D., Nix, A., and Gaskell, M. G. (1995) Phonological variation in lexical access: abstractness, inference and English place assimilation. *Language and Cognitive Processes,* 10: 285–308.

Marslen-Wilson, W. D., and Tyler, L. K. (1980) The temporal structure of spoken language understanding. *Cognition*: 8, 1–71.

Marslen-Wilson, W., and Warren, P. (1994) Levels of perceptual representation and process in lexical access: words, phonemes, and features. *Psychological Review,* 101: 653–75.

Marslen-Wilson, W., and Zwitserlood, P. (1989) Accessing spoken words: the importance of word onsets. *Journal of Experimental Psychology: Human Perception and Performance,* 15: 576–85.

Mattys, S. L. (2004) Stress versus coarticulation: towards an integrated approach to explicit speech segmentation. *Journal of Experimental Psychology: Human Perception and Performance,* 30: 397–408.

Mattys, S. L., White, L., and Melhorn, J. F. (2005) Integration of multiple speech segmentation cues: a hierarchical framework. *Journal of Experimental Psychology: General,* 134: 477–500.

McClelland, J. L. (1979) On the time relations of mental processes: an examination of systems of processes in cascade. *Psychological Review,* 86: 287–330.

McClelland, J. L., and Elman, J. L. (1986) The TRACE model of speech perception. *Cognitive Psychology,* 10: 1–86.

McLennan, C. T., and Luce, P. A. (2005) Examining the time course of indexical specificity effects in spoken word recognition. *Journal of Experimental Psychology: Learning, Memory, and Cognition,* 31: 306–21.

McLennan, C. T., Luce, P. A., and Charles-Luce, J. (2003) Representation of lexical form. *Journal of Experimental Psychology: Learning, Memory, and Cognition,* 29: 539–53.

McMurray, B., Tanenhaus, M. K., and Aslin, R. N. (2002) Gradient effects of within-category phonetic variation on lexical access. *Cognition,* 86: B33–42.

McQueen, J. M. (1998) Segmentation of continuous speech using phonotactics. *Journal of Memory and Language,* 39: 21–46.

McQueen, J. M. (2003) The ghost of Christmas future: didn't Scrooge learn to be good? Commentary on Magnuson, McMurray, Tanenhaus and Aslin (2003) *Cognitive Science,* 27: 795–9.

McQueen, J. M. (2005) Speech perception. In K. Lamberts and R. Goldstone (eds), *The Handbook of Cognition,* pp. 255–75. Sage, London.

McQueen, J. M., Norris, D., and Cutler, A. (1994) Competition in spoken word recognition: spotting words in other words. *Journal of Experimental Psychology: Learning, Memory, and Cognition,* 20: 621–38.

McQueen, J. M., Norris, D., and Cutler, A. (1999) Lexical influence in phonetic decision making: evidence from subcategorical mismatches. *Journal of Experimental Psychology: Human Perception and Performance,* 25: 1363–89.

McQueen, J. M., Otake, T., and Cutler, A. (2001) Rhythmic cues and possible-word constraints in Japanese speech segmentation. *Journal of Memory and Language,* 45: 103–32.

Milberg, W., Blumstein, S. E., and Dworetzky, B. (1988) Phonological factors in lexical access: evidence from an auditory lexical decision task. *Bulletin of the Psychonomic Society,* 26: 305–8.

Miller, J. L., Green, K., and Schermer, T. (1984) On the distinction between the effects of sentential speaking rate and semantic congruity on word identification. *Perception and Psychophysics,* 36: 329–37.

Mirman, D., McClelland, J. L., and Holt, L. L. (2005) Computational and behavioral investigations of lexically induced delays in phoneme recognition. *Journal of Memory and Language,* 52: 416–35.

Mitterer, H., and Blomert, L. (2003) Coping with phonological assimilation in speech perception: evidence for early compensation. *Perception and Psychophysics,* 65: 956–69.

Mitterer, H., Csépe, V., and Blomert, L. (2006) The role of perceptual integration in the perception of assimilation word forms. *Quarterly Journal of Experimental Psychology*: 1395–424.

Mitterer, H., and Ernestus, M. (2006) Listeners recover /t/'s that speakers reduce: evidence from /t/-lenition in Dutch. *Journal of Phonetics,* 34: 73–103.

Morton, J. (1969) The interaction of information in word recognition. *Psychological Review,* 76: 165–78.

Moss, H. E., and Marslen-Wilson, W. D. (1993) Access to word meanings during spoken language comprehension: effects of sentential semantic context. *Journal of Experimental Psychology: Learning, Memory & Cognition,* 19: 1254–76.

Moss, H. E., McCormick, S. F., and Tyler, L. K. (1997) The time course of activation of semantic information during spoken word recognition. *Language and Cognitive Processes,* 10: 121–36.

Nakatani, L. H., and Dukes, K. D. (1977) Locus of segmental cues for word juncture. *Journal of the Acoustical Society of America,* 62: 714–9.

Norris, D. (1994) Shortlist: a connectionist model of continuous speech recognition. *Cognition,* 52: 189–234.

Norris, D., Cutler, A., McQueen, J. M., and Butterfield, S. (2006) Phonological and conceptual activation in speech comprehension. *Cognitive Psychology,* 53: 146–53.

Norris, D., McQueen, J. M., and Cutler, A. (1995) Competition and segmentation in spoken word recognition. *Journal of Experimental Psychology: Learning, Memory, and Cognition,* 21: 1209–28.

Norris, D., McQueen, J. M., and Cutler, A. (2000) Merging information in speech recognition: feedback is never necessary. *Behavioral and Brain Sciences,* 23: 299–325.

Norris, D., McQueen, J. M., and Cutler, A. (2003) Perceptual learning in speech. *Cognitive Psychology,* 47: 204–38.

Norris, D., McQueen, J. M., Cutler, A., and Butterfield, S. (1997) The possible-word constraint in the segmentation of continuous speech. *Cognitive Psychology,* 34: 191–243.

Norris, D., McQueen, J. M., Cutler, A., Butterfield, S., and Kearns, R. (2001) Language-universal constraints on speech segmentation. *Language and Cognitive Processes,* 16: 637–60.

Oden, G. C., and Spira, J. L. (1983) Influence of context on the activation and selection of ambiguous word senses. *Quarterly Journal of Experimental Psychology,* 35: 51–64.

Onifer, W., and Swinney, D. A. (1981) Accessing lexical ambiguities during sentence comprehension: effects of frequency of meaning and contextual bias. *Memory and Cognition,* 9: 225–36.

Otake, T., Hatano, G., Cutler, A., and Mehler, J. (1993) Mora or syllable? Speech segmentation in Japanese. *Journal of Memory and Language,* 32: 358–78.

Otake, T., Yoneyama, K., Cutler, A., and Lugt, A., van der (1996) The representation of Japanese moraic nasals. *Journal of the Acoustical Society of America,* 100: 3831–42.

Pallier, C., Sebastián-Gallés, N., Felguera, T., Christophe, A., and Mehler, J. (1993) Attentional allocation within the syllable structure of spoken words. *Journal of Memory and Language,* 32: 373–89.

Patterson, D., and Connine, C. M. (2001) Variant frequency in flap production: a corpus analysis of variant frequency in American English flap production. *Phonetica,* 58: 254–75.

Pitt, M. A., and McQueen, J. M. (1998) Is compensation for coarticulation mediated by the lexicon? *Journal of Memory and Language,* 39: 347–70.

Radeau, M., and Morais, J. (1990) The uniqueness point effect in the shadowing of spoken words. *Speech Communication,* 9: 155–64.

Radeau, M., Morais, J., Mousty, P., and Bertelson, P. (2000) The effect of speaking rate on the role of the uniqueness point in spoken word recognition. *Journal of Memory and Language,* 42: 406–22.

Radeau, M., Mousty, P., and Bertelson, P. (1989) The effect of the uniqueness point in spoken word recognition. *Psychological Research,* 51: 123–8.

Salverda, A. P., Dahan, D., and McQueen, J. M. (2003) The role of prosodic boundaries in the resolution of lexical embedding in speech comprehension. *Cognition,* 90: 51–89.

Samuel, A. G. (1981) Phonemic restoration: Insights from a new methodology. *Journal of Experimental Psychology: General,* 110: 474–94.

Samuel, A. G. (2001) Knowing a word affects the fundamental perception of the sounds within it. *Psychological Science,* 12: 348–51.

Samuel, A. G., and Pitt, M. A. (2003) Lexical activation (and other factors) can mediate compensation for coarticulation. *Journal of Memory and Language,* 48: 416–34.

Scharenborg, O., Norris, D., den Bosch, L., and McQueen, J. M. (2005) How should a speech recognizer work? *Cognitive Science,* 29: 867–918.

Sebastián-Gallés, N., Dupoux, E., Seguí, J., and Mehler, J. (1992) Contrasting syllabic effects in Catalan and Spanish. *Journal of Memory and Language,* 31: 18–32.

Seidenberg, M. S., Tanenhaus, M. K., Leiman, J. M., and Bienkowski, M. (1982) Automatic access of the meanings of ambiguous words in context: Some limitations of knowledge-based processing. *Cognitive Psychology,* 14: 489–537.

Shattuck-Hufnagel, S., and Turk, A. E. (1996) A prosody tutorial for investigators of auditory sentence processing. *Journal of Psycholinguistic Research,* 25: 193–247.

Shatzman, K. B. (2006) Sensitivity to detailed acoustic information in word recognition. Ph.D. dissertation, Radboud University Nijmegen (MPI Series in Psycholinguistics, 37). Wageningen: Ponsen & Looijen.

Shatzman, K. B., and McQueen, J. M. (2006a) Segment duration as a cue to word boundaries in spoken word recognition. *Perception and Psychophysics,* 68: 1–16.

Shatzman, K. B., and McQueen, J. M. (2006b) Prosodic knowledge affects the recognition of newly-acquired words. *Psychological Science,* 17: 372–7.

Shillcock, R. C. (1990) Lexical hypotheses in continuous speech. In G. T. M. Altmann (ed.), *Cognitive Models of Speech Processing: Psycholinguistic and Computational Perspectives,* pp. 24–49. MIT Press, Cambridge, MA.

Simpson, G. B. (1981) Meaning dominance and semantic context in the processing of lexical ambiguity. *Journal of Verbal Learning and Verbal Behavior,* 20: 120–36.

Smits, R., Warner, N., McQueen, J. M., and Cutler, A. (2003) Unfolding of phonetic information over time: a database of Dutch diphone perception. *Journal of the Acoustical Society of America,* 113: 563–74.

Soto-Faraco, S., Sebastián-Gallés, N., and Cutler, A. (2001) Segmental and suprasegmental mismatch in lexical access. *Journal of Memory and Language,* 45: 412–32.

Spinelli, E., McQueen, J. M., and Cutler, A. (2003) Processing resyllabified words in French. *Journal of Memory and Language,* 48: 233–54.

Spivey, M. J., Grosjean, M., and Knoblich, G. (2005) Continuous attraction toward phonological competitors. *Proceedings of the National Academy of Sciences,* 102: 10393–8.

Stevens, K. N. (2002) Toward a model for lexical access based on acoustic landmarks and distinctive features. *Journal of the Acoustical Society of America,* 111: 1872–91.

Streeter, L. A., and Nigro, G. N. (1979) The role of medial consonant transitions in word perception. *Journal of the Acoustical Society of America,* 65: 1533–41.

Suomi, K., McQueen, J. M., and Cutler, A. (1997) Vowel harmony and speech segmentation in Finnish. *Journal of Memory and Language,* 36: 422–44.

Swinney, D. (1979) Lexical access during sentence comprehension: (re)consideration of context effects. *Journal of Verbal Learning and Verbal Behavior,* 18: 645–59.

Tabossi, P. (1988a) Effects of context on the immediate interpretation of unambiguous nouns. *Journal of Experimental Psychology: Learning, Memory, and Cognition,* 14: 153–62.

Tabossi, P. (1988b) Accessing lexical ambiguity in different types of sentential contexts. *Journal of Memory and Language,* 27: 324–40.

Tabossi, P., Burani, C., and Scott, D. (1995) Word identification in fluent speech. *Journal of Memory and Language,* 34: 440–67.

Tabossi, P., Collina, S., Mazzetti, M., and Zoppello, M. (2000) Syllables in the processing of spoken Italian. *Journal of Experimental Psychology: Human Perception and Performance,* 26: 758–75.

Tabossi, P., and Zardon, F. (1993) Processing ambiguous words in context. *Journal of Memory and Language,* 32: 359–72.

Tanenhaus, M. K., and Donenwerth-Nolan, S. (1984) Syntactic context and lexical access. *Quarterly Journal of Experimental Psychology,* 36A: 649–61.

Tanenhaus, M. K., Leiman, J. M., and Seidenberg, M. S. (1979) *Journal of Verbal Learning and Verbal Behavior,* 18: 427–40.

Tyler, L. K. (1984) The structure of the initial cohort: evidence from gating. *Perception and Psychophysics,* 62: 1297–1311.

Tyler, L. K., and Wessels, J. (1983) Quantifying contextual contributions to word-recognition processes. *Perception and Psychophysics,* 34: 409–20.

Utman, J. A., Blumstein, S. E., and Burton, M. W. (2000) Effects of subphonetic and syllable structure variation on word recognition. *Perception and Psychophysics,* 62: 1297–1311.

Van Petten, C., Coulson, S., Rubin, S., Plante, E., and Parks, M. (1999) Time course of word identification and semantic integration in spoken language. *Journal of Experimental Psychology: Learning, Memory, and Cognition,* 25: 394–417.

Vitevitch, M. S. (2002) Influence of onset density on spoken word recognition. *Journal of Experimental Psychology: Human Perception and Performance,* 28: 270–8.

Vitevitch, M. S., and Luce, P. A. (1998) When words compete: levels of processing in spoken word recognition. *Psychological Science,* 9: 325–9.

Vitevitch, M. S., and Luce, P. A. (1999) Probabilistic phonotactics and neighborhood activation in spoken word recognition. *Journal of Memory and Language,* 40: 374–408.

Vroomen, J., and de Gelder, B. (1995) Metrical segmentation and lexical inhibition in spoken word recognition. *Journal of Experimental Psychology: Human Perception and Performance,* 21: 98–108.

Vroomen, J., and de Gelder, B. (1997) Activation of embedded words in spoken word recognition. *Journal of Experimental Psychology: Human Perception and Performance,* 23: 710–20.

Vroomen, J., and de Gelder, B. (1999) Lexical access of resyllabified words: evidence from phoneme monitoring. *Memory and Cognition,* 27: 413–21.

Vroomen, J., Tuomainen, J., and de Gelder, B. (1998) The roles of word stress and vowel harmony in speech segmentation. *Journal of Memory and Language,* 38: 133–49.

Vroomen, J., van Zon, M., and de Gelder, B. (1996) Cues to speech segmentation: evidence from juncture misperceptions and word spotting. *Memory and Cognition,* 24: 744–55.

Warner, N., Kim, J., Davis, C., and Cutler, A. (2005) Use of complex phonological patterns in speech processing: evidence from Korean. *Journal of Linguistics,* 41: 353–87.

Warner, N., Smits, R., McQueen, J. M., and Cutler, A. (2005) Phonological and statistical effects on timing of speech perception in Dutch: insights from a database of Dutch diphone perception. *Speech Communication,* 46: 53–72.

Warren, P., and Marslen-Wilson, W. (1987) Continuous uptake of acoustic cues in spoken word recognition. *Perception and Psychophysics,* 41: 262–75.

Warren, P., and Marslen-Wilson, W. (1988) Cues to lexical choice: discriminating place and voice. *Perception and Psychophysics,* 43: 21–30.

Weber, A. (2001) Help or hindrance: how violation of different assimilation rules affects spoken-language processing. *Language and Speech,* 44: 95–118.

Weber, A., and Cutler, A. (2006) First-language phonotactics in second-language listening. *Journal of the Acoustical Society of America,* 119: 597–607.

Whalen, D. H. (1984) Subcategorical phonetic mismatches slow phonetic judgments. *Perception and Psychophysics,* 35: 49–64.

Whalen, D. H. (1991) Subcategorical phonetic mismatches and lexical access. *Perception and Psychophysics,* 50: 351–60.

Whitney, P., McKay, T., Kellas, G., and Emerson, W. A. (1985) Semantic activation of noun concepts in context. *Journal of Experimental Psychology: Learning, Memory, and Cognition,* 11: 126–35.

Zwitserlood, P. (1989) The locus of the effects of sentential-semantic context in spoken word processing. *Cognition,* 32: 25–64.

Zwitserlood, P., and Schriefers, H. (1995) Effects of sensory information and processing time in spoken word recognition. *Language and Cognitive Processes,* 10: 121–36.

CHAPTER 4

Statistical and connectionist models of speech perception and word recognition

M. Gareth Gaskell

4.1 Introduction

In Terminator 2, Arnold Schwarzenegger confidently informed the human race: "My CPU is a neural net processor, a learning computer" (Cameron, 1991). This was a good reflection of the degree to which connectionist models had penetrated mainstream culture by that time. A brighter future—with neural networks in our toasters—was promised. A decade and a half later, my chapter looks at whether this promise has been delivered on, not in terms of toaster technology, but in terms of the modeling of human language. Where have these theories left us, how have they progressed, and is Arnie now due for an upgrade? This chapter will review the current impact of connectionism in the area of speech perception and spoken word recognition.

The inclusion of statistical models in the title of this chapter is an attempt to address one aspect of the influence of connectionist models in this area. A major advance that connectionism provided was to highlight the value and power of statistical models of language processing, which have partly as a consequence been rejuvenated. Therefore, some types of statistical model—particularly those stressing statistical learning—will be reviewed alongside connectionist theories.

Section 4.2 will provide a brief introduction to some of the major models and modeling styles that have been influential in speech perception. This will provide the necessary background for the bulk of the chapter, which is dedicated to the issues that these models have addressed. In section 4.3, I examine how connectionist models represent speech pre-lexically, and how such representations might develop and adapt to fit the requirements of the perceptual system. Section 4.4 looks at the process of segmentation, again addressing both acquisition issues and the degree to which connectionist models can explain performance in the adult system. Finally, in section 4.5, I will examine the process of word recognition, as modeled in terms of lexical competition. Key issues here include whether distributed models can cope with the specific properties that are imposed by the speech medium, such as the drawn-out nature of the input, and the consequent requirement to entertain multiple hypothesis (parallel activation) during recognition. This section also examines the interaction between levels of processing during recognition.

It would be difficult, and rather bizarre, to discuss models of human function without any mention of data on human performance. On the other hand, there is no way in which this chapter can provide complete coverage of the empirical data in the space available. Instead, I have chosen to relate the models to recent experiments that in my view are particularly relevant or discriminating. For a fuller picture of the current state of research, the reader is referred to Pisoni and Levi (Chapter 1 this volume), and McQueen (Chapter 3 this volume).

4.2 Modeling styles

4.2.1 Interactive activation and competition (IAC)

IAC models have been applied to aspects of recognition and perception for some considerable time (e.g. Grossberg, 1978; McClelland and Rumelhart, 1981), and build on a tradition of modeling stretching back further still (Morton, 1969; Selfridge, 1959). They typically consist of multiple hierarchical levels, in which nodes representing hypotheses about the nature of the input become activated. This activation level is a key concept in IAC models, being a dynamically changing representation of the strength of a particular hypothesis. In the simplest form, all nodes within a level represent mutually exclusive hypotheses, necessitating a competition between the activated nodes in order for recognition to take place. This competition is normally instantiated by linking together competing nodes with inhibitory connections, allowing strongly activated nodes to suppress weaker ones.

The TRACE model (McClelland and Elman, 1986) is a classic example of an IAC model, with an input layer representing phonetic features, and two further layers representing hypotheses about phonemes and words. Connections are inhibitory within the phoneme and word levels, and excitatory between levels for compatible hypotheses (e.g. between the /t/ phoneme node and the "torch" word node). This simple architecture has provided the basis for modeling numerous aspects of speech perception, particularly relating to phoneme perception (e.g. Dahan, Magnuson, Tanenhaus and Hogan, 2001; Elman and McClelland, 1988), lexical competition (e.g. Allopenna et al., 1998) and word segmentation (e.g. Gow and Gordon, 1995). This continued influence is notable particularly in view of the fact that the model has rarely been revised or adapted by its authors in the two decades following publication of the original research (although cf. McClelland et al., 2006).

Shortlist (Norris, 1994) makes use of similar principles in terms of modeling word segmentation and lexical competition in terms of a competitive activation network at the word levels, but differs from TRACE in a number of key respects. First the lower levels of the TRACE network were replaced by a computational matching process, which assigns a goodness-of-fit measure to each word in the lexicon in a non-dynamic fashion. Unlike TRACE, the implementation of this measure does not involve any feedback mechanism for word activations to influence phoneme detectors, but does make use of a direct cost in cases where input mismatches the phonemic representation of the word. A useful aspect of the word-level competition network in Shortlist is that only the word nodes with the strongest activation at any time point are linked into the competition network. This dramatically reduces the computational load involved in simulation, allowing realistically sized lexicons to be employed rather than a small sample of words.

A final noteworthy model of this type is the PARSYN model (Luce et al., 2000). Compared to TRACE, Shortlist can be thought of as a shift from a pure connectionist model to a more mathematical hybrid. The PARSYN model goes in the opposite direction, taking a mathematical model (NAM; Pisoni and Luce, 1998) and providing a connectionist implementation. This model resembles TRACE and Shortlist at a word level, but representations at input and intermediate layers are of allophones rather than features or phonemes. More importantly, the model implements effects of sublexical phonotactic probabilities directly, through links between temporally adjacent allophone nodes (implementing transitional probabilities), and through resting levels of allophone nodes (simple occurrence probabilities). These features allow the model to capture effects of phonotactic frequency on spoken word recognition (e.g. Luce and Large, 2001).

4.2.2 Error-driven learning networks

A second strand of connectionist modeling involves training (i.e. teaching) a network to perform a mapping from an input pattern (activations of a set of input nodes) to an output representation. One or more sets of *hidden units* often mediate between these layers, increasing the computational power available for performing the mapping. Training consists of activating the input nodes with an input pattern and allowing activation to percolate through the system to the output units, then adjusting the weights in the network to increase the similarity between the current output of the network and the desired output (often using backpropagation of error; Rumelhart et al., 1986).

The fact that these networks incorporate learning is one of their major appeals. Training the network avoids possibly arbitrary hand-coding of connection weights. More importantly, the behavior of the trained network reflects the structure inherent in the set of input-output mappings provided. Models of this nature often assume relatively little in the way of pre-existing psychological structure, testing the hypothesis that the environment provides the basis for learning the necessary structure (e.g. McClelland and Rumelhart, 1985).

For models relating to speech perception a principal requirement is to incorporate the continuous nature of the medium. IAC models typically achieve this by linking together large numbers of subnetworks, with each new "chunk" of the speech stream (often a phoneme) being handled by a new sub-network. Simple recurrent networks (SRNs: Elman, 1990) make use of error-driven learning, but carry out the reduplication at the hidden-unit level. For these networks the speech stream is fed into the same input layer, one chunk at a time, but an additional context layer feeds the state of the hidden units at the previous time-step into the hidden units alongside each new input. The result, computationally, is a rather weak memory system for sequences (Servan-Schreiber et al., 1991). Scientifically though, the impact of these extremely simple network models has been vast, with at the time of writing over 900 journal citations of the original 1990 article.

Elman's original simulations addressed the acquisition of structured internal (hidden unit) representations when trained on a "next item" prediction task for sequences of letters and words. Gaskell and Marslen-Wilson (1997) applied the SRN architecture to a mapping from a representation of speech input (phonetic feature bundles) onto a distributed representation of lexical content (form and meaning). This is the only model discussed so far that does not have a localist (i.e. single node) representation of words, with instead recognition of a word being intimately tied in with activation of the word's meaning and form. The model is also distinctive in terms of not relying on an explicit segmental (e.g. phonemic or allophonic) prelexical representation of speech for the purposes of lexical access.

4.2.3 Statistical models

One of the consequences of Elman's (1990) SRN simulations was to promote the value of statistical learning as applied to the speech stream. When trained on sequences of letters without any spaces between words, the accuracy of a network's predictions followed a seesaw pattern. Accuracy would improve towards the ends of words (where transitional probability information provides valuable information about the upcoming letter), but prediction error would peak at a word boundary, due to the unpredictability of the first letter of a word.

Framed in this way, we can think of an SRN model as a specific instance of a wider class of statistical models, in which statistical regularities are employed in order to discover linguistic structure (e.g. Harris, 1955). There is a wealth of empirical data demonstrating statistical learning in both infants and adults (e.g. Saffran et al., 1996; Saffran et al., 1997; see Gómez, Chapter 36 this volume). Recent statistical models of language learning and processing (e.g. Cairns et al., 1997; Swingley, 2005) have addressed these data by proposing that infants act as statistical learning devices, calculating statistics such as co-occurrence frequencies of phonemes in order to determine the identity of higher-level units. These models have an advantage over connectionist learning models in that they allow more powerful and less opaque learning algorithms to be applied to the training set, facilitating larger-scale simulation. Some connectionist studies have made use of a hybrid approach, combining pure statistical analyses with distributed connectionist representations (e.g. Gaskell and Marslen-Wilson, 1999).

4.2.4 Adaptive resonance theory (ART)

The final major connectionist approach to have proved influential in speech perception has been the ART theory of Grossberg (Carpenter and Grossberg, 1991). This form of modeling relies on the development of *resonant links* between items in working memory and higher-level list chunks. In the domain of speech perception, two models are particularly relevant. ARTPHONE (Grossberg et al., 1997) relates to the perception of phonemes, whereas ARTWORD (Grossberg and Myers, 2000) models spoken word recognition. In both these domains, ART has proved effective in modeling fine-grained temporal processes (e.g. Repp et al., 1978). In terms of its relationship to other models of spoken word recognition, ARTWORD has much in common with TRACE, in that it emphasizes feedback between word and prelexical levels, and uses inhibitory links between word nodes to implement lexical competition. Unlike TRACE, however, ART models make use of *masking* as a means of allowing larger list chunks to inhibit smaller ones. Vitevitch and Luce (1999) have utilized this property to model the interactions between lexical and sublexical (e.g. syllabic) units in word recognition. They argue that the multilevel approach supported by ART accommodates the contrasting effects of neighbourhood density on words and non-words (although cf. Lipinski and Gupta, 2005).

4.3 Prelexical representations of speech

As the previous section has indicated, connectionist and statistical models of spoken word recognition have tended to rely on the assumption that at least one pre-lexical representation of speech is extracted from the speech waveform and made available to the word recognition process. This greatly reduces the scope of the task faced by these models, but the choice of unit has functional implications for the model. In this section I will discuss the types of representation that have been promoted, and look at the extent to which learning models can help to explain how representations of speech develop.

4.3.1 Representation and dynamics in pre-lexical processing

The phoneme unit features in many models of speech perception, being the key prelexical level of representation in TRACE (McClelland and Elman, 1986) and Shortlist (Norris, 1994), and prominent in Grossberg's ART models (Grossberg et al., 1997; Grossberg and Myers, 2000). The advantages of the phoneme as a unit are many. It is a relatively simple unit, with only forty or so different phonemes required to describe all words in a particular language. It is also a unit that listeners have some awareness of (Morais and Kolinsky, 1994). It would be extremely surprising if the phoneme did not have an important role to play in speech perception at some level or other. However, it is possible that phoneme representations become prominent as a consequence of learning to read an alphabetic language (cf. Treiman and Kessler, Chapter 40 this volume). Indeed, adults' judgements about phonological form are often heavily influenced by their knowledge of a word's spelling (e.g. Hallé et al., 2000). Consequently, questions have been raised over whether the phoneme is a plausible unit for the key mediating role in the access to lexical representations in word recognition. Marslen-Wilson and Warren (1994) examined listeners' percepts of cross-spliced speech in which cues to the identity of syllable-final consonants mismatched. For example, the initial consonant and vowel (containing coarticulatory cues) from *job* were spliced onto the final release of *jog*. They argued that the pattern of inhibitory effects these mismatches had on perception, particularly with reference to the contrasting effects of word and non-word components of the cross-spliced speech, could not be explained in a model such as TRACE, in which phoneme representations intervened in the word recognition process. Although later data and simulations (Dahan, Magnuson, Tanenhaus, and Hogan, 2001) indicated that TRACE can adequately explain these mismatch effects, the Marslen-Wilson and Warren (1994) results do neatly demonstrate the fact that *resolution* of any sub-phonemic conflict is not necessary prior to word recognition. The clearest demonstration of this was the fact that cross-spliced non-words containing conflicting information about the identity of the final consonant did not delay a lexical decision "no" response. Models in which some hard decision must be made on the identity of phonemes prior to initiating word recognition would predict that anything delaying the evaluation of phonemic identity would of necessity pass the delay on to the lexical level.

The data on sub-phonemic mismatch do not rule out a phonemic level, but they do imply that any mediating phoneme level should be *cascaded* (passing on activation to the next level continuously, rather than completing processing at each level in a serial order), and that phoneme level activation functions should be *continuous* rather than discrete. This characterisation fits well with many of the connectionist models in the area (e.g. TRACE, Shortlist).

The avoidance of hard decisions at a pre-lexical level of representation makes discrimination between phonemic units of representation and more fine-grained representations surprisingly difficult. The DCM (Gaskell and Marslen-Wilson, 1997) employs a featural pre-lexical representation, partly as a response to Marslen-Wilson and Warren (1994) and other data showing effects of sub-phonemic detail on lexical access in spoken word recognition (e.g. Andruski et al., 1994). However, any fine-grained detail (e.g. voice onset time) that helps to discriminate between two phonemes can just as easily be represented at a phonemic level as a small shift in the activation of a phoneme. All the same, there are a few studies that suggest that some aspects of speech that do not discriminate between phonemes are used to discriminate between words. Davis et al. (2002; cf. Salverda et al., 2004) demonstrated that sub-phonemic information (most likely vowel duration) can be used to discriminate between embedding and embedded words (e.g. *captain* and *cap*) before any contrasting phonemic information is perceived. These data are unlikely to resolve the issue of choice of pre-lexical representation on their own, but they do suggest that some fine-grained detail is preserved in whatever representation serves in the process of word recognition.

4.3.2 Emergence of phonological representations

An attractive aspect of the learning-based connectionist approach, and one that has been somewhat neglected in this area so far, is that there may be no need for the researcher to select any particular unit of speech representation. Instead, the representational structure can emerge at the hidden unit level in response to the language environment and mapping on which the network is trained. Plaut and Kello (1999) sketched out a model of both the perception and production of speech in which a common phonology is an emergent property of the learned mapping. Their overall framework for modeling phonological development involves a phonological level of representation that mediates in two types of mapping: from semantics to articulation (in speech production) and from acoustics to semantics (in speech perception). Within this framework semantics are assumed to be derived from interactions with other modalities (e.g. vision) and acoustic representations are provided by the auditory system. The language learner also has a range of different articulations that are available before learning begins.

The key question Plaut and Kello (1999) addressed was how the phonological representations are learned. Network training was relatively straightforward for the comprehension side of things (acoustics to semantics) because of the availability of an independent semantic representation to generate a training error signal to propagate back through the network. However, the situation for production (semantics to articulation) was more complicated, because the equivalent training signal was not available. The solution to this problem was to rely on a learned direct association between articulation and acoustics: the *forward model*, which could be trained using a form of "babbling" in which random articulations generated sounds that were then translated to acoustic representations via the auditory system. This provided the information required to learn the forward model, which closes the loop in the Plaut and Kello (1999) model. The training signal for the production mapping can then be derived from perception, by propagating error signals back through the learned forward model in order to adjust weights in the production network.

This ambitious model holds great promise, in terms of allowing the structure of phonological representations to be defined by the combined requirements of speech perception and production. However, although the forward model has been fleshed out (Kello and Plaut, 2004), the full model remains in relatively early stages of development.

Monaghan and Shillcock (2003) studied the emergent representation of phonology, with more modest but also more concrete aims. They wished to examine the extent to which dissociations in the representation of vowels and consonants (as observed in aphasic data; Caramazza et al., 2000) could be an emergent property of learning speech mappings. They trained back-propagation networks to encode phonetic feature representations of phonemes using a corpus of speech. Some degree of specialization in hidden unit representations was encouraged in two different ways. In one simulation, two sets of hidden units were used with different distortions of the featural input applied to each set. In a second simulation, the hidden units differed in terms of the segmental context that was available on the encoding of each feature bundle. One set of hidden units was *fine-coded* in that only the feature bundle itself was fed into the hidden units, whereas in the *coarse-coded* set the featural representations of the preceding and following segments were available on the encoding of each item. Neither of these dissociations caused a hard division of labor between the processing of vowels and consonants in the two sets of hidden units. Nonetheless, both methods encouraged some kind of asymmetry in the processing of vowels and consonants between the two hidden unit sets. For example, the coarse-coded units developed representation more suitable to the encoding of vowels, whereas the fine-coded units developed representations more amenable to consonant encoding. The weak, emergent modularization in these models thus provided a potential explanation of the dissociations found in the patient data. The Monaghan and Shillcock (2003) simulations demonstrated that there is structure available both in featural representations of phonemes and in their segmental context that a learning model can utilize when processing speech, leading to some degree of functional specialization.

The phonological representations that we employ in the perception of speech must be robust in the face of sometimes quite wide variations in the phonological form of words (cf. Hawkins, 2003). Gaskell et al. (1995) again made use of the SRN architecture to model the perception of a typical form of variation—place assimilation—in which the surface form of coronal consonants depends on their following context. For example, *run* could be articulated as something approximating *rum* in *run back* or more like *rung* in the context of *run carefully*. Gaskell et al. (1995; see also Gaskell, 2003) trained an SRN to map from a representation of the surface (variant) form of the speech waveform onto an underlying representation in which these variations had been resolved. The network was able to learn to make use of following context in determining the underlying place of articulation of potential variants. In effect the network learned to reverse the "rules" of assimilation in the course of perception. This context-sensitivity has been demonstrated empirically in a number of studies (Gaskell and Marslen-Wilson, 1996; 1998; Gow, 2003; Mitterer and Blomert, 2003). A more controversial aspect of this model is that it predicts that the listener's sensitivities to context are learned, and vary depending on the listener's native language (because languages differ in terms of the assimilation phenomena they support). The evidence relating to language specificity is mixed (Darcy, 2003; Gow and Im, 2004; Mitterer et al., 2006), although experiments focusing on comprehension rather than low-level form appear to give the best evidence in favor of language-specific processing (Darcy et al., forthcoming).

4.3.3 Evolution of phonological representations

Because learning is so prominent in back-propagation-style models, they are often thought to reject any role for innate knowledge. A fairer reflection of the connectionist paradigm is that emergent structure is the null hypothesis—a parsimonious stance that is adopted in the absence of contradictory evidence. However, it is true that few connectionists have addressed how innate organization might interact with learning mechanisms in human development. Nakisa and Plunkett (1998) explored this combined approach in examining the rapid development of phonological skills in early infancy. They assumed that the infant is born with a learning mechanism that can be applied to acoustic input in order to learn a rudimentary phonological representation that can categorize speech segments. However, the precise architecture of this network (e.g. connectivity and type of learning rules) was assumed to be innately specified. Nakisa and Plunkett (1998) simulated the evolution of this "genome" using a genetic algorithm that allowed the gradual selection of an architecture particularly suited to the job of phonological development. The evolved network was then able to categorize adequately after only a couple of minutes of training. The innate specification was not language-specific, in that the network would learn to categorize given any one of a range of different languages as speech training, and the training element remained an important component of the procedure (although note that training on white noise produced reasonable categorization of speech). In sum, the Nakisa and Plunkett research demonstrates how evolved parameters can be integrated into connectionist accounts of speech perception.

4.4 Word segmentation

Research papers on word segmentation typically open with the statement that speech contains no equivalent of the blank space that separates words on a page. This modality division is stated a little too starkly, given that some acoustic cues (including silence) can be used as boundary markers, and in some cases handwritten text can obscure boundaries. Nonetheless, there remains a significant problem to be solved in identifying spoken word boundaries, both in terms of language development and in the adult steady state.

4.4.1 Bottom-up approaches

In many areas of psycholinguistics there are heated debates as to the relative importance of nature and nurture in the development of language skills. In the case of segmentation, however, there are no doubts as to the prominence of learning in the process. Adult listeners show marked differences in their use of speech rhythm in segmenting speech depending on their native language (Cutler et al., 1988; Otake and Cutler, 1993), and developmental studies have demonstrated that these language-specific biases are observable within the first year of an infant's life (Echols et al., 1997; Polka and Sundara, 2003). Not surprisingly, given this situation, statistical and connectionist learning models have been particularly influential in helping to understand how the segmentation skills of a listener develop.

Following Elman's (1990) demonstration of the ability of SRNs to pick up useful information about word boundaries, other researchers have carried out larger-scale analyses of the utility of phoneme co-occurrence statistics in segmentation. Cairns et al. (1997) employed *n-gram* and recurrent network models to carry out unsupervised learning of a prediction task for a phonemic transcription of a large corpus of English speech. The n-gram (bigram and trigram) models relied on the probabilistic assumption that across a large corpus of speech relatively rare sequences of two or three phonemes are likely to span word boundaries. These models were moderately successful, with the bigram model able to identify 38 percent of the word boundaries with a 0.85:1 ratio of hits to false alarms. A variant on the SRN, applied to the same learning task, produced similar performance. Interestingly, this model performed best at prediction of boundaries preceding metrically strong syllables (i.e. containing unreduced vowels), providing a potential explanation for the development of the metrical segmentation strategy (Cutler and Norris, 1988) in adult perception of English.

Christiansen et al. (1998) extended the SRN methodology to incorporate information available from lexical stress and utterance boundary cues, alongside phonotactic knowledge. The plausibility of the approach was tested by training their network on a phonemically transcribed corpus of child-directed speech. Rather than simply rely on predictability troughs in the speech stream, the use of an "utterance boundary" prediction unit provided an explicit indicator of a potential boundary. The development of reliable boundary predictions here was predicated on the assumption that sequences containing a word boundary would be relatively similar to sequences containing an utterance boundary. The added cues available in the Christiansen et al. (1998) simulations, which are easily extracted from the speech stream, showed further benefit in terms of word boundary identification. Indeed, even this set of cues would most likely constitute a small fraction of the types of non-lexical cues available in the speech stream to aid segmentation. The attraction of the connectionist/statistical approach is that in principle any number of different cues can be combined and utilized by the same processor, without the need for any specialized mechanisms.

4.4.2 Lexical approaches

Conventionally, there has been a very clear distinction between bottom-up, or pre-lexical, segmentation strategies (e.g. Cutler and Norris, 1988) and lexical ones. Models like TRACE and Shortlist exemplify the lexical approach, in which word-level competition generates an implicit segmentation of the speech stream as part of the lexical competition process. The reason these models have such a property is that word nodes at different time-steps inhibit each other only to the extent that they compete for "ownership" of the same stretch of speech. This means that the network is likely to settle into a solution for which all activated words are non-overlapping. Empirical evidence for this competition between overlapping words was provided by McQueen et al. (1994). Although such competition prevents activation patterns in which activated words overlap, it is less able to inhibit segmentation solutions in which activated words leave an unattributed "gap" in the speech stream. An additional constraint was added to Shortlist (Norris et al., 1997), penalizing segmentation solutions with a residual gap only if that residue could not be a "possible word" (i.e. did not contain a vowel). Cross-linguistic research (Cutler et al., 2002) suggested that this segmentation constraint, unlike many in this area, was common to users of all languages rather than tailored to the specific properties of the listener's native language.

When it comes to learning models, the lexical/pre-lexical distinction becomes somewhat murky. Models based on co-occurrence statistics can use this information to predict word boundaries, as discussed under "Bottom-up approaches" above; but if this information is reliable, the predicted boundaries can then be used to demarcate potential lexical items, and the store of lexical items can then be used to further inform word boundary hypotheses. Swingley (2005) presented a statistical learning model that segments through discovery of potential word candidates. Although superficially similar to the Cairns et al. (1997) model, sequence probabilities were calculated at the level of the syllable rather than the phoneme (cf. Saffran et al. 1996). Sequences of syllables in a child-directed speech corpus were evaluated on the basis of their occurrence frequency and *mutual information* (a measure of the likelihood of the syllable sequence weighted according to the frequency of the individual components), with sequences above threshold values being treated as words. The identification of these words in a sequence of speech then allowed word boundaries to be hypothesized.

As in related studies, the trained model demonstrated modest success in identifying word boundaries. Once again, there was an interesting tendency for the model, trained on either Dutch or English speech, to show a segmentation bias in line with the metrical segmentation strategy (Cutler and Norris, 1988).

Whether determined in terms of phonemes (Cairns et al., 1997) or syllables (Swingley, 2005) it seems that sequence probabilities can be used in a simplistic and unsupervised manner to extract structure relevant to the segmentation of one's native language.

A rather different slant on the use of statistics in word learning in acquisition and segmentation was provided by Brent and colleagues (Brent, 1999; Brent and Cartwright, 1996). Their methodology was related to the *minimum description length* concept, which has found applications in a wide range of areas including engineering, computing, and biological science (Rissanen, 1978; see also Goldsmith, 2001). In all cases, the basic idea is that a set of data can be compressed by looking for recurring patterns within the data, and replacing the most common recurring patterns with symbols. For speech, the data would be a corpus of phonemically transcribed speech, and the recurring patterns, with a bit of luck, would be words.

Although this theory in its purest form is rather abstract and difficult to relate to psycholinguistic data, Brent (1999) developed an implementation that had more attractive properties, in that it could be applied in an incremental way to a sequence of speech in order to extract potential lexical units in an "online" fashion (see also Perruchet and Vinter, 1998). One prediction based on this model is that if people hear a sequence in isolation (e.g. *passit*), that sequence should be lexicalized and subsequently used to parse a longer stretch of speech (e.g. *passit#downthewing*). This prediction was confirmed in a study of adult learning (Dahan and Brent, 1999).

The learning models discussed in section 4.4 have taken a particularly low-level, minimalist approach to segmentation, in which speech is examined in isolation from the wider context of the visual world. The final model discussed here (Davis, 2003) examines the role that semantics extracted from the visual domain might have on learning to segment. The idea behind this SRN model was that a child might hear a sentence such as *Look at that cat drinking the milk* in the context of seeing a cat, some milk, a saucer, and so on. However, without any prior knowledge of word boundaries or lexical items, there is no way in which the sequence *milk* can be associated with the white stuff the child sees. In other words, this many-to-many mapping does not provide the information required to perform segmentation. However, across a series of episodes (*Don't spill that milk, Pass me the milk, please*, etc.) the listener may extract the common sequence of phonemes linked with the recurring semantic representation of *milk*. Davis (2003) demonstrated that this cross-sentence comparison could be modeled using an SRN trained on the mapping between phoneme strings and multiple lexical items. Over time, the model was able to identify which lexical items were associated with which phoneme sequences, gradually leading to "cohort-like" competition between onset matching lexical nodes (Marslen-Wilson and Welsh, 1978).

This model, like many others in this section, focused on a single potential cue to the segmentation of speech. These models may appear unrealistic or inadequate when faced with the complexity of human language, and when compared with the enormously proficient human language system. The power in these approaches, however, is that they can be combined with relative ease (cf. Christiansen et al., 1998). There is evidence to support both pre-lexical and lexical strategies in adult processing (McQueen et al., 1994), and there is evidence that multiple strategies are employed in the acquisition of human languages (Johnson et al., 2003; Mattys and Jusczyk, 2001; Saffran et al., 1996). Thus, these models may not be best thought of as competing models, but as complementary ones, highlighting the flexibility of the segmentation system for speech.

4.5 Lexical representation and competition

There is near-unanimity in the view that spoken word recognition relies on a competitive process involving direct inhibition between lexical candidates. In this section I will look at this competition process in more detail, outlining the positions of the main connectionist models in this respect.

4.5.1 Granularity of representation

The role of connectionism in cognition has been hotly disputed throughout the period since connectionist models returned to favor in the mid-1980s. However, a somewhat different, but equally fierce, debate has been conducted in the last decade *within* the connectionist community over the granularity of representation in connectionist models. Learning models employing distributed representations had become increasingly popular towards the end of the twentieth century, but strong critiques of this style of modeling, and defences of the more traditional localist representations, emerged in the years following the turn of the century (e.g. Page, 2000; Bowers, 2002). Many aspects of this debate are discussed by Seidenberg (Chapter 14 this volume) with respect to reading, and Goldrick (Chapter 31 this volume) with respect to speech production. Here I focus on the relevance of this debate to the specific issues in spoken word recognition.

As laid out in section 4.1, many of the models of spoken word recognition (e.g. TRACE, Shortlist, and PARSYN) are essentially localist in terms of word recognition, whereas the DCM relies on distributed representations of words. Both modeling styles are able to implement inhibitory competition at the word level (Gaskell and Marslen-Wilson, 1999), but notable differences between their properties exist. The kind of competition envisaged in TRACE is typical of the localist solution, in which each word node maintains an activation level representing the strength of that word hypothesis, and directly competing nodes inhibit one another according to their activation.

In the DCM, direct competition is an obligatory aspect of the representational system. Words do not have individual nodes, but are instead represented as a unique pattern of activity across a set of nodes. Therefore, any attempt to activate words in parallel results in a blend of the different representations. This problem has been described as the *superposition catastrophe* (von der Malsburg, 1986; Bowers, 2002). A blend can weakly represent multiple lexical items inasmuch as it is relatively similar to some words and dissimilar to others. This apparently unpromising state of affairs was examined in detail by Gaskell and Marslen-Wilson (1999; 2002). We found that the limit on parallel activation depended on a range of factors, such as the number of elements in the distributed vector and the degree of sparseness, but that none of these factors could radically improve the ability to represent different items in parallel. Nonetheless, the superposition of distributed representations provided a good model for the degree of semantic and form-based priming afforded by word fragments of differing length and ambiguity. Although the distributed model is not particularly powerful in terms of parallel activation, it may well be that in this case the human system has the same "weaknesses", at least as measured via priming.

On the subject of catastrophes, Page (2000) argued that one of the principal disadvantages of distributed models was their potential to induce *catastrophic interference* in learning. This phenomenon occurs for some types of mapping when a network is trained on new information without any further presentation of previously learned information. Interleaving new and old information and making use of relatively slow learning will circumvent this problem, but there are cases where exploitation of new information is required quickly, and interleaving is not an option. A good example of this situation is the learning of a new spoken word (Gaskell and Dumay, 2003; Dumay et al., 2004).

Gaskell and Dumay (2003) showed that if adults learn a pseudo-word like *cathedruke* there are immediate consequences for memory in that these items can be recognized with ease, and recalled with a little prompting. Most critically, though, there is little to suggest that these items engage in lexical competition at this early timepoint. Nonetheless, without further exposure, these items do show lexical competition effects a day later (e.g. learning the "novel word" *cathedruke* causes slower recognition of the word *cathedral* through heightened lexical competition). One might imagine that the time between exposure and test could provide an opportunity for interleaving the new information with the existing items in lexical memory, simply through listening to everyday speech. However, what seems to be most important is a period of sleep, without any explicit exposure to novel or existing words. Dumay and Gaskell (2007) compared learning of novel words either in the morning or in the evening, with tests of lexical competition effects twelve and twenty-four hours later. For participants presented with novel words in the evening, the novel items appeared to have engaged in lexical competition twelve hours later, after a period of sleep. On the other hand, for items learned in the morning, there was no lexical competition effect after twelve hours (prior to sleep), but this effect emerged the following morning (after twenty-four hours). The delayed, sleep-associated emergence of lexical competition lends credence to the possibility that avoiding catastrophic interference during the integration of novel items in the mental lexicon requires some kind of short-term, episodic partitioning from the existing information. Interleaving can then occur overnight, perhaps as a consequence of reactivation of episodic knowledge during sleep (cf. McClelland et al., 1995; Robins and McCallum, 1999).

A possible advantage of localist models in this area is that activations can be easily converted into predicted response times in tasks such as lexical decision. Because there is no unique node representing any single word, it is less obvious how recognition decisions might be simulated in a distributed model (Page, 2000). One solution is to monitor the degree to which activations are close to their extremes (Plaut, 1997), since extreme values imply a lack of ambiguity in the response of the network. Nonetheless, it is fair to say that solutions of this kind are not always implemented, with a tendency to rely on the similarity to training patterns as an equivalent of localist activation.

On a related note, Coltheart (2004) has argued that distributed models of recognition lack the flexibility required to explain the range of deficits found in aphasic patients. For speech, Coltheart stressed the dissociation between *word-form deafness*, where patients are unable to understand or make lexical decisions about words, and *word meaning-deafness*, in which patients rarely understand the meanings of words but nonetheless have relatively preserved lexical decision performance. Coltheart argued that this latter pattern was particularly difficult to accommodate in a distributed model where lexical decisions are made primarily on the basis of semantic activation (Gaskell and Marslen-Wilson, 1997).

A number of points relate to this criticism. First, the debate is not really a localist vs. distributed debate. Although Coltheart (2004) identified a localist phonological lexicon as the means for accommodating word identification without access to meaning, the thrust of the argument is simply that for some of these patients, lexical decision can be carried out in some way independently of semantic activation (for example, a "phonological input lexicon" or other structure could operate using distributed representations that do not correspond to lexical semantics). A second point is that even for the patients with relatively spared ability to make lexical decisions, their performance was often poorer than matched controls in terms either of speed of response (Tyler and Moss, 1997) or of accuracy (Hall and Riddoch, 1997). Losing access to spoken word meaning seems to cause some problems in lexical decision—in some cases severe and in other cases not. Most significantly, though, it may well be the case that even a severely damaged semantic system could provide the basis for performing lexical decisions reasonably well. This is because if lexical decision relies on a measure of the degree to which semantic activations are extreme (Plaut, 1997), then there is no need to monitor all units in order to make a lexical decision—if a small sample of these units all show extreme values (reflecting a lack of ambiguity in terms of the meaning of those features) then it is highly likely that the remaining features are also extreme. Thus, even if a large proportion of the semantic system in spoken word recognition is obliterated, as long as there are a reasonable number of semantic nodes responding normally, the system could provide a good basis for lexical decision (cf. Plaut and Booth, 2006). This argument could equally be applied to other preserved units representing lexical content, such as orthographic or syntactic information.

In sum, the dissociation between word-meaning and word-form deafness does not provide a means of ruling out distributed models. Generally speaking, both localist and distributed representations appear to be able to operate to support lexical competition in word recognition. Interestingly, though, some of the limitations that are characteristic of distributed models, such as weak parallel activation and delayed consolidation, also appear to reflect human processing in this area.

4.5.2 Dynamics of lexical competition

As mentioned, there is a general reliance on direct inhibition between lexical items in order to resolve competition. There is also a growing empirical acceptance of the involvement of word frequency in the competition process (Dahan, Magnuson, and Tanenhaus, 2001; Cleland et al., 2006), although this has not been implemented in all models. The original TRACE simulations did not make use of word frequency, but Dahan, Magnuson, and Tanenhaus (2001) evaluated a range of implementations making use of word frequency. In a simulation of eye-tracking data showing early effects of frequency in recognition, they showed that using frequency to scale the weights between phoneme and word nodes provided the closest fit to their data. The DCM model incorporates frequency effects as a consequence of the differences between words in terms of exposure level during training. The network responds to these by weighting high-frequency words more strongly than low-frequency words in states of ambiguity. This frequency effect is largely transient and reliant on ambiguity, but a smaller effect remains even after ambiguity is resolved (Gaskell and Marslen-Wilson, 1997).

The accommodation of frequency weighting to reflect conditional probability is a desirable property, as it provides some convergence between psycholinguistic models and automatic speech recognition (ASR) systems, which commonly make use of probabilistic mathematical models. A further step in this direction was provided by

Scharenborg et al. (2005), who examined the implementation of a psycholinguistic model using ASR components. Their SpeM model made use of a probabilistic search mechanism, to derive the equivalent of lexical activations from the analysis of real speech. This model is valuable because it provides an opportunity for much more direct comparisons between human and simulation data, given that exactly the same speech files can be presented to both.

The role of feedback in the dynamics of spoken word recognition has been a subject of particular dispute. TRACE (McClelland and Elman, 1986) and models based on ART (Grossberg and Myers, 2000; Vitevitch and Luce, 1999) employ feedback links between word levels and subword levels so that lexical information is able to influence phoneme activations. In TRACE, for example, the excitatory feedback from word to phoneme level provides a simple explanation of the fact that lexical status can influence participants' judgements of the identity of ambiguous phonemes (Ganong, 1980). However, Norris et al. (2000) presented a strong defence of bottom-up models based on an alternative model, Merge, which made no use of top-down connections. Merge incorporates Shortlist (Norris, 1994) to explain normal spoken word recognition alongside a decisional system dedicated to judgements about phonological form. This decisional level integrates information from both lexical and pre-lexical levels, allowing lexical information to influence decisions without any feedback between lexical and phoneme nodes.

Both these models allow pre-lexical and lexical information to interact in the evaluation of speech, so they have been difficult to distinguish empirically. One criticism of TRACE levelled by Norris et al. (2000) was that it predicted lexically induced inhibitory effects on phoneme monitoring, when targets were embedded in incompatible lexical contexts (e.g. monitoring for /t/ in *vocabutary*). In these circumstances, there should be top-down excitation of the phoneme node congruent with the embedding word (e.g. /l/), and this should cause inhibition of the target phoneme node (e.g. /t/), leading to delayed recognition. Two previous empirical studies (Frauenfelder et al., 1990; Wurm and Samuel, 1997) had found no such inhibition. However, Mirman et al. (2005) showed that this inhibitory effect does arise in cases where the lexically compatible phoneme and the target phoneme are acoustically similar (e.g. *epidemit*, where /t/ and /k/ are similar). Simulations showed that in these circumstances (and not in the circumstances described above), TRACE does predict some inhibitory effect. However, this result does not provide a means of discriminating TRACE and Merge, because Merge can also accommodate this finding.

The clearest division between the predictions of TRACE and Merge relates to the question of whether lexical information can induce effects that are perceptual in nature. Elman and McClelland (1998) showed that lexically "restored" ambiguous phonemes can trigger *compensation for coarticulation* in neighbouring segments (Mann and Repp, 1981). This low-level indirect effect of lexical knowledge can be accommodated by TRACE but not by Merge, because of Merge's stipulation that lexical information can only affect high-level decisional processes. However, Pitt and McQueen (1998) contrasted lexical and transitional probability biases towards the restoration of the ambiguous phoneme in this paradigm, concluding that transitional probabilities are the key source of bias in this case.

The question of whether true lexical information can induce compensation for coarticulation is probably not settled, but the balance of evidence (cf. Magnuson et al., 2003a; 2003b; McClelland et al., 2006; McQueen, 2003; Samuel and Pitt, 2003) is now in its favor. Furthermore, Norris et al. (2003) have argued for lexical feedback with a longer time-course, to support the fine-tuning of phonetic category boundaries when faced with atypical speech (see also McQueen, Chapter 3 this volume).

4.6 **Conclusion**

It should be evident from the preceding review that we have clear-cut answers to some of the questions we might ask about the relevance of statistical and connectionist models of the perception of speech. Do these models help to explain how we perceive and understand speech? Undoubtedly so. Indeed, some of their properties have been so fully integrated into current theorizing that it is difficult to think of a current model in this area that could not be thought of as at least influenced by the class of models under discussion. The big question one might now ask is: what kind of statistical/connectionist model is best at explaining the behavior observed in human speech perception? Here, unfortunately, there are no clear answers. IAC-style models have been the most influential in terms of modeling larger-scale aspects of word recognition, with TRACE continuing to grow in terms of influence and prominence. Among its strengths are its simplicity and its portability, with easy-to-use implementations of the original model available in many computer operating systems (e.g. Strauss et al., forthcoming).

Meanwhile, learning-style connectionist models and their statistical relatives have tended to be applied in a more piecemeal way, addressing smaller aspects of speech perception in more detail. There have been notable successes in the application of these models, for example to the problem of word segmentation, but few models that are able to address the range of data that models such as TRACE or Shortlist accommodate. This is an indication of the greater challenges that this style of model faces, and to some extent a weakness of the learning algorithms that have been applied to the training data.

As to the future, there appears to be a progression towards further fractionation of modeling styles, with hybrid approaches becoming increasingly promising (e.g. Gaskell and Marslen-Wilson, 1999; Scharenborg et al., 2005). In principle, these models can cherry-pick the most attractive aspects of the range of models currently on offer. One would want perhaps the activation metaphor and ease of implementation of the IAC-style models coupled with the emergent representations and the application to development of the error-driven models, alongside the scalability of statistical models. Perhaps this is too much to ask for; but the preliminary work of Scharenborg et al. (2005) marks a significant step forward in the explicitness of relations between behavioral data and computational theory.

Acknowledgements

Preparation of this chapter was supported by grants awarded by the Medical Research Council and Biotechnology and Biological Sciences Research Council. Thanks are due to Padraic Monaghan and Mark Seidenberg for comments on an earlier version of this chapter, and to Mark Seidenberg for photographic evidence relating to the issue of Arnie's need for an upgrade.

References

Allopenna, P. D., Magnuson, J. S., and Tanenhaus, M. K. (1998) Tracking the time course of spoken word recognition using eye movements: evidence for continuous mapping models. *Journal of Memory and Language*, 38: 419–39.

Andruski, J. E., Blumstein, S. E., and Burton, M. (1994) The effect of subphonetic differences on lexical access. *Cognition*, 52: 163–87.

Bowers, J. S. (2002) Challenging the widespread assumption that connectionism and distributed representations go hand-in-hand. *Cognitive Psychology*, 45: 413–45.

Brent, M. R. (1999) Speech segmentation and word discovery: a computational perspective. *Trends in Cognitive Sciences*, 3: 294–301.

Brent, M. R., and Cartwright, T. A. (1996) Distributional regularity and phonotactic constraints are useful for segmentation. *Cognition*, 61: 93–125.

Cairns, P., Shillcock, R., Chater, N., and Levy, J. (1997) Bootstrapping word boundaries: a bottom-up corpus based approach to speech segmentation. *Cognitive Psychology*, 33: 111–53.

Cameron, J. (producer/director) (1991) *Terminator 2: Judgement Day*. United States: Tri-Star Pictures, USA.

Caramazza, A., Chialant, D., Capasso, R., and Miceli, G. (2000) Separable processing of consonants and vowels. *Nature*, 403: 428–30.

Carpenter, G. A., and Grossberg, S. (1991) *Pattern recognition by self-organising neural networks*. MIT Press, Cambridge, MA.

Christiansen, M. H., Allen, J., and Seidenberg, M. S. (1998) Learning to segment speech using multiple cues: a connectionist model. *Language and Cognitive Processes*, 13: 221–68.

Cleland, A. A., Gaskell, M. G., Quinlan, P. T., and Tamminen, J. (2006) Frequency effects in spoken and visual word recognition: evidence from dual-task methodologies. *Journal of Experimental Psychology: Human Perception and Performance*, 32: 104–19.

Coltheart, M. (2004) Are there lexicons? *Quarterly Journal of Experimental Psychology Section A: Human Experimental Psychology*, 57: 1153–71.

Cutler, A., Demuth, K., and McQueen, J. M. (2002) Universality versus language-specificity in listening to running speech. *Psychological Science*, 13: 258–62.

Cutler, A., Mehler, J., Norris, D., and Segui, J. (1988) Phoneme identification and the lexicon. *Cognitive Psychology*, 19: 141–77.

Cutler, A., and Norris, D. (1988) The role of strong syllables in segmentation for lexical access. *Journal of Experimental Psychology: Human Perception and Performance*, 14: 113–21.

Dahan, D., and Brent, M. R. (1999) On the discovery of novel wordlike units from utterances: an artificial-language study with implications for native-language acquisition. *Journal of Experimental Psychology: General*, 128: 165–85.

Dahan, D., Magnuson, J. S., and Tanenhaus, M. K. (2001) Time course of frequency effects in spoken-word recognition: evidence from eye movements. *Cognitive Psychology*, 42: 317–67.

Dahan, D., Magnuson, J. S., Tanenhaus, M. K., and Hogan, E. M. (2001) Subcategorical mismatches and the time course of lexical access: evidence for lexical competition. *Language and Cognitive Processes*, 16: 507–34.

Darcy, I. (2003) Assimilation phonologique et reconnaissance des mots. Ph.D. thesis, Ecole des Hautes Etudes en Science Sociales, Paris.

Darcy, I., Peperkamp, S., and Dupoux, E. (forthcoming) Plasticity in compensation for phonological variation:

the case of late second language learners. In J. Cole and J. I. Hualde (eds), *Laboratory Phonology 9*. Mouton de Gruyter, Berlin.

Davis, M. H. (2003) Connectionist modelling of lexical segmentation and vocabulary acquisition. In P. Quinlan (ed.), *Connectionist Models of Development: Developmental Processes in Real and Artificial Neural Networks*. Psychology Press, Hove, UK.

Davis, M. H., Marslen-Wilson, W. D., and Gaskell, M. G. (2002) Leading up the lexical garden path: segmentation and ambiguity in spoken word recognition. *Journal of Experimental Psychology: Human Perception and Performance*, 28: 218–44.

Dumay, N., and Gaskell, M. G. (2007) Sleep-associated changes in the mental representation of spoken words. *Psychological Science*, 18: 35–9.

Dumay, N., Gaskell, M. G., and Feng, X. (2004) A day in the life of a spoken word. In K. Forbus, D. Gentner, and T. Regier (eds), *Proceedings of the Twenty-Sixth Annual Conference of the Cognitive Science Society*, pp. 339–44. Erlbaum, Mahwah, NJ.

Echols, C. H., Crowhurst, M. J., and Childers, J. B. (1997) The perception of rhythmic units in speech by infants and adults. *Journal of Memory and Language*, 36: 202–25.

Elman, J. (1990) Finding structure in time. *Cognitive Science*, 14: 179–211.

Elman, J. L., and McClelland, J. L. (1988) Cognitive penetration of the mechanisms of perception: compensation for coarticulation of lexically restored phonemes. *Journal of Memory and Language*, 27: 143–65.

Frauenfelder, U. H., Segui, J., and Dijkstra, T. (1990) Lexical effects in phonemic processing: facilitory or inhibitory. *Journal of Experimental Psychology: Human Perception and Performance*, 16: 77–91.

Ganong, W. F. (1980) Phonetic categorisation in auditory word perception. *Journal of Experimental Psychology: Human Perception and Performance*, 6: 110–25.

Gaskell, M. G. (2003) Modelling regressive and progressive effects of assimilation in speech perception. *Journal of Phonetics*, 31: 447–63.

Gaskell, M. G., and Dumay, N. (2003) Lexical competition and the acquisition of novel words. *Cognition*, 89: 105–32.

Gaskell, M. G., Hare, M., and Marlsen-Wilson, W. D. (1995) A connectionist model of phonological representation in speech perception. *Cognitive Science*, 19: 407–39.

Gaskell, M. G., and MarslenWilson, W. D. (1996) Phonological variation and inference in lexical access. *Journal of Experimental Psychology: Human Perception and Performance*, 22: 144–58.

Gaskell, M. G., and Marslen-Wilson, W. D. (1997) Integrating form and meaning: a distributed model of speech perception. *Language and Cognitive Processes*, 12: 613–56.

Gaskell, M. G., and Marslen-Wilson, W. D. (1998) Mechanisms of phonological inference in speech perception. *Journal of Experimental Psychology: Human Perception and Performance*, 24: 380–96.

Gaskell, M. G., and Marslen-Wilson, W. D. (1999) Ambiguity, competition, and blending in spoken word recognition. *Cognitive Science*, 23: 439–62.

Gaskell, M. G., and Marslen-Wilson, W. D. (2002) Representation and competition in the perception of spoken words. *Cognitive Psychology*, 45: 220–66.

Goldsmith, J. (2001) Unsupervised learning of the morphology of a natural language. *Computational Linguistics*, 27: 153–98.

Gow, D. W. (2003) Feature parsing: feature cue mapping in spoken word recognition. *Perception and Psychophysics*, 65: 575–90.

Gow, D. W., and Gordon, P. C. (1995) Lexical and prelexical influences on word segmentation: evidence from priming. *Journal of Experimental Psychology: Human Perception and Performance*, 21, 344–59.

Gow, D. W., and Im, A. M. (2004) A cross-linguistic examination of assimilation context effects. *Journal of Memory and Language*, 51: 279–96.

Grossberg, S. (1978) Do all neural models really look alike? *Psychological Review*, 85: 592–6.

Grossberg, S., Boardman, I., and Cohen, M. (1997) Neural dynamics of variable-rate speech categorization. *Journal of Experimental Psychology: Human Perception and Performance*, 23: 481–503.

Grossberg, S., and Myers, C. W. (2000) The resonant dynamics of speech perception: Interword integration and duration-dependent backward effects. *Psychological Review*, 107: 735–67.

Hall, D. A., and Riddoch, M. J. (1997) Word meaning deafness: spelling words that are not understood. *Cognitive Neuropsychology*, 14: 1131–64.

Hallé, P. A., Chéreau, C., and Segui, J. (2000) Where is the /b/ in "absurde" [apsyrd]? It is in French listeners' minds. *Journal of Memory and Language*, 43: 618–39.

Harris, Z. S. (1955) From phoneme to morpheme. *Language*, 31: 190–222.

Hawkins, S. (2003) Roles and representations of systematic fine phonetic detail in speech understanding. *Journal of Phonetics*, 31: 373–405.

Johnson, E. K., Jusczyk, P. W., Cutler, A., and Norris, D. (2003) Lexical viability constraints on speech segmentation by infants. *Cognitive Psychology*, 46: 65–97.

Kello, C. T., and Plaut, D. C. (2004) A neural network model of the articulatory-acoustic forward mapping trained on recordings of articulatory parameters. *Journal of the Acoustical Society of America*, 116: 2354–64.

Lipinski, J., and Gupta, P. (2005) Does neighborhood density influence repetition latency for nonwords? Separating the effects of density and duration. *Journal of Memory and Language*, 52: 171–92.

Luce, P. A., Goldinger, S. D., Auer, E. T., and Vitevitch, M. S. (2000) Phonetic priming, neighborhood activation, and PARSYN. *Perception and Psychophysics*, 62: 615–25.

Luce, P. A., and Large, N. R. (2001) Phonotactics, density, and entropy in spoken word recognition. *Language and Cognitive Processes*, 16, 565–81.

Luce, P. A., and Pisoni, D. B. (1998) Recognizing spoken words: the neighborhood activation model. *Ear and Hearing*, 19, 1–36.

Magnuson, J. S., McMurray, B., Tanenhaus, M. K., and Aslin, R. N. (2003a) Lexical effects on compensation for coarticulation: a tale of two systems? *Cognitive Science*, 27: 801–5.

Magnuson, J. S., McMurray, B., Tanenhaus, M. K., and Aslin, R. N. (2003b) Lexical effects on compensation for coarticulation: the ghost of Christmash past. *Cognitive Science*, 27: 285–98.

Malsburg, C., von der (1986) Am I thinking assemblies? In G. Palm and A. Aertsen (eds), *Brain Theory*, 161–76. Springer, Berlin.

Mann, V. A., and Repp, B. H. (1981) Influence of preceding fricative on stop consonant perception. *Journal of the Acoustical Society of America*, 69: 548–58.

Marslen-Wilson, W., and Warren, P. (1994) Levels of representation and process in lexical access. *Psychological Review*, 101: 653–75.

Marslen-Wilson, W. D., and Welsh, A. (1978) Processing interactions and lexical access during word recognition in continuous speech. *Cognitive Psychology*, 10, 29–63.

Mattys, S. L., and Jusczyk, P. W. (2001) Do infants segment words or recurring contiguous patterns? *Journal of Experimental Psychology: Human Perception and Performance*, 27: 644–55.

McClelland, J. L., and Elman, J. L. (1986) The TRACE model of speech perception. *Cognitive Psychology*, 18: 1–86.

McClelland, J. L. Mirman, D., and Holt, L. L. (2006) Are there interactive processes in speech perception? *Trends in Cognitive Sciences*, 10: 363–9.

McClelland, J. L., McNaughton, B. L., and O' Reilly, R. C. (1995) Why there are complementary learning-systems in the hippocampus and neocortex: insights from the successes and failures of connectionist models of learning and memory. *Psychological Review*, 102: 419–57.

McClelland, J. L., and Rumelhart, D. E. (1981) An interactive activation model of context effects in letter perception, part 1: An account of basic findings. *Psychological Review*, 88: 375–407.

McClelland, J. L., and Rumelhart, D. E. (1985) Distributed memory and the representation of general and specific information. *Journal of Experimental Psychology: General*, 114: 159–188.

McQueen, J. M. (2003) The ghost of Christmas future: didn't Scrooge learn to be good? Commentary on Magnuson, McMurray, Tanenhaus, and Aslin (2003). *Cognitive Science*, 27: 795–9.

McQueen, J. M., Norris, D., and Cutler, A. (1994) Competition in spoken word recognition: spotting words in other words. *Journal of Experimental Psychology: Learning Memory and Cognition*, 20: 621–38.

Mirman, D., McClelland, J. L., and Holt, L. L. (2005) Computational and behavioral investigations of lexically induced delays in phoneme recognition. *Journal of Memory and Language*, 52: 416–35.

Mitterer, H., and Blomert, L. (2003) Coping with phonological assimilation in speech perception: evidence for early compensation. *Perception and Psychophysics*, 65: 956–69.

Mitterer, H., Csépe, V., and Blomert, L. (2006) The role of perceptual integration in the recognition of assimilated word forms. *Quarterly Journal of Experimental Psychology*, 59, 1395–1424.

Monaghan, P., and Shillcock, R. (2003) Connectionist modelling of the separable processing of consonants and vowels. *Brain and Language*, 86: 83–98.

Morais, J., and Kolinsky, R. (1994) Perception and awareness in phonological processing: the case of the phoneme. *Cognition*, 50: 287–97.

Morton, J. (1969) The interaction of information in word recognition. *Psychological Review*, 76: 165–78.

Nakisa, R. C., and Plunkett, K. (1998) Evolution of a rapidly learned representation for speech. *Language and Cognitive Processes*, 13: 105–27.

Norris, D. (1994) Shortlist: a connectionist model of continuous speech recognition. *Cognition*, 52: 189–234.

Norris, D., McQueen, J. M., and Cutler, A. (2000) Merging information in speech recognition: feedback is never necessary. *Behavioral and Brain Sciences*, 23: 299–370.

Norris, D., McQueen, J. M., and Cutler, A. (2003) Perceptual learning in speech. *Cognitive Psychology*, 47: 204–38.

Norris, D., McQueen, J. M., Cutler, A., and Butterfield, S. (1997) The possible-word constraint in the segmentation of continuous speech. *Cognitive Psychology*, 34: 191–243.

Otake, T., Hatano, G., Cutler, A., and Mehler, J. (1993) Mora or syllable: speech segmentation in Japanese. *Journal of Memory and Language*, 32: 258–78.

Page, M. (2000) Connectionist modelling in psychology: a localist manifesto. *Behavioral and Brain Sciences*, 23: 443–67.

Perruchet, P., and Vinter, A. (1998) PARSER: a model for word segmentation. *Journal of Memory and Language*, 39: 246–63.

Pitt, M. A., and McQueen, J. M. (1998) Is compensation for coarticulation mediated by the lexicon? *Journal of Memory and Language*, 39: 347–370.

Plaut, D. C. (1997) Structure and function in the lexical system: insights from distributed models of word reading and lexical decision. *Language and Cognitive Processes*, 12: 765–805.

Plaut, D. C., and Booth, J. R. (2006) More modeling but still no stages: reply to Borowsky and Besner. *Psychological Review*, 113: 196–200.

Plaut, D. C., and Kello, C. T. (1999) The emergence of phonology from the interplay of speech comprehension and production: a distributed connectionist approach. In B. MacWhinney (ed.), *The Emergence of Language*, pp. 381–415. Erlbaum, Mahwah, NJ.

Polka, L., and Sundara, M. (2003) Word segmentation in monolingual and bilingual infant learners of English and French. In M. J. Solé, D. Recasens, and J. Romero (eds), *Proceedings of the 15th International Congress of Phonetic Sciences*, pp. 1021–4. Causal Productions, Adelaide.

Repp, B. H., Liberman, A. M., Eccardt, T., and Pesetsky, D. (1978) Perceptual integration of acoustic cues for stop, fricative and affricate manner. *Journal of Experimental Psychology: Human Perception and Performance*, 4: 621–7.

Rissanen, J. (1978) Modelling by shortest data description. *Automatica*, 14: 465–71.

Robins, A., and McCallum, S. (1999) The consolidation of learning during sleep: comparing the pseudorehearsal and unlearning accounts. *Neural Networks*, 12: 1191–1206.

Rumelhart, D. E., Hinton, G. E., and McClelland, J. L. (1986) A general framework for parallel distributed processing. In D. E. Rumelhart and J. L. McClelland (eds), *Parallel Distributed Processing: Explorations in the Microstructure of Cognition*, vol. 1: *Foundations*. MIT Press/Bradford Books, Cambridge, MA.

Saffran, J. R., Aslin, R. N., and Newport, E. L. (1996) Statistical learning by 8-month old infants. *Science*, 274: 1926–8.

Saffran, J. R., Newport, E. L., Aslin, R. N., Tunick, R. A., and Barrueco, S. (1997) Incidental language learning: listening (and learning) out of the corner of your ear. *Psychological Science*, 8, 101–5.

Salverda, A. P., Dahan, D., and McQueen, J. M. (2003) The role of prosodic boundaries in the resolution of lexical embedding in speech comprehension. *Cognition*, 90: 51–89.

Samuel, A. G., and Pitt, M. A. (2003) Lexical activation (and other factors) can mediate compensation for coarticulation. *Journal of Memory and Language*, 48: 416–34.

Scharenborg, O., Norris, D., ten Bosch, L., and McQueen, J. M. (2005) How should a speech recognizer work? *Cognitive Science*, 29, 867–918.

Selfridge, O. G. (1959) Pandemonium: a paradigm for learning. In *Symposium on the Mechanisation of Thought Processes*. HMSO, London.

Servan-Schreiber, D., Cleeremans, A., and McClelland, J. L. (1991) Graded state machines: the representation of temporal contingencies in simple recurrent networks. *Machine Learning*, 7: 161–93.

Strauss, T. D., Harris, H. D., and Magnuson, J. S. (forthcoming) jTRACE: a reimplementation of the TRACE model of speech perception and spoken word recognition. *Behavior Research Methods*.

Swingley, D. (2005) Statistical clustering and the contents of the infant vocabulary. *Cognitive Psychology*, 50: 86–132.

Tyler, L. K., and Moss, H. E. (1997) Functional properties of concepts: studies of normal and brain-damaged patients. *Cognitive Neuropsychology*, 14: 511–45.

Vitevitch, M. S., and Luce, P. A. (1999) Probabilistic phonotactics and neighborhood activation in spoken word recognition. *Journal of Memory and Language*, 40: 374–408.

Wurm, L. H., and Samuel, A. G. (1997) Lexical inhibition and attentional allocation during speech perception: evidence from phoneme monitoring. *Journal of Memory and Language*, 36: 165–87.

CHAPTER 5

Visual word recognition

Kathleen Rastle

5.1 Introduction

> Because the emissary, his mouth (being) heavy, was not able to repeat (it),
> The lord of Kulaba patted clay and wrote the message like (on a present-day) tablet—
> Formerly, the writing of messages on clay was not established—
> Now, with Utu's bringing forth the day, verily this was so...
>
> (from *Enmerkar and the Lord of Arrata*, cited in Schmandt-Besserat, 1996: 2)

This Sumerian epic provides the oldest known account of the development of a system for writing language (Schmandt-Besserat, 1996). It tells the story of an emissary sent by Enmerkar, lord of Kulaba, to negotiate the purchase of timber, metals, and precious stones from the lord of a distant land. Following many rounds of difficult negotiations, a day came that the emissary was unable to commit Enmerkar's full instructions to memory. Enmerkar dealt remarkably effectively with this problem: He invented a system for writing language, which he used to inscribe his instructions onto a clay tablet. On that day, Enmerkar perhaps unwittingly also provided the foundation for what was to become a cognitive skill central to life in modern society: reading.

Though the contribution of Enmerkar himself is dubious, the Sumerians of Mesopotamia are generally credited with the invention of writing, and by implication reading, at the end of the 4th millennium BC. Thus, unlike our inborn capacity to use spoken language, reading must be seen as a cultural phenomenon that constitutes an astonishing form of expertise. Understanding the mechanisms underlying skilled reading is at the center of modern psycholinguistics, and has been a topic of considerable interest since the beginnings of psychology as a scientific discipline (e.g. Cattell, 1886; Huey, 1908). This brief chapter considers some of the theoretical and empirical issues that have shaped our understanding of one specific aspect of skilled reading—the recognition of single printed words—focusing in particular on aspects of this problem that are the subject of significant recent inquiry.

5.2 Orthographic representations

Our discussion begins with a term used in early psycholinguistic theories to denote a mental dictionary thought to package together all of the orthographic (spelling), semantic (meaning), and phonological (pronunciation) information about known words: the mental lexicon. This term still surfaces in the literature on the recognition of printed words, and it is not particularly out of the ordinary to see references to "lexical access" or "access to the mental lexicon" from the visual stimulus. These types of references are ambiguous, however, because it has been thought for many years that information about the orthographic forms of words is stored separately from information about the phonological forms of words and from information about the meanings of words (see e.g. Allport and Funnell, 1981; Baron, 1977; Borowsky and Besner, 2006; Coltheart, 2004; Coltheart et al., 2001; Forster and Davis, 1984; Grainger and Jacobs, 1996; Morton, 1979; Morton and Patterson, 1980). Implemented models of skilled reading such as the interactive-activation model (McClelland and Rumelhart, 1981; Rumelhart and McClelland, 1982), the DRC model (Coltheart et al., 2001), the SOLAR model (Davis, 1999), the MROM model (Grainger and Jacobs, 1996), and the distributed-connectionist models (Harm and Seidenberg, 2004; Plaut, 1997; Plaut et al., 1996;

Seidenberg and McClelland, 1989; see Seidenberg, Chapter 14 this volume) thus postulate bodies of orthographic knowledge, which are distinct from bodies of semantic knowledge and bodies of phonological knowledge. Visual word recognition begins with these orthographic representations; and so too, this chapter begins by considering three key issues about their nature.

5.2.1 Orthographic input coding: letters and letter positions

The earliest theories of visual word recognition (Cattell, 1886) posited that words are recognized not in terms of their component letters but as wholes, on the basis of their shapes. Though this hypothesis continues to engender fascination (e.g. Pelli et al., 2003; Perea and Rosa, 2002; Saenger, 1997), most modern theories suggest that word recognition is based on the analysis of letters. There is a broad consensus, based on evidence from behavioral (see e.g. Bowers, 2000) and neuropsychological (Coltheart, 1981; see also Rapp et al., 2001) studies, that these representations are *abstract letter identities*. They are abstract in the sense that they are independent of surface properties such as case, position, font, color, retinal location, or size. Thus, for example, the stimuli in Figure 5.1 all map onto the same abstract letter identity.[1] Mapping the visual stimulus onto abstract letter representations enables skilled readers to recognize words rapidly, even though they may appear in surface contexts (e.g. handwriting, typeface) of which the reader has no experience.

Representations of orthographic form need to encode more than abstract letter identities, however. They also need to encode information about the position of the letters in the stimulus. Otherwise, readers would not be able to detect the difference between anagram stimuli like *top*, *pot*, and *opt*, which share all the same letters. The interactive-activation model (McClelland and Rumelhart, 1981; Rumelhart and McClelland 1982), along with its subsequent variants including the DRC model (Coltheart et al., 2001) and the MROM model (Grainger and Jacobs, 1996), solves this problem through the use of slot-based coding. In this scheme, there are slots for each letter position in a stimulus, and each of these slots is filled with a separate set of letter units (one unit for each letter of the alphabet). For example, the word CLAM would be represented by selecting C in the first slot, L in the second slot, A in the third slot, and M in the fourth slot ($C_1L_2A_3M_4$). The distributed-connectionist models, by contrast, have solved the letter position problem in a variety of ways. These include slot-based coding schemes (e.g. Harm and Seidenberg, 2004) and Wickelcoding (Seidenberg and McClelland, 1989)—a scheme in which a word is represented by triplets of letters (e.g. CLAM would be represented as #CL, CLA, LAM, AM#).

Figure 5.1 Example visual stimuli thought to map onto a single abstract letter identity.

Recent research has begun to highlight the inadequacies of these types of schemes for coding letter order, however. The general problem is that stimuli that are perceptually very similar may be represented by very different slot-based codes or Wickelcodes (see Davis, 1999; Davis, 2005; Plaut et al., 1996). Consider the text presented below, which was taken from an email message circulated globally that purported to address the mechanisms underlying letter position coding.

> Aoccdrnig to rseearch at Cmabrigde Uinervtisy, it deosn't mttaer in waht oredr the ltteers in a wrod are, the olny iprmoetnt tihng is taht the frist and lsat ltteer be at the rghit pclae.

Though the specific idea expressed in this passage does not entirely stand up to research (see M. H. Davis, 2003; Grainger and Whitney, 2004 for discussion), the text does illustrate one major problem with these coding schemes. To be specific, one reason that we can read this passage so easily is that stimuli with letter transpositions (e.g. WAHT) are perceived as being very similar to their base words. Forster et al. (1987) used a masked form priming technique (see below) to explore this issue. They found that identity primes (e.g. what-WHAT) and transposition primes (e.g. waht-WHAT) produced equivalent levels of facilitation on lexical decision

[1] Some may wonder how information from the printed stimulus maps onto these abstract letter identities. The received view is that letter identification is based on the detection of feature primitives (e.g. horizontal bar, curve that opens to the right) stored in memory. Even despite variations in letter presentation, it turns out that many orthographies can be described with relatively few features and are thus amenable to an approach based on feature analysis (see e.g. Neisser, 1967 for a discussion).

latency; and further, that both of these prime types produced more facilitation than substitution primes (e.g. whut-WHAT; see also Perea and Lupker, 2003 for an extension of this finding to associative priming, e.g. jugde-COURT versus judge-COURT and judpe-COURT). Despite the perceptual similarity of WAHT to WHAT demonstrated by these experiments, the slot codes for WAHT and WHAT overlap by only 50 percent (W_1T_4). The situation is even worse with Wickelcoding, because on that scheme the codes for WAHT (#WA, WAH, AHT, HT#) are entirely different from the codes for WHAT (#WH, WHA, HAT, AT#; Davis,1999). Thus, neither of these letter coding schemes appears to provide an adequate explanation for these findings.

Further difficulties for slot-based coding schemes arise when "deletion neighbors" are considered (Davis, 2005). Deletion neighbors are words that can be derived from other words by removing one or two letters (e.g. PLUCK-LUCK; REPLAY-PLAY). On a left-aligned slot-based coding scheme, the words PLUCK ($P_1L_2U_3C_4K_5$) and LUCK ($L_1U_2C_3K_4$) share no overlap whatsoever, and should thus be perceived as highly dissimilar. Research using masked form priming (De Moor and Brysbaert, 2000; Drews and Zwitserlood, 1995; Schoonbaert and Grainger, 2004) and simple lexical decision (Davis and Taft, 2005) has, however, indicated that these types of letter strings are instead perceived as being highly similar. These and related findings (e.g. Davis and Bowers, 2004) have laid bare the inadequacies of existing schemes for coding letter position, and have made the search for a letter position coding scheme that better captures perceptual similarity among words one of the most interesting problems in visual word recognition research today (see also Dehaene et al., 2005, for a discussion of this problem from a neurobiological angle). Leading theories of position encoding include the open bigram coding scheme (Grainger and Van Heuven, 2003; Schoonbaert and Grainger, 2004; Whitney and Berndt, 1999; Whitney, 2001) and the spatial coding scheme as used in the SOLAR model (Davis, 1999). Unlike slot-based coding, which codes the absolute position of letters in the stimulus (e.g. the H in WHAT is in position 2), both of these coding schemes capture the *relative* position of letters in the stimulus (e.g. the H comes after the W in WHAT). Research is currently under way to adjudicate between these alternatives (see Davis, 2005 for a review).

5.2.2 Local and distributed word representations

Though all implemented models of visual word recognition postulate an orthographic body of knowledge that encodes letters and letter order, the form of this knowledge differs across models. Classical models of visual word recognition based on the interactive-activation model (McClelland and Rumelhart, 1981; Rumelhart and McClelland, 1982), such as the DRC model (Coltheart et al., 2001) and the MROM model (Grainger and Jacobs, 1996), postulate multiple levels of orthographic representation, one of which is an *orthographic lexicon* within which known words are represented locally (i.e. one unit stands for one word). The more spellings that are in someone's vocabulary, the more individual units that person will have in their orthographic lexicon. Distributed-connectionist theories, in contrast, deny the existence of an orthographic lexicon—or indeed, any lexicon (e.g. Harm and Seidenberg, 2004; Plaut, 1997; Plaut and Booth, 2000; Plaut et al., 1996; Seidenberg and McClelland, 1989; see Seidenberg, Chapter 14 this volume). These theories propose instead that the orthographic information about known words is coded in a distributed manner as learned patterns of activation over a large body of units. There are no individual units for known words in these models. This distinction between local and distributed lexical representations is a fundamental one for modeling skilled reading, and has been an issue of considerable debate over the last fifteen years of research.

The primary manner in which researchers have explored this distinction is in terms of the lexical decision task. Lexical decision is one of the most elementary abilities of the skilled reader. *Given sufficient time*, skilled readers can decide with a remarkable degree of accuracy (perhaps 100 percent) whether a visually presented letter string (e.g. BALSE, FALSE) is a known word or a non-word. Classical models of visual word recognition provide a natural account of lexical decision by virtue of their local representations of known words: if the visually-presented stimulus is represented in the orthographic lexicon, then it is a word. Further, both the DRC and MROM models have been able to simulate a wide range of human lexical decision data (Coltheart et al., 2001; Grainger and Jacobs, 1996). One may wonder, however, how the distributed-connectionist models are able to perform the lexical decision task, given that there are no local representations of known orthographic forms in these models. Indeed, this has been an issue of significant concern to distributed-connectionist modellers for some time (see Plaut, 1997; Seidenberg and McClelland, 1989), and has been discussed at length in the literature on visual word recognition (see e.g. Borowsky and Besner, 2006; Besner et al., 1990; Coltheart et al., 1993; Coltheart, 2004; Coltheart et al., 2001; Rastle and Coltheart, 2006).

The answer appears to be that these models can't perform this task—at least not in the manner that human readers can perform it. Rastle and Coltheart (2006) explained that the only way in which these models have been able to simulate the word/non-word discrimination with any degree of accuracy is on the basis of *semantic information* (Plaut, 1997; Plaut and Booth, 2000; see also Bullinaria, 1995). Seidenberg and McClelland (1989) claimed that their model could make this discrimination without consulting a semantic system; but closer inspection (Besner et al., 1990; Fera and Besner, 1992) revealed significant problems with the model's performance of the lexical decision task, "[calling] into question the ... claim that words can be distinguished from non-words by a distributed system lacking word-specific representations" (Plaut, 1997: 787). The problem with making lexical decisions on the basis of semantic information is that it renders these models incapable of explaining how patients with severe acquired semantic damage can perform the lexical decision task at levels of accuracy comparable to those of skilled readers without brain damage. Coltheart (2004) described several such neuropsychological cases. Irrespective of how unimpaired readers perform the lexical decision task (i.e. whether they use semantic information in making their decisions), the cases described by Coltheart (2004) demonstrate that readers *can* perform the lexical decision task without the use of semantic information. This is exactly what models without local representations of words have difficulty doing (see also Rastle and Coltheart, 2006).[2]

The most recent work on lexical decision in distributed-connectionist models was undertaken by Harm and Seidenberg (2004), who explored the use of two sources of *orthographic* information—orthographic stress and orthographic distance—for simulating the word/-non-word discrimination. Understanding exactly how these measures were computed is not important for the purposes of this chapter; what is important is that each of these measures reflects information about the state of orthographic units in a distributed-connectionist network following presentation of a visual stimulus. Harm and Seidenberg (2004) demonstrated that average orthographic distance and orthographic stress measures computed during stimulus processing differed for groups of words and non-words, and claimed that "these variables produce results that provide a basis on which lexical decisions could be made." One problem with this conclusion, however, is that Harm and Seidenberg (2004) did not report the *accuracy* with which their network could make the word/-non-word discrimination (Rastle and Coltheart, 2006). Even though the *groups* of words and non-words produced different *average* stress and distance values, it is not apparent from Harm and Seidenberg (2004) whether there is a value of stress and/or distance that reliably discriminates words from non-words to the level of accuracy achieved by skilled readers under non-speeded conditions.[3] Perhaps an even larger problem is that the orthographic information consulted in these simulations was computed on the basis of an orthographic representation regenerated from a semantic representation.[4] Thus, Rastle and Coltheart (2006) argued that this approach to lexical decision is still not immune to the neuropsychological evidence presented by Coltheart (2004), since any damage to semantic representations would impair the regenerated orthographic representations.

None of these are "in principle" arguments against the position that orthographic lexical

[2] I am grateful to Ken Forster for observing that another piece of evidence that skilled readers *can* make lexical decisions without the use of semantic information is the experience of knowing that a particular letter string is a word without having any idea of what it means. I have this experience with the word *aver*, for example.

[3] These words and non-words would, of course, have to be matched on orthographic structure. Plaut and Booth (2000) attempted a simulation of lexical decision based on semantic information in which they compared trained letter strings with a CVC structure against untrained letter strings with a VCV structure. The VCV structure had not been encountered previously by the network. Borowsky and Besner (2006) highlight the folly of simulating the task in this manner: in an equivalent experiment with human readers, the decision could be made with 100% accuracy simply by classifying the initial letter as a vowel or consonant.

[4] In this simulation, orthographic units activated semantic units, and the activated semantic pattern was used to compute a secondary orthographic representation. It was this secondary orthographic representation (reconstructed from the activated semantic pattern) that was used to calculate the orthographic stress and orthographic distance values.

knowledge is represented in a distributed manner. However, in fifteen years of study, models with distributed representations have yet to produce an acceptable account of one of the most basic abilities of skilled readers: deciding under non-speeded conditions whether a visually presented letter string is a known word. One must take a cautious approach in drawing inductive inferences about the reading system from this failure; indeed, these models may yet produce an acceptable account of this most elementary ability. However, at least at present, it appears that a great irony of distributed-connectionist modeling is that it has helped to demonstrate the importance of local orthographic representations in the visual word recognition system.

5.2.3 Frequency, cumulative frequency, and age of acquisition

The most powerful determinant of the time taken to recognize a word is the frequency with which it occurs (see e.g. Monsell, 1991; Murray and Forster, 2004 for reviews). Effects of word frequency have been reported in lexical decision (e.g. Forster and Chambers, 1973; Balota et al., 2004) along with every other task thought to contact the orthographic representations involved in visual word recognition. These include, for example, perceptual identification (e.g. Broadbent, 1967), reading aloud (e.g. Balota and Chumbley, 1984), and eye fixation times in reading (e.g. Inhoff and Rayner, 1986; Schilling et al., 1998). Though some have questioned whether frequency effects might be exaggerated in the lexical decision task (Balota and Chumbley, 1984), there is widespread agreement that one's experience with words is somehow encoded in (local) orthographic representations of known words and thus influences the ease with which those words are recognized. The interactive-activation model (McClelland and Rumelhart, 1981; Rumelhart and McClelland, 1982) and its subsequent variants (Coltheart et al., 2001; Grainger and Jacobs, 1996), for example, conceptualize frequency effects in terms of the resting activation of local orthographic representations of words: Units representing words that occur frequently in print have higher resting levels of activation than units representing words that occur only rarely in print, and thus reach a criterion for recognition more quickly.

Recently, an interesting debate has emerged in the literature, which questions exactly how our experience with words is encoded into the orthographic representations supporting visual word recognition. Previous research has always suggested that the frequency with which a particular printed word occurs in the language provides a good estimate of our experience with words, and thus influences recognition time (e.g. Forster and Chambers, 1973). These frequency estimates are normally gathered through the analysis of large corpora of adult text, in which the occurrences of individual words are counted (e.g. Baayen et al., 1993; Kucera and Francis, 1967; Zeno et al., 1995). However, more recent research has suggested that the age at which we acquire a word may also be an important determinant of our experience with words (e.g. Brysbaert et al., 2000; Morrison and Ellis, 1995; Gerhand and Barry, 1999). Might this information also be encoded in representations of orthographic form? Research attempting to manipulate these factors orthogonally seems to suggest that there may indeed be independent effects of printed frequency and age of acquisition (Morrison and Ellis, 1995; Gerhand and Barry, 1999) on visual word recognition: the time taken to recognize a word is reduced both when that word has a high printed frequency and when that word was acquired early in life.

A closer look, however, reveals the methodological difficulties inherent in conducting these studies (Zevin and Seidenberg, 2002). For one thing, the age of acquisition measures typically used in these studies is based on subjective estimates from adults of the age at which certain words were acquired (Gilhooly and Logie, 1980). Though these measures correlate with objective measures of the age at which children acquire object names (Morrison et al., 1997), they are estimates nonetheless. Measures of printed word frequency are also estimates, and these estimates differ depending on the size and nature of the corpus used (Zevin and Seidenberg, 2002). Pairing these measurement issues with the fact that printed word frequency and age of acquisition are so highly related (high-frequency words are those most likely to be learned early; $r = -.68$, Carroll and White, 1973) can render it very difficult to design experiments that examine independent effects of these variables. Indeed, Zevin and Seidenberg (2002) demonstrated that recent studies of age of acquisition have typically confounded the age of acquisition variable with at least one of the available counts of printed word frequency.

Further—and this is also a critical point—it might be the case that printed frequency and age of acquisition are actually two dimensions of a single variable: cumulative frequency (i.e. the frequency with which an individual is exposed to a particular word over their lifetime; e.g.

Lewis et al., 2001; Zevin and Seidenberg, 2002). It is certainly not unlikely that our experience with words (and the representation of this experience in the recognition system) accrues over our lifetimes; indeed, the view that cumulative frequency provides a better description of our experience with words than printed word frequency is now fairly uncontroversial (see Brysbaert and Ghyselinck, 2006). The difficult question of interest and debate at present is whether cumulative frequency can account fully for the age of acquisition effect observed on visual word recognition. Recent research using experimental (Stadthagen-Gonzales et al., 2004) and regression (Brysbaert and Ghyselinck, 2006; Ghyselinck et al., 2004) approaches suggests that the answer is probably "no": the age at which a word was acquired also seems to play a role in its recognition. Clearly, however, further empirical and computational research is necessary in this important area, which promises to give us insight into the mechanisms by which we acquire experience with printed words and represent this experience in the recognition system.

5.3 Processing dynamics and mechanisms for selection

Thus far, our discussion has homed in on a theory of visual word recognition that consists of multiple levels of orthographic representation. The visual stimulus is analyzed in terms of its features; these features map onto a level of representation that codes abstract letter identity as well as letter position; and these letters map onto a level of representation at which the orthographic forms of known words are represented locally and somehow coded for our experience with them. However, this theory so far consists only of the architecture. How is information transmitted through these levels of representation? Further, what is the mechanism by which a single local word unit corresponding to the target is selected? These are the questions that are considered in this section.

5.3.1 The interactive-activation model

Two empirical findings, the word superiority effect (Reicher, 1969; Wheeler, 1970) and the pseudo-word superiority effect (Carr et al., 1978; McClelland and Johnston, 1977) were crucially important in constraining early accounts of visual word recognition. In the Reicher-Wheeler experiments, a word (e.g. WORK) or a non-word (e.g. OWRK) was flashed very briefly and then replaced by a pattern mask. Participants were then forced to decide which of two letters (e.g. D or K), presented adjacent to the position of the previous target letter, was in the stimulus. Results showed that letter identification was more accurate when letters had been presented within word stimuli than within non-word stimuli. Further experiments (Carr et al., 1978; McClelland and Johnston, 1977) demonstrated that the letter-identification benefit seen with words extends to pronounceable non-words (e.g. K is identified with greater accuracy in TARK than in ATRK). These findings provided benchmark phenomena for the development of the interactive-activation model (McClelland and Rumelhart, 1981; Rumelhart and McClelland, 1982), which many still consider to be the cornerstone of our understanding of processing and selection in visual word recognition (see e.g. Coltheart et al., 2001; Davis, 2003; Grainger and Jacobs, 1996; but see Forster, 2005; Murray and Forster, 2004 for important criticisms). The model is depicted in Figure 5.2.

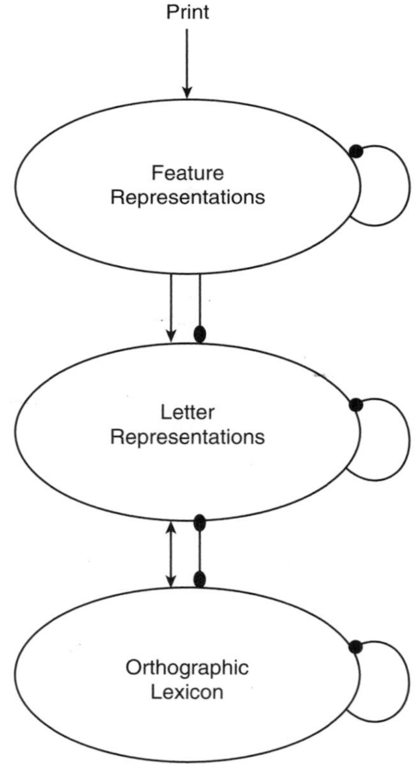

Figure 5.2 The interactive-activation model of visual word recognition (McClelland and Rumelhart, 1981; Rumelhart and McClelland, 1982).

In the model, information from the visual stimulus flows through feature, letter, and word levels of representation. Each of these levels of representation consists of individual units called nodes. The connections between these adjacent levels of representation are both excitatory and inhibitory: nodes at every level excite nodes at adjacent levels with which they are consistent and inhibit nodes at adjacent levels with which they are inconsistent. For example, the initial letter T in a stimulus will activate word nodes for TAKE, TALL, and TREE while inhibiting word nodes for CAKE, MALL, and FREE. Information flows continuously (i.e. in "cascade"; McClelland, 1979) through these levels of representation. Unlike the logogen models that preceded it (e.g. Morton, 1969; 1979), information at one level of representation does not have to reach a threshold before being passed on to another level of representation (see Coltheart et al., 2001 for a discussion).

Information flows between adjacent layers of the model in a bidirectional manner (e.g. information travels from letters to words and also from words to letters). It is through these bidirectional connections that the model explains how knowledge of a higher-level unit (e.g. a word) can influence the processing of a lower-level unit (e.g. a letter). Letters embedded in words are particularly easy to recognize (i.e. the word superiority effect) because they enjoy top-down support from nodes activated by the stimulus at the word level. Letters embedded in pronounceable pseudo-words (i.e. the pseudo-word superiority effect) may also enjoy top-down support through these bidirectional connections. Even though pseudo-words are not represented by nodes at the word level, they too can activate (and derive support from) nodes at this level that represent visually-similar words (e.g. TARK activates and derives support from nodes for PARK, DARK, TURK, etc.).

The discussion so far has indicated that printed letter strings (whether words or non-words) can activate multiple nodes at the word level. For example, the stimulus CAKE activates the node for CAKE at the word level, but also activates nodes for visually similar alternatives like CARE, FAKE, CAPE, RAKE, and COKE. When the printed stimulus corresponds to a word, nodes for alternative candidates will be activated more weakly than the node for the target, but will be activated nonetheless. How, then, does the recognition system select the node corresponding to the target from these multiple candidates? One possible mechanism is search. Both the search model (Forster, 1976; Murray and Forster, 2004) and the activation-verification model (Paap et al., 1982; Paap and Johansen, 1994) posit that target selection is achieved through a frequency-ordered serial search or verification process that seeks to establish which candidate provides the best fit to the stimulus.[5] The interactive-activation model solves this target selection problem in a different manner, however: through competition. In the model, inhibitory connections between word nodes enable the most active node (typically that of the target) to drive down the activation of multiple alternative candidates. Of course, the presence of many competing candidates will also make it difficult for the target to reach a critical recognition threshold, since inhibition emanating from those competing candidates will act to drive down activation of the target (see e.g. Andrews, 1997; Davis, 2003; Davis and Lupker, 2006; Grainger and Jacobs, 1993; Grainger et al., 1989 for a discussion of competitive mechanisms in target selection).

5.3.2 Neighborhood (N) effects

The general problem of selecting a representation of the target stimulus from multiple candidates has provided the impetus for a significant body of research on lexical similarity effects in word recognition. Coltheart et al. (1977) defined the neighborhood size of a stimulus (N) as the number of words that can be created by changing one letter of that stimulus. Using this metric of lexical similarity, the word CAKE, for example, has a very large neighborhood (e.g. BAKE, LAKE, CARE, COKE, CAVE, etc). Coltheart et al. (1977) reported that high-N non-words (e.g. PAKE) were rejected more slowly in lexical decision than low-N non-words (e.g. PLUB), an effect now replicated by a number of investigators (e.g. Davis and Taft, 2005; Forster and Shen, 1996; McCann et al., 1988). It is not hard to see why high-N non-words should be difficult to reject in lexical decision. Such non-words activate many nodes at the word level (i.e. they look like many actual words), and this total activation makes it difficult to decide that the stimulus is not a word. However, Coltheart et al. (1977) also reported no effect of N on the YES response in lexical decision: high-N and low-N words were recognized with similar latencies. This result is interesting, since it is inconsistent with both of the mechanisms for target selection

[5] Both of these models have played a very important part in the development of our understanding of visual word recognition over the past 30 years. However, they are described only briefly in this chapter because they play a far more limited role than the interactive-activation model in driving research at present.

described above (i.e. search and competition). These mechanisms would seem to predict that a large N should be detrimental to the recognition of words, since a large N implies the activation of many competing candidates.

This issue surfaced again ten years later, when Andrews (1989) observed that high-N words are *easier* to recognize in lexical decision than are low-N words, especially when these words are of a low printed frequency. Simultaneously, however, Grainger et al. (1989) reported inhibitory effects of neighborhood frequency on lexical decision. They found that words with at least one higher-frequency neighbor are recognized more slowly than are words with no higher-frequency neighbors, an effect seemingly in line with the predictions of competitive network models like the interactive-activation model. These findings would appear to be contradictory, since words with many neighbors usually have at least one higher-frequency neighbor—presumably all that it takes to delay lexical decision (Sears et al., 1995). Thus, the first three examinations of the effect of N on the recognition of words seem to have produced the three logically possible results: no effect (Coltheart et al., 1977); facilitation (Andrews, 1989); and inhibition (Grainger et al., 1989). Empirical findings over the next fifteen years have not especially clarified this matter (see Andrews, 1997 for a review). Several investigators have continued to report facilitatory effects of N on the YES response in lexical decision (Andrews, 1992; Balota et al., 2004; Forster and Shen, 1996; Sears et al., 1995), while several others have continued to report inhibitory effects of neighborhood frequency in this task (Carreiras et al., 1997; Grainger, 1990; Grainger et al., 1992; Grainger and Jacobs, 1996; Grainger and Segui, 1990; Huntsman and Lima, 1996; Perea and Pollatsek, 1998). This issue is central to our understanding of mechanisms for target selection in visual word recognition, and so these inconsistencies must be resolved.

Three types of explanation have been offered for these inconsistent effects. The first explanation relates to the fact that while most of the facilitatory neighborhood findings have been reported using English stimuli (but see Davis and Taft, 2005), most of the inhibitory findings have been reported using French, Spanish, or Dutch stimuli (Andrews, 1997). One possibility (Ziegler and Perry, 1998) is that the direction of the neighborhood effect is determined by the relative balance of two opposing effects: inhibition due to competition from neighbors and facilitation due to overlap with larger sublexical units (e.g. bodies, rimes[6]). N is positively correlated with these larger sublexical units, such that a word with many neighbors will usually also consist of highly frequent sublexical units (Andrews, 1997). Because larger units play a more important role in English than in other languages (see Ziegler and Goswami, 2005 for discussion), one would expect to find facilitatory N effects in English and inhibitory N effects in other languages—precisely the pattern normally observed.

The second explanation for the inconsistent neighborhood findings was proposed by Grainger and Jacobs (1996), who argued that the inhibitory pattern might be the "true" pattern and that the facilitatory pattern may result from strategic processes involved in the decision component of the lexical decision task. They postulated a "fast guess" decision mechanism whereby the "YES" response in the lexical decision task can be made on the basis of the total activity of units in the orthographic lexicon (see also Coltheart et al., 2001). It is through this fast guess mechanism that the facilitatory effects of neighborhood size are deemed to arise. This theory has received support from observations that the direction of the neighborhood effect can be shifted from inhibition to facilitation by stressing accuracy or speed in task instructions (De Moor et al., 2005; Grainger and Jacobs, 1996). Situations in which participants are instructed to be very accurate typically produce inhibitory neighborhood effects, presumably because participants in these situations have to access a specific lexical node undergoing competition from other nodes. Conversely, situations in which participants are instructed to be very fast typically produce facilitatory neighborhood effects, presumably because participants in these situations can make their decision on the basis of the strategic fast guess mechanism, and do not have to access a specific lexical node undergoing competition.

The third explanation for the inconsistent neighborhood findings is due to Davis and Taft (2005). These authors have recently suggested that these inconsistencies may be a consequence of the fact that the N-metric as defined by Coltheart et al. (1977) is overly restrictive. This metric is based on a slot-based scheme for coding letter position, and therefore excludes transposed-letter neighbors and deletion neighbors

[6] The body or rime of a syllable consists of its vowel plus its final consonants, where the body refers to the syllable's orthography and the rime refers to its phonology. For example, the body of MOOT is -OOT and the rime of /mut/ is /ut/.

of target words—neighbors that are perceptually similar to target words (see discussion above). Thus, items like ACRE (which have no higher-frequency neighbors, as defined on Coltheart's N-metric) may have been used inappropriately as experimental controls in many of the studies of neighborhood frequency, even despite the fact that they have higher-frequency transposed-letter neighbors (e.g. CARE) and higher-frequency deletion neighbors (e.g. ARE). Davis and Taft (2005) speculate that if the neighborhoods of such target words had been properly defined in previous studies, the true inhibitory pattern might have emerged. It is not difficult to see that each of these three explanations for the inconsistent neighborhood findings provides exciting possibilities for future research on a problem that is fundamental to our understanding of selection mechanisms in visual word recognition.

5.3.3 Masked form priming effects

Masked form priming effects are another important source of evidence concerning selection mechanisms in visual word recognition. Masked form priming is a technique in which a briefly presented lower-case prime (e.g. 50 ms) is sandwiched between a forward pattern mask and an upper-case target presented for some type of lexical processing task (including lexical decision, reading aloud, semantic categorization, perceptual identification; e.g. Evett and Humphreys, 1981; Forster and Davis, 1984; Forster et al., 1987; Forster and Davis, 1991). Because participants in these experiments do not have conscious experience of the prime (they normally report seeing a flash or nothing at all prior to the target), it is normally argued that masked priming provides a highly-desirable situation in which neither strategic nor episodic factors can be invoked to explain the priming effects observed (but see Bodner and Masson, 2001). Researchers using this technique over the past twenty years have normally sought to determine how the recognition of a target word is influenced by the prior presentation of a visually similar word or non-word prime.

Priming in the interactive-activation model is conceptualized as a balance between facilitation and inhibition (Davis, 2003; Ziegler et al., 2000). Primes activate visually similar targets, thus producing savings in the time it takes for those targets to reach a critical recognition threshold of activation. However, primes can also activate word nodes that compete with targets for recognition. Davis (2003) therefore suggested that prime lexicality (i.e. the word/non-word status of a prime) should be a particularly influential factor in determining the magnitude of form priming effects. Non-word primes (e.g. azle–AXLE) should typically produce robust facilitation, because these primes activate nodes for their corresponding targets without also activating any strongly competitive nodes. In contrast, word primes (e.g. able–AXLE) activate nodes for their corresponding targets but also activate their own nodes, which compete with the target nodes for recognition. The interactive-activation model therefore predicts that word primes should facilitate target recognition to a much lesser degree than non-word primes (Davis, 2003). Search models (e.g. Forster et al., 1987; Forster and Veres, 1998), on the other hand, predict facilitation of visually similar masked primes on target recognition because these models propose that visually similar primes (whether words or non-words) constrain the area of the orthographic lexicon that is searched.

Broadly speaking, data from masked form priming seem to show support for the interactive-activation model. First of all, masked non-word primes facilitate lexical decisions to target words (e.g. bontrast–CONTRAST). This result was first obtained by Forster and Davis (1984), and has since been replicated numerous times (e.g. Davis and Lupker, 2006; Forster et al., 1987; Forster et al., 2003; Forster and Veres, 1998; Perea and Lupker, 2003). In contrast, most of the experiments that have examined the effects of masked word primes on target recognition have revealed inhibitory effects or null effects (e.g. de Moor and Brysbaert, 2000; Davis, and Lupker, 2006; Drews and Zwitserlood, 1995; Forster and Veres, 1998; Grainger et al., 1991; Grainger and Ferrand, 1994; Segui and Grainger, 1990). That said, for reasons not yet totally clear (Davis and Lupker, 2006), facilitatory effects in this situation are sometimes obtained (Forster et al., 1987; Forster and Veres, 1998). Further research is needed if these findings are to be reconciled with the interactive-activation model.

There is also one special case in which masked word primes *always facilitate* the recognition of visually similar targets: the case in which primes comprise a *morphological surface structure*. Stimuli that have a morphological surface structure are those that can be parsed into known morphemes (i.e. stems and affixes) on the basis of their orthography (Rastle and Davis, 2003). For example, the stimuli DARKNESS and CORNER both have a morphological surface structure (even despite the fact that only one of the stimuli,

DARKNESS, is genuinely morphologically complex) because they can both be parsed into stems and suffixes (DARK+NESS; CORN+ER). Now, previous research (De Moor and Brysbaert, 2000) has demonstrated that the recognition of a target word is normally inhibited when that target word is preceded by a masked word prime that constitutes an "addition neighbor" (e.g. brothel-BROTH). These inhibitory effects are not observed, however, if that addition neighbor has a morphological surface structure (e.g. brother-BROTH; Rastle et al. 2004). In these circumstances, robust facilitation of the magnitude typically obtained by identity primes is instead observed (Longtin et al., 2003; Rastle and Davis, 2003; Rastle et al., 2004). Furthermore, there is no effect of the lexicality of the prime on the magnitude of priming (Longtin and Meunier, 2005). Primes with a morphological surface structure facilitate recognition of their embedded targets, irrespective of whether those primes are words or non-words. One explanation for this set of results is that morphological surface structure enables a rapid perceptual segmentation of a prime, which disables that prime's ability to activate a word node that would normally compete against the target for recognition. For example, the prime BROTHER may be rapidly segmented into {BROTH} + {ER}, thus enabling activation of the word node for the target (BROTH) without activating the competing word node for the prime (BROTHER). Primes such as BROTHEL cannot be segmented because they do not constitute a morphological surface structure (i.e. -EL never functions as an English suffix), and thus end up competing with the target for recognition (see also Marslen-Wilson, Chapter 11 this volume).

5.4 **Word recognition and the reading system**

Our discussion so far has centered on the architecture and mechanics of the recognition components of the reading system. However, the reading system also comprises pathways for the computation of meaning and for the computation of phonology (i.e. reading aloud). These latter pathways in particular have been studied in great detail from behavioral, neuropsychological, and computational perspectives (see Coltheart et al., 2001 for a review), and it is well beyond the scope of this chapter to review this literature. However, this final section of the chapter does consider the effects that these pathways to meaning and phonology may have on the recognition of printed words. Indeed, though visual word recognition is normally conceptualized as being driven primarily by the analysis of orthography, it is now indisputable that semantic and phonological information *can* contribute to this process. My discussion of these issues is necessarily brief. Further more detailed discussion can be found in several of the chapters in this volume including those of Frost and Ziegler (7), Lupker (10), Moss, Tyler, and Taylor (13), and Seidenberg (14).

5.4.1 **The DRC model**

One theory of skilled reading that may help us to understand phonological and semantic influences on visual word recognition is the DRC model (Coltheart et al., 2001). DRC is the most comprehensive theory of visual word recognition *and* reading aloud described to date, and it has been studied extensively (see Coltheart et al., 2001 for a review). The model takes its architecture, depicted in Figure 5.3, from many years of theoretical development on the nature of the skilled reading system dating back to Morton (1979), Morton and Patterson (1980), Harris and Coltheart (1986), and Patterson and Shewell (1987). Further, the model retains the processing and selection mechanisms of the interactive-activation model, which have been so successful in helping us to understand visual word recognition. Lexical decisions in the model are based on an analysis of activation of nodes in the orthographic lexicon.

This model, along with its capabilities for simulating phenomena concerning visual word recognition reading aloud, has been described extensively elsewhere (e.g. Coltheart et al., 2001; Rastle and Coltheart, 1999). Briefly, there are three processing pathways in the model: (a) a non-lexical pathway through which a printed letter string is translated to sound by rule (e.g. VIB → /vIb/); (b) a lexical pathway through which the phonological form of a word is retrieved directly following its activation in the orthographic lexicon; and (c) a second lexical pathway through which the phonological form of a word is retrieved via its meaning representation. Information about the printed stimulus flows through all of these pathways in cascade. Thus, semantic and phonological representations for a printed stimulus can be activated well before the activation of a node in the orthographic lexicon has reached a critical recognition threshold.

The crucial feature of this model for our discussion of visual word recognition is that it postulates

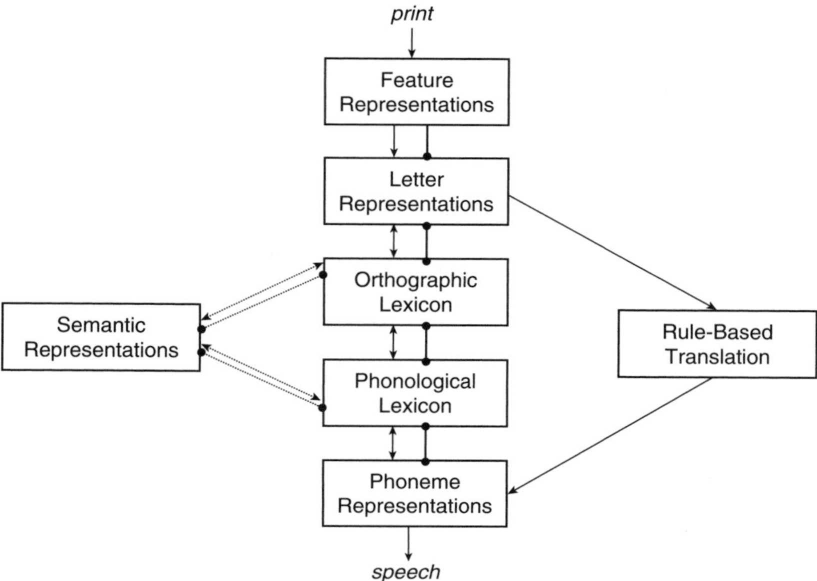

Figure 5.3 The DRC model of visual word recognition and reading aloud (Coltheart et al., 2001) Dashed lines indicate components of the model that have not yet been implemented.

bidirectional connections between semantic, phonological, and orthographic bodies of knowledge. These bidirectional connections provide an opportunity for phonological and semantic information to influence the rise of activation of nodes in the orthographic lexicon (the source of information monitored in the recognition of printed words; see above). For example, the stimulus COAT will activate its own node in the orthographic lexicon through feedforward activation from the letter nodes. However, the orthographic node for COAT will also receive supporting activation from semantic nodes (activated via phonological nodes and/or via orthographic nodes) and from phonological nodes (activated via orthographic nodes, semantic nodes, and/or phoneme nodes). Though semantic and phonological information can influence the rise of activation in orthographic nodes, an important claim of this model is that neither semantic nor phonological information is a *necessary* condition for the recognition of a printed word. This postulate of the theory is based on considerable data from neuropsychological patients demonstrating that the recognition of printed words remains possible even in the face of severe semantic and/or phonological damage (see e.g. Coltheart, 2004; Coltheart and Coltheart, 1997; Coltheart et al., 1980/1987; Coltheart et al., 2001 for discussion). If there are bidirectional connections between orthography, semantics, and phonology, then what types of semantic and/or phonological influences might we observe on the recognition of printed words?

5.4.2 Semantic influences on recognition

The specific influences of semantic variables on the recognition of single printed words have been challenging to pin down because of the need to exercise control over numerous highly related variables (see e.g. Balota et al., 1991; Balota, 1994; Gernsbacher, 1984 for discussion). However, it now seems reasonably clear that printed words with particularly rich semantic representations are recognized more quickly than words with more impoverished semantic representations—though it is not yet known exactly how semantic richness is best conceptualized. Potential candidates include, for example, imageability (Balota et al., 2004), number of semantic features (Pexman et al., 2002), semantic neighborhood density (Buchanan et al., 2001; Locker et al., 2003), number of meanings (Hino and Lupker, 1996), number of related meanings (Azuma and Van Orden, 1997), and number of related senses (Rodd et al., 2002; see Lupker, Chapter 10 this volume for a full review). Irrespective of the exact nature of the semantic effect on recognition, researchers in this area have typically explained their findings in terms of interactivity between semantic and orthographic bodies of knowledge.

Priming studies also reveal semantic influences on visual word recognition. Meyer and Schvaneveldt (1971) were the first to demonstrate that lexical decisions to words (e.g. DOCTOR) are significantly shorter when they are preceded by semantically related words (e.g. NURSE) than when they are preceded by unrelated words (e.g. BREAD). This finding, which has been replicated numerous times, has motivated a literature of its own that is much too great to treat in this chapter (see e.g. Balota, 1994; Hutchison, 2003; Lucas, 2000; Neely, 1991 for reviews). The dominant metaphor for explaining semantic priming is spreading activation (e.g. Collins and Loftus, 1975; Neely, 1977). The idea is that the orthographic representation of the prime activates a semantic node, which then sends positive activation to related nodes (including the target) at the semantic level of representation. If the semantic node for the target is activated by the prime through spreading activation, then that semantic node may send activation back to its corresponding node in the orthographic lexicon—influencing the time it takes for that target orthographic node to reach a recognition threshold. Here again, we see the importance of bidirectional connections between orthography and semantics for explaining core phenomena in visual word recognition.

5.4.3 Phonological influences on recognition

Rubenstein et al. (1971) presented homophonic words (e.g. MAID, SALE), non-homophonic words (e.g. PAID, RAIL), pseudo-homophones (e.g. BURD, KOAT), and non-pseudo-homophonic non-words (e.g. GURD, WOAT) to participants for lexical decision. They observed that "YES" responses were slower for homophones than they were for non-homophonic words, and that "NO" responses were slower for pseudo-homophones than they were for non-pseudo-homophonic non-words. Both of these effects on lexical decision—the homophone effect and the pseudo-homophone effect—have been replicated (homophone effect: Ferrand and Grainger, 2003; Pexman et al., 2001; pseudo-homophone effect: Besner and Davelaar, 1983; Coltheart et al., 1977; McCann et al., 1988; McQuade, 1981; Vanhoy and Van Orden, 2001; Ziegler et al., 2001). On the theory pictured in Figure 5.3, the homophone effect could be understood in terms of an effect of feedback from nodes in the phonological lexicon to nodes in the orthographic lexicon (Pexman et al., 2001). For example, the stimulus MAID activates the phonological node for /meId/ in the phonological lexicon; and this node subsequently sends activation back not only to the orthographic node for MAID but also to the competitor orthographic node for MADE. The pseudo-homophone effect can also be understood in terms of feedback from phonological levels of representation to nodes in the orthographic lexicon. For example, on the theory in Figure 5.3, the stimulus KOAT will be translated by rule to /kəʊt/; this phonemic representation will then activate the phonological node for /kəʊt/ and subsequently the orthographic node for COAT. Rejecting this stimulus in lexical decision will be particularly difficult because of the activation of the orthographic node COAT.

Priming studies also reveal an influence of phonology on the recognition of printed words. Some of the most interesting work in this domain comes from the use of the masked form priming technique (see above). Numerous studies have now revealed that target recognition is speeded by the prior brief presentation of a masked pseudo-homophone prime (e.g. koat–COAT) relative to an orthographic control (e.g. poat–COAT). This benefit from phonology is observed in lexical decision (e.g. Drieghe and Brysbaert, 2002; Ferrand and Grainger, 1992; Lukatela et al., 1998; Rastle and Brysbaert, 2006) as well as a multitude of other tasks that tap recognition components of the reading system (e.g. Perfetti et al., 1988; Perfetti and Bell, 1991; see Rastle and Brysbaert, 2006, for a review). These findings indicate not only that phonology influences the recognition of printed words, but that phonological influences become apparent very early in processing. This evidence for "fast" phonology has led a number of researchers (e.g. Drieghe and Brysbaert, 2002; Frost, 1998; Lukatela and Turvey, 1994; Xu and Perfetti, 1999) to suggest that phonological recoding of a printed stimulus plays a leading role in its recognition, a role much more central to that allowed by theories such as the DRC model. Indeed, it remains to be seen whether these fast phonological effects can be explained by such a theory, in which the recognition of words is driven primarily by orthographic form and in which phonological effects on recognition are explained solely in terms of a feedback mechanism (Rastle and Brysbaert, 2006).

5.5 Conclusion

The printed word presents the skilled reader with a challenging problem. Letters often appear in surface contexts (e.g. fonts, sizes) with which they are unfamiliar. These letters form a limited array that renders distinct words highly confusable (e.g. SALT, SLAT). Information about the spellings, sounds, and meanings of these words must be stored; and one form of information must be accessed rapidly from the other. Further, these challenges present themselves to an organism that is not endowed with special hardware for reading. The skilled reader solves all these problems remarkably well. Skilled reading is not only highly accurate but also effortless; and we have seen evidence in this chapter that decoding a printed stimulus begins even before we are aware of its existence. Much has been learned over the past 125 years about the mechanisms that underlie this astonishing form of expertise, though it should be clear that there is still much, much more to learn.

Acknowledgements

I am grateful to Marc Brysbaert, Max Coltheart, Gareth Gaskell, and Johannes Ziegler for comments on an earlier draft of this chapter.

References

Allport, D. A., and Funnell, E. (1981) Components of the mental lexicon. *Philosophical Transactions of the Royal Society of London*, B295: 397–410.

Andrews, S. (1989) Frequency and neighborhood effects on lexical access: activation or search? *Journal of Experimental Psychology: Learning, Memory, and Cognition*, 15: 802–14.

Andrews, S. (1992) Frequency and neighborhood effects on lexical access: lexical similarity or orthographic redundancy. *Journal of Experimental Psychology: Learning, Memory, and Cognition*, 18: 234–54.

Andrews, S. (1997) The effect of orthographic similarity on lexical retrieval: resolving neighborhood conflicts. *Psychonomic Bulletin and Review*, 4: 439–61.

Azuma, T., and Van Orden, G. (1997) Why safe is better than fast: the relatedness of a word's meaning affects lexical decision times. *Journal of Memory and Language*, 36: 484–504.

Baayen, R. H., Piepenbrock, R., and van Rijn, H. (1993) *The CELEX lexical database (CD-ROM)* Linguistic Data Consortium, University of Pennsylvania, Philadelphia, PA.

Balota, D. A. (1994) Visual word recognition: the journey from features to meaning. In M.A. Gernsbacher (ed.), *Handbook of Psycholinguistics*, pp. 303–48. Academic Press, San Diego, CA.

Balota, D. A., and Chumbley, J. I. (1984) Are lexical decisions a good measure of lexical access? The role of word frequency in the neglected decision stage. *Journal of Experimental Psychology: Human Perception and Performance*, 10: 340–57.

Balota, D. A., Cortese, M. J., Sergent-Marshall, S. D., Spieler, D. H., and Yap, M.J. (2004) Visual word recognition of single-syllable words. *Journal of Experimental Psychology: General*, 133: 283–316.

Balota, D. A., Ferraro, F. R., and Connor, L. T. (1991) On the early influence of meaning in word recognition: a review of the literature. In P. J. Schwanenflugel (ed.), *The Psychology of Word Meanings*, pp. 187–222. Erlbaum, Hillsdale, NJ.

Baron, J. (1977) Mechanisms for pronouncing printed words: use and acquisition. In D. LaBerge and S. J. Samuels (eds), *Basic Processes in Reading: Perception and Comprehension*. Erlbaum, Hillsdale, NJ.

Besner, D., and Davelaar, E. (1983) Suedohomofoan effects in visual word recognition: evidence for phonological processing. *Canadian Journal of Psychology*, 37: 300–5.

Besner, D., Twilley, L., McCann, R. S., and Seergobin, K. (1990) On the connection between connectionism and data: are a few words necessary? *Psychological Review*, 97: 432–46.

Bodner, G. E., and Masson, M. J. (2001) Prime validity affects masked repetition priming: evidence for an episodic resource account of priming. *Journal of Memory and Language*, 45: 616–47.

Borowsky, R., and Besner, D. (2006) Parallel distributed processing and lexical-semantic effects in visual word recognition: are a few stages necessary? *Psychological Review*, 113: 181–95.

Bowers, J. S. (2000) In defence of abstractionist theories of repetition priming and word identification. *Psychonomic Bulletin and Review*, 7: 83–99.

Broadbent, D. E. (1967) Word-frequency effects and response bias. *Psychological Review*, 74: 1–15.

Brysbaert, M. (2001) Prelexical phonological coding of visual words in Dutch: automatic after all. *Memory and Cognition*, 29: 765–73.

Brysbaert, M. and Ghyselinck, M. (2006) The effect of age-of-acquisition: partly frequency-related partly frequency-independent. *Visual Cognition*, 13: 992–1011.

Brysbaert, M., Lange, M., and Van Wijnendaele, I. (2000) The effects of age-of-acquisition and frequency-of-occurrence in visual word recognition: further evidence from the Dutch language. *European Journal of Cognitive Psychology*, 12: 65–85.

Buchanan, L., Westbury, C., and Burgess, C. (2001) Characterizing semantic space: neighborhood effects in word recognition. *Psychonomic Bulletin and Review*, 8: 531–44.

Bullinaria, J. (1995) Modeling lexical decision: who needs a lexicon? In J. G. Keating (ed.), *Neural computing research and applications III: Proceedings of the fifth Irish neural networks conference*, pp. 62–9. St Patrick's College, Maynooth, Ireland.

Carr, T. H., Davidson, B. J., and Hawkins, H. L. (1978) Perceptual flexibility in word recognition: strategies affect orthographic computation but not lexical access.

Journal of Experimental Psychology: Human Perception and Performance, 4: 674–90.

Carreiras, M., Perea, M., and Grainger, J. (1997) Effects of the orthographic neighborhood in visual word recognition: cross-task comparisons. *Journal of Experimental Psychology: Learning, Memory, and Cognition*, 23: 857–71.

Carroll, J. B. and White, M. N. (1973) Word frequency and age of acquisition as determiners of picture naming latencies. *Quarterly Journal of Experimental Psychology*, 24: 85–95.

Cattell, J. (1886) The time it takes to see and name objects. *Mind*, 11: 63–65.

Collins, A. M. and Loftus, E. F. (1975) A spreading-activation theory of semantic processing. *Psychological Review*, 82: 407–28.

Coltheart, M. (1981) Disorders of reading and their implications for models of normal reading. *Visible Language*, 15: 245–86.

Coltheart, M. (2004) Are there lexicons? *Quarterly Journal of Experimental Psychology*, 57A: 1153–71.

Coltheart, M., and Coltheart, V. (1997) Reading comprehension is not exclusively reliant upon phonological representation. *Cognitive Neuropsychology*, 14: 167–75.

Coltheart, M., Curtis, B., Atkins, P., and Haller, M. (1993) Models of reading aloud: dual-route and parallel-distributed-processing approaches. *Psychological Review*, 100: 589–608.

Coltheart, M., Davelaar, E., Jonasson, J. T., and Besner, D. (1977) Access to the internal lexicon. In S. Dornic (ed.), *Attention and Performance*, VI, pp. 535–55. Erlbaum, Hillsdale, NJ.

Coltheart, M., Patterson, K., and Marshall, J. C. (1980/1987) *Deep Dyslexia*. Routledge & Kegan Paul, London.

Coltheart, M., Rastle, K., Perry, C., Langdon, R., and Ziegler, J. (2001) DRC: A dual route cascaded model of visual word recognition and reading aloud. *Psychological Review*, 108: 204–56.

Davis, C. J. (1999) The Self-Organising Lexical Acquisition and Recognition (SOLAR) model of visual word recognition. Doctoral dissertation.

Davis, C. J. (2003) Factors underlying masked priming effects in competitive network models of visual word recognition. In S. Kinoshita and S. J. Lupker (eds), *Masked Priming: The State of the Art*, pp. 121–70. Psychology Press, Hove, UK.

Davis, C. J. (2005) Orthographic input coding: a review of behavioural data and current models. In S. Andrews (ed.), *From Inkmarks to Ideas: Challenges and Controversies about Word Recognition and Reading*. Psychology Press, Hove, UK.

Davis, C. J., and Bowers, J. S. (2004) What do letter migration errors reveal about letter position coding in visual word recognition? *Journal of Experimental Psychology: Human Perception and Performance*, 30: 923–41.

Davis, C. J., and Lupker, S. J. (2006) Masked inhibitory priming in English: evidence for lexical inhibition. *Journal of Experimental Psychology: Human Perception and Performance*, 32: 668–87.

Davis, C. J. and Taft, M. (2005) More words in the neighborhood: interference in lexical decision due to deletion neighbors. *Psychonomic Bulletin and Review*, 12: 904–10.

Davis, M. H. (2003) Scrambled letters in reading. Downloaded from http://www.mrc-cbu.cam.ac.uk/~matt.davis/Cambridge/index.html on 19 Aug. 2005.

Dehaene, S., Cohen, L., Sigman, M., and Vinckier, F. (2005) The neural code for written words: a proposal. *Trends in Cognitive Sciences*, 9: 335–41.

De Moor, W., and Brysbaert, M. (2000) Neighborhood frequency effects when primes and targets are of different lengths. *Psychological Research*, 63: 159–62.

De Moor, W., Verguts, T., and Brysbaert, M. (2005) Testing the "multiple" in the multiple read-out model of visual word recognition. *Journal of Experimental Psychology: Learning, Memory, and Cognition*, 31: 1502–8.

Drews, E., and Zwitserlood, P. (1995) Morphological and orthographic similarity in visual word recognition. *Journal of Experimental Psychology: Human Perception and Performance*, 21: 1098–116.

Drieghe, D., and Brysbaert, M. (2002) Strategic effects in associative priming with words, homophones, and pseudohomophones. *Journal of Experimental Psychology: Learning, Memory, and Cognition*, 28: 951–61.

Evett, L. J., and Humphreys, G. W. (1981) The use of abstract graphemic information in lexical access. *Quarterly Journal of Experimental Psychology*, 33A, 325–50.

Fera, P., and Besner, D. (1992) The process of lexical decision: more words about a parallel distributed processing model. *Journal of Experimental Psychology: Learning, Memory, and Cognition*, 18: 749–64.

Ferrand, L., and Grainger, J. (1992) Phonology and orthography in visual word recognition: evidence from masked non-word priming. *Quarterly Journal of Experimental Psychology*, 45A: 353–72.

Ferrand, L., and Grainger, J. (2003) Homophonic interference effects in visual word recognition. *Quarterly Journal of Experimental Psychology*, 56A: 403–19.

Forster, K. I. (1976) Accessing the mental lexicon. In R. J. Wales and E. C. T. Walker (eds), *New Approaches to Language Mechanisms*, pp. 257–87. North-Holland, Amsterdam.

Forster, K. I. (2005) Five challenges for activation models. In S. Andrews (ed.), *From Inkmarks to Ideas: Challenges and Controversies about Word Recognition and Reading*. Psychology Press, Hove, UK.

Forster, K. I., and Chambers, S. (1973) Lexical access and naming time. *Journal of Verbal Learning and Verbal Behaviour*, 12: 627–35.

Forster, K. I., and Davis, C. (1984) Repetition priming and frequency attenuation in lexical access. *Journal of Experimental Psychology: Learning, Memory, and Cognition*, 10: 680–89.

Forster, K. I., and Davis, C. (1991) The density constraint on form-priming in the naming task: interference effects from a masked prime. *Journal of Memory and Language*, 30, 1–25.

Forster, K. I., Davis, C., Schoknecht, C., and Carter, R. (1987) Masked priming with graphemically related forms: repetition or parallel activation? *Quarterly*

Journal of Experimental Psychology: Human Experimental Psychology, 39A: 211–51.

Forster, K. I., Mohan, K., and Hector, J. (2003) The mechanics of masked priming. In S. Kinoshita and S. J. Lupker (eds), *Masked Priming: The State of the Art*, pp. 3–37. Psychology Press, Hove, UK.

Forster, K. I., and Shen, D. (1996) No enemies in the neighborhood: Absence of inhibitory neighborhood effects in lexical decision and semantic categorization. *Journal of Experimental Psychology: Learning, Memory, and Cognition*, 22: 696–713.

Forster, K. I., and Veres, C. (1998) The prime lexicality effect: form priming and a function of prime awareness, lexical status, and discrimination difficulty. *Journal of Experimental Psychology: Learning, Memory, and Cognition*, 24: 498–514.

Frost, R. (1998) Toward a strong phonological theory of visual word recognition: true issues and false trails. *Psychological Bulletin*, 123: 71–99.

Gerhand, S., and Barry, C. (1999) Age of acquisition, word frequency, and the role of phonology in the lexical decision task. *Memory and Cognition*, 27: 592–602.

Gernsbacher, M. A. (1984) Resolving 20 years of inconsistent interactions between lexical familiarity and orthography, concreteness, and polysemy. *Journal of Experimental Psychology: General*, 113: 256–81.

Ghyselinck, M., Lewis, M. B., and Brysbaert, M. (2004) Age of acquisition and the cumulative-frequency hypothesis: a review of the literature and a new multi-task investigation. *Acta Psychologica*, 115: 43–67.

Gilhooly, K. J., and Logie, R. H. (1980) Age-of-acquisition, imagery, concreteness, familiarity, and ambiguity measures for 1,944 words. *Behavior Research Methods, Instruments, and Computers*, 12: 395–427.

Grainger, J. (1990) Word frequency and neighborhood frequency effects in lexical decision and naming. *Journal of Memory and Language*, 29: 228–44.

Grainger, J., Cole, P., and Segui, J. (1991) Masked morphological priming in visual word recognition. *Journal of Memory and Language*, 30: 370–84.

Grainger, J., and Ferrand, L. (1994) Phonology and orthography in visual word recognition: effects of masked homophone primes. *Journal of Memory and Language*, 33: 218–33.

Grainger, J., and Jacobs, A. M. (1993) Masked partial-word priming in visual word recognition: effects of positional letter frequency. *Journal of Experimental Psychology: Human Perception and Performance*, 19: 951–64.

Grainger, J., and Jacobs, A. M. (1996) Orthographic processing in visual word recognition: a multiple read-out model. *Psychological Review*, 103: 518–65.

Grainger, J., O'Regan, J. K., Jacobs, A. M., and Segui, J. (1989) On the role of competing word units in visual word recognition: the neighborhood frequency effect. *Perception and Psychophysics*, 51: 49–56.

Grainger, J., O'Regan, J. K., Jacobs, A. M., and Segui, J. (1992) Neighborhood frequency effects and letter visibility in visual word recognition. *Perception and Psychophysics*, 45: 189–95.

Grainger, J., and Segui, J. (1990) Neighborhood frequency effects in visual word recognition: a comparison of lexical decision and masked identification latencies. *Perception and Psychophysics*, 47: 191–98.

Grainger, J., and Van Heuven, W. J. B. (2003) Modeling letter position coding in printed word perception. In P. Bonin (ed.), *The Mental Lexicon*. Nova Science, New York.

Grainger, J., and Whitney, C. (2004) Does the huamn mnid raed wrods as a wlohe? *Trends in Cognitive Sciences*, 8: 58–9.

Harm, M., and Seidenberg, M. S. (2004) Computing the meanings of words in reading: cooperative division of labor between visual and phonological processes. *Psychological Review*, 111: 662–720.

Harris, M., and Coltheart, M. (1986) *Language Processing in Children and Adults: An Introduction*. Routledge & Kegan Paul, London.

Hino, Y., and Lupker, S. J. (1996) Effects of polysemy in lexical decision and naming: an alternative to lexical access accounts. *Journal of Experimental Psychology: Human Perception and Performance*, 22: 1331–56.

Huey, E. B. (1908) *The Psychology and Pedagogy of Reading*. Repr. 1968. MIT Press, Cambridge, MA.

Huntsman, L. A., and Lima, S. D. (1996) Orthographic neighborhood structure and lexcial access. *Journal of Psycholinguistic Research*, 25: 417–29.

Hutchison, K. A. (2003) Is semantic priming due to association strength or feature overlap? A *micro*-analytic review. *Psychonomic Bulletin and Review*, 10: 785–813.

Inhoff, A. W., and Rayner, K. (1986) Parafoveal word processing during eye fixations in reading: effects of word frequency. *Perception and Psychophysics*, 40: 431–9.

Kucera, H., and Francis, W. N. (1967) Computational analysis of present-day American English. Brown University Press, Providence, RI.

Lewis, M. B., Gerhand, S., and Ellis, H. D. (2001) Re-evaluating age-of-acquisition effects: are they simply cumulative frequency effects? *Cognition*, 72: 189–205.

Locker, L., Simpson, G. B., and Yates, M. (2003) Semantic neighborhood effects on the recognition of ambiguous words. *Memory and Cognition*, 31: 505–15.

Longtin, C. M., and Meunier, F. (2005) Morphological decomposition in early visual word processing. *Journal of Memory and Language*, 53: 26–41.

Longtin, C. M., Segui, J., and Halle, P. (2003) Morphological priming without morphological relationship. *Language and Cognitive Processes*, 18: 313–34.

Lucas, M. (2000) Semantic priming without association: a meta-analytic review. *Psychonomic Bulletin and Review*, 1: 618–30.

Lukatela, G., Frost, S. J., and Turvey, M. T. (1998) Phonological priming by masked non-word primes in the lexical decision task. *Journal of Memory and Language*, 39: 666–83.

Lukatela, G., and Turvey, M. T. (1994) Visual lexical access is initially phonological, 1: Evidence from associative priming by words, homophones, and pseudohomophones. *Journal of Experimental Psychology: General*, 123: 107–28.

McCann, R. S., Besner, D., and Davelaar, E. (1988) Word recognition and identification: do word-frequency effects reflect lexical access? *Journal of Experimental Psychology: Human Perception and Performance*, 14: 693–706.

McClelland, J. L. (1979) On the time relations of mental processes: a framework for analyzing processes in cascade. *Psychological Review*, 86: 287–330.

McClelland, J. L., and Johnston, J. C. (1977) The role of familiar units in perception of words and non-words. *Perception and Psychophysics*, 22: 249–61.

McClelland, J. L., and Rumelhart, D. E. (1981) An interactive activation model of context effects in letter perception, part 1: An account of basic findings. *Psychological Review*, 88: 375–407.

McQuade, D. V. (1981) Variable reliance on phonological information in visual word recognition. *Language and Speech*, 24: 99–109.

Meyer, D. E., and Schvaneveldt, R. W. (1971) Facilitation in recognizing pairs of words: evidence of a dependence between retrieval operations. *Journal of Experimental Psychology*, 90: 227–34.

Monsell, S. (1991) The nature and locus of word frequency effects in reading. In D. Besner and G. W. Humphreys (eds), *Basic Processes in Reading: Visual Word Recognition*. Erlbaum, Hillsdale, NJ.

Morrison, C. M., and Ellis, A. W. (1995) Roles of word frequency and age of acquisition in word naming and lexical decision. *Journal of Experimental Psychology: Learning, Memory, and Cognition*, 21: 116–33.

Morrison, C. M., Ellis, A. W., and Chappell, T. D. (1997) Age of acquisition norms for a large set of object names and their relation to adult estimates and other variables. *Quarterly Journal of Experimental Psychology*, 50A: 528–59.

Morton, J. (1969) Interaction of information in word recognition. *Psychological Review*, 76: 165–78.

Morton, J. (1979) Facilitation in word recognition: experiments causing change in the logogen model. In P. A. Kolers, M. E. Wrolstad, and H. Bouma (eds), *Processing of Visible Language*, vol. 1, Plenum Press, New York.

Morton, J., and Patterson, K. (1980) A new attempt at an interpretation, or, an attempt at a new interpretation. In Coltheart et al. (1980/1987).

Murray, W. S., and Forster, K. I. (2004) Serial mechanisms in lexical access: the rank hypothesis. *Psychological Review*, 111: 721–56.

Neely, J. H. (1977) Semantic priming and retrieval from lexical memory: roles of inhibitionless spreading activation and limited-capacity attention. *Journal of Experimental Psychology: General*, 106: 226–54.

Neely, J. H. (1991) Semantic priming effects in visual word recognition: a selective review of current findings and theories. In D. Besner and G. W. Humphreys (eds), *Basic Processes in Reading: Visual Word Recognition*, pp. 264–336. Erlbaum, Hillsdale, NJ.

Neisser, U. (1967) *Cognitive Psychology*. Appleton-Century-Crofts, New York.

Paap, K. R., and Johansen, L. S. (1994) The case of the vanishing frequency effect: a retest of the verification model. *Journal of Experimental Psychology: Human Perception and Performance*, 20: 1129–57.

Paap, K. R., Newsome, S. L., McDonald, J. E., and Schvaneveldt, R. W. (1982) An activation-verification model for letter and word recognition: the word-superiority effect. *Psychological Review*, 89: 573–94.

Patterson, K. d and Shewell, C. (1987) Speak and spell: Dissociations and word class effects. In M. Coltheart, G. Sartori, and R. Job (eds), *The Cognitive Neuropsychology of Language*, pp. 273–94. Erlbaum, London.

Pelli, D. G., Farell, B., and Moore, D. C. (2003) The remarkable inefficiency of word recognition. *Nature*, 423: 752–6.

Perea, M., and Lupker, S. J. (2003) Does jugde activate COURT? Transposed-letter similarity effects in masked associative priming. *Memory and Cognition*, 31: 829–41.

Perea, M., and Pollatsek, A. (1998) The effects of neighborhood frequency in reading and lexical decision. *Journal of Experimental Psychology: Human Perception and Performance*, 24: 767–79.

Perea, M., and Rosa, E. (2002) Does "whole word shape" play a role in visual word recognition? *Perception and Psychophysics*, 64: 785–94.

Perfetti, C. A., and Bell, L. C. (1991) Phonemic activation during the first 40 ms of word identification: evidence from backward masking and priming. *Journal of Memory and Language*, 30: 473–85.

Perfetti, C. A., Bell, L. C., and Delaney, S. M. (1988) Automatic (prelexical) phonetic activation in silent word reading: evidence from backward masking. *Journal of Memory and Language*, 27: 59–70.

Pexman, P. M., Lupker, S. J., and Hino, Y. (2002) The impact of feedback semantics in visual word recognition: number of features effects in lexical decision and naming tasks. *Psychonomic Bulletin and Review*, 9: 542–9.

Pexman, P. M., Lupker, S. J., and Jared, D. (2001) Homophone effects in lexical decision: *Journal of Experimental Psychology: Learning, Memory, and Cognition*, 22: 139–56.

Plaut, D. C. (1997) Structure and function in the lexical system: insights from distributed models of word reading and lexical decision. *Language and Cognitive Processes,* 12: 767–808.

Plaut, D. C., and Booth, J. R. (2000) Individual and developmental differences in semantic priming: empirical and computational support for a single-mechanism account of lexical processing. *Psychological Review*, 107: 786–823.

Plaut, D. C., McClelland, J. L., Seidenberg, M. S., and Patterson, K. (1996) Understanding normal and impaired word reading: computational principles in quasi-regular domains. *Psychological Review*, 103: 56–115.

Rapp, B. (1992) The nature of sublexical orthographic organization: the bigram trough hypothesis examined. *Journal of Memory and Language*, 31: 33–53.

Rapp, B., Folk, J. R., and Tainturier, M. J. (2001) Word reading. In B. Rapp (ed.), *The Handbook of Cognitive Neuropsychology*, pp. Psychology Press, Hove, UK.

Rastle, K., and Brysbaert, M. (2006) Masked phonological priming effects in English: are they real? do they matter? *Cognitive Psychology*, 53: 97–145.

Rastle, K., and Coltheart, M. (1999) Serial and strategic effects in reading aloud. *Journal of Experimental Psychology: Human Perception and Performance*, 25: 461–81.

Rastle, K., and Coltheart, M. (2006) Is there serial processing in the reading system; and are there local representations? In S. Andrews (ed.), *From Inkmarks to Ideas: Current Issues in Lexical Processing*, pp. 3–24. Psychology Press, Hove, UK.

Rastle, K., and Davis, M. (2003) Reading morphologically complex words: some thoughts from masked priming. In S. Kinoshita and S. J. Lupker (eds), *Masked Priming: The State of the Art*, pp. 279–305. Psychology Press, Hove, UK.

Rastle, K., Davis, M., and New, B. (2004) The broth in my brother's brothel: morpho-orthographic segmentation in visual word recognition. *Psychonomic Bulletin and Review*, 11: 1090–98.

Reicher, G. M. (1969) Perceptual recognition as a function of meaningfulness of stimulus material. *Journal of Experimental Psychology*, 81: 274–80.

Rodd, J., Gaskell, G., and Marslen-Wilson, W. (2002) Making sense of semantic ambiguity: semantic competition in lexical access. *Journal of Memory and Language*, 46: 245–66.

Rogers, T. T., Lambon Ralph, M. A., Hodges, J. R., and Patterson, K. (2004) Natural selection: the impact of semantic impairment on lexical and object decision. *Cognitive Neuropsychology*, 21: 331–52.

Rubenstein, H., Lewis, S. S., and Rubenstein, M. A. (1971) Evidence for phonemic recoding in visual word recognition. *Journal of Verbal Learning and Verbal Behavior*, 10: 645–57.

Rumelhart, D. E., and McClelland, J. L. (1982) An interactive activation model of context effects in letter perception, part 2: The contextual enhancement effect and some tests and extensions of the model. *Psychological Review*, 89: 60–94.

Saenger, P. H. (1997) *Space between Words: The Origins of Silent Reading*. Stanford University Press, Stanford, CA.

Schilling, H. E. H., Rayner, K., and Chumbley, J. I. (1998) Comparing naming, lexical decision, and eye fixation times: word frequency effects and individual differences. *Memory and Cognition*, 26: 1270–81.

Schmandt-Besserat, D. (1996) *How Writing Came About*. University of Texas Press, Austin.

Schoonbaert, S., and Grainger, J. (2004) Letter position coding in printed word perception: effects of repeated and transposed letters. *Language and Cognitive Processes*, 19: 333–67.

Sears, C. R., Hino, Y., and Lupker, S. J. (1995) Neighborhood size and neighborhood frequency effects in word recognition. *Journal of Experimental Psychology: Human Perception and Performance*, 21: 876–900.

Segui, J., and Grainger, J. (1990) Priming word recognition with orthographic neighbors: effects of relative prime-target frequency. *Journal of Experimental Psychology: Human Perception and Performance*, 16: 65–76.

Seidenberg, M. S. (1987) Sublexical structures in visual word recognition: access units or orthographic redundancy? In M. Coltheart (ed.), *Attention and Performance 12*, Erlbaum, Hillsdale, NJ.

Seidenberg, M. S., and McClelland, J. L. (1989) A distributed, developmental model of word recognition and naming. *Psychological Review*, 96: 523–68

Stadthagen-Gonzales, H., Bowers, J. S., and Damian, M. F. (2004) Age-of-acquisition effects in visual word recognition: evidence from expert vocabularies. *Cognition*, 93: B11–B26.

Vanhoy, M., and Van Orden, G. C. (2001) Pseudohomophones and word recognition. *Memory and Cognition*, 29: 522–9.

Wheeler, D. D. (1970) Processes in visual word recognition. *Cognitive Psychology*, 1: 59–85.

Whitney, C. (2001) How the brain encodes the order of letters in a printed word: the SERIOL model and selective literature review. *Psychonomic Bulletin and Review*, 8: 221–43.

Whitney, C., and Berndt, R. S. (1999) A new model of letter string encoding: simulating right neglect dyslexia. In J. A. Reggia, E. Ruppin, and D. Glanzman (eds), *Progress in Brain Research*, vol. 121, pp. 143–63. Elsevier, Amsterdam.

Xu, B., and Perfetti, C. A. (1999) Nonstrategic subjective thresholds in phonemic masking. *Memory and Cognition*, 27: 26–36.

Zeno, S., Ivens, S., Millard, R., and Duvvuri, R. (1995) *The Educator's Word Frequency Guide*. Touchstone Applied Science Associates, Brewster, NY.

Zevin, J. D., and Seidenberg, M. S. (2002) Age of acquisition effects in word reading and other tasks. *Journal of Memory and Language*, 47: 1–29.

Ziegler, J. C., Ferrand, L., Jacobs, A. M., Rey, A., and Grainger, J. (2000) Visual and phonological codes in letter and word recognition: evidence from incremental priming. *Quarterly Journal of Experimental Psychology*, 53A: 671–92.

Ziegler, J. C., and Goswami, U. C. (2005) Reading acquisition, developmental dyslexia and skilled reading across languages: a psycholinguistic grain size theory. *Psychological Bulletin*, 131: 3–29.

Ziegler, J. C., Jacobs, A. M., and Kluppel, D. (2001) Pseudohomophone effects in lexical decisions: still a challenge for current word recognition models. *Journal of Experimental Psychology: Human Perception and Performance*, 27: 547–559.

Ziegler, J. C., and Perry, C. (1998) No more problems in Coltheart's neighborhood: resolving neighborhood conflicts in the lexical decision task. *Cognition*, 68: B53–B62.

CHAPTER 6

Eye movements and visual word recognition

Richard Shillcock

In this chapter we look at the relationship between eye movements and word recognition, moving from what we know about isolated word recognition to the reading of text. There are clear points of contact between behavior in laboratory tasks with iso lated words and word recognition in text; for instance, Schilling et al. (1998) have shown consistent word frequency effects in naming, lexical decision, and fixation times in silent reading. However, there are also major differences between these two domains. Radach and Kennedy (2004) cite "integration with work on single word recognition" as an issue for future reading research. Equally, though, research on isolated visual word recognition can benefit from a consideration of normal reading; when a word is processed in isolation its normal context has been replaced by a "null" context. This chapter complements Staub and Rayner's review (Chapter 19 this volume) of lexical influences on word recognition, and concentrates on some of the anatomical and computational principles governing access to the mental lexicon. We begin by considering eye movements in reading isolated words.

6.1 Words in isolation

When viewing a page, the eyes are either relatively stable (fixating) or moving between fixations (saccading) When the eyes are moving, we still experience perceptual stability—a phenomenon known as saccadic suppression. This suppression of information uptake occurs in the retina (Roska and Werblin, 2003) and in the cortex (Thiele et al., 2002), and to the extent that it is cortical we might expect it to have cognitive implications. Saccadic suppression does indeed seem to interfere with tasks involving, for instance, counting (Matin et al., 1993), mental rotation (Irwin and Carlson-Radvansky, 1996), and attending to the global aspects of shapes (Brockmole et al., 2002). Irwin and Brockmole (2004) claim that saccadic suppression disproportionately affects dorsal-stream visual processing, with potential implications for concurrent spatial computation. Such suppression may also have an effect, albeit smaller, arising from the movements that occur during a fixation, given that sensitivity is reduced during the early part of a fixation (Ishida and Ikeda, 1989).

Although the eyes are relatively stable during a fixation, small movements—nystagmus (tremor), drift and microsaccades (flicks)—all serve to refresh the image across the photoreceptors; the nervous system typically processes change and ignores stasis, so it is important not to let the image stay too still on the retina. (Although Gilchrist et al. (1997) report an ophthalmoplegic subject, with no eye movements since birth, who only exhibited drift, but who read effectively.) These three movements differ in scale and in potential relevance to cognition. Nystagmus operates at the level of single photoreceptors and may be independent in the two eyes; drift occurs across several photoreceptors and may be correlated in the two eyes (Spauschus et al., 1999); and microsaccades, although involuntary, are the size of small voluntary saccades (Martinez-Conde et al., 2004) Whether or not the same type of movement is coordinated across the two eyes has implications for binocular processing and for cortical control. Both drift and microsaccades seem to help maintain fixation, with cognitive consequences.

Engbert and Kliegl (2003; 2004) have shown that microsaccades are responsive to changes in covert attention, that they also help refresh the image on a short timescale (up to 20 ms), and overall that they act to reduce the disparity between the two eyes' fixations. In general, the three types of movement interact in a complex way with the nature of the task; furthermore, different circumstances obtain at the periphery and in the fovea (the part of the retina most involved with fixation), so that the implications for reading text (with its foveal and non-foveal components) may be more complex than for isolated visual word recognition.

These movements within a fixation are evolutionarily early, but may have become specialized by the presence of a fovea and some at least partially involve cognition; for instance, microsaccades can be voluntarily suppressed or delayed (Winterson and Collewijn, 1976; Engbert and Kliegl, 2003). Although not specific to reading, such movements may help us understand certain reading problems caused by their impairment, and they may speak to issues of levels of processing during reading if they are under cortical control. Even their complete absence may inform us about word recognition: the most constrained conditions for word recognition involve fixating a single word with no eye movements permitted. Various retinal stabilization techniques can keep the image of a word exactly stable on the retina (Martinez-Conde et al., 2004; Pritchard, 1961), with seemingly provocative phenomenological results. Pritchard (1961) reported that letters and parts of letters are lost to perception, with BEER becoming BEEP or PEE, for instance; the same happened for clearly demarcated regions of line drawings. Strict experimental controls are necessary to gauge the level at which any effect is occurring, but Inhoff and Topolski (1994) claim that morpheme boundaries in semantically transparent compound words like *cowboy* can affect the pattern of loss during retinal stabilization in a way that cannot be explained by differential forgetting or guessing bias; *cowboy* tended to become *cow* or *boy*, although most of the image loss was of outer letters and presumably had a more visuospatial explanation. Image loss in retinal stabilization occurs after word recognition, and can speak only to the maintenance of the perception of a word. The psychological reality of word-internal morpheme boundaries has been addressed by other techniques, generally with more ecological validity, from the reading of text in agglutinating languages (Hyönä and Pollatsek, 2000) to the priming of scrambled words (Christianson et al., 2005) and the retinal stabilization data reinforce these findings. As a final comment on these data, the fact that the human fovea is precisely vertically split (see below) means that fixating six-letter words centrally may invite apparent morphological splitting by projecting their two halves initially to different cerebral hemispheres.

6.1.1 Controlling fixation in word recognition

Most trials in isolated word recognition experiments begin with subjects fixating a designated point on the screen. Jordan et al. (1998) have shown that this standard procedure can mean participants fixating slightly right of the presented fixation point. Their goal was to assess the reliability of instructing participants to fixate centrally as opposed to monitoring their fixations with an eye-tracking device (see also Jordan and Patching, 2006). They found that the right visual field (RVF) advantage for words was robust but could be affected by deviations in fixation of only 15′ of arc (a single letter subtended about 12′), demonstrating the rapid decline in acuity from the center of the fovea. They recommend that researchers track fixations to ensure accuracy in visual field experiments. In fact, typical experimental practice rarely exceeds using a subsidiary task, such as recognizing a very small number presented precisely at the fixation point. As we will see when we consider binocularity, below, the issue of exactly where a participant is fixating may be even more vexed than appears from the Jordan et al. studies.

Notwithstanding these observations, paradigms controlling the initial fixation point of an isolated word have been widely used to study a word's optimal viewing position (OVP), following O'Regan (1981). The participant fixates a point, and an isolated word is projected relative to that point. The participant is then fixating a particular position within the word and may be asked to recognize the briefly presented stimulus, or make a lexical decision or naming response. This paradigm has revealed multiple influences on word recognition, and provides a baseline perspective for interpreting eye movements to different parts of a word in reading text.

Plotting the probability of recognition against fixation position in an isolated word gives an asymmetric curve. At the ends of words, performance is superior in the RVF, initially projecting to the left hemisphere (LH), compared with the LVF; the OVP, which gives the best performance, is usually left of the middle of the word for left-to-right alphabetic languages. The whole curve is an inverted U-shape, and emerges in lexical decision and word naming (O'Regan and Jacobs, 1992; O'Regan et al., 1984) and perceptual identification (Brysbaert et al., 1996; Stevens and Grainger, 2003).

In learning to read, the OVP appears early, even at the end of the first year (Aghababian and Nazir, 2000; Ducrot et al., 2003). Compared with children of normal reading ability, dyslexic children produce a more symmetric OVP curve (Ducrot et al., 2003).

Several characteristics intrinsic to the word interact with the OVP effect. Low-frequency words are less effectively processed at fixation points away from the OVP (O'Regan and Jacobs, 1992). Longer words have a more marked OVP curve, although performance at the OVP itself is comparable for longer and shorter words; for long words there is a sharper drop from the OVP to the poorest processing, which occurs at the right end of the word (Nazir, 2000). There is no OVP effect in lexical decision for non-words even when they are wordlike (Nazir et al., 2004). The distribution of information within a word affects its OVP, such that it is to the left of the middle of the word for words with rare initial trigrams and moves closer to the middle for words with rare final trigrams (Brysbaert et al., 1996).

The OVP effect interacts with orthographic conventions. In Japanese Hiragana, there is an OVP effect both for horizontally and vertically displayed words, with the curve being more prominent in the former (Kajii and Osaka, 2000). In Arabic and Hebrew, with their right-to-left orthography (both within the word and across the page), there is a more symmetrical OVP curve compared with left-to-right languages; the prefixes and suffixes in Arabic move the OVP leftwards and rightwards, respectively (Farid and Grainger, 1996; Deutsch and Rayner, 1999). There seem to have been no OVP experiments using single Chinese characters, probably because researchers have assumed (possibly erroneously) that the small visual angle subtended by a single character allows no differential processing across the horizontal extent of its foveal representation. According to Yang and McConkie (1999), Chinese readers do not exhibit a tendency to land in a particular position within a multi-character word (the preferred viewing location, PVL; Rayner, 1979), although Tsai et al. (2005) report preferential landing on the first character of two-character words. In Chinese, reading behavior is probably subject to interacting effects of information from the word (an unsegmented string of one or more—usually two—characters), from the character and from the constituents of the character. Although Chinese orthography is radically different from alphabetic orthographies, anatomical constraints on reading are universal, and the distribution of information across even a single character should have a measurable effect; note that the right-hand side of a Chinese character, typically providing pronunciation information, tends to be more informative than its left-hand side (see e.g. Hsiao and Shillcock, 2005).

In addition, total time spent fixating a word is shortest at the OVP (O'Regan et al., 1984), although the duration of the first fixation in a two-fixation inspection of an isolated word tends to be greatest at the middle of the word (O'Regan and Levy-Schoen, 1987: 374). Nazir et al. (1998) show no dramatic processing advantage from progressively magnifying the letters further away from fixation—producing a "butterfly" effect—suggesting that reduced legibility of outer letters is not the major determinant of the OVP effect. (Rather, Nazir et al. pursued an explanation based on perceptual learning.) Brysbaert et al. (1996) have shown that the effectiveness of the perceptual identification of a word falls off continuously, on a Gaussian distribution, when words are presented foveally (fixated on the first, middle, or last letter) and parafoveally (fixated four or two character spaces left or right of the word). This distribution had its mode to the left of the middle of the word, resembling the standard OVP curve, leading Brysbaert et al. to name it the extended optimal viewing position (EOVP) effect.

Researchers have pursued a variety of theoretical accounts of the basic OVP data (Brysbaert and Nazir, 2005). One approach has involved the implications of the precise vertical splitting of the human fovea (Shillcock et al., 2000). A fixation to the left of the center of a word (in a left-to-right language) tends to divide the word at its informational midpoint, thereby giving each hemisphere an equally good chance of recognizing the word, and dividing the labor equally between the right and left hemispheres (RH and LH); computational studies of such hemisphere-based competition produce OVP-like behavior. One of the closest fits between a model's behavior and the central human data is reported by Stevens and Grainger (2003), whose model distinguishes between three letter positions—first, last, and inner—and specifies for a given word how much each letter in those positions contributes to the identity of that word when experimentally derived visibility for letter positions is taken into account. In summary, the OVP effect is multiply determined, chiefly by the information profile across the letters of the word, the special role of the LH, and the decrease in acuity from the center of the fovea.

Most discussions of isolated visual word recognition ignore the realities of reading text, such as the fact that most processing of a particular word involves some parafoveal preview of that word on the previous fixation(s). Radach et al. (2004) tested the same participants to compare PVL in text and OVP in isolated visual word recognition, and found that performance in one task does not predict performance in the other. Thus, although OVP data speak to information processing of the isolated word, more factors are in play in the reading of text.

6.2 **Binocularity**

We have seen that there are complex issues regarding the movements inside a fixation, and that the precise point to which the reader moves to fixate a word has important processing implications. Like most psycholinguists, we have largely ignored the fact that we read with two eyes. For instance, no OVP study seems to have involved a check that both eyes were fixating the relevant point, or required participants to read with only one eye. Similarly, most experimenters conducting eye-tracking experiments have recorded from only the right eye, assuming (erroneously) that the two eyes fixate the same position, and/or that priority attaches to the sighting/dominant eye (often the right eye) (see Mapp et al., 2003 for a review of this last issue). Accordingly, most models/theories of word recognition have been implicitly cyclopean.

Psycholinguists have assumed that the two eyes fixate the same place because constraints on binocular fusion have been shown to be severe. Some small disparity between the images presented to the two eyes is useful for depth perception (see e.g. Howard, 2005); when there is only a small disparity—perhaps 8–15 arc-min at the fovea (Ogle, 1952; Yeshurun and Schwartz, 1999)—a single fused image results; otherwise binocular rivalry has been seen as the only alternative, with one eye's image being perceived and then replaced piecemeal by the other eye's image over several seconds (see Alais and Blake, 2005). (In reality, stimuli of particular types can elicit a range of fusion-based perceptions.) What happens to the "non-preferred" input? Zimba and Blake (1983) found no semantic facilitation from a word presented to the temporarily suppressed eye, but Fang and He (2005) show action- related information (e.g. relating to tools) reaching dorsal cortex. Thus, high-level lexical information is seemingly lost when there is a substantial mismatch between the two eyes, but the door is left open for the processing of information relevant to eye movements in reading.

Binocularity in reading has been shown to be a rich issue in recent years; see, for instance, eye-tracking studies by Hendriks (1996) and Heller and Radach (1999). We concentrate on two questions relevant to reading. First, are the eyes closely coordinated? Second, if not, how is the disparate information managed?

The eyes seem to be a lot less coordinated in reading than had been thought. There is variation between readers; how much variation exists within individual readers is still an unfolding issue, and will be answered by corpus-reading studies and by developments in the neglected area of reading for different purposes. The key observation is that on a substantial proportion of fixations the two eyes fixate positions in the text that are beyond what have been traditionally taken to be the limits of fusion, but diplopia (double vision) is not reported or experienced. Heller and Radach report fixation disparities of one to three letters. Subsequent research (Juhasz et al., 2006; Liversedge et al., 2007; Liversedge et al., 2006; Rayner and Liversedge, 2004; see also the Potsdam Corpus, Kliegl et al., 2004) has confirmed binocular fixation disparity in reading. In recent studies, the proportion of fixations on which the two eyes' fixation points were more than one character apart (i.e. not expected to be fused) varies considerably. For instance, Liversedge et al. (2006) report that 47 percent of fixations overall were one character or more apart at the end of a fixation. It is difficult to assess the precise implications of such a figure, as a one-letter disparity (perhaps .25°) puts a lot of these disparities on the cusp of fusability. However, the important datum is that a non-trivial proportion of fixations is seemingly beyond fusion, with no diplopia.

Research comparing the saccades of the two eyes has typically been with non-reading tasks, such as saccading to points of light (Collewijn et al., 1988); similarly, studies concerned with the spatial limits of binocular fusion have mostly used very constrained stimuli, such as point stimuli. Fewer studies have involved realistic scenes or relatively free viewing conditions; those that have (see e.g. Cornell et al., 2003) show a divergence between the two eyes during the first part of the saccade and a convergence in the second part that may not have brought the two eyes back together by the end, and Enright (1998) reports fast *monocular* fixating when both version and vergence movements are required (although see also Liversedge et al.'s claims regarding cyclopean representation). The conclusion seems to be that we should perhaps not be surprised at the rather mixed picture of binocular coordination in reading that emerges from recent research.

How does the brain deal with disparity between the two eyes? At the anatomical level, binocular coordination begins with the huge recurrent connectivity from area V1 to the lateral geniculate nucleus (LGN); Sillito et al. (1994) suggest that such recurrence synchronizes activity in the cortex, LGNs, and retinas. The management of retinal image disparities extends far into cortical processing (Lee, 2004). Such processing needs to be flexible, above all. First, there are differences between the abducting (away from the nose) and the adducting eye in speed of movement in a saccade. Second, uneven development, injury, and aging may place the eyes out of kilter. Third, our anatomy makes parts of the visual field monocular, binocular, or blind. Fourth, a close, cluttered scene contains many monocular regions behind edges, contributing to depth perception; the representational space employed cannot be a simple linear one. Blake and Camisa (1978) show that where corresponding points on each retina receive a fuseable image, then fusion occurs; both images typically contribute to the perception. Elsewhere suppression necessarily happens to resolve large interocular conflicts, and to account for our monocular perception of such instances (cf. the "sighting eye"; Leopold et al., 2004). For more marginal instances, there is "ocular prevalence" (Kommerell et al., 2003), in which one or other of a pair of fused images contributes more to the perception. In addition, fusion is more robust with distance from the center of the fovea; the strict spatial limits on fusion are relaxed towards the periphery (Schwartz, 1977). Furthermore, fusion is more robust at low spatial frequencies (coarser visual transitions); there is a division of labor between different frequency channels (Felton et al., 1972). One large blurry object in an empty scene is readily resolved even with disparate retinal images (see e.g. Kulikowski, 1978). Because real objects contain information at a range of frequencies, and because they are perceived as coherent, the implication seems to be that there is an interaction that emphasizes coarse-grain over fine-grain processing, a longstanding concept in vision science (see Marr and Poggio, 1979; Farell et al., 2004; Watt, 1987). The upshot of these observations is that even in the normal inspection of close scenes we should not be surprised at departures from the abstract characterization of fusion as requiring strict adherence to the activation of geometrically corresponding points on the two retinas. In short, the eyes do not necessarily fixate the same point in text. We should not be surprised—the brain probably copes by using a complex and flexible combination of fusion and suppression to create the optimal perception of the text.

So, if the eyes are not aligned, what is the nature of their non-alignment? They may be "crossed" with the left eye's fixation pointing to the right of the right eye's, or they may be "uncrossed" (ignoring any vertical discrepancy). At the time of writing, the data are conflicting. Liversedge et al. report a majority of uncrossed fixations and a variable minority of crossed fixations, whereas Kliegl et al. (2004) and others observe an overwhelming majority of crossed fixations. Blythe et al. (2006) report that the proportion of crossed fixations in reading diminishes as children develop. It is currently premature to say much about the proportions of crossed and uncrossed fixations in reading, but we may note three issues.

First, there may be a sex difference in processing disparate retinal images. Zaroff et al. (2003) report such a difference in the retinal disparity at which optimal fusion of simple random-dot stereograms occurs. Females tended to have optimal fusion when conditions were such that the lines of sight from the two eyes crossed before the plane of fixation (i.e. as if participants were converging in front of the object), and conversely for males. Zaroff et al. also remark that fixation disparity in the normal population may be more prevalent than previously reported (2003: 891).

Second, Toosy et al. (2001) report a general contralateral preference in the projections from the retina to the cortex: although each eye projects directly to both hemispheres, the contralateral projections (left eye to RH, right eye to LH) are stronger. This prioritizes the processing and representation of the left visual field (LVF) for the left eye, and the RVF for the right eye. Initial results from stereoscopic reading experiments in our own laboratory suggest that this projection bias may affect reading—at least of single words—with differing implications depending on the mutual location of the two eyes' fixations points. Managing binocular processing in reading is complex and may allow different perceptual "strategies" with varying advantages for different reading tasks. Ultimately, we need to be able to say why reading with two eyes is better than reading with one, for normal readers (Heller and Radach, 1999); the issues we have outlined here should be relevant to understanding the summation of the two eye's inputs. The fact that dyslexics may achieve some amelioration from monocular occlusion (Stein et al., 2000) is also relevant. For a long time researchers have suggested that at least some dyslexics have magnocellular impairments (Stein and Talcott, 1999), and/or that they have atypical transmission across the corpus callosum (Davidson and Saron, 1992; Shillcock and Monaghan, 2001). The present sketch of binocular processing implicates callosal connectivity as a way of coordinating hemifield representations, and a suppression mechanism that probably involves magnocellular pathways for large spatial frequency processing.

Third, to the extent that fixations in corpora of eye movements in reading can be modeled in terms of informational, psychological, and anatomical constraints (see e.g. Kliegl et al., 2006; McDonald and Shillcock, 2005), different data from the right and the left eye should provide a better or worse fit to current models of eye movements in reading. Such corpus data can be partitioned to explore particular hypotheses about the potential division of labor between the two eyes. For instance, the relative locations of the eyes' fixation points, or the direction of movement of the saccade, may be important in prioritizing the role of one or other eye. Similarly, left-to-right and right-to-left orthographies may yield pervasive preferences. However, rapid interactions between the two eyes and very flexible interdependencies in processing may mean that an approach based on traditional experimentation, as opposed to correlational analyses of corpora, may be required to explore binocularity fully.

If we cannot assume that both eyes are fixating the same letter, or even the same word, in reading text, there are potentially important implications for eye movement methodologies and analyses that rely on small, discrete partitioning of the text being read, the best outcome being that small amounts of non-directional noise are added by binocularity. Participants are routinely screened for problems with vision and language, but subtle visual abnormalities may be important, such as slight strabismus, differential goodness of vision in the two eyes, or a latent ocular misalignment that is normally checked by fusion. However, the fact remains that the majority of people read with a substantial proportion of disparate binocular fixations and without double vision; a theory of eye movements in reading has to accommodate this fact, rather than speculating about readers with "perfect" vision. Indeed, the very flexibility of binocular processing may reflect the variety of factors involved. At this level of analysis of eye movements and word recognition, individual differences between readers seem to become more important, and it is hard to exclude a role in explanations of behavior for data such as participants' eye dominance, sex, and the visual capabilities of each eye. Moreover, in standard experiments on isolated visual word recognition, we cannot assume that the disparity has been reduced to a trivial distance while the subject views the fixation point. Monocular occlusion is one response to the issue, but we have seen that reading is less effective under such conditions; atypical compensations may result. As ever, if an aspect of behavior cannot be adequately controlled, the best response may be its detailed exploration.

6.3 **Words in text**

Having considered some of the lower-level constraints on how visual information reaches the cortex, we now look at some of the large literature on eye movements during text reading (see also Rayner 1978; 1998; Staub and Rayner, Chapter 19 this volume) We will explore some of the factors affecting the fixation of a word, and illustrate the range of types of relevant information and the spatial range over which they operate. Historically many psycholinguists have approached the field of eye movements in reading from the direction of higher-level processing, such as the syntactic and discoursal processing of text. Parsimony dictates that explanations of eye movements in reading text are best grounded, wherever possible, in given anatomical constraints, in non-reading behaviors arising in evolution, and in terms that may be applied to any orthography. How we look at words and recognize them is constrained *computationally* by the abstract nature of the problem: how do words differ from each other? What is the relationship between orthographic form, phonological form, and meaning? How much text does a person see when learning to read, and over a lifetime? ... In this respect, a key theoretical assumption is that the brain has probably devised the best solution to the problem of reading (cf. Anderson, 1991; Legge et al., 1997; Pelli et al., 2003). However, reading is also constrained *algorithmically* by the nature of the processing substrate, the anatomical and physiological nature of the visual system. Where and when does all of the letter information from a word come together? Is there a faster processing route for certain types of visual information? At what granularity can the brain reliably encode the letter and word statistics observed in text? How does the cortex store and modify information over a lifetime? ... These computational and algorithmic constraints are sufficient to ensure a surprising, if noisy, consistency in reading and its impairments, across individuals and across languages; at the same time, divergences and individual differences are also revealing.

Within the reading process there is a wealth of structure and of levels of description. At the visual level, there is the physical form of the text. How long is the next word? How familiar are the next few letters? How far back in the text was the word *cat*?... At the cognitive level there is linguistic structure and the interpretation of individual words. Is the next word an adjective or noun? Which meaning of *bank* is intended? What is the antecedent of *he*?... This distinction between the visual and cognitive levels defines the principal research orientations within research on eye movements in reading—between oculomotor theories and cognitive theories (cf. Rayner and Liversedge, 2004). In the former, the emphasis is on basic oculomotor behavior—as might be observed in non-linguistic tasks; in the latter, researchers are concerned with the role that might be played by the cognitive/linguistic demands of the task. Overall, cognitive effects are seen as having little or no effect on the "where" of eye movements—the precise locations of fixations—and more effect on the "when"—their durations. This oculomotor/cognitive distinction is somewhat correlated with a corpus/correlation-based versus experiment-based distinction between research paradigms, between the analysis of eye movements produced in the relatively naturalistic reading of extended texts, and in reading shorter, carefully manipulated stimulus materials, often coupled with ingenious presentational techniques. In each case, the simple dependent variables are the location and duration of fixations, and the length and direction of saccades. Perhaps the largest part of the variance in eye movement data is noise—the result of stochastic processing in a system that, overall, only needs to be accurate enough to serve the apparently very flexible higher-level processing. Indeed, computational models of reading typically incorporate some version of such stochastic processing. Overall, a surprising amount of the data seems able to be captured in low-level oculomotor terms, but cognitive factors are still implied by some of the data; in between is disputed territory.

As a convenient way of sampling this large literature, we will look at the processing of a word in text before, during, and after its fixation. However, it should be noted that eyemovements in reading are the result of a complex set of constraints from different levels of representation and processing: Kliegl et al. (2006) note eighteen different variables significantly contributing to the variance in fixation duration of the currently fixated word in a regression analysis (though the lion's share of the variance goes to rather fewer variables). In the light of such data, the role of regression analyses of large corpora of eye movements can only increase, although the continuing importance of factorial experiments with carefully manipulated independent variables is assured.

6.3.1 Before a word is fixated

Following work by McConkie and Rayner (1975) and Rayner (1975), the perceptual span has been a key theoretical construct, referring to the view the reader has of the fixated text, and particularly of the word(s) following the fixated word. When a word is fixated, information about letter identity declines in quality with distance from the fixation point, both within the word and within the line of text; there is even a close-to-linear decline with distance from the center of the fovea (Weymouth et al., 1928). How large such a window is, and how processing is distributed within it, are critical research issues: to what extent are the words within the window processed sequentially—either in strict left-to-right order, or not—or in parallel? At first sight, strictly sequential processing seems to be an appropriate analog of speech processing, which is prior to reading and which has necessarily linearized language. Clear speech *is* processed incrementally, with any audible phonetic cue affecting linguistic processing virtually instantaneously. However, less clear, spontaneous speech is comprehended in a less strictly incremental fashion, with some short strings of (typically, short, unstressed) words being unrecognized or misrecognized and then recognized conjointly, along with their subsequent context (Bard et al., 1988). Equally, listeners use information such as the length of the first syllable to predict the length of the whole word (Davis et al., 2002; Lehiste, 1960). The parallels between incremental processing in speech perception and reading may lie as much in their departures from strictly sequential processing as in their observance of it.

If words are made available "gaze-contingently" around where the reader fixates, and the rest of the text is meaningless, then such a window onto the text can be decreased until reading begins to be impaired (McConkie and Rayner, 1975; Rayner, 1975; 1978). The effective processing window thus defined for English is typically three or four letters left of fixation and fourteen or fifteen letters right of fixation, but with accurate recognition of only seven or eight letters to the right. This perceptual span generalizes to other alphabetic languages, but it is substantially smaller for informationally denser orthographies, such as Chinese (Inhoff and Liu, 1998), Japanese (Ikeda and Saida, 1978), or Hebrew; in Hebrew, the span is skewed leftwards, in the direction of reading (Pollatsek et al., 1981).

Researchers have drawn on different mechanisms to characterize the variation in processing difficulty inside the perceptual span. For instance, Henderson and Ferreira (1990) proposed that the size of this window is affected by foveal processing difficulty: the more demanding the fixated word, the less effectively the reader processes text in the rest of the perceptual span. In other perspectives, this effect has been explained by a variety of resource allocation arguments (see also Inhoff and Liu, 1998; Rayner, 1986) or other mechanisms.

At the retinal level, reduced acuity reflects the density of photoreceptors and ganglion cells; in each eye there is an asymmetry in acuity, in that these cells are more densely packed in the nasal hemiretina (Perry and Cowey, 1985). At the cognitive level, accurate report of letter information reflects attention (see e.g. Pollatsek et al., 1993). Between the peripheral and the cognitive, there may be more task-related effects on facility of letter processing, stemming from the information structure of the words of the mental lexicon, for instance, or from perceptual learning acquired during reading (Ahissar and Hochstein, 1996; 1997; Seitz and Watanabe, 2005). Claims about whether acuity is asymmetrical across the two visual hemifields need to be assessed with respect to the task (cf. Nazir, 2000). As acuity falls, high spatial frequency information is lost, but low spatial frequency information remains, so that the spatial extent of words will be visible when letter identity is uncertain. Although readers can cope well with unspaced text (and Chinese and Thai do not mark lexical boundaries explicitly), word identification and the control of eye movements are not completely normal for such text (Rayner et al., 1998).

When word *n* is fixated, some or all of word *n+1* may be projected to the LH (or the RH in a right-to-left language). If word *n+1* is short, then some or all of the letters of word *n+2* may also be in the parafoveal preview. Given the LH's special status in language processing (cf. Brysbaert, 1994; Cohen et al., 2000), the implication is that there is a fortuitous natural advantage for left-to-right orthographies. The leftmost (and rightmost) parts of a word, temporarily considered independently, have also been seen as salient in models of word recognition based on the functional splitting of the foveal projection either side of the fixation point (Shillcock et al., 2000; Whitney, 2001), meaning that the parafoveally previewed beginning letters may be an effective access code to the word.

Parafoveally acquired information about a word benefits the reading of that word when it comes to be directly fixated; reading is more difficult without such advance information (Rayner and Bertera, 1979; Rayner et al., 1982). What sort of information is available parafoveally? We might expect low-level visual information to be more available than high-level cognitive information, and indeed several studies have shown that length information about an upcoming word is available prior to its fixation. Vitu (1991) proposed a center of gravity effect with text, such that the eyes landed on the position in a test word corresponding to the weighted center of gravity of the peripherally presented word. Reilly and O'Regan (1998) make a claim for saccades being directed to the longest word within the twenty letters to the right of fixation. Inhoff et al. (2003) report that, surprisingly, parafoveal length information does not seem to constrain subsequent lexical processing—information about length of word *n+1* is useful but its effects are additive with respect to other types of information. White et al. (2005) show that length information interacts with predictability of the previewed word to determine fixation duration and word skipping.

Orthographic information in the form of what letters are visible in word *n+1* is important (Lima and Inhoff, 1985; Rayner et al., 1982); the beginning letters seem to be more useful than other letters (Briihl and Inhoff, 1995), but information about the latter also has an effect (Rayner et al., 1982). It seems that the relative informativeness of the beginning letters with respect to lexical access (cf. Bryden et al., 1990) plays a role here.

The predictability of words in text affects ease of processing (Ehrlich and Rayner, 1981; Rayner and Well, 1996; Stanovich and West, 1983). A number of relationships may exist between successive words in text, ranging from frozen expressions (*wreak havoc, of course*), function word sequences (*I am*), to frequent phrases and compounds (*careful driver, garage door*), some of which may be lexicalized (*onto, waterbird*), to strings with high Cloze predictability (measured by completions given to a truncated string). The predictability inherent in such strings affects eye movements; in agglutinating languages such as Finnish or Turkish, lexical structure itself is involved.

One of the simplest measures of predictability is transitional probability—the corpus-derived probability that word *n* follows word *n-1*. McDonald and Shillcock (2003a; 2003b), on the basis of corpus analysis and a sentence-reading experiment, claim that several measures of fixation duration on word *n* are influenced by transitional probability, if sufficient letter or length information is available from word *n* on the previous fixation. The implication is that the brain stores detailed statistics about the conjunctions of words in text and can access those statistics on the basis of a partial match with the current text. Note that it is the surface form of the words that is being recognized, not the associated meanings; the full activation and integration of the meanings of words in text could still be relatively sequential, even though lower-level aspects of word recognition were occurring in parallel. For an experiment contesting these data on transitional probability, see Frisson et al. (2005).

Higher-order, Cloze predictability embodies the whole range of discoursal and real world understanding. Its effects on the initial fixation position in words have been disputed; Lavigne et al. (2000) present evidence for such an effect, and Rayner et al. (2001) present evidence against. Again, the larger implication is for or against parallel processing of words in text.

Word skipping is a reading behavior that speaks strongly to the issue of parafoveal preview (Brysbaert et al., 2005; Drieghe and Brysbaert, 2004; Drieghe et al., 2005). Depending on the text, the task, and the language, around one third of words may not receive a direct fixation, yet they contribute to the reader's understanding. A word may be skipped in part simply because it is short and/or occurs close to the current fixation (Brysbaert and Vitu, 1998; Rayner and McConkie, 1976; Rayner et al., 1996). Brysbaert et al. (1998) claim that the length of word *n+1* determines some 90 percent of word skipping. Thus word length is perhaps the most influential aspect of the word to have effects prior to the word being fixated. However, predictability plays a part in accounting for the remaining variance.

We have seen that if information about word *n* is available, then the statistics of the transition between words *n* and *n-1* are relevant, implying that parafoveal preview allows access to those statistics—a "parafoveal-on-foveal effect". McDonald and Shillcock (2003b) show that *backwards* transitional probability in a corpus (the probability of word *n* given *word n+1*) is relevant to measures of fixation on word *n*; this effect clearly implicates the parafoveal preview of word *n+1* in the processing of word *n*, but again it need only be the surface form that is accessed, not the interpreted meaning. For claims regarding pragmatic parafoveal effects, see Kennedy et al. (2004), in which the authors report effects of the pragmatic plausibility of the verb on the processing of the first noun in a noun–verb–noun sequence; they also report longer-range sublexical parafoveal effects. The relatively artificial nature of some of the tasks involved, such as sentence matching, has been criticized by Rayner and Juhasz (2004). See Rayner et al. (2004) for a demonstration of the immediate effect of an anomalous word but a delayed effect of an implausible word.

Finally, phonological information appears to be implicated in parafoveal preview. Ashby et al. (2006) report that the nature of the vowel in a previewed word conditions the processing of that word when fixated: if a contingent change technique is used to present a phonologically identical vowel in parafoveal preview there is facilitation when that word is fixated—*raff*, but not *rall*, will prime *rack*. This facilitation occurs even when the prime is not orthographically identical—*cherg*, but not *chorg*, will prime *chirp*.

In summary, a range of types of lexical information are in play ahead of a word being directly fixated. Such demonstrations indicate greater parallelism, if not departures from strictly serial processing of consecutive words in text.

6.3.2 When a word is fixated

Word recognition in text and in isolation at least appear to be comparable; both require the reader to fixate to take up maximally useful letter information with the limited span available. O'Regan (1990) proposed a strategy-tactics model of word recognition in text, in which a "risky" strategy fixates only the OVP and a less risky strategy follows a non-OVP fixation with a saccade towards the end of the word and thereby maximizes the chances of identifying the word. These two routes to recognition reflect the nature of the problem of identifying strings of possibly unknown length with more information typically towards their beginnings. Eye movements in text usually show the reader landing on a preferred viewing location (PVL) (Rayner, 1979; Underwood et al., 1990), a position typically left of the OVP. If the previous fixation is quite far from word *n* and word *n* is quite long, then a refixation within word *n* is more likely. See McDonald and Shillcock (2004) for a suggestion that the PVL might partly represent a population of (possibly preplanned) refixations (see also Doré-Mazars et al., 2003).

Demonstrating that refixations are preplanned, rather than generated on the fly in response to the result of each saccade, remains a challenge; the window within which a saccade may be open to revision is perhaps the first two-thirds of the 150 ms necessary for its initiation. One way in which researchers have sought to disentangle this issue has been with the double-step paradigm, in which the text moves fractionally during the saccade. Using this technique, Beauvillain et al. (2000) show that even though a refixation within a word may be preplanned, there still appears to be scope for it to be cancelled depending on the outcome of the first saccade; they further show that when the second saccade is to the next word, then a recalculation occurs. Thus, there seems to be sufficient flexibility within reading behavior to precompile eye movements and possibly revise the sequence if time permits.

The claim that the precise vertical division of the human fovea projects the two parts of the word contralaterally to the two hemispheres (see Brysbaert, 2004; Shillcock et al., 2000), may imply relatively independent processing in the two hemispheres in reading. It may also imply that an equitable hemispheric division of labor is desirable, meaning that fixations should aim to bisect the information content of a word. As well as potentially explaining OVP data for isolated words, this approach applies to the recognition of words in text and to the generation of eye movements even when some part of each word may have been visible in parafoveal preview at the previous fixation (McDonald and Shillcock, 2005; McDonald et al., 2005; Shillcock and McDonald, 2005). The importance of this hemispheric analysis is reinforced by the finding that dyslexics fixate significantly closer to the beginning of the word than normal readers, thereby sending more letters to the LH (Kelly et al., 2004).

The duration of the fixation of the current word is affected by length, frequency, and predictability of the word, all factors with a central role in lexical processing (for representative data, see Kliegl et al., 2004). An aspect of eye movement behavior which resisted initial explanation in terms of lexical or contextual factors is the duration of the fixation at different points within the word. Vitu et al. (2001) first reported an inverted optimal viewing position (IOVP) effect, whereby first and single fixations were longest at positions closest to word center. The OVP effect in isolated word recognition suggests the opposite—faster, more efficient processing at word center. To date, two potential explanations have been offered, based on misplaced fixations (Nuthmann et al., 2005) and on competing build-up in the LH and RH to initiate a saccade (McDonald et al., 2005).

In summary, both the location and the duration of fixation on a word are constrained by the intrinsic qualities of the word, its context, and aspects of the architecture of the processor.

6.3.3 After a word is fixated

Rayner (1977; 1978) suggested a general cognitive lag in which higher-level processing relevant to a word continues after fixation has moved on to the next word (see also Bouma and DeVoogd, 1974). Thus the recognition of a difficult word may spill over and be reflected in the fixation of word *n+1* (Rayner and Duffy, 1986). This effect may be mediated by the length of word *n-1*; one way of interpreting such a length effect is that there is a reduced parafoveal preview benefit due simply to the saccade to word *n* being longer. The duration of the fixation on word *n-1* may affect processing of word *n*, given that a shorter fixation on the previous word affords less chance of parafoveal processing of word *n* (Schroyens et al., 1999). There are thus complex, and often conflicting, possibilities concerning the effects of the previous word; these include allowing that attentional processing may also act to constrict the current perceptual span (Henderson and Ferreira, 1990).

These effects apply when the saccades are progressive ones, but words in text are frequently regressively refixated. This fact raises methodological issues regarding the best measure of lexical processing in reading; what is the relationship between total fixation time on a word and the duration of the first fixation on that word, for instance, and which measure is more relevant to a particular research question? (See e.g. Radach and Kennedy, 2004; Rayner, 1998.) Regressions are more likely to occur in difficult text or during reinterpretation (Frazier and Rayner, 1982), but short regressions may also occur apparently to correct oculomotor error, given that a longer forward saccade is more likely to elicit a regression (Vitu et al., 1998). Thus both lower- and higher-level factors seem to elicit a return to a previously fixated word.

Occasionally the reader needs to refer to an earlier point in the line, outside the perceptual span, or to even more distant regions in the text, perhaps to resolve an ambiguity or establish the antecedent of a referring expression. In this case, a spatial memory of the line of text seems to be available, which is more (Kennedy and Murray, 1987; Kennedy et al., 2003) or less (Inhoff and Weger, 2005) accurate. Thus, once a word has left the perceptual window, and has been incorporated into the discourse, it may still exist in the reader's lower-level processing. Interestingly, there may also be an interaction between conceptual and spatial aspects of the word's representation: Murray (2005) has shown that long regressive fixations that cross a pronoun seem to embody the orthographic length of the antecedent of the pronoun: a longer saccade is programmed to cross *it* referring to *chimpanzee* than to *it* referring to *ape*.

Overall, although the contents of the perceptual span to the left of fixation (in left-to-right languages) and beyond have far less influence on ongoing processing than the contents to the right, they are not lost to cognition.

6.4. **Conclusions**

One approach to understanding reading behavior is to consider the relevant anatomical constraints, which include details of the pathways from retina to cortex, and the issues raised by binocularity. This approach is inherently interdisciplinary. Indeed, because of the clarity of the anatomical distinctions in the visual pathways, the known dimensions of the problem of word recognition, and the multiplicity of levels of representation in written language, understanding reading provides us with an invaluable avenue to understanding cognition. Gilchrist et al.'s (1997) ophthalmoplegic subject with no eye movements could read well by simulating saccadic movements with her whole head; the nature of the reading task and the relevant visual pathways remained the same, and she arrived at the same visual sampling solution as normal readers, but using different muscles.

It has only been possible here to sample from the eye movement literature, but current concerns in the field are clear.

Can binocularity be incorporated into models of reading? The story is rapidly unfolding, and promises to expand the domain of data relevant to reading isolated words and text.

To what degree are words in text processed non-sequentially or in parallel? This central question continues to be answered in the direction of greater flexibility for parallel, if not non-sequential, processing. The medium of speech has fundamentally linearized language in a way that prioritizes the communication of meaning, at the level of information within monomorphemic words (Bryden et al., 1990), polymorphemic words (Hawkins and Cutler, 1988), and complex noun phrases (Vendler, 1968), so we should expect this directionality to assert itself more at the highest cognitive levels.

How are competing theories to be judged? The complexity of the data militates in favor of implemented computational models: E-Z Reader (Rayner et al., 1998; Reichle et al., 2003), SWIFT (Engbert et al., 2005), SERIF (McDonald et al., 2005), the Competition/Interaction theory (Yang and McConkie, 2001), Glenmore (Reilly and Radach, 2003). These models involve radically different assumptions regarding, for instance, degree of parallelism, attentional processing, or explicit lexical information, and they account for closely comparable amounts of the data. Criteria for preferring one model might involve, for instance, number of parameters, applicability to different orthographies, or continuity with non-linguistic visual processing. These criteria are themselves controversial. Defining free parameters in different types of model is not straightforward. Regarding different orthographies, see Li et al. (2005) for data on fixation behaviors of Chinese and English readers in pictorial and visual search tasks, and the suggestion that substantially different models of reading may be required for alphabetic and non-alphabetic languages. At issue here is the extent to which a model is seen as a purely functional architecture dealing with particular representational levels, or as embodying psychological universals.

What are the critical data? Analysis of large corpora of eye movements in naturalistic reading will be increasingly important in assessing the relative roles of large numbers of variables.

What is the relationship between lower-level, more peripheral oculomotor processing and higher-level, more central cognitive processing? Psycholinguists have long debated the status of top-down interaction in language processing (Norris et al., 2000). The brain seems adept at using lower-level proxies of higher-level representations, in reading: *d-*, *dw-*, *dwi*, *dwin-* signal with increasing probability the presence of *dwindle*, and the frequency of occurrence of *dwin* and *dwi* becomes interchangeable with the frequency of *dwindle*. Thus, a processor running on letter strings may appear to be guided by higher-level lexical processing. Fodor (1983) notes this issue, seeing associative priming as a "quick but dirty" approach to semantic relevance. Nazir (2000) captures the notion with the phrase "traces of print along the visual pathway" to describe perceptual learning. Reading affords rich possibilities for such proxies, simulating cognitive involvement and obscuring levels of processing. Occam's Razor dictates that bottom-up, data-driven explanations should be exhaustively explored before adopting top-down, or at least cognitively driven, explanations. Clearly higher-level cognition *can* impact on reading—we can consciously adopt different reading strategies—but the brain will automate the process as much as possible using the simplest data and the subtlest real-world statistics, extracted from years of reading experience. If and when higher-level supervision is required, it may be that inhibition of automated lower-level processes by higher-level processes is the norm, if other domains of cortical processing are any indication (cf. Brazelli and Spinnler, 1998). Distinct from—but complementary to—this view, we may argue for *embodied* lexical processing, with perceptual representations of words differing according to the specific context in which they are encountered in the text and according to the cerebral hemisphere to which they are initially projected. In this view, such perceptions retain the processing signature specific to those contexts (cf. Ito, 2001), so that the perception of *chair* in the RH is different from the perception of *chair* in the LH and may have different implications for further processing. For instance, we may see examples of successive views of a word in text failing to combine information, apparently encapsulating different types of information (cf. Lima and Inhoff, 1985).

In conclusion, eye movements in reading present a rare interdisciplinary opportunity to study the range of processing from retina to cortex, from oculomotor to cognitive, and demand clear metatheoretical principles for capturing explanations of behavior.

References

Aghababian, V., and Nazir, T. A. (2000) Developing normal reading skills: aspects of the visual processes underlying word recognition. *Journal of Experimental Child Psychology*, 76: 123–50.

Ahissar, M., and Hochstein, S. (1996) Learning pop-out detection: specificities to stimulus characteristics. *Vision Research*, 36: 3487–500.

Ahissar, M., and Hochstein, S. (1997) Task difficulty and the specificity of perceptual learning. *Nature*, 387: 401–6.

Alais, D., and Blake, R. (2005) *Binocular Rivalry*. MIT Press, Cambridge.

Anderson, J. R. (1991) Is human cognition adaptive? *Behavioral and Brain Sciences*, 14: 471–517.

Andrews, S., Miller, B., and Rayner, K. (2004) Eye movements and morphological segmentation of compound words: there is a mouse in mousetrap. *European Journal of Cognitive Psychology*, 16: 285–311.

Ashby, J., Treiman, R., Kessler, B., and Rayner, K. (2006) Vowel processing during silent reading: evidence from eye movements. *Journal of Experimental Psychology: Learning, Memory and Cognition*, 32: 416–24.

Bard, E.G., Shillcock, R. C., and Altmann, G. T. M. (1988) The recognition of words after their acoustic offsets in spontaneous speech: effects of subsequent context. *Perception and Psychophysics*, 44: 395–408.

Beauvillain, C., Doré, K., and Baudoin, V. (1996) The 'centre of gravity' of words: evidence for an effect of the word initial letters. *Vision Research*, 36: 589–603.

Beauvillain, C., Vergilino, D., and Dukic, T. (2000) Planning two saccade sequences in reading. In A. Kennedy, R. Radach, D. Heller, and J. Pynte (eds), *Reading as a Perceptual Process*, pp. 327–54. Elsevier, Amsterdam.

Becker, W. (1989) Metrics. In R. H., Wurtz, and M. E., Goldberg, eds *The Neurobiology of Saccadic Eye Movements*, pp. 13–61. Elsevier, Amsterdam.

Binder, K. S., Pollatsek, A., and Rayner, K. (1999) Extraction of information to the left of the fixated word in reading. *Journal of Experimental Psychology: Human Perception and Performance*, 25: 1162–72.

Blake, R., and Camisa, J. (1978) Is binocular vision always monocular? *Science*, 200: 1497–9.

Blythe, H., Liversedge, S., Joseph, H., White, S., Findlay, J., and Rayner, K. (2006) The binocular co-ordination of eye movements during reading in adults and children *Vision Research*, 46: 3898–908.

Bouma, H., and de Voogd, A. H. (1974) On the control of eye saccades in reading. *Vision Research*, 14: 273–284.

Brazelli, M., and Spinnler, H. (1998) An example of lack of frontal inhibition: the 'utilization behaviour'. *European Journal of Neurology*, 5: 347–53.

Briihl, D. S., and Inhoff, A. (1995) Integrating information across fixations during reading: the use of orthographic bodies and of exterior letters. *Journal of Experimental Psychology: Learning, Memory, and Cognition*, 21: 55–67.

Brockmole, J. R., Carlson, L. A., and Irwin, D. E. (2002) Inhibition of attended processing during saccadic eye movements. *Perception and Psychophysics*, 64: 867–81.

Bryden, M. P., Mondor, T. A., Loken, M., Ingleton, M., and Bergstrom, K. (1990) Locus of information in words and the right visual field effect. *Brain and Cognition*, 14: 44–58.

Brysbaert, M. (1994) Interhemispheric transfer and the processing of foveally presented stimuli. *Behavioural Brain Research*, 64: 151–61.

Brysbaert, M. (2004) The importance of interhemispheric transfer for foveal vision: a factor that has been overlooked in theories of visual word recognition and object perception. *Brain and Language*, 88: 259–67.

Brysbaert, M., Drieghe, D., and Vitu, F. (2005) Word skipping: implications for theories of eye movement control in reading. In G. Underwood (ed.), *Cognitive Processes in Eye Guidance*, pp. 53–77. Oxford University Press, Oxford.

Brysbaert, M., and Nazir, T. (2005) Visual constraints in written word recognition: evidence from the optimal viewing position effect. *Journal of Research in Reading*, 28: 216–28.

Brysbaert, M., and Vitu, F. (1998) Word skipping: implications for theories of eye movement control in reading. In G. Underwood (ed.), *Eye Guidance in Reading and Scene Perception*, pp. 125–47. Elsevier, Amsterdam.

Brysbaert, M., Vitu, F., and Schroyens, W. (1996) The right visual field advantage and the optimal viewing position effect: on the relation between foveal and parafoveal word recognition. *Neuropsychology*, 10: 385–95.

Burkhalter, A., and Van Essen, D. C. (1986) Processing of color, form and disparity information in visual areas VP and V2 of ventral extrastriate cortex in the macaque monkey. *Journal of Neuroscience*, 6: 2327–51.

Carpenter, P. A., and Just, M. A. (1983) What your eyes do while your mind is reading. In K. Rayner (ed.), *Eye Movements in Reading: Perceptual and Language Processes*, pp. 275–307. Academic Press, New York.

Christianson, K., Johnson, R. L., and Rayner, K. (2005) Letter transpositions within and across morphemes. *Journal of Experimental Psychology: Learning, Memory, and Cognition*, 31: 1327–39.

Ciuffreda, K. J., and Tannen, B. (1995) *Eye Movement Basics for the Clinician*. St Louis: Mosby Year Book.

Cohen, L., Dehaene, S., Naccache, L., Lehericy, S., Dehaene-Lambertz, G., Henaff, M.A., Michel, F. (2000) The visual word form area: spatial and temporal characterization of an initial stage of reading in normal subjects and posterior split-brain patients. *Brain*, 123: 291–307.

Collewijn, H., Erkelens, C. J., and Steinman, R. M. (1988) Binocular co-ordination of human horizontal eye movements. *Journal of Physiology*, 404: 157–82.

Cornell, E. D., Macdougall, H. G., Predebon, J., and Curthoys, I. S. (2003) Errors of binocular fixation are common in normal subjects during natural conditions. *Optometry and Vision Science*, 80: 764–71.

Davidson, R. J., and Saron, C. D. (1992) Evoked potential measures of interhemispheric transfer time in reading disabled and normal boys. *Developmental Neuropsychology*, 8: 261–77.

Davis, M. H., Marslen-Wilson, W. D., and Gaskell, M. G. (2002) Leading up the lexical garden-path: segmentation and ambiguity in spoken word recognition. *Journal of Experimental Psychology: Human Perception and Performance*, 28: 218–44.

Deutsch, A., and Rayner, K. (1999) Initial fixation location effects in reading Hebrew words. *Language and Cognitive Processes*, 14: 393–421.

Doré-Mazars, K., Vergilino-Perez, D., and Collins, T. (2003) Are there two populations of refixations in the reading of long words? Commentary on Reichle et al., "The E-Z Reader model of eye movement control in reading: comparisons to other models." *Behavioral and Brain Sciences*, 26: 480–1.

Drieghe, D., and Brysbaert, M. (2004) Word skipping in reading: on the interplay of linguistic and visual factors. *European Journal of Cognitive Psychology*, 16: 79–103.

Drieghe, D., Rayner, K., and Pollatsek, A. (2005) Eye movements and word skipping during reading revisited. *Journal of Experimental Psychology: Human Perception and Performance*, 31: 954–69.

Ducrot, S., Lété, B., Sprenger-Charolles, L., Pynte, J., and Billard, C. (2003) The optimal viewing position effect in beginning and dyslexic readers. *Current Psychology Letters*, 10, special issue on Language Disorders and Reading Acquisition. http://cpl.revues.org/document99.html

Ehrlich, S. F., and Rayner, K. (1981) Contextual effects on word recognition and eye movements during reading. *Journal of Verbal Learning and Verbal Behavior*, 20: 641–55.

Engbert, R., and Kliegl, R. (2003) Microsaccades uncover the orientation of covert attention. *Vision Research*, 43: 1035–45.

Engbert, R., and Kliegl, R. (2004) Microsaccades keep the eyes' balance during fixation. *Psychological Science*, 15: 431–6.

Engbert, R., Nuthmann, A., Richter, E. M., and Kliegl, R. (2005) SWIFT: a dynamical model of saccade generation during reading. *Psychological Review* 112: 777–813.

Enright, J. T. (1998) Monocularly programmed human saccades during vergence changes? *Journal of Physiology*, 512: 235–50.

Fang, F., and He, S. (2005) Cortical responses to invisible objects in the human dorsal and ventral pathways. *Nature Neuroscience*, 8: 1380–5.

Farell, B., Li, S., and McKee, S. P. (2004) Disparity increment thresholds for gratings. *Journal of Vision*, 4: 156–68.

Farid, M., and Grainger, J. (1996) How initial fixation position influences visual word recognition: a comparison of French and Arabic. *Brain and Language*, 53: 351–68.

Felton, T. B., Richards, W., and Smith, R. A. Jr (1972) Disparity processing of spatial frequencies in man. *Journal of Physiology*, 225: 349–62.

Fisher, D. F., and Shebiske, W. L. (1985) There is more than meets the eye than the eye-mind assumption.In R Groner, G. W. McConkie, and C. Menz (eds), *Eye Movements and Human Information Processing*, pp. 149–58. North Holland, Amsterdam.

Fodor, J. (1983) *The Modularity of Mind: An Essay on Faculty Psychology*. Bradford, Cambridge, MA.

Frazier, L., and Rayner, K. (1982) Making and correcting errors during sentence comprehension: eye movements in the analysis of structurally ambiguous sentences. *Cognitive Psychology*, 14: 178–210.

Frisson, S., Rayner, K., and Pickering, M. J. (2005) Effects of contextual predictability and transitional probability on eye movements during reading. *Journal of Experimental Psychology: Learning, Memory, and Cognition*, 31: 862–77.

Gilchrist, I. D., Brown, V., and Findlay, J. M. (1997) Saccades without eye movements. *Nature*, 390: 130–1.

Hawkins, J.A., and Cutler, A. (1988). Psycholinguistic factors in morphological asymmetry. In J. A. Hawkins (ed.),

Explaining Language Universals, pp. 281–317. Blackwell, Oxford.

Heller, D., and Radach, R. (1999) Eye movements in reading: are two eyes better than one? In W. Becker, H. Deubel, and T. Mergner (eds), *Current Oculomotor Research: Physiological and Psychological Aspects*. Plenum Press, New York.

Henderson, J. M., and Ferreira, F. (1990) Effects of foveal processing difficulty on the perceptual span in reading: implications for attention and eye movement control *Journal of Experimental Psychology: Learning, Memory, and Cognition*, 16: 417–29.

Hendriks, A. W. (1996) Vergence eye movements during fixations in reading. *Acta Psychologica*, 92: 131–51.

Howard, I. P. (2005). Binocular rivalry and the perception of depth. In D. Alais and R. Blake (eds), *Binocular Rivalry*, pp. 169–86. MIT Press, Cambridge, MA.

Hsiao, J. H., and Shillcock, R. (2005) Foveal splitting causes differential processing of Chinese orthography in the male and female brain. *Cognitive Brain Research*, 25: 531–6.

Hyönä, J. (1995) Do irregular letter combinations attract readers' attention? Evidence from fixation locations in words. *Journal of Experimental Psychology: Human Perception and Performance*, 21: 68–81.

Hyönä, J. Bertram, R., and Pollatsek, A. (2005) Identifying compound words in reading: an overview and a model. In G. Underwood (ed.), *Eye Guidance in Reading and Scene Perception*, pp. 80–103. Elsevier Science, Amsterdam.

Hyönä, J., and Pollatsek, A. (2000) Reading Finnish compound words: eye fixations are affected by component morphemes. *Journal of Experimental Psychology: Human Perception and Performance*, 24: 1612–27.

Ikeda, M., and Saida, S. (1978) Span of recognition in reading. *Vision Research*, 18: 83–8.

Inhoff, A. W., and Liu, W. (1998) The perceptual span and oculomotor activity during the reading of Chinese sentences. *Journal Experimental Psychology: Human Perception and Performance*, 24: 20–34.

Inhoff, A. W., Pollatsek, A,, Posner, M. I., and Rayner, K. (1989) Covert attention and eye movements during reading. *Quarterly Journal of Experimental Psychology*, 41: 63–89.

Inhoff, A. W., and Radach, R. (1998). Definition and computation of oculomotor measures in the study of cognitive processes. In G. Underwood (ed.), *Eye Guidance in Reading and Scene Perception*, pp. 29–53. Elsevier Science, Amsterdam.

Inhoff, A. W., Radach, R., Eiter, B., and Juhasz, B. (2003) Parafoveal processing in reading: distinct subsystems for spatial and linguistic information. *Quarterly Journal of Experimental Psychology*, 56A: 803–27.

Inhoff, A. W., and Topolski, R. (1994) Seeing morphemes: loss of visibility during the retinal stabilization of compound and pseudocompound words. *Journal of Experimental Psychology: Human Perception and Performance*, 20: 840–53.

Inhoff, A. W., and Weger, U. (2005) Memory for word location during reading: eye movements to previously read words are spatially selective but not precise. *Memory and Cognition*, 33: 447–61.

Irwin, D. E., and Brockmole, J. R. (2004) Suppressing *Where* but not *What*: the effect of saccades on dorsal- and ventral-stream visual processing. *Psychological Science*, 15: 467–73.

Irwin, D. E., and Carlson-Radvansky, L. A. (1996) Suppression of cognitive activity during saccadic eye movements. *Psychological Science*, 7: 83–8.

Ishida, T., and Ikeda, M. (1989) Temporal properties of information extraction studied by a text-mask replacement technique. *Journal of the Optical Society of America*, 6: 1624–32.

Ito, Y. (2001) Hemispheric asymmetry in the induction of false memories. *Laterality: Asymmetries of Body, Brain, and Cognition*, 6: 337–46.

Jordan, T. R., and Patching, G. R. (2006) Assessing effects of fixation demands on perception of lateralized words: a visual window technique for studying hemispheric asymmetry. *Neuropsychologia*, 44: 686–92.

Jordan, T. R., Patching, G. R., and Milner, A. D. (1998) Central fixations are inadequately controlled by instructions alone: implications for studying cerebral asymmetry. *Quarterly Journal of Experimental Psychology*, 51A: 371–91.

Juhasz, B. J., Liversedge, S. P., White, S. J., and Rayner, K. (2006) Binocular coordination of the eyes during reading: word frequency and case alternation affect fixation duration but not fixation disparity. *Quarterly Journal of Experimental Psychology*, 59: 1614–25.

Kajii, N., and Osaka, N. (2000) Optimal viewing position in vertically and horizontally presented Japanese words. *Perception and Psychophysics*, 62: 1634–44.

Kelly, M. L., Jones, M. W., McDonald, S. A., and Shillcock, R. C. (2004) Dyslexics' eye fixations may accommodate to hemispheric desynchronisation. *NeuroReport*, 15: 2629–32.

Kennedy, A., Brooks, R., Flynn, L.-A., and Prophet, C. (2003) The reader's spatial code. In J. Hyönä, R. Radach and H. Deubel (eds), *The Mind's Eye: Cognitive and Applied Aspects of Eye Movement Research*, pp. 413–27. Elsevier Science, Amsterdam.

Kennedy, A., and Murray, W. S. (1987) Spatial coding and reading: some comments on Monk (1985) *Quarterly Journal of Experimental Psychology*, 39: 649–718.

Kennedy, A., Murray, W. S., and Boissiere, C. (2004) Parafoveal pragmatics revisited. *European Journal of Cognitive Psychology*, 16: 128–53.

Kliegl, R., and Engbert, R. (2005) Fixation durations before word skipping in reading. *Psychonomic Bulletin and Review*, 12: 132–8.

Kliegl, R., Grabner, E., Rolfs, M., and Engbert, R. (2004) Length, frequency and predictability effects of words on eye movements in reading. *European Journal of Cognitive Psychology*, 16: 262–84.

Kliegl, R., Nuthmann, A., and Engbert, R. (2006) Tracking the mind during reading: the influence of past, present, and future words on fixation durations. *Journal of Experimental Psychology: General*, 135: 12–35.

Kliegl, R., Olson, R. K., and Davidson, B. J. (1983) On problems of unconfounding perceptual and language processes. In K. Rayner (ed.), *Eye Movements in Reading and Perceptual and Language Processes*, pp. 333–43. Academic Press, New York.

Kommerell, G., Schmitt, C., Kromeier, M., and Bach, M. (2003) Ocular prevalence versus ocular dominance. *Vision Research*, 43: 1397–403.

Kulikowski, J. J. (1978) Limit of single vision in stereopsis depends on contour sharpness. *Nature*, 275: 126–7.

Lang, J. (1994) Die sensorischen und standespolitischen Schwachstellen der Prismenverordnung am Polatest. *Klinische Monatsblätter für Augenheilkunde*, 204: 378–80.

Lavidor, M., and Walsh, V. (2004) The nature of foveal representation. *Nature Reviews Neuroscience*, 5: 729–735.

Lavigne, F., Vitu, F., and d'Ydewalle, G. (2000) The influence of semantic context on initial landing sites in words. *Acta Psychologica*, 104: 191–214.

Lee, S.-H. (2004) Binocular battles on multiple fronts. *Trends in Cognitive Sciences*, 8: 148–51.

Legge, G. E., Klitz, T. S., and Tjan, B. S. (1997) Mr. Chips: an ideal-observer model of reading. *Psychological Review*, 104: 524–53.

Lehiste, I. (1960) *An Acoustic-Phonetic Study of Internal Open Juncture*. Basel: Buchdruckerei National-Zeitung.

Leopold, D. A., Maier, A., Wilke, M., and Logothetis, N. K. (2004) Binocular rivalry and the illusion of monocular vision. In D. Alais and R. Blake (eds), *Binocular Rivalry and Perceptual Ambiguity*. MIT Press, Cambridge, MA.

Li, X., Rayner, K., Williams, C. C., and Cave, K. R. (2005) Differences in picture processing and its relation with reading performance for Chinese and English readers. Talk presented at ECEM 13, Bern, Switzerland, August 2005.

Lima, S. D., and Inhoff, A. W. (1985) Lexical access during eye fixations in reading: effects of word-initial letter sequence. *Journal of Experimental Psychology: Human Perception and Performance*, 11: 272–85.

Liversedge, S. P., Rayner, K, White, S. J., Findlay, J. M., and McSorley, E. (2007) Binocular coordination of the eyes during reading. *Current Biology*, 16: 1726–9.

Liversedge, S. P., White, S. J., Findlay, J. M., and Rayner, K. (2006) Binocular coordination of eye movements during reading. *Vision Research*, 46: 2363–74.

Mapp, A. P., Ono, H., and Barbeito, R. (2003) What does the dominant eye dominate? A brief and somewhat contentious review. *Perception and Psychophysics*, 65: 310–17.

Marr, D., and Poggio, T. (1979) A computational theory of human stereo vision. *Proceedings Royal Society London*, B(204): 301–28.

Martinez-Conde, S., Macknik, S. L., and Hubel, D. H. (2004) The role of fixational eye movement in visual perception. *Nature Reviews, Neuroscience*, 5: 229–40.

Matin, E., Shao, K., and Boff, K. (1993) Saccadic overhead: information-processing time with and without saccades. *Perception and Psychophysics*, 53: 372–80.

McConkie, G. W., Kerr, P. W., Reddix, M. D., and Zola, D. (1988) Eye movement control during reading, I: the location of initial eye fixations on words. *Vision Research*, 28: 1107–18.

McConkie, G. W., and Rayner, K. (1975) The span of the effective stimulus during a fixation in reading. *Perception and Psychophysics*, 17: 578–86.

McDonald, S. A., Carpenter, R. H. S., and Shillcock, R. C. (2005) An anatomically constrained, stochastic model of eye movement control in reading. *Psychological Review*, 112: 814–40.

McDonald, S. A., and Shillcock, R. C. (2003a) Eye movements reveal the on-line computation of lexical probabilities. *Psychological Science*, 14: 648–52.

McDonald, S. A. and Shillcock, R. C. (2003b) Low-level predictive inference in reading: the influence of transitional probabilities on eye movements. *Vision Research*, 43: 1735–51.

McDonald, S. A. and Shillcock, R. C. (2004) The contribution of preplanned refixations to the preferred viewing location. *Perception and Psychophysics*, 66: 1033–44.

McDonald, S. A., and Shillcock, R. C. (2005) The implications of foveal splitting for saccade planning in reading. *Vision Research*, 45: 801–20.

Murray, W (2005) The reader's conception of space. Talk presented at the *Thirteenth European Conference on Eye Movements ECEM13*, Bern, August 2005.

Nazir, T. A. (2000) Traces of print along the visual pathway. In A. Kennedy, R. Radach, D. Heller, and J. Pynte (eds), *Reading as a Perceptual Process*, pp. 3–22. Elsevier, Oxford.

Nazir, T. A., Ben-Boutayab, N., Decoppet, N., Deutsch, A., and Frost, R. (2004) Reading habits, perceptual learning, and recognition of printed words. *Brain and Language*, 88: 294–311.

Nazir, T. A., Jacobs, A. M., and O'Regan, J. K. (1998) Letter legibility and visual word recognition. *Memory and Cognition*, 26: 810–21.

Norris, D., McQueen, J. M., and Cutler, A. (2000) Merging information in speech recognition: feedback is never necessary. *Behavioral and Brain Sciences*, 23: 352–63.

Nuthmann, A., Engbert, R., and Kliegl, R. (2005) Mislocated fixations during reading and the inverted optimal viewing position effect. *Vision Research*, 45: 2201–17.

Ogle, K. N. (1952) Disparity limits of stereopsis. *Archives of Ophthalmology*, 48: 50–60.

O'Regan, J. K. (1981) The convenient viewing position hypothesis. In D. F. Fisher, R. A. Monty, and J. W. Senders (eds), *Eye Movements, Cognition, and Visual Perception*, pp. 289–98. Erlbaum, Hillsdale, NJ.

O'Regan, J. K. (1990) Eye movements and reading. In E. Kowler (ed.), *Reviews of Oculomotor Research*, vol. 4: *Eye Movements and Their Role in Visual and Cognitive Processes*, pp. 395–453. Elsevier, Amsterdam.

O'Regan, J. K. and Jacobs, A. M. (1992) Optimal viewing position effect in word recognition: a challenge to current theory. *Journal of Experimental Psychology: Human Perception and Performance*, 18: 185–97.

O'Regan, J. K., and Lévy-Schoen, A. (1987) Eye movement strategy and tactics in word recognition and reading. In M. Coltheart (ed.), *Attention and Performance XII: The Psychology of Reading*, pp. 363–83. Erlbaum, Hillsdale, NJ.

O'Regan, J. K., Lévy-Schoen, A., Pynte, J., and Brugaillère, B. (1984) Convenient fixation location within isolated words of different lengths and structure. *Journal of Experimental Psychology: Human Perception and Performance*, 10: 250–7.

Pelli, D. G., Farell, B., and Moore, D. C. (2003) The remarkable inefficiency of word recognition. *Nature*, 423: 752–6.

Perry, V. H., and Cowey, A. (1985) The ganglion cell and cone distributions in the monkey's retina: implications for central magnification factors. *Vision Research*, 25: 1795–810.

Pollatsek, A., Bolozky, S., Well, A. D., and Rayner, K. (1981) Asymmetries in the perceptual span for Israeli readers. *Brain and Language*, 14: 174–80.

Pollatsek, A., Raney, G. E., LaGasse, L., and Rayner, K. (1993) The use of information below fixation in reading and in visual search. *Canadian Journal of Experimental Psychology*, 47: 179–200.

Pritchard, R. M. (1961) Stabilized images on the retina. *Scientific American*, 204: 72–8.

Radach, R., and Kennedy, A. (2004) Theoretical perspectives on eye movements in reading: past controversies, current issues and an agenda for future research. *European Journal of Cognitive Psychology*, 16: 3–26.

Radach, R., Reilly, R., and Vorstius, C. (2004) Causes and consequences of the preferred viewing position in reading. Talk presented at the Sixth European Workshop on Language Comprehension, Oléron, France.

Rayner, K. (1975) The perceptual span and peripheral cues during reading. *Cognitive Psychology*, 7: 65–81.

Rayner, K. (1977) Visual attention in reading: eye movements reflect cognitive processes. *Memory and Cognition*, 4: 443–48.

Rayner, K. (1978) Eye movements in reading and information processing. *Psychological Bulletin*, 85: 618–60.

Rayner, K. (1979) Eye guidance in reading: fixation locations within words. *Perception*, 8: 21–30.

Rayner, K. (1986) Eye movements and the perceptual span in beginning and skilled readers. *Journal of Experimental Child Psychology*, 41: 211–36.

Rayner, K. (1998) Eye movements in reading and information processing: 20 years of research. *Psychological Bulletin*, 124: 373–422.

Rayner, K., and Bertera, J. H. (1979) Reading without a fovea. *Science*, 206: 468–9.

Rayner, K., Binder, K S., Ashby, J., and Pollatsek, A. (2001) Eye movement control in reading: word predictability has little influence on initial landing positions in words. *Vision Research*, 41: 943–54.

Rayner, K., and Duffy, S. A. (1986) Lexical complexity and fixation times in reading: effects of word frequency, verb complexity, and lexical ambiguity. *Memory and Cognition*, 14: 191–201.

Rayner, K., Fischer, M., and Pollatsek, A. (1998) Unspaced text interferes with both word identification and eye movement control. *Vision Research*, 38: 1129–44.

Rayner, K., and Juhasz, B. (2004) Eye movements in reading: old questions and new directions. *European Journal of Cognitive Psychology*, 16: 340–52.

Rayner, K., and Liversedge, S. (2004) Visual and linguistic processing during eye fixations in reading. In J. M. Henderson and F. Ferreira (eds), *The Interface of Language, Vision and Action: Eye Movements in the Visual World*. Psychology Press, Hove, UK.

Rayner, K., and McConkie, G. W. (1976) What guides a reader's eye movements? *Vision Research*, 16: 829–37.

Rayner, K., Reichle, E. D., and Pollatsek, A. (1998) Eye movement control in reading: an overview and model. In G. Underwood (ed.), *Eye Guidance in Reading and Scene Perception*, pp. 243–68. Elsevier Science, Oxford.

Rayner, K., Sereno, S. C., and Raney, G. E. (1996) Eye movement control in reading: a comparison of two types of models. *Journal of Experimental Psychology: Human Perception and Performance*, 22: 1188–200.

Rayner, K., Warren, T., Juhasz, B., and Liversedge, S. (2004) The effects of plausibility on eye movements in reading. *Journal of Experimental Psychology: Learning, Memory and Cognition*, 30: 1290–301.

Rayner, K., and Well, A. D. (1996) Effects of contextual constraint on eye movements in reading: a further examination. *Psychonomic Bulletin and Review*, 3: 504–9.

Rayner, K., Well, A. D., Pollatsek, A., and Bertera, J. H. (1982) The availability of useful information to the right of fixation in reading. *Perception and Psychophysics*, 31: 537–50.

Reichle, E. D., Rayner, K., and Pollatsek, A. (2003) The E–Z Reader model of eye movement control in reading: comparisons to other models. *Behavioral and Brain Sciences*, 26: 445–526.

Reilly, R., and O'Regan, J. K. (1998) Eye-movement control in reading: a simulation of some word-targeting strategies. *Vision Research*, 38: 303–17.

Reilly, R., and Radach, R. (2003) Glenmore: An interactive activation model of eye movement control in reading. In J. Hyönä, R. Radach and H. Deubel (eds), *The Mind's Eye: Cognitive and Applied Aspects of Eye Movement Research*. Elsevier, Amsterdam.

Roska, B., and Werblin, F. (2003) Rapid global shifts in natural scenes block spiking in specific ganglion cells. *Nature Neuroscience*, 6: 600–8.

Schilling, H. E., Rayner, K., and Chumbley, J. I. (1998) Comparing naming, lexical decision, and eye fixation times: word frequency effects and individual differences. *Memory and Cognition*, 26: 1270–81.

Schroyens, W., Vitu, F., Brysbaert, M., and d'Ydewalle, G. (1999) Eye movement control during reading: foveal load and parafoveal processing. *Quarterly Journal of Experimental Psychology*, 52: 1021–46.

Schwartz, E. L. (1977) Afferent geometry in the primate visual cortex. *Biological Cybernetics*, 28: 1–24.

Seitz, A. R., and Watanabe, T. (2005) A unified model for perceptual learning, *Trends in Cognitive Science*, 9: 329–34.

Shillcock, R., Ellison, T. M., and Monaghan, P. (2000) Eye-fixation behaviour, lexical storage and visual word recognition in a split processing model. *Psychological Review*, 107: 824–51.

Shillcock, R. C., and McDonald, S. A. (2005) Hemispheric division of labour in reading. *Journal of Research in Reading*, 28: 244–57.

Shillcock, R. C., and Monaghan, P. (2001) Connectionist modelling of surface dyslexia based on foveal splitting: impaired pronunciation after only two half *pints*. *Proceedings of the 23rd Annual Conference of the Cognitive Science Society*, pp. 916–21. Lawrence Erlbaum Associates, Edinburgh.

Sillito, A. M., Jones, H. E., Gerstein, G. L., and West, D. C. (1994) Corticofugal feedback in the visual system produces stimulus dependent correlation. *Nature*, 369: 479–82.

Spauschus, A., Marsden, J., Halliday, D. M., Rosenberg, J. R., and Brown, P. (1999) The origin of ocular microtremor in man. *Experimental Brain Research*, 126: 556–62.

Stanovich, K. E., and West, R. F. (1983) On priming by a sentence context. *Journal of Experimental Psychology: General*, 112: 1–36.

Stein, J., Fowler, M. S., and Richardson, A. J. (2000) Monocular occlusion can improve binocular control and reading in dyslexics. *Brain*, 123: 164–70.

Stein, J. F., and Talcott, J. B. (1999) Impaired neuronal timing in developmental dyslexia: the magnocellular hypothesis. *Dyslexia*, 5: 59–78.

Stevens, M., and Grainger, J. (2003) Letter visibility and the viewing position effect in visual word recognition. *Perception and Psychophysics*, 65: 133–51.

Thiele, A., Henning, P., Kubischik, M., and Hoffmann, K. P. (2002) Neural mechanisms of saccadic suppression. *Science*, 295: 2460–2.

Toosy, A. T., Werring, D. J., Plant, G. T., Bullmore, E. T., Miller, D. H., and Thompson, A. J. (2001) Asymmetrical activation of human visual cortex demonstrated by functional MRI with monocular stimulation. *Neuroimage*, 14: 632–41.

Tsai, J.-L., Lee, C.-Y., Hung, D. L., and Tseng, O. J.-L. (2005) Eye movement guidance without word space: the preferred landing location in reading Chinese text. Presented at the 11th European Conference on Eye Movements, ECEM11, Turku, Finland.

Underwood, G., Clews, S., and Everatt, J. (1990) How do readers know where to look next? Local information distributions influence eye fixations. *Quarterly Journal of Experimental Psychology*, 42: 39–65.

Vendler, Z. (1968) *Adjectives and nominalizations*. Mouton, The Hague.

Vitu, F. (1991) The existence of a centre of gravity effect during reading. *Vision Research*, 31: 1289–313.

Vitu, F., McConkie, G. W., Kerr, P., and O'Regan, J. K. (2001) Fixation location effects on fixations during reading: an inverted optimal viewing position effect. *Vision Research*, 41: 3513–33.

Vitu, F., McConkie, G. W., and Zola, D. (1998) About regressive saccades in reading and their relation to word identification. In G. Underwood (ed.), *Eye Guidance in Reading and Scene Perception*, pp. 101–24. Elsevier, Oxford.

Watt, R. J. (1987) Scanning from coarse to fine spatial scales in the human visual system after the onset of a stimulus. *Journal of the Optical Society of America A*, 4: 2006–21.

Weymouth, F. W., Hines, D. C., Acres, L. H., Raaf, J. E., and Wheeler, M. C. (1928) Visual acuity within the area centralis and its relation to eye movements and fixation. *American Journal of Ophthalmology*, 11: 947–60.

White, S., Rayner, K., Liversedge, S., and Simon, P. (2005) The influence of parafoveal word length and contextual constraint on fixation durations and word skipping. *Psychological Bulletin and Review*, 12: 466–71.

Whitney, C. (2001) How the brain encodes the order of letters in a printed word: the SERIOL Model and selective literature review. *Psychonomic Bulletin and Review*, 8: 221–43.

Winterson, B. J., and Collewijn, H. (1976) Microsaccades during finely guided visuomotor tasks. *Vision Research*, 16: 1387–90.

Yang, H. M., and McConkie, G. W. (1999) Reading Chinese: some basic eye movement characteristics. In J. Wang, A. Inhoff, and H. C. Chen (eds), *Reading Chinese Script: A Cognitive Analysis*, pp. 207–22. Erlbaum, Hillsdale, NJ.

Yang, S.-N., and McConkie, G. W. (2001) Eye movements during reading: a theory of saccade initiation times. *Vision Research*, 41: 3567–85.

Yeshurun, Y., and Schwartz, E. L. (1999) Cortical hypercolumn size determines stereo fusion limits. *Biological Cybernetics*, 80: 117–129.

Zaroff, C. M., Knutelska, M., and Frumkes, T. E. (2003) Variation in stereoacuity: normative description, fixation disparity, and the roles of aging and gender. *Investigative Ophthalmology and Visual Science*, 44: 891–900.

Zimba, L., and Blake, R. (1983) Binocular rivalry and semantic processing: out of sight, out of mind. *Journal of Experimental Psychology: Human Perception and Performance*, 9: 807–15.

CHAPTER 7

Speech and spelling interaction: the interdependence of visual and auditory word recognition

Ram Frost and Johannes C. Ziegler

7.1 Introduction

In literate cultures, linguistic abilities involve not only perception, comprehension, and production of speech but also reading and writing of print. Language acquisition initially entails the association of spoken words with meanings. However, as literacy is attained, not only does the spoken word lexicon continue to expand both in size and detail, but an orthographic system begins to develop as well (for a review, see Ziegler and Goswami, 2005). This orthographic system appends to the existing connections between spoken words and semantic meanings. A simple model of these processes is presented in Figure 7.1.

According to this framework, word recognition is based on a correlation between orthographic, phonological, and semantic units (Seidenberg and McClelland, 1989; Van Orden and Goldinger, 1994). Note that the schematic model of Figure 7.1 does not specify the size or nature of orthographic, phonological, or semantic units. Hence, in principle, this framework is consistent with classical localist models, such as the Interactive Activation Model (McClelland and Rumelhart, 1981), or parallel-distributed connectionist models (Plaut et al., 1996; Seidenberg and McClelland, 1989).

Although Figure 7.1 appears to present a symmetrical and equilateral triangle in which orthographic, phonological, and semantic representations map onto one another, it is important to note a major bias of this system: since orthography is primarily designed to represent the spoken language rather than directly represent meaning, the relations between orthography and phonology (the O–P connections representing associations of letters or letter clusters with phonemes or syllables) are highly systematic (see Frost, 2005 for a discussion of writing systems). By contrast, the relations between orthographic and semantic sub-units (the O–S connections) are basically arbitrary. Consequently, the orthography–phonology associations are necessarily stronger than the orthography–semantics associations. As an illustration, consider the following example: the letter D is always pronounced /d/ but knowing that a word starts with the letter D does not tell you much about its meaning. As a rule, in all alphabetic writing systems the mapping between orthographic sub-units and semantic features is inconsistent and unpredictable (with the possible exception of morphophonemic units such as prefixes and suffixes, or other morphological derivations

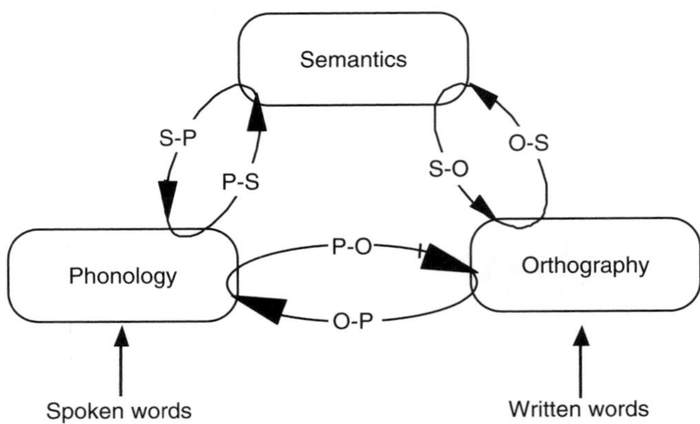

Figure 7.1 A simple interactive framework for written and spoken word recognition.

which are in fact mediated by phonological structures). Consequently, we assume that, at least in alphabetic orthographies, meaning cannot be recovered without explicit instructions that focus on the way the graphic signs represent the surface phonetic units of the spoken language and their matching phonological lexical representations. Van Orden and Goldinger (1994) label this state of affairs "the phonological coherence constraint."

Our ability to effortlessly read printed words aloud, spell spoken words correctly, and automatically retrieve the meaning of both spoken and printed words further suggests that information does not flow in only one direction. Thus, a critical feature of interactive networks is the bidirectional flow of activation (Frost and Katz, 1989; McClelland and Rumelhart, 1981; Stone and Van Orden, 1994; Van Orden and Goldinger, 1994). In an interactive model, *cross-code consistency* is crucial (see Grainger and Ziegler, 2005). Cross-code consistency, in both feed-forward and feed-back directions, guarantees stable and fast learning. Consistent symmetrical relations result in stable and fast activation. Inconsistent and asymmetrical relations are necessarily more slowly resolved than consistent and symmetrical ones (Tuller et al., 1994; Van Orden, 2002; Van Orden et al., 1997; Van Orden et al., 1990; Ziegler, Van Orden, and Jacobs, 1997). Again, the phonological coherence constraint puts a major emphasis on the correlations between orthographic and phonological subunits of the system.

This framework makes a number of intriguing predictions with regard to spelling-to-phonology interactions. First, it predicts that phonology should routinely be involved in visual word recognition. Second, it predicts that inconsistency in the mapping between orthography and phonology should hurt word recognition. Third, it predicts that inconsistency should matter not only between spelling and phonology but also between phonology and spelling ("feedback consistency"). Finally, it predicts that feedback consistency effects should not only occur in reading but also in spoken word recognition. In the present chapter, we will summarize the empirical evidence in favor of these predictions, we will review the behavioral data regarding speech and spelling interactions, and we will discuss to what extent current computational models of word recognition are able to account for these effects.

7.2 **The importance of phonology in reading**

As described in our schematic model above, printed words could, in principle, directly map onto meanings, thus bypassing the computation of phonology. However, the past twenty years of research have shown that this is not the case. It is now well established that the recovery of phonological structure is a mandatory phase of print processing, and that a phonological code is used as a routine procedure for lexical access and for accessing meaning. The necessary role of phonological computation in visual word perception is acknowledged today by many studies, with a wide array of experimental paradigms, and across many orthographic systems. These experimental procedures were especially designed for the purpose of monitoring the very early phases of visual word recognition.

In the backward masking paradigm (Perfetti et al., 1988), for example, a target word is presented for a very short duration (usually 15–30 msecs).

The target word is followed (i.e. masked) by a pseudo-word that appears for 15–60 msecs and is then replaced by a simple pattern mask (#####). The pseudo-word which masks the target can be phonemically similar to the target (e.g. *raik* masking *rake*), graphemically similar (e.g. *ralk* masking *rake*), or a dissimilar control (e.g. *bont* masking *rake*). The subjects' task is to report in writing what they have perceived. Typically, subjects perceive only one event, the target word, and do not have any conscious recollection of the non-word mask. The short exposures characteristic of the masking paradigm allow the on-line processing of the non-word masks to merge with the incomplete processing of the word targets. Thus, in spite of the fact that the non-word masks are not consciously perceived, they exert some influence on the detection of the target. Research in English, Dutch, Chinese, and Hebrew has consistently demonstrated that the phonological information extracted from the masks contributed to the reinstatement of the phonological properties of the targets (e.g. Brysbaert, 2001; Grunau and Frost, 1997; Perfetti et al., 1988; Tan et al., 1996).

In the forward masking paradigm (Forster and Davis, 1984), a pattern mask is presented before the prime, with a very brief temporal interval between the onset of the priming stimulus and the subsequent target stimulus. Because the prime is presented briefly and is masked by a combination of forward and backward masking (the latter coming from the target), the prime itself is usually unavailable for report. Research in English, Dutch, French, and Hebrew has shown that a pseudo-homophone mask (*klip*) facilitated the recognition of the homophonic target (*clip*) even at very short Stimulus Onset Asynchronies (SOAs; e.g. Ferrand and Grainger, 1993; 1994; Lukatela et al., 1998; Brysbaert, 2001; Frost et al., 2003; Ziegler et al., 2000). Using similar procedures, Lukatela and Turvey (1994) examined semantic and phonological priming at various exposure durations, consistently demonstrating that the phonological properties of the primes were always recoded, contributing to the recognition of the targets.

In the letter-search task, subjects are required to identify a pre-specified target letter in a briefly presented masked letter string. Ziegler and Jacobs (1995) have shown that subjects made more false alarms in detecting *i* in *brane* relative to *brate*, presumably because *i* appears in the word *brain* which is homophonic with the visually presented *brane*. This seems to suggest that the phonological structure of the pseudohomophonic target *brane* invoked the lexical entry and the orthographic form of the homophonic word *brain*, thus falsely producing the searched-after letter (see also Ziegler, Van Orden, and Jacobs, 1997). Finally, a series of studies monitoring eye movements in readers of English and Chinese (e.g. Pollatsek et al., 1992; Pollatsek et al., 2000) showed that the phonological structure of a given word was often obtained even before it was fixated, this taking place during a window of the first 50 msecs of the first fixation on that word.

From a developmental perspective, the beneficial effect of phonological awareness and phonics instruction during reading acquisition seems to be uncontested as well. Learning to read was found to be most successful when young readers are informed about the manner in which graphemes represent the sounds of their language. Visual learning based on matching whole printed words to the meaning they convey was not found to represent a viable alternative to the segmentation of words into smaller units (e.g. Share, 1995).

Taken together, the converging evidence that emerges from this vast research consistently demonstrates that the computation of phonology is a necessary component of processing printed words, even when explicit pronunciation is not required, and phonological activation seems to be the rule rather than the exception (see Frost, 1998 for an extensive review, and a discussion of the Strong Phonological Theory). The immediate implication of these findings is that factors that are related to the resonance between the orthographic and phonological systems should have an important influence on the processing of printed words and on reading performance. The first to consider in the present context is the *consistency* with which the phonology of a given word can be computed from print.

7.3 The importance of spelling-to-phonology consistency

> Beware of heard, a dreadful word
> That looks like beard and sounds like bird
> And dead: it's said like bed, not bead;
> For goodness sake, don't call it deed.

Given the fundamental role of phonology in reading, one obvious consequence is that spelling–phonology consistency effects should be ubiquitous. As nicely illustrated by the above lines, spelling-to-phonology inconsistency is common in English. Spelling-to-phonology inconsistency occurs when an orthographic pattern (e.g.-EARD) is pronounced differently in different words (e.g. *beard* vs. *heard*). Note that most research in English has manipulated consistency at the level of the orthographic rime (e.g. Jared, 1997). However, inconsistency can be defined at any level (e.g. graphemes, rimes, or syllables). Note also that consistency is sometimes differentiated from the concept of *regularity* (e.g. Coltheart et al., 2001). An irregular word is one that violates grapheme-phoneme rules (e.g. *yacht*). To define an irregular or exception word, one obviously has to know what the "rules" are. For the concept of consistency, it does not matter what the rules are. The pure existence of a word that is spelt similarly to other words but yet pronounced differently renders the neighborhood of that word inconsistent.

Glushko (1979) was the first to demonstrate that inconsistent words take longer to name than consistent words of similar frequency. He focused on the spelling-to-phonology consistency of orthographic rimes, the orthographic rime being everything that is left after removing the initial onset in a monosyllabic word. For instance, a word like *pint* is inconsistent because most of the English words that end in *-int* rime with *mint*, *lint*, *tint*, or *print*. In fact, Glushko (1979) compared two groups of words that were both *regular* according to grapheme–phoneme correspondence rules but differed in consistency. For example, the pronunciation of a regular inconsistent word such as *wave* can be correctly determined by the application of grapheme-to-phoneme rules. However, *wave* is, nevertheless, inconsistent because the *-ave* rime is pronounced differently than in *have*. Glushko's finding of a consistency effect was very important because it showed that the pronunciation of a word is influenced by the knowledge of other, similarly spelled, words.

Subsequent research replicated the existence of consistency effects in naming and demonstrated that the size of the consistency effect depends on the ratio of "friends" (words pronounced in a similar way) to "enemies" (words pronounced differently; Jared, 1997; 2002). For a word like *mint*, for example, *hint* and *lint* are "friends" while *pint* is an "enemy." *Mint* is more consistent than *pint* because it has a higher ratio of friends to enemies (for statistical analyses, see Ziegler, Stone, and Jacobs, 1997). Although it was initially believed that consistency effects could only be seen in low-frequency words (i.e. the consistency by frequency interaction), Jared (1997) argued that this may not be due to word frequency per se, but rather to the fact that most high-frequency words also have fewer enemies of a higher frequency. Jared (1997; 2002) ran several experiments in which frequency, regularity, and the number of friends/enemies were manipulated in an orthogonal fashion. The data showed that, for both low- and high-frequency words, words with fewer friends than enemies were read aloud significantly more slowly than their controls. Thus, these data show that when the friend/enemy ratio is controlled for, the consistency effect for high-frequency words can be similar to that of low-frequency words (Jared, 1997). What matters is how many friends and enemies any given word has. These findings support the generality and importance of the spelling-to-phonology consistency effects in visual word recognition.

7.4 **Consistency effects across languages**

Most of the studies that investigated consistency effects were conducted in English. However, we should note that the transparency of the relation between spelling and phonology varies widely between orthographies, and writing systems differ in the degree of inconsistency encountered by the native speaker of the language. Thus, alphabetic orthographies can be classified according to the transparency of their letter-to-phonology correspondence. This aspect of the writing system is usually referred to as "orthographic depth" (Liberman et al., 1980; Lukatela et al., 1980; Katz and Feldman, 1981). An orthography that represents its phonology unequivocally following simple grapheme–phoneme correspondences is considered "shallow," while an orthography in which the relation of orthography to phonology is more opaque is labeled "deep." Orthographic depth is often regarded as a continuum, and according to this view languages can be ordered such that a given language is considered deeper than some but shallower than others (e.g. Frost et al., 1987; and see Frost, 2005 for a review and discussion).

According to this classification, a number of languages are considered shallow, including Italian, Spanish, German, Greek, Turkish, Finnish, and Serbo-Croatian. In these languages, learning a set of grapheme-to-phoneme conversion rules enables readers to read most words without errors. In contrast, English represents probably one of the most inconsistent orthographies amongst Indo-European languages (for a review see Ziegler and Goswami, 2005). A recent study investigated to what extent consistency differences across languages affect reading development (European Concerted Action on Learning Disorders as a Barrier to Human Development). Participating scientists from fourteen European Community countries developed a matched set of items of simple real words and non-words. These items were then given to children from each country during their first year of reading instruction (for details see Seymour et al., 2003). The most striking finding from the study was that the children who were acquiring reading in orthographically consistent languages (Greek, Finnish, German, Italian, Spanish) were close to ceiling in both word and non-word reading by the middle of first grade. In contrast, English-speaking children performed extremely poorly (34 percent correct). Danish (71 percent correct), Portuguese (73 percent correct), and French (79 percent correct) children showed somewhat reduced levels of recoding accuracy, which is in line with the reduced consistency of these languages. Analogous results were obtained in smaller-scale studies, comparing French, Spanish, and English (Goswami et al., 1998), and English and German (Goswami et al., 2001; 2003). Altogether, then, it is not only consistency at an item-level that matters but also system-wide consistency. That is, in a writing system with many inconsistencies, reading and spelling development will be delayed. Furthermore, fundamental reading processes in an inconsistent orthography might differ from those in a consistent orthography not only in terms of efficiency but also in terms of grain size and flexibility (Frost et al., 1987; Frost, 1998; Ziegler and Goswami, 2005; Ziegler et al., 2001).

7.5 **The bidirectional nature of consistency**

In the context of the term "orthographic depth", languages may be fairly consistent in their relations of spelling to phonology, but may be inconsistent in their relations of phonology to spelling. A good example is French, which is characterized by fairly transparent grapheme-to-phoneme conversion rules (see Ziegler, Perry, and Coltheart, 2003), but has several permissible graphemes for the same pronunciation (e.g. the phoneme /o/ may appear in print as O, OT, OS, AU, AUX, EAU, EAUX, etc.). The empirical question is whether this form of inconsistency affects reading. Most research on consistency in visual word recognition typically manipulated consistency only between spelling and phonology, but not between phonology and spelling. The exclusive focus on "one-way consistency effects" was probably due to the fact that, in traditional information-processing models, information only flows downstream, as from spelling to phonology. However, as our schematic framework proposes (Figure 7.1), the bidirectional flow of activation between the orthographic and phonological systems is a major determinant of the system.

Stone et al. (1997) were the first to challenge the "one-way-consistency" perspective in reading. They demonstrated that performance in a visual lexical decision task was not only influenced by inconsistency in the spelling-to-phonology mapping (*pint* versus *mint*) but also by inconsistency in the phonology-to-spelling mapping. The latter kind of inconsistency was called "feedback inconsistency." For example, the word *heap* is "feedback-inconsistent" because *heap*'s pronunciation rime /_E:p/ has more than one conventional spelling (compare *_eap*, as in *heap*, versus *_eep* as in *deep*). Indeed, Stone et al. (1997) showed that feedback-inconsistent words, such as *heap*, produced slower correct "yes" responses in lexical decision than feedback-consistent words, that is, words with phonological rimes that could only be spelled one way (e.g. /Uk/ as in *duck* or *luck*).

Subsequent to the original report, the pattern of feed-forward and feedback consistency effects was replicated in French (Ziegler, Montant, and Jacobs, 1997; but see Peereman et al., 1998, for a different account of consistency effects in French). Feedback consistency effects have been replicated in other studies, which controlled their material for subjective rated familiarity (Perry, 2003; Lacruz and Folk, 2004).

Considering again the triangular model of Figure 7.1, feedback consistency effects have been found not only between phonology and orthography but also between semantics and orthography. On the basis of an interactive model with a bidirectional connection between orthography and meaning, Pecher (2001) predicted that performance should be worse for words that are feedback-inconsistent (words with a synonym, such as *jail*) than for words that are feedback-consistent (words without a synonym, such as *milk*). Pecher (2001) has indeed demonstrated that both naming and lexical decision responses were faster and more accurate for consistent than for inconsistent words. These results thus provide additional support for models that allow feedback activation between phonology, orthography, and semantics.

7.6 The influence of orthography on spoken language

We now come to the most important demonstration of speech and spelling interaction, as we examine how spelling affects auditory word recognition. Since consistency concerns the manner by which the printed graphemes represent a phonological structure, it should have an effect during reading but not necessarily during auditory word recognition. However, if the processing of spoken and printed forms is interactive, and word recognition results from the recurrent flow of activation within a highly interactive network, then one might predict that orthography affects spoken word recognition as much as phonology has been shown to affect visual word recognition (see section 7.2).

Indeed, we have known for many years that certain meta-phonological skills, such as our capacity to consciously manipulate phonemes (phonological awareness), are largely dependent on literacy (Morais et al., 1979). For example, a person who has never acquired an orthographic system may find it relatively difficult to delete a phoneme at the beginning of a word or a nonword. In contrast, literate people do not have any difficulties with this task. Bentin et al. (1991) have shown that the effect of learning to read in the first year of school on a phonemic awareness test is far more influential than the mere chronological increase in age by one year. Thus, it is the mere exposure to the orthographic principle which enables the mastering of this phonological ability. Similarly, Alegria et al. (1982) reported that children who learned to read by analytic methods emphasizing letter–sound correspondences performed better on tests of phonemic segmentation than children who learned by holistic methods.

Once reading is acquired, orthographic influences appear to be strong enough to further affect purely phonological tasks. For example, Ehri and Wilce (1980) have shown that literate children find it difficult to count the same number of phonemes in /rItS/ and /pItS/ because the spellings of these words contain a different number of letters (rich vs. pitch). The influence of orthography on spoken word recognition and production has been demonstrated not only with children or illiterates but also with completely literate college students. For example, skilled adults find it harder to judge whether two spoken words rime when their rimes are spelled differently (e.g. *rye/tie*) then when their rimes are spelled the same (Seidenberg and Tanenhaus, 1979). Similarly, Frauenfelder et al. (1990) showed that phoneme detection in spoken French words took longer for the phoneme /k/ than for the phoneme /p/, supposedly because the phoneme /k/ in French has more orthographic realizations C, CC, K, CK, QU, etc.) than the phoneme /p/ (see Dijkstra et al., 1995 for a similar finding in Dutch). Halle et al. (2000) recently demonstrated that French listeners were more likely to misperceive the phoneme /p/ in /apsyrd/ than in /lapsys/, because *absurd* is spelled with the letter "B" whereas *lapsus* LAPSUS is spelled with the letter P.

Because many of these orthographic effects were obtained in tasks with a strong metaphonological component (e.g. phoneme search, phoneme deletion, phoneme counting), Ziegler and Ferrand (1998) manipulated the orthographic consistency of spoken words in a simple auditory lexical decision task. Half of the words were inconsistent, that is, their phonological rimes could be spelt in multiple ways (e.g. /E:p/ may be spelt -EAP or -EEP); the other half was consistent, that is, their rimes could be spelled in only one way (e.g. /-Uk/ may only be spelled -UCK). Results showed that inconsistent words produced slower correct "yes" responses and more errors than did consistent words. This effect has now been replicated a number of times in French (Ziegler et al., 2004) and in other languages (English: Miller and Swick, 2003; Portuguese: Ventura et al., 2004). The existence of an orthographic consistency effect suggests that orthographic information is automatically processed during the recognition of spoken words.

An intriguing demonstration of how reading proficiency in different writing systems affects simple phonemic segmentation was reported by Ben-Dror et al. (1995). In this study Ben-Dror et al. presented native speakers of Hebrew and English with printed CVC segments that had a meaning in both languages (e.g. /gUn/ meaning "gun" in English and "garden" in Hebrew). Subjects were required to delete the first phoneme of the word (/g/) and pronounce the remaining utterance (/Un/) as fast as possible. Whereas in English each phoneme is represented by a discrete letter, in unpointed printed Hebrew, most vowels are not conveyed in print. Thus the vowel /U/ in /gUn/ is not printed, and /gUn/ is, therefore, a two-letter word, where the initial letter represents a CV segment. Ben Dror et al. found that Hebrew speakers deleted the initial CV segment instead of the initial consonant more often than English speakers for both Hebrew and English words. Moreover, even when only correct deletions were considered, Hebrew speakers were significantly slower than English speakers in correctly deleting the initial phoneme, and faster in deleting the whole syllable. These results demonstrate the long-lasting effects of reading experience on a pure phonemic segmentation task (but see Share and Blum, 2005 for a discussion of the joint combination of orthography and phonology in syllabic segmentation in Hebrew).

7.7 Direct investigation of print–speech interaction

The studies discussed so far have looked at literacy effects on spoken word recognition without ever presenting orthographic information. An intriguing way to examine how print and speech interact online during word recognition is by way of a simultaneous presentation of visual and auditory stimuli. An example of such an experimental procedure is the "matching task." In the matching task subjects are simultaneously presented with a printed word (or a non-word) on a computer screen and with a spoken word (or a non-word) via headphones. The subject is asked to decide as fast as possible whether or not the stimuli presented in the visual and the auditory modalities are the same (positive response), or whether they are different (negative response). The working hypothesis underlying the matching task is that the simultaneous presentation of visual and auditory words produces separate activations of the orthographic and the phonological lexical systems that are, at least initially, independent. The matching of an orthographic form to a spoken word might be performed in at least two different ways: one possibility is that at the first stage, functionally independent and complete phonological representations of the printed word and the spoken stimulus are constructed. These two representations are then further compared at a subsequent stage. A second possibility is that the process of mapping the print into phonology and the process of mapping the spoken stimulus into the same abstract phonological structure are interactive. According to this alternative, the two processes share information, and by doing so they affect each other's processing. Whether the processing of orthographic and phonological information is interactive or not is, obviously, an empirical question.

Frost and Katz (1989) have offered a method to directly examine the interactive processing of print and speech by monitoring effects of visual or auditory degradation in the matching task, while orthographic transparency is manipulated. In this study Frost and Katz examined how the different relations between spelling and phonology in the deep English and the shallow Serbo-Croatian orthographies are reflected in the ability of subjects to match printed and spoken stimuli. They presented subjects simultaneously with words or non-words in the matching task. Performance was measured in three experimental conditions: (1) clear print and clear speech, (2) clear print and speech degraded by signal-correlated noise, and (3) clear speech and degraded print. Within each language, the effects of visual and auditory degradation were measured relative to the baseline of undegraded presentation. If the systems for processing of print and speech interact and exchange information, when the visual or the auditory inputs are degraded, subjects are able to restore the partial information in one modality by matching it to the clear information in the other modality. When subjects are presented with speech alone, restoration of degraded speech components has been shown to be an automatic lexical process. However, in addition to this ipsimodal restoration mechanism, subjects in the Frost and Katz experiment had the additional possibility of a compensatory exchange of speech and print information. Thus, the technique of simultaneous visual and auditory presentation along with degradation provided insight concerning the interaction of orthography and phonology in the two languages.

The results showed that for Serbo-Croatian, visual degradation had a stable slowing effect relative to the baseline condition (about 20 msecs), regardless of stimulus frequency. For the English subjects, the effect of visual degradation was three to four times stronger than for the Serbo-Croatians. The inter-language differences that were found for visual degradation were almost identically replicated for auditory degradation; the degradation effects in English were again three to four times greater than in Serbo-Croatian. Thus, the overall pattern of results demonstrated that although the readers of English were efficient in matching print to speech under normal conditions, their efficiency deteriorated substantially under degraded conditions relative to the readers of Serbo-Croatian.

The different effects of degradation obtained in English and Serbo-Croatian were explained by Frost and Katz (1989) as cross-code consistency effects, emerging from a bidirectional flow of activation. According to this architecture, seeing print and forming a partial phonological representation of it can confirm (or contradict) a match to the accumulating phonological information being received via speech. In a complementary way, the rapid accumulation of information about which phonemes could be represented by the print can be influenced by the phonological information that is being received simultaneously via the auditory channel. Frost and Katz argued that the effects of visual or auditory degradation were greater for English than for Serbo-Croatian, because the simple isomorphic connections between the orthographic and the phonologic systems in the shallower orthography enabled subjects to restore both the degraded phonemes from the print and the degraded graphemes from the phonemic information, with ease. This is because, in a shallow system, partial phonemic information can correspond to only one, or at worst, a few graphemic alternatives, and vice versa. In contrast, in the deeper orthography, because the degraded information in one system was usually consistent with several alternatives in the other system, the build-up of sufficient information for a unique solution to the matching judgement was delayed, and the matching between print and degraded speech, or between speech and degraded print, was slowed. Overall, these findings provide a clear demonstration as to how the orthographic and phonological systems interact to exchange information during visual and auditory word recognition.

7.8 **Modeling speech and print interaction**

The first generations of word recognition models were purely orthographic (Grainger and Jacobs, 1996; Paap et al., 1982; McClelland and Rumelhart, 1981; for review see Jacobs and Grainger, 1994). Because their focus was on simulating what has been long thought of as purely "orthographic effects," such as the effects of word superiority or orthographic neighborhood, these early models neglected the role of phonology and spelling-to-sound interactions. In contrast, capturing spelling-to-sound interactions has been a major preoccupation in more recent modeling approaches (e.g. Coltheart et al., 2001; Harm and Seidenberg, 1999; 2004; Plaut et al., 1996; Zorzi et al., 1998). Not surprisingly, all of the recent computational models can simulate consistency or regularity effects which reflect interactions between spelling and sound. More problematic for some of the models are fast phonology effects. For example, the DRC model of reading has serious problems of accounting for masked phonological priming. At present, at least to our knowledge, none of the above mentioned models has been tested on feedback consistency effects in visual and auditory word recognition.

A model that appears highly compatible with all of the above mentioned effects is the bi-modal interactive activation (BIA) model described in Figure 7.2. The earliest version, (although schematic and purely descriptive), has been proposed by Frost and Katz (1989) to account for their effects of visual and phonological degradation in the matching task (see above). Frost and Katz have suggested a lexical structure which rationalizes the relationship between the orthographic and phonologic systems in terms of lateral connections between the systems at all of their levels. The structure of these lateral connections was determined by the relationship between spelling and phonology in the language: simple isomorphic connections between graphemes and phonemes in shallow orthographies, but more complex, many-to-one connections in deep orthographies. Since then a more detailed bimodal interactive model has been developed by Grainger and colleagues (Grainger and Ferrand, 1994; 1996; Grainger et al., 2005; Jacobs, et al., 1998; Ziegler, Muneaux and Grainger, 2003).

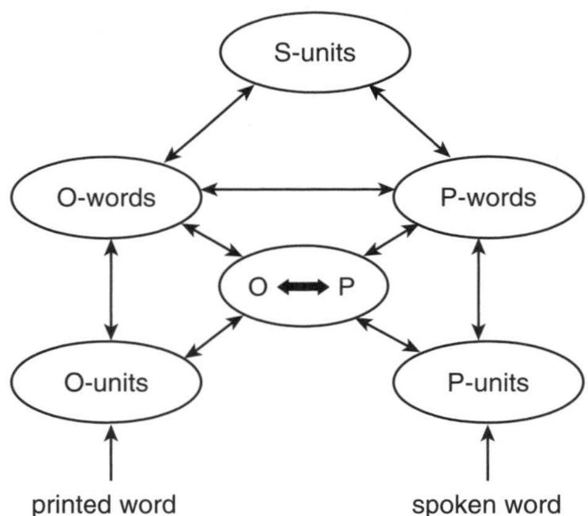

Figure 7.2 Architecture of a bimodal interactive activation model of word recognition (Grainger and Ferrand, 1994; 1996). In this architecture, orthography and phonology communicate directly at the level of whole-word representations (O-words, P-words), and also via a sublexical interface (O ⇔ P). Semantic representations (S-units) receive activation from whole-word orthographic and phonological representations (the details of inhibitory within-level and between-level connections are not shown).

In the BIA model, a printed word stimulus activates a sublexical orthographic code (O-units). This early orthographic code then sends activation onto the central interface between orthography and phonology (O ⇔ P) that allows sublexical orthographic representations to be mapped onto their corresponding phonological representations, and vice versa. Thus a printed word stimulus rapidly activates a set of sublexical phonological representations (phonemes in transparent alphabetic languages) that can influence the course of visual word recognition via their interaction with sublexical orthographic representations, or via the activation of whole-word phonological representations. Differences in orthographic transparency across languages will have a major impact at this processing level. It is this central interface between orthography and phonology that provides the mechanism to account for fast phonology and feedback consistency effects (for simulations of these effects, see Jacobs et al., 1998). Most importantly, because of its symmetrical structure across modalities, the BIA model predicts orthographic effects on spoken word recognition that should mirror phonological effects in visual word recognition. Such effects have indeed been found (Grainger et al., 2005; Ziegler, Muneaux, and Grainger, 2003). Yet these effects have not yet been simulated with the BIA model or any other model. Note, however, that traditional models of spoken word recognition (e.g. TRACE, McClelland and Elman, 1986) are not able to simulate orthographic effects on spoken word recognition because they lack an orthographic interface.

7.9 Summary and conclusions

Although printed and spoken words are associated with semantic features and result in the retrieval of word meaning, the most systematic resonance in reading is the one between orthographic and phonological units. Several decades of research on visual word recognition have revealed that the recovery of phonological information is the primary mechanism by which we retrieve meaning. Hence, during literacy acquisition, the printed and spoken forms of letters, letter clusters, and whole words become tightly interconnected such that they could be considered as the two faces of the same coin.

We suggest that the only viable theoretical approach to lexical architecture is to regard the orthographic and phonological systems as closely interconnected networks whereby the flow of information is not constrained to one direction, but is bidirectional, regardless of the source of the input, whether it is print or speech. This architecture predicts a symmetry with respect to how phonological structure affects print processing, and how orthographic structure affects auditory word recognition.

The empirical evidence supporting print and speech interaction is abundant. First, we have shown how the consistency with which the phonological structure of a given word is conveyed in print, or the consistency with which a spoken form can be spelt, affects reading. In general, inconsistent words are found to hinder visual word recognition. Similarly, reading acquisition in shallow orthographies, which are characterized by transparent relations between orthography and phonology, is easier than learning to read in deep orthographies. We reviewed evidence demonstrating that consistency effects are bidirectional: inconsistent words not only affect reading performance but also affect performance in pure phonological tasks such as phonemic segmentation, or auditory word recognition. Finally, we discussed evidence showing how print and speech interact when visual and auditory verbal stimuli are presented simultaneously.

The interaction of print and speech provides then another demonstration of how a bidirectional flow of activation between two processing systems favors fast and stable learning. It is the consistent and symmetrical connection between the visual and auditory modalities that is the basis for our linguistic ability to effortlessly match printed forms with spoken ones, and vice versa.

Authors' note

This study was supported in part by National Institute of Child Health and Human Development Grant HD-01994 to Haskins Laboratories.

References

Alegria, J., Pignot, E., and Morais, J. (1982) Phonetic analysis of speech and memory codes in beginning readers. *Memory and Cognition*, 10: 451–6.

Ben-Dror, I., Frost, R., and Bentin, S. (1995) Orthographic representation and phonemic segmentation in skilled readers: a cross-language comparison. *Psychological Science*, 6: 176–80.

Bentin, S., Hammer, R., and Cahan, S. (1991) The effects of aging and first grade schooling on the development of phonological awareness. *Psychological Science*, 2: 271–4.

Brysbaert, M. (2001) Prelexical phonological coding of visual words in Dutch: automatic after all. *Memory and Cognition*, 29: 765–73.

Coltheart, M., Rastle, K., Perry, C., Langdon, R., and Ziegler, J. C. (2001) DRC: a dual route cascaded model of visual word recognition and reading aloud. *Psychological Review*, 108(1): 204–56.

Dijkstra, T., Roelofs, A., and Fieuws, S. (1995) Orthographic effects on phoneme monitoring. *Canadian Journal of Experimental Psychology*, 49(2): 264–71.

Ehri, L. C., and Wilce, L. S. (1980) The influence of orthography on readers' conceptualization of the phonemic structure of words. *Applied Psycholinguistics*, 1(4): 371–85.

Ferrand, L., and Grainger, J. (1993) The time course of orthographic and phonological code activation in the early phases of visual word recognition. *Bulletin of the Psychonomic Society*, 31(2): 119–22.

Ferrand, L., and Grainger, J. (1994) Effects of orthography are independent of phonology in masked form priming. *Quarterly Journal of Experimental Psychology: Human Experimental Psychology*, 47A(2): 365–82.

Forster, K.I., and Davis, C. (1984) Repetition priming and frequency attenuation in lexical access. *Journal of Experimental Psychology: Learning, Memory, and Cognition*, 10: 680–98.

Frauenfelder, U. H., Segui, J., and Dijkstra, T. (1990) Lexical effects in phonemic processing: facilitatory or inhibitory? *Journal of Experimental Psychology: Human Perception and Performance*, 16(1): 77–91.

Frost, R. (1998) Toward a strong phonological theory of visual word recognition: true issues and false trails. *Psychological Bulletin*, 123(1): 71–99.

Frost, R. (2005) Orthographic systems and skilled word recognition processes in reading. In C. Hulme and M. Snowling (eds) *The Science of Reading: A Handbook*, pp. 272–95. Blackwell, Oxford.

Frost, R., Ahissar, M., Gotesman, R., and Tayeb, S. (2003) Are phonological effects fragile? The effect of luminance and exposure duration on form priming and phonological priming. *Journal of Memory and Language*, 48(2): 346–78.

Frost, R., and Katz, L. (1989) Orthographic depth and the interaction of visual and auditory processing in word recognition. *Memory and Cognition*, 17: 302–11.

Frost, R., Katz, L., and Bentin, S. (1987) Strategies for visual word recognition and orthographical depth: a multilingual comparison. *Journal of Experimental Psychology: Human Perception and Performance*, 13: 104–15.

Glushko, R. J. (1979) The organization and activation of orthographic knowledge in reading aloud. *Journal of Experimental Psychology: Human Perception and Performance*, 5(4): 674–91.

Goswami, U., Gombert, J. E., and de Barrera, L. F. (1998) Children's orthographic representations and linguistic transparency: nonsense word reading in English, French, and Spanish. *Applied Psycholinguistics*, 19(1): 19–52.

Goswami, U., Ziegler, J. C., Dalton, L., and Schneider, W. (2001) Pseudohomophone effects and phonological recoding procedures in reading development in English and German. *Journal of Memory and Language*, 45(4): 648–64.

Goswami, U., Ziegler, J. C., Dalton, L., and Schneider, W. (2003) Nonword reading across orthographies: how flexible is the choice of reading units? *Applied Psycholinguistics*, 24: 235–47.

Grainger, J., and Ferrand, L. (1994) Phonology and orthography in visual word recognition: effects of masked homophone primes. *Journal of Memory and Language*, 33(2): 218–33.

Grainger, J., and Ferrand, L. (1996) Masked orthographic and phonological priming in visual word recognition and naming: cross-task comparisons. *Journal of Memory and Language*, 35: 623–47.

Grainger, J., and Jacobs, A. M. (1996) Orthographic processing in visual word recognition: a multiple read-out model. *Psychological Review*, 103(3): 518–65.

Grainger, J., and Jacobs, A.M. (1998) On localist connectionism and psychological science. In J. Grainger and A. M. Jacobs (eds), *Localist Connectionist Approaches to Human Cognition*. Erlbaum, Mahwah, NJ.

Grainger, J., Muneaux, M., Farioli, F., and Ziegler, J. C. (2005) Effects of phonological and orthographic neighbourhood density interact in visual word recognition. *Quarterly Journal of Experimental Psychology*, 58A: 981–98.

Grainger, J., and Ziegler, J. C. (2005) Cross-code consistency effects in visual word recognition. In E. L. Grigorenko and A. Naples (eds), *Single-Word Reading: Biological and Behavioral Perspectives*, Lawrence Erlbaum Associates, Mahwah, NJ.

Gronau, N., and Frost, R. (1997) Prelexical phonologic computation in a deep orthography: evidence from backward masking in Hebrew. *Psychonomic Bulletin and Review*, 4: 107–12.

Halle, P. A., Chereau, C., and Segui, J. (2000) Where is the /b/ in "absurde" [apsyrd]? It is in French listeners' minds. *Journal of Memory and Language*, 43(4): 618–39.

Harm, M. W., and Seidenberg, M. S. (1999) Phonology, reading acquisition, and dyslexia: insights from connectionist models. *Psychological Review*, 106(3): 491–528.

Harm, M. W., and Seidenberg, M. S. (2004) Computing the meanings of words in reading: cooperative division of labor between visual and phonological processes. *Psychological Review*, 111(3): 662–720.

Jacobs, A. M., and Grainger, J. (1994) Models of visual word recognition: sampling the state of the art. *Journal of Experimental Psychology: Human Perception and Performance*, 20(6): 1311–334.

Jacobs, A. M., Rey, A., Ziegler, J. C., and Grainger, J. (1998) MROM-p: an interactive activation, multiple readout model of orthographic and phonological processes in visual word recognition. In J. Grainger and A. M. Jacobs (eds), *Localist Connectionist Approaches to Human Cognition*, pp. 147–88. Lawrence Erlbaum Associates, Mahwah, NJ.

Jared, D. (1997) Spelling-sound consistency affects the naming of high-frequency words. *Journal of Memory and Language*, 36(4): 505–29.

Jared, D. (2002) Spelling-sound consistency and regularity effects in word naming. *Journal of Memory and Language*, 46: 723–50.

Katz, L., and Feldman L.B. (1981) Linguistic coding in word recognition. In A.M. Lesgold and C.A. Perfetti (eds), *Interactive Processes in Reading*, pp. 85–105. Erlbaum, Hillsdale, NJ.

Lacruz, I., and Folk, J.R. (2004) Feedforward and feedback consistency effects for high- and low-frequency words in lexical decision and naming. *Quarterly Journal of Experimental Psychology*, 57A: 1261–84.

Liberman, I. Y., Liberman, A. M., Mattingly, I. G., and Shankweiler, D. (1980) Orthography and the beginning reader. In J. F. Kavanagh and R. L. Venezky (eds), *Orthography, Reading, and Dyslexia*, pp. 137–53. Pro-Ed. Austin, TX.

Lukatela, G., Popadic, D., Ognjenovic, P., and Turvey, M. T. (1980) Lexical decision in a phonologically shallow orthography. *Memory and Cognition*, 8: 415–23.

Lukatela, G., and Frost, S., and Turvey, M. T. (1998) Phonological priming by masked nonword primes in the lexical decision task. *Journal of Memory and Language*, 39: 666–83.

Lukatela, G., and Turvey, M. T. (1994) Visual access is initially phonological, 2: evidence from phonological priming by homophones, and pseudohomophones. *Journal of Experimental Psychology: General*, 123: 331–53.

McClelland, J. L., and Elman, J. L. (1986) The TRACE model of speech perception. *Cognitive Psychology*, 18(1): 1–86.

McClelland, J. L., and Rumelhart, D. E. (1981) An interactive activation model of context effects in letter perception, 1: an account of basic findings. *Psychological Review*, 88(5): 375–407.

Morais, J., Cary, L., Alegria, J., and Bertelson, P. (1979) Does awareness of speech as a sequence of phones arise spontaneously? *Cognition*, 7(4): 323–31.

Miller, K. M., and Swick, D. (2003) Orthography influences the perception of speech in alexic patients. *Journal of Cognitive Neuroscience*, 15(7): 981–90.

Paap, K. R., Newsome, S. L., McDonald, J. E., and Schvaneveldt, R. W. (1982) An activation-verification model for letter and word recognition: the word-superiority effect. *Psychological Review*, 89(5): 573–94.

Pecher, D. (2001) Perception is a two-way junction: feedback semantics in word recognition. *Psychonomic Bulletin and Review*, 8(3): 545–51.

Peereman, R., Content, A., and Bonin, P. (1998) Is perception a two-way street? The case of feedback consistency in visual word recognition. *Journal of Memory and Language*, 39(2): 151–74.

Perfetti, C. A., Bell, L. C., and Delaney, S. M. (1988) Automatic (prelexical) phonetic activation in silent word reading: evidence from backward masking. *Journal of Memory and Language*, 27: 59–70.

Perry, C. (2003) A phoneme-grapheme feedback consistency effect. *Psychonomic Bulletin and Review*, 10(2): 392–97.

Plaut, D. C., McClelland, J. L., Seidenberg, M. S., and Patterson, K. (1996) Understanding normal and impaired word reading: computational principles in quasi-regular domains. *Psychological Review*, 103(1): 56–115.

Pollatsek, A., Lesch, M. F., Morris, and Rayner, K. (1992) Phonological codes are used in integrating information across saccades in word identification and reading. *Journal of Experimental Psychology: Human Perception and Performance*, 18: 148–62.

Pollatsek, A., Tan, L. H., and Rayner, K. (2000) The role of phonological codes in integrating information across saccadic eye movements in Chinese character identification. *Journal of Experimental Psychology: Human Perception and Performance*, 26(2): 607–33.

Seidenberg, M. S., and McClelland, J. L. (1989) A distributed, developmental model of word recognition and naming. *Psychological Review*, 96(4): 523–68.

Seidenberg, M. S., and Tanenhaus, M. K. (1979) Orthographic effects on rime monitoring. *Journal of Experimental Psychology: Human Learning and Memory*, 5(6): 546–54.

Seymour, P. H. K., Aro, M., and Erskine, J. M. (2003) Foundation literacy acquisition in European orthographies. *British Journal of Psychology*, 94: 143–74.

Share, D. L. (1995) Phonological recoding and self-teaching: sine qua non of reading acquisition. *Cognition*, 55(2): 151–218.

Share, D. L., and Blum, P. (2005) Syllable splitting in literate and preliterate Hebrew speakers: onsets and rimes or bodies and codas? *Journal of Experimental Child Psychology*, 92(2): 182–202.

Stone, G. O., and Van Orden, G. C. (1994) Building a resonance framework for word recognition using design and system principles. *Journal of Experimental Psychology: Human Perception and Performance*, 20(6): 1248–68.

Stone, G. O., Vanhoy, M., and Van Orden, G. C. (1997) Perception is a two-way street: feedforward and feedback phonology in visual word recognition. *Journal of Memory and Language*, 36(3): 337–59.

Tan, L. H., Hoosain, R., and Siok, W. W. T. (1996) The activation of phonological codes before access to character meaning in written chinese. *Journal of Experimental Psychology: Learning, Memory, and Cognition*, 22: 865–82.

Tuller, B., Case, P., Ding, M., and Kelso, J. A. (1994) The nonlinear dynamics of speech categorization. *Journal of Experimental Psychology: Human Perception and Performance*, 20(1): 3–16.

Van Orden, G. C. (2002) Nonlinear dynamics and psycholinguistics. *Ecological Psychology*, 14(1–2): 1–4.

Van Orden, G. C., and Goldinger, S. D. (1994) Interdependence of form and function in cognitive systems explains perception of printed words. *Journal of Experimental Psychology: Human Perception and Performance*, 20(6): 1269–91.

Van Orden, G. C., Jansen op de Haar, M. A., and Bosman, A. M. T. (1997) Complex dynamic systems also predict dissociations, but they do not reduce to autonomous components. *Cognitive Neuropsychology*, 14(1): 131–65.

Van Orden, G. C., Pennington, B. F., and Stone, G. O. (1990) Word identification in reading and the promise of subsymbolic psycholinguistics. *Psychological Review*, 97(4): 488–522.

Ventura, P., Morais, J., Pattamadilok, C., and Kolinsky, R. (2004) The locus of the orthographic consistency effect in auditory word recognition. *Language and Cognitive Processes*, 19(1): 57–95.

Ziegler, J. C., and Ferrand, L. (1998) Orthography shapes the perception of speech: the consistency effect in auditory word recognition. *Psychonomic Bulletin and Review*, 5(4): 683–9.

Ziegler, J. C., Ferrand, L., Jacobs, A. M., Rey, A., and Grainger, J. (2000) Visual and phonological codes in letter and word recognition: evidence from incremental priming. *Quarterly Journal of Experimental Psychology: Human Experimental Psychology*, 53A(3): 671–92.

Ziegler, J. C., Ferrand, L., and Montant, M. (2004) Visual phonology: the effects of orthographic consistency on different auditory word recognition tasks. *Memory and Cognition*, 32(5): 732–41.

Ziegler, J. C., and Goswami, U. (2005) Reading acquisition, developmental dyslexia, and skilled reading across languages: a psycholinguistic grain size theory. *Psychology Bulletin*, 131(1): 3–29.

Ziegler, J. C., and Jacobs, A. M. (1995) Phonological information provides early sources of constraint in the processing of letter strings. *Journal of Memory and Language*, 34(5): 567–93.

Ziegler, J. C., Montant, M., and Jacobs, A. M. (1997) The feedback consistency effect in lexical decision and naming. *Journal of Memory and Language*, 37(4): 533–54.

Ziegler, J. C., Muneaux, M., and Grainger, J. (2003) Neighborhood effects in auditory word recognition: phonological competition and orthographic facilitation. *Journal of Memory and Language*, 48(4): 779–93.

Ziegler, J. C., Perry, C., and Coltheart, M. (2003) Speed of lexical and nonlexical processing in French: the case of the regularity effect. *Psychonomic Bulletin and Review*, 10(4): 947–53.

Ziegler, J. C., Perry, C., Jacobs, A. M., and Braun, M. (2001) Identical words are read differently in different languages. *Psychological Science*, 12(5): 379–84.

Ziegler, J. C., Stone, G. O., and Jacobs, A. M. (1997) What is the pronunciation for -ough and the spelling for /u/? A database for computing feedforward and feedback consistency in English. *Behavior Research Methods, Instruments and Computers*, 29: 600–18.

Ziegler, J. C., Van Orden, G. C., and Jacobs, A. M. (1997) Phonology can help or hurt the perception of print. *Journal of Experimental Psychology: Human Perception and Performance*, 23(3): 845–60.

Zorzi, M., Houghton, G., and Butterworth, B. (1998) Two routes or one in reading aloud? A connectionist dual-process model. *Journal of Experimental Psychology: Human Perception and Performance*, 24(4): 1131–61.

Correspondence should be addressed to Ram Frost, Department of Psychology, The Hebrew University, Jerusalem, 91905, Israel.
Email: frost@mscc.huji.ac.il

CHAPTER 8

Word processing in the brain as revealed by neurophysiological imaging

Friedemann Pulvermüller

8.1 Neurophysiological research in psycholinguistics

Psycholinguistics has classically focused on button press tasks and reaction time experiments from which cognitive processes are being inferred. The advent of neuroimaging opened new research perspectives for the psycholinguist as it became possible to look at the neuronal mass activity that underlies language processing. Studies of brain correlates of psycholinguistic processes can complement behavioral results, and in some cases, as will be argued here, can lead to direct information about the basis of psycholinguistic processes.

Even more importantly, the neuroscience move in psycholinguistics made it possible to advance language theorizing to the level of the brain. The theorist was no longer restricted to box–arrow diagrams: a range of models that spell out language in terms of neuron circuitry became directly testable in psychophysiological and psycholinguistic experiments. The methodological advance thus inspired and consolidated an advance at the level of theory building.

This chapter focuses on neurophysiological imaging with electroencephalography (EEG) and magnetoencephalography (MEG). The reason for this focus lies in the great temporal resolution of these methods. They allow following brain processes in real time, in the millisecond range, a property necessary for testing theories that make predictions about exact time courses. Metabolic imaging methods, in contrast, have a much lower time resolution and therefore make it difficult to decide whether two processes are simultaneous or serial, or to pin down the time delay between the two in real time. Given the importance of the "when?" question in psycholinguistics, the question of *where* in the brain certain processes happen will naturally be somewhat in the background in the present chapter. The "where" issue is best addressed by a combination of EEG/MEG and metabolic imaging work (cf. Pulvermüller, 2005).

After early pioneering work (Friedman et al., 1975; Molfese et al., 1975; Sherrard, 1969; Walter, 1965), cortical electrophysiology with EEG started to be used on a broader scale to address linguistic questions in the 1980s (e.g. Bentin, 1989; Bentin and Feinsod, 1983; Kutas and Hillyard, 1980; Neville et al., 1982; Picton and Stuss, 1984; Rugg and Dickens, 1982), and later on, in the 1990s, also magnetoencephalography (MEG) was first used to address linguistic questions (e.g. Eulitz et al., 1995b; Hari, 1991; Pulvermüller et al., 1996; Salmelinet al., 1994). The idea was to use these methods, which allow one to reveal the electric potentials and magnetic fields produced by the near-simultaneous activation of thousands of nerve cells in the cortex (Coles and Rugg, 1995; Fabiani et al., 2000; Levine and Orrison, 1995a; 1995b), to look directly at the neuronal substrate of psycholinguistic processes.

In principle, neurophysiological and behavioral measures can tap into the same cognitive processes, although at different levels of the causal chain (Henson, 2005; Rugg and Coles, 1995). Still, reaction time and neurophysiological experiments have different advantages and limitations. The relation between signal and noise (signal-to-noise ratio, SNR) is low in both cases, and this requires that averages over numerous trials, ideally 50 to 200, are calculated to obtain average reaction times and average event-related brain response. Averaging minimizes non-systematic variance (noise) and emphasizes stimulus and task-related variance (signal relative to the noise). Whereas behavioral press-button tasks just deliver two measures, reaction time and accuracy, an experiment using event-related potentials (ERPs) leads to a time series of measurement points. These represent activation values that can be informative about different stages of stimulus or task-related processing. Such monitoring of different stages is more difficult to achieve in reaction time experiments, although it is possible. However, it requires application of special techniques, for example the consecutive presentation of multiple stimuli at different stimulus onset asynchronies. Although it is possible to relate neurophysiological and behavioral results of time course studies (see e.g. Mohr and Pulvermüller, 2002), it appears that, in behavioral reaction time studies, the monitoring of temporal dynamics of stimulus-related process is costly, whereas it comes out for free from EEG and MEG studies. The output, the time series of activation values locked to stimulus presentation or, as an alternative, to response onset, can be so thinly sliced that steps of 1 ms are monitored. The method allows it to relate physiological changes revealed during the recording period to properties of a stimulus, response, or task (for an introduction to event-related potentials and fields, see Coles and Rugg, 1995; Fabiani et al., 2000; Levine and Orrison, 1995a; 1995b).

As information can be obtained time-slice by time-slice, this implies a unique opportunity to obtain definitive information about *when* the brain processes differ between stimulus categories, response types, or tasks. As an example, Figure 8.1 shows averaged MEG responses to meaningful words and phonologically legal pseudo-words, and it can be seen that these eventrelated field

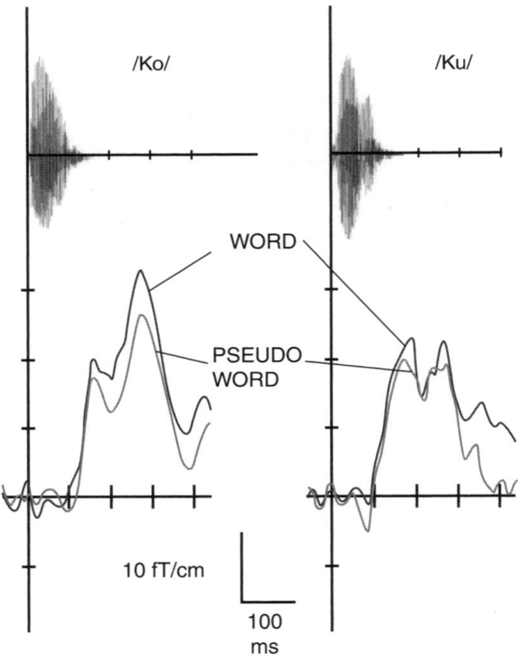

Figure 8.1 The Mismatch negativity (MMN) elicited by the same syllables presented in contexts where they completed a meaningful word of Finnish or a meaningless pseudo-word. The syllable-elicited MMN was larger in word context than in pseudo-word context (after Pulvermüller et al., 2001). See Plate 1 for a color version of this figure.

(ERF) curves diverge at around 150 ms, therefore showing that the brain processes elicited by words and pseudo-words are different at this latency. The critical zero point in the experiment was the onset of the word final syllables. Thirty ms after onset of these word final syllables, the words could be unambiguously recognized. The result therefore indicates that word and pseudo-word processes differ within 120 ms after the point of word recognition (Marslen-Wilson, 1987). Behavioral responses cannot provide equivalent information, as the initiation of a behavioral response always requires time, and usage of the earliest reaction time at which responses to different stimulus types differ therefore implies an overestimation of the psycholinguistic processing time targeted. Therefore, differences between conditions, but not absolute reaction times, can be interpreted. Also in this sense the neurophysiological measures are therefore closer to the cortical mechanisms than are behavioral responses.

An additional limitation of psycholinguistic reaction time experiments comes from the fact that responses of the usual types can only be obtained if a behavioral task is administered. A button must be pressed to one type of word, letter or stimulus feature—or at the least, taking the example of an eye monitoring task where also overt motor responses are studied, the gaze must follow a string of words in the context of an attentive reading task. Neurophysiological recordings can also be taken while linguistic or other cognitive tasks are being performed, but, importantly, they can also be obtained while subjects rest and do not focus their attention on the critical stimuli that elicit the brain response. In the extreme, they may focus their attention on a demanding distraction task while language stimuli they are asked to ignore are investigated with regard to the brain-internal effects they bring about. This opens opportunities to look at processes elicited by language stimuli independent of the subjects' task-related strategies and without subjects paying attention to them. In the mismatch negativity (MMN) paradigm (Näätänen, 2001), for example, subjects can attend to a silent video film while spoken language stimuli are played to them, and subjects are instructed to ignore the language input and focus their attention on the film. This makes it possible to look at the physiological correlates of language processes elicited by stimuli that are not the target of an attention-demanding task ("outside the focus of attention"[1]). In behavioral reaction time experiments, unattended stimuli can also be presented, but the responses (button presses) collected are, in this case, always to the attended material, and therefore only reveal indirect information about the unattended one.

The necessary link between behavioral task, attention to language materials, and the dependent measure obtained—the finger movement pushing the button—implies a limitation of behavioral experiments from which neurophysiological research can escape: tasks can be undertaken with different strategies. A word response in a lexical decision task can be made at different levels of certainty, and before responding with a word or pseudo-word (or high- or low-frequency word) button press, different amounts of effort can be invested into the search for possible word candidates. Different accuracies and reaction times may reflect this, and it may be difficult to disentangle the possible contribution of differences in processing strategies between stimulus types from factors intrinsically related to stimulus information. In contrast, neurophysiological responses do not require a task or attention to stimuli. They "come for free", can even be recorded while subjects engage in something else and critical stimuli are played in the background, and still can give the researcher important information about brain processes related to language. Also in this sense, it seems, neurophysiological responses can get closer to language mechanisms, here by providing clues as to which features of processing may be stimulus-related and which, on the other hand, may be task- and strategy-dependent.

In summary, neuropsychological experiments provide an important upgrade to the experimental toolkit available in psycholinguistics and can be helpful in addressing specific brain- and language-theoretical questions.

8.2 Behavioral and neurophysiological evidence in psycholinguistic research: lexical class membership and word frequency

Most psycholinguists would probably agree that the frequency with which a given word form

[1] The MMN paradigm has its own limitations, too. For example, it implies that the critical "deviant stimulus" occurs rarely within a uniform sequence of frequently repeated standard stimuli. The monotony of the experiment and the frequent repetitions limit this approach to the investigation of more automatic processes.

occurs in standard text and the word type it belongs to are important variables determining psycholinguistic processes. Here, word form frequency, or standardized lexical frequency, and lexical class membership will be used to illustrate psycholinguistc research perspectives opened by neurophysiological imaging.

It is common to divide the lexicon into word classes or "lexical categories" such as nouns, verbs, prepositions, auxiliaries, and determiners; and the proposal that these category distinctions are reflected by the mental machinery and also by the biological substrate therefore has some plausibility. The most general lexical category distinction is between the word classes comprising content and function words, where the meaningful contentful categories of nouns, verbs, adjectives, adverbs, and spatial prepositions are contrasted with the word groups with mainly grammatical function, including determiners, conjunctions, auxiliaries, and so on. Although psycholinguistic theories have made postulates about the two main lexical classes that could not be confirmed (Bradley, 1983; Gordon and Caramazza, 1982), clear evidence for the relevance of this distinction comes from aphasia types characterized by a predominant impairment in processing either function or content words, i.e. agrammatism and anomia (Caplan et al., 1996; Pick, 1913; Pulvermüller, 1995).

One psycholinguistic reaction time experiment performed by Bradley provided behavioral evidence for a word category difference that was supported by subsequent research. In this experiment, Bradley and colleagues presented words from the two categories either to the left or right visual half field (LVF and RVF), from where stimulus information is directly relayed to the contralateral hemisphere of the cortex (from LVF to the right hemisphere, RH, and from RVF to the left hemisphere, LH—Bradley and Garrett, 1983). While all words showed a right visual field advantage (RVFA)—that is, more effective processing when presented on the right as compared with left visual field presentation—this effect differed between function words and content words. The RVFA for words generally observed in right-handed native speakers of a language is best explained by left hemispheric specialization for language processes (Zaidel, 1989) or an imbalance towards the left hemisphere of distributed neuronal ensembles processing lexical items (Pulvermüller and Mohr, 1996). A differential laterality of content and function words processing could also be documented by other researchers using tachistoscopic stimulus presentation in the left and right visual half-fields (Chiarello and Nuding, 1987; Mohr et al., 1994), although not all studies confirmed the effect. The result provides some support for the idea of different lexicons for function and for content words, and is even suggestive regarding the responsible mechanisms. As function words showed a greater RVFA than content words, it may be that the cortical networks processing the former are more strongly lateralized than those of the latter (Mohr et al., 1994).

Susan Garnsey performed a pioneering psychophysiological study addressing the issues of different brain correlates of content and function words directly (Garnsey, 1985; Garnsey and Chapman, 1985). She found a differentiation between frequency-matched content and function words of similar length in ERP recordings, an effect present around 500 ms after the onset of written word presentations. These differences appeared in a lexical decision task, i.e. in the same task also used by Bradley and others.

In a further EEG experiment, Neville and colleagues presented words in normal sentence context and averaged activity elicited by content and function words separately (Neville et al., 1992). Here for the first time, pronounced differences in laterality of the ERPs to content and function words were seen, which in this case appeared at latencies around 300 ms. The function words elicited an "N280" component, which was left-lateralized, whereas content words gave rise to a so-called "N350" component, which was symmetrical over the hemispheres. However, this study, along with a replication work published by Nobre and McCarthy (1994), used content and function words not matched for word frequency, so that the different lateralities of N280 and N350 might tentatively be related to the word frequency factor, rather than to vocabulary type.

This suspicion was in fact nurtured by subsequent work reporting a shift of ERP latency with word frequency. Similarly to the lexical decision responses, which decrease in latency with increasing word frequency, the latency of a negative component of the ERP was found to be shorter to more frequent words (King and Kutas, 1998; Osterhout et al., 1997). In these experiments, numerous sentences included very highly frequent function words and also rare (mostly content) words. It is possible that the high-frequency items were more often presented in the experiment than were the low-frequency ones, so that the latency shift seen for high-frequency words relative to low-frequency items could be related to the number of item repetitions. Major efforts to replicate the ERP frequency effect failed when only content words were presented in randomized sequences and each item only appeared once; (Assadollahi and Pulvermüller, 2001; 2003; Hauk and Pulvermüller, 2004a) but see Embick et al., 2001). In Hauk's and Assadollahi's studies, words with high and low frequency elicited event-related potentials with different magnitudes starting already 150–200ms after written word onset, but a shift of peak amplitude with frequency could not be confirmed. Consistent with this work, amplitude modulations of early and late ERPs have been found by a range of studies (see Polich and Donchin, 1988: sections 3.1, 3.2; Rugg, 1990; Sereno et al., 1998; Smith and Halgren, 1987; Van Petten and Kutas, 1990).

Given the possible manifestation of word frequency in the event-related potential, the neurophysiological correlate of function and content words needs to be investigated for word groups matched for word frequency and length, as in Garnsey's early seminal work (Garnsey, 1985). As low-frequency function word are sometimes considered exceptional and atypical, it appears advantageous to restrict the range of content and function words from which experimental stimuli are taken to high frequencies, where function words, such as *rather* and *further* reside beside content words such as *mother* and *music.* To further reduce stimulus variance in both word groups, it is possible to restrict the length range of the materials, for example by selecting words of two syllables only. Presentation of such low-variance frequency- and length-matched word groups led to ERPs that revealed a significant hemisphere by word class interaction: there was a great and significant laterality difference in the ERPs to function words, but a reduced or even absent laterality of the ERPs to content words (Pulvermüller et al., 1995). Remarkably, the vocabulary type difference in ERPs emerged in the N160 response, an early negative component peaking ~160 ms after stimulus onset overlaying the positive wave following the initial large negativity called N100 (see section 8.2). Although a range of studies reported differential laterality of event-related brain responses to the two main vocabulary types (Brown et al., 1999; Neville et al., 1992; Nobre and McCarthy, 1994; Pulvermüller et al., 1995; Weber-Fox and Neville, 2001), other studies reported ERPs that did not support a fundamental difference in brain processes related to the two word classes, except for a sometimes larger late negative ERP (N400 component: see section 8.3.1) to content words compared with function words (Friederici et al., 2000; Kutas and Hillyard, 1983; Munte et al., 2001; Van Petten and Kutas, 1991).

In sum, combined evidence from some psycholinguistic studies—both behavioral and psychophysiological—suggests that there may be a fundamental vocabulary type difference (Figure 8.2). This difference has been observed in behavioral responses to lateralized tachistoscopic word presentation, as a greater RVFA to function words compared with content words, and in neurophysiological experiments as well, in this case as a more strongly lateralized neurophysiological responses to function words than to content words. These results indicate a match between behavioral and neurophysiological methods. Both suggest more strongly lateralized mechanism for function words than for content words. As one possibility, distributed neuronal memory networks for function words may be strongly lateralized to the left perisylvian language cortex (Figure 8.3), whereas those for content words are more equally distributed over both hemispheres of the forebrain, a feature attributable to the bihemispheric processing of referential semantic information linked to content words (Pulvermüller and Mohr, 1996). It should, however, be emphasized once again that the results on vocabulary differences are controversial and, if replicable at all, small and strongly dependent on psycholinguistic stimulus matching.

In contrast to word class differences, the word frequency effect is easily replicable and clearly apparent in behavior and in neurophysiology as well. Although ERP latency shifts are controversial, several laboratories reported early (100–200 ms) and late (>200 ms) manifestations of word frequency in the electric and magnetic brain response, which commonly materialized as amplitude modulation of ERP and ERF components. These effects, along with the behavioral data, may be related to differences in internal connection strengths of neuronal ensembles processing high- and low-frequency words (Pulvermüller, 1999).

8.3 Event-related potentials indicating language processing

This section attempts to give a brief introduction to language-related components of the event-related brain potential (ERP) and field (ERF) and to relate them to psycholinguistic models and information types. A typical ERP shows an early positive peak at about 100 ms, the so-called P100, closely followed by a negative peak, the N100, and, subsequently, positive

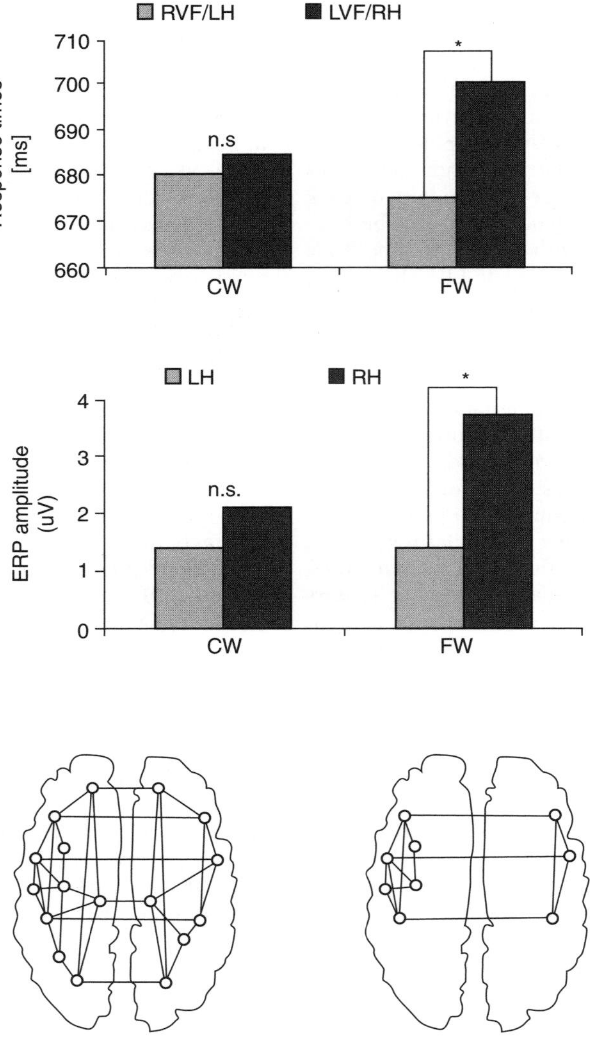

Figure 8.2 Differential laterality of content and function word (cw, fw) processing as indicated by behavioral and neurophysiological experiments. The diagram at the top shows response times of lexical decision responses to content and function words presented either in the right or left visual field, therefore respectively reaching the left or right hemisphere (LVF, RVF, Mohr et al., 1994). The middle diagram presents event-related potentials, ERPs, to content and function words recorded over the left and right hemisphere (Pulvermüller et al., 1995). In both the behavioral and ERP data, there was differential laterality with stronger interhemispheric differences for function words than for content words matched for word length and frequency (significant differences are indicated by an asterisk). These results are explained by the differential laterality model shown at the bottom, according to which the neuronal assemblies that process function words are strongly lateralized, but those for content words show a reduced laterality degree, due to the bihemispheric addition of semantic networks (Pulvermüller and Mohr, 1996).

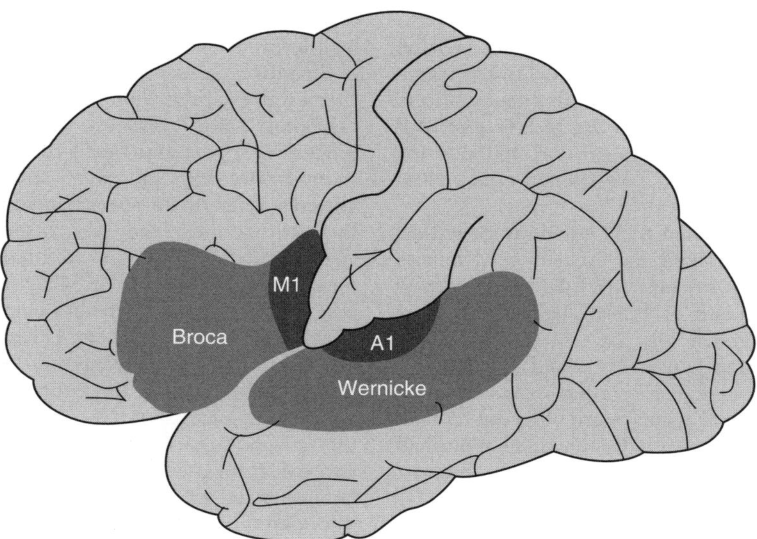

Figure 8.3 Language areas of the human brain: the left perisylvian cortex, especially Broca's and Wernicke's areas in the vicinity of the primary articulatory motor (M1) and auditory (A1) cortex, is essential for–and becomes active during–the processing of phonological, syntactic and lexical information. It may be of particular relevance for processing function words and inflectional affixes.

and negative deflection named by the polarity—N for negative or P for positive—and the approximate latency of the peak of the wave in milliseconds, e.g. 160, 200, 300, 350, 400. Some of these waves or components are early, and occur irrespective of whether subjects pay attention to the stimuli. These include the positive and negative peaks up to about 200 ms after stimulus onset, also including the so-called mismatch negativity (MMN). Later components, in particular the P300 component and the N400, are attention-dependent, and some of their sub-components, for example a late part of the P300 called P300b, disappear entirely if subjects do not attend to the stimulus perceived.

8.3.1 Late language potentials

Late language components still tend to be better known than the earlier ones, and they are therefore discussed first. A broader overview of these can be found in the chapter by Kutas and Federmeier (Chapter 23 this volume).

The N400 component is perhaps the most famous language component of the ERP. Kutas and Hillyard found that it is elicited by "senseless sentences," more precisely words presented in a sentence context where they are grammatically possible but semantically unexpected (Kutas and Hillyard, 1980), e.g. *He drank tea with sugar and socks*, where the last word elicits a pronounced N400. In contrast, a semantically expected final word, such as *milk*, would only elicit a reduced or even absent N400. This component has therefore been interpreted as an index of semantic context integration and semantic memory use (Kutas and Federmeier, 2000), although it may also indicate a range of other stimulus-induced cognitive processes, for example phonological ones (Rugg, 1984).

The magnitude of the N400 response also reflects psycholinguistic properties of single words presented in random lists, where each word is, quite naturally, difficult to predict. As mentioned in section 8.2, the late negativity decreases with increasing word frequency and was reported to be smaller for function words than for content words. Concreteness and imageability of words may be reflected in its size and topography (Kounios and Holcomb, 1994; Paller et al., 1988; Smith and Halgren, 1987; West and Holcomb, 2000). Semantic and lexical word categories, such as animal and tool names or nouns and verbs, seem also to elicit slightly different N400 typographies (Federmeier et al., 2000; Kiefer, 2001; Pulvermüller, Mohr, and Schleichert, 1999). Further psycholinguistic properties, which will be discussed in section 8.3.2, have also been found to influence the N400 or related late event-related potentials and fields. For example, neighborhood size and frequency effects have been reported to modulate ERP and ERF components at latencies around 300–400 ms (Holcomb et al., 2002; Pylkkanen et al., 2004; Stockall et al., 2004).

Positivities related to linguistic information processing that exhibited even longer latencies than the N400 were observed following Garnsey's original observations (1985). Single words of low frequency (Polich and Donchin, 1988; Rugg, 1990; Rugg and Doyle, 1992) and, intriguingly, words placed in sentence contexts where they violated the rules of syntax, were observed to elicit pronounced late positivities maximal about half a second after critical word onset (P600, Hagoort et al., 1993; Osterhout and Holcomb, 1992).

8.3.2 Early language potentials

Acoustic and visual stimulus information is transmitted to the cortex within 20–50 ms or even faster (e.g. Maunsell and Gibson, 1992; Pelizzone et al., 1987). However, the first big cortical response in the average event-related potential and field appears as late as around 100 ms after stimulus onset. At this latency, activity may already have spread through numerous synapses; or the moderately fast conducting fibers, which form the majority in cortical-cortical long-distance fibre tracts (Aboitiz et al., 1992), could have led activity once or twice from posterior cortex to the front and back (for discussion, see Pulvermüller, 2000). The lateness of all major cortical components of the ERP, including what we call here the "early" ones, i.e. P100, N100, P200, N200 and P200, is therefore surprising. Considering the well-known rapid progression of neuronal activity in the central nervous system, it appears an even greater mystery that language processing per se should be reflected by components of maximal amplitude following stimulation only at around half a second. The biological advantage of language in the phylogenetic development of the species lies in the rapid transmission of information between individuals, which it makes possible. This rapid information transmission is at odds with the lateness of brain potentials such as the N400 and P600 components. It therefore appears that neuro-anatomical and neurophysiological data as well as phylogenetic considerations suggest a search for early brain responses related to language. If a reliable neurophysiological correlate of early psycholinguistic information access can be demonstrated, late responses carrying the same information must be interpreted as the reflection of a second step in the processing sequence.

It is well established that the neurophysiological reflections of phonetic and phonological processing appear in the early cortical responses, around 100–150 ms after stimulus onset. Differences between speech sounds and non-linguistic sounds, and even between specific speech sounds or syllables of a language, were seen in the N100 and the MMN and in their magnetic correlates (Dehaene-Lambertz, 1997; Eulitz et al., 1995a; Eulitz and Lahiri, 2004; Hari, 1991; Molfese, 1978; Näätänen et al., 1997; Obleser, Elbert, Lahiri, and Eulitz, 2003; Obleser, Lahiri, and Eulitz, 2003). It could even be shown that psycholinguistic phenomena such as the perceptual magnet effect for phoneme variants (Aaltonen et al., 1997) and language-specific phonotactic constraints (Eulitz and Lahiri, 2004) have a neural correlate in the early brain response. This makes early brain responses at around 100–200 ms after stimulus onset a fruitful tool for addressing phonological questions.

Early neurophysiological responses related to linguistic levels "above" phonological processing had already occasionally been observed in the 1980s. Among these are Rugg's report that lexicality (or "wordness"), the difference between meaningful words and regular pseudo-words, is first reflected in the N100–P200 complex (Rugg, 1983), and the observation by Bentin et al. (1985) of an early effect of semantic priming at ~200 ms after visual word onset. In the early 1990s, Helen Neville and colleagues first saw a left-lateralized early negativity for syntactic violations, especially violations of phrase structure rules (Neville et al., 1991). Supporting evidence for an early syntactic negativity was found with both visual and auditory sentence presentation (Friederici and Kotz, 2003; Friederici et al., 1993). The original hope that differences in syntactic violation types might become distinguishable on the basis of the brain responses these violations elicit could not be fulfilled. Some violation types thought to be bound to relatively late ERP effects, for example violations of rules of agreement, could later be demonstrated to have an early brain reflection in a left anterior negativity as well (Deutsch and Bentin, 2001; Shtyrov et al., 2003). It thus appears that the P600 response is preceded by earlier responses reflecting syntactic processes.

Early reflections of lexical and semantic processing in the ERP and ERF have been reported more recently. The differences in the N160 response between frequency matched content words and function words presented in random lists have already been mentioned in section 8.2 (Pulvermüller et al., 1995). An early left-lateralized response was seen not only for grammatical function words but also for grammatical word parts, inflectional morphemes such as the past and plural affixes *-ed* or *-s* in *sealed* and *houses*. This was so when morphologically complex words were presented in random lists, and also when they were placed in a context where their occurrence violated morphological or syntactic rules and therefore was unexpected for grammatical reasons (Friederici et al., 1993; Penke et al., 1997; Shtyrov and Pulvermüller, 2002; Weyerts et al., 1997). In contrast, irregular inflected word forms, for example *stole* or *mice*, also presented in ungrammatical contexts elicited a symmetrical ERP response over the hemisphere (Penke et al., 1997; Weyerts et al., 1997). The early-lateralized brain response to grammatical words and regular inflectional affixes agrees well with the suggestion that memory traces of these non-referential members of the mental lexicon are housed primarily in the left hemispheric perisylvian language areas of the human brain (see section 8.2).

Correspondingly, other lexical-semantic categories became neurophysiologically manifest before and around 200ms after visual word onset. Nouns and verbs, which differ in their lexical category membership, but also in their semantics—because they tend to relate to objects and actions respectively—were found to elicit P200 and N200 responses with different topographies over the scalp and presumably underlying generator constellations (Brown and Lehmann, 1979; Dehaene, 1995; Koenig and Lehmann, 1996; Molfese et al., 1996; Preissl et al., 1995; Pulvermüller et al., 1999). Fine-grained semantic differences between word groups also became manifest in the brain response at short latencies (Koenig et al., 1998; Skrandies, 1998). Verbs referring to actions involving different parts of the body—as, for example, *lick, pick* and *kick*, which relate to face, arms, and legs respectively—led to diverging ERPs already at 200 ms after visual word onset (Pulvermüller et al., 2000). Estimates of the cortical generators underlying these ERP differences pointed to a differential involvement of sources in or close to the motor cortex where face, arms, and legs are represented in a somatotopic fashion (Hauk et al., 2004; Hauk and Pulvermüller 2004b; Pulvermüller et al., 2005; Shtyrov et al., 2004). It thus appears that the memory networks for meaningful words that refer to objects and actions may extend into brain areas outside the classic language areas, and that the storage of information about the referential meaning of words is distributed over a range of areas involved in the processing of referent objects and actions (Pulvermüller, 2005). Differences in word frequency (Sereno et al., 1998), have also been found within the first 200 ms (section 8.2).

As pointed out in section 8.3.1, semantic context expectancy violation has classically been linked to the N400 component. More recent studies, however, showed differences in early ERPs related to the semantic expectedness of a word and its sentence and discourse context. Brown and colleagues showed an effect of story coherence appearing already around 100 ms after onset of spoken words (Brown et al., 2000). Sereno and her co-workers found a semantic context effect at 100–200ms after the violating word appeared (Sereno et al., 2003). Martin-Loeches, Hinojosa, and their colleagues reported a similar effect slightly later (Hinojosa et al., 2004; Martin-Loeches et al., 2004). This is neurophysiological evidence for early processing of all types of psycholinguistic information, across phonological, lexical, semantic, syntactic, and discourse levels.

Penolazzi and colleagues (Penolazzi et al., 2007) found that early semantic context effects depended on the length of the critical words violating semantic expectations. This new finding may provide a clue for explaining why, generally, many early studies found their neurophysiological correlates of linguistic differences at long latencies but not within the first 200 ms after stimuli became uniquely identifiable. An explanatory key feature may be the variance of stimulus parameters. To compare the neurophysiological processes underlying two sets of linguistic stimuli—for example sentences, words or phonemes—it is necessary to match the two sets for possible differences that are reflected in the neurophysiological response but are not in the focus of the study. In a study of semantic context effects, for example, it is important to match the critical words used to probe the semantic effects, e.g. the critical words *sugar* and *sock* in the context *he drank his tea with milk and* ______); for word length, as short and long words elicit different N100 responses; for word frequency, as frequent words tend to elicit small ERPs (see section 8.1.3, 8.4); and for a variety of other psycholinguistic variables (section 8.3.2). Such necessary stimulus-matching was not undertaken in all early studies (e.g. Kutas and Hillyard, 1980). But even if the matching is perfect, it may be that a large variance on one parameter works against the appearance of early neurophysiological effects. Early ERPs with latency <200 ms are short-lived and focal, whereas long latency responses are widespread and long-lasting. Variations in the stimulus set reflected in the latency and topography of electrophysiological activity are therefore in danger of reducing or even annihilating the early average event-related response. As the late components are long-lasting and widespread, the same spatio-temporal variance will affect them less. For obtaining early linguistic effects in the ERP, it therefore appears necessary to match stimulus groups for relevant psycholinguistic and physical variables, and, in addition, to keep stimulus variance to a minimum (Pulvermüller, 1999). The study by Penolazzi showed that early on, within the first 200 ms after onset of the critical word, the neurophysiological effect of a congruent or incongruent context differed between short and long words, so that it disappeared in the average over all words tested. In contrast, late semantic-context effects in the N400 range did not depend on stimulus word length. To see the early effects, it therefore indeed appears to be necessary that stimulus variance (here: word length) is kept low—a feature that may help to explain why it was only very recently that the early effects could be discovered. Later sections will discuss a range of psycholinguistic variables in detail that might be of relevance for psycholinguistic stimulus-matching.

8.3.3 Early and late language potentials and their implications for psycholinguistics

The early and late context effects observed in the history of psycholinguistic neurophysiology—or neurophysiological psycholinguistics—have been interpreted as evidence for two classes of cognitive models.

One type of model is rooted in early serial processing theories (e.g. Fromkin, 1973; Garrett, 1976), and posits a sequence of stages for the processing of different kinds of psycholinguistic information. Friederici, for example, envisages the process of spoken language understanding to be separable into strictly consecutive stages related to the identification of phonemes, word forms, syntactic word categories, and word meanings, finally followed by reprocessing and reanalysis of syntactic structure (Friederici, 2002). This view can be bolstered by referring to early word category and syntactic effects, which are followed by the semantic N400 and the syntactic P600 (section 8.3.1; Figure 8.4, left diagram).

A different view is rooted in early psycholinguistic models of parallel psycholinguistic information processing according to which lexical, semantic, phonological, and contextual information are available near-simultaneously early on (e.g. Marslen-Wilson and Tyler, 1975; Marslen-Wilson, 1987). This view is strengthened by early near-simultaneous neurophysiological reflection of lexical and semantic features of language, and by the similar latencies of syntactic and semantic context effects (section 8.3.2). The early neurophysiological components related to different psycholinguistic information types are perhaps best captured by a model according to which a lexical entry is selected and fully activated, along with all psycholinguistic information attached to it, at 100–200 ms after stimulus information is sufficient for its identification (Pulvermüller, 2001). This activation process would, accordingly, be influenced from its very start by previous activation sparked by the lexical items in the preceding sentence and discourse context (Figure 8.4, right diagram).

Although both approaches have their strengths, there are also weaknesses. The serial model leaves the early lexical and semantic effects largely unexplained, whereas the parallel model suggests that late neurophysiological effects brought about by semantically and syntactically unexpected word strings are related to cognitive processes not necessarily of a linguistic nature, which follow early contextual integration. It is clear that the two kinds of theoretical approach can also be viewed as complementary, so that the simultaneous early processing of linguistic information types would be followed by later stages of linguistic reprocessing.

An attempt to integrate both approaches into an ultimate brain processing model of language may fruitfully use the concept of near-simultaneous early access to all types of linguistic information. At the early access and selection stage, within 200 ms after the critical lexical item can be recognized, minor delays in the range of tens of milliseconds are related to the time required for neuronal activity to travel between cortical area (see Pulvermüller, 2005; Pulvermüller and Shtyrov, 2006). Subsequent to early access, there may be two major steps of reprocessing psycholinguistic information. The reprocessing of semantic and phonological information at ~400 ms may be followed by syntactic reanalysis around half a second past information intake.

8.4 The universe of psycholinguistic variables and its neurophysiological reality

In the light of serial and parallel models of psycholinguistic information access, it becomes relevant to look at the full range of psycholinguistic

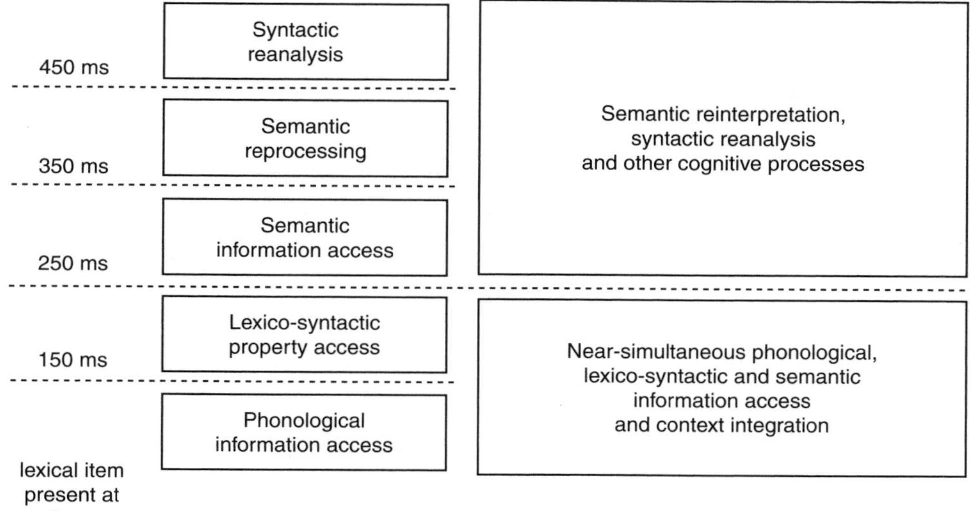

Figure 8.4 Serial vs. parallel models of language processing. The time scale on the left gives the approximate delay after the information in the input allows for unique recognition of a critical stimulus word. Box diagram on the left: A serial model of word and sentence comprehension and the approximate time when it suggests access to and processing of linguistic information of particular types. Box diagram on the right: An integrated model of psycholinguistic information access taking into account early neurophysiological manifestations of psycholinguistic processes puts near-simultaneous access and integration of all types of psycholinguistic information, followed by secondary reanalysis processes.

variables and ask when each variable becomes neurophysiologically manifest. This can provide a neurophysiological test to brain-based theories of psycholinguistic information access.

Psycholinguistic research led to meticulous descriptions of features of lexical items most of which may have a significant correlate in the cognitive and brain processes of word production or perception. Superficially, words written in black on a white background can be different in their length, luminance, or number of black pixels. Regarding their higher cognitive features, one may ask whether they occur frequently or have imageable meaning. These variables, word frequency and imageability, which have clear behavioral correlates (Howes and Solomon, 1951; Paivio et al., 1968; Rubin, 1980; Solomon and Howes, 1951; Whaley, 1978), can be broken down further, for example by answering the following questions. If a word form occurs frequently, does this also apply to its stem? And as for its entire family—all the words that can be derived from it by adding derivational affixes—how big is this family, how many members has it, and what is the cumulative frequency of all the family members? An entire written or spoken word may be frequent, but what about its parts, letters and phonemes, or so-called bigrams or trigrams, i.e. letter/phoneme pairs or triplets? How likely is it that, by changing a single letter, one obtains a different meaningful word out of a source word? How many lexical neighbors does it therefore have? How many other words would start with the same phoneme, syllable, or longer word fragments, and how big therefore is the word's co-activated cohort of competitors at different time points during spoken word understanding? Imageability can be viewed as multimodal (Paivio, 1986). What about visual imageability and, contrasting with it, the imageability related to other modalities including odors, tastes, sounds, somato-sensory sensations, actions, and emotions? It appears possible to break down imageability into different modalities, resulting in a multimodal space of conceptual and referential semantic aspects. And further: does the word have meaning in the referential sense at all, is it related semantically to objects and actions, or is it a rather abstract carrier of meaning, a grammatical functional word in the extreme (section 8.1.2)? Also, when has the word been learned and got its meaning? Very early in life, or rather by the end of school education, after almost the entire vocabulary had been established? Finally, does the word have one or more different usage types and meanings (*car* vs. *bark*), and can it be regularly used as member of one or more lexical categories?

Questions of this type proliferate, and it is therefore not surprising that psycholinguists and language psychologists have come up with a large number of descriptions for psycholinguistic features of lexical items. These include surface form frequency or standardized lexical frequency, stem frequency, age of acquisition (Carroll and White, 1973; Ellis and Morrison, 1998), family size (Nivja et al., 2000), cumulative family frequency, bigram frequency and trigram frequency (Zesiger et al., 1993), neighborhood size for printed words (Coltheart et al., 1977) and cohort sizes for spoken ones (Marslen-Wilson, 1987), the strength of visual, gustatory, auditory, tactile, and action-related semantic associations (Paivio, 1986), arousal and valance (Osgood et al., 1975; Rubin, 1980), abstractness and concreteness, and the number of meanings and syntactic category memberships of a word form, to name only some.

Given this overwhelming universe of psycholinguistic features, and given that many of them are highly inter-correlated, how can we possibly find out about the specific brain correlates of any of these properties? Taking a critical position, attempts like those reviewed in section 8.1.2 may be considered to be doomed to fail, as they have varied one variable, may have controlled for another few, but ignored the rest. It cannot generally, therefore, be concluded that what appears to be a word form frequency effect in a given study (e.g. Hauk and Pulvermüller, 2004a; Osterhout et al., 1997) is not in fact related to stem frequency, bigram frequency, age of acquisition, imageability, or the strength with which action knowledge is semantically linked to the word form. There is therefore much left to do in the cognitive neuroscience of language at the level of studies on individual lexical items.

However, the situation is not as hopeless as it may appear. Mike Ford ran principal component analysis over large corpora of words for all of which a substantial number (twenty) of psycholinguistic parameters had been obtained (Ford, 2004; Hauk et al., 2006). The good news was that most of the psycholinguistic variance could be captured by four principal components. These loaded on the following clusters of psycholinguistic features:

1. surface features, including word length, which inversely relate to neighborhood size;
2. sublexical frequency, including bigram and trigram frequency;
3. lexical frequency, including stem and word form frequency; and finally,
4. semantic family coherence, a new meaning-related variable indicating the degree of semantic relatedness within the derivational family of a word.

These results were obtained from words taken from a corpus, without preselecting items. When investigating non-preselected corpora, it therefore appears feasible to study these four compound variables to get a first impression of major psycholinguistic effects. In a second experimental step, it may then be possible to disentangle those variables that are merged into one of the four clusters of features (e.g. word length and family size).

As mentioned in sections 8.2 and 8.3, two of these major variables have been investigated in earlier neurophysiological studies: Osterhout and colleagues and King and Kutas looked at words that exhibited a strong inverse correlation of the length and lexical frequency factors (King and Kutas, 1998; Osterhout et al., 1997). As these authors reported a relationship between word form frequency and latency of components of the ERP, it is not entirely clear whether a similar relationship may exist between ERP latency and word length. In Assadollahi's and Hauk's work, word length and lexical frequency were varied orthogonally (Assadollahi and Pulvermüller, 2001; 2003; Hauk and Pulvermüller, 2004a) and no ERP latency shift with lexical frequency was found. However, neurophysiological manifestation of the surface variable word length was found at 100 ms after written-word onset—a difference which could be attributed to early sensory levels (stimulation of the retina and subsequent brain structures) or, alternatively, to subsequent levels of visual or language processing. The cortical localization of this effect in the inferior temporal cortex is consistent with the idea that properties of the visual word form were crucial (Assadollahi and Pulvermüller, 2003). The word frequency effect became manifest at 150–200 ms and was due to more widely dispersed left lateralized sources. This indicates that at least two of the main features of words, which are also characteristic of two of the four main feature clusters of Ford, have their real-time neurophysiological correlates in visual word recognition within the first 200 ms after information in the input is sufficient for identifying words.

In a recent experiment, Hauk, Davis, Ford, Pulvermüller, and Marslen-Wilson looked at the entire set of four clusters and their manifestation in neurophysiological recordings during a lexical decision experiments (Hauk et al., 2006a).

A regression technique was used whereby, for each subject, the EEG activity elicited by individual word stimuli was correlated with psycholinguistic variables for these words, and correlation coefficients obtained for each subject and recording electrode were analyzed statistically over the entire subject group.

The main results were the following. The neurophysiological correlates of the surface-related feature clusters, i.e. word length and sublexical frequency, appeared early, at about 100 ms, whereas the lexical frequency correlate appeared slightly later, finally followed by the brain reflection of semantic family coherence at ~160 ms. This indicates early near-simultaneous access to information immanent and bound to a lexical item, and, in addition, within the early processes, a fine-grained activation sequence orchestrating the retrieval of specific types of psycholinguistic information. Form features seem to be accessed first, followed by lexical and semantic features. All this appears to be going on within 200 ms of the appearance of a written word. A tentative explanation might be that in visual word recognition the near-synchroneous initial full activation, or "ignition," of lexico-semantic networks starts in the inferior temporal cortex, where form information is first processed, then spreads to the perisylvian cortex, where the lexical networks have the lion's share of their neurons, and near-simultaneously propagates to areas contributing to semantic analysis (Pulvermüller, 2005; Pulvermüller and Shtyrov, 2006).

Using more conventional ERP measures, Hauk et al. (2006b) also found early near-simultaneous serial effects of sublexical bi/trigram frequency (also called typicality) and lexicality within the first 160 ms after written-word onset. Together with other studies, these results provide further support for early near-simultaneous access to sublexical and lexical information in written-word recognition (for further discussion, see Sereno and Rayner, 2003).

8.5 What makes speech special? Laterality of neurophysiological activity interpreted as the critical brain feature of language

What is the specific feature of language that sets apart humans from the animal kingdom? Not surprisingly, different researchers have answered this question by emphasizing different abilities, all of which may be considered to be critical for language and speech, including the following:

- building a sheer endless repertoire of sentences out of a limited vocabulary and rule set;
- creating new meaning by assembling old words;
- learning, storing, and using huge vocabularies of thousands of meaningful units, words, and morphemes;
- learning, storing, and using lexical items that primarily serve a grammatical function, i.e. function words and inflectional and derivational affixes;
- using a phonological inventory of about fifty articulatory gestures and firmly linking these gestures to acoustic patterns, so that the corresponding gesture can be immediately identified whenever a given sound has been perceived;
- discriminating rich acoustic stimuli that only minimally differ in the spectro-temporal features.

At the level of the brain, the specificity of language translates into a neurophysiological feature: left-hemispheric dominance. In physiology, left dominance means stronger activation of the left cortex compared with the right, and such laterality is frequently observed in various language tasks. It is usually elicited by written- and spoken-language stimuli in right-handed subjects who are native speakers of the experimental language, and can be revealed with all imaging methods alike, including MEG, EEG, fMRI, and PET.

Not surprisingly, left laterality has been postulated to be the hallmark of a number of features that have been thought to make language special: for the detection of rapid changes in spectrally rich sounds (Zatorre et al., 2002), the mapping between acoustic and articulatory phonological information (Liberman and Whalen, 2000), for functional lexical items, function words, and functional affixes, which are known to distinguish human from all animal languages (section 8.1.2), for word meaning (Patterson and Hodges, 2001), and, of course, for syntax (Kaan and Swaab, 2002). Should we therefore conclude that all these aspects of language are equally lateralized, and – related to this – equally characteristic of and critical for human language?

A remark is necessary here. The brain-physiological features cannot, for principled reasons, tell us about which aspects of language are of importance, relevance, or interest. What can be done, however, is to link specific aspects of language processing to brain-physiological features that are to a degree specific to language and therefore special. If we find that left laterality is linked to linguistic aspect X, this may suggest (but not prove) that X is critical for language mechanisms. A firm statement about this would also need to be anchored in psycholinguistic and brain theory.

One way of addressing the laterality question, i.e. the question of which aspects of language and speech are functionally related to laterality, is the study of development. Surprisingly, babies show strong laterality of ERP responses, spoken syllables, and words shortly after birth, long before they start to speak (Dehaene-Lambertz et al., 2002). Even more surprisingly, laterality is not specific to language stimuli at that stage, but also characterizes non-linguistic acoustic stimuli (Dehaene-Lambertz, 2000). This may suggest that the crucial mechanisms that lead to the specific laterality of language and the symmetrical or predominantly right-hemispheric processing of other materials is established at later stages.

The evidence for laterality of syntactic processes is manifold. fMRI and EEG/MEG studies indicate that left inferior frontal and/or superior temporal cortex are most actively responding when syntactic processing demands are high—in the case both of the processing of syntactic violations and of complex sentences (Caplan et al., 2000; Caplan et al., 2002; Friederici and Kotz, 2003; Neville et al., 1991). However, if function words and inflectional affixes are already posing stronger processing demands to the left perisylvian cortex than to its homotopic area in the right hemisphere, the laterality of syntax is most economically explained on the basis of the laterality of functional lexical items (Pulvermüller, 1995). Still, the origin of laterality could be located at an even more elementary cognitive level. Liberman's motor theory of speech perception posits that the links between speech sounds and their corresponding articulatory gestures are laid down in the left hemisphere (Liberman, 1967; Liberman and Whalen, 2000) and, along these lines, the laterality of all "higher" language processes, be they related to syntax, lexical items, or semantics, could be an epiphenomenon of phonological processes. (Note, however, that a complementary explanation of laterality of sign languages would be required in this case.) A most parsimonious explanation of language-related laterality phenomena is possible on the basis of physical features of speech. Fast temporal changes in spectrally rich sounds could be at the basis of language laterality across all psycholinguistic levels (Zatorre and Belin, 2001; Zatorre et al., 2002).

To find out experimentally at which level the pronounced laterality observable for language occurs, it is necessary to compare the levels with each other, step by step.

Zatorre and Belin presented subjects with rapidly changing spectrally rich sounds and compared this condition with one where the same stimuli were presented with a slow rate of change (Zatorre and Belin, 2001). This led to left laterality only in the case of rapid changes. The same stimuli changing more slowly over time did not evoke left-lateralized fMRI responses. This could have been the end of the story of the neurophysiological laterality of language, had there not been other studies leading to somewhat different results: Scott and colleagues presented spoken sentences to their subjects along with noise stimuli derived from and matched to the sentences for acoustic features (Scott et al., 2000; Scott and Johnsrude, 2003). Only the intelligible spoken sentences elicited lateralized brain activity. This suggests that the dominance of Zatorre's rapidly changing stimuli might not be a general feature of all spectrally rich fast changing sounds.

Scott's data show that speech made up of intelligible phonemes, with syntactic structure and semantic content, produces laterality. However, these results do not reveal which of these features—phoneme content, syntactic structure, or semantic meaning—is specifically related to laterality. Also, neuro-metabolic studies have general limitations in psycholinguistic research, as they do not distinguish early stimulus-related from possible late secondary processes. We cannot, therefore, be sure whether Zatorre's and Scott's fMRI data reveals immediate, perhaps automatic, stimulus processing or secondary thought about the stimuli—which could always take the form of thinking in sentences.

Studies using neurophysiological methods, especially MEG, demonstrated left-lateralized activity to a range of phonemes and syllables (Eulitz et al., 1995a; Molfese, 1978; Näätänen et al., 1997; Rinne et al., 1999). This lateralized activity to phonemes and syllables usually emerges early, within 100–200 ms after stimulus onset, and one may therefore argue that the observed laterality of the speech perception process can be attributed to the phonological level. Using the Mismatch Negativity (MMN), some of these studies could show that laterality to CV syllables even occurs if subjects are instructed to ignore the incoming speech and focus their attention elsewhere, suggesting an automatic early lateralized process of phonological analysis of the speech input. Interestingly, Shtyrov and colleagues tested speech-like stimuli that shared important spectro-temperal characteristics with

CV syllables, and showed that these rapidly changing spectrally rich sounds did not produce lateralized MMN responses (Shtyrov et al., 2000). This research argues for laterality at the phonological level, but not below.

However, sounds that have the status of a phoneme in a language did not always elicit lateralized brain responses. This does not only apply to the EEG—where laterality to acoustic stimuli is sometimes difficult to achieve, as generators in both left and right superior temporal lobes may produce the strongest ERP deflections at fronto-central recording electrodes—but also to MEG work. Shtyrov, Pihko, and Pulvermüller (2005) recorded the MMN to the same chirp-like sound presented in the context of noise and in linguistic contexts, in the context either of pseudo-words or of Finnish words. The critical sound was perceived as a chirp noise when presented in the context of other noises, but it was perceived as a [t] sound in both word and pseudo-word contexts (see Liberman, 1996). If perceived as noise, the MMN elicited an MMN symmetrical over the hemispheres. Surprisingly, this was also true if the chirp noise was perceived as an instance of the phoneme [t] at the end of the CVC pseudo-word (ryot), therefore failing to support cortical laterality of phonological processing. It was only when the [t] appeared at the end of words, where it had the status of an inflectional affix, that it produced statistically significant laterality of the neurophysiological response measured (Figure 8.5).

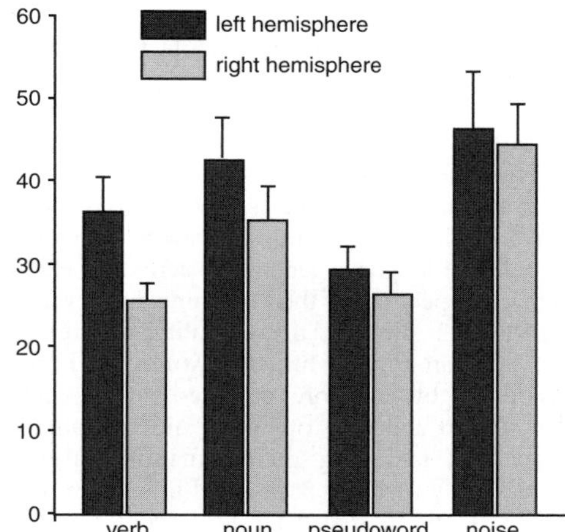

Figure 8.5 Different degrees of laterality of neuromagnetic activity elicited by a chirp noise presented in four different contexts, in that of noise, pseudo-words, or as an inflectional affix attached to a noun or verb. The magnetic MMN showed a significant context x laterality interaction. Lateralized brain responses were specific to the word contexts (Shtyrov et al., 2005).

Shtyrov et al.'s result challenges established views on phonological laterality. In this case the phonological status of a spectrally rich, rapidly changing sound was not sufficient to elicit lateralized processing in the human brain. One may therefore hypothesize that an additional feature, in addition to acoustic complexity and phonological status, is necessary for language laterality. This feature may be sought in the previous usage of a phoneme in a particular context. Most previous studies revealing phonological laterality used vowels or CV syllables as stimuli. Vowels alone are used in early language development by the infant, during the stage of cooing, where they constitute complete utterances, pre-speech acts, so to speak. CV syllables form the main pre-speech repertoire and are produced repeatedly or in isolation during the babbling phase between months 6 and 12 (Locke, 1993). It may therefore be that vowels and CV syllables lateralize because they are acoustically complex, have phonological status, and have been repeatedly produced before. The syllable structure tested in Shtyrov et al.'s experiment, CVC syllables with the diphthong [yö] as the vowel in the middle, is rarely observed in cooing or babbling and this may be the reason why the syllable-final phoneme failed to elicit cerebral laterality in this very context (Shtyrov et al., 2005). In contexts, as the [t] sound usually occurs as an inflectional affix, and therefore has been used as such repeatedly in the context of various verb stems, laterality emerges in this case. As an alternative possibility, the differential laterality observed may be related to the status of the [t] as an inflectional affix and thus, similarly to function words, as a lexical item with predominantly grammatical and syntactic function (Pulvermüller et al., 1995).

Shtyrov et al.'s results concerning the absence of a laterality effect to pseudo-words (Figure 8.5) should not be over interpreted: after all, there cannot be strong support for a null hypothesis not rejected by an experiment. What their results demonstrate is that the degree of cortical laterality is significantly stronger for phonemes presented in a context where they are frequently used as inflectional affixes compared with a context where they occur rarely. Thus, there is a determinant of laterality above the level of phonological representation. Whether this critical feature is the status of the phoneme as a frequently used large unit, or whether it relates to the grammatical or syntactic function of the inflectional morphemes represented by the phoneme in this case, remains to be clarified.

As there is strong laterality of brain responses to phonemes with the status of an inflectional affix attached to a word (see also Shtyrov and Pulvermüller, 2002), one may ask whether the laterality of language generalizes across all lexical items, independent of their meaning. However, as section 8.2 focused on laterality differences between content and function words, the impression might therefore emerge that laterality depends to a degree on word and morpheme properties, including their semantic features. Consistently with this, a range of imaging results indicates differential laterality depending on word type, and one explanation of this relates the laterality of brain responses to semantic features. Whereas well-imageable concrete content words, for example, fail to elicit laterality or may even tend to lateralize to the right hemisphere, abstract words with low imageability tend to exhibit left laterality (Binder et al., 2005; Kounios and Holcomb, 1994; Kujala et al., 2002; Pulvermüller et al., 2004). Although the differential laterality issue is still under discussion, it appears in general that at the semantic level there is evidence for bihemispheric involvement and variable laterality. The laterality of language to the left hemisphere might therefore best be traced to phonological, lexical, or syntactic origins.

In summary, the evidence for left laterality of the processing of spectrally rich, rapidly changing sounds seems to be mixed, but CV syllables seem to exhibit reliable left-hemispheric dominant brain responses. An important factor in the enhanced degree of laterality is the status of a phoneme as part of a previously used language unit, for example as an inflectional affix attached to word stems. Strong laterality is also obvious for syntactic processes, although it could be argued that it is possible to explain at least some aspects of the laterality of syntax on the basis of the laterality of inflectional affixes and function words. Semantic processing seems to involve both hemispheres, and it may be that semantic features of lexical items determine the degree to which the two hemispheres become involved in processing them (Pulvermüller and Shtyrov, 2006).

8.6 Summary and outlook

This chapter has highlighted the contribution of neurophysiological imaging with EEG and MEG to psycholinguistics, focusing on the question of how words and morphemes are processed in the brain. After introducing neurophysiological perspectives in psycholinguistics, brain correlates of word frequency and lexical categories were discussed, illustrating how behavioral and neurophysiological research mutually fertilized each other in past decades. The main section, 8.3, started with an overview of language components of the event-related potential and field, and related them to serial and parallel models of psycholinguistic processing. Section 8.4 reviewed recent work on early brain reflections of a range of psycholinguistic variables. In the last section, 8.5, a major brain index of language processing, laterality to the left language-dominant hemisphere, was discussed and related to psycholinguistic information processing.

This tour around selected areas of neurophysiological psycholinguistics may provide evidence for the following three points. First, we are in a position to study language with physiological tools. There are organic manifestations of the "mental processes" that constitute and contribute to language processing. Distinct brain correlates have been revealed for the different psycholinguistic levels of physical, phonological, lexical, morphological, semantic, syntactic, and dialogue-related information. Second, as we have available these neurophysiological correlates, we can use them to improve our understanding of language processes and language mechanisms. Illustrations were given that neurophysiological evidence may contribute to psycholinguistic discussions emerging on the basis of reaction time studies, for example the time course of information access in word recognition. Third, and possibly most importantly, the neurophysiological study of psycholinguistic processes may propel the field toward a goal which may always have been the long-distance target of language science (cf. de Saussure, 1916), but may sometimes have been lost from sight: an understanding of the brain mechanisms that make language possible. We can, of course, look at neurophysiological data to draw conclusions about box-and-arrow models of language functions; however, as we have data about brain function available, it becomes possible, and actually desirable, to theorize about the mechanistic neuronal circuits that realize psycholinguistic processes at the level of the brain (Pulvermüller, 2003). This crucial theoretical step redefines psycholinguistics as a core discipline of human brain research.

Acknowledgements

I would like to thank Marion Ormandy and Susan Howell for their help in preparing this manuscript, and Ram Frost, Gareth Gaskell, Olaf Hauk, William Marslen-Wilson, Yury Shtyrov, and an anonymous referee for comments on earlier versions of the text. This work was supported by the Medical Research Council (UK), by the European Community under the Information Society Technologies Programme (IST-2001-35282), and by NEST (Nestcom project).

References

Aaltonen, O., Eerola, O., Hellstrom, A., and Uusipaikka, E. (1997) Percpetual magnet effect in the light of behavioral and psychophysiological data. *Journal of the Acoustic Society of America*, 101: 1090–105.

Aboitiz, F., Scheibel, A. B., Fisher, R. S., and Zaidel, E. (1992) Fiber composition of the human corpus callosum. *Brain Research*, 598: 143–53.

Assadollahi, R., and Pulvermüller, F. (2001) Neuromagnetic evidence for early access to cognitive representations. *Neuroreport*, 12(2): 207–13.

Assadollahi, R., and Pulvermüller, F. (2003) Early influences of word length and frequency: a group study using MEG. *Neuroreport*, 14(8): 1183–7.

Bentin, S. (1989) Electrophysiological studies of visual word perception, lexical organization, and semantic processing: a tutorial review. *Language and Speech*, 32(3): 205–20.

Bentin, S., and Feinsod, M. (1983) Hemispheric asymmetry for word perception: behavioral and ERP evidence. *Psychophysiology*, 20(5): 489–97.

Bentin, S., McCarthy, G., and Wood, C. C. (1985) Event-related potentials, lexical decision and semantic priming. *Electroencephalography and Clinical Neurophysiology*, 60: 343–55.

Binder, J. R., Westbury, C. F., McKiernan, K. A., Possing, E. T., and Medler, D. A. (2005) Distinct brain systems for processing concrete and abstract concepts. *Journal of Cognitive Neuroscience*, 17(6): 905–17.

Bradley, D. C. (1983) *Computational distinctions of vocabulary type*. Indiana University Linguistics Club: Bloomington.

Bradley, D. C., and Garrett, M. F. (1983) Hemisphere differences in the recognition of closed and open class words. *Neuropsychologia*, 21: 155–9.

Brown, C. M., Hagoort, P., and ter Keurs, M. (1999) Electrophysiological signatures of visual lexical processing: open- and closed-class words. *Journal of Cognitive Neuroscience*, 11(3): 261–81.

Brown, C. M., van Berkum, J. J., and Hagoort, P. (2000) Discourse before gender: an event-related brain potential study on the interplay of semantic and syntactic information during spoken language understanding. *Journal of Psycholinguistic Research*, 29(1): 53–68.

Brown, W. S., and Lehmann, D. (1979) Verb and noun meaning of homophone words activate different cortical generators: a topographic study of evoked potential fields. *Experimental Brain Research*, 2: 159–68.

Caplan, D., Alpert, N., Waters, G., and Olivieri, A. (2000) Activation of Broca's area by syntactic processing under conditions of concurrent articulation. *Human Brain Mapping*, 9(2): 65–71.

Caplan, D., Hildebrandt, N., and Makris, N. (1996) Location of lesions in stroke patients with deficits in syntactic processing in sentence comprehension. *Brain*, 119(3): 933–49.

Caplan, D., Vijayan, S., Kuperberg, G., West, C., Waters, G., Greve, D., and Dale, A. M. (2002) Vascular responses to syntactic processing: event-related fMRI study of relative clauses. *Human Brain Mapping*, 15(1): 26–38.

Carroll, J. B., and White, M. N. (1973) Word frequency and age-of-acquisition as determiners of picture-naming latencies. *Quarterly Journal of Experimental Psychology*, 25: 85–95.

Chiarello, C., and Nuding, S. (1987) Visual field effects for processing content and function words. *Neuropsychologia*, 25: 39–548.

Coles, M. G. H., and Rugg, M. D. (1995) Event-related brain potentials. In M. D. Rugg and M. G. H. Coles (eds), *Electrophysiology of Mind: Event-Related Brain Potentials and Cognition*, pp. 1–26. Oxford University Press, Oxford.

Coltheart, M., Davelaar, E., Jonasson, J., and Besner, D. (1977) Access to the internal lexicon. In S. Dornic (ed.), *Attention and Performance VI*, pp. 535–55. Academic Press, London.

Dehaene, S. (1995) Electrophysiological evidence for category-specific word processing in the normal human brain. *Neuroreport*, 6(16): 2153–2157.

Dehaene-Lambertz, G. (1997) Electrophysiological correlates of categorical phoneme perception in adults. *NeuroReport*, 8: 919–924.

Dehaene-Lambertz, G. (2000) Cerebral specialization for speech and non-speech stimuli in infants. *Journal of Cognitive Neuroscience*, 12(3): 449–60.

Dehaene-Lambertz, G., Dehaene, S., and Hertz-Pannier, L. (2002) Functional neuroimaging of speech perception in infants. *Science*, 298(5600): 2013–15.

Deutsch, A., and Bentin, S. (2001) Syntactic and semantic factors in processing gender agreement in Hebrew: evidence from ERPs and eye movements. *Journal of Memory and Language*, 45: 200–24.

Ellis, A. W., and Morrison, C. M. (1998) Real age-of-acquisition effects in lexical retrieval. *J Journal of Experimental Psychology: Learning, Memory and Cognition*, 24(2): 515–23.

Embick, D., Hackl, M., Schaeffer, J., Kelepir, M., and Marantz, A. (2001) A magnetoencephalographic component whose latency reflects lexical frequency. *Brain Research: Cognitive Brain Research*, 10(3): 345–48.

Eulitz, C., Diesch, E., Pantev, C., Hampson, S., and Elbert, T. (1995a) Magnetic and electric brain activity evoked by the processing of tone and vowel stimuli. *Journal of Neuroscience*, 15: 2748–55.

Eulitz, C., Diesch, E., Pantev, C., Hampson, S., and Elbert, T. (1995b) Magnetic and electric brain activity evoked by the processing of tone and vowel stimuli. *Journal of Neuroscience*, 15(4): 2748–55.

Eulitz, C., and Lahiri, A. (2004) Neurobiological evidence for abstract phonological representations in the mental lexicon during speech recognition. *Journal of Cognitive Neuroscience*, 16(4): 577–83.

Fabiani, M., Gratton, G., and Coles, M. G. H. (2000) Event-related brain potentials. In J. T. Cacioppo, L. G. Tassinary, and G. G. Berntson (eds), *Handbook of Psychophysiology*, pp. 53–84. Cambridge University Press: Cambridge.

Federmeier, K. D., Segal, J. B., Lombrozo, T., and Kutas, M. (2000) Brain responses to nouns, verbs and class-ambiguous words in context. *Brain*, 123: 2552–66.

Ford, M. A. (2004) Morphology in the mental lexicon: frequency, productivity and derivation. Doctoral dissertation, Cambridge University.

Friederici, A. D. (2002) Towards a neural basis of auditory sentence processing. *Trends in Cognitive Sciences*, 6(2): 78–84.

Friederici, A. D., and Kotz, S. A. (2003) The brain basis of syntactic processes: functional imaging and lesion studies. *NeuroImage*, 20 Suppl. 1, S8–17.

Friederici, A. D., Opitz, B., and von Cramon, D. Y. (2000) Segregating semantic and syntactic aspects of processing in the human brain: an fMRI investigation of different word types. *Cerebral Cortex*, 10(7): 698–705.

Friederici, A. D., Pfeifer, E., and Hahne, A. (1993) Event-related brain potentials during natural speech processing: effects of semantic, morphological and syntactic violations. *Cognitive Brain Research*, 1(3): 183–92.

Friedman, D., Simson, R., Ritter, W., and Rapin, I. (1975) Cortical evoked potentials elicited by real speech words and human sounds. *Electroencephalography and Clinical Neurophysiology*, 38: 13–19.

Fromkin, V. A. (1973) The non-anomalous nature of anomalous utterances. In V. A. Fromkin (ed.), *Speech Errors as Linguistic Evidence*, pp. 215–42. Mouton, Paris and The Hague.

Garnsey, S. M. (1985) Function words and content words: reaction time and evoked potential measures of word recognition. Doctoral dissertation, University of Rochester, NY.

Garnsey, S. M., and Chapman, R. M. (1985) Function and content word reaction times and evoked potentials during lexical decisions. In *BABBLE: Annual Conference Reporting Research in the Neuropsychology of Language*, pp. 1–20. Ontario.

Garrett, M. (1976) Syntactic processes in sentence production. In R. Wales and E. Walker (eds), *New Approaches to Language Mechanisms*, pp. 231–56. North- Holland: Amsterdam.

Gordon, B., and Caramazza, A. (1982) Lexical decision for open- and closed-class words: failure to replicate differential frequency sensitivity. *Brain and Language*, 15: 143–60.

Hagoort, P., Brown, C., and Groothusen, J. (1993) The syntactic positive shift (SPS) as an ERP-measure of syntactic processing. *Language and Cognitive Processes*, 8(4): 439–83.

Hari, R. (1991) Activation of the human auditory cortex by speech sounds. *Acta Otolaryngol* Suppl. 491, 132–7; discussion 138.

Hauk, O., Davis, M. H., Ford, M., Pulvermüller, F., and Marslen-Wilson, W. (2006a) The time course of visual word-recognition as revealed by linear regression analysis of ERP data. *NeuroImage*, 30(4): 1383–400.

Hauk, O., Johnsrude, I., and Pulvermüller, F. (2004) Somatotopic representation of action words in the motor and premotor cortex. *Neuron*, 41: 301–7.

Hauk, O., Patterson, K., Woollam, A., Watling, L., Pulvermüller, F., and Rogers, T. T. (2006b) [Q:] When would you prefer a SOSSAGE to a SAUSAGE? [A:] At about 100 ms. ERP correlates of orthographic typicality and lexicality in written word recognition. *Journal of Cognitive Neuroscience*, 18: 818–32.

Hauk, O., and Pulvermüller, F. (2004a) Effects of word length and frequency on the human event-related potential. *Clinical Neurophysiology*, 115(5): 1090–103.

Hauk, O., and Pulvermüller, F. (2004b) Neurophysiological distinction of action words in the fronto-central cortex. *Human Brain Mapping*, 21(3): 191–201.

Henson, R. (2005) What can functional neuroimaging tell the experimental psychologist? *Quarterly Journal of Experimental Psychology Section A Human Experimental Psychology*, 58(2): 193–233.

Hinojosa, J. A., Martin-Loeches, M., Munoz, F., Casado, P., and Pozo, M. A. (2004) Electrophysiological evidence of automatic early semantic processing. *Brain and Language*, 88(1): 39–46.

Holcomb, P. J., Grainger, J., and O'Rourke, T. (2002) An electrophysiological study of the effects of orthographic neighborhood size on printed word perception. *Journal of Cognitive Neuroscience*, 14(6): 938–50.

Howes, D. H., and Solomon, R. L. (1951) Visual duration threshold as a function of word-probability. *Journal of Experimental Psychology*, 41(6): 401–10.

Kaan, E., and Swaab, T. Y. (2002) The brain circuitry of syntactic comprehension. *Trends in Cognitive Science*, 6(8): 350–6.

Kiefer, M. (2001) Perceptual and semantic sources of category-specific effects: event-related potentials during picture and word categorization. *Memory and Cognition*, 29: 100–16.

King, J. W., and Kutas, M. (1998) Neural plasticity in the dynamics of human visual word recognition. *Neuroscience Letters*, 244: 61–4.

Koenig, T., Kochi, K., and Lehmann, D. (1998) Event-related electric microstates of the brain differ between words with visual and abstract meaning. *Electroencephalography and Clinical Neurophysiology*, 106: 535–46.

Koenig, T., and Lehmann, D. (1996) Microstates in language-related brain potential maps show noun-verb differences. *Brain and Language*, 53: 169–82.

Kounios, J., and Holcomb, P. J. (1994) Concreteness effects in semantic priming: ERP evidence supporting dual-coding theory. *Journal of Experimental Psychology: Lerning, Memory and Cognition*, 20: 804–23.

Kujala, A., Alho, K., Valle, S., Sivonen, P., Ilmoniemi, R. J., Alku, P., and Näätänen, R. (2002) Context modulates processing of speech sounds in the right auditory cortex of human subjects. *Neuroscience Letters*, 331(2): 91–4.

Kutas, M., and Federmeier, K. D. (2000) Electrophysiology reveals semantic memory use in language comprehension. *Trends in Cognitive Science*, 4(12): 463–70.

Kutas, M., and Hillyard, S. A. (1980) Reading senseless sentences: brain potentials reflect semantic incongruity. *Science*, 207(4427): 203–5.

Kutas, M., and Hillyard, S. A. (1983) Event-related brain potentials to grammatical errors and semantic anomalies. *Memory and Cognition*, 11: 539–50.

Levine, J. D., and Orrison, W. W., Jr. (1995a) Clinical electroencephalography and event-related potentials. In W. W. Orrison Jr, J. D. Levine, J. A. Sanders, and M. F. Hartshorne (eds), *Functional Brain Imaging*, pp. 327–68. Mosby: St Louis.

Levine, J. D., and Orrison, W. W., Jr. (1995b) Magnetoencephalography and magnetic source imaging. In W. W. Orrison, Jr., J. D. Levine, J. A. Sanders, and M. F. Hartshorne (eds), *Functional Brain Imaging*, pp. 369–418. Mosby: St Louis.

Liberman, A. M. (1996) *Speech: A Special Code*. MIT Press: Cambridge, MA.

Liberman, A. M., Cooper, F. S., Shankweiler, D. P., and Studdert-Kennedy, M. (1967) Perception of the speech code. *Psychological Review*, 74: 431–61.

Liberman, A. M., and Whalen, D. H. (2000) On the relation of speech to language. *Trends in Cognitive Science*, 4(5): 187–96.

Locke, J. L. (1993) *The Child's Path to Spoken Language*. Harvard University Press: Cambridge, MA.

Marslen-Wilson, W., and Tyler, L. K. (1975) Processing structure of sentence perception. *Nature*, 257(5529): 784–6.

Marslen-Wilson, W. D. (1987) Functional parallelism in spoken word-recognition. *Cognition*, 25(1-2): 71–102.

Martin-Loeches, M., Hinojosa, J. A., Casado, P., Munoz, F., and Fernandez-Frias, C. (2004) Electrophysiological evidence of an early effect of sentence context in reading. *Biological Psychology*, 65(3): 265–80.

Maunsell, J. H., and Gibson, J. R. (1992) Visual response latencies in striate cortex of the macaque monkey. *Journal of Neurophysiology*, 68(4): 1332–44.

Mohr, B., and Pulvermüller, F. (2002) Redundancy gains and costs in cognitive processing: effects of short stimulus onset asynchronies. *Journal of Experimental Psychology: Learning, Memory and Cognition*, 28(6): 1200–23.

Mohr, B., Pulvermüller, F., and Zaidel, E. (1994) Lexical decision after left, right and bilateral presentation of content words, function words and non-words: evidence for interhemispheric interaction. *Neuropsychologia*, 32: 105–24.

Molfese, D. L. (1978) Left and right hemisphere involvement in speech perception. *Perception and Psychophysics*, 23: 237–43.

Molfese, D. L., Burger-Judisch, L. M., Gill, L. A., Golinkoff, R. M., and Hirsch-Pasek, K. A. (1996) Electrophysiological correlates of noun-verb processing in adults. *Brain and Language*, 54: 388–413.

Molfese, D. L., Freeman, R. B., and Palermo, D. S. (1975) The ontogeny of brain lateralization for speech and nonspeech stimuli. *Brain and Language*, 2: 356–68.

Munte, T. F., Wieringa, B. M., Weyerts, H., Szentkuti, A., Matzke, M., and Johannes, S. (2001) Differences in brain potentials to open and closed class words: class and frequency effects. *Neuropsychologia*, 39(1): 91–102.

Näätänen, R. (2001) The perception of speech sounds by the human brain as reflected by the mismatch negativity (MMN) and its magnetic equivalent (MMNm) *Psychophysiology*, 38(1): 1–21.

Näätänen, R., Lehtokoski, A., Lennes, M., Cheour, M., Huotilainen, M., Iivonen, A., Valnio, A., Alku, P., Ilmoniemi, R. J., Luuk, A., Allik, J., Sinkkonen, J., and Alho, K. (1997) Language-specific phoneme representations revealed by electric and magnetic brain responses. *Nature*, 385: 432–4.

Neville, H., Nicol, J. L., Barss, A., Forster, K. I., and Garrett, M. F. (1991) Syntactically based sentence processing classes: evidence from event-related brain potentials. *Journal of Cognitive Neuroscience*, 3: 151–65.

Neville, H. J., Kutas, M., and Schmidt, A. (1982) Event-related potential studies of cerebral specialization during reading, I: Studies of normal adults. *Brain and Language*, 16(2): 300–15.

Neville, H. J., Mills, D. L., and Lawson, D. S. (1992) Fractionating language: different neural subsystems with different sensitive periods. *Cerebral Cortex*, 2: 244–58.

Nivja, H., Schreuder, R., and Baayen, R. H. (2000) The morphological family size effect and morphology. *Language and Cognitive Processes*, 15(4–5): 329–65.

Nobre, A. C., and McCarthy, G. (1994) Language-related EPRs: scalp distributions and modulation by word type and semantic priming. *Journal of Cognitive Neuroscience*, 6: 233–55.

Obleser, J., Elbert, T., Lahiri, A., and Eulitz, C. (2003) Cortical representation of vowels reflects acoustic dissimilarity determined by formant frequencies. *Brain Research: Cognitive Brain Research*, 15(3): 207–13.

Obleser, J., Lahiri, A., and Eulitz, C. (2003) Auditory-evoked magnetic field codes place of articulation in timing and topography around 100 milliseconds post syllable onset. *NeuroImage*, 20(3): 1839–47.

Osgood, C., Suci, G., and Tannenhaus, P. (1975) *The Measurement of Meaning*. University of Illinois: Urbana, IL.

Osterhout, L., Bersick, M., and McKonnon, R. (1997) Brain potentials elicited by words: word length and frequency predict the latency of an early negativity. *Biological Psychology*, 46: 143–68.

Osterhout, L., and Holcomb, P. J. (1992) Event-related brain potentials elicited by syntactic anomaly. *Journal of Memory and Language*, 31: 785–806.

Paivio, A. (1986) *Mental Representations: A Dual Coding Approach*. Oxford University Press, Oxford.

Paivio, A., Yuille, J. C., and Madigan, S. A. (1968) Concreteness, imagery, and meaningfulness values for 925 nouns. *Journal of Experimental Psychology*, 76(1), Suppl:1–25.

Paller, K. A., Kutas, M., Shimamura, A. P., and Squire, L. R. (1988) Brain responses to concrete and abstract words reflect processes that correlate with later performance on test of recall and stem-completion priming. In R. Johnson, J. Rohrbaugh, and R. Parasuraman (eds), *Current Trends in Brain Potential Research*, pp. 360–5. Elsevier, Amsterdam.

Patterson, K., and Hodges, J. R. (2001) Semantic dementia. In R. F. Thompson and J. L. McClelland (eds), *International Encyclopaedia of the Social and Behavioral sciences: Behavioral and Cognitive Neuroscience Section*, pp. 3401–5. Pergamon Press, New York.

Pelizzone, M., Hari, R., Mäkelä, J. P., Huttunen, J., Ahlfors, S. P., and Hämäläinen, M. (1987) Cortical origin of middle-latency auditory evoked responses in man. *Neuroscience Letters*, 82(3): 303–7.

Penke, M., Weyerts, H., Gross, M., Zander, E., Munte, T. F., and Clahsen, H. (1997) How the brain processes complex words: an event-related potential study of German verb inflections. *Brain Research: Cognitive Brain Research*, 6(1): 37–52.

Penolazzi, B., Hauk, O., and Pulvermüller, F. (forthcoming). Early semantic context integration and lexical access as revealed by event-related brain potentials. *Biological Psychology*, 74(3): 374–88.

Pick, A. (1913) *Die agrammatischen Sprachstörungen: Studien zur psychologischen Grundlegung der Aphasielehre*. Springer, Berlin.

Picton, T. W., and Stuss, D. T. (1984) Event-related potentials and the study of speech and language: a critical review. In D. Caplan, A. R. Lecours, and A. Smith (eds), *Biological Perspectives on Language*. MIT Press, Cambridge, MA.

Polich, J., and Donchin, E. (1988) P300 and the word frequency effect. *Electroencephalography and Clinical Neurophysiology*, 70: 33–45.

Preissl, H., Pulvermüller, F., Lutzenberger, W., and Birbaumer, N. (1995) Evoked potentials distinguish nouns from verbs. *Neuroscience Letters*, 197: 81–3.

Pulvermüller, F. (1995) Agrammatism: behavioral description and neurobiological explanation. *Journal of Cognitive Neuroscience*, 7: 165–81.

Pulvermüller, F. (1999) Words in the brain's language. *Behavioral and Brain Sciences*, 22: 253–336.

Pulvermüller, F. (2000) Cell assemblies, axonal conduction times, and the interpretation of high-frequency dynamics in the EEG and MEG. In R. Miller (ed.), *Time and the Brain*, pp. 241–9. Harwood Academic Publishers, Newark, NJ.

Pulvermüller, F. (2001) Brain reflections of words and their meaning. *Trends in Cognitive Sciences*, 5(12): 517–24.

Pulvermüller, F. (2003) *The Neuroscience of Language*. Cambridge University Press, Cambridge.

Pulvermüller, F. (2005) Brain mechanisms linking language and action. *Nature Reviews Neuroscience*, 6(7): 576–82.

Pulvermüller, F., Eulitz, C., Pantev, C., Mohr, B., Feige, B., Lutzenberger, W., Elbert, T., and Birbaumer, N. (1996) High-frequency cortical responses reflect lexical processing: an MEG study. *Electroencephalography and Clinical Neurophysiology*, 98: 76–85.

Pulvermüller, F., Härle, M., and Hummel, F. (2000) Neurophysiological distinction of verb categories. *Neuroreport*, 11(12): 2789–93.

Pulvermüller, F., Kujala, T., Shtyrov, Y., Simola, J., Tiitinen, H., Alku, P., Alho, K., Martinkauppi, S., Ilmoniemi, R. J., and Näätänen, R. (2001) Memory traces for words as revealed by the mismatch negativity. *NeuroImage*, 14(3): 607–16.

Pulvermüller, F., Lutzenberger, W., and Birbaumer, N. (1995) Electrocortical distinction of vocabulary types. *Electroencephalography and Clinical Neurophysiology*, 94: 357–70.

Pulvermüller, F., Lutzenberger, W., and Preissl, H. (1999) Nouns and verbs in the intact brain: evidence from event-related potentials and high-frequency cortical responses. *Cerebral Cortex*, 9: 498–508.

Pulvermüller, F., and Mohr, B. (1996) The concept of transcortical cell assemblies: a key to the understanding of cortical lateralization and interhemispheric interaction. *Neuroscience and Biobehavioral Reviews*, 20: 557–66.

Pulvermüller, F., Mohr, B., and Schleichert, H. (1999) Semantic or lexico-syntactic factors: What determines word-class specific activity in the human brain? *Neuroscience Letters*, 275: 81–4.

Pulvermüller, F., and Shtyrov, Y. (2006) Language outside the focus of attention: the mismatch negativity as a tool for studying higher cognitive processes. *Progress in Neurobiology*, 79(1): 49–71.

Pulvermüller, F., Shtyrov, Y., and Ilmoniemi, R. J. (2005) Brain signatures of meaning access in action word recognition. *Journal of Cognitive Neuroscience*, 17(6): 884–92.

Pulvermüller, F., Shtyrov, Y., Kujala, T., and Näätänen, R. (2004) Word-specific cortical activity as revealed by the mismatch negativity. *Psychophysiology*, 41(1): 106–12.

Pylkkanen, L., Feintuch, S., Hopkins, E., and Marantz, A. (2004) Neural correlates of the effects of morphological family frequency and family size: an MEG study. *Cognition*, 91(3): B35–45.

Rinne, T., Alho, K., Alku, P., Holi, M., Sinkkonen, J., Virtanen, J., Bertrand, O., and Naatanen, R. (1999) Analysis of speech sounds is left-hemisphere predominant at 100–150ms after sound onset. *Neuroreport*, 10(5): 1113–17.

Rubin, D. C. (1980) 51 properties of 125 words: A unit analysis of verbal behavior. *Journal of Verbal Learning and Verbal Behavior*, 19: 736–55.

Rugg, M. D. (1983) Further study of the electrophysiological correlates of lexical decision. *Brain and Language*, 19: 142–52.

Rugg, M. D. (1984) Event-related potentials and the phonological processing of words and non-words. *Neuropsychologia*, 22: 435–43.

Rugg, M. D. (1990) Event-related potentials dissociate repetition effects of high- and low-frequency words. *Memory and Cognition*, 18: 367–79.

Rugg, M. D., and Coles, M. G. H. (1995) The ERP and cognitive psychology: Conceptual issues. In M. D. Rugg and M. G. H. Coles (eds), *Electrophysiology of Mind: Event-Related Brain Potentials and Cognition*, pp. 27–39. Oxford University Press, Oxford.

Rugg, M. D., and Dickens, A. M. J. (1982) Dissociation of alpha and theta activity as a function of verbal and visuospatial tasks. *Electroencephalography and Clinical Neurophysiology*, 53: 201–7.

Rugg, M. D., and Doyle, M. C. (1992) Event-related potentials and recognition memory for low- and high-frequency words. *Journal of Cognitive Neuroscience*, 4: 69–79.

Salmelin, R., Hari, R., Lounasmaa, O. V., and Sams, M. (1994) Dynamics of brain activation during picture naming. *Nature*, 368: 463–5.

Saussure, F., de (1916) *Cours de linguistique generale.* Payot, Paris.

Scott, S. K., Blank, C. C., Rosen, S., and Wise, R. J. (2000) Identification of a pathway for intelligible speech in the left temporal lobe. *Brain*, 123(12): 2400–06.

Scott, S. K., and Johnsrude, I. S. (2003) The neuroanatomical and functional organization of speech perception. *Trends in Neurosciences*, 26(2): 100–7.

Sereno, S. C., Brewer, C. C., and O'Donnell, P. J. (2003) Context effects in word recognition: evidence for early interactive processing. *Psychological Science*, 14(4): 328–33.

Sereno, S. C., and Rayner, K. (2003) Measuring word recognition in reading: eye movements and event-related potentials. *Trends in Cognitive Sciences*, 7(11): 489–93.

Sereno, S. C., Rayner, K., and Posner, M. I. (1998) Establishing a time line for word recognition: evidence from eye movements and event-related potentials. *NeuroReport*, 13: 2195–200.

Sherrard, G. (1969) Findings of a study devoted to the analysis of averaged EEG responses to words and language. *Electroencephalography and Clinical Neurophysiology*, 27(7): 667.

Shtyrov, Y., Hauk, O., and Pulvermüller, F. (2004) Distributed neuronal networks for encoding category-specific semantic information: the mismatch negativity to action words. *European Journal of Neuroscience*, 19(4): 1083–92.

Shtyrov, Y., Kujala, T., Palva, S., Ilmoniemi, R. J., and Näätänen, R. (2000) Discrimination of speech and of complex nonspeech sounds of different temporal structure in the left and right cerebral hemispheres. *NeuroImage*, 12(6): 657–63.

Shtyrov, Y., Pihko, E., and Pulvermüller, F. (2005) Determinants of dominance: is language laterality explained by physical or linguistic features of speech? *NeuroImage*, 27(1): 37–47.

Shtyrov, Y., and Pulvermüller, F. (2002) Memory traces for inflectional affixes as shown by the mismatch negativity. *European Journal of Neuroscience*, 15: 1085–91.

Shtyrov, Y., Pulvermüller, F., Näätänen, R., and Ilmoniemi, R. J. (2003) Grammar processing outside the focus of attention: an MEG study. *Journal of Cognitive Neuroscience*, 15(8): 1195–206.

Skrandies, W. (1998) Evoked potential correlates of semantic meaning: a brain mapping study. *Cognitive Brain Research*, 6: 173–83.

Smith, M. E., and Halgren, E. (1987) Event-related potentials during lexical decision: effects of repetition, word frequency, pronounceability, and concreteness. In R. Johnson, Jr., J. W. Rohrbaugh, and R. Parasuraman (eds), *Current Trends in Event-Related Potential Research*, pp. 417–21. Elsevier, New York.

Solomon, R. L., and Howes, D. H. (1951) Word frequency, personal values, and visual duration thresholds. *Psychological Review*, 58: 256–70.

Stockall, L., Stringfellow, A., and Marantz, A. (2004) The precise time course of lexical activation: MEG measurements of the effects of frequency, probability, and density in lexical decision. *Brain and Language*, 90(1–3): 88–94.

Van Petten, C., and Kutas, M. (1990) Interaction between sentence context and word frequency in event-related brain potentials. *Memory and Cognition*, 18: 380–93.

Van Petten, C., and Kutas, M. (1991) Influences of semantic and syntactic context on open- and closed-class words. *Memory and Cognition*, 19: 95–112.

Walter, W. G. (1965) Brain responses to semantic stimuli. *Journal of Psychosomaatic Research*, 9(1): 51–61.

Weber-Fox, C., and Neville, H. J. (2001) Sensitive periods differentiate processing of open- and closed-class words: an ERP study of bilinguals. *Journal of Speech, Language and Hearing Research*, 44(6): 1338–53.

West, W. C., and Holcomb, P. J. (2000) Imaginal, semantic, and surface-level processing of concrete and abstract words: an electrophysiological investigation. *Journal of Cognitive Neuroscience*, 12(6): 1024–37.

Weyerts, H., Penke, M., Dohrn, U., Clahsen, H., and Münte, T. (1997) Brain potentials indicate differences between regular and irregular German plurals. *NeuroReport*, 8: 957–62.

Whaley, C. P. (1978) Word-nonword classification time. *Journal of Verbal Learning and Verbal Behavior*, 17: 143–54.

Zaidel, E. (1989) Hemispheric independence and interaction in word recognition. In C. von Euler, I. Lundberg, and G. Lennerstrand (eds), *Brain and Reading*, pp. 77–97. Macmillan: Hampshire.

Zatorre, R. J., and Belin, P. (2001) Spectral and temporal processing in human auditory cortex. *Cerebral Cortex*, 11(10): 946–53.

Zatorre, R. J., Belin, P., and Penhune, V. B. (2002) Structure and function of auditory cortex: music and speech. *Trends in Cognitive Science*, 6(1): 37–46.

Zesiger, P., Mounoud, P., and Hauert, C. A. (1993) Effects of lexicality and trigram frequency on handwriting production in children and adults. *Acta Psychol. (Amst)*, 82(1–3): 353–65.

CHAPTER 9

Word recognition in aphasia

Sheila E. Blumstein

9.1 Introduction

A crucial aspect of language understanding is word recognition—the ability to map sound structure on to a lexical representation. Such abilities are often compromised in aphasia, and, as such, provide insight into the nature not only of the cognitive architecture of the speech-lexical processing system but also of the neural systems underlying them. It is the goal of this chapter to review current knowledge about the nature of auditory word recognition deficits in aphasia.

Aphasia is the study of language and speech deficits pursuant to brain injury. Although both children and adults may have aphasia, the focus of this chapter will be on word recognition deficits in adults. In this way, it is assumed that the language functioning of these individuals was normal prior to sustaining brain injury, and that their word recognition system was intact. As a consequence, the study of aphasia provides a window into how and in what ways the word recognition system may fragment. It also provides insight into how damage to particular areas of the brain affects speech and language processing, and thus provides a crucial step in mapping out the neural systems underlying speech and language processing. To this end, much of the chapter will focus on word recognition deficits in Broca's and Wernicke's aphasics, two clinical syndromes that have provided the basis for much of the study of the neural basis of language.

Clinically, Broca's aphasics have a profound expressive impairment in the face of relatively good auditory language comprehension. Their speech output is typically non-fluent and often agrammatic, and their production of the sound structure of language is compromised. The lesions that give rise to this syndrome typically involve left frontal brain structures including the inferior frontal gyrus (also called Broca's area, which includes Brodmann's areas (BA) 44 and 45) (see Bornkessel, Schlesewsky, and Friederici, Chapter 24 this volume, Figures 24.1 and 24.2), as well as the premotor and motor regions posterior and superior to the inferior frontal gyrus, extending to the white matter below and including the basal ganglia and insula (Damasio 1998). Wernicke's aphasics, in contrast, have fluent, well-articulated speech in the context of a dense auditory language comprehension impairment. Nonetheless, the content of their speech output is compromised. Their speech tends to be semantically empty and includes inappropriately juxtaposed words and grammatical structure. Typically these patients have lesions that involve left posterior brain structures including the posterior region of the superior temporal gyrus (also called Wernicke's area or BA 22) (see Figures 24.1 and 24.2 this volume) often extending into parietal structures such as the angular gyrus (BA 39) or supramarginal gyrus (BA 40) (see Figure 24.2e) (Damasio 1998).

Although the clinical symptoms and associated lesions described above characterize the classical syndromes of Broca's and Wernicke's aphasia, it is worth noting that there is considerable variability in performance on a patient by patient basis. This variability reflects a number of factors. Perhaps first and foremost, no two patients have exactly the same lesion. Given that the language deficits of these patients are presumably a consequence of damage to particular neural systems, it would be expected that the performance of the patients would vary as a function of both the severity and the extent of the lesion. Second, patients are typically tested at different times post insult. As a consequence, they may be at different trajectories in the recovery process. Moreover, some patients appear to show more substantial recovery than others, and the factors underlying that recovery process are unclear. These caveats notwithstanding, the particular language behaviors giving rise to the characterization of a patient as a Broca's or Wernicke's aphasic are typically present, and the associated lesions typically involve the neural areas described. Thus, to a first approximation, the aphasia syndromes allow for inferences regarding the correspondence between brain and behavior. Nonetheless, focusing on the behavioral/cognitive deficits underlying the clinical syndromes is only a starting point, and integrating the results of behavioral studies with those of neuroimaging studies with normal subjects is essential. As a consequence, in this chapter neuroimaging findings will also be considered as they relate to word recognition deficits in aphasia.

As a first step in consideration of word recognition deficits in aphasia, it is important briefly to outline a theoretical framework. All research, whether experimental or descriptive, is built on a set of theoretical assumptions. We take as our starting point a functional architecture of the speech-lexical processing system consisting of multiple stages of processing required to access a word, as shown in Figure 9.1. In order for a word to be recognized, auditory input goes through a number of transformations that progressively map the raw acoustic signal onto more abstract properties of speech. The auditory input from the peripheral auditory system is transformed into a spectral representation based on the extraction of more generalized auditory patterns or properties from the acoustic signal. This representation is in turn converted to a more abstract phonetic-phonological representation corresponding to the phonetic categories of speech. This phonetic-phonological representation maps onto lexical form (i.e. a word in the lexicon) where a particular lexical entry is selected from the potential set of lexical candidates.

Most current models of word recognition assume that the word recognition system is characterized by a network-like architecture with properties of activation, inhibition, and competition (Gaskell and Marslen-Wilson, 1999; McClelland and Elman, 1986; McClelland and Rumelhart, 1986). There are several consequences of this functional architecture. First, there is *graded activation*. That is, activation patterns at a particular level of representation are not all-or-none but are graded. For example, the activation of a phonetic category such as [t] is influenced by the goodness of the acoustic-phonetic input.

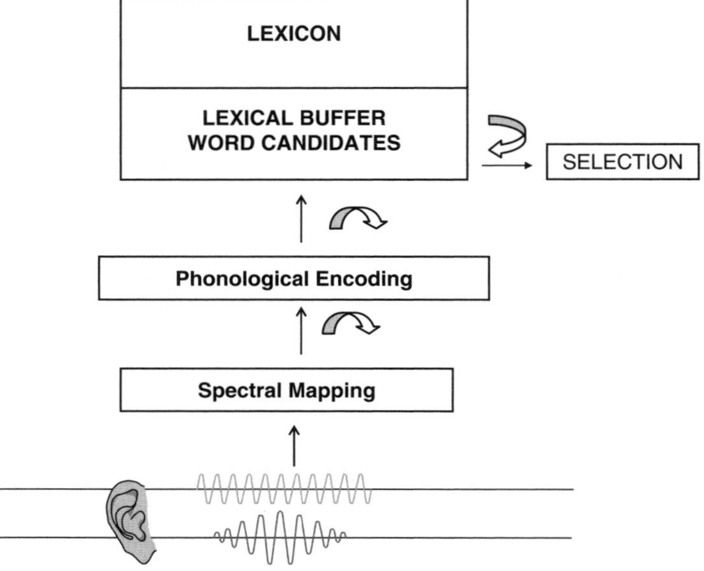

Figure 9.1 A model of auditory word recognition.

Second, there is *competition* among potential candidates within a particular level of representation, i.e. there is competition within the phonetic-phonological and lexical levels of representation. The extent of competition influences the time course and patterns of activation at each of the levels of representation, and ultimately, the performance of the network. Third, although more controversial (cf. Levelt, 1992; Levelt et al., 1999; Rapp and Goldrick, 2000), it is assumed that processing stages interact with each other such that activation patterns at one level will influence those at other levels (McClelland, 1979; Gaskell and Marslen-Wilson, 1999). For example, a poor acoustic-phonetic exemplar of a word will affect not only the activation of its phonetic-phonological category representation but also its activation at the lexical level, i.e. the representation of that word in the lexicon.

In the course of this chapter we will consider the various stages of word recognition and potential impairments to these stages. We will also consider the extent to which the computational properties of the system may be compromised, with particular focus on graded activation, the effects of competition on word recognition, and the extent to which deficits at one level of processing influence processing at other stages of processing.

9.2 **Deficits in processing the sound structure of language**

Most models of word recognition do not focus on the early stages of processing in which the auditory input is converted to a more abstract phonetic-phonological form. Rather, they typically assume that the acoustic-phonetic input is appropriately mapped to a phonological representation. In theory, however, deficits in such speech perception processes could have direct consequences on word recognition. If the sound structure of language were not properly extracted and transformed from the raw acoustic signal into more generalized acoustic parameters and subsequently mapped onto more abstract phonetic-phonological properties of speech, then the activation of lexical candidates should be compromised. Thus, impairments in either processing the acoustic-phonetic parameters of speech or the processing of the phonological aspects of speech could underlie or contribute to word recognition impairments. For this reason, it is important to consider the extent to which aphasic patients show deficits in the processes related to speech perception.

9.2.1 **Deficits in auditory/phonetic processing**

A number of studies have investigated the perception of the acoustic cues used by the listener in perceiving the phonetic categories of speech. Particular focus has been on two acoustic parameters associated with perceiving stop consonants [p t k b d g], one relating to the perception of voicing and the other relating to the perception of place of articulation (Basso et al., 1977; Blumstein, Cooper, Zurif, and Caramazza, 1977; Blumstein, et al., 1984; Caplan et al., 1995; Carpenter and Rutherford, 1973; Gandour and Dardarananda, 1982; Gow and Caplan, 1996; Leeper et al., 1986). In these studies, acoustic continua are created which parametrically vary the acoustic cue in question. Listeners are asked either to discriminate pairs of stimuli from the continua or, alternatively, to identify or categorize individual stimuli as belonging to a particular phonetic category. For the perception of voicing, studies have investigated a temporal parameter of speech, voice-onset time, which corresponds to the timing relation between the release of the stop closure and the onset of vocal cord vibration. And for place of articulation, studies have investigated the spectral properties associated with frequency changes of the formant transitions.

Results show that in general all aphasic patients regardless of their clinical type have difficulty in performing these tasks. Thus, Broca's aphasics with damage including anterior brain structures such as the inferior frontal gyrus and Wernicke's aphasics with damage including posterior brain structures such as the superior temporal and middle temporal gyrus show deficits in processing the acoustic parameters of speech. Both groups tend to make more errors in categorizing the stimuli than in discriminating them. However, for those patients who are able to perform the discrimination task, the discrimination functions are similar in shape to those of neurologically intact subjects. That is, functions show peaks of discrimination at the phonetic boundaries, and chance performance discriminating within category stimuli. These findings suggest that these patients can extract spectral representations from the auditory input and map them onto phonetic category structure. Thus, the locus of their speech perception deficit does not appear to be auditory/phonetic, but rather may reflect an inability to map sound structure to a phonetic label (i.e. name the stimuli) or to process the stimuli phonologically (see section 9.2.2). That patients with lesions involving either anterior or posterior brain structures show speech perception deficits challenges the classical view that there is a structural/functional dichotomy between anterior and posterior brain structures, with anterior structures involved in expressive aspects of speech-language and posterior structures involved in receptive aspects of speech-language. Recent neuroimaging experiments also show that the perception of the acoustic properties of speech recruits a broad neural system. In particular, both anterior and posterior brain structures show sensitivity to voice-onset time differences of 10 ms and to the details of phonetic category structure (Blumstein et al., 2005; for a review see Scott and Johnsrude, 2003 and Scott and Wise, 2004).

That aphasic patients show deficits in processing the acoustic-phonetic properties of speech might suggest that such impairments would be predictive of impairments in word recognition. Interestingly, however, this appears not to be the case. Performance on labeling and discrimination tasks does not correlate with the severity of auditory language comprehension impairment (Basso et al., 1977; Blumstein, Cooper, Zurif, and Caramazza, 1977; Blumstein et al., 1984; Leeper et al., 1986), nor does it appear to be predictive of word discrimination performance (Csepe et al., 2001). Taken together, these results suggest that while aphasic patients have some impairments in processing the auditory/phonetic parameters of speech, the locus of word recognition deficits does not appear to be in the early stages of acoustic-phonetic processing.

9.2.2 Deficits in phonological processing

Deficits have emerged in studies exploring patients' abilities to perceive the sound segments of language and particularly to perceive a particular phonetic feature when presented in an array of phonetic competitors. In some experiments, patients have been asked to discriminate pairs of naturally produced words or non-words distinguished by one or several phonetic features, e.g. *pear* vs. *bear*, distinguished by voicing, and *tear* vs. *bear*, distinguished by voicing and place of articulation. In other studies, they have been asked to point to the appropriate picture corresponding to a target stimulus which is presented in an array of pictures whose names are phonologically similar to the target word. Typically, these studies explore segmental distinctions which have phonemic (contrasting) status in the language. However, in addition, several studies have explored the perception of tone contrasts which serve as lexical, i.e. phonemic, cues in the language (cf. Gandour and Daradarananda, 1983 for Thai and Naeser and Chan, 1980 for Chinese).

Similar patterns of results to those found in the perception of acoustic-phonetic properties of speech have emerged in studies investigating the perception of phonological contrasts. Nearly all aphasic patients display some deficits (Blumstein, Baker, and Goodglass, 1977; Jauhiainen and Nuutila, 1977; Miceli et al., 1978; 1980). Typically, patients have considerably more difficulty in tasks in which they must categorize (or name) the test stimuli than in discrimination tasks in which they must decide whether two stimuli are the same or different (Baum, 2001; Gow and Caplan, 1996). Although there are more errors in the perception of nonsense syllables than real words, the overall patterns of performance are similar: the perception of consonants is worse than that of vowels; more consonant perception errors occur when the test stimuli contrast by a single phonetic feature than when they contrast by two or more features; and among the various types of feature contrasts, the perception of place of articulation contrasts and the perception of voicing contrasts are particularly vulnerable (Baker et al., 1981; Blumstein, Baker, and Goodglass, 1977; Gow and Caplan, 1996; Miceli et al., 1978; Sasanuma et al., 1976).

Similar impairments in the perception of phonological properties have emerged even in the absence of an overt response by the patient (Csepe et al., 2001). Both Broca's and Wernicke's have shown impairments in the detection of changes of phonetic category voicing and place of articulation as measured by evoked-related responses using mismatch negativity. These same patients are normal in the processing of non-speech tone stimuli, indicating that the deficit is not a generalized auditory impairment but relates to the perception of the properties of speech.

Taken together, these results suggest that aphasic patients have a deficit in the activation of the phonological representations of the sound structure of language that occurs at the phonological encoding stage of perception. These deficits appear to be distinct from lower-level deficits in extracting the spectral-temporal acoustic properties of speech. As a result, phonologically similar competitors, e.g. /pa/ vs. /ba/, may inappropriately reach the threshold of activation, rather than the phonologically appropriate stimulus. That at least part of the deficit lies in phonological encoding, and not in the mapping of these phonological representations onto the lexicon, is supported by the similar patterns of deficit in the perception of both words and nonsense syllables. The processing advantage for words over non-words for aphasic patients is not surprising, given that a word not only matches a phonological entry in the lexicon but also has a meaning representation. Hence, there may be different resting levels of activation for words vs. non-words (words presumably have a higher resting activation) and words also have a perceptual advantage afforded by top-down influences from the lexicon back to the stage of phonological encoding (see section 9.4).

The processes involved in phonological encoding appear to have a distributed neural basis, one that involves the perisylvian regions of the left hemisphere. The pattern of errors does not appear to differ significantly as a function of type of aphasia and underlying neuropathology. To be sure, Wernicke's aphasics make a large number of phoneme-perceptual errors, more so than Broca's aphasics, and there is evidence that damage to the left supramarginal gyrus and the bordering parietal operculum is highly correlated with speech perception deficits (Caplan et al., 1995). However, anterior aphasics show perceptual impairments as well (Baker et al., 1981; Blumstein, Baker, and Goodglass, 1977; Miceli et al., 1978; Sasanuma et al., 1976). Consistent with these findings are the results from neuroimaging studies investigating the perception of speech in neurologically intact individuals which show that both anterior and posterior brain structures are involved in the perception of phonological contrasts (Burton, 2001; Poeppel, 1996).

That anterior and posterior brain structures are involved in such processing does not mean that they contribute in the same way. In fact, most neuroimaging studies propose a functional division within the neural system, a division that relates not only to the level of processing of sound structure but also to the nature of task demands and the cognitive requirements to perform a particular task (Binder and Price, 2001; Burton, 2001; Hickok and Poeppel, 1996; Poeppel, 1996; Scott and Johnsrude, 2003). In particular, the primary auditory cortex and auditory association areas (STG) bilaterally have been implicated in early stages of acoustic-phonetic processing (Belin et al., 1999; Price et al., 1992; Zatorre et al., 1996) (see Figure 24.2 this volume). Phonological processing and tasks that require short-term phonological store have shown activation of left inferior parietal areas (Awh et al., 1996; Jonides et al., 1998; Paulesu et al., 1993). And executive decisions and tasks that involve overt segmentation of the speech signal activate frontal regions, particularly the IFG and to a lesser extent the MFG (Burton et al., 2000; Demonet et al., 1992; 1994; Zatorre et al., 1992; 1996). To date, results from the studies of speech processing in aphasia have not allowed for an elaboration of this proposed functional division—in large measure because lesions in aphasic patients tend to be fairly large, making it difficult to attribute a function to a particular focal region of the brain.

Nonetheless, similar to the results for the processing of the auditory-phonetic parameters of speech, deficits in phonological processing in patients with either anterior or posterior damage do not correlate with either auditory comprehension or word discrimination tasks. Patients with good auditory comprehension skills have shown impairments in speech processing; conversely, patients with severe auditory language comprehension deficits have shown minimal speech perception deficits (Baker et al., 1981; Basso et al., 1977; Blumstein, Baker, and Goodglass, 1977; Blumstein, Cooper, Zurif, and Caramazza, 1977; Csepe et al., 2001; Jauhiainen and Nuutila, 1977; Metz-Lutz et al., 1992; Miceli et al., 1980; Yeni-Komshian and Lafontaine, 1983). The high-level redundancy of language may help compensate for weakly activated phonological representations. Thus, although it is likely that deficits in encoding phonological representations may contribute to deficits in word recognition in aphasia, they do not appear to be the basis of such impairments.

9.3 Deficits in processes contributing to word recognition

As discussed above, although it is the case that aphasic patients show deficits in processing the sound structure of language, such deficits do not appear to underlie word recognition impairments in aphasia. And aphasic patients appear to be able to map the auditory input onto lexical form. Tyler (1992) investigated this issue using a gating paradigm. In this paradigm, participants are presented with increasingly larger auditory fragments of words. After the presentation of each fragment, they are asked to say what word they think is being presented. In this way, it is possible for the examiner to determine at what point the participant uniquely identifies a word. Results of this study, which included non-fluent and fluent aphasic patients, showed a similar pattern to that of age-matched controls. The patients were able to identify the word well before its offset; they recognized the word at approximately the same point as the age-matched controls; and they produced a similar set of candidate words, called cohort words, for a particular fragment of a word. These findings suggest that there are minimal problems in auditory word recognition in aphasic patients. However, as we shall elaborate below, deficits in word recognition do emerge for two groups of patients, Broca's and Wernicke's aphasics, under a number of experimental conditions. Their patterns of performance suggest that their deficits reside in the processes that map sound structure to the lexicon and to the subsequent activation of lexical candidates.

9.3.1 Graded activation of the lexicon

The cognitive architecture of the speech-lexical processing system suggests that activation of the lexicon from phonetic-phonological form may be graded. That is, the extent of activation of a lexical candidate may vary with the degree of activation a function of the goodness of fit between the phonetic-phonological input and its lexical representation. A number of models of lexical access allow for graded activation of phonetic and phonological features and lexical competition via interactive activation in mapping from sound structure to lexical form. These include the Cohort model (Gaskell and Marslen-Wilson, 1999; Marslen-Wilson, 1987; Marslen-Wilson and Welsh, 1978), TRACE (Elman and McClelland, 1986; McClelland and Elman, 1986), and Shortlist (Norris, 1994).

Evidence consistent with this view comes from studies using two research methodologies, one using semantic priming in a lexical decision task and the other picture-pointing in an eye-tracking paradigm. In the lexical decision priming paradigm, subjects are required to maker a lexical decision to a stimulus. Reaction-time latencies are faster if a word target is preceded by a prime stimulus that is semantically related to it than if the target is preceded by a semantically unrelated word or a non-word. Thus, *cat* primes *dog* and *pear* primes *fruit*. The question is whether alterations of the phonetic category structure of a prime stimulus will affect the magnitude of semantic priming. Results show that within-category differences in voice-onset time (VOT) do affect the magnitude of semantic priming in a lexical decision task (Andruski et al., 1994). That is, there is a significant reduction in the magnitude of semantic priming when the VOT of the initial consonant of the prime stimulus is reduced; acoustically modified [k] in the prime stimulus *cat* results in less priming to the semantically related target word *dog* compared to a good exemplar of the prime stimulus *cat*.

Why does this effect emerge? Presumably because shortening the VOT of an initial voiceless stop consonant of the prime stimulus renders it a poorer exemplar of the voiceless phonetic category and closer in acoustic-phonetic space to the voiced-voiceless phonetic category boundary. It also results in a prime stimulus that is a poorer match to its lexical representation. Thus, the graded activation of phonetic category structure influences the extent of activation of a lexical entry. Similar graded effects of semantic priming emerge with manipulations to phonetic category structure in initial, medial, and final position and with different types of acoustic manipulations (Utman, 1997; Utman et al., 2001).

Graded activation of lexical candidates has also been shown using an eye-tracking methodology in which subjects are asked to point to one of four named pictures as their eye movements are measured. In this study (McMurray et al., 2002), stimuli consisted of words which varied in VOT of the initial stop consonant. As stimuli approached the phonetic boundary between voiced and voiceless lexical competitors, e.g. *bear/pear*, fixation times increased in a gradient fashion. Although subjects pointed to the appropriate target, they showed increasingly more looks to the picture corresponding to *bear* as the VOT of the target word *pear* was reduced and approached the phonetic boundary, and similarly they showed increasingly more looks to the picture corresponding to *pear* as the VOT of the target word *bear* was increased and the stimulus approached the phonetic boundary.

Both the lexical decision and eye-tracking experiments suggest that the lexicon is sensitive to phonetic category structure. Phonetic category structure information including within-phonetic category variation appears to affect initial contact with the lexicon in a graded fashion. Thus, a poor exemplar of a phonetic category affects mapping to the lexicon such that a lexical candidate that is a poor exemplar fails to activate a lexical entry to the same degree as a good one. This initial reduction in activation not only has effects on the lexical candidate; it but also influences activation levels within the lexical network itself, including potential lexical competitors (as shown by the eye-tracking paradigm) and the lexical semantic network (as shown by the lexical decision paradigm).

The question is whether aphasic patients also show graded activation of the lexicon. A study investigating this question with Broca's aphasics indicated that indeed Broca's aphasics do show graded activation of the lexicon. Presentation of prime stimuli in which the VOT of the initial voiceless stop consonant is reduced (*c*at-dog*) or the glottal phonation in the closure interval of voiced final stops is replaced by silence of equal duration (*tub*-wash*) resulted in a reduction in the magnitude of semantic priming in a lexical decision task just as it did for normal controls (Utman et al., 2001). Thus, not only do these patients show sensitivity to phonetic category structure, but the processes that activate word recognition and access to the lexical-semantic network appear to be normal.

To date, Wernicke's aphasics have not been tested in these experiments. However, in other studies exploring the effects of phonological distortion on lexical access, both Broca's and Wernicke's aphasics have shown impairments. Normal subjects show monotonically less priming for *cat-dog* when the initial segment of non-words differs from the phonologically related word prime by one phonetic feature, e.g. *gat-dog*, or several phonetic features, e.g. *wat-dog* (Connine et al., 1993; 1997; Milberg et al., 1988a). Similar to the results investigating the effects of phonetic category structure on lexical access, these findings also indicate that activation of the lexicon is graded. Non-words activate the lexicon, with the extent of activation a function of the phonological distance between the sound structure of the non-word and the phonological representation of a lexical candidate. Although Broca's and Wernicke's aphasics show semantic priming in a lexical decision task, e.g. *cat* primes *dog*, both groups of patients show pathological performance when the initial consonant of the prime stimulus is phonologically altered (Milberg et al., 1988b). Broca's aphasics fail to show priming under conditions of phonological modification, i.e. although *cat* primes *dog*, both *gat* and *wat* fail to prime *dog*. In contrast, Wernicke's aphasics show a similar magnitude of priming under all conditions, i.e. *cat-dog*, *gat-dog*, and *wat-dog* all show an equal magnitude of semantic priming. The presence of semantic priming in both Broca's and Wernicke's aphasics when the prime stimulus consists of a good phonological exemplar suggests that both groups of patients can map the sound structure input onto lexical form. and that the lexical representation activates the lexical-semantic network. However, the failure of the non-word stimuli to activate the lexicon in the Broca's aphasics and to overactivate the lexicon in the Wernicke's aphasics suggests that both groups of patients have deficits in the dynamics of lexical activation (Blumstein and Milberg, 2000; cf. also Del Toro, 2000).

While there is agreement in the literature that aphasic patients do have deficits in the dynamics of lexical activation, there is disagreement about the exact nature of the deficit. One view is that the deficit for Broca's and Wernicke's aphasics lies in the degree of activation of lexical candidates. In this view, it is hypothesized that the overall activation in the lexicon is reduced in Broca's aphasics, and that it is either increased in Wernicke's aphasics or there is a failure to inhibit lexical competitors (McNellis and Blumstein, 2001; Blumstein and Milberg, 2000; Janse, 2006). An alternative hypothesis focusing on the basis of the impairment in Broca's aphasics is that for these patients there is a delay in the time course of activation. Activation is delayed, leading to a slower than normal rise time (Prather et al., 1997; Swinney et al., 1989; 2000). These two hypotheses will be discussed further later in the chapter. However, whichever hypothesis is correct, a deficit in the dynamics of lexical activation should have particular consequences for word recognition under condition of lexical competition. It is to this issue that we now turn.

9.3.2 Lexical competition

As described in the model of word recognition, the activation of a lexical candidate also activates lexical entries that are similar in their sound shape. Both the number and frequency of occurrence of these lexical competitors influence word recognition processes. For example, it has been shown that the extent of form (phonological) overlap between a prime and a target stimulus influences reaction-time latencies to the target. Overlap in the onsets of such stimuli leads to slowed reaction-time latencies to the target. When two stimuli are highly similar at onset, both candidates are activated. However, as more phonological information comes in and the lexical candidate is uniquely isolated, the activation of the lexical candidate is boosted while at the same time the activation of the lexical competitor is inhibited. Thus, the presentation of words that share at least two phonemes at onset results in slowed reaction-time latencies to the second word, presumably because of inhibition effects (Monsell and Hirsch, 1998; Slowiaczek and Hamburger, 1992; Slowiaczek and Pisoni, 1986).

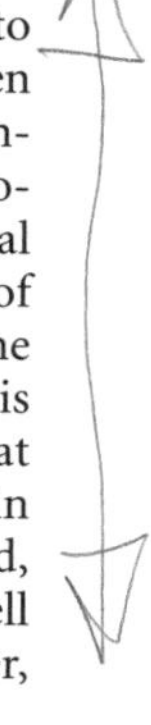

A recent study (Janse, 2006) explored the sensitivity of Broca's and Wernicke's aphasics to such competitor effects using an auditory lexical decision priming paradigm. In contrast to neurologically intact subjects who showed the expected inhibitory effect, both Broca's and Wernicke's aphasics showed impairments. However, their patterns of performance were different. Wernicke's aphasics showed a significant priming effect. That is, their response latencies were not slowed down, as was the case for neurologically intact individuals, but they were *faster* for lexical targets presented in the context of stimuli that had onset competitors. This pattern of results is consistent with the hypothesis that there is overactivation of the lexicon with a failure to inhibit lexical competitors.

In contrast to the Wernicke's aphasics and normal participants, Broca's aphasics showed a weak, but non-significant, inhibitory effect. The interpretation of this effect is less clear, since there was considerable variability of performance among the subjects. Nevertheless, the findings suggest that there is a deficit in the processes of lexical activation. With weakly activated lexical entries (McNellis and Blumstein, 2001) or a delay in the time course of activation (Prather et al., 1997), the system is unable to select a "winner" among competitors. As a consequence, inhibition processes in the context of a lexical competitor are reduced. As we shall elaborate below, similar patterns of performance emerge under conditions of onset competition using the eye-tracking paradigm in which subjects are asked to point to one of four pictures given an auditorily presented target (Yee, 2005; Yee et al., 2004; forthcoming). Importantly, these findings indicate that the effects of competition influence not only lexical form but also access to its lexical-semantic representation.

Lexical competition is based on the extent to which the phonological form of a word shares phonological attributes with other words in the lexicon. Thus, in theory, lexical competition effects should emerge not only when lexical candidates share onsets but also when lexical candidates share rimes. Indeed, normal individuals show auditory rhyme priming effects (Burton, 1989; Hillinger, 1980; Schacter and Church, 1992). Several studies investigating rhyme priming in aphasic patients have been conducted (Baum, 1997; Blumstein et al., 2000; Gordon and Baum, 1994). However, the results are not consistent across studies, making it difficult to draw any definitive conclusions.

Given that aphasic patients appear to have deficits under conditions of lexical competition, such deficits may be exacerbated when the auditory input is a poor acoustic-phonetic match to its lexical representation. That is, if activation of lexical form is graded and the extent of that activation varies as a function of the goodness of fit of the sound shape with its lexical representation, then a poor exemplar that is closer in acoustic-phonetic space to a lexical competitor should affect word recognition processes.

As described earlier, Broca's aphasics showed, as did normal subjects, graded activation of the lexicon (Utman et al., 2001). However, deficits for these patients emerged under conditions of lexical competition. When the VOT of an initial voiceless stop consonant of a prime stimulus was reduced and the prime stimulus had a voiced lexical competitor, semantic priming was lost. That is, although phonetically altered *cat* (which does not have a voiced lexical competitor) showed a significant reduction in the magnitude of priming for *dog*, phonetically altered *pear* (with the lexical competitor *bear*) failed to show priming for the semantically related word *fruit*. Thus, the presence of a lexical competitor resulted in the *loss* of semantic priming when the prime stimulus was a poorer exemplar of the phonetic category. In addition, unlike normal subjects, where the effects of the acoustic manipulation were short-lived, emerging at 50 ms and disappearing at 250 ms, the effects of the acoustic manipulations persisted. That is, the failure of acoustically manipulated *pear* to show semantic priming emerged at both interstimulus (ISI) intervals.

These findings suggest that Broca's aphasics do not have a slower than normal rise time in activation, but rather a reduction in activation. Nonetheless, it is possible that the ISI intervals were too short to show a delay in activation. Findings from eye-tracking experiments described below allow for a closer examination of the time course of lexical activation.

Importantly, in a separate post-test, the same patients perceived the initial consonant of the acoustically modified prime stimuli as voiceless, indicating that the failure to show semantic priming under conditions of lexical competition was not because the patients misperceived the manipulated prime stimuli as the voiced lexical competitor. Consistent with these results were the findings of a second experiment (Utman et al., 2001) which investigated the effects of degrading phonetic category structure in word final position. The glottal phonation in the closure interval of final voiced stop consonants was replaced by silence of equal duration in a series of prime stimuli, e.g. *robe*, and the magnitude of priming to a semantically related target, e.g. *dress*, was explored. Half of the prime stimuli had voiceless competitors, e.g. *robe* with the competitor *rope*, and half did not, e.g. *tub*. Again, Broca's aphasics showed different patterns of performance as a function of whether the prime stimulus had a lexical competitor or not.

A final study in this series of experiments investigated the effects that the acoustic-phonetic structure of a stimulus exerts on the processes by which lexical candidates compete for activation (Misiurski et al., 2005). Consistent with models of lexical processing that allow for interaction between phonological and semantic levels of processing (Allopenna et al., 1998; Dell et al., 1997; Gaskell and Marslen-Wilson, 1997; Peterson and Savoy, 1998), alterations in the VOT of an initial voiceless stop consonant in a real word should not only influence the activation of the lexical candidate itself and its lexical-semantic network, but should also influence the activation of its voiced lexical competitor and its lexical-semantic network. An auditory lexical decision paradigm was used to investigate whether shortening the VOT of an initial voiceless stop consonant in a real word results in the activation of the lexical-semantic network of its voiced competitor, i.e. does acoustically modified *t*ime* with the voiced lexical competitor *dime* prime *penny*? Neurologically intact subjects showed such mediated priming, i.e. *t*ime* primes *penny* via *dime*, but the magnitude of priming for *penny* was significantly less than it was for *dime-penny*. Although Broca's aphasics showed priming for semantically related *dime-penny*, they failed to show mediated priming.

That Broca's aphasics' priming patterns are "pathological" only under conditions of lexical competition is consistent with the view that the basis of their impairment resides in initial activation levels of the lexicon. Given the low activation levels for word candidates in Broca's aphasics, a stimulus that is a poor phonetic exemplar of the lexical candidate may fail to override the activation of lexical competitors. As a result, it may take longer for the lexical processing system to settle on the most compatible lexical candidate and ultimately select a "winner," resulting in a loss of semantic priming that persists over longer time intervals (cf. McNellis and Blumstein, 2001; Prather et al., 1991; 1997; Swinney et al., 2000; Utman et al., 2001). Nonetheless, the lexical decision paradigm is unable to capture the time course of these word recognition processes. However, the eye-tracking paradigm is uniquely suited to provide such evidence. Moreover, it may provide a means of examining whether the basis of Broca's aphasic deficit is in the extent of lexical activation or the time course of lexical activation.

In recent years, the eye-tracking paradigm has been developed and applied to investigate the time course of spoken word recognition and to explore the effects of lexical competition on such processing (Tanenhaus et al., 1995). This paradigm has several advantages in testing aphasic participants: task requirements are natural and easy, even for patients with severe auditory language comprehension impairments; performance can be monitored for the same stimulus when lexical competitors are present and when they are absent in the stimulus array; and it allows for a detailed tracking of the time course of lexical activation.

This paradigm was used in a series of experiments with Broca's and Wernicke's aphasics and older normal controls examining effects of semantic relatedness, onset competition, and semantically mediated onset competition (Yee, 2005; Yee et al., 2004; forthcoming). In this paradigm, participants' eye movements are monitored as they hear a word and select the matching picture from a four picture display. When normal subjects hear a word (e.g. *hammock*), initially, they are more likely to fixate on a picture of a distractor object whose name is an onset competitor (e.g. *hammer*) of the uttered word than on unrelated distractors (Allopenna et al., 1998). Furthermore, normal subjects show onset-mediated semantic competitor effects in that they preferentially fixate on a distractor object that is *semantically* related to an onset competitor of the uttered word, despite the fact that the onset competitor itself is absent from the display. For example, when subjects hear *hammock*, they preferentially fixate on *nail*, even though there is no *hammer* in the display (Yee and Sedivy, 2006). If Broca's aphasics indeed have deficits in the dynamics of lexical activation, then the (limited) amount of acoustic input that matches the onset competitor should weakly activate the onset competitor's lexical representation. If this is true, then Broca's aphasics should show both a smaller onset competitor effect and a smaller onset-mediated semantic competitor effect than normal subjects (i.e. when Broca's aphasics hear *hammock*, they should be less likely to fixate on *hammer*, and also less likely to fixate on *nail* compared to normal subjects). In contrast, if Wernicke's aphasics have abnormally high levels of lexical activation or fail to inhibit competitors, even the (limited) amount of acoustic input that matches the onset competitor might be enough to strongly activate the onset competitor's lexical representation. If this is true, then Wernicke's aphasics should show both a larger onset competitor effect and a larger onset-mediated semantic competitor effect than normal subjects.

As predicted, Broca's aphasics failed to show an onset competitor effect: they were no more likely to fixate on onset competitors of the uttered word than on unrelated distractor pictures. They also failed to show a mediated competitor effect. In particular, they did not show a preference to fixate on distractors that were semantically related to the onset competitor.

In contrast to the Broca's aphasics, the Wernicke's aphasics showed competitor effects. They were significantly more likely to fixate on onset competitors of the uttered word than on unrelated distractors, and they also preferentially fixated on distractors that were semantically related to the onset competitor. Nonetheless, although the Wernicke's aphasics showed competitor effects, the patterns of these effects were pathological. Not only did they look at the competitor more often, as shown by their proportion of fixations, but the temporal course of their fixations lasted longer than those of age-matched control subjects.

The findings from the eye-tracking experiments are important for a number of reasons. First, the failure to show competitor effects for Broca's aphasics using the eye-tracking paradigm replicates the results using the auditory lexical decision paradigm, providing converging evidence across very different experimental methodologies. Second, the eye-tracking results show that deficits in auditory word recognition in Broca's aphasics emerge under conditions of lexical competition even in the context of stimuli that are phonetically good exemplars. Thus, the acoustic-phonetic manipulations used in the lexical decision experiments are not in themselves the basis for the failure to show semantic priming under conditions of lexical competition. Rather, it is the presence of a lexical competitor which gives rise to the impaired performance of the patients. The eye-tracking results also indicate that Broca's aphasics do not show a delayed time course of activation, i.e. the patients do not show a slower than normal rise time as shown by the proportion of their fixations to the competitor. Instead, they show a similar time course but a reduced magnitude of activation compared to normal controls. And Wernicke's aphasics show continued activation of competitors over a longer duration than normal controls, consistent with the view that that they are unable to inhibit the activation of lexical competitors.

The competitor effects that emerged for Broca's aphasics dovetail with both the theoretical and experimental findings from the functional neuroimaging literature. In particular, it has been suggested that the left inferior frontal gyrus is involved in the selection of information from among competing alternatives (Thompson-Schill et al., 1997; 1998; 1999). In a series of studies, Thompson-Schill has shown increased activation in the IFG under conditions of increased semantic competition. She has proposed that this increased activation of the IFG reflects selection between competing alternatives rather than merely semantic retrieval. Consistent with these predictions, Broca's aphasics with damage including the inferior frontal gyrus should show lexical processing impairments under conditions of lexical competition.

9.4 Interaction effects on word recognition in aphasia

As discussed earlier, it has generally been assumed that the speech-lexical processing system is interactive. Not only is there an influence of lower levels of processing on higher levels of processing, but there is also influence of higher levels of processing on lower levels of processing. In what follows, we consider interactivity effects on word recognition in aphasia by examining how word recognition influences lower-level speech processing, on the one hand, and how word recognition is influenced by higher level sentence processing, on the other. There is not an extensive literature in this area, but the results provide some insight into the extent to which the functional architecture of the word recognition system is impaired in aphasia.

9.4.1 Influence of word recognition on speech processing

Even though both Broca's and Wernicke's aphasics show word recognition deficits, there is no question that they are sensitive to the lexical status of the auditory input. There is a large body of literature that shows that aphasic patients, even those with language comprehension deficits, are able to perform a lexical decision task, a task which requires them to make a decision about the lexical status of a word (Blumstein et al., 1982; Hagoort, 1993; 1997; Milberg and Blumstein, 1981; Swinney et al., 1989). However, what is less clear is whether word recognition processes have a cascading effect on other levels of processing, as appears to be the case in normal subjects. For example, it has been shown in neurologically intact individuals that the perception of the phonetic categories of speech is influenced by the lexical status of a stimulus. In particular, the locus of the phonetic boundary of a VOT word–non-word continuum varies as a function of whether the endpoint stimulus is a word or not. Thus, subjects perceive more [p]s in a *peace–beace* continuum and more [b]s in a *peef–beef* continuum even though they are asked only to categorize the first consonant of the stimuli as either [p] or [b]. This phenomenon has been called the "lexical effect" (Ganong, 1980). While there is some debate in the literature about whether the lexical effect reflects the influence of higher-level lexical information on lower-level speech perception processes or post-lexical decision-related processes as subjects are required to categorize ambiguous stimuli (see Pitt, 1995 for a review), in either case the results show how lexical status may affect phonetic category structure in speech perception.

What about aphasic patients? Will they also show a lexical bias in the perception of an acoustic-phonetic continuum? Indeed, both fluent and non-fluent aphasics show a lexical effect (Boyczuk and Baum, 1999). However, the fluent and nonfluent classification for aphasic patients includes various clinical types of patient. Although Broca's aphasics are typically classified as nonfluent and Wernicke's aphasics are typically classified as fluent, there are other patient types subsumed in the nonfluent/fluent classification schema. Thus, the question remains whether Broca's and Wernicke's aphasics will show a lexical bias.

The presence of a lexical effect was explored in a study comparing Broca's and Wernicke/Conduction aphasics to that of age-matched controls (Blumstein et al., 1994). Broca's aphasics showed a greater lexical effect than did the control subjects, suggesting not only that they were sensitive to the lexical status of a word but that they had a very strong lexical bias. That Broca's aphasics can use lexical information to enhance processing further downstream was shown in another study investigating the ability of aphasic patients to recognize auditorily presented CV syllables in various types of contexts. Broca's aphasics were able to use lexical information to enhance syllable recognition. In particular, similar to normal participants, they showed faster reaction-time latencies in recognizing a target auditory CV syllable embedded in a word when the syllable occured in word final position compared to either word-initial or word-medial position (Metz-Lutz et al., 1992).

In contrast to Broca's aphasics, who showed a strong lexical effect, Wernicke/Conduction aphasics failed to show a lexical effect (Blumstein et al., 1993). If, as proposed, the word recognition system is overactivated in Wernicke's aphasics, then non-words may fail to be quickly and efficiently inhibited as potential lexical candidates, resulting in the absence of a lexical bias effect in the perception of a VOT continuum. The failure of non-words to be inhibited by Wernicke's aphasics was shown in a study described earlier investigating whether non-words that are phonologically similar to real words show graded priming effects (Milberg et al., 1988b). It will be recalled that Wernicke's aphasics showed an equal magnitude of semantic priming for non-word primes that were phonologically similar to real words. That is, the non-words *gat* and *wat* showed an equal magnitude of priming for *dog* as did the prime word *cat*. Thus, the overactivation of the lexical system results in a failure to inhibit lexical candidates, including non-words.

9.4.2 **Influence of sentential context on word recognition**

Although both Broca's and Wernicke's aphasics evidence word recognition deficits, it appears that the functional architecture of the speech-lexical processing system is fundamentally intact. That is, the word recognition system for both groups of aphasics shows graded activation and, as well, is influenced by lexical competition. The question is whether higher-level information from sentential context influences word recognition processes as it does in neurologically intact individuals, and whether it may even serve to override the word recognition deficits shown for these patients.

Little research has been done in this area. However, a few studies have suggested that indeed aphasic patients can take advantage of higher-level information in the processes of word recognition. Metz-Lutz et al. (1992) showed that recognition of a word-final target CV syllable was faster when the word was in a sentential context than when it was presented in isolation. These results emerged for high-comprehending Broca's aphasics and for normal controls. Thus, sentence context enhanced word recognition in these patients. And Baum (2001) showed an influence of a biasing sentence context on the perception of a VOT continuum in both fluent and nonfluent aphasics. A word–word VOT continuum was constructed and the target stimulus was preceded by a sentence context. Subjects' task was to identify the initial segment of the target stimulus. The question was whether the locus of the voiced/voiceless phonetic boundary would change as a function of the biasing context. For example, subjects received a *path–bath* continuum preceded by a neutral context such as *She is not thinking of the* __ , or by a biasing context such as *She needs hot water for the*__ . The patients who were able to perform the categorization task showed sensitivity to the biasing context. In fact, Baum showed that for a number of both fluent and nonfluent aphasics, there was an overriding effect of the biasing sentence context such that the perception of the initial consonant of *all* the stimuli on the VOT continuum was consistent with the biasing context. For example, these subjects perceived all the stimuli on a *path–bath* continuum, including the exemplar [p] stimulus, as beginning with [b] in the context of *She needs hot water for the ___*. Thus, higher-level sentence information influences word recognition processes in aphasic patients.

9.5 Conclusions and future directions

This chapter has attempted to examine current knowledge about word recognition deficits in aphasia. The studies reviewed have shown a rich tapestry of impairments and spared abilities in the processes contributing to word recognition. The results of this research suggest that there is a broad neural network involved in such processing extending throughout the perisylvian areas of the left hemisphere. Of particular significance, the findings suggest that the cognitive architecture of the word recognition system is largely intact, and deficits appear to result from impairments in the dynamics of lexical activation. However, we have much more to learn.

The aphasia studies reviewed in this chapter have typically taken either a syndrome-based approach, as in the analysis of deficits in Broca's aphasics or Wernicke's aphasics, or a symptom-based approach, as in the analysis of deficits in fluent or nonfluent aphasics. In both cases there is a *range* of lesions that may give rise to a given syndrome or that give rise to a given symptom, making it difficult to generalize about the neural systems underlying a particular deficit. In fact, many studies in the aphasia literature do not systematically report or analyze the lesions of their patients, and those that report lesions typically describe them qualitatively rather than quantitatively. However, voxel-based lesion analysis techniques are now available, allowing for the same level of localization specificity as in functional neuroimaging (Rorden and Karnath, 2004; Bates et al., 2003). As a consequence, it is possible to map out quantitatively the nature and extent of a patient's lesion as a means of delineating the functional networks underlying particular deficits.

It is also the case that lesions tend to be large in residual aphasic patients, making it difficult to pinpoint exactly what focal area is responsible for the impairment. Functional neuroimaging studies have some of the same challenges. Although they provide a rich source of data about the neural areas activated in word recognition tasks, they typically show clusters of activation that encompass a range of areas not only within the left hemisphere but also within the right hemisphere and in midline structures bilaterally. As a consequence, given the activation of multiple clusters in a particular study, it is impossible to determine the *functional* role of a particular activated area or even if that area plays a *necessary* role in the performance of the task (cf. Price et al., 1999; Rorden and Karnath, 2004). However, a potential solution to this problem lies in determining whether behavioral deficits will emerge with damage to those areas of activation identified in functional neuroimaging studies with neurologically intact individuals. Such research requires that lesion studies and functional neuroimaging studies be done programmatically and in concert with each other. They need to focus on similar questions and use similar tasks and stimulus materials, so that direct comparisons and links can be made across these different methods of study.

A lesion-based approach to the study of word recognition deficits in aphasia has its strength in providing not only a means of specifying brain–behavior relations but also a window into how and in what ways the functional architecture of the word recognition system may break down. More research is needed to provide the details of this breakdown. How do activation and inhibition processes interact and intersect with each other in word recognition processes? Is it possible that Broca's aphasics do not have a deficit characterized by a reduction in lexical activation or in the time course of activation, as proposed currently, but rather a deficit in inhibitory processes, such that potential competitors are inhibited more than normal? Is the basis of the deficit for Wernicke's aphasics in overactivation of the lexicon or the processes that inhibit potential competitors? In fact, is it really the case that, as proposed, word recognition deficits in aphasic patients reside in the dynamics of lexical activation, leaving the functional architecture of the word recognition system intact? These are only a few of the questions remaining to be answered, but together they set a research agenda for future research on word recognition deficits in aphasia.

Acknowledgements

This research was supported in part by NIH Grant DC00314 to Brown University and DC0081 to the Boston University School of Medicine.

References

Allopenna, P. D., Magnuson, J. S., and Tanenhaus, M. K. (1998) Tracking the time course of spoken word recognition using eye movements: evidence for continuous mapping models. *Journal of Memory and Language*, 38: 419–39.

Andruski, J.E., Blumstein, S. E., and Burton, M. (1994) The effect of subphonetic differences on lexical access. *Cognition*, 52: 163–87.

Awh, E., Jonides, J., Smith, E., Schumacher, W., Koeppe, R., and Katz, S. (1996) Dissociation of storage and rehearsal in verbal working memory: evidence from PET. *Psychological Science*, 7: 25–31.

Baker, E., Blumstein, S.E., and Goodglass, H. (1981) Interaction between phonological and semantic factors in auditory comprehension. *Neuropsychologia*, 19: 1–16.

Basso, A., Casati, G., and Vignolo, L. (1977) Phonemic identification defects in aphasia. *Cortex*, 13: 84–95.

Bates, E., Wilson, S. M., Saygin, A. P., Dick, F., Sereno, M. I., Knight, R. T., and Dronkers, N. F. (2003) Voxel-based lesion-symptom mapping. *Nature Neuroscience*, 6: 448–50.

Baum, S. R. (1997) Phonological, semantic, and mediated priming in aphasia. *Brain and Language*, 60: 347–59.

Baum, S. R. (2001) Contextual influences on phonetic identification in aphasia: the effects of speaking rate and semantic bias. *Brain and Language*, 76: 266–81.

Belin, P., Zatorre, R. J., Hoge, R., Evans, A. C., and Pike, B. (1999). Event-related fMRI of the auditory cortex. *NeuroImage*, 10: 417–29.

Binder, J. R., and Price, C. J. (2001) Functional neuroimaging of language. In R. Cabeza and A. Kingstone (eds), *Handbook of Functional Neuroimaging*, pp.187–254. MIT Press, Cambridge, MA.

Blumstein, S. E., Baker, E., and Goodglass, H. (1977) Phonological factors in auditory comprehension in aphasia. *Neuropsychologia*, 15: 19–30.

Blumstein, S. E., Burton, M., Baum, S., Waldstein, R., and Katz, W. (1994) The role of lexical status on the phonetic categorization of speech in aphasia. *Brain and Language*, 46: 181–97.

Blumstein, S. E., Cooper, W. E., Zurif, E. B., and Caramazza, A. (1977) The perception and production of voice-onset time in aphasia. *Neuropsychologia*, 15: 371–83.

Blumstein, S. E., and Milberg, W. P. (2000) Language deficits in Broca's and Wernicke's aphasia: a singular impairment. In Y. Grodzinsky, L. Shapiro, and D. Swinney (eds), *Language and the Brain: Representations and Processing*, pp. 167–84. Academic Press, New York.

Blumstein, S. E., Milberg, W., Brown, T., Hutchinson, A., Kurowski, K., and Burton, M. (2000) The mapping from sound structure to the lexicon: evidence from rhyme and repetition priming. *Brain and Language*, 72: 75–99.

Blumstein, S. E., Milberg, W., and Shrier, R. (1982) Semantic processing in aphasia: evidence from an auditory lexical decision task. *Brain and Language*, 17: 301–15.

Blumstein, S. E., Myers, E. B., and Rissman, J. (2005) The perception of voice onset time: an fMRI investigation of phonetic category structure. *Journal of Cognitive Neuroscience*, 17: 1353–66.

Blumstein, S. E., Tartter, V. C., Nigro, G., and Statlender, S. (1984) Acoustic cues for the perception of place of articulation in aphasia. *Brain and Language*, 22: 128–49.

Boyczuk, J. P., and Baum, S. R. (1999). The influence of neighborhood density on phonetic categorization in aphasia. *Brain and Language*, 67: 46–70.

Burton, M. W. (1989) Associative, mediated, and rhyme priming: a study of lexical processing. Doctoral dissertation, Brown University.

Burton, M. W. (2001) The role of inferior frontal cortex in phonological processing. *Cognitive Science*, 25: 695–709.

Burton, M. W., Small, S. L., and Blumstein, S. E. (2000) The role of segmentation in phonological processing: an fMRI investigation. *Journal of Cognitive Neuroscience*, 12: 679–90.

Caplan, D., Gow, D., and Makris, N. (1995) Analysis of lesions by MRI in stroke patients with acoustic-phonetic processing deficits. *Neurology*, 45: 293–8.

Carpenter, R. L., and Rutherford, D. R. (1973) Acoustic cue discrimination in adult aphasia. *Journal of Speech and Hearing Research*, 16: 534–44.

Connine, C. M., Blasko, D. G., and Titone, D. A. (1993) Do the beginnings of spoken words have a special status in auditory word recognition? *Journal of Memory and Language*, 32: 193–210.

Connine, C. M., Titone, D., Dellman, T., and Blasko, D. (1997) Similarity mapping in spoken word recognition. *Journal of Memory and Language*, 37: 463–80.

Csepe, V., Osman-Sagi, J., Molnar, M., and Gosy, M. (2001) Impaired speech perception in aphasic patients: event-related potential and neuropsychological assessment. *Neurospychologia*, 39: 1194–208.

Damasio, H. (1998) Neuroanatomical correlates of the aphasias. In M. T. Sarno (ed.), *Acquired Aphasia*, pp. 43–70. Academic Press, New York.

Del Toro, J. F. (2000) An examination of automatic versus strategic semantic priming in Broca's aphasia: how controlled processing produces inhibitory semantic priming. *Brain and Language*, 55: 264–88.

Dell, G. S., Schwartz, M. F., Martin, N., Saffran, E. M., and Gagnon, D. A. (1997) Lexical access in aphasic and nonaphasic speakers. *Psychological Review*, 104: 801–38.

Demonet, J. F., Chollet, F., Ramsay, S., Cardebat, D., Nespoulous, J. L., Wise, R., Rascol, A., and Frackowiak, R. (1992) The anatomy of phonological and semantic processing in normal subjects. *Brain*, 115: 1753–68.

Demonet, J. F.C., Price, C., Wise, R., and Frackowiak, R. (1994) Differential activation of right and left sylvian regions by semantic and phonological tasks: a positron-emission tomography study in normal human subjects. *Neuroscience Letters*, 182: 25–8.

Elman, J., and McClelland, J. (1986) Exploring lawful variability in the speech waveform. In S. Perkell and D. H. Klatt (ed.), *Invariance and Variability in Speech Processing*, pp. 360–85. Erlbaum, Hillsdale, NJ.

Gandour, J., and Dardarananda, R. (1982). Voice onset time in aphasia: Thai, I: Perception. *Brain and Language*, 17: 24–33.

Gandour, J., and Dardarananda, R. (1983) Identification of tonal contrasts in Thai aphasic patients. *Brain and Language*, 17: 24–33.

Ganong, F. (1980) Phonetic categorization in auditory word recognition. *Journal of Experimental Psychology: Human Perception and Performance*, 6: 110–25.

Gaskell, M. G., and Marslen-Wilson, W. D. (1997) Integrating form and meaning: a distributed model of speech perception. *Language and Cognitive Processes*, 12: 613–56.

Gaskell, M. G. and Marslen-Wilson, W. D. (1999) Ambiguity, competition, and blending in spoken word recognition. *Cognitive Science*, 23: 439–62.

Gordon, J. K., and Baum, S. R. (1994) Rhyme priming in aphasia: the role of phonology in lexical access. *Brain and Language*, 47: 661–83.

Gow, D. W., and Caplan, D. (1996) An examination of impaired acoustic-phonetic processing in aphasia. Brain and Language, 52: 386–407.

Hagoort, P. 1993. Impairments of lexical-semantic processing in aphasia: evidence from the processing of lexical ambiguities. *Brain and Language*, 45: 189–232.

Hagoort, P. 1997. Semantic priming in Broca's aphasia: no support for an automatic access deficit. *Brain and Language*, 56: 287–300.

Hickok, G., and Poeppel, D. (2000) Towards a functional neuroanatomy of speech perception. *Trends in Cognitive Science*, 4: 131–8.

Hickok, G., and Poeppel, D. (2004) Dorsal and ventral streams: a framework for understanding aspects of the functional anatomy of language. *Cognition*, 92: 67–99.

Hillinger, M. L. (1980) Priming effects with phonemically similar words: the encoding-bias hypothesis reconsidered. *Memory and Cognition*, 8: 115–23.

Janse, E. (2006) Lexical competition effects in aphasia: deactivation of lexical candidates in spoken word processing, *Brain and Language*, 97: 1–11.

Jauhiainen, T., and Nuutila, A. (1977) Auditory perception of speech and speech sounds in recent and recovered aphasia. *Brain and Language*, 4: 572–9.

Jonides, J., Schumacher, E. H., Smith, E. E., et al. (1998) The role of parietal cortex in verbal working memory. *Journal of Neuroscience*, 18: 5026–34.

Leeper, H. A. Jr., Shewan, C., and Booth, J. C. (1986) Altered acoustic cue discrimination in Broca's and Conduction aphasics. *Journal of Communication Disorders*, 19: 83–103.

Levelt, W. J. M. (1992) Accessing words in speech production: stages, processes, and representations. *Cognition*, 42: 1–22.

Levelt, W. J. M., Roelofs, A., and Meyer, A. S. (1999) A theory of lexical access in speech production. *Behavioral and Brain Sciences*, 22: 1–75.

Marslen-Wilson, W. (1987) Functional parallelism in spoken word-recognition. *Cognition*, 25: 71–102.

Marslen-Wilson, W., and Welsh, A. (1978) Processing interactions and lexical access during word recognition in continuous speech. *Cognitive Psychology*, 10: 29–63.

McClelland, J. L. (1979) On the time relations of mental processes: an examination of systems of processes in cascade. *Psychological Review*, 86: 287–330.

McClelland, J. L., and Elman, J. (1986) The TRACE model of speech perception. *Cognitive Psychology*, 18: 1–86.

McClelland, J. L., and Rumelhart, D. 1986. *Parallel Distributed Processing*, vol. 2: *Psychological and Biological Models*. MIT Press, Cambridge, MA.

McMurray, B., Tanenhaus, M. K., and Aslin, R. N. (2002) Gradient effects of within-category phonetic variation on lexical access. *Cognition*, 86: B33–B42.

McNellis, M. G., and Blumstein, S. E. (2001) Self-organizing dynamics of lexical access in normals and aphasics. *Journal of Cognitive Neuroscience*, 13: 151–70.

Metz-Lutz, M.-N., Wioland, F., and Brock, G. (1992) A real time approach to spoken language processing in aphasia. *Brain and Language*, 43: 565–82.

Miceli, G., Caltagirone, C., Gainotti, G., and Payer-Rigo, P. (1978) Discrimination of voice versus place contrasts in aphasia. *Brain and Language*, 2: 434–50.

Miceli, G., Gainotti, G., Caltagirone, C., and Masullo, C. (1980) Some aspects of phonological impairment in aphasia. *Brain and Language*, 11: 159–69.

Milberg, W., and Blumstein, S. E. (1981) Lexical decision and aphasia: evidence for semantic processing. *Brain and Language*, 14: 371–85.

Milberg, W., Blumstein, S., and Dworetzky, B. 1988a. Phonological factors in lexical access: evidence from an auditory lexical decision task. *Bulletin of the Psychonomic Society*, 26: 305–8.

Milberg, W., Blumstein, S., and Dworetzky, B. (1988b) Phonological processing and lexical access in aphasia. *Brain and Language*, 34: 279–93.

Misiurski, C., Blumstein, S. E., Rissman, J., and Berman, D. (2005) The role of lexical competition and acoustic-phonetic structure in lexical processing: evidence from normal subjects and aphasic patients. *Brain and Language*, 93: 64–78.

Monsell, S., and Hirsch, K. W. (1998) Competitor priming in spoken word recognition. *Journal of Experimental Psychology: Learning, Memory, and Cognition*, 24: 1495–520.

Naeser, M. A., and Chan, S. W.-C. (1980) Case study of a Chinese aphasic with the Boston Diagnostic Aphasia Examination. *Neuropsychologia*, 18: 389–410.

Norris, D. (1994) Shortlist: a connectionist model of continuous speech recognition. *Cognition*, 52: 189–234.

Paulesu, E., Frith, C. D., and Frackowiak, R. S. J. (1993) The neural correlates of the verbal component of working memory. *Nature*, 362: 342–5.

Peterson, R. R., and Savoy, P. (1998) Lexical selection and phonological encoding during language production: evidence for cascaded processing. *Journal of Experimental Psychology: Learning, Memory, and Cognition*, 24: 539–57.

Plaut, D. (1995) Semantic and associative priming in a distributed attractor network. *Proceedings of the 17th Annual Conference of the Cognitive Science Society*, 37–42.

Poeppel, D. (1996) A critical review of PET studies of phonological processing. *Brain and Language*, 55: 317–51.

Prather, P., Shapiro, L., Zurif, E. B., and Swinney, D. (1991) Real-time examinations of lexical processing in aphasic patients. *Journal of Psycholinguistic Research*, 20: 271–81.

Prather, P. A., Zurif, E., Love, T., and Brownell, H. (1997) Speed of lexical activation in nonfluent Broca's aphasia and fluent Wernicke's aphasia. *Brain and Language*, 59: 391–411.

Price, C. J., Mummery, C., Moore, C. J., Frackowiak, J. C., and Friston, K. J. (1999) Delineating necessary and sufficient neural systems with functional imaging of studies with neuropsychological patients. *Journal of Cognitive Neuroscience*, 11: 371–82.

Price, C., Wise, R., Ramsey, S., Friston, K., Howard, D., and Patterson, K. (1992) Regional response differences within the human auditory cortex when listening to words. *Neuroscience Letters*, 146: 179–82.

Rapp, B., and Goldrick, M. (2000) Discreteness and interactivity in spoken word production. *Psychological Review*, 107: 460–99.

Rorden, C., and Karnath, H.-K. (2004) Using human brain lesions to infer function: a relic from a past era in the fMRI age. *Nature Reviews Neuroscience*, 5: 813–19.

Sasanuma, S., Tatsumi, I. F., and Fujisaki, H. (1976) Discrimination of phonemes and word accent types in Japanese aphasic patients. *XVIth International Congress of Logopedics and Phoniatrics*, 403–8.

Schacter, D. L., and Church, B. A. (1992) Auditory priming: implicit and explicit memory for words and voices. *Journal of Experimental Psychology: Learning, Memory, and Cognition*, 18: 915–30.

Scott, S. K., and Johnsrude, I. S. (2003) The neuroanatomical and functional organization of speech perception. *Trends in Neuroscience*, 26: 100–7.

Scott, S. K., and Wise, R. J. S. (2004) The functional neuroanatomy of prelexical processing in speech perception. *Cognition*, 92: 13–45.

Slowiaczek, L. M., and Hamburger, M. (1992) Prelexical facilitation and lexical interference in auditory word recognition. *Journal of Experimental Psychology: Learning, Memory, and Cognition*, 13: 64–75.

Slowiaczek, L. M., and Pisoni, D. B. (1986) Effects of phonological similarity on priming in auditory lexical decision. *Memory and Cognition*, 14: 230–7.

Swinney, D., Prather, P., and Love, T. (2000) The time-course of lexical access and the role of context: converging evidence from normal and aphasic processing. In Y. Grodzinsky, L. Shapiro, and D. Swinney (eds), *Language and the Brain: Representations and Processing*, pp. 273–92. Academic Press, New York.

Swinney, D., Zurif, E., and Prather, P. (1989) The effects of focal brain damage on sentence processing: an examination of the neurological organization of a mental module. *Journal of Cognitive Neuroscience*, 1: 25–37.

Tanenhaus, M. K., Spivey-Knowlton, M. J., Eberhard, K. M., and Sedivy, J. C. (1995) Integration of visual and linguistic information in spoken language comprehension. *Science*, 268: 632–4.

Thompson-Schill, S. L., D'Esposito, M., Aguirre G. K., and Farah M. J. (1997) Role of the left inferior prefrontal cortex in retrieval of semantic knowledge: a reevaluation. *Proceedings of the National Academy of Sciences*, 94: 14792–7.

Thompson-Schill, S. L., D'Esposito, M., and Kan, I. P. (1999) Effects of repetition and competition on activation in left prefrontal cortex during word generation. *Neuron*, 23: 513–22.

Thompson-Schill, S. L., Swick, D., Farah, M.J., D'Esposito, M., Kan, I. P., and Knight R. T. (1998) Verb generation in patients with focal frontal lesions: a neuropsychological test of neuroimaging findings. *Proceedings of the National Academy of Sciences, USA*, 95: 15855–60.

Tyler, L. K. (1992) *Spoken Language Comprehension*, pp. 77–84. MIT, Cambridge, MA.

Utman, J. A. (1997) Effects of subphonetic acoustic differences in lexical access in neurologically intact adults and patients with Broca's aphasia. Doctoral dissertation, Brown University.

Utman, J. A., Blumstein, S. E., and Sullivan, K. (2001) Mapping from sound to meaning: reduced lexical activation in Broca's aphasics, *Brain and Language*, 79: 444–72.

Yee, E. (2005) The time course of lexical activation during spoken word recognition: evidence from unimpaired and aphasic individuals. Doctoral dissertation, Brown University.

Yee, E., Blumstein, S. E., and Sedivy, J. (2004) The time course of lexical activation in Broca's and Wernicke's aphasia: evidence from eye movements. *Program for the 42nd Annual Meeting of the Academy of Aphasia. Brain and Language*, 91: 62–3.

Yee, E., Blumstein, S. E., and Sedivy, J. (forthcoming) Lexical activation in Broca's and Wernicke's aphasia: an eye movement study.

Yee, E., and Sedivy, J. (2006) Eye movements to pictures reveal transient semantic activation during spoken word recognition. *Journal of Experimental Psychology: Learning, Memory and Cognition*, 32: 1–14.

Yeni-Komshian, G., and LaFontaine, L. (1983) Discrimination and identification of voicing and place contrasts in aphasic patients. *Canadian Journal of Psychology*, 37: 107–31.

Zatorre, R. J., Evans, A. C., Meyer, E., and Gjedde, A. (1992) Lateralization of phonetic and pitch discrimination in speech processing. *Science*, 256: 846–9.

Zatorre, R., Meyer, E., Gjedde, A., and Evans, A. (1996) PET studies of phonetic processing of speech: Review, replication, and reanalysis. *Cerebral Cortex*, 6: 21–30.

SECTION II

The mental lexicon

CHAPTER 10

Representation and processing of lexically ambiguous words

Stephen J. Lupker

> John and Pat looked over at their friend Bob. Both of them sighed. John turned to Pat and said, "You know, Bob could use a belt."

Readers of this passage are confronted with a basic problem common not only in English but also in many other languages. Words are inherently ambiguous in that most have multiple legitimate meanings. What does Bob actually need here, something to hold his pants up? A good smack? A stiff drink? Or, perhaps Bob is a down-on-his-luck developer who could get back on his feet if he could just get his hands on a patch of undeveloped land. In the end, context will help readers determine which of these things Bob's friends think he needs. Without context, however, one, some or all of these possible meanings may have been activated and considered by readers. It is that process, the process by which readers (and listeners) activate meanings and, ultimately, resolve ambiguities that is the topic of the present chapter.

Much of the work on this topic, particularly prior to 1990, was directed at the questions of: (1) whether all meanings of an ambiguous word were initially activated even if context favored only one (Glucksberg et al., 1986; Onifer and Swinney, 1981; Simpson, 1981; Swinney, 1979; Seidenberg et al., 1982; Tabossi, 1988; Tabossi et al., 1987; Tanenhaus et al., 1979); and (2) whenever more than one meaning was activated, whether the dominant meaning was activated more rapidly (Hogaboam and Perfetti, 1975; Simpson, 1981; Simpson and Burgess, 1985; Swinney, 1979). Much of this work involved priming paradigms. Essentially, ambiguous words were presented in sentences with or without preceding, disambiguating context. Latencies to respond to words related to one or the other meaning of the ambiguous word were then evaluated.

Some of these studies are reviewed at the end of the chapter. The main focus of the chapter, however, is the impact of ambiguity on word processing out of context, mostly in single word presentation tasks. These tasks should give us the best chance of uncovering the basic principles underlying how these words are represented in memory and how that memory representation is accessed. (See also Rastle, Chapter 5 this volume, for a discussion of the word recognition literature based on these types of experiments.) A discussion of the key phenomenon is followed by a discussion of attempts to model that phenomenon based on some possible ways that ambiguous words might be represented in memory. Next, more recent attempts to distinguish between different types of ambiguous words are discussed and what that research might have to say about the representation question. Finally, we examine a prediction of all current models by considering data from other, neutral-context tasks before turning to the question of the impact of context.

10.1 The ambiguity advantage

10.1.1 Rubenstein and colleagues

Intuitively, the expectation most people have is that ambiguous words, like *belt*, would be harder to process than unambiguous words. Indeed, most models of the process implicitly or explicitly make exactly that prediction. The story, however, is more complicated. Ambiguity can also have benefits depending on what the reader is attempting to do with the word.

Rubenstein et al. (1970) appear to have been the first researchers to compare the processing of ambiguous vs. unambiguous words (or, in their terms, homographs vs. non-homographs). The homographic status of each word was derived from a subjective rating procedure carried out by twenty independent raters. The experimental task was a lexical decision task. The results were straightforward: lexical decisions were faster to ambiguous words than to unambiguous words matched on frequency and concreteness. Subsequently, Rubenstein et al. (1971) reported that this ambiguity advantage was essentially restricted to those ambiguous words that had two, unrelated, equiprobable meanings. That is, ambiguous words like *glue*, which means both "a strong adhesive substance" and "to cause to stick tightly with glue," showed much less of an advantage.

The explanation these authors offered was based on the idea that ambiguous words have more lexical entries (essentially one for each distinct, known meaning) than unambiguous words. According to Rubenstein and colleagues, the identification of a word involves a search of lexical memory. That search is essentially random; however, it involves only those words that have some orthographic resemblance to the presented word. Because ambiguous words have more lexical entries, the chance of discovering one of these entries early in processing is heightened. As a result, word identification is more rapid.

10.1.2 Clark's (1973) response

These results did not, of course, go unchallenged. The most influential challenge was offered by Clark (1973). Clark's now well-known argument is that in order to be able to generalize results from experiments contrasting two sets of stimuli (e.g. ambiguous words and unambiguous words) one has to carry out an analysis in which inter-item variability is considered. In Clark's original paper, his recommended analysis was a quasi-F (F') procedure in which the error terms in ANOVAs involved both subject and item variability. When Clark applied this technique to Rubenstein and colleagues' data, their ambiguity advantages became non-significant.

Although Clark's (1973) approach has received considerable criticism (Cohen, 1976; Keppel, 1976; Raaijmakers et al., 1999; Smith, 1976; Wike and Church, 1976), using item variability when analyzing data from language experiments is now common practice. More importantly, Clark's analysis reopened the question of the existence of an ambiguity advantage. Papers published soon thereafter did nothing to remedy the problem. Forster and Bednall (1976) found small and non-significant ambiguity effects with both equiprobable and unequiprobable ambiguous words ("balanced" and "unbalanced" respectively). (Categorization of words into the various conditions was again done by subject ratings.) In contrast, Jastrzembski and Stanners (1975) and Jastrzembski (1981), using meaning counts from dictionaries to determine ambiguity, did observe an ambiguity advantage in a series of experiments, even using Clark's very conservative F' procedure.

10.1.3 Gernsbacher's (1984) challenge

The story, however, took another twist when Gernsbacher (1984) argued convincingly that using meaning counts from dictionaries is not a good way to determine the number of meanings a word has. Using *gauge*, *cadet*, and *fudge* as examples, she noted that the former actually has thirty dictionary definitions while the others each have fifteen. In her informal survey of college professors, she discovered that they could "on average provide only 3 definitions of the word *fudge*, 2 of the word *gauge*, and 1 of the word *cadet*" (p. 272). In general, it's clear that the match between dictionary definitions and what people actually know about a word isn't very good. More importantly for her purposes, she also noted that in none of the previous demonstrations of an ambiguity advantage had the researchers equated their stimuli on "experiential familiarity," a variable that she had demonstrated to be very important in lexical decision tasks. (See Gernsbacher, 1984 for a discussion of the experiential familiarity concept.) Using stimuli in which rated experiential familiarity was controlled, Gernsbacher found no evidence of an ambiguity advantage.

10.1.4 Firmly establishing the effect

Gernsbacher's (1984) arguments caused Millis and Button (1989) to re-evaluate the issue. Recognizing that people's knowledge about words' meanings is often different than what is contained in dictionaries, they created three different subjective ratings of the number of available meanings. The first involved having subjects record the first meaning that came to mind when reading a word (essentially, the procedure of Rubenstein et al., 1970). The second involved having subjects record all the meanings that came to mind when reading a word and counting the total number of meanings across all subjects. The third also involved having subjects record all meanings that came to mind when reading a word, but what was counted was the average number of meanings generated per subject. Few-meaning and multiple-meaning words were selected using each of these measures (equating word sets on experiential familiarity). Lexical decision results showed an ambiguity advantage when ambiguity was defined using either the second or third measure and a large (87 ms) but non-significant advantage using the first measure (using Clark's 1973 F′ procedure).

Although Millis and Button (1989) failed to replicate Gernsbacher's (1984) null effect, their results do underline one of Gernsbacher's main points. Word properties should be measured by determining how those properties are actually represented in subjects' minds. Since Millis and Button's paper most researchers have done exactly that, and the existence of the ambiguity advantage is now reasonably well documented. For example, Kellas et al. (1988) demonstrated an ambiguity advantage in two lexical decision experiments when familiarity was controlled and ambiguity was measured by using a procedure those authors developed. In this procedure, subjects are asked to rate words as to whether they have no meaning (0), one meaning (1), or more than one meaning (2). Hino and Lupker (1996), using Kellas et al.'s procedure to select stimuli, showed an ambiguity advantage for both high- and low-frequency words in lexical decision tasks and for low-frequency words in naming tasks. Borowsky and Masson (1996) also observed an ambiguity advantage in lexical decision when using Kellas et al.'s procedure, although they didn't observe an advantage in their naming task. Nonetheless, ambiguity advantages in naming have been reported by Gottlob et al. (1999), Hino et al. (1998a), Hino et al. (1998b), Lichacz et al. (1999), and Rodd (2004).

Rodd's (2004) data provide a likely explanation for the difference between Borowsky and Masson's (1996) results and those reported elsewhere. Rodd showed that the effect size grows as function of the difficulty of the words being named (i.e. the effect existed for exception words but not for easy-to-name regular words). Certainly, Borowsky and Masson's words were short, typically regular, and produced mean naming latencies between 494 and 508 ms, suggesting that any ambiguity advantage would have been quite small for those stimuli. This analysis is also consistent with Hino and Lupker's (1996) observation that, in naming, there was no ambiguity advantage for high frequency words.

10.2 **Explaining the ambiguity advantage**

10.2.1 **Models based on multiple lexical units**

The first attempt to explain the ambiguity advantage in lexical decision was Rubenstein et al.'s (1970) search model. Because Rubenstein et al. did not observe an interaction between frequency and ambiguity, they proposed that the two variables affected separate processing stages. Frequency affected the "marking" process, the process by which lexical units were designated for further evaluation. The higher a word's frequency the sooner it gets marked and enters the set of words available for evaluation. The ambiguity effect, in contrast, emerged because, as noted earlier, each meaning of a word has a separate lexical entry. Thus, on average, the random search through the marked entries would locate one of the multiple lexical entries for an ambiguous word more rapidly than the single lexical entry for an unambiguous word.

No computational version of this model was, of course, created and, hence, it is not entirely clear that the model actually does explain Rubenstein et al.'s (1970) results. For example, if each meaning of an ambiguous word has a separate lexical entry, the frequency values of those lexical entries would, presumably, represent the frequency with which that particular meaning had been previously activated. These frequency values would be less than the frequency value of a matched unambiguous word because that word's single meaning would have been activated every time the word was processed. As such, it is more likely that an unambiguous word would be entered into the marked set early in processing. If so, the result would be an ambiguity disadvantage rather than an ambiguity advantage.

The second attempt to explain the ambiguity advantage was proposed by Jastrzembski (1981), who did observe an interaction between frequency and ambiguity. Jastrzembski's account was an activation account based on Morton's (1969) logogen model. According to this model, each word in a reader's lexicon is represented by a logogen. In reading, word identification occurs when the activation of its logogen reaches a threshold value. The activation threshold for each logogen is a function of the word's frequency: higher-frequency words have lower thresholds and hence reach threshold more rapidly. Jastrzembski's idea, like Rubenstein et al.'s (1970), was that ambiguous words have multiple entries (i.e. multiple logogens). Hence, the chance of one of them reaching threshold early would be higher than the chance of the single logogen of an unambiguous word reaching threshold early.

Again, no computational version of the model was available, and thus it is not entirely clear that it does explain Jastrzembski's (1981) results. The problem is the same as with Rubenstein et al.'s model. The separate multiple logogens for each meaning of an ambiguous word would, presumably, have threshold values appropriate to the frequency of that particular meaning. So the thresholds for all logogens of an ambiguous word would be higher than the single threshold for the logogen of a frequency-matched unambiguous word. If so, it seems unlikely that an ambiguity advantage would emerge.

Forster and Bednall's (1976) results provide an additional problem for these types of account. Forster and Bednall asked subjects to decide whether a word had multiple meanings or not. They found that "yes" responses to ambiguous words were faster than "no" responses to unambiguous words, presumably due to the fact that exhaustive searches were necessary in order to be able to say "no" to unambiguous words. What they didn't find was the expected difference between ambiguous words with balanced and unbalanced meanings. Presumably, in order to respond "yes" readers must find both meanings (in a search context) or have both meanings activated over threshold (in an activation context). Thus, the frequency of the less probable meaning should determine response latency. Words with unbalanced meanings should, therefore, suffer in contrast to words with balanced meanings. For high-frequency words there was no difference between the two ambiguous words types. For low-frequency words, the words with unbalanced meanings showed a nonsignificant 37 ms advantage.

10.2.2 Models based on distributed representations

To this point, the models discussed have all been "localist" models. The term "localist" in this context refers to the assumption that a unit in memory represents a full meaning. More recently, localist models have become less popular and there has been an explosion of models based on distributed representations. According to these types of models, meanings are represented as a pattern of activation across a set of meaning units. Similarly, a word's orthography is represented as pattern of activation across a set of orthographic units and a word's phonology is represented as a pattern of activation across a set of phonological units. These units are interconnected and, through a learning process, the connections come to be weighted in a way that reflects the appropriate relationships among the units.

When a word is visually presented, a set of orthographic units is initially activated. This activation then spreads to semantic units through the weighted connections. Most importantly, the degree to which the connection weights come to represent those connections is a function of the consistency of the connections. That is, a set of orthographic units that always activates a specific set of semantic units will produce strong connections among those units (i.e. having 1:1 "feedforward" connections from orthography to meaning builds strong connections). Ambiguous words do not facilitate the development of strong connections because ambiguous words, by necessity, activate different semantic units (i.e. meanings) in different situations (i.e. 1:many "feedforward" connections are weaker). As a result, the general expectation derived from a model with this type of architecture is that meaning activation for ambiguous words will be slower and more error-prone than that for ambiguous words.

10.2.3 The problem for distributed representation models

Joordens and Besner (1994) provided one of the first investigations of this issue using Masson's (1991) parallel distributed processing (PDP) model of semantic memory. Their simulation results showed that, typically, this model was unsuccessful in activating a semantic pattern appropriate to any single meaning, instead activating and ultimately settling into a "blend state," a combination of the semantics from the two meanings. When the simulations were successful (e.g. typically when the two meanings of the ambiguous word had quite different frequencies), there was no ambiguity effect. Joordens and Besner also reported that when Hinton and Shallice's (1991) model was examined, performance was actually noticeably better for unambiguous words than for ambiguous words (in terms of error scores).

Kawamoto (1993) and Kawamoto et al. (1994) reported similar results using their PDP model. That is, the time (i.e. the number of processing cycles) taken to activate an appropriate semantic code was longer and the settling process was more error-prone for ambiguous words than for unambiguous words. Similarly, Borowsky and Masson (1996), using Masson's (1995) model, reported that full semantic activation was slower and more error-prone for ambiguous words than for unambiguous words.

10.2.4 The solutions for distributed representation models

In order to explain the ambiguity advantage, both Kawamoto et al. (1994) and Borowsky and Masson (1996) assumed that lexical decision-making is not based on the time to activate the appropriate semantic codes (see also Besner and Joordens, 1995, Masson and Borowsky, 1995; Piercey and Joordens, 2000; Rueckl, 1995). Kawamoto et al. assumed that lexical decisions were made on the basis of orthographic activity. They also noted that when their semantic system was trained in a particular way (i.e. using the "least mean square" (LMS) error-correction algorithm rather than the Hebbian learning algorithm), the model could account for the ambiguity advantage. The reason was that when using the LMS algorithm, the orthographic-semantic inconsistencies for ambiguous words caused the connections in the orthographic system to become stronger (essentially making up for the weak orthographic-semantic connections). Thus, processing at the orthographic level was better for ambiguous words than for unambiguous words. (A similar argument could be applied to the phonological connections, allowing the model to explain the ambiguity advantage reported by Hino and Lupker (1996), Lichacz et al. (1999), and Rodd (2004) in the naming task.)

A slightly different account was offered by Borowsky and Masson (1996). These authors suggested that lexical decision-making was based on computing the sum of energy at the orthographic and semantic levels. When that sum reached a criterion value, a positive decision could be made. Indeed, ambiguous words, due to the semantic activation they produce, do reach this criterion faster in their model, allowing it to predict an ambiguity advantage. Note, however, the model does not predict an ambiguity advantage in naming (i.e. phonological units are activated at the same rate for both ambiguous and unambiguous words). This is intentional. As noted, Borowsky and Masson did not observe an ambiguity advantage in naming. Thus, various parameters of the model (i.e. those reflecting the phonological-semantic linkages) were set so that the model would not produce an effect. In fact, before doing this, the model tended to predict an ambiguity disadvantage in naming. Reducing the weightings on these parameters nullified this disadvantage. It is not impossible that further reductions would allow the model to explain the ambiguity advantage in naming observed by Hino and Lupker (1996), Lichacz et al. (1999), and Rodd (2004).

Our work in this area (Hino and Lupker, 1996; Hino et al., 2002; Hino et al., 2006; Pexman et al., 2004; Pexman and Lupker, 1999) has produced a third account of the ambiguity advantage, what we call the "feedback account." The framework we have used is a PDP framework, although the principles could also be applied to localist frameworks like Coltheart et al.'s (2001) dual-route model. The main requirement is that the system be highly interactive. The idea is that once an orthographic representation starts to become active, semantic activation (and phonological activation) follows rapidly. This semantic activation then feeds back to the orthographic level (and forward to the phonological level) to help stabilize the activity there. Because ambiguous words, by definition, have multiple meanings, on average they would have more substantial semantic representations. Thus, the semantic feedback (and feedforward) activation they provide will be stronger than that from unambiguous words, allowing the orthographic and phonological activation for ambiguous words to stabilize more rapidly. Under the assumption that orthographic activation drives performance in the lexical decision task while phonological activation drives performance in the naming task, the prediction is an ambiguity advantage in both tasks.

Although there is as yet no implemented version of the model, the general principle that feedback plays a major role in word recognition (see Balota et al., 1991) does have considerable support. For example, the principle provides a ready explanation of the homophone disadvantage in lexical decision (e.g. Pexman et al., 2001), the synonym disadvantage in lexical decision (Hino et al., 2002; Pecher, 2001), and the lexical decision and naming advantages for words with larger numbers of features (Pexman et al., 2002). Thus, at present, of all the accounts mentioned above, the feedback account appears to be the most successful.

10.3 A reconsideration of the concept of ambiguity

10.3.1 The meaning/sense distinction

In the above discussion the concept of ambiguity has been regarded as unidimensional. Words have some number of alternative meanings, and readers need to pick the right meaning in order to understand the writer's story. In the linguistics literature, however, the concept of ambiguity is considered to be more complicated (e.g. Caramazza and Grober, 1976; Nunberg, 1979; Tuggy, 1993). In particular, a clear distinction is made between words that are homonyms, i.e. words that have multiple unrelated meanings, and words that are polysemous, i.e. words with multiple senses based on the same original meaning. Homonyms are essentially accidents of history. *Bank*, the classic example of an ambiguous word, is a homonym. The fact that it means a place to keep your money and the side of a river is a result of two independent contributions to the English language (probably Germanic and Scandinavian, respectively). *Roll*, on the other hand, is polysemous. The fact that it means a list of names, any of various food preparations rolled up for cooking or serving, a flight maneuver, a heavy reverberatory sound, etc. is not an accident. Each of these senses is derived from the core meaning of the word *roll*.

The idea is that because the multiple senses of polysemous words are derived from the same core meaning, the representation of the different senses in semantic memory should be somewhat intertwined (e.g. they will share features). The same is not true for homonyms, which should have two (or more) distinct representations in semantic memory. As a result, the two types of ambiguous words may have different processing implications. In particular, from a PDP perspective, polysemous words would be less likely to cause the blend state problem that seems to occur when words with two distinct meanings are processed (Joordens and Besner, 1994). One could even hypothesize that researchers who found an ambiguity advantage may have done so because they tended to use polysemous words as their ambiguous words, while the failures to find an ambiguity advantage could be attributed to the use of homonyms.

10.3.2 Processing implications? Klein and Murphy (2001; 2002)

The question of whether this linguistic distinction is psychologically real is, of course, a crucial one. To many, the distinction between *bank* and *roll* noted above seems rather artificial. Most of the meanings/senses listed for both words seem to represent quite different meanings. In fact, readers are encouraged to reconsider the example at the beginning of this chapter. Is *belt* a homonym or a polysemous word? The answer is provided near the end of this section of the chapter.

One attempt to directly assess the psychological reality of this distinction was provided by Klein and Murphy (2001; 2002). The main task Klein and Murphy (2001) used was a "sensicality judgment task." Word pairs (e.g. *daily paper*, *yellow lecture*) were presented and subjects had to decide whether the word combination made sense. The key manipulation involved sequential trials in which the second word was repeated (e.g. *daily paper – wrapping paper*). On half of these trials, the first word in the two pairs evoked the same sense of the second word (e.g. *daily paper – liberal paper*). On the other half, it evoked a different sense (e.g. *wrapping paper – liberal paper*). The idea was that if all the senses of a concept are stored together in memory, both *daily paper* and *wrapping paper* should activate the semantic information necessary to process *liberal paper* effectively. If the senses of *paper* were stored separately, however, pairs evoking the same sense would be much more effective "primes." Across a number of experiments, Klein and Murphy (2001) found a large advantage for same-sense primes. In fact, the advantages for same-sense primes were essentially the same size as the advantage for same meaning primes when homonyms were used (e.g. *commercial bank – savings bank* vs. *creek bank – savings bank*). They concluded "the main empirical result is the finding that different senses have little functional overlap—about the same as the unrelated meanings of homonyms" (p. 277).

Klein and Murphy (2002) reached a similar conclusion based on results in a similarity judgement task. In this task, subjects were asked to judge which of two two-word phrases was most similar to a target phrase (e.g. *daily paper*). One phrase used the same second word as the target phrase but had a first word that evoked a different sense for the second word (e.g. *shredded paper*). The other phrase did not repeat words; however, the phrase was related to the concept in the target phrase either taxonomically (e.g. *evening news*) or thematically (e.g. *smart editor*). Subjects rarely chose second phrases that shared a word with the target phrase (<20 percent of the time). In fact, they only chose the second phrase which shared the target word slightly more often in the polysemous word condition than in the homonym condition (e.g. target: *national bank*, options: *river bank* and *checking account*). Klein and Murphy concluded that "different senses of a word are probably related but are not generally similar" (p. 566). In essence, what Klein and Murphy's (2001; 2002) research suggests is that the different senses of a word are represented much more distinctly in memory than one might have imagined.

10.3.3 **Processing implications? Azuma and Van Orden (1997)**

In spite of Klein and Murphy's (2001; 2002) findings, it seems reasonable that there could be at least some processing differences for polysemous words vs. homonyms, or at least for ambiguous words with related vs. unrelated meanings. Azuma and Van Orden (1997) appear to have provided the first specific examination of this question as it relates to the ambiguity advantage in the lexical decision task. In their experiments, Azuma and Van Orden factorially manipulated number of meanings and the relatedness of those meanings. Following Gernsbacher's (1984) arguments that the best way to know what's going on in a subject's mind is to ask, Azuma and Van Orden obtained number-of-meaning and relatedness-of-meaning measures by asking subjects to rate words on both dimensions. To determine the number of meanings, they used Millis and Button's (1989) total meanings metric. In this procedure, subjects write down all the meanings that they can think of for each word. Each meaning is compared against a dictionary definition and a count is made of how many of the dictionary meanings are listed by at least one subject. To determine the relatedness of meanings, they selected each word's dominant meaning and asked subjects to rate how strongly it was related to each of the subordinate meanings (on a seven-point scale). They then calculated the average of these ratings.

Using standard non-words (i.e. the type used in virtually every other experiment investigating these issues in the prior literature. e.g. *prane*) in their lexical decision task, Azuma and Van Orden got a non-significant 8 ms number-of-meanings effect and no hint of a relatedness effect. Using pseudo-homophones (non-words that, when pronounced, sound like words, e.g. *brane*), however, they got a large interaction. The few-meanings, low-relatedness words had much slower latencies than the other three word types, which had equivalent latencies. A second lexical decision experiment, using a new set of words and pseudo-homophones as non-words, produced a similar interaction.

Interpreting the slower latency in the few-meanings, low-relatedness condition in terms of either of the two experimental factors is somewhat difficult. One could interpret this result as implying that when the relatedness of the various meanings is low, having multiple meanings is quite beneficial (the standard ambiguity advantage). Only when there is strong relatedness is there no ambiguity advantage. Alternatively, one could interpret this result as meaning that there is a relatedness effect when the number of meanings is low but not when the number of meanings is high. (In Experiment 1, a multiple regression analysis suggested that the number-of-meanings effect was slightly stronger than the relatedness effect. In Experiment 2, a similar analysis suggested exactly the opposite.) Azuma and Van Orden (1997) chose to interpret the result as showing a relatedness effect but no number-of-meanings effect. That is, they felt that the way they measured relatedness (ratings of how related each subordinate meaning is to the dominant meaning) did not adequately capture the relatedness among meanings of multiple-meaning words (because the relatedness among subordinate meanings was not considered). Thus, the data from the few-meanings conditions, showing a relatedness advantage, should be taken more seriously than the data from the multiple-meanings condition.

Following Azuma and Van Orden's (1997) logic and only considering the data from the few-meanings conditions creates an obvious problem. There is no way to evaluate the ambiguity (i.e. number-of-meanings) effect. That is, there is no comparison available to determine whether multiple-meaning words are easier to process than few-meaning words. However, the paper does raise two important points. First, relatedness of meanings might be important in lexical decision even if it is not in Klein and Murphy's (2001; 2002) tasks. Second, the nature of the non-words used may be important. Indeed, using consonant strings (e.g. *prvnt*) as non-words inevitably reduces overall latencies and shrinks the size of virtually any effect (Borowsky and Masson, 1996; Stone and Van Orden, 1993). Not surprisingly, when the discrimination is easy there is little time for variables that normally affect processing to show an impact. In contrast, when pseudo-homophones are used, latencies are longer, and often the impact of variables increases. Indeed, Pexman and Lupker (1999) demonstrated this to be the case for the ambiguity advantage.

Azuma and Van Orden (1997) suggested, however, that pseudo-homophones do more than simply make the task more difficult. Supposedly, they also get subjects to attend more to semantic information which can, potentially, provide a better window on the nature of semantic representations. Thus, the argument is that the interaction showed up in Azuma and Van Orden's pseudo-homophone condition not because the task was more difficult, but because the qualitative nature of the process of distinguishing between words and non-words changed. Speaking against this argument, however, is the fact that non-semantic effects also grow in the presence of pseudo-homophones. For example, the homophone effect (low-frequency homophones like *maid* have longer latencies than non-homophonic control words) also grows when pseudo-homophones are used as non-words (Pexman and Lupker, 1999; Pexman et al., 2001). Thus, whether pseudo-homophones do cause subjects to recruit more semantic information or not, that clearly is not the only thing they do.

10.3.4 **Processing implications? Rodd et al. (2002)**

Working on the principles postulated by Azuma and Van Orden (1997), Rodd et al. (2002) took the argument one step further. They postulated that it is only the "senses" of a word that produce the ambiguity advantage. In line with what PDP models typically predict, they further proposed that multiple unrelated meanings actually cause difficulty for activating the appropriate semantic information, and hence inhibit lexical decision-making.

Rodd et al. (2002) used the Wordsmyth dictionary, rather than subjective ratings, to determine both how many unrelated meanings and how many senses each of their words had. In their Experiment 2, they factorially manipulated the number of meanings (one or two) and number of senses (few or many—summed over both meanings for two-meaning words) while using pseudo-homophones as their non-words. Rodd et al. observed a significant 14 ms number-of-senses advantage and a non-significant 6 ms number-of-meanings disadvantage. Based on these results, they claimed that number of senses is the key to the ambiguity advantage and that multiple meanings do cause the types of problem predicted by PDP models. (More recently, Beretta et al., 2005, using Rodd et al.'s stimuli, have reported a number-of-meanings disadvantage (16 ms) that was significant over subjects although not over items.)

In their Experiment 3, Rodd et al. used most of the same words in an auditory lexical decision task. In this task, both main effects were now significant and essentially equivalent in size. The most interesting (and novel) aspect of these results is, of course, the significant ambiguity disadvantage. Although there have been failures to replicate the ambiguity advantage in the literature (e.g. Forster and Bednall, 1976; Gernsbacher, 1984), there seems to be no result even hinting at an ambiguity disadvantage in the lexical decision task. What must be kept in mind, however, is that the auditory lexical decision task is somewhat novel in the word recognition literature. At this point in time, it is less than clear whether the processes involved in making auditory vs. visual lexical decisions are similar or not.

This concern emerges more clearly when one reconsiders the issue of the type of non-words used in these tasks. As noted, Azuma and Van Orden (1997) claimed that their effects (which Rodd et al., 2002 argued are sense effects) only emerge when pseudo-homophones are used. Rodd et al. appeared to accept Azuma and Van Orden's argument, which led to their use of pseudo-homophones in their Experiments 1 and 2. In fact, Rodd et al. reported in a footnote that when they didn't use pseudo-homophones with the words from their Experiment 2, their pattern was even weaker. Pseudo-homophones, of course, cannot be used in auditory lexical decision tasks. If it sounds like a word, it is a word. Thus, standard non-words had to be used in Rodd et al.'s Experiment 3, which presumably should have made it harder, rather than easier, to get their effects. The fact that the ambiguity disadvantage was significant only in Experiment 3 does imply that the visual and auditory lexical decision tasks are based on somewhat different processes.

What should also be noted is that Rodd et al. (2002) faced a daunting task in defining their independent variables. First of all, as noted previously, Gernsbacher (1984) provided a rather compelling argument against using dictionary based measures of the number of meanings. The same argument would certainly apply to the count of the number of senses. To return to the earlier question, is *belt* polysemous or a homonym? Are the definitions of *belt* noted earlier separate meanings or different senses? According to Wordsmyth, Rodd et al.'s source, *belt*, one of Rodd et al.'s words, is polysemous. Those apparently different meanings are actually different senses. It's far from clear that human raters would agree. Equally importantly, defining the "sense" variable in Rodd et al.'s manipulation itself is a challenge. Should an ambiguous word with two separate meanings, each with six senses, be thought of as having twelve senses, as

Rodd et al. assumed? (How about an ambiguous word with twelve separate meanings, each having only one sense?) If so, the matching word in the unambiguous condition should also have twelve senses. However, if one wishes to argue, as Rodd et al. do, that what produces the ambiguity advantage is the nature of the representation of the meaning that ultimately is settled on, then that meaning (whichever one it is) only has six senses. Thus, the matching word in the unambiguous condition should only have six senses. Methodologically, it is not clear that there actually is a solution to this problem (although see Jastrzembski, 1981 for a notable attempt).

10.3.5 A model: Rodd et al. (2004)

Rodd et al. (2004) proposed a PDP model of semantic processing that, with the right assumptions, produces a sense advantage and an ambiguity disadvantage. The idea is that if semantic processing does not have to be completed, as may be the case in the lexical decision task, there is a time period when many sense words would show an advantage due to the nature of their semantic representations while multiple-meaning words would show a disadvantage due to the competition created by having separate semantic representations. Thus, lexical decisions made at this point in time would show both a sense advantage and an ambiguity disadvantage. As processing continues, however, even many sense words should start to show a disadvantage due to the fact that the multiple senses ultimately compete with one another as well. Interestingly, the problem of equating words on the total number of senses (discussed in the last paragraph) was handled differently in the model simulation than it was in Rodd et al.'s (2002) experiments. In the model simulation, all meanings with multiple senses were assumed to have the same number of senses per meaning. As a result, two-meaning (i.e. ambiguous) multiple-sense words had twice as many total senses as unambiguous multiple-sense words.

With respect to predictions, the model does produce both a sense advantage and an ambiguity disadvantage. The ambiguity disadvantage, however, was far larger (156 cycles) than the sense advantage (108 cycles) in the simulations reported by Rodd et al. (2004). In their Experiment 2, Rodd et al. (2002) had observed exactly the opposite relationship, while in their Experiment 3 the two effects were nearly the same size. Whether the model can be altered to account for these discrepancies is a matter for future research.

10.4 Ambiguity effects in semantic tasks

10.4.1 Looking for an ambiguity disadvantage

One thing shared by all the models discussed above is that they predict an ambiguity disadvantage in semantically based tasks (i.e. tasks that require complete, or nearly complete, activation of semantics). That is, although an ambiguity (or sense) advantage might be observed in lexical decision if responding can be accomplished without completing semantic processing, things are different in semantically based tasks. In localist models, when an ambiguous word is processed, the wrong meaning may be activated, which should hinder performance. In PDP models, ambiguous words produce a competition between meanings, slowing the semantic activation process. Thus, a key question is whether there is an ambiguity disadvantage in such tasks.

There appear to be three types of experimental paradigms that have been used to address this question. The general finding has been, as predicted, an ambiguity disadvantage. The first paradigm involves a standard reading task. Various eye behaviors are monitored as subjects read sentences containing either ambiguous or unambiguous words. At present, consider only situations where the preceding context is purposely neutral so as not to bias the reader toward one meaning of the ambiguous word (e.g. *He thought that the punch/cider* was a little sour).

Using this procedure, Rayner and Duffy (1986) (see also Duffy et al., 1988; Rayner and Frazier, 1989) demonstrated that gaze durations on both the target word and the following words were longer when the target word was ambiguous (i.e. *punch* vs. *cider*), however, this difference was only observed if the two meanings of the target word were approximately balanced. When one meaning dominated, the difference in target processing disappeared, although the difference for post-target words did not. The reason for the post-target difference was that the post-target context was always set up to be supportive of the less dominant meaning of the ambiguous word. The conclusion, therefore, is that typically there is an ambiguity disadvantage when reading for meaning. Only when one meaning is quite dominant (and appropriate) could it, and subsequent text, be read without cost.

The second paradigm is the association (or relatedness) judgement task. In this task, two words (e.g. *bat–vampire*) are presented and subjects must decide whether the words are related. Using sequential presentations with the ambiguous word (e.g. *bat*) as either the first or second presented word, Gottlob et al. (1999) demonstrated that it took longer to determine that two words were related when one was ambiguous (see also Piercey and Joordens, 2000). Again, the conclusion is that when the meaning of ambiguous words must be determined, there is a cost.

The third paradigm is the semantic categorization task. Subjects must determine whether each presented word is a member of a designated semantic category. Hino et al. (2002) demonstrated that it was more difficult to categorize ambiguous, vs. unambiguous, words as being non-living things in a two-choice (living/non-living) task. Ambiguity was not manipulated for the living-thing stimuli. These results also support the claim that when the meaning of ambiguous words must be determined, there is a cost.

10.4.2 **Explaining the ambiguity disadvantage**

Unfortunately, answers are never this simple. In all of these tasks, not only must meaning be activated, subjects must also engage decision processes. Thus, in order to determine whether or not having multiple meanings slows the meaning activation process, as both localist and PDP type models would have it, the potential impact of competition during decision-making must be considered. For example, when one fixates on an ambiguous word in text with no prior context to disambiguate it, time and effort would be required to decide which meaning the writer had in mind (unless one meaning is highly dominant, in which case, as noted above, the fixation is short). When an ambiguous word (e.g. *bat*) is presented as the first word in a relatedness judgment task, the selection of the meaning unrelated to the second word (i.e. baseball) would certainly lead to a response delay when the second word (i.e. *vampire*) is presented, as the subject goes back and evaluates alternative meanings of *bat*. When the ambiguous word is presented second, as it was in Gottlob et al.'s (1999) Experiment 3, a slightly different problem arises. The activation of two meanings for *bat* early in processing would presumably cause a response conflict. The animal meaning of *bat* suggests that it is related to *vampire*; however, the baseball meaning suggests that a negative response is required. In all cases, an ambiguity disadvantage would emerge—but, not necessarily because of competition during meaning activation, rather because of problems created during decision-making.

Indeed, Rayner and Duffy (1986) did propose that the ambiguity disadvantage in gaze duration for unbiased ambiguous words in their experiments may have been due to decision/selection difficulties (see also Frazier and Rayner, 1990). When there is no context, which of the multiple activated meanings do subjects select? With respect to the relatedness judgment task, Pexman et al. (2004) have provided clear evidence that the ambiguity disadvantage observed in that task is a response bias effect. Using both sequential and simultaneous presentations of word pairs, Pexman et al. replicated Gottlob et al.'s (1999) and Piercey and Joordens's (2000) ambiguity disadvantage on positive trials; however, they found no evidence of a disadvantage on negative trials (e.g. *bat–door*). The important aspect of negative trials is that ambiguous words create no response conflict on these trials. Both meanings are unrelated to the meaning of the paired word. If the ambiguity disadvantage were due to difficulty activating the meaning for *bat*, there should have been a disadvantage on these trials as well. The implication is that the disadvantage on positive trials is due to response conflict.

The one set of results seemingly immune to this problem is Hino et al.'s (2002) demonstration of an ambiguity disadvantage on negative (non-living) trials in a semantic categorization task. However, as noted, answers are almost never simple. Forster (1999) reported no evidence of any ambiguity effect on negative trials in a different semantic categorization task (i.e. animal/non-animal). More recently, Hino et al. (2006) re-examined this issue and discovered that Forster's results are the more typical results. That is, Hino et al. (2006) discovered that there is no ambiguity disadvantage when the task involves small, well-defined categories (e.g. vegetables or animals) and, further, even when using larger, ill-defined categories (e.g. living things), the disadvantage only emerges when considering homonyms (words with unrelated meanings).

If the ambiguity disadvantage were due to difficulty during the meaning activation process, it should show up whenever semantic processing of an ambiguous word is required. The fact that it had such a limited role in Hino et al.'s (2006) experiments is more consistent with a decision-making/meaning-selection explanation. That is, only when two (or more) completely unrelated meanings become activated in a complicated decision-making process (e.g. *bank*—is it living?) does a delay occur because each meaning has to be thoroughly considered. When the multiple meanings are more closely related or when the categorization task is easier (e.g. animal/non-animal, vegetable/non-vegetable), a more parallel analysis of the multiple meanings can be done. Thus, no ambiguity disadvantage emerges. The implication, of course, is that the prediction of both localist and PDP models is wrong. There is not an ambiguity disadvantage whenever the semantic activation process must be completed.

This conclusion does produce a rather unfortunate state of affairs. Hopefully, more sophisticated theories will soon emerge to allow for a reasonable explanation of how multiple meanings of a word are represented and activated. One possible basis for such a theory is the work of H. Damasio and colleagues (Damasio, 2001; Damasio et al., 1996; Tranel, Damasio and Damasio, 1997; 1998). This work suggests that different types of semantic information (e.g. nouns vs. verbs, different categories of concrete objects) are localized in different neural regions. Activation in each region could certainly arise independently. Thus, when processing a multiple-meaning word, the interaction among semantic units that leads to the prediction of a delay in semantic activation may not inevitably exist because the linkages between those units may not exist (i.e. the two meanings are stored quite separately). Obviously, this is also an issue for future research.

10.5 Ambiguity in context

10.5.1 Implications from priming experiments

As noted, a major issue in the psychological investigation of ambiguity has been the impact of context. Can a biasing context alter the meaning activation process for either the biased or unbiased meaning (or are effects of context merely decision-making/meaning-selection effects?) and is this process affected by the dominance relationship between meanings? Although a number of experimental paradigms have been used to investigate these issues (e.g. phoneme monitoring: Foss, 1970; Foss and Jenkins, 1973, or memory tasks involving rapid serial visual presentations of words: Holms et al., 1977), the most compelling types of experiments are those that tap more closely into on-line processing. Most of these are "priming" experiments in which an ambiguous word is presented in either a neutral or biasing context and is followed by a target that is related to one of the meanings. Subjects are required to make either a lexical decision, naming or color-naming response to the target. We will also consider experiments, like those discussed above, in which eye movements are monitored while people read ambiguous words.

10.5.1.1 Multiple meaning activation independent of context

Possibly the classic paper in this "priming" literature was Conrad's (1974). Conrad used a modified Stroop (1935) color-naming task. An ambiguous final word in a spoken sentence was followed immediately by a target word written in a color. Subjects were required to name the color. Color-naming latencies were longer for words related to either meaning of the ambiguous word than to matched control words, regardless of whether the context was biased toward one meaning or not. Similar results were obtained by Whitney et al. (1985). The implication is that all meanings of an ambiguous word appear to be activated when that word is read even if the context is biased toward one of those meanings. As Oden and Spira (1983) demonstrated, however, when there is a delay before the target is presented, context does start to play a role, with targets related to the biased meaning producing larger effects.

Swinney (1979) reported similar results using a lexical decision task. Swinney's subjects listened to sentences over headphones, while from time to time letter strings would appear on the screen for a lexical decision response. The sentence contained an ambiguous word that served as a prime. Immediately following the offset of the ambiguous word, the lexical decision target appeared on the screen. When the sentence was essentially neutral (*The man was not surprised when he found several bugs in the corner of his room*), responses to targets related to either meaning of the ambiguous word (e.g. *spy* or *ant*) were faster than responses to unrelated words. Once again, an important finding was that the same result arose even when the sentence was biased (*The man was not surprised when he found several spiders, roaches, and other bugs in the corner of his room*). When the target was delayed three syllables, however, the priming remained for the target appropriate for the context but disappeared for the target that was inappropriate for the context.

Swinney's (1979) (and Conrad's, 1974) basic pattern has now been replicated many times. For example, Blutner and Sommer (1988) provided a direct replication of Swinney's results. Kintsch and Mross (1985), Till et al. (1988), and Elston-Güttler and Friederici (2005) reported similar results using visual presentations of context sentences. Tanenhaus et al. (1979) reported similar results using auditory presentations and a target-naming task, while Onifer and Swinney (1981) showed that the priming occurred in an immediate target condition even when the sentence was biased toward the dominant meaning and the target was related to the subordinate meaning. (The dominance factor had been uncontrolled in Swinney, 1979.)

10.5.1.2 Evidence that context can affect meaning activation

The implication of all these results is that initially all meanings are automatically activated, with context playing virtually no role in that process. Again, however, answers are never that simple—contradictory results have also been reported. For example, Simpson (1981) showed that when one used a strong prior context, there was only priming for associates of the intended meaning of the ambiguous word, regardless of whether the targets were associated with the dominant or subordinate meaning. Simpson and Krueger (1991) obtained similar results in a naming task.

Although Simpson's (1981) experiment was criticized because there was a 120 ms lag between the prime word and the target, allowing, in theory, time for context to deactivate the inappropriate meaning, results reported by Tabossi et al. (1987), Tabossi (1988), and Tabossi and Zardon (1993) (see also Experiment 2 in Seidenberg et al., 1982) do not appear to have this problem. Using essentially the same paradigm as Swinney (1979), Tabossi et al. showed that a prior context biased toward the dominant meaning of the ambiguous target only primed associates of the dominant meaning. A parallel type of prior context biased toward the subordinate meaning primed both types of targets. Tabossi further produced data suggesting that getting selective priming of dominant meaning associates required having a context that "makes salient a characteristic feature of it" (Tabossi, 1988: p. 334). Other types of context produced essentially equivalent priming of associates of both dominant and subordinate meanings.

On the basis of the results of Simpson and colleagues (Simpson, 1981; Simpson and Kreuger, 1991) and Tabossi and colleagues (Tabossi et al., 1987; Tabossi, 1988; Tabossi and Zardon, 1993), it appears that, although multiple meanings of ambiguous words are normally activated, it is not impossible for context to suppress activation of the subordinate meaning. However, given the restricted conditions under which such a result has been obtained and the fact that context seems to have no impact on activation of the dominant meaning, a second conclusion would be that the ability of context to influence the meaning activation process is minimal at best.

10.5.2 Measuring eye movements

At first glance, the conclusion that context has an extremely limited role in the meaning activation process may appear to be at odds with the results in the eye movement literature. In particular, the results of Rayner and colleagues (Duffy et al., 1988; Rayner and Duffy, 1986; Rayner and Frazier, 1989; Rayner et al., 1994; Staub and Rayner, Chapter 19 this volume) clearly indicate that context does affect fixation times. In the experiments of Rayner and colleagues, although balanced ambiguous words appearing in neutral contexts produced longer fixations (compared to control words), a biasing context eliminated this effect. In addition, although ambiguous words with a dominant meanings were read just as rapidly as unambiguous words when the prior context was neutral, when the prior context was biased toward the subordinate meaning there was a cost when reading the ambiguous word. These results appear to be consistent with the idea that context does affect activation of both dominant and subordinate meanings.

As noted earlier, however, it is unclear whether effects of this sort are due to meaning activation or meaning-selection/decision processes. That is, it is possible that the context does affect how rapidly the contextually appropriate meaning is activated. However, it is also possible that the context preceding a balanced ambiguous word merely biases the reader's decision process toward the selection of the intended meaning, eliminating the ambiguity disadvantage. It is also possible that, when viewing an unbalanced ambiguous word, a context biased toward the subordinate meaning makes it difficult to ignore that meaning initially, creating decision problems. Thus, while Rayner and colleagues' results certainly speak to the complexity of the reader's ambiguity resolution process, at present it is not possible to rule out either an activation-based or a decision-based explanation of those results.

10.5.3 Finding a resolution

In deciding how to determine which explanation is the best explanation of the impact of context, a couple of points should be considered. First, the priming experiments with the shortest prime-target intervals would seem to provide the best window on the activation process because they have the best chance of tapping into the process before a decision has been made (i.e. while all meanings might still be active). Second, as noted, the far more typical finding in those experiments is that, even in biased contexts, both meanings of ambiguous words are activated (e.g. Blutner and Sommer, 1988; Conrad, 1974; Elston-Güttler and Friederici, 2005; Kintsch and Mross, 1985; Onifer and Swinney, 1981; Swinney, 1979; Tanenhaus et al., 1979; Till et al., 1988). Third, as Hino et al. (1997) have noted, in those priming experiments in which there was little evidence of activation for words related to the subordinate meaning (e.g. Simpson 1981; Simpson and Burgess, 1985), typically no effort was made to equate the strengths of association between the ambiguous word primes and the targets that were related to the dominant vs. subordinate meanings. When Hino et al. did make such an effort in a single word priming experiment, they showed equivalent priming for the two types of visual targets at a 0 ms interstimulus interval (using auditory primes in a lexical decision task). It is therefore certainly possible that even in the experiments in which it did appear that the context suppressed activation of the subordinate meaning, the effect was simply due to using stronger associates in the dominant meaning condition. Everything considered, it seems more likely that the effects in the eye movement literature are due to decision/selection processes rather than to context affecting the meaning activation process.

10.6 Further thoughts on the activation/selection distinction

Using the eye movement paradigm, Pickering and Frisson (2001) recently reported no cost on initial gaze durations for ambiguous words having two verb meanings (in contrast to Rayner and Duffy's, 1986, results using ambiguous words with two noun meanings). The cost showed up later in the sentence. Pickering and Frisson explained these results by suggesting that because verbs are harder to interpret than nouns and their meanings are often dependent on subsequent words in the sentence, readers will delay meaning selection until they have seen some of those other words.

The noun/verb differences that Pickering and Frisson (2001) reported (see also Seidenberg et al., 1982, and Folk and Morris, 2003) obviously represent an interesting avenue for future research. More importantly, because these results suggest that meaning selection can be delayed when it is useful to do so, they underline the point that theories of ambiguity resolution need to distinguish between activation and selection processes. Many of the early researchers in the field, virtually all of whom were working with localist frameworks, were careful to make the activation/selection distinction. For example, the nonselective priming at short prime-target intervals discussed above was typically taken as being informative about the meaning activation process, while the selective priming at longer prime-target intervals was taken as being informative about the meaning selection process.

To implement this activation/selection distinction within a localist framework, one has to assume that multiple lexical units are activated initially and that they then maintain their activation (and hence their candidacy) during the selection process. One would also need to assume that intralexical inhibition processes are not so strong that they cause competing candidates to be inhibited. For PDP models (e.g. Rodd et al., 2004), the situation appears to be slightly more complicated. For these types of models, the activation process is, inherently, a process of deactivating competitors. Once the activation process runs to completion, the set of semantic units that have been activated defines the meaning that must be selected. Only if the system ends up in a "blend state" (a situation that PDP modelers have assumed represents a failure of the model) are there competitors to select among. Thus, PDP models may have some difficulty with the idea that multiple meanings are maintained for a period of time awaiting the context that allows an accurate selection. In the end, however, it seems clear that what can be thought of as "selection processes" must play a major role in the ambiguity resolution process. Any successful model of that process will need to explain not only how multiple meanings come to be activated but also how readers use context to (usually) successfully select the meaning the writer intended.

10.7 Final thought

Semantic ambiguity is a fact of life for readers/speakers of most languages. The fact that our processing systems seem to allow resolution of these ambiguities so rapidly that we hardly notice them is testimony to a very sophisticated set of language skills. Any successful model of the processes will have to be rather sophisticated as well. The challenge of explaining the ambiguity advantage in lexical decision and naming has certainly provided a strong impetus to the development of those models. The challenge of explaining the impact of context provides an additional impetus and should continue to do so. The path ahead has many theoretical twists and methodological turns, and successes will be measured in small increments. Nevertheless, the puzzle of understanding how readers deal with ambiguity is one that researchers will continue to find irresistible.

Acknowledgements

Much of the author's research discussed in this chapter was supported by Natural Sciences and Engineering Research Council of Canada Grant A6333. I would like to thank Yasushi Hino, Sachiko Kinoshita, and Penny Pexman for their contributions to that research and for their helpful comments on earlier versions of this chapter.

References

Azuma, T., and Van Orden, G. C. (1997) Why SAFE is better than FAST: the relatedness of a word's meanings affects lexical decision times. *Journal of Memory and Language*, 36: 484–504.

Balota, D. A., Ferraro, R. F., and Connor, L. T. (1991) On the early influence of meaning in word recognition: a review of the literature. In P. J. Schwanenflugel (ed.), *The Psychology of Word Meanings*, pp. 187–221. Erlbaum, Hillsdale, NJ.

Beretta, A., Fiorentina, R., and Poeppel, D. (2005) The effects of homonymy and polysemy on lexical access: an MEG study. *Cognitive Brain Research*, 24: 57–65.

Besner, D., and Joordens, S. (1995) Wrestling with ambiguity—further reflections: reply to Masson and Borowsky (1995) and Rueckl (1995). *Journal of Experimental Psychology: Learning, Memory, and Cognition*, 21: 515–19.

Blutner, R., and Sommer, R. (1988) Sentence processing and lexical access: the influence of the focus-identifying task. *Journal of Memory and Language*, 27: 359–67.

Borowsky, R., and Masson, M. E .J. (1996) Semantic ambiguity effects in word identification. *Journal of Experiment Psychology: Learning, Memory, and Cognition*, 22: 63–85.

Caramazza, A., and Grober, E. (1976) Polysemy and the structure of the subjective lexicon. In C. Rameh (ed.), *Georgetown University Roundtable on Languages and Linguistics. Semantics: Theory and Application*, pp.181–206. Georgetown University Press, Washington, DC.

Clark, H. H. (1973) The language-as fixed-effect fallacy: a critique of language statistics in psychological research. *Journal of Verbal Learning and Verbal Behavior*, 12: 335–59.

Cohen, J. (1976) Random means random. *Journal of Verbal Learning and Verbal Behavior*, 15: 261–2.

Collins, A. M., and Loftus, E. F. (1975) A spreading activation theory of semantic processing. *Psychological Review*, 82: 407–28.

Coltheart, M., Rastle, K., Perry, C., Langdon, R., and Ziegler, J. (2001) DRC: A dual route cascaded model of visual word recognition and reading aloud. *Psychological Review*, 108: 204–56.

Conrad, C. (1974) Context effects in sentence comprehension: a study of the subjective lexicon. *Memory and Cognition*, 2: 130–8.

Damasio, H. (2001) Words and concepts in the brain. In J. Branquinho (ed.), *The Foundations of Cognitive Science*, pp. 109–20. Oxford University Press, Oxford.

Damasio, H., Grabowski, T. J., Tranel, D., Hichwa, R. D., and Damasio, A. (1996) A neural basis for lexical retrieval. *Nature*, 380: 499–505.

Duffy, S. A., Morris, R. K., and Rayner, K. (1988) Lexical ambiguity and fixation times in reading. *Journal of Memory and Language*, 27: 429–46.

Elston-Güttler, K. E., and Friederici, A. D. (2005) Native and L2 processing of homonyms in sentential context. *Journal of Memory and Language*, 52: 256–83.

Folk, J. R., and Morris, R. K. (2003) Effects of syntactic category assignment on lexical ambiguity resolution in reading: an eye-movement analysis, *Memory and Cognition*, 31: 87–99.

Forster, K. I. (1999, November) Beyond lexical decision: lexical access in categorization tasks. Paper presented at the 40th Annual Meeting of the Psychonomic Society, Los Angeles, CA.

Forster, K. I., and Bednall, E. S. (1976) Terminating and exhaustive search in lexical access. *Memory and Cognition*, 4: 53–61.

Foss, D. J. (1970) Some effects of ambiguity upon sentence comprehension. *Journal of Verbal Learning and Verbal Behavior*, 9: 699–706.

Foss, D. J., and Jenkins C. M. (1973) Some effects of context on the comprehension of ambiguous sentences. *Journal of Verbal Learning and Verbal Behavior*, 12: 577–89.

Frazier, L., and Rayner, K. (1990) Taking on semantic commitments: processing multiple meanings vs. multiple senses. *Journal of Memory and Language*, 29: 181–200.

Gernsbacher, M. A. (1984) Resolving 20 years of inconsistent interactions between lexical familiarity and orthography, concreteness, and polysemy. *Journal of Experimental Psychology: General*, 113: 256–81.

Glucksberg, S., Kreuz, F. J., and Rho, S. H. (1986) Context can constrain lexical access: implications for models of language comprehension. *Journal of Experimental Psychology: Learning, Memory, and Cognition*, 12: 323–35.

Gottlob, L. R., Goldinger, S. D., Stone, G. O., and Van Orden, G. C. (1999) Reading homographs: orthographic, phonologic, and semantic dynamics. *Journal of Experimental Psychology: Human Perception and Performance*, 25: 561–74.

Hino, Y., and Lupker, S. J. (1996) Effects of polysemy in lexical decision and naming: an alternative to lexical access accounts. *Journal of Experimental Psychology: Human Perception and Performance*, 22: 1331–56.

Hino, Y., Lupker, S. J., and Besner D. (1998a) Polysemy effects in the naming of Japanese Katakana words and their Hiragana transcriptions. Paper presented at the 39th Annual Meeting of the Psychonomic Society, Dallas, TX.

Hino, Y., Lupker, S. J., and Pexman, P. M. (2001) Effects of polysemy and relatedness of meanings in lexical decision and semantic categorization tasks. Paper presented at the 42nd Annual Meeting of the Psychonomic Society, Orlando, FL.

Hino, Y., Lupker, S. J., and Pexman, P. M. (2002) Ambiguity and synonymy effects in lexical decision, naming and semantic categorization tasks: Interactions between orthography, phonology and semantics. *Journal of Experimental Psychology: Learning, Memory, and Cognition*, 28: 686–713.

Hino, Y., Lupker, S. J., and Sears, C. R. (1997) The effects of word association and meaning frequency in a cross-modal lexical decision task: is the priming due to "semantic" association? *Canadian Journal of Experimental Psychology*, 51: 195–210.

Hino, Y., Lupker, S. J., Sears, C. R., and Ogawa, T. (1998b) The effects of polysemy for Japanese katakana words. *Reading and Writing: An Interdisciplinary Journal*, 10: 395–424.

Hino, Y., Pexman, P. M., and Lupker, S. J. (2006) Ambiguity and relatedness effects in semantic tasks: are they due to semantic coding? *Journal of Memory and Language*, 55: 247–73.

Hinton, G. E., and Shallice, T. (1991) Lesioning an attractor network: Investigations of acquired dyslexia. *Psychological Review*, 98: 74–95.

Hogaboam, T. W., and Perfetti, C. A. (1975) Lexical ambiguity and sentence comprehension. *Journal of Verbal Learning and Verbal Behavior*, 14: 265–74.

Holmes, V. M., Arwas, R., and Garrett, M. F. (1977) Prior context and the perception of lexically ambiguous sentences. *Memory and Cognition*, 5: 103–10.

Jastrzembski, J. E. (1981) Multiple meanings, number of related meanings, frequency of occurrence, and the lexicon. *Cognitive Psychology*, 13: 278–305.

Jastrzembski, J. E., and Stanners, R. F. (1975) Multiple word meanings and lexical search speed. *Journal of Verbal Learning and Verbal Behavior*, 14: 534–537.

Joordens, S., and Besner, D. (1994) When banking on meaning is not (yet) money in the bank: explorations in connectionist modeling. *Journal of Experimental Psychology: Learning, Memory, and Cognition*, 20: 1051–62.

Kawamoto, A. H. (1993) Nonlinear dynamics in the resolution of lexical ambiguity: a parallel distributed processing account. *Journal of Memory and Language*, 32: 474–516.

Kawamoto, A. H., Farrar W. T., and Kello, C. (1994) When two meanings are better than one: modeling the ambiguity advantage using a recurrent distributed network. *Journal of Experimental Psychology: Human Perception and Performance*, 20: 1233–47.

Kellas, G., Ferraro, F. R., and Simpson G. B. (1988) Lexical ambiguity and the timecourse of attentional allocation in word recognition. *Journal of Experimental Psychology: Human Perception and Performance*, 14: 601–9.

Keppel, G. (1976) Words as random variables. *Journal of Verbal Learning and Verbal Behavior,* 15: 263–5.

Kintsch, W., and Mross, E. F. (1985) Context effects in word identification. *Memory and Cognition*, 24: 336–49.

Klein, D. E., and Murphy, G. L. (2001) The representation of polysemous words. *Journal of Memory and Language*, 45: 259–82.

Klein, D. E., and Murphy, G. L. (2002) Paper has been my ruin: conceptual relations of polysemous senses. *Journal of Memory and Language*, 47: 548–70.

Lichacz, F. M., Herdman, C. M., Lefevre, J.-A., and Baird B. (1999) Polysemy effects in word naming. *Canadian Journal of Experimental Psychology*, 53: 189–93.

Masson, M. E. J. (1991) A distributed memory model of context effects in word identification. In D. Besner and G. Humphreys (eds), *Basic Processes in Reading: Visual Word Recognition*, pp. 233–63. Erlbaum, Hillsdale, NJ.

Masson, M. E. J. (1995) A distributed memory model of semantic priming. *Journal of Experimental Psychology: Learning, Memory, and Cognition*, 21: 3–23.

Masson, M. E. J., and Borowsky, R. (1995) Unsettling comments about semantic ambiguity in connectionist models: comments on Joordens and Besner (1994). *Journal of Experimental Psychology: Learning, Memory, and Cognition*, 21: 509–14.

Millis, M. L., and Button, S. B. (1989) The effect of polysemy on lexical decision time: now you see it, now you don't. *Memory and Cognition*, 17: 141–7.

Morton, J. (1969) Interaction of information in word recognition. *Psychological Review*, 76: 165–78.

Nunberg, G. (1979) The non-uniqueness of semantic solutions: polysemy. *Linguistics and Philosophy*, 3: 143–84.

Oden, G. C., and Spira, J. L. (1983) Influence of context on the activation and selection of ambiguous word senses. *Quarterly Journal of Experimental Psychology*, 35: 51–64.

Onifer, W., and Swinney, D. A. (1981) Accessing lexical ambiguities during sentence comprehension: effects of frequency of meaning and contextual bias. *Memory and Cognition*, 15: 225–36.

Pecher, D. (2001) Perception is a two-way junction: feedback semantics in word recognition. *Psychonomic Bulletin and Review*, 8: 545–51.

Pexman, P. M., Hino, Y., and Lupker, S. J. (2004) Semantic ambiguity and the process of generating meaning from print. *Journal of Experimental Psychology: Learning, Memory and Cognition*, 30: 1252–70.

Pexman. P. M., and Lupker S. J. (1999) Ambiguity and visual word recognition: can feedback explain both homophone and polysemy effects? *Canadian Journal of Experimental Psychology*, 53: 323–34.

Pexman, P. M., Lupker, S. J., and Hino, Y. (2002) The impact of feedback semantics in visual word recognition: number of features effects in lexical decision and naming tasks. *Psychonomic Bulletin and Review*, 9: 542–9.

Pexman, P. M., Lupker, S. J., and Jared, D. (2001) Homophone effects in lexical decision. *Journal of Experimental Psychology: Learning, Memory, and Cognition*, 27: 139–56.

Pickering, M. J., and Frisson, S. (2001) Processing ambiguous verbs: evidence from eye movements. *Journal of Experimental Psychology: Learning, Memory, and Cognition*, 27: 556–73.

Piercey, C. D., and Joordens, S. (2000) Turning an advantage into a disadvantage: ambiguity effects in lexical decision versus reading tasks. *Memory and Cognition*, 28: 657–66.

Raaijmakers, J. G. W., Schrijnemakers, J. M. C., and Gremmen, F. (1999) How to deal with "the language-as-fixed-effect fallacy": common misconceptions and alternative solutions. *Journal of Memory and Language*, 41: 416–26.

Rayner, K., and Duffy, S. A. (1986) Lexical complexity and fixation times in reading: effects of word frequency, verb complexity, and lexical ambiguity. *Memory and Cognition*, 14: 191–201.

Rayner, K., and Frazier, L. (1989) Selection mechanisms in reading lexically ambiguous words. *Journal of Experimental Psychology: Learning, Memory, and Cognition*, 15: 779–90.

Rayner, K., Pacht, J. M., and Duffy, S. A. (1994) Effects of prior encounter and global discourse bias on the processing of lexically ambiguous words. *Journal of Memory and Language*, 33: 527–44.

Rodd, J. M. (2004) The effect of semantic ambiguity on reading aloud: a twist in the tale. *Psychonomic Bulletin and Review*, 11: 440–5.

Rodd, J. M., Gaskell, G., and Marslen-Wilson, W. D. (2002) Making sense of semantic ambiguity: semantic competition in lexical access. *Journal of Memory and Language*, 46: 245–66.

Rodd, J. M., Gaskell, M. G., and Marslen-Wilson, W. D. (2004) Modelling the effects of semantic ambiguity in word recognition. *Cognitive Science*, 28: 89–104.

Rubenstein, H., Garfield, L., and Millikan, J. A. (1970) Homographic entries in the internal lexicon. *Journal of Verbal Learning and Verbal Behavior*, 9: 487–94.

Rubenstein, H., Lewis, S. S., and Rubenstein, M. A. (1971) Evidence for phonemic recoding in visual word recognition. *Journal of Verbal Learning and Verbal Behavior*, 10: 645–57.

Rueckl, J. G. (1995) Ambiguity and connectionist networks: still settling into a solution—commentary on Joordens and Besner (1994). *Journal of Experimental Psychology: Learning, Memory, and Cognition*, 21: 501–8.

Seidenberg, M. S., Tanenhaus, M. K., Leiman, J. M. & Bienkowski, M. (1982). Automatic access of meanings of ambiguous words in context: Some limitations of knowledge-based processing. *Cognitive Psychology*, 14: 489–537.

Simpson, G. B. (1981) Meaning dominance and sementic context in the processing of lexical ambiguity. *Journal of Verbal Learning and Verbal Behavior*, 20: 120–36.

Simpson, G. B., and Burgess, C. (1985) Activation and selection processes in the recognition of ambiguous words. *Journal of Experimental Psychology: Human Perception and Performance*, 11: 28–39.

Simpson, G. B., and Krueger, M. A. (1991) Selective access of homograph meanings in sentence context. *Journal of Memory and Language*, 30: 627–43.

Smith J. E. K. (1976) The assuming-will-make-it-so fallacy. *Journal of Verbal Learning and Verbal Behavior*, 15: 262–3.

Stone, G. O., and Van Orden, G. C. (1993) Building a resonance framework for words recognition using design and system principles. *Journal of Experimental Psychology: Human Perception and Performance*, 20: 1248–68.

Stroop, J. R. (1935) Studies of interference in serial verbal reactions. *Journal of Experimental Psychology*, 18: 643–62.

Swinney, D. A. (1979) Lexical access during sentence comprehension: (re)consideration of context effects. *Journal of Verbal Learning and Verbal Behavior*, 18: 645–59.

Tabossi, P. (1988) Accessing lexical ambiguity in different types of sentential context. *Journal of Memory and Language*, 27: 324–40.

Tabossi, P., Colombo, L., and Job, R. (1987) Accessing lexical ambiguity: effects of context and dominance. *Psychological Research*, 49: 161–7.

Tabossi, P., and Zardon, F. (1993) Processing ambiguous words in context. *Journal of Memory and Language*, 32: 359–72.

Tanenhaus, M. K., Leiman, J. M., and Seidenberg, M. S. (1979) Evidence for multiple stages in the processing of ambiguous words in syntactic contexts. *Journal of Verbal Learning and Verbal Behavior*, 18: 427–40.

Till, R. E., Mross, E. F., and Kintsch, W. (1988) Time course of priming for associate and inference words in a discourse context. *Memory and Cognition*, 16: 283–98.

Tranel, D., Damasio, H., and Damasio, A. (1997) A neural basis for the retrieval of conceptual knowledge. *Neuropsychologia*, 35: 1319–27.

Tranel, D., Damasio, H., and Damasio, A. (1998) The neural basis of lexical retrieval. In R. W. Parks, D. S. Levine, and D. L. Long (eds), *Fundamentals of Neural Network Modeling: Neuropsychology and Cognitive Neuroscience*, pp. 271–96. The MIT Press, Cambridge, MA.

Tuggy, D. (1993) Ambiguity, polysemy, and vagueness. *Cognitive Linguistics*, 4: 273–90.

Whitney, P., McKay, T., Kellas, G., and Emerson, WA Jr. (1985) Semantic activation of noun concepts in context. *Journal of Experimental Psychology: Learning, Memory, and Cognition*, 11: 126–35.

Wike, E. L., and Church, J. D. (1976) Comments on Clark's "The Language-as-Fixed-Effect Fallacy." *Journal of Verbal Learning and Verbal Behavior*, 15: 249–55.

CHAPTER 11

Morphological processes in language comprehension

William D. Marslen-Wilson

11.1 Introduction

A psycholinguistic account of human communication must explain how linguistic inputs and outputs are structured to convey the speaker's intended meaning. The concept of a "mental lexicon" plays a key role in standard conceptions of this process, referring to the learned representations that mediate between the spoken utterance (or written text) and the interpretation computed by the listener or reader.

The organization of these representations needs to reflect, broadly speaking, two kinds of linguistic information being communicated: semantic information, about meanings in the world, and a wide range of syntactic information, specifying grammatical relations, tense, aspect, and so forth. These different kinds of linguistic information are associated with specific lexical entities—words and morphemes—which are assembled together, in different ways in different languages, to convey the necessary mix of semantic and syntactic cues to intended meaning as the speech input is heard over time (or as a written text is read). The cognitive status of these entities—where the morpheme is defined as the minimal meaning-bearing unit in the language, and where the word is generally defined as the graphical dictionary word (cf. Grosjean and Gee, 1987)—has become a major focus of psycholinguistic research.

In a language like English, a high proportion of semantic and syntactic morphemes can occur as phonologically separate entities—that is, as individual function and content words like *the* or *dog*—so that the distinction between word and morpheme is neutralized. Nonetheless, this is by no means the case for the language as a whole, with the frequent occurrence of complex words made up of the combination of different morphemes, especially those involving bound morphemes. These latter are grammatical morphemes, like {-ness} or {-s}, which cannot occur as words on their own, but only in combination with content word stems, as in forms like *darkness* ({dark} + {-ness}) or *smiles* ({smile} + {-s}).

In common with many other languages, English offers three modes of complex word formation: *inflectional* and *derivational morphology*, where a stem is combined with either a derivational or an inflectional morpheme (as in the *darkness* and *smiles* examples), and *compounding*, where two stems are combined together, as in words like *teapot* or *ceasefire*. In this chapter I will focus on inflectional and derivational morphology.

These possibilities for complex word formation—the packaging of morphemes into larger lexical units—raise basic questions about the representational and processing consequences of this salient linguistic phenomenon, and more generally about lexical representations themselves. How are complex words of different types represented in the mental lexicon, and how are they comprehended and produced? Are complex forms stored as complete units, as if they were simple words, or are they stored in partially or fully decomposed morphemic format? How is the information captured by these forms accessed from spoken or written inputs, and how is this information made available to the rest of the psycholinguistic system?

A fully explanatory answer to these questions will have two principal characteristics. It will be a cognitive neuroscience account which embeds computationally specific cognitive accounts of the functional properties of the system in a specific analysis of the neural systems underlying these properties, and it will be strongly cross-linguistic—English is an unusual language in many respects, but especially so in the morphological domain (Blevins, 2006).

We are far from being able, at the time of writing, to put such an explanatory account into place. Although there is a plethora of cognitive theories of different aspects of the lexical system, and although these are increasingly cross-linguistic in scope, the cognitive neuroscience of these systems is still in its infancy, and especially weak cross-linguistically. The area of research that is most advanced in integrating these elements is inflectional morphology, where an exceptional degree of scientific interest and resource has been directed at a single morphological sub-process (the English past tense), addressing its properties in a multidisciplinary manner from computational, linguistic, behavioral, and neural perspectives. This is where I will focus the next part of this chapter, before turning to a review of research into derivational morphology.

11.2 Inflectional morphology

Inflectional morphology is the combination of a stem with one or more inflectional affixes; in English, examples are regular noun plurals (*cats* – {cat} + {-s}) and the regular past tense (*walked* – {walk}+ {-ed}). Although the precise definition of an inflectional morphological process (as opposed to a derivational one) is theory- and language-dependent, and a continued source of controversy in linguistics (cf. Bickel and Nichols, 2006), some core properties of inflectional morphology are generally accepted, and are of critical significance to a proper psycholinguistic approach.

First, inflectional morphology does not, by definition, create new words requiring new lexical entries. Rather, the prototypical inflectional functions—marking number, tense, aspect, gender, case, and so forth—produce new forms of the same word, and not new different words. Inflectional variants like *cat* and *cats* or *walk* and *walked* are not listed as separate headwords in standard dictionaries. If inflectional morphemes do modify the semantics of a word—as in the noun plural—they do not change the basic meaning of the stem to which they attach, nor do they change its grammatical category. The word *cats* is still a noun, and all that the morpheme {-s} adds to the meaning of the base form *cat* is the information that there is more than one of them.

The second key characteristic of inflections is that they are responsive, in a regular and predictable way, to the properties of the grammatical environment in which they occur (e.g. Anderson, 1992; Bickel and Nichols, 2006). This is clear, for example, where inflectional morphemes express agreement—as in the third person singular {-s} for English verbs (*he walks*), or, in many other languages, when morphological case is used to express the grammatical role of a noun as subject, object, indirect object, and so forth. Similarly, the presence of the regular past tense in English verbs (*they walked*) is dictated by the role of the verb in the context of the utterance and its wider temporal and aspectual properties. This means, on the one hand, that whether and how a given stem will be inflected depends on the environment in which it occurs, and, on the other, that the information carried by the inflection is not just about the stem itself, but about the processes of phrasal and sentential interpretation to which that stem relates.

These two functional properties—of meaning preservation and context sensitivity—clearly divide inflectional morphology from the other two principal mechanisms of complex word formation: derivational morphology and compounding. Both of these latter processes do change the meaning (and often the syntactic category) of the stems involved, and both processes are lexical in character and operate independently of the grammatical contexts in which their products might occur.

11.2.1 English inflectional morphology: the past-tense debate

Issues in the representation and processing of inflectionally complex words have reached a very wide audience in the context of the "Words and Rules" debate that has been prominent in the cognitive sciences since the mid-1980s. This debate took English regular and irregular inflectional morphology as its main empirical focus, as a way of addressing fundamental questions about whether rule-like behavior should be explained in terms of symbolic computation (Pinker, 1999; Pinker and Ullman, 2002), or in terms of connectionist learning systems, containing neither rules nor symbols (Rumelhart and McClelland, 1986;

McClelland and Patterson, 2002). The reason why the English past tense is relevant here is because of the sharp contrast that it offers between a classically rule-like process—the procedure for forming the regular past tense by combining a phonologically unchanged stem with an inflectional suffix (as in *jump/jumped, agree/agreed*, etc.)—and an idiosyncratic set of irregular forms where there is no predictable relationship between the stem and its inflected past tense form (as in *bring/brought, give/gave*, etc.), and no basis for segmentation of these irregular forms into a concatenative stem + affix format.

Leaving aside questions about the nature of mental computation, these same properties of the English past tense allow us to contrast whole-word and morphemic approaches to lexical representation in an exceptionally direct manner. Both regular and irregular forms express the same underlying combination of semantic and syntactic information (carried by the verb stem and by the past tense inflection). But in the regular case this combination is morphophonologically overt, with a phonologically unchanged verb stem concatenated with an inflectional suffix, thereby constituting a prime candidate, on many accounts, for morphological decomposition in processing and representation. In the irregular case this combination is morphophonologically hidden, with a non-decomposable whole form that conveys the same linguistic information but which cannot straightforwardly be decomposed into a stem and an affix.

Almost all approaches to English inflectional morphology agree that these irregular forms[1] must be learned, represented, and processed as undecomposable whole forms (though see Marantz and colleagues (Halle and Marantz, 1993; Stockall and Marantz, 2006) for a contrasting view). In fact, in the Words and Rules debate, both sets of protagonists agree not only that this is the case, but also that the irregulars are acquired and processed by essentially the same connectionist learning mechanisms.

Where the divergence comes is in the treatment of the regular past-tense forms. The connectionist school, over the two decades spanning the original Rumelhart and McClelland paper in 1986, the Plunkett and Marchman (1993) and the Joanisse and Seidenberg (1999) models, and the recent restatement by McClelland and Patterson (2002), has consistently held to the view that regular and irregular past tense forms are handled by a single, integrated mechanism, dependent jointly on constraints from phonology and semantics. This approach denies the existence of separable stem and inflectional morphemes, and argues instead that inflected forms are learned and represented as overlapping whole forms sharing certain semantic and phonological similarities. Any behavioral (or neural) differences between regular and irregular forms simply reflect differences in the distribution of these similarities, and the implications of these for how the system as a whole is learned.

The competing views, though varying in many other respects, all take the view that regular inflected forms do differ qualitatively from the irregular forms, and that different cognitive and neural mechanisms are implicated in the processing and representation of each type of form. The approach taken by Pinker, Ullman, Marcus, Clahsen and colleagues, argued vigorously in several papers over the years (e.g. Pinker and Prince, 1988; Pinker, 1999; Pinker and Ullman, 2002), is primarily focused on arguments for the role of rule-based symbolic computation in regular inflectional processes. Here I will focus on the lexical processing systems invoked by regular and irregular forms in English (and other languages), and on the neural systems underlying these processes.

Because English regular and irregular forms contrast whole-word and potentially decomposable representations in such a direct manner, the key empirical question has been to track the similarities and differences in the way these forms are represented and processed, and to determine, where differences are found, whether these can be attributed to distributional differences in a single-system framework, or whether they reflect genuine underlying qualitative distinctions. The first decade of research addressed to these questions, based primarily on observational and behavioral data, examined the detailed properties of the acquisition of regular and irregular forms (e.g. Marcus et al., 1992), the relative merits of different models of these processes (e.g. Pinker and Prince, 1988; Plunkett and Marchman, 1993), and the processing of such forms in the adult mental lexicon (e.g. Marslen-Wilson et al., 1993). However, it is fair to say that a clear resolution, either way, did not emerge. When differences are found between regular and irregular forms—for example in priming studies with adult speakers—it is hard to exclude single mechanism accounts of these regularities, given the many distributional differences

[1] Even though a subset of irregular forms have an identifiable remnant of the regular suffix, as in forms like *slept, fled, built*, etc., the unpredictability of these forms seems to require that they too are treated as whole forms, without a decomposable internal structure.

between the two kinds of forms (see Seidenberg and Hoeffner, 1998).

Since the mid-1990s, however, the character of research into these questions has changed considerably, with increased emphasis on techniques targeting the underlying neural systems that support the representation and processing of regular and irregular forms. Taken as a whole, this research provides strong evidence against claims for a single underlying neural system supporting both regular and irregular forms in English, and, more generally, against the claim that inflectionally complex words, with a morphophonologically overt structure, are handled by the same set of processes that are invoked by non-decomposable whole forms.

This evidence comes from several sources. The first is neuropsychological in nature, asking whether injury to the brain can lead to behavioral dissociations between processes involving regular and irregular inflected forms (cf. Shallice, 1988). There is now compelling evidence that such dissociations do occur, pointing to the separability of the neural systems required for the production and perception of English regular and irregular inflected forms. This is most clearly the case for regular inflectional morphology, where selective deficits for the regulars are associated with damage to the left hemisphere perisylvian language system—in particular left inferior frontal cortex and superior temporal cortex. Selective deficits for the irregulars, while less well neuro-anatomically specified, seem to be associated with medial and inferior temporal lesions, in patients who often also have semantic deficits. This has been shown in a variety of neuropsychological studies probing the comprehension and production of the regular and irregular past tense (e.g. Longworth et al., 2005; Marslen-Wilson and Tyler, 1997, 1998; Miozzo, 2003; Patterson et al., 2001; Tyler, Randall, and Marslen-Wilson, 2002; Tyler, de Mornay Davies et al., 2002; Ullman et al., 1997; 2005).

To cope with this growing neuropsychological evidence for neural differentiation, Joanisse and Seidenberg (1999) proposed a revised single mechanism model, where a central connectionist core is linked to phonological and semantic subsystems, such that performance on irregulars is more dependent on links to semantics, and performance on regulars is more sensitive to phonological factors. Damage to either subsystem leads to apparently selective deficits for regulars or irregulars, but in this context the presence of such selectivity does not allow the inference that there are underlying dissociations in processing mechanisms.

It turns out, however, that the key claims made by this model are empirically incorrect: namely, that the relationship between irregulars and their stems is predominantly semantic while between regulars and their stems it is predominantly phonological, and that in neither case is the relationship morphological. The first problem is that the model makes the wrong predictions about the role of semantics in the relationship between an irregular past tense form and its stem. Marslen-Wilson and Tyler (1997; 1998) were the first to report a correlation between semantic deficits and impaired performance on the English irregular past tense. But subsequent studies with normal adults, designed to probe this implied causal link, show that the underlying relationship between irregular forms and their stems is morphological rather than semantic. Pairs like *gave/give* and *jumped/jump* are related because they share a common morpheme, in contrast to semantically related pairs (*cello/violin*) which do not have a common morpheme and are lexically separate. In a delayed repetition priming experiment, designed to separate semantic from morphological effects, priming of regular and irregular pairs was equally well preserved over time, while semantic priming rapidly dissipated (Marslen-Wilson and Tyler, 1998).[2] In an ERP study, the patterns of brain activity associated with regular and irregular cross-modal repetition priming were almost identical, with both showing left anterior negativities standardly associated with linguistic processing, while semantic primes showed only a centrally distributed N400-type effect (Marslen-Wilson et al., 2000).

This evidence suggests that the co-occurrence of semantic deficits and of disrupted access to irregular past tense forms is accidental rather than causal in nature. This conclusion is supported by the report of an anomic patient with a selective deficit for the irregular past tense but no semantic deficit (Miozzo, 2003), and by subsequent reports that semantic deficits are not necessarily associated with irregular past tense deficits (Tyler et al., 2004).

The second problematic aspect of the Joanisse and Seidenberg model is that it seeks to explain poor performance with the regular past tense purely in terms of general phonological processing deficits, and rejects the possibility of a deficit specific to morphological or morphophonological factors. These predictions are inconsistent with a recent study, using a speeded same-different

[2] This held even when judged semantic relatedness was matched across conditions.

judgement task, where participants are asked to detect differences between the past tense and stem of regular (*played/play*) and irregular (*taught/teach*) past tense verbs, phonologically matched pseudo-regular and irregular pairs (*trade/tray*; *port/peach*), and similarly matched sets of non-words (Tyler, Randall, and Marslen-Wilson, 2002). Non-fluent left-hemisphere patients performed consistently worse on the regular past-tense pairs than on the matched pseudo-regular and non-word pairs. Furthermore, performance on the task did not correlate with the patients' phonological processing difficulties, which ranged from very mild to severe (though see Lambon Ralph et al., 2005).

The second type of evidence—and the result which seems to refute most directly the Joanisse and Seidenberg (1999) model—comes from a recent study using a lesion-behavior correlational technique (Tyler, Marslen-Wilson, and Stamatakis, 2005). This is a new methodology, which directly relates brain structure to neuropsychological function by correlating voxel-level variations in signal intensity across the entire brains of brain-damaged patients with their behavioral scores in reaction-time (and similar) tasks. If a brain region is important for a given function, then damage to this region (as reflected in reduced signal density) should correlate with relevant changes in performance. This study correlated structural imaging measures for twenty-two right-handed brain-damaged patients with their performance on a priming study, using lexical decision, which contrasted regular and irregular inflected test pairs (*jumped/jump*, *slept/sleep*) with prime-target pairs related only in phonological form (*pillow/pill*) or only in meaning (*card/paper*).

Different neural regions correlated with behavioral priming scores in each of these four conditions. Priming for regularly inflected past tense words showed a strong positive correlation with signal intensity in left inferior frontal cortex (Broca's area). At a lower threshold this cluster extended, via the arcuate fasciculus, to include all of Wernicke's area (in left temporal cortex). Disrupted performance on phonologically related pairs, in contrast, did not correlate with damage to the same areas, and was linked instead with damage to a more medial left-hemisphere structure, the insula, which is known to be involved in phonological processing mechanisms. Critically, damage in this brain area did not correlate with performance on the regulars. This is not consistent with the view that the regular inflectional relationship is phonologically mediated. In the irregular past-tense condition, priming correlated with signal intensity in very different neural regions (mainly posterior temporo-parietal), which in turn were quite distinct from the areas correlating with performance on the pure semantic priming task.

This seems to be direct evidence that regular and irregular past-tense forms activate different neural substrates, and that in neither case can the activation pattern be reduced just to phonological or semantic subsystems. In the context of the broader issues being considered here, it is also compelling evidence that the processing of morphemically decomposable inflectional forms depends on different (or additional) neural mechanisms to the processing of whole forms that are not morphemically decomposable. This in turn raises the question of how to characterize these differences in mechanism and process.

11.2.2 A neurocognitive approach to regular inflectional morphology

The neuropsychological evidence summarized above, coupled with converging evidence from fMRI studies of the intact, normal brain (e.g. Tyler, Stamatakis et al., 2005b), leads to a preliminary sketch of the functional and neural systems underlying regular inflectional morphology in English—as well as, prima facie, cross-linguistically. This account, which is also consistent with several EEG and MEG studies of morphological function, distinguishes three types of interdependent processing activity triggered by a regularly inflected stem combined with an inflectional affix. These are processes of stem and affix access, of morphophonological segmentation of the original complex form, and of morphosyntactic interpretation of the grammatical implications of the inflectional affix.[3]

This set of processes reflect the primary function of inflectional morphology: to provide grammatical information of various types to guide the interpretation of the semantic (and syntactic) information carried by the stems to which these morphemes attach. The analysis of forms like *played* requires the simultaneous access of the lexical content associated with the stem *play*, and of the grammatical implications of the {-ed} morpheme. Unless these different morphemic components of the word are assigned to their appropriate processing destinations, effective

[3] The emphasis here is on the systems supporting speech comprehension, reflecting the predominance of spoken inputs in the research with patients and in neuroimaging. Similar principles apply to the processing of written materials, though the input system will be different (see section 11.3.1. below).

on-line processing of such forms is disrupted, as demonstrated in the priming studies mentioned earlier (Longworth et al., 2005; Marslen-Wilson and Tyler, 1997; Tyler, de Mornay Davies et al., 2002).

These functions are distributed over a left-lateralized fronto-temporal language system, with some differentiation of function between frontal and temporal areas.[4] Access to lexico-semantic content is mediated by temporal lobe structures, centered around the posterior superior and middle temporal gyri, and linking sensory inputs to stem-based representations of morphemic form and meaning (cf. Binder et al., 2000; Wise et al., 2001). If these brain regions are intact, we see preserved phonological and semantic processing both of monomorphemic forms (like *jump* or *dog*) and of irregular forms (like *gave* or *taught*) that have to be accessed as whole forms. Critically, this holds even for patients who are significantly impaired in processing regularly inflected forms (e.g. Longworth et al., 2005). This means that the relevant access representations—the perceptual targets for the initial access process—cannot be the inflected whole forms (such as *jumped* or *dogs*) of the stems in question. Otherwise there would be no reason for access to fail for the regular inflected forms when it was succeeding for the irregular forms. What seem to be stored instead, for the regular inflectional morphology, are just the access representations corresponding to the uninflected stems, like *jump* and *dog*.[5]

When a form like *jumped* is encountered, therefore, it does not fully match with a stored access representation. Instead, such forms depend on a further process of morphophonological parsing, which segments potential complex forms into stems and grammatical affixes (Marslen-Wilson and Tyler, 1998; Tyler, Randall, and Marslen-Wilson, 2002; Tyler et al., 2005). This segmentation, on the one hand, allows the isolated stem to access successfully the appropriate stem representation and, on the other, allows the inflectional affix to access the representations and processes relevant to its successful interpretation. The processes supporting this parsing process, as well as the full morphosyntactic interpretation of the information carried by inflectional morphemes, seem to require intact left inferior frontal cortex, and intact processing links between these areas and posterior temporal cortex. This is consistent with recent analyses of functional connectivity between these regions (Stamatakis et al., 2005).

A striking feature of these segmentation processes is that they are apparently triggered by any input, word or non-word, that shares the diagnostic properties of an inflectional affix in English, which I have labeled as the "inflectional rhyme pattern."[6] Pseudo-regular forms like *trade* or *snade*, which terminate with the phonetic pattern typical of English regular inflection, also seem to stimulate morphophonological segmentation processes that coactivate frontal and temporal regions, as reflected in data both from patients (Tyler, Randall, and Marslen-Wilson, 2002) and from normals (Tyler et al., 2005b). This, again, is consistent with stem-based access representations. The system cannot rule out, without decompositional analysis, the possibility that the pseudo-regular *trade* is actually the morpheme *tray* in the past tense, or that *snade* is the past tense of the potential real stem *snay*.

The basic claim here—that regularly inflected forms trigger a left-lateralized process of segmentation and analysis that involves interactions between temporal and inferior frontal areas—is consistent with evidence from studies using EEG and MEG techniques. These techniques (see Pulvermüller, Chapter 8 this volume) allow us to track brain events with millisecond temporal accuracy, though with limited spatial resolution. Research across a variety of languages shows additional left fronto-temporal activity associated with the presence of grammatical morphemes. This holds for contrasts between isolated

[4] For a discussion of fronto-temporal contributions to language processing from a different theoretical perspective, see the chapter by Ullman (Ch. 16 this volume).

[5] This is not to say that language users may not also have a stored episodic trace of frequently encountered individual inflected forms (e.g. Stemberger and MacWhinnney, 1986). But these traces are not the same, on this account, as the access representations (and associated processes) which operate to decomposed inflected forms into stems and affixes (Clahsen, 1999). However, the fact that irregular past tenses, arguably stored as whole forms (*pace* Marantz and colleagues), function seamlessly to convey inflectional information in on-line language processing does provide a precedent for the possibility that some high-frequency regular forms might move into the same whole-word category. What would militate against this is that such forms would nonetheless be obligatorily subject to decompositional analysis, as argued below.

[6] This characteristic phonetic pattern is defined as the presence of a word-final coronal consonant (d, t, s, z) which agrees in voice with the preceding segment. Thus *trade* is a potential past tense form of *tray*, but *trait* is not (since the word-final (t) does not agree in voice with the preceding vowel). Similar constraints seem to apply to English (-s) inflection, where forms like *place* or *lace* are not potential plural forms.

function and content words (e.g. Pulvermüller and Mohr, 1996), and for several EEG studies examining the effects of morphological violations involving regular and irregular inflected forms, typically as they occur in sentence contexts.

The common finding for these violation studies, conducted in languages that include English, German, Catalan, and Spanish, is that so-called "default overapplications" seem to be treated as combinatorial violations. These are cases where a regular inflectional suffix is applied to a verb or noun that requires an irregular inflection—in English, *gived* rather than *gave*. These elicit a pattern of electrophysiological activity, peaking in left fronto-temporal scalp regions, that is similar to the left anterior negativity (or LAN) effects seen for syntactic violations (e.g. Lück et al., 2006; Münte et al., 1999; Rodriguez-Fornells et al., 2001). The contrary case, where a stem that takes a regular affix is given an irregular ending—an English example might be *filt* rather than *filled*—does not elicit these LAN-type effects, and seems instead to be processed as if it were a lexical violation without a combinatorial component.

Recent MEG experiments using the Mismatch Negativity (MMN) paradigm demonstrate with considerable spatial as well as temporal precision the dynamic properties of the fronto-temporal links underpinning inflectional processes. Pulvermüller et al. (2006), for example, show that a left superior temporal burst of activation, triggered by successful word recognition, is followed within tens of milliseconds by a second burst of activity in left inferior temporal regions. This is for inflected verbal forms in Finnish, where a stem like {tuo-} is accompanied by the inflectional suffix {-t}, giving the surface form *tuot* 'you bring'. Other MEG research using the MMN paradigm indicates that this left frontal activation reflects the status of the final phoneme as an inflectional affix (e.g. Shtyrov and Pulvermüller, 2002; Shtryov et al., 2005). These MEG and EEG results, in turn, are consistent with the fMRI research mentioned earlier (Tyler, Stamatakis et al., 2005), where bilateral activation of superior temporal areas is triggered by all word (and word-like) stimuli, but where additional temporal activity (especially on the left), together with a marked increase in left inferior frontal activation, is stimulated by the presence of a real or a potential inflectional affix.[7]

In summary, research into the processing of regular inflectional morphology reveals a fronto-temporal neural system that dynamically separates the speech input into complementary processing streams, on the one hand extracting information about meaning, conveyed by nouns and verb stems such as *house* or *run*, and on the other information about grammatical structure, conveyed in part by inflectional morphemes such as the English past tense {-d}. Obligatory decompositional processes map the syntactic and semantic information carried by different types of morpheme onto brain regions with separable but interdependent functions in the on-line interpretation process (Tyler and Marslen-Wilson, forthcoming). In the next section I consider how far such an model is applicable to other types of morphological process.

11.3 Derivational morphology

The core functions of derivational morphology are arguably quite different from those of inflectional morphology. Whereas inflectional morphemes result in different forms of the same word, adjusted to the requirements of its current phrasal and sentential environment, derivational processes produce new words—in linguistic terms, new lexemes with new lexical entries (Matthews, 1991)—whose meaning and syntactic function is much more context-independent. A key dimension here is whether the resulting complex form is to be regarded as a stored form in the mental lexicon, or whether it is computed "on the fly" in comprehension and production.

[7] I have not considered here the growing body of neuroimaging studies (e.g. Beretta et al., 2003; Dhond et al., 2003; Jaeger et al., 1996; Joanisse and Seidenberg, 2005; Lavric et al., 2001) looking at the neural substrates of regular and irregular past-tense production (these are all covert elicitation tasks, where participants are given a stem as a prompt and are asked to generate its past tense form, but without saying it aloud). This is partly because my focus here is on comprehension rather than production, and partly because the interpretation of these results is not straightforward (cf. Seidenberg and Arnoldussen, 2003; Seidenberg and Hoeffner, 1998). Interestingly, however, the Joanisse and Seidenberg (2005) study is consistent with our claims here for the role of the inflectional rhyme pattern. They separate out the irregulars into what they call true irregulars (like *took* and *gave*) and pseudo-irregulars—the latter being a small set of cases like *slept* and *heard* which they describe as phonologically similar to regulars. In fact these are irregular forms which either fully or partially match the inflectional rhyme pattern, but which are irregular because of a change in the stem (as in *sleep/slept*). Looking at activation for regulars, irregulars, and pseudo-irregulars, they find significantly stronger effects for both regulars and pseudo-irregulars in inferior frontal cortex, especially on the left. This seems to parallel, in language production, the LIFG effects for the inflectional rhyme pattern that we see in language comprehension (Tyler et al., 2005).

Inflectional morphology falls at one end of this continuum, where regularly inflected forms are arguably not stored. These are forms whose grammatical properties and meaning are fully compositional, in the sense of being completely predictable from the combination of the morphemes out of which they are constructed. This follows from their functional role, where the inflectional morpheme does not interact with the meaning of the stem to which it attaches, but rather with the structural context in which the stem occurs, and with the stem's relationship to that context.

The link between a derivational morpheme and its stem is a much tighter and more intralexical relationship, where the resulting product takes on a linguistic life of its own. When the adjectival stem {dark}, for example, combines with the suffix {-ness} to form the abstract noun *darkness*, this creates a new lexical entity with its own grammatical properties and meaning. Depending on its history in the language, and on the transparency and the productivity of the morphemes involved, each derivational product will vary enormously in its predictability and compositionality, and hence in the degree to which any given form can be regarded as a candidate for decompositional or stored representation. This range of variation creates a parallel, in the derivational domain, to the questions about storage and decomposition that have dominated the study of English regular and irregular inflectional morphology.

The history of psycholinguistic research into derivational morphology can be seen as a series of attempts to come to terms with this rather disparate set of phenomena, not always with the clearest and most systematic outcomes.[8] This is reflected in the great variety of theoretical positions in this area, ranging from fully *decompositional* accounts, assuming morphologically structured lexical representations which are accessed by decomposing complex forms into their constituent morphemes (e.g. Taft and Forster, 1975; Taft, 2004), through *dual-route* accounts, where complex forms can be accessed both as whole forms and in a decomposed format (e.g. Schreuder and Baayen, 1995; Burani and Caramazza, 1987; Clahsen et al., 2003), to *non-decompositional* or "full-listing" accounts, where morphological organization is claimed not to play an independent role in either central representation or in access to these representations (e.g. Bybee, 1995; Rueckl and Raveh, 1999; Seidenberg and Gonnerman, 2000).

These accounts tend to ally themselves with a range of different computational assumptions—whether they are based on distributed representations or on a network of interacting localist nodes. Decompositional and dual-route models typically assume localist accounts, where the form and meaning associated with a given word—or with its decompositional components—is represented in terms of labeled symbolic nodes, and where lexical access and selection depends on excitatory and inhibitory interactions between these nodes. Current non-decompositional models, in contrast, typically assume distributed connectionist accounts of lexical representation and processing, where complex forms are learned and represented as overlapping patterns of activity sharing certain similarities in form and meaning. Morphological relations between words, whether inflectional or derivational in nature, are captured as sub-regularities in the form-to-meaning mapping process, and are not assigned any independent status in the system. Nonetheless, to the extent that these sub-regularities are assigned a componential function in the operations of the network—as proposed by Plaut and Gonnerman (2000) and Ruekl and Raveh (1999)—then they seem to take on many of the functional roles of morphemes in competing localist accounts.

Against the background of these theoretical contrasts, and given the differences in emphasis between derivational and inflectional morphological processes, we can then return to the question posed earlier: to what extent does the kind of model proposed for inflectional morphology hold for derivational morphology. Do we see the same processes of obligatory decomposition during the lexical access process, and how far are representations of derived forms also decompositional? More generally, is there evidence that morphological effects in the derivational domain are distinguishable from the overlap of form and meaning?

11.3.1 Frequency, repetition priming, and decompositional access

Research into derivational morphology has mainly been behavioral. Unlike the research into inflectional morphology, there are only scattered neuropsychological studies, and neuroimaging research into derivational systems is still in its infancy. In the behavioral domain, one of the main tools in the attempt to distinguish decompositional and whole-form accounts has been

[8] Especially when derivational and inflectional processes are not distinguished.

research into the patterning of base- and surface-frequency effects.

The frequency of occurrence of a lexical entity affects speed and accuracy of response in a timed recognition task such as lexical decision. In a hierarchically organized representational system, it is argued that frequency effects will collect at specific points of the system. For example, if there is a lemma level of representation, into which feed all of the inflectional variants of a given noun or verb stem—and if the lemma level controls performance for a given task—then the frequency effects for each of these variants should follow the summed (or base) frequency across the lemma, rather than being driven by the frequency of occurrence of each surface form separately.

Research along these lines has been a principal input, for example, into the dual-route model developed by Baayen, Schreuder, and others, building on earlier work by Caramazza and his colleagues (e.g. Baayen et al., 1997; Caramazza et al., 1988). The first stage of this type of model consists of access representations both of words as a whole and of their morphemic components (so that *bake*, *baker*, and *-er* are all separately represented), and where complex forms are recognized either through a whole-word route or through a decompositional route. The specific patterning of response times to simple (e.g. *bake*) and complex forms (e.g. *baker*), as a function of their respective surface frequencies and of their summed base frequency, is then used to deduce whether the derived forms are recognized by direct look-up via these whole-word access representations, or whether recognition is based on decompositional parsing into morphemic components. These questions have been pursued for both inflectional and derivational morphology across a range of languages, although the story has become very intricate as the notion of frequency has itself become increasingly complex (cf. Ford et al., 2003).

Although this distributional, frequency-based approach has had major successes, most notably where the concept of morphological family size is concerned (e.g. Schreuder and Baayen, 1997; Moscoso del Prado Martin et al., 2005), its central assumption—that whole-word and decompositional access can be distinguished on the basis of surface and base frequency effects—seems increasingly open to question. Both empirical and theoretical considerations suggest that variations in lexical decision reaction time between sets of stimuli can rarely be unambiguously attributed just to the frequency differences between these sets (cf. Järvikivi et al., 2006; Taft, 2004). A case in point is the series of experiments in this framework testing claims about the role of affixal homonymy: the English suffix {-er}, for example, is homonymic between an agentive suffix, as in *baker*, and a comparative suffix, as in *slower*.

The underlying claim here is that the choice between "storage" and "computation"—i.e. between whole-form or decompositional access—is tipped towards storage by any characteristics of the complex derived (or inflected) form which would make it relatively slower to access in decomposed format (Bertram, Laine, et al., 2000). One such factor is affix homonymy, which would introduce additional competition into a decompositional access process, since the ambiguous morpheme would need to be evaluated against two sets of grammatically different possibilities—is the {-er} in *slower*, for example, agentive or comparative?

This claim has been extensively evaluated, focusing on Finnish, Dutch, and English, using the base/surface frequency methodology to ask whether various affixal factors affected the perceptual analysis of derived forms in the two languages. The counterintuitive result was that Finnish derived forms (and some inflected forms) behaved as if they were stored and accessed as full forms—with weak base frequency effects and strong surface frequency effects—while English derived forms (such as *friendship* and *childhood*) showed strong base frequency effects, consistent with decompositional access (Bertram, Laine et al., 2000; Vannest et al., 2002). This was an a-priori unlikely outcome, given the implausibility of a full-listing approach for a language like Finnish, with its productive and combinatorial morphological system (Hankamer, 1989). In fact, these results in Finnish seem to reflect a further dimension of suffix variation (suffix allomorphy[9]) that was not taken into account in the earlier research. When this is controlled for, base frequency effects duly begin to emerge (Järvikivi et al., 2006).

More generally, as Taft (2004) argues, the presence or absence of base frequency effects can also be accommodated in a fully decompositional framework and not just in a dual-route model. The typical reaction-time effect—usually a failure of high base-frequency items to show the response advantage predicted by their frequency of occurrence—could equally well, Taft points out, reflect difficulties in a post-access

[9] Allomorphy means changes in the surface form of a suffix in different environments. In Finnish, several suffixes vary unpredictably in form as a function of case (Järvikivi et al., 2006).

compositional process, where decomposed stems and affixes are combined in the process of recognition or production. This is quite consistent with the emphasis in the dual-route literature on the role of affix properties in determining whether a form is stored or not. Variations in affixal properties such homonymy, productivity, and allomorphy could all, in different ways, affect the stem/affix composition process, leading to a slowing in reaction time and the reduction of any processing advantage for high base-frequency cases. This possibility undermines any purely frequency-based claims for whole-form as opposed to decompositional access (and vice versa). Furthermore, as Davis et al. (2003) have demonstrated, it is possible to capture at least some base/surface frequency contrasts in a single mechanism connectionist model, where the storage/decomposition dichotomy no longer applies.

These considerations suggest that claims about lexical organization and processing derived from frequency contrasts need to be complemented by inputs from other techniques. The most salient of these is the armory of priming paradigms in the current literature, based on the phenomenon of "repetition priming" (typically in speeded recognition tasks). The rationale for this approach is that if two words share a common element at some level of representation—for example, the pair *darkness* and *dark* may share the morpheme {dark}—then the activation of this element by the prime word will affect responses to a target word sharing the same element. Prima facie, this can form the basis for claims about compositionality; for example, Marslen-Wilson et al. (1994) have used a cross-modal immediate repetition priming task to argue for a partially decompositional account of English derivational morphology, where semantic transparency plays a major role in determining whether central lexical representations are morphologically structured or not.

The priming task is of course subject to its own methodological caveats. One difficulty is that words which share morphemes will also tend to share phonological, orthographic, and semantic properties as well, as in the pair *darkness/dark*. It therefore becomes critical—especially in the context of connectionist claims that derivational morphology is reducible to form and meaning overlap—to determine whether a priming effect between morphologically related words is anything more than overlap along these other dimensions. A second problem, especially where overt priming tasks are used (so that both prime and target are fully visible or audible to the participant), is the possibility both for strategic effects and for episodic effects, so that responses reflect episodic memories of previously presented stimuli, rather than the relatedness of lexical representations (e.g. Fowler et al., 1985).

Nonetheless, from the large body of priming research that has been conducted over the last twenty-five years, a number of basic properties of derivational morphological processing have emerged. The most recent of these—and directly relevant to the questions we are asking here—is the compelling evidence that all potentially morphologically complex words undergo an initial obligatory process of segmentation into their morphemic components, irrespective of whether the words actually are morphologically complex. Although this obligatory early decomposition was initially proposed over thirty years ago (Taft and Forster, 1975), the recent wider acceptance of this view reflects new experiments, across a range of languages, using the masked priming technique (and hence focusing on visual rather than auditory word recognition).

Masked priming is an experimental situation where a visual prime word (preceded by a pattern mask and followed by a visual target) is presented so briefly that the reader is not aware that the prime is present, and simply makes a lexical decision to the target (Forster and Davis, 1984). From a methodological point of view, this greatly reduces the potential for both strategic and episodic effects. Several sets of experiments using this task provide converging evidence for the dominance of morphological factors in the early stages of lexical access.

There is, first, strong cross-linguistic evidence that morphological decomposition in early visual access can be demonstrated independently of the effects of form or meaning overlap between prime and target. Working in English, for example, Forster and Azuma (2000) show robust priming for pairs like *permit/submit*, which share the bound morpheme {-mit}, but where there is no semantic relationship between prime and target, and where orthographic control pairs (such as *rodent/student*) show no priming. The effects for the bound-stem pairs are in fact just as strong as those for semantically transparent pairs involving free stems, such as *unhappy/happy*.

Similar phenomena can be seen in Semitic languages (such as Hebrew and Arabic), which provide a striking cross-linguistic contrast in the types of word-formation processes that they employ. Instead of the "concatenative" processes which dominate in languages like English, Finnish, or French, where successive morphemes are linked together in a linear sequence, these Semitic languages are based on a non-concatenative morphology, where the surface phonetic form is constructed by interleaving two or more abstract morphemes: the consonantal root, carrying semantic information, and a word pattern which specifies the syntactic category and the phonological structure of the surface form.[10] These are abstract, bound morphemes, which never surface as phonetic forms on their own.

Several masked priming studies, both in Hebrew (e.g. Frost et al., 1997; Deutsch et al., 1998) and Arabic (e.g. Boudelaa and Marslen-Wilson, 2005) demonstrate priming between pairs that share the same consonantal root—for example, the Arabic prime word /ʔidxaalun/ ('inserting') speeds responses to the target /duxuulun/ ('entering'), where prime and target have in common the root {dxl}. Similarly to Forster and Azuma's results, priming is just as strong when the prime is semantically opaque, as in the form /mudaax-alatun/ ('interference'), which also shares the root {dxl} with the target /duxuulun/, but where the meaning of the form is not semantically transparent. This preservation of root priming under conditions of semantic opacity shows up consistently in both Arabic and Hebrew. Morphologically driven priming is also found between pairs that share the same word pattern but have different roots and different meanings—to take an Arabic example, for pairs like [ħaziinun]/[kariimun] ('sad/generous') which share the word pattern {faʕiilun}—and where orthographic effects have quite different characteristics (Boudelaa and Marslen-Wilson, 2004a; 2005). In general, the results for Semitic languages provide clear examples of decompositional lexical processing, with abstract morphemes combining to produce the surface form, and being separated out in the process of recognition.

The dominant role of morphological factors in the early analysis of derivational complex forms is underlined by a further series of experiments, also using masked priming, which show that this early segmentation is conducted independently not only of semantic factors, but also of the stored lexical properties of the forms in question. Studies in English, for example, by Rastle et al. (2000; 2005), show strong priming not only between transparent pairs like *bravely/brave*, which are genuinely morphologically related, but also between pairs like *hardly/hard*, which are not compositionally related in modern English, and even for pseudo-derived pairs like *corner/corn*, where *corner* clearly has no morphological interpretation as {corn + -er}. The process underlying these effects is nonetheless morphologically sensitive, since pairs like *scandal/scan*, where *-dal* is not a derivational affix in English, do not show priming (even though the amount of orthographic overlap is identical to the morphological cases). Dominguez et al. (2002) report related effects for Spanish, although in the inflectional rather than the derivational domain.

Similar patterns are reported for French by Longtin and colleagues, where transparent pairs like *gaufrette/gaufre* ('wafer/waffle') and pseudo-stem pairs like *baguette/bague* ('bread stick/ring') both prime robustly, but pairs like *auberge/aube*[11] ('inn/dawn') do not (Longtin et al., 2003). In a second set of experiments Longtin and Meunier (2005) go on to show that non-word primes (such as *rapidifier*) can prime their real word pseudo-stem (*rapide* 'rapid') just as well as transparent real-word primes (*rapidement* 'rapidly'), but only if the pseudo-stem co-occurs with an existing French suffix. Thus *rapiduit*, where *-uit* is not a possible suffix in French, does not prime *rapide*. These results not only support a lexically blind early segmentation account of masked morphological priming (non-words, by definition, cannot have a stored lexical representation), but also confirm that this early segmentation is sensitive to morphological factors. Only if the potential stem is paired with an actual suffix in the language do we see priming.

In summary, these masked priming results point to an initial modality-specific phase of the access process, where all morphologically decomposable surface forms are segmented into potential stems and affixes by a process which is blind to semantic factors, and even to higher-order lexical structure (cf. McKinnon et al., 2003; Shallice and Saffran, 1986). Given the ample evidence for masked priming between inflectionally related pairs (e.g. Drews and Zwitserlood, 1995; Forster et al., 1987; Pastizzo and Feldman, 2002), this undoubtedly extends to inflectionally complex forms as well. This is a picture that is generally consistent with both dual-route and decompositional approaches, but does not seem to follow naturally from the properties or the architecture of current non-decompositional models.

In terms of the neural substrate for these early segmentation processes, a strong candidate is

[10] For example, the surface form [xarʒa] ('go out') consists of the root morpheme {xrʒ}, with the general semantic load 'going out', combined with the word pattern {faʕala} with the syntactic reading 'singular', 'active'.

[11] The prime *auberge* does not have a morphologically plausible segmentation into {aube} plus an affix.

the left fusiform gyrus—a left-hemisphere brain region known as the visual word form area (cf. Cohen et al., 2002; McCandliss et al., 2003), which is believed to play an important role in the early interpretation of orthographic inputs. Consistent with this, a recent paper by Devlin et al. (2004) reports masked priming effects in exactly this area, using an event-driven fMRI approach, for a mixture of semantically opaque and pseudo-derived stimuli (such as *apartment/apart*, *homely/home*, and *corner/corn*). The behavioral priming effect for these materials (Devlin et al., 2006) was identical in size to the effect for morphologically transparent pairs like *teacher/teach*, consistent with the existing masked priming literature. The neural priming effect, however, was stronger in the visual word form area for the opaque and pseudo-stem pairs than for the transparent pairs, consistent with the view that activation at this level primarily reflects pre-lexical segmentation processes.[12]

Neuroimaging data from a different study (Bozic et al., forthcoming) indicates that the effects of these early analyses propagate more widely than the data from Devlin et al. (2004) would suggest. Using delayed repetition priming in an event-related fMRI paradigm, Bozic compared effects for transparent and opaque morphologically decomposable pairs (*bravely/brave*, *archer/arch*) with appropriate form and meaning controls (*harpoon/harp*, *accuse/blame*). Second presentations of morphologically related words produced significantly reduced activation in left inferior frontal regions, whether the pairs were semantically transparent or opaque. No effects were observed for the form and meaning control conditions. The appearance of these frontal morphologically driven effects at long repetition delays, for opaque as well as for transparent pairs (though see Vannest et al., 2005), suggests that potential morphemic segmentations are widely evaluated in the neural language system.

[12] Devlin et al. (2004) themselves interpret these results quite differently, since they regard their pseudo-derived/semantically opaque condition (*homely/home*, *corner/corn*) as a purely orthographic control for their morphologically related condition (*teacher/teach*). From this perspective, the weaker priming for *teacher/teach* vs *corner/corn* in the fusiform gyrus is thought to reflect the dominance of orthographic factors in explaining apparent morphological effects. In fact, this inference is not valid, given the ample evidence for the morphologically driven processing elicited by opaque and pseudo-derived pairs. A genuine orthographic control would have to be prime/target pairs that are not open to potential morphological decomposition because they do not end in potential derivational or inflectional affixes, as in Rastle et al. (2000), Longtin et al. (2003), or Bozic et al. (forthcoming).

11.3.2 Morphological decomposition and lexical representation

The research reviewed so far allows us to answer two of the main questions posed earlier. There is clear evidence for decompositional analysis in the early stages of processing of complex derivational forms, and there seems little doubt that these effects are distinguishable from the overlap of form and meaning. This brings into sharper focus the properties of "central" lexical representations—the core morphosemantic representations that are accessed via these early decompositional processes. To what extent are these also decompositional in nature? And if they are decompositional, in the sense of preserving their morphological organization, then how far are they stored as distinct lexical units?

In considering these issues, an important cue is provided by the differences between masked priming and overt priming, where the prime is fully visible or audible to the participant. Morphological masked priming seems to be driven almost entirely by the properties of early segmentation processes, and is not influenced by the lexical properties of the forms involved (cf. Marslen-Wilson et al., forthcoming). Overt priming, in contrast, seems to be primarily driven by the properties of central lexical representations of complex forms (and their component morphemes). For languages like English, French, and Polish, overt priming tasks paint a much more restricted picture of morphological decomposability than is revealed in masked priming. Robust priming between derived forms and their stems is only obtained if the relationship between them is semantically transparent in current language use.

Marslen-Wilson et al. (1994), using a cross-modal repetition priming task, where a spoken prime is immediately followed by a visual probe, report significant priming only for pairs like *darkness/dark* or *unhappy/happy*. Semantically opaque pairs like *department/depart* or *restrain/strain* consistently fail to prime, as do bound stem pairs like *submit/permit*. In the Rastle et al. (2000) masked priming paper, opaque pairs like *apartment/apart* and pseudo-stem pairs like *belly/bell*, which prime significantly at an SOA of 43 ms, show no sign of priming at an SOA of 250 ms, where the prime is fully visible to the participant (see also Feldman and Soltano, 1999), while priming for transparent pairs is not affected. In the research by Longtin et al. (2003), opaque pairs like *dentelle/dent* ('lace/tooth') and pseudo-stem pairs like *baguette/bague* ('bread stick/ring'), both of which prime strongly under masked conditions, show no priming in the cross-modal task, with a spoken prime and visual target.

In all of these studies (and there are many further examples, e.g. Feldman, 2000) the common factor in conditions where priming is preserved is the semantic transparency of the morphological relationship between the derived form and its stem. This must reflect the stored properties of central lexical representations, and the relationships between these representations. At this level of the lexical system, words like *strain* and *restrain*, or *department* and *depart*, are treated as lexically and semantically separate, capturing the fact that they are distinct and unrelated words in the language—and even more so for words like *corner* and *corn* or *belly* and *bell*. For this reason, no facilitatory priming is seen in tasks which tap into the relatedness (or not) of these stored representations. Although *bell* and *belly* may be co-activated when either one of them is seen or heard, they function as cohort competitors, generating slower responses to each other in tasks like lexical decision.

This contrasts with transparently derivationally related pairs like *darkness* and *dark* or *happy* and *unhappy*, which are rated in morphosemantic judgement tasks as being closely related, and which show strong facilitatory priming in a range of experimental paradigms. These words do not behave like cohort competitors; instead, hearing or seeing the one should always speed the recognition of the other. Marslen-Wilson et al. (1994), in a widely cited analysis, interpreted this pattern of contrasts as being driven by shared morphemic representations in stems and transparent derived forms. On this account, the reason *darkness* primes *dark* (and vice versa) is because prime and target share the morpheme {dark}, so that when either form is heard or seen the same underlying element is activated, generating savings in the appropriate response tasks.

This is an explicitly combinatorial account of lexical representation, where the same morpheme combines with other morphemes across the transparent members of a morphological family (cf. Marslen-Wilson, 1999). The morpheme {dark} in *darkness* is the same lexical and cognitive entity as the {dark} in *darkly*. Similarly, the derivational morpheme {-ness} in *darkness* is argued to be the same as the {-ness} in *toughness*, as suggested by experiments showing robust priming between semantically unrelated prime/target pairs which share the same affix, as in *darkness/toughness* and *rebuild/rethink* (Marslen-Wilson, Ford, et al., 1996). These affix-priming effects are strongest for productive affixes, and are consistent with claims for the combinatorial reuse of the same bound morpheme in prime and target. A combinatorial account of lexical representation is also suggested by the phenomenon of suffix/suffix interference. This is the interference effect observed between semantically transparent pairs sharing the same stem but different suffixes, as in *darkness/darkly* (Marslen-Wilson et al., 1994; Marslen-Wilson, Zhou, and Ford, 1996; Marslen-Wilson and Zhou, 1999). The absence of priming between these highly semantically and morphologically related pairs is interpreted as interference between two affixes competing for linkage to the same stem.

The co-occurrence of stem-priming, affix-priming, and suffix/suffix interference can be taken as diagnostic of decompositional and combinatorial lexical representations, and can be used to explore how far other languages share similar word-formation systems and processing procedures. One case study is for Polish, a Slavic language with a rich morphological system, where essentially all surface forms are morphologically complex, combining a bound stem with one or more affixes. Thus the word *przybiegłam* 'I run up' consists of the stem *bieg-*, the derivational-aspectual prefix *przy-*, and the inflectional suffixes *-ł* and *-am*, indicating the past tense and first person singular feminine. The profile of results for Polish turns out to be very similar overall to English (Reid and Marslen-Wilson, 2003). There is robust stem and affix priming, and the same strong effects as in English of semantic transparency in overt priming tasks that tap into central representations. These parallels suggest that Polish and English both fit an overall template that is consistent with a morphemically organized and combinatorial mental lexicon.

These and other results (e.g. the evidence provided by Clahsen et al., 2003 for decompositional processes in German productive derivation) make a convincing case that a substantial proportion of derived words, across a variety of languages, are centrally represented in a format which preserves the origins of these words as combinations of morphemes. This seems to hold primarily for words where the morphological relationship between derived form and stem is semantically transparent, although some cases of overt priming have been reported for opaque forms (e.g. Bozic et al., forthcoming; Zwitserlood et al., 2005). This in turn raises the question of whether decomposability and morphemic combination should be equated with the absence of storage, similarly to regular inflectional morphology.

It is unlikely this can be true across the board. For one thing, as Clahsen et al. (2003) point out, the fundamental difference between inflection and derivation is that derivation creates new words—which means new lexical entries (cf. Blevins, 1999). This implies that even highly transparent forms, made up of productive stems and affixes, and whose meaning is fully compositional, will be stored as entities at some level of the system. Clahsen et al. (2003) in fact suggest a three-way distinction that treats regular inflection, together with transparent and productive derivation, as the result of combinatorial operations, but which associates productive derivation with stored entries (which preserve this combinatorial structure). Irregular inflected items, and opaque derived forms also have stored entries, but without a decompositional morphemic structure.

In dealing with derived forms, however, we have to deal with the representation of meaning as well as with the representation of morphological organization. Even if the meaning of some derived forms is transparently compositional, a large proportion of derived forms have clearly slipped down the gradient of compositionality, with meanings that become increasingly unpredictable just from the combination of their constituent morphemes. When compositionality does not hold, then the meaning of the form must be stored separately.

These issues are brought into sharp focus by results for the Semitic languages, Arabic and Hebrew. Unlike the languages we have been discussing above, here there is no sharp distinction between masked and overt priming. As noted earlier, masked root priming in Hebrew (Deutsch et al., 1998; Frost et al., 1997) is as strong for semantically opaque prime-target pairs as it is for transparent pairs. When the same stimuli are run in a cross-modal task, with an overt auditory prime, there are still robust priming effects for the opaque pairs (Frost et al., 2000). In Arabic, several studies have consistently found priming effects for semantically opaque pairs, whether they use masked or overt priming (e.g. Boudelaa and Marslen-Wilson, 2001; 2004b). Similarly, word-pattern priming effects in both languages, which are purely morphological in nature, and where there is no semantic relationship between prime and target, are equally strong under both masked and overt conditions (e.g. Frost et al., 2000; Boudelaa and Marslen-Wilson, 2004a; 2005).

These results seem to demonstrate the separability of morphological combination from the computation and representation of meaning. If we take the familiar Arabic triconsonantal root {ktb} with the general meaning of 'write', this gives rise to many different derivational forms, which are all related to the core meaning of {ktb}, such as [kaataba] 'correspond', [maktabatun] 'library', and so forth. For these words, a compositional account of their meaning, putting together the meaning of the root and the morphosyntactic valence of the word pattern, seems plausible. For the same root, however, we also have synchronically opaque surface forms like [katiibatun], meaning 'squadron', whose meaning cannot be compositionally extracted from the meaning of the root and the word-pattern, but where, nonetheless, strong root priming is obtained between pairs like [katiibatun]/[kaataba] ('squadron/correspond').

This is a situation where the priming results tell us that the same underlying root is being accessed in the processing of the prime and the target, but where the semantic properties of at least one member of the prime/target pair cannot be derived compositionally from the meaning of that root. The specific meaning of the form [katiibatun], and many other similar forms in Arabic, must be stored separately from the morphological system. This suggests a more general separation of morphological operations from the representation and generation of the meaning of derivational forms. This in itself is not so surprising: almost all approaches to morphology assume a level of conceptual semantic representation which is distinct from processes of morphological combination (e.g. Zwitserlood et al., 2005). What is less clear is why these different aspects of lexical representation and access play out so differently in languages like Arabic from how they do in English and Polish (and similar languages). This may reflect the special properties of non-concatenative morphology, interacting with the demands of different kinds of priming task.

Either way, these considerations do not leave us with any single answer to the question posed at the beginning of this section about the balance of decomposition and storage in the representation of derived forms. In fact, it is likely that there is no single answer. For West Germanic languages like English, Dutch, or German, we may have the kind of situation sketched by Clahsen et al. (2003), where all derived forms have, by definition, a "lexical entry" in the neurocognitive language system, but where only a subset of these, based on transparent and productive word-formation processes, are stored in a decomposed and combinatorial format. It would only be this subset, then, that could support the kinds of lexicon-wide representational linkages that we pick up in overt priming tasks—and perhaps also the same subset that accounts for most of the variance in studies of morphological family size. For a language like Arabic, in contrast, it is possible that all complex forms are stored in a morphemically decomposed format, so that there are not the same variations in accessibility to a word's morphemic components as a function of priming task and semantic transparency. But a great deal of further research is needed to flesh out these speculations.

11.4 Conclusions

At the beginning of this chapter, I framed the problem of morphological processing in the broader context of how linguistic inputs are structured to convey the speaker's intended meaning, and how the sequential packaging of syntactic and semantic morphemes was central to this process. The empirical picture that is emerging, in the domains of inflectional and derivational morphology, underlines the importance of morpheme-level analysis in the language comprehension process. It seems to be one of the highest priorities of the system, as soon as orthographic or phonological information starts to accumulate, to identify possible stems and possible grammatical morphemes. There is substantial evidence from neurocognitive and behavioral sources that this is true for both inflectional and derivational morphology.

In the case of inflectional morphology, where the neurocognitive picture is better established, the basic process of lexical access for stems interacts with morphophonological parsing processes which identify the presence of potential grammatical morphemes. Regular inflected forms do not seem to participate in language comprehension as whole forms, but rather as bearers of inflectional morphemes relevant to basic phrasal and sentential interpretation, and of stem morphemes conveying further semantic and syntactic information.

For derivational morphology, we again see very early identification of morphemic structure, for both transparent and opaque derived forms, but it is unlikely that this leads to a disassembly of the complex form into its morphemic components for the purposes of subsequent analysis. This would require the meaning of such forms to be fully compositional, and this could only be true for the most recently created forms in the language. Instead, the information made available by identifying the presence of a derivational morpheme may be relevant to the appropriate syntactic treatment of the whole word in its sentential context: detecting the presence of the affix {-ness} means that the adjectival stem {dark} is now syntactically a noun, while the presence of {-er} indicates that the verb {build} is functioning as an agentive noun, and so forth. Unlike regular inflected forms, derivational forms do seem to be stored, but with considerable variation cross-linguistically both in the degree to which these stored representations are themselves morphologically organize, and in the criteria that determine whether or not this is the case.

The neurocognitive interpretation of these functional arrangements is still fragmentary and preliminary, but a picture is beginning to emerge of basic, morphologically tuned input systems in the auditory and visual domains, projecting onto separable fronto-temporal processing streams, that link the different combinations of brain areas that support the grammatical and semantic analysis of the utterance being heard or the sentence being read (Tyler and Marslen-Wilson, forthcoming). The functional architecture of the system reflects this emerging neural architecture, which seems to be largely inherited from general primate systems for complex auditory and visual object processing. Traditional cognitive models, in contrast, whether the classic dual route and decompositional varieties or current connectionist models, seem increasingly less adequate as vehicles for building explanatory models of the morphological processing systems at the heart of human language function.

Acknowledgements

I thank Tim Shallice, Lorraine Tyler, Gareth Gaskell, and an anonymous reviewer for their helpful comments on earlier drafts. The writing of this chapter was supported by the UK Medical Research Council.

References

Anderson, S. R. (1992) *A-morphous morphology*. Cambridge University Press, Cambridge.

Baayen, R. H., Dijkstra, T., and Schreuder, R. (1997) Singulars and plurals in Dutch: evidence for a parallel dual-route model. *Journal of Memory and Language*, 37: 94–117.

Beretta, A., Campbell, C., Carr, T. H., et al. (2003) An ER-fMRI investigation of morphological inflection in German reveals that the brain makes a distinction between regular and irregular forms. *Brain and Language*, 85: 67–92.

Bertram, R., Laine, M., Baayen, R. H., Schreuder, R., and Hyönä, J. (2000) Affixal homonymy triggers full-form storage, even with inflected words, even in a morphologically rich language. *Cognition*, 74: B13–B25.

Bertram, R., Schreuder, R., and Baayen, R. H. (2000) The balance of storage and computation in morphological processing: the role of word formation type, affixal homonymy, and productivity. *Journal of Experimental Psychology: Learning, Memory, and Cognition*, 26: 489–511.

Bickel, B., and Nichols, J. (2006) Inflectional morphology. In T. Shopen (ed.), *Language Typology and Syntactic Description*. Cambridge University Press, Cambridge.

Binder, J. R, Frost, T. A., Hammeke P. S. F., Bellgowan, P. S. F., Springer, J. A., Kaufman J. N., and Possing, E. T. (2000) Human temporal lobe activation by speech and nonspeech sounds. *Cerebral Cortex*, 10: 512–28.

Blevins, J. P. (1999) Productivity and exponence. *Brain and Behavioral Sciences*, 22: 1015–16.

Blevins, J. P. (2006) English inflection and derivation. In B. Aaarts and A. M. MacMahon (eds), *Handbook of English Linguistics*, pp. 507–36. Oxford: Blackwell.

Boudelaa, S., and Marslen-Wilson, W. D. (2001) Morphological units in the Arabic mental lexicon. *Cognition*, 81: 65–92.

Boudelaa, S., and Marslen-Wilson, W. D. (2004a) Abstract morphemes and lexical representation: the CV-Skeleton in Arabic. *Cognition*, 92: 271–303.

Boudelaa, S., and Marslen-Wilson, W. D. (2004b) Allomorphic variation in Arabic: consequences for lexical processing and lexical architecture. *Brain and Language*, 90: 106–16.

Boudelaa, S., and Marslen-Wilson, W. D. (2005) Discontinuous morphology in time: incremental masked priming in Arabic. *Language and Cognitive Processes*, 20: 207–60.

Bozic, M., Marslen-Wilson, W. D., Stamatakis, E., Davis, M. H., and Tyler, L. K. (forthcoming) Differentiating morphology, form, and meaning: neural correlates of morphological complexity. *Journal of Cognitive Neuroscience.*

Burani, C., and Caramazza, A. (1987) Representation and processing of derived words. *Language and Cognitive Processes*, 2: 217–27.

Bybee, J. (1995) Regular morphology and the lexicon. *Language and Cognitive Processes*, 10: 425–55.

Caramazza, A., Laudanna, A., and Romani, C. (1988) Lexical access and inflectional morphology. *Cognition*, 28: 297–332.

Clahsen, H. (1999) Lexical entries and rules of language: a multidisciplinary study of German inflection. *Behavioral and Brain Sciences*, 22: 991–1060.

Clahsen, H., Sonnenstuhl, I., and Blevins, J. P. (2003) Derivational morphology in the German mental lexicon: a dual mechanism account. In R. H. Baayen and R. Schreuder (eds), *Morphological Structure in Language Processing*, pp. 125–55. Mouton de Gruyter: Berlin.

Cohen, L., Lehericy, S., Chochon, F., Lemer, C., Rivard, S., and Dehaene, S. (2002) Language-specific tuning of visual cortex? Functional properties of the visual word form area. *Brain*, 125: 1054–69.

Davis, M. H., van Casteren, M., and Marslen-Wilson, W. D. (2003) Frequency effects in the processing of inflectional morphology: a distributed connectionist account. In R. H. Baayen and R. Schreuder (eds), *Morphological Structure in Language Processing*, pp. 427–62. Mouton de Gruyter: Berlin.

Deutsch, A, Frost, R., and Forster, K. I. (1998) Verbs and nouns are organised and accessed differently in the mental lexicon: evidence from Hebrew. *Journal of Experimental Psychology: Learning, Memory, and Cognition*, 24: 1238–55.

Devlin, J. T., Jamison, H. L., Gonnerman, L. M., and Matthews, P. M. (2006) The role of the posterior fusiform gyrus in reading. *Journal of Cognitive Neuroscience*, 18: 911–22.

Devlin, J. T., Jamison, H. L., Matthews, P. M., and Gonnerman, L. (2004) Morphology and the internal structure of words. *Proceedings of the National Academy of Sciences*, 101: 14984–88.

Dhond, R. P., Marinkovic, K., Dale, A. M., Witzel, T., and Halgren, E. (2003) Spatiotemporal maps of past-tense verb inflection. *NeuroImage*, 19: 91–100.

Dominguez, A., Cuetos, F., and Segui, J. (2002) Representation and processing of inflected words in Spanish: masked and unmasked evidence. *Linguistics*, 40: 235–59.

Drews, E., and Zwitserlood, P. (1995) Effects of morphological and orthographic similarity in visual word recognition. *Journal of Experimental Psychology: Human Perception and Performance*, 21: 1098–116.

Feldman, L. B. (2000) Are morphological effects distinguishable from the effects of shared meaning and shared form? *Journal of Experimental Psychology: Learning, Memory, and Cognition*, 26: 1431–444.

Feldman, L. B., and Soltano, E. G. (1999) Morphological priming: the role of prime duration, semantic transparency, and affix position. *Brain and Language*, 68: 33–9.

Ford, M. A., Marslen-Wilson, W. D., and Davis, M. H. (2003) Morphology and frequency: contrasting methodologies. In R. H. Baayen and R. Schreuder (eds), *Morphological Structure in Language Processing*, pp. 89–124. Mouton de Gruyter: Berlin.

Forster, K. I., and Azuma, T. (2000) Masked priming for prefixed words with bound stems: does *submit* prime *permit*? *Language and Cognitive Processes*, 14: 539–61.

Forster, K. I., and Davis, C. (1984) Repetition priming and frequency attenuation in lexical access. *Journal of Experimental Psychology: Learning, Memory, and Cognition*, 10: 680–98.

Forster, K. L, Davis, C., Schoknecht, C., and Carter, R. (1987) Masked priming with graphemically related forms: repetition or partial activation? *Quarterly Journal of Experimental Psychology*, 39A: 211–51.

Fowler, C. A., Napps, S. E., and Feldman, L. B. (1985) Relations among regular and irregular morphologically related words in the lexicon as revealed by repetiton priming. *Memory and Cognition*, 13: 241–55.

Frost, R., Deutsch, A., Gilboa, A., Tannenbaum, M., and Marslen-Wilson, W. D. (2000) Morphological priming: dissociation of phonological, semantic, and morphological factors. *Memory and Cognition*, 28: 1277–88.

Frost, R., Forster, K. I., and Deutsch, A. (1997) What can we learn from the morphology of Hebrew? A masked-priming investigation of morphological representation. *Journal of Experimental Psychology: Learning, Memory, and Cognition*, 23: 829–56.

Grosjean, F., and Gee, J. P. (1987) Prosodic structure and spoken word recognition. In U. H. Frauenfelder and L. K. Tyler (eds), *Spoken Word Recognition*, pp. 135–55. MIT Press, Cambridge, MA.

Halle, M., and Marantz, A. (1993) Distributed morphology and the pieces of inflection. In K. Hale and S. J. Keyser (eds), *The View from Building* 20: pp. 111–76. MIT Press, Cambridge, MA.

Hankamer, J. (1989) Morphological parsing and the lexicon. In W. D. Marslen-Wilson (ed.), *Lexical Representation and Process*, pp. 392–408. MIT Press, Cambridge, MA.

Jaeger, J., Lockwood, A., Kemmerer, D., Van Valin, R., Murphy, B., and Khalak, H. (1996) A positron emission tomography study of regular and irregular verb morphology in English. *Language*, 72: 451–97.

Järvikivi, J., Bertram, R., and Niemi, J. (2006) Affixal salience and the processing of derivational morphology: the role of suffix allomorphy. *Language and Cognitive Processes*, 21: 394–431.

Joanisse, M. F., and Seidenberg, M. S. (1999) Impairments in verb morphology after brain injury. *Proceedings of the National Academy of Sciences*, 96: 7592–7.

Joanisse, M. F., and Seidenberg, M. S. (2005) Imaging the past: neural activation in frontal and temporal regions during regular and irregular past-tense processing. *Cognitive, Affective, and Behavioral Neuroscience*, 5: 282–96.

Lambon Ralph, M. A., Braber, N., McClelland, J. L., and Patterson, K. (2005) What underlies the neuropsychological pattern of irregular > regular past-tense verb production? *Brain and Language*, 93: 106–19.

Lavric, A., Pizzzagalli, D., Forstmeier, S., and Rippon, G. (2001) A double-dissociation of English past-tense production revealed by event-related potentials and low-resolution electro-magnetic tomography (LORETA). *Clinical Neurophysiology*, 112: 833–49.

Longworth, C. E., Marslen-Wilson, W. D., Randall, B., and Tyler, L. K. (2005) Getting to the meaning of the regular past tense: evidence from neuropsychology. *Journal of Cognitive Neuroscience*, 17: 1087–97.

Longtin, C.-M., and Meunier, F. (2005) Morphological decomposition in early visual word processing. *Journal of Memory and Language*, 53: 26–41.

Longtin, C.-M., Segui, J., and Hallé, P. A. (2003) Morphological priming without morphological relationship. *Language and Cognitive Processes*, 18: 313–34.

Lück, M., Hahne, A., and Clahsen, H. (2006) Brain potentials to morphologically complex words during listening. *Brain Research*, 1077: 144–52.

Marcus, G. F., Pinker, S., Ullman, M., Hollander, M., Rosen. T., and Xu, F. (1992) Overregularization in language acquisition. *Monographs of the Society for Research in Child Development*, 57: 1–165.

Marslen-Wilson, W. D. (1999) Abstractness and combination: the morphemic lexicon. In S. Garrod and M. Pickering (eds), *Language Processing*, pp 101–19. Psychology Press, Hove, UK.

Marslen-Wilson, W. D., Bozic, M., and Randall, B. (forthcoming) Early decomposition in visual word recognition: dissociating morphology, form and meaning. *Language and Cognitive Processes*.

Marslen-Wilson, W., Csibra, G., Ford, M., Hatzakis, H., Gaskell, G., and Johnson, M. H. (2000) Associations and dissociations in the processing of regular and irregular verbs: electrophysiological evidence. *Journal of Cognitive Neuroscience: Annual Meeting Suppl.*, 117: 55E.

Marslen-Wilson, W. D., Ford, M., Older, L., and Zhou, X. (1996) The combinatorial lexicon: priming derivational affixes. In G. Cottrell (ed.), *Proceedings of the 18th Annual Conference of the Cognitive Science Society*, pp. 223–7. LEA, Mahwah, NJ.

Marslen-Wilson, W. D., Hare, M., and Older, L. (1993) Inflectional morphology and phonological regularity in the English mental lexicon. *Proceedings of the 15th Annual Meeting of the Cognitive Science Society*. Erlbaum, Mahwah, NJ.

Marslen-Wilson, W. D., and Tyler, L. K. (1997) Dissociating types of mental computation. *Nature*, 387: 592–4.

Marslen-Wilson, W. D., and Tyler, L. K. (1998) Rules, representations, and the English past tense. *Trends in Cognitive Science*, 2: 428–35.

Marslen-Wilson, W. D., and Tyler, L. K. (2004) The lexicon, grammar, and the past tense: dissociation revisited. In M. Tomasello and D. Slobin (eds), *Beyond Nature-Nurture: Essays in Honor of Elizabeth Bates*, pp. 263–79. Erlbaum, Mahwah, NJ.

Marslen-Wilson, W. D., Tyler, L. K., Waksler, R., and Older, L. (1994) Morphology and meaning in the English mental lexicon. *Psychological Review*, 101: 3–33.

Marslen-Wilson, W. D., and Zhou, X-L. (1999) Abstractness, allomorphy, and lexical architecture. *Language and Cognitive Processes*, 14: 321–52.

Marslen-Wilson, W. D., Zhou, X., and Ford, M. (1996) Morphology, modality, and lexical architecture. In G. Booij and J. van Marle (eds), *Yearbook of Morphology*, pp. 117–34. Kluwer, Dordrecht.

Matthews, P. H. (1991) *Morphology* (2nd edn). Cambridge University Press, Cambridge.

McCandliss, B. D., Cohen, L., and Dehaene, S. (2003) The visual word form area: expertise for reading in the fusiform gyrus. *Trends in Cognitive Sciences*, 7: 2003.

McClelland, J., and Patterson, K. (2002) Rules or connections in past-tense inflections: what does the evidence rule out? *Trends in Cognitive Sciences*, 6: 465–72.

McKinnnon, R., Allen, M., and Osterhout, L. (2003) Morphological decomposition involving non-productive morphemes: ERP evidence. *Neuroreport*, 14: 883–6.

Miozzo, M. (2003) On the processing of regular and irregular forms of verbs and nouns: evidence from neuropsychology, *Cognition*, 87: 101–27.

Moscoso del Prado Martin, F., Deutsch, A., Frost, R., Schreuder, R., De Jong, N. H., and Baayen, R. H. (2005) Changing places: a cross-language perspective on frequency and family size in Dutch and Hebrew. *Journal of Memory and Language*, 53: 496–512.

Münte, T. F., Say, T., Schiltz, K., Clahsen, H., and Kutas, M. (1999) Decomposition of morphologically complex words in English: evidence from event-related brain potentials. *Cognitive Brain Research*, 7: 241–53.

Pastizzo, M. J., and Feldman, L. B. (2002) Discrepancies between orthographic and unrelated baselines in masked priming undermine a decompositional account of morphological facilitation. *Journal of Experimental Psychology: Learning, Memory, and Cognition*, 28: 244–9.

Patterson, K., Lambon Ralph, M. A., Hodges, J. R., and McClelland, J. L. (2001) Deficits in irregular past-tense verb morphology associated with degraded semantic knowledge. *Neuropsychologia*, 39: 709–24.

Pinker, S. (1999) *Words and Rules: The Ingredients of Language*. HarperCollins, New York.

Pinker, S., and Prince, A. (1988) On language and connectionism: analysis of a parallel distributed processing model of language acquisition. *Cognition*, 28: 73–193.

Pinker, S., and Ullman, M. (2002) The past and future of the past tense. *Trends in Cognitive Sciences*, 6: 456–63.

Plaut, D. C., and Gonnerman, L. M. (2000) Are non-semantic morphological effects incompatible with a distributed connectionist approach to lexical processing? *Language and Cognitive Processes*, 15: 455–486.

Plunkett, K., and Marchman, V. A. (1993) From rote learning to system building: acquiring verb morphology in children and connectionist nets. *Cognition*, 48: 21–69.

Pulvermüller, F., and Mohr, B. (1996) The concept of transcortical cell assemblies: a key to the understanding of cortical localisation and interhemispheric interaction. *Neuroscience and Biobehavioral Reviews*, 20: 557–66.

Pulvermüller, F., Shtyrov, Y., Ilmoniemi, R., and Marslen-Wilson, W. D. (2006) Tracking speech comprehension in space and time. *NeuroImage*, 31: 1297–305.

Rastle, K., Davis, M. H., Marslen-Wilson, W. D., and Tyler, L. K. (2000) Morphological and semantic effects in visual word recognition: a time-course study. *Language and Cognitive Processes*, 15: 507–37.

Rastle, K., Davis, M. H., and New, B. (2005) The broth in my brother's brothel: morpho-orthographic segmentation in visual word recognition. *Psychonomic Bulletin and Review*, 11: 1090–8.

Reid, A. A., and Marslen-Wilson, W. D. (2003) Lexical representation of morphologically complex words: evidence from Polish. In R. H. Baayen and R. Schreuder (eds), *Morphological Structure in Language Processing*, pp. 287–336. Mouton de Gruyter, Berlin.

Rodriguez-Fornells, A., Clahsen, H., Lleo, C., Zaake, W., and Münte, T. F. (2001) Event-related brain responses to morphological violations in Catalan. *Cognitive Brain Research*, 11: 47–58.

Rueckl, J. G., and Raveh, M. (1999) The influence of morphological regularities on the dynamics of a connectionist network. *Brain and Language*, 68: 110–17.

Rumelhart, D. E., and McClelland, J. L. (1986) On learning the past tenses of English verbs. In D. E. Rumelhart, J. L. McClelland, and P. R. Group (eds), *Parallel Distributed Processing: Explorations in the Microstructure of Cognition*, vol. 2. MIT Press, Cambridge, MA.

Schreuder, R., and Baayen, R. H. (1995) Modeling morphological processing. In L. Feldman (ed.), *Morphological Aspects of Language Processing*, pp. 131–54. Erlbaum, Hillsdale, NJ.

Schreuder, R., and Baayen, R. H. (1997) How complex simplex words can be. *Journal of Memory and Language*, 37: 118–39.

Seidenberg, M. S., and Arnoldussen, A. (2003) The brain makes a distinction between hard and easy stimuli: comments on Beretta et al. *Brain and Language*, 85: 527–30.

Seidenberg, M. S., and Gonnerman, L. M. (2000) Explaining derivational morphology as the convergence of codes. *Trends in Cognitive Sciences*, 4: 353–61.

Seidenberg, M. S., and Hoeffner, J. (1998) Evaluating behavioral and neuroimaging evidence about past tense processing. *Language*, 74: 104–22.

Shallice, T. (1988) *From Neuropsychology to Mental Structure*. Cambridge University Press, Cambridge.

Shallice, T., and Saffran, E. (1986) Lexical processing in the absence of explicit word identification: evidence from a letter-by-letter reader. *Cognitive Neuropsychology*, 3: 429–58.

Shtyrov, Y., Pihko, E., and Pulvermüller, F. (2005) Determinants of dominance: is language laterality determined by physical or linguistic features of speech? *Neuroimage*, 27: 37–47.

Shtyrov, Y., and Pulvermuller, F. (2002) Memory traces for inflectional affixes as shown by the mismatch negativity. *European Journal of Neuroscience*, 15: 1085–91.

Stamatakis, E. A., Marslen-Wilson, W. D., Tyler, L. K., and Fletcher, P. C. (2005) Cingulate control of fronto-temporal integration reflects linguistic demands: a three-way interaction in functional connectivity. *NeuroImage*, 15: 115–21.

Stemberger, J., and MacWhinney, B. (1986) Frequency and the lexical storage of regularly inflected forms. *Memory and Cognition*, 14: 17–26.

Stockall, L., and Marantz, A. (2006) A single route, full decomposition model of morphological complexity. *Mental Lexicon*, 1: 85–124.

Taft, M. (2004) Morphological decomposition and the reverse base frequency effect. *Quarterly Journal of Experimental Psychology*, 57A, 745–65.

Taft, M., and Forster, K. I. (1975) Lexical storage and retrieval of prefixed words. *Journal of Verbal Learning and Verbal Behavior*, 15: 638–47.

Tyler, L. K., and Marslen-Wilson, W. D. (forthcoming) Fronto-temporal brain systems supporting spoken language comprehension. *Philosophical Transactions of the Royal Society Series B*.

Tyler, L. K., Marslen-Wilson, W. D., and Stamatakis, E. A. (2005) Differentiating lexical form, meaning and structure in the neural language system. *Proceedings of the National Academy of Sciences*, 102: 8375–80.

Tyler, L. K., de Mornay Davies, P., Anokhina, R., Longworth, C., Randall, B., and Marslen-Wilson, W. D. (2002) Dissociations in processing past tense morphology: neuropathology and behavioral studies. *Journal of Cognitive Neuroscience*, 14: 79–95.

Tyler, L. K., Randall, B., and Marslen-Wilson, W. D. (2002) Phonology and neuropsychology of the English past tense. *Neuropsychologia*, 40: 1154–66.

Tyler, L. K., Stamatakis, E. A., Jones, R., Bright, P., Acres, K., and Marslen-Wilson, W. D. (2004) Deficits for semantics and the irregular past tense: a causal relationship? *Journal of Cognitive Neuroscience,* 16: 1159–72.

Tyler, L. K., Stamatakis, E. A., Post, B., Randall, B., and Marslen-Wilson, W. D. (2005) Temporal and frontal systems in speech comprehension: an fMRI study of past tense processing. *Neuropsychologia,* 43: 1963–74.

Ullman, M. T., Corkin, S., Coppola, M., et al. (1997) A neural dissociation within language: evidence that the mental dictionary is part of declarative memory and that grammatical rules are processed by the procedural system. *Journal of Cognitive Neuroscience,* 9: 266–76.

Ullman, M. T., Pancheva, R., Love, T., Yee, E., Swinney, D., and Hickok, G. (2005) Neural correlates of lexicon and grammar: evidence from the production, reading, and judgement of inflection in aphasia. *Brain and Language,* 93: 185–238.

Vannest, J., Bertram, R., Järvikivi, J., and Niemi, J. (2002) Counter-intuitive cross-linguistic differences: more morphological computation in English than in Finnish. *Journal of Psycholinguistic Research,* 31: 83–106.

Vannest, J., Polk, T. A., and Lewis, R. L. (2005) Dual-route processing of complex words: new fMRI evidence from derivational suffixation. *Cognitive, Affective, and Behavioral Neuroscience,* 5: 67–76.

Wise, R., Scott, S., Blank, C., Mummery, C., Murphy, K., and Warburton, E. (2001) Separate neural systems within "Wernicke's area." *Brain,* 124: 83–95.

Zwitserlood, P., Bolwiender, A., and Drews, E. (2005) Priming morphologically complex verbs by sentence contexts: effects of semantic transparency and ambiguity. *Language and Cognitive Processes,* 20: 395–415.

CHAPTER 12

Semantic representation

Gabriella Vigliocco and David P. Vinson

THIS chapter deals with how word meaning is represented by speakers of a language, reviewing psychological perspectives on the representation of meaning. We start by outlining four key issues in the investigation of word meaning, then we introduce current theories of semantics, and we end with a brief discussion of new directions.

Meaning representation has long interested philosophers (since Aristotle) and linguists (e.g. Chierchia and McConnell-Ginet, 2000; Dowty, 1979; Pustejovsky, 1993; see Jackendoff, 2002), in addition to psychologists, and a very extensive literature exists in these allied fields. However, given our goal to discuss how meaning is represented in speakers' minds/brains, we will not be concerned with theories and debates arising primarily from these fields except where the theories have psychological or neural implications (as for example the work by linguists such as Jackendoff, 2002; Kittay, 1987; Lakoff, 1987; 1992). Moreover, the discussion we present is limited to the meaning of single words; it will not concern the representation and processing of the meaning of larger linguistic units such as sentences and text.

12.1 Key issues in semantic representation

When considering how meaning is represented, four fundamental questions to ask are: (1) How are word meanings related to conceptual structures? (2) How is the meaning of each word represented? (3) How are the meanings of different words related to one another? (4) Can the same principles of organization hold in different content domains (e.g. words referring to objects, words referring to actions, words referring to properties)? With few exceptions, existing theories of semantic organization have made explicit claims concerning the representation of each meaning and the relations among different word meanings, while the relation between conceptual and semantic structures is often left implicit, and the issue of whether different principles are needed for representation of different content domains is often neglected. Let us address these questions in turn.

12.1.1 How are word meanings related to concept ual knowledge?

Language allows us to share experiences, needs, thoughts, desires, etc.; thus, word meanings need to map into our mental representations of objects, actions, properties, etc. in the world. Moreover, children come to the language learning task already equipped with substantial knowledge about the world (based on innate biases and concrete experience; e.g. Bloom, 1994; Gleitman, 1990); thus, word meanings (or semantics) must be grounded in conceptual knowledge (mental representations of objects, events, etc. that are non-linguistic). This claim is certainly uncontroversial in the cognitive sciences and neuroscience: it is not so unusual, in fact, for researchers to assume (explicitly, or more often implicitly) that concepts and word meanings are the same thing, or at least are linked on a one-to-one mapping (e.g. Humphreys et al., 1999). It has also been discussed in bilingualism research (Grosjean, 1998) where this issue has important ramifications for theories of the representation of meaning in multiple languages.

In the concepts and categorization literature, scholars treat semantics and concepts as entirely interchangeable. Typically, experiments on the structure of conceptual knowledge use words as stimuli but the findings are discussed in terms of concepts, under the tacit assumption that the use of words in a given task should produce comparable results to nonlinguistic stimuli (e.g. pictures, or artificial categories). In other words, it is often assumed that the conceptual system is entirely responsible for categorizing entities in the world (physical, mental), whereas the assignment of a name to a conceptual referent (and its retrieval) is a transparent and straightforward matter.

Obviously, word meanings and concepts must be tightly related, and when we activate semantic representations we also activate conceptual information. One striking demonstration of the fact that comprehending language entails activation of information beyond linguistic meaning comes from imaging studies showing that primary motor areas are activated when speakers see or hear sentences or even single words referring to motion, in comparison to sentences referring to abstract concepts (Tettamanti et al., 2005), non-words (Hauk et al., 2004), or spectrally rotated speech (Vigliocco et al., 2006). These activations indicate that the system engaged in the control of action is also automatically engaged in understanding language related to action. Because of this tight link between conceptual structure and word meanings, research into the latter cannot dispense with the former. The issue that we must address is whether concepts and word meanings can be treated as completely interchangeable, as is often assumed.

12.1.1.1 Concepts and word meanings: do we need to draw a line?

As discussed in Murphy (2002), effects of category membership and typicality are well established in both the concepts and categorisation literature (for concepts) (e.g. Rosch, 1978) and in the psycholinguistic literature (for words) (e.g. Federmeier and Kutas, 1999; Kelly et al., 1986). Moreover, properties that have been argued to have explanatory power in the structure of conceptual knowledge and its breakdown in pathological conditions (e.g. semantic dementia) such as correlation among conceptual features, shared and distinctive features (e.g. Gonnerman et al., 1997; McRae and Cree, 2002; McRae et al., 1997; Tyler et al., 2000; see Moss, Tyler, and Taylor, Chapter 13 this volume), have also been shown to predict semantic effects such as semantic priming among words (e.g. McRae and Boisvert, 1998; Vigliocco et al., 2004). For example, McRae and Boisvert (1998) showed that previously conflicting patterns of results from semantic priming studies could be accounted for in terms of featural overlap and featural correlation between prime and target word.

Thus, if the factors that affect conceptual structures also affect semantic representations, it would seem to be parsimonious to consider conceptual and semantic representations to be the same thing, or at least to be linked on a one-to-one basis.

However, the relation between concepts and word meanings may not be so straightforward. First, word meanings and concepts cannot be the same thing, because speakers of any language have far many more concepts than words. Murphy (2002) provides the following example of a concept familiar to many of us but which is not lexicalized, at least amongst most English speakers: "the actions of two people maneuvering for one armrest in a movie theatre or airplane seat." The distinction between concepts and word meanings is also supported by findings in the neuropsychological literature which document semantic deficits, for example, impairments limited to a given semantic field of knowledge, such as fruits and vegetables (Hart and Gordon, 1992) or artifacts (Cappa et al., 1998), only in linguistic tasks (such as naming) and not in non-verbal tasks. These findings suggest that a distinction must be drawn between concepts and word meanings. They do not, however, preclude a system in which concepts and word meanings are mapped to each other on a one-to-one basis, and in which only a subset of concepts are lexicalized (as discussed below with regards to holistic theories of semantic representation). It is difficult, however, to provide a suitable account of polysemy in this way; while it is reasonable to assume that there are two distinct word meanings for the two senses of an ambiguous word like *bank* (Cruse, 1986; Lyons, 1977), it is extremely difficult to apply a similar approach to the multiple senses of polysemous words (e.g. *move* used in the context of moving objects, or moving houses; see Lupker, Chapter 10 this volume). These issues become even more complicated if we also consider cross-linguistic variability in which conceptual properties are mapped into lexical entries, as we discuss in the following section.

12.1.1.2 Concepts and word meanings: universality and language specificity

Vigliocco and Filipovic (2004), following Gentner and Goldin-Meadow (2003) and Levinson (2003), describe the dominant position within cognitive psychology for the last few decades as one in which: (i) the conceptual structure of humans is relatively constant in its core features across cultures, and (ii) conceptual structure and semantic structure are closely coupled. Levinson (2003) terms one version of such a position "Simple Nativism", according to which "linguistic categories are a direct projection of universal concepts that are native to the species" (p. 28).

Languages, however, map conceptual domains onto linguistic domains in different ways (see e.g. Kittay, 1987). To take very simple examples, English and Italian speakers both have different words for the body parts *foot* (It. *piede*) and *leg* (It. *gamba*), while Japanese speakers have a single word (*ashi*) which refers to both foot and leg. By the same token, English and Hebrew speakers have a large repertoire of verbs corresponding to different manners of jumping (leap, hop, spring, bounce, caper, vault, hurdle, galumph, and so on), whereas Italian and Spanish speakers do not (Slobin, 1996b). Surely, Japanese speakers can conceptualize "foot" as distinct from "leg", and there do not appear to be obvious cultural reasons (independent of language) to explain why Spanish or Italian speakers have fewer verbs to describe the manner of motion. To consider a further example, given the universality of human spatial abilities and the concrete relation between spatial terms and real-world referents, it might be expected that spatial categories should be similar cross-linguistically. However, spatial categories differ even among closely related languages such as Dutch and English; for example, where English has two terms (*on* and *in*), Dutch has three (*aan*, *in*, and *op*) (see Bowerman and Choi, 2003).

Under the assumption that linguistic categories are a projection of conceptual categories, cases of cross-linguistic variability like the above have important implications. If people have different semantic structures in their languages, they may also have different conceptual structures, *contra* the universality of conceptual structures. This claim is represented in the literature as the "linguistic relativity" hypothesis (Davidoff et al., 1999; Levinson, 1996; Lucy, 1992; Roberson et al., 2000; Sapir, 1921; Sera et al., 2002; Slobin, 1992; 1996a; 1996b; Whorf, 1956). Under the strongest versions of this hypothesis, proponents maintain the assumption of a one-to-one mapping between concepts and lexico-semantic representations, and thus maintain that differences in lexical semantics would lead to differences in conceptual representations for speakers of different languages (Davidoff et al., 1999; Levinson, 1996; Lucy, 1992; Sera et al., 2002; Sapir, 1921; Whorf, 1956). Weaker versions also exist in which a one-to-one mapping is not assumed but instead, linguistic categories affect conceptualization (processing) during verbal tasks (e.g. the "thinking for speaking" hypothesis put forward by Slobin, 1992; 1996a).

Assuming that cross-linguistic differences can arise in semantic rather than conceptual representation allows for (at least some) universality of conceptual structures while at the same time allowing for cross-linguistic variability of semantic representations (Vigliocco et al., 2004). It does not, however, preclude the possibility that language-specific properties can play a role in shaping conceptual representation (at least during development). For example, in the domain of color perception, Roberson et al. (2000) found differences between speakers of English and Berinmo (spoken in Papua, New Guinea). Berinmo lacks a linguistic distinction between green and blue, but contains a distinction not present in English (*nol*, approximately covering English yellow, orange, and brown; and *wor*, green, yellow-green, blue, and purple). This distinction led to differences in performance on a variety of non-linguistic tasks, suggesting that the perceptual categories we impose on colors may in part be affected by the language spoken.

Language-specific effects have also been demonstrated for properties of events. Kita and Özyürek (2003) investigated the spontaneously produced gestures of speakers co-occurring with speech referring to motion events, in order to assess whether these co-speech gestures would differ according to language differences. The co-speech gestures of interest in the study were so-called "iconic" gestures, namely gestures that iconically resemble properties of the event. These gestures encode the same message being produced in speech and are time-locked with speech, but crucially they also encode imagistic aspects of the event being described that are not encoded in the speech (as discussed below; see also McNeill, 1992), indicating that their origin is non-linguistic. Languages of the world differ with respect to whether they preferentially encode the path (direction) or the manner of motion in the verb stem (Talmy, 1986); whereas English speakers encode manner in the verb stem, Japanese and Turkish speakers encode path. Gestures produced by speakers of English (a manner language) were compared to gestures produced by speakers of Japanese and Turkish (path languages). While speakers of English tended to produce gestures that conflated manner and path (for example, producing a left-to-right arc gesture while talking about a left-to-right "swinging" event), speakers of Japanese and Turkish instead tended to produce successive gestures separating path from manner (e.g. producing first a straight left-to-right gesture and then an arc gesture) for the same swinging event. Kita and Özyürek argued that the finding that gestures, in all languages, encoded properties of the events that were not encoded in speech (e.g. the left-to-right direction of the movement was universally present in the gestures and absent in the speech) indicates that gestures are generated at a prelinguistic (conceptual) level. The finding that these gestures were affected by the lexicalization patterns of specific languages thus indicates that linguistic features can affect conceptual structures.

However, there are also studies investigating other language-specific properties that report effects that appear to be strictly limited to semantic representations, being present only in tasks that require verbalization (Brysbaert et al., 1998; Malt et al., 1999; Vigliocco et al., 2005). Brysbaert et al. (1998) showed that the time to perform mental calculations were affected by whether speakers' language required them to produce number words in forms like "four-and-twenty" (Dutch) or "twenty-four" (French), but these differences disappeared when participants were asked to type their responses rather than saying the numbers aloud. Vigliocco et al. (2005) investigated grammatical gender of Italian words (e.g. *tigre* 'tiger' is feminine in Italian regardless of whether it refers to a male or female tiger), and found that Italian words referring to animals sharing the same grammatical gender were judged to be semantically more similar; and were more likely to replace one another in semantically related slips of the tongue than words that did not share the same gender, compared to an English baseline. Although grammatical gender of nouns is a syntactic, relatively arbitrary property of words, the findings from this study suggest that it has semantic consequences. Crucially, these language-specific effects of grammatical gender disappeared when the task did not require verbalization (similarity judgements upon pictures rather than words), indicating that the effect was semantic rather than conceptual.

Together these results seem to demand a theoretical distinction between conceptual and semantic levels of representation. As we will see below, one way in which this distinction can be realized in models is by assuming that concepts comprise distributed featural representations and that lexical-semantics binds these distributed representations for the purpose of language use (Damasio et al., 2004; Vigliocco et al., 2004). Before we discuss this architectural possibility, let us consider different ways in which conceptual and lexico-semantic information can be represented.

12.1.2 How is the meaning of each word represented?

Theories of semantic organization starting from the 1960s and 1970s can be divided into those theories that consider each word's meaning as holistic, and are concerned with the types of relations between meanings (e.g. Anderson and Bower, 1973; Collins and Loftus, 1975), and theories that instead consider meanings as decomposable into features, and discuss semantic similarity in terms of featural properties such as feature overlap, among others (e.g. Minsky, 1975; Norman and Rumelhart, 1975; Rosch and Mervis, 1975; Smith et al., 1974). It is important here to note that, despite our aim of discussing semantic representations, in both types of theory the issue of decomposition vs. non-decomposition applies more directly to conceptual structures. It is necessary, however, to consider it here, as this issue has direct consequences for any attempt to describe semantic representations (concerning those conceptual structures which are, or can be, lexicalixed). In the case of non-decompositional views, word meanings are characterized as *lexical concepts* (i.e. a part of conceptual structures that represents holistic concepts each of which corresponds to a word in a given language). In the case of decompositional views, word meanings are conceived as combining a set of conceptual features (Jackendoff, 1992; Vigliocco et al., 2004), which are bound into lexical representations in order to interface with other linguistic information such as phonology (e.g. Damasio et al., 1996; Damasio et al., 2004; Rogers et al., 2004; Vigliocco et al., 2004).

12.1.2.1 Holistic views

In non-decompositional, holistic views, lexical concepts correspond to the meanings of words (Fodor, 1976; Fodor et al., 1980; Levelt, 1989; Levelt et al., 1999; Roelofs, 1997). In these views the mental representation for each thing, event, property, etc., in the world that can be lexicalized in a language is represented in a unitary and abstract way in a speaker's conceptual system. These representations can be innate, at least in some instances (for concepts that do not require combinations of different concepts) or learned via association among different features. The fact that certain concepts can be learned via association between features does not undermine the non-decompositional nature of adult representations: it is assumed that conceptual processing for adult language users does not entail retrieval of constituent properties, but instead that the assembled properties develop into a single (non-decompositional) lexical concept during language acquisition (Roelofs, 1997). Thus, for example, the concept "spinster" for the adult language user does not imply the retrieval of features such as "female" although this feature played a role in its acquisition (Levelt, 1989; Roelofs, 1997). The manner in which lexical concepts representing a sub-component of conceptual knowledge are linked to other aspects of conceptual knowledge as well as to the sensory-motor systems is not specified (but see Levelt, 1989 for a sketch).

Moreover, in holistic views, the conceptual system must include among its entries all the lexical concepts that are lexicalized and can be lexicalized in all possible languages, in order to preserve universality of conceptual representation in the face of the existence of cross-linguistic variability (Levinson, 2003). This is because the assumption of holistic lexical concepts implies a strict one-to-one mapping between concepts and lexical representations. If this is the case, cross-linguistic differences in lexical representations must then correspond to differences in concepts. Universality in conceptual structures can thus be defended only by assuming that conceptual structures comprise more entries than lexical representations and, crucially, that they comprise all lexical concepts that are (or can be) lexicalized in all existing languages.

12.1.2.2 Featural views

Initial "feature list" theories, such as the Feature Comparison Model (Smith et al., 1974) assumed that word meanings could be conceived as a combination of "defining" and "characteristic" conceptual features. Approaches of this type, however, underwent strong criticisms in the 1980s and 1990s that led to their disappearance. For example, Fodor et al. (1975) and Fodor et al., (1980) argue for the impossibility of identifying defining features for all meanings.

Another argument that has been raised against decompositionality is the so-called "hyponym/hyperonym" problem (Roelofs, 1997; Levelt et al., 1999): if word meanings were to be decomposed, nothing could stop a speaker from erroneously producing the word *animal* every time s/he wants to say *dog*. This is because all the features of *animal* are also features of *dog* (which has additional features not part of the representation of animal). This issue, however, can be computationally solved, as has been shown by Bowers (1999; see also Caramazza, 1997), who demonstrates that lateral inhibitory connections between lexical units allow the correct production of both subordinates (hyponyms) and superordinates (hyperonyms).

In the recent literature, two alternative types of featural proposal have been developed. On one hand, in the linguistic literature we find proposals such as those by Jackendoff (1983; 1990; 1992; 2002), who argues for abstract conceptual primitive features as underlying word meanings, some of which can be mapped into syntactic properties across languages (THING, EVENT, STATE, PLACE, PATH, PROPERTY). These abstract conceptual features include high-level abstract perceptual rendering of concrete things (along the lines of 3D models: Marr, 1982).

In cognitive science and neuroscience a different featural approach has developed, starting primarily from work in neuropsychology (Allport, 1985; Warrington and Shallice, 1984) and computational neuroscience (Farah and McClelland, 1991). Here, conceptual features are not abstract, but grounded in perception and action at least to some extent. In other words, conceptual features, the building blocks of semantic representation, are *embodied* in our concrete interactions with the environment. In a number of proposals, one important dimension along which concepts in different semantic fields differ is the type of conceptual feature, with some concepts relying primarily on sensory-related properties; and others relying primarily on motor-related properties (e.g. Barsalou et al., 2003; Cree et al., 1999; Damasio et al., 2004; Gallese and Lakoff, 2005; Rogers et al., 2004; Vigliocco et al., 2004).

In order to gain insight into these conceptual features some authors have used "feature norms" obtained by asking speakers of a language to provide a list of the features they believe to be important in describing and defining the meaning of a given word (Cree and McRae, 2003; McRae et al., 1997; Vigliocco et al., 2004; Vinson and Vigliocco, 2002).[1] Example of features produced for four words (two referring to objects, two referring to actions) are given in Table 12.1. These feature norms have been shown to be useful not only in giving some leverage into identifying the relative proportions of different featural types underlying each word's meaning,

[1] These differ crucially from association norms (in which participants are typically given a target word and asked to produce the first word that comes to mind), which can be considered holistic in nature because they provide only links between words, rather than revealing conceptual elements of the meanings of individual words.

Table 12.1 Sample of speaker-generated features for two nouns referring to objects and two verbs referring to actions. Weights reflect the number of speakers (max = 20) who generated that feature for a given word (from Vinson and Vigliocco, 2002).

the-grapefruit		the-hatchet		to-blink		to-pound	
feature	**weight**	**feature**	**weight**	**feature**	**weight**	**feature**	**weight**
fruit	18	sharp	14	use-eye	16	hit	14
pink	17	cut	13	close	14	beat	8
yellow	13	tool	13	involuntary	11	hard	6
sour	11	wood	9	open	8	force	5
juice	8	axe	8	action	7	noise	5
eat	7	chop	7	protect	7	use-fist	5
breakfast	6	handle	7	fast	5	anger	4
round	6	metal	7	move	5	action	3
citrus	4	blade	6	use-eyelid	5	contact	3
large	4	small	4	reflex	4	flat	3
orange	4	for-humans	3	intentional	3	loud	3
food	3	weapon	3	sudden	3	move	3
seed	3	danger	2	by-animal	2	object	3
sweet	3	survive	2	by-humans	2	physical	3
bitter	2			natural	2	punch	3
healthy	2					use-hammer	3
						violent	3

as illustrated in Figure 12.1, but also in providing information concerning featural properties shared by different words. The latter is discussed below.

Among the evidence in support of embodied views are imaging studies (like the ones we have mentioned earlier) that show differential activations for example in naming entities from different semantic fields (e.g. Damasio et al., 1996; Martin and Chao, 2001) and entities vs. actions (Damasio et al., 2001; Tranel et al., 2001). In addition, a number of recent behavioral studies have shown the importance of embodied knowledge in guiding comprehension (for an extended discussion, see Glenberg, this volume). For example, Glenberg and Kaschak (2002) presented participants with sentences depicting transfer events between *you* and another person (both concrete, e.g. *Courtney handed you the notebook*, and abstract, e.g. *You told Liz the story*) and asked participants to indicate whether the sentences were sensible by pressing buttons. Crucially, the buttons were arranged so that a response (yes or no) was either consistent or inconsistent with the (implied) direction of the transfer (towards or away from the body). Participants' response times were sensitive to the relation between the direction of the transfer and the position of the "yes" response button, demonstrating that comprehension of sentences depicting transfer events had consequences for manual responses. Richardson et al., (2003) also found a relationship between perceived language and spatial information processing by acoustically presenting participants with sentences whose verbs reflected either horizontal or vertical motion schemas (e.g. *push* vs. *lift*) and asking them to perform non-linguistic tasks for which the horizontal or vertical axes were relevant (visual discrimination, pictorial memory) at the same time. Performance on these tasks differed depending on the direction of the motion implied by the sentences, again consistent with the influence of embodied knowledge upon comprehension.[2]

[2] We will return to this issue in section 12.3, where we will discuss how embodied views of representation may be able to account for the representations of abstract words.

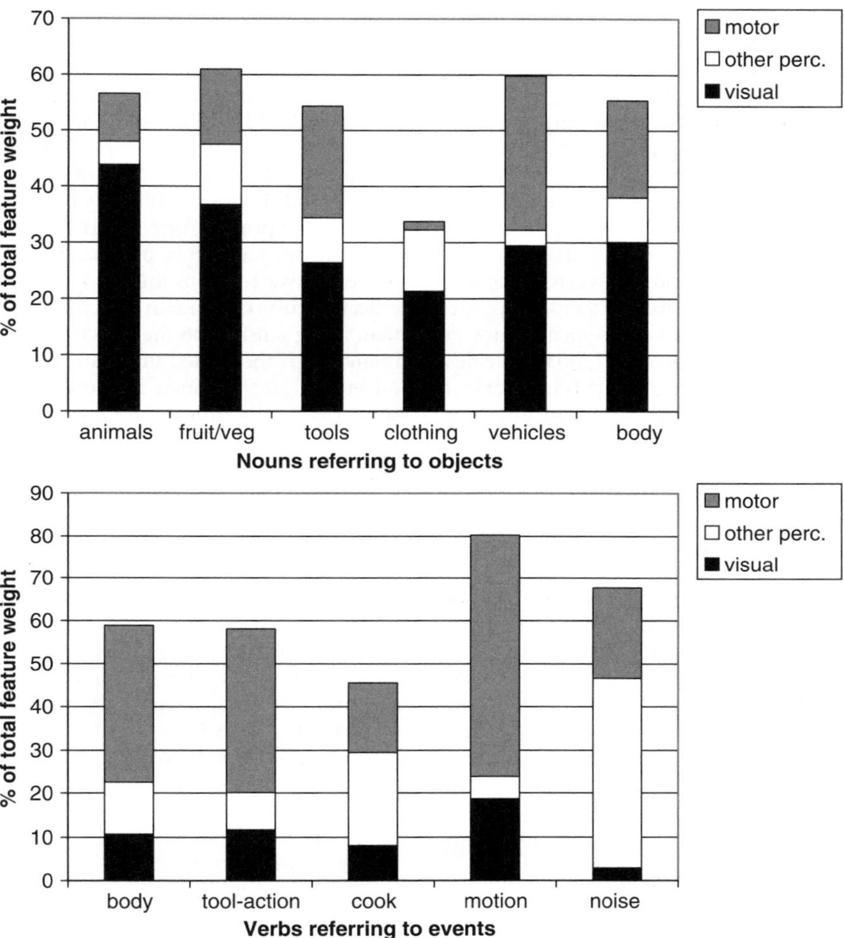

Figure 12.1 Distribution of features of different types across some semantic fields: nouns referring to objects and verbs referring to events. Black sections depict features related to the visual modality (e.g. <red>); white sections depict features related to other perceptual modalities (e.g. <loud>, <hot>); gray sections depict features related to motion (e.g. <fast>, <awkward>).

Taken together, the imaging and behavioral studies suggest that concrete aspects of our interaction with the environment (sensory-motor features) are automatically retrieved as part of sentence comprehension. Note that under assumptions of holistic lexical concepts or abstract featural representations, these findings can only be explained by invoking strategic (i.e. extralinguistic) processes. Although such a possibility cannot be completely dismissed on the basis of the current evidence, it appears to be unsatisfactory because of the difficulty of identifying clear reasons for why these processes should be engaged.

Interestingly, within the general embodiment framework, until recently researchers have assumed some degree of abstraction (i.e. supramodality). For example, on the basis of imaging studies in which participants were asked to name different types of entity, Martin and colleagues concluded that featural conceptual information related to sensory-motor modality is represented in the brain in areas adjacent to, but not overlapping with, perceptual associative areas (Martin and Chao, 2001). In a very recent and highly provocative paper, however, Gallese and Lakoff (2005) present the possibility that featural representations are literally sensory-motor, engaging the same cortical networks used in perception and motion (including primary sensory and motor areas) without the need to invoke additional, more abstract representations.

Among the reasons why it has been argued that conceptual features must be abstract, rather than embodied in perception and action, Jackendoff (1983) suggests that a featural view in which the features are directly linked to perception and action cannot underlie the representation of conceptual *types* (representations of a class of objects, such as various types of drills, rather than of specific exemplars or *tokens*, i.e. specific instances of drills). However, Barsalou et al. (2003) provide a possible solution, presenting a framework in which type representations are able to arise from modality-related perceptual symbol systems.

Figure 12.2 provides a schematic representation of the basic differences between the holistic and featural views. To summarize, although both holistic and featural views are represented in the current literature, it appears that the weight of the evidence is in favor of featural views (see also Moss, Tyler, and Taylor, Chapter 13 this volume) and, more specifically, embodied views. Taking this perspective, language is seen as more similar to other cognitive systems than it has been considered to be in traditional psycholinguistic views in which language was considered an abstract system *par excellence*.

12.1.3 How are meanings of different words related to each other?

Semantic similarity effects are powerful and well documented in the word recognition literature (semantic priming, Neely, 1991); word production literature (semantic substitution errors, Garrett, 1984; 1992; 1993; interference effects in the picture-word interference paradigm, Glaser and Düngelhoff, 1984; Schriefers et al., 1990) and neuropsychological literature (patients who make only semantic errors in their speech, e.g. Caramazza and Hillis, 1990; Ruml et al., 2000; patients who cannot name entities in specific semantic fields, e.g. Hart et al., 1985; see Vinson et al., 2003 for a review). These similarity effects must reflect principles of semantic organization, and must be accounted for by theories of semantic representation.

Let us consider first semantic effects in psycholinguistic experiments. Semantic priming refers to the robust finding that speakers typically respond faster to a target word when it is preceded by a semantically related word than when it is preceded by an unrelated word (Meyer and Schvaneveldt, 1971). Semantic priming in lexical decision tasks (word/non-word decision) or in naming tasks has been largely investigated because it has been considered to directly reflect the organization of semantic memory (e.g. Anderson, 1983; Collins and Loftus, 1975; Cree et al., 1999; McRae and Boisvert, 1998). Especially relevant are the results of Cree et al. (1999), and McRae and Boisvert (1998), who found that priming for prime/target words from the same semantic category can be observed in the absence of associative relations among items (the latter reflecting co-occurrence in speech and text, rather than being sensitive to the structure of semantic memory), if the related items are selected based on empirically obtained measures of semantic similarity. Furthermore, they also reported these priming effects to be symmetrical (e.g. *turkey* primes *goose* as much as *goose* primes *turkey*).

Whereas in word recognition the presentation of a semantically related prime facilitates the recognition of a target word, the presentation of a semantically related word immediately before a picture which must be named slows down naming latencies, compared to an unrelated word. Studies using this picture-word interference paradigm have established that the time course of these semantic effects for categorically related distractors/targets ranges from slightly before picture onset (SOA–200 milliseconds) up to very slightly after the picture onset (SOA +50 ms) (Glaser and Düngelhoff, 1984).

The contrast between the interference effect in the picture-word interference experiments and the priming effect in word recognition experiments may be explained in terms of differences between the processes involved in the two tasks. In particular, in the picture naming task, a specific word must be selected for naming with no additional support from orthography (because the input is a picture). In this case, other co-activated lexical representations could slow down the process by competing for selection. The lexical decision task, instead, requires recognition rather than selection; furthermore, additional support from the orthographic form is available (because the input is a word). In this case, co-activation of other words would not create costs because the task only requires participants to decide whether the presented string is a word or not, rather than to select that specific word from among competitors. Hence, in both cases, the prime/distractor word would have similar effects upon lexico-semantic processing; however, because of task differences the effect is facilitatory in one case (priming in lexical decision) and inhibitory in the other (picture-word interference).

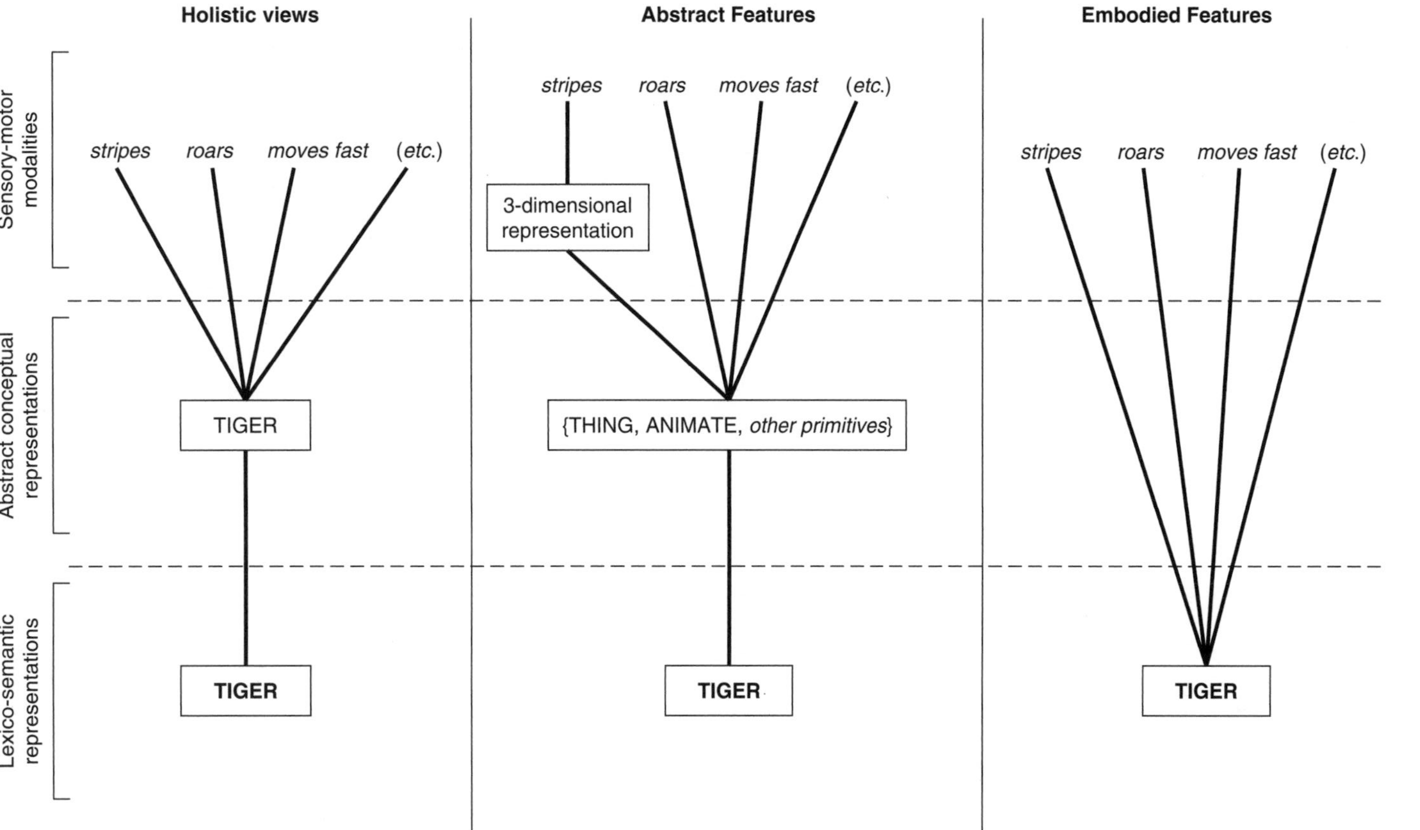

Figure 12.2 Schematic representation of the differences between holistic views (left panel), featural views based upon abstract conceptual features (center panel), and featural views based on sensory-motor experience (right panel).

Under a holistic view, these semantic effects are accounted for in terms of spreading of activation in the lexical network (Collins and Loftus, 1975; Roelofs, 1997). Holistic lexical concepts are linked to each other on the basis of different links, representing different types of relationship among concepts. With respect to words referring to concrete objects (with few exceptions the only type of word investigated in the literature), the links represent hyperonymy and hyponymy (identification of hierarchical structure of superordinates and subordinates), meronymy (parts of), and various other relations depending on the specific theoretical framework.

Under a featural view, the semantic effects are accounted for in terms of featural properties: the semantic relation between words can be determined on the basis of the featural overlap (between individual features, but also between sets of correlated features) (Cree et al., 1999; Masson, 1995; Plaut, 1995; Vigliocco et al., 2004). Using featural norms, McRae and Boisvert (1998) evaluated previous studies which failed to find semantic priming in the absence of associative relations (Shelton and Martin 1992), discovering that these studies employed prime/target pairs that were not sufficiently semantically similar despite being from the same semantic category.

Semantic effects can be *graded* even for complex semantic categories such as objects, not just for categories that naturally extend along a single dimension (numbers) or only a few dimensions (colors) in both word recognition and picture naming (Vigliocco et al., 2004). These effects will be discussed in some more detail in section 12.2. Here we would like to point out that finding graded effects is somewhat problematic for holistic theories. Take for example *cucumber* and *pumpkin*. Both words are from the same semantic category as *celery* (vegetables, at least according to Wordnet). Priming from *cucumber* and *pumpkin* to *celery* in holistic theories would come about because both prime words would activate the superordinate term *vegetable* via hyperonym links. Because *cucumber* and *pumpkin* are co-hyponyms, they should activate the superordinate to the same extent, and would therefore spread an equal amount of activation to other co-hyponyms of the primes such as the target *celery*. The amount of priming should not differ between these conditions, unless additional assumptions are implemented, such as, for example, the assumption that priming reflects category typicality (for example, by allowing the strength of hyponym links to vary as a function of typicality), or that other types of link are also relevant in determining the amount of priming. Featural views, instead, can easily account for such effects: the degree of featural overlap (and hence the degree of co-activation) is higher between *cucumber* and *celery* (which share many specific features like <crisp>, <green>, <healthy>, <salad>, <watery>, etc.) than between *cucumber* and *pumpkin* (which mainly share only the basic features common among most vegetables; see Vigliocco et al., 2004).

Featural views also seem to offer a more promising account than holistic views for semantic-relatedness effects reported in the neuropsychological literature. Because this literature is treated at length elsewhere (Moss et al., Chapter 13 this volume), we limit our discussion here to the implications of "category-related deficits" (deficits limited to a domain of knowledge or to a single category) for holistic and featural views of semantic representation. Most current accounts of category-related deficits assume featural representations and explain the observed dissociations either in terms of impairments of a given type of features (sensory or functional, e.g. Warrington and McCarthy, 1983; 1987; Borgo and Shallice, 2001) or in terms of different featural properties characterizing different categories (e.g. Devlin et al., 1998; Gonnerman et al., 1997; McRae and Cree, 2002; Tyler et al., 2000; Vinson et al., 2003). These accounts are in line with the general finding that the category-related deficits are usually graded rather than all-or-none for a specific category, compatible with distributed neural representation of knowledge. It is unclear how these findings could be explained within holistic views.

Thus, although semantic priming in word recognition and semantic interference in the picture-word interference task can be accounted for by both holistic and featural views, some results—in particular the indication that the semantic effects may be graded—are more naturally accounted for within featural accounts. This is also the case for category-related deficits reported in the neuropsychological literature. Before we discuss in some detail some of the current holistic and featural theories of semantic organization, it is important to consider the final key issue: whether words from different content domains should be represented following the same principles or not.

12.1.4 **Are words from different conceptual domains represented in the same way?**

This issue has received relatively little attention, perhaps because much of the behavioral research aimed at assessing models of semantic representation has focused upon nouns referring to concrete objects. As Miller and Fellbaum (1991) put it, "When psychologists think about the organisation of lexical memory it is nearly always the organisation of nouns they have in mind" (p. 204). We can further add that most research has been limited not only to investigating nouns, but more precisely nouns referring to concrete objects.

Words referring to objects differ from words referring to other content domains along a number of dimensions. Because the content domain of words referring to actions/events is the only other domain beyond words referring to concrete objects that has received appreciable attention, our discussion below is primarily limited to contrasting these two domains. For work on the semantic representation of adjectives see Gross et al. (1989); for a short discussion of the representation of abstract words see section 12.3 below. A first intuitive difference between objects and actions/events is that objects can be understood in isolation, while events are relational in nature. One implication of this difference is that words referring to events are more abstract than words referring to objects (Bird et al., 2000; Breedin et al., 1994). Some authors have also argued that words referring to objects and events differ in featural properties (Graesser et al., 1987; Huttenlocher and Lui, 1979). For words referring to objects there would be more features referring only to narrow semantic fields (e.g. <domesticated> vs. <wild> for animals) than for words referring to events. For these latter, instead, more features would apply to members of diverse semantic fields (e.g. <intentionality>, <involves motion>). Furthermore, features would tend to be more strongly correlated within semantic fields for objects (e.g. <having a tail>, and <having four legs> for mammals) than for events. Such differences are indeed observed within feature norms; see Table 12.2, which reports a number differences in terms of featural properties between objects and events (from Vinson and Vigliocco, 2002).

It is intuitively clear that while distinguishing between different levels (superordinate, basic, subordinate; Rosch and Mervis, 1975) is relatively simple and fruitful for object concepts (and especially natural kinds); the situation is different for events. Nonetheless, there have been attempts to define basic level actions (Lakoff, 1987; Morris and Murphy, 1990), and hierarchical representations for events have been offered in the literature (Jackendoff, 1990; Keil, 1989). Differences between the domains, however, persist. For example, in Keil (1989), the hierarchical organization for objects and events is described as being different, with event categories being represented by fewer levels (generally two) and with fewer distinctions at the superordinate level. Other attempts to capture a level of organization for events have included distinctions between "light" (e.g. *do*) and "heavy" (e.g. *construct*) verbs (Jespersen, 1965; Pinker, 1989) and distinctions between "general" (e.g. *move*) and "specific" (e.g. *run*) verbs (Breedin et al., 1998). However, the light/heavy dichotomy only allows us to draw a distinction between verbs used as auxiliaries and other verbs; while where to draw the line between "general" and "specific" verbs is not an easy or agreed-upon exercise.

Words referring to objects and words referring to events also differ in dimensions crossing the boundary between semantics and syntax. The syntactic information associated with event words is richer than for object words. It has been argued that the lexico-semantic representations for actions contain the "core" meaning (the action or the process denoted) and the thematic roles specified (e.g. the verb "to kick" implies striking out with the foot, and thematic roles that refer to the roles played by the verb in terms of "who did what to whom"). Strictly related to the thematic roles are the number and kind of arguments the verb can take (argument structure and subcategorization) (Grimshaw, 1991; Jackendoff, 1990; Levin, 1993). These different kinds of information seem to be strongly related to each other within a language (Fisher, 1994), and can differ between languages.

Also relevant here are imaging studies which provide some evidence for distinct neural substrates for processing the meanings of words referring to objects and actions. For words referring to objects, multimodal areas of the basal temporal cortex are involved in semantic processing (Price, 1998), while semantic processing of words referring to actions involves left primary motor and premotor areas (Hauk et al., 2004; Tettamanti et al., 2005; Vigliocco et al., 2006) and left middle temporal areas (Tranel et al., 2004).

In the very few existing models that have addressed the semantic representation of objects and events, researchers have decided either to embed different or the same organizational principles. In Wordnet, a holistic model of semantic representation (Miller and Fellbaum (1991) has been developed using the strategy of deciding a priori diagnostic properties of the different domains, with different types of relational links for objects and events. For nouns referring to objects, relations such as synonymy, hyponymy

Table 12.2 Summary of feature-based distinctions between words referring to objects and words referring to actions and events (Vinson and Vigliocco, 2002). All differences are significant at $p<.01$. Analyses of properties of individual features and feature types consider all 456 words in the feature-norm database; properties of multiple features consider a set of animals, artefacts and actions matched for concept familiarity (reported in Vinson et al., 2003).

	Objects	**Actions**
Properties of individual features:		
Number of features/word	29.8	26.8
Summed feature weights/word	113.3	86.3
Feature types:		
Visual/perceptual features (%)	39.1%	23.7%
Functional features (%)	17.0%	12.5%
Motoric features (%)	12.7%	30.7%
Properties of multiple features:		
Shared features[a]	44.9	32.9
Feature correlation (r)[b]	0.133	0.081

[a]Shared features were defined as those features shared by 15% or more of the exemplars within a semantic field. The values given here are the average summed weight of all the "shared" features per word in the test set.

[b]Average correlation of feature pairs for each word in the test set, calculated on the basis of correlations with all feature pairs across the entire set of 456 words.

(e.g. *dog* is a hyponym of *animal*), and meronymy (e.g. *mouth* is part of *face*) are argued to play a prime role in describing the semantic organization. For verbs, instead, the authors propose that relational links among verb concepts include troponymy (i.e. hierarchical relation in which the term at a level below, e.g. *crawling*, is a manner of a term at a level above, e.g. *travel/go/move/locomote*), entailment (e.g. *snoring* entails *sleeping*), and antonymy (e.g. *coming* is the opposite of *going*), while relations such as meronymy would not apply.

In the Featural and Unitary Semantic Space Hypothesis (FUSS, Vigliocco et al., 2004) the strategy, instead, has been not to decide a priori upon criteria to distinguish the object and the event domains, but to model both types of word within the same lexico-semantic space using the same principles. This strategy has also been used by global co-occurrence memory models such as Latent Semantic Analysis (LSA, Landauer and Dumais, 1997) and Hyperspace Analogue to Language (HAL, Burgess and Lund, 1997).

In the following section, we consider in more detail the general assumptions underlying these different theories.

12.2 Theories of semantic representation

Theories of semantic representation can be described as falling into these two general classes: those in which a word's meaning is represented in terms of its relation to other words, and those in which a words meaning is, instead, represented in terms of separable aspects of meaning, which taken together constitute the meaning of each word.

12.2.1 Theories based on relations among words

Holistic theories

Early theories of this type were framed as *semantic networks* in which different words are represented as nodes, and semantic relationships are expressed by labelled connections between nodes.

Within such views a word's meaning is expressed by the links it has to other words: which other words it is connected to, what types of connection are involved, etc. Of paramount importance for network-based theories is the type, configuration, and relative contribution of the links that exist between words. Numerous alternative frameworks have been developed (see Johnson-Laird et al., 1984 for a review) which differ along these crucial dimensions. Importantly, these models have in common a focus upon (explicit) intensional relations, and a necessity to explicitly designate those relations that are implemented within the network.

Perhaps the most extensive model which implements distinct representational themes is Wordnet (Miller and Fellbaum, 1991), a network model of the representations of a large number of nouns, verbs, and adjectives in English. In Wordnet, "nouns, adjectives and verbs each have their own semantic relations and their own organisation determined by the role they must play in the construction of linguistic messages" (p. 197). These relations and organization are constructed by hand on the basis of the relations that are believed to be relevant within a given class of words. For nouns, the most important roles are typically played by relations including synonymy, hierarchical relations, and part–whole relations. For verbs, instead, dominant are troponymy (hierarchical relations related to specificity in manner), entailment, causation, and antonymy. Some evidence compatible with a different role of relations, such as cohyponymy and antonymy for nouns and verbs, comes from spontaneously occurring semantic substitution errors. In an analysis of semantic substitution errors from the MIT/AZ corpus, Garrett (1992) reports that for nouns (n = 181) the large majority of substitutions involve category coordinates (n = 137); with opposites being present but far less common (n = 26). For verbs (n = 48), the preferred semantic relationship between target and intruding words is different from that for nouns, with opposite pairs (e.g. *go/come*; *remember/forget*) being more represented (n = 30) than non-contrastive categorical relations (*drink/eat*; *looks/sounds*).

Like network models, semantic field theory (originating with Trier, 1931; see Lehrer, 1974; Kittay, 1987) considers semantic representations as arising from relationships among the meanings of different words. Semantic fields are considered to be a set of words that are closely related in meaning. The meaning of a word within a field is determined entirely in terms of contrast to other words within the given semantic field. Crucially, unlike network models this approach does not require overtly defining the particular relations that are involved in general; but in order to allow evaluation of such views it is necessary to identify which principles of contrast apply within a field. For example, the semantic field of color words is largely distinguished by the continuous properties of hue and brightness (Berlin and Kay, 1969); kinship terms by dimensions like age, sex, degree of relation (Bierwisch, 1969); cooking terms by factors like heat source, utensils involved, and materials cooked (Lehrer, 1974); body parts by function and bodily proximity (Garrett, 1992). Such factors have been demonstrated to have behavioral consequences, for example, Garrett (1992) showed that spontaneously occurring semantic substitution errors reflect minimal contrasts along the relevant dimensions within a semantic field (errors involving body parts are largely related by physical proximity; while errors involving artefacts are much more likely to share function). One crucial difference with network models is that semantic field theory allows for flexibility in representation, and therefore a word can be a member of multiple semantic fields at once.

12.2.2 Beyond holistic theories

All of the above theories depend upon deciding which relationships or characteristics are most relevant in representing meaning (either at a broad level, like network models, or within finer-grained domains of meaning, like semantic field theory), and then deciding upon a manner of implementation based on them. An entirely different relational approach, however, seeks to discover representations of words in terms of their relationship to other words, without making any a priori assumptions about which principles are most important. This approach can be found in global co-occurrence models such as Latent Semantic Analysis (LSA, Landauer and Dumais, 1997) and Hyperspace Analogue to Language (HAL, Burgess and Lund, 1997). These models take advantage of computational techniques, using large corpora of texts in order to compute aspects of a word's meaning on the basis of those other words found in the same linguistic contexts. As such, representations are purely abstract, denoting a word's similarity to other words without revealing which aspects of meaning or relation are responsible in one case or another. Measures of similarity based on these models have been demonstrated to predict behavioral performance to some extent. For example (Landauer and Dumais, 1997; see also Burgess and Lund, 1997), LSA similarity measures (cosines) derived from encyclopedia text were applied to a set of synonym questions from the Test of English as a Foreign Language (TOEFL). In these questions, a target word is presented along with four possible choices, one of which is a synonym to the target. On this task, LSA similarity measures identified the correct answer 64.4 percent of the time, comparable to the performance of individuals from non-English-speaking countries who took the test (64.5 percent). Results like these suggest that abstract representations derived from words' contexts (e.g. LSA and HAL) reflect patterns of similarity that have some psychological plausibility.

These abstractionist theories, however, have in common a serious flaw in that they focus only upon relationships among words and are not grounded in perception and action. As Johnson-Laird et al. (1984) wrote, "The meanings of words can only be properly connected to each other if they are properly connected to the world" (p. 313). Although specifically criticizing semantic network models, this statement is equally relevant to any theory of representation that is not embodied in experience to some extent.

12.2.3 Featural theories

A variety of theories (e.g. Rosch and Mervis, 1975; Smith et al., 1974; Collins and Quillian, 1969; Jackendoff, 1990; Minsky, 1975; Norman and Rumelhart, 1975; Shallice, 1993; Smith and Medin, 1981) considers the representation of meaning not in terms of the relationships among words but in terms of feature lists: those properties of meaning which, taken together, express the meaning of a word. As discussed above, models differ with respect to whether these features are considered to be abstract or embodied as they are descriptors of sensory/motor experience with the world. Whereas some authors' research agenda concerns the identification of those primitive features that represent the *actual* decompositional components of meaning (e.g. Jackendoff, 1983), other authors have attempted to gain insight into those dimensions of meaning that are considered to be psychologically salient by speakers by using feature norms (e.g. McRae et al., 1997; Rogers and McClelland, 2004; Vigliocco et al., 2004). These feature norms are considered to provide a window into conceptual representation. Nonetheless, properties of such features have been shown to account for effects of meaning similarity (Cree et al., 1999; Vigliocco et al., 2004), and have been used as the basis to develop models of impaired performance (Vinson et al., 2003) and to generate prediction for imaging experiments (Vigliocco et al., 2006).

Several models of semantic representations based on speaker-generated features have been implemented, differing mainly in the manner in which semantic representations are derived from a set of feature norms. One class of models employs connectionist frameworks which develop representations from semantic input informed by feature norms, often in order to demonstrate how particular patterns of semantic impairment can be observed as a consequence of differential featural composition. This approach typically entails training a connectionist network with input that, although not directly obtained from speakers, is informed by particular characteristics of feature norms that are hypothesized to play a role. For example, Farah and McClelland (1991) constructed a model in which words referring to living or non-living entities were associated with different proportions of visual-perceptual vs. functional features (the former predominant for living things, the latter predominant for non-living entities), consistent with evidence from feature-generation tasks. Differential category-related effects were found when the model was lesioned (damaged in order to simulate impaired performance), depending upon whether the lesion targeted the visual-perceptual or functional features. A similar approach was taken by Devlin et al. (1998), who addressed the differential impairment over time for living or non-living things as a consequence of Alzheimer's dementia. Instead of distinguishing between the two on the basis of feature types of individual items, Devlin et al., implemented semantic representations that were based upon the relationship between entities in a particular domain: intercorrelated features (those features which frequently co-occur with each other) and distinguishing features (those which best enable similar entities to be distinguished from each other). While living things typically have many intercorrelated features but few distinguishing ones, the situation is reversed for non-living entities (McRae et al., 1997). These differences in the composition of living and non-living entities were sufficient to explain the progression of relative impairment in distinguishing living and non-living things as a consequence of Alzheimer's dementia, even within a single representational system (see also Rogers et al., 2004).

In these examples, however, semantic representations are based on features whose distribution is informed by the properties generated by speakers (e.g. more visual-perceptual features for living things, as in Farah and McClelland, 1991; more intercorrelated but fewer distinguishing features, as in Devlin et al., 1998). Such approaches, however, require making a priori assumptions about the particular properties that are relevant to explain a particular pattern of data (e.g. difference in correlated features between living and non-living entities). An alternative approach has been to assemble sets of words and decide a priori upon their features. Such an approach was taken by Hinton and Shallice (1991; see also Plaut and Shallice, 1993), who created a set of semantic features which capture intuitive properties of common objects (e.g. <has-legs>, <hard>, <made-of-metal>, <part-of-limb>), then used those features to train an attractor network to learn the mapping between orthography and semantics. Lesioning this network produced semantic, visual, and combined visual/semantic errors consistent with patterns of performance in deep dyslexia. In a similar vein, Plaut (1995) used the same approach to investigate double dissociations between reading concrete and abstract words, using a set of empirical semantic features underlying the meanings of concrete and abstract words. One particular aspect of these representations was that abstract words had fewer features overall; this broad difference in featural properties between concrete and abstract domains (perhaps in conjunction with other differences) translated into differential consequences when different aspects of the model were damaged: abstract words were more impaired when the feedforward connections were lesioned, while concrete words were more impaired when the recurrent connections were lesioned.

A common property of these models, however, is the fact that the semantic features used are chosen a priori by the investigators, and may not reflect the full range of properties of meaning that may be relevant to the representations of the words in question. It is therefore an important additional step to assess comparable feature information that is produced by speakers who are naive about the research questions involved (i.e. feature norms). This allows the investigation of issues like featural properties, distribution of features across different sensory modalities, etc. using entirely empirically derived measures. By collecting features of meaning from multiple naive speakers, we also gain a fine-grained measure of featural salience, as a feature's relative contribution to a word's meaning can be weighted according to the number of speakers who produced that word (while the above approaches used binary features which are either part of a word's representation or not). See Moss et al. (Chapter 13 this volume) for a discussion of the relevance of feature variables, established on the basis of feature norms, to the representation of concepts.

Two main models of semantic representations based directly upon speaker-generated feature norms have been implemented (McRae et al., 1997; Vigliocco et al., 2004). These models differ mainly in their composition (McRae et al., including a substantially larger set of object nouns; Vigliocco et al., including object nouns but also nouns and verbs referring to actions and events), and the specific manner in which semantic representations are derived from a set of feature norms (dimensionality reduction techniques in both cases; McRae et al., through attractor networks, Vigliocco et al., through self-organizing maps; Kohonen, 1997). Here we focus upon Vigliocco et al.'s (2004) Featural and Unitary Semantic Space (FUSS) model in order to address the semantic representation of both words referring to objects and words referring to events. Conceptual features (of which feature norms are a proxy) are bound into a separate level of lexico-semantic representations which serves to mediate between concepts and other linguistic information (syntax and word form), in line with Damasio et al.'s (2001) idea of "convergence zones" (see also Simmons and Barsalou, 2003). The organization at this level arises through an unsupervised learning process (implemented using self-organizing maps; Kohonen, 1997; see Vinson and Vigliocco, 2002; Vigliocco et al., 2004 for complete details of implementation) which is sensitive to properties of the featural input, such as the number of features for each concept, how salient a given feature is for a concept (feature weight), features that are shared among different concepts, and features that are correlated. Thus it is not necessary to specify in advance which aspects of the input should be reflected in lexico-semantic organization; this process also allows different properties to exert different influences depending upon the characteristics of a given semantic field (see Table 12.2 for resulting differences between objects and actions; see also Cree and McRae, 2003), giving rise, for example, to the different smoothness of the space for objects (organized in a "lumpy" manner) with semantic field boundaries being well-defined, and events (organized "smoothly") in which there are no clear boundaries among fields (see Figure 12.3).

This model, which uses the same representational principles for the organization of objects and events, has been shown to account for graded semantic effects in both domains (Vigliocco et al., 2002; Vigliocco et al., 2004). In these studies graded effects were assessed by varying the semantic distance between words (operationalized as the Euclidean distance between two units, in the resulting composite output map, best responding to the input vectors corresponding to the features of two different words). Importantly, these graded effects were found both in production (semantic errors and naming latencies in picture word interference experiments) and word recognition; crucially, they were found both for words referring to objects and for words referring to events (Vigliocco et al., 2004). Finally, especially in the object domain, these effects were found both within and across categories (see Vigliocco et al., 2002),

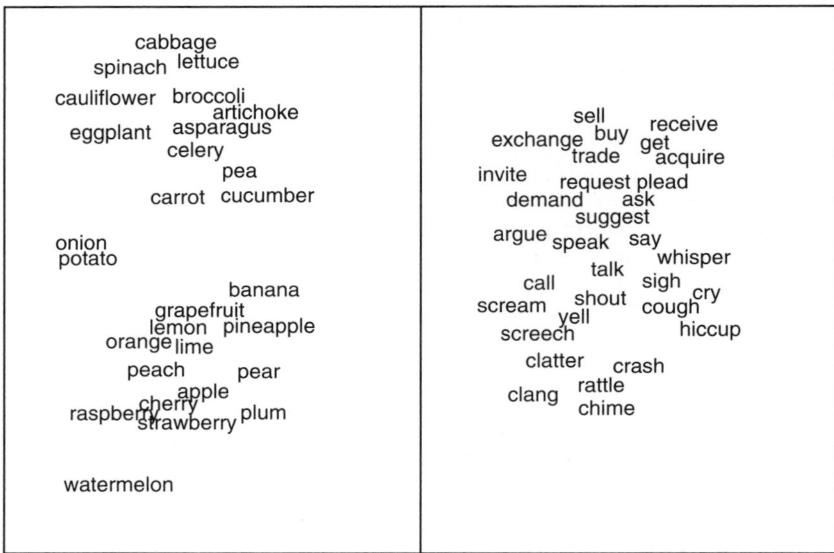

Figure 12.3 Two-dimensional representation of semantic proximity in FUSS (Vinson and Vigliocco, 2002; Vigliocco et al., 2004) illustrating the different clustering tendencies among some object nouns (left panel) and action verbs (right panel).

suggesting that there are no boundaries between categories. These findings suggest that some important aspects of words' meanings can be captured using feature norms and the same principles across domains, despite the differences between objects and events that we have discussed above, and the greater context dependency of words referring to events than words referring to objects.

12.2.4 Comparison between theories

How do these various models compare with each other? The results of experiments by Barsalou et al., (2003), Glenberg and Kaschak (2002), and Richardson et al. (2003) demonstrate the importance of grounding representations in experience in some manner, and the evidence from cognitive neuroscience (e.g. Hauk et al., 2004; Martin and Chao, 2001; Tettamanti et al., 2005; Vigliocco et al., 2006) shows that brain areas related to sensory-motor modalities are activated even in the most abstract linguistic tasks. But beyond this call for grounding, models can also be directly contrasted with each other in the extent to which their semantic representations predict performance on behavioral tasks involving the same items, provided the models have sufficient breadth.

Athough most models are not implemented to the extent which would allow such comparisons (e.g. most network models, semantic field theory, and the embodied views of Glenberg and Barsalou), this is possible with Wordnet, global co-occurrence models, and featural models. Vigliocco et al. (2004) contrasted similarity measures extracted from three models, one derived from each class (Wordnet, LSA, FUSS), assessing the extent to which similarity measures predicted performance on behavioral tasks sensitive to semantic similarity (lexical substitution errors in speeded picture naming; semantic interference effects on picture naming latencies from distracter words; semantic priming in lexical decision), both for words referring to objects and for words referring to events. In these studies, the feature-based model (FUSS) consistently performed the best in predicting semantic effects. LSA measures of similarity were also strong predictors in general, though not to the extent of FUSS. Wordnet's performance for objects was also strong, but for events it performed particularly poorly, as the limited degree of hierarchical organization led to a lack of fine-grained differentiation among large numbers of loosely related events. Within the current implementations, these findings highlight the importance of grounding semantic representations, although it remains to be seen whether more sophisticated assumptions related to co-occurrence or large-scale network structure may improve the performance of those classes of models.

12.3 **New directions: representation of abstract words**

We have said above that most research has focused primarily or exclusively on the representation of words referring to objects, and that only very few studies have addressed the semantic organization of words from other content domains, such as events and properties. More generally, however, even when events and properties have been addressed, much of the work has been limited to exploring the organization of *concrete* concepts/words. Notable exceptions are studies in neuropsychology that have documented a double dissociation between concrete and abstract words (Breedin et al., 1994), and have offered an account for the greater degree of impairment of abstract rather than concrete words in terms of differences in featural richness of semantic representations, with concrete words having richer representations and therefore being more resistant to damage than abstract words, whose representation would instead be characterized by fewer features (Plaut, 1995).

On the basis of analyses of speaker-generated features for the concepts of "truth", "freedom", and "invention", Barsalou and Wiemer-Hastings (2005) suggest that an important distinction between abstract and concrete words is which situations are more salient for the two types of word. Whereas for objects, attention focuses on the specific object against a background, for abstract notions, attention focuses on social context, events, and introspective properties. For example, for *true*, the focus would include the speaker's claim, the listener's representation of the claim, and the listener's assessment of the claim, rendering abstract words more complex than concrete ones.

An interesting proposal concerning the representation of abstract words has been developed within cognitive linguistics by Lakoff and colleagues (Lakoff, 1992; Lakoff and Johnson, 1980; see also Coulson, 2000; Turner and Fauconnier, 2000). Abstract knowledge is viewed as originating in conceptual metaphors (i.e. the use of a concrete conceptual domain of knowledge to describe an abstract conceptual domain). For example, English consistently uses language concerning *throwing* and *catching* to describe communication of ideas; and words such as *in front* and *behind* to describe the passage of time. It has been argued that these patterns of metaphorical language use reflect the manner in which we think about abstract concepts (Boroditsky, 2001). In this view, learning and representation of abstract concepts in the mind/brain is grounded in the learning and representation of concrete knowledge, which in turn is grounded in our bodily experience of the world (see also Taub, 2001, who presents an excellent discussion of iconicity in American Sign Language as a window into the concrete dimensions expressed in conceptual metaphors). Some initial evidence for a role of conceptual metaphors in representing abstract words comes from the study by Richardson et al. (2003) presented in section 12.1, who showed that speakers were sensitive to the direction of motion implied in abstract words such as *respect* (upward motion, linked to the metaphor of "looking up" to someone who ones respects). This hypothesis suggests continuity between the representation of concrete and abstract words, both of which would be grounded in our experiences with the physical world.

An alternative possibility, however, is that the meaning of abstract words is more highly dependent upon language than the meaning of concrete words: concepts corresponding to concrete things and events could develop in a manner that is to a large extent driven by innate predispositions and direct experience with the world (and then generalization of these experiences). Abstract words, however, are learned later and are learned primarily via language. These facts suggest that, compared to the acquisition of concrete words, the acquisition of abstract words is more dependent upon implicit learning mechanisms like those underlying models such as LSA and HAL (i.e. that inferences about meaning originate from the fact that words sharing similar meaning tend to be found in similar sentences). They further suggest that mechanisms such as syntactic bootstrapping (e.g. Gleitman et al., 2005) underlie the development and thus the representation of abstract words more than concrete words. We are not aware of any empirical study that has addressed this possibility. It is interesting to note, however, that in the model comparison carried out by Vigliocco et al. (2004) and described above in section 12.2.3, LSA, a global co-occurrence model whose representations were developed solely from linguistic input, provided better predictions of graded semantic effects for words referring to events (which are more abstract) than for words referring to concrete objects.

Of course, the two possibilities outlined above are not necessarily mutually exclusive; whereas conceptual metaphors may be part of the semantic representation for at least some words, implicit learning mechanisms based on extracting similarity in meaning from similarity in linguistic context may also play an important part. As abstract words also appear to be more susceptible to cross-linguistic variability (and cross-cultural variability too) than concrete words, investigations of this domain of knowledge may provide important information on how conceptual universal biases may interact with language-specific factors in determining the organization of the semantic system. It is a challenge for future research to explore these issues in a systematic manner.

Acknowledgments

While writing this chapter, Gabriella Vigliocco and David Vinson were supported by an ESRC research grant (RES000230038).

References

Allport, P. (1985) Distributed memory, modular subsystems and dysphasia. In S. K. N. R. Epstein (ed.), *Current Perspectives in Dysphasia*, pp. 32–60. Churchill Livingstone, Edinburgh.

Anderson, J. (1983) *The Architecture of Cognition*. Harvard University Press, Cambridge, MA.

Anderson, J. R., and Bower, G. H. (1973) *Human Associative Memory*. Winston, Washington, DC.

Barsalou, L. W., Simmons, W. K., Barbey, A. K., and Wilson, C. D. (2003) Grounding conceptual knowledge in the modality-specific systems. *Trends in Cognitive Sciences*, 7: 84–91.

Barsalou, L. W., and Wiemer-Hastings, K. (2005) Situating abstract concepts. In D. Pecher and R. Zwaan (eds), *Grounding Cognition: The Role of Perception and Action in Memory, Language, and Thought*, pp. 129–63. Cambridge University Press, New York.

Berlin, B., and Kay, P. (1969) *Basic Color Terms: Their Universality and Uvolution*, University of California Press, Berkeley.

Bierwisch, M. (1969) Strukturelle Semantik. *Deutsch als Fremdsprache*, 6: 66–71.

Bird, H., Lambon Ralph, M. A., Patterson, K., and Hodges, J. R. (2000) The rise and fall of frequency and imageability: noun and verb production in semantic dementia. *Brain and Language*, 73: 17–49.

Bloom, P. (1994) Possible names: the role of syntax–semantics mappings in the acquisition of nominals. *Lingua*, 92: 297–329.

Borgo, F., and Shallice, T. (2001) When living things and other "sensory-quality" categories behave in the same fashion: a novel category-specific effect. *Neurocase*, 7: 201–20.

Boroditsky, L. (2001) Does language shape thought? Mandarin and English speakers' conception of time. *Cognitive Psychology*, 43: 1–22.

Bowerman, M., and Choi, S. (2003) Space under construction: language-specific spatial categorization in first language acquisition. In D. Gentner and S. Goldin-Meadow (eds), *Language in Mind*, pp. 387–428. MIT Press, Cambridge, MA.

Bowers, J. S. (1999) Grossberg and colleagues solved the hyperonym problem over a decade ago. *Behavioral and Brain Sciences*, 22: 38.

Breedin, S. D., Saffran, E. M., and Coslett, H. B. (1994) Reversal of the concreteness effect in a patient with semantic dementia. *Cognitive Neuropsychology*, 11: 617–60.

Breedin, S. D., Saffran, E. M., and Schwartz, M. F. (1998) Semantic factors in verb retrieval: an effect of complexity. *Brain and Language*, 63: 1–31.

Brysbaert, M., Fias, W., and Noel, M. P. (1998) The Whorfian hypothesis and numerical cognition: is "twenty-four" processed in the same way as "four-and-twenty"? *Cognition*, 66: 51–77.

Burgess, C., and Lund, K. (1997) Modeling parsing constraints with high-dimensional context space. *Language and Cognitive Processes*, 12: 177–210.

Cappa, S. F., Frugoni, M., Pasquali, P., Perani, D., and Zorat, F. (1998) Category-specific naming impairment for artifacts: a new case. *Neurocase*, 4: 391–7.

Caramazza, A. (1997) How many levels of processing are there in lexical access? *Cognitive Neuropsychology*, 14: 177–208.

Caramazza, A., and Hillis, A. E. (1990) Where do semantic errors come from? *Cortex*, 26: 95–122.

Chierchia, G., and McConnell-Ginet, S. (2000) *Meaning and Grammar*. MIT Press, Cambridge, MA.

Collins, A. C. and Loftus, E. F. (1975) A spreading-activation theory of semantic processing. *Psychological Review*, 82: 407–28.

Collins, A. M., and Quillian, M. R. (1969) Retrieval time from semantic memory. *Journal of Verbal Learning and Verbal Behavior*, 12: 240–7.

Coulson, S. (2000) *Semantic Leaps: Frame-Shifting and Conceptual Blending in Meaning Construction*. Cambridge University Press, Cambridge.

Cree, G. S., McRae, K., and McNorgan, C. (1999) An attractor model of lexical conceptual processing: simulating semantic priming. *Cognitive Science*, 23: 371–414.

Cree, G. S., and McRae, K. (2003) Analyzing the factors underlying the structure and computation of the meaning of chipmunk, cherry, chisel, cheese and cello (and many other such concrete nouns). *Journal of Experimental Psychology: General*, 132: 163–201.

Cruse, D. A. (1986) *Lexical Semantics*. Cambridge University Press, Cambridge.

Damasio, H., Grabowski, T. J., Tranel, D., Hichwa, R. D., and Damasio, A. R. (1996) A neural basis for lexical retrieval. *Nature*, 380: 499–505.

Damasio, H., Grabowski, T. J., Tranel, D., Ponto, L. L. B., Hichwa, R. D., and Damasio, A. R. (2001) Neural correlates of naming actions and of naming spatial relations. *NeuroImage*, 13: 1053–64.

Damasio, H., Tranel, D., Grabowski, T. J., Adolphs, R., and Damasio, A. R. (2004): Neural systems behind word and concept retrieval. *Cognition*, 92: 179–229.

Davidoff, J., Davies, I., and Roberson, D. (1999) Colour categories in a stone-age tribe. *Nature*, 398: 203–4.

Devlin, J. T., Gonnerman, L. M., Andersen, E. S., and Seidenberg, M. S. (1998) Category-specific semantic deficits in focal and widespread brain damage: a computational account. *Journal of Cognitive Neuroscience*, 10: 77–94.

Dowty, D. R. (1979) *Word Meaning and Montague Grammar: The Semantics of Verbs and Times in Generative Semantics and in Montague's PTQ*. Dordrecht: Reidel.

Farah, M. J., and McClelland, J. L. (1991) A computational model of semantic memory impairment: modality-specificity and emergent category specificity. *Journal of Experimental Psychology: General*, 120: 339–57.

Federmeier, K. D., and Kutas, M. (1999) A rose by any other name: long-term memory structure and sentence processing. *Journal of Memory and Language*, 41: 469–95.

Fisher, C. (1994) Structure and meaning in the verb lexicon: input for a syntax-aided verb learning procedure. *Cognitive Psychology*, 5: 473–517.

Fodor, J. (1976) *The Language of Thought*. Harvester Press, Brighton, UK.

Fodor, J., Fodor, J. A., and Garrett, M. (1975) The psychological unreality of semantic representations. *Linguistic Inquiry*, 6: 515–35.

Fodor, J. A., Garrett, M. F., Walker, E. C.T., and Parkes, C. H. (1980) Against definitions. *Cognition*, 8: 263–367.

Gallese, V., and Lakoff, G. (2005) The brain's concepts: the role of the sensory-motor system in conceptual knowledge. *Cognitive Neuropsychology*, 22: 455–79.

Garrett, M. F. (1984) The organization of processing structure for language production: applications to aphasic speech. In D. Caplan, A. R. Lecours, and A. Smith (eds), *Biological Perspectives on Language*, pp. 172–93. MIT Press, London.

Garrett, M. F. (1992) Lexical retrieval processes: semantic field effects. In E. Kittay and A. Lehrer (eds), *Frames, Fields and Contrasts: New Essays in Semantic and Lexical Organization*, pp. 377–95. Erlbaum, Hillsdale, NJ.

Garrett, M. F. (1993) Errors and their relevance for models of language production. In G. Blanken, J. Dittman, H. Grim, J. Marshall, and C. Wallesch (eds), *Linguistic Disorders and Pathologies*, pp. 72–92. de Gruyter, Berlin.

Gentner, D., and Goldin-Meadow, S. (2003) *Language in Mind: Advances in the Study of Language and Thought*. MIT Press, Cambridge, MA.

Glaser, W. R., and Düngelhoff, R. J. (1984) The time course of picture-word interference. *Journal of Experimental Psychology: Human Perception and Performance*, 10: 640–54.

Gleitman, L. R. (1990) The structural sources of verb learning. *Language Acquisition*, 1: 3–55.

Gleitman, L. R., Cassidy, K., Nappa, R., Papafragou, A., and Trueswell, J. C. (2005) Hard words. *Language Learning and Development*, 1: 23–64.

Glenberg, A., and Kaschak, M. (2002) Grounding language in action. *Psychonomic Bulletin and Review*, 9: 558–65.

Gonnerman, L. M., Andersen, E. S., Devlin, L. T., Kempler, D., and Seidenberg, M. (1997) Double dissociation of semantic categories in Alzheimer's disease. *Brain and Language*, 57: 254–79.

Graesser, A. C., Hopkinson, P. L., and Schmid, C. (1987) Differences in interconcept organization between nouns and verbs. *Journal of Memory and Language*, 26: 242–53.

Grimshaw, J. (1991) *Argument Structure*. MIT Press, London.

Grosjean, F. 1998. Studying bilinguals: methodological and conceptual issues. *Bilingualism: Language and Cognition* 1:131–49.

Gross, D., Fischer, U., and Miller, G. A. (1989) Antonymy and the representation of adjectival meanings. *Journal of Memory and Language* 28: 92–106.

Hart, J., Berndt, R. S., and Caramazza, A. (1985) Category-specific naming deficit following cerebral infarction. *Nature*, 316: 439–40.

Hart, J., and Gordon, B. (1992) Neural subsystems for object knowledge. *Nature*, 359: 60–4.

Hauk, O., Johnsrude, I., and F. Pulvermüller, F. (2004). Somatotopic representation of action words in human motor and premotor cortex. *Neuron*, 41: 301–7.

Hinton, G. E., and Shallice, T. (1991) Lesioning an attractor network: investigations of acquired dyslexia. *Psychological Review*, 98: 74–95.

Humphreys, G. W., Price, C. J., and Riddoch, M. J. (1999) From objects to names: a cognitive neuroscience approach. *Psychological Research*, 62: 118–130.

Huttenlocher, J., and Lui, F. (1979) The semantic organization of some simple nouns and verbs. *Journal of Verbal Learning and Verbal Behavior*, 18: 141–79.

Jackendoff, R. (1983) *Semantics and Cognition*. MIT Press, Cambridge, MA.

Jackendoff, R. (1990) *Semantic Structures*. MIT Press, Cambridge, MA.

Jackendoff, R. (1992) *Languages of the Mind*. MIT Press, Cambridge, MA.

Jackendoff, R. (2002) *The Foundations of Language*. Oxford University Press, Oxford.

Jespersen, O. (1965) *A Modern English Grammar Based on Historical Principles*. Allen & Unwin, London.

Johnson-Laird, P. N., Herrmann, D. J., and Chaffin, R. (1984) Only connections: a critique of semantic networks. *Psychological Bulletin*, 96: 292–315.

Keil, F. C. (1989) *Concepts, Kinds, and Cognitive Development*. MIT Press, Cambridge, MA.

Kelly, M. H., Bock, J. K., and Keil, F. C. (1986) Prototypicality in a linguistic context: effects on sentence structure. *Journal of Memory and Language*, 25: 59–74.

Kita, S., and Özyürek, A. (2003) What does cross-linguistic variation in semantic coordination of speech and gesture reveal? Evidence for an interface representation of spatial thinking and speaking. *Journal of Memory and Language*, 48: 16–32.

Kittay, E. F. (1987) *Metaphor: Its Cognitive Force and Linguistic Structure*. Clevender Press, Oxford.

Kohonen, T. (1997) *Self-Organizing Maps*. Springer, New York.

Lakoff, G. (1987) *Women, Fire, and Dangerous Things: What Categories Reveal about the Mind*. University of Chicago Press, Chicago.

Lakoff, G. (1992) The contemporary theory of metaphor. In Andrew Ortony (ed.), *Metaphor and Thought* (2nd edn.), pp. 202–51. Cambridge University Press, Cambridge.

Lakoff, G., and Johnson, M. (1980) *Metaphors We Live By*. University of Chicago Press, Chicago.

Landauer, T. K., and Dumais, S. T. (1997) A solution to Plato's problem: the Latent Semantic Analysis theory of acquisition, induction and representation of knowledge. *Psychological Review*, 104: 211–40.

Lehrer, A. (1974) *Semantic Fields and Lexical Structure*. North-Holland, Amsterdam.

Levelt, W. J. L. (1989) *Speaking: From Intention to Articulation*. MIT Press, Cambridge, MA.

Levelt, W. J. M., Roelofs, A., and Meyer, A. S. (1999) A theory of lexical access in speech production. *Behavioral and Brain Sciences*, 22: 1–38.

Levin, B. (1993) *English Verb Classes and Alternations: A Preliminary Investigation*. University of Chicago Press, Chicago.

Levinson, S. C. (1996) Frames of reference and Molyneux's question: crosslinguistic evidence. In P. Bloom, M. Peterson, L. Nadel, and M. Garrett (eds), *Language and Space*, pp. 109–69. MIT Press, Cambridge, MA.

Levinson, S. C. (2003) Language and mind: let's get the issue straight! In D. Gentner and S. Goldin-Meadow (eds), *Language in Mind: Advances in the Study of Language and Thought*, pp. 25–46. MIT Press, Cambridge, MA.

Lucy, J. A. (1992) *Grammatical Categories and Cognition: A Case Study of the Linguistic Relativity Hypothesis*. Cambridge University Press, Cambridge.

Lyons, J. (1977) *Semantics*, vol. 2. Cambridge University Press, Cambridge.

Malt, B., Sloman S., Gennari S., Shi M., and Wang Y. (1999) Knowing versus naming: similarity and linguistic categorization of artifacts. *Journal of Memory and Language*, 40: 230–62.

Marr, D. (1982) *Vision*. Freeman, San Francisco.

Martin, A., and Chao, L. L. (2001) Semantic memory and the brain: structure and processes. *Current Opinion in Neurobiology*, 11: 194–201.

Masson, M. E. J. (1995) A distributed memory model of semantic priming. *Journal of Experimental Psychology: Learning, Memory and Cognition*, 21: 3–23.

McNeill, D. (1992) *Hand and Mind*. University of Chicago Press, Chicago.

McRae, K., and Boisvert, S. (1998) Automatic semantic similarity priming. *Journal of Experimental Psychology: Learning, Memory and Cognition*, 24: 558–72.

McRae, K., and Cree, G. S. (2002) Factors underlying category-specific semantic deficits. In E. M. E. Forde and G. W. Humphreys (eds), *Category-Specificity in Brain and Mind*, pp. 211–50. Psychology Press, Hove, UK.

McRae, K., de Sa, V., and Seidenberg, M. C. (1997) On the nature and scope of featural representations of word meaning. *Journal of Experimental Psychology: General*, 126: 99–130.

Meyer, D. E., and Schvaneveldt, R. W. (1971) Facilitation in recognizing pairs of words: evidence of a dependence between retrieval operations. *Journal of Experimental Psychology*, 90: 227–34.

Miller, G. A., and Fellbaum, C. (1991) Semantic networks of English. *Cognition*, 41: 197–229.

Minsky, M. (1975) A framework for representing knowledge. In P. H. Winston (ed.), *The Psychology of Computer Vision*, pp. 211–77. McGraw-Hill, New York.

Morris, M. W., and Murphy, G. L. (1990) Converging operations on a basic level in event taxonomies. *Memory and Cognition*, 18: 407–18.

Murphy, G. L. (2002) *The Big Book of Concepts*. MIT Press, Cambridge, MA.

Neely, J. H. (1991) Semantic priming effects in visual word recognition: a selective review of current findings and theories. In D. Laberge and S. J. Samuels (eds), *Basic Processes in Reading: Perception and Comprehension*, pp. 264–336. Erlbaum, Hillsdale, NJ.

Norman, D. A., and Rumelhart, D. E. (1975) *Explorations in Cognition*. Freeman, San Francisco.

Pinker, S. (1989) *Learnability and Cognition: The Acquisition of Argument Structure*. MIT Press, Cambridge, MA.

Plaut, D. C. (1995) Semantic and associative priming in a distributed attractor network. *Proceedings of the Seventeenth Annual Conference of the Cognitive Science Society*, 17: 37–42.

Plaut, D. C.,and Shallice, T. (1993) Deep dyslexia: a case study of connectionist neuropsychology. *Cognitive Neuropsychology*, 10: 377–500.

Price, C. J. (1998) The functional anatomy of word comprehension and production. *Trends in Cognitive Sciences*, 2: 281–8.

Pustejovsky, J. (1993) *Semantics and the Lexicon*. Kluwer Academic, Boston, MA.

Richardson, D., Spivey, M., McRae, K., and Barsalou, L. (2003) Spatial representations activated during real-time comprehension of verbs. *Cognitive Science*, 27: 767–80.

Roberson, D., Davies I., and Davidoff, J. (2000) Color categories are not universal: Replications and new evidence from a Stone-age culture. *Journal of Experimental Psychology*: General, 129: 369–98.

Roelofs, A. (1997) The WEAVER model of word-form encoding in speech production. *Cognition*, 64: 249–84.

Rogers, T. T., Lambon Ralph, M. A, Garrard, P., Bozeat, S., McClelland, J. L., Hodges, J. R., and Patterson, K. (2004) The structure and deterioration of semantic memory: A neuropsychological and computational investigation. *Psychological Review*, 111: 205–35.

Rogers, T. T., and McClelland, J. L. (2004) *Semantic Cognition: A Parallel Distributed Processing Approach*. MIT Press, Cambridge, MA.

Rosch, E. (1978) Principles of categorization. In E. Rosch and B. Lloyd (eds), *Cognition and Categorization*, pp. 27–48. Erlbaum, Hillsdale, NJ.

Rosch, E., and Mervis, C. B. (1975) Family resemblance: studies in the internal structure of categories. *Cognitive Psychology*, 7: 573–605.

Ruml, W., Caramazza, A., Shelton, J. R., and Chialant, D. (2000) Testing assumptions in computational theories of aphasia. *Journal of Memory and Language*, 43: 217–48.

Sapir, E. (1921) *Language*, Harcourt, Brace, & World, New York.

Schriefers, H., Meyer, A. S., and Levelt, W. J. M. (1990) Exploring the time course of lexical access in language production: picture–word interference studies. *Journal of Memory and Language*, 29: 86–102.

Sera, M., Elieff, C., Forbes, J., Burch, M. C., Rodriguez, W., and Dubois, D. P. (2002) When language affects cognition and when it does not: an analysis of grammatical gender and classification. *Journal of Experimental Psychology: General*, 131: 377–97.

Shallice, T. (1993) Multiple semantics: whose confusion? *Cognitive Neuropsychology*, 10: 251–61.

Shelton, J. R., and Martin, R. C. 1992. How semantic is automatic semantic priming? *Journal of Experimental Psychology: Learning, Memory and Cognition*, 18: 1191–210.

Simmons, W. K., and Barsalou, L. W. (2003) The similarity-in-topography principle: reconciling theories of conceptual deficits. *Cognitive Neuropsychology*, 20: 451–86.

Slobin, D. I. (1992) *The Cross-Linguistic Study of Language Acquisition*. Erlbaum, Hillsdale, NJ.

Slobin, D. I. (1996a) From "thought and language" to "thinking for speaking". In J. Gumperz and S. Levinson (eds), *Rethinking Linguistic Relativity*, pp. 70–6. Cambridge University Press, Cambridge, MA.

Slobin, D. I. (1996b) Two ways to travel: verbs of motion in English and Spanish. In M. Shibatani and S. A. Thompson (eds), *Grammatical Constructions: Their Form and Meaning*. Clarendon Press, Oxford.

Smith, E. E., and Medin, D. L. (1981) *Categories and Concepts*. Harvard University Press, Cambridge, MA.

Smith, E. E., Shoben, E. J., and Rips, L. J. (1974) Structure and process in semantic memory: featural model for semantic decisions. *Psychological Review*, 81: 214–41.

Talmy, L. (1986) Lexicalization patterns: semantic structure in lexical forms. In T. Shopen (ed.), *Language Typology and Syntactic Description*, vol. III: *Grammatical Categories and the Lexicon*, pp. 57–150. Cambridge University Press, Cambridge.

Taub, S. F. (2001) *Language from the Body: Iconicity and Metaphor in American Sign Language*. Cambridge University Press, Cambridge.

Tettamanti, M., Buccino, G., Saccuman, M. C., Gallese, V., Danna, M., Scifo, P. Fazio, F., Rizzolatti, G., Cappa, S. F., and Perani, D. (2005) Listening to action-related sentences activates fronto-parietal motor circuits. *Journal of Cognitive Neuroscience*. 17: 273–81.

Tranel, D., Adolphs, R., Damasio, H., and Damasio, A. R. (2001) A neural basis for the retrieval of words for actions. *Cognitive Neuropsychology*, 18: 655–70.

Trier, J. (1931) *Der Deutsche Wortschatz im Sinnbezirk des Verstandes*. Winter, Heidelberg.

Turner, M., and Fauconnier, G. (2000) Metaphor, metonymy, and binding. In A. Barcelona (ed.), *Metonymy and Metaphor at the Crossroads*, pp. 133–45. de Gruyter, New York.

Tyler, L. K., Moss, H. E., Durrant-Peatfield, M., and Levy, J. (2000) Conceptual structure and the structure of categories: a distributed account of category-specific deficits. *Brain and Language*, 75: 195–231.

Vigliocco, G., and Filipovic, L. (2004) From mind in the mouth to language in the mind. *Trends in Cognitive Science*, 8: 5–7.

Vigliocco, G., Vinson, D. P., Damian, M. F., and Levelt, W. (2002) Semantic distance effects on object and action naming. *Cognition*, 85: B61–B69.

Vigliocco, G., Vinson, D. P, Lewis, W., and Garrett, M. F. (2004) The meanings of object and action words. *Cognitive Psychology*, 48: 422–88.

Vigliocco, G., Vinson, D. P., Paganelli, F., and Dworzynski, K. (2005) Grammatical gender effects on cognition: implications for language learning and language use. *Journal of Experimental Psychology: General* 134: 501–20.

Vigliocco, G., Warren, J., Siri, S., Arciuli, J., Scott, S., and Wise, R. (2006) The role of semantics and grammatical class in the neural representation of words. *Cerebral Cortex*, 16: 1790–6.

Vinson, D. P., and Vigliocco, G. (2002) A semantic analysis of noun–verb dissociations in aphasia. *Journal of Neurolinguistics*, 15: 317–51.

Vinson, D. P., Vigliocco, G., Cappa, S. F., and Siri, S. (2003) The breakdown of semantic knowledge: insights from a statistical model of meaning representation. *Brain and Language*, 86: 347–65.

Warrington, E. K., and McCarthy, R. (1983) Category specific access dysphasia. *Brain* 106: 859–78.

Warrington, E. K., and McCarthy, R. (1987) Categories of knowledge: further fractionations and an attempted integration. *Brain* 110: 1273–96.

Warrington, E. K., and Shallice, T. (1984) Category specific semantic impairments. *Brain*, 107: 829–54.

Whorf, B. (1956) *Language, Thought, and Reality: Selected Writing of Benjamin Lee Whorf*, ed. J. B. Carroll, MIT Press, Cambridge, MA.

CHAPTER 13

Conceptual structure

Helen E. Moss, Lorraine K. Tyler, and Kirsten I. Taylor

13.1 Introduction

Concepts lie at the heart of our mental life, supporting cognitive functions from language comprehension and production to reasoning, remembering, and recognizing objects. Therefore, the study of the representation and processing of conceptual knowledge has been a central activity across many disciplines, traditionally in the realm of philosophy, and more recently psycholinguistics, neuropsychology, and neuroscience. Given the context of the present Handbook, we will focus here on the role of concepts—and conceptual structure—in the comprehension and production of language, although we will consider evidence from beyond the traditional boundaries of psycholinguistics, in particular from cognitive neuropsychology. Brain-damaged patients with deficits in one category or domain of knowledge have provided valuable insights into the nature of conceptual representations, and represent an alternative study population with which to test the claims of psycholinguistically motivated theories of conceptual knowledge. A detailed consideration of relevant neuroimaging research is beyond the scope of the current chapter, but can be found in Taylor et al. (forthcoming). We believe that converging evidence from different approaches and methodologies provides the greatest potential for progressing our understanding of this central but challenging subject.

13.1.1 Concepts and meanings

Conceptual representations are essential to express and understand information about the world, so must capture a rich variety of knowledge about objects, abstract ideas, mental states, actions, and the relations among all of these. A distinction has frequently been made in the psycholinguistic literature between a much smaller set of definition-like semantic information stored as part of the mental lexicon, and richer "world knowledge" or "encyclopedic" information (e.g. Miller, 1978). In this chapter we do not make such a distinction, instead assuming the position taken by Jackendoff (1983; 1989) in his Conceptual Semantic approach, in which there is no clear lexical/encyclopedic boundary, with both kinds of information being "cut from the same cloth" (Jackendoff, 1983). According to Jackendoff, semantic structures (i.e. the semantic content in the mental lexicon) are simply a subset of conceptual structures which can be verbally expressed. Critically, conceptual representations form an interface between lexical information and other domains such as sensory and motor systems. This function introduces several constraints on the nature of these representations: irrespective of their content, they must be in a format that is readily accessible by both a range of linguistic and non-linguistic modalities of input and output; they must permit processing rapid enough to support on-line production and comprehension of meaningful speech at a rate of several words per second and to support rapid and appropriate motor responses to meaningful sensory stimuli in the environment; and they must enable flexibility of meaning across different contexts of use (see Moss and Gaskell, 1999). For a more detailed discussion and an alternative approach to the relationship between concepts and word meanings, see Vigliocco and Vinson (Chapter 12 this volume).

13.1.2 Componentiality

In this chapter we explore the representation of concepts within a theoretical framework that stresses the importance of the internal structure of those representations. We will discuss several specific models within this framework, but present the Conceptual Structure Account (Durrant-Peatfield et al., 1997, Moss, McCormick, and Tyler, 1997; Moss et al., 2002, Tyler and Moss, 2001, Tyler, Moss, et al., 2000; Moss and Tyler, 2000; Taylor et al., forthcoming) in greater detail as one example of this class of accounts. While competing perspectives on conceptual representation can be found in the literature, an extensive discussion of these is not within the purview of this chapter (see e.g. Barsalou et al., 1999; Murphy and Medin, 1985; Vigliocco and Vinson, Chapter 12 this volume; Glenberg, Chapter 21).

The notion that concepts *have* an internal structure rests on the critical assumption that conceptual representations are componential in nature, i.e. that they are made up of smaller elements of meaning, variously referred to as properties, features or attributes (or in the connectionist literature, as microfeatures). Although agreement on this point has by no means been unanimous, with several theorists arguing that meanings are unanalyzable wholes (e.g. Fodor and Fodor, 1980; see also de Almeida, 1999), componentiality is now quite widely assumed in the psycholinguistic literature. Thus, many current models of concept representation (e.g. classical, prototype, and exemplar theories) share the assumption that concepts are made up of attributes, and that categorization is possible to the extent that instances of a concept can be grouped together according to the similarity or overlap of these attributes. Although these models differ with respect to the nature of the attributes they consider and the similarity computations they hypothesize, with classical models considering only necessary and sufficient features while prototype and exemplar models additionally account for characteristic, non-defining features, all share the assumptions of componentiality and similarity (see Smith and Medin, 1981; Komatsu, 1992 for reviews and Vigliocco and Vinson, Chapter 12 this volume for further discussion of this issue).

The componential approach has gained popularity in recent years, in part due to the rise of parallel distributed processing models of cognitive functions including those of the conceptual system (e.g. Durrant-Peatfield et al., 1997; Hinton et al., 1986; Plaut and Shallice, 1993; Rogers and Plaut, 2002; Rogers et al., 2004; Moss et al., 2000). Such models instantiate conceptual knowledge in neural networks in which simple processing nodes correspond to components of meaning, and where individual concepts are captured as patterns of activation over large sets of these microfeatures. Although many of the models were developed to show a "proof of concept" and were thus based on small, arbitrarily chosen feature sets, more recent models have grounded their semantic representations in more realistic, empirically derived datasets (e.g. Greer et al., 2001; McRae et al., 1997; Devlin et al., 1998; see below for further details). These distributed models on the whole appear to account for psycholinguistic and neuropsychological phenomena as well as or better than earlier localist models, in which concepts are represented as a single node, with semantic content captured in activation links among related nodes (e.g. Collins and Loftus, 1975). For example, distributed models can easily perform generalizations to novel stimuli and pattern completions (Hinton et al., 1986), and show a gradual degradation of performance when damaged, reminiscent of that shown following brain damage in humans (e.g. Hinton and Shallice, 1991; Plaut and Shallice, 1993; Devlin et al., 1998; Tyler, Moss, et al., 2000; Rogers et al., 2004). Although localist semantic network models have been extremely influential as a framework for interpreting psycholinguistic phenomena (most notably semantic priming, e.g. McNamara, 1992), priming effects can also be readily accommodated within the distributed framework (e.g. Masson, 1995; McRae et al., 1997; Tyler et al., 2002; Cree et al., 1999; Vigliocco et al., 2004; Randall et al., 2004). Moreover, the finer-grained effects of conceptual structure can more readily be accommodated within the distributed framework, including the flexibility of meaning over different contexts (e.g. Tabossi, 1988; Moss and Marslen-Wilson, 1993; Kawamoto, 1993), the effects of the number of semantic features associated with a concept (e.g. Plaut and Shallice, 1993; Pexman et al., 2003; Tyler, Moss, et al., 2000) and the varying time courses of activation of different features of a word's meaning (McRae et al., 1997; Randall et al., 2004; McCormick, and Tyler, 1997). In summary, a distributed componential model seems to be a well-founded and plausible framework for understanding and studying conceptual representations and their internal structures.

13.2 The conceptual structure framework

We turn now to the recent literature on conceptual structure, which builds on the basic assumptions of the componential account, aiming to specify the internal structures of various classes of concepts and to determine the processing consequences of these proposed representational characteristics. This is a cyclical process. Given that we cannot observe the content of mental representations directly, we draw inferences about their likely nature on the basis of empirical observations of conceptual processing over a range of tasks and stimuli, from both healthy and impaired language users. These inferences can then be used to construct a hypothetical account of the structure of the underlying concepts, on the basis of which further predictions about the potential processing consequences can be generated—often with the help of a computational model—which in turn can be tested in behavioral studies. Recently it has become possible to test hypotheses concerning the potential neural bases of conceptual representations with neuroimaging techniques, although the relationship between activations in different areas of the brain and the content and structure of individual concepts remains a controversial one (Caramazza and Mahon, 2003; Moss and Tyler, 2003; Tyler et al., 2003; Tyler and Moss, 2001).

13.2.1 Structure and features

At the heart of the conceptual structure approach is the claim that a given concept can be defined in terms of the features that make up its meaning, and that the quantity and quality of these features, as well as featural interrelationships—its internal structure—determines how a concept is activated during normal language comprehension and production, as well as the way that it is affected by damage to the system. Within the general term "structure" we will discuss those variables that have been shown to have the most prominent effects: the total number of features a concept has, whether those features are shared with many other concepts or are highly distinctive, the relationships between those features, most critically the degree of correlation among them, and the kind of information specified by the features, both in terms of their derivation (e.g. whether they are based on sensory information or are functional in nature), and their salience (whether they are critical or peripheral to the concept). While this list of factors is no doubt incomplete, it captures the main areas of investigation pursued in our own work in this area and that of other researchers with similar interests.

13.2.2 Structure and domain

Most models of this type also propose that the internal structure of conceptual representations varies systematically across different categories or domains of knowledge, for example between living and non-living things, abstract and concrete words, or verbs and nouns—a proposal that has been of particular relevance in the neuropsychological literature, where there has been lively debate as to the bases of category-specific semantic deficits. Patients with this type of disorder show dissociations in their degree of impairment for different categories/domains; for example, living and non-living things (Bunn et al., 1998; Moss et al., 1998; de Renzi and Lucchelli, 1994; Hart and Gordon, 1992; Hillis and Caramazza, 1991; Warrington and Shallice, 1984; see Forde and Humphreys, 1999 for a review), with verbs and nouns (Caramazza and Hillis, 1991; Silveri and Di Betta; 1997, Zingeser and Berndt, 1990; Laiacona and Caramazza, 2004) or concrete and abstract words (Franklin, 1989; Warrington and Shallice, 1984; Breedin et al., 1994).[1] Other patients have demonstrated deficits for specific categories within domains, for example for animals (e.g. EW; Caramazza and Shelton, 1998) or fruit and vegetables (e.g. FAV; Crutch and Warrington, 2003). Some researchers have suggested that these deficits are evidence for the existence of modular neural subsystems for concepts in different domains which can be independently impaired as a result of brain damage (e.g. Caramazza and Shelton, 1998; Caramazza and Mahon, 2003). However, the conceptual structure framework suggests an alternative approach in which category-specific semantic deficits do not necessarily result from damage to modular neural subsystems (e.g. selective damage to the animal subsystem). Rather, patterns of preserved and impaired conceptual knowledge may emerge within a unitary distributed system—one without explicit boundaries into separate categories or domains. This is possible because the effects of neural damage will vary as a function of the internal structure of concepts, which can be shown to vary systematically across different categories, as will be described in further detail below (Durrant-Peatfield et al., 1997; Moss et al., 1998; Moss et al., 2002;

[1] There is considerable variation in the literature as to the use of the terms "category" and "domain." Here, we use "domain" to refer to a high-level grouping of concepts into e.g. living and non-living things or abstract and concrete words, and reserve the term "category" to denote specific superordinate classes within those domains (e.g. animals, vehicles, motion verbs). However, we acknowledge these are working definitions, and that there are other ways in which the conceptual space may potentially be subdivided.

Tyler, Moss, et al., 2000; Tyler and Moss, 2001; Gonnerman et al., 1997; Devlin et al., 1998; McRae et al., 1997; McRae and Cree, 2002; Garrard et al., 2001; Caramazza et al., 1990; Cree and McRae, 2003).

13.2.3 **Models in the conceptual structure framework**

Several models could be described as belonging within the general framework of the conceptual structure approach, with the earliest forerunner perhaps being the OUCH (organized unitary content hypothesis) model proposed by Caramazza et al. (1990) as an account of category-specific deficits in neuropsychological patients. According to the OUCH model, concepts are represented as patterns of activation over "microfeatures within a distributed semantic system". Damage to this kind of unitary, distributed system can potentially affect one category of concepts more than another because similar concepts are represented close together in semantic space—they have overlapping patterns of activation (see Caramazza et al., 1990; Dixon et al., 1997; Forde et al., 1997; Humphreys et al., 1988 for related similarity-based models).

13.2.3.1 The conceptual structure account

Our own model, which has acquired the name Conceptual Structure Account (CSA), has been developed over the last decade (Durrant-Peatfield et al., 1997; Moss, McCormick, and Tyler, 1997; Moss et al., 2002; Tyler and Moss, 2001; Tyler, Moss, et al., 2000; Moss and Tyler, 2000; Taylor et al., forthcoming), building on empirical results from our own studies as well as the findings of other research teams who have proposed similar accounts of conceptual structure, albeit with some critical differences (McRae et al., 1997; Gonnerman et al., 1997; Devlin et al., 1998; Cree and McRae, 2003; Vinson et al., 2003). Like Caramazza et al.'s OUCH model, the CSA was initially proposed to try to account for the nature of category-specific semantic deficits, largely in response to the limitations of modular accounts which hypothesized separate neural subsystems for either conceptual domains or types of featural knowledge. Modular accounts are those which propose that there are topographically distinct regions of the brain underpinning representations of specific domains of knowledge (e.g. animals or plants, as in the Caramazza and Shelton (1998) account mentioned above) or specific types of conceptual feature, such as sensory vs. motor features (e.g. Warrington and McCarthy, 1983; 1987; Warrington and Shallice, 1984; Borgo and Shallice, 1994; Farah et al., 1989; Farah and McClelland, 1991; Saffran, 2000; and see section 13.3.1 for further discussion of the representation of different feature types). We present the CSA here as an illustrative example of one model within the theoretical framework of the conceptual structure approach.

On the CSA, not only do similar concepts tend to activate overlapping sets of semantic features, but there are also systematic differences in the *internal structure* of concepts in different categories and domains. Like some other accounts, we claim that *correlation*—the degree to which properties co-occur—is a key relation among semantic properties (see also Garrard et al., 2001; Vinson et al., 2003). In a distributed connectionist system, correlated properties like *has eyes* and *can see* support each other with mutual activation and so are more resilient to damage than are those that are more weakly correlated. Hence, different patterns of correlation among properties within a concept will lead to different patterns of loss and preservation of information, given the same degree of overall damage.

In this framework category-specific deficits arise because the structure of concepts in the living and non-living domains differs in systematic ways. Importantly, the most common type of category-specific deficit is an impairment for living things relative to non-living things. On the basis of well-supported claims in the psychological literature, we proposed that living things (and most typically animals) have many properties and many of these are shared among all members of a category (e.g. all mammals *breathe, move, have eyes, can see, have live young, eat*, and so on). Moreover, these shared properties co-occur frequently and so are strongly correlated (Keil, 1986; 1989). Living things also have distinctive properties that are informative in distinguishing one category member from another (e.g. *having stripes* vs. *having spots*), although these tend to be weakly correlated with other properties and so are vulnerable to damage. Artefacts have fewer properties in total, and they tend to be relatively more distinctive, with a smaller pool of information shared across all members of a category. Moreover, unlike living things, the distinctive properties of artefacts tend to be more highly correlated. The result of these structural differences is that brain damage will tend to adversely affect the distinctive properties of living things (because they are weakly correlated) to a greater extent than those of artefacts (because they are more strongly correlated), so making living-thing concepts difficult to differentiate, leading to the typical pattern of semantic deficit for living things. On the CSA account, the variables of distinctiveness and intercorrelation also interact with feature *type*, allowing more complex differences across categories to emerge. This is based on the widely held premise that concepts (at least those referring to concrete entities) contain a mix of different types of feature, including both perceptually based (e.g. color, shape) and more abstract, or functional information (e.g. behavior, use). The amount and salience of different feature types appears to differ systematically across categories (Cree and McRae, 2003; Warrington and McCarthy, 1983; Warrington and McCarthy, 1987; Warrington and Shallice, 1984). We propose that patterns of interactions among these variables also differ: for example, while concepts in the animal category have strong correlations among shared perceptual and "biological" functional properties of (e.g. between *has eyes* and *can see*, *has a mouth* and *eats food*), concepts in artefact categories such as tools have strong correlations among distinctive form (perceptual) and functional properties (Tyler, Moss, et al., 2000; Tyler and Moss, 1997; 2001; see de Renzi and Lucchelli, 1994 for related accounts).

Thus, although there are differences between specific theories, the common theme of conceptual structure based accounts is that the combined effects of structural variables predict *both* processing consequences that are picked up as psycholinguistic phenomena in lexical and semantic tasks, as well as the consequences of damage to the conceptual system in terms of the patterns of loss and preservation of different kinds of semantic information.

Most recently, the approach has also been applied to the study of the neural basis of conceptual knowledge (Tyler et al., 2004; Tyler and Moss, 2001; Moss et al., 2005; Bright et al., 2005; Raposo et al., 2004; Taylor et al., forthcoming). Although many other factors potentially reflect important aspects of conceptual representation (see Tranel et al., 1997 for discussion of many other candidates, including familiarity, age of acquisition, and manipulability), the four variables referred to in the previous paragraph appear to be critically important to the internal structure of a concept: number of features, distinctiveness of those features, patterns of correlation among them, and the interactions of these variables with feature type. In the following section we consider the theoretical development and empirical support for the role of each of these variables in turn.

13.3 Conceptual structure variables: theoretical development and empirical data

13.3.1 Type of semantic feature: perceptual, functional, and beyond

The distinction between perceptually grounded features and more abstract or "functional" features is a critical one in accounts of both the development (e.g. Madole et al., 1993; Mandler, 1992; Tyler, Moss, et al., 2000) and the final structure of the conceptual system (see Miller and Johnson-Laird, 1976; Barsalou, 1999). Warrington and colleagues were amongst the first to explore distinctions among feature types in relation to the neural basis of semantic memory and the effects of damage to that system. They suggested that some categories, such as food and living things, are primarily differentiated in terms of their perceptual/sensory properties, while manmade objects are more reliant on their core functional properties. On the assumption that different types of feature are stored in separate subsystems within semantic memory, which is reflected in the topographical organization of the neural substrate (Allport, 1985), Warrington and colleagues proposed that focal brain damage may disrupt one type of feature more than another, indirectly causing a greater impairment for any category of concept for which that feature type is particularly important (Warrington and McCarthy, 1983; Warrington and McCarthy, 1987; Warrington and Shallice, 1984; Borgo and Shallice, 1994; Farah et al., 1989; Farah and McClelland, 1991; Saffran, 2000).

These assumptions were instantiated in a connectionist model by Farah and McClelland (1991), although the difference between living things and non-living things was captured by the relative *amount* of functional and perceptual features for each concept, rather than their relative importance for differentiating members of the two domains, as had been proposed by Warrington and colleagues. Based on empirical data from a property identification study, the model's representations of non-living things contained similar numbers of functional and perceptual features, while living things had a far higher proportion of perceptual to functional features. When functional features were removed from the model, its performance was more impaired with artefacts than with living things, while the reverse was true when perceptual features were removed from the model, demonstrating that category-specific deficit can emerge from a system organized by feature type rather than category per se.

Distinctions between feature types may have implications for on-line processing of conceptual information in the intact, as well as the impaired system; in a priming study, Moss, McCormick, and Tyler (1997) found greater facilitation for targets denoting functional features of prime concepts (e.g. *tractor–farm*) than for targets denoting perceptual features (e.g. *tractor–wheels*), at least for artefact concepts such as tools and vehicles (primes referring to living things were not included in this study). This suggests more rapid activation of functional features, consistent with the notion that this type of feature is especially important for artefact concepts (see also Barton and Komatsu, 1989; Tyler and Moss, 1997). However, the interaction with other critical factors such as feature distinctiveness and correlation were not manipulated in this study. Moreover, although this sensory/functional or sensory/motor account of semantic memory has received considerable support from neuropsychological studies of patients with category-specific deficits for living things (e.g. Borgo and Shallice, 2001; de Renzi and Lucchelli, 1994; Basso et al., 1988; Sartori and Job, 1988; Moss, Tyler, and Jennings, 1997; see Saffran and Schwartz, 1994 for a review) and from neuroimaging studies suggesting a topographical organization of feature types in the brain (e.g. Martin and Chao, 2001; Martin et al., 2000; Hauk et al., 2004; Pecher et al., 2004; Pulvermüller, 1999), there have also been a number of important challenges to this approach. Many patients have been reported whose patterns of deficit appear inconsistent with the predicted associations between feature type and category, including those with a living-things deficit who are impaired for both functional and perceptual properties (Caramazza and Shelton, 1998; Lambon Ralph et al., 1998; Moss et al., 1998), and those with deficits for visual properties who are not disproportionately impaired for living over non-living things (Lambon Ralph et al., 1998; see Capitani et al., 2003). Moreover, data from imaging studies concerning the proposed neural regions for different types of semantic feature are not consistent.

Finally, it is important to note that the broad distinction between perceptual and functional features is at best a convenient shorthand for the differentiation that may exist, based on multiple sensory, motor, and associative sources of information. Finer-grained distinctions have been proposed, both in the original proposals of Warrington and colleagues and more recently (e.g. Crutch and Warrington, 2003; Cree and McRae, 2003; McRae and Cree, 2002; Tyler and Moss, 1997). For example, Barsalou et al. (1999, cited in McRae and Cree, 2002) developed a taxonomy of twenty-eight "knowledge-types" which were broadly classified as "entity," "situation," "introspective," and "taxonomic." Cree and McRae (2003), using a slightly modified version of this taxonomy, coded the knowledge type of features belonging to concepts in thirty-four categories spanning the living and non-living domains. A principal components analysis revealed that eight of these knowledge types accounted for most of the variance in the distribution of feature types across categories: six "entity" knowledge types ("entity behaviors," e.g. *clock–ticks*, "external components," e.g. *tricycle–has pedals*, "made-of" features, e.g. *sink–made of enamel*, "internal surface properties," e.g. *fridge–is cold*, "external surface properties," e.g. *apple–is red*, and "internal components," e.g. *cherry–has a pit*), and two "situation" knowledge types ("functions," e.g. *tomato–eaten*, and "locations," e.g. *cupboard–found in kitchens*, and "entity" feature types). Moreover, the group of "creature" categories could be distinguished from non-living things based on the greater importance of entity behaviors to creatures and the greater importance of "function" and "made of" properties for non-living things. However, while sensory features ("external components") were highly important to the representation of creatures, they did not distinguish between creatures and non-living things—surprisingly, considering the effects of sensory feature type shown in previous studies noted above. Perhaps more importantly, it is unclear how these knowledge types would pattern onto neural systems, as many refer to multi-componential cognitive processes (Cree and McRae, 2003). Nevertheless, the notion that there are different kinds of feature which may contribute in different ways to the structure of concepts across various categories remains an important insight and variable within the conceptual structure framework, whether the assumption of neural organization along this dimension is explicitly preserved (e.g. Devlin et al., 1998) or not (e.g. Tyler, Moss, et al., 2000). Moreover, the role of features that are grounded in the perceptual and motor systems has been critical in the development of recent "embodied theories" of conceptual representation (see Barsalou, 1999; see also Vinson and Vigliocco, Chapter 12, and Glenberg, Chapter 21 this volume).

13.3.2 Number of features: from complexity to semantic richness

Perhaps the most basic claim of the conceptual structure framework is that some concepts contain more features than others. Theoretical linguistic analyses suggest, for example, that the concept *man* contains the features [+male +adult +human], while *bachelor* contains all these and [+unmarried]. A series of early memory and verification time studies failed to find any support for the prima facie prediction that words containing many features should be at a processing disadvantage compared to those with few features due to the additional complexity of their representations (e.g. Kintsch, 1974). In a classic study, Fodor et al. (1980) also failed to find evidence for decomposition, although they used a task in which subjects judged the relatedness of sentence elements as the index of complexity for simple (e.g. *to die*) vs complex verbs (e.g. *to kill* [i.e. to cause to die]), rather than a measure of on-line processing cost (see also Pitt, 1999 for a critique of the logic of this task).The early results were quickly challenged on a number of grounds. Most importantly, it is not necessarily the case that a greater number of features should be problematic if we assume parallel rather than serial processing—indeed, if the features have a high degree of connectivity among them, this may even facilitate processing (Gentner, 1981, and see discussion of correlations among features below).

More recently, it has become apparent that having more semantic features may indeed be beneficial to conceptual and lexical processing. Various empirical feature generation studies have demonstrated that concrete words typically have more features than do abstract words (e.g. de Mornay Davies and Funnell, 2000; Tyler et al., 2002). This difference has been instantiated in a connectionist model designed to account for the effects of abstractness on the reading performance of patients with deep dyslexia (Plaut and Shallice, 1993). In this model, concrete words are represented over a greater number of microfeatures than are abstract words, and the activation of those features is also more consistent over different occurrences of the word. This leads to more stable patterns of activation, providing a basis for the better performance on concrete than abstract words when the input to the system is noisy, as in patients with deep dyslexia (Plaut and Shallice, 1993) or word meaning deafness (Tyler and Moss, 1997). Conversely, it is also possible that in some cases concrete nouns may be impaired to a greater extent than abstract nouns and verbs: since the latter concepts contain fewer semantic features (especially perceptually based ones), they may be less adversely affected by damage to the semantic system (Breedin et al., 1994; Saffran and Sholl, 1999).

The "richer" semantic representations for concrete words also provide an account of the processing advantage for these words in the normal system when coupled with a model of word recognition which allows activation from the semantic level to feed back to facilitate processing at lower levels (e.g. McClelland and Elman, 1986; Marslen-Wilson and Welsh, 1978; Balota et al., 1991). It follows that the greater number of features activated for a given concept, the greater the amount of activation at the semantic level to facilitate semantic processing, and the more semantic activation is fed back to the orthographic and phonological levels to facilitate processing here (Tyler, Voice, and Moss, 2000). These claims have recently been tested in greater detail in a series of studies by Pexman and colleagues (Pexman et al., 2002; 2003). For example, Pexman et al. (2003) showed that semantic (concrete/abstract) decisions to words with a greater number of features (NoF) were faster than to low-NoF words, a finding attributed to the greater semantic activation of high NoF words. The purported facilitatory effects of semantic feedback activation were confirmed in naming and lexical decision tasks, in which reaction times were faster to high- than to low-NoF words (Pexman et al., 2002), and to polysemous than non-polysemous words (Hino and Lupker, 1996). However, semantic feedback activation is not always advantageous: words with many synonyms purportedly result in a large amount of semantic activation which feeds back to several different orthographic representations, creating *competition* at this level. Indeed, lexical decisions to words with many synonyms are slower than to words without synonyms (Pecher, 2001). Taken together, these elegant series of studies provide compelling evidence for a distributed, componential semantic system in which NoF plays an important role. However, it should be noted that most of the evidence on this point comes from the study of noun concepts; similar results have yet to be demonstrated for other form classes, including verbs. In fact, one recent study suggests (*contra* Fodor et al., 1980) that there may indeed be a processing cost for complex-event verbs over simple-state verbs in reading and lexical decision times (Gennari and Poeppel, 2003).

Although semantic richness or number of features is clearly an important aspect of conceptual structure, it can only be part of the story. As discussed above, concrete words typically have a greater number of features than do abstract words, affording several processing advantages in the healthy system, and providing greater feedback compensation when lexical systems are damaged. However, within the domain of concrete words, living things typically have more features than do artefacts, as shown in property generation norms (Randall et al., 2004; Garrard et al., 2001; Greer et al., 2001). Whether living things show a consistent processing advantage over non-living things in the intact system is debatable (Pilgrim et al., 2005; Laws and Neve, 1999; Gaffan and Heywood, 1993). The pattern varies with task demands; for example, in studies using pictures, living things are disadvantaged when fine-grained distinctions among similar items are needed, but this effect can be removed or even reversed when color and texture information is added to the picture—features that are highly informative for living things (Price and Humphreys, 1989; Moss et al., 2005). Similarly, level of categorization is important, with an advantage for living things often revealed for category-level identification, but a disadvantage for basic-level naming (Humphreys et al., 1988; Lloyd-Jones and Humphreys, 1997; see Moss et al., 2005 for a discussion of potential neural bases of these differences). For brain-damaged patients, however, there is commonly a clear disadvantage for living things, which remains even when familiarity and other potentially confounding factors are taken into account. Thus, a high number of features alone does *not* protect these concepts. The basis for this discrepancy between the concrete/abstract dissociation and the living/artefact dissociation may lie in the contrasting loci of damage in these patients (both functionally and neurally). Many patients with deficits for abstract words have impairments affecting lexical systems, often limited to a specific modality of input or output (e.g. deep dyslexia, word meaning deafness). Their patterns of performance over semantic domains can be accounted for as the relative success of feedback from a largely intact semantic system to an impaired lexical system; concepts with many features providing greater support. Patients with living-things deficits, on the other hand, typically have impairments to central conceptual systems, not limited to a specific modality of input or output. Although living-things concepts have many features, it is the nature of those features, both in terms of their distinctiveness (or lack thereof) and their correlations, that make them vulnerable to damage, as discussed in the following sections (see also Chapter 12 above for a related discussion of differences in the representation of abstract and concrete words).

13.3.3 Feature distinctiveness: from cue validity to relevance

"Feature distinctiveness" essentially refers to the number of concepts in which a feature appears, ranging from one (e.g. *has an udder*, which is true of cows) to very many (e.g. *has eyes*, true of all animals). This factor can be traced back to the notion of cue validity—the conditional probability with which a feature signals a specific concept (Rosch and Mervis, 1975). Similarly, Devlin et al. (1998) characterize features in terms of their informativeness: features occurring for very few concepts are highly informative in identifying specific concepts, while those occurring for many concepts place few constraints on the range of possible concepts to which the feature belongs.

Although distinctiveness can be readily captured in distributed connectionist models of conceptual structure in terms of the overlap of activation of feature units within concept representations (e.g. Devlin et al., 1998; Durrant-Peatfield et al., 1997; Tyler, Moss, et al., 2000; Greer et al., 2001), distinctiveness has also been an important issue within the very different framework of localist hierarchical models of semantic memory. Here, the drive for cognitive economy suggested that features shared by all members of a category be stored at higher levels of the hierarchy only, being "inherited" by concepts within that category, rather than duplicated for each member. Distinctive features, on the other hand, would need to be represented individually for each feature at lower levels (Collins and Loftus, 1975; see Moss and Marslen-Wilson, 1993 for a discussion). This was the framework in which Warrington (1975) initially interpreted the finding that patients with semantic deficits have more difficulty with distinctive than general properties, claiming that access to semantic memory may proceed in a "top-down" manner starting with the general information stored at the category level, culminating in the most distinctive properties at the ends of the branches—these later, more detailed retrieval processes being more susceptible to disruption.

Although the weight of evidence does not support the claim of general to specific access

(Rapp and Caramazza, 1989) or the hierarchical model more generally (see section 13.1), the key finding that distinctive properties are more vulnerable to damage than are shared properties has proved to be a defining characteristic of semantic impairments (e.g. Bub et al., 1988; Hodges et al., 1995; Moss, McCormick, and Tyler, 1997; Moss et al., 1998; Hart and Gordon, 1992; Tippett et al., 1995). This general pattern can be accounted for within a distributed connectionist framework, given that distinctive features are experienced less frequently than are highly shared properties (which occur with many different objects), resulting in weaker connection strengths over all.

However, effects of distinctiveness are unlikely to be uniform across the conceptual system. First, there is considerable evidence that concepts differ in terms of the distinctiveness of their features; specifically, living things appear to have a higher proportion of shared to distinctive features than do artefact concepts. For example, Randall et al. (2004) analyzed the distribution of the distinctiveness of properties generated by a group of participants to ninety-three concepts from the categories of animals, fruit, tools, and vehicles. We measured the distinctiveness of a feature as an inverse function of the number of concepts for which it is generated. Each feature has a distinctiveness value associated with it ranging from 1 (highly distinctive) to 0 (not distinctive). As predicted, the mean distinctiveness of features within artefact concepts was significantly greater than that for living things. This effect has been found in a number of property generation studies, although the cut-off between distinctive and shared properties is defined in various ways across studies (Devlin et al., 1998; Garrard et al., 2001; McRae and Cree, 2002; Vinson and Vigliocco, 2002), and although the precise proportions vary across studies, largely due to the tendency for participants to under-produce highly shared features unless encouraged to do so (see Rogers et al., 2004 for a comparison across studies which highlights the potential for variation in resulting feature sets). While this domain difference in shared/distinctive feature ratio has important consequences for the effect of damage on the conceptual system, the precise consequences of the ratio of distinctive to shared properties across domains cannot be considered in isolation from other factors with which it interacts, most importantly feature type and feature correlation.

Recently, Sartori and Lombardi (2004) have proposed a new feature variable of semantic relevance. Although very similar to the notion of distinctiveness, this variable is weighted according to the importance of the feature for the meaning of the concept (as derived from the number of responses in a property generation study and calculated using a relevance matrix). Thus, while distinctiveness is a concept-independent measure (the distinctiveness of a feature will be the same for all those concepts in which it occurs), relevance is concept-dependent (the same feature may be more relevant for one concept than another: e.g. in Sartori and Lombardi's dataset, the relevance of *has a beak* is greater for the concept *duck* than *swan*, largely reflecting the fact that more participants listed this feature for duck in the generation study). Sartori and Job's analyses of the distribution of feature relevance values across categories suggest a similar pattern to that found for distinctiveness in the earlier studies; most importantly, features of living things (and especially fruit and vegetables) had significantly lower relevance values than those of non-living things. The relevance measure may be an important development on the notion of distinctiveness, as it captures the relationship between a concept and its features as a graded one, rather than in an all-or-none manner (see also Vinson and Vigliocco, 2002 for a related approach to weighting features by salience).

13.3.4 **Feature correlation: clusters and mutual activation**

Rosch et al. (1976) observed that properties of natural categories, rather than being independent, tend to cluster together—for example, that creatures with feathers generally have wings and beaks and lay eggs. Certain combinations of properties occur together much more frequently than do others. In a series of studies, Keil (1986) demonstrated that clusters of properties are larger and more densely intercorrelated for concepts within the domain of living things than of man-made objects. This notion of correlation of properties, and their variation across domains of concepts, is a central tenet of the conceptual structure approach.

However, early studies of the role of property correlation in real-world categories (as opposed to learning artificial concepts) were rather mixed. Malt and Smith (1984) generated a property correlation matrix for a set of basic level concepts, based on participants' responses in feature generation and verification studies. They found that the incidence of property correlations was much greater than would be expected by chance, with about a third of all potential pairs correlated at greater than the .05 level. However, it was less clear that participants actually used this information to perform concept processing tasks: for example, adding property correlation information to a simple family resemblance-weighted sum model significantly improved predictions of ratings in a typicality rating task only under certain conditions—when highly salient correlations were considered and explicit comparisons between correlated and uncorrelated pairs were required. This finding, along with other empirical results showing that correlations among features had little or no effects on explicit off-line category learning tasks (Murphy and Wisniewski, 1989), led to claims that conceptual processing is not typically sensitive to statistical regularities such as feature correlation, but rather that correlations tend only to be noticed when they are explicitly pointed out, or when participants are aware of a theoretical basis for why certain properties might co-occur (Murphy and Medin, 1985).

This rather negative view of the role of correlation has recently been challenged by a number of studies demonstrating the importance of intercorrelation and distinctiveness in conceptual structure, in predicting both patterns of semantic impairment following brain damage and on-line activation of information in the intact system. In each case, the theoretical proposals have also been implemented in distributed connectionist models to test the validity of the major assumptions (McRae et al., 1997; McRae et al., 1999; McRae and Cree, 2002; Devlin et al., 1998; Durrant-Peatfield et al., 1997; Moss et al., 1998; Tyler, Moss, et al., 2000; Tyler and Moss, 2001).

McRae and colleagues (McRae et al., 1997; McRae et al., 1999) suggest that correlations among semantic features play a role in the early computation of word meaning in on-line tasks—in contrast to the more metalinguistic conceptual reasoning tasks that had been used in earlier studies, in which higher-level theoretical knowledge may be more relevant (e.g. Keil, 1989; Rips, 1989). To investigate this issue, McRae et al. compared the impact of featural variables in fast on-line tasks (e.g. semantic priming, speeded feature verification) with that in slower, untimed tasks, more akin to those used in earlier studies (e.g. similarity and typicality ratings). Featural variables for concepts were established in a large-scale property generation study. Analysis of these norms supported the claim that living things have a significantly greater number of correlated properties than do artefacts (Keil, 1989), although the overall number of features did not differ across domains in this cohort.

Results from the on-line semantic tasks suggested that the initial computation of word meaning is indeed highly sensitive to the distributional statistics of features within concepts. For example, in a short SOA priming task, facilitation increased as a function of the overlap in individual features for artefact pairs (i.e. number of shared features, e.g. *pistol–rifle*), while overlap specifically in correlated features predicted facilitation for living things (e.g. *eagle–hawk*). However, in an untimed similarity rating task, the effect of correlation for living things disappeared, suggesting that this factor affects initial activation of the meaning rather than the eventual stable state. A similar pattern was shown in a feature verification paradigm: participants were asked to indicate whether a feature was true of a concept (e.g. *deer–hunted by people*). Feature correlation was manipulated such that half of the features were highly correlated with other features of the concept (e.g. *hunted by people* is correlated with many other properties of *deer*), while for the other half of the stimuli the features were presented with concepts where they were weakly correlated with other features (e.g. *duck–hunted by people*). Feature correlation was a significant predictor of reaction times, over and above other important factors such as conceptual familiarity and production frequency of the feature. This finding was replicated by McRae et al. (1999), who also found a significant, albeit smaller effect of correlation strength at a longer SOA, and by Randall et al. (2004), who reported significantly slower reaction times to the weakly correlated, distinctive features of living things than to the shared properties of living things and the relatively strongly intercorrelated properties of non-living things in a speeded feature verification task. However, correlation strength was not a significant predictor of typicality ratings in an untimed task (McRae et al., 1999) nor an unspeeded feature verification task (Randall et al., 2004). Finally, McRae et al. simulated the main effects of these two empirical studies in a distributed connectionist model which mapped from word form units to semantic representations which were distributed over feature units, directly reflecting the structure of concepts derived from the property generation study. In a simulation of the priming study, the model replicated the behavioral results, showing an early effect of overlap of correlated features for living things, but of individual feature similarity for artefacts. These findings suggest that null effects of correlation in the earlier category learning studies may have been due at least in part to their extended time course, which would not pick up the early effects on meaning activation that were so clearly revealed in priming and speeded feature verification tasks.

13.4 **Conceptual structure account revisited: correlation, distinctiveness, feature type, and domain**

Our CSA model described earlier in this chapter also stresses the combined contribution of feature correlations and distinctiveness in determining conceptual structure. A critical difference between our approach and that of Gonnerman and colleagues (Gonnerman et al., 1997; Devlin et al., 1998) and McRae and colleagues (McRae et al., 1997; Cree and McRae, 2003) is that we incorporate a set of claims about how these variables interact with differences in feature type—specifically form (perceptual properties) and function—in the living and non-living domains. These claims draw on the developmental literature, which investigates how children learn the relations among properties of concepts. We claim that an essential aspect of conceptual structure is the pattern of correlations between form and function (Tversky and Hemenway, 1984). If a perceptual form is consistently observed performing a function, then a system which is sensitive to co-occurrences will learn that a specific form implies a specific function (Madole et al., 1993; Mandler, 1992). The nature of these form–function relations distinguishes between living things and artefacts. Artefacts have distinctive forms, which are consistently associated with the functions for which they were created (de Renzi and Lucchelli, 1994; Keil, 1986; 1989, see also Caramazza et al.'s (1990) claim of privileged relations among properties for a similar view). Artefacts are generally designed to perform a single distinctive function so that their form is as distinctive as the function. In contrast, living things tend to "do" similar things and they tend to resemble each other, and thus they share many features. Individual variations in form tend not to be functionally significant (e.g. *a lion's mane*). Even so, living things (like artefacts) also have form–function correlations. But whereas the form–function correlations for artefacts involve distinctive properties, for living things it is the shared properties (e.g. *eyes*, *legs*) that are involved in form–function correlations (e.g. *eye–see*; *legs–move*). We refer to these as biological functions (Durrant-Peatfield et al., 1997; Tyler, Moss, et al., 2000; Tyler and Moss, 1997). Unlike the sensory/functional account, we do not claim that functional information is more important for artefacts than for living things, but rather that there is a difference across domains in the *kind* of functional information that is most strongly correlated—and therefore most robust to damage. Living things have many, very important functional properties, but the most significant ones concern biological activities that are frequently shared across most or all members of a category, rather than their intended use or purpose in relation to human beings (Tyler and Moss, 1997). These predictions were supported by the analysis of property generation norms (Randall et al., 2004). First, living-things concepts had more significantly correlated features than did concepts in the non-living domain—a finding that has also been reported for several other property norm studies (McRae et al., 1997; Garrard et al., 2001; Vinson et al., 2003; Devlin et al., 1998). Most importantly for the CSA account, the distinctiveness of features that participated in form–function correlations (e.g. has *a blade–is used for cutting)* was significantly greater for concepts in the non-living than in the living domain. However, this finding has not been replicated in other property norm studies. Garrard et al. (2001) and Vinson et al. (2003) both reported a greater number of correlated features for living than non-living things, but also reported that distinctive properties of living things were more, rather than less, correlated than those of non-living things. While it is possible that both these studies were limited by the small number of concepts entered into the analyses, and by the underestimation of shared properties overall, it will clearly be important to establish in future studies whether the interaction between distinctiveness, correlation, and domain is a robust one, as claimed by the CSA.

13.4.1 **The conceptual structure account and semantic deficits**

Taken together, the assumptions of the CSA predict that patients with category-specific deficits for living things will show a particular pattern of loss and preservation of features; specifically, that they will have the greatest problem with the distinctive properties of living things, due to the inherently weak correlations of this type of information. Since most semantic tasks require within-category discriminations that rely on intact knowledge of distinctive properties, this will generally show up as a deficit for living things, even though knowledge of the highly correlated shared information may be intact—indeed, in some cases may be superior to knowledge of shared information about manmade objects. This pattern was demonstrated in a detailed single-case study of a patient with a deficit for living things following Herpes Simplex Encephalitis (HSE). Across a range of tasks, including property verification, sorting and naming to definition, RC showed selective difficulties with the distinctive properties of living things, but no apparent difficulty with shared properties. We have reported similar findings for other patients with living things deficits with an etiology of HSE (Tyler and Moss, 2001; Moss et al., 2002). Other authors have also reported relatively preserved knowledge of shared properties and impaired knowledge of distinctive properties of living things for patients with category-specific deficits (e.g. patient EW; Caramazza and Shelton, 1998). For most other patients in the literature, the appropriate contrasts between distinctive and shared information were not tested, so it is not possible to determine whether these patients were more impaired with the distinctive properties of living things. In several reports, however, there are hints that this is the case (e.g. Sartori and Job, 1988). Similarly, Sartori and Lombardi (2004) report evidence which suggests that the typically low semantic relevance of features of living things cause patients' difficulties with concepts in this domain: when relevance was controlled across domain, living-thing deficits were reduced or even reversed.

13.4.2 The conceptual structure account and speed of intact processing

The CSA also makes predictions for the speed with which different types of feature become activated during normal on-line processing in the intact system. This includes the prediction that there will be a disadvantage in rapidly activating the distinctive properties of living things relative to other kinds of feature, due to their lack of correlation with other information—even in the normal conceptual system—on the premise that mutual activation produces faster initial processing times for correlated features. For shared properties we predicted little difference across domains, since both living and non-living things have groups of correlated shared properties; if anything, the pattern should be in the opposite direction, as living things have a greater number of shared properties. These predictions were supported by the results of a speeded feature verification task, which was designed to tap into the early stages of semantic activation, with short presentation times, backward masking, and a response deadline at only 450 msec SOA. There was a significant interaction between distinctiveness and domain; feature verification for distinctive features of living things was disproportionately slow and error-prone, while there was no difference between living and non-living things for shared features (Randall et al., 2004). These results were simulated in a distributed connectionist model, which mapped orthographic word form units, via a set of hidden units, onto semantic representations which were distributed over semantic feature units, directly reflecting the structure of the concepts derived from our property generation study. The model replicated the domain by distinctiveness interaction in the speeded feature verification results, showing that the distinctive properties of living things were more error-prone and took longer to settle than the distinctive properties of non-living things, while there were no domain differences for shared properties. These results demonstrated that processing differences across domains arise on the basis of differences in the correlational structure of concepts within domains.

13.5 Challenges for the conceptual structure framework

Conceptual structure accounts have taken us a long way in understanding the psychology and neuropsychology of conceptual representation and processing. However, as with any model of conceptual representation, this account faces several challenges. For example, the CSA makes clear predictions about the relationship between the severity of impairment and the degree of deficit for living and non-living things. Based on the results of our computational simulations, we predicted that at most levels of damage, living things would be most impaired, but when damage was very severe, and overall performance very inaccurate, that living things would have a slight processing advantage over artefacts (Tyler, Moss, et al., 2000; Greer et al., 2001). We have argued that this pattern is due to the large number of highly intercorrelated shared properties for living things, which constitute the only information that can withstand a high degree of damage, allowing a small percentage of living-things trials to be correct (see Moss and Tyler, 2000 for further details). Our own longitudinal studies of patients with degenerative diseases affecting the semantic system have supported this hypothesis (Moss and Tyler, 2000; Moss et al., 2002). Moreover, some of the handful of patients reported with artefact deficits do seem to have very severe deficits, consistent with this view (e.g. VER and YOT; Warrington and McCarthy, 1983; 1987). However, data from cross-sectional studies of groups of Alzheimer's patients are mixed, with some showing no relationship between severity and domain effects (Garrard et al., 1998). Other patients with category-specific semantic impairments for non-living things have been reported that were not severely impaired in other domains (Hillis and Caramazza, 1991; Sacchett and Humphreys, 1992). The domain by severity interaction thus remains controversial (Garrard et al., 1998; Caramazza and Mahon, 2003).

A further challenge to distributed conceptual structure accounts such as the CSA is to reconcile their claim of a unitary semantic system with the behavioral and functional neuroimaging evidence for a sensory-motor organisation of features (e.g. Warrington and Shallice, 1984; Chao et al., 1999; Martin et al., 2000). Some authors have addressed this issue by proposing a hybrid model of conceptual structure which includes a sensory-motor distribution of semantic features (e.g. the Featural and Unitary Semantic Space (FUSS) model; Vigliocco et al., 2004; Cree and McRae, 2003, where knowledge types play a critical role alongside conceptual structure variables). According to the FUSS model, semantic representations of object (and action) knowledge are represented at two levels: a conceptual feature space organized by sensory-motor feature type, and a second, "lexico-semantic" space organized by the conceptual structure factors of feature salience, sharedness/distinctiveness, and intercorrelation, which binds features from the conceptual feature space. This architecture allows for isolated impairments of specific kinds of sensorimotor feature and thus category for which these features are particularly important, as well as patterns of deficits consistent with a conceptual structure approach, by hypothesizing damage to the conceptual feature and lexico-semantic space, respectively. Further studies will need to determine the extent to which the FUSS's two-tiered model of conceptual representation is supported by functional-neuroanatomical activation patterns.

Simmons and Barsalou (2003) likewise argued that a more comprehensive and powerful model of semantic memory may be achieved by integrating conceptual structure and sensory-functional or sensory-motor accounts, and in this vein developed their Conceptual Topography Theory (CTT). The CTT draws heavily on the non-human primate literature on object processing, as well as on Damasio's (1989) convergence zone theory of human object processing. It postulates that each sensory and motor system contains "feature maps" processing the respective elementary object features. These sensory and motor features are bound together into increasingly complex feature conjunctions from posterior to anterior regions in a hierarchical system of "convergence zones" (association areas) in each sensory and motor stream. It is proposed that the anteromedial temporal lobe plays a special role in object processing, in that it purportedly processes the most complex conjunction of visual features as well as the multimodal feature conjunctions. The CTT makes two additional assumptions about the neural code of conceptual similarity. Specifically, it postulates that the proximity of neurons in a convergence zone increases as a function of the similarity of the features they conjoin (the "similarity-in-topography principle"), and that clumps of conjunctive neurons representing category members become more dispersed as the similarity of the represented category members decreases (the "variable dispersion principle"). Thus, the CTT's sensory and motor feature maps correspond to these feature representations in the sensory-functional and sensory-motor accounts (Warrington and McCarthy, 1983; Warrington and McCarthy, 1987; Martin and Chao, 2001; and Martin et al., 2000 respectively). The CTT also instantiates distinctiveness in neural space: concepts which share many features (e.g. living things) would be represented close together in the convergence zone (the "similarity-in-topography principle"), while the representations of concepts which share fewer features (e.g. non-living things) would be more dispersed in the convergence zone (the "variable dispersion principle").

We recently tested the central claims of this "neurocognitive" account in a series of functional neuroimaging studies (Tyler et al., 2004; Moss et al., 2005). Healthy participants were instructed to perform two different picture-naming tasks with the same picture stimuli. In a domain-level naming task, participants silently named the domain (i.e. *living, manmade*) to which pictured objects belonged, while a basic-level naming task with the same picture stimuli required participants to silently name the pictured object (e.g. *tiger*). We hypothesized that the domain-level naming task would require relatively simple visual feature conjunctions (e.g. curvature) mediated by more posterior regions in the visual object processing stream to differentiate living from non-living things, while the basic-level naming task would require relatively more complex visual feature conjunctions mediated by more anterior regions in the visual object processing stream in order to distinguish the pictured object from other, visually similar objects (e.g. a tiger from a lion). Consistent with these hypotheses, domain-level naming was associated with more posterior ventral occipito-temporal and basic-level naming additionally with more antero-medial temporal lobe activity (Tyler et al., 2004). We next hypothesized that, since living things are characterized by many shared and relatively few distinctive features while non-living things typically have a greater proportion of distinctive to shared features, the identification of living things would be more visually demanding, requiring more complex visual feature conjunctions compared to the basic-level naming of non-living things. As predicted, we found greater antero-medial temporal lobe activity, presumably reflecting complex visual feature conjunctions during the basic-level naming of living compared to matched sets of non-living things—a finding confirmed in behavioral studies with patients with brain damage including the antero-medial temporal lobe (Moss et al., 2005).

The ultimate challenge to conceptual structure accounts may be to explain how conceptual knowledge is instantiated in the brain. Neurocognitive accounts, which integrate psycholinguistically and neuropsychologically verified principles of conceptual structure with a hierarchical object-processing model developed in non-human primates, may have the capacity to meet this challenge. We hope that future psycholinguistic, neuropsychological, and neuroimaging research on conceptual structure will continue to be conducted in parallel, mutually enriching each other's findings, to determine how feature types, number of features, distinctiveness, intercorrelation, and the combination of these factors are behaviorally and neurally represented and processed.

Acknowledgements

This work was supported by an MRC programme grant to LKT and a grant from the Roche Research Foundation and Olga Mayenfisch Foundation to KIT.

References

Allport, D. A. (1985) Distributed memory, modular subsystems and dysphasia. In S. K. Newman and R. Epstein (eds), *Current Perspectives in Dysphasia*, pp. 32–60. Churchill Livingstone, Edinburgh.

Almeida, R. G. de (1999) What do category-specific semantic deficits tell us about the representation of lexical concepts? *Brain and Language*, 68: 241–8.

Balota, D. A., Ferraro, R. F., and Connor, L. T. (1991) On the early influence of meaning in word recognition: a review of the literature. In P. J. Schwanenflugel (ed.), *The Psychology of Word Meanings*, pp. 187–218. Erlbaum, Hillsdale, NJ.

Barsalou, L. W. (1999) Perceptual symbol systems. *Behavioral and Brain Sciences*, 22: 577–609.

Barsalou, L. W., Solomon, K. O., and Wu, L. L. (1999) Perceptual simulation in conceptual tasks. In M. K. Hiraga, C. Sinha, and S. Wilcox (eds), *Cultural, Typological, and Psychological Perspectives in Cognitive Linguistics: Proceedings of the 4th Conference of the International Cognitive Linguistics Association.* Benjamins, Amsterdam.

Barton, M. E., and Komatsu, L. (1989) Defining features of natural kinds and artefacts. *Journal of Psycholinguistic Research*, 18: 433–47.

Basso, A., Capitani, E., and Laiacona, M. (1988) Progressive language impairment without dementia: a case with isolated category specific semantic defect. *Journal of Neurology, Neurosurgery and Psychiatry*, 51: 1201–7.

Borgo, F., and Shallice, T. (1994) When living things and other "sensory quality" categories behave in the same fashion: a novel category specificity effect. *Neurocase*, 7: 201–20.

Borgo, F., and Shallice, T. (2001) When living things and other sensory quality categories go together: a novel category-specific effect. *Neurocase*, 7: 201–20.

Breedin, S., Saffran, E., and Coslett, H. (1994) Reversal of the concreteness effect in a patient with semantic dementia. *Cognitive Neuropsychology*, 11: 617–60.

Bright, P., Moss, H. E., Stamatakis, E. A., and Tyler, L. K. (2005) The anatomy of object processing: the role of anteromedial temporal cortex. *Quarterly Journal of Experimental Psychology, Section B*, 58: 361–77.

Bub, D. N., Black, S. E., Hampson, E., and Kertesz, A. (1988) Semantic encoding of pictures and words: some neuropsychological observations. *Cognitive Neuropsychology*, 5: 27–66.

Bunn, E. M., Tyler, L. K., and Moss, H. E. (1998) Category-specific semantic deficits: The role of familiarity and property type reexamined. *Neuropsychology*, 12: 367–9.

Capitani, E., Laiacona, M., Mahon, B., and Caramazza, A. (2003) What are the facts of semantic category-specific deficits? A critical review of the clinical evidence. *Cognitive Neuropsychology*, 20: 213–61.

Caramazza, A., and Hillis, A. E. (1991) Lexical organisation of nouns and verbs in the brain. *Nature*, 349: 788–90.

Caramazza, A., Hillis, A. E., Rapp, B. C., and Romani, C. (1990) The multiple semantics hypothesis: multiple confusions? *Cognitive Neuropsychology*, 7: 161–89.

Caramazza, A., and Mahon, B. Z. (2003) The organization of conceptual knowledge: the evidence from category-specific semantic deficits. *Trends in Cognitive Sciences*, 7: 354–61.

Caramazza, A., and Shelton, J. R. (1998) Domain-specific knowledge systems in the brain: the animate–inanimate distinction. *Journal of Cognitive Neuroscience*, 10: 1–34.

Chao, L. L., Haxby, J. V., and Martin, A. (1999) Attribute-based neural substrates in temporal cortex for perceiving and knowing about objects. *Nature Neuroscience*, 2: 913–19.

Collins, A. M., and Loftus, E. F. (1975) A spreading activation theory of semantic processing. *Psychological Review*, 82: 407–28.

Cree, G. S., and McRae, K. (2003) Analyzing the factors underlying the structure and computation of the meaning of chipmunk, cherry, chisel, cheese, and cello (and many other such concrete nouns). *Journal of Experimental Psychology: General*, 132: 163–201.

Cree, G. S., McRae, K., and McNorgan, C. (1999) An attractor model of lexical conceptual processing: simulating semantic priming. *Cognitive Science*, 23: 371–414.

Crutch, S. J., and Warrington, E. K. (2003) The selective impairment of fruit and vegetable knowledge: a multiple processing channels account of fine-grain category specificity. *Cognitive Neuropsychology*, 20: 355–72.

Damasio, A. R. (1989) Time-locked multi-regional retro-activation: a systems-level proposal for the neural substrates of recall and recognition. *Cognition*, 33: 25–62.

Devlin, J. T., Gonnerman, L. M., Andersen, E. S., and Seidenberg, M. S. (1998) Category-specific semantic deficits in focal and widespread brain damage: a computational account. *Journal of Cognitive Neuroscience*, 10: 77–94.

Dixon, M., Bub, D. N., and Arguin, M. (1997) The interaction of object form and object meaning in the identification performance of a patient with category-specific visual agnosia. *Cognitive Neuropsychology*, 14: 1085–130.

Durrant-Peatfield, M. R., Tyler, L. K., Moss, H. E., and Levy, J. P. (1997) The distinctiveness of form and function in category structure: a connectionist model. In Shafto, M. G., and Langley, P. (eds), *Proceedings of the19th Annual Conference of the Cognitive Science Society.* Erlbaum, Mahwah, NJ.

Farah, M. J., Hammond, K. M., Mehta, Z., and Radcliff, G. (1989) Category-specificity and modality-specificity in semantic memory. *Neuropsychologia*, 27: 193–200.

Farah, M. J., and McClelland, J. L. (1991) A computational model of semantic memory impairment: modality specificity and emergent category specificity. *Journal of Experimental Psychology: General*, 120: 339–57.

Fodor, J. A., and Fodor, J. D. (1980) Functional structure, quantifiers and meaning postulates. *Linguistic Inquiry*, 11: 4.

Fodor, J. A., Garrett, M. F., Walker, E. C. T., and Parkes, C. H. (1980) Against definitions. *Cognition*, 8: 263–367.

Forde, E. M. E., Francis, D., Riddoch, M. J., Rumiati, R. I., and Humphreys, G. W. (1997) On the links between visual knowledge and naming: a single case study of a patient with a category-specific impairment for living things. *Cognitive Neuropsychology*, 14: 403–58.

Forde, E. M. E., and Humphreys, G. W. (1999) Category-specific recognition impairments: a review of important case studies and influential theories. *Aphasiology*, 13: 169–93.

Franklin, S. (1989) Dissociations in auditory word comprehension: evidence from 9 "fluent" aphasic patients. *Aphasiology*, 3: 189–207.

Gaffan, D., and Heywood, C. A. (1993) A spurious category-specific visual agnosia for living things in normal human and non-human primates. *Journal of Cognitive Neuroscience*, 5: 118–28.

Garrard, P., Lambon, Ralph, M. A., Hodges, J. R., and Patterson, K. (2001) Prototypicality, distinctiveness, and intercorrelation: analyses of the semantic attributes of living and nonliving concepts. *Cognitive Neuropsychology*, 18: 125–74.

Garrard, P., Patterson, K., Watson, P. C., and Hodges, J. R. (1998) Category-specific semantic loss in dementia of the Alzheimer's type: functional-anatomical correlations from cross-sectional analyses. *Brain*, 121: 633–46.

Gennari, S., and Poeppel, D. (2003) Processing correlates of lexical semantic complexity. *Cognition*, 89: 27–41.

Gentner, D. (1981) Some interesting differences between nouns and verbs. *Cognition and Brain Theory*, 4: 161–78.

Gonnerman, L. M., Andersen, E. S., Devlin, J. T., Kempler, D., and Seidenberg, M. S. (1997) Double dissociation of semantic categories in Alzheimer's disease. *Brain and Language*, 57: 254–79.

Greer, M. J., van Casteren, M., and McLellan, J., et al. (2001) The emergence of semantic categories from distributed featural representations. In J. D. Moore and K. Stenning (eds), *Proceedings of the 23rd Annual Conference of the Cognitive Science Society*, pp. 358–63. Erlbaum, London.

Hart, J., and Gordon, B. (1992) Neural subsystems for object knowledge. *Nature*, 359: 60–64.

Hauk, O., Johnsrude, I., and Pulvermüller, F. (2004) Somatotopic representation of action words in human motor and premotor cortex. *Neuron*, 41: 301–7.

Hillis, A. E., and Caramazza, A. (1991) Category-specific naming and comprehension impairment: a double dissociation. *Brain*, 114: 2081–94.

Hino, Y., and Lupker, S. J. (1996) Effects of polysemy in lexical decision and naming: an alternative to lexical access accounts. *Journal of Experimental Psychology: Human Perception and Performance*, 22: 1331–56.

Hinton, G. E., McClelland, J. L., and Rumelhart, D. E. (1986) Distributed representations. In J. L. McClelland and D. E. Rumelhart (eds), *Parallel Distributed Processing: Explorations in the Microstructure of Cognition*, pp. 77–109. MIT Press, Cambridge, MA.

Hinton, G. E., and Shallice, T. (1991) Lesioning an attractor network: investigations of acquired dyslexia. *Psychological Review*, 98: 74–95.

Hodges, J. R., Graham, N., and Patterson, K. (1995) Charting the progression in semantic dementia: implications for the organisation of semantic memory. *Memory*, 3: 463–495.

Humphreys, G. W., Riddoch, M. J., and Quinlan, P. (1988) Cascade processes in picture identification. *Cognitive Neuropsychology*, 5: 67–103.

Jackendoff, R. (1983) *Semantics and Cognition*. MIT Press, Cambridge, MA.

Jackendoff, R. (1989) What is a concept, that a person can grasp it? *Mind and Language*, 4: 68–102.

Kawamoto, A. H. (1993) Nonlinear dynamics in the resolution of lexical ambiguity: a parallel distributed processing account. *Journal of Memory and Language*, 32: 474–516.

Keil, F. C. (1986) The acquisition of natural kind and artifact terms. In W. Domopoulous and A. Marras (eds), *Language Learning and Concept Acquisition*, pp. 133–53. Ablex, Norwood, NJ.

Keil, F. C. (1989) *Concepts, Kinds and Cognitive Development*, MIT Press, Cambridge, MA.

Kintsch, W. (1974) *The Representation of Meaning in Memory*, Lawrence Erlbaum, Hillsdale, NJ.

Komatsu, L. K. (1992) Recent views on conceptual structure. *Psychological Bulletin*, 112: 500–526.

Laiacona, M., and Caramazza, A. (2004) The noun/verb dissociation in language production: varieties of causes. *Cognitive Neuropsychology*, 21: 103–23.

Lambon Ralph, M. A., Howard, D., Nightingale, G., and Ellis, A. W. (1998) Are living and non-living category-specific deficits causally linked to impaired perceptual or associative knowledge? Evidence from a category-specific double dissociation. *Neurocase*, 4: 311–38.

Laws, K. R., and Neve, C. (1999) A "normal" category-specific advantage for naming living things. *Neuropsychologia*, 37: 1263–9.

Lloyd-Jones, T., and Humphreys, G. W. (1997) Categorizing chairs and naming pears: category differences in object processing as a function of task and priming. *Memory and Cognition*, 25: 606–24.

Madole, K. L., Oakes, L. M., and Cohen, L. B. (1993) Developmental changes in infants' attention to function and form–function correlations. *Cognitive Development*, 8: 189–209.

Malt, B. C., and Smith, E. (1984) Correlated properties in natural categories. *Journal of Verbal Learning and Verbal Behavior*, 23: 250–69.

Mandler, J. M. (1992) How to build a baby II: conceptual primitives. *Psychological Review*, 99: 587–604.

Marslen-Wilson, W. D., and Welsh, A. (1978) Processing interactions and lexical access during word-recognition in continous speech. *Cognitive Psychology*, 10: 29–63.

Martin, A., and Chao, L. L. (2001) Semantic memory and the brain: structure and processes. *Current Opinion in Neurobiology*, 11: 194–201.

Martin, A., Ungerleider, L. G., and Haxby, J. V. (2000) Category-specificity and the brain: the sensory-motor model of semantic representations of objects. In M. S. Gazzaniga (ed.), *The Cognitive Neurosciences* (2nd edn), pp. 1023–46. MIT Press, Cambridge, MA.

Masson, M. (1995) A distributed memory model of semantic priming. *Journal of Experimental Psychology: Learning, Memory, and Cognition*, 21: 3–23.

McClelland, J., and Elman, J. (1986) The TRACE model of speech perception. *Cognitive Psychology*, 18: 1–86.

McNamara, T. P. (1992) Priming and constraints it places on theories of memory and retrieval. *Psychological Review*, 99: 650–62.

McRae, K., and Cree, G. S. (2002) Factors underlying category-specific semantic deficits. In E. M. E. Forde and G. W. Humphreys (eds), *Category-Specificity in Brain and Mind*. Psychology Press, Hove, UK.

McRae, K., Cree, G. S., Westmacott, R., and de Sa, V. R. (1999) Further evidence for feature correlations in semantic memory. *Canadian Journal of Experimental Psychology*, 53: 360–73.

McRae, K., de Sa, V. R., and Seidenberg, M. S. (1997) On the nature and scope of featural representations of word meaning. *Journal of Experimental Psychology: General*, 126: 99–130.

Miller, G., and Johnson-Laird, P. N. (1976) *Language and Perception*. Harvard University Press, Cambridge, MA.

Miller, G. A. (1978) Semantic relations among words. In M. Halle, J. Bresnan, and G. A. (eds), *Linguistic Theory and Psychological Reality*, pp. 60–118. MIT Press, Cambridge, MA.

Mornay, Davies, P. de, and Funnell, E. (2000) Semantic representation and ease of predication. *Brain and Language*, 73: 92–119.

Moss, H. E., and Gaskell, M. G. (1999) Lexical semantic processing during speech. In S. Garrod and M. Pickering (eds), *Language Processing*, pp. 59–99. Psychology Press, Hove, UK.

Moss, H. E., and Marslen-Wilson, W. D. (1993) Access to word meanings during spoken language comprehension: effects of sentential semantic context. *Journal of Experimental Psychology: Learning, Memory, and Cognition*, 19: 1254–76.

Moss, H. E., McCormick, S. F., and Tyler, L. K. (1997) The time-course of activation of semantic information during spoken word recognition. *Language and Cognitive Processes*, 12: 695–732.

Moss, H. E., Rodd, J. M., Stamatakis, E. A., Bright, P., and Tyler, L. K. (2005) Anteromedial temporal cortex supports fine-grained differentiation among objects. *Cerebral Cortex*, 15: 616–27.

Moss, H. E., and Tyler, L. K. (2000) A progressive category-specific semantic deficit for non-living things. *Neuropsychologia*, 38: 60–82.

Moss, H. E., and Tyler, L. K. (2003) Weighing up the facts of category-specific semantic deficits: a reply to Caramazza and Mahon. *Trends in Cognitive Sciences*, 7: 480–1.

Moss, H. E., Tyler, L. K., and Devlin, J. (2002) The emergence of category specific deficits in a distributed semantic system. In E. Forde and G. W. Humphreys (eds), *Category-Specificity in Brain and Mind*, pp. 115–48. Psychology Press, Hove, UK.

Moss, H. E., Tyler, L. K., Durrant-Peatfield, M., and Bunn, E. M. (1998) "Two eyes of a see-through": impaired and intact semantic knowledge in a case of selective deficit for living things. *Neurocase*, 4: 291–310.

Moss, H. E., Tyler, L. K., and Jennings, F. (1997) When leopards lose their spots: knowledge of visual properties in category-specific deficits for living things. *Cognitive Neuropsychology*, 14: 901–50.

Murphy, G. L., and Medin, D. L. (1985) The role of theories in conceptual coherence. *Psychological Review*, 92: 289–316.

Murphy, G. L., and Wisniewski, E. J. (1989) Feature correlations in conceptual representations. In G. Tiberghien (ed.), *Advances in Cognitive Science: Theory and Applications*, pp. 23–45. Ellis Horwood, Chichester, UK.

Pecher, D. (2001) Perception is a two-way junction: feedback semantics in word recognition. *Psychonomic Bulletin and Review*, 8: 545–51.

Pecher, D., Zeelenberg, R., and Barsalou, L. W. (2004) Sensorimotor simulations underlie conceptual representations: modality-specific effects of prior activation. *Psychonomic Bulletin and Review*, 11: 164–7.

Pexman, P. M., Holyk, G. G., and Monfils, M. H. (2003) Number-of-features effects and semantic processing. *Memory and Cognition*, 31: 842–55.

Pexman, P. M., Lupker, S. J., and Hino, Y. (2002) The impact of feedback semantics in visual word recognition: number-of-features effects in lexical decision and naming tasks. *Psychonomic Bulletin and Review*, 9: 542–9.

Pilgrim, L. K., Moss, H. E., and Tyler, L. K. (2005) Semantic processing of living and nonliving domains of knowledge across the cerebral hemisphere. *Brain and Language*, 94: 86–93.

Pitt, D. (1999) In defence of definitions. *Philosophical Psychology*, 12: 139–59.

Plaut, D. C., and Shallice, T. (1993) Deep dyslexia: a case study of connectionist neuropsychology. *Cognitive Neuropsychology*, 10: 377–500.

Price, C. J., and Humphreys, G. W. (1989) The effects of surface detail on object categorisation and object naming. *Quarterly Journal of Experimental Psychology*, 41A: 797–828.

Pulvermüller, F. (1999) Words in the brain's language. *Behavioral and Brain Sciences*, 22: 253–79.

Randall, B., Moss, H. E., Rodd, J. M., Greer, M., and Tyler, L. K. (2004) Distinctiveness and correlation in conceptual structure: behavioral and computational studies. *Journal of Experimental Psychology: Learning, Memory, and Cognition*, 30: 393–406.

Raposo, A., Stamatakis, E. A., Moss, H. E., and Tyler, L. K. (2004) Interactions between processing demands and conceptual structure in object recognition: an event-related fMRI study. *Journal of Cognitive Neuroscience*, 16: B82.

Rapp, B., and Caramazza, A. (1989) General to specific access to word meaning: a claim re-examined. *Cognitive Neuropsychology*, 6: 251–72.

Renzi, E., de, and Lucchelli, F. (1994) Are semantic systems separately represented in the brain? The case of living category impairment. *Cortex*, 30: 3–25.

Rips, L. J. (1989) Similarity, typicality, and categorization. In S. Vosniadou and A. Ortony (eds), *Similarity and Analogical Reasoning*, pp. 21–59. Cambridge University Press, Cambridge.

Rogers, T. T., Lambon Ralph, M. A., Garrard, P, et al. (2004) Structure and deterioration of semantic memory: a neuropsychological and computational investigation. *Psychological Review*, 111: 205–35.

Rogers, T. T., and Plaut, D. C. (2002) Connectionist perspectives on category-specific deficits. In E. Forde and G. W. Humphreys (eds), *Category-Specificity in Brain and Mind*, pp. 251–90. Psychology Press, Hove, UK.

Rosch, E., and Mervis, C. B. (1975) Family resemblances: studies in the internal structure of categories. *Cognitive Psychology*, 7: 573–605.

Rosch, E., Mervis, C. B., Gray, W. D., Johnson, D. M., and Boyes-Braem, P. (1976) Basic objects in natural categories. *Cognitive Psychology*, 8: 382–439.

Sacchett, C., and Humphreys, G. W. (1992) Calling a squirrel a squirrel but a canoe a wigwam: a category-specific deficit for artefactual objects and body parts. *Cognitive Neuropsychology*, 9: 73–86.

Saffran, E. M. (2000) The organization of semantic memory: in support of a distributed model. *Brain and Language*, 71: 204–12.

Saffran, E. M., and Schwartz, M. F. (1994) Of cabbages and things: semantic memory from a neuropscyhological point of view—a tutorial review. In C. Umilta and M. Moscovitch (eds), *Attention and Performance*, pp. 507–36. Cambridge University Press, Cambridge.

Saffran, E. M. and Sholl, A. (1999) Clues to the functional and neural architecture of word meaning. In C. M. Brown and P. Hagoort (eds), *The Neurocognition of Language*, pp. 241–71. Oxford University Press, Oxford.

Sartori, G., and Job, R. (1988) The oyster with four legs: a neuropsychological study on the interaction of visual and semantic information. *Cognitive Neuropsychology*, 5: 105–32.

Sartori, G., and Lombardi, L. (2004) Semantic relevance and semantic disorders. *Journal of Cognitive Neuroscience*, 16: 439–52.

Silveri, M. C., and Di Betta, A. M. (1997) Noun–verb dissociations in brain-damaged patients: Further evidence. *Neurocase*, 3: 477–88.

Simmons, W. K., and Barsalou, L. W. (2003) The similarity-in-topography principle: reconciling theories of conceptual deficits. *Cognitive Neuropsychology*, 20: 451–86.

Smith, E. E., and Medin, D. L. (1981) *Categories and Concepts*. Harvard University Press, Cambridge, Mass.

Tabossi, P. (1988) Effects of context on the immediate interpretation of unambiguous nouns. *Journal of Experimental Psychology: Learning, Memory, and Cognition*, 14: 153–62.

Taylor, K. I., Moss, H. E., and Tyler, L. K. (forthcoming) The conceptual structure account: a cognitive model of semantic memory and its neural instantiation. In J. Hart and M. Kraut (eds), *The Neural Basis of Semantic Memory*. Cambridge University Press, Cambridge.

Tippett, L. J., McAuliffe, S., and Farah, M. J. (1995) Preservation of categorical knowledge in Alzheimer's disease: a computational account. *Memory*, 3: 519–534.

Tranel, D., Logan, C. G., Frank, R. J., and Damasio, A. R. (1997) Explaining category-related effects in the retrieval of conceptual and lexical knowledge for concrete entities: operational and analysis of factors. *Neuropsychologia*, 35: 1329–40.

Tversky, B., and Hemenway, K. (1984) Objects, parts, and categories. *Journal of Experimental Psychology: General*, 113: 169–93.

Tyler, L. K., Bright, P., Dick, E., et al. (2003) Do semantic categories activate distinct cortical regions? Evidence for a distributed neural semantic system. *Cognitive Neuropsychology*, 20: 541–59.

Tyler, L. K., and Moss, H. E. (1997) Functional properties of concepts: studies of normal and brain-damaged patients. *Cognitive Neuropsychology*, 14: 511–45.

Tyler, L. K., and Moss, H. E. (2001) Towards a distributed account of conceptual knowledge. *Trends in Cognitive Sciences*, 5: 244–52.

Tyler, L. K., Moss, H. E., Durrant-Peatfield, M. R., and Levy, J. P. (2000) Conceptual structure and the structure of concepts: a distributed account of category-specific deficits. *Brain and Language*, 75: 195–231.

Tyler, L. K., Moss, H. E., Galpin, A., and Voice, J. K. (2002) Activating meaning in time: the role of imageability and form-class. *Language and Cognitive Processes*, 17: 471–502.

Tyler, L. K., Stamatakis, E. A., Bright, P., et al. (2004) Processing objects at different levels of specificity. *Journal of Cognitive Neuroscience*, 16: 351–62.

Tyler, L. K., Voice, J. K., and Moss, H. E. (2000) The interaction of meaning and sound in spoken word recognition. *Psychonomic Bulletin and Review*, 7: 320–6.

Vigliocco, G, Vinson, D. P., Lewis, W., and Garrett, M. F. (2004) Representing the meanings of object and action words: the featural and unitary semantic space hypothesis. *Cognitive Psychology*, 48: 422–88.

Vinson, D. P., and Vigliocco, G. (2002) A semantic analysis of grammatical class impairments: semantic representations of object nouns, action nouns and action verbs. *Journal of Neurolinguistics*, 15: 317–51.

Vinson, D. P., Vigliocco, G., Cappa, S., and Siri, S. (2003) The breakdown of semantic knowledge: insights from a statistical model of meaning representation. *Brain and Language*, 86: 347–65.

Warrington, E. K. (1975) The selective impairments of semantic memory. *Quarterly Journal of Experimental Psychology*, 27: 635–57.

Warrington, E. K., and McCarthy, R. (1983) Category-specific access dysphasia. *Brain*, 106: 859–78.

Warrington, E. K., and McCarthy, R. A. (1987) Categories of knowledge: further fractionations and an attempted integration. *Brain*, 110: 1273–96.

Warrington, E. K., and Shallice, T. (1984) Category specific semantic impairments. *Brain*, 107: 829–54.

Zingeser, L. B., and Berndt, R. S. (1990) Retrieval of nouns and verbs in agrammatism and anomia. *Brain and Language*, 39: 14–32.

CHAPTER 14

Connectionist models of reading

Mark S. Seidenberg

14.1 Introduction

Much of what we know about the acquisition and use of language has resulted from close analyses of normal and disordered behavior. Since the late 1980s, another tool has been available: the building of connectionist computational models. These models have been extensively used in the study of reading: how children learn to read, skilled reading, and reading impairments (dyslexia). The models are computer programs that simulate detailed aspects of behavior. So, for example, a reading model might be taught to recognize letter strings and compute their meanings or pronunciations. Such models provide a way of developing and testing ideas about how people read, in the service of developing a general theory. The purpose of this chapter is to provide an overview of connectionist models of reading, with an emphasis on the "triangle" framework developed by Seidenberg and McClelland (1989), Plaut et al. (1996), and Harm and Seidenberg (1999; 2004).

14.2 Basic elements of connectionist models of reading

The term "connectionism" refers to a broad, varied set of ideas, loosely connected (so to speak) by an emphasis on the notion that complexity, at different grain sizes or scales ranging from neurons to overt behavior, emerges from the aggregate behavior of large networks of simple processing units. Our focus is on the parallel distributed processing (PDP) variety developed by Rumelhart, McClelland, and Hinton (1986). These models consist of large networks of simple neuron-like processing elements that learn to perform tasks such as reading words or recognizing objects. Our reading models were used to explore a more general theory of how lexical knowledge is acquired and used in performing several communicative tasks (speaking, listening, reading, writing), based on PDP principles. The reading models differ in detail but all conform to a common theoretical framework, the main elements of which will be summarized briefly.

14.2.1 Task orientation

The models are designed to perform tasks such as computing the meanings or pronunciations of words. The goal is to develop a theory that explains how people learn to perform such tasks, given their perceptual, cognitive, and learning capacities. The models are a tool for developing and evaluating such a theory, in conjunction with behavioral studies and evidence concerning brain function-derived neuroimaging, and psychophysiological methods, and studies of impaired individuals. The modeling methodology involves endowing a model with capacities and types of knowledge that approximate what a beginning reader possesses, and providing it with similar experiences. For example, our reading models were constructed with the capacity to represent different lexical codes (orthography, phonology, semantics) as well as the capacity to learn. This knowledge may itself have been learned, and may depend on other capacities (e.g. perceptual, motoric, conceptual) that can be explored in other models.

In practice, model performance is greatly influenced by properties of the input and output representations. The intent is for these representations to accurately reflect children's capacities and the state of their knowledge at a particular point in development (e.g. a beginning reader); however, this ideal can only be approximated in an implemented model. Such limitations eventually show up as deviations between the performance of model and human. For example, the early model by Seidenberg and McClelland (1989) used a phonological representation that limited the model's capacity to support generalization (pronunciation of non-words such as JINJE; Besner et al., 1990). This limitation was addressed in later models using phonological representations that incorporated additional theoretical insights (Plaut et al., 1996; Harm and Seidenberg, 1999). Every model makes simplifications about some issues in order to be able to explore other ones. Eventually the simplifications themselves become the focus of further research.

14.2.2 Distributed representations

The models use distributed representations in which a particular type of information is represented by a finite set of units, with each unit participating in many patterns (Hinton et al., 1986). For example, a model might include units that correspond to phonemes or phonetic features, each of which is activated for all the words that contain that sound. This type of representation contrasts with "localist" ones in which units correspond to higher-order entitites such as words (e.g. McClelland and Rumelhart, 1981; Grainger and Jacobs, 1994).

There is a literature debating the relative virtues of distributed vs. localist representations (see e.g. Page, 2000), but I think it is misguided. A representation is localist or distributed only in relation to other entities. For example, in McClelland and Rumelhart's interactive activation model, the representations at the letter level are localist with respect to letters (each unit corresponds to one letter) but distributed with respect to words (each word corresponds to many letters; each letter unit contributes activation to many words). Harm and Seidenberg's (2004) model used localist representations of letters, phonetic features, and semantic features, but distributed representations of the spellings, sounds, and meanings of words. The contrast is not between models employing localist vs. distributed representations, because all of the above models include both. Rather, there is a contrast between models that are committed to the specific claim that there are localist representations of *words* (e.g. Coltheart et al., 2001) and models for which there are no representations at this level. In keeping with common practice, I will use the term "localist" to refer to models with word representations, although the term is not literally accurate.

Both types of models have proved useful in past research. The choice of model depends on the state of current knowledge (often localist models are employed in early explorations of phenomena), and the question being asked (e.g. the distributed models have said more about how lexical knowledge is acquired). The use of distributed representations in our models was a theoretical choice: we think they capture basic facts about how lexical codes are represented and they are relevant to capturing various behavioral phenomena (such as consistency effects; see below). Like other aspects of the theoretical framework, the use of distributed representations is also motivated by the desire to use mechanisms that are consistent with evidence about brain function, in this case the use of large networks of simple cells to encode information.[1]

14.2.3 Learning

Units are linked to one another to form a network; units are activated (e.g. by presenting a letter string as input) and activation spreads to other units (e.g. units representing phonological information). The connections between units carry weights that determine how activation is passed along. The goal is to find a set of weights that allows the model to perform the task accurately and efficiently. Learning involves adjusting the weights on the basis of experience. The reading models to date have used a learning procedure ("backpropagation") in which the output that the model produces for a word is compared to the correct, target pattern (Rumelhart et al., 1986b). Adjustments to the weights are made on the basis of the discrepancy between the two. Backpropagation is a procedure for adjusting the weights efficiently: weights that contribute a great deal to the discrepancy are adjusted more than weights that contribute less. Performance improves gradually as the weights assume values that minimize this discrepancy ("error").

Backpropagation is one of a class of "supervised" learning algorithms in which the output

[1] Interestingly, Quiroga et al. (2005) reported that single cells in human visual cortex responded to highly specific information, such as a picture of a particular famous actress. This indicates that individual cells become highly specialized, but it does not mean that the representation of Jennifer Aniston is localist. There is no reason to think the Aniston information is represented by a single neuron rather than a network, and this network may well include many neurons that are not as highly specialized.

that the model computes is compared to a target pattern (see Hinton, 1989 for a review). The use of backpropagation raises two important issues. One arises at the neurophysiological level: do neurons perform anything like the backpropagation of error? They apparently do not, but there are various proposals for how the same effects could be achieved in a biologically realistic way (see O'Reilly, 1996). So, the algorithm may be accurately capturing what the brain is doing but at a level that abstracts away from the neurophysiology. A second issue arises at the behavioral level: does human learning involve anything like comparing one's behavior to a target that fully specifies the correct response? Taken literally, backpropagation suggests that learning only takes place when a person generates a response that is corrected by an omnipresent teacher. The algorithm is clearly an idealization, but the extent to which it deviates from normal experience, and which conclusions are affected by this idealization, need to be considered carefully. One way to formulate this issue is to ask: is there a basis in the child's experience (e.g. in learning to read) for the teaching signal that automatically provided by the learning algorithm? In fact, there may be several (Harm and Seidenberg, 2004):

- A literal teacher. For tasks such as reading, for which there is explicit instruction (usually), a target is often provided by a human teacher. In fact, children typically receive more types of explicit feedback than are used in training our models; whereas the models receive feedback about the pronunciations of words, children are explicitly taught names and sounds for letters and the pronunciations of groups of letters (such as onsets and rimes). This observation illustrates a general methodological point: many of the simplifications demanded in implementing a model create a more difficult learning problem than the one confronting the child. Given these simplifications, one might find it remarkable that the models approximate people's performance even as well as they do.[2]
- Self-generating the target. The fact that an individual can both comprehend and produce language creates the opportunity for generating one's own teaching signal. Consider learning to pronounce a word aloud. Assume the child generates a pronunciation based on the current state of his/her knowledge. The child's own output (on the production side) is also an input (on the comprehension side). If the word is pronounced correctly, then it should also produce coherent patterns if passed through the comprehension system. That is, the word will generate corresponding phonological, semantic, or even orthographic codes. All of these computations would provide a basis for deciding if the letter string had been pronounced correctly. If it is pronounced incorrectly (e.g. because the child has regularized an exception such as *have* or *pint*), then it cannot be comprehended; the failure to activate semantics would itself provide a strong error signal. This procedure is not exactly like backpropagation: it provides the correct target when the word has been pronounced correctly, but when it is mispronounced, there is only a signal that an error was made, not a specification of the correct answer. In the latter case, the child may attempt another pronunciation that succeeds, or may require an explicit teaching signal. Learning an exception does, after all, require having the correct pronunciation provided by an external source, such as a teacher or dictionary. Jorm and Share (1983) described a similar "self-teaching" mechanism: the child learns by pronouncing a letter string and matching the computed output to a word that the individual has learned from using speech. Elman (1991) also discussed the role of confirming or disconfirming predictions about upcoming events in learning.

There are other ways in which the child may determine the correct output without explicitly being told; for example, the word may be remembered from previous exposure to the text in which it occurs, or the context may provide the target information (e.g. reading the word *bear* in a picture book about a boy's beloved toy bear).

Clearly, however, the child's learning process is not like backpropagation insofar as complete feedback about the correct target is not available on every learning occasion. Feedback may be partial or wholly absent; the child may know that a word was misread but not how; the child may learn from his/her own computed output, whether correct or not. Backpropagation does not capture these varied circumstances. An obvious step for future research would be to

[2] This is why I found Besner et al.'s (1990) critique of the original Seidenberg and McClelland (1989) model surprising. The model performed more poorly than people on difficult nonwords such as JINJE, but the miraculous thing, for me, was that it captured as much about word reading as it did without fiddling. Still, surprise factor aside, identifying where a model's performance degrades is informative and part of a normal cycle in which the limitations of one model provide the focus for additional research thereby advancing the theoretical enterprise (Seidenberg, 2005).

examine learning under these more variable conditions, with different types of feedback (ranging from complete target specification to no feedback) on different occasions. My experience is that models that more closely embody naturalistic conditions tend to perform better and in ways that correspond more closely to people; in modeling, verisimilitude is good. I think it likely that merely providing fully specified targets on relatively few trials would have a disproportionately large effect on performance. It takes a few exposures to learn a word like *have*, but once the word is learned only intermittent feedback is required to retain it (Hetherington and Seidenberg, 1989; Zevin and Seidenberg, 2002). Providing the correct target on every trial is not ideal; it encourages the development of word-specific knowledge, whereas what is needed is a representation of what is known in a way that supports generalization (e.g. sounding out novel words). Adding imprecision to the target pattern (e.g. not fully specifying it on every trial) may support more robust learning and better generalization.

Note that the same may be true with respect to the input and output representations themselves. In our models, each word is represented by single orthographic and phonological representations. Of course, the forms of words vary; accounting for how people are able to recognize spoken words despite variability across instances (due to variation in pitch, rate, and many other properties) is a serious, unresolved computational and theoretical issue. The same problem exists on the input (orthographic) side, insofar as letters and printed words are recognized despite variations in font, style, size, handwriting, and other factors. Our models ignore these generalization issues, in the service of addressing other concerns. Thus the problem confronting the model is simpler than that confronting a child, and so caution is warranted with respect to whether such simplified models capture basic phenomena that are also observed in the more difficult, general case. Note, however, that although learning to cope with orthographic or phonological variability creates a more difficult task, it may yield more robust results. Again, what is a "simplification" from the perspective of implementation may create a task that is actually more difficult than the one facing the human learner. This is an important area for future research.

14.2.4 Hidden units

The reading models include pools of units that encode orthography, phonology, and semantics. As in the model shown in Figure 14.1, there are additional "hidden" units that mediate the computations between codes. These units allow the network to encode more complex mappings. In practice, a pattern is presented to the network (e.g. over the orthographic units), and activation spreads to the hidden layer, resulting in a pattern of activation over those units. Activation also passes to the output layer (e.g. phonology). The hidden units increase the computational power of the network, i.e. the range and complexity of problems the model can solve (Rumelhart, Hinton, and Williams, 1986). However, the hidden units also have an interesting theoretical interpretation: they are the model's basis for developing underlying representations that abstract away from surface features of the input and output codes. Thus learning in such systems is not merely the creation of associations between patterns. The hidden layer allows such generalizations to be learned; the patterns of activation over the hidden units are a reduced, intermediate code formed by this abstraction process. The existence of these intermediate units gives the networks a different character than older approaches in which behavior was construed as simple stimulus–response associations or associative chains (see Bower and Hilgard, 1981 for discussion of such approaches).

14.2.5 Experience

The other major factor that determines the model's behavior is how it is trained, i.e. how it learns from experience. The procedure used in

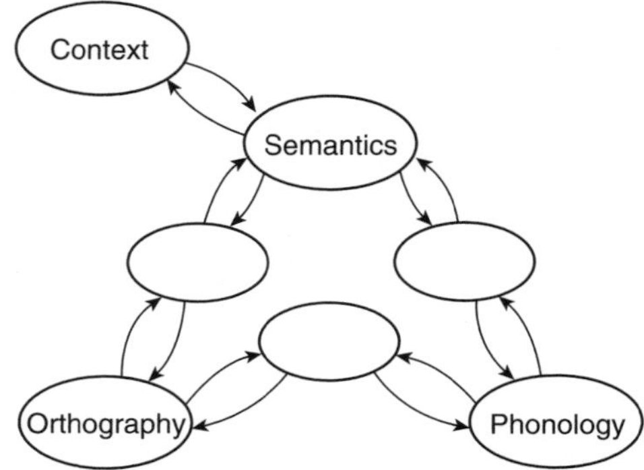

Figure 14.1 The framework developed by Seidenberg and McClelland (1989). Early models focused on the orthography to phonology computation. A later model by Harm and Seidenberg (2004) addressed the computation of meaning, using a variant of this architecture.

training the model is intended to capture basic elements of the child's experience, although like other aspects of the models, it is simplified in many respects. Like children learning to read, the models learn through exposure to many examples. In the Seidenberg and McClelland (1989) model, for example, there was a training corpus consisting of about 2,900 monosyllabic words. On each training trial, a word would be selected from the corpus, the model would compute its phonological output, the output would be compared to the target, and the weights would be adjusted by the learning algorithm. This process was repeated for many words. Words were sampled such that the probability of being selected was a function of a word's frequency. Thus higher-frequency words such as *the* were presented more often than lower frequency words such as *singe*. The theory here is that learning the correspondences between spelling and sound involves picking up on the statistical structure of this mapping as instantiated across a large pool of words. The models pick up on this implicit structure and encode it in the weights. What the model learns from exposure to one word, such as *save*, carries over to other, partially overlapping words such as *gave* and *sale*. This results from two properties of the model: (a) the use of distributed representations, and (b) the fact that the same weights are used in processing all words. Thus, changes to the weights that are beneficial for *save* also benefit performance on *gave* and many other words. The regularities in English exist at many different grain sizes. Some occur across relatively small units (e.g. initial *b* is always pronounced /b/), others involve larger units such as rimes (e.g. the *-ave* in *gave*, *save*, and *pave*) or complex contingencies among non-adjacent letters. The weights can also encode the atypical spelling–sound correspondences that occur in words such as *have* and *pint*.

Our models treat learning the correspondences between spelling and sound as a statistical learning problem. This approach contrasts with the approach instantiated by dual-mechanism theories (e.g. Coltheart et al., 2001; Pinker, 1994). Such theories hold that knowledge which is generative (i.e. can be extended to novel cases) is encoded by rules. Examples include the spelling–sound correspondences of English, or the rules governing inflectional morphology (in English, the formation of the tenses on verbs and number on nouns). The rules afford generalization: being able to pronounce a novel letter string such as *nust* or create a novel past tense or plural (*nusted*, *nusts*). There are many forms that violate the nominal rules; words such as *give* and *done* have irregular pronunciations (they should rhyme with *five* and *bone*, respectively), and words such as *took* and *men* have irregular morphology (they should be *taked* and *mans*). Dual-mechanism theories postulate a second mechanism to handle these exceptions. They are thought to be learned by a different process (e.g. rote memorization) and processed by a different mechanism (e.g. an "associative network," Pinker, 1994; a localist connectionist network, Coltheart et al., 2001). The merits of these different approaches have been discussed elsewhere (e.g. McClelland and Patterson, 2002; Seidenberg and Plaut, 2006). They are also discussed below in the section about quasi-regularity.

The nature of the correspondences between input and output codes varies. In alphabetic orthographies, orthography and phonology are highly correlated: letters and letter patterns represent sounds. The degree to which they are correlated (the consistency of the mapping across words) varies in alphabetic writing systems. For example, English contains more irregular correspondences than in the writing system for Serbian, in which letter–sound correspondences are much more predictable. The network will pick up on these regularities to whatever extent they are present in the ensemble of training items, subject to any limitations imposed by the choice of input and output representations. Thus, the same network architecture and learning procedure are thought to be involved in learning the mappings in different writing systems (Seidenberg, 1992). These principles are also assumed to apply to learning the mapping between orthography and semantics, which has a somewhat different character (Van Orden et al., 1990). For monosyllabic, monomorphemic words in English, orthography is highly predictive of phonology but not semantics. The mapping between spelling and meaning is often said to be arbitrary but the relation is actually more complicated (Seidenberg and Gonnerman, 2000). The observation is largely true of monomorphemic words; however, morphemes are orthographic-phonological units that make systematic contributions to the meanings of many words (e.g. *teach*, *teacher*, *teaching*). Again, the model will pick up on whatever regularities exist. Learning the mapping between two correlated codes such as orthography and phonology will proceed more rapidly than learning the mapping between orthography and semantics, but the latter can be learned with sufficient experience. These differences in ease of learning play an important role in models of the development of skilled reading (Harm and Seidenberg, 2004; see below).

Again one can easily see that the model is a simplification insofar as it does not capture many elements of the child's actual experience (e.g. in a classroom). Of course, nothing prevents one from developing a model that more closely matches this experience. I've already noted that schooling includes experiences that benefit the child but are not available to existing models. However, two other issues should be noted. One is that, in the absence of a cognitive or perceptual deficit, the exact details of many aspects the child's experience may not matter a great deal. For example, we construe learning the correspondences between spelling and sound as a statistical learning problem. Because the correspondences are systematic, there is considerable redundancy: only some combinations of letters and pronunciations are permitted, and patterns are repeated across many words. Given this redundancy, individuals can converge on the same knowledge despite considerable differences in experience. For example learning the standard pronunciation of *-ave* depends on exposure to words like *save*, *gave*, and *cave*, but the exact order or relative frequencies of exposure is less important. This suggests that it may not be necessary for a model to simulate any given child's exact experience in order to capture basic facts about the learning process. The situation would be different if the goal were to simulate an individual child's performance, or perhaps the order in which words are learned averaged across many children, but that is not the grain of the phenomena to which our models are addressed.

A second issue is this: how does the experience of the child in an instructional setting correspond to what happens in a model—or more importantly, in the child's brain? Consider the situation in which a teacher provides explicit instruction about how spellings are pronounced (e.g. pointing out the fact that there is the same vowel sound in the words *train*, *cake*, and *play*). Clearly we could approximate this situation in a model by providing training trials on these words. The more interesting question is how the explicit instruction of the teacher is translated into events that are realized at computational and neuronal levels. It is interesting to observe that there may be significant gaps between what a teacher thinks he/she is teaching (e.g. a rule about how a vowel is pronounced, which is an explicit type of knowledge) and what is occurring at these other levels (which are implicit). Would a teaching method that is more closely modeled on what we think is occurring at these other levels be more effective? I don't know the answer or think it is by any means obvious. Here I would just note there are differences between learning (in the neural network model sense) and instruction (in the pedagogical sense), and that a complete theory of how children learn would explain how the effects of instruction are mediated.

14.3 Why connectionist models?

The modeling approach involves implementing, training, and testing a model, comparing the model's behavior to data concerning human performance, and analyzing the model's behavior, among other steps. The technical aspects of the models are daunting to the many psychologists and reading researchers who are more comfortable with an informal style of theorizing in which reading mechanisms and learning procedures are described in general rather than computational terms. Moreover, we can now study reading and its brain bases using neuroimaging techniques. Neuroimaging also plays more to cognitive psychologists' traditional strengths in experimental design and data analysis. Given these circumstances, it is important to consider why it is worth building such models at all. Several of the main reasons will be considered briefly (see Seidenberg, 1993; 2005 for further discussion).

14.3.1 Intuition and beyond

Connectionist models are a source of ideas about how reading is accomplished. The approach incorporates ways of thinking about how knowledge is represented, acquired, and used that deviate in many respects from intuitive, folk-psychological accounts of cognitive phenomena. As an example, people's knowledge of words is usually assumed to be stored in a dictionary-like mental lexicon with entries for individual words. In models employing distributed representations (e.g. Figure 14.1), there are no lexical entries; each word is represented as a pattern of activation over sets of units encoding different codes. These models nonetheless capture phenomena previously thought to require lexical entries (e.g. frequency effects) and generate novel predictions (e.g. about effects of the consistency of spelling–sound mappings on reading aloud). This step beyond intuition is an important one. The ways we usually think about reading are closely tied to intuitions about how the process works derived from extensive personal experience. As in other areas of science, however, intuitions only provide a starting point for an investigation; often what makes a theoretical idea insightful or exciting is that it departs from intuition but nonetheless manages to provide a better account of something. Often intuitions are systematically misleading (e.g. in the well-studied case of naïve theories of physics). The need to transcend intuition is particularly acute in the case of reading because the mechanisms we are trying to explain are largely unconscious. People are aware of the outcome of this process—that words are understood—not the mental operations involved in achieving it. Connectionist models address the nature of underlying mechanisms at a level that intuition does not easily penetrate.

14.3.2 Explanatory value

Connectionist models provide the basis for developing theories that provide a deeper explanation of behavioral phenomena such as reading. Here there are two points of comparison. One is the informal style of theorizing that dominated research in neuropsychology in the 1970s and 1980s (see Patterson et al., 1985, for examples). The other is the computational model of reading developed by Coltheart and his colleagues (Coltheart et al., 1993, 2001), which employs a different modeling methodology and thereby raises questions about the goals of the modeling enterprise.

14.3.2.1 Informal models

A considerable amount of theorizing in cognitive psychology is pitched at a level that I would term "informal modeling." Computational models were first applied to psychological issues by Newell and Simon (1963). Many psychologists adopted the terminology of such "information processing" models but abandoned the computational aspect. In the 1970s and 1980s there were many models that consisted of verbal descriptions of hypothesized mental operations, coupled to flow charts that broadly characterized the types of knowledge representations and processing operations that the theorist envisioned. These models were extensively used in cognitive neuropsychology as a way of characterizing the "functional architecture" of the cognitive system (see chapters in Coltheart et al., 1987, and Patterson et al., 1985, for examples). There are two main problems with this informal style of theorizing (Seidenberg, 1988; 1993). One is that mechanisms are often invented in response to particular behavioral phenomena and so run the risk of being little more than redescriptions of them. Our approach is different: the principles that govern connectionist models of reading are not specific to this task; they are thought to reflect more general principles that govern many aspects of language and cognition and their brain bases. In this respect the approach is consistent with the fact that reading, a cultural artefact created very recently in human history, makes use of capacities (language, vision, learning, thinking) that evolved for other purposes. The other problem with more informal approaches is that it is not always clear whether the proposed mechanisms will work in the intended ways. For example, saying that words are recognized by "accessing" their entries in the mental lexicon begs difficult questions about how the lexicon is organized and how it could be searched accurately and efficiently. Implementing a connectionist or other type of computational model requires that such concepts be stated in explicit mechanistic terms, and running the model provides a way of assessing their adequacy.

14.3.2.2 Modeling as data fitting

Several types of computational model have been used in cognitive science and neuroscience; in the reading area, the main alternative is the Dual-Route Cascade model of Coltheart and colleagues (see Rastle, Chapter 5 this volume). Coltheart et al. (2001) correctly stress that their modeling methodology is different from ours (they term their approach "Old Cognitivism"). The DRC model can be seen as part of a bottom-up, data-driven approach to modeling that has a long history in cognitive psychology; Many mathematical models have this character, as well as the "information processing" models of the 1970s. These models aspire to what Chomsky (1965) termed "descriptive adequacy." Researchers conduct experiments and models are developed to "fit" the data. The main criterion for evaluating a model is the range of phenomena the model fits. Thus Coltheart et al. (2001) emphasized the twenty-some different phenomena they simulated using a single version of DRC. Our approach is different insofar as the models are only a means to an end. The goal is a theory that explains behavior (e.g. reading) and its brain bases. The models are a tool for developing and exploring the implications of a set of hypotheses concerning the neural basis of cognition. Models are judged not only with respect to their ability to account for robust findings in a particular domain such as reading but also with respect to considerations that extend beyond a single domain. These include the extent to which the underlying computational principles apply across domains, the extent to which these principles can unify phenomena previously thought to be governed by different principles, the ability of the models to explain how behavior might arise from a neurophysiological substrate, and so on. Such models aspire to what Chomsky termed "explanatory adequacy."

Seidenberg and Plaut (2006) provide a detailed comparison of these approaches. To summarize briefly, the data-fitting approach appears to be better suited to capturing the results of individual studies, because that is the major goal of the approach. A model such as DRC thus seems satisfying because it accords with the intuition that accounting for a broad range of behavioral phenomena is always a good thing. However, when one examines DRC more closely, problems with the approach emerge. The extent to which a model developed in this manner actually fits the data is questionable. As Seidenberg and Plaut (2006) point out, DRC exhibits a striking pattern: for almost all phenomena that were studied, the model accurately simulates the results of a single experiment (e.g. the interaction of frequency and regularity; Paap and Noel, 1991) but then produces anomalous results for other studies of the same behavioral phenomenon (e.g. Seidenberg, 1985; Taraban and McClelland, 1987). Fitting the results of one study but not others in a series is a problem; one could as well choose to report a different study and conclude that the model is inadequate. The data-fitting strategy encourages tailoring a model to reproduce the results of specific studies. This results in overfitting and a failure to generalize to other studies. This is a sign that the model does not instantiate the correct principles underlying the phenomena.

14.3.2.3 Principle-based modeling

Whereas the DRC approach is data-driven, the PDP approach is more theory-driven because the models derive from a set of principles concerning neural computation and behavior. These principles are themselves motivated by computational, behavioral, and neurophysiological evidence. The models are responsive to data insofar as they need to capture patterns that reflect basic characteristic of people's behavior, particularly with regard to phenomena about which the models make different predictions. The primary goal is not to implement the model that fits the most possible data; rather, it is to use evidence provided by the model, in conjunction with other evidence (e.g. about brain organization or neurophysiology; about other types of behavior) to converge on the correct theory of the phenomena. In fact, we could always achieve better fits to particular data sets than we have reported, but at the cost of using unmotivated "tweaks" and at the risk of overfitting. In practice there is considerable feedback between modeling, theorizing, and empirical (behavioral and, more recently, neuroimaging) research. The connectionist framework provides a set of principles and concepts out of which theories can be constructed. An implemented model instantiates some of the basic principles of the theory, for the purpose of assessing their adequacy as applied to a particular domain. At the same time, exploring a computational model typically generates new insights about underlying mechanisms and novel predictions about behavior, which can result in modifications to the theory or the general principles themselves.

Of course, this approach has its own limitations. Any given model is an imperfect instantiation of the theory on which it is based. Limitations on scope are inevitable because models become too complex to run in reasonable time or too complex to analyze and because our understanding of many phenomena is too limited. This kind of simplification and idealization is common in other areas of science, but it complicates the task of assessing a model's behavior and its theoretical implications. At some level of detail every model is necessarily false; part of the science involves determining whether the model's failures are for interesting reasons (e.g. because some aspect of the theory on which it is based is wrong) or uninteresting ones (e.g. because some phenomena are outside the scope of the model). This can be determined by experimenting with the model and comparing it to other models. Again, the limitations of a given model generate questions that inspire the next generation of research. See Seidenberg (1989) and Seidenberg and Plaut (2006) for extensive discussion.

The extent to which connectionist models contribute to progress in understanding language and cognitive is controversial; see, for example, the exchange between McCloskey (1991) and Seidenberg (1993). McCloskey's main concern was that connectionist models did not explain phenomena in a satisfactory way. A model might behave in accordance with human behavior but a reader might not understand why, because the models were too complex to analyze and the secret to the model's behavior was buried in a mass of weights and connections. I think

McCloskey was wrong to assume that these concerns are specific to connectionist modeling; in fact they arose almost contemporaneously with Newell and Simon's pioneering work (see Miller et al., 1960). But perhaps the problems are real nonetheless. My own feeling is that people tend to overestimate the difficulty of understanding how such models work. As I described in the 1993 paper, they can be analyzed at multiple levels, each of which contributes to understanding, in deep way, "how it works." Note that the goal is to develop a theory, phrased in terms of general principles, that explains the phenomena; this involves abstracting away from the details of any given model, as in other areas of science (Putnam, 1972). I also think one can point to examples in the literature where researchers have attempted to explain how their models work in some detail; Seidenberg and McClelland (1989), Plaut et al. (1996), and Harm and Seidenberg (1999; 2004) come to mind. I think McCloskey put his finger on a real problem, but his diagnosis of its source was not correct. The problem is not with modeling as a tool or connectionism as a theoretical framework. Rather, understanding such models requires having background knowledge that many psychologists, linguists and other cognitive scientists have lacked. Thus the models made demands on readers who were more comfortable with other approaches. Backpropagation is indeed hard to explain to someone who is not familiar with the relevant mathematics. I think this is more a reflection on the state of theoretical psychology and how researchers are trained than on connectionist science. Still, it means that many people will indeed find the models unsatisfying. A further consequence is that many people's understanding of the models is limited to that provided by commentators (e.g. Pinker, 1999) rather than a reading of the original sources.

14.3.3 **Establishing causal effects**

Models provide a unique way to test causal hypotheses about the bases of normal and disordered reading. To illustrate this point, consider the issue of developmental reading impairments (dyslexia). Many hypotheses about the causes of dyslexia have been proposed: that it is secondary to impaired processing of speech (Liberman and Shankweiler, 1985); that it is secondary to deficits in the processing of visual information (e.g. Livingstone et al., 1991); that it can be caused by a learning impairment that is not specific to reading (Manis and Morrison, 1985), and there are others. The evidence for these hypotheses is largely correlational. For example, poor readers tend to be poor at spoken language tasks that involve the manipulation or comparison of phonological codes (see Blachman, 2000, for a review); similarly, some poor readers exhibit deficits on visual perception tasks such as motion detection (Eden et al., 1996; but see Sperling et al., 2006), and so on for other hypotheses. These correlations are highly suggestive, but it is difficult to establish a causal relationship between the hypothesized deficit and impaired reading. What is required is to show how a given type of impairment produces specific dyslexic behaviors. For example, what is nature of the phonological deficit and why would it affect reading in specific ways? Similarly, how would a deficit in some aspect of visual processing affect learning to read and pronounce words? It is often unethical or impractical to conduct the kinds of controlled experiments that might establish more direct causal connections between deficits and behavior.

In contrast, testing causal hypothesis in a computational model is simple. Several models have focused on learning to map from orthography to phonology and the task of naming words and non-words. Many dyslexic children (often called "phonological dyslexics") are impaired on these tasks and also on spoken-language tasks that involve the use of segmental phonological information (Snowling, 1996). The hypothesis that this pattern of poor reading derives from a phonological deficit can be tested in the following way. Take a model of normal performance and, before training has begun, introduce a phonological impairment. Harm and Seidenberg (1999) did this by introducing anomalies that affected the model's capacity to represent phonological structure. They introduced either mild or severe phonological impairments and then trained the model in the normal fashion. The purpose was to examine how learning proceeds in the presence of this "congenital anomaly." The impaired models learned more slowly but, importantly, some aspects of reading were more affected than others. With a great deal of training the models could learn the pronunciations of many words but they consistently performed poorly on the task of pronouncing novel letter strings (non-words) such as *glorp*. This behavior closely resembles that of phonological dyslexics, in whom non-word naming impairments are prominent. These children have difficulty discovering the systematic relationships between orthographic patterns and phonology (i.e. the alphabetic principle); degrading the phonological representations in the model has this effect. Studies of adults with childhood diagnoses of dyslexia (e.g. Bruck, 1998) are consistent with this picture: after many years of practice, many of the dyslexics that Bruck studied had attained considerable proficiency in reading words; however, their knowledge of phonological structure and their ability to sound out non-words continued to be limited.

Our understanding of dyslexia is still limited, and the picture is changing rapidly, with recent research focusing on the fact that dyslexics often present with multiple impairments, not just a phonological one. The outstanding question is what kind of deficit (or deficits) could underlie these various problems (see Sperling et al., 2005, for one suggestion). My point here is only that our models provide a unique way to test hypotheses about the causes of dyslexia and how they give rise to characteristic behavioral deficits. This is possible because the models are inherently developmental: they simulate the acquisition of knowledge, which can be studied under normal and atypical conditions.

14.4 **Insights from connectionist models**

Against this background, let us consider some of the insights to have emerged from connectionist models of reading. Several generations of models have been developed, and they continue to evolve as researchers address the inherent limitations of existing models and extend the range of phenomena they address. The two issues discussed below are central ones that any adequate theory of word reading must address. Space limitations do not permit considering others, such as the bases of individual differences and of different types of cognitive impairments following brain injury.

14.4.1 **Quasiregularity**

The first issue that we addressed was how knowledge of the correspondences between the written and spoken forms of language is acquired, represented, and used. This initial focus was motivated by two considerations. First, a large body of research suggests that this knowledge plays important roles in both learning to read and skilled reading (Rayner et al., 2001). Second, learning the correspondences between the written and spoken forms of language presents an interesting computational problem, the study of which is potentially revealing about broader issues concerning learning and memory. English has an alphabetic orthography in which written symbols represent sounds. The most intuitive way to characterize the correspondences between the two is in terms of rules, a particular kind of knowledge representation. The classic evidence for rule-based knowledge is the capacity to generalize; in the reading domain, this means generating pronunciations for non-words. Learning to read is thought to involve learning spelling–sound rules, an assumption that is widely reflected in how reading is taught. The interesting observation is that the correspondences in English are not completely consistent; there are many words (such as *have*, *give*, *said*, *was*, *were*, *pint*, *once*, *aisle*) whose pronunciations deviate from what would be expected if the system were strictly rule-governed. In standard approaches, these words are treated as exceptions that must be learned by rote. This is the core idea underlying dual-route theories.

Note, however, that the exceptions are not arbitrary. *Have* is not pronounced "glorp;" it overlaps with many other words including *hat*, *has*, and *hive*. Thus, the spelling–sound correspondences of English can be said to be rule-governed only if the rules are not obliged to apply in all cases; the system admits many forms that deviate from these central tendencies in differing degrees. Seidenberg and McClelland (1989) introduced the term "quasiregular" to describe bodies of knowledge that have this character, which include many aspects of language (e.g. inflectional and derivational morphology: Seidenberg and Gonnerman, 2000).

Connectionist networks are intrinsically well-suited to the problem of learning in quasiregular domains. A connectionist network learns to map between codes (e.g. orthography and phonology). The weights reflect the aggregate effects of training on a large corpus of words. The weights simultaneously encode both the "rule-governed" cases and the "exceptions." Seidenberg and McClelland (1989), Plaut et al. (1996), and Harm and Seidenberg (1999) presented models that acquired spelling–sound knowledge in this manner and showed that the models could account for many phenomena associated with the task of reading letter strings aloud.

Three main aspects of this research should be noted. First, it is important to recognize how much of a departure this approach represents. Prior to the development of the connectionist framework, there was little alternative to the rules plus exceptions view. If someone had asked in 1985 what kind of lexical processing system could encode both rule-governed cases and exceptions, the question would have been treated as a non sequitur. The models challenge the deep-seated intuition that behavior is rule-governed, by demonstrating that a wholly different type of mechanism can account for the phenomena, one that is consistent with other facts about learning and its brain basis. In the connectionist framework, the characterization of language as rule-governed is taken as an informal characterization of some aspects of the underlying processing system, convenient perhaps but not accurate in detail.

Second, the approach provides an alternative way of thinking about generalization: it involves using the weights that were trained on the basis of exposure to words. Thus the weights come to encode the regularities underlying *must*, *dust*, and *nut*, which allows the model to correctly pronounce non-words such as *nust* the first time they are presented. Generalization had previously been thought to require rules and, indeed to provide the strongest evidence for their existence. Whether this approach will be able to account for generalization in many other domains is not known, but it invites reconsideration of the kinds of evidence standardly taken as evidence for rules.

A third point is that this approach to spelling–sound knowledge makes different predictions than the dual-route model. Our approach holds that performance is affected by the consistency of the mappings between spelling and sound. Consistency is a statistical notion, in contrast to the dual-route approach's categorical distinction between rule-governed forms and exceptions. The two theories therefore make different predictions about words such as *gave*, which are rule-governed (according to DRC) but inconsistent (according to PDP) because of irregular neighbors such as *have*. Many studies have now replicated Glushko's (1979) original findings that spelling–sound consistency affects word and non-word pronunciation. The DRC model does not capture these phenomena correctly. According to Coltheart et al. (2001), consistency effects are mostly an artefact: many of the inconsistent words used in previous studies are actually exceptions according to DRC. They also claim that consistency effects arise from "whammies" (misanalyses of words) that occur more often in inconsistent words than rule-governed ones. However, several studies have shown that consistency effects cannot be reduced to these factors (Jared, 2002; Cortese and Simpson, 2000). When tested on the words in these studies, DRC does not reproduce the human pattern of results.

14.4.2 Division of labor

The early reading models were largely concerned with the computation of phonology. Harm and Seidenberg (2004) turned to the question of how meanings are computed. They used a variant of the model in Figure 14.1 in which there were computations from orthography to semantics, orthography to phonology, and phonology to semantics. The model also incorporated Zorzi et al.'s (1998) use of direct connections between the outer layers (e.g. orthography and semantics; semantics and phonology; orthography and phonology).[3] Given an orthographic pattern as input, the model had to compute its meaning. The model was used to address a longstanding debate concerning the role of phonological information in silent reading. Intuitions about whether this information plays any useful role in word reading vary greatly, with plausible a priori arguments on both sides. Deriving the meanings of words directly from print seems to involve fewer steps than recoding letter strings into phonological representations and then using that information to compute meaning. On the other hand, learning the mapping from orthography to semantics may be more difficult because, as previously noted, it is more arbitrary. The pendulum has swung between "direct" and "phonologically mediated" theories with considerable regularity over the past hundred years. The Harm and Seidenberg (2004) model offers a way to break this cycle, by treating the issue as a computational one: given the above architecture, how does the model learn to compute meanings quickly and accurately? That is,

[3] Zorzi et al. developed a connectionist reading model that included both the orthography-hidden-phonology structure of the Seidenberg and McClelland (1989) model and an additional set of direct connections from orthography to phonology. They characterized their model as a connectionist implementation of the dual-route model, with the direct connections corresponding to a sublexical route and the hidden unit pathway corresponding to a lexical route. However, as Harm and Seidenberg (2004) noted, this characterization is not wholly accurate. The direct connections did perform well on regular words and non-words, and poorly on exceptions, similar to the traditional "nonlexical" route. When this route is lesioned, the remaining route is not able to produce correct pronunciations for either regular or exception words. Thus, exceptions required input from both pathways to be read correctly. Unlike the standard dual-route model, damage to the nonlexical route in the Zorzi et al. model would not produce phonological dyslexia (relatively preserved word reading, impaired generalization), because the "lexical" route cannot independently read any words. The addition of direct connections between input and output layers does facilitate learning, but it does not cause the model to adopt the standard dual-route model's division of labor between lexical and nonlexical processes.

what division of labor does the model converge on, given the availability of both pathways?

The simple answer is that the model uses input from both sources for most words. The pattern that emerges over the semantics reflects the joint of effects of both pathways; what one pathway contributes depends on the capacity of the other pathway. This property contrasts with models in which the orthography → semantics and orthography → phonology → semantics pathways are independent, with the process that finishes first determining the access of meaning. The connectionist model performs more efficiently using both pathways than either one in isolation; thus it is not a question of which pathway wins the race, but rather how they cooperatively solve the problem. Early in training, semantic activation is largely driven by input from the orthography → phonology → semantics pathway. The phonology → semantics component was trained prior to the introduction of orthography on the view that pre-readers possess this knowledge from their use of spoken language. The orthography → phonology mapping is easy to learn because the codes are highly correlated; the orthography → semantics pathway takes longer to become established because the mapping is more arbitrary. Over time, however, orthography → semantics begins to exert its influence, particularly for higher-frequency words that get trained more often. Two main factors contribute to the development of the orthography → semantics pathway. First, it is needed to disambiguate homophones such as *bear–bare*. Second, the pathway develops in response to the requirement to compute meanings quickly. The orthography → semantics association is more arbitrary but the pathway also involves fewer intermediate steps. If the model is given subtle pressure to respond quickly, more of the work gets taken over by orthography → semantics. Note, however, that what changes is the relative division of labor between the two pathways; there is some input from both pathways for most words.

The model is consistent with many previous assertions about word reading but also differs from them in virtue of its specific computational properties. Previous researchers have noted the tradeoffs involved in using direct orthography → semantics associations (arbitrary, but no intermediate step) vs. using phonological mediation (orthography → phonology is nonarbitrary but an additional step). The model instantiates these tradeoffs but shows that an efficient solution results if the pathways jointly determine the output, with the division of labor determined by their complementary computational properties. This account is consistent with the results of behavioral studies of homophones and pseudohomophones (e.g. Van Orden et al., 1988).

14.5 Future directions

As I have noted throughout this chapter, the models to date are limited in scope and many basic phenomena remain to be addressed. In closing I want to mention two areas in particular.

14.5.1 Lexical semantics

The models to date have barely touched on issues concerning word meaning. This is not to minimize the significance of work such as Plaut and Booth's (2000) model of semantic priming, or the Harm and Seidenberg (2004) division-of-labor model. However, there is a large body of excellent research on lexical semantics that has yet to be assimilated within the computational framework. This research would include the following.

14.5.1.1 Studies of the semantics of verbs

Whereas much of the research on semantic priming has focused on overlap between words at the featural level (e.g. *bread–cake*), verbs can be similar in meaning but participate in different sentence structures (e.g. *give–donate*). One concern about semantic feature representations is that they seem ad hoc, but theoretical work such as Levin's (1993) and empirical work such as McRae et al.'s (2005) provide a basis for motivated representations that can do a lot of work.

14.5.1.2 Context effects

We continue to treat meanings as fixed entities—distributed perhaps but nonetheless unvarying. This is grossly misleading. Of course words have multiple meanings and senses, but even the meaning of a seemingly concrete word such as *piano*, which is merely the name for a kind of keyboard instrument, varies as a function of the context in which it occurs (e.g. pushing a piano vs. playing one). It would not be difficult to implement models in which different semantic patterns are computed for words as a function of contexts that pick out different features. There is also a literature on conceptual combination suggesting how people interpret novel phrases such *mountain magazine* (Gagne and Shoben, 1997; see also Clark and Clark, 1979, regarding novel uses of nouns).

14.5.1.3 Grounding representations in perception, action, affect

There is a large body of empirical research showing that word meanings are closely tied to ("grounded in") sensory, affective, and motor experience (e.g. Glenberg, Chapter 21 this volume). The extent to which grasping a ball activates the same brain circuits as the literal act and whether such activation is necessary for comprehension remain to be determined, but there is clearly some non-trivial overlap, possibly arising from how the verb was learned. (More interesting is whether figurative uses of language such as *grasping an idea* retain any sensory-motoric-affective basis). When a model includes units representing features such as "yellow" or "sour" there is an implicit assumption that this knowledge was acquired through interaction with the world. One can think of the semantic representations in the network as hidden units that mediate between perceiving, acting, and perhaps other ways of interacting with the world. Similarly, phonological representations are actually hidden units that mediate between hearing and producing sounds; orthographic representations are hidden units that mediate between seeing letters and writing them. This yields a picture like the one illustrated in Figure 14.2. These hidden unit representations will not have exactly the same properties as the feature-based representations used in existing models.

14.5.2 Connecting model and brain

In areas such as reading, considerable evidence is accumulating concerning the brain bases of the skill. The time is ripe for a reconciliation of the computational models and this evidence. I view these approaches as complementary: each approach can inform the other and together converge on the theory of behavior and its brain bases that we all want. The models have progressed to the point where they provide strong leads for what to look for in the brain (e.g. cooperative division of labor) and generate testable hypotheses (e.g. Frost et al., 2005). At the same time, neuroimaging research is yielding evidence to which the models must be responsive. For example, there is considerable evidence about the brain bases of visual aspects of reading, including the functions of the so-called visual word form area (McCandliss et al., 2004). This aspect of reading has been sorely neglected in the computational models. On the other hand, whereas neuroimaging evidence has begun to identify areas that support the identification of letters despite variation in size, font, and style, computational models could contribute to understanding how this is accomplished. It also

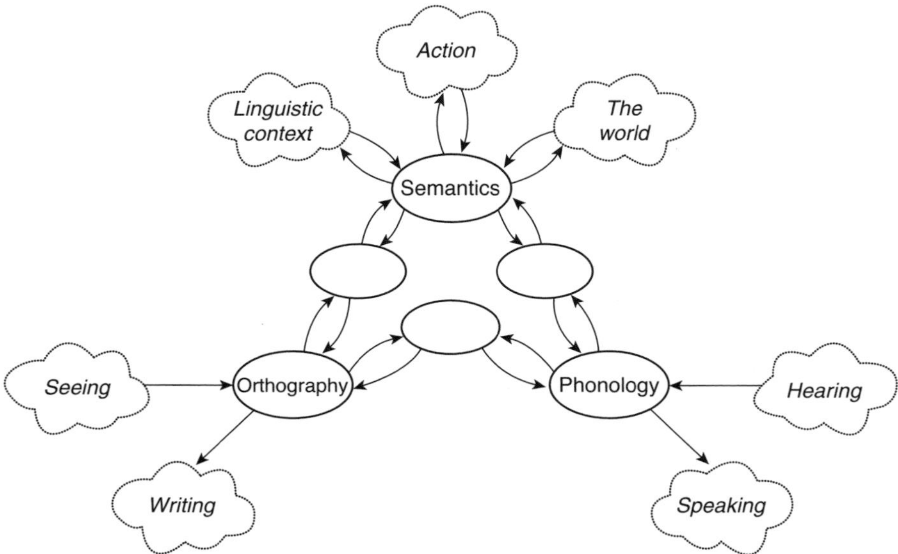

Figure 14. 2 Lexical codes as hidden unit representations. The semantic, phonological, and orthographic codes in existing models are simplifications; they can be seen as hidden unit representations mediating the illustrated inputs and outputs.

appears that processing in this region is not limited to orthographic information; it is also activated by phonological properties of words (Sandak et al., 2004). Thus it appears to function like a hidden unit representation mediating computations between visual and phonological codes, rather than as a strictly letter-based code.[4] Placing the modeling and neuroimaging in a feedback relation, in which each constrains the other, seems like a powerful approach that could yield more understanding than either method in isolation. The goal of developing an integrated account of reading behavior and its brain bases, with computational models providing the interface between the two, seems a realistic one and likely to be the focus of considerable attention.

[4] These findings suggest that the Harm and Seidenberg (2004) model imposes too strong a distinction between orthography and phonological processes. If orthographic representations are themselves shaped by phonology, the mapping from "orthography to semantics" is not strictly orthographic. This would be consistent with the claim that there is partial activation of phonological information via both pathways. The division of labor issues remain essentially the same; the mapping from this representation to semantics is largely arbitrary, whereas the mapping to phonology is systematic.

References

Besner, D., Twilley, L., McCann, R., and Seergobin, K. (1990) On the connection between connectionism and data: are a few words necessary? *Psychological Review*, 97: 432–46.

Blachman, B. A. (2000) Phonological awareness. In M. L. Kamil and P. B. Mosenthal (eds), *Handbook of Reading Research*, vol. III, pp. 483–502. Erlbaum, Mahwah, NJ.

Bower, G., and Hilgard, E. (1981) *Theories of Learning*. Prentice-Hall, Englewood Cliffs, NJ.

Bruck, M. (1998) Outcomes of adults with childhood histories of dyslexia. In C. Hulme, and R. M. Joshi (eds), *Reading and Spelling: Development and Disorders*, pp. 179–200. Erlbaum, Mahwah, NJ.

Chomsky, N. (1965) *Aspects of the Theory of Syntax.* MIT Press, Cambridge, MA.

Clark, E. and Clark, H. (1979) When nouns surface as verbs. *Language*, 55(4), 767–811.

Coltheart, M., Curtis, B., Atkins, P., and Haller, M. (1993) Models of reading aloud: dual-route and parallel distributed processing approaches. *Psychological Review*, 100: 589–608.

Coltheart, M., Rastle, K., and Perry, C. (2001) DRC: a dual route cascaded model of visual word recognition and reading aloud. *Psychological Review*, 108: 204–56.

Coltheart, M., Sartori, G., and Job, R. (eds) (1987), *Cognitive Neuropsychology of Language*. Erlbaum, London.

Cortese, M. J., and Simpson, G. B. (2000) Regularity effects in word naming: what are they? *Memory and Cognition*, 28: 1269–76.

Eden, G. F., Van Meter, J. W., and Rumsey, J. M. (1996) Abnormal processing of visual motion in dyslexia revealed by functional brain imaging. *Nature*, 382: 66–9.

Elman, J. (1990) Finding structure in time. *Cognitive Science*, 14: 179–211.

Frost, S. J., Einar Mencl, W., Sandak, R., Moore, D. L., Rueckl, J. G., Katz, L., Fulbright, R. K., and Pugh, K. R. (2005) A functional mgnetic resonance imaging study of the tradeoff between semantics and phonology in reading aloud. *Neuroreport*, 16: 621–4.

Gagné, C. L., and Shoben, E. J. (1997) Influence of thematic relations on the comprehension of modifier–noun combinations. *Journal of Experimental Psychology: Learning, Memory, and Cognition*, 23(1): 71–87.

Glushko, R. J. (1979) The organization and activation of orthographic knowledge in reading aloud. *Journal of Experimental Psychology: Human Perception and Performance*, 5: 674–91.

Grainger, J., and Jacobs, A. M. (1994) Orthographic processing in visual word recognition. *Psychological Review*, 103: 518–65.

Harm, M., McCandliss, B., and Seidenberg, M. S. (2003) Modeling the successes and failures of interventions for disabled readers. *Journal of the Society for the Scientific Study of Reading*, 7: 155–82.

Harm, M., and Seidenberg, M. S. (1999) Reading acquisition, phonology, and dyslexia: insights from a connectionist model. *Psychological Review*, 106: 491–528.

Harm, M. W., and Seidenberg, M. S. (2004) Computing the meanings of words in reading: cooperative division of labor between visual and phonological processes. *Psychological Review*, 111: 662–720.

Hetherington, P., and Seidenberg, M. S. (1989) Is there "catastrophic interference" in connectionist networks? *Proceedings of the Cognitive Science Society Conference*, 26–33.

Hinton, G. (1989) Connectionist learning procedures. *Artificial Intelligence*, 40: 185–234.

Hinton, G. E., McClelland, J. L., and Rumelhart, D. E. (1986) Distributed representations. In D. E. Rumelhart and J. L. McClelland (eds), *Parallel Distribute Processing: Explorations in the Microstructure of Cognition*, vol. 1. MIT Press, Cambridge, MA.

Jared, D. (2002) Spelling–sound consistency and regularity effects in word naming. *Journal of Memory and Language*, 46: 723–50.

Jorm, A. F., and Share, D. L. (1983) Phonological recoding and reading acquisition. *Applied Psycholinguistics*, 4: 103–47.

Levin, B. (1993) English Verb Classes and Alternations: A Preliminary Investigation. University of Chicago Press, Chicago.

Liberman, I. Y., and Shankweiler, D. (1985) Phonology and the problems of learning to read and write. *Remedial and Special Education*, 6(6): 8–17.

Livingstone, M., Rosen, G., Drislane, F., and Galaburda, A. (1991) Physiological and anatomical evidence for a magnocellular defect in developmental dyslexia. *Proc. National Academy of Sciences USA*, 88: 7943–47.

Manis, F., and Morrison, F. J. (1985) Reading disability: A deficit in rule learning? In L. S. Siegel and F. J. Morrison (eds), *Cognitive Development in Atypical Children*, pp. Springer, New York.

McCandliss, B. D., Cohen, L., and Dehaene, S. (2003) The visual word form area: Expertise for reading in the fusiform gyrus. *Trends in Cognitive Sciences*, 7: 293–9.

McClelland, J. L., and Patterson, K. (2002) Rules or connections in past-tense inflections: what does the evidence rule out? *Trends in Cognitive Sciences*, 6(11): 465–72.

McClelland, J. L., and Rumelhart, D. E. (1981) An interactive activation model of context effects in letter perception, part 1: An account of basic findings. *Psychological Review*, 86: 287–330.

McCloskey, M. (1991) Networks and theories: the place of connectionism in cognitive science. *Psychological Science*, 2: 387–95.

McRae, K., Cree, G. S., Seidenberg, M. S., and McNorgan, C. (2005) Semantic feature production norms for a large set of living and nonliving things. Special issue of *Behavioral Research Methods*, 37: 547–59.

Miller, G., Galanter, E., and Pribram, K. (1960) Plans and the structure of behavior. Holt, Rinehart, & Winston, New York.

Newell, A., and Simon, H. (1963) GPS, a program that simulates human thought. In E. A. Feigenbaum and J. Feldman (eds), *Computers and Thought*, pp. 279–93. McGraw-Hill, New York.

O'Reilly, R. C. (1996) Biologically plausible error-driven learning using local activation differences: the generalized recirculation algorithm. *Neural Computation*, 8(5), 895–938.

Page, M. (2000) Connectionist modeling in psychology: A localist manifesto. *Behavioral and Brain Sciences*, 23: 443–512.

Patterson, K., Marshall, J. C., and Coltheart, M. (1985) Surface Dyslexia: Cognitive and Neuropsychological Studies of Phonological Reading. Erlbaum, London.

Pinker, S. (1994) *The Language Instinct*. Morrow, New York.

Pinker, S. (1999) *Words and rules: The ingredients of language*. Basic Books, New York.

Plaut, D. C., and Booth, J. R. (2000) Individual and developmental differences in semantic priming: empirical and computational support for a single-mechanism account of lexical processing. *Psychological Review*, 107: 786–823.

Plaut, D. C., McClelland, J. L., Seidenberg, M. S., and Patterson, K. E. (1996) Understanding normal and impaired word reading: computational principles in quasi-regular domains. *Psychological Review*, 103: 56–115.

Putnam, H. (1972) Reduction and the nature of psychology. *Cognition*, 2: 131–46.

Quiroga, R. Q., Reddy, L., Kreiman, G., Koch, C. and Fried, I. (2005) Invariant visual representation by single neurons in the human brain. *Nature*, 435: 1102–07.

Rayner, K., Foorman, B. R., Perfetti, E., Pesetsky, D., and Seidenberg, M. S. (2001) How psychological science informs the teaching of reading. *Psychological Science in the Public Interest Monograph*, 2: 31–74.

Rumelhart, D., Hinton, G., and McClelland, J. L. (1986) A general framework for parallel distributed processing. In D. Rumelhart and J. McClelland (eds), *Parallel Distributed Processing*, vol. 1. MIT Press, Cambridge, MA.

Rumelhart, D., Hinton, G., and Williams, R. (1986) Learning internal representations by error propagation. In D. Rumelhart and J. McClelland (eds), *Parallel Distributed Processing*, vol. 1. MIT Press, Cambridge, MA.

Sandak, R., Einar Mencl, W., and Frost, S. J. (2004) The neurobiology of adaptive learning in reading: a contrast of different training conditions. *Cognitive, Affective, and Behavioral Neuroscience*, 4: 67–88.

Seidenberg, M. S. (1985) The time course of phonological code activation in two writing systems. *Cognition*, 19: 1–10.

Seidenberg, M. S. (1988) Cognitive neuropsychology and language: the state of the art. *Cognitive Neuropsychology*, 5: 403–26.

Seidenberg, M. S. (1989) Word recognition and naming: a computational model and its implications. In W. D. Marlsen-Wilson (ed.), Lexical representation and process. MIT Press, Cambridge, MA.

Seidenberg, M. S. (1992) Beyond orthographic depth in reading: equitable division of labor. In R. Frost and L. Katz (eds), *Orthography, Phonology, Morphology, and Meaning*, pp. 85–118. North-Holland, Oxford.

Seidenberg, M. S. (1993) Connectionist models and cognitive theory. *Psychological Science*, 4: 228–35.

Seidenberg, M. S. (1995) Visual word recognition. In J. L. Miller and P. D. Eimas (eds), *Handbook of Perception and Cognition*, vol. 11: *Speech, Language and Communication*, pp. 137–79. Academic Press, San Diego, CA.

Seidenberg, M. S. (2005) Connectionist models of reading. *Current Directions in Psychological Science*, 14: 238–42.

Seidenberg, M. S., and Gonnerman, L. (2000) Explaining derivational morphology as the convergence of codes. *Trends in Cognitive Sciences* 4: 353–61.

Seidenberg, M. S., and McClelland, J. L. (1989) A distributed, developmental model of word recognition and naming. *Psychological Review*, 96: 523–68.

Seidenberg, M. S. and Plaut, D. C. (2006) Progress in understanding word reading: data fitting versus theory building. In S. Andrews (ed.), *From Inkmarks to Ideas: Current Issues in Lexical Processing*. Psychology Press, Hove, UK.

Snowling, M. J. (1996) Contemporary approaches to the teaching of reading. *Journal of Child Psychology and Psychiatry*, 37(2): 139–48.

Sperling, A. J., Lu, Z.-L., Manis, F. R., and Seidenberg, M. S. (2005) Deficits in perceptual noise exclusion in developmental dyslexia. *Nature Neuroscience,* 8: 862–3.

Sperling, A. J., Lu, Z.-L., Manis, F. R., and Seidenberg, M. S. (2006) Motion perception deficits in reading impairment: it's the noise, not the motion. *Psychological Science,* 17: 1047–53.

Taraban, R., and McClelland, J. L. (1987) Conspiracy effects in word recognition. *Journal of Memory and Language,* 26: 608–31.

Van Orden, G. C., Johnston, J. C., and Hale, B. L. (1988) Word identification in reading proceeds from spelling to sound to meaning. *Journal of Experimental Psychology: Learning, Memory, and Cognition,* 14: 371–86.

Van Orden, G. C., Pennington, B. F., and Stone, G. O. (1990) Word identification in reading and the promise of a subsymbolic psycholinguistics. *Psychological Review,* 97: 488–522.

Zevin, J. D., and Seidenberg, M. S. (2002) Age of acquisition effects in reading and other tasks. *Journal of Memory and Language,* 47: 1–29.

Zorzi, M., Houghton, G., and Butterworth, B. (1998) Two routes or one in reading aloud? A connectionists dual-process model. *Journal of Experimental Psychology: Human Perception and Performance,* 24(4): 1131–61.

CHAPTER 15

The multilingual lexicon

Ton Dijkstra

15.1 Introduction

As contacts between nations increase due to economical, political, and technological developments, so does the importance of being able to speak and understand a different language from one's own. One part of the world where this is strongly felt is the European Union. At the end of 2005, 56 percent of all civilians indicated that they could speak a foreign language well enough to converse in it, whereas this was the case for about 80 percent of students (Eurobarometer 243; see also De Swaan, 2001: 202). For about one third of the inhibitants of the Union, this second language was English, and this proportion has certainly increased since then. Over 90 percent of the Dutch speak English as a second language (exceptions are older people and children under 11 years old), and, in fact, the majority of them should be called "multilingual" rather than "bilingual," because they speak German and/or French in addition to Dutch and English. Although precise numbers are lacking, in the world at large there may be more multilinguals than monolinguals when we define "multilingualism" as the regular use of two or more languages.

This prominence of multilingualism in the world has its consequences, of course, for educational systems (e.g. with respect to foreign language teaching), but also for psycholinguistic research, because the language processing system might be differently organized in monolinguals and bilinguals. In fact, research might miss out on important characteristics or limitations of the language processing system when the workings of only one language (often English) are investigated.

The study of the multilingual lexicon raises some unique and fundamental questions. First, there is a *structure-oriented* issue: Are the words a multilingual knows stored in one or more databases? A second, *process-oriented*, question is: can the retrieval of a word in one language be affected by (word candidates in) another language? These questions are closely related and hard to disentangle (Van Heuven et al., 1998).

How can we determine if the vocabularies of different languages are in a common database or not? If words from different languages are in one and the same database, a presented input (letter string or spoken word) should at least be able to activate those words simultaneously. However, such co-activation might even occur when the items are located in different stores. More convincing therefore would be the finding that words from different languages compete during identification. If we can demonstrate that the retrieval of a word in one language is affected by word candidates in another language, this clearly supports the assumption of a shared multilingual lexicon.

There is a third question to be asked, with respect to the role of *context and cognitive control* in multilingual word recognition. Might the retrieval of a target word be restricted to only one lexicon under certain circumstances, even when the mental lexicon is integrated across languages? Certain types of context, task, or participant strategy might change the degree of cross-linguistic influence. For instance, multilinguals might exert a certain degree of cognitive control on the activation of words of different languages when they switch from one language to another.

In the following we will consider these structural, process, and context/control issues with respect to the multilingual lexicon, addressing the following questions:

- How are words stored in the mental lexicon of multilinguals? (section 15.2)

- How does a multilingual retrieve words in reading, listening, and speaking? (15.3–15.5)
- What is the effect of context and cognitive control on multilingual processing? (15.6)
- What models have been proposed to account for the available data? (15.7)
- What can cognitive neuroscience contribute to bilingualism? (15.8)

15.2 The storage of words in the multilingual lexicon

It is estimated that monolinguals possess a mental lexicon of 50,000 words or more, from which they can retrieve a word within a third of a second in comprehension and production (see Aitchison, 1987: 5–7; Rastle, Chapter 5 this volume). Multilinguals who are reasonably fluent in other languages as well must, therefore, have stored tens of thousands of additional words for their second language, and the number of extra words from yet other languages is often considerable. And yet the cost associated with the ability to process more than one language in terms of processing time and error rate seems to be relatively mild. In their comparison of bilingual and monolingual performance in different tasks, Ransdell and Fischler (1987: 400) concluded: "Becoming fluent in a second language appears to have only slight impact on the ability to process the first." They observed, for instance, that bilinguals made English lexical decisions on words that were only about 125 ms slower than those of monolinguals (given RTs of 700–900 ms), but just as accurate. How can multilinguals retrieve the right words from their mental lexicon so quickly?

The mental lexicon stores a language user's knowledge with respect to words. All words must be represented with respect to spelling (orthography), sound (phonology), meaning (concepts/semantics), and several other characteristics, including the language to which a word belongs (language membership information), morphology, and pragmatics. The mental lexicon is usually considered as a multidimensional storage space set up along these dimensions. During reading, the entry dimension and first activated code is orthographic in nature; during listening, it is phonological; and during speaking, it is some kind of conceptual or semantic message specification.

Each word can be specified with respect to these various dimensions and has its own unique position in multidimensional space. On average, words belonging to the same language will be located more closely to other words of that language than to words from other languages. Thus, words of a particular language will cluster in certain regions of space that only partly overlap for different languages. The greater the differences between two languages in terms of their word characteristics, the greater the *language distance*.

Because the orthographic similarity of words from within a language is on average larger than that between languages, the number of words that are similar to a target word increases relatively slowly when a new language is added to the first one (Dijkstra, 2003: 18). Factors that increase the distance between (words of different) languages include differences in script, morphology, diacritical markers, bigram frequencies, phonological repertoire, and phonotactics.

Although many words have an orthographic or phonological form that is unique, there are exceptions. Within English, for instance, the orthographic word form BANK refers to a financial institution or the edge of a river, and word forms like COLONEL and KERNEL are to considerable extent ambiguous in terms of their phonology (cf. Lupker, Chapter 10 this volume). The two item types are referred to as, respectively, intralingual homographs and intralingual homophones. There is an analogous case of ambiguity across languages. Here *interlingual homographs* exist, words that share their orthographic word form across languages, but may be different in meaning and phonology. A Dutch–English example is a letter string like BOND; a French–English example is COIN. In contrast, *interlingual homophones* are very similar in terms of their phonological representation. An example is an English word like AID relative to Dutch EED ('oath'). Note that the members of such pairs may differ in their frequency of usage in the two languages. Interlingual homographs and homophones are sometimes referred to by the general term "false friends."

Another special type of words are translation equivalents with word forms that are similar or identical across languages. Such items, like HOTEL, ECHO, and DEMOCRACY (with the same meaning across languages), are called "cognates." Note that, in contrast to linguists, psycholinguists use this term irrespective of etymological relationship. For example, Dutch VIJF and French CINQ are historically related, but psychologists would not call these items cognates, because the form relationship has largely been lost.

For closely related language pairs like Dutch and English, the number of cognates and false friends is considerable. Van Hell (1998: 14) found that about half of the 200 most frequent English words were closely similar in sound or spelling to their Dutch translation equivalents. Lemhöfer et al. (2007) reported that in an English list of 1,025 three-to-five-letter content words, 137 items could be considered as orthographically identical cognates and 65 as non-cognate interlingual homographs, a total of nearly 20 percent. The number of identical cognates between English and German may be somewhat smaller, but Friel and Kennison (2001: 257) also considered 19.9 percent of the translation pairs for 563 nouns as English–German cognates. Of course, for language combinations with different scripts, all orthographic forms may be language-specific, but even for combinations like English with Korean or Chinese there may be interlingual (near-)homophones.

Interlingual homographs, interlingual homophones, and cognates are favorite stimulus materials of researchers in multilingualism, because their special cross-linguistic characteristics can be used to investigate whether words from different languages are activated during comprehension or production. This will become evident in the next section, in which we discuss the multilinguals' word retrieval processes in detail.

15.3 **The process of multilingual word recognition: visual modality**

Research on monolingual word recognition indicates that upon the presentation of a letter string, representations of all words in the mental lexicon that are similar to the input letter string become activated (see Chapter 5 above). It is not completely clear how the similarity between input and activated internal representations should be characterized. A *similarity metric* often found in the literature on visual word recognition is that of the *neighborhood* (Coltheart et al., 1977). To the neighborhood of a target word belong all *competitor* words that differ in only one letter position. For instance, GIN has neighbors like BIN, GUN, and GIG. According to this definition, GINA is not a neighbor. For languages that share scripts, the activated neighbors during reading might, of course, derive from different languages. For instance, in a Dutch–English bilingual GIN might activate not only the neighbors from their second language English (L2), but also neighbors from their native language Dutch (L1), like VIN, GEN, and GIL.

Evidence that neighbors from both languages are activated upon the presentation of a word that belongs uniquely to one language would support language-non-specific access to the mental lexicon (the *process issue*). Furthermore, if neighbors from both languages affect target word identification latencies as well, they apparently compete during the recognition process, revealing that the multilingual lexicon is integrated across languages (*structural issue*). Van Heuven et al. (1998) showed that word candidates from both languages are indeed activated in parallel, and that they both affect target word recognition. They manipulated the number of orthographic neighbors of the target words in the same and the other language of the bilinguals in a series of progressive demasking and lexical decision experiments involving Dutch–English bilinguals. Increasing the number of Dutch orthographic neighbors systematically slowed responses to English target words. Within the target language itself, an increase in neighbors consistently produced inhibitory effects for Dutch target words and facilitatory effects for English target words. Monolingual English readers also showed facilitation due to English neighbors, but no effects of Dutch neighbors. Highly correlated and very similar result patterns were obtained for one-language (pure) and two-languages (mixed) experiments. Simulations with a computer model of bilingual word recognition (the BIA model) suggested that the opposite effects of English (facilitation) and Dutch (inhibition) neighbors were due to differences in the specific organization of the English and Dutch lexicons. The activation of neighbors from both the same and the other language during the presentation of a target word indicates that the orthographic lexicon of bilinguals is integrated and language non-selective in nature.

It also indicates that the bilingual's recognition of isolated words, like his/her monolingual counterpart, basically proceeds in a bottom-up manner and automatically. Item characteristics in the language of the target word rather than participant expectations determine the identification process. This view is further supported by a recent large-scale progressive demasking study by Lemhöfer et al. (2007) with bilinguals having Dutch, German, or French as their L1. In a regression analysis on data for 1,025 English items, Lemhöfer et al. found that L2 target item characteristics like English frequency, word length, number and frequency of L2 neighbors, and bigram frequency were the major determinants of the identification process, rather than the L1 characteristics. Cross-linguistic effects occurred mainly for "special" items with form-and/or meaning-overlap across languages, such as false friends and cognates.

Note that the target words in these neighborhood studies exist in one language only. This is different for false friends, which have either an orthographic form (interlingual homographs) or a phonological form (interlingual homophones) that exists as a word in more than one language. False friends have two important characteristics: their relative frequency in the two languages, and their cross-linguistic overlap in terms of orthography and/or phonology. Let us consider the impact of each factor on word recognition.

In a series of closely related experiments, Dijkstra et al. (1998) manipulated the *relative frequency* of the two members of interlingual homograph pairs. In a first experiment, Dutch–English participants performed an English lexical decision task including interlingual homographs and cognates, as well as exclusively English control words. The English–Dutch homographs were of high or low frequency in either language, leading to four frequency combinations. For instance, an item like RAMP had a low frequency in English and a high frequency in Dutch (where it means 'disaster'). Under these circumstances, Dutch–English bilinguals responded more or less equally fast to interlingual homographs and exclusively English matched controls (and faster to cognates). This happened irrespective of the frequency of the English and Dutch members of the homograph pair.

In a second experiment, purely Dutch words were added to the stimulus list, but the task remained English lexical decision. Participants responded "no" to these Dutch items, because they were not existing English words. RTs were much slower now for interlingual homographs than for the matched controls, especially when the homographs were low-frequency in English and high-frequency in Dutch. Dijkstra et al. attributed these inhibition effects to a frequency-dependent competition between the two readings of the homographs, where the non-target language reading of the interlingual homograph could not be ignored by the participants. Other studies observed similar inhibitory or null effects for interlingual homographs relative to one-language control words in tasks like translation recognition, repetition priming, and word naming (e.g. De Groot et al., 2000; Gerard and Scarborough, 1989; Smits et al., 2006 Von Studnitz and Green, 1997).

A third experiment tested the hypothesis that the recognition of the interlingual homograph could be conceived of in terms of a "race to recognition" between its two readings. In a generalized lexical decision task, participants were instructed to "say yes to English and/or Dutch words," implying they could in principle respond as soon as either of the two readings of a homograph became available. As the result of a "race" between the two readings of the homograph, a facilitation effect of homographs relative to control items should arise. This was indeed what was found. The size of the facilitation effect depended on the frequency of both the English and the Dutch readings of the homograph. The largest benefit to the RT was observed for the homographs with low-frequency English and high-frequency Dutch readings. Participants were apparently able to respond to either reading of an interlingual homograph. The three experiments in this study lead to the insight that stimulus list composition and task demands affect performance in a systematic but complex way, resulting in null effects, inhibition effects, or facilitation effects depending on the exact empirical circumstances. The importance of task and context factors in bilingualism has recently attracted much more interest (see section 15.6 below).

Another look at this study reveals another interesting but neglected issue, namely whether *language membership* is stored in the lexicon as a characteristic of words, and, if so, at which level of representation. The bilinguals in Experiment 2 performed an English lexical decision task, in which English and Dutch words were included, as well as non-words. In this situation, Dutch items had to be rejected, because they did not belong to the target language (English). To reject them, participants had to retrieve information about the language to which the words belonged. Nevertheless, the RTs to control words in this experiment were about as fast as in Experiment 1, in which no Dutch words were included. These findings suggest that participants can retrieve language information quite quickly, before they arrive at the meaning of an word. At the same time, however, they apparently could not use such information in time to ignore the non-target readings of interlingual homographs. In all, the data suggest that language membership information becomes available directly following word identification (possibly at the lemma level: see section 15.4).

Identical *cognates* (e.g. AVION in French and Spanish) are usually processed faster than one-language control items in many experimental situations. In two progressive demasking experiments involving French–Spanish bilinguals,

Font (2001), in collaboration with Lavaur, found a facilitation effect for orthographically identical cognates relative to one-language items. The facilitation decreased considerably for non-identical cognates in which the last letter was different across languages (as in TEXTE–TEXTO) and tended to inhibition when an internal letter was changed (as in USUEL–USUAL). Similar patterns of results were found in L1 and L2 processing.

A recent English lexical decision study by Dijkstra, Baayen, et al. (2007) with Dutch-English bilinguals led to facilitation effects of 40 ms for form-identical cognates relative to English controls (e.g. ALARM–ALARM), decreasing to 25 ms for cognates that are one letter different between languages ("neighbor cognates," like BAKER and BAKKER), and to even less for cognates different in more letters (relative to an overall RT of about 540 ms). However, a different pattern of results was found for progressive demasking, indicating that cognate effects may be task-sensitive, just like interlingual homograph effects. It has been suggested (e.g. Sánchez-Casas and García-Albea, 2005) that cognates may have a special representation that may be morphemic in nature.

Van Hell and Dijkstra (2002) had trilinguals with Dutch as their L1, English as their L2, and French as their L3 perform a word association task or a lexical decision task in their native language. Stimulus words were (mostly) non-identical *cognates* such as TOMAAT or non-cognates. Shorter association and lexical decision times were observed for Dutch–English cognates than for non-cognates. For trilinguals with a higher proficiency in French, lexical decision responses were faster for both Dutch–English and Dutch–French cognates. Thus, even when their orthographic and phonological overlap across languages is incomplete, cognates may still be recognized faster than non-cognates in the *native* language.

Dijkstra, Grainger, and Van Heuven (1999) examined the effects of different types of *code overlap* in cognate and interlingual homograph processing. Dutch–English bilinguals performed an English lexical decision task with English words varying in their degree of semantic (S), orthographic (O), and phonological (P) overlap with Dutch words. Three groups of cognates (+S) and three groups of false friends (–S) were selected that varied in the degree of orthographic and phonological overlap. Items were, for instance, SPORT (overlap in S, O, and P codes), CHAOS (SO), WHEEL (SP; Dutch item: WIEL), PINK (OP), GLAD (O), and CORE (P; Dutch item: KOOR). Lexical decisions were facilitated by cross-linguistic orthographic and semantic overlap relative to control words that belonged only to English. In contrast, phonological overlap produced inhibitory effects. A very similar pattern of results was found using a different task (progressive demasking), but no systematic differences between test and control conditions arose for American English monolinguals. Later studies suggested that the size and direction of the phonological effect may depend on stimulus list composition. Nevertheless, phonological effects have been observed in various experimental situations (Van Wijnendaele and Brysbaert, 2002) and even when there are script differences between the involved languages (Gollan et al., 1997; Kim and Davis, 2003).

To summarize, the great majority of empirical studies in the visual domain support the view of language non-selective lexical access into a mental lexicon that is integrated across languages. The observed cross-linguistic orthographic and phonological effects depend on the similarity or identity of lexical representations rather than on their language membership. To put it another way, language membership does not appear to be an important factor in organizing the multilngual lexicon; language information probably becomes available at a relatively late stage of processing.

15.4 **The process of multilingual word recognition: auditory modality**

In spoken word recognition, the input must be represented using sublexical and lexical phonology. Just like in the visual modality, it is assumed that in the initial stage of processing, a number of word candidates are activated (see McQueen, Chapter 3 this volume). In the auditory modality, this set of competitors is called a "(word-initial) cohort." All words in the cohort have the same beginning, but they may differ in length (note that this leads to a different competitor set from the neighborhood). For example, upon presentation of the English word CAP, activated lexical items may include CAP, CAPTAIN, CAPTIVE, and CAPITAL. As in the visual modality, we can ask to what extent the activation of word candidates is limited to the language of the target word. We may note that, differently from the visual modality, from onset on, the auditory signal may contain sublexical and subphonemic cues (e.g. in terms of specific phonemes, like /th/ or /ae/, or phoneme features, like aspiration) that indicate the presented word belongs to one language and not another. So far, most auditory studies have examined and found sublexical effects of L1 on L2, which can be understood from the clear dominance of L1 in terms of phonemic repertoire and word frequency. Only a limited number of studies have investigated effects at the lexical level.

Spivey and Marian (1999) demonstrated that lexical competitors of a target word from several languages can become active during bilingual auditory word recognition. In one study, a head-mounted eyetracker registered the eye movements of participants to particular objects presented on a display. Russian–English bilinguals received a spoken instruction in English or Russian to move a particular target object. The name properties of the objects on the display were varied systematically. Sometimes, there were two objects with names in English or Russian that shared the same initial phonemes. For instance, a target object with the English name *speaker* could be presented together with an object with the English name *spear* (within-language competitor), or with the object "matches," having the Russian name *speachki* (between-language competitor). Participants were found to fixate more often on distractor objects with target-similar names than on other unrelated objects. This was true for competitors from the same and the other language. Both within- and between-language competitors in the instruction led to more eye movements to the between-language competitor objects than to the control objects. These data support the language non-selective access view. Bilingual listeners do not appear to be able to deactivate words from the lexicon that is irrelevant in the task situation at hand, even if the situation is purely monolingual and even if it is restricted to the native language (also see Weber and Cutler, 2004).

Pallier, Colomé, and Sebastián-Gallés (2001) showed that bilinguals are differentially sensitive to specific phoneme contrasts in their first language (L1) or their second language (L2). Using Spanish–Catalan and Catalan–Spanish bilinguals as participants, they compared repetition priming effects to word pairs that were identical or minimally different in a contrast existing only in Catalan. For instance, in Catalan the length difference in the first vowel of the words /netə(/ ('granddaughter') and /nɛtə(/ ('clean') leads to a meaning difference (the words are *minimal pairs*), but this specific contrast does not exist in Spanish. When auditorily presented words were repeated, the standard repetition priming effect was found, i.e. the lexical decision times to the second presentation of the words were faster than to its first presentation. However, the repetition priming effect for the minimal pairs was found to depend on the language dominance of the bilingual participants. Spanish–Catalan bilinguals (maternal language Spanish) showed equivalent priming effects for minimal pairs and identical words, demonstrating that they did not perceive the phoneme contrast that was specific to Catalan. However, Catalan–Spanish bilinguals did not show the repetition effect for the minimal pairs, although they did for the identical words. Apparently, Spanish-dominant bilinguals, but not Catalan-dominant bilinguals, treated the Catalan-specific minimal pairs as homophones. The study by Pallier et al. indicates that bilingual participants may not be optimally equipped to make phoneme distinctions that are irrelevant in their mother tongue. This conclusion is also a key concept in Flege's (1987) Speech Learning model, which intends to account for the bilingual acquisition of common and unique phonemes in a new language.

Nevertheless, there is evidence that bilinguals may be sensitive at least to some sublexical differences. In a bilingual gating study, Grosjean (1988) explored how "guest words" in sentences are processed by bilingual listeners (cf. Li, 1996). Guest words are words from another language that are brought into the main language of ongoing communication or "base language." Grosjean investigated whether, in sentence context, guest words that have close homophones in the main language are identified more slowly than other guest words. English–French examples of such guest words are *pick* (*piquer*), *cool* (*couler*), and *knot* (*noter*). Participants heard increasingly long fragments of words and "made a guess" from which words the fragments were derived and how confident they were of their judgement. Each target word was embedded in a carrier sentence, namely *Il faudrait qu'on ...* . An example of a complete sentence is *Il faudrait qu'on PICK les bons chiffres* ('We should pick the right numbers') with *PICK* as the code-switched element.

The isolation (identification) of interlingual homophones required a longer speech segment than other words (if they were identified at all). Importantly, code-switched homophones were isolated sooner than borrowed homophones, apparently because isolation was sensitive to phonetic cues indicating the language of the fragment. The relative frequencies of the homophone competitors from the two languages were also relevant.

Schulpen et al. (2003) replicated and extended Grosjean's results by means of a gating task involving English and Dutch words without sentence context. They also examined the role of language-specific information in bilingual auditory word recognition in two cross-modal priming experiments. Dutch–English bilinguals made lexical decisions to visually presented target words accompanied by auditory distractor words that were sometimes *interlingual homophones*. An example is the English item /leaf/, which sounds similar (but not identical) to the Dutch word /li:f/, meaning "nice." The visual targets differed in their amount of form overlap with the auditory primes (e.g. possible distractors for the visual target LEAF could be /leaf/, li:f/, or /bike/). Visual lexical decisions to words accompanied by the auditory version of an interlingual homophone (e.g. /leaf/ [English]–LEAF and /lief/ [Dutch]–LEAF) were faster than to words accompanied by unrelated primes (e.g. /bike/–LEAF). This was the case not only for the English version of the homophone, but also for the Dutch version. This indicates that both representations of the interlingual homophone were activated and affected visual target processing, even the one that was not directly presented. Because the effects of English and Dutch homophones on visual processing differed in size, it further appears that participants used sublexical cues to differentiate the two versions of a homophone after language non-selective access occurred.

A study by Akker and Dijkstra (forthcoming) shows that with respect to the *relative frequency* of the word candidates, the same mechanisms appear to underlie competition between interlingual homophones as between interlingual homographs in visual lexical decision and word naming. In an auditory lexical decision study, slower RTs relative to controls were found for interlingual homophones that were low-frequency in English and low- or high-frequency in Dutch (examples of such items were STAIN, with the Dutch reading of STEEN "stone") and DOSE, Dutch DOOS "box"). As in the visual modality, these results can be understood as the consequence of competition between the English and Dutch members of the homophonic pair.

Zwitserlood et al. (2007) examined the process of spoken word recognition in bilinguals with respect to code overlap in interlingual homophones. German–Dutch bilinguals performed a German lexical decision experiment in which auditorily presented Dutch prime words were completely included in longer visual German targets. Experimental conditions differed in the semantic and phonological cross-linguistic overlap between primes and targets. For instance, in one (cognate) condition there was overlap of both types (+S +P) between auditory prime and visual target. An example of this condition is the Dutch prime *bril* followed by the German target word *Brille*. Other conditions did not have semantic overlap but did have phonological overlap (–S +P), for instance, prime *beer*–target *Beere*, or clear differences in both (e.g. prime *gat*–target *Gatte*, with a different pronunciation and meaning). Latencies in the test conditions differed systematically from those in the control conditions. Overlap in both semantics and phonology led to strong facilitation effects, while differences in both factors led to strong inhibition. Overlap in only one of the codes resulted in small facilitation effects in the case of phonologically similar but semantically unrelated conditions, and no effect in the case of phonological dissimilarity but semantic overlap.

We can easily summarize the results of this section, because (leaving aside complications due to modality differences) it appears that similar mechanisms of parallel activation and response competition play a role in the auditory and visual domain. Indeed, the last study we reviewed indicates that visual and auditory lexical representations of different languages can affect each other on-line. This suggests that there is a shared lexical workspace irrespective of modality or language.

15.5 Multilingual word production

According to monolingual standard theories of language production, the input for speaking is a preverbal message of conceptual nature. During the production process this conceptual representation is turned into a phonological representation and then into an articulatory one (see Costa, Alario, and Sebastián-Gallés, Chapter 32 this volume). Some researchers propose that a concept is immediately recoded into a phonological representation (e.g. Caramazza, 1997), while others assume an intermediary level of representation, called the *lemma* (e.g. Levelt et al., 1999).

To ensure that bilinguals express their preverbal messages in the desired language of utterance, it must contain not only the concepts to be expressed, but also a *language cue*. Poulisse and Bongaerts (1994) suggested that conceptual information and the language cue together activate lemmas of the appropriate meaning and language. La Heij (2005) argued that this simple model is sufficient to account for bilingual speech production phenomena if it is assumed that the language cue "boosts" the lemma candidates of the appropriate language, leading to a correct selection in almost all cases.

This view should not be taken to imply that non-target language candidates are not activated at all during bilingual word production. On the contrary, the available empirical data indicate that word candidates from non-target and target languages are activated in parallel. Hermans et al. (1998) conducted a series of picture–word interference experiments, in which Dutch–English bilinguals were named pictures in their L2 while ignoring auditory distractor words in L1 or L2. In one condition, the distractor word was phonologically related to the target's translation. For example, if the speaker had to name a picture of a mountain in English (*mountain*), the distractor word was phonologically related to the target's translation (*berm* related to *berg*, the translation of *mountain*). If activation from the conceptual level flows to the target's translation in the non-response language (*berg*), lexical selection should be harder when the translation word receives extra activation from the distractor word (i.e. when the distractor word is phonologically related, e.g. *berm*) than when it does not (i.e. when the distractor word in phonologically unrelated, e.g. *kaars*). Naming latencies were indeed slower in the former condition, supporting the predictions. It was concluded that word candidates from both languages are indeed activated in parallel.

Kroll et al. (1999) used a cued picture-naming paradigm in which bilinguals named pictures in one of their two languages following the presentation of a tone cue. In the mixed-language condition, the tone could vary from trial to trial, signalling one target language (high tone) or the other (low tone). Kroll et al. found that cognates were named faster than matched controls in this condition for both L1 and L2. When picture-naming was blocked, however, cognate facilitation was restricted to L2 and occurred only at short SOAs relative to picture onset. Thus, the selection process appears to be context-sensitive and variable in time. In addition, it was found that interlingual homophones such as the English word *leaf*, sounding like the Dutch word *lief*, were named more slowly in L2 than in non-homophonic controls. This suggests that even the phonology of items was co-activated cross-linguistically, pointing to cross-linguistic effects up to a late stage of processing. Overall, the results support a language non-selective model of lexical access in which a combination of factors determines the time course and locus of selection.

A different approach was taken by Costa et al. (2000). These authors hypothesized that if during picture-naming the phonological representation of the target's translation is activated, then the retrieval of the phonological properties of the target word should be easier for cognates than for one-language items. A non-identical Spanish–English cognate like *guitarra* would receive activation from both its own lexical representation (*guitarra*) and its English counterpart (*guitar*). In contrast, purely Spanish words would receive activation from one source only, because their lexical node and their translation would activate different phonological representations. This prediction was confirmed, because naming latencies were indeed faster for pictures with cognate than with non-cognate names. This supports the view of language-non-specific activation in the production system, leading to a phonological co-activation of lexical nodes in the non-target language.

In the phoneme monitoring paradigm used by Colomé (2001), fluent Catalan–Spanish bilinguals indicated whether a certain phoneme was in the Catalan name of a picture. Phonemes could be part of the Catalan word, its Spanish translation, or absent from both nouns. For instance, for a picture of *taula* (the Catalan word for 'table'), they had to decide if an /m/ (present in *mesa*, the Spanish word for 'table') or an /f/ (not in *taula* or *mesa*) occurred. Participants took longer to reject the phoneme appearing in the Spanish word than in the control word, again indicating that the phonology of target and non-target language were simultaneously activated.

How can words from the non-target language become activated up to the phonological level even though the language intention is already available at the conceptual level? According to Costa and Caramazza, a distinction must be made between the word activation process and target word selection. They suggest that, while word candidates from both languages are activated in processing, the word *selection* process is language-specific. By this they mean that lexical nodes belonging to the non-response language do not enter the competition process during lexical selection (Costa and Caramazza, 1999). However, Costa et al. do not specify how and when language membership information is used to restrict the word selection process.

A solution to this problem could be derived from the comprehension domain. The empirical studies reviewed above suggest that language membership information becomes available relatively late (after word identification). Language membership information might therefore be stored as an item property at the lemma level (storing it only as a conceptual feature does not seem enough, because it is the word forms and not their meanings that are language-specific). If this language membership information, stored with each lexical item, is looked up in the course of the word production process, language-specific selection can occur by matching it to the "intended language" information at the conceptual level. Such a matching process might take time, during which strongly activated lemma representations could already spread activation to their linked phonological representations.

This assumption accounts for some phenomena in the acquisition process of a new language, for instance, the finding that phonological representations of cognates in both languages may become active. It also explains why even for a weaker target language (with subjectively lower-frequency representations) and a low language proficiency, lexical selection and translation processes may proceed properly: by matching the concept- and lexicon-based language membership codes. Finally, consider the following example. Learning Italian, I cannot suppress French words when I wish to utter similar Italian items. Apparently my intention to select words from my very small Italian vocabulary fails. This problem could be ascribed to a lack of "boosting" my Italian words; but another solution is to consider it as a word-selection problem at the lemma or phonological level. French items are becoming too active relative to Italian ones, and the language membership of the weakly activated Italian words is not known in time to serve as a cue for item selection.

However this may be, the results of various word production studies can be summarized in similar terms as in the comprehension domain. There appears to be parallel lexical activation across languages, followed by (response) competition and late selection. Language membership information appears to play a relatively late role in processing.

15.6 **Context effects and cognitive control**

Our review of studies so far indicates that lexical access to the multilingual lexicon is generally not language-specific, i.e. it is not restricted to one language. Thus, the architecture of the bilingual word retrieval system must at least *allow* language nonselective access. Possibly, lexical access is *always* language non-selective. In this case, target item selection might take place on the basis of task- and context-dependent decision criteria. However, another possibility is that word retrieval proceeds in a language-selective or non-selective way depending on the situation. Two variants of this viewpoint relate to the concepts of relative language activation and cognitive control. Relative language activation entails that (words from) different languages may be activated to different extent (cf. Grosjean's language mode hypothesis). For instance, the relative activation of Dutch would be higher in an experiment including stimuli from both English and Dutch, compared to a purely English experiment. Note that an effect of relative language activation implies that the presentation of some words from a particular language changes the activation of *any* word from that language. The second concept, cognitive control, in one interpretation holds that multilinguals can modulate the relative language activation by themselves. This would allow them to optimize their response behavior in different experimental situations (e.g. by ignoring undesired word candidates from a non-target language). This type of top-down control implies that particular selection criteria (like language membership) can be applied at will earlier or later in processing.

Dijkstra, De Bruijn, et al. (2000) investigated the role of cognitive control as a non-linguistic context factor. Dutch–English bilinguals performed an English lexical decision task consisting of two parts. They were informed that purely Dutch items could be presented, which required a "no" response. However, part 1 of this study in fact included only English words and non-words. In this part, the RTs of the participants to interlingual homographs were just as fast as to English control items. In part 2, Dutch items were introduced that led to clear inhibition effects for interlingual homographs relative to controls. The responses to English control items, however, were only marginally affected by the transition from part 1 to part 2, indicating little change in lexical activation. The combined results indicate that expectations on the basis of instructions apparently do not lead to a reduction of non-target language activation even when that would be profitable (cf. Dijkstra, Timmermans, and Schriefers, 2000). Because stimulus list composition (without/with Dutch items) and not instruction was the effective factor, the data pattern was largely determined by factors outside the participants' cognitive control. Furthermore, because the control conditions were comparable across parts, in spite of the change in the relative proportion of items from English and Dutch, there was apparently no change in relative language activation. Instead, the results can be accounted for by a language non-selective acccess view that assumes that participants changed their response criteria in the second part of the experiment.

A more extensive consideration of different studies suggests that, although differences in stimulus list composition do affect word recognition performance, performance changes do not arise as the result of changes in relative language activation (see Dijkstra and Van Heuven, 2002 for a review). For instance, the pure and mixed variants of the progressive demasking experiments by Van Heuven et al. (1998) led to neighborhood density effects that were correlated above .90. Furthermore, regression analyses indicate that RTs for items of different frequency ranges in control conditions do not reflect changes in the proportion of items from different languages. As yet, there is no convincing evidence that suppression on the basis of expectations or strategies occurs during reading. Of course, participant strategies may speed word recognition, but apparently this is done by adapting decision criteria or task schemas, rather than L1/L2 lexical activation.

At the same time, task differences and stimulus list composition may modify the bilingual performance patterns to considerable extent. We already discussed the task-dependent patterns of results in Dijkstra et al. (1998). De Groot et al. (2002) investigated the commonalities between different tasks such as (delayed) word-naming, perceptual identification, and lexical decision in L1 and L2, and found that bilingual performance was quite task-dependent. For instance, in an English lexical decision task performed by Dutch–English bilinguals, frequency had a major impact, whereas in English naming onset was most important. Thus, the bilingual word recognition process can be understood properly only if one takes into account both the item characteristics and task demands. It is likely that task and stimulus list are also factors affecting the word production process; but research into these matters has only just begun.

Linguistic context factors like sentence context appear to be able to modify lexical processing patterns as well (Altarriba et al., 1996; Schwartz and Kroll, 2006; see also Kutas and Federmeier, Chapter 23 this volume). Dijkstra, Van Hell, and Brenders (2007) found that in Dutch–English bilinguals the processing of the English version of Dutch–English non-identical cognates like *doctor* (which is *dokter* in Dutch) was affected by the language of the preceding sentence context (Dutch or English) and the semantic constraint it exerted (relative to purely English control words). More than in the RTs, this was visible in the simultaneously recorded Event-Related Potentials (ERPs).

The issue of cognitive control over bilingual processing has also been investigated by means of *language-switching* tasks. As early as the 1960s it was found that bilinguals took more time to read mixed-language texts than texts in one language (Kolers, 1966) and were slower to name numbers in two languages than in one language (Macnamara et al., 1968). Grainger and Beauvillain (1987) obtained similar results in a general lexical decision task. When participants had to decide if the letter string which appeared was a word or not in any language, the RTs for words in mixed lists were significantly longer than for words in pure lists.

Meuter and Allport (1999) found asymmetrical language switch costs in bilingual participants, using a number-naming paradigm. Participants had to name a number appearing on the screen. If the background screen was *red* they named the number in English, if it was *blue* they named it in their second language, for instance, German or French. Somewhat counterintuively, switch costs were higher when participants switched into their first language rather than their second language. The authors explained these asymmetrical switch costs in terms of the different strength of the bilingual's languages. Participants took more time to switch into their first language, because the first and stronger language would be inhibited more by the second weaker language, and this inhibition would persist in processing in the next trial.

Costa and Santesteban (2004) compared the switching performance of highly proficient Spanish–Catalan bilinguals to that of Catalan learners with a Spanish native language and Spanish learners with Korean native language in a picture-naming task. Participants named pictures in Spanish or Catalan depending on the background color of the stimuli. Comparable to Meuter and Allport (1999), the switch costs for Catalan learners were higher when the participants switched into their first language. However, highly proficient bilinguals showed approximately equal switch costs in both directions. Thus, the switching performance of bilinguals may be affected by their proficiency in the second language. When highly proficient Spanish–Catalan speakers were tested in their weakest third language, symmetrical switch costs were found as well. Apparently, symmetrical switch costs extend to the third language when participants have a high proficiency in the first and second language. The authors proposed that for L2 learners, inhibition of the non-relevant language took place, resulting in asymmetrical switch costs. However, in highly proficient bilinguals lexical access would be sensitive to the activation level of the intended language but would not be inhibited (at a later age, attrition effects on language switching might come in: see Hernandez and Kohnert, 1999).

15.7 **Models of bilingual word processing**

The multilingual research discussed above has led to the development of both verbal and implemented models for multilingual word recognition, production, and L2 acquisition. In the visual modality, both localist and distributed connectionist models have been proposed. Localist models like the Bilingual Interactive Activation (BIA) model and its successor BIA+ (Dijkstra and Van Heuven, 1998; 2002) have implemented a language-non-selective mechanism of lexical access and proposed a functional distinction between a word identification mechanism and a task/decision system. These computational models have successfully simulated a large number of empirical studies, involving different stimulus types processed in various tasks. Distributed models, like those of French (1998) and of Li and Farkas (2000), have concentrated on aspects of bilingual acquisition. French (1998) has shown that a simple recurrent network was able to represent and separate words from two micro-languages after these were presented in sentences that switched from one language to the other from time to time, as in: *boy pushes book femme soulève stylo…* The SOMBIP model of Li and Farkas (2000) consists of two interconnected, self-organizing neural networks, coupled with a recurrent network that computes lexical co-occurrence constraints. After a Hebbian learning phase involving the presentation of transcribed recordings of bilingual conversations, this model was able to distinguish words of different languages (Chinese–English in this case), had acquired meaningful lexical-semantic categories, and accounted for a variety of priming effects in bilinguals differing in proficiency and working memory capacity.

A localist connectionist model for bilingual auditory word recognition is the BIMOLA model (Léwy et al., 2005). The model is similar to the BIA model in terms of its Interactive Activation structure, with different layers for symbolic units like features, phonemes (letters in BIA), and words. However, it also implements a number of different assumptions about bilingual auditory word recognition. While the feature level is shared by the two languages, the phoneme and word levels are organized in language-specific subsets (still in the same extended system). Language activation or selection takes place via top-down connections representing global language activation and higher linguistic information, and via within-language connections at phoneme and word levels (items from the same language support each other). The top-down connections allow the model to preactivate lexical information from one language at the expense of the other. For instance, upon the presentation of an interlingual homophone (e.g. English /leaf/ and Dutch /li:f/ "nice", both lexical representations may be activated, but top-down information from the language context, in combination with language-specific sublexical information, will lead to an inhibition of the lexical representation in the non-target language.

In the domain of bilingual word production, a number of competing models exists as well. De Bot (1992; 2004) and Poulisse and Bongaerts (1994) formulated models that have been inspired by the monolingual language production model by Levelt (1989). An interesting aspect of these models is the presence of a language cue in the conceptual input, which might achieve a selection of words in a target language by activating one subset of word candidates and deactivating another (see La Heij, 2005). In contrast, some other production models do not believe in such inhibitory processes but consider the available empirical results in terms of task-dependent decision processes (Costa and Caramazza, 1999; Costa and Santesteban, 2004).

A model that accounts for lexical development in first and second language processing is the Revised Hierarchical Model (RHM), developed by Kroll and Stewart (1994). In its original form, this model held that the lexical representations of two languages are independent at the lexical level but shared at the conceptual level. On the basis of more recent empirical data, it is now assumed that the lexical level also consists of representations shared across languages (Kroll et al., 2002). In the bilingual lexicon, links between lexical forms and conceptual links are active, but the strength of such links differs as a function of L2 fluency. Relatively strong *lexical form* links map L2 words onto L1 words during the early stages of second language acquisition (e.g. *horse* to *Pferd*), whereas the form links from L1 to L2 are relatively weak. This leads to a processing asymmetry in studies investigating the translation from L1 into L2 and vice versa (Kroll et al., 2002; Kroll and Stewart, 1994; Sholl et al., 1995). Early in L2 acquisition, the *conceptual* links between L1 words and concepts are already in place, but those between L2 items and concepts must be developed and are strengthened as bilinguals become more fluent in their L2. Thus both lexical and conceptual links are bidirectional, but they differ in strength in the two directions. A number of predictions of the RHM have been validated by empirical data (see Kroll and De Groot, 1997 for a review), but some researchers have criticized the model in terms of its predictions regarding the directionality of processing at the conceptual level (Altarriba and Mathis, 1997; La Heij et al., 1996).

Finally, a model that focuses on bilingual cognitive control in both bilingual production and comprehension is the Inhibitory Control model of Green (1998). This model has been applied to translation data and language switching. More recently, Green has developed his ideas on cognitive control in terms of brain activity as well (e.g. Abutalebi and Green, forthcoming).

15.8 **Contributions of cognitive neuroscience**

All studies discussed so far are concerned with behavioral data mainly involving reaction times of some sort. However, new studies in cognitive neuroscience are quickly delivering evidence from a completely different kind: where in the brain cognitive functions are performed and how they interrelate in terms of their processing components. Due to space limitations, we can consider only a few of the available studies that demonstrate how techniques involving Event-Related Potentials (ERPs) and fMRI may lead to insights into bilingual processing.

Rodriguez-Fornells et al. (2002) conducted a study involving ERP and fMRI data for Spanish–Catalan bilinguals. In this study, bilinguals appeared to avoid accessing the meaning of words from a non-target language while they were processing target language words by inhibiting the direct access route from lexical orthography to semantics in the lexicon. Instead, they were thought to apply a specific set of sublexical grapheme-to-phoneme spelling rules, leading to an activation only of word candidates from the target language. This view was supported by an observed insensitivity of the bilingual ERPs to word frequency variation in the non-target language, and an increased fMRI activation of areas implicated in phonological and pseudo-word processing, such as the posterior inferior frontal cortex and the planum temporale. In addition, there was evidence of increased activation in an anterior prefrontal area (BA45/9) implicated in the selection of relevant information and interference resolution. In all, the results were interpreted as supporting a language-selective access hypothesis; and they thus deviated from the great majority of available reaction time studies that support language-*non*-selective access.

However, in direct contrast to this study, Kerkhofs et al. (2006) and Van Heuven et al. (2007) obtained neuroscientific data for interlingual homographs processed by Dutch–English bilinguals that *did* support language-non-selective access. In the study by Kerkhofs et al., Dutch–English bilinguals performed an English lexical decision task in which homographs like STEM (meaning 'voice' in Dutch) were preceded by primes like ROOT or FOOL that were semantically related or unrelated to the English target reading. Homographs were responded to faster following semantically related primes than following unrelated primes. As predicted, responses were modulated by the relative frequencies of homograph readings: They were faster when English word frequency was high or Dutch word frequency was low. In the ERPs, N400 effects, indicative of semantic integration, were found for interlingual homographs preceded by related primes. The amplitude of the N400 effect was modulated by relative word frequency in L1 and L2. The effects of Dutch and English frequency on the ERPs were in opposite directions.

Van Heuven et al. (2007) contrasted the RT and fMRI patterns for interlingual homographs processed by Dutch–English bilinguals for three lexical decision tasks. In a language-specific lexical decision task, a Dutch–English homograph like STEM can be interpreted as an English word requiring a "Yes" response, and as a Dutch word requiring a "No" response. The fMRI data revealed language conflicts, because greater activation for homographs than for control words was found in the dorsal anterior cingulate cortex (dACC) and the left inferior/middle frontal gyrus. Both these brain regions are associated with cognitive control. Importantly, the dACC was not activated in a generalized lexical decision task, where a "Yes" response is correct for both the Dutch and the English reading of the homograph. This suggests that the dACC is involved only when language conflict occurs at response level.

These results are compatible with the BIA+ model (see also Dijkstra and Van Heuven, 2006).

It will be clear that the studies we considered led to opposite results. Given the relative novelty of the field, it may be unavoidable that complex studies which differ in various respect may temporarily reach apparently incompatible conclusions that must somehow be reconciled in the future.

15.9 **Conclusion**

Although the phenomenon of multilingualism has only recently begun to attract the attention of psycholinguistic researchers, the available studies on multilingual lexical processing in comprehension and production have already touched upon several issues that may have important consequences for monolingual processing views or are theoretically relevant in their own right. The available functional models so far have focused mainly on lexical retrieval itself. In the near future, they will have to find ways to account for effects of linguistic and non-linguistic context, task demands, and stimulus composition as well. The models will also need to be extended or reformulated to include information about when, where, and how in the brain context-sensitive lexical processing takes place. Because of the brain's complexity, it will take time before the various factors involved are disentangled and the goal of a unified bilingual processing model can be reached. Nevertheless, it is encouraging that by and large the available empirical evidence involving various types of stimulus, modality, task, and language combinations appears to reflect similar underlying processing mechanisms.

References

Abutalebi, J., and Green, D. (forthcoming) Bilingual language production: The neurocognition of language representation and control. *Brain and Language.*

Aitchison, J. (1987) Words in the Mind: An Introduction to the Mental Lexicon. Blackwell, Oxford.

Akker, E., and Dijkstra, A. (forthcoming) Interlingual homophone effects in bilingual auditory word recognition. [working title]

Altarriba, J., Kroll, J. F., Sholl, A., and Rayner, K. (1996) The influence of lexical and conceptual constraints on reading mixed-language sentences: evidence from eye fixations and naming times. *Memory and Cognition,* 24: 477–92.

Altarriba, J., and Mathis, K. M. (1997) Conceptual and lexical development in second language acquisition. *Journal of Memory and Language,* 36: 550–68.

Caramazza, A. (1997) How many levels of processing are there in lexical access? *Cognitive Neuropsychology,* 14: 177–208.

Colomé, A. (2001) Lexical activation in bilinguals' speech production: language-specific or language-independent? *Journal of Memory and Language,* 45: 721–36.

Coltheart, M., Davelaar, E., Jonasson, J. T., and Besner, D. (1977) Access to the internal lexicon. In S. Dornic (ed.), *Attention and Performance,* vol. VI, pp. 535–55. Academic Press, New York.

Costa, A., and Caramazza, A. (1999) Is lexical selection in bilingual speech production language specific? Further evidence from Spanish-English and English-Spanish bilinguals. *Bilingualism: Language and Cognition,* 3: 231–43.

Costa, A., Caramazza, A., and Sebastián-Gallés, N. (2000) The cognate facilitation effect: Implications for models of lexical access. *Journal of Experimental Psychology: Learning, Memory, and Cognition,* 26: 1283–96.

Costa, A., and Santesteban, M. (2004) Lexical access in bilingual speech production: evidence from language switching in highly proficient bilinguals and L2 learners. *Journal of Memory and Language,* 50: 491–511.

Cristoffanini, P., Kirsner, K., and Milech, D. (1986) Bilingual lexical representation: the status of Spanish–English cognates. *Quarterly Journal of Experimental Psychology,* 38A: 367–93.

De Bot, K. (1992) A bilingual production model: Levelt's "Speaking" model adapted. *Applied Linguistics,* 13: 1–24.

De Bot, K. (2004) The multilingual lexicon: modeling selection and control. *International Journal of Multilingualism,* 1: 17–32.

De Groot, A. M. B., Borgwaldt, S., Bos, M., and Van den Eijnden, E. (2002) Lexical decision and word naming in bilinguals: language effects and task effects. *Journal of Memory and Language,* 47: 91–124.

De Groot, A. M. B., Delmaar, P., and Lupker, S. J. (2000) The processing of interlexical homographs in a bilingual and a monolingual task: support for nonselective access to bilingual memory. *Quarterly Journal of Experimental Psychology,* 53: 397–428.

De Swaan, A. (2001) *Woorden van de wereld: het mondiale talenstelsel* [Words of the World: The Global Language System]. Amsterdam: Bert Bakker & Leonoor Broeder.

Dijkstra, A. (2003) Lexical processing in bilinguals and multilinguals: the word selection problem. In J. Cenoz, B. Hufeisen, and U. Jessner (eds), *The Multilingual Lexicon,* pp. 11–26. Kluwer Academic, Dordrecht.

Dijkstra, A., Baayen, H., Brummelhuis, B., and Lemhöfer, K. (2007) Orthographic and phonological cross-linguistic similarity affects cognate processing in a task-dependent way. MS.

Dijkstra, A., De Bruijn, E., Schriefers, H. J., and Ten Brinke, S. (2000) More on interlingual homograph recognition: language intermixing versus explicitness of instruction. *Bilingualism: Language and Cognition,* 3: 69–78.

Dijkstra, A., Grainger, J., and Van Heuven, W. J. B. (1999) Recognition of cognates and interlingual homographs: the neglected role of phonology. *Journal of Memory and Language,* 41: 496–518.

Dijkstra, A., Timmermans, M., and Schriefers, H. (2000) On being blinded by your other language: effects of task demands on interlingual homograph recognition. *Journal of Memory and Language,* 42: 445–64.

Dijkstra, A., Van Hell, J. G., and Brenders, P. (2007) Recognition of non-identical cognates in L1 and L2 sentence contexts: RT and ERP data. MS.

Dijkstra, A., and Van Heuven, W. J. B. (1998) The BIA model and bilingual word recognition. In J. Grainger and A. M. Jacobs (eds), *Localist Connectionist Approaches to Human Cognition*, pp. 189–225. Erlbaum, Mahwah, NJ.

Dijkstra, A., and Van Heuven, W. J. B. (2002) The architecture of the bilingual word recognition system: from identification to decision. *Bilingualism: Language and Cognition,* 5: 175–97.

Dijkstra, A., and Van Heuven, W. J. B. (2006) On language and brain! Or on (psycho)linguists and neuroscientists? Comments on A. Rodriguez-Fornells et al., in *Language Learning,* 56: 191–8.

Dijkstra, A., Van Jaarsveld, H., and Ten Brinke, S. (1998) Interlingual homograph recognition: effects of task demands and language intermixing. *Bilingualism: Language and Cognition,* 1: 51–66.

Flege, J. E. (1987) The production of "new" and "similar" phones in a foreign language: evidence for the effect of equivalence classification. *Journal of Phonetics,* 15: 47–65.

Font, N. (2001) Rôle de la langue dans l'accès au lexique chez les bilingues: influence de la proximité orthographique et sémantique interlangue sur la reconnaissance visuelle de mots. Doctoral thesis, Université Paul Valéry, Montpellier, France.

French, R. M. (1998) A Simple Recurrent Network model of bilingual memory. In *Proceedings of the Twentieth Annual Cognitive Science Society Conference*, pp. 368–73. Erlbaum, Mahwah, NJ.

Friel, B. M., and Kennison, S. M. (2001) Identifying German–English cognates, false cognates, and non-cognates: methodological issues and descriptive norms. *Bilingualism: Language and Cognition,* 4: 249–74.

Gerard, L. D., and Scarborough, D. L. (1989) Language-specific lexical access of homographs by bilinguals. *Journal of Experimental Psychology: Learning, Memory and Cognition,* 15: 305–13.

Gollan, T., Forster, K. I., and Frost, R. (1997) Translation priming with different scripts: masked priming with cognates and noncognates in Hebrew–English bilinguals. *Journal of Experimental Psychology: Learning, Memory, and Cognition,* 23: 1122–39.

Grainger, J., and Beauvillain, C. (1987) Language blocking and lexical access in bilinguals. *Quarterly Journal of Experimental Psychology,* 39A, 295–319.

Green, D. W. (1998) Mental control of the bilingual lexico-semantic system. *Bilingualism: Language and Cognition,* 1: 67–81.

Grosjean, F. (1988) Exploring the recognition of guest words in bilingual speech. *Language and Cognitive Processes,* 3: 233–74.

Hermans, D., Bongaerts, T., De Bot, K., and Schreuder, R. (1998) Producing words in a foreign language: can speakers prevent interference from their first language? *Bilingualism: Language and Cognition,* 1: 213–29.

Hernandez, A. E. and Kohnert, K. (1999) Aging and language switching in bilinguals. *Aging, Neuropsychology, and Cognition,* 6: 69–83.

Jared, D. (2005) Phonological activation in bilingual word recognition. Paper presented at 5th International Symposium on Bilingualism, Barcelona, March.

Kerkhofs, R., Dijkstra, A., Chwilla, D. J., and De Bruijn, E. R. A. (2006) Testing a model for bilingual semantic priming with interlingual homographs: RT and ERP effects. *Journal of Cognitive Brain Research,* 1068: 170–83.

Kim, J., and Davis, C. (2003) Task effects in masked cross-script translation and phonological priming. *Journal of Memory and Language,* 49: 484–99.

Kolers, P. A. (1966) Reading and talking bilingually. *American Journal of Psychology,* 79: 357–77.

Kroll, J. F. and De Groot, A. (1997) Lexical and conceptual memory in the bilingual: mapping form to meaning in two languages. In A. M. B. De Groot and J. F. Kroll (eds), *Tutorials in Bilingualism: Psycholinguistic Perspectives,* pp. 169–99. Erlbaum, Mahwah, NJ.

Kroll, J. F., and Dijkstra, A. (2002) The bilingual lexicon. In R. Kaplan (eds), *Handbook of Applied Linguistics,* pp. 301–21. Oxford University Press, Oxford.

Kroll, J. F., Dijkstra, A, Janssen, N., and Schriefers, H. J. (1999) Cross-language lexical activity during production: evidence from cued picture naming. In A. Vandierendonck, M. Brysbaert, and K. Van der Goten (eds), *Proceedings of the 11th Congress of the European Society for Cognitive Psychology*, p. 92. ESCOP/ Academic Press, Ghent.

Kroll, J. F., Michael, E., Tokowicz, N., and Dufour, R. (2002) The development of lexical fluency in a second language. *Second Language Research,* 18: 137–71.

Kroll, J. F., and Stewart, E. (1994) Category interference in translation and picture naming: evidence for asymmetric connections between bilingual memory representations. *Journal of Memory and Language,* 33: 149–74.

La Heij, W. (2005) Selection processes in monolingual and bilingual lexical access. In J. F. Kroll and A. M. B. De Groot (eds), *Handbook of Bilingualism: Psycholinguistic Approaches*, pp. 289–307. Oxford University Press, Oxford.

La Heij, W., Kerling, R., and Van der Velden, E. (1996) Nonverbal context effects in forward and backward translation: evidence for concept mediation. *Journal of Memory and Language,* 35: 648–65.

Lemhöfer, K., Dijkstra, A., Schriefers, H., Grainger, J., and Zwitserlood, P. (207) Native language influences on word recognition in a second language: a mega-study. MS.

Levelt, W. J. M., Roelofs, A., and Meyer, A. S. (1999) A theory of lexical access in speech production. *Behavioral and Brain Sciences,* 21: 1–38.

Léwy, N., Grosjean, F., Grosjean, L., Racine, I., and Yersin, C. (2005) Un modèle psycholinguistique informatique de la reconnaissance des mots dans la chaîne parlée du français. *French Language Studies,* 15: 25–48.

Li, P. (1996) Spoken word recognition of code-switched words by Chinese-English bilinguals. *Journal of Memory and Language,* 35: 757–74.

Li, P., and Farkas, I. (2000) A self-organizing connectionist model of bilingual processing. In R. Heredia and J. Altarriba (eds), *Bilingual Sentence Processing*, pp. 59–98. North-Holland/ Elsevier Science, Amsterdam.

MacNamara, J., Krauthammer, M., and Bolgar, M. (1968) Language switching in bilinguals as a function of stimulus and response uncertainty. *Journal of Experimental Psychology*, 78: 208–15.

Meuter, R. F. I., and Allport, A. (1999) Bilingual language switching in naming: asymmetrical costs of language selection. *Journal of Memory and Language*, 40: 25–40.

Pallier, Ch., Colomé, A., and Sebastián-Gallès, N. (2001) The influence of native-language phonology on lexical access: exemplar-based versus abstract lexical entries. *Psychological Science*, 12: 445–9.

Poulisse, N., and Bongaerts, T. (1994) First language use in second language production. *Applied Linguistics*, 15: 36–57.

Ransdell, S. E., and Fischler, I. (1987) Memory in a monolingual mode: when are bilinguals at a disadvantage? *Journal of Memory and Language*, 26: 392–405.

Rodriguez-Fornells, A., Rotte, M., Heinze, H.-J., Nösselt, T., & Münte, T. F. (2002) Brain potential and functional MRI evidence for how to handle two languages with one brain. *Nature*, 415: 1026–9.

Sánchez-Casas, R., and García-Albea, J. E. (2005) The representation of cognate and noncognate words in bilingual memory: can cognate status be characterized as a special kind of morphological relation? In J. F. Kroll and A. M. B. De Groot (eds), *Handbook of Bilingualism: Psycholinguistic Approaches*, pp. 226–50. Oxford University Press, Oxford.

Schulpen, B., Dijkstra, A., Schriefers, H. J., and Hasper, M. (2003) Recognition of interlingual homophones in bilingual auditory word recognition. *Journal of Experimental Psychology: Human Perception and Performance*, 29: 1155–78.

Schwartz, A. I., and Kroll, J. F. (2006). Bilingual lexical activation in sentence context. *Journal of Memory and Language*, 55: 197–212.

Sholl, A., Sankaranarayanan, A., and Kroll, J. F. (1995) Transfer between picture naming and translation: a test of asymmetries in bilingual memory. *Psychological Science*, 6: 45–9.

Smits., E., Martensen, H., Dijkstra, A., and Sandra, D. (2006) Naming interlingual homographs: variable competition and the role of the decision system. *Bilingualism: Language and Cognition*, 9: 281–97.

Spivey, M. J. and Marian, V. (1999) Cross talk between native and second languages: partial activation of an irrelevant lexicon. *Psychological Science*, 10: 281–4.

Thomas, M. S. C. and Allport, A. (2000) Language switching costs in bilingual visual word recognition. *Journal of Memory and Language*, 43: 44–66.

Van Hell, J. G. (1998) Cross-language processing and bilingual memory organization. Doctoral thesis, University of Amsterdam.

Van Hell, J. G., and Dijkstra, A. (2002) Foreign language knowledge can influence native language performance in exclusively native contexts. *Psychonomic Bulletin and Review*, 9: 780–9.

Van Heuven, W. J. B., Dijkstra, A., and Grainger, J. (1998) Orthographic neighborhood effects in bilingual word recognition. *Journal of Memory and Language*, 39: 458–83.

Van Heuven, W. J. B., Schriefers, H. J., Dijkstra, A., and Hagoort, P. (2007) Language conflict in the bilingual brain. MS.

Van Wijnendaele, I., and Brysbaert, M. (2002) Visual word recognition in bilinguals: phonological priming from the second to the first language. *Journal of Experimental Psychology: Human Perception and Performance*, 28: 616–27.

Von Studnitz, R. E., and Green, D. W. (1997) Lexical decision and language switching. *International Journal of Bilingualism*, 1: 3–24.

Weber, A., and Cutler, A. (2004) Lexical competition in non-native spoken-word recognition. *Journal of Memory and Language*, 50: 1–25.

Zwitserlood, P., Dijkstra, A., and Lemhöfer, K. (2007) Separate contributions of form and meaning in bilingual word recognition: Evidence from auditory priming. MS.

CHAPTER 16

The biocognition of the mental lexicon

Michael T. Ullman

16.1 Introduction

The mental lexicon is rooted in the biology of the brain. Therefore, understanding the biological bases of the lexicon is critical for a full understanding of the lexicon itself. The vast majority of research on the biology of the mental lexicon and other aspects of language has thus far focused on the level of structural brain anatomy. However, the roles of many other substrates, from cells to molecules to genes, must also be elucidated. Moreover, the study of the biology of language should be complemented by and integrated with investigations of language acquisition; psycholinguistic studies of how language is actually used as we speak and understand; and the theoretical linguistic examination of the architecture of language. Finally, because evidence suggests that important language and *non*-language functions are subserved by common neurocognitive substrates, our vast *independent* knowledge of the biology of the brain and its role in other cognitive functions in both humans and animals is likely to lead to novel predictions about language—predictions that would be far less likely to be entertained in the isolated study of language alone. Taken together, the integrated investigation of these different aspects of language and non-language functions should lead to a full understanding of the biocognitive (that is, neurocognitive, across all biological levels) bases of the mental lexicon and other aspects of language.

One can ask a number of different questions about the biocognition of the mental lexicon. Here we focus on four broad issues, most—but not all—of which have been and continue to be major areas of research: biological substrates, separability, redundancy, and domain-specificity. (Other important issues are covered in other chapters; see e.g. Indefrey, Chapter 33 this volume, for discussion of the spatio-temporal dynamics of lexical processing, i.e. which brain structures perform which functions in which time periods during real-time lexical processing.) In each case, we first examine the nature of the issue and then summarize evidence relevant to the mental lexicon and discuss competing theoretical explanations that have been proposed to account for this evidence. Because a variety of methods can be used to examine the biological bases of language, and because each method has a different set of strengths and weaknesses, it is imperative to examine whether different methods point to the same conclusion. Therefore findings from multiple methodological approaches are presented throughout the chapter.

16.2 Biological substrates

What anatomical structures, cytoarchitectonic regions, brain networks, neuron types, neurotransmitters, hormones, receptors, genes, and other biological substrates does the mental lexicon depend on, and what specific functional roles does each substrate play? This wide-ranging question reflects the many levels at which the *functional biology* of the lexicon can and should be investigated.

Although the biological substrates of the lexicon can be studied at all of these levels, the *functional neuroanatomy* of language has been by far the most intensively examined. The goal here is to *map* language, or particular aspects of language such as the lexicon, to the brain. Because different parts of the brain underlie different cognitive functions, this mapping enterprise generally involves trying to localize particular language functions to particular brain regions. The most common approach is to map language and other cognitive functions to anatomical structures such as specific gyri, sulci, or subcortical structures in one or the other hemisphere. Indeed, a variety of methods—such as the lesion method (examining impaired and spared functions in individuals with brain damage), Positron Emission Tomography (PET), and functional Magnetic Resonance Imaging (fMRI)—lend themselves quite well to such structure–function mapping.

In principle one can also map language to particular cytoarchitectonic regions in the brain such as those designated by Brodmann's areas (BAs). (Cytoarchitechtonic regions are distinguished by their cellular makeup, i.e. the types and distributions of the nerve cells found within them.) However, the lack of appropriate methods for identifying cytoarchitectonics in a living brain generally precludes this approach. Note that while BAs are widely referred to in the functional neuroanatomy literature, they are almost always used as convenient labels for structural brain regions rather than as actual cytoarchitectonic claims.

The molecular substrates of language, such as the specific types of hormones, neurotransmitters, receptors, and genes that underlie lexical and other linguistic functions, can also be examined. Moreover, evidence suggests that many of these substrates have particular regional distributions in the brain. For example, the *FOXP2* gene, which plays an important role in certain aspects of language (Marcus and Fisher, 2003; Ullman and Pierpont, 2005; Vargha-Khadem et al., 2005), seems to be expressed particularly in the caudate nucleus in the basal ganglia, especially in the developing brain (Bruce and Margolis, 2002; Lai et al., 2003; Takahashi et al., 2003). Similarly, the neurotransmitter dopamine is particularly prevalent in frontal cortex, the basal ganglia, and certain other structures. Thus one can also localize the molecular substrates of language. Importantly, because much is known about the biology of molecules in the brain, and their roles in non-language functions in both humans and animals, one can make novel predictions about their potential roles in lexical functioning—including pharmacological (drug) effects, which are especially important for the remediation of language disorders.

16.2.1 The temporal lobes are critical for the mental lexicon

The use of lexical knowledge depends heavily on the temporal lobes, mainly but not exclusively in the left hemisphere. Focal brain damage from acute lesions has long pointed to this important role of temporal cortex (Alexander, 1997; Damasio, 1992; Dronkers et al., 2000; Farah and Grossman, 1997). Patients whose damage is relatively restricted to the temporal lobes from degenerative disease, such as in Alzheimer's disease and semantic dementia, also have severe lexical deficits (Bozeat et al., 2000; Nebes, 1997; Ullman, 2004). Numerous PET and fMRI neuroimaging studies have reported activation in temporal-lobe regions during tasks which involve processing word forms or meanings, or even word-specific grammatical knowledge such as argument structure (Bookheimer et al., 1993; Damasio et al., 1996; Kuperberg et al., 2000; Martin et al., 2000; Newman et al., 2001; Wise et al., 1991). Temporal lobe activation in neuroimaging studies is observed during lexical tasks both in receptive language (listening or reading) and in expressive language (speaking), such as when subjects name pictures of objects. In event-related potential (ERP) studies, manipulations of lexical factors such as word frequency or meaning affect the "N400" component, which has been tied to temporal lobe structures (Friederici et al., 1998; Hagoort and Kutas, 1995; Kutas and Hillyard, 1980; Segalowitz and Chevalier, 1998a; 1998b). For example, larger N400s are generated by lower-frequency words (those that have been heard or seen less often, e.g. *newt* as compared to *frog*) and words that are more concrete (e.g. *raccoon* as compared to *country*) (Rugg, 1990; West and Holcomb, 2000). Direct brain recording and magnetoencephalography (MEG) have shown that lexical processing depends on neural activity in various temporal lobe regions (McCarthy et al., 1995; Nobre et al., 1994; Simos et al., 1997). Evidence from brain stimulation has also implicated the temporal lobes. For example, a recent study reported that direct brain stimulation of certain temporal-lobe areas impaired the naming of objects and actions (Corina et al., 2005). In another experiment, the repetitive transcranial magnetic stimulation (rTMS) of Wernicke's area (generally taken to correspond to the posterior portion of left superior temporal cortex) actually speeded up performance in a picture naming task (Mottaghy et al., 1999).

However, not all lexically related functions depend on the same set of temporal lobe structures.

The use of phonological word forms, and perhaps phonological and/or phonetic processing more generally, relies heavily on mid-to-posterior superior temporal cortex (i.e. mid-to-posterior BA 22; see Figures 16.1 and 16.2; Hickok and Poeppel, 2004; Indefrey and Cutler, 2004; Scott and Wise, 2004). This region has been implicated in these functions in both hemispheres. Although it is commonly assumed that the left hemisphere is dominant for all aspects of phonological processing, a number of studies have shown that left-hemisphere dominance varies with the task being carried out. Thus while phonological processing in speech production appears to be left-dominant, both left and right superior temporal regions are involved during auditory comprehension—although the two sides seem to play somewhat different roles. For example, some research suggests that the left side detects rapid acoustic changes such as those found in formants, whereas the right is more important for detecting slow changes, like those that often occur in prosody (Hickok and Poeppel, 2004).

The use of conceptual-semantic knowledge, as well as of non-phonological lexical information stored in lexical entries, seems to be supported by cortical areas largely distinct from the superior temporal region that underlies word forms and phonology. These conceptual/lexical areas include temporal cortex in front of and below the phonological region, with a somewhat greater role on the left than the right side (Indefrey and Cutler, 2004; Martin and Chao, 2001). For example, in neuroimaging studies this cortical area is activated bilaterally, but especially on the left, by processing real words, whereas the phonological region is engaged by pseudo-words like *blick*, whose phonological word forms are presumably not accompanied by meanings or lexical entries (Indefrey and Cutler, 2004).

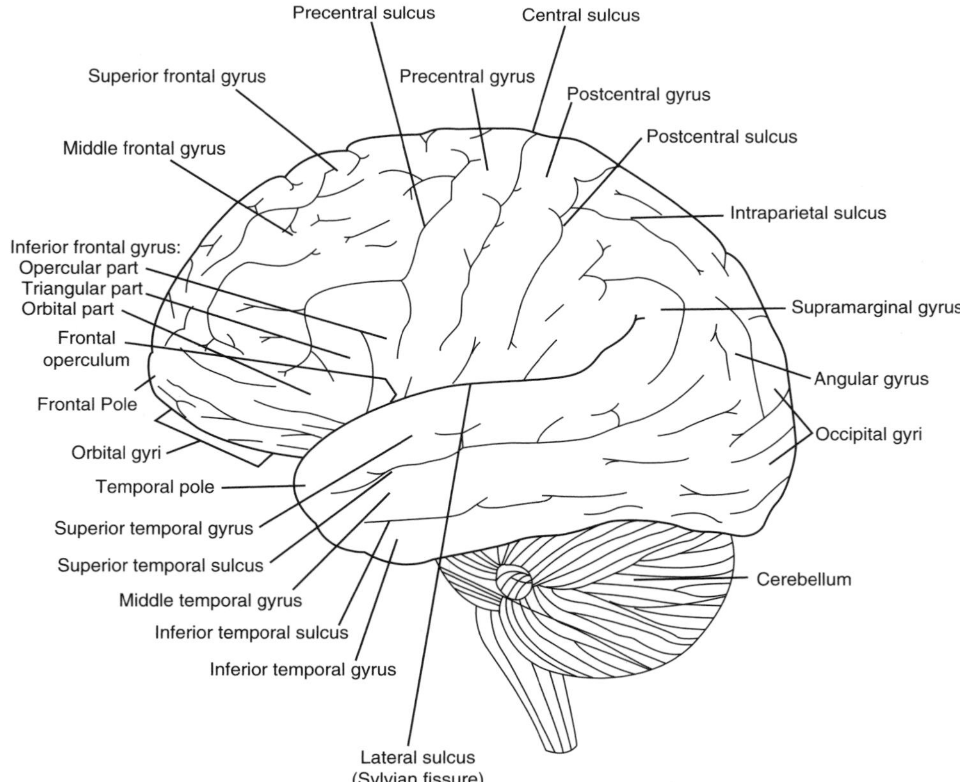

Figure 16.1 A lateral view of anatomical structures in the left hemispheres of the cerebrum and the cerebellum. The same structures are found on the right side.

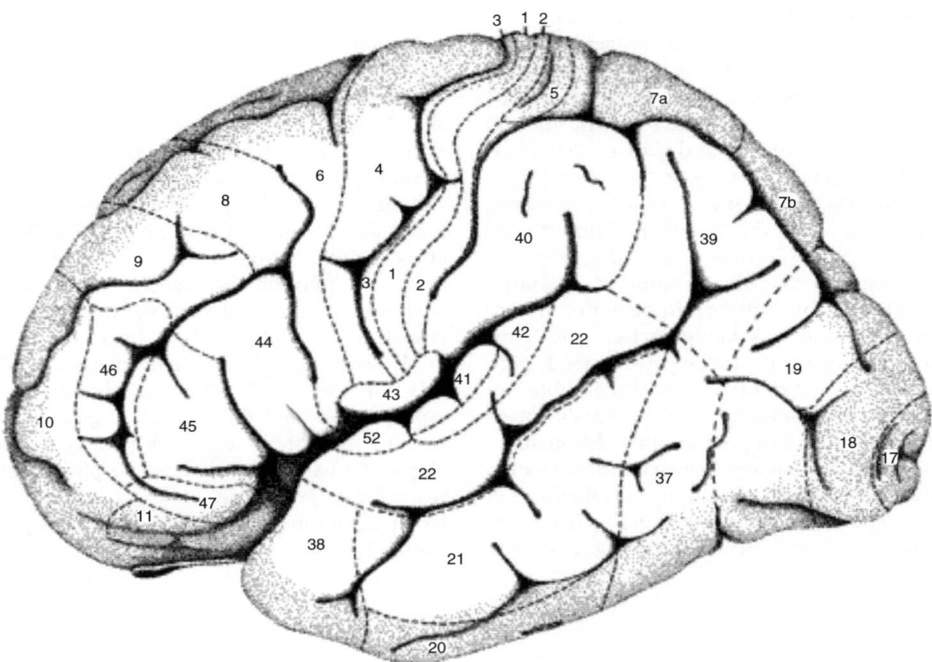

Figure 16.2 Brodmann's areas of the lateral part of the left hemisphere. The same areas are found in the right hemisphere. Not shown are Brodmann's areas in the ventral and medial portions of the cerebrum.

16.2.2 Beyond the temporal lobes: the role of other brain structures

The temporal lobes are not the only brain structures that underlie aspects of lexically related knowledge and processing. Evidence suggests that phonological word forms and phonology depend not just on mid-to-posterior superior temporal cortex, but also on nearby cortex in the supramarginal gyrus (BA40), as well as a frontal region near the boundary of BA6 and BA44 that seems to play a role in phonological working memory (holding and rehearsing information actively in mind, such as one might do with a phone number after looking it up and before dialing it) (Martin et al., 2003; McDermott et al., 2003).

Other cortical as well as subcortical and cerebellar structures seem to play other functional roles in lexical processing. The right cerebellum (which is closely connected to the left rather than the right hemisphere of the cerebrum) may underlie searching for lexical knowledge (Desmond and Fiez, 1998). Retrieving or selecting this knowledge instead appears to depend on portions of the basal ganglia and the inferior frontal gyrus—i.e. BA47 and Broca's area (which is generally taken to correspond to the opercular and triangular parts of the inferior frontal gyrus, which in turn largely correspond to BA44 and BA45, respectively) (Buckner, 2000; Fiez, 1997; Friederici, 2002; Poldrack et al., 1999; Thompson-Schill et al., 1997; Ullman, 2006b). Additionally, a much more anterior frontal region (BA10) may be involved in the verification or monitoring of retrieved items (Buckner et al., 1998).

Evidence that these structures underlie these lexical functions has been provided by a variety of methodological approaches, including PET and fMRI neuroimaging (Buckner, 2000; Fiez, 1997; Halgren et al., 2002; Poldrack et al., 1999; Thompson-Schill et al., 1997). For example, in one fMRI experiment subjects were instructed to complete word fragments like STA___ or PSA___. Fragments with few possible completions, like PSA___, elicited more right cerebellar activation than fragments with many possible completions, like STA___, possibly reflecting the difficulty in searching for an appropriate word (Desmond et al., 1998). Investigations of both adult-onset brain damage and developmental disorders also support these functional roles. For example, individuals with acute lesions to inferior frontal cortex, and patients with Parkinson's disease (who suffer from the degeneration of neurons that project to frontal and basal ganglia structures), generally have word-finding trouble, but have less difficulty in recognizing words, consistent with a role for these regions in lexical selection or retrieval (Alexander, 1997; Matison et al., 1982). Similarly, children with Specific Language Impairment, in which Broca's area and the basal ganglia are abnormal, have trouble recalling words but are largely spared in their lexical knowledge (Ullman and Pierpont, 2005).

Interestingly, *within* inferior frontal cortex, BA44 might play a role in selecting competing lexical alternatives, while the more anterior/ventral area (BA45/47) underlies their retrieval (Thompson-Schill et al., 1997). For example, BA44 has been found to be activated more during the selection of words that have more competing alternatives—for example, trying to think of a verb that relates to *wheel*, where there are many alternatives (*turn*, *spin*, *roll*, etc.), as compared to thinking of a verb that relates to *scissors* (for which most people think of *cut*) (Thompson-Schill et al., 1997). It has also been suggested that BA 45/47 may be involved more broadly in retrieving and maintaining lexical and semantic representations in working memory (Gabrieli et al., 1998; Wagner, 1999).

16.2.3 Of lions and tigers and hammers

Evidence suggests that words from different conceptual categories depend on different networks of brain structures (Damasio et al., 1996; Martin and Chao, 2001; Warrington and Shallice, 1984). Specifically, word meanings seem to depend on cortex adjacent to areas that underlie the sensory or motor functions that are linked to these meanings. These cortical regions are also activated by *non*-linguistic tasks, such as object recognition or even mental imagery, related to the same concepts. For example, words denoting items with strong visual attributes such as form or color involve a temporal-occipital ventral area just in front of visual cortex. In fact, specific subregions of this area, and even individual neurons associated with it, seem to be specialized for different types of categories in which visual form is important, such as animals (e.g. lions and tigers), faces, and houses (Chao et al., 1999; Kreiman et al., 2000; Martin and Chao, 2001).

Similarly, posterior lateral temporal regions just in front of an area implicated in motion perception are activated by naming tools (such as hammers), actions, and verbs, as well as simply perceiving or remembering these items (Chao et al., 1999; Martin and Chao, 2001; Martin et al., 1995). Moreover, patients with damage to this area (Damasio et al., 1996), or subjects with direct brain stimulation in this region (Corina et al., 2005), have particular trouble naming these types of items. Interestingly, within this posterior temporal region, an area around the superior temporal sulcus may play a role for items with biological motion, such as animals or humans, whereas an area just below it in middle temporal cortex may be more important for items with non-biological motion, such as tools (Martin and Chao, 2001).

Motor and premotor regions are also important in processing movement related words. In neuroimaging studies, naming tools and actions activate ventral premotor cortex, around BA6 and BA44, a region that is also involved in actual movement, as well as in the mental imagery of movement (Gerardin et al., 2000; Grafton et al., 1996; Martin and Chao, 2001). Additionally, in high-resolution electroencephalography (EEG) studies, action verbs have been found to elicit brain activity over motor regions that represent the body parts involved in those actions. For example, leg-related verbs like *walk* elicit activity around the leg area of motor cortex, whereas speaking-related verbs like *talk* elicit activity around the mouth area of motor cortex (Pulvermuller et al., 2001).

16.2.4 Nouns and verbs in the brain

A neuroanatomical difference appears to exist between nouns and verbs (Gainotti, 1998; Pulvermuller et al., 1996; Shapiro and Caramazza, 2004). Whereas verbs are strongly linked to left frontal cortex, nouns depend on more posterior regions, in left temporal or occipital regions. For example, patients with frontal lesions often have more difficulty producing verbs, whereas the opposite holds for those with left temporal damage (Gainotti, 1998; Shapiro and Caramazza, 2004). The reasons for this dichotomy are not yet clear, and may involve one or more factors, including lexical, conceptual-semantic, and grammatical differences between nouns and verbs. The *lexical-grammatical* hypothesis argues that lexical knowledge in the brain is organized anatomically according to grammatical word category, such as noun and verb (Caramazza and Hillis, 1991; Miceli et al., 1984). *Semantic* hypotheses suggest instead that the dissociations reflect differences in the conceptual semantics of nouns and verbs rather than the word category distinction itself. For example, the dissociation may reflect the fact that verbs tend to represent actions (which are associated with frontal motor regions; see above), whereas nouns often represent visualizable objects (which are associated with temporal lobe regions; see above) (Damasio and Tranel, 1993). Alternatively, *morphosyntactic* hypotheses suggest that verbs and nouns differentially depend on morphosyntactic processes that involve frontal lobe structures (Shapiro and Caramazza, 2004; Tyler et al., 2004). It remains to be seen which of these perspectives, or perhaps others, will ultimately explain the data best.

16.2.5 Do proper names depend on a different brain region?

Evidence from both lesion and neuroimaging studies suggest that anterior temporal regions, in particular the temporal pole (BA38), may play a particularly important role in the use of proper nouns, such as people's names (Damasio et al., 1996). Although it is not yet clear what best accounts for this observation, it may be due (at least in part) to a specialization of this region for unique or subordinate level conceptual knowledge, including not just individuals, but also broader subordinate categories such as golden retriever (as opposed to dog or animal) or Phillips screwdriver (as opposed to tool) (Gauthier et al., 1997).

16.2.6 Learning words involves medial temporal lobe structures

Evidence suggests that word learning depends on medial temporal lobe structures, including the hippocampus. Neuroimaging studies show that activation increases in these regions while people are learning words (Breitenstein et al., 2005). Patients with anterograde amnesia, which is associated with damage to the hippocampus and other medial temporal lobe structures, are impaired at learning new word forms or meanings. For example, the well-studied amnesic patient H.M., most of whose medial temporal lobe structures were surgically removed from both hemispheres, has profound deficits learning new word forms and new conceptual knowledge. Thus, he does not appear to have any knowledge of words like *nerd*, *granola*, or *bikini* which entered the English language after his surgery in 1953 (Postle and Corkin, 1998).

16.2.7 Acetylcholine and estrogen modulate aspects of the lexicon and conceptual semantics

The neurotransmitter acetylcholine, which plays an important role in hippocampal function, seems to be implicated in aspects of word learning. For example, the drug scopolamine, which blocks acetylcholine, impairs the ability to memorize word forms, while leaving working memory and the processing of previously learned lexical-semantic knowledge relatively intact (Curran, 2000; Hasselmo et al., 1996; Nissen et al., 1987). Patients with Alzheimer's disease, which involves a severe loss of acetylcholine activity in the hippocampus, are particularly impaired at learning new word forms and meanings (Nebes, 1997). However, giving these patients acetylcholinesterase inhibitors, which increase the amount of acetylcholine in synapses, improves these learning abilities (Freo et al., 2002).

Evidence suggests that estrogen also modulates aspects of the acquisition and processing of lexical and conceptual-semantic knowledge. Estrogen therapy can improve the ability of postmenopausal women to remember word forms and to generate lists of words in a category (verbal fluency; e.g. "in the next thirty seconds, name all the words you can think of that start with the letter S") (Grodstein et al., 2000; Resnick et al., 1998). Neuroimaging studies have linked such improvements to medial temporal lobe structures (Maki and Resnick, 2000). Giving estrogen to men can also help them at these tasks (Miles et al., 1998). And prior to menopause, women are better at such lexical tasks when they are at high estrogen levels in their menstrual cycle than at low levels (Hampson, 1990; Kimura, 1999).

These and related estrogen effects may be at least partly explained via the action of acetylcholine (Packard, 1998; Shughrue et al., 2000) and/or brain derived neurotrophic factor (BDNF) (Scharfman and MacLusky, 2005). Indeed, this protein, which plays an important role in memory-related modifications in the hippocampus (i.e. long-term potentiation, or LTP) (Poo, 2001), has been directly implicated in verbal memory. For example, individuals with the *val* as opposed to the *met* allele of the val66met single nucleotide polymorphism in the BDNF gene have been found to show superior performance at remembering new verbal material (Egan et al., 2003; Hariri et al., 2003; Pezawas et al., 2004).

16.3 Separability

A major question in the study of language is whether different language functions depend on distinct or common biocognitive substrates. This question tends to divide researchers into contrasting camps of "splitters" and "lumpers." The splitters argue that different aspects of language depend on distinct biocognitive correlates. Various researchers have suggested a wide range of language splits, including grammar vs. lexicon, morphology vs. syntax, syntactic knowledge vs. syntactic processing, and lexical acquisition vs. lexical knowledge. According to the splitters, these various linguistic domains or functions are *separable*. That is, each one depends largely on its own biocognitive substrates, which can operate for the most part independently from the substrates that subserve other language functions. In contrast, lumpers deny separability, and suggest instead that different aspects of language share common neurocognitive correlates.

Of course many intermediate positions can be taken between the far-lumpers and the far-splitters. For example, one view admits the existence of distinct biocognitive substrates for distinct language or language-related functions, such as phonology and semantics, but argues that these interact to such an extent that they are functionally inseparable with respect to their computational roles in many language functions (McClelland and Patterson, 2002). Alternatively, it has been suggested that there exists a major neurocognitive split between lexical memory and rule-governed grammatical combination, and that this split holds *across* multiple aspects of language, including syntax, morphology, and phonology (see below, and Ullman, 2001c; 2004; Ullman and Pierpont, 2005).

We have seen above that there is substantial separability *within* the mental lexicon, namely between different types of lexically related functions. Thus we saw that there appear to be different temporal-lobe regions for phonological word forms vs. lexical-conceptual and abstract lexical knowledge; distinct brain structures, including inferior frontal, basal ganglia, and cerebellar structures, for lexical retrieval, selection, and search; separate cortical regions for words that represent different conceptual categories, based on the categories' sensory and motor attributes; frontal regions for verbs vs. temporal/occipital regions for nouns (or some sort of analogous conceptual or grammatical distinction); and medial temporal structures for the acquisition of lexical knowledge vs. neocortical regions for the storage or processing of that knowledge after it has been learned. So, even when we restrict our focus to the lexicon, there appears to be substantial separability among different linguistic functions. However, it is important to keep in mind that this separability does *not* imply that any of the brain structures that underlie these various lexical functions subserve *only* these functions (see discussion of domain-specificity below, section 16.5).

Evidence also indicates at least some degree of separability *between* lexical abilities and certain other linguistic functions. Thus the neurocognitive data suggest at least some separability between syntactic processing on the one hand and lexical/semantic and phonological processing on the other (Friederici, 2002; Ullman, 2004; 2006a). However, given the fact that these latter functions are *also* required in syntactic processing, they are likely to be engaged in syntactic processing studies as well. Therefore, clear neurocognitive dissociations between syntax and these lexically related functions are not always expected. For example, whereas BA45/47 and anterior temporal cortex are critical in lexical and semantic processing, they also play roles in sentence processing, albeit roles that seem to reflect their apparently core lexical and semantic functions (Friederici, 2002; Ullman, 2004; 2006b).

16.3.1 Regular and irregular morphology

Because of the difficulty in distinguishing syntactic from lexical processes, much recent attention has focused on the distinction between regular and irregular morphophonology. According to "dual-system" hypotheses, irregular inflected and derived forms (e.g. *kept*, *mice*, *solemnity*) depend on representations that are stored in the mental lexicon, whereas regular forms (e.g. *walked*, *rats*, *happiness*) can be (but are not necessarily; see discussion below on redundancy) computed by neurocognitively distinct rule-governed processes that combine discrete elements, and may also underlie composition in syntax (Clahsen, 1999; Pinker, 1999; Pinker and Ullman, 2002; Ullman, 2001c).

In contrast, "single-mechanism" hypotheses deny such a morphological distinction between storage and composition, arguing instead that all forms depend on the same computational mechanisms—i.e. statistical learning mechanisms that can be modeled by connectionist ("neural network") simulations (Joanisse and Seidenberg, 1999; Plunkett and Marchman, 1991;

Rumelhart and McClelland, 1986). On this view, both regular and irregular forms may be thought of as being learned, represented, and processed in lexical memory. For example, according to one single-mechanism model, regulars and irregulars both depend on closely interconnected networks that underlie phonological and semantic processing (Bird et al., 2003; Joanisse and Seidenberg, 1999; McClelland and Patterson, 2002). In this model it is posited that the inconsistent phonological patterns of irregulars result in their computation relying more on semantics than on phonology. Regulars, in contrast, are not expected to show this bias, and novel verbs should actually show the opposite pattern, relying for their computation on phonology but not on semantics.

These two opposing views make at least partly distinct predictions, and thus can be empirically distinguished. Whereas dual-system hypotheses predict double dissociations between regulars and irregulars (Pinker and Ullman, 2002; Ullman et al., 1997), single-mechanism models do not, once other differences between the word types (e.g. their phonological complexity and real-world frequencies) are controlled for (Bird et al., 2003; Joanisse and Seidenberg, 1999; McClelland and Patterson, 2002). Although the data have not yet unambiguously distinguished between these two perspectives, accumulating evidence favors a dual-system view.

First of all, double dissociations between regular and irregular inflected forms have repeatedly been found, in particular between patients with temporal-lobe and frontal/basal ganglia damage. Patients with temporal-lobe lesions have greater difficulty producing, recognizing and reading irregular than regular inflected forms (e.g. *dug*, *kept*, or *mice* vs. *walked*, *played*, or *rats*). This pattern has been found for English inflectional morphology in patients with focal lesions in temporal-lobe regions as well as in patients with Alzheimer's disease or semantic dementia (Patterson et al., 2001; Ullman, forthcoming; Ullman et al., 1997; Ullman et al., 2005). The pattern has also been observed for Italian irregular vs. regular inflected forms in Italian Alzheimer's patients (Cappa and Ullman, 1998; Walenski, Sosta, et al., forthcoming). In contrast, damage to frontal and/or basal ganglia structures—in patients with focal lesions as well as in those with Parkinson's disease or Huntington's disease—has often (but not always) been found to affect regulars more than irregulars, even controlling for factors such as the frequency and phonological complexity of the inflected forms (Coslett, 1986; 1988; Marin et al., 1976; Marslen-Wilson and Tyler, 1997; Tyler et al., 2002; Ullman, forthcoming; Ullman et al., 1997; Ullman et al., 2005). Interestingly, despite these patients' greater difficulty with regulars, irregulars can also be somewhat problematic. In particular, evidence suggests that patients with frontal/basal ganglia damage have trouble *retrieving* irregular inflected forms, while the recognition of these forms is spared, consistent with a role for certain frontal and basal ganglia structures in lexical retrieval (see above; and Ullman, 2006b; Ullman et al., 2005). Finally, recent studies have reported that irregular impairments can be found in the absence of semantic deficits, and conversely, that semantic deficits do not necessarily lead to irregular impairments, contrary to the predictions of the single mechanism model described above (Miozzo, 2003; Tyler, 2004).

ERP studies of receptive language in English, German, and Italian also support a dual-system view (Gross et al., 1998; Newman et al., 1999; Newman et al., 2007 Penke et al., 1997; Weyerts et al., 1997). Whereas the inappropriate presence or absence of irregular inflection (e.g. *Yesterday I <u>dig</u> a hole*) often elicits N400s (which depend on temporal lobe structures; see above), the inappropriate presence or absence of regular affixation (e.g. *Yesterday I <u>walk</u> over there*) generally leads to left anterior negativities (LANs), which are linked to automatic rule-based computation (Friederici et al., 1996; Hahne and Friederici, 1999) and to left frontal structures (Friederici et al., 1998; Friederici et al., 1999).

ERP and MEG studies of expressive language have also reported dissociations between regular and irregular inflected forms. One ERP and two MEG studies have examined the time course of English past tense production (Dhond et al., 2003; Lavric et al., 2001; Rhee et al., 1999). These three studies elicited largely similar patterns. In all three, the production of irregular past tenses (e.g. *dug*) elicited left temporal-lobe activation between 250 and 340 ms following presentation of the stem (e.g. *dig*, which is used to prompt the subject). Interestingly, this pattern of left temporal-lobe activation is very similar to the pattern of activation found between 250 and 330 ms in left temporal cortex for the retrieval of phonological word forms in picture naming tasks (Indefrey and Levelt 2004; Levelt, 2001). Regulars (e.g. *walked*) also showed consistency across the three studies, eliciting activation in frontal cortex—specifically localized to Broca's area in one study—between 310 and 470 ms after stem presentation in all three studies. Again, this pattern is very similar to that found in picture naming, in which Broca's area has been found to subserve the *combination* of sound patterns, including morphemes, between 330 and 455 ms after stimulus presentation (Indefrey and Levelt 2004; Levelt, 2001).

In neuroimaging studies, irregulars have elicited particular activation in a broad range of structures, including the left middle temporal gyrus, other temporal and parietal regions, and the cerebellum (Beretta et al., 2003; Jaeger et al., 1996; Sach et al., 2004). In contrast, a number of studies have reported that regular morphological forms elicit activation in Broca's region and the basal ganglia. For example, a PET study of Finnish, a morphologically very rich and productive language, found greater activation in Broca's area while subjects listened to regular inflected nouns as compared to monomorphemic forms (e.g. like *cat* in English) (Laine et al., 1999). Similarly, an fMRI study of English inflectional and derivational morphology reported that the visual presentation of regular inflected forms (*-ed* or *-ing* suffixed) and regular derivational forms (with productive affixes, such as *-ness* and *-less*) elicited greater activation in Broca's area and the caudate nucleus of the left basal ganglia than irregular derivational forms (with relatively unproductive affixes, such as *-ity* and *-ation*) and monomorphemic words (Vannest et al., 2005).

Thus the evidence suggests that, in both expressive and receptive language, irregulars and regulars depend on largely different brain structures, with the former relying heavily on temporal-lobe regions, while the latter depend more on frontal cortex, especially Broca's region, as well as basal ganglia structures. These and other data are at least somewhat problematic for single-mechanism hypotheses, while supporting a dual-system view and the separability between lexical and at least certain compositional linguistic processes (Pinker and Ullman, 2002; Ullman, 2001c).

16.4 **Redundancy**

In the study of language, as in the investigation of many other areas of cognition, there is often a focus on revealing "the" mechanism for a given function, or on discovering how such a mechanism develops, how it evolved, or where it is located in the brain. For example, controversies are centered on asking whether language, or some aspect of language such as syntax or the lexicon, is computed or represented or learned in this *or* that way. That is, the debate is usually framed in terms of mutually exclusive competing hypotheses.

However, many problems are solved in *more than one* way. For example, if we want to write, we can use a pencil or a pen or a computer. If we want to warm up we can put on more clothes, make a fire, or eat a bowl of hot soup. Crucially, redundant mechanisms are also widespread in biological systems. Biological solutions for thermal regulation include fur, fat, size (larger animals lose heat more slowly), evaporation (a panting dog, a sweating athlete), various metabolic processes, and even anti-freeze molecules.

Although such redundancy can be costly (it takes more energy to make both fur and fat), it also confers important advantages. Different mechanisms are likely to have different and complementary characteristics. Thus the ability to depend on more than one system can lead to a wide variety of functional advantages, based on the complementary advantages of each system. In addition, such mechanistic redundancy inherently confers increased reliability in overall functionality. If one mechanism isn't working properly, others are there to take its place, providing a straightforward means for compensation.

So it is somewhat surprising that the notion of redundant mechanisms is often ignored in the study of language and other areas of cognition. Research rarely focuses on examining whether more than one mechanism can play the same functional role in language, or what factors within or across individuals may result in changes in the relative dependence on different systems serving the same function.

It is not that the assumption of a single mechanism for a given linguistic function is unreasonable. As noted above, redundant mechanisms can be costly, so one might expect them to be unlikely. William of Ockham's original Razor—*Pluralitas non est ponenda sine necessitate*, or "Plurality should not be posited without necessity"—suggests a preference for assuming the parsimony of a single mechanism rather than multiple ones. Even if one accepts the possibility of more than one mechanism, it may be easier to study them one at a time. And it may be that redundant mechanisms yield identical or similar linguistic behaviors, making it very difficult to distinguish them.

However, given the advantages of redundant mechanisms, and their prevalence in biological systems, it would be surprising *not* to find them in the mind and brain, including in the domain of language. Such redundancy seems particularly likely given both the computational flexibility of the brain and the importance of this organ. So the Anti-Razors such as Liebniz, Kant and Menger ("Entities must not be reduced to the point of inadequacy" and "It is vain to do with fewer what requires more"), should be taken seriously. In fact, the discovery of redundant biocognitive mechanisms may help to resolve controversies that have been framed in mutually exclusive terms. That is, in some cases more than one view may be right, with different explanatory mechanisms playing mutually supportive rather than mutually exclusive roles.

Using various methods that can reveal underlying computational and biological mechanisms, research has begun to demonstrate the presence of redundant mechanisms in the neurocognition of language (Caramazza et al., 1988; Coltheart et al., 1993; Pinker, 1999; Ullman, 2004; 2005b; Ullman et al., 1997). Here we will focus on one aspect of language in which such redundancy has been observed. As we have seen above, an important issue in the study of language is how complex forms such as *walked* or *the cat* are learned, represented, and computed. Although many explanatory accounts have been proposed, the basic theoretical debate contrasts the two apparently mutually exclusive perspectives set out briefly above: On one side are those who argue that complex forms are put together from their memorized parts (*walk*, *-ed*, *the*, *cat*) by a rule-governed grammatical system that is distinct from the mental lexicon. On the other side are those who argue that complex forms are in principle no different from simple lexicalized forms like *walk* and *cat*, and that all linguistic forms are learned and processed by the same neurocognitive mechanisms.

On the one hand, as we have seen above, it does indeed appear to be the case that there are (at least) two distinct systems: a lexical system for memorizing pieces of information, and another system that underlies rule-governed composition. However, the existence of these two systems does not require that all regulars and other rule-governed forms are necessarily and always computed by the system that subserves composition. In particular, accumulating evidence suggests that while regular inflected forms can be and in fact often are computed by the compositional system, they can *also* be stored and processed in the mental lexicon, consistent with at least some aspects of single-mechanism claims. Importantly, on the surface the forms do not seem to be any different. Thus when we hear or say *walked*, we could be doing it either way—even though on the surface the forms appear the same.

Together, these lexical and compositional neurocognitive systems appear to work better and more robustly in processing complex forms than either system could on its own. In some cases one system seems to have the upper hand, whereas in other cases the other does. For example, complex forms that we encounter more frequently are—not surprisingly—more likely to be memorized than those that we encounter less frequently, which tend to be composed (Alegre and Gordon, 1999; Baayen, 1992; Baayen et al., 1997; Frauenfelder and Schreuder, 1992; Prado and Ullman, forthcoming; Stemberger and MacWhinney, 1986; Ullman, Walenski, et al., forthcoming). So we are more likely to retrieve *walked* from memory, while we tend to put together *balked* from its parts. Recent data also suggests that regularly inflected forms of verbs with higher mental imagery are more likely to be stored (Prado and Ullman, forthcoming)—a finding that follows from previous evidence suggesting that more imageable words are better remembered (Balota et al., 2004; Mellet et al., 1998; Paivio, 1963; 1967).

Additionally, people who have better memories are more likely to use stored complex forms than people with worse memories. Thus females, who have an estrogen-related advantage at remembering verbal material (Kimura, 1999; Ullman, Miranda, and Travers, forthcoming), appear more likely than males to retrieve complex forms from memory, and correspondingly less likely to compose forms in the grammatical system (it is important to emphasize that, like other cognitive sex differences, this is not a categorical but a probabilistic sex difference) (Hartshorne and Ullman, 2006; Prado and Ullman, forthcoming; Steinhauer and Ullman, 2002; Ullman and Estabrooke, 2004; Ullman et al., 2002; Ullman, Maloff, et al., forthcoming; Ullman, Walenski, et al., forthcoming; Walenski, Mostofsky, et al., forthcoming). Interestingly, these sex differences interact with item-specific factors such as frequency. For example, studies of English past tense have revealed that women but not men show frequency and imageability effects (suggesting storage) of higher frequency regular past-tense forms, whereas neither sex shows signs of storage of lower frequency regulars (Prado and Ullman, forthcoming; Ullman, Maloof, et al., forthcoming; Ullman, Walenski, et al., forthcoming).

It is not just that regularly inflected forms can be stored as chunks. Their storage also appears to lead to at least some degree of *productivity* within the lexicon. In a recent study, girls were found to over-regularize at a significantly higher rate than boys (indeed, at more than twice the rate) (Hartshorne and Ullman, 2006). Phonological neighborhood analyses suggested that girls were over-regularizing by generalizing in an associative lexical memory over already-stored regulars, while boys did not, suggesting that they resorted to the compositional system: girls over-regularized more on those irregular verbs whose over-regularized form has more regular neighbors in the language (e.g. *throwed*, cf. *flowed*, *rowed*, *stowed*, vs. *digged*, cf. *rigged*), whereas boys showed no such correlation.

Evidence also suggests that weaknesses in the grammatical system can lead to compensatory storage in memory. For example, an increased dependence on lexical memory for complex forms, including memorized regulars, is found both in adults learning a foreign language (Brovetto and Ullman, 2001; Ullman, 2001b; 2005a) and in children with disorders that affect grammar, such as Specific Language Impairment (Ullman and Pierpont, 2005) and autism (Walenski et al., 2006). For example, individuals with Specific Language Impairment or related developmental language disorders show frequency effects for regularly inflected forms (Oetting and Horohov, 1997; Oetting and Rice, 1993; Ullman and Gopnik, 1994; 1999; van der Lely and Ullman, 2001).

In sum, it does in fact appear that regulars and other complex forms can be subserved not only by a neurocognitive system that underlies compositional aspects of grammar, but also by the mental lexicon. Thus these forms can be processed by distinct neurocognitive mechanisms, which work together to confer both flexibility and reliability. Importantly, this redundancy seems to reveal the false dichotomy of the debate between dual-system and single-mechanism views. Rather, the dependence of regulars on either compositional or lexical processes suggests that both perspectives are at least partly correct. Moreover, the data suggest the significance of the mental lexicon and its biocognitive substrates as a redundant mechanism for compensation (e.g. in Specific Language Impairment, and even in normal adult language learning), as well as the importance of variation across individuals and groups in *how* we do it, even ifon the surface our behavior looks identical.

16.5 Domain-specificity

Are the biological substrates that subserve the mental lexicon or other aspects of language dedicated exclusively to these linguistic functions? That is, are they domain-specific? Or are they domain-general in that they *also* subserve other, non-language functions? This issue is related to, but distinct from, the issue of separability. In the case of separability, we are asking whether two or more aspects of *language*, such as two lexical functions, or lexical and grammatical abilities, rely on the same or different substrates. In contrast, here we are asking whether language depends on substrates that also subserve *non-language* functions, such as attention, memory, or movement.

Just as with separability, here too we find lumpers and splitters, as well as those in between. The far-splitters argue that language, or specific language functions, depend on substrates that are dedicated solely to these functions (Fodor, 1983; Grodzinsky, 2000; van der Lely, 2005). The far-lumpers argue instead that there is nothing special at all about language, and that all aspects of language depend on domain-general systems or mechanisms (Elman et al., 1996; McClelland et al., 1986; Seidenberg, 1997). In between we find a number of positions, such as the suggestion that lexical and grammatical abilities depend on distinct brain systems that each subserves a particular type of memory (see below, and Ullman, 2001c; 2004; Ullman et al., 1997).

It is important to keep in mind that the question of domain-specificity is distinct from that of another issue, that of species-specificity. In the case of domain-specificity, we are asking whether language depends on neurocognitive substrates that also underlie other functions *in humans*. In the case of species-specificity, one is generally asking whether language, or particular language abilities, depend on substrates that underlie analogous functions in *other* animals. For example, it has recently been argued that recursion is uniquely human (but possibly dependent on domain-general mechanisms in humans), whereas other aspects of language, such as learning concepts, rely on substrates that are also found in other species (Hauser et al., 2002).

Finally, note that it is very difficult in principle to demonstrate domain-specificity. For example, one might show double dissociations between lexical processing and attention, between lexical processing and motor function, between lexical processing and ... the list goes on. How can we test every possible function, with every possible task? Not surprisingly, there is little if any good evidence that the biocognitive substrates of lexical abilities are dedicated to language.

16.5.1 Lexical memory depends on declarative memory

In contrast, there *is* increasing evidence for biocognitive associations between lexical and non-linguistic conceptual-semantic functions, suggesting that these functions depend on common biocognitive substrates. For example, we have seen above that the same neural substrates are activated by words from a given conceptual category and by non-linguistic tasks that tap the same concepts. Other evidence also supports a common basis for lexical and conceptual-semantic functions (see below). These and other data have led to the proposal that lexical memory depends on *declarative memory*, a brain system that underlies the learning and use of knowledge about facts and events (Ullman, 2001c; 2004; 2005a; Ullman et al., 1997).

This proposal has been made in the context of a broader proposal—referred to as the Declarative/Procedural model or theory—that posits that language depends on *two* well-studied brain memory systems, both of which have been implicated in specific non-language functions in animals and humans (Ullman, 2001a; 2001c; 2004; 2005a; Ullman et al., 1997). The declarative memory system subserves the learning, representation, and use of knowledge about facts and events, such as the fact that chairs are for sitting on, or that you had pumpkin and sage ravioli for dinner last night (Eichenbaum and Cohen, 2001; Mishkin et al., 1984; Squire and Knowlton, 2000). Knowledge is rapidly learned in this system, with as little as a single exposure being necessary for retention. The learned knowledge is at least partly (but not completely; Chun, 2000) explicit—that is, available to conscious awareness. The hippocampus and other medial temporal structures consolidate and retrieve new memories, which eventually come to depend largely on neocortical regions, particularly in the temporal lobes (Eichenbaum and Cohen, 2001; Hodges and Patterson, 1997; Martin et al., 2000; Squire and Knowlton, 2000). Other brain structures play a role in declarative memory as well, including Broca's region (i.e. Broca's area and BA47; Ullman, 2006a), which underlies the selection or retrieval of declarative memories (Buckner and Wheeler, 2001). Declarative memory and hippocampal function can be enhanced by estrogen (McEwen et al., 1998; Resnick et al., 1998; Sherwin, 1988), perhaps via the modulation of acetylcholine (Packard, 1998) and/or BDNF (Scharfman and MacLusky, 2005), both of which play important roles independent of estrogen in declarative memory functionality (Egan et al., 2003; Freo et al., 2002; Hariri et al., 2003; Pezawas et al., 2004). Indeed, individuals with the *val* as opposed to the *met* allele of the val66met single nucleotide polymorphism in the BDNF gene have not only superior verbal memory performance (see above) but also larger hippocampal grey matter volumes (Egan et al., 2003; Hariri et al., 2003; Pezawas et al., 2004).

The procedural memory system underlies the gradual implicit (non-conscious) learning of new, and control of long-established, motor and cognitive "skills" and "habits," especially those involving rules or sequences (Mishkin et al., 1984; Squire and Knowlton, 2000; Ullman, 2004; Willingham, 1998). The system is composed of a network of interconnected brain structures. The network is rooted in frontal/basal ganglia circuits, including portions of the premotor cortex and BA44 within frontal cortex, but also encompasses portions of superior temporal cortex, the cerebellum, and other structures (Ullman, 2004; Ullman, 2006b). The neurotransmitter dopamine plays a particularly important role in aspects of procedural learning (Harrington et al., 1990; Nakahara et al., 2001). Note that the term "procedural memory" is used here to refer *only* to one type of implicit, non-declarative, memory system (Squire and Zola, 1996), *not* to all such systems. Additionally, both the declarative and procedural memory systems refer here to the *entire* systems involved in the learning and use of the relevant knowledge or skills (Eichenbaum, 2000), not just to those structures or mechanisms underlying the learning of new knowledge or skills.

The two memory systems interact, yielding both cooperative and competitive learning and processing (Packard and Knowlton, 2002; Poldrack and Packard, 2003; Ullman, 2004). First, the two systems can complement each other in acquiring the same or analogous knowledge, including knowledge of sequences. The declarative memory system may acquire knowledge initially, thanks to its rapid acquisition abilities, while the procedural system gradually learns analogous knowledge. Thus, at least to some extent, declarative and procedural memory can play redundant functional roles (Ullman, 2004; 2005b; Ullman and Pierpont, 2005; Walenski et al., 2006). Second, animal and human studies suggest that the two systems also interact competitively (Packard and Knowlton, 2002; Poldrack and Packard, 2003; Ullman, 2004). This leads to a "see-saw effect" (Ullman, 2004), such that a dysfunction of one system can enhance learning in the other, or that learning in one system may depress the functionality of the other.

According to the Declarative/Procedural model, each of the two memory systems plays analogous roles in its non-linguistic and linguistic functions. The distinction between declarative and procedural memory largely parallels the distinction between the mental lexicon on the one hand and the rule-governed mental grammar that underlies the composition of complex linguistic forms on the other. Thus declarative memory underlies the mental lexicon, which contains not only all idiosyncratic word-specific knowledge but also memorized complex forms. The hippocampus and other medial-temporal lobe structures underlie the consolidation of all types of linguistic and non-linguistic knowledge learned in this system. Once this knowledge is established, it depends largely on neocortical regions, with different neocortical regions responsible for different types of knowledge. For example, as we have seen above, visually related conceptual and linguistic knowledge depend on areas in or near visual cortex. Similarly, visual word forms (e.g. the letter string *cat*) rely on left ventral temporal-occipital regions (McCandliss et al., 2003; Turkeltaub et al., 2002). Various types of categorical and related linguistic knowledge (e.g. for animals) are localized in different temporal-lobe regions (see above, sections 16.2.3 and 16.2.4). Subordinate-level conceptual and associated linguistic knowledge may rely on anterior temporal lobe regions (see above, section 16.2.5). In contrast, superior temporal regions appear to subserve phonological word form knowledge and perhaps stored complex linguistic forms (Ullman, 2004). In fact, portions of superior temporal cortex may serve as one type of interface between the declarative and procedural systems (Ullman, 2004; 2005a).

In contrast, the procedural memory system underlies aspects of the mental grammar, in particular the rule-governed sequential and hierarchical computation of complex linguistic structures. This system plays computationally analogous roles across grammatical subdomains, including syntax and regular morphology (Ullman, 2004). Finally, the two memory systems are expected to interact both cooperatively and competitively in language, just as they do in non-language domains. For example, young children should initially store complex as well as idiosyncratic forms in declarative memory, while the procedural system gradually acquires the grammatical knowledge underlying rule-governed combination.

A wide range of neurocognitive evidence, from developmental, psycholinguistic, neurological, electrophysiological, and neuroimaging studies, seem to support this view. Here we only briefly summarize evidence relevant to the dependence of the mental lexicon on declarative memory. For additional evidence and discussion, both on the relation between lexical and declarative memory and on the relation between grammar and procedural memory, see Ullman et al. (1997) and Ullman (2001c; 2004; 2005a).

Alzheimer's disease, which affects both medial and neocortical temporal-lobe structures, leaving frontal and basal ganglia structures relatively spared, is associated not only with impairments at learning new and using previously learned knowledge of facts, events, and words (e.g. irregulars), but also with relatively spared motor function, procedural learning, and compositional aspects of language such as regular inflection (see above, and Beatty et al., 1994; Gabrieli et al., 1993; Grossman et al., 1998; Nebes, 1997; Sagar et al., 1988; Saint-Cyr et al., 1988; Ullman et al., 1997). Moreover, across patients, error rates at object naming and fact retrieval correlate with error rates at producing irregular, but not regular or *-ed*-suffixed, novel past tenses, directly linking lexical processing with conceptual but not compositional processes (Ullman, forthcoming; Ullman et al., 1997).

Patients with semantic dementia, who have progressive and severe degeneration of inferior and anterior temporal-lobe regions, suffer from a loss of lexical and non-linguistic conceptual knowledge, have more difficulty with irregular than regular inflected forms (see above), and are relatively spared at syntax and motor function (Bozeat et al., 2000; Graham et al., 1999; Mummery et al., 2000; Patterson et al., 2001). However, unlike patients with Alzheimer's disease, those with semantic dementia, who do not have medial temporal-lobe damage, are able to learn new declarative knowledge (Graham and Hodges, 1997; Hodges and Patterson, 1997). In contrast, H.M. and other amnesics with medial-temporal damage are severely impaired at remembering not only new words (see above) but also new facts (e.g. that the Soviet Union does not exist any more) and personally experienced events (e.g. that he met you five minutes ago) (Squire et al., 2004).

On the other hand, Parkinson's disease, which is associated with the degeneration of dopaminergic neurons (especially in the basal ganglia) but the relative sparing of temporal-lobe regions (particularly early in disease progression), leads to impairments of regularly inflected forms, syntactic processing, motor function, and procedural learning, leaving relatively intact the knowledge (but not the retrieval) of facts and words (see above, and Dubois et al., 1991, Ullman, 2004, Ullman et al., 1997, Willingham, 1998, Young and Penney, 1993). Likewise, individuals with Specific Language Impairment, a disorder that is associated with abnormalities of Broca's area and the basal ganglia (see above), have impairments at syntax, regular morphology, and motor functioning (especially of sequences), but have relatively spared lexical and conceptual knowledge (but not retrieval), and learning in declarative memory (see above, Ullman and Pierpont, 2005).

Evidence for the proposal that lexical memory depends on declarative memory also comes from electrophysiological, neuroimaging, and endocrine studies. The N400 ERP component is elicited not just by lexical manipulations but also to non-linguistic conceptual stimuli (Barrett and Rugg, 1990; Olivares et al., 1994). Medial and neocortical temporal lobe activation in neuroimaging studies is found not only for lexical processing but also for conceptual processing (Bookheimer et al., 1993; Damasio et al., 1996; Kuperberg et al., 2000; Martin et al., 1995; Martin et al., 2000; Martin et al., 1996; Newman et al., 2001; Wise et al., 1991). For example, medial temporal lobe structures are activated both by word learning (see above), and by memorizing visual material such as complex scenes (Brewer et al., 1998). Finally, estrogen and its underlying molecular mechanisms also play a role in both linguistic and non-linguistic knowledge. For example, in one study, which examined the effects of estrogen replacement in post-menopausal women, medial temporal lobe activation was found to increase with estrogen not just for learning words but also for learning novel abstract visual images (Maki and Resnick, 2000).

16.6 Summary and conclusion

At the beginning of this chapter, we emphasized that every aspect of the biology of the mental lexicon should be considered, from brain structures down to neurons, molecules, and genes, and that the examination of all of these biological substrates should be complemented by and integrated not only with the study of the acquisition, processing, and representation of language but also with the investigation of non-language functions, particularly those which may share their biocognitive bases with language.

In this context we discussed four major questions that have been asked about the biology of the mental lexicon:

1. What are the biological substrates of the learning, knowledge, and processing of the mental lexicon? That is, which anatomical structures, hormones, genes, and other substrates underlie lexical functions?
2. Do different lexical and other linguistic functions depend on distinct biological substrates? In other words, are lexical functions separable from each other and from other linguistic functions?
3. Can the mental lexicon act as a redundant mechanism for functions otherwise subserved by distinct neurocognitive correlates, in particular those that underlie compositional aspects of language, and in what circumstances might it do so?
4. Are the biological substrates of the mental lexicon dedicated exclusively to this linguistic function (domain-specific), or do they also subserve non-language functions (domain-general)?

For each of these questions we discussed the nature of the issue; we presented relevant findings from multiple methodologies, allowing us to examine whether converging evidence was obtained; and we discussed alternative theoretical perspectives in light of those findings.

The study of the biology of the mental lexicon and other aspects of language is just beginning. In fact, most of the evidence presented above was reported within the past ten years. The recent emergence of many of the techniques referred to here, as well as others that are likely to appear soon, will lead to an ever-larger explosion of research on the biological bases of the lexicon and other aspects of language. Moreover, as attention increasingly turns from neuroanatomy to cellular, molecular, and genetic levels, and as the study of all the biological bases of language is increasingly integrated with the investigation of non-language functions, our understanding of the biocognition of the mental lexicon, and of language more generally, will grow dramatically. We are just at the beginning of an extremely exciting period of discovery.

Acknowledgements

This chapter was written with support for the author from NIH R01 HD049347 and NIH R03 HD050671.

References

Alegre, M., and Gordon, P. (1999) Frequency effects and the representational status of regular inflections. *Journal of Memory and Language*, 40: 41–61.

Alexander, M. P. (1997) Aphasia: clinical and anatomic aspects. In T. E. Feinberg and M. J. Farah (eds), *Behavioral Neurology and Neuropsychology*, pp. 133–50. McGraw-Hill, New York.

Baayen, R. H. (1992) Quantitative aspects of morphological productivity. In G. E. Booij and J. von Marle (eds), *Yearbook of Morphology 1991*, pp. 109–49. Kluwer Academic, Dordrecht.

Baayen, R. H., Dijkstra, T., and Schreuder, R. (1997) Singulars and plurals in Dutch: evidence for a parallel dual-route model. *Journal of Memory and Language*, 37: 94–117.

Balota, D. A., Cortese, M. J., Sergent-Marshall, S. D., Spieler, D. H., and Yap, M. J. (2004) Visual word recognition of single-syllable words. *Journal of Experimental Psychology: General*, 133: 283–316.

Barrett, S. E., and Rugg, M. D. (1990) Event-related potentials and the semantic matching of pictures. *Brain and Cognition*, 14: 201–12.

Beatty, W. W., Winn, P., Adams, R. L., Allen, E. W., Wilson, D. A., Prince, J. R., Olson, K. A., Dean, K., and Littleford, D. (1994) Preserved cognitive skills in dementia of the Alzheimer type. *Archives of Neurology*, 51: 1040–46.

Beretta, A., Campbell, C., Carr, T. H., Huang, J., Schmitt, L. M., Christianson, K. and Cao, Y. (2003) An ER-fMRI investigation of morphological inflection in German reveals that the brain makes a distinction between regular and irregular forms. *Brain and Language*, 85: 67–92.

Bird, H., Lambon Ralph, M. A., Seidenberg, M. S., McClelland, J. L., and Patterson, K. (2003) Deficits in phonology and past tense morphology: what's the connection? *Journal of Memory and Language*, 48: 502–26.

Bookheimer, S. Y., Zeffiro, T. A., Gaillaird, W., and Theodore, W. (1993) Regional cerebral blood flow changes during the comprehension of syntactically varying sentences. *Society for Neuroscience Abstracts*, 19: 843.

Bozeat, S., Lambon Ralph, M. A., Patterson, K., Garrard, P., and Hodges, J. R. (2000) Non-verbal impairment in semantic dementia. *Neuropsychologia*, 38: 1207–14.

Breitenstein, C., Jansen A., Deppe, M., Foerster, A.-F., Sommer, J., Wolbers, T., and Knecht, S. (2005) Hippocampus activity differentiates good from poor learners of a novel lexicon. *NeuroImage*, 25: 958–68.

Brewer, J. B., Zhao, Z., Desmond, J. E., Glover, G. H., and Gabrieli, J. D. (1998) Making memories: brain activity that predicts how well visual experience will be remembered. *Science*, 281: 1185–7.

Brovetto, C., and Ullman, M. T. (2001) First vs. second language: a differential reliance on grammatical computations and lexical memory. Paper presented at the CUNY 2001 Conference on Sentence Processing, Philadelphia, PA.

Bruce, H. A., and Margolis, R. L. (2002) FOXP2: novel exons, splice variants, and CAG repeat length stability. *Human Genetics*, 111: 136–44.

Buckner, R. L. (2000) Neuroimaging of memory. In M. S. Gazzaniga (ed.), *The New Cognitive Neurosciences*, pp. 817–28. MIT Press, Cambridge, Mass.

Buckner, R. L., Koutstaal, W., Schacter, D. L., Dale, A. M., Rotte, M., and Rosen, B. R. (1998) Functional-anatomic study of episodic retrieval, II: Selective averaging of event-related fMRI trials to test the retrieval success hypothesis. *NeuroImage*, 7: 163–75.

Buckner, R. L., and Wheeler, M. E. (2001) The cognitive neuroscience of remembering. *Nature Reviews Neuroscience*, 2: 624–34.

Cappa, S., and Ullman, M. T. (1998) A neural dissociation in Italian verbal morphology. *Journal of Cognitive Neuroscience*, Supplement 63.

Caramazza, A., and Hillis A. E. (1991) Lexical organization of nouns and verbs in the brain. *Nature*, 349: 788–90.

Caramazza, A., Laudanna, A., and Romani, C. (1988) Lexical access and inflectional morphology. *Cognition*, 28: 297–332.

Chao, L. L., Haxby, J. V., and Martin, A. (1999) Attribute-based neural substrates in temporal cortex for perceiving and knowing about objects. *Nature Neuroscience*, 2: 913–9.

Chun, M. M. (2000) Contextual cueing of visual attention. *Trends in Cognitive Sciences*, 4: 170–178.

Clahsen, H. (1999) Lexical entries and rules of language: a multidisciplinary study of German inflection. *Behavioral and Brain Sciences*, 22: 991–1060.

Coltheart, M., Curtis, B., Atkins, P., and Haller, M. (1993) Models of reading aloud: dual-route and parallel-distributed-processing approaches. *Psychological Review*, 100: 589–608.

Corina, D. P., Gibson, E. K., Martin, R., Poliakov, A., Brinkley, J., and Ojemann, G. A. (2005) Dissociation of action and object naming: evidence from cortical stimulation mapping. *Human Brain Mapping*, 24: 1–10.

Coslett, H. B. (1986) Dissociation between reading of derivational and inflectional suffixes in two phonological dyslexics. Paper presented at the Academy of Aphasia, Nashville.

Coslett, H. B. (1988) A selective morphologic impairment in writing: Evidence from a phonological dysgraphic. Paper presented at the Academy of Aphasia, Montreal.

Curran, H. V. (2000) Psychopharmacological approaches to human memory. In M. S. Gazzaniga (ed.), *The New Cognitive Neurosciences*, pp. 797–804. MIT Press, Cambridge, MA.

Damasio, A. R., (1992) Aphasia. *New England Journal of Medicine*, 326: 531–539.

Damasio, H., Grabowski, T. J., Tranel, D., Hichwa, R. D., and Damasio, A. R. (1996) A neural basis for lexical retrieval. *Nature*, 380: 499–505.

Damasio, A. R., and Tranel, D. (1993) Nouns and verbs are retrieved with differently distributed neural systems. *Proceedings of the National Academy of Science*, 90: 4957–60.

Desmond, J. E., and Fiez, J. A. (1998) Neuroimaging studies of the cerebellum: language, learning, and memory. *Trends in Cognitive Sciences*, 2: 355–62.

Desmond, J. E., Gabrieli, J. D. E., and Glover, G. H. (1998) Dissociation of frontal and cerebellar activity in a cognitive task: evidence for a distinction between selection and search. *NeuroImage*, 7: 368–76.

Dhond, R. P., Marinkovic, K., Dale, A. M., Witzel, T., and Halgren, E. (2003) Spatiotemporal maps of past-tense verb inflection. *NeuroImage*, 19: 91–100.

Dronkers, N. F., Redfern, B. B. and Knight, R. T. (2000) The neural architecture of language disorders. In M. S. Gazzaniga (ed.), *The New Cognitive Neurosciences*, pp. 949–958. MIT Press, Cambridge, MA.

Dubois, B., Boller, F., Pillon, B., and Agid, Y. (1991) Cognitive deficits in Parkinson's disease. In F. Boller and J. Grafman (eds), *Handbook of Neuropsychology*, vol. 5, pp. 195–240. Elsevier, Amsterdam.

Egan, M. F., Kojima, M., Callicott, J. H., Goldberg, T. E., Kolachana, B. S., Bertolino, A., Zaitsev, E., Gold, B., Goldman, D., Dean, M., Lu, B., and Weinberger, D. R. (2003) The BDNF val66met polymorphism affects activity-dependent secretion of BDNF and human memory and hippocampal function. *Cell*, 112: 257–69.

Eichenbaum, H. (2000) A cortical-hippocampal system for declarative memory. *Nature Reviews Neuroscience*, 1: 41–50.

Eichenbaum, H. and Cohen, N. J. (2001) *From Conditioning to Conscious Recollection: Memory Systems of the Brain.* Oxford University Press, New York.

Elman, J. L., Bates, E. A., Johnson, M. H., Karmiloff-Smith, A., Parisi, D. and Plunkett, K. (1996) *Rethinking Innateness: A Connectionist Perspective on Development.* MIT Press, Cambridge, MA.

Farah, M. J., and Grossman, M. (1997) Semantic memory impairments. In T. E. Feinberg and M. J. Farah (eds), *Behavioral Neurology and Neuropsychology*, pp. 473–477. McGraw-Hill, New York.

Fiez, J. A. (1997) Phonology, semantics, and the role of the left inferior prefrontal cortex. *Human Brain Mapping*, 5: 79–83.

Fodor, J. A. (1983) *The Modularity of Mind: An Essay on Faculty Psychology*. MIT Press, Cambridge, MA.

Frauenfelder, U. H. and Schreuder, R. (1992) Constraining psycholinguistic models of morphological processing and representation: the role of productivity. In G. Booij and J. van Marle (eds), *Yearbook of Morphology 1991*, pp. 165–83. Kluwer Academic, Dordrecht.

Freo, U., Pizzolato, G., Dam, M., Ori, C., and Battistin, L. (2002) A short review of cognitive and functional neuroimaging studies of cholinergic drugs: implications for therapeutic potentials. *Journal of Neural Transmission*, 109: 857–70.

Friederici, A. D. (2002) Towards a neural basis of auditory sentence processing. *Trends in Cognitive Sciences*, 6: 78–84.

Friederici, A. D., Hahne, A., and Mecklinger, A. (1996) The temporal structure of syntactic parsing: early and late effects elicited by syntactic anomalies. *Journal of Experimental Psychology: Learning, Memory, and Cognition*, 22: 1219–48.

Friederici, A. D., Hahne, A., and von Cramon, D. Y. (1998) First-pass versus second-pass parsing processes in a Wernicke's and a Broca's aphasic: electrophysiological evidence for a double dissociation. *Brain and Language*, 62: 311–41.

Friederici, A. D., von Cramon, D. Y., and Kotz, S. A. (1999) Language related brain potentials in patients with cortical and subcortical left hemisphere lesions. *Brain*, 122: 1033–47.

Gabrieli, J. D., Poldrack, R. A., and Desmond, J. E. (1998) The role of left prefrontal cortex in language and memory. *Proceedings of the National Academy of Sciences USA*, 95: 906–13.

Gabrieli, J. D. E., Corkin, S., Mickel, S. F., and Growdon, J. H. (1993) Intact acquisition and long-term retention of mirror-tracing skill in Alzheimer's disease and in global amnesia. *Behavioral Neuroscience*, 107: 899–910.

Gainotti, G. (1998) Category-specific disorders for nouns and verbs: a very old and very new problem. In B. Stemmer and H. A. Whitaker (eds), *Handbook of Neurolinguistics*, pp. 3–11. Academic Press, San Diego, CA.

Gauthier, I., Anderson, A. W., Tarr, M. J., Skudlarski, P., and Gore, J. C. (1997) Levels of categorization in visual recognition studied using functional magnetic resonance imaging. *Current Biology*, 7: 645–51.

Gerardin, E., Sirigu, A., Lehericy, S., Poline, J. B., Gaymard, B., Marsault, C., Agid, Y., and Le Bihan, D. (2000) Partially overlapping neural networks for real and imagined hand movements. *Cerebral Cortex*, 10: 1093–104.

Grafton, S. T., Arbib, M. A., Fadiga, L., and Rizzolatti, G. (1996) Localization of grasp representations in humans by positron emission tomography, 2: Observation compared with imagination. *Experimental Brain Research*, 112: 103–11.

Graham, K. S., and Hodges, J. R. (1997) Differentiating the roles of the hippocampal complex and the neocortex in long-term memory storage: evidence from the study of semantic dementia and Alzheimer's disease. *Neuropsychology*, 11: 77–89.

Graham, K. S., Patterson, K., and Hodges, J. R. (1999) Episodic memory: new insights from the study of semantic dementia. *Current Opinion in Neurobiology*, 9: 245–50.

Grodstein, F., Chen, J., Pollen, D. A., Albert, M. S., Wilson, R. S., Folstein, M. F., Evans, D. A., and Stampfer, M. J. (2000) Postmenopausal hormone therapy and cognitive function in healthy older women. *Journal of the American Geriatrics Society*, 48: 746–52.

Grodzinsky, Y. (2000) The neurology of syntax: language use without Broca's area. *Behavioral and Brain Sciences*, 23: 1–71.

Gross, M, Say, T., Kleingers, M., Münte, T. F., and Clahsen, H. (1998) Human brain potentials to violations in morphologically complex Italian words. *Neuroscience Letters*, 241: 83–6.

Grossman, M., Payer, F., Onishi, K., D'Esposito, M., Morrison, D., Sadek, A., and Alavi, A. (1998) Language comprehension and regional cerebral defects in frontotemporal degeneration and Alzheimer's disease. *Neurology*, 50: 157–63.

Hagoort, P. and Kutas, M. (1995) Electrophysiological insights into language deficits. In F. Boller and J. Grafman (eds), *Handbook of Neuropsychology*, vol. 10, pp. 105–34. Elsevier, Amsterdam.

Hahne, A., and Friederici, A. D., (1999) Electrophysiological evidence for two steps in syntactic analysis: early automatic and late controlled processes. *Journal of Cognitive Neuroscience*, 11: 194–205.

Halgren, E., Dhond, R. P., Christensen, N., Van Petten, C., Marinkovic, K., Lewine, J. D., and Dale, A. M. (2002) N400-like magnetoencephalography responses modulated by semantic context, word frequency, and lexical class in sentences. *NeuroImage*, 17: 1101–16.

Hampson, E. (1990) Variations in sex-related cognitive abilities across the menstrual cycle. *Brain Cognition*, 14: 26–43.

Hariri, A. R., Goldberg, T. E., Mattay, V. S., Kolachana, B. S., Callicott, J. H., Egan, M. F., and Weinberger, D. R. (2003) Brain-derived neurotrophic factor val66met polymorphism affects Human memory-related hippocampal activity and predicts memory performance. *Journal of Neuroscience*, 23: 6690–4.

Harrington, D. L., Haaland, K. Y., Yeo, R. A., and Marder, E. (1990) Procedural memory in Parkinson's disease: impaired motor but not visuoperceptual learning. *Journal of Clinical and Experimental Neuropsychology*, 12: 323–39.

Hartshorne, J. K., and Ullman, M. T. (2006) Why girls say 'holded' more than boys. *Developmental Science*, 9: 21–32.

Hasselmo, M. E., Wyble, B. P., and Wallenstein, G. V. (1996) Encoding and retrieval of episodic memories: role of cholinergic and GABAergic modulation in the hippocampus. *Hippocampus*, 6: 693–708.

Hauser, M. D., Chomsky, N., and Fitch, W. T. (2002) The faculty of language: what is it, who has it, and how did it evolve? *Science*, 298: 1569–79.

Hickok, G., and Poeppel, D. (2004) Dorsal and ventral streams: a framework for understanding aspects of the functional anatomy of language. *Cognition*, 92: 67–99.

Hodges, J. R., and Patterson, K. (1997) Semantic memory disorders. *Trends in Cognitive Sciences*, 1: 68–72.

Indefrey, P., and Cutler, A. (2004) Prelexical and lexical processing in listening. In M. S. Gazzaniga (ed.), *The Cognitive Neurosciences*, pp. 759–74. MIT Press, Cambridge, MA.

Indefrey, P., and Levelt, W. J. (2004) The spatial and temporal signatures of word production components. *Cognition*, 92: 101–44.

Jaeger, J. J., Lockwood, A. H., Kemmerer, D. L., Van Valin, Jr. R. D., Murphy, B. W., and Khalak, H. G. (1996) A positron emission tomographic study of regular and irregular verb morphology in English. *Language*, 72: 451–97.

Joanisse, M. F., and Seidenberg, M. S. (1999) Impairments in verb morphology after brain injury: a connectionist model. *Proceedings of the National Academy of Sciences of the United States of America*, 96: 7592–7.

Kimura, D. (1999) *Sex and Cognition*. MIT Press, Cambridge, MA.

Kreiman, G., Koch, C., and Fried, I. (2000) Category-specific visual responses of single neurons in the human medial temporal lobe. *Nature Neuroscience*, 3: 946–53.

Kuperberg, G. R., McGuire, P. K., Bullmore, E. T., Brammer, M. J., Rabe-Hesketh, S., Wright, I. C., Lythogoe, D. J., Williams, S. C. R., and David, A. S. (2000) Common and distinct neural substrates for pragmatic, semantic, and syntactic processing of spoken sentences: an fMRI study. *Journal of Cognitive Neuroscience*, 12: 321–41.

Kutas, M., and Hillyard, S. A. (1980) Reading senseless sentences: brain potentials reflect semantic incongruity. *Science*, 207: 203–5.

Lai, C., Gerrelli, D., Monaco, A., Fisher, S., and Copp, A. (2003) FOXP2 expression during brain development coincides with adult sites of pathology in a severe speech and language disorder. *Brain*, 126: 2455–62.

Laine, M., Rinne, J. O., Krause, B. J., Teras, M., and Sipila, H. (1999) Left hemisphere activation during processing of morphologically complex word forms in adults. *Neuroscience Letters*, 271: 85–8.

Lavric, A., Pizzagalli, D., Forstmeier, S., and Rippon, G. (2001) A double-dissociation of English past-tense production revealed by event-related potentials and low-resolution electromagnetic tomography (LORETA). *Clinical Neurophysiology*, 112: 1833–49.

Levelt, W. J. M. (2001) Spoken word production: a theory of lexical access. *Proceedings of the National Academy of Science*, 98: 13464–71.

Maki, P. M., and Resnick, S. M. (2000) Longitudinal effects of estrogen replacement therapy on PET cerebral blood flow and cognition. *Neurobiology of Aging*, 21: 373–83.

Marcus, G., and Fisher, S. (2003) FOXP2 in focus: what can genes tell us about speech and language? *Trends in Cognitive Sciences*, 7: 257–62.

Marin, O. S. M., Saffran, E. M., and Schwartz, M. F. (1976) Dissociations of language in aphasia: implications for normal function. *Annals of the New York Academy of Sciences*, 280: 868–84.

Marslen-Wilson, W. D., and Tyler, L. K. (1997) Dissociating types of mental computation. *Nature*, 387: 592–4.

Martin, A., and Chao, L. L. (2001) Semantic memory and the brain: structure and processes. *Current Opinion in Neurobiology*, 11: 194–201.

Martin, A., Haxby, J. V., Lalonde, F. M., Wiggs, C. L., and Ungerleider, L. G. (1995) Discrete cortical regions associated with knowledge of color and knowledge of action. *Science*, 270: 102–5.

Martin, A., Ungerleider, L. G., and Haxby, J. V. (2000) Category specificity and the brain: the sensory/motor model of semantic representations of objects. In M. S. Gazzaniga (ed.), *The Cognitive Neurosciences*, pp. 1023–36. MIT Press, Cambridge, MA.

Martin, A., Wiggs, C., Ungerleider, L. and Haxby, J. (1996) Neural correlates of category-specific knowledge. *Nature*, 379: 649–52.

Martin, R. C., Wu, D., Freedman, M., Jackson, E. F., and Lesch, M. (2003) An event related fMRI investigation of phonological versus semantic short-term memory. *Journal of Neurolinguistics*, 16: 341–60.

Matison, R., Mayeux, R., Rosen, J., and Fahn, S. (1982) 'Tip-of-the-tongue' phenomenon in Parkinson's disease. *Neurology*, 32: 567–70.

McCandliss, B., Cohen, L., and Dehaene, S. (2003) The visual word form area: expertise for reading in the fusiform gyrus. *Trends in Cognitive Sciences*, 7: 293–9.

McCarthy, G., Nobre, A. C., Bentin, S., and Spencer, D. D. (1995) Language-related field potentials in the anterior-medial temporal lobe, I: Intracranial distribution and neural generators. *Journal of Neuroscience*, 15: 1080–9.

McClelland, J. L., and Patterson, K. (2002) Rules or connections in past-tense inflections: what does the evidence rule out? *Trends in Cognitive Sciences*, 6: 465–72.

McClelland, J. L., Rumelhart, D. E. and the PDP Research Group (1986) *Parallel Distributed Processing: Explorations in the Microstructure of Cognition*. Bradford Books/MIT Press, Cambridge, MA.

McDermott, K. B., Petersen, S. E., Watson, J. M., and Ojemann, J. G. (2003) A procedure for identifying regions preferentially activated by attention to semantic and phonological relations using functional magnetic resonance imaging. *Neuropsychologia*, 41: 293–303.

McEwen, B. S., Alves, S. E., Bulloch, K., and Weiland, N. G. (1998) Clinically relevant basic science studies of gender differences and sex hormone effects. *psychopharmacology Bulletin*, 34: 251–9.

Mellet, E., Tzourio, N., Denis, M., and Mazoyer, B. (1998) Cortical anatomy of mental imagery of concrete nouns based on their dictionary definition. *NeuroReport*, 9: 803–8.

Miceli, G., Silveri, M. C., Villa, G., and Caramazza, A. (1984) On the basis for the agrammatic's difficulty in producing main verbs. *Cortex*, 20: 207–20.

Miles, C., Green, R., Sanders, G., and Hines, M. (1998) Estrogen and memory in a transsexual population. *Hormones and Behavior*, 34: 199–208.

Miozzo, M. (2003) On the processing of regular and irregular forms of verbs and nouns: evidence from neuropsychology. *Cognition*, 87: 101–127.

Mishkin, M., Malamut, B., and Bachevalier, J. (1984) Memories and habits: two neural systems. In G. Lynch, J. L. McGaugh, and N. W. Weinburger (eds), *Neurobiology of Learning and Memory*, pp. 65–77. Guilford Press, New York.

Mottaghy, F. M., Hungs, M., Brugmann, M., Sparing, R., Boroojerdi, B., Foltys, H., Huber, W., and Topper, R. (1999) Facilitation of picture naming after repetitive transcranial magnetic stimulation. *Neurology*, 53: 1806–12.

Mummery, C. J., Patterson, K., Price, C. J., Ashburner, J., Frackowiak, R. S., and Hodges, J. R. (2000) A voxel-based morphometry study of semantic dementia: relationship between temporal lobe atrophy and semantic memory. *Annals of Neurology*, 47: 36–45.

Nakahara, H., Doya, K., and Hikosaka, O. (2001) Parallel cortico-basal ganglia mechanisms for acquisition and execution of visuomotor sequences: a computational approach. *Journal of Cognitive Neuroscience*, 13: 626–47.

Nebes, R. D. (1997) Alzheimer's disease: cognitive neuropsychological aspects. In T. E. Feinberg and M. J. Farah (eds), *Behavioral Neurology and Neuropsychiatry*, pp. 545–50. McGraw-Hill, New York.

Newman, A., Izvorski, R., Davis, L., Neville, H., and Ullman, M. T. (1999) Distinct electrophysiological patterns in the processing of regular and irregular verbs. *Journal of Cognitive Neuroscience*, Supplement 47.

Newman, A. J., Pancheva, R, Ozawa, K, Neville, H. J., and Ullman, M. T. (2001) An event-related fMRI study of syntactic and semantic violations. *Journal of Psycholinguistic Research*, 30: 339–64.

Newman, A. J., Ullman, M. T., Pancheva, R., Waligura, D. L., and Neville, H. J. (2007) An ERP study of regular and irregular English past tense inflection. *Neuroimage*, 34: 435–45.

Nissen, M. J., Knopman, D. S., and Schacter, D. L. (1987) Neurochemical dissociation of memory systems. *Neurology*, 37: 789–94.

Nobre, A. C., Allison, T., and McCarthy, G. (1994) Word recognition in the human inferior temporal lobe. *Nature*, 372: 260–3.

Oetting, J. B., and Horohov, J. E. (1997) Past tense marking by children with and without specific language impairment. *Journal of Speech and Hearing Research*, 40: 62–74.

Oetting, J. B., and Rice, M. (1993) Plural acquisition in children with specific language impairment. *Journal of Speech and Hearing Research*, 36: 1236–48.

Olivares, E., Bobes, M. A., Aubert, E., and Valdes-Sosa, M. (1994) Associative ERP effects with memories of artificial faces. *Cognitive Brain Research*, 2: 39–48.

Packard, M. G. (1998) Posttraining estrogen and memory modulation. *Hormones and Behavior*, 34: 126–39.

Packard, M. G., and Knowlton, B. J. (2002) Learning and memory functions of the basal ganglia. *Annual Review of Neuroscience*, 25: 563–93.

Paivio, A. (1963) Learning of adjective-noun paired associates as a function of adjective-noun word order and noun abstractness. *Canadian Journal of Psychology*, 17: 370–9.

Paivio, A. (1967) Paired-associate learning and free recall of nouns as a function of concreteness, specificity, imagery, and meaningfulness. *Psychological Reports*, 20: 239–45.

Patterson, K., Lambon Ralph, M. A., Hodges, J. R., and McClelland, J. L. (2001) Deficits in irregular past-tense verb morphology associated with degraded semantic knowledge. *Neuropsychologia*, 39: 709–24.

Penke, M., Weyerts, H., Gross M., Zander, E., Munte, T. F., and Clahsen, H. (1997) How the brain processes complex words: an ERP-study of German verb inflections. *Essex Research Reports in Linguistics*, 14: 1–41.

Pezawas, L., Verchinski, B. A., Mattay, V. S., Callicott, J. H., Kolachana, B. S., Straub, R. E., Egan, M. F., Meyer-Lindenberg, A., and Weinberger, D. R. (2004) The brain-derived neurotrophic factor val66met polymorphism and variation in human cortical morphology. *Journal of Neuroscience*, 24: 10099–102.

Pinker, S. (1999) *Words and Rules: The Ingredients of Language*. Basic Books, New York.

Pinker, S., and Ullman, M. T. (2002) The past and future of the past tense. *Trends in Cognitive Sciences*, 6: 456–63.

Plunkett, K., and Marchman, V. (1991) U-shaped learning and frequency effects in a multi-layered perceptron: Implications for child language acquisition. *Cognition*, 38: 43–102.

Poldrack, R. A., and Packard, M. G. (2003) Competition among multiple memory systems: converging evidence from animal and human brain studies. *Neuropsychologia*, 41: 245–51.

Poldrack, R. A., Wagner, A. D., Prull, M. W., Desmond, J. E., Glover, G. H., and Gabrieli, J. D. (1999) Functional specialization for semantic and phonological processing in the left inferior prefrontal cortex. *NeuroImage*, 10: 15–35.

Poo, M. (2001) Neurotrophins as synaptic modulators. *Nature Reviews Neuroscience*, 2: 24–32.

Postle, B. R., and Corkin, S. (1998) Impaired word-stem completion priming but intact perceptual identification priming with novel words: evidence from the amnesic patient H. M. *Neuropsychologia*, 15: 421–440.

Prado, E., and Ullman, M. T. (forthcoming) Can imageability help us draw the line between storage and composition?

Pulvermuller, F., Harle, M., and Hummel, F. (2001) Walking or talking? Behavioral and neurophysiological correlates of action verb processing. *Brain and Language*, 78: 143–68.

Pulvermuller, F., Preissl, H, Lutzenberger, W., and Birbaumer, N. (1996) Brain rhythms of language: nouns versus verbs. *European Journal of Neuroscience*, 8: 937–41.

Resnick, S., Maki, P., Golski, S., Kraut, M., and Zonderman, A. (1998) Effects of estrogen replacement therapy on PET cerebral blood flow and neuropsychological performance. *Hormones and Behavior*, 34: 171–82.

Rhee, J., Pinker, S., and Ullman, M. T. (1999) A magnetoencephalographic study of English past tense production. *Journal of Cognitive Neuroscience*, Supplement, 47.

Rugg, M. D. (1990) Event-related brain potentials dissociate repetition effects of high- and low-frequency words. *Memory and Cognition*, 18: 367–79.

Rumelhart, D. E., and McClelland, J. L. (1986) On learning the past tenses of English verbs. In J. L. McClelland, D. E. Rumelhart, and PDP Research Group (eds), *Parallel Distributed Processing: Explorations in the Microstructures of Cognition*, vol. 2: *Psychological and Biological Models*, pp. 272–326. Bradford Books/MIT Press, Cambridge, MA.

Sach, M., Seitz, J., and Indefrey, P. (2004) Unified inflectional processing of regular and irregular verbs: a PET study. *NeuroReport*, 15: 533–7.

Sagar, H. J., Cohen, N. J., Sullivan, E. V., Corkin, S., and Growdon, J. H. (1988) Remote memory function in Alzheimer's and Parkinson's disease. *Brain*, 111: 185–206.

Saint-Cyr, J. A., Taylor, A. E., and Lang, A. E. (1988) Procedural learning and neostriatal dysfunction in man. *Brain*, 111: 941–59.

Scharfman, H. E., and MacLusky, N. J. (2005) Similarities between actions of estrogen and BDNF in the hippocampus: coincidence or clue? *TRENDS in Neurosciences*, 28.

Scott, S. K., and Wise, R. J. S. (2004) The functional neuroanatomy of prelexical processing in speech perception. *Cognition*, 92: 13–45.

Segalowitz, S. J., and Chevalier, H. (1998a) Event-related potential (ERP) research in neurolinguistics, part I: Techniques and applications to lexical access. In B. Stemmer and H. A. Whitaker (eds), *Handbook of Neurolinguistics*, pp. 95–109. Academic Press, San Diego, Calif.

Segalowitz, S. J., and Chevalier, H. (1998b) Event-related potential (ERP) research in neurolinguistics, part II: Language processing and acquisition. In B. Stemmer and H. A. Whitaker (eds), *Handbook of Neurolinguistics*, pp. 111–23. Academic Press, San Diego, Calif.

Seidenberg, M. S. (1997) Language acquisition and use: learning and applying probabilistic constraints. *Science*, 275: 1599–1603.

Shapiro, K. A., and Caramazza, A. (2004) The organization of lexical knowledge in the brain: the grammatical dimension. In M. S. Gazzaniga (ed.), *The Cognitive Neurosciences*, pp. 803–14. MIT Press, Cambridge, MA.

Sherwin, B. B. (1988) Estrogen and/or androgen replacement therapy and cognitive functioning in surgically menopausal women. *Psychoneuroendocrinology*, 13: 345–57.

Shughrue, P. J., Scrimo, P. J., and Merchenthaler, I. (2000) Estrogen binding and estrogen receptor characterization (ERalpha and ERbeta) in the cholinergic neurons of the rat basal forebrain. *Neuroscience*, 96: 41–9.

Simos, P. G., Basile, L. F. H., and Papanicolaou, A. C. (1997) Source localization of the N400 response in a sentence-reading paradigm using evoked magnetic fields and magnetic resonance imaging. *Brain Research*, 762: 29–39.

Squire, L. R., Clark, R. E., and Bayley, P. J. (2004) Medial temporal lobe function and memory. In M. S. Gazzaniga (ed.), *The Cognitive Neurosciences*, pp. 691–708. MIT Press, Cambridge, MA.

Squire, L. R., and Knowlton, B. J. (2000) The medial temporal lobe, the hippocampus, and the memory systems of the brain. In M. S. Gazzaniga (ed.), *The New Cognitive Neurosciences*, pp. 765–80. MIT Press, Cambridge, MA.

Squire, L. R., and Zola, S. M. (1996) Structure and function of declarative and nondeclarative memory systems. *Proceedings of the National Academy of Science USA*, 93: 13515–22.

Steinhauer, K., and Ullman, M. T. (2002) Consecutive ERP effects of morph-phonology and morpho-syntax. *Brain and Language*, 83: 62–5.

Stemberger, J. P. and MacWhinney, B. (1986) Frequency and the lexical storage of regularly inflected forms. *Memory and Cognition*, 14: 17–26.

Takahashi, K., Liu, F.-C., Hirokawa, K., and Takahashi, H. (2003) Expression of Foxp2, a gene involved in speech and language, in the developing and adult striatum. *Journal of Neuroscience Research*, 73: 61–72.

Thompson-Schill, S. L., D'Esposito, M., Aguirre, G. K., and Farah, M. J. (1997) Role of left inferior prefrontal cortex in retrieval of semantic knowledge: a reevaluation. *Proceedings of the National Academy of Science USA*, 94: 14792–7.

Turkeltaub, P., Eden, G., Jones, K., and Zeffiro, T. (2002) Meta-analysis of the functional neuroanatomy of single-word reading: method and validation. *NeuroImage*, 16: 765.

Tyler, L., Bright, P., Fletcher, P., and Stamatakis, E. (2004) Neural processing of nouns and verbs: the role of inflectional morphology. *Neuropsychologia*, 42: 512–23.

Tyler, L., Randall, B., and Marslen-Wilson, W. (2002) Phonology and neuropsychology of the English past tense. *Neuropsychologia*, 40: 154–1166.

Tyler, L. K. (2004) Deficits for semantics and the irregular past tense: a causal relationship? *Journal of Cognitive Neuroscience*, 16: 1159–72.

Ullman, M. T. (2001a) The declarative/procedural model of lexicon and grammar. *Journal of Psycholinguistic Research*, 30: 37–69.

Ullman, M. T. (2001b) The neural basis of lexicon and grammar in first and second language: the declarative/procedural model. *Bilingualism: Language and Cognition*, 4: 105–22.

Ullman, M. T. (2001c) A neurocognitive perspective on language: the declarative/procedural model. *Nature Reviews Neuroscience*, 2: 717–26.

Ullman, M. T. (2004) Contributions of memory circuits to language: the declarative/procedural model. *Cognition*, 92: 231–70.

Ullman, M. T. (2005a) A cognitive neuroscience perspective on second language acquisition: the declarative/rocedural Model. In C. Sanz (ed.), *Mind and Context in Adult Second Language Acquisition: Methods, Theory and Practice*, pp. 141–78. Georgetown University Press, Washington, DC.

Ullman, M. T. (2005b) More is sometimes more: redundant mechanisms in the mind and brain. *APS Observer*, 18: 7–46.

Ullman, M. T. (2006a) Language and the brain. In J. Connor-Linton, and R. W. Fasold (eds), *An Introduction to Language and Linguistics*, pp. 235–74. Cambridge University Press, Cambridge.

Ullman, M. T. (2006b) Is Broca's area part of a basal ganglia thalamocortical circuit? *Cortex* 42: 480–5.

Ullman, M. T. (forthcoming) Evidence that lexical memory is part of the temporal lobe declarative memory, and that grammatical rules are processed by the frontal/basal-ganglia procedural system. *Brain and Language*.

Ullman, M. T., Corkin, S., Coppola, M., Hickok, G., Growdon, J. H., Koroshetz, W. J., and Pinker, S. (1997) A neural dissociation within language: evidence that the mental dictionary is part of declarative memory, and that grammatical rules are processed by the procedural system. *Journal of Cognitive Neuroscience*, 9: 266–76.

Ullman, M. T., and Estabrooke, I. V. (2004) Grammar, tools and sex. *Journal of Cognitive Neuroscience*, Supplement, 67.

Ullman, M. T., Estabrooke, I. V., Steinhauer, K., Brovetto, C., Pancheva, R., Ozawa, K., Mordecai, K., and Maki, P. (2002) Sex differences in the neurocognition of language. *Brain and Language*, 83: 141–3.

Ullman, M. T., and Gopnik, M. (1994) The production of inflectional morphology in hereditary specific language impairment. In J. Matthews (ed.), *The McGill Working Papers in Linguistics: Linguistic Aspects of Familial Language Impairment*, vol. 10, pp. 81–118. McGill University, Montreal.

Ullman, M. T., and Gopnik, M. (1999) Inflectional morphology in a family with inherited specific language impairment. *Applied Psycholinguistics*, 20: 51–117.

Ullman, M. T., Maloof, C. J., Hartshorne, J. K., Estabrooke, I. V., Brovetto, C., and Walenski, M. (forthcoming) Sex, regularity, frequency and consistency: a study of factors predicting the storage of inflected forms.

Ullman, M. T., Miranda, R. A., and Travers, M. L. (forthcoming). Sex differences in the neurocognition of language. In J. B. Becker, K. J. Berkley, N. Geary, E. Hampson, J. Herman, and E. Young (eds), *Sex on the Brain: From Genes to Behavior*. Oxford University Press, New York, NY.

Ullman, M. T., Pancheva, R., Love, T., Yee, E., Swinney, D., and Hickok, G. (2005) Neural correlates of lexicon and grammar: evidence from the production, reading, and judgment of inflection in aphasia. *Brain and Language*, 93: 185–238.

Ullman, M. T., and Pierpont, E. I. (2005) Specific language impairment is not specific to language: the procedural deficit hypothesis. *Cortex*, 41: 399–433.

Ullman,M. T., Walenski M, Prado, E. L., Ozawa, K., and Steinhauer, K. (forthcoming) The compositionality and storage of inflected forms: evidence from working memory effects. *Cognition*.

van der Lely, H. K. J. (2005) Domain-specific cognitive systems: insight from Grammatical-SLI. *Trends in Cognitive Sciences*, 9: 53–59.

van der Lely, H. K. J., and Ullman, M. T. (2001) Past tense morphology in specifically language impaired and normally developing children. *Language and Cognitive Processes*, 16: 177–217.

Vannest, J., Polk, T. A., and Lewis, R. L. (2005) Dual-route processing of complex words: new fMRI evidence from derivational suffixation. *Cognitive, Affective and Behavioral Neuroscience*, 5: 67–76.

Vargha-Khadem, F., Gadian, D. G., Copp, A., and Mishkin, M. (2005) FOXP2 and the neuroanatomy of speech and language. *Nature Reviews Neuroscience*, 6: 131–8.

Wagner, A. D. (1999) Working memory contributions to human learning and remembering. *Neuron*, 22: 19–22.

Walenski, M., Mostofsky, S. H., Larson, J. C. G., and Ullman, M. T. (forthcoming) Enhanced picture naming in autism.

Walenski, M., Sosta, K., Cappa, S., and Ullman, M. T. (forthcoming) Deficits on irregular verb morphology in Italian-speaking Alzheimer's disease patients: evidence from present tense and past participle production.

Walenski, M., Tager-Flusberg, H., and Ullman, M. T. (2006) Language in Autism. In S. O. Moldin and J. L. R. Rubenstein (eds), *Understanding Autism: From Basic Neuroscience to Treatment*, pp. 175–203. Taylor & Francis, Boca Raton, FL.

Warrington, E. K., and Shallice, T. (1984) Category-specific semantic impairments. *Brain*, 107: 829–54.

West, W. C., and Holcomb, P. J. (2000) Imaginal, semantic, and surface-level processing of concrete and abstract words: an electrophysiological investigation. *Journal of Cognitive Neuroscience*, 12: 1024–37.

Weyerts, H., Penke, M., Dohrn, U., Clahsen, H., and Münte, T. F. (1997) Brain potentials indicate differences between regular and irregular German plurals. *NeuroReport*, 8: 957–62.

Willingham, D. B. (1998) A neuropsychological theory of motor skill learning. *Psychological Review*, 105: 558–584.

Wise, R., Chollet, F., Hadar, U., Friston, K., and Hoffner, E. (1991) Distribution of cortical neural networks involved in word comprehension and word retrieval. *Brain*, 114: 1803–17.

Young, A. B. and Penney, J. B. (1993) Biochemical and functional organization of the basal ganglia. In J. Jankovic and E. Tolosa (eds), *Parkinson's Disease and Movement Disorders*, pp. 1–11. Williams & Wilkins, Baltimore, MD.

SECTION III

Comprehension and discourse

CHAPTER 17

Syntactic parsing

Roger P. G. van Gompel and Martin J. Pickering

17.1 Introduction

A crucial part of understanding a sentence is to construct its syntactic structure. Without this, it would be very difficult for language users to determine that sentences with different word orders, such as *The man sees the woman* and *The woman sees the man* have different interpretations, or explain why sentences such as *The hunter killed the poacher with the rifle* have two possible interpretations. The processes involved in constructing syntactic structures during language comprehension are commonly referred to as *parsing* or *syntactic processing*.

Sentence processing research has shown that parsing is largely incremental, i.e. language comprehenders incorporate each word into the preceding syntactic structure as they encounter it; they do not delay syntactic structure building until, for instance, the end of the sentence or phrase (e.g. Marslen-Wilson, 1973; 1975). Evidence for incrementality comes from numerous studies that show that language comprehenders experience difficulty with temporarily ambiguous sentences well before the end of the sentence. For example, many experiments have shown that readers slow down in the region *by the lawyer* in (1) (e.g. Clifton et al., 2003; Ferreira and Clifton, 1986; Rayner et al., 1983; Trueswell et al., 1994).

1. The defendant examined by the lawyer turned out to be unreliable.

This sentence is temporarily ambiguous at *examined*, because this verb could be part of a *reduced relative structure*, in which it is a past participle, or part of a *main clause structure*, in which it is a past tense verb. The finding that people experience difficulty at *by the lawyer* is normally interpreted as evidence that people initially favor the main clause analysis, and experience difficulty because *by the lawyer* rules out this analysis. The difficulty that people experience in such a case is often referred to as a "garden-path effect" (Bever, 1970).

There is considerable controversy about when people use different sources of information during sentence processing. Most controversially, do they immediately use all relevant sources of information, or are some sources of information delayed relative to others? Sentence processing theories can roughly be divided into *interactive* accounts, in which all relevant information can be used immediately, and *modular* accounts, in which some information can be used immediately but some information cannot.

17.2 Modular models

Modular models assume that the mind consists of modules that perform very specific processes (e.g. Fodor, 1983). These processes are informationally encapsulated: they use only information represented within this module. In sentence processing research, this has led to the question of whether syntactic processes are separable from other processes such as semantic and discourse processing.

Modularity and informational encapsulation in sentence processing have usually been investigated using (temporarily) ambiguous sentences. In unambiguous sentences, syntactic information provides an extremely strong structural cue, so even according to models that are not modular, non-syntactic factors are unlikely to have much of an effect on processing. Therefore, most sentence processing studies have investigated how different sources of information are employed during the processing of globally and temporarily ambiguous sentences, where syntactic cues allow multiple interpretations.

According to by far the most influential modular account of syntactic ambiguity resolution, the garden-path model (e.g. Frazier, 1987), the sentence processor initially employs only information about the syntactic structure of the sentence to adopt a single analysis in (temporarily) ambiguous sentences. Other, non-structural sources of information such as semantics, context, and frequency of the structures are employed during later stages of processing (e.g. Frazier, 1987; Rayner et al., 1983). When the initial analysis is inconsistent with information that becomes available later, the processor has to reanalyze, and processing difficulty ensues.

The garden-path model stipulates that the principles of minimal attachment and of late closure determine people's initial analysis of (temporarily) ambiguous sentences. These principles are language-universal, so they apply to all ambiguities in any language. According to minimal attachment, the processor incorporates an ambiguous phrase into the preceding syntactic tree structure using the fewest number of nodes. This explains the garden-path effect in sentences such as (1). Figure 17.1a shows a simplified tree structure of the reduced relative analysis (Frazier, 1979), while Figure 17.1b shows the tree structure of the main clause analysis. At *examined*, the reduced relative analysis requires more nodes (the circled NP and S nodes) than the main clause analysis, so the main clause analysis is initially adopted. However, this analysis is inconsistent with the disambiguation at *by the lawyer*, so the processor cannot attach this phrase (as indicated in Fig. 17.1b) and has to reanalyze. Hence, (1) is harder to process than an unambiguous relative clause containing *that was* preceding the verb *examined* (e.g. Ferreira and Clifton, 1986; Trueswell et al., 1994). The minimal attachment principle also explains people's parsing preferences in many other syntactic ambiguities across different languages.

If two analyses of an ambiguous structure have an equal number of tree structure nodes, the late closure principle applies. It predicts that people attach an ambiguous phrase to the currently processed phrase. The late closure principle accounts for parsing preferences in many other ambiguities. For example, it predicts that in (2), the relative clause *that was tasty* prefers to attach low to the most recent noun phrase *the sauce*

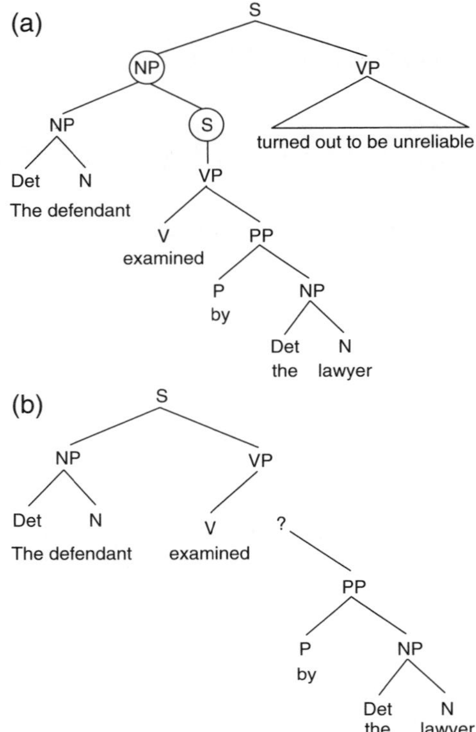

Figure 17.1 (a) Simplified tree structure of the reduced relative analysis for *The defendant examined by the lawyer turned out to be unreliable.* (b) Simplified tree structure of the main clause analysis.

rather than high to *the steak* (e.g. Traxler et al., 1998; Gilboy et al., 1995).

2. The steak with the sauce that was tasty didn't win a prize.

In many cases, late closure results in a preference for attachment to the most recent phrase in the preceding part of the sentence, and therefore it makes predictions similar to those of recency principles in other theories (Gibson, 1998; Kimball, 1973; Stevenson, 1994). Proponents of the garden-path model have conducted several studies that showed evidence for garden-path effects predicted by minimal attachment and late closure (e.g. Ferreira and Clifton, 1986; Frazier and Rayner, 1982; Rayner et al., 1983).

The garden-path account assumes a third parsing principle, known as the "active filler strategy," which accounts for the way in which people process unbounded dependencies, as found in relative clauses and questions such as (3).

3. Who did the housekeeper from Germany urge the guests to consider?

Following transformational grammars (e.g. Chomsky, 1981), the garden-path theory assumes that the filler *who* has been moved from its original direct object position and leaves a gap. The active filler strategy predicts that the processor fills the gap as early as possible. Because the gap following *urge* (as in *The housekeeper from Germany urged who?*) occurs earlier than following *consider* (the correct interpretation), the active filler strategy predicts a misanalysis in (3), resulting in processing difficulty. Several experiments have provided evidence consistent with this strategy (e.g. Frazier and Clifton, 1989; Frazier and Flores D'Arcais, 1989), though the data are also compatible with accounts without gaps (Traxler and Pickering, 1996); see also Phillips and Wagers (Chapter 45 this volume).

Although the garden-path model has been the dominant modular account, a number of alternative accounts also claim that the processor initially ignores certain sources of information. Most of these assume that the processor prefers analyses that involve a thematic relationship; in other words, it prefers arguments, which receive a thematic role from another word in the sentence (e.g. a verb), over adjuncts, which do not (e.g. Abney, 1989; Crocker, 1995; Pritchett, 1992). In support of this, Schütze and Gibson (1999) found that minimal attachment of the adjunct phrase *for a month* to the verb phrase containing *considered* in (4a) was harder to process than non-minimal argument of the argument phrase *for a raise* to the noun phrase *employee demands* in (4b).

4a. The company lawyers considered employee demands for a month but they did not act.
4b. The company lawyers considered employee demands for a raise but they did not act.

17.3 **Reanalysis**

An important question in modular accounts is what happens once the processor discovers that the initial analysis is inconsistent with subsequently processed disambiguating information and has to reanalyze (i.e., it has to construct an alternative analysis). We will discuss reanalysis before we move on to interactive models, because it plays such an essential role in modular models. Modular accounts are generally serial models, so they assume that the processor adopts only a single analysis at any one time. Reanalysis occurs when the initial analysis is inconsistent with later information. Detection of the misanalysis and the subsequent reanalysis of the initial structure result in processing difficulty.

It is usually assumed that reanalysis occurs when the initially adopted analysis is inconsistent with later syntactic information, i.e. syntactic information makes the initial analysis ungrammatical. Implausibility of the initial analysis may also be able to trigger reanalysis (Pickering and Traxler, 1998). However, there is little evidence for reanalysis when the initial choice remains syntactically possible and semantically plausible, but other sources of information (e.g. recency) favor the alternative analysis (Schneider and Phillips, 2001; Sturt et al., 2001).

Models of reanalysis provide an explanation for why some types of reanalysis appear to be more difficult than others (e.g. Gorrell, 1995; Pritchett, 1992; Sturt and Crocker, 1996). These theories have often relied on intuitive judgements about reanalysis difficulty, but there are also a number of experimental studies that have tested different factors affecting reanalysis cost. For example, Sturt et al. (1999) compared reanalysis cost in object/complement clause ambiguities such as (5a) with that in object/null complement ambiguities such as (5b).

5a. The Australian woman saw the famous doctor had been drinking quite a lot.
5b. Before the woman visited the famous doctor had been drinking quite a lot.

Although the ambiguities were controlled for non-syntactic factors such as lexical frequency preferences, processing difficulty with (5b) was larger than with (5a). Pritchett's (1992) explanation of this difference is that *the famous doctor* has to move out of the thematic domain of *visited* in (5b), whereas it remains within the domain of *saw* in (5a). Alternatively, both Gorrell (1995) and Sturt and Crocker (1996) proposed that the parser has to change hierarchical relations in the tree structure in (5b) but not in (5a).

Several other studies have shown that the length of the temporarily ambiguous phrase (e.g. *the famous doctor* in (5)) affects reanalysis cost (e.g. Ferreira and Henderson, 1991; Tabor and Hutchins, 2004). Ferreira and Henderson (1991) argued that the further the head noun (e.g. *doctor*) is from the point of disambiguation, the stronger the processor commits to a thematic analysis, and the harder reanalysis is. Finally, Sturt et al. (2002) showed that during reanalysis, attachment to a recent phrase is preferred to attachment to a more distant phrase, suggesting that reattachment to a distant phrase is costly.

However, experiments by Christianson et al. (2001) suggested that people do not always successfully abandon their initial analysis after encountering a syntactic disambiguation, contrary to the assumptions implicit in most reanalysis models. Christianson et al. showed that following temporarily ambiguous sentences such as (6), participants usually answered the question *Who spit up on the bed?* correctly, suggesting that they had correctly analyzed *the baby* as the subject of *spit up*.

6. While Anna dressed the baby that was small and cute spit up on the bed.

The more striking result was that following sentences such as (6), participants more often answered *yes* to the question *Did Anna dress the baby?* than following sentences that were disambiguated by a comma following *dressed*. Hence, Christianson et al. concluded that readers adopted the subject analysis for *the baby*, while at the same time they retained the (incorrect) analysis on which this phrase was the object of the preceding verb.

One possibility is that these results are due to strategic processes that occur when people have to answer the question. However, in a reading study, Kaschak and Glenberg (2004) showed that incorrectly adopted structures affect the reading of subsequent utterances in cases where the correct alternative is a newly learned structure. Furthermore, van Gompel et al. (2006) showed that the initially adopted but incorrect analysis primes the production of subsequent sentences. Hence, these results suggest that the initial analysis retains activation even if the disambiguation is inconsistent with it.

17.4 **Interactive models**

In contrast to modular models, interactive accounts assume that the processor immediately draws upon all possible sources of information during sentence processing, including semantics, discourse context, and information about the frequency of syntactic structures. Current interactive models are usually called *constraint-based theories* (e.g. MacDonald et al., 1994; McRae et al., 1998; Trueswell et al., 1994) and follow from earlier interactive accounts (e.g. Tyler and Marslen-Wilson, 1977). They generally assume that all syntactic alternatives are activated in parallel, with the analysis receiving most support from the various sources of information or constraints being activated most. When one analysis has a much higher activation than its alternative(s), processing is easy, but when two analyses have an approximately equal activation, competition occurs, and this results in processing difficulty. For example, when the constraints at the beginning of the sentence highly activate one analysis, but disambiguating information later in the sentence activates an alternative analysis, the two analyses have a similar activation at the point of disambiguation. In such a case, it takes a long time before the correct analysis wins the competition and before the incorrect (but initially highly activated) analysis is inhibited. This results in processing difficulty. Note that there is no true reanalysis in this type of model, because both analyses are activated from the onset of the ambiguity, so disambiguation does not necessitate the construction of an analysis that was not initially considered.

Most constraint-based models are lexicalist: they assume that syntactic information is associated with words. For example, it is generally assumed that all verbs contain information about the frequency with which they occur in particular argument frames and that this type of information is used during syntactic ambiguity resolution. Hence, many models assume that there is a tight correspondence between sentence comprehension and production preferences: structures that are frequently produced should be easier to process than structures than are infrequent. One possible way to determine frequency constraints is to experimentally elicit production preferences by asking participants to complete sentence fragments. Constraint-based theories claim that parsing preferences should correlate with such completion preferences (e.g. Garnsey et al., 1997; McRae et al., 1998; Trueswell et al., 1993).

Constraint-based theorists have implemented computational models to explain how various sources of information interact during the processing of reduced relative clause ambiguities. One such model was proposed by McRae et al. (1998) and Spivey and Tanenhaus (1998). In their model, contextual information, semantic constraints, and information about the structures' frequency determine the activation levels of alternative syntactic analyses. At each word, the syntactic analyses compete until one reaches a threshold level of activation and the others are sufficiently inhibited. The longer it takes one analysis to reach threshold, the longer processing times are. Hence, processing is slow when two analyses receive approximately equal support from the different constraints and fast when one analysis receives much more support than its alternative(s). McRae et al. showed that this model accurately predicted processing difficulty in reduced relatives.

Tabor and Tanenhaus (1999; Tabor et al., 1997) reported a different type of constraint-based model that learns to predict sentence fragment continuations using sentences generated by a grammar which employs information about the frequency with which structures occur. The sentence fragments are represented in a multidimensional space, with fragments which have similar continuations forming clusters that function as attractors. Tabor and colleagues assume that processing times for ambiguous sentences can be modeled as the time it takes for a representation of a sentence fragment to drift to one of the attractors in the space: the more similar a sentence fragment representation is to those in a single cluster and the denser that cluster is, the faster it reaches the attractor. The model predicts that the faster the attractor is reached, the faster processing should be. Because the clusters reflect both syntactic and semantic similarities between sentence fragments, both sources of information should be used immediately during syntactic ambiguity resolution. Tabor and Tanenhaus (1999) showed that in this way reading times for reduced relatives could be accurately modelled.

17.5 Semantic effects

Semantic information often provides strongly constraining information for syntactic analysis, so an important question has been whether this information is used immediately to guide sentence processing. According to constraint-based models, semantic information should have an immediate effect on sentence processing, whereas according to modular models, the use of this information should be delayed.

A number of studies have investigated the reduced relative/main clause ambiguity in (7) (see above).

7a. The defendant examined by the lawyer turned out to be unreliable.
7b. The evidence examined by the lawyer turned out to be unreliable.

When people encounter *examined* in (7a), both the main clause and the reduced relative analysis are plausible. All studies show that reading times for *by the lawyer* are longer than for the same region in unambiguous sentences containing *that was* preceding *examined*, suggesting that people initially adopt the main clause analysis, and have to revise this when they reach the disambiguation. The crucial question is whether similar difficulty occurs in (7b), where semantic or animacy information rules out the main clause analysis (evidence cannot examine anything). Some eye-movement reading studies found no immediate effects of semantics, so (7b) did not differ from (7a) (Ferreira and Clifton, 1986; Rayner et al., 1983), whereas another found no sign of difficulty with (7b) at all, in comparison to an unambiguous control (Trueswell et al., 1994). However, a more recent study by Clifton et al. (2003), which used more materials and additional eye-movement measures, did observe difficulty with (7b). Similarly, experiments on different types of ambiguity also show that semantic information fails to override syntactic preferences (e.g. Hoeks et al., 2006; Schriefers et al., 1995). Hence, it appears that, if anything, semantics has only a weak effect on sentence processing.

However, this is not necessarily inconsistent with constraint-based models, so long as semantics provides a fairly weak constraint. Other methods may therefore be more helpful in discriminating between the models. Using a speed/accuracy trade-off method (in which participants are forced to respond quickly whether or not they are confident of the appropriate response), McElree and Griffith (1995) showed that semantics had a slower effect on grammaticality judgements than syntax, even though both provided equally strongly constraining information. Furthermore, in an ERP study, Hagoort (2003) showed that semantic effects, reflected by an N400 ERP response, were larger when the sentence contained a syntactic violation. In contrast, syntactic effects, reflected by a P600 response, were unaffected by semantic violations. Together, these results suggest that syntax affects semantic interpretation and therefore that syntax functionally precedes semantics. In conclusion, most evidence seems to suggest that semantics does not constrain initial syntactic analysis. This is most consistent with modular models.

17.6 Frequency effects

Constraint-based theories assume that people make immediate use of information about structural frequency. However, there are different possibilities here. Mitchell et al. (1995) distinguished between fine-grained, lexical frequency information, which takes into account how often specific words (especially verbs) occur in particular structures, and coarse-grained information, which simply considers the frequency of the structure itself. They argued that a coarse-grained frequency account might explain why different languages have different relative clause attachment preferences in sentences such as (8).

8a. The journalist interviewed the daughter of the colonel who had the accident.
8b. El periodista entrevisto a la hija del coronel que tuvo el accidente.

In the English sentence (8a) and its Spanish translation (8b), the relative clause *who had the accident* may be attached to either *the daughter* (high in the tree structure) or to *the colonel* (low). Cuetos and Mitchell (1988) found a low attachment preference in English, but a high attachment preference in Spanish. More recent studies have shown either no preference or a weak low attachment preference in English (e.g. Carreiras and Clifton, 1993; 1999; Traxler et al., 1998), whereas many other languages, such as Spanish, Dutch, and French, show a preference for high attachment (e.g. Brysbaert and Mitchell, 1996; Carreiras and Clifton, 1993; 1999; Zagar et al., 1997). Mitchell et al. (1995) argued that attachment preferences may be different between languages because in some languages, high relative clause attachment is most frequent, whereas in a language like English, low attachment is most frequent.

Cross-linguistic differences in relative clause attachment present a problem for the garden-path theory, because late closure predicts a universal preference for low attachment. Hence, Frazier and Clifton (1996) proposed that the garden-path theory only holds for *primary phrases* (roughly, arguments), and that non-structural information can have an immediate effect on the processing of other phrases. Essentially, this implies that the processor is no longer modular for non-primary phrases such as relative clauses.

However, the coarse-grained frequency account has difficulty explaining why there is a high attachment relative clause preference in Dutch (Brysbaert and Mitchell, 1996) even though low attachment is more frequent (Mitchell and Brysbaert, 1998). Furthermore, relative clause attachment preferences are strongly affected by particular words. For example, languages show a strong low attachment preference when the preposition in the noun phrase is *with* (e.g. *the colonel with the daughter*), but either no preference or a much weaker preference with *of* (Gilboy et al., 1995; Traxler et al., 1998); and attachment preferences are also affected by animacy and concreteness (e.g. Desmet et al., 2006). A frequency-based model therefore has to assume that the processor takes more fine-grained frequency information into account.

Many constraint-based theories assume that the processor employs both coarse-grained and fine-grained lexical frequency information (e.g. McRae et al., 1998; Tabor and Tanenhaus, 1999), but tests of the theories have largely focused on the latter. Trueswell et al. (1993) tested sentences such as (9), where *the solution* is temporarily ambiguous between an object analysis (the student forgot the solution) and the correct complement-clause analysis.

9a. The student forgot the solution was in the book.
9b. The student hoped the solution was in the book.

The verb *forgot* occurs more frequently with an object, whereas *hoped* occurs most frequently with a complement clause. Trueswell et al. observed that (9a) took longer to read than sentences disambiguated by *that* following the critical verb, whereas there was no difference for sentences such as (9b). This suggests that people use lexical frequency information during syntactic ambiguity resolution (see also Garnsey et al., 1997; Mitchell and Holmes, 1985; Trueswell, 1996). These results are difficult to reconcile with structurally based models such as the garden-path model unless one assumes that frequency information can be used very rapidly to revise initial structural decisions (e.g. Frazier, 1987; 1995). However, a number of studies suggest that lexical frequency information is not used to guide initial processing (e.g. Kennison, 2001; Mitchell, 1987; Pickering et al., 2000). For example, Pickering et al. showed that readers experienced difficulty in (10) shortly after *her exercises* (an implausible object) even though the verb *realised* is biased towards the complement clause analysis.

10. The young athlete realised her exercises one day might make her a world-class sprinter.

One way of explaining these conflicting results is to assume that the verb bias facilitates the complement-clause analysis, but does not completely rule out the object analysis. Therefore, there is some difficulty when the object analysis is implausible.

17.7 Discourse effects

Crain and Steedman (1985) argued that many parsing preferences occur because the sentences are presented in isolation. In the absence of a context, people initially prefer to attach the prepositional phrase *with the dynamite/new lock* in (11) to the verb phrase containing *blew open* rather than to the noun phrase *the safe* (Rayner et al., 1983).

11a. The burglar blew open the safe with the dynamite and made off with the loot.
11b. The burglar blew open the safe with the new lock and made off with the loot.

But when the same sentences are presented with specific discourse contexts, the preferences may change. Altmann and Steedman (1988) had participants first read a context sentence that referred to either one or two safes. If only one safe had been mentioned, then the complex noun phrase *the safe with the new lock* is unnecessarily specific, so the prepositional phrase *with the new lock* took a long time to read. But if two safes had been mentioned, then the simple noun phrase *the safe* fails to pick out a particular safe, and so the phrase *with the dynamite* took a long time to read. Altmann and Steedman claimed that people initially adopt whichever analysis is compatible with the discourse context, attaching the prepositional phrase to the verb phrase when one safe has been mentioned, but to the noun phrase when two safes have been mentioned. In the absence of any context, verb-phrase attachment is preferred because the processor has to assume one unmentioned safe, which is easier than assuming more than one unmentioned safe. The findings from Altmann and Steedman's (1988) study are consistent with several other studies investigating referential context effects (e.g. Altmann et al., 1992; Van Berkum et al., 1999). However, it appears that one important factor is the strength of the bias when the syntactically ambiguous sentence is presented in the absence of a context. Several studies suggest that referential contexts may affect the processing of weakly biased structures, but not of more strongly biased structures (Altmann et al., 1998; Britt, 1994; Britt et al., 1992; Spivey and Tanenhaus, 1998). In particular, Britt (1994) showed that referential contexts neutralized the preference to attach a prepositional phrase to the verb phrase if the prepositional phrase was an optional argument of the verb (12a, b), but not if it was an obligatory argument (12c, d).

12a. He dropped the book on the chair before leaving.
12b. He dropped the book on the battle onto the chair.
12c. He put the book on the chair before leaving.
12d. He put the book on the battle onto the chair.

According to constraint-based theories, discourse information is just one of the many factors that affect sentence processing, so one might assume that it is overridden by other factors in ambiguities that are strongly biased towards one analysis. In such ambiguities, discourse effects may be relatively weak and may therefore show up in later measures of processing. In weakly biased ambiguities, by contrast, discourse may overpower other factors, so discourse effects should be clearer.

Spivey et al. (2002) argued that information from the linguistic context may be forgotten or may not be salient, so it may exert a relatively weak effect on sentence processing. They investigated whether information provided by a visual context that is present during the auditory presentation of a sentence affects processing. They asked people to follow auditory instructions such as (13).

13a. Put the apple on the towel in the box.
13b. Put the apple that's on the towel in the box.

Spivey et al. used the *visual world eye-movement method* (Tanenhaus et al., 1995). People's eye movements were monitored while they were presented with either a one-referent scene containing a single apple on a towel, or a two-referent scene containing two apples, one of which was on a towel. Both scenes also contained an empty towel without an apple, and a box. When viewing the one-referent scene, people looked more often at the empty towel when hearing (13a) than when hearing (13b). Hence, they appeared to initially misinterpret the prepositional phrase *on the towel* in the temporarily ambiguous sentence (13a) as modifying the verb *put* and took it as the destination for the apple, rather than as the modifier of *the apple*, which is the correct interpretation. But most importantly, in the two-referent scene, no such difference was observed, suggesting that participants immediately interpreted *on the towel* as a modifier of *the apple*. Hence, Spivey et al. argued that visual referential context immediately affected syntactic ambiguity resolution. Chambers et al. (2004) showed that the use of visual context during syntactic ambiguity resolution is affected by action-relevant properties of objects, termed *affordances*. If the only one of the referents in the two-referent scene could be picked up (e.g. the scene contained a liquid and a solid egg), people misinterpreted the temporarily ambiguous prepositional phrase as modifying the verb, so they essentially processed the sentence as in a one-referent scene.

Results from Knoeferle et al. (2005) indicate that people also use visual information that provides cues about the event roles in the sentence. They tested word order ambiguities in German and showed that depicted actions influenced whether people analyzed an ambiguous noun phrase as an agent (the subject) or a patient (the object) of the verb. However, Snedeker and Trueswell (2004) found less strong effects of visual context with ambiguities that were only slightly different from (13). They showed that visual context influenced syntactic ambiguity resolution, but that it did not completely eliminate the preference for the verb modifier analysis. Interestingly, Trueswell et al. (1999) and Snedeker and Trueswell (2004) found no evidence that children use the visual-world context at all during syntactic ambiguity resolution.

Recent research has also investigated other discourse effects on parsing. Hoeks et al. (2002) proposed that people adopt the simplest possible topic structure. They showed that when a sentence occurs in a neutral context, people preferred the analysis that introduces the fewest number of sentence topics. But when the discourse had already introduced these topics, this preference was neutralized.

Altmann et al. (1998; see also Liversedge et al., 1998) showed that contexts created by indirect questions also affected syntactic ambiguity resolution. In the absence of a question, reading times for *next week* in (14a) were longer than for *last week* in (14b), indicating that readers prefer to attach the temporal phrase to the second verb phrase (*she proposed to the committee*) rather than to the first (*She'll implement the plan*).

14a. She'll implement the plan she proposed to the committee next week, they hope.
14b. She'll implement the plan she proposed to the committee last week, they hope.

But when these sentences were preceded by an indirect question such as (15), which creates the expectation that the first clause is modified, reading times were longer for (14b) than (14a).

15. The committee members wonder when Fiona will implement the plan she proposed.

Hence, it appears that indirect questions can set up a context that affects sentence processing.

An interesting issue is whether the processing of word order ambiguities in languages with flexible word order is affected by discourse factors. Functional linguistic theories assume that different word orders reflect different information structures of the sentence (e.g. Givón, 1984; 1990). Non-canonical word orders should be straightforward when justified by prior context but difficult otherwise. In accord with this, Kaiser and Trueswell (2004) showed that sentences with non-canonical object–verb–subject order in Finnish took longer to read than canonical subject–verb–object sentences (see also Hyönä and Hujanen, 1997), but this effect was reduced when the context introduced the object. A visual-world eye-movement experiment suggested that the residual difficulty associated with object–verb–subject sentences was due to people anticipating new information: before hearing the postverbal noun, participants looked more often at new information following object–verb–subject than following subject–verb–object sentences.

In sum, it appears that discourse information often has a very early influence on sentence processing, though it does not always completely override parsing preferences that exist in the absence of a context. If the use of discourse information is delayed, as claimed by modular models, then the delay must be very short—too short to be detected by current psycholinguistic methods.

17.8 **Testing other properties of the models**

In addition to the distinction between modularity and interaction, the dominant models in the sentence processing literature differ in other ways. Most modular models are serial models, i.e. they assume that the processor adopts only a single analysis at a time, whereas most constraint-based models assume that syntactic analyses are activated in parallel in cases of ambiguity. Unfortunately, it has been notoriously difficult to test whether the processor is serial or parallel (e.g. Gibson and Pearlmutter, 2000; Lewis, 2000), because both serial accounts and ranked parallel accounts (in which one analysis is initially favored over others) predict comparable garden-path effects.

A more fruitful way of discriminating between the models is to investigate whether processing difficulty is due to reanalysis, as claimed by the garden-path model and other two-stage accounts, or competition, as claimed by most constraint-based theories. Van Gompel et al. (2005) compared the processing of globally ambiguous sentences such as (16a), where either the bodyguard or the governor may be retiring, with semantically disambiguated sentences (16b/c) and unambiguous sentences (16d).

16a. I read that the bodyguard of the governor retiring after the troubles is very rich.
16b. I read that the governor of the province retiring after the troubles is very rich.

16c. I read that the province of the governor retiring after the troubles is very rich.
16d. I read quite recently that the governor retiring after the troubles is very rich.

According to constraint-based competition models, strong competition should occur in (16a), because the constraints equally support both analyses: they are equally plausible and roughly equally preferred. In contrast, competition should be much weaker in (16b/c), because plausibility should immediately affect syntactic ambiguity resolution. However, (16a) was actually *easier* to process than (16b) and (16c) and in fact did not differ from (16d). These results also present difficulty for the garden-path model, which cannot explain why low attachment sentences such as (16c) are harder than globally ambiguous sentences such as (16a). Van Gompel et al. (2005) accounted for these results in terms of the "unrestricted race model" (Van Gompel et al., 2001). This model claims that when there is syntactic ambiguity, the possible analyses are engaged in a race, and that the analysis which is constructed fastest is adopted. The more strongly syntactic and non-syntactic information prior to the point of ambiguity (at *retiring* in (16)) support an analysis, the faster it is constructed, and therefore the more likely it is to be adopted. For balanced ambiguities such as (16), the processor initially adopts each analysis about half the time, because both analyses are about equally preferred. It therefore has to reanalyze about half the time in (16b) and (16c), because plausibility information at *retiring* is inconsistent with the initial analysis. However, it never has to reanalyze when both analyzes are plausible, as in (16a), or when the sentence is unambiguous, as in (16d) (see also Traxler et al., 1998; Van Gompel et al., 2001).

Recently, Green and Mitchell (2006) have argued that Van Gompel et al.'s (2005) results can be explained by the competition-integration model proposed by McRae et al. (1998) and Spivey and Tanenhaus (1998), even though this model assumes competition. To make this model work, Green and Mitchell postulated that competition between high and low attachment in (16) occurs from the very first word in the sentence. By the time the relative clause is encountered, only a single analysis is highly activated. Therefore, there should be no competition in the globally ambiguous sentences. In the disambiguated sentences, by contrast, the highly activated analysis may be implausible, and this should result in difficulty. However, given that an infinite number of structures for the rest of the sentence is possible at the beginning of the sentence, the construction of all these structures should result in a massive working memory load. Because there is no evidence for extreme difficulty at the beginning of the sentence, this assumption seems implausible.

To conclude, there is no reason to assume that competition occurs during syntactic ambiguity resolution. Instead, the results are more consistent with the unrestricted race model, which claims that a single analysis is adopted in a probabilistic fashion, and that difficulty occurs when the initial analysis is implausible. This model also fits well with research showing that non-syntactic information has an early influence on syntactic ambiguity resolution, as it claims that both syntactic and non-syntactic information affect the chance with which an analysis is adopted.

17.9 Working memory capacity

Although much research on sentence processing has investigated modularity and interaction, several other issues have also been prominent over the years, and several new strands of research have recently started to emerge. One issue that has been the focus of much interest is the role of working memory capacity in sentence processing. Much debate has centered around the question of whether the working memory resources employed during syntactic processing are different from the working memory resources used for other, more conscious verbal tasks. Just and Carpenter (1992) proposed a *shared resources account* of working memory, in which all linguistic processes draw upon the same limited pool of working memory resources. When people's working memory capacity is exceeded, because either storage or processing demands are very high, this should result in either a processing slow down or a failure to maintain linguistic information in memory. They claimed that individual differences in people's verbal working memory lead to individual differences in sentence processing. These differences can be assessed with a *reading span test* (e.g. Daneman and Carpenter, 1980), which determines how many unrelated words people can remember while reading sentences.

In contrast, Caplan and Waters (1999) proposed the *dedicated resources account*, which assumes that the working memory resources dedicated to obligatory and automatic linguistic processes such as sentence processing are different from those used for more strategic and controlled linguistic processes such as those used in the reading span test.

In one study, King and Just (1991) tested subject and object relative clauses such as (17) in order to investigate whether sentence complexity effects were larger for people with a low reading span than for people with a high reading span.

17a. The reporter who attacked the senator admitted the error publicly after the meeting.

17b. The reporter who the senator attacked admitted the error publicly after the meeting.

As predicted by the shared resources account, there was an interaction between reading span and sentence complexity such that low-span readers experienced more difficulty with object relatives (as compared to subject relatives) than high-span readers. However, subsequent experiments did not replicate these results (Traxler et al., 2005; Waters and Caplan, 2004), and therefore support the dedicated resources account.

Just and Carpenter (1992) also claimed that their theory has important implications for the debate on modularity and interaction. They argued that syntactic processing for low-capacity readers is essentially modular, because their working memory capacity is not sufficiently large to use non-syntactic information immediately. In contrast, people with a larger working memory capacity have sufficient resources to use both syntactic and non-syntactic information immediately, so syntactic processing is essentially interactive. As evidence for this claim, Just and Carpenter reported an experiment investigating the use of animacy in reduced relative ambiguities such as (7). The results showed that high-span readers experienced less difficulty with reduced relatives with an inanimate first noun phrase (7b) than with an animate first noun phrase (7a), but that animacy did not affect how low-span readers processed these sentences. However, as pointed out by Waters and Caplan (1996), exactly the same effects occurred with unambiguous controls containing *that was* following the initial noun phrase *defendant/ evidence*. Hence, there was no evidence that during syntactic ambiguity resolution, high- and low-span readers used animacy information differently.

Finally, MacDonald et al. (1992) claimed that readers with a high working memory span retain syntactic analyses in parallel, whereas people with a low span do not. However, a subsequent study by Pearlmutter and MacDonald (1995) suggested that the difference in the size of the ambiguity effect for high- and low-span readers was due to their different sensitivity to subtle plausibility constraints, rather than due to a difference in their ability to retain syntactic analyzes in parallel, while Caplan and Waters (1999) failed to replicate MacDonald et al.'s results.

More recently, MacDonald and Christiansen (2002) argued that interactions between reading span and sentence processing effects can be explained as effects of experience. They claimed that people with a high reading span tend to read more than people with a low reading span, and that the difference in processing difficulty between subject and object relatives decreases with people's reading experience. Because the word order in object relative clauses is rare, people who read little (especially complex sentences) have insufficient experience with these sentences, so they should find them relatively hard to process. In contrast, people with more reading experience should find them relatively easy. However, Caplan and Waters (2002) found no evidence that people with a low reading span read less than high-span readers, casting doubt on the claim that reading experience could explain any interactions between reading span and sentence processing effects. Furthermore, as we have seen, many studies have failed to find evidence that reading span interacts with processing difficulty, which is problematic for both Just and Carpenter's (1992) and MacDonald and Christiansen's (2002) accounts. On balance then, the results seem most compatible with the dedicated resources account.

17.10 Structural complexity

A number of current theories provide accounts of which structures should result in a high working memory load. Probably the most influential and detailed of these is Gibson's (1998) *syntactic prediction locality theory* (SPLT) (see Lewis, 1996; Stabler, 1994 for other accounts; see also Phillips and Wagers, Chapter 45 this volume). It claims that two factors result in memory load: syntactic storage and integration. Both occur when there is a syntactic dependency between two linguistic elements in a sentence. Integration costs occur when a linguistic element has to be integrated with another element with which it forms a dependency. For example, unbounded dependencies incur an integration cost when the moved phrase (e.g. a *wh*-phrase) is integrated with its trace position. Storage costs occur while a linguistic element has to be retained in memory before it can be integrated with the element with which it forms a dependency. The SPLT claims that the more discourse referents (i.e. an entity that is referred to with a referring expression) intervene between two elements which form a syntactic dependency, the larger both integration and storage costs are.

A number of experiments have provided evidence for storage costs. Chen et al. (2005) showed that reading times for regions intervening a syntactic dependency were longer than similar regions in sentences where there was no such syntactic dependency. Fiebach et al. (2002) and Phillips et al. (2005) showed evidence for a sustained negativity in the ERP signal during sentence regions that intervened between a syntactic dependency and argued that this was due to syntactic storage costs. Other studies have provided evidence for integration costs. For example, in another ERP experiment, Kaan et al. (2000) observed a larger P600 effect at a position in the sentence where an unbounded dependency had to be formed than in a comparable sentence without such a dependency (see also Fiebach et al., 2002; Phillips et al., 2005).

Gibson (1998) claimed that object relatives such as (17a) are harder to process than subject relatives such as (17b) because both storage and integration costs are higher in object relatives. Essentially, this is because the dependency between *who* and *attacked* in (17b) crosses the discourse referent *the senator*, whereas the dependencies in (17a) do not. Warren and Gibson (2002) argued that the extent to which object relatives cause processing difficulty depends on the discourse status of this noun phrase: if the noun phrase (e.g. an indefinite or definite noun phrase) tends to refer to an inaccessible or new referent, object relatives are very hard to process, whereas they are relatively easy if the noun phrase (e.g. a pronoun) tends to refer to highly accessible information. They provided evidence for this in grammaticality judgement experiments.

However, there are different explanations for the effect of type of noun phrase. Kaan (2001) argued that discourse referents which are highly accessible tend to be syntactic subjects (e.g. Keenan and Comrie, 1977). When the referent in the object relative clause is a pronoun (as in *the reporter who you attacked admitted the error*) and therefore tends to refer to highly accessible referents, it is easy to associate it with the subject role, so processing is easy. In contrast, if the referent is a definite noun phrase and therefore tends to refer to inaccessible antecedents, associating it with the subject role is difficult. Although Kaan proposed this explanation to account for the processing of relative clauses in Dutch, where subject and object relative clauses are often ambiguous, this account may also explain Warren and Gibson's findings in English.

Gordon et al. (2001; 2004) proposed that processing difficulty in object relative clauses is due to interference between the noun phrases (e.g. *reporter* and *senator*) while they have to be retained in memory (see Lewis and Vasishth, 2005 for a different type of interference-based account). They argued that when the two noun phrases are of the same type (e.g. both are definite noun phrases) interference is larger than when the two noun phrases are of a different type (e.g. a definite noun phrase and a pronoun). This explains Warren and Gibson's (2002) finding that difficulty with object relatives is much reduced if the noun phrase in the relative clause is a pronoun (see also Gordon et al., 2001). Similarly, it explains why object relatives such as (18a), in which one of the noun phrases is a definite noun phrase and the other a proper name, are easier to process than object relatives with two noun phrases, such as (18b) (Gordon et al., 2001; 2004).

18a. It was John that the lawyer saw in the parking lot.

18b. It was the barber that the lawyer saw in the parking lot.

This latter finding is inconsistent with Gibson's SPLT, because the noun phrase *the lawyer*, which crosses the dependency between the *relative pronoun* and the verb *saw* in the relative clause, is identical. Finally, Gordon et al. (2004) showed that difficulty with object relatives is unaffected by whether this noun phrase is definite or indefinite. This is difficult for both the SPLT and Kaan's (2001) account to explain, because both claim that the difference in accessibility of the discourse entities that definite and indefinite noun phrases refer to should affect processing.

An important question is whether the processing of subject and object relative clauses is only affected by differences in working memory demands. Several studies have shown that semantic factors also play a role. That is, object relatives tend to be easier to process when semantics rules out the subject relative clause interpretation than when it is consistent with both the object and subject relative interpretation (Mak et al., 2002; Traxler et al., 2005). However, results by Traxler et al. (2002) in English and Schriefers et al. (1995) in German suggest that semantic information does not completely eliminate difficulty with object relatives, and therefore that it does not entirely neutralize difficulty resulting from working memory demands.

17.11 **Adopting ungrammatical syntactic structures**

A major challenge for parsing theories comes from recent findings suggesting that the processor may sometimes adopt ungrammatical syntactic structures. Gibson and Thomas (1999) observed that in sentences with multiple object-relative embeddings, people preferred incomplete sentences to complete sentences. Furthermore, Christianson et al.'s (2001) data discussed above suggest that people may retain two incompatible syntactic structures in parallel. Tabor et al. (2004) showed that people had difficulty with reduced relatives such as in (19) even though the prior syntactic structure made the alternative main clause analysis ungrammatical.

19. The bandit worried about the prisoner transported the whole way by the capricious guards.

Research by Ferreira (2003) suggests that people may even misanalyze sentences that are not locally ambiguous. She showed that people often misanalyzed passive sentences such as (20) as an active sentence meaning *the dog bit the man*.

20. The dog was bitten by the man.

Ferreira argued that the processor uses a strategy to interpret the first noun phrase as the agent and the second as the patient, despite the fact that this is ungrammatical (see also Townsend and Bever, 2001). According to Ferreira, this strategy is particularly strong if plausibility information supports this analysis. Ferreira used an offline task where participants had to identify the "doer" and the "acted-on" nouns in the sentences. This task may be sensitive to strategic effects, so it will be important to examine whether these effects also occur during online processing.

Interestingly, on-line evidence from ERP studies suggests that people may sometimes misanalyze active sentences as passives. Kim and Osterhout (2005) presented readers with sentences such as (21):

21a. The hearty meal was devouring by the kids.
21b. The dusty tabletops were devouring thoroughly.

At *devouring* in (21a), a P600 effect occurred (relative to plausible control conditions), which is normally associated with syntactic incongruency (e.g. Kutas and Federmeier, Chapter 23 this volume), whereas in (21b) an N400 effect, associated with semantic incongruency, occurred. Kim and Osterhout argued that because *hearty meal* is a plausible theme of *devour*, readers analyze it as the subject of a passive, despite the fact that this is ungrammatical. In Kim and Osterhout's study, it is possible that readers initially analyzed the sentence as a passive because this analysis is grammatically possible and the most plausible analysis until they encounter the inflection *-ing*. However, Van Herten et al. (2005; Kolk et al., 2003) tested Dutch implausible sentences such as (22) and also showed a P600 effect at *joeg* 'hunted' (relative to plausible counterparts).

22. De vos die op de stroper joeg sloop door het bos.
The fox that at the poacher hunted stalked through the woods.
'The fox that hunted the poachers stalked through the woods.'

Here, the plausible analysis (the poacher hunted the fox) becomes syntactically impossible at *op* 'at' before *joeg* 'hunted'. Van Herten et al. (2005) proposed that readers use a plausibility heuristic in parallel with syntactic analysis, and that the conflict between the two results in a P600 effect. Hence, in contrast to Kim and Osterhout (2005), they do not assume that semantic plausibility causes syntactic misanalysis. Still, both accounts are inconsistent with the traditional view that the processor does not consider ungrammatical structures. However, this conclusion may not be necessary. Kuperberg et al. (2003) observed very similar results for sentences such as *For breakfast the eggs would eat toast and jam*, and argued that the P600 occurs because the agent role that is assigned by the verb is inconsistent with the inanimate subject. On this account, the processor does not initially consider the ungrammatical analysis.

In fact, research on unbounded dependencies (e.g. McElree and Griffith, 1998; Stowe, 1986; Traxler and Pickering, 1996) suggests that the processor does adhere to grammatical constraints known as *island constraints* (e.g. Ross, 1967). For example, Traxler and Pickering (1996) showed that people did not analyze *the book* as the theme of *wrote* in sentences similar to (23).

23. We like the book that the author who wrote unceasingly saw.

This suggests a very tight link between grammar and processor, in sharp contrast to studies like Ferreira (2003). It is likely that future research will try to reconcile these seemingly different results, and will lead to more detailed models of whether and how people construct ungrammatical syntactic representations.

17.12 Conclusions and future directions

We have seen that one of the important aims in sentence processing research has been to investigate whether the parser is modular or interactive. This research has revealed many of the factors that affect sentence processing. It appears that non-syntactic information often has a very rapid effect on sentence processing, especially discourse and frequency information, though the use of semantic plausibility information appears to be less rapid. Overall, the findings on the use of non-syntactic information seem most compatible with interactive accounts such as constraint-based theories (e.g. MacDonald et al., 1994; McRae et al., 1998; Trueswell et al., 1994). They can straightforwardly account for the rapid use of non-syntactic information, and many of the findings that show a delayed use of non-syntactic information may be explained by assuming that this information is too weak to override strong syntactic biases. Modular theories (e.g. Ferreira and Clifton, 1986; Frazier, 1987; Rayner et al., 1983) may account for the rapid use of non-syntactic information by assuming that the delay in the use of non-syntactic information is extremely short, and undetectable with our current methods. However, this raises the question of why one needs to postulate a two-stage processor to explain current data.

The very rapid use of non-syntactic information provides support for constraint-based theories, but not all findings are compatible with these theories. In particular we have seen that, contrary to the predictions of most constraint-based theories, there is evidence that competition during syntactic ambiguity resolution does not occur (e.g. Van Gompel et al., 2005). To explain the absence of competition (Green and Mitchell, 2006), one needs to resort to assumptions that seem implausible and for which there is certainly no evidence. Rather, the results suggest that the processor employs multiple sources of information to select an analysis, and processing difficulty occurs when reanalysis has to occur (rather than when two analyses compete).

Although the debate between modular and interactive models has dominated research on sentence processing, several other issues have also been the focus of attention. One important strand of research has investigated how working memory load affects processing. As we have discussed, it is clear that people use working memory during sentence processing, but the working memory resources used for sentence processing are likely to be different from those used for verbal tasks to assess working memory capacity such as the reading span task (e.g. Caplan and Waters, 1999; Waters and Caplan, 1996; but cf. Just and Carpenter, 1992). Other researchers have started to develop detailed models about the type of sentences that result in a high working memory load (e.g. Gibson, 1998). This has led to research investigating the processing of largely unambiguous sentences, which suggests that working-memory related factors such as storage cost, integration cost, and memory interference play important roles in the processing of sentences that involve long distance dependencies.

In the last couple of years, several new themes have started to emerge. We expect that future research will study sentence processing within a much broader perspective. For instance, the use of the visual-world eye-movement method (e.g. Tanenhaus et al., 1995) has opened up many possibilities for exploring the interaction between sentence and visual processing. As discussed in section 17.7 on discourse effects, it is already clear that the visual context has a strong influence on sentence processing (e.g. Chambers et al., 2004; Spivey et al., 2002). Furthermore, research on anticipations in sentence processing indicates that people look at objects in a scene which are likely to be mentioned in the upcoming part of the sentence (e.g. Altmann and Kamide, 1999; Kamide et al., 2003). It is probable that in the near future much progress will be made in research that investigates the interaction between language and vision.

Researchers have also become more and more interested in natural conversation. Until recently, most research focused on how people process perfectly constructed sentences, mostly during reading. However, the sentences produced during natural conversation are generally very different from those in well-constructed texts. During natural conversation, speakers often produce marginally grammatical sentences and disfluencies such as speech errors, corrections, repetitions, and pauses; so one challenge for sentence processing research is to investigate how people process sentences with such imperfections. As we have seen, several recent studies have investigated the processing of ungrammatical sentences (e.g. Ferreira, 2003; Kim and Osterhout, 2005). Researchers have also started to investigate how people process sentences with disfluencies. Bailey and Ferreira (2003) investigated sentences such as (24), where the noun phrase *the waiter* is temporarily ambiguous, because it can initially be part of a conjoined noun phrase (as in *Sandra bumped into the busboy and the waiter*) or the subject of a conjoined clause, as in the correct analysis for (24).

24. Sandra bumped into the busboy and the waiter told her to be careful.

Bailey and Ferreira observed that participants more often considered sentences such as (24) grammatical when a disfluency (*uh uh*) preceded *waiter* than when it preceded *busboy*. Similar effects occurred with disruptions consisting of environmental noises (e.g. barking, ringing telephone), but not with adjectives preceding the *waiter* or *busboy*. This indicates that interruptions affect sentence processing, but that the parser is insensitive to the type of interruption.

In another study on disfluencies, Lau and Ferreira (2005) investigated the effect of speech errors and subsequent self-corrections on sentence processing. Participants listened to sentences such as (25), which contained a speech error (*chosen*) and a self-correction (*selected*).

25. The little girl chosen, uh, selected for the role celebrated with her parents and friends.

When the speech error was an unambiguous past participle, as in (25), and therefore ruled out the main clause analysis, the sentence was judged as grammatical more often than when the speech error was ambiguous and could either be a past participle or a past tense (e.g. *picked*). Hence, processing of the reduced relative clause is affected by the speech error, indicating that the syntactic structure that is adopted when hearing the speech error is not entirely overwritten by the subsequent self-correction.

Finally, research has started to explore the relationship between sentence comprehension and production. In terms of representational economy, it seems plausible to assume that the syntactic representations drawn upon during comprehension and production are shared. Evidence for this comes from a structural priming study by Branigan et al. (2000). *Structural priming* refers to the finding that the processing of a structure is facilitated by very recent prior exposure to the same or a similar structure. Such an effect has been well documented in the sentence production literature (e.g. Bock, 1986; see Pickering and Branigan, 1999). Branigan et al. (2000) showed that people tended to produce sentences using the same structure as the structure in the immediately preceding sentence that they had just comprehended. They argued that because priming occurs from comprehension to production, people employ the same syntactic representations when they comprehend sentences as when they produce them. Pickering and Garrod (2004) argued that this alignment of representations between production and comprehension is particularly important in dialogue, because it facilitates both production and comprehension processes.

There is evidence that structural priming also affects comprehension processes (Arai et al., forthcoming; Branigan et al., 2005; Frazier et al., 1984; Mehler and Carey, 1967; Noppeney and Price, 2004). For example, in Arai et al., participants read prime sentences with a prepositional object structure such as (26a) or a double object structure such as (26b) Next, they listened to prepositional or double object target sentences such as (27a) and (27b) while they saw pictures of the nouns.

26a. The assassin will send the parcel to the dictator.
26b. The assassin will send the dictator the parcel.

27a. The pirate will send the necklace to the princess.
27b. The pirate will send the princess the necklace.

At the target verb in (27), participants looked more often at the necklace following prepositional object than following double object primes, and more often at the princess following double object than prepositional object primes. This indicates that people anticipate the first argument following the verb, and that this anticipation is primed by the structure of the preceding sentence. Given that syntactic priming occurs in both production and comprehension, this suggests that some of the mechanisms involved in comprehension and production are similar. However, there may be important differences too: Arai et al. and Branigan et al. only observed priming when the verb in prime and target was the same (e.g. *send* in (26) and (27)), but not when it was different. By contrast, priming in production occurs even when the verb is not repeated (Bock, 1986).

We anticipate that future research will consider sentence processing in a wider context. New research is likely to shed more light on the relationship between comprehension and production and on the interaction between language and visual context, and will explore sentence processing in natural conversation in more detail. We expect that study of these issues will feed back to more traditional questions in parsing, such as determining the role played by working memory constraints and working out which sources of information are used in selecting among potential analyses.

Acknowledgements

Roger van Gompel was supported by ESRC award RES-000-23-1363 and Martin Pickering by a British Academy Research Readership while writing this chapter. We thank Gerry Altmann, Gareth Gaskell, and Don Mitchell for comments on a previous version of this chapter.

References

Abney, S. P. (1989) A computational model of human parsing. *Journal of Psycholinguistic Research*, 18: 129–44.

Altmann, G., and Steedman, M. (1988) Interaction with context during human sentence processing. *Cognition*, 30: 191–238.

Altmann, G. T. M., Garnham, A., and Dennis, Y. (1992) Avoiding the garden path: eye movements in context. *Journal of Memory and Language*, 31: 685–712.

Altmann, G. T. M., and Kamide, Y. (1999) Incremental interpretation at verbs: restricting the domain of subsequent reference. *Cognition*, 73: 247–64.

Altmann, G. T. M., van Nice, K. Y., Garnham, A., and Henstra, J.A. (1998) Late closure in context. *Journal of Memory and Language*, 38: 459–84.

Arai, M., Van Gompel, R. P. G., and Scheepers, C. (forthcoming) Priming ditransitive structures in comprehension. *Cognitive Psychology*.

Bailey, K. G. D., and Ferreira, F. (2003) Disfluencies affect the parsing of garden-path sentences. *Journal of Memory and Language*, 49: 183–200.

Bever, T. G. (1970) The cognitive basis for linguistic structures. In J. R. Hayes (ed.), *Cognition and the Development of Language*, pp. 279–352. Wiley, New York.

Bock, J. K. (1986) Syntactic persistence in language production. *Cognitive Psychology*, 18: 355–87.

Branigan, H. P., Pickering, M. J., and Cleland, A. A. (2000) Syntactic co-ordination in dialogue. *Cognition*, 75: B13–B25.

Branigan, H. P., Pickering, M. J., and McLean, J. F. (2005) Priming prepositional-phrase attachment during comprehension. *Journal of Experimental Psychology: Learning, Memory, and Cognition*, 31: 468–81.

Britt, M. A. (1994) The interaction of referential ambiguity and argument structure in the parsing of prepositional phrases. *Journal of Memory and Language*, 33: 251–83.

Britt, M. A., Perfetti, C. A., Garrod, S., and Rayner, K. (1992) Parsing in discourse: context effects and their limits. *Journal of Memory and Language*, 31: 293–314.

Brysbaert, M., and Mitchell, D. C. (1996) Modifier attachment in sentence parsing: evidence from Dutch. *Quarterly Journal of Experimental Psychology*, 49A: 664–95.

Caplan, D., and Waters, G. S. (1999) Verbal working memory and sentence comprehension. *Behavioral and Brain Sciences*, 22: 77–126.

Caplan, D., and Waters, G. (2002) Working memory and connectionist models of parsing: a reply to MacDonald and Christiansen (2002). *Psychological Review*, 109: 66–74.

Carreiras, M., and Clifton, C. (1993) Relative clause interpretation preferences in Spanish and English. *Language and Speech*, 36: 353–72.

Carreiras, M., and Clifton, C. (1999) Another word on parsing relative clauses: eyetracking evidence from Spanish and English. *Memory & Cognition*, 27: 826–33.

Chambers, C. G., Tanenhaus, M. K., and Magnuson, J. S. (2004) Actions and affordances in syntactic ambiguity resolution. *Journal of Experimental Psychology: Learning, Memory, and Cognition*, 30: 687–96.

Chen, E., Gibson, E., and Wolf, F. (2005) Online syntactic storage costs in sentence comprehension. *Journal of Memory and Language*, 52: 144–69.

Chomsky, N. (1981) *Lectures on Government and Binding*. Foris, Dordrecht.

Christianson, K., Hollingworth, A., Halliwell, J. F., and Ferreira, F. (2001) Thematic roles assigned along the garden path linger. *Cognitive Psychology*, 42: 368–407.

Clifton, C., Traxler, M. J., Mohamed, M. T., Williams, R. S., Morris, R. K., and Rayner, K. (2003) The use of thematic role information in parsing: syntactic processing autonomy revisited. *Journal of Memory and Language*, 49: 317–34.

Crain, S., and Steedman, M. (1985) On not being led up the garden path: the use of context by the psychological syntax processor. In D. R. Dowty, L. Karttunen, and A. M. Zwicky (eds), *Natural Language Parsing: Psychological, Computational and Theoretical Perspectives*, pp. 320–58. Cambridge University Press, Cambridge.

Crocker, M. W. (1995) *Computational Psycholinguistics: An Interdisciplinary Approach to the Study of Language*. Kluwer, Dordrecht.

Cuetos, F., and Mitchell, D. C. (1988) Cross-linguistic differences in parsing: restrictions on the use of the Late Closure strategy in Spanish. *Cognition*, 30: 73–105.

Daneman, M., and Carpenter, P. A. (1980) Individual differences in working memory and reading. *Journal of Verbal Learning and Verbal Behavior*, 19: 450–66.

Desmet, T., De Baecke, C., Drieghe, D., Brysbaert, M., and Vonk, W. (2006) Relative clause attachment in Dutch: on-line comprehension corresponds to corpus frequencies when lexical variables are taken into account. *Language and Cognitive Processes*, 21: 453–85.

Ferreira, F. (2003) The misinterpretation of noncanonical sentences. *Cognitive Psychology*, 47: 164–203.

Ferreira, F., and Clifton, C. (1986) The independence of syntactic processing. *Journal of Memory and Language*, 25: 348–368.

Ferreira, F., and Henderson, J. M. (1991) Recovery from misanalyses of garden-path sentences. *Journal of Memory and Language*, 30: 725–45.

Fiebach, C. J., Schlesewsky, M., and Friederici, A. D. (2002) Separating syntactic memory costs and syntactic integration costs during parsing: the processing of German WH-questions. *Journal of Memory and Language*, 47: 250–72.

Fodor, J. A. (1983) *The Modularity of Mind*. MIT Press, Cambridge, MA.

Frazier, L. (1979) On comprehending sentences: syntactic parsing strategies. Ph.D. dissertation, University of Connecticut.

Frazier, L. (1987) Sentence processing: a tutorial review. In M. Coltheart (ed.), *Attention and Performance XII: The Psychology of Reading*, pp. 559–86. Erlbaum, Hillsdale, NJ.

Frazier, L. (1995) Constraint satisfaction as a theory of sentence processing. *Journal of Psycholinguistic Research*, 24: 437–68.

Frazier, L., and Clifton, C. (1989) Successive cyclicity in the grammar and the parser. *Language and Cognitive Processes*, 4: 93–126.

Frazier, L., and Clifton, C., Jr (1996) *Construal*. MIT Press, Cambridge, MA.

Frazier, L., and Flores D'Arcais, G. B. (1989) Filler driven parsing: a study of gap filling in Dutch. *Journal of Memory and Language*, 28: 331–44.

Frazier, L., and Rayner, K. (1982) Making and correcting errors during sentence comprehension: eye movements in the analysis of structurally ambiguous sentences. *Cognitive Psychology*, 14: 178–210.

Frazier, L., Taft, L., Roeper, T., Clifton, C., and Ehrlich, K. (1984) Parallel structure: a source of facilitation in sentence comprehension. *Memory & Cognition*, 12: 421–30.

Garnsey, S. M., Pearlmutter, N. J., Myers, E., and Lotocky, M. A. (1997) The contributions of verb bias and plausibility to the comprehension of temporarily ambiguous sentences. *Journal of Memory and Language*, 37: 58–93.

Gibson, E. (1998) Linguistic complexity: locality of syntactic dependencies. *Cognition*, 68: 1–76.

Gibson, E., and Pearlmutter, N. J. (2000) Distinguishing serial and parallel parsing. *Journal of Psycholinguistic Research*, 29: 231–40.

Gibson, E., and Schütze, C. T. (1999) Disambiguation preferences in noun phrase conjunction do not mirror corpus frequency. *Journal of Memory and Language*, 40: 263–79.

Gibson, E., and Thomas, J. (1999) Memory limitations and structural forgetting: the perception of complex ungrammatical sentences as grammatical. *Language and Cognitive Processes*, 14: 225–48.

Gilboy, E., Sopena, J. M., Clifton, C., and Frazier, L. (1995) Argument structure and association preferences in Spanish and English complex NPs. *Cognition*, 54: 131–67.

Givón, T. (1984) *Syntax: A Functional-Typological Approach*, vol. 1. Benjamins, Amsterdam.

Givón, T. (1990) *Syntax: A Functional-Typological Approach*, vol. 2. Benjamins, Amsterdam.

Gordon, P. C., Hendrick, R., and Johnson, M. (2001) Memory interference during language processing. *Journal of Experimental Psychology: Learning, Memory, and Cognition*, 27: 1411–23.

Gordon, P. C., Hendrick, R., and Johnson, M. (2004) Effects of noun phrase type on sentence complexity. *Journal of Memory and Language*, 51: 97–114.

Gorrell, P. (1995) *Syntax and Parsing*. Cambridge University Press, Cambridge.

Green, M. J., and Mitchell, D. C. (2006) Absence of real evidence against competition during syntactic ambiguity resolution. *Journal of Memory and Language*, 55: 1–17.

Hagoort, P. (2003) Interplay between syntax and semantics during sentence comprehension: ERP effects of combining syntactic and semantic violations. *Journal of Cognitive Neuroscience*, 15: 883–99.

Hoeks, J., Hendriks, P., Vonk, W., Brown, C., and Hagoort, P. (2006) Processing NP- versus S-coordination ambiguity: thematic information does not completely eliminate processing difficulty. *Quarterly Journal of Experimental Psychology A*, 59: 1581–99.

Hoeks, J. C. J., Vonk, W., and Schriefers, H. (2002) Processing coordinated structures in context: the effect of topic-structure on ambiguity resolution. *Journal of Memory and Language*, 46: 99–119.

Hyönä, J., and Hujanen, H. (1997) Effects of case marking and word order on sentence parsing in Finnish: an eye fixation analysis. *Quarterly Journal of Experimental Psychology A*, 50: 841–58.

Just, M. A., and Carpenter, P. A. (1992) A capacity theory of comprehension: individual differences in working memory. *Psychological Review*, 99: 122–49.

Kaan, E. (2001) Effects of NP type on the resolution of word-order ambiguities. *Journal of Psycholinguistic Research*, 30: 529–47.

Kaan, E., Harris, A., Gibson, E., and Holcomb, P. (2000) The P600 as an index of syntactic integration difficulty. *Language and Cognitive Processes*, 15: 159–201.

Kaiser, E., and Trueswell, J. C. (2004) The role of discourse context in the processing of a flexible word-order language. *Cognition*, 94: 113–47.

Kamide, Y., Altmann, G. T. M., and Haywood, S. L. (2003) The time-course of prediction in incremental sentence processing: evidence from anticipatory eye movements. *Journal of Memory and Language*, 49: 133–56.

Kamide, Y., Scheepers, C., and Altmann, G. T. M. (2003) Integration of syntactic and semantic information in predictive processing: cross-linguistic evidence from German and English. *Journal of Psycholinguistic Research*, 32: 37–55.

Kaschak, M. P., and Glenberg, A. M. (2004) This construction needs learned. *Journal of Experimental Psychology: General*, 133: 450–67.

Keenan, E. L., and Comrie, B. (1977) Noun phrase accessibility and universal grammar. *Linguistic Inquiry*, 8: 63–99.

Kennison, S. M. (2001) Limitations on the use of verb information during sentence comprehension. *Psychonomic Bulletin & Review*, 8: 132–8.

Kim, A., and Osterhout, L. (2005) The independence of combinatory semantic processing: evidence from event-related potentials. *Journal of Memory and Language*, 52: 205–25.

Kimball, J. (1973) Seven principles of surface structure parsing in natural language. *Cognition*, 2: 15–47.

King, J., and Just, M. A. (1991) Individual differences in syntactic processing: the role of working memory. *Journal of Memory and Language*, 30: 580–602.

Knoeferle, P., Crocker, M. W., Scheepers, C., and Pickering, M. J. (2005) The influence of the immediate visual context on incremental thematic role-assignment: evidence from eye-movements in depicted events. *Cognition*, 95: 95–127.

Kolk, H. H. J., Chwilla, D. J., Van Herten, M., and Oor, P. J. W. (2003) Structure and limited capacity in verbal working memory: a study with event-related potentials. *Brain and Language*, 85: 1–36.

Kuperberg, G. R., Sitnikova, T., Caplan, D., and Holcomb, P. J. (2003) Electrophysiological distinctions in processing conceptual relationships within simple sentences. *Cognitive Brain Research*, 17: 117–29.

Lau, E. F., and Ferreira, F. (2005) Lingering effects of disfluent material on comprehension of garden path sentences. *Language and Cognitive Processes*, 20: 633–66.

Lewis, R. L. (1996) Interference in short-term memory: the magical number two (or three) in sentence processing. *Journal of Psycholinguistic Research*, 25: 93–115.

Lewis, R. L. (2000) Falsifying serial and parallel parsing models: empirical conundrums and an overlooked paradigm. *Journal of Psycholinguistic Research*, 29: 241–248.

Lewis, R. L., and Vasishth, S. (2005) Activation-based model of sentence processing as skilled memory retrieval. *Cognitive Science*, 29: 375–419.

Liversedge, S. P., Pickering, M. J., Branigan, H. P., and Van Gompel, R. P. G. (1998) Processing arguments and adjuncts in isolation and context: the case of by-phrase ambiguities in passives. *Journal of Experimental Psychology-Learning Memory and Cognition*, 24: 461–75.

MacDonald, M. C., and Christiansen, M. H. (2002) Reassessing working memory: comment on Just and Carpenter (1992) and Waters and Caplan (1996). *Psychological Review*, 109: 35–54.

MacDonald, M. C., Just, M. A., and Carpenter, P. A. (1992) Working memory constraints on the processing of syntactic ambiguity. *Cognitive Psychology*, 24: 56–98.

MacDonald, M. C., Pearlmutter, N. J., and Seidenberg, M. S. (1994) The lexical nature of syntactic ambiguity resolution. *Psychological Review*, 101: 676–703.

Mak, W. M., Vonk, W., and Schriefers, H. (2002) The influence of animacy on relative clause processing. *Journal of Memory and Language*, 47: 50–68.

Marslen-Wilson, W. (1973) Linguistic structure and speech shadowing at very short latencies. *Nature*, 244: 522–3.

Marslen Wilson, W. (1975) Sentence perception as an interactive parallel process. *Science*, 189: 226–8.

McElree, B., and Griffith, T. (1995) Syntactic and thematic processing in sentence comprehension: evidence for a temporal dissociation. *Journal of Experimental Psychology: Learning, Memory, and Cognition*, 21: 134–57.

McElree, B., and Griffith, T. (1998) Structural and lexical constraints on filling gaps during sentence comprehension: a time-course analysis. *Journal of Experimental Psychology: Learning, Memory, and Cognition*, 24: 432–60.

McRae, K., Spivey-Knowlton, M. J., and Tanenhaus, M. K. (1998) Modeling the influence of thematic fit (and other constraints) in on-line sentence comprehension. *Journal of Memory and Language*, 38: 283–312.

Mehler, J., and Carey, P. (1967) Role of surface and base structure in the perception of sentences. *Journal of Verbal Learning and Verbal Behavior*, 6: 335–8.

Mitchell, D. C. (1987) Lexical guidance in human parsing: locus and processing characteristics. In M. Coltheart (ed.), *Attention and Performance XII: The Psychology of Language*, pp. 601–18. Erlbaum, Hillsdale, NJ.

Mitchell, D. C., and Brysbaert, M. (1998) Challenges to recent theories of crosslinguistic variations in parsing: evidence from Dutch. In D. Hillert (ed.), *Sentence Processing: A Crosslinguistic Perspective*, pp. 313–35. Academic Press, San Diego, CA.

Mitchell, D. C., Cuetos, F., Corley, M. M. B., and Brysbaert, M. (1995) Exposure-based models of human parsing: evidence for the use of coarse-grained (nonlexical) statistical records. *Journal of Psycholinguistic Research*, 24: 469–88.

Mitchell, D. C., and Holmes, V. M. (1985) The role of specific information about the verb in parsing sentences with local structural ambiguity. *Journal of Memory and Language*, 24: 542–59.

Noppeney, U., and Price, C. J. (2004) An fMRI study of syntactic adaptation. *Journal of Cognitive Neuroscience*, 16: 702–13.

Pearlmutter, N. J., and MacDonald, M. C. (1995) Individual differences and probabilistic constraints in syntactic ambiguity resolution. *Journal of Memory and Language*, 34: 521–42.

Phillips, C., Kazanina, N., and Abada, S. H. (2005) ERP effects of the processing of syntactic long-distance dependencies. *Cognitive Brain Research*, 22: 407–28.

Pickering, M., and Branigan, H. (1999) Syntactic priming in language production. *Trends in Cognitive Sciences*, 3: 136–41.

Pickering, M. J., and Garrod, S. (2004) Toward a mechanistic psychology of dialogue. *Behavioral and Brain Sciences*, 27: 169–225.

Pickering, M. J., and Traxler, M. J. (1998) Plausibility and recovery from garden paths: an eye-tracking study. *Journal of Experimental Psychology: Learning, Memory, and Cognition*, 24: 940–61.

Pickering, M. J., Traxler, M. J., and Crocker, M. W. (2000) Ambiguity resolution in sentence processing: evidence against frequency-based accounts. *Journal of Memory and Language*, 43: 447–75.

Pritchett, B. L. (1992) *Grammatical Competence and Parsing Performance*. University of Chicago Press, Chicago.

Rayner, K., Carlson, M., and Frazier, L. (1983) The interaction of syntax and semantics during sentence processing: eye movements in the analysis of semantically biased sentences. *Journal of Verbal Learning and Verbal Behavior*, 22: 358–74.

Ross, J. R. R. (1967) Constraints on variables in syntax. PhD thesis, MIT.

Schneider, D., and Phillips, C. (2001) Grammatical search and reanalysis. *Journal of Memory and Language*, 45: 308–36.

Schriefers, H., Friederici, A. D., and Kühn, K. (1995) The processing of locally ambiguous relative clauses in German. *Journal of Memory and Language*, 34: 499–520.

Schütze, C. T., and Gibson, E. (1999) Argumenthood and English prepositional phrase attachment. *Journal of Memory and Language*, 40: 409–31.

Snedeker, J., and Trueswell, J. C. (2004) The developing constraints on parsing decisions: the role of lexical-biases and referential scenes in child and adult sentence processing. *Cognitive Psychology*, 49: 238–99.

Spivey, M. J., and Tanenhaus, M. K. (1998) Syntactic ambiguity resolution in discourse: modeling the effects of referential context and lexical frequency. *Journal of Experimental Psychology: Learning, Memory, and Cognition*, 24: 1521–43.

Spivey, M. J., Tanenhaus, M. K., Eberhard, K. M., and Sedivy, J. C. (2002) Eye movements and spoken language comprehension: effects of visual context on syntactic ambiguity resolution. *Cognitive Psychology*, 45: 447–81.

Stabler, E. P. (1994) The finite connectivity of linguistic structures. In C. Clifton, Jr, L. Frazier, and K. Rayner (eds), *Perspectives on Sentence Processing*, pp. 303–36. Erlbaum, Hillsdale, NJ.

Stevenson, S. (1994) Competition and recency in a hybrid network model of syntactic disambiguation. *Journal of Psycholinguistic Research*, 23: 295–322.

Stowe, L. A. (1986) Parsing WH-constructions: evidence for on-line gap location. *Language and Cognitive Processes*, 1: 227–45.

Sturt, P. and Crocker, M. W. (1996) Monotonic syntactic processing: a cross-linguistic study of attachment and reanalysis. *Language and Cognitive Processes*, 11: 449–94.

Sturt, P., Pickering, M. J., and Crocker, M. W. (1999) Structural change and reanalysis difficulty in language comprehension. *Journal of Memory and Language*, 40: 136–50.

Sturt, P., Pickering, M. J., Scheepers, C., and Crocker, M. W. (2001) The preservation of structure in language comprehension: is reanalysis the last resort? *Journal of Memory and Language*, 45: 283–307.

Sturt, P., Scheepers, C., and Pickering, M. (2002) Syntactic ambiguity resolution after initial misanalysis: the role of recency. *Journal of Memory and Language*, 46: 371–90.

Tabor, W., Galantucci, B., and Richardson, D. (2004) Effects of merely local syntactic coherence on sentence processing. *Journal of Memory and Language*, 50: 355–70.

Tabor, W., and Hutchins, S. (2004) Evidence for self-organized sentence processing: digging-in effects. *Journal of Experimental Psychology: Learning, Memory, and Cognition*, 30: 431–50.

Tabor, W., Juliano, C., and Tanenhaus, M. K. (1997) Parsing in a dynamical system: an attractor-based account of the interaction of lexical and structural constraints in sentence processing. *Language and Cognitive Processes*, 12: 211–71.

Tabor, W., and Tanenhaus, M. K. (1999) Dynamical models of sentence processing. *Cognitive Science*, 23: 491–515.

Tanenhaus, M. K., Spivey Knowlton, M. J., Eberhard, K. M., and Sedivy, J. C. (1995) Integration of visual and linguistic information in spoken language comprehension. *Science*, 268: 1632–4.

Townsend, D. J., and Bever, T. G. (2001) *Sentence Comprehension: The Integration of Habits and Rules*. MIT Press, Cambridge, MA.

Traxler, M. J., Morris, R. K., and Seely, R. E. (2002) Processing subject and object relative clauses: evidence from eye movements. *Journal of Memory and Language*, 47: 69–90.

Traxler, M. J., and Pickering, M. J. (1996) Plausibility and the processing of unbounded dependencies: an eye-tracking study. *Journal of Memory and Language*, 35: 454–75.

Traxler, M. J., Pickering, M. J., and Clifton, C. (1998) Adjunct attachment is not a form of lexical ambiguity resolution. *Journal of Memory and Language*, 39: 558–92.

Traxler, M. J., Williams, R. S., Blozis, S. A., and Morris, R. K. (2005) Working memory, animacy, and verb class in the processing of relative clauses. *Journal of Memory and Language*, 53: 204–24.

Trueswell, J. C. (1996) The role of lexical frequency in syntactic ambiguity resolution. *Journal of Memory and Language*, 35: 566–85.

Trueswell, J. C., Sekerina, I., Hill, N. M., and Logrip, M. L. (1999) The kindergarten-path effect: studying on-line sentence processing in young children. *Cognition*, 73: 89–134.

Trueswell, J. C., Tanenhaus, M. K., and Garnsey, S. M. (1994) Semantic influences on parsing: use of thematic role information in syntactic ambiguity resolution. *Journal of Memory and Language*, 33: 285–318.

Trueswell, J. C., Tanenhaus, M. K., and Kello, C. (1993) Verb-specific constraints in sentence processing: separating effects of lexical preference from garden-paths. *Journal of Experimental Psychology: Learning, Memory, and Cognition*, 19: 528–53.

Tyler, L. K., and Marslen-Wilson, W. D. (1977) The on-line effects of semantic context on syntactic processing. *Journal of Verbal Learning and Verbal Behavior*, 16: 683–92.

Van Berkum, J. J. A., Brown, C. M., and Hagoort, P. (1999) Early referential context effects in sentence processing: evidence from event-related brain potentials. *Journal of Memory and Language*, 41: 147–82.

Van Gompel, R. P. G., Pickering, M. J., Pearson, J., and Jacob, G. (2006) The activation of inappropriate analyses in garden-path sentences: evidence from structural priming. *Journal of Memory and Language*, 55: 335–62.

Van Gompel, R. P. G., Pickering, M. J., Pearson, J., and Liversedge, S. P. (2005) Evidence against competition during syntactic ambiguity resolution. *Journal of Memory and Language*, 52: 284–307.

Van Gompel, R. P. G., Pickering, M. J., and Traxler, M. J. (2001) Reanalysis in sentence processing: evidence against current constraint-based and two-stage models. *Journal of Memory and Language*, 45: 225–58.

Van Herten, M., Kolk, H. H., and Chwilla, D. J. (2005) An ERP study of P600 effects elicited by semantic anomalies. *Cognitive Brain Research*, 22: 241–55.

Warren, T., and Gibson, E. (2002) The influence of referential processing on sentence complexity. *Cognition*, 85: 79–112.

Waters, G. S., and Caplan, D. (1996) The capacity theory of sentence comprehension: critique of Just and Carpenter (1992) *Psychological Review*, 103: 761–72.

Waters, G. S., and Caplan, D. (2004) Verbal working memory and on-line syntactic processing: evidence from self-paced listening. *Quarterly Journal of Experimental Psychology A*, 57: 129–63.

Zagar, D., Pynte, J., and Rativeau, S. (1997) Evidence for early-closure attachment on first-pass reading times in French. *Quarterly Journal of Experimental Psychology A*, 50: 421–38.

CHAPTER 18

Spoken language comprehension: insights from eye movements

Michael K. Tanenhaus

18.1 Introduction

Eye movements have been one of the most widely used response measures in studies of written word recognition and sentence reading since the classic work of McConkie and Rayner (1976), Frazier and Rayner (1982), and Just and Carpenter (1980) (for review see Staub and Rayner, Chapter 19 this volume). More recently, eye movements have become a widely used response measure for studying spoken language processing in both adults and children, in situations where participants comprehend and generate utterances about a circumscribed "Visual World" while fixation is monitored, typically using a free-view eye-tracker.

Psycholinguists now use the Visual World eye-movement method to study both language production and language comprehension, in studies that run the gamut of current topics in language processing. Eye movements are a response measure of choice for addressing many classic questions about spoken language processing in psycholinguistics, for example: Is the processing of stop consonants categorical (McMurray et al., 2002)? Does context influence the earliest moments of temporary lexical and syntactic ambiguity resolution (Dahan and Tanenhaus, 2004; Spivey et al., 2002)? What is the locus of frequency effects in spoken word recognition (Dahan, Magnuson, and Tanenhaus, 2001)? What factors influence the time course with which anaphoric expressions such as pronouns are resolved (Arnold et al., 2000)? How are sentences with long-distance dependencies processed (Sussman and Sedivy, 2003)? And, for bilingual speakers, does a word spoken in one language activate the lexical representations of similar sounding words in the other language (Spivey and Marian, 1999; Ju and Luce, 2004)?

The use of eye movements has also opened up investigations of relatively uncharted territory in language comprehension and language production. In comprehension this includes real-time sentence processing in children (Trueswell et al., 1999); how and when interlocutors take into account each others knowledge and intentions in on-line processing (Keysar et al., 2000; Hanna, Tanenhaus, and Trueswell, 2003; Nadig and Sedivy; 2002; Tanenhaus and Brown-Schmidt, 2008); whether listeners make use of disfluencies in real-time language processing (Arnold et al., 2004; Ferreira and Bailey, forthcoming); how participants in a conversation coordinate their referential domains (Brown-Schmidt et al., 2005; Tanenhaus and Brown-Schmidt, 2008). In production, eye movements are being used to assess the locus of disfluency effects (Griffin, 2004) and the interface between message formulation and utterance planning (Bock et al., 2003; Griffin and Bock, 2000; Brown-Schmidt and Tanenhaus, 2008) and the relationship between language and thought. The Visual World approach has also spawned a new family of studies investigating the interface between action and language (Chambers, Tanenhaus, and Magnuson, 2004; Chambers, Tanenhaus, Eberhard, Filip, and Carlson, 2002) and between vision and language (Spivey et al., 2002; Spivey and Geng, 2001; Altmann, 2004; Altmann and Kamide, 2004; Knoeferle and Crocker, 2006; Knoeferle, Crocker, Scheepers, and Pickering, 2005).

This chapter reviews the burgeoning Visual World literature on language comprehension, highlighting some of the seminal studies, and examining how the Visual World approach has contributed new insights to our understanding of spoken word recognition, parsing, reference resolution, and interactive conversation. We consider some of the methodological issues that come to the fore when psycholinguists use eye movements to examine spoken language comprehension. Finally, we highlight some issues that are likely to become increasingly important in future research using the Visual World paradigm.

18.2 **Foundational studies**

18.2.1 **Comprehension**

Roger Cooper (1974) pioneered using eye movements as a tool for studying spoken language comprehension. Cooper tracked participant's eye movements as they listened to stories while looking at a display of pictures. He found that listeners looked at pictures which were named in the stories, as well as pictures associated to words in the story. Moreover, fixations were often generated before the end of the word.

Tanenhaus et al. (1995) initiated the recent wave of Visual World studies, taking advantage of the advent of accurate, lightweight, head-mounted eye-trackers. Tanenhaus et al. examined eye movements as participants followed instructions to perform simple tasks with objects in a workspace. They found that varying the number of potential referents for a temporarily ambiguous prepositional phrase (e.g. *Put the apple on the towel...*) determined whether the phrase was initially parsed as a goal argument (where to put the apple) or as a modifier (the location of the apple to be moved), as predicted by Altmann and Steedman (1988). A more complete report of the Tanenhaus et al. study is presented in Spivey et al. (2002).

Trueswell et al. (1999) replicated the Tanenhaus et al. (1995) study with adults, and more importantly extended it to 5- and 8-year-old children. They found important developmental differences in how children weight lexical and referential constraints on sentence parsing, laying the foundation for the rapidly expanding field of online sentence processing in preliterate children (Trueswell and Gleitman, Chapter 39 this volume).

Eberhard et al. (1995) demonstrated that fixations to entities referred to in an instruction are remarkably time-locked to the unfolding utterance. Fixations to a target referent among a display of competitors occurred as soon as continuous integration of constraints provided by both the unfolding speech and the visual display could, in principle, distinguish the referent from its competitors. These results obtained both for simple instructions (*Touch the starred red square*) and complex instructions (*Put the five of hearts that's below the eight of clubs above the three of diamonds*). This "point-of disambiguation" logic is now widely used in studies of reference resolution.

Sedivy initiated an influential line of research demonstrating that pre-nominal scalar adjectives, such as *tall*, affect the point of disambiguation of potential referents in referential expressions, such as *the tall glass*. Speakers use, and listeners interpret, scalar adjectives contrastively, i.e. to distinguish between two or more objects of the same type (Sedivy et al., 1999; Sedivy, 2003). For example, in a display with a tall glass, a speaker will typically not use the adjective *tall*, unless the display contains, as a potential contrast, another, smaller glass (Sedivy, 2003). Eye movements show that at *tall* listeners immediately interpret *the tall glass* as referring to the taller of two glasses, even when another taller object, e.g. a *pitcher*, is present, whereas in the absence of a potential contrast, fixations to the glass do not begin until after the listener hears *glass* (Sedivy et al., 1999). Listeners also typically look at the contrast member several hundred ms after fixating the referent. In addition to being interesting in their own right, the processing of pre-nominal adjectives has become an important methodological tool for addressing a range of issues in language processing (e.g. Hanna et al. 2003; Grodner and Sedivy, forthcoming; Brown-Schmidt and Tanenhaus, 2006).

Building on initial results by Spivey-Knowlton (1996), Allopenna et al. (1998) demonstrated that the timing of fixations to a pictured referent, and competitors with different types of phonological overlap, was sufficiently time-locked to the input to trace the time course of lexical access. Allopenna et al. had participants follow instructions to click on and move one of four pictures presented in a display with four geometric shapes in the corners (e.g. *Click on the beaker. Now put it below the triangle*). Allopenna et al. also showed that a simple linking hypothesis could be used to map fixations onto computational models of lexical activation, thus laying the foundation for the growing body of work that uses the Visual World paradigm to study spoken word recognition.

Altmann and Kamide (1999) made a seminal contribution to the Visual World paradigm by demonstrating that listeners make linguistically mediated, anticipatory eye movements using a task like Cooper's in which participants listened to a description of an upcoming event involving entities depicted in a display. As participants heard sentences such as *The boy will eat the cake*, they would look to a picture of a cake before the offset of *eat* (the other depicted objects were not edible). Anticipatory eye movements are now widely used as a dependent measure, typically with non-action-based variants of the Visual World paradigm (e.g. Boland, 2005).

In an ingenious experiment Keysar et al. (Keysar et al., 2000) used eye movements to evaluate when in the time course of comprehension listeners take into account common ground information, i.e. information that is shared with an interlocutor. A confederate speaker, the director, instructed a naive participant, the matcher, to move objects in a box with cubbyholes. Most objects could be seen by both the speaker and the matcher, and thus were in common ground by virtue of physical co-presence (Clark and Marshall, 1981). However, some objects were blocked from the speaker's view by an opaque barrier, and were therefore only in the matcher's privileged ground. Nonetheless, the matcher looked at these objects when they, along with an object in common ground, were consistent with the speaker's referential description. This study has laid the groundwork for an ongoing debate about when interlocutors do and do not make use of each other's likely knowledge and intentions in real-time language processing (Keysar et al., 2003; Nadig and Sedivy, 2002; Hanna et al., 2003; Hanna and Tanenhaus, 2004).

18.2.2 Production

Although the focus of this review is on language comprehension, psycholinguists are now using eye movements to examine a range of issues in language production. Two studies laid the foundation for using eye movements to study language production. Meyer et al. (1998) had participants name sequences of objects. Eye gaze was tightly coordinated with the speech. Participants fixated a to-be-named object about 1 sec prior to the onset of naming, shifting their gaze to the next object about 150 ms after utterance onset.

Griffin and Bock (2000) presented participants with a simple event rendered as a line drawing that could be described with either an active or passive sentence, such as a woman shooting a man. The sequence of eye movements reflected the order of constituents in the utterance. Speakers looked at pictured objects about 800 ms to 1 sec before naming them. Once speaking began, the sequence and timing of fixations was controlled by the utterance, rather than perceptual properties of the input, suggesting that the speaker had completed message planning prior to beginning to speak (also see Bock et al., 2003).

18.3 Methodological issues

18.3.1 Linking hypothesis

The assumption linking fixations to real-time comprehension processes is that as the linguistic input unfolds, the listener's attention will shift to potential referents in the display as they become relevant. A shift in attention will typically be followed by a saccadic eye movement. Because saccades are rapid, low-cost, low-threshold responses, a small proportion of saccades will be generated by even small changes in the state of the system. The likelihood of a shift in attention resulting in a fixation to a particular picture or object is then a function of the response strength of that picture relative to the other pictures at a particular point in time.

Allopenna et al. (1998) formalized a linking hypothesis between word recognition and eye movements using the Luce choice rule and computing response strengths from activations generated by the TRACE model of spoken word recognition (McClelland and Elman, 1986). For examples, see also Dahan et al (2001a), Dahan, Magnuson, Tanehaus, and Hogan (2001b), Dahan et al. (2002), and Magnuson et al. (2003). The Allopenna et al. formalization is only an approximation to what would be a more accurate formalization of the linking hypothesis which would predict the probability that a saccade would be generated at a particular point in time, contingent upon (a) the location of the previous fixation (and perhaps the several preceding fixations; (b) time from the onset of the last fixation; and (c) the current goal state of the listener's task—which can be ignored in a simple "click" task like the Allopenna et al. paradigm. Knoeferle and Crocker (2006) present a model linking listener's fixations to potential referents in display as they listen to descriptive sentences.

18.3.2 Data analysis

Each saccade is a discrete event. However, the probabilistic nature of saccades ensures that with sufficient numbers of observations, the results will begin to approximate a continuous measure (see Spivey et al., 2005, and Magnuson, 2005). Aggregating looks to pictures over time across subjects and trials results in a summary profile of the timing and pattern of eye movements, which is often displayed as "proportion of fixation curve."

A window of interest is often defined for purposes of analysis. For example, one might want to focus on the fixations to the target and cohort in the region from 200 ms after the onset of the spoken word to the point in the speech stream where disambiguating phonetic information first arrives. The proportion of fixations to pictures or objects and the time spent fixating on the alternative pictures (essentially the area under the curve, which is a simple transformation of proportion of fixations) can then be analyzed. Because each fixation is likely to be 150–250 ms, the proportion of fixations in different time windows is not independent. One way of increasing the independence is to restrict the analysis to the proportion of new saccades generated to pictures within a region of interest. Another is to compare fixation ratios between conditions to chance. A third approach explored by Magnuson and colleagues is to apply growth curve analyses—which are designed for data with time-dependent measures—to fixation proportion curves (Magnuson et al., 2007).

18.3.2.1 Action-contingent analyses

One useful feature of combining eye movements with an action is that the behavioral responses reveal the participant's interpretation. This allows for "interpretation-contingent" analyses in which fixations are analyzed separately for trials on which participants choose a particular interpretation (McMurray et al., 2002; Runner et al., 2003; Brown-Schmidt et al., 2005; Brown-Schmidt and Tanenhaus, 2006). Fixations can also be analyzed contingent upon prior looks to pictures or objects.

18.3.3 Task variables

As the eye movement literature on spoken language comprehension has developed, researchers have begun to vary the sorts of task given to their participants. The effects of these variations are important to evaluate and track from experiment to experiment, since, as discussed in the opening of this chapter, eye movement patterns are heavily task- and goal-dependent (i.e. we shift our attention to *task-relevant* regions of the world). It would be a mistake, for instance, to assume that the "task" involved in the studies discussed in this chapter can be monolithically described as "spoken language comprehension" or worse still "use of language." Very similar issues of task variation arise in reading eye movement studies; eye movement patterns over identical sequences of text will differ substantially depending on whether readers are "skimming," "understanding," "memorizing," or "proofing." Much greater opportunity for task variability appears to be possible in Visual World studies because of the wide range of ways that participants can be asked to interact with the world. However, it is precisely this variability which provides experimenters with the leverage to make the Visual World paradigm useful for such a wide range of questions.

One important task dimension is whether or not the linguistic stimuli used in the study involve instructions to act on the world. This variable is likely to be crucial because eye fixation plays an important role in visually guided reaching (see Hayhoe and Ballard, 2005). At one extreme, imperative sentences are commonly used, such that participants are required to manipulate the objects (e.g. *Pick up the ball. Put it inside the cup*). At the other extreme, participants listen to declarative sentences, while looking at visually co-present referents. Here the reference is intended to be non-deictic (*The boy picked up the ball. Then he put it inside the cup*).

Action-based studies offer several advantages in that participants are required in a natural way to remain engaged with their referent world; planning to execute a response requires calculating the spatial location of referents and presumably increases the time-locked nature of the relationship between linguistic interpretation and eye fixation. One clear limitation of the action-based paradigm, however, is that the linguistic stimuli must be embedded in instructions, which can limit the experimenter's degrees of freedom. The non-action-based listening procedure places far fewer constraints on both the experimenter and the participant. Decoupling fixations from action planning may also increase the proportion of anticipatory eye movements, which are extremely useful for inferring expectations generated by the listener.

Indeed, many of the most important applications of non-action based listening have explored and documented referential expectations, starting with research initiated by Altmann and colleagues, who showed that listeners can anticipate upcoming reference based on the semantic requirements of verbs and/or whole predicates (e.g. Altmann and Kamide, 1999; Kamide et al., 2003).

Studies building upon this on this work include Boland (2005), who compared verb-based expectations for adjuncts and arguments, and Knoeferle and Crocker (2006), who studied the effects of visually based information on expectation about thematic role assignment.

We should note that this non-action paradigm is sometimes referred to as "passive listening," and some investigators (e.g. Boland, 2005) have proposed that differences between fixations in action and passive listening tasks might be used to separate fixations that are controlled by language from those that are controlled by action. We are skeptical for several reasons. First, it is becoming increasingly clear that perception and action are inextricably intertwined in most perceptual domains, and we expect that this is also likely to be the case for language. Second, interpreting sequences of fixations in the absence of an explicit task are likely to prove problematic for reasons eloquently articulated by Viviani (1990). We note, however, that many non-action task studies provide listeners with a well-defined task, typically so as to increase engagement with the scene and decrease variability. For instance, Kaiser and Trueswell (2004) and Arnold et al. (2000) asked listeners to judge whether the depicted image on a trial matched the spoken description/story.

More generally, it is important to keep in mind the following considerations. First, all saccadic eye movements involve some attentional resources (Kowler, 1995). Second, the concept of passive listening leaves the underlying goals of the listener up to the listener. Thus, each listener may adopt different goals—or worse, all listeners might adopt a pragmatically appropriate goal that was unforeseen by the experimenter. In short, there is no such thing as a taskless task. We therefore consider the notion of passive listening as akin to the notion of the null context, which is problematic for reasons articulated by Crain and Steedman (1985) and Altmann and Steedman (1988). Third, and perhaps most importantly, the difference between action-based (or perhaps more appropriately manipulation-based) and non-action based variants of the Visual World paradigm is really a subset of a more general question about the goal structures which control the moment-by-moment attentional state of the participants. In tasks with complex goal structures, e.g. a task-oriented dialogue, multiple layers of goals will contribute to fixations, some of which may be are tied to expectations about upcoming linguistic input, some to the current sub-goal, and some to higher-level planning.

To date, relatively few studies have compared action and non-action tasks. However, to a first approximation, it appears that when anticipatory eye movements are excluded, the timing of fixations to potential referents may be slightly delayed in listening tasks compared to action-based tasks. The data from simple action-based tasks with imperatives (tasks where participants follow a sequence of instructions) is also somewhat cleaner than the data from non-action-based tasks with declaratives, most likely because a higher proportion of the fixations are likely to be task-relevant.

18.3.4 **Comparing Visual World and eye-movement reading studies**

Many of the issues that have been investigated for decades using eye movements in reading—in particular issues in lexical processing and sentence processing—are now being investigated using eye movements with spoken language. Although some aspects of these processes will differ in reading and spoken language because of intrinsic differences between the two modalities, psycholinguists investigating issues such as syntactic ambiguity resolution and reference resolution using eye movements in reading and eye movements in spoken language believe they are testing theoretical claims about these processes that transcend the modality of the input. Thus, the psycholinguistic community will increasingly be faced with questions about how to integrate results from Visual World studies with results from studies of eye movements in reading, and sometimes how to reconcile conflicting results.

18.3.4.1 Processing load vs. representational measures

In comparing reading studies to Visual World studies it is useful to make a distinction between behavioral measures of language processing which measure processing difficulty and measures which probe representation. The distinction is more of a heuristic than a categorical distinction, because many response measures combine aspects of both. Processing load measures assess transient changes in process complexity, and then use these changes to make inferences about the underlying processes and representations. Representational measures examine when during processing a particular type of representations emerges, and then use that information to draw inferences about the underlying processes and representations. Neither class of measure or its accompanying experimental logic is intrinsically preferable to the other; the nature of the question under investigation determines which type of response measure is more appropriate.

The majority of studies that use eye movements to examine reading make use of eye movements as a processing load measure. The primary dependent measure is fixation duration. The linking hypothesis between fixation duration and underlying processes is that reading times increase when processing becomes more difficult. In contrast, the majority of Visual World studies use eye movements as a representational measure. The primary dependent measure is when and where people fixate as the utterance unfolds.

18.3.5 Effects of display

The single factor that most complicates the interpretation of Visual World studies of language processing is the need to present either real objects in a workspace or pictures in a display on a computer screen. For example, the timing of looks to a potential referent at point *t* could be affected by whether or not that referent has been fixated on during time *t–x*, either during preview or as the sentence unfolds. Thus the likelihood of a fixation may be contingent on both the input and the pattern of prior fixations. This, of course, has the potential to complicate inferences about time-course, in much the same way that rereading after a regression can complicate the interpretation of fixation duration data in eye-movement reading studies. Recent studies have begun to examine how having fixated a potential referent in a display during preview affects the likelihood that it will be fixated when it is temporarily consistent with the input (Dahan et al., forthcoming).

In addition, use of a display with a small number of pictured referents or objects and a limited set of potential actions creates a more restricted environment than language processing in most natural contexts, while at the same time imposing more demands on the participant than most psycholinguistic tasks. In order to address these closed-set issues, we consider two cases: the first from spoken word recognition, the second from reference resolution.

18.3.5.1 Spoken word recognition: closed-set concerns

In the Allopenna et al. paradigm, the potential response set on each trial is limited to four pictured items. If participants adopted a task-specific verification strategy, such as implicitly naming the pictures, then the unfolding input might be evaluated against these activated names, effectively bypassing the usual recognition process, and leading to distorted results. Even if participants do not adopt such a strategy, the Visual World methodology might be limited if the effects of the response alternatives mask effects of non-displayed alternatives (e.g. neighborhood effects in the entire lexicon). This would restrict its usefulness for investigating many issues in spoken word recognition, in particular issues about the effects of lexical neighborhoods, i.e. the set of words in the lexicon that are similar to the target word. Here, an analogy might be helpful. Researchers often use lexical priming paradigms to probe for whether an exemplar of a particular class of lexical competitor is active, for example, cohorts or rhymes. However, paradigms that probe for activation of word related to the target word are not well suited for asking questions about the aggregate effects of the number and frequency of potential competitors. In order to investigate this class of question, researchers have found it more useful to measure response time to a target word—for example, auditory lexical decision—which more closely approximates a processing load measure (but cf. Gaskell and Marslen-Wilson, 2002).

Implicit naming. The issue of implicit naming has been addressed most directly by Dahan and Tanenhaus (2005) in a study that varied the amount of preview time, 300 or 1,000 ms, for four-picture displays with minimal phonological overlap between the names of the distractors and the target. On a subset of the trials, two of the pictures were visually similar (e.g. a picture of a snake and a coiled rope) and the instruction referred to one of the pictures (e.g. *click on the snake*). The particular pictures chosen as the two referents shared some features associated with a prototypical visual representation of one or both word. For example, the pair *snake–rope* was selected because the picture of a coiled rope shares some features with the visual representation most often associated with the concept of a snake. When selecting pictures, Dahan and Tanenhaus (2005) sought to minimize their visual similarity so that the objects could be easily differentiated. For example, they chose a snake in a non-coiled position. Thus, visual similarity was maximized between the prototypical visual representation of one of the concepts, the referent, and the picture associated with the other concept, the competitor, and minimized between the competitor picture and the picture of the referent concept.

Several aspects of the results provide strong evidence against implicit naming. The naming hypothesis predicts that visual similarity effects should be eliminated or weakened with preview, because the encoded name of the picture would not match the unfolding target. However, visually similar competitors attracted more looks than other distractors with dissimilar names. Moreover, the magnitude of the visual similarity effect was not affected by preview even when participants fixated the visually dissimilar competitor during preview. In addition, similarity effects were larger when the target had a competitor which was chosen to share visual features of its prototype representation compared to when that competitor was the referent. Thus visual similarity effects were due to the fit between the picture and the conceptual representation of the picture, not simply surface visual confusability. This last result suggests that mapping of the word onto its referent picture is mediated by a visual/conceptual match between the activated lexical form of the target and the picture. Additional evidence against implicit naming comes from a study by Salverda and Altmann (2005), who demonstrated that a spoken word triggers looks to pictures even when a participant is engaged in a visual search task to identify the location of a dot that appeared in a random location within a schematic scene. In this task, it seems highly unlikely that participants would encode the names of the pictures in the display.

Sensitivity to hidden competitors. Perhaps the strongest test of the sensitivity of Visual World studies comes from studies that look for effects of non-displayed or "hidden competitors." For example, Magnuson et al. (2007) examined the temporal dynamics of neighborhood effects using two different metrics: neighborhood density, a frequency-weighted measure defined by the Neighborhood Activation Model (NAM), and a frequency-weighted measure of cohort density. The referent was displayed along with three semantically unrelated pictures, with names that had little phonological overlap with the referent (all names were monosyllabic). Crucially, none of the referent's neighbors were either displayed or named throughout the course of the experiment. The results showed clear effects of both cohort and neighborhood density, with cohort density effects dominating early in the recognition process and neighborhood effects emerging relatively late.

These results demonstrate that the processing neighborhood for a word changes dynamically as the word unfolds. It also establishes the sensitivity of the paradigm to the entire lexicon. To a first approximation, then, when competitors are displayed, the paradigm can be used to probe specific representations; however, the aggregate effects of competitors can best be observed in the timing of fixations to the target referent.

Magnuson et al.'s results complement those of the Dahan, Magnuson, et al. (2001) finding that the misleading coarticulatory information delays recognition more when it renders the input temporarily consistent with a (non-displayed) word, compared to when it does not. Crucially, simulations using the Allopenna et al. linking hypothesis successfully captured differences between the effects of misleading coarticulatory information with displayed and non-displayed competitors. Whether the non-displayed competitor logic can be extended to higher-level sentence processing remains to be seen.

18.3.5.2 Sentence processing

Much trickier issues about the effects of the display come into play in higher-level processing. For example, in the Tanenhaus et al. (1995) study, displaying an apple on a towel and an apple on a napkin might increase the salience of a normally less accessible structure compared to circumstances where the alternative referents are introduced linguistically. One could make a similar argument about the effects of action on the rapidity with which object-based affordances influence ambiguity resolution in studies by Chambers and colleagues (Chambers et al., 2002; Chambers et al., 2004). In these studies, the issue of implicit naming seems *prima facie* to be less plausible. However, one might be concerned about task-specific strategies. For example, in Chambers et al. (2002), participants were confused, as indexed by fixations, when they were told to *Pick up the cube. Now put the cube in the can,* and there were two cans. The confusion was reduced or eliminated, however, when the cube would only fit in one of the cans. Because only one action was possible, one might attribute this to problem-solving and not, as Chambers et al. argued, to the effects of action and affordance on referential domains. However, the manipulation had opposite effects for instructions that used an indefinite article, e.g. *Pick up the cube. Now put it in a can.* Here participants were confused when the cube would only fit in one of the cans. This strategy of pitting linguistic effects against potential problem-solving strategies is crucial for evaluating the impact of strategies due to the display and the task.

Perhaps the most general caution for researchers using the Visual World paradigm in both production and comprehension is to be aware that while the Visual World displays entities that can be used to infer the representations that the listener is developing, it also serves as a context for the utterance itself. Note that the fact that information in a display affects processing is not itself any more problematic than the observation that reference resolution, for example, is affected by whether or not potential referents are introduced linguistically in a prior discourse. The crucial question is whether the nature of the interactions with the display shed light on language processing, or whether they introduce strategies that mislead or obscure the underlying processes.

Two examples might help illustrate this point. The first is taken from Tanenhaus et al. (2004; see also Tanenhaus and Brown-Schmidt, 2008) and illustrates how the Visual World paradigm has clarified our understanding of the comprehension of pre-nominal scalar adjectives and definite reference. The second uses a hypothetical scenario to illustrate what kind of effect might demonstrate that the display is distorting "normal" language comprehension.

Prior to Visual World studies, a standard psycholinguistic account of the processing of the sentence *After putting the pencil below the big apple, James moved the apple onto the towel* would have gone something like this. When the listener encounters the scalar adjective *big,* interpretation is delayed because a scalar dimension can only be interpreted with respect to the noun it modifies (e.g. compare a big building and a big pencil). As *apple* is heard, lexical access activates the apple concept, a prototypical apple. The apple concept is then modified, resulting in a representation of a BIG APPLE. When *apple* is encountered in the second clause, lexical access again results in activation of a prototypical APPLE concept. Because *apple* was introduced by a definite article, this representation would need to be compared with the memory representation of the BIG APPLE to decide whether the two corefer.

Now, consider how real-time interpretation proceeds in a context which includes a pencil, two apples—one, a small prototypical, red apple, the other a large, misshapen green apple—and a towel, taking into account recent results from Visual World studies. At *big*, the listener's attention would be drawn to the larger of the two apples, because a scalar adjective signals a contrast among two or more entities of the same semantic type (Sedivy et al., 1999). Thus *apple* will be immediately interpreted as the misshapen green apple, even though a more prototypical red apple is present in the display. And when *the apple* is encountered in the second clause, the red apple would be ignored in favor of the large green apple, because the green apple has been introduced into the discourse, but not as the most salient entity and thus would not be referred to with a pronoun (Dahan et al., 2002).

The standard account does not make sense when we try to generalize it to processing in the context of concrete referents. In contrast, the account which emerges from Visual World research does generalize to processing in the absence of a more specific context. In particular, the scalar *big* would still be interpreted as the member of a contrast set picked out by size; it's just that the content of contrast set are not instantiated until the noun, *apple*, has been heard. And any increase in processing difficulty when *the apple* is processed would not reflect an inference to establish that the referent is the big apple, but rather the shift in discourse focus from the previously focused entity (the pencil) to a previously mentioned entity (the apple). In this example, then, the display clearly changes processing, but in ways that clarify (but do not distort) the underlying processes.

Now consider the discourse: *The man returned home and greeted his pet dog. It/ The beast/A beast then began to lick/attack him.* Well-understood principles of reference assignment mandate that *it* should refer to the dog, and *a beast* to an animal other than the dog. Now imagine the same discourse in the context of a display containing a man standing in front of an open door to a hut in a jungle village, a dog with a collar, a tiger, and a rabbit. Compared to appropriate control conditions, we would expect a pattern of looks indicating that *it* was interpreted as the dog, and *a beast* as the tiger, regardless of whether the verb was *lick* or *attack*. If, however, *it* were interpreted as the tiger when the verb was *attack*, or if *a beast* were to be interpreted as the dog for *lick,* then we would have a clear case of the display distorting the comprehension process. This conclusion would be merited because these interpretations *would* violate well-understood principles of reference resolution. Now consider the definite noun phrase, *the beast*. This referential expression could either refer to the mentioned entity, the pet dog, or it could introduce another entity. In the discourse-alone condition, a listener or reader would most likely infer that *the beast* refers to the dog, because no other entity has been mentioned. However, in the discourse with display condition, a listener might be more likely to infer that *the beast* refers to the tiger. Here the display changes the interpretation, but it does *not* change the underlying process; the display simply makes accessible a potential unmentioned referent, which is consistent with the felicity conditions for the type of definite reference used in the discourse. Indeed, we would expect the same pattern of interpretation if the tiger had been mentioned in the discourse.[1]

Thus far, investigations of the effects of using a display and using a task have not uncovered any evidence that the display or the task is distorting the underlying processes. However, it will be crucial in further work to explore the nature of the interactions between the display, the task, and linguistic processing in much greater detail. Moreover, the ability to control and understand the context in which the language is being produced and understood, which is one of the most powerful aspects of the Visual World paradigm, depends in large part on developing a better understanding of these interactions.

18.4 **Applications to issues in language comprehension**

We now briefly review work in domains where using eye movements is beginning to have a major impact on our understanding of spoken language processing. We begin with issues in speech, spoken word recognition, and prosody that can be addressed by using variations of the procedure introduced by Allopenna et al. (1998). We then focus on questions about sentence processing, including classic issues concerning the role of context in syntactic ambiguity resolution, and assorted issues about referential domains. These issues are addressed by taking advantage of various features of the Visual World paradigm, including having an implicit measure that can be used with simple tasks and spoken language, having a co-present referential world, and the capability of monitoring real-time processing in paradigms that bridge the language-as-product and language- as-action traditions.

18.4.1 **Spoken word recognition and prosody**

18.4.1.1 Spoken word recognition

Visual World studies have helped resolve some controversial issues within spoken word recognition by combining its sensitivity to fine-grained acoustic/phonetic detail and information about time-course with an explicit linking hypothesis. For example, Dahan, Magnuson, and Tanenhaus (2001) established that word frequency affects the earliest moments of lexical access. Moreover, within a localist network the time-course of emerging frequency effects is best modeled as arising from differences in connection strength, rather than differences in resting activation levels or response bias. Dahan, Magnuson, et al. (2001) showed that useful and misleading information about upcoming place of articulation affected spoken word recognition, with a time-course that was more consistent with TRACE than with models incorporating strong bottom-up mismatch (Marslen-Wilson and Warren; 1994; Norris et al., 2000). Creel et al. (2008) showed that speaker-specific indexical effects arise early rather than late in lexical processing.

The Allopenna et al (1998) procedure has also proved extremely useful for addressing questions about how listeners use sub-phonetic information in word recognition. Examples include the McMurray et al. (2002) study described earlier, which used looks to competitors to demonstrate gradient sensitivity to within-category variation, and work by Dahan, Magnuson, and Tanenhaus (2001), Dahan, Magnuson, et al. (2001) and Gow and McMurray (2007) on listener's use of coarticulatory information. And, in an important study, Salverda, Dahan, and McQueen (2003) demonstrated that listeners exploit small systematic differences in vowel duration in processing of words such as *captain*, which begin with a phonetic sequence that is itself a word, e.g. *cap* (the vowel in a monosyllabic word is typically longer than the same vowel in a polysyllabic word). Examining looks to cohort competitors to words embedded in utterances has also proved useful for examining spoken word recognition in bilinguals. For example, Spivey and Marian (1999) used looks to cohorts to demonstrate that bilingual speakers following instructions in one language briefly consider potential referents with names that are cohort competitor in their second language (see also Ju and Luce, 2004). Finally, studies that use eye movements to measure processing of artificial lexicons and languages, initiated by Magnuson and his colleagues (Magnuson et al., 2003) have proved useful for addressing a range of issues in spoken word recognition and lexical learning (Creel, Tanenhaus and Aslin 2006; Shatzman and McQueen 2006).

18.4.1.2 Prosody

Visual World studies are beginning to have an increasingly significant impact on research

[1] This observation is due to Gerry Altmann. The example presented here is adapted from one presented by Simon Garrod in a presentation at the 2003 Meetings of the CUNY Sentence Processing Conference.

investigating how listeners process information about prosody, which is carried by the pattern and type of pitch accents and realized acoustically as changes in duration, intensity, and pitch excursion on stressed vowels. Differences in vowel duration between monosyllabic and polysyllabic words vary with the prosodic environment; they are smallest in the middle of a phrase, and largest at the end of a phrase. Salverda (2005) demonstrated that prosodic factors modulate the relative degree to which different members of a neighborhood will be activated in different environments; in medial position a polysyllabic carrier word such as *captain* is a stronger competitor than *cat* for the target *cap*, whereas the opposite pattern obtains in utterance-final position.

Cohort manipulations, in particular, are well suited for examining pitch accents because one can examine effects that are localized to the vowel that carries the pitch accent. Dahan et al. (2002) examined the timing of looks to targets and cohort competitors for accented and unaccented words which referred to discourse given and discourse new entities (e.g. *Put the candle above the triangle. Now put the CANDY/candy…*). Dahan et al. found that listeners use information about pitch accent as the vowel unfolds, initially assuming that nouns in definite referring expression with unaccented vowels refer to the most salient entity (the subject/focus) of the previous sentences, whereas words with accented vowels refer to a non-focused given entity if available, or, if not, a new entity.

Arnold and colleagues (2004) adapted the Dahan et al. cohort design to evaluate the hypothesis that a disfluent production of a noun phrase (*thee uh CANDY*) would bias listeners to expect reference to a discourse-new entity. With fluent productions, Arnold et al. replicated Dahan et al.'s finding that an accented noun was preferentially interpreted as referring to a non-focused entity. However, with a disfluent production, the preference shifted to the discourse new entity. Watson and his colleagues (e.g. Watson et al., 2006) have also used cohort competitors to test hypotheses about the interpretation of different pitch accents, focusing on potential differences between the H* (presentational) and L+H* (contrastive) pitch accents (Pierrehumbert and Hirschberg, 1990).

Ito and Speer (described in Speer and Ito, forthcoming) have also investigated presentational and contrastive accents, combining eye movements with a "targeted language game." The director, a naive participant, instructs a confederate about how to decorate a Christmas tree using ornaments that need to be placed on the tree in a specified sequence. Ornaments differ in type, e.g. bells, hats, balls, houses, and in color, e.g. orange, silver, gold, blue. Recordings demonstrated that participants typically used a presentational accent (H*) when a color was new to the local discourse. For example, *orange* typically received a presentational accent in the instruction *First, hang an orange ball on the left* when an orange ornament was being mentioned for the first time) for a particular row. However, if the instruction to place the orange ball followed placement of a ball of a different color, e.g. a silver ball, then "orange" was more likely to be produced with a contrastive accent (L+H*). Ito and Speer showed that the recordings using the preferred pitch accent pattern used by naive participants facilitated listeners' time to identify the correct ornament, as measured by eye movements.

18.4.2 Sentence processing: syntactic ambiguity resolution

In a series of classic papers, Crain (1981), Crain and Steedman (1985), and Altmann and Steedman (1988) argued that many of the systematic preferences that readers and listeners exhibit when resolving temporary syntactic ambiguity are not due to differences in syntactic complexity between the alternative structures, but rather to differences in referential implications. A well-known example comes from prepositional (PP) attachment ambiguities as illustrated in sentences such as *Anne hit the thief with the wart* is one such example. The strong initial preference to consider *with the wart* (erroneously) as the instrument of *hit* rather than as a restrictive modifier of *the thief* could in part be due to the fact the restrictive modifier is most felicitous in a context in which multiple thieves are present, one of which has a wart. In the absence of such a context, there is little reason for considering the modification analysis. Indeed, some (but not all) eye movement studies with text have found that this referential factor (i.e. the presence/absence of referential ambiguity) has immediate effects on real-time syntactic ambiguity resolution in reading (e.g. Altmann and Steedman, 1988; Britt, 1994; Sedivy, 2003; Spivey-Knowlton and Sedivy, 1995; Spivey and Tanenhaus, 1998; but for discussion of studies finding weak or delayed effects of referential context see Staub and Rayner, this volume, and Rayner and Liversedge, 2004).

Introducing a referential world that is co-present with the unfolding language, naturally highlights these and other questions about reference. Indeed, the initial action-based Visual World study (Tanenhaus et al., 1995, described earlier) examined how referential ambiguity (i.e. the presence of multiple apples in a scene) influences the listeners' initial bias when encountering a sentence with a temporarily ambiguous prepositional phrase (*Put the apple on the towel in the box.*). Recall that the presence of two apples in the scene shifted listeners' initial preference to interpret *on the towel* from a goal preference to a modifier preference. This study confirms that something like Crain's Referential Principle (Crain and Steedman, 1985) is an important factor when listeners interpret spoken language in the context of visually co-present referents.

Subsequent work by Snedeker and Trueswell (2004) confirmed the importance of referential context, but importantly established that high-level expectations *contribute* to but do not solely *determine* the outcome of ambiguity resolution in visual contexts. A multiple constraint view of sentence processing predicts that lower level linguistic factors, such as verb argument preferences, contribute simultaneously to the ambiguity resolution process. Snedeker and Trueswell (2004) confirmed this prediction in a study using globally ambiguous sentences such as *Tickle the pig with the fan,* in which they manipulated the bias that the verb has for an instrument when it is followed by a *with*-phrase along with the referential context. The eye movement and action data revealed simultaneous effects of both the referential context (one and two-referent) and verb argument preferences; the presence of multiple pigs reduced looks to, and use of, the potential instrument; likewise degree of verb-bias systematically affected looks and actions involving the potential Instrument. Crucially, these verb effects were observed in both scenes with one and two potential referents, suggesting that the mere presence of multiple referents does not solely determine attachment preferences for listeners.

It remains something of a puzzle why the effects of referential context seem so much stronger in studies examining the PP-attachment ambiguities involving goals versus modifiers (*Put the apple on the towel*) compared to Instrument versus modifiers (*Tickle the frog with the feather*) given that *put* is a verb that has a strong goal-bias. For some speculation about possible explanations, see Snedeker and Trueswell (2004); Spivey et al. (2002); Tanenhaus and Trueswell (2005); Trueswell and Gleitman (2004); and Engelhardt, Bailey, and Ferreira (2006).

18.4.3 Circumscribing referential domains

The studies reviewed thus far made the simplifying assumption that the referential domain for a linguistic expression comprises all the salient entities in the environment which are temporarily consistent with the referring expression as it unfolds. However, speakers—at least in their own productions—consider real-world constraints like the proximity and relevance of potential referents, the relevance of other estimations of the knowledge that the listener has of the world, and several other factors (Clark, 1992; Levelt, 1989; Lyons, 1981; Stone and Webber, 1998). Put more concretely, a speaker's decision to refer to an object as *the ball, the red ball, the ball closer to you, the slightly asymmetric sphere, it, that one*, or *that* clearly depends on this wide range of spatial, perceptual, social, and cognitive factors.

A central theme of research using the Visual World paradigm has been to understand how and when these factors impinge on decisions made by listeners and speakers (Chambers et al., 2002; Sedivy, 2003; Sedivy et al., 1999; Grodner and Sedivy, forthcoming; Keysar et al., 2000; Keysar and Barr, 2005; Brown-Schmidt et al., 2005; Brown-Schmidt and Tanenhaus, 2006). For instance, we have already discussed some studies demonstrating that listeners dynamically update referential domains, integrating information from the unfolding utterance in conjunction with the entities in the workspace (Chambers et al., 2002; Chambers et al., 2004; Eberhard et al., 1995) and generating expectations about upcoming referents (Altmann and Kamide, 1999; Kamide et al., 2003), especially those that are likely to be realized as arguments (Boland, 2005). And, in an ingenious series of eye movement studies, Altmann and colleagues have recently demonstrated that actions described or implied in a narrative influence expectations about how the location of objects will change in the listener's mental model of the scene, as determined by looks to locations in the scene (Altmann et al., 2004).

A listener's referential domain is also affected by intended actions and the affordances of potential objects that are relevant to those actions (Chambers et al., 2002). These affordances also affect the earliest moments of syntactic ambiguity resolution, challenging the claim that language processing includes a syntactic subsystem (module) that is informationally encapsulated, and thus isolated from high-level non-linguistic expectations (Coltheart, 1999; Fodor, 1983).

For example, Chambers et al. (2004) showed that in a two-referent context that includes a liquid egg in a bowl and a liquid egg in a glass, participants will initially treat the PP *in the bowl* as a modifier with an instruction such as *pour the egg in the bowl over the flour.* However, when the egg in the bowl is solid and thus cannot be poured, then participants initially misinterpret *in the bowl* as the Goal. These results cannot be attributed to constraints lexically encoded within the linguistic representation of the verb *pour*; Chambers et al. found the same pattern of results with the verb *put* when the affordances were introduced non-linguistically by handing the participant an instrument.

18.4.3.1 Scalar implicatures

Earlier we reviewed Sedivy's finding that listeners assume that the referential domain includes a contrast set when they hear a pre-nominal scalar adjective, such as *tall.* These results are particularly striking because they represent one case in which listeners immediately generate a pragmatic inference based on a generalized implicature. There is an emerging debate about when listeners generate these types of inference; whether they apply differently to different classes of scales—especially those that involve potential contrasts between a so-called logical interpretation (e.g. logical or inclusive *OR* versus pragmatic or exclusive *OR*) where there are claims that logical *OR* is computed (obligatorily) prior to pragmatic *OR*; and how these inferences are modulated by context (see Noveck and Sperber, 2005). Visual World eye movement studies are beginning to feature prominently in research in this arena, though this work had not yet begun to appear in the literature as this chapter went to press.

Eye movement research using pre-nominal adjectives is beginning to shed light on inference under other circumstances. Although any adjective can appear post-nominally, either in a restrictive relative clause (*the glass* ***that is tall***) or in a prepositional phrase (*The glass* <u>*with spots*</u>), some adjectives are typically used pre-nominally (e.g. scalar adjectives and color adjectives), others are nearly always used post-nominally (*the shape* <u>*with diamonds*</u>), and others occur equally often in pre-nominal and post-nominal positions (e.g. *striped, with stripes*). Using a point of disambiguation logic, Edwards and Chambers (2003) have shown that listeners make rapid use of the *absence* of a pre-nominal modifier to rule out candidate referents. Grodner and Sedivy (forthcoming) have established that listeners rapidly adjust to how reliably a speaker uses scalar adjectives contrastively, including making adjustments based on metalinguistic information provided by an experimenter. Arnold et al. (2007) report similar results with metalinguistic information provided about a disfluent speaker. These results bear on questions about when in the time-course of processing, and under what circumstances, speakers and listeners consider the likely knowledge and intentions of their interlocutors—a topic we will return to shortly.

18.4.4 Word order variation, discourse, and information structure

The Visual World paradigm has proved to be a useful tool in investigating how discourse and pragmatic factors related to information structure influence reference resolution and parsing. Languages with highly flexible word orders are invaluable for examining these questions because word order communicates information structure and discourse status (e.g. given/new distinctions). Kaiser and Trueswell (2004) used the Visual World paradigm to explore how reference resolution in Finnish, a flexible word order language with canonical SVO order and no articles. The non-canonical order OVS marks the object as given and the subject as new; SVO is more flexible, being used in multiple contexts. In the study, the eye gaze of Finnish listeners was tracked as they heard spoken descriptions of simple pictures, so as to test whether listeners use this knowledge of information structure to their advantage, to increase the efficiency with which visual information is collected. That is, upon hearing an OV ... sequence, Finnish listeners should expect the upcoming noun to be discourse-new, whereas an SV ... sequence makes no such prediction. The results confirmed these predictions. As compared to SVO, OVS sentences caused listeners to launch anticipatory eye movements to a discourse-new referent at the second noun onset, even before participants had enough acoustic information to recognize this word. The findings illustrate that in a flexible word order language, a non-canonical order can result in anticipatory processes regarding the discourse status of a yet-to-be-heard constituent.

18.4.5 Pronouns and other referring expressions

Psycholinguists are also using the Visual World paradigm to study how syntax and information structure interact with the type of referring expressions, e.g. definite noun phrases, and different types of pronouns (Arnold et al., 2000; Järvikivi, 2005; Brown-Schmidt et al., 2005;

Runner et al., 2003; Runner et al., 2006). The visual paradigm is particularly useful for addressing these questions because the looks to potential referents, especially when combined with a decision, allow for strong inferences about which potential referents are being considered and which referent is selected.

Several studies have examined how the order in which characters in a scene are mentioned influence the interpretation of utterances with both ambiguous and unambiguous pronouns. Arnold et al. (2000) found that English listeners, upon hearing a sentence beginning with an ambiguous pronoun (*he*), preferentially looked to the character that had been mentioned first in the previous sentence. Kaiser and Trueswell (forthcoming) showed that this preference, at least in Finnish, reflects a preference for pronouns to refer to the grammatical subject of the previous sentence, not the object (but see also Järvikivi et al., 2005). Preferences depend, though, on the type of pronoun used in Finnish: another class of pronouns (demonstratives) preferentially selects referents on the basis of surface word order rather than grammatical role. Brown-Schmidt and colleagues (2005) used eye movements and actions to demonstrate differences in the interpretation of *it* and *that,* following an instruction such as *Put the cup on the saucer. Now put it/that* ... Addressees preferentially interpret *it* as referring to the theme (the cup), whereas *that* is preferentially interpreted as referring to the composite created by the action (the cup on the saucer), which does not have a linguistic antecedent (*the cup on the saucer* is not a constituent in the instruction). Finally, the Visual World paradigm is being used to examine the interplay between structural constraints (e.g. binding constraints), discourse, and type of referring expression for pronouns and reflexives (Runner et al., 2003; Runner et al., 2006).

18.4.6 Common ground, alignment, and dialogue

Until recently, most psycholinguistic research on spoken language comprehension could be divided into one of two traditions, each with its own theoretical concerns and dominant methodologies (Clark, 1992; Trueswell and Tanenhaus, 2005). The product tradition examined the individual cognitive processes by which listeners recover linguistic representations, typically by examining moment-by-moment processes in real-time language processing, using carefully controlled stimuli scripted materials and fine-grained online measures.

In contrast, the action tradition focused on how people use language to perform acts in conversation. Many of the characteristic features of conversation emerge only when interlocutors have joint goals and when they participate in a dialogue both as a speaker and as an addressee. Thus research within the action tradition typically examines unscripted interactive conversation involving two or more participants engaged in a cooperative task, typically with real-world referents and well-defined behavioral goals.

Recently the language processing community has begun to show increased interest in bridging the product and action traditions (Pickering and Garrod, 2004; Garrod and Pickering, Chapter 26 this volume; Trueswell and Tanenhaus, 2005). However, research which aims to bridge the two traditions has rarely combined on-line measures—the methodological cornerstone of the product tradition, with unscripted cooperative conversation—the central domain of inquiry in the action tradition. (see Brennan, 1990; 2005 for a notable exception). Research monitoring eye movements in unscripted conversation is likely to play a central role in addressing at least two fundamental questions which are becoming the focus of much current research. The first is at what temporal grain interlocutors monitor each other's likely knowledge and intentions. The second is to what degree, and at what temporal grain, the representations of interlocutors become ***aligned*** during interactive conversation (Pickering and Garrod, 2004; Garrod and Pickering, Chapter 26 this volume; Richardson et al., 2007).

With respect to common ground, although keeping track of what is known, and not known, to the individual participants in a discourse would seem to be fundamental for coordinating information flow (Brennan and Hulteen, 1995; Clark, 1992; 1996), computing common ground by building, maintaining, and updating a model of a conversational partner's beliefs could be memory-intensive (thus interlocutors may not consider common ground during initial processing; Keysar and Barr, 2005). Some supporting evidence comes from eye movement studies showing that addressees often fail to reliably distinguish their own knowledge from that of their interlocutor when interpreting a partner's spoken instructions (Keysar et al., 2000; Keysar et al., 2003; but cf. Nadig and Sedivy, 2002; Hanna et al., 2003). However, these studies have used confederates which restricts the nature of the interaction (Metzing and Brennan, 2003), including the degree to which common goals are negotiated, and, perhaps most importantly, the types of construction that are used in the conversation. This could mask effects of perspective taking (for discussion and supporting evidence see Tanenhaus and Brown-Schmidt, 2008).

With respect to alignment, Pickering and Garrod (2004) propose that successful dialogue requires interlocutors to arrive at similar (aligned) representations across multiple linguistic and conceptual levels. They further propose that priming provides a mechanism by which alignment occurs, noting, for example, that syntactic persistence—the tendency for speakers to choose a structure they have previously heard or produced— appears to be particularly robust in dialogue (Branigan et al., 2000). Even if Pickering and Garrod are correct in identifying priming as an important mechanism for alignment, priming studies will have to be supplemented by real-time measures that probe the representations of interlocutors. Otherwise, priming is being called upon to serve both as a proposed mechanism for alignment and as a diagnostic for alignment, raising concerns about circularity.

In recent work, Brown-Schmidt and colleagues have demonstrated that it is possible to use eye movements to monitor real-time processes in task- oriented dialogues with complex tasks and naive participants (Brown-Schmidt et al., 2005; Brown-Schmidt, 2005; Brown-Schmidt and Tanenhaus, and Brown-Schmidt, 2008). For example, Brown-Schmidt et al. used a referential communication task in which participants separated by a barrier cooperated to replace stickers with blocks to match the placement of the blocks in their respective boards They adopted a "targeted language game" approach, placing stickers to maximize the likelihood that conditions approximating those that might be incorporated in a standard factorial design would emerge. Despite the complexity of the dialogue, they were able to see point-of-disambiguation effects for referring expressions that mirror effects observed in studies with scripted instructions and simple displays. In particular, as a speaker's referring expression unfolded, the addressee's fixations to the referent increased, and fixations to potential competitors decreased, about 200 ms after the place in the speech stream where the input first disambiguated the referent. Additional results showed that the interlocutor's referential domains became closely aligned. For example, when proximal competitors that did not match the immediate task goals were not part of the speaker's referential domain (as inferred by the form of the referring expression), they were also not considered as potential referents by the addressee (as inferred from fixations). Related results come from ingenious studies by Richardson, Dale, and colleagues demonstrating that eye movements of interlocutors become closely coordinated and, more strikingly, the degree of temporal coordination is correlated with comprehension (Richardson and Dale, 2005; Richardson et al., forthcoming).

18.5 Closing remarks

This chapter has provided an overview of the rapidly growing literature on eye movements and spoken language processing, focusing on applications to spoken language comprehension. We have reviewed some of the foundational studies, discussed issues of data analysis and interpretation, and discussed issues that arise in comparing eye movement reading studies to Visual World studies. We have also reviewed some of the major lines of research which are utilizing this method, focusing on topics in language comprehension, including spoken word recognition, use of referential constraints in parsing, interactive conversation, and the development of language processing abilities in children.

It should be clear from this review that the Visual World paradigm is being employed in most traditional areas of inquiry within psycholinguistics. And in each of these areas, the Visual World approach is encouraging psycholinguists to investigate uncharted theoretical and empirical issues. Within the study of spoken sentence comprehension, issues about reference have taken center stage, in part because the Visual World methodology makes it possible to connect research on real-time reference resolution with social and cognitive research on pragmatics and conversation. Within the study of spoken word recognition, the time-locked nature of this measure has allowed researchers to explore phonemic, sub-phonemic, and prosodic contributions to word recognition in utterances at a level of detail not possible with traditional methods. Most generally, the Visual World approach is part of a larger movement toward connecting language and action in rich goal-directed tasks using increasingly rich and complex data arrays to understand the dynamics of comprehension and production in conversation. This approach is likely to have an increasingly important influence on theoretical development in natural language, just as it as it has begun to enrich theories in other areas of perception and cognition (Ballard et al., 1997; Barsalou, 1999; Hayhoe and Ballard, 2005; Land, 2004).

References

Allopenna, P. D., Magnuson, J. S., and Tanenhaus, M. K. (1998) Tracking the time course of spoken word recognition: evidence for continuous mapping models. *Journal of Memory and Language*, 38: 419–39.

Altmann, G. T. M. (2004) Language-mediated eye movements in the absence of a Visual World: the 'blank screen paradigm'. *Cognition*, 93: B79–B87.

Altmann, G. T. M., and Kamide, Y. (1999) Incremental interpretation at verbs: restricting the domain of subsequent reference. *Cognition*, 73: 247–64.

Altmann, G. T. M., and Kamide, Y. (2004) Now you see it, now you don't: mediating the mapping between language and the visual world. In J. M. Henderson and F. Ferreira (eds), *The Interface of Language, Vision, and Action: Eye Movements and the Visual World*, pp. 279–318. Psychology Press, New York.

Altmann, G. T. M., and Steedman, M. J. (1988) Interaction with context during human sentence processing. *Cognition*, 30: 191–238.

Arnold, J. E., Eisenband, J. G., Brown-Schmidt, S., and Trueswell, J. C. (2000) The rapid use of gender information: evidence of the time course for pronoun resolution from eyetracking. *Cognition*, 76: B13–B26.

Arnold, J. E., Hudson Kam, C. L., and Tanenhaus, M. K. (2007) If you say *thee uh-* you're describing something hard: the on-line attribution of disfluency during reference comprehension. *Journal of Experimental Psychology: Learning, Memory & Cognition*, 33: 914–30.

Arnold, J. E., Tanenhaus, M. K., Altmann, R. J., and Fagnano, M. (2004) The old and thee, uh, new: disfluency and reference resolution. *Psychological Science*, 15: 578–82.

Ballard, D. H., Hayhoe, M. M., Pook, P. K., and Rao, R. P. N. (1997) Deictic codes for the embodiment of cognition. *Behavioral and Brain Sciences*, 20: 723–67.

Barsalou, L. (1999) Language comprehension: archival memory or preparation for situated action? *Discourse Processes*, 28: 61–80.

Bock, K., Irwin, D. E., and Davidson, D. J. (2004) Putting first things first. In J. M. Henderson and F. Ferreira (eds), *The Interface of Language, Vision, and Action: Eye Movements and the Visual World*, pp. 249–78. Psychology Press, New York.

Bock, J. K., Irwin, D. E., Davidson, D. J., and Levelt, W. J. M. (2003) Minding the clock. *Journal of Memory and Language*, 48: 653–85.

Boland, J. E. (2005) Visual arguments. *Cognition*, 95: 237–74.

Branigan, H. P., Pickering, M. J., and Cleland, A. A. (2000) Syntactic co-ordination in dialogue. *Cognition*, 75: B13–B25.

Brennan, S.E. (1990) Seeking and providing evidence for mutual understanding. Doctoral dissertation, Stanford University.

Brennan, S.E. (2005) How conversation is shaped by visual and spoken evidence. In J. C. Trueswell and M. K. Tanenhaus (eds) *Approaches to studying world-situated language use: Bridging the language-as-product and language-as-action traditions*, pp. 95–130. MIT Press, Cambridge, MA.

Brennan, S. E. and Hulteen, E. (1995) Interaction and feedback in a spoken language system: A theoretical framework. *Knowledge-Based Systems*, 8: 143–51.

Britt, M.A. (1994) The interaction of referential ambiguity and argument structure in the parsing of prepositional phrases. *Journal of Memory and Language*, 33: 251–83.

Brown-Schmidt, S. (2005) Language processing in conversation. Unpublished Doctoral dissertation, University of Rochester.

Brown-Schmidt, S., Byron, D. K., and Tanenhaus, M. K. (2005) Beyond salience: interpretation of personal and demonstrative pronouns. *Journal of Memory and Language*, 53: 292–313.

Brown-Schmidt, S., Campana, E., and Tanenhaus, M. K. (2005) Real-time reference resolution in a referential communication task. In J. C. Trueswell and M. K. Tanenhaus (eds), *Approaches to studying world-situated language use: Bridging the language-as-product and language-as-action traditions*, pp. 153–72. MIT Press, Cambridge, MA.

Brown-Schmidt, S. and Tanenhaus, M. K. (2006) Watching the eyes when talking about size: an investigation of message formulation and utterance planning. *Journal of Memory and Language*, 54: 592–609.

Brown-Schmidt S. and Tanenhaus, M. K. (2005) Real-time interpretation of referential expressions in unscripted interactive conversations. MS submitted.

Chambers, C. G., Tanenhaus, M. K., Eberhard, K. M., Filip, H., and Carlson, G. N. (2002) Circumscribing referential domains during real-time language comprehension. *Journal of Memory and Language*, 47: 30–49.

Clark, H. H. (1996) *Using Language*. Cambridge University Press, Cambridge, UK.

Clark, H. H. (1992) *Arenas of Language Use*. University of Chicago Press, Chicago.

Chambers, C.G., Tanenhaus, M. K., and Magnuson, J. S. (2004) Action-based affordances and syntactic ambiguity resolution. *Journal of Experimental Psychology: Learning, Memory and Cognition*, 30: 687–96.

Coltheart, M. (1999). Modularity and cognition. *Trends in Cognitive Sciences*, 3: 115–20.

Cooper, R. M. (1974) The control of eye fixation by the meaning of spoken language: a new methodology for the real-time investigation of speech perception, memory, and language processing. *Cognitive Psychology*, 6: 84–107.

Crain, S. (1981) Contextual Constraints on Sentence Comprehension. Ph.D. dissertation. University of California, Irvine.

Crain, S. and Steedman, M. (1985) On not being led up the garden path: the use of context by the psychological parser. In D. Dowty, L., Karttunen, and A. Zwicky (eds), *Natural Language Parsing: Psychological, Computational, and Theoretical Perspectives*, pp. 320–58. Cambridge University Press, Cambridge.

Creel, S. C., Aslin, R. N., and Tanenhaus, M. K. (2008) Heeding the voice of experience: the role of talker variation in lexical access. *Cognition*, 106: 633–64.

Creel, S. C., Tanenhaus, M. K., and Aslin, R. N. (2006) Consequences of lexical stress on learning an artificial lexicon. *Journal of Experimental Psychology: Learning, Memory, and Cognition*, 32: 15–32.

Dahan, D., Magnuson, J. S., and Tanenhaus, M. K. (2001) Time course of frequency effects in spoken-word recognition: evidence from eye movements. *Cognitive Psychology*, 42: 317–67.

Dahan, D., Magnuson, J. S., Tanenhaus, M. K., and Hogan, E. M. (2001) Subcategorical mismatches and the time course of lexical access: evidence for lexical competition. *Language and Cognitive Processes*, 16: 507–34.

Dahan, D., and Tanenhaus, M. K. (2004) Continuous mapping from sound to meaning in spoken-language comprehension: evidence from immediate effects of verb-based constraints. *Journal of Experimental Psychology: Learning, Memory and Cognition*, 30: 498–513.

Dahan, D. and Tanenhaus, M. K. (2005) Looking at the rope when looking for the snake: conceptually mediated eye movements during spoken-word recognition. *Psychonomic Bulletin and Review*, 12: 453–59.

Dahan, D., Tanenhaus, M. K., and Chambers, C. G. (2002) Accent and reference resolution in spoken-language comprehension. *Journal of Memory and Language*, 47: 292–314.

Dahan, D., Tanenhaus, M. K., and Salverda, A. P. (forthcoming) The influence of visual processing on phonetically driven saccades in the "Visual World" paradigm. In R. P. G. Van Gompel, M. H. Fischer, W. D. Murray, and R. L. Hill (eds) *Eye movements: A Window on Mind and Brain*. Elsevier, Oxford.

Eberhard, K. M., Spivey-Knowlton, M. J., Sedivy, J. C., and Tanenhaus, M. K. (1995) Eye-movements as a window into spoken language comprehension in natural contexts. *Journal of Psycholinguistic Research*, 24: 409–36.

Edwards, J. D., and Chambers, C. G. (2003) Codability differences influence on-line referential interpretation. Poster presented at the Sixteenth Annual CUNY Conference on Human Sentence Processing, Cambridge, MA.

Engelhardt, P. E., Bailey, K. G. D., and Ferreira, F. (2006) Do speakers and listeners observe the Gricean Maxim of Quantity? *Journal of Memory and Language*, 54: 554–573.

Ferreira, F. and Bailey, K.G.B. (forthcoming) The processing of filled pause disfluencies in the visual world. In R. P. G. Van Gompel, M. H. Fischer, W. S. Murray, and R. L. Hill (eds), *Eye Movements: A Window on Mind and Brain*. Elsevier, Oxford.

Fodor, J. A. (1983) *Modularity of Mind*. Bradford Books, Cambridge, MA.

Gaskell, M. G., and Marslen-Wilson, W. D. (2002) Representation and competition in the perception of spoken words. *Cognitive Psychology*, 45: 220–66.

Gow, D. W. and McMurray, B. (2007) Word recognition and phonology: the case of English coronal place assimilation. J.S. Cole & J. Hualdo (eds), *Papers in Laboratory Phonology 9*, pp. 173–200. Mouton de Gruyter, New York.

Griffin, Z. M. (2004) The eyes are right when the mouth is wrong. *Psychological Science*, 15: 814–21.

Griffin, Z. M. and Bock, J. K. (2000) What they eyes say about speaking. *Psychological Science*, 11: 274–9.

Grodner, D. and Sedivy, J. (forthcoming) The effect of speaker-specific information on pragmatic inferences. In N. Pearlmutter and E. Gibson (eds), *The Processing and Acquisition of Reference*. MIT Press, Cambridge, MA.

Hanna, J. E. and Tanenhaus, M. K. (2004) Pragmatic effects on reference resolution in a collaborative task: evidence from eye movements. *Cognitive Science: A Multidisciplinary Journal*, 28 (1): 105–15.

Hanna, J. E., Tanenhaus, M. K., and Trueswell, J. C. (2003) The effects of common ground and perspective on domains of referential interpretation. *Journal of Memory and Language*, 49: 43–61.

Hayhoe, M. and Ballard, D. (2005) Eye movements in natural behavior. *Trends in Cognitive Sciences*, 9: 188–94.

Henderson J. M.,and Ferreira, F. (eds) (2004) *The Interface of Language, Vision, and Action: Eye Movements and the Visual World*. Psychology Press, New York.

Järvikivi, J., van Gompel, R. P. G., Hyönä, J., and Bertram, R. (2005) Ambiguous pronoun resolution: contrasting the first-mention and subject-preference accounts. *Psychological Science*, 16: 260–4.

Ju, M. and Luce, P.A. (2004) Falling on sensitive ears: constraints on bilingual lexical activation. *Psychological Science*, 15: 314–18.

Just, M. A. and Carpenter, P. A. (1980) A theory of reading: from eye fixations to comprehension. *Psychological Review*, 87: 329–54.

Kaiser, E. and Trueswell, J. C. (2004) The role of discourse context in the processing of a flexible word-order language. *Cognition*, 94: 113–47.

Kaiser, E. and Trueswell, J.C. (forthcoming) The referential properties of Dutch pronouns and demonstratives: is salience enough? In M. Weisgerber (ed.), *Proceedings of Sinn und Bedeutung 8*. University of Konstanz linguistics working papers.

Kamide, Y., Altmann, G. T. M., and Haywood, S. L. (2003) The time-course of prediction in incremental sentence processing: evidence from anticipatory eye movements. *Journal of Memory and Language*, 49: 133–56.

Keysar, B. and Barr, D. (2005) Coordination of action and belief in conversation. In J. C. Trueswell and M. K. Tanenhaus (eds), *Approaches to studying world-situated language use: Bridging the language-as-product and language-as-action traditions*. MIT Press, Cambridge, MA.

Keysar, B., Barr, D. J., Balin, J. A., and Brauner, J. S. (2000) Taking perspective in conversation: the role of mutual knowledge in comprehension. *Psychological Science*, 11: 32–8.

Keysar, B., Lin, S., and Barr, D. J. (2003) Limits on theory of mind use in adults. *Cognition*, 89: 25–41.

Knoeferle, P., and Crocker, M.W. (2006) The coordinated interplay of scene, utterance, and world knowledge: evidence from eye tracking. *Cognitive Science*, 30(3): 481–529.

Knoeferle, P., Crocker, M. W., Scheepers, C., and Pickering, M. J. (2005) The influence of the immediate visual context on incremental thematic role-assignment: evidence from eye- movements in the depicted events. *Cognition*, 95: 95–127.

Kowler, E. (1995) Eye movements. In S. M. Kosslyn, and D. N. Osherson (eds), *Visual Cognition: An Invitation to Cognitive Science*, 2nd edn, vol. 2, pp. 215–66. MIT Press, Cambridge, MA.

Land, M. (2004) Eye movements in daily life. In L. Chalupa and J. Werner (eds), *The Visual Neurosciences*, vol. 2, pp. 1357–68. MIT Press, Cambridge, MA.

Levelt, W. J. M. (1989) *Speaking: From Intention to Articulation*. MIT Press, Cambridge, MA.

Lucas, M. (1999) Context effects in lexical access: a meta-analysis. *Memory and Cognition*, 27: 385–398.

Luce, D. R. (1959) *Individual Choice Behavior*. Wiley, Oxford.

Lyons, J. (1981) *Language, meaning, and context*. Collins/Fontana, London.

Magnuson, J. S. (2005) Moving hand reveals dynamics of thought. *Proceedings of the National Academy of Sciences*, 102: 9995–6.

Magnuson, J. S., Dixon, J. A., Tanenhaus, M. K., and Aslin, R. N. (2007) The dynamics of lexical competition in spoken word recognition. *Cognitive Sciences*, 31: 131–56.

Magnuson, J. S., Tanenhaus, M. K., Aslin, R. N., and Dahan, D. (2003) Time course of spoken word learning and recognition: studies with artificial lexicons. *Journal of Experimental Psychology: General*, 132: 202–27.

Marslen-Wilson, W. D. and Warren, P. (1994). Levels of perceptual representation and process in lexical access: Words, phonemes, and features. *Psychological Review*, 101: 653–75.

McClelland, J. L., and Elman, J. L. (1986) The TRACE model of speech perception. *Cognitive Psychology*, 18: 1–86.

McConkie, G. W., and Rayner, K. (1976) Asymmetry of the perceptual span in reading. *Bulletin of the Psychonomic Society*, 8: 365–8.

McMurray, B., Tanenhaus, M. K., and Aslin, R. N. (2002) Gradient effects of within-category phonetic variation on lexical access. *Cognition*, 86: B33–B42.

Metzing, C., and Brennan, S. E. (2003) When conceptual pacts are broken: partner-specific effects on the comprehension of referring expressions. *Journal of Memory and Language*, 49: 201–13.

Meyer, A. S., Sleiderink, A. M., and Levelt, W. J. M. (1998) Viewing and naming objects: eye movements during noun phrase production. *Cognition*, 66: B25–B33.

Nadig, A., and Sedivy, J. C. (2002). Evidence of perspective-taking constraints in children's on-line reference resolution. *Psychological Science*, 13(4): 329–36.

Norris, D., McQueen, J. M., and Cutler, A. (2000). Merging information in speech recognition: Feedback is never necessary. *Behavioral and Brain Sciences*, 23(3): 299–370.

Noveck, J., and Sperber, D. (eds) (2005) *Experimental Pragmatics*. Oxford University Press, Oxford.

Pickering, M. J., and Garrod, S. C. (2004) Towards a mechanistic theory of dialog. *Behavioral and Brain Sciences*, 7: 169–90.

Pierrehumbert, J., and Hirschberg, J. (1990) The meaning of intonational contours in the interpretation of discourse. In P. R. Cohen, J. L. Morgan, and M. E. Pollack (eds), *Intentions in Communication*, pp. 271–311. MIT Press, Cambridge, MA.

Rayner, K., and Liversedge, S. P. (2004) Visual and linguistic processing during eye fixations in reading. In J. M. Henderson, and F. Ferreira (eds), *The Interface of Language, Vision, and Action: Eye Movements and the Visual World*, pp. 59–104. Psychology Press, New York.

Richardson, D. C., and Dale, R. (2005) Looking to understand: the coupling between speaker's and listener's eye movements and its relationship to discourse comprehension. *Cognitive Science*, 29: 1045–60.

Richardson, D. C., Dale, R., and Kirkham, N. Z. (2007) The art of conversation is coordination: common ground and the coupling of eye movements during dialogue. *Psychological Science*, 18: 407–13.

Runner, J. T., Sussman, R. S., and Tanenhaus, M. K. (2003) Assignment of reference to reflexives and pronouns in picture noun phrases: evidence from eye movements. *Cognition*, 89: B1–B13.

Runner, J. T., Sussman, R. S., and Tanenhaus, M. K. (2006) Assigning referents to reflexives and pronouns in picture noun phrases: experimental tests of binding theory. *Cognitive Science*, 30: 1–49.

Salverda, A. P. (2005) Prosodically-conditioned detail in the recognition of spoken words. Ph.D. dissertation, Max Planck Institute for Psycholinguistics, Nijmegen.

Salverda, A. P., and Altmann, G. (2005) Cross-talk between language and vision: interference of visually-cued eye movements by spoken language. Poster presented at the AMLaP Conference, Ghent, Belgium.

Salverda, A. P., Dahan, D., and McQueen, J. M. (2003) The role of prosodic boundaries in the resolution of lexical embedding in speech comprehension. *Cognition*, 90: 51–89.

Sedivy, J. C. (2003) Pragmatic versus form-based accounts of referential contrast: evidence for effects of informativity expectations. *Journal of Psycholinguistic Research*, 32: 3–23.

Sedivy, J. C., Tanenhaus, M. K., Chambers, C. G., and Carlson, G. N. (1999) Achieving incremental semantic interpretation through contextual representation. *Cognition*, 71: 109–47.

Sereno, S. C. and Rayner, K. (1992) Fast priming during eye fixations in reading. *Journal of Experimental Psychology: Human Perception and Performance*, 18: 173–184.

Shatzman, K. B., and McQueen, J. M. (2006) Prosodic knowledge affects the recognition of newly acquired words. *Psychological Science*, 17: 372–7.

Snedeker, J., and Trueswell, J. C. (2004) The developing constraints on parsing decisions: the role of lexical-biases and referential scenes in child and adult sentence processing. *Cognitive Psychology*, 49: 238–99.

Speer, S. R. and Ito, K. (2006) Using interactive tasks to elicit natural dialogue production. In S. Sudhoff, D. Lenertov·, R. Meyer, S. Pappert, P. Augurzky, I. Mleinek, N. Richter, and J. Schliefler (eds), *Methods in Empirical Prosody Research*, Berlin: Walter de Gruyter, 229–57.

Spivey, M., and Geng, J. (2001). Oculomotor mechanisms activated by imagery and memory: Eye movements to absent objects. *Psychological Research*, 65: 235–41.

Spivey, M. J., Grosjean, M., and Knoblich, G. (2005) Continuous attraction toward phonological competitors. *Proceedings of the National Academy of Sciences*, 102: 10393–8.

Spivey, M. J., and Marian, V. (1999) Cross talk between native and second languages: partial activation of an irrelevant lexicon. *Psychological Science*, 10: 281–4.

Spivey, M. J., and Tanenhaus, M. K. (1998) Syntactic ambiguity resolution in discourse: modeling the effects of referential context and lexical frequency. *Journal of Experimental Psychology: Learning, Memory, and Cognition*, 24: 1521–43.

Spivey, M. J., Tanenhaus, M. K., Eberhard, K. M., and Sedivy, J. C. (2002) Eye movements and spoken language comprehension: effects of visual context on syntactic ambiguity resolution. *Cognitive Psychology*, 45: 447–81.

Spivey-Knowlton, M. J. (1996) Integration of visual and linguistic information: human data and model simulations. Ph.D. dissertation, University of Rochester.

Spivey-Knowlton, M. and Sedivy, J. C. (1995) Resolving attachment ambiguities with multiple constraints. *Cognition*, 55: 227–67.

Stone, M., and Webber, B. (1998) Textual economy through close coupling of syntax and semantics. In *Proceedings of 9th biennial International Workshop on Natural language Generation (INLG)*, pp. 178–187 Niagra-on-the-lake, Ontario, Canada.

Sussman, R. S., and Sedivy, J. C. (2003). The time-course of processing syntactic dependencies: Evidence from eye movements. *Language and Cognitive Processes*, 18(2): 143–63.

Tanenhaus, M. K., and Brown-Schmidt, S. (2008). Language processing in the natural world. In Moore, B. C. M., Tyler, L. K. & Marslen-Wilson, W. D. (eds), The perception of speech: from sound to meaning, *Philosophical Transactions of the Royal Society B: Biological Sciences*, 363: 1105–22.

Tanenhaus, M. K., Chambers, C. G., and Hanna, J. E. (2004) Referential domains in spoken language comprehension: Using eye movements to bridge the product and action traditions. In J. M. Henderson and F. Ferreira (eds), *The Interface of language, vision, and action: Eye movements and the Visual World*,. Psychology Press, New York. 279–318.

Tanenhaus, M. K., Spivey-Knowlton, M. J., Eberhard, K., and Sedivy, J. (1995) Integration of visual and linguistic information in spoken language comprehension. *Science*, 286: 1632–4.

Tanenhaus, M. K. and Trueswell, J. C. (2005). Using eye movements to bridge the language as action and language as product traditions. In J. C. Trueswell and M. K. Tanenhaus, (eds), *Approaches to studying world-situated language use: Bridging the language-as-product and language-as-action traditions*, pp. 3–38. Edited Volume. MIT Press, Cambridge, MA.

Trueswell, J. C. and Gleitman, L. (2004) Children's eye movements during listening: developmental evidence for a constraint-based theory of sentence processing. In J. M. Henderson, and F. Ferreira (eds), *The Interface of Language, Vision, and Action: Eye Movements and the Visual World*, pp. 319–460. Psychology Press, New York.

Trueswell, J. C., Sekerina, I., Hill, N., and Logrip, M. (1999) The kindergarten-path effect: studying on-line sentence processing in young children. *Cognition*, 73: 89–134.

Trueswell, J. C. and Tanenhaus, M. K. (eds) (2005) *Approaches to studying world-situated language use: Bridging the language-as-product and language-as-action traditions*. MIT Press, Cambridge, MA.

Viviani, P. (1990) Eye movements in visual search: cognitive, perceptual and motor control aspects. In E. Kowler (ed.), *Eye Movements and Their Role in Visual and Cognitive Processes*, vol. 4: *Reviews of Oculomotor Research*, pp. 253–393. Elsevier, Amsterdam.

Watson, D., Gunlogson, C., and Tanenhaus, M. K. (2006) Online methods for the investigation of prosody. In I. Mleinek (ed.), *Methods in Empirical Prosody Research*. Mouton de Gruyter, Berlin.

CHAPTER 19

Eye movements and on-line comprehension processes

Adrian Staub and Keith Rayner

19.1 Introduction

Reading is a rather complex process in which comprehension at a number of levels is essential. In this chapter, we will provide an overview of how different kinds of variables influence eye movements. We want to stress at the outset that eye movement data are highly informative with respect to understanding reading. They provide a moment-to-moment indicator of the ease (or the difficulty) with which readers are able to comprehend the text that they read. Because eye movements are a natural part of the reading process, secondary tasks are not needed to make inferences about reading comprehension. Rather, information about where readers fixate in the text and how long they look at different part of the text provides remarkably reliable data about comprehension at a number of levels.

We will begin with a brief overview of the characteristics of eye movements during reading, which will include a discussion of the different eye movement measures that are typically employed in reading research (these issues are discussed in greater detail in Rayner, 1998, and in Rayner and Pollatsek, 2006). We will then discuss in turn: (1) effects of lexical processing on eye movements, (2) effects of syntactic processing on eye movements, and (3) effects of discourse processing on eye movements. Thus, these sections focus on comprehension at the word level, at the level of syntax, and at the level of higher-level discourse. Shillcock (Chapter 6 this volume) also discusses eye movements and word recognition.

19.2 Basic characteristics of eye movements during reading

On the basis of introspection, it can appear that the eyes move smoothly across the text as one reads. In fact, the eyes move in a series of jumps, remaining relatively stationary between these jumps. The jumps, known as "saccades," typically require 20–40 ms. The durations of the stationary periods, known as "fixations," comprise a somewhat right-skewed normal distribution with the mean at around 200–250 ms and minimum and maximum at about 50–100 ms and about 500 ms, respectively. Meaningful information is extracted from the text only during fixations; during saccades, the visual system does not register the information picked up by the retina.

In normal English reading, the eyes move about 7–9 letter spaces on the average saccade. However, there is great variability in saccade size, with some saccades ranging over twenty characters, and others moving the reader's eyes by only a single character. In skilled readers, about ninety percent of saccades move the eyes forward, with the rest moving the eyes backward in the text, either to resolve comprehension difficulty or to correct error in the programming of forward saccades (these backward eye movements are known as "regressions"). How many fixations a reader makes on a word is, unsurprisingly, related to a word's length, and very short words are frequently skipped altogether (Brysbaert and Vitu, 1998; Rayner and McConkie, 1976).

Function words such as determiners and prepositions, which tend to be quite short, are in fact skipped more than half of the time (Carpenter and Just, 1983; Rayner and Duffy, 1988).

Based on the anatomy of the eye, it is possible to divide the text that is visible on each fixation into three regions. The "foveal" region consists of the text within about 1° of visual angle on either side of the fixation point; at a normal viewing distance, this is about 3–4 letters to the left and right of fixation. Beyond this region, visual acuity drops off rapidly, but readers are still able to obtain some letter identity information in the "parafoveal" region, which extends up to about 5° of visual angle to either side of the fixation point. Beyond the parafovea, in "peripheral" vision, readers are usually only aware of the general shape of the text, such as where a line ends.

Interestingly, the area of text from which readers obtain useful information is not symmetric. Studies that have carefully controlled the amount of text the reader can see (e.g. McConkie and Rayner, 1975; Rayner and Bertera, 1979) have shown that for readers of English, this region extends 14–15 character spaces to the right of fixation, but only 3–4 characters to the left. Given the limits of visual acuity, the region in which readers can actually identify words (the "perceptual span") extends only 7–8 characters to the right of fixation, though this varies as a function of text difficulty. It has also been shown that readers do not make use of information from the lines of text below the one they are fixating (Pollatsek et al., 1993). Readers of languages in which a great deal of information is conveyed by each character (e.g. Chinese) have a considerably smaller perceptual span, one character to the left of fixation to 2–3 characters to the right when reading from left to right (Inhoff and Liu, 1998); readers of languages that are read right to left (e.g. Hebrew) have a span that is larger to the left of fixation than to the right (Pollatsek et al., 1981). These findings show that the size and shape of the perceptual span are in fact determined by complex attentional and information-processing factors, not just by perceptual limitations.

It is clear from the foregoing discussion that on a given fixation, a reader of English is likely to obtain useful word identity information primarily about the word that is currently being fixated and the word immediately to the right of this word. Experiments that have manipulated the visibility of the word to the right of fixation (so-called "boundary change" experiments; Rayner, 1975) have shown that readers do indeed obtain useful information about this word, and that in fact this word is typically read 30–40 ms faster when it was visible on the previous fixation than when it was not (Hyönä et al., 1998; Rayner, 1998). Many studies have explored the nature of the information that the reader extracts about the word to the right of fixation; it appears that readers generally have access to information about the specific letters in this word (Briihl and Inhoff, 1995; Inhoff et al., 1987; Johnson, 2007; Johnson et al., 2007; Rayner et al., 1980; Rayner et al., 1982) and about the phonological or sound codes in the word (Ashby and Clifton, 2005; Ashby and Rayner, 2004; Ashby et al., 2006; Chace et al., 2005; Henderson et al., 1995; Miellet and Sparrow, 2004; Pollatsek et al., 1992; Sparrow and Miellet, 2002). On the other hand, neither information about a word's meaning (Altarriba et al., 2001; Rayner et al., 1986) nor information about the word's morphological composition (Inhoff, 1989; Kambe, 2004; Lima, 1987) is usually available before the word is fixated directly.

As noted above, short words tend to be skipped more frequently. This may be partly because short words are more likely to be identified while the eyes are still fixated on the previous word. This explanation is consistent with results showing that words are also skipped more often when they are easy to identify either because they are predictable in context (Gautier et al., 2000; Rayner and Well, 1996) or because they are very frequent (Rayner et al., 1996). (We have more to say below on the role of these lexical factors in controlling eye movements.) Interestingly, the duration of the fixation prior to a skip is inflated (Drieghe et al., 2005; Kliegl and Engbert, 2005; Pollatsek et al., 1986; Pynte et al., 2004).

Though linguistic factors clearly play a role in word skipping, in general it seems that low-level visual information is the most important input to decisions about where to move the eyes. Rayner and Pollatsek (1981) conducted an experiment in which the amount of text that the reader could see varied randomly from fixation to fixation, and found that the less text was visible to the right of fixation, the shorter the reader's saccades. Subsequent research has shown that the spaces between words are of primary importance (Morris et al., 1990; Pollatsek and Rayner, 1982; Rayner, Fischer, and Pollatsek, 1998), with readers tending to make their first fixation on a word between the beginning and middle of the word (McConkie et al., 1988; Rayner, 1979; Rayner et al., 1996), and using the information provided by spaces to execute a saccade of the appropriate length. Interestingly, when the initial fixation on a word is near the beginning or end of the word, it tends to be relatively short (Vitu et al., 2001). Nuthmann et al. (2005) have recently demonstrated that this is largely because these fixations reflect errors in saccade programming that the reader rapidly corrects.

Compared to decisions about *where* to move the eyes next, decisions about *when* to move the eyes (or, looked at another way, decisions about how long to remain focused on a given point in the text before moving on) are quite strongly affected by cognitive factors related to text comprehension. It is these factors that are the focus of the remaining sections of this chapter. The fact that such cognitive processes are of great importance in these *when* decisions is perhaps demonstrated most clearly by the experimental finding that when each word disappears as soon as 50–60 ms after it is first fixated, reading proceeds quite normally (Ishida and Ikeda, 1989; Rayner et al., 1981), with fixation durations still being affected by factors such as word frequency (Liversedge et al., 2004; Rayner, Liversedge, and White, 2006; Rayner et al., 2003). In other words, most of the time devoted to each fixation is not needed for low-level perceptual processing, but is instead used for higher-level linguistic or conceptual processing.

Given that fixation duration is more sensitive than saccade length to linguistic factors, it is not surprising that the most commonly used measures of processing difficulty in psycholinguistic studies are temporal measures (though probability of skipping a word and regressing to it are typically also reported). In studies in which the critical region of text is a single target word, the measures most often used are "first fixation duration" (the duration of the first fixation on the word), "single fixation duration" (the time spent on a word on those trials on which only a single fixation was made on the word), and "gaze duration" (the sum of the durations of all fixations on the word before leaving the word). In addition, "total time" on the word (the time spent on the word including re-reading) is often reported, as is "go-past time," also known as "regression path duration" (the time from first fixating the word to first moving past the word to the right, including time spent in rereading earlier parts of the sentence). Less frequently, "second pass time" (the time spent rereading the word) is also reported. When larger regions of text are being examined, the first fixation duration is often not a meaningful measure, but the other measures mentioned above are all commonly reported (though when a region comprises multiple words, the term "first pass time" is used instead of gaze duration). With multiple-word regions, researchers also frequently report the percentage of trials on which readers made a regressive eye movement out of the region on their first pass through the region. On occasion they also report the percentage of trials on which readers made a regressive eye movement *into* the region.

Measures such as first fixation duration and gaze duration/first pass time are often referred to as "early" measures, while total time and second pass time are "late" measures. While it is important to define, in a given theoretical context, exactly what is meant by this distinction (see Clifton et al., 2006), careful examination of the point in the eye movement record at which the effect of some linguistic manipulation first appears can be highly informative about the nature of the underlying cognitive processes involved.

This brings us to a final issue introduced by Just and Carpenter (1980), referred to as the "eye–mind span": how big of a lag is there between the eyes and the mind. When we read out loud, if the lights in the room are turned off, we are still able to produce two or three words after the lights go out. This is because there is an eye–voice span where the eyes are ahead of the voice by a few words. Analogously, is there an eye–mind span where the eyes are ahead of the mental processing associated with each word, or is the link rather tight? As we'll see in the next section, there is quite a bit of evidence that various lexical properties of a word influence the amount of time that the eyes remain on that word. The link isn't perfect, as there are preview effects (i.e. when readers have a valid preview of the next word to the right of fixation, they look at it for about 30–50 ms less time than if they have no preview of the word) and spillover effects (i.e. the processing associated with a given word can sometimes spillover onto the next word in the text). But it is generally the case that how long readers look at a word is a fairly good reflection of the processing time associated with that word.

19.3 **Effects of lexical processing on eye movements**

In this section we review how eye movements in reading are affected by properties of individual words. This general topic can be divided fairly naturally into two subtopics. First, we discuss the role of factors such as frequency, morphology, and lexical ambiguity, which we call "intrinsic" lexical factors. We then discuss how the fit between a word and its context influences eye movements, under the heading of "relational" lexical factors.

19.3.1 Intrinsic lexical factors

Rayner (1977) and Just and Carpenter (1980) first reported that readers look longer at words that are used relatively infrequently. Not surprisingly, frequency is confounded with word length; however, Rayner and Duffy (1986) and Inhoff and Rayner (1986) controlled for differences in word length, and found that there was still a strong frequency effect both on the first fixation on a word and on gaze duration. These basic findings have now been replicated many times (see Rayner, 1998; Reichle et al., 2003 for summaries). In addition, high-frequency words are skipped more often (O'Regan, 1979; Rayner et al., 1996), and reading time on the word after a low-frequency word is inflated (Rayner and Duffy, 1986). However, reading time on a low-frequency word decreases dramatically when it is repeated in a text (Rayner et al., 1995).

Word frequency is determined by counting the occurrences of a word in a corpus of printed or spoken materials, but word familiarity is determined by a norming procedure in which participants rate how familiar they are with a given word. Familiarity has an effect on reading time that is independent of frequency (Chaffin et al., 2001; Juhasz and Rayner, 2003; Williams and Morris, 2004). Age of acquisition (Juhasz, 2005), which is determined by both corpus counts and subjective ratings, also has an independent effect (Juhasz and Rayner, 2003; 2006).

Recently, several studies have examined effects of the morphological structure of a word on reading time. Studies of long and morphologically complex Finnish words (Hyönä and Pollatsek, 1998; Pollatsek and Hyönä, 2005; Pollatsek et al., 2000) have demonstrated that the frequency of the first morpheme (and, to a lesser extent, the second morpheme) in a two-morpheme word influences fixation durations, suggesting that these words are decomposed into their constituent morphemes as they are analyzed. Interestingly, this is true both of transparent compound words, in which the meaning of the whole is systematically related to the meaning of the parts, and of opaque ones. Morphological decomposition has also been demonstrated in English (Andrews et al., 2004; Juhasz et al., 2003).

Another word-intrinsic factor that has a significant influence on fixation times is meaning ambiguity (Rayner and Duffy, 1986; Duffy et al., 1988; Rayner and Frazier, 1989; Sereno et al., 2006). When a word has two meanings that are approximately equal in frequency, and the word is encountered in a neutral context, fixation durations are inflated compared to an unambiguous control word matched on length and overall frequency. If the word has one dominant meaning, on the other hand, there is no increase in reading time; evidently, competition from the subordinate meaning does not slow processing. Not surprisingly, if information later in the sentence reveals the subordinate meaning to be the relevant one, disruption appears in the form of long fixations and regressive eye movements. When disambiguating information precedes a balanced ambiguous word, reading time on the word is no longer inflated, compared to an unambiguous control; but when preceding information disambiguates a biased ambiguous word toward the subordinate meaning, reading time on the word is increased (this is known as the "subordinate bias effect"). Rayner et al. (2006) have shown that even a single biasing adjective preceding a target noun can produce this effect. However, Folk and Morris (2003) found that the subordinate bias effect disappears when the two meanings of a word are in different syntactic categories (e.g. *rose*), and only one of these categories provides a syntactically legal continuation of the sentence.

Other forms of ambiguity result in distinct patterns in the eye movement record. Frazier and Rayner (1987) found that when a word is ambiguous between two syntactic categories, and either category could appear in the sentence context (e.g. the word *trains* could be either a noun or a verb in the sentence *I know that the desert trains*...), slowdown does not appear on the ambiguous word itself, but only later in the sentence (see also Pickering and Frisson, 2001). Similarly, Frazier and Rayner (1990) found that when a word has two senses, rather than two distinct meanings (e.g. the word *newspaper* can refer either to a physical object or to an institution), there is no slowdown on the word itself. On the other hand, fixation durations are increased when a single spelling corresponds to two distinct, and differently pronounced, words (e.g. *tear*; Carpenter and Daneman, 1981; Folk, 1999), and when a word is a homonym of a more frequent word (e.g. *chute/shoot*; Jared et al., 1999; Rayner, Pollatsek, and Binder, 1998). In sum, it seems likely that fixation times are increased when an ambiguity results in competition between alternative lexical representations, though the nature of the mechanisms underlying these various effects is under debate.

19.3.2 Relational lexical factors

A considerable body of research has demonstrated that reading time decreases as the predictability of a word, based on the preceding context, increases. Predictability (also called "contextual constraint") is usually defined in terms of Cloze probability, which is the probability that informants will produce the target word as the likely next word in the sentence, given the sentence up to that point. Ehrlich and Rayner (1981) first demonstrated the effect of predictability on reading time, and this effect has now been confirmed many times (Ashby et al., 2005; Balota et al., 1985; Frisson et al., 2005; Rayner, Ashby, et al., 2004; Rayner and Well, 1996). Readers are also more likely to skip words that are highly predictable in context. Recently, it has also been reported (MacDonald and Shillcock, 2003a; 2003b) that the transitional probability between two words, based on corpus counts, has an independent effect on reading time on the second word. However, subsequent work (Frisson et al., 2005) has suggested that when overall predictability is well controlled, transitional probability may not have an independent effect.

Fixation durations on a word are also affected by semantic priming from a specific preceding word (or words). Morris (1994) reported shorter first fixation and gaze durations on a target word that was semantically associated with a preceding word in the sentence, even though the target word was not predictable; e.g. on the word *moustache* in the sentence *The friend talked to the barber and trimmed the moustache after lunch* (cf. Carroll and Slowiaczek, 1986, who argued that the associate must be within the same clause in order for semantic priming to have an effect on fixation times). Morris and Folk (1998) reported that this facilitation depends in part on whether the semantic associate of the target word is in linguistic focus.

At the extreme low end of the predictability continuum are cases in which the target word does not even make sense in its context. Several studies have examined how readers process such semantic anomalies. Though the processing of anomalies is probably not directly informative about normal reading, it does help to reveal the time course with which meaning-related factors influence eye movements. At least three studies (Braze et al., 2002; Murray and Rowan, 1998; Rayner, Warren, et al., 2004) have found that when a word is implausible given the preceding context, first fixation or gaze duration on the word is inflated. The study by Rayner, Warren, et al. (2004) suggests, however, that the processing of semantic anomaly is not a unitary phenomenon. Rayner et al. reported increased gaze duration on the direct object when it was essentially an impossible theme for the verb (e.g. *carrots* in *John used a pump to inflate the large carrots for dinner*) but only a go-past effect on this word when it was an implausible theme given the combination of verb and instrument (e.g. *John used an axe to chop the large carrots for dinner*), coupled with a first pass effect on the next region. Anomaly never significantly increased the first fixation on the word, leading Rayner et al. to conclude that this early measure reflects primarily lexical processing itself, rather than higher-level integrative processing.

Finally, several studies have reported that specific kinds of semantic processing have measurable effects on reading time. Traxler, McElree, et al. (2005) and Traxler et al. (2002) investigated the effect on readers' eye movements when the context forces a noun with no intrinsic temporal component to be interpreted as an event, as in the phrase *finish the book*, and found increased go-past time on the critical word or increased first pass time on the next region (see also Frisson and Pickering, 1999). Frisson and Frazier (2005) found that when a mass noun appears with plural morphology (e.g. *some beers*) or a count noun appears in the singular with a plural determiner (e.g. *some banana*), there is an increase in the duration of the first fixation on the critical word.

Summing up this section, we point out that recent models of eye movement control in reading (e.g. E-Z Reader: Pollatsek et al., 2006; Reichle et al., 1998; Reichle et al., 2006; Reichle et al., 2003, and SWIFT: Engbert et al., 2005) have accounted for a large portion of the variance in fixation durations by focusing exclusively on the kinds of lexical factor discussed above. Specifically, it appears that in addition to word length, frequency and predictability are especially good predictors of the amount of time the eyes will spend on a word. However, a very large literature has now demonstrated that some kinds of higher-level linguistic factors can also exert a strong influence. The next two sections are devoted to a discussion of these factors.

19.4 Effects of syntactic processing on eye movements

It is clear from several decades of psycholinguistic research that as a sentence is read, the reader constructs an analysis of the sentence's syntactic structure in a highly incremental manner, usually on a word-by-word basis (Frazier and Rayner, 1982; Just and Carpenter, 1980; see Pickering, 1999 for discussion). In this section we focus on the question of how this process of incremental syntactic analysis affects eye movements in reading.

In most experiments examining the effects of syntactic processing on eye movements, participants read sentences that are temporarily ambiguous between two syntactic structures. In sentence (1) below, for example, the region in italics could initially be analyzed either as part of the subordinate clause or as the subject of the main clause:

1. Since Jay always jogs *a mile and a half* seems like a very short distance to him. (Frazier and Rayner, 1982)

In light of the findings reviewed in the last section, an obvious question is whether syntactic ambiguity has an effect similar to lexical ambiguity. Does the presence of two possible syntactic analyses result in slower reading times, similar to the manner in which reading times are slowed when an individual word has two meanings that are roughly similar in frequency? A second question is how a reader's eye movements are affected when subsequent material reveals that the reader's initial analysis of a syntactic ambiguity is incorrect. If, for example, a reader initially analyzes the ambiguous region of (1) as part of the subordinate clause, what happens when the reader encounters the word *seems*, since this word cannot be attached into the sentence on this analysis?

Of the very large number of published eye movement studies dealing with syntactic ambiguity (approximately seventy, according to a recent review by Clifton et al., 2007), the vast majority have not reported any statistically significant effects on reading time in the ambiguous region itself. A small number of studies (Frazier and Rayner, 1982; Traxler et al., 1998; Van Gompel et al., 2005; Van Gompel et al., 2001) reported experiments in which an ambiguous region was in fact read more quickly than the corresponding region of an unambiguous control sentence. Three of these (Traxler et al., 1998; Van Gompel et al., 2001; van Gompel et al., 2005) were explicit attempts to answer the question of whether competition between multiple syntactic analyses results in slower processing (e.g. MacDonald et al., 1994; McRae et al., 1998), so it is worth discussing their results in some detail. Traxler et al. (1998) compared reading times for sentences like the following:

2a. The driver of the car with the moustache was pretty cool.
2b. The car of the driver with the moustache was pretty cool.
2c. The son of the driver with the moustache was pretty cool.

Sentence (2c) is globally ambiguous: it is never clear whether the prepositional phrase *with the moustache* is a modifier of the first noun phrase (*the son*) or the second noun phrase (*the driver*). Across three experiments, Traxler et al. found that gaze duration on the word *moustache* was shorter in condition (c) than in conditions (a) or (b). Van Gompel et al. (2005) demonstrated a similar effect for attachment of adverbial phrases. They tested sentences like (3a–c):

3a. The carpenter sanded the shelves he will attach onto the kitchen wall yesterday morning ...
3b. The carpenter will sand the shelves he attached onto the kitchen wall yesterday morning ...
3c. The carpenter sanded the shelves he attached onto the kitchen wall yesterday morning ...

Sentence (3c) is again globally ambiguous, since *yesterday morning* could modify either the first verb (*sanded*) or the second one (*attached*). This phrase must modify the first verb in (3a), and the second in (3b). The adverbial phrase or the next region was read faster in (3c) than in (3a) or (3b).

A few studies have also reported a slowdown in the ambiguous region compared to an unambiguous control (Clifton et al., 2003; Kennison, 2001; Ni et al., 1996; Paterson et al., 1999; Schmauder and Egan, 1998). However, an explanation other than ambiguity is often available. For example, Clifton et al. (2003) examined sentences like (4a, b):

4a. The ransom paid by the parents was unreasonable.
4b. The ransom that was paid by the parents was unreasonable.

Clifton et al. found longer first fixation durations on the verb (*paid*) in sentences like (4a), in which this verb could be either the main verb of the sentence or the beginning of a relative clause, than in (4b), in which this verb is unambiguously part of a relative clause. However, when participants were reading under normal conditions (there was also a condition in which the amount of visible text was restricted), this effect was due almost entirely to those sentences in which the subject was inanimate. In these sentences, the normally preferred main verb analysis (on which e.g. the ransom is paying somebody or something) is implausible, so readers may have taken longer to read this verb in (4a) because they had to revise their initial analysis at this point. In another study on the reduced relative/main verb ambiguity, Ni et al. (1996) found slower reading times on the relative clause verb when it was morphologically ambiguous (e.g. *raced*) than when it was an unambiguous passive participle (e.g. *ridden*). However, these verb forms were not equated for other factors known to affect reading times.

In sum, there are very few, if any, solid experimental results indicating that syntactic ambiguity causes a slowdown in reading, and there seem to be circumstances in which ambiguity leads to especially fast reading times. Evidently readers either do not consider multiple syntactic analyses in parallel (Frazier, 1978; 1987), or if they do, competition between these analyses does not disrupt processing (Van Gompel et al., 2001; 2005). This conclusion stands in contrast with the conclusion from studies of the processing of lexical ambiguity, in which it has been clearly shown that competition between multiple word meanings does slow reading times.

Research using other paradigms has sometimes revealed apparent effects of syntactic ambiguity on on-line processing (e.g. Fiebach et al., 2004; Frisch et al., 2002; Stowe et al., 2004). Frisch et al. (2002) conducted an event-related potential (ERP) experiment with German readers in which the P600 waveform (which is usually associated with syntactic processing difficulty) appeared when a sentence-initial noun phrase was ambiguous between subject and object. Fiebach et al. (2004) and Stowe et al. (2004) both report distinct patterns of brain activation associated with the processing of syntactic ambiguity in functional magnetic resonance imaging (fMRI) studies. However, we think that several methodological issues need to be addressed before drawing theoretical conclusions on the basis of these results. In all these studies, sentences were presented to participants in a segmented manner at an extremely slow rate, with at least 500 ms between word onsets. In the ERP experiment, each participant saw a total of 160 sentences, of which 80 had an ambiguous initial noun phrase, raising the possibility that participants became aware of the experimental manipulation and adopted task-specific strategies. In the fMRI experiments, the observed increase in activation could only be approximately time-locked to the ambiguity itself. In sum, more research is needed to determine the theoretical significance of these findings from other paradigms.

In most studies of syntactic effects on eye movements, the primary focus is the region of a sentence that resolves a temporary ambiguity. The logic of these studies is simple: if normal reading is disrupted when a reader reaches this material (in the form of longer reading times, more regressive eye movements, or both) it is reasonable to infer that this disambiguating material is inconsistent with the reader's initial syntactic analysis. In other words, the reader has been "garden-pathed" (Bever, 1970). In this way, the eye movement record provides a tool for uncovering the parser's initial structural choices.

The first study to examine systematically the effect on eye movements when an initial syntactic analysis is disconfirmed was by Frazier and Rayner (1982; see also Rayner and Frazier, 1987). They examined ambiguities like that in (1) above, as well as ambiguities like that in (5):

5. The second wife will claim the entire family inheritance belongs to her.

As the reader progresses through this sentence, *the entire family inheritance* could initially be analyzed either as the direct object of *claim* or as the subject of an embedded clause. Upon reaching the verb *belongs*, it becomes clear that the latter analysis is the correct one. Abstracting away from the details of the analyses, what Frazier and Rayner found was that the very first fixation on the disambiguating region was lengthened in sentences like (1) and (5), compared to control sentences in which the correct analysis was signaled earlier in the sentence. This disruption persisted for several fixations, and readers were also more likely to make regressive eye movements to earlier regions of the sentence.

Rapidly appearing effects of syntactic disambiguation have also been shown when this disambiguation takes the form of implausibility, rather than ungrammaticality. In another early study, Rayner et al. (1983) tested sentences like (6a, b):

6a. The kid hit the girl with a whip before he got off the subway.
6b. The kid hit the girl with a wart before he got off the subway.

They found increased first pass reading time beginning with the word *wart* in sentences like (6b), where this word indicates that the prepositional phrase is not a plausible argument or modifier of the verb. This suggests that readers' initial parsing preference is indeed to attach the prepositional phrase to the verb, rather than to the noun that is the verb's direct object.

Eye movement experiments have now been used to investigate the parser's preferred analysis of many types of temporary ambiguity; an extensive list of references organized by the type of ambiguity under investigation appears in Clifton et al. (2006). Because there are reliable signs of disruption in the eye movement record when an initial syntactic analysis is disconfirmed, researchers have been able to test subtle and linguistically sophisticated hypotheses about the strategies and principles that the parser employs. For example, eye movement experiments have helped to reveal that the parser adopts a very "eager" strategy for resolving so-called long-distance dependencies, in which a phrase appears some distance from the element from which it gets its thematic role, as in a question like *Which boy did the teacher reward?*, where *which boy* is the theme of the verb *reward* (Pickering and Traxler, 2001; 2003; Traxler and Pickering, 1996). They have also helped to reveal that the processor is sensitive to a phrase's status as an argument or adjunct of a verb, and prefers to attach incoming material as an argument (Clifton et al., 1991; Kennison, 2002; Liversedge et al., 1998; Liversedge et al., 2003; Speer and Clifton, 1998).

A central question for parsing theories is whether factors such as plausibility, appropriateness in context, and lexical preferences play a role in determining the initial analysis that the parser constructs (e.g. MacDonald et al., 1994; Trueswell et al., 1994), or whether this initial analysis is constructed entirely on the basis of structural preferences (e.g. Ferreira and Clifton, 1986; Frazier, 1987), with other factors affecting only a later stage of processing (Binder et al., 2001; Frazier et al., 2006; Rayner et al., 1992). For example, Ferreira and Clifton (1986), Trueswell et al. (1994), and Clifton et al. (2003) have all conducted eye movement studies of the processing of sentences like (4a, b) above, with the goal of determining whether there is a brief period during which the parser's structural preferences lead it to adopt the implausible main verb analysis of sentences like (4a), in which, for example, the ransom is paying someone or something. In this chapter we will not attempt to settle the substantive question of whether the parser does in fact adopt such an analysis, since a review of the relevant evidence would constitute a chapter in itself. Instead, we merely point out that questions about the fine details of the time course of syntactic analysis are most likely to be settled by eye tracking experiments, in contrast to, say, self-paced reading (see Mitchell, 2004 for discussion). In the latter paradigm, participants must press a button to reveal each new word or phrase, resulting in unnaturally slow reading times (often 400–600 ms per word). This may make it difficult, if not impossible, to determine exactly when a particular factor has its effect, and it may be impossible to detect real, if short-lived, syntactic misanalyses. Because ERP experiments can reveal fine temporal details of brain activity in response to syntactic manipulations, they are likely to be useful in this regard, though in this paradigm as well the stimulus is usually presented at a very slow rate that does not approximate real-world uptake of either written or spoken language.

We note that there are continuing questions about the details of the relationship between eye movements and syntactic disambiguation. For example, it is unclear whether disruption due to disconfirmation of an initial syntactic analysis generally results in movement upwards of the entire reading time distribution, or whether it sometimes affects only a subset of trials, but affects these to such a great extent that the overall differences between conditions are statistically significant (see Clifton et al., 2006 for discussion of this issue). There are also open questions about the circumstances under which disambiguation results in a slowing down of forward saccades, regressive eye movements, or both (Altmann, 1994; Altmann et al., 1992; Rayner and Sereno, 1994a; 1994b). However, both Frazier and Rayner (1982) and Meseguer et al. (2002) have presented evidence that when readers do make regressive eye movements, they do not do so randomly. Instead, the landing position of these regressions reflects some awareness of the point at which the reader's initial, incorrect analysis diverged from the correct analysis.

Not all experiments examining the effects of syntactic processing on eye movements have employed syntactic ambiguities. Several articles have focused on the time-course with which grammatical information affects eye movements by studying the effects of syntactic anomaly (Braze et al., 2002; Deutsch and Bentin, 2001; Ni et al., 1998; Pearlmutter et al., 1999). For example, Pearlmutter et al. (1999) had participants read sentences in which the verb either did or did not agree with the subject (*key* in (7) below) in number. In addition, an irrelevant noun that intervened between the subject and the verb could either agree with the verb or not:

7. The key to the cabinet/cabinets was/were rusty from many years of disuse.

Pearlmutter et al. found that on the word following the verb, ungrammaticality and mismatch in number with the irrelevant distractor resulted in an approximately equal increase in gaze duration. Surprisingly, the manipulations had no effect on the verb itself, except in late measures such as total reading time. Deutsch and Bentin (2001), on the other hand, found that when the gender of the verb in Hebrew sentences explicitly mismatched the gender of the subject, there was a first pass effect on the verb itself. Sturt (2003) also found that when an anaphor (*himself, herself*) did not match the stereotypical gender of its antecedent, this increased the duration of the very first fixation on the anaphor. Clearly, more research is required in order to understand the processing principles underlying these apparently conflicting results.

There are additional questions about the relationship between syntactic processing and eye movements which have received relatively little investigation. One question is whether syntactic complexity has an effect on reading time, in the absence of ambiguity (e.g. Hyönä and Vainio, 2001). Does a sentence take longer to read if its structure is syntactically complex, as measured by, for example, the number of nodes in the sentence's phrase structure diagram? Another question is whether constraints related to working memory have an effect on syntactic processing. While research from other paradigms such as self-paced reading (see Gibson, 1998 for discussion), speed–accuracy tradeoff (McElree et al., 2003), and ERP (Fiebach et al., 2002; Kaan et al., 2000; Vos et al., 2001) suggests that syntactic processing is influenced by memory load, very few eyetracking studies have focused specifically on this issue (though see Traxler et al., 2005). Still another question is whether syntactic effects on eye movements interact with lower-level effects (e.g. lexical frequency and predictability effects), or whether these are two independent sources of variability in the eye movement record. Finally, a question that we have recently begun to investigate in our own laboratory is whether reading is speeded when a sentence's structure can be predicted in advance (see also Altmann et al., 1998). For example, we have recently found (Staub and Clifton, 2006; Staub et al., 2006) that the presence of the word *either* significantly speeds reading of coordinate structures that make use of the word *or*, even in the absence of ambiguity, and that a direct object that appears to the right of its usual position adjacent to the verb is read more quickly when the verb is obligatorily transitive (e.g. *John praised from the stands his daughter's attempt to shoot a basket*) than when the verb is optionally transitive (e.g. *John watched from the stands his daughter's attempt to shoot a basket*).

Finally, an additional interesting finding, which has been replicated on several occasions (Just and Carpenter, 1980; Rayner et al., 2000; Rayner et al., 1989), is that fixation durations on a word are inflated when the word ends a clause or sentence. Because the sentences in these experiments are typically identical through the target word (with the only difference being whether additional material follows this word), it is likely that this extra reading time is due to integrative processing that takes place at clause and sentence boundaries. Rayner et al. (2000; see also Hill and Murray, 2000) found, however, that readers tended to make longer saccades following these extended fixations on sentence- and clause-final words. This suggests that once readers have completed their integrative processing, it is as if they have emptied a buffer and now have extra processing resources available. Hirotani et al. (2006) have also recently demonstrated that implicit prosody (i.e. sentence phrasing and intonation) plays a role in these wrap-up effects, though this prosody is actually imposed by the reader.

19.5 Effects of discourse processing on eye movements

In order to comprehend a text, the reader must not only recognize individual words and analyze the grammatical structure of each sentence; he or she must also maintain a representation of the entities and events that have been mentioned, and relate the information that is currently being processed to this stored representation. This involves, for example, determining which entities pronouns (e.g. *she*) and definite descriptions (e.g. *the fisherman*) refer to. It also involves making inferences about relationships between events and entities, including explanatory, causal, and chronological relationships. Compared to the large number of eye movement studies of syntactic parsing, relatively few studies have examined how such discourse processing affects eye movements in reading; we suspect that this may be a growth area in the next several years. In this section, we review the literature that now exists.

In ordinary spoken language, an anaphoric element such as a pronoun or a reflexive typically has an antecedent. Blanchard (1987) found that the process of identifying this antecedent could be so easy that it left no trace in the eye movement record. However, it is now clear that if the antecedent violates a gender stereotype (e.g. if the reflexive *herself* refers to *the pilot*), reading time on the pronoun is inflated (Duffy and Keir, 2004; Sturt, 2003; Sturt and Lombardo, 2005). In addition, the distance between an anaphor and its antecedent influences fixation times; when the antecedent is relatively far back in the text, fixations on the pronoun, as well as the next few fixations, tend to be longer (Ehrlich and Rayner, 1983; Garrod et al., 1994; O'Brien et al., 1997). Fixation times are also inflated when the antecedent is a low-frequency word (Van Gompel and Majid, 2004). Albrecht and Clifton (1998) and Moxey et al. (2004) also demonstrated increased reading time on a pronoun when it refers to one member of a conjoined NP (e.g. *John and Mary painted the room. He really liked the color*), and Moxey et al. found that reading time on the plural pronoun *they* was reduced when the reference was a conjoined NP.

Though it is sometimes felicitous to use a definite description without specifying an antecedent (which is essentially never the case with a pronoun or reflexive), it appears that readers also identify antecedents for definite descriptions on-line, and that doing so carries some processing cost. Duffy and Rayner (1990) found evidence of increased reading time on a definite description when the antecedent was distant (though unlike the case with anaphors, this effect was localized to the NP itself; see also Van Gompel and Majid, 2004).

Establishing the referent of a pronoun or definite NP can be seen as a form of inference. A potentially more difficult, but no less common, form of inference takes place when readers draw conclusions that have not been explicitly stated in the text. Eye movement experiments have shown that when readers make such "elaborative" inferences, processing is slowed. O'Brien et al. (1988) had participants read passages followed by a critical sentence in which a target word appeared. An example is shown below; the target word is *knife*:

8. He threw the knife into the bushes, took her money, and ran away.

The preceding passage could explicitly mention a knife (*he stabbed her with his knife*), strongly suggest the existence of a knife (*he stabbed her with his weapon*), or make only rather general reference to a category of which a knife is but one exemplar (*he assaulted her with his weapon*). Gaze duration on the target word did not differ between the first two conditions, but was longer in the third condition. Evidently, in this last condition readers needed time to complete the inference that the weapon mentioned earlier in the passage was in fact a knife. However, O'Brien et al. also found that such an inference tended to be made only when a sentence preceding the target sentence invited one, and a follow-up study by Garrod et al. (1990) found evidence for such inferences only when the target noun co-referred with a preceding noun. Myers et al. (2000) also found that when a category name was introduced in one sentence and an exemplar of the category was introduced in a later sentence, both the typicality of the exemplar and the distance between the two words influenced fixation times. Other studies (Cook and Myers, 2004; Garrod and Terras, 2000) have found that a target word is read more quickly when it fills a thematic role that is left open in the preceding discourse; for example, if the preceding sentence makes reference to *driving*, the word *car* would be read particularly quickly.

19.6 **Summary**

In this chapter, we have provided a brief review of issues and studies related to on-line comprehension processes. As we pointed out earlier, it is fairly clear that variables related to lexical processing (such as frequency, age of acquisition, and predictability) have a major impact on eye movements, and particularly the decision of when to move the eyes. Models of eye movement control in reading (Engbert et al., 2005; McDonald et al., 2005; Pollatsek et al., 2006; Reichle et al., 1998; Reichle et al., 2003; Reichle et al., 2006; Reilly and Radach, 2006) do a fairly good job of accounting for how such variables influence eye movements and how the decision is made concerning where to move the eyes next. But, as should be clear from our review, higher-level syntactic and discourse level variables also influence eye movements. Current models do not do a good job of accounting for the impact of these variables on decisions about when and where to move the eyes.

In fact, a reasonable account of eye movements in reading would be to suggest that lexical variables are the primary engine driving the eyes through text (and they primarily influence fixation times), and that higher-level variables typically (though not always) exert their influence later in processing. Thus, the higher-level variables may primarily serve to slow down processing (and increase fixation times) when something doesn't compute well (as in the case with garden path effects, anomaly effects, and when a discourse referent is difficult to locate). Future research and further modeling work is needed to more fully explicate exactly when and how these higher order variables exert their influence.

Acknowledgments

Preparation of this chapter was supported by grants HD26765 and HD17246 from the National Institute of Health to the second author. The first author was supported by a University of Massachusetts Fellowship. Thanks to two reviewers for their helpful comments.

References

Albrecht, J. E., and Clifton, C., Jr. (1998) Accessing singular antecedents in conjoined phrases. *Memory and Cognition*, 26: 599–610.

Altarriba, J., Kambe, G., Pollatsek, A., and Rayner, K. (2001) Semantic codes are not used in integrating information across eye fixations in reading: evidence from fluent Spanish-English bilinguals. *Perception and Psychophysics*, 63: 875–90.

Altmann, G. T. M. (1994) Regression-contingent analyses of eye movements during sentence processing: Reply to Rayner and Sereno. *Memory and Cognition*, 22: 286–90.

Altmann, G. T. M., Garnham, A., and Dennis, Y. (1992) Avoiding the garden path: eye movements in context. *Journal of Memory and Language*, 31: 685–712.

Altmann, G. T. M., van Nice, K. Y., Garnham, A., and Henstra, J.-A. (1998) Late closure in context. *Journal of Memory and Language*, 38: 459–484.

Andrews, S., Miller, B., and Rayner, K. (2004) Eye movements and morphological segmentation of compound words: there is a mouse in mousetrap. *European Journal of Cognitive Psychology*, 16: 285–311.

Ashby, J., and Clifton, C., Jr.(2005) The prosodic property of lexical stress affects eye movements during silent reading. *Cognition*, 96: B89–B100.

Ashby, J., and Rayner, K. (2004) Representing syllable information during silent reading: evidence from eye movements. *Language and Cognitive Processes*, 19: 391–426.

Ashby, J., Rayner, K., and Clifton, C., Jr. (2005) Eye movements of highly skilled and average readers: differential effects of frequency and predictability. *Quarterly Journal of Experimental Psychology*, 58A: 1065–86.

Ashby, J., Treiman, R., Kessler, B., and Rayner, K. (2006) Vowel processing in silent reading: evidence from eye movements. *Journal of Experimental Psychology: Learning, Memory, and Cognition*, 32: 416–24.

Balota, D. A., Pollatsek, A., and Rayner, K. (1985) The interaction of contextual constraints and parafoveal visual information in reading. *Cognitive Psychology*, 17: 364–88.

Bever, T. G. (1970) The cognitive basis for linguistic structures. In J. R. Hayes (ed.), *Cognition and the Development of Language*, pp. 279–352. Wiley, New York.

Binder, K. S., Duffy, S. A., and Rayner, K. (2001) The effects of thematic fit and discourse context on syntactic ambiguity resolution. *Journal of Memory and Language*, 44: 297–324.

Blanchard, H. E. (1987) Pronoun processing during fixations: effects on the time course of information utilization. *Bulletin of the Psychonomic Society*, 25: 171–4.

Braze, D., Shankweiler, D., Ni, W., and Palumbo, L. C. (2002) Readers' eye movements distinguish anomalies of form and content. *Journal of Psycholinguistic Research*, 31: 25–44.

Briihl, D., and Inhoff, A. W. (1995) Integrating information across fixations in reading: the use of orthographic bodies and of exterior letters. *Journal of Experimental Psychology: Learning, Memory, and Cognition*, 21: 55–67.

Brysbaert, M., and Vitu, F. (1998) Word skipping: implications for theories of eye movement control in reading. In G. Underwood (ed.), *Eye Guidance in Reading and Scene Perception*. pp. 125–48. Elsevier, Oxford.

Carpenter, P. A., and Daneman, M. (1981) Lexical retrieval and error recovery in reading: a model based on eye fixations. *Journal of Verbal Learning and Verbal Behavior*, 28: 138–60.

Carpenter, P. A., and Just, M. A. (1983) What your eyes do while your mind is reading. In K. Rayner (ed.), *Eye Movements in Reading: Perceptual and Language Processes*, pp. 275–307. Academic Press, New York.

Carroll, P. J., and Slowiaczek, M. L. (1986) Constraints on semantic priming in reading: a fixation time analysis. *Memory and Cognition*, 14: 509–22.

Chace, H. E., Rayner, K., and Well, A. D. (2005) Eye movements and phonological preview benefit: effects of reading skill. *Canadian Journal of Experimental Psychology*, 59: 209–17.

Chaffin, R., Morris, R. K., and Seely, R. E. (2001) Learning new word meanings from context: a study of eye movements. *Journal of Experimental Psychology: Learning, Memory and Cognition*, 27: 225–35.

Clifton, C., Jr., Speer, S., and Abney, S. (1991) Parsing arguments: phrase structure and argument structure as determinants of initial parsing decisions. *Journal of Memory and Language*, 30: 251–71.

Clifton, C., Jr., Staub, A., and Rayner, K. (2007) Eye movements in reading words and sentences. In R. P. G. Van Gompel, M. H. Fischer, W. S. Murray, and R. L. Hill (eds), *Eye Movements: A Window on Mind and Brain*, pp. 341–72. Elsevier, Oxford.

Clifton, C., Jr., Traxler, M., Mohamed, M. T., Williams, R. S., Morris, R. K., and Rayner, K. (2003) The use of thematic role information in parsing: syntactic processing autonomy revisited. *Journal of Memory and Language*, 49: 317–334.

Cook, A. E., and Myers, J. L. (2004) Processing discourse roles in scripted narratives: the influences of context and world knowledge. *Journal of Memory and Language*, 50: 268–88.

Deutsch, A., and Bentin, S. (2001) Syntactic and semantic factors in processing gender agreement in Hebrew: evidence from ERPs and eye movements. *Journal of Memory and Language*, 45: 200–24.

Drieghe, D., Rayner, K., and Pollatsek, A. (2005) Eye movements and word skipping during reading revisited. *Journal of Experimental Psychology: Human Perception and Performance*, 31: 954–69.

Duffy, S., and Keir, J. A. (2004) Violating stereotypes: eye movements and comprehension processes when text conflicts with world knowledge. *Memory and Cognition*, 32: 551–9.

Duffy, S. A., Morris, R. K., and Rayner, K. (1988) Lexical ambiguity and fixation times in reading. *Journal of Memory and Language*, 27: 429–46.

Duffy, S. A., and Rayner, K. (1990) Eye movements and anaphor resolution: effects of antecedent typicality and distance. *Language and Speech*, 33: 103–19.

Ehrlich, S. F., and Rayner, K. (1981) Contextual effects on word perception and eye movements during reading. *Journal of verbal Learning and Verbal Behavior*, 20: 641–55.

Ehrlich, K., and Rayner, K. (1983) Pronoun assignment and semantic integration during reading: eye movements and immediacy of processing. *Journal of Verbal Learning and Verbal Behavior*, 22: 75–87.

Engbert, R., Nuthmann, A., Richter, E., and Kliegl, R. (2005) SWIFT: a dynamical model of saccade generation during reading. *Psychological Review*, 112: 777–813.

Ferreira, F., and Clifton, C. (1986) The independence of syntactic processing. *Journal of Memory and Language*, 25: 348–68.

Fiebach, C. J., Schlesewsky, M., and Friederici, A. D. (2002) Separating syntactic memory costs and syntactic integration costs during parsing: the processing of German wh-questions. *Journal of Memory and Language*, 47: 250–72.

Fiebach, C. J., Vos, S. H., and Friederici, A. D. (2004) Neural correlates of syntactic ambiguity in sentence comprehension for low and high span readers. *Journal of Cognitive Neuroscience*, 16: 1562–75.

Folk, J. R. (1999) Phonological codes are used to access the lexicon during silent reading. *Journal of Experimental Psychology: Learning, Memory, and Cognition*, 25: 892–906.

Folk, J. R., and Morris, R. K. (2003) Effects of syntactic category assignment on lexical ambiguity resolution in reading: an eye movement analysis. *Memory and Cognition*, 31: 87–99.

Frazier, L. (1978) On comprehending sentences: syntactic parsing strategies. Doctoral dissertation, University of Connecticut, Storrs.

Frazier, L. (1987) Sentence processing: a tutorial review. In M. Coltheart (ed.), *Attention and Performance XII*, pp. 559–86. Erlbaum, Hillsdale, NJ.

Frazier, L., Carminatti, M. N., Cook, A. E., Majewski, H., and Rayner, K. (2006) Semantic evaluation of syntactic structure: evidence from eye movements. *Cognition*, 99: B53–B62.

Frazier, L., and Rayner, K. (1982) Making and correcting errors during sentence comprehension: eye movements in the analysis of structurally ambiguous sentences. *Cognitive Psychology*, 14: 178–210.

Frazier, L., and Rayner, K. (1987) Resolution of syntactic category ambiguities: eye movements in parsing lexically ambiguous sentences. *Journal of Memory and Language*, 26: 505–26.

Frazier, L., and Rayner, K. (1990) Taking on semantic commitments: processing multiple meanings vs. multiple senses. *Journal of Memory and Language*, 29: 181–200.

Frisch, S., Schlesewsky, M., Saddy, D., and Alpermann, A. (2002) The P600 as an indicator of syntactic ambiguity. *Cognition*, 85: B83–B92.

Frisson, S., and Frazier, L. (2005) Carving up word meaning: portioning and grinding. *Journal of Memory and Language*, 53: 277–91.

Frisson, S., and Pickering, M. J. (1999) The processing of metonymy: evidence from eye movements. *Journal of Experimental Psychology: Learning, Memory, and Cognition*, 25: 1366–83.

Frisson, S., Rayner, K., and Pickering, M. J. (2005) Effects of contextual predictability and transitional probability on eye movements during reading. *Journal of Experimental Psychology: Learning, Memory, and Cognition*, 31: 862–77.

Garrod, S., Freudenthal, S., and Boyle, E. (1994) The role of different types of anaphor in the on-line resolution of sentences in a discourse. *Journal of Memory and Language*, 33: 39–68.

Garrod, S., O'Brien, E. J., Morris, R. K., and Rayner, K. (1990) Elaborative inferencing as an active or passive process. *Journal of Experimental Psychology: Learning, Memory, and Cognition*, 16: 250–7.

Garrod, S., and Terras, M. (2000) The contribution of lexical and situational knowledge to resolving discourse roles: bonding and resolution. *Journal of Memory and Language*, 42: 526–44.

Gautier, V., O'Regan J. K., and Le Gargasson, J.-F. (2000) 'The-skipping' revisited in French: programming saccades to skip the article *les*'. *Vision Research*, 40: 2517–31.

Gibson, E. (1998) Linguistic complexity: locality of syntactic dependencies. *Cognition*, 68: 1–76.

Henderson, J. M., Dixon, P., Petersen, A., Twiley, L. C., and Ferreira, F. (1995) Evidence for the use of phonological representations during transaccadic word recognition. *Journal of Experimental Psychology: Human Perception and Performance*, 21: 82–97.

Hill, R. L., and Murray, W. S. (2000) Commas and spaces: effects of punctuation on eye movements and sentence parsing. In A. Kennedy, R. Radach, D. Heller, and J. Pynte (eds), *Reading as a Perceptual Process*, pp. 565–90. Elsevier, Oxford.

Hirotani, M., Frazier, L., and Rayner, K. (2006) Punctuation and intonation effects on clause and sentence wrap-up: evidence from eye movements. *Journal of Memory and Language*, 54: 425–43.

Hyönä, J., Bertram, R., and Pollatsek, A. (1998) Are long compound words identified serially via their constituents? Evidence from an eye-movement-contingent display change study. *Memory and Cognition*, 32: 523–32.

Hyönä, J., and Pollatsek, A. (1998) Reading Finnish compound words: eye fixations are affected by component morphemes. *Journal of Experimental Psychology: Human Perception and Performance*, 24: 1612–27.

Hyönä, J., and Vainio, S. (2001) Reading morphologically complex clause structures in Finnish. *European Journal of Cognitive Psychology*, 13: 451–74.

Inhoff, A. W. (1989) Lexical access during eye fixations in reading: are word access codes used to integrate lexical information across interword fixations? *Journal of Memory and Language*, 28: 444–61.

Inhoff, A. W., and Liu, W. (1998) The perceptual span and oculomotor activity during the reading of Chinese sentences. *Journal of Experimental Psychology: Human Perception and Performance*, 24: 20–34.

Inhoff, A. W., Pollatsek, A., Posner, M. I., and Rayner, K. (1987) Covert attention and eye movements during reading. *Quarterly Journal of Experimental Psychology*, 41A: 63–89.

Inhoff, A. W., and Rayner, K. (1986) Parafoveal word processing during eye fixations in reading: effects of word frequency. *Perception and Psychophysics*, 40: 431–9.

Ishida, T., and Ikeda, M. (1989) Temporal properties of information extraction in reading studied by a text-mask replacement technique. *Journal of the Optical Society A: Optics and Image Science*, 6: 1624–32.

Jared, D., Levy, B. A., and Rayner, K. (1999) The role of phonology in the activation of word meanings during reading: evidence from proofreading and eye movements. *Journal of Experimental Psychology: General*, 128: 219–64.

Johnson, R. L. (2007) The flexibility of letter coding: Nonadjacent letter transposition effects in the parafovea. In R. Van Gompel, M. Fischer, W. Murray, and R. L. Hill (eds), *Eye Movements: A Window on Mind and Brain*, pp. 425–40. Elsevier, Oxford.

Johnson, R. L., Perea, M., and Rayner, K. (2007) Transposed-letter effects in reading: evidence from eye movements and parafoveal preview. *Journal of Experimental Psychology: Human Perception and Performance*, 33: 209–29.

Juhasz, B. J. (2005) Age-of-acquisition effects in word and picture processing. *Psychological Bulletin*, 131: 684–712.

Juhasz, B. J., and Rayner, K. (2003) Investigating the effects of a set of intercorrelated variables on eye fixation durations in reading. *Journal of Experimental Psychology: Learning, Memory, and Cognition*, 29: 1312–18.

Juhasz, B. J., and Rayner, K. (2006) The role of age-of-acquisition and word frequency in reading: evidence from eye fixation durations. *Visual Cognition*, 13: 846–63.

Juhasz, B. J., Starr, M. S., Inhoff, A. W., and Placke, L. (2003) The effects of morphology on the processing of compound words: evidence from naming, lexical decisions and eye fixations. *British Journal of Psychology*, 94: 223–44.

Just, M. A., and Carpenter, P. (1980) A theory of reading: from eye fixations to comprehension. *Psychological Review*, 85: 109–30.

Kaan, E., Harris, A., Gibson, E., and Holcomb, P. (2000) The P600 as an index of syntactic integration difficulty. *Language and Cognitive Processes*, 15: 159–2001.

Kambe, G. (2004) Parafoveal processing of prefixed words during eye fixations in reading: evidence against morphological influences on parafoveal preprocessing. *Perception and Psychophysics*, 66: 279–92.

Kennison, S. M. (2001) Limitations on the use of verb information during sentence comprehension. *Psychonomic Bulletin and Review*, 8: 132–8.

Kennison, S. M. (2002) Comprehending noun phrase arguments and adjuncts. *Journal of Psycholinguistic Research*, 31: 65–81.

Kliegl, R., and Engbert, R. (2005) Fixation durations before word skipping in reading. *Psychonomic Bulletin and Review*, 12: 132–8.

Lima, S. D. (1987) Morphological analysis in reading. *Journal of Memory and Language*, 26: 84–99.

Liversedge, S. P., Pickering, M. J., Branigan, H. P., and Van Gompel, R. P. G. (1998) Processing arguments and adjuncts in isolation and context: the case of by-phrase ambiguities in passives. *Journal of Experimental Psychology: Learning, Memory, and Cognition*, 24: 461–75.

Liversedge, S. P., Pickering, M., Clayes, E. L., and Branigan, H. P. (2003) Thematic processing of adjuncts: evidence from an eye-tracking experiment. *Psychonomic Bulletin and Review*, 10: 667–75.

Liversedge, S. P., Rayner, K., White, S. J., Vergilino-Perez, D., Findlay, J. M., and Kentridge, R. W. (2004) Eye movements when reading disappearing text: is there a gap effect in reading? *Vision Research*, 44: 1013–24.

MacDonald, M. C., Pearlmutter, N. J., and Seidenberg, M. S. (1994) The lexical nature of syntactic ambiguity resolution. *Psychological Review*, 101: 676–703.

McConkie, G. W., Kerr, P. W., Reddix, M. D., and Zola, D. (1988) Eye movement control during reading, I: The location of initial eye fixations in words. *Vision Research*, 28: 1107–18.

McConkie, G. W., and Rayner, K. (1975) The span of the effective stimulus during a fixation in reading. *Perception and Psychophysics*, 17: 578–86.

McDonald, S. A., Carpenter, R. H. S., and Shillcock, R.C. (2005) An anatomically- constrained, stochastic model of eye movement control in reading. *Psychological Review*, 112: 814–40.

McDonald, S. A., and Shillcock, R. (2003a) Eye movements reveal the on-line computation of lexical probabilities during reading. *Psychological Science*, 14: 648–52.

McDonald, S.A., and Shillcock, R.C. (2003b) Low-level predictive inference in reading: the influence of transitional probabilities on eye movements. *Vision Research*, 43: 1735–51.

McElree, B., Foraker, S., and Dyer, L. (2003) Memory structures that subserve sentence comprehension. *Journal of Memory and Language*, 48: 67–91.

McRae, K., Spivey-Knowlton, M. J., and Tanenhaus, M. K. (1998) Modeling the influence of thematic fit (and other constraints) in on-line sentence comprehension. *Journal of Memory and Language*, 38: 283–312.

Meseguer, E., Carreiras, M., and Clifton, C. (2002) Overt reanalysis strategies and eye movements during the reading of mild garden path sentences. *Memory and Cognition*, 30: 551–61.

Miellet, S., and Sparrow, L. (2004) Phonological codes are assembled before word fixation: evidence from boundary paradigm in sentence reading. *Brain and Language*, 90: 299–310.

Mitchell, D. C. (2004) On-line methods in language processing: introduction and historical review. In M. Carreiras and C. Clifton, Jr (eds), *The On-line Study of Sentence Comprehension: Eyetracking, ERPs, and Beyond*, pp. 15–32. Psychology Press, New York.

Morris, R. K. (1994) Lexical and message-level sentence context effects on fixation times in reading. *Journal of Experimental Psychology: Learning, Memory, and Cognition*, 20: 92–103.

Morris, R. K., and Folk. J. R. (1998) Focus as a contextual priming mechanism in reading. *Memory and Cognition*, 26: 1313–22.

Morris, R.K., Rayner, K., and Pollatsek, A. (1990) Eye movement guidance in reading: the role of parafoveal letter and space information. *Journal of Experimental Psychology: Human Perception and Performance*, 16: 268–81.

Moxey, L. M., Sanford, A. J., Sturt, P., and Morrow, L. I. (2004) Constraints on the formation of plural reference objects: the influence of role, conjunction, and type of description. *Journal of Memory and Language*, 51: 346–64.

Murray, W. S., and Rowan, M. (1998) Early, mandatory, pragmatic processing. *Journal of Psycholinguistic Research*, 27: 1–22.

Myers, J. L., Cook, A.E., Kambe, G., Mason, R. A., and O'Brien, E. J. (2000) Semantic and episodic effects on bridging inferences. *Discourse Processes*, 29: 179–200.

Ni, W., Crain, S., and Shankweiler, D. (1996) Sidestepping garden paths: assessing the contributions of syntax, semantics, and plausibility in resolving ambiguities. *Language and Cognitive Processes*, 11: 283–334.

Ni, W., Fodor, J. D., Crain, S., and Shankweiler, D. (1998) Anomaly detection: eye movement patterns. *Journal of Psycholinguistic Research*, 27: 515–39.

Nuthmann, A., Engbert, R., and Kliegl, R. (2005) Mislocated fixations during reading and the inverted optimal viewing position effect. *Vision Research*, 45: 2201–17.

O'Brien, E. J., Raney, G. E., Albrecht, J. E., and Rayner, K. (1997) Processes involved in the resolution of explicit anaphors. *Discourse Processes*, 23: 1–24.

O'Brien, E. J., Shank, D. M., Myers, J. L., and Rayner, K. (1988) Elaborative inferences during reading: do they occur on-line? *Journal of Experimental Psychology: Learning, Memory, and Cognition*, 14: 410–20.

O'Regan, J. K. (1979) Eye guidance in reading: evidence for the linguistic control hypothesis. *Perception and Psychophysics*, 25: 501–9.

Paterson, K. B., Liversedge, S. P., and Underwood, G. (1999) The influence of focus operators on syntactic processing of short relative clause sentences. *Quarterly Journal of Experimental Psychology: Human Experimental Psychology*, 52A: 717–37.

Pearlmutter, N. J., Garnsey, S. M., and Bock, K. (1999) Agreement processes in sentence comprehension. *Journal of Memory and Language*, 41: 427–56.

Pickering, M. J. (1999) Sentence comprehension. In S. Garrod and M. J. Pickering (eds), *Language Processing*, pp. 123–53. Psychology Press, Hove, UK.

Pickering, M.J., and Frisson, S. (2001) Processing ambiguous verbs: evidence from eye movements. *Journal of Experimental Psychology: Learning, Memory, and Cognition*, 27: 556–73.

Pickering, M. J., and Traxler, M. J. (2001) Strategies for processing unbounded dependencies: lexical information and verb-argument assignment. *Journal of Experimental Psychology: Learning, Memory, and Cognition*, 27: 1401–10.

Pickering, M. J., and Traxler, M. J. (2003) Evidence against the use of subcategorisation frequencies in the processing of unbounded dependencies. *Language and Cognitive Processes*, 18: 469–503.

Pollatsek, A., Bolozky, S., Well, A. D., and Rayner, K. (1981) Asymmetries in the perceptual span for Israeli readers. *Brain and Language*, 14: 174–80.

Pollatsek, A., and Hyönä, J. (2005) The role of semantic transparency in the processing of Finnish compound words. *Language and Cognitive Processes*, 20: 261–90.

Pollatsek, A., Hyönä, J., and Bertram, R. (2000) The role of morphological constituents in reading Finnish compound words. *Journal of Experimental Psychology: Human Perception and Performance*, 26: 820–33.

Pollatsek, A., Lesch, M., Morris, R. K., and Rayner, K. (1992) Phonological codes are used in integrating information across saccades in word identification and reading. *Journal of Experimental Psychology: Human Perception and Performance*, 18: 148–62.

Pollatsek, A., Raney, G. E., LaGasse, L., and Rayner, K. (1993) The use of information below fixation in reading and in visual search. *Canadian Journal of Experimental Psychology*, 47: 179–200.

Pollatsek, A., and Rayner, K. (1982) Eye movement control in reading: the role of word boundaries. *Journal of Experimental Psychology: Human Perception and Performance*, 8: 817–33.

Pollatsek, A., Rayner, K., and Balota, D. A. (1986) Inferences about eye movement control from the perceptual span in reading. *Perception and Psychophysics*, 40: 123–30.

Pollatsek, A., Reichle, E. D., and Rayner, K. (2006) E-Z Reader: Testing the interface between cognition and eye movement control in reading. *Cognitive Psychology*, 52: 1–56.

Pynte, J., Kennedy, A., and Ducrot, S. (2004) The influence of parafoveal typographical errors on eye movements in reading. *European Journal of Cognitive Psychology*, 16: 178–202.

Rayner, K. (1975) The perceptual span and peripheral cues in reading. *Cognitive Psychology*, 7: 65–81.

Rayner, K. (1977) Visual attention in reading: eye movements reflect cognitive processes. *Memory and Cognition*, 4: 443–8.

Rayner, K. (1979) Eye guidance in reading: Fixation locations within words. *Perception*, 8: 21–30.

Rayner, K. (1998) Eye movements in reading and information processing: 20 years of research. *Psychological Bulletin*, 124: 372–422.

Rayner, K., Ashby, J., Pollatsek, A., and Reichle, E. (2004) The effects of frequency and predictability on eye fixations in reading: implications for the E-Z Reader model. *Journal of Experimental Psychology: Human Perception and Performance*, 30: 720–32.

Rayner, K., Balota, D. A., and Pollatsek, A. (1986) Against parafoveal semantic processing during eye fixations in reading. *Canadian Journal of Psychology*, 40: 473–83.

Rayner, K., and Bertera, J. H. (1979) Reading without a fovea. *Science*, 206: 468–9.

Rayner, K., Carlson, M., and Frazier, L. (1983) The interaction of syntax and semantics during sentence processing: eye movements in the analysis of semantically biased sentences. *Journal of Verbal Learning and Verbal Behavior*, 22: 358–74.

Rayner, K., Cook, A. E., Juhasz, B. J., and Frazier, L. (2006) Immediate disambiguation of lexically ambiguous words during reading: evidence from eye movements. *British Journal of Psychology*, 97: 467–82.

Rayner, K., and Duffy, S. (1986) Lexical complexity and fixation times in reading: effects of word frequency, verb complexity, and lexical ambiguity. *Memory and Cognition*, 14: 191–201.

Rayner, K., and Duffy, S. A. (1988) On-line comprehension processes and eye movements in reading. In M. Daneman, G. E. MacKinnon, and T. G. Waller (eds), *Reading Research: Advances in Theory and Practice*, pp. 13–66. Academic Press, New York.

Rayner, K., Fischer, M. H., and Pollatsek, A. (1998) Unspaced text interferes with both word identification and eye movement control. *Vision Research*, 38: 1129–44.

Rayner, K., and Frazier, L. (1987) Parsing temporarily ambiguous complements. *Quarterly Journal of Experimental Psychology*, 39A: 657–73.

Rayner, K., and Frazier, L. (1989) Selection mechanisms in reading lexically ambiguous words. *Journal of Experimental Psychology: Learning, Memory, and Cognition*, 15: 779–90.

Rayner, K., Garrod, S., and Perfetti, C. A. (1992) Discourse influences during parsing are delayed. *Cognition*, 45: 109–39.

Rayner, K., Inhoff, A. W., Morrison, R. E., Slowiaczek, M. L., and Bertera, J. H. (1981) Masking of foveal and parafoveal vision during eye fixations in reading. *Journal of Experimental Psychology: Human Perception and Performance*, 7: 167–79.

Rayner, K., Kambe, G., and Duffy, S. A. (2000) The effect of clause wrap-up on eye movements during reading. *Quarterly Journal of Experimental Psychology*, 53A: 1061–80.

Rayner, K., Liversedge, S. P., and White, S. J. (2006) Eye movements when reading disappearing text: the importance of the word to the right of fixation. *Vision Research*, 46: 310–23.

Rayner, K., Liversedge, S. P., White, S. J., and Vergilino-Perez, D. (2003) Reading disappearing text: cognitive control of eye movements. *Psychological Science*, 14: 385–9.

Rayner, K., and McConkie, G. W. (1976) What guides a reader's eye movements? *Vision Research*, 16: 829–37.

Rayner, K., McConkie, G. W., and Zola, D. (1980) Integrating information across eye movements. *Cognitive Psychology*, 12: 206–26.

Rayner, K., and Pollatsek, A. (1981) Eye movement control during reading: evidence for direct control. *Quarterly Journal of Experimental Psychology*, 33A: 351–73.

Rayner, K., and Pollatsek, A. (2006) Eye movement control in reading. In M. Traxler and M. Gernsbacher (eds), *Handbook of Psycholinguistics*, pp. 613–57. Elsevier, Amsterdam.

Rayner, K., Pollatsek, A., and Binder, K. (1998) Phonological codes and eye movements in reading. *Journal of Experimental Psychology: Learning, Memory, and Cognition*, 24: 476–97.

Rayner, K., Raney, G., and Pollatsek, A. (1995) Eye movements and discourse processing. In R. F. Lorch and E. J. O'Brien (eds), *Sources of Coherence in Reading*, pp. 9–36. Erlbaum, Hillsdale, NJ.

Rayner, K., and Sereno, S. C. (1994a) Regressive eye movements and sentence parsing: on the use of regression-contingent analyses. *Memory and Cognition*, 22: 281–85.

Rayner, K., and Sereno, S. C. (1994b) Regression-contingent analyses: a reply to Altmann. *Memory and Cognition*, 22: 291–2.

Rayner, K., Sereno, S., Morris, R., Schmauder, R., and Clifton, C. J. (1989) Eye movements and on-line language comprehension processes. *Language and Cognitive Processes*, 4: SI 21–50.

Rayner, K., Sereno, S. C., and Raney, G. E. (1996) Eye movement control in reading: a comparison of two types of models. *Journal of Experimental Psychology: Human Perception and Performance*, 22: 1188–200.

Rayner, K., Warren, T., Juhasz, B. J., and Liversedge, S. P. (2004) The effect of plausibility on eye movements in reading. *Journal of Experimental Psychology: Learning, Memory and Cognition*, 30: 1290–301.

Rayner, K., and Well, A. D. (1996) Effects of contextual constraint on eye movements in reading: a further examination. *Psychonomic Bulletin and Review*, 3: 504–9.

Rayner, K., Well, A. D., Pollatsek, A., and Bertera, J. H. (1982) The availability of useful information to the right of fixation in reading. *Perception and Psychophysics*, 31: 537–50.

Reichle, E. D., Pollatsek, A., Fisher, D.L., and Rayner, K. (1998) Toward a model of eye movement control in reading. *Psychological Review*, 105: 125–57.

Reichle, E. D., Pollatsek, A., and Rayner, K. (2006) E-Z Reader: a cognitive-control, serial-attention model of eye-movement behavior during reading. *Cognitive Systems Research*, 7: 4–22.

Reichle, E. D., Rayner, K., and Pollatsek, A. (2003) The E-Z Reader model of eye-movement control in reading: comparisons to other models. *Behavioral and Brain Sciences*, 26: 445–76.

Reilly, R. G., and Radach, R. (2006) Some empirical tests of an interactive activation model of eye movement control in reading. *Cognitive Systems Research*, 7: 34–55.

Schmauder, A. R., and Egan, M. C. (1998) The influence of semantic fit on on-line sentence processing. *Memory and Cognition*, 26: 1304–12.

Sereno, S. C., O'Donnell, P. J., and Rayner, K. (2006) Eye movements and lexical ambiguity resolution: investigating the subordinate bias effect. *Journal of Experimental Psychology: Human Perception and Performance*, 32: 335–50.

Sparrow, L., and Miellet, S. (2002) Activation of phonological codes during reading: evidence from error detection and eye movements. *Brain and Language*, 81: 509–16.

Speer, S. R., and Clifton, C., Jr. (1998) Plausibility and argument structure in sentence comprehension. *Memory and Cognition*, 26: 965–78.

Staub, A., and Clifton, C., Jr. (2006) Syntactic prediction in language comprehension: evidence from *either ... or*. *Journal of Experimental Psychology: Learning, Memory, and Cognition*, 32: 425–36.

Staub, A., Clifton, C., Jr., and Frazier, L. (2006) Heavy NP shift is the parser's last resort: evidence from eye movements. *Journal of Memory and Language*, 54: 389–406.

Stowe, L. A., Paans, A. M. J., Wijers, A. A., and Zwarts, F. (2004) Activations of "motor" and other non-language structures during sentence comprehension. *Brain and Language*, 89: 290–9.

Sturt, P. (2003) The time course of the application of binding constraints in reference resolution. *Journal of Memory and Language*, 48: 542–62.

Sturt, P., and Lombardo, V. (2005) Processing coordinated structures: incrementality and connectedness. *Cognitive Science*, 29: 291–305.

Traxler, M., McElree, B., Williams, R. S., and Pickering, M. (2005) Context effects in coercion: evidence from eye movements. *Journal of Memory and Language*, 53: 1–26.

Traxler, M. J., and Pickering, M. J. (1996) Plausibility and the processing of unbounded dependencies: an eye-tracking study. *Journal of Memory and Language*, 35: 454–75.

Traxler, M. J., Pickering, M. J., and Clifton, C. (1998) Adjunct attachment is not a form of lexical ambiguity resolution. *Journal of Memory and Language*, 39: 558–92.

Traxler, M., Pickering, M. J., and McElree, B. (2002) Coercion in sentence processing: evidence from eye movements and self-paced reading. *Journal of Memory and Language*, 47: 530–48.

Traxler, M., Williams, R. S., Blozis, S. A., and Morris, R. K. (2005) Working memory, animacy, and verb class in the processing of relative clauses. *Journal of Memory and Language*, 53: 204–24.

Trueswell, J. C., Tanenhaus, M. K., and Garnsey, S. M. (1994) Semantic influences on parsing: use of thematic role information in syntactic disambiguation. *Journal of Memory and Language*, 33: 285–318.

van Gompel, R. P. G., and Majid, A. (2004) Antecedent frequency effects during the processing of pronouns. *Cognition*, 90: 255–64.

van Gompel, R. P. G., Pickering, M. J., Pearson, J., and Liversedge, S. P. (2005) Evidence against competition during syntactic ambiguity resolution. *Journal of Memory and Language*, 52: 284–307.

van Gompel, R. P. G., Pickering, M. J., and Traxler, M. J. (2001) Reanalysis in sentence processing: evidence against current constraint-based and two-stage models. *Journal of Memory and Language*, 45: 225–58.

Vitu, F., McConkie, G. W., Kerr, P., and O'Regan, J. K. (2001) Fixation location effects on fixation durations during reading: an inverted optimal viewing position effect. *Vision Research*, 41: 3513–33.

Vos, S. H., Gunter, T. C., Schriefers, H., and Friederici, A. D. (2001) Syntactic parsing and working memory: the effects of syntactic complexity, reading span, and current load. *Language and Cognitive Processes*, 16: 65–103.

Williams, R. S., and Morris, R. K. (2004) Eye movements, word familiarity, and vocabulary acquisition. *European Journal of Cognitive Psychology*, 16: 312–39.

CHAPTER 20

Inference processing in discourse comprehension

Murray Singer

20.1 Introduction

Discourse understanding has been systematically studied within the framework of modern cognitive psychology for fewer than forty years. The inferences that accompany discourse comprehension have been a central focus of this field. One reason for this is that virtually every aspect of language comprehension is inferential. An inference is required to judge that *The mathematician consulted the table* refers to a chart rather than an article of furniture. The current linguistic context must be consulted to infer whether *They are eating apples* refers to some fruit or some people. For the sentence *Mary beat Helen at cards because she was a skillful player*, complex inferences of syntax and semantics are required to decide that *she* probably refers to Mary. Examples of this sort are inexhaustible.

Among these many inferential phenomena, this chapter will focus on those that involve augmenting explicitly stated discourse ideas with implied concepts and relations. In this regard, understanding *The tooth was drilled* might promote an inference about the participation of a dentist. A full understanding of *The lightning struck. The hut collapsed* might include inferring the relation that the first event caused the second. It is noteworthy that these inferences are typically based on people's ordinary world knowledge rather than on technical expertise or logical deductions.

The principles that have emerged from research in this field are generally considered to apply to both written and spoken messages (Just and Carpenter, 1984). The term "discourse" refers to coherent messages in either of these modalities. In practice, however, a majority of the research has scrutinized reading comprehension. It is also noted that researchers have inspected numerous genres of discourse, including narratives, expositions, recipes, instruction lists, and poetry.

20.2 Scientific background

20.2.1 Theoretical framework

20.2.1.1 The construction-integration model

Progress in the field of language understanding has been accompanied by the evolution of comprehensive theoretical analyses of this domain. The construction-integration model of Kintsch (1988) is a noteworthy instance of such analyses, providing an effective framework for integrating scientific findings concerning discourse inferences. Construction-integration is based on modern information processing principles of process and representation, and has the capacity to clarify those principles (Kintsch, 1998).

According to the model, the understander analyzes discourse in units informally called "chunks." Processing comprises the stages of construction and integration. During "construction," mental processes ranging from word recognition to syntactic parsing result in the extraction of the fundamental semantic units underlying the message (Clark and Clark, 1977), termed "propositions." Each proposition consists of a predicate plus one or more arguments (e.g. Kintsch, 1972). The predicate corresponds to relational terms in the current chunk or clause, such as verbs, adjectives, and adverbs. The arguments correspond to the nouns, and each argument bears a different semantic relationship to the predicate. Thus, underlying the sentence *The bugs ate the sweet jelly* are the propositions (EAT, AGENT:BUGS, OBJECT:JELLY) and (SWEET, JELLY). The propositions are assembled into a network on the basis of shared arguments, such as JELLY (e.g. Anderson, 1976; Kintsch and van Dijk, 1978). During this construction stage, the network is augmented by several categories of ideas (Kintsch, 1988): relevant and irrelevant close associates of text concepts, such as both the insect and spying connotations of "bugs;" generalizations of the sentence ideas, such as that the kitchen needed an exterminator; and ideas that contribute to the coherence of the message, such as that the first event caused the second in *The lightning struck. The hut collapsed.*

This constructed network is probably somewhat jumbled and cluttered. This problem is resolved by the second stage of processing, "integration." This term refers to what is computationally termed the "settling of activation" in the constructed network. The concepts and propositions in the network that are most highly interconnected receive the greatest amount of activation. As a result, the associate "insect" of *The bugs ate the sweet jelly* would retain moderate activation but the otherwise unconnected associate, "spying," would retain little or none. In formal cognitive theories, the settling of activation is accomplished by complex computational algorithms (Anderson, 1993; Kintsch, 1998; Rumelhart and McClelland, 1986). Integration is critical to the coherence of the resulting representation: It would be counterproductive for the representation of a sentence about foraging bugs to include reference to spying.

20.2.1.2 Memory representations

Memory functions are critical to language comprehension. Each construction-integration cycle of processing modifies an evolving memory representation of the message in long-term memory (Kintsch and Welsch, 1991). In addition, a small number of recent and important ideas are retained in working memory and therefore participate in the processing of the ensuing chunk (Fletcher, 1981; Kintsch and van Dijk, 1978). The constructed network of the next chunk is based appreciably on the connections among its ideas plus those retained in working memory.

The resulting long-term representation of the message is considered to consist of multiple levels of representation (Kintsch et al., 1990; van Dijk and Kintsch, 1983). First, the surface representation captures features such as the specific wording and grammatical constructions of the message. Second, the textbase refers to the integrated network of text propositions. Finally, and arguably most importantly, the situation model (or mental model) represents the situation to which the text refers (Johnson-Laird, 1983; van Dijk and Kintsch, 1983; Zwaan and Radvansky, 1998). It captures the complex relations that link the discourse entities with one another and with relevant world knowledge (Sanford and Garrod, 1998). As such, the situation model comprises numerous dimensions, including those pertaining to cause, motivation, narrative character, space, and time (Zwaan et al., 1995). The multiple-levels hypothesis is supported by observations of systematic differences among the levels. For example, the situation model is the level most resistant to forgetting in most reading contexts (Kintsch et al., 1990).

Unlike the surface and textbase representations, the situation model need not reflect the original form of the message. For example, the situation model of *The squirrel was older than the fox. The fox was older than the bear* might capture the relative ages of the animals. However, the reader might not remember which pairs of animals were explicitly compared or whether the text used the term *older* or *younger* throughout (Potts, 1972).

20.2.1.3 Memory processes

There is accumulating evidence that passive memory processes guide the course of discourse comprehension. According to this "memory-based text processing analysis," the current discourse chunk reminds the reader of (a) related ideas mentioned earlier (or "antecedents") and (b) relevant world knowledge. These ideas are said to resonate (Ratcliff, 1978) on the basis of their overlap with the current chunk (Greene et al., 1994; Myers and O'Brien, 1998). Resonance is affected by the similarity and the text-distance between the current clause and the antecedent, the degree of elaboration of the antecedent (Albrecht and Myers, 1995; O'Brien and Albrecht, 1991; O'Brien et al., 1995), and the distinctiveness of the cuing text (Albrecht and Myers, 1998; McKoon and Ratcliff, 1992). As a result, resonating ideas, like ideas that have been carried over in working memory, participate in the computations of comprehending the current text.

Researchers have identified the contribution of memory resonance to numerous complex phenomena of language comprehension, including anaphoric (e.g. pronoun) resolution (O'Brien and Albrecht, 1991); and, particularly important for this chapter, the detection of implicit relations among text ideas (Albrecht and Myers, 1995; Klin, 1995). The coherence of ordinary language messages is critically dependent on such processes.

It is noteworthy that a resonating idea may actually be irrelevant to the gist of that text. For example, the return of a character to the narrative action may remind the reader of many associated ideas. Likewise, both "insect" and "spying" may resonate to *bugs*. However, among the resonating ideas, only pertinent ones will be inferentially linked to the current clause in an enduring manner (Kintsch, 1988; McKoon et al., 1996). As such, resonance may be characterized as a necessary but not sufficient condition for antecedent text ideas and world knowledge to be encoded in a robust representation of the current clause.

20.2.2 Measuring inference processing

The full range of methods of cognitive psychology has been applied to the study of discourse inference processes. Researchers frequently measure understanders' *memory*, on the rationale that this reflects people's interpretation of a message. In free recall, participants are given either limited or unlimited time to report everything that they remember about the discourse (e.g. Kintsch and van Dijk, 1978). In cued recall, participants encounter the stimulus message and are later presented with a small portion of it as a prompt to remember other parts (Black and Bern, 1981; Corbett and Dosher, 1978). Tests of recognition determine whether the understander can distinguish portions of the original message from contrasting "distractors" (Kintsch and Bates, 1977; Sulin and Dooling, 1974). Recognition tests have the capacity to portray the encoded representation while placing fewer demands on people's memory than does recall. Furthermore, timing people's recognition judgments can allow assessment of the relative status of different ideas in the representation (Singer, 1980). In a variation of recognition, test items appear in the form of ordinary questions (e.g. *Was the fox was older than the bear?*) rather than a recognition phrase (*The fox was older than the bear*).

A widely understood limitation of memory measures is that the message representation may change between reading and test (Kintsch and van Dijk, 1978). Therefore, researchers routinely evaluate readers' behavior during the course of comprehension, by means of "on-line" measures. Probably most commonly, researchers measure the time that people take to read the words, phrases, or sentences of a message. Reading time is considered to clarify people's ongoing discourse processing (Forster, 1970; Haviland and Clark, 1974). A sophisticated and incisive method of measuring reading time involves tracking the location of people's eye fixations while they read a message (Just and Carpenter, 1980; Staub and Rayner, Chapter 19 this volume). Furthermore, there is evidence that a "moving window" technique of measuring reading time while the reader proceeds through a computer-screen message, most of which is obscured at any moment, provides a reasonable first approximation of eyetracking (Just et al., 1982; cf. Magliano et al., 1993).

A different approach to the on-line assessment of language comprehension is to interrupt reading and measure the time of judging or otherwise responding to words that bear various relations to the message. In recognition, the participant judges whether the word appeared in the preceding portion of the message. In lexical decision, people indicate whether letter-strings (e.g. non-words like SNARF and message-relevant and -irrelevant words), constitute English words. In naming, the participant simply articulates the interrupting stimulus, and the time that they take to do so is registered using a voice-activated relay. The logic underlying these methods is that response time reflects the degree of activation of the corresponding concept at that point in the message (e.g. Potts et al., 1988). The use of these measures has not been without controversy. First, there are differing views about the capacity of recognition, lexical decision, and naming to reflect the status of the different levels of text representation that were discussed earlier (Keenan et al., 1990; Magliano and Graesser, 1991; McKoon and Ratcliff, 1990). Second, by disrupting reading, the measures may alter the comprehension processes that they were devised to evaluate (Masson, 1984). Furthermore, it is arguable as to whether these measures meet the "on-line" criterion. Although the stimuli are judged during the message, they literally appear after reading, however briefly.

Cognitive neuroscientists now use a battery of brain-imaging techniques to quantify neural activity during language processing. The method of event-related potentials (ERPs) measures the electrical activity of the brain, fractions of a second after the presentation of a crucial stimulus (Kutas and Federmeier, Chapter 23 this volume). Using functional magnetic resonance imaging (fMRI), researchers assess activity of different brain regions in terms of their relative degree of oxygen uptake during mental processing (Bornkessel-Schlesewsky and Friederici, Chapter 24 this volume). These measures are already being applied to language comprehension in general and inference processing in particular (Reichel and Mason, forthcoming).

In the evaluation of people's inference processes, researchers originally used their own intuitions to identify the likely implications of a message. A preferable technique involves measuring, prior to experimental testing, native speakers' insights about the inferences that one might derive from a message. These measurements take the form of ratings or norms. For example, a group of participants may be asked to specify the most likely unstated agent, object, instrument, or outcome of a stimulus event (Singer, 1980; Singer and Ferreira, 1983). A refinement of this procedure involves asking the norming participants to identify possible implications of a message either intermittently or continually while they inspect a message (Olson et al., 1984; Trabasso and Suh, 1993). If the research emphasis is a particular category of inference, the participant may be asked to generate only implications of that sort (Graesser and Murachver, 1985; Graesser et al., 1981).

In conclusion, researchers avail themselves of a wide variety of methodologies and measures. To the extent that any given procedure may have limitations, it is optimal to evaluate a phenomenon using a battery of methods (Klin, 1995; Magliano and Graesser, 1991).

20.3 **Bridging inferences**

A quality of discourse which exerts a considerable impact on inference processing is coherence. Coherence refers to the presence of connections among the parts of a message. Sequence (1) seems incoherent because its sentences appear to be unconnected:

1. The dentist drilled the tooth. The broom was tattered.

   Sequence (2), in contrast, is coherent.

2. The worker swept the floor. The broom was tattered.

However, the coherence of (2) depends on an inference on the part of the reader. Without detecting the relation between *broom* and *swept*, (2) would be as incoherent as (1).

Central to the psychological analysis of coherence, in turn, is the distinction between given and new sentence information. For example, the grammatical structure of *What the mathematician consulted was a table* conveys as "given" that the mathematician consulted something and as "new" that a table was consulted (Halliday and Hasan, 1976). For comprehension to proceed, the reader must distinguish the given and new ideas of the current text chunk, retrieve information from the memory of the preceding text that corresponds to the given idea (the antecedent or referent of the given information), and link the new information to the referent (Clark and Haviland, 1977; Kintsch, 1974). The successful retrieval of the referent of the given information preserves discourse coherence.

Detecting the referent of the given information frequently requires an inference. In a classic study, Haviland and Clark (1974) showed that people need less time to read *The beer was warm* in the sequence *We got some beer out of the trunk. The beer was warm* than in *We checked the picnic supplies. The beer was warm*. They attributed the difference to the extra time needed determine that *picnic supplies* is a satisfactory referent for *beer*: i.e. to infer, on the basis of world knowledge, that beer is a sensible component of picnic supplies. This inference bridges the sentences of the *picnic supplies* sequence, so Haviland and Clark labeled it a "bridging inference." Thirty years of subsequent research strongly favors the encoding of many bridging inferences during comprehension.

20.3.1 **Anaphoric bridging inferences**

An anaphor is a linguistic expression that refers to an antecedent in the message. The pronoun is the prototypical anaphor. In *But this prince was always unhappy. He spent his days staring into space*, detecting that *he* refers to the prince serves to bridge the two sentences. More complex is the sequence *A king had an only son. But the prince spent his days staring into space*. The definite article *the* signals that the noun it modifies is given; the reader must therefore identify a referent of *the prince*. However, the prior sentence does not mention a prince. Resolving this anaphoric definite noun phrase therefore depends on accessing the knowledge that the son of a king is a prince.

Pronouns in English vary in gender (e.g. *she/he*), number (e.g. *she/they*), and person (e.g. *she/I*). Comprehension proceeds more readily when these characteristics unambiguously signal only one possible referent as opposed to multiple referents. Single-referent pronouns are understood more quickly (Caramazza et al., 1977; Vonk, 1985), and sentences such as (3) take less time to read than ones like (4) (Ehrlich, 1980; Frederiksen, 1981; Springston, 1975).

3. Sally rewarded Ron because *he* was on time.
4. Tom rewarded Ron because *he* was on time.

These results indicate that the reader resolves the pronoun during the consideration of the current phrase or clause: If not, reading time for sentences (3) and (4) would be identical. The evidence thus suggests that the reader is executing an anaphoric bridging inference during comprehension.

20.3.2 Semantic bridging inferences

Bridging the sentences of *A king had an only son. But the prince was always unhappy* requires detecting that the referent of *prince* is *son*. Consider again, in contrast, sequence (2):

2. The worker swept the floor. The broom was tattered.

The first sentence of (2) includes no referent at all for *broom*. Rather, bridging the sentences of (2) requires detecting that *broom* plays a typical but unstated role in the act of sweeping. There is evidence that this type of bridging inference is more cognitively demanding than (a) detecting coreference on the basis of repetition (*beer–beer*) (Haviland and Clark, 1974), (b) comprehending sentences that require that a referent be retrieved from long-term memory (Lesgold et al., 1979), and (c) comprehending sentences which present misleading distinctions between given and new sentence information (Yekovich et al., 1979).

Bridging inferences of the sort underlying sequence (2) have been extensively scrutinized. Consider the idea that the tourist used a camera with reference to the materials of Table 20.1 (Singer, 1980). That idea is stated explicitly in the explicit passage, requires a bridging inference in the bridging version, and is plausible but does not serve a bridging function in the "elaborative inference" passage. The time that the experimental participants needed to verify (judge the truth of) *The tourist used a camera* after reading the passage was approximately equal in the explicit and bridging conditions and about 0.25 sec. longer in the elaborative condition (Singer, 1980; Singer and Ferreira, 1983).[1] This suggested that the crucial bridging inference accompanied comprehension and that it was encoded in the resulting message representation. Consistently with that conclusion, single words are responded to more quickly in lexical decision and naming tasks when they capture bridging inferences than when they appear in a suitable control context (Potts et al., 1988).

Table 20.1 Three versions of sample experimental passage plus test sentence of Singer (1980).

Explicit	The tourist took the picture with the camera. The scene was more beautiful than he remembered.
Bridging inference	The tourist took the picture of the church. The camera was the best he had ever owned.
Elaborative inference	The tourist took the picture of the church. The scene was more beautiful than he remembered.
Test sentence	The tourist used a camera.

Thus, numerous findings suggested that coherence-preserving bridging inferences reliably accompany comprehension. Discourse clauses can be inferentially bridged with regard to many semantic relations, such as instruments (see sequence 2 above), agents, and objects. However, no relation has received as much attention in this realm as causation.

20.3.2.1 Causal bridging inferences

The ideas communicated by many text genres are interrelated by relations of physical, motivational, and psychological causation. A warm sun can cause a snowman to melt and, analogously, being short of money can cause someone to seek a job. It has been proposed that, in discourse comprehension, the reader evaluates candidate causes with reference to several criteria. Upon reading *The sun came out and the snowman melted*, both the sufficiency and especially the "necessity in the circumstances" of the sun coming out are important for establishing this as the cause of the snowman melting (Trabasso et al., 1989; van den Broek, 1990). Necessity in the circumstances means that, had the sun not come out, the snowman would not have melted.

There is considerable evidence that people draw causal bridging inferences during comprehension. For a sequence such as (5), it is apparent that the first event caused the second.

5. The boy walked over to the refrigerator, bumping a bowl he had left on the table. Suddenly, it fell off the edge and broke.

[1] For the moment, the version labelled "elaborative inference" may be viewed as a control passage.

Congruent with that causal observation, after one reads the two sentences of (5), the sentences cue the recall of one another more effectively than do two similar sentences linked only by temporal relations (Black and Bern, 1981). This suggests that the reader has encoded the implicit causal relation between the sentences of (5).

Further evidence for the on-line drawing of causal bridging inferences emerged from the study of sequences such as (6) and (7) (Keenan et al., 1984; Myers et al., 1987).

6. Tony's friend suddenly pushed him into a pond. He walked home, soaking wet, to change his clothes.
7. Tony met his friend near a pond in the park. He walked home, soaking wet, to change his clothes.

According to rating data, the sentences of (6) are causally closer than those of (7) (Myers et al., 1987). Concomitantly, people read *He walked home, soaking wet, to change his clothes* faster in sequence (6) than sequence (7) (Keenan et al., 1984; Myers et al., 1987). This suggests that readers strive to detect the causal relations between the sentences of a discourse.

Furthermore, it is possible either: (a) that understanding sequence (7) simply requires more or more difficult inferences than sequence (6); or that (b) sequence (7) demands the consideration of more candidate inferences than (6) but that none of these candidates satisfactorily connects the sentences of (7). The results of an fMRI study tended to support the second view. Mason and Just (2004) reported that fMRI activity in bilateral (left and right brain hemispheres) regions of the prefrontal cortex increased systematically with causal distance. However, fMRI responses in certain right-hemisphere temporal-cortex areas were conspicuously higher for the close-causal than the distant-causal sequences. Mason and Just considered this right-hemisphere difference to indicate that causal inferences were successfully integrated only in the close-causal (sequence 6) condition (see also Myers and Duffy, 1990).

Causal bridging inferences ultimately depend on routine world knowledge. A proper understanding of sequence (6) requires the knowledge that ponds contain water and that water is wet. Direct evidence for this conjecture stems from a study in which people read causal or temporal sequences such as (8) and (9), respectively.

8. Dorothy poured the bucket of water on the bonfire. The bonfire went out. [causal]
9. Dorothy placed the bucket of water by the bonfire. The bonfire went out. [temporal]

Answer time for a mundane question such as *Does water extinguish fire?* was less after sequence (8) than (9) (Singer et al., 1992). It was concluded that world knowledge accessed during the course of drawing a bridging inference is temporarily activated, and perhaps linked to the text representation (Halldorson and Singer, 2002).

Expository as well as narrative texts have been inspected in research concerning causal bridging inferences. According to the "principle of explanation" (Graesser et al., 1994), readers of expositions ought to infer the causes of physical outcomes. Consistent with this hypothesis, there is evidence that lexical decisions about words that represent candidate causes of expository outcomes are faster than comparable judgments in control conditions (Graesser and Bertus, 1998; Millis and Graesser, 1994). For example, lexical decisions for the cause word *gravity* were faster shortly after a discourse sentence describing the collapse of a star than after a sentence of an unrelated passage (Millis and Graesser, 1994). In another project, sentence sequences analogous to the bonfire examples (8) and (9) above were presented in expository passages derived from an encyclopedia. Reading times for target sentences in the texts and answer times for questions about ideas that sanctioned bridging inferences suggested that the readers engaged in bridging processes similar to those that accompany narrative comprehension (Singer et al., 1997; Singer and O'Connell, 2003). However, sufficiently complex expository text can thwart such inferences (Noordman et al., 1992).

20.3.2.2 Bridging inferences: other situational dimensions

Bridging inferences pertaining to physical and motivational cause have received extensive attention because of the central contribution of causal relations to most text genres. As discussed earlier, causation and motivation constitute dimensions of the situation model. More recently, empirical evidence has indicated that the space and time dimensions of the situation model likewise contribute to bridging inference.

The importance of the physical location of entities coupled with people's knowledge about locations jointly permit readers to monitor the spatial features of discourse situation models (Morrow et al., 1987; Wilson et al., 1993). This capacity may be limited by the detail and functionality of spatial information (Zwaan and van Oostendorp, 1993). That is, the spatial phrase *standing under the bridge* may be encoded differently in the functional context, *starting to rain*, than the less relevant context *blocking the moonlight* (Radvansky and Copeland, 2000).

Ordinarily, however, readers are quite sensitive to the conspicuous spatial relations among entities. In one study (O'Brien and Albrecht, 1991), participants read about a character's location, as in (10a) and (10b).

10a. Jane waited inside the door of her health club, waiting for the instructor.
10b. Jane waited outside the door of her health club, waiting for the instructor.

Later in the story, the reader encountered (11).

11. The instructor came in.

The results indicated that the participants were aware of the spatial inconsistency of (10b) and (11): Reading time was greater for sentence (11) in the context of (10b) than (10a). Among the many relations that might inferentially bridge (11) to the versions of (10), only the monitoring of the spatial situation could account for this result.

Temporal (i.e. time) relations are also central to discourse meaning. Indeed, linguistic markers ranging from adverbs to verb tense explicitly signify these relations continually. Readers detect temporal inconsistencies much as they do spatial ones. Thus, reading time for (12b) is greater when one has read the "after" than the "before" version of (12a) (Rinck et al., 2001).

12a. Claudia's train arrived in Dresden on time (before/after) Markus's train.
12b. Claudia was already waiting for him when he got off the train with his huge bag.

Recent intense focus on readers' inferential construction of the situation model has highlighted a subtle difference among bridging inferences. In an prototype bridging sequence such as *The worker swept the floor. The broom was tattered*, the two sentences are ostensively locally incoherent: There is no antecedent for *broom* in the first sentence. In contrast, the second sentence of sequence (6), considered earlier, includes the pronoun *he* that clearly refers to Tony.

6. Tony's friend suddenly pushed him into a pond. He walked home, soaking wet, to change his clothes.

Therefore, the inference that the first event of (6) caused the second event bridges the two sentences with reference to the causal situation model but does not literally serve to repair local incoherence (Keenan et al., 1984; Schmalhofer, McDaniel, and Keefe, 2002). Upon consideration, it is observed that many of the inferences that contribute to the situation model connect text ideas with reference to numerous situational dimensions, but only a subset of them repair outright instances of local incoherence.

20.3.3 Theoretical considerations of bridging inference

20.3.3.1 Construction-integration analyses

The robust encoding of bridging inferences has been addressed in the framework of Kintsch's (1988; 1998) construction-integration theory (Schmalhofer et al., 2002; Singer and Halldorson, 1996; Singer and Kintsch, 2001). At the construction stage (see construction-integration overview, earlier), the concepts and relations that contribute to bridging inferences are encoded in the textbase either because the text explicitly mentions them (see the bridging inference sequence of Table 20.1) or because they enhance text coherence (Fincher-Kiefer and D'Agostino, 2004; Kintsch, 1988; Schmalhofer et al., 2002). In addition, bridging ideas find expression in the situation model, because they pertain to situational dimensions such as cause or time (Schmalhofer et al., 2002) and because they involve world knowledge (Kintsch and Welsch, 1991; Singer, 1996). The encoding of these ideas at multiple levels of representation results in their being highly interconnected. Therefore, at the integration phase of processing, relatively high levels of activation settle upon the concepts and propositions that bridge other text ideas. This high activation is the manifestation of their inclusion in the text representation.

It has been proposed that the apparent status of an idea in the text representation predominantly reflects its level of activation in the situation model, as opposed to lower levels of representation. From this perspective, both explicit text ideas and bridging inferences may have strong levels of activation but for different reasons (Schmalhofer et al., 2002). Explicit ideas at the situational level may be mainly interconnected with their corresponding propositions in the textbase. The interconnections of bridging inferences, in contrast, may be predominantly with other situation model elements.

Hypothetical distinctions between the comprehension processes of construction and integration ought to be reflected by profiles of neural response. In one study that evaluated this hypothesis, fMRI was measured when text coherence-breaks ought to have initiated inferential bridges (Virtue et al., forthcoming). Virtue et al. particularly scrutinized the data of readers high in working-memory capacity, who exhibit more effective bridging processes (Just and Carpenter, 1992). They detected certain fMRI responses that were stronger in the implicit than explicit experimental conditions. These differences were generally consistent with the construction-integration distinction. First, Virtue et al. reported such an implicit/explicit difference in the left and right superior temporal gyri, areas that they associated with the generation of inferences (akin to the construction of construction-integration). Second, there was an enhanced response in the left inferior frontal gyrus (IFG), an area that the investigators associated with the resolution of a coherence break (the integration of construction-integration). Virtue et al. interpreted these patterns as corroborating hypothetical inference sub-processes but also offered the caution that the IFG "resolution" response might reflect processing effort or difficulty rather than incisive inference computation.

Further to these neuroscientific results, Beeman (2005) has proposed that the relatively diffuse connections of the right-hemisphere language areas suggests distinct contributions of the right hemisphere (vs. the left hemisphere) to inference computation. In this vein, Beeman noted that right-hemisphere priming for relatively distant semantic relations is stronger than that of the left hemisphere; and that the right hemisphere is relatively more involved than the left in arduous text comprehension (e.g. in the absence of a theme or title). However, existing neural evidence in this realm requires careful scrutiny. For example, the resolution of bridging inferences was most strongly associated with a right-hemisphere cortical region by Mason and Just (2004) but with a left-hemisphere region (left IFG) by Virtue et al. (forthcoming).

20.3.3.2 Memory-based vs. constructionist interpretations

The phenomena of bridging inference processes have sometimes been claimed to distinctively favour one of two theoretical positions: either the memory-based text processing analysis (see section 20.2.1.3) or constructionism (e.g. Bransford et al., 1972; Graesser et al., 1994). A central principle of constructionism is that understanders engage in a search after meaning (Graesser et al., 1994). Two assumptions associated with this principle are that readers monitor coherence at all levels of the discourse representation and that they seek explanations for the outcomes described in text.

Memory-based theorists have presented findings that they have sometimes claimed to challenge constructionism. A sample text of one study (Albrecht and Myers, 1995) described Mary as needing to finalize an air reservation before midnight. She either succeeds or fails to do so, and then undertakes a different task. In this context, reading time for a subsequent target sentence describing Mary as going to bed is greater in the fail than the succeed condition. This is analogous to the spatial and temporal inconsistency effects discussed earlier (section 20.3.2.2). However, this result is observed only when the target sentence bears some relatively superficial overlap with the antecedent text, such as mentioning that Mary sat on a leather sofa. Albrecht and Myers proposed that the absence of superficial overlap should not have thwarted the constructionist search after meaning from detecting that going to bed was inconsistent with failing to make an air reservation. Also cited as contradicting constructionism has been the finding that the availability of a (physically) nearby candidate cause of a story outcome prevented readers from detecting a more distant cause (Rizzella and O'Brien, 1996).

In support of constructionism, in contrast, it has frequently been shown that readers capitalize on situational structures of cause and goal that span moderate to great text distances. Importantly, these studies have controlled the degree of superficial overlap between the target region of the story and the critical antecedent text (Long et al., 1992; Long et al., 1996; Richards and Singer, 2001; Singer and Halldorson, 1996; Suh and Trabasso, 1993; van den Broek and Lorch, 1993). These results suggest that constructionist mechanisms do a good job of accounting for understanders' inferential processing. Other studies have offered evidence claimed to refute specific memory-based postulates, such as that the amount of text intervening between target and antecedent should affect inference processing (Lutz and Radvansky, 1997).

The prevailing approach to this debate is currently conciliatory, an attitude reflected by a recent special issue of the journal *Discourse Processes* (Gueraud and O'Brien, 2005). On one hand, constructionism, while emphasizing situational and global levels of representation, has explicitly embraced the impact of the passive retrieval processes of the memory-based analysis (Singer et al., 1994). On the other, memory-based analyses increasingly address higher-level processes and situational representations (Albrecht and Myers, 1998; Cook et al., 2001; Myers and O'Brien, 1998; Rizzella and O'Brien, 1996).

A likely basis of the ostensive differences between memory-based processing and constructionism is that situational structures are much harder to characterize than surface and textbase representations. As a result, it has been difficult to specify how situational representations mediate the memory-based retrieval of relevant causal, spatial, and temporal discourse information. For example, exactly how is the knowledge that a girl has previously failed to obtain a birthday present for her mother made available at the moment that one reads that she neatly folds a sweater that she has knitted (Suh and Trabasso, 1993)?

However, appreciable progress is already being achieved in answering this question. Investigators have demonstrated that, in the comprehension of sentences, subtle situational implications have a considerable impact on measures of readers' performance. A classic result in experimental psychology is the fan effect: that is, the outcome that fact-judgment time increases systematically with the number of facts known about a concept (Anderson, 1974). The fan effect is abolished when multiple facts can integrated into a coherent situation model (Smith et al., 1978). In this regard, there is evidence that multiple facts that convey an integrated situation on the dimension of goal, space, or time do not generate a fan effect (Radvansky, 1998; Radvansky et al., 1997; see also Sharkey and Bower, 1987). For example, when an event such as the falling of a vase serves as the basis for integrating varying numbers of activities that occurred at the same *time* (temporal relation), there is no fan effect: answer time to questions about the core event does not vary systematically with the number of coinciding activities (Radvansky et al., 1998). To specify exactly how complex messages, rather than sentence lists, give rise to comparable effects is an important challenge to researchers.

20.4 Elaborative inferences

Even the simplest sentence bears innumerable implications of varying probabilities. *The mother read to her daughter* implies that an adult read to a child, an adult human read to a young human, the mother read to her female offspring, the mother read a book to her daughter, and the mother wanted to entertain the daughter. In the realm of discourse comprehension, reasonable extrapolations of explicit text ideas that stem from world knowledge are called "elaborative inferences."

Investigators initially offered the hypothesis that elaborative inferences of high probability might be drawn during comprehension (Johnson et al., 1973). However, evidence subsequently converged from measures of cued recalled, answer times, speeded word judgements, and event-related (brain) potentials (ERPs) on the conclusion that elaborative inferences are frequently weakly encoded in the representation of discourse meaning (Corbett and Dosher, 1978; McKoon and Ratcliff, 1986; Potts et al., 1988; Singer, 1980; Singer and Ferreira, 1983). For example, consider again the elaborative sequence in Table 20.1, *The tourist took the picture of the church. The scene was more beautiful than he remembered.* In this context, the concept that the tourist used a camera is an elaborative inference. It was discussed earlier, that, having read the elaborative sequence, people needed about 0.25 sec more to judge that "the tourist used a camera" was probably true than in the comparable explicit and bridging inference conditions (Singer, 1980). This tends to deny the enduring representation of the elaborative inference.

Evidence stemming from an electrophysiological study is consistent with the latter analysis. In this study, ERPs were measured when readers encountered a critical target sentence in text (St. George et al., 1997). These targets expressed ideas that (a) represented either bridging inferences or elaborative inferences previously afforded by the text or (b) functioned as controls. The researchers measured a brain response called N400, which is an index the degree to which newly encountered text material seems unexpected (Kutas and Hilyard, 1980; van Berkum et al., 2003; St George et al., 1997). The N400 potentials were lower in the bridging condition than in the elaborative and control conditions, although this pattern was most prominent for readers with relatively low working memory capacity (cf. Just and Carpenter, 1992). The low N400 value suggests that bridging-inference targets were *not* unexpected in the text, which in turn is consistent with the notion that the corresponding bridging inference had already been computed during the comprehension of the antecedent text. Conversely, the elaborative inference targets were somewhat unexpected.

These empirical results are consistent with the proposal that the encoding of all reasonable elaborative inferences during reading would overwhelm limited cognitive resources (Charniak, 1975; Rieger, 1975). Nevertheless, early findings concerning elaborative inferences promoted at least two systematic programs of research, which will be considered next.

20.4.1 Highly constrained elaborative inferences

Elaborative inferences may be more permanently encoded in discourse representations when they are highly constrained by semantic context than otherwise. Evidence for this proposal arises from many types of inference and many dependent measures. In this regard, *They carved the bird for Thanksgiving* makes a stronger implication that the bird was a turkey than that it was a robin. Experiments examining people's reading of continuation sentences, timed judgements about inference-related words, and cued recall (e.g. does the implication "turkey" remind the reader of the sentence?) suggested that readers encoded the elaborative inference that the bird was a turkey (Anderson et al., 1976; Dubois and Denis, 1988; Garrod et al., 1990; McKoon and Ratcliff, 1989; O'Brien et al., 1988; Whitney, 1986).

There is evidence that people infer relevant properties of discourse concepts, such as that a tomato is (a) round when it is described as rolling and (b) red when one paints a picture of it (McKoon and Ratcliff, 1988). Readers infer implied themes, such as that *The townspeople were amazed to find that all the buildings had collapsed except the mint* connotes an earthquake (Till et al., 1988).

Some of the effects in this domain are very subtle. In sequence (13), the conclusion that Bill used a broom is an elaborative inference rather than a bridging inference, because no phrase in (13b) has an anaphoric function.

13a. There was a broom in the closet next to the kitchen.
13b. Bill swept the floor every week on Saturday.

In spite of this, readers made faster decisions about *broom* than about suitable control words immediately after (13b) (Lucas et al., 1990). The authors concluded that this inference is promoted by the ready availability of the concept "broom" (see also McKoon and Ratcliff, 1992). Similarly subtle is that certain linguistic expressions promote the encoding of elaborative inferences about implied semantic roles, but without specifying the concept that fulfills the role. For example, the capitalized "rationale" in *The game show wheel was spun TO WIN A PRIZE* results in an inference about the involvement of an unknown agent who spun the wheel (Mauner et al., 1995).

20.4.2 Predictive inferences

Researchers have persevered in evaluating the status of certain elaborative inferences that are not highly constrained. Two likely reasons for this are that we might expect that perceiving any psychological context ought to facilitate the processing of its elements (e.g. Miller, 1980); and, as active problem solvers (Black and Bower, 1980), readers might intentionally generate predictions about the contents of discourse.

Accordingly, researchers have carefully scrutinized elaborative inferences about the predicted consequences of text events, and a generally stable portrayal has emerged from these investigations. Example (14) is one sentence of a story originating in materials that have been widely inspected (e.g. Keefe and McDaniel, 1993; Klin et al., 1999; McKoon and Ratcliff, 1986; Murray et al., 1993).

14a. No longer able to control his fury, the husband hurled the delicate porcelain vase against the wall.
14b. He had been feeling upset for weeks, but had refused to seek help.

Sentence (14a) implies the consequence that the vase broke. Shortly after the reading of (14a), response times (naming, lexical decisions, recognition) to the corresponding inference word, *broke*, are lower than after a control sentence that uses similar words but that does not make this implication. Such facilitation has been measured both for physical consequences (sentence 14a) and for the consequences of people's goals and motives (Murray et al., 1993). Inference activation takes relatively long to accumulate: On the basis of carefully regulating the time from which the implication is first available, estimates of inference-activation time of 1.25 seconds have been presented (Calvo and Castillo, 1996; Calvo et al., 1999; see also Till et al., 1988).

Under ordinary circumstances, however, this activation of inferences about predicted consequences appears transient. When sentence (14b) intervenes between sentence (14a) and its test word, response time is *not* lower in the inference condition than the control condition (Keefe and McDaniel, 1993; Potts et al., 1988; see also

McKoon and Ratcliff, 1986). Inferences about predicted consequences are somewhat fragile in other ways as well. In one study, one version of the story context preceding sentence (14a) included the "distractor consequence" that if the husband had another temper tantrum, his wife would leave him. Therefore, sentence (14a) had two conspicuous consequences. In the presence of the distractor consequence, *broke* did not exhibit facilitation when the typical half-second interval intervened between (14a) and the test word (Klin et al., 1999); although it was facilitated after 1500 ms (Weingartner et al., 2003).

Generally congruent conclusions have emerged from the study of other predictive inferences. Consider set (15).

15a. Jimmy's friends taught him a fun game that involved throwing (rocks/ sponge balls) at a target to get points.
15b. <intervening sentences>
15c. Jimmy missed, though, and he accidentally hit the door of a new car.

The *rock* version of sequence (15a–c) implies that the car door would be dented whereas the *ball* version does not (Cook et al., 2001). Within 500 ms after the reading of (15c), people's naming time for the test word *dent* was lower in the implicational (*rock*) condition than the control condition. Cook et al. emphasized that, by contrast with other studies of predicted consequences, their target inferences were not specifically related to the meaning of other words in the discourse. They concluded that the context defined by the situation model could activate predictive inferences. They agreed with other researchers, however, that the inferences in question might not be robustly encoded: In another experiment, they found that the time to read a subsequent target sentence which mentioned the prediction was greater in the implicational condition than when the outcome was explicitly mentioned. This suggests that the crucial inference was either computed or recomputed at the time of reading the target sentence.

Numerous issues in this domain continue to receive close attention. There is evidence that the encoding of predictive inferences about consequences is enhanced by instructions to (a) read discourse with the aim of thinking about what might occur next or (b) monitor the discourse situation (Albritton, 2004; Schmalhofer et al., 2002; see also Perrig and Kintsch, 1985; Schmalhofer and Glavanov, 1986; Singer and Halldorson, 1996). A novel hypothesis in the predictive-inference realm is that inferences about predicted consequences might be encoded as hypothetical facts (Campion, 2004). In this regard, Campion showed that people needed less time, after reading, to assess the truth of statements about predicted consequences when the statements were phrased hypothetically than as certainties; whereas the opposite was true for deductive inferences derived from text.

It is noteworthy that these investigations of predictive elaborative inferences have focused on causal consequences. This is understandable and legitimate, in view of the centrality of causal relations to many discourse genres. However, caution needs to be exercised in generalizing these findings to other inferential relations.

20.4.3 Theoretical considerations of elaborative inference

20.4.3.1 Construction-integration analyses

Like bridging inferences, people's derivation of elaborative inferences from discourse has been addressed within the construction-integration framework (Kintsch, 1988; 1998). In one treatment, Schmalhofer et al. (2002) inspected patterns of activation of predictive inferences about causal consequences in the framework of a unified treatment of both elaborative and bridging inferences. Consider again sequence (14).

14a. No longer able to control his fury, the husband hurled the delicate porcelain vase against the wall.
14b. He had been feeling upset for weeks, but had refused to seek help.

The focus was on the possible elaboration, upon reading that the vase was thrown, that it broke. Insofar as breaking is not explicitly mentioned in (14a), the plausible predictive inference that the vase broke is encoded in the situation model but not in the surface or textbase representations. The situational encoding, marked by ample connections between this elaboration and other text ideas, results in a reasonable degree of activation of this inference. The gist of (14b), however, does not result in the construction of propositions pertaining to breakage. After (14b), therefore, the vase's destruction accumulates meagre activation, because it is closely connected neither with other situational ideas nor with the textbase. This analysis meshes closely with the naming-time facilitation of a broke elaboration immediately after (14a) but not subsequently (Keefe and McDaniel, 1993).

Consistent with the latter analysis, Fincher-Kiefer and D'Agostino (2004) proposed that, to the extent that predictive inferences are represented exclusively in the situation model, their encoding ought to require perceptual processing. This is because, from the cognitive embodiment position (Barsalou, 1999), the construction of situation models is a fundamentally perceptual process. In a series of experiments, Fincher-Kiefer and D'Agostino's participants read messages while holding in memory a 4×4 spatial configuration of dots. Under this concurrent visuo-spatial memory load, data patterns that reflect the drawing of predictive inferences were abolished. The outcome was detected both for lexical decision and for sentence reading-time measures. The results mesh with Schmalhofer et al.'s (2002) proposals about the situational representation of predictive inferences.

Construction-integration has likewise been applied to people's encoding of elaborations concerning the relevant properties of text concepts, such as the roundness of a tomato described as rolling (Kintsch and Welsch, 1991; McKoon and Ratcliff, 1988). Again, this analysis emphasized the construction, in the text situation model, of ideas derived from pertinent world knowledge; followed by the settling of appreciable activation on those ideas during the integration stage of processing.[2]

The joint construction-integration analysis of bridging and elaborative inferences offered by Schmalhofer et al. (2002) prompted them to suggest that bridging inferences may originate as elaborative inferences which are later consolidated, depending on the gist of the ensuing discourse. This characterization may be apt when a tentative elaborative inference is almost immediately recruited, by the following clause, to preserve coherence. There are many other circumstances, however, in which the transient activation of a tentative elaborative inference will have decayed before the bridge-inducing text is encountered (Keefe and McDaniel, 1993). Effectively, that elaborative inference is no longer encoded in the message representation. The bridging inference in question can still be computed (Suh and Trabasso, 1993; van den Broek and Lorch, 1993), but would not stem from an existing elaborative inference.

20.5 **Conclusions**

The mandatory nature of discourse inference-processing is elegantly reflected by the following dialogue from the movie *Shadowlands* (Attenborough and Nicholson, 1993), in which the characters Jack and Joy are having a spat:

Jack: I'm not lying, why should I be?
Joy: It's just that you don't say it all, do you?
Jack: Well, one can't say it all, it would take too long.

For communication to proceed, the speaker must assume that the listener can access ordinary world knowledge known to both parties. Conversely, were speakers required to specify every relevant detail of the pertinent situation, discourse would collapse under the weight of myriad boring details. This is captured by Adams's satiric presentation of a narrative character's preparation for bed (1985: 130–1):

> Arthur Dent went to bed. He went up the stairs, all fifteen of them, opened the door, went into his room, took off his shoes and socks and then all the rest of his clothes one by one and left them in a neatly crumpled heap on the floor. He put on his pyjamas, the blue ones with the stripe. He washed his face and hands, cleaned his teeth, went to the lavatory, realized that he had once again got this all in the wrong order, had to wash his hands again and went to bed.

Consistent with these observations, thirty-five years of research has confirmed the fundamentally inferential nature of discourse comprehension (Schank, 1976). These investigations have identified many of the discourse and comprehender factors (Goetz, 1979) that guide inference computation. More importantly, they have situated the empirical results in the context of detailed theoretical statements about language comprehension.

This noteworthy progress should be viewed as setting the stage for further advances in understanding discourse-inference processing, rather than as constituting definitive solutions to these scientific problems. There are numerous contemporary influences that will imminently shape, if not dramatically alter, our understanding of these issues. During the past decade, theorists have advanced novel proposals about the representation both of general knowledge and of specific texts in the form of high-dimensional semantic spaces (Burgess et al., 1998; Landauer and Dumais, 1997). It has been hypothesized that discourse meaning is characterized more aptly in the form of perceptual representations than amodal, propositional ones (Barsalou, 1999; Glenberg and Robertson, 2000; Glenberg, Chapter 21 this volume). Methods of brain imaging inform cognitive theory in a manner not possible fifteen years ago (Bornkessel and

[2] Kintsch and Welsch's (1991) discussion of this example mainly invoked the discourse textbase, but their posited representation met their own situational definition of fusing text information and general knowledge.

Friederici, Chapter 24 this volume; Kutas and Federmeier, Chapter 23 this volume). These advances and controversies strongly suggest that our understanding of inference processing will change appreciably during the coming years.

Acknowledgements

This research was supported by Discovery Grant OGP9800 from the Natural Sciences and Engineering Research Council of Canada. I am grateful to Doug Alards-Tomalin for technical assistance in the preparation of the manuscript.

References

Adams, D. (1985) *So Long and Thanks for All the Fish*. Pan, London.

Albrecht, J. E., and Myers, J. L. (1995) The role of context in accessing distant information during reading. *Journal of Experimental Psychology: Learning, Memory, and Cognition*, 21: 1459–68.

Albrecht, J. E., and Myers, J. L. (1998) Accessing distant text information during reading: effects of contextual cues. *Discourse Processes*, 26: 87–108.

Albritton, D. (2004) Strategic production of predictive inferences during comprehension. *Discourse Processes*, 38: 309–22.

Anderson, J. R. (1974) Retrieval of propositional information from long-term memory. *Cognitive Psychology*, 4: 451–74.

Anderson, J. R. (1976) *Language, Memory, and Thought*. Erlbaum, Hillsdale, NJ.

Anderson, J. R. (1993) *Rules of the Mind*. Erlbaum, Hillsdale, NJ.

Anderson, R. C., Pichert, J. V., Goetz, E. T., Schallert, D. L., Stevens, K. V., and Trollip, S. R. (1976) Instantiation of general terms. *Journal of Verbal Learning and Verbal Behavior*, 15: 667–79.

Attenborough, R. (producer/director) and Nicholson, W. (writer) (1993) *Shadowlands* (motion picture). HBO Studios, USA.

Barsalou, L. W. (1999) Perceptual symbol systems. *Behavioral and Brain Sciences*, 220: 577–660.

Beeman, M. J. (2005) Bilateral brain processes for comprehending natural language. *Trends in Cognitive Sciences*, 9: 512–18.

Black, J. B., and Bern, H. (1981) Causal inference and memory for events in narratives. *Journal of Verbal Learning and Verbal Behavior*, 20: 267–75.

Black, J. B., and Bower, G. H. (1980) Story understanding as problems solving. *Poetics*, 9: 223–50.

Bransford, J. D., Barclay, J. R., and Franks, J. J. (1972) Semantic memory: a constructive versus interpretive approach. *Cognitive Psychology*, 3: 193–209.

Burgess, C., Livesay, K., and Lund, K. (1998) Explorations in context space: words, sentences and discourse. *Discourse Processes*, 25: 211–57.

Calvo, M. G., and Castillo, M. D. (1996) Predictive inferences occur on-line but with delay: convergence of naming and reading times. *Discourse Processes*, 22: 57–78.

Calvo, M. G., Castillo, M. D., and Estevez, A. (1999) On-line predictive inferences in reading: processing time during versus after the priming context. *Memory and Cognition*, 27: 834–43.

Campion, N. (2004) Predictive inferences are represented as hypothetical facts. *Journal of Memory and Language*, 50: 149–54.

Caramazza, A., Grober, E., Garvey, C., and Yates, J. (1977) Comprehension of anaphoric pronouns. *Journal of Verbal Learning and Verbal Behavior*, 16: 601–9.

Charniak, E. (1975) Organization and inference in a frame-like system of common sense knowledge. In R. Schank and B. Nash-Webber (eds), *Theoretical Issues in Natural Language Processing: An Interdisciplinary Workshop*. Massachusetts Institute of Technology, Cambridge, MA.

Clark, H. H., and Clark, E. V. (1977) *Psychology and Language*. Harcourt Brace Jovanovich, New York.

Clark, H. H., and Haviland, S. E. (1977) Comprehension and the given-new contract. In R. Freedle (ed.), *Discourse Production and Comprehension*, Erlbaum, Hillsdale, NJ.

Cook, A. E., Limber, J. E., and O'Brien, E. J. (2001) Situation-based context and the availability of predictive inferences. *Journal of Memory and Language*, 44: 220–34.

Corbett, A. T., and Dosher, B. A. (1978) Instrument inferences in sentence encoding. *Journal of Verbal Learning and Verbal Behavior*, 17: 479–92.

Dubois, D., and Denis, M. (1988) Knowledge organization and instantiation of general terms in sentence comprehension. *Journal of Experimental Psychology: Learning, Memory, and Cognition*, 14: 604–11.

Ehrlich, K. (1980) The comprehension of pronouns. *Quarterly Journal of Experimental Psychology*, 32: 247–56.

Fincher-Kiefer, R., and D'Agostino, P. R. (2004) The role of visuospatial resources in generating predictive and bridging inferences. *Discourse Processes*, 37: 205–24.

Fletcher, C. R. (1981) Short-term memory processes in text comprehension. *Journal of Verbal Learning and Verbal Behavior*, 20: 564–74.

Forster, K. I. (1970) Visual perception of rapidly presented word sequences of varying complexity. *Perception and Psychophysics*, 8: 215–21.

Frederiksen, J. R. (1981) Understanding anaphora: rules used by readers in assigning pronominal referents. *Discourse Processes*, 4: 323–47.

Garrod, S., O'Brien, E. J., Morris, R. K., and Rayner, K. (1990) Elaborative inferences as an active or passive process. *Journal of Experimental Psychology: Learning, Memory, and Cognition*, 16: 250–7.

Glenberg, A. M., and Robertson, D. A. (2000) Symbol grounding: a comparison of high-dimensional and embodied theories of mean. *Journal of Memory and Language*, 43: 379–401.

Goetz, E. T. (1979) Inferring from text: some factors influencing which inferences will be made. *Discourse Processes*, 2: 179–95.

Graesser, A. C., and Bertus, E. L. (1998) The construction of causal inferences while reading expository texts on science and technology. *Scientific Studies of Reading*, 2: 247–69.

Graesser, A. C., and Murachver, T. (1985) Symbolic procedures of question answering. In A. Graesser and J. Black (eds), *The Psychology of Questions*, pp. 15–88. Erlbaum, Hillsdale, NJ.

Graesser, A. C., Robertson, S. P., and Anderson, P. A. (1981) Incorporating inferences in narrative representations: a study of how and why. *Cognitive Psychology*, 13: 1–26.

Graesser, A. C., Singer, M., and Trabasso, T. (1994) Constructing inferences during narrative text comprehension. *Psychological Review*, 101: 371– 95.

Greene, S. B., Gerrig, R. J., McKoon, G., and Ratcliff, R. (1994) Unheralded pronouns and management by common ground. *Journal of Memory and Language*, 35: 511–26.

Gueraud, S., and O'Brien, E. J. (2005) Components of comprehension: a convergence between memory-based processes and explanation-based processes. Special issue, *Discourse Processes*, 39(2–3).

Halldorson, M., and Singer, M. (2002) Inference processes: integrating relevant knowledge and text information. *Discourse Processes*, 34: 145–62.

Halliday, M. A. K., and Hasan, R. (1976) *Cohesion in English*. Longman, London.

Haviland, S. E., and Clark, H. H. (1974) What's new? Acquiring new information as a process in comprehension. *Journal of Verbal Learning and Verbal Behavior*, 13: 512–21.

Johnson, M. K., Bransford, J. D., and Solomon, S. K. (1973) Memory for tacit implications of sentences. *Journal of Experimental Psychology*, 98: 203–5.

Johnson-Laird, P. N. (1983) A computational analysis of consciousness. *Cognition and Brain Theory*, 6: 499–508.

Just, M. A., and Carpenter, P. A. (1980) A theory of reading: from eye fixations to comprehension. *Psychological Review*, 87: 329–54.

Just, M. A. and Carpenter, P. A. (1984) Reading skills and skilled reading in the comprehension of text. In H. Mandl, N. Stein, and T. Trabasso (eds), *Learning and Comprehension of Text*, Erlbaum, Hillsdale, NJ.

Just, M. A., and Carpenter, P. A. (1992) A capacity theory of comprehension: individual differences in working memory. *Psychological Review*, 99: 122–49.

Just, M. A., Carpenter, P. A., and Wooley, J. D. (1982) Paradigms and processes in reading comprehension. *Journal of Experimental Psychology: General*, 111: 228–38.

Keefe, D. E., and McDaniel, M. (1993) The time course and durability of predictive inferences. *Journal of Memory and Language*, 32: 446–63.

Keenan, J. M., Baillet, S. D., and Brown, P. (1984) The effects of causal cohesion on comprehension and memory. *Journal of Verbal Learning and Verbal Behavior*, 23: 115–26.

Keenan, J. M., Potts, G. R., Golding, J. M., and Jennings, T. M. (1990) Which elaborative inferences are drawn during reading? A question of methodologies. In D. Balota, G. Flores d'Arcais, and K. Rayner (eds), *Comprehension Processes in Reading*, pp. 377–402. Erlbaum, Hillsdale, NJ.

Kintsch, W. (1972) Notes on structure of semantic memory. In E. Tulving and W. Donaldson (eds), *Organization of Memory*, Academic Press, New York.

Kintsch, W. (1974) *The Representation of Meaning in Memory*. Erlbaum, Hillsdale, NJ.

Kintsch, W. (1988) The role of knowledge in discourse comprehension: a construction-integration model. *Psychological Review*, 95: 163–82.

Kintsch, W. (1998) *Comprehension*. Cambridge University Press, New York.

Kintsch, W. and Bates, E. (1977) Recognition memory for statements from a classroom lecture. *Journal of Experimental Psychology: Human Learning and Memory*, 3: 150–9.

Kintsch, W., and van Dijk, T. A. (1978) Toward a model of text comprehension and production. *Psychological Review*, 85: 363–94.

Kintsch, W., and Welsch, D. M. (1991) The construction-integration model: a framework for studying memory for text. In W. E. Hockley and S. Lewandowsky (eds), *Relating Theory and Data: Essays on Human Memory in honor of Bennet B. Murdock*, pp. 367–85. Erlbaum, Hillsdale, NJ.

Kintsch, W., Welsch, D., Schmalhofer, F., and Zimny, S. (1990) Sentence memory: a theoretical analysis. *Journal of Memory and Language*, 29: 133–59.

Klin, C. M. (1995) Causal inferences in reading: from immediate activation to long term memory. *Journal of Experimental Psychology: Learning, Memory, and Cognition*, 21: 1483–94.

Klin, C. M., Guzman, A. E., and Levine, W. H. (1999) Prevalence and persistence of predictive inferences. *Journal of Memory and Language*, 40: 593–604.

Kutas, M., and Hilyard, S. A. (1980) Reading senseless sentences: brain potentials reflect semantic incongruity. *Science*, 207: 203–5.

Landauer, T. K., and Dumais, S. T. (1997) A solution to Plato's problem: the latent semantic analysis theory of acquisition induction and representation of knowledge. *Psychological Review*, 104: 211–40.

Lesgold, A. M., Roth, S. F., and Curtis, M. E. (1979) Foregrounding effects in discourse comprehension. *Journal of Verbal Learning and Verbal Behavior*, 18: 291–308.

Long, D. L., Golding, J. M., and Graesser, A. C. (1992) A test of the on-line status of goal-related elaborative inferences. *Journal of Memory and Language*, 31: 634–47.

Long, D. L., Seely, M. R., and Oppy, B. J. (1996) The availability of causal information during reading. *Discourse Processes*, 22: 145–70.

Lucas, M. M., Tanenhaus, M. K., and Carlson, G. N. (1990) Levels of representation in the interpretation of anaphoric reference and instrument inference. *Memory and Cognition*, 18: 611–31.

Lutz, M. F., and Radvansky, G. A. (1997) The fate of completed goal information. *Journal of Memory and Language* 36: 293–310.

Magliano, J. P., and Graesser, A. C. (1991) A three-pronged method for studying inference generation in literary texts. *Poetics*, 20: 193–232.

Magliano, J. P., Graesser, A. C., Eymard, L. A., Haberlandt, K., and Gholson, B. (1993) Locus of interpretive and inference processes during text comprehension: a comparison of gaze durations and word reading times. *Journal of Experimental Psychology: Learning, Memory, and Cognition*, 19: 704–9.

Mason, R. A., and Just, M. A. (2004) How the brain processes causal inferences in text. *Psychological Science*, 15: 1–7.

Masson, M. E. J. (1984) Priming word identification with rapidly presented sentences. Paper presented at the annual meeting of the Psychonomic Society, San Antonio, TX.

Mauner, G. Tanenhaus, M. K., and Carlson, G. N. (1995) Implicit arguments in sentence processing. *Journal of Memory and Language*, 34: 357–82.

McKoon, G. Gerrig, R. J., and Greene, S. B. (1996) Pronoun resolution without pronouns: some consequences of memory based text processing. *Journal of Experimental Psychology: Learning, Memory, and Cognition*, 22: 919–32.

McKoon, G. and Ratcliff, R. (1986) Inferences about predictable events. *Journal of Experimental Psychology: Learning, Memory, and Cognition*, 12: 82–91.

McKoon, G., and Ratcliff, R. (1988) Contextually relevant aspects of meaning. *Journal of Experimental Psychology: Learning, Memory, and Cognition*, 14: 331–43.

McKoon, G., and Ratcliff, R. (1989) Inferences about contextually defined categories. *Journal of Experimental Psychology: Learning, Memory, and Cognition*, 15: 1134–46.

McKoon, G., and Ratcliff, R. (1990) Textual inferences: models and measures. In D. Balota, G. Flores d'Arcais, and K. Rayner (eds), *Comprehension Processes in Reading*, pp. 403–21. Erlbaum, Hillsdale, NJ.

McKoon, G., and Ratcliff, R. (1992) Inference during reading. *Psychological Review*, 99: 440–66.

Miller, J. R. (1980) The role of knowledge and text structure in prose comprehension. MS, Department of Psychology, University of Colorado, Boulder.

Millis, K. K., and Graesser, A. C. (1994) The time-course of constructing knowledge-based inferences for scientific texts. *Journal of Language and Memory*, 33: 583–99.

Morrow, D. G., Greenspan, S. L., and Bower, G. H. (1987) Accessibility and situation models in narrative comprehension. *Journal of Memory and Language*, 2: 165–87.

Murray, J. D., Klin, C., M. and Myers, J. L. (1993) Forward inferences about specific events in reading. *Journal of Memory and Language*, 32: 464–73.

Myers, J. L., and Duffy, S. A. (1990) Causal inferences and text memory. In A. Graesser and G. Bower (eds), *Psychology of Learning and Motivation*, 25: 159–73.

Myers, J. L., and O'Brien, E. J. (1998) Accessing the discourse representation during reading. *Discourse Processes*, 26: 131–58.

Myers, J. L., Shinjo, M., and Duffy, S. A. (1987) Degree of causal relatedness and memory. *Journal of Verbal Learning and Verbal Behavior*, 26: 453–65.

Noordman, G. M., Vonk, W., and Kempff, H. J. (1992) Causal inferences during the reading of expository texts. *Journal of Memory and Language*, 31: 573–90.

O'Brien, E. J., and Albrecht, J. E. (1991) The role of context in accessing antecedents in text. *Journal of Experimental Psychology: Learning, Memory, and Cognition*, 17: 94–102.

O'Brien, E. J., Albrecht, J. E., Hakala, C. M., and Rizzella, M. L. (1995) Activation and suppression of antecedents during reinstatement. *Journal of Experimental Psychology: Learning, Memory, and Cognition*, 21: 626–34.

O'Brien, E. J., Shank, D. M., Myers, J. L., and Rayner, K. (1988) Elaborative inferences during reading: do they occur on-line? *Journal of Experimental Psychology: Learning, Memory, and Cognition*, 14: 410–20.

Olson, G. M., Duffy, S. A., and Mack, R. L. (1984) Thinking-out-loud as a method for studying real-time comprehension processes. In D. Kieras and M. Just (eds), *New methods in reading comprehension research*, pp. 253–86. Erlbaum, Hillsdale, NJ.

Perrig, W., and Kintsch, W. (1985) Propositional and situational representations of text. *Journal of Memory and Language*, 24: 503–18.

Potts, G. R. (1972) Information-processing strategies used in the encoding of linear orders. *Journal of Verbal Learning and Verbal Behavior*, 11: 727–40.

Potts, G. R., Keenan, J. M., and Golding, J. M. (1988) Assessing the occurrence of elaborative inferences: lexical decision versus naming. *Journal of Memory and Language*, 27: 399–415.

Radvansky, G. A. (1998) The organization of information retrieved from situation models. *Psychonomic Bulletin and Review*, 5: 283–9.

Radvansky, G. A., and Copeland, D. E. (2000) Functionality and spatial relations in memory and language. *Memory and Cognition*, 28: 987–92.

Radvansky, G. A., Wyer, R. S., Jr, Curiel, J. M., and Lutz, M. F. (1997) Situation models and abstract ownership relations. *Journal of Experimental Psychology: Learning, Memory, and Cognition*, 23: 1233–46.

Radvansky, G. A., Zwaan, R. A., Federico, T., and Franklin, N. (1998) Retrieval from temporally organized situation models. *Journal of Experimental Psychology: Learning, Memory, and Cognition*, 24: 1224–37.

Ratcliff, R. (1978) A theory of memory retrieval. *Psychological Review*, 85: 59–108.

Rayner, K. (1983) The perceptual span and eye movement control during reading. In K. Rayner (ed.), *Eye Movements in Reading: Perceptual and Language Processes*, Academic Press, New York.

Reichel, E. D., and Mason, R. A. (forthcoming) The neural signatures of causal inferences. In F. Schmalhofer and C. Perfetti (eds), *Higher Level Language Processes in the Brain: Inference and Comprehension Processes.* Erlbaum, Mahwah, NJ.

Richards, E., and Singer, M. (2001) Representation of complex goal structures in narrative comprehension. *Discourse Processes*, 31: 111–35.

Rieger, C. (1975) The commonsense algorithm as a basis for computer models of human memory, inference, belief, and contextual language comprehension. In R. Schank and B. Nash-Webber (eds), *Theoretical Issues in Natural Language Processing: An Interdisciplinary Workshop*. MIT Press, Cambridge, MA.

Rinck, M., Hahnel, A., and Becker, G. (2001) Using temporal information to construct, update, and retrieve situation models of narratives. *Journal of Experimental Psychology: Learning, Memory, and Cognition*, 27: 67–80.

Rizzella, M. L., and O'Brien, E. J. (1996) Accessing global causes during reading. *Journal of Experimental Psychology: Learning, Memory, and Cognition*, 22: 1208–18.

Rumelhart, D. E., and McClelland, J. L. (1986) *Parallel Distributed Processing: Explorations in the Microstructure of Cognition*, vol 1. MIT Press, Cambridge, MA.

Sanford, A. J., and Garrod, S. (1998) The role of scenario mapping in text comprehension. *Discourse Processes*, 26: 159–90.

Schank, R. C. (1976) The role of memory in language processing. In C. Cofer (ed.), *The Nature of Human Memory*. Freeman, San Francisco, CA.

Schmalhofer, F., and Glavanov, D. (1986) Three components of understanding a programmer's manual: verbatim, propositional, and situation representations. *Journal of Memory and Language*, 25: 279–94.

Schmalhofer, F., McDaniel, M. A., and Keefe, D. E. (2002) A unified model for predictive and bridging inferences. *Discourse Processes*, 33: 105–32.

Sharkey, N. E., and Bower, G. H. (1987) A model of memory organization for interacting goals. In P. Morris (ed.), *Modelling Cognition*, pp. 231–48. Wiley, Chichester, UK.

Singer, M. (1980) The role of case-filling inferences in the coherence of brief passages. *Discourse Processes*, 3: 185–201.

Singer, M. (1996) Comprehending consistent and inconsistent causal text sequences: a construction-integration analysis. *Discourse Processes*, 21: 1–21.

Singer, M., and Ferreira, F. (1983) Inferring consequences in story comprehension. *Journal of Verbal Learning and Verbal Behavior*, 22: 437–48.

Singer, M., Graesser, A. C., and Trabasso, T. (1994) Minimal or global inference in reading. *Journal of Memory and Language*, 33: 421–41.

Singer, M., and Halldorson, M. (1996) Constructing and validating motive bridging inferences. *Cognitive Psychology*, 30: 1–38.

Singer, M., Halldorson, M., Lear, J. C., and Andrusiak, P. (1992) Validation of causal bridging inferences. *Journal of Memory and Language*, 31: 507–24.

Singer, M., Harkness, D., and Stewart, S. T. (1997) Constructing inferences in expository text comprehension. *Discourse Processes*, 24: 199–228.

Singer, M., and Kintsch, W. (2001) Text retrieval: a theoretical exploration. *Discourse Processes*, 31: 27–59.

Singer, M., and O'Connell, G. (2003) Robust inference processes in expository text comprehension. *European Journal of Cognitive Psychology*, 15: 607–31.

Smith, E. E., Adams, N., and Schorr, D. (1978) Fact retrieval and the paradox of interference. *Cognitive Psychology*, 10: 438–64.

Springston, F. J. (1975) Some cognitive aspects of presupposed coreferential anaphora. Doctoral dissertation, Stanford University.

St George, M., Mannes, S., and Hoffman, J. E. (1997) Individual differences in inference processing. *Journal of Cognitive Neuroscience*, 9: 776–87.

Suh, S., and Trabasso, T. (1993) Inferences during reading: converging evidence from discourse analysis talk-aloud protocols and recognition priming. *Journal of Memory and Language*, 32: 279–300.

Sulin, R. A., and Dooling, D. J. (1974) Intrusion of a thematic idea in retention of prose. *Journal of Experimental Psychology*, 103: 255–62.

Till, R. E., Mross, E. F., and Kintsch, W. (1988) Time course of priming for associate and inference words in a discourse context. *Memory and Cognition*, 16: 283–98.

Trabasso, T., and Suh, S. (1993) Understanding text: achieving explanatory coherence through on-line inferences and mental operations in working memory. *Discourse Processes*, 16: 3–34.

Trabasso, T., van den Broek, P., and Suh, S. Y. (1989) Logical necessity and transitivity of causal relations in stories. *Discourse Processes*, 12: 1–25.

van Berkum, J. J. A., Zwiterslood, P., Hagoort, P., and Brown, C. (2003) When and how do listeners relate a sentence to the wider discourse? Evidence from the N400 effect. *Cognitive Brain Research*, 17: 701–18.

van den Broek, P. (1990) Causal inferences and the comprehension of narrative texts. In A. Graesser and G. Bower (eds), *The Psychology of Learning and Motivation*, vol. 25: pp. 175–96. Academic Press, New York.

van den Broek, P., and Lorch, Jr R. F. (1993) Network representations of causal relations in memory for narrative texts: evidence from primed recognition. *Discourse Processes*, 16: 75–98.

van Dijk, T. A., and Kintsch, W. (1983) Strategies of discourse comprehension. Academic Press, New York.

Virtue, S., Haberman, J., Clancy, Z., Parrish, T., and Beeman, M. J. (forthcoming) Neural activity during inference generation. *Cognitive Brain Research*.

Vonk, W. (1985) The immediacy of inferences in the understanding of pronouns. In G. Rickheit and H. Strohner (eds), *Advances in Psychology 29: Inferences in Text Processing*, pp. 205–18. North-Holland, Amsterdam.

Weingartner, K. M., Guzman, A. E., Levine, W. H., and Klin, C. M. (2003) When throwing a vase has multiple consequences: minimal encoding of predictive inferences. *Discourse Processes*, 36: 131–46.

Whitney, P. (1986) Processing category terms in context: instantiations as inferences. *Memory and Cognition*, 14: 39–48.

Wilson, S. G., Rinck, M., McNamara, T. P., Bower, G. H., and Morrow, D. G. (1993) Mental models and narrative comprehension: some qualifications. *Journal of Memory and Language*, 32: 141–54.

Yekovich, F. R.,Walker, C. H., and Blackman, H. S. (1979) The role of presupposed and focal information in integrating sentences. *Journal of Verbal Learning and Verbal Behavior*, 18: 535–48.

Zwaan, R. A., Magliano, J. P., and Graesser, A. C. (1995) Dimensions of situation-model construction in narrative comprehension. *Journal of Experimental Psychology: Learning, Memory, and Cognition*, 21: 386–97.

Zwaan, R. A., and Radvansky, G. A. (1998) Situation models in language comprehension and memory. *Psychological Bulletin*, 123: 162–85.

Zwaan, R. A., and van Oostendorp, H. (1993) Do readers construct spatial representations in naturalistic story comprehension? *Discourse Processes*, 16: 125–43.

CHAPTER 21

Language and action: creating sensible combinations of ideas

Arthur M. Glenberg

COULD two topics be less related than language and action? Both historical (e.g. Descartes, 1992) and contemporary (e.g. Fodor, 1975) philosophers have argued that language is separate from perception and action, that it is a higher faculty, or that it is what separates human from animal. The data, however, present an overwhelming case in favor of an intimate relation between language and action. Much of the data and theory derive from considerations of embodied cognition, and so this chapter begins with a brief overview of that notion. Then, the relation between language and action is considered from the perspectives of neuroscience, cognitive development, and behavioral research. The chapter will conclude with a theoretical rationale for the relation: the mechanism of action planning is the mechanism that allows us to sensibly combine meanings across words and sentences.

21.1 Embodied cognition

The embodied cognition framework has been applied to variety of areas including memory (e.g. Glenberg, 1997), concepts (Barsalou, 1999), language (Glenberg and Kaschak, 2004; Lakoff, 1987; Zwaan, 2004), social psychology (Barsalou et al., 2003), and development (Thelen and Smith, 1994). A common theme that runs through these endeavors is that facts of the body (e.g. morphology, perceptual processes) play a prominent role in cognition. Glenberg et al. (forthcoming) characterize embodied approaches to language:

> Linguistic symbols are embodied to the extent that a) the meaning of the symbol ... depends on activity in systems also used for perception, action, and emotion, and b) reasoning about meaning, including combinatorial processes of sentence understanding, requires use of those systems.

At first blush, the notion that language calls upon processes of perception, action, and so on would seem to flounder on the apparent fact that language deals with abstractions such as the meanings of a words, grammatical categories, and generalized syntactic processes (see Vigliocco and Vinson, Chapter 12 this volume). In contrast, Barsalou (1999) discusses conceptual systems built from perceptual symbols. Perceptual symbols are collections of neural activity based on attended aspects of experience, such as shape, sound, and so on. Repeated experience results in different aspects being attended and hence greater knowledge. Importantly, the neural activities which compose perceptual symbols are maintained in the neural systems originally used in perceiving and acting. Thus, for example, the shape of an airplane is represented as a trace of neural activity in the visual system, whereas the sound of the airplane is represented in the auditory system. Perceptual symbols can enter into simulations of various situations, such as an airplane landing or taking off. These simulations are a type of imagery, although there is no requirement that the imagery be consciously experienced, particularly when dealing with familiar situations which may have resulted in simulations becoming automated. Furthermore, Barsalou discusses how a conceptual system based on perceptual symbols and simulators has the power to account for inferences, abstract ideas such as negation, and compositionality. Thus, perceptual symbols constitute a fully functional conceptual system.

The idea that conceptual processes are embodied is supported by several types of data. First, work in the neurosciences demonstrates that language comprehension results in activation in many areas of the brain that bear a systematic relation to the content of the language. For example, language about visual motion produces activation in those areas of the brain (MT/V5) strongly associated with the perception of visual motion (Tettamanti et al., 2005). If language were purely symbolic and divorced from bodily mechanisms such as perception, then this systematicity would have to be treated as an amazing coincidence. Second, behavioral work has demonstrated interactions between language comprehension and tasks that are demonstrably related to perception, action, and emotion. Finally, work in language development shows strong links between bodily mechanisms and language acquisition. We turn to these sources of evidence now.

21.2 **The neuroscience of language and action**

Neuroscience has provided multiple demonstrations of the overlap between areas of the brain contributing to language and those contributing to action (particularly useful reviews are provided by Pulvermuller, 2005, and Rizzolatti and Craighero, Chapter 47 this volume). What happens in our brains when we hear words such as *pick*, *kick*, and *lick*? Of course, there is activation in the left temporal lobe (e.g. Wernicke's area) traditionally associated with language perception. Somewhat surprisingly, there is also activation in the prefrontal area (e.g. Broca's region) normally thought of as contributing to speech production (e.g. Fadiga et al., 2002). The big surprise, however, concerns activation in areas of the brain associated with motor activity. For example, Hauk et al. (2004) used functional magnetic resonance imagery (fMRI) to record brain activity while people listened to verbs. When they were listening to verbs referring to leg actions, regions of the motor cortex that control the leg were particularly active, when they were listening to verbs referring to hand actions, regions of the motor cortex that control the hand were particularly active, and so on. Similarly, Tettamanti et al. (2005) tracked areas of activation while people listened to sentences using verbs requiring mouth actions (e.g. *I eat an apple*), hand actions (e.g. *I grasp the knife*), and leg actions (e.g. *I kick the ball*). As predicted by the embodiment position, these sentences selectively activated areas of the brain associated with mouth, hand, and leg actions, respectively.

The fMRI findings can be interpreted in several ways. The data could indicate that understanding these verbs requires activity in motor areas of the brain. Or the results might simply reflect a habit of envisioning action after hearing action verbs. The balance of the research points strongly to the first interpretation. For example, Pulvermuller et al. (2003) demonstrated that activity in the motor areas occurs very soon (e.g. 20 msec) after the word produces peak activation in areas of the brain traditionally associated with language. The speed of activation would appear to rule out a conscious or optional process. Pulvermüller et al. (2005) activated motor areas using transcranial magnetic stimulation (TMS). When left-hemisphere leg motor areas were activated, people were fast at identifying leg-related words, and when left-hemisphere arm motor areas were activated, people were fast at identifying arm-related words. Finally, Buccino et al. (2005) reported related findings for whole sentences. That is, when people listened to sentences describing leg (or arm) movements while TMS was applied to leg (or arm) motor centers, there was differential modulation of electrical activity recorded in the legs (or arms). Thus, there are strong connections between language and action that can be found in the brain and that extend out to the periphery of the body. The time-course of the effect is too quick, and the causal pathways demonstrated by TMS too convincing, to believe that the link between language and action is optional.

Another finding from the neuroscience literature helps to cement the relation between language and action. Rizzolatti and Arbib (1998) review data on the mirror neuron system and the relation between that system and language. Mirror neurons were first discovered in an area of monkey prefrontal cortex (F5). The mirror neurons in this area respond when the animal takes a particular action, such as ripping a sheet of paper. The same neuron will respond when the animal observes another monkey or a human performing the same action. In fact, the neuron will also respond when the animal simply hears paper being ripped (Kohler et al., 2002). The mirror neuron system has been associated with the ability to recognize the intent of a conspecific's actions (e.g. you understand the intent of another person's gesture because the mirror neurons firing are those that would fire when you take action with the same intent), and hence the system is thought to be particularly important for empathy and social interaction (Gallese et al., 2004).

The story becomes more interesting for the connection between language and action because area F5 in the monkey brain is a homolog of Broca's area (which is involved in speech production) in the human brain. Once this correspondence was noted, research demonstrated that the human Broca's area also contains neurons with mirror-like properties (Fadiga et al., 1995), and that parts of Broca's area control not just the speech articulators but also the hand (Binkofski et al., 1999). From these various correspondences, Rizzolatti and Arbib (1998) suggest that oral language developed from the ability to recognize the communicative intent of actions and gestures. That is, Broca's area evolved into a language area because of its prior usefulness in gestural communication.

The tremendous overlap between neural structures contributing to language and hand/arm movement may help to explain the prevalence of hand gesture in language (McNeill, 1992). Gestures while speaking are nearly universal. Even congenitally blind people speaking to blind listeners gesture (Iverson and Golden-Meadow, 2001), so gesture is unlikely to be something learned or consciously planned for the benefit of the listener. Nonetheless, gestures do enhance communication (e.g. Valenzeno et al., 2003; Kelly et al., 1999). With two assumptions, it becomes clear why gestures are so prevalent while speaking. The first assumption is that much of meaning is based on action, i.e. what a sentence means to a listener consists of how that sentence describes, suggests, or modulates actions. Data supporting this assumption is reviewed in section 21.4. The second assumption is that meaning can only be determined by utilizing the motor system (section 21.5.2). Thus, sentences convey meanings which have action at their core, and many of our humanly important actions involve the hand (e.g. giving, eating, threatening, or appeasing). Broca's area controls both the speech articulators (e.g. lips, tongue) and the hand. Thus, there can be near-simultaneous activation of the speech apparatus and the hand in the service of the same message.

21.3 Developmental support for the language and action connection

Several recent reports in the language acquisition literature provide confirmation of the relation between language and action. One particularly interesting set of studies was reported by Smith (2005), who documented the causal relations amongst action, naming, and categorization in children between 24 and 35 months old. In one experiment, children were given a graspable toy shaped roughly like an asymmetric barbell—i.e. there were bumps on both ends, but one bump was larger. The children were told that the object was a *wug*. Half the children were taught to hold the wug using both hands, with one hand on each bump, and to play with it by rotating the wrists. Note that this activity treats the wug in a symmetrical manner. The other children were taught to hold the wug by using one hand to grasp the smaller bump and to wave the wug about. This activity treats the wug in an asymmetrical manner. Following these activities, children were shown other objects that were either more symmetrical or less symmetrical than the original, and were asked to determine which were wugs. Children who acted on the original wug in a symmetrical manner were more likely to classify symmetrical variations as wugs than were the children who acted on the original in an asymmetrical manner, and the reverse was found for the asymmetrical variations. In other words, how the children interacted with the original wug helped to determine what other objects would be called the same name.

21.4 Behavioral support for the connection between language and action

Behavioral work with adults has also produced strong evidence for the interaction of action and language across multiple levels of language processing: grammatical, basic word meaning, and the meanings of sentences about concrete and abstract situations, as well as the interpretation of extended dialog (Noice and Noice, forthcoming; Ochs et al. 1996; Roth, 1999). An important concept that occurs throughout this work is that of an "affordance." Gibson (1979) coined the term to refer to possible interactions between biological and physical systems. Thus, a chair affords sitting for organisms with the right sort of body morphology (e.g. humans, but not elephants). Some types of chair also afford hiding under for toddlers, but not for adults, whereas some chairs afford throwing in anger by adults, but not by toddlers because they are not strong enough. In brief, what an object affords depends on the body of the organism interacting with the object. Gibson proposed that the function of perceptual systems is to detect affordances that direct action.

Chambers et al. (2004) used the concept of affordances to show the relation between action and grammatical parsing. In their experiments, participants were faced with real situations, such as that illustrated in Figure 21.1, and they heard instructions regarding how to move the objects. One instruction was *Put the whistle on the folder in the box*. Note that there are two whistles in the situation. Thus, clear communication must use some sort of language (or gesture) to discriminate between the two whistles, and that is exactly the function of the phrase *on the folder*. That is, which whistle should be moved? The whistle that is *on the folder*. In another condition, people held a hook and used it to move objects. In this condition, even though both whistles were physically present, there was only one whistle that afforded moving, namely the one with the lanyard that can be grabbed with the hook. Thus, when holding the hook, there is really only one whistle to consider, and the phrase *on the folder* is redundant at best (indicating which whistle to move, but we already know that it is the one with the lanyard) or easily misinterpreted at worst. That is, when holding the hook and listening to the sentence *Put the whistle on the folder...*, people could reasonably interpret *on the folder* as a phrase indicating where the (afforded) whistle might be moved. In fact, when holding the hook, people tended to look at the empty folder (as if they were preparing to move the whistle there) much more frequently than when they were not holding the hook. The point is that the affordances of the situation determined how people parsed the phrase *on the folder*. With the "no-hook" affordances, the phrase was parsed as a reduced relative clause indicating which whistle to move; with the "hook" affordances, the phrase was parsed as a prepositional phrase describing where the whistle was to be moved.

Borghi et al. (2004) also used the concept of affordances to demonstrate that the basic meaning of a word taps action. In one of their experiments, participants read a sentence that mentioned an object, e.g. *There is a car in front of you*. Then, the participant pressed the middle button of a vertically oriented three-button panel. Pressing this button revealed a target word such as *roof*, *wheel*, or *road*. At that point, the participant was to determine if the target was a part of the object named in the sentence (yes for *roof* and *wheel*) or not (for *road*). Note that interacting with the roof of a car normally requires action directed upwards, whereas interacting with the wheel of a car normally requires action directed downwards. Suppose that these different affordances are part of the basic meanings of *car*, *roof*, and *wheel*. That is, suppose that just thinking of the meaning of a word such as *roof* prepares one to act upwards. In this case, participants required to move upwards to the top response button to indicate "yes," should respond faster to a target such as *roof* than participants required to move downwards to indicate "yes." In contrast, for a target word such as *wheel*, those participants required to move downwards should respond faster. This is exactly what Borghi et al. (2004) found. Apparently, when we think about

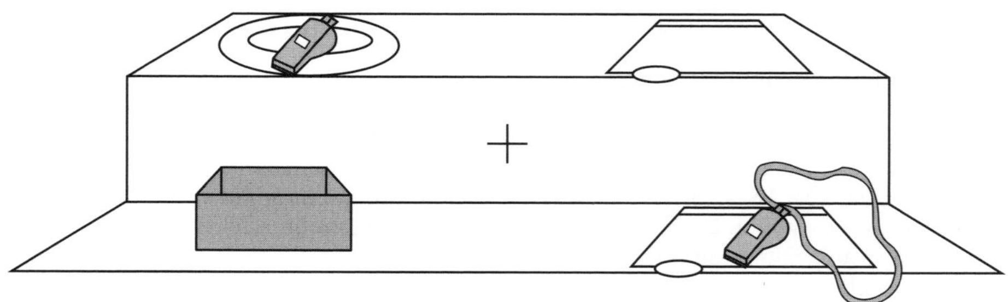

Figure 21.1 Illustration of one environment used in Chambers et al. (2004). Reprinted from *Journal of Experimental Psychology: Learning, Memory, and Cognition*, vol. 30: C. G. Chambers, M. K. Tanenhaus, and J. S. Magnuson, 'Actions and affordances in syntactic ambiguity resolution', pp. 687–96 (copyright © 2004), with permission from the American Psychological Association.

the meaning of a word, at least part of that meaning is in terms of how to act on the object named by the word.

Glenberg and Kaschak (2002) used a similar methodology to determine the contribution of action to the interpretation of whole sentences. The task was to judge if a sentence was sensible (e.g. *Courtney handed you the notebook* or *You handed Courtney the notebook*) or nonsense (e.g. *You drank the house to Joe*). The sensible judgement was made by moving to a button requiring movement away from the body (in one condition) or toward the body (in the other condition). As with the *Courtney* sentences, half of the sensible sentences described action toward the reader and half away. If sentence understanding requires a determination of direction using action systems, then readers literally moving a hand toward the body to make the "sensible" judgement should respond faster to sentences describing action toward the body than to sentences describing action away. The opposite should be found for those readers required to respond "sensibly" by a moving a hand away from the body. This interaction was found, thus demonstrating a contribution of action to sentence comprehension.

The data described so far involve language about concrete objects and activities. But language can also be used to describe abstract feelings, events, transitions, and so on. At first glance, it would appear that action could not possibly contribute to understanding language of this sort; but the data indicate otherwise. One such illustration comes from the Glenberg and Kaschak (2002). In addition to sentences describing the transfer of concrete objects, some described transfer of information from one person to another, e.g. *Liz told you the story* or *You told Liz the story*. The same interaction of transfer direction and literal response direction was found, implying a contribution of mechanisms of action to language understanding of at least some abstract situations.

More impressive are the data from Matlock (2004). Her participants first read descriptions of terrains, for example of a desert described as smooth and flat or as rocky and hilly. Matlock then timed the participants' reading of target sentences such as *A fence runs through it.* These sentences describe "fictive" motion (Talmy, 1996), i.e. nothing mentioned in the sentence is literally moving. Nonetheless, Matlock observed that people took substantially longer to read target sentences describing fictive motion through complex terrains than through simple terrains. That is, people seemed to be simulating movement through the terrain as they cognitively followed the fence. See Vigliocco and Vinson (Chapter 12 this volume) for further discussion of the representation of abstract knowledge.

21.5 Language as an opportunistic system

The data from a variety of literatures are convincing: contrary to first impressions, there are strong connections between language and action. Why? The Indexical Hypothesis (Glenberg and Robertson, 1999; 2000; Kaschak and Glenberg, 2000) begins to answer this question. According to the Indexical Hypothesis, language understanding makes use of three processes (none of which need be consciously experienced). The first process is using words and phrases to index (i.e. map to) objects and events in the world or their perceptual symbols. That is, upon hearing a sentence such as *Courtney handed you the pizza*, one indexes *the pizza* to a real pizza in the environment or to a perceptual symbol of a pizza. Second, one derives affordances from the indexed objects. Note that affordances cannot be derived directly from words because words do not have affordances in the traditional sense of supporting bodily interaction; only objects do. Any object, however, may have a tremendously large number of affordances, so which are considered? Derivation of the affordances is controlled in part by syntax. According to construction grammar (e.g. Goldberg, 1995), many sentence forms carry with them information about goals. For example, double-object sentences, such as the one about Courtney (the two objects are *you* and *the pizza*), carry the goal of transfer. Therefore, in deriving affordances for objects mentioned in a double-object sentence, the focus is on those affordances that might be relevant to transfer, in contrast, say, to eating.

The third process specified by the Indexical Hypothesis is combining, or meshing, affordances as specified by syntax. As just noted, the double-object syntax indicates that the pizza is transferred to *you* from Courtney by means of handing. The third process determines how the affordances can be integrated to satisfy the goals (e.g. transfer) and specifications (to you from Courtney) provided by syntax. Only when all three processes—indexing, derivation of appropriate affordances, and meshing—are successful is the sentence understood. For example, if you happen to have a dog named Courtney and you indexed *Courtney* to your dog, you would have difficulty understanding the sentence because dogs do not have the body morphology that allows the affordance of handing. As another example, the sentence *You drank the house to Joe* is difficult to understand because people do not have the body morphology for drinking to transfer a solid object from one person to another. In a world inhabited by creatures with long, large, and flexible digestive systems, however, the sentence might be perfectly acceptable.

Given the power of other approaches to meaning (see Vigliocco and Vinson, Chapter 12 this volume), it is difficult to incisively demonstrate the operation of affordances and mesh. Kaschak and Glenberg (2000) attempted to do so by using innovative language. Because innovations are made up and interpreted on the fly, it is unlikely that the words have long-term semantic representations; instead, meaning must be derived from the situation. Kaschak and Glenberg (2000), asked participants to understand sentences containing innovative denominal verbs. Denominal verbs are made from nouns, such as *to bicycle*. Innovative denominal verbs such as *porched* in *The newsboy porched the paper* (Clark and Clark, 1979) appear to be understood with little effort. Kaschak and Glenberg investigated the hypothesis that people will only understand a sentence with an innovative denominal verb when the object named by the verb has the affordances needed to accomplish the goal specified by the syntactic construction. For example, consider this scenario with two alternative endings:

> A man with a broken leg was eating a hard-boiled egg on a park bench when a soccer ball rolled up from a game being played by school girls. He crutched the girls the ball/He egg-shelled the girls the ball.

Note that neither *to crutch* nor *to egg-shell* is a verb in standard English. Thus, on many accounts, both versions should be seen as nonsense. Nonetheless, the first alternative ending is comprehensible whereas the second is not. Kaschak and Glenberg's (2000) interpretation makes use of the Indexical Hypothesis. The double-object syntax carries the goal of transfer. Here, the soccer ball is transferred from the man to the girls. In the case of *to crutch*, the mechanism of transfer is a crutch, and crutches have the right affordances to transfer a soccer ball. Hence, the affordances can be meshed, as directed by syntax, into a smooth and coherent set of actions that accomplish the goal of transfer, and the sentence is understood. In contrast, egg-shells do not afford transfer of soccer balls. Consequently, comprehension fails for the egg-shell sentence.

21.5.1 **Why language and action are related: an evolutionary argument**

Whereas the Indexical Hypothesis helps us to understand how action systems are used in language comprehension, it does not provide a reason for the intimate connection between language and action. Did it have to be this way? There are two ways to answer this question in the affirmative: yes because of evolutionary pressure; and yes because of function. The evolutionary idea was briefly noted before. Rizzolatti and Arbib (1998) begin with the observation that mirror neurons are a type of communicative device in that they allow signals, i.e. actions produced by one animal, to be comprehended by another. Furthermore, mirror neurons are found in what was to evolve into Broca's area. Finally, there is some evidence (see Craighero and Rizzolatti, this volume) that hand shapes used to grasp large objects invoke an opening of the mouth consistent with vowels used in words designating large objects, and hand shapes used to grasp small objects invoke an opening of the mouth consistent with vowels used in words designating tiny objects. Thus, Craighero and Rizzolatti speculate that oral sounds began to accompany gestures automatically by virtue of the overlap between hand and mouth control in Broca's area. Then, the system of oral communication advanced with evolutionary pressure to communicate quickly, accurately, and under circumstances where gesture is not useful, such as in the dark.

21.5.2 **Why language and action are related: a functional argument**

The functional answer to the question of why language and action are related is based on three conjectures. First, language is a system that depends on combinations of parts (e.g. words). Second, language is opportunistic, i.e. it will use whatever brain mechanisms are available to accomplish the task. Third, action planning is the brain's most well-developed system for producing effective, goal-directed combinations of parts, namely combinations of actions to accomplish a goal.

The first conjecture does not need much defense. Language makes use of a relatively small number of words and rules to create a very large number of meanings and communications. The key is to combine these parts in the right ways.

To what extent is language opportunistic? This chapter has already reviewed data demonstrating that language calls upon action systems. The case can also be made for language calling on perception and emotion systems. For example,

Kaschak et al. (2005) had participants listen to and judge the sensibility of sentences conveying motion in specific directions such as toward an observer (e.g. *The car approached you*) or away (e.g. *The squirrel scurried away*). Simultaneously, the participant looked at a spiral spinning so as to convey visual motion toward or away. Kaschak et al. found that sensibility judgements were slowed by the visual stimulus conveying motion in the same direction as implied by the sentence. Apparently, the same visual processing system required for perceiving the spiral motion was also required for understanding the sentence. Because that system was engaged, sentence understanding was slowed (see Tettamanti et al., 2005 for neural imaging data demonstrating activation of visual processing areas in understanding language about actions).

The case can also be made that language is opportunistic in regard to emotion. Glenberg et al. (2005) report an effect of emotion on the ease of language comprehension. They induced emotions using the Strack et al. (1988) procedure. Participants were asked to hold a pen using only their teeth (inducing a smile and a pleasant emotional state) or lips (inducing a frown or pout and a negative emotional state). Concurrently, participants read sentences describing pleasant situations (e.g. *Your lover chases you playfully around the bedroom*) or unpleasant situations. The pleasant sentences were read more quickly when the participant was smiling than when frowning, and sentences describing negative situations were read more quickly when frowning than when smiling. (The question of when embodied states facilitate language comprehension, as in Glenberg et al., 2005, and when they interfere, as in Kaschak et al., 2005, remains to be answered.) Thus, understanding language about emotional situations may call upon neural systems controlling emotion.

Is language an opportunistic system? Although the case for language being opportunistic is just starting to be made, in fact, wherever psychologists and neuroscientists have looked, they have found neural systems that evolved for one purpose (e.g. action, perception, emotion) being used for language comprehension.

The third conjecture is that the action planning system is the brain's best-developed system for producing effective, goal-directed combinations of parts. That is, even simple transitive actions (e.g. picking up a coffee cup and moving it to the lips) requires combinations of multiple muscles (e.g. in the hand and arm) and muscle systems (e.g. those muscles controlling eye movements and posture). Consider further that the goals of similar actions can be tremendously variable (a coffee cup can be picked up for drinking, for throwing, for admiring, for trapping an insect, etc.). Apparently, actions cannot be based solely on fixed routines; instead, the action components need to be flexibly combined. Thus, action planning systems are ready made for the sort of flexible combinations demanded for language comprehension (for a related idea, see Steedman, 2002). Furthermore, the action planning system has learned to avoid the combination of actions that would be physically impossible. Thus, if language were to use this system, there would be a mechanism for determining (at least in part) when sentences do not make sense, or when one is misunderstanding: when the parts cannot be successfully combined to satisfy the goal.

Kaschak and Glenberg's (2000) work with innovative denominal verbs is one demonstration of flexibility in combining novel affordances (actions) in the service of language. Another example is provided by Glenberg and Robertson (2000). They presented participants with sentences describing novel situations which ended in one of three ways, and the participants judged the sentences as sensible or nonsense. For example:

> *Bill needed to paint the top of his barn wall so he stood on his ...*
>
> afforded and associated: *ladder*
> afforded: *tractor*
> non-afforded: hammer

The objects named in the "afforded and associated condition" afforded accomplishing the goal and were the usual object used to do so. In the "afforded" condition, the object had the right affordances to accomplish the goal, but an unusual use of the object was required. In the "non-afforded" condition, the object could not be used to accomplish the goal. Participants easily judged the non-afforded condition as nonsensical and the others as sensible, but how? Many of the procedures standardly invoked for determining sensible combinations do not work here. For example, note that both tractors and hammers are tools, both are common words, neither are animate, etc. That is, the afforded and non-afforded objects are equivalent on many of the standard linguistic criteria used to determine if a word combines with its context. Also, because most people have never attempted to paint the top of a barn wall, differential familiarity with the situation cannot contribute to the judgement. Third, it is unlikely that people go through a complex logical reasoning process to determine that a tractor can be used but not a hammer, because participants read and judged the "afforded" sentences in about the same time as they read and judged the "afforded and associated" sentences. Finally, note that there is nothing intrinsically impossible about standing on a hammer (e.g. *The braggart stood on his hammer to show off his sense of balance*); however, standing on a hammer does not afford lifting the body to accomplish the goal of painting the top of a wall. Thus, many of the linguistic processes that we might invoke do not seem to discriminate between, on the one hand, sensible sentences (the "afforded and associated" and the "afforded") and, on the other, nonsense sentences (the "non-afforded"). Instead, the judgement seems to be made by using action planning systems to determine if the components of the sentence can be combined to describe coherent action.

A possible mechanism for this sort of action planning is the forward model. Forward models have been proposed (e.g. Wolpert and Kawato, 1998) as a solution to the feedback problem in motor control. The problem arises because the time required to sense feedback from actions often exceeds the time needed to make the movement. Thus, the sensory feedback arrives too late to help correct quick movements. Grush (2004) extended the formal work of Wolpert and Kawato by proposing an articulated, organism/environment forward model. The model is articulated in the sense that it takes into account the joints, masses, strengths, etc. of the real body. The model is an organism/environment model in that it takes into account "some number of objects and surfaces, their rough sizes and shapes, their dynamical properties (especially movements), and their egocentric locations" (Grush, 2004: 391). When the model is fed the same motor commands as are issued to the real body, it can be run fast enough to provide quick feedback both to correct action and to aid in interpretation of the actual sensory feedback (Wilson and Knoblich, 2005). Grush discusses how such a model can be used for motor control, to aid perception, and as a source of motor and visual imagery.

Grush also speculates on how the forward model (or "emulator," as he calls it) can be used in language comprehension. For example, consider how it can be combined with the Indexical Hypothesis to analyze understanding of two sentences, *You kicked Joe the telephone/skyscraper*. Upon hearing *kicked*, the motor system related to the leg becomes active (Hauk et al., 2004; Tettamanti et al., 2005). Upon hearing *the* it is clear that a second noun phrase will be encountered. Thus, the sentence is likely to be a double-object sentence implying transfer of a second object named by the noun phrase (*the telephone* or *the skyscraper*) to the first (*Joe*). Once a perceptual symbol for the second object is inserted into the model (through the indexing process), there is enough information to begin an emulation, namely using a kicking action to transfer the object to Joe. The articulated model will reveal that it is possible (albeit quite unusual) to transfer the telephone by kicking, but that it is not possible to transfer the skyscraper this way (at least not if indexing inserted a realistically sized skyscraper into the model).

Clearly, this is a very speculative account. It has the advantage, however, of being highly testable. For example, the model predicts that many aspects of motor control (e.g. the common coding principle; Hommel et al., 2001) should apply to language understanding. Also, forward models need to be updated or recalibrated to take into account the current sensorimotor environment. When using a tool, for example, literal movement in one direction can cause an effect in another direction. Would such a recalibration affect language comprehension? Or, if one fatigues an effector system through repeated use, and presumably the forward model is updated to reflect this fatigue, will that fatigue affect language comprehension about that effector (e.g. about kicking a telephone)? Whereas the scientific literature currently offers no answers to these question, it is easy to envision how they might be answered.

21.6 Conclusions

Advances in scientific understanding have come at the cost of demoting humans from a unique position in the universe. We no longer believe that the sun revolves around the earth, or that humans are unrelated to other animals. A corollary of the belief that humans are unrelated to other animals is that the mechanisms of language constitute a higher faculty unrelated to our bodily nature. That corollary is also succumbing to the weight of the data. For example, language seems to be related to mirror systems found in other primates. Furthermore, language uses neural systems highly evolved in many animal species.

Clearly, much work needs to be done to secure the ideas (a) that language is opportunistic in the sense described above and (b) that the mechanisms of action control provide the basis for combining ideas conveyed by language. For example, as currently formulated, the Grush emulator account is far from being able to handle the majority of what is known about syntax. Nonetheless, because clear and novel predictions can be derived from embodied accounts, it is certain that they will be tested and lead to a clearer understanding of the close relationship between language and action.

Acknowledgements

This work was supported by NSF grant BCS-0315434 to Arthur Glenberg. Any opinions, findings, and conclusions or recommendations expressed in this material are those of the authors and do not necessarily reflect the views of the National Science Foundation.

References

Barsalou, L.W. (1999) Perceptual symbol systems. *Behavioral and Brain Sciences*, 22: 577–660.

Barsalou, L. W., Niedenthal, P. M., Barbey, A., and Ruppert, J. (2003) Social embodiment. In B. Ross (ed.), *The Psychology of Learning and Motivation*, vol. 43, pp. 43–92. Academic Press, San Diego, Calif.

Binkofski, F., Buccino, G., Stephan, K. M., Rizzolatti, G., Seitz, R. J., and Freund, H.-J. (1999). A parieto-premotor network for object manipulation: evidence from neuroimaging. *Experimental Brain Research*, 128: 21–31.

Borghi, A. M., Glenberg, A. M., and Kaschak, M. P. (2004) Putting words in perspective. *Memory and Cognition*, 32: 863–73.

Buccino, G., Riggio, L., Melli, G., Binkofski, F., Gallese, V., and Rizzolatti, G. (2005) Listening to action-related sentences modulates the activity of the motor system: a combined TMS and behavioral study. *Cognitive Brain Research*, 24: 355–63.

Chambers, C. G., Tanenhaus, M. K., and Magnuson, J. S. (2004) Actions and affordances in syntactic ambiguity resolution. *Journal of Experimental Psychology: Learning, Memory, and Cognition*, 30: 687–96.

Clark, E. V., and Clark, H. H. (1979) When nouns surface as verbs. *Language*, 55: 767–811.

Descartes, R. (1992 [1641]) *Meditations on first philosoph : in which the existence of God and the distinction of the human soul from the body are demonstrated.* Translated by G. Heffernan. University of Notre Dame Press, Notre Dame, IN.

Fadiga, L., Craighero, L., Buccino, G., and Rizzolatti, G. (2002) Speech listening specifically modulates the excitability of tongue muscles: a TMS study. *European Journal of Neuroscience*, 15: 399–402.

Fadiga, L., Fogassi, L., Pavesi, G., and Rizzolatti, G. (1995) Motor facilitation during action observation: a magnetic stimulation study. *Journal of Neurophysiology*, 73: 2608–11.

Fodor, J. A. (1975) *The Language of Thought*. Harvard University Press, Cambridge, MA.

Gallese, V., Keysers, C., and Rizzolatti, G. (2004) A unifying view of the basis of social cognition. *Trends in Cognitive Sciences*, 8: 396–403.

Gibson, J. J. (1979) *The Ecological Approach to Visual Perception*. Houghton Mifflin, New York.

Glenberg, A. M. (1997) What memory is for. *Behavioral and Brain Sciences*, 20: 1–55.

Glenberg, A. M., de Vega, M., and Graesser, A. C. (forthcoming) Framing the debate. In M. de Vega, A. M. Glenberg, and A. C. Graesser (eds.), *Symbol Embodiment, and Meaning.* Oxford, UK: Oxford University Press.

Glenberg, A. M., Havas, D. A., Becker, R., and Rinck, M. (2005) Grounding language in bodily states: the case for emotion. In R. Zwaan and D. Pecher (eds), *The Grounding of Cognition: The Role of Perception and Action in Memory, Language, and Thinking*, pp. 115–28. Cambridge University Press, Cambridge.

Glenberg, A. M., and Kaschak, M. P. (2002) Grounding language in action. *Psychonomic Bulletin and Review*, 9: 558–65.

Glenberg, A. M., and Robertson, D. A. (1999) Indexical understanding of instructions. *Discourse Processes*, 28: 1–26.

Glenberg, A. M. and Robertson, D. A. (2000) Symbol grounding and meaning: a comparison of high-dimensional and embodied theories of meaning. *Journal of Memory and Language*, 43: 379–401.

Goldberg, A. E. (1995). *Constructions: A Construction Grammar Approach to Argument Structure*. University of Chicago Press, Chicago.

Grush, R. (2004) The emulation theory of representation: motor control, imagery, and perception. *Behavioral and Brain Sciences,* 27: 377–442.

Hauk, O., Johnsrude, I., and Pulvermüller, F. (2004) Somatotopic representation of action words in human motor and premotor cortex. *Neuron*, 41: 301–7.

Hommel, B., Muesseler, J., Aschersleben, G., and Prinz, W. (2001) The theory of event coding (TEC): a framework for perception and action planning. *Behavioral and Brain Sciences*, 24: 849–78.

Iverson, J. M., and Goldin-Meadow, S. (2001) The resilience of gesture in talk: gesture in blind speakers and listeners. *Developmental Science*, 4: 416–22.

Kaschak, M. P., and Glenberg, A. M. (2000) Constructing meaning: the role of affordances and grammatical constructions in sentence comprehension. *Journal of Memory and Language*, 43: 508–29.

Kaschak, M. P., Madden, C. J., Therriault, D. J., Yaxley, R. H., Aveyard, M., Blanchard, A., and Zwaan, R. A. (2005) Perception of motion affects language processing. *Cognition*, 94: B79–B89.

Kelly, S. D., Barr, D. J., Church, R. B., and Lynch, K. (1999) Offering a hand to pragmatic understanding: the role of speech and gesture in comprehension and memory. *Journal of Memory and Language*, 40: 577–92.

Kohler, E., Keysers, C., Umiltá, M. A., Fogassi, L., Gallese, V., and Rizzolatti, G. (2002) Hearing sounds, understanding actions: action representation in mirror neurons. *Science*, 297: 846–8.

Lakoff, G. (1987) *Women, Fire, and Dangerous Things: What Categories Reveal about the Mind.* University of Chicago Press, Chicago.

Matlock, T. (2004) Fictive motion as cognitive simulation. *Memory and Cognition*, 32: 1389–1400.

McNeill, D. (1992) *Hand and Mind: What Gestures Reveal about Thought.* University of Chicago Press, Chicago.

Noice, T., and Noice, H. (2006) What studies of actors and acting can tell us about memory and cognitive functioning. *Current Directions in Psychological Science*, 15: 14–18.

Ochs, E., Gonzales, P., and Jacoby, S. (1996) "When I come down I'm in the domain state": grammar and graphic representation in the interpretive activity of physicists. In E. A. Schegloff and S. A. Thompson (eds), *Interaction and Grammar*, pp. 328–69. Cambridge University Press, Cambridge.

Pulvermüller, F. (2005) Brain mechanisms linking language and action. *Nature Reviews Neuroscience*, 6: 576–82.

Pülvermuller, F., Hauk, O., Nikulin, V. V., and Ilmoniemi, R. J. (2005) Functional links between motor and language systems. *European Journal of Neuroscience*, 21: 793–97.

Pulvermüller, F., Shtyrov, Y., and Ilmoniemi, R. J. (2003) Spatio-temporal patterns of neural language processing: an MEG study using Minimum-Norm Current Estimates. *Neuroimage*, 20: 1020–5.

Roth, W.-M. (1999) Discourse and agency in school science laboratories. *Discourse Processes*, 28: 27–60.

Rizzolatti, G., and Arbib, M. A. (1998) Language within our grasp. *Trends in Neuroscience*, 21: 188–94.

Smith, L. B. (2005) Action alters shape categories. *Cognitive Science*, 29: 665–79.

Steedman, M. (2002) Plans, affordances, and combinatory grammar. *Linguistics and Philosophy*, 25: 723–53.

Strack, F., Martin, L. L., and Stepper, S. (1988) Inhibiting and facilitating condition of facial expressions: a non-obtrusive test of the facial feedback hypothesis. *Journal of Personality and Social Psychology*, 54: 768–77.

Talmy, L. (1996) Fictive motion in language and "ception." In P. Bloom, M. A. Peterson, L. Nadel, and M. F. Garrett (eds), *Language and Space*, pp. 211–76. MIT Press, Cambridge, MA.

Tettamanti, M., Buccino, G., Saccuman, M. C., Gallese, V., Danna, M., Scifo, P. Fazio, F., Rizzolatti, G., Cappa, S. F., and Perani, D. (2005) Listening to action-related sentences activates fronto-parietal motor circuits. *Journal of Cognitive Neuroscience*, 17: 273–81.

Thelen, E., and Smith, L. B. (1994*) A Dynamic Systems Approach to the Development of Cognition and Action.* MIT Press, Cambridge, MA.

Valenzeno, L., Alibali, M. W., and Klatzky, R. (2003) Teachers' gestures facilitate students' learning: a lesson in symmetry. *Contemporary Educational Pscyhology*, 28: 187–204.

Wilson, M., and Knoblich, G. (2005) The case for motor involvement in perceiving conspecifics. *Psychological Bulletin*, 131: 460–73.

Wolpert, D. M., and Kawato, M. (1998) Multiple paired forward and inverse models for motor control. *Neural Networks*, 11: 1317–29.

Zwaan (2004) The immersed experiencer: toward an embodied theory of language comprehension. In B. Ross (ed.), *The Psychology of Learning and Motivation*, vol. 44: pp. 35–62. Academic Press, San Diego, CA.

CHAPTER 22

Bilingual sentence processing

Arturo E. Hernández, Eva M. Fernández, and Noemí Aznar-Besé

22.1 Introduction

Bilinguals live, by definition, in two linguistic worlds. Given the different demands of each language, one might think that each system functions independently. However, as Grosjean (1992) and Paradis (1987) have pointed out, bilinguals do not behave like two monolingual speaker/listeners housed in a single brain. Instead, the evidence to date suggests that the characteristics of bilingual language processing may appear to be "in between" the individual's two codes (Cutler et al., 1992; Hernandez et al., 1994; Kilborn, 1989; Kilborn and Ito, 1989; Liu et al., 1992; Vaid and Pandit, 1991).

Studies in bilingual sentence processing have focused on phenomena related to how semantic or syntactic representations are built. This chapter reviews data consistent with the view of interdependence between the two languages of the bilingual, using evidence from the literature on bilingual sentence processing. To do this, we will discuss processing at the semantic and syntactic level. Studies in both the semantic and syntactic domain reveal that bilinguals almost always use a unitary mechanism that accesses two separately represented grammars. We will also see that the study of bilingual sentence processing can also offer insights to our understanding of human language processing in general, because bilinguals offer opportunities to examine sentence processing effects in within-participant designs, impossible to carry out with monolinguals.

22.2 Semantic processing

One of the fundamental questions for researchers studying bilingual sentence processing is the nature of language representation. Does a bilingual store both sets of words in the same lexicon or there is a separate lexicon for each language? For many years, researchers addressed this issue by using traditional memory methodologies involving free recall or recognition (see Heredia and McLaughlin, 1992 for a review) and it was not until the 1990s that investigators turned to the semantic priming paradigm. At the single-word level, researchers looked at whether cross-language priming is an automatic process and thus the product of strong intra-lexical priming. These studies found that, depending on circumstances, priming across languages may either be automatic (Altarriba, 1991; 1992; Tzelgov and Eben-Ezra, 1992), controlled (Grainger and Beauvillain, 1988), or both (Hernandez et al., 1996; Keatley and de Gelder, 1992), thus providing insufficient evidence to clearly resolve the two-lexicon debate.

One factor that has emerged as a possible explanation for the strength of within- or between-language priming is order of acquisition. For example, Kroll and Sholl (1992) looked at the size of lexical priming from bilinguals' first language to their second language (L1 to L2) and from bilinguals' second language to their first language (L2 to L1) across a set of studies. In general, most such studies demonstrate that the priming effect is larger from L1 to L2 than vice versa. Kroll and colleagues (Kroll, 1994; Kroll and Sholl, 1992; Kroll and Stewart, 1994) suggest that the results from studies investigating within- and between-language lexical priming fit very well within their revised hierarchical model, a model that was initially designed to address the nature of second-language acquisition. First of all, it is posited that there are two lexical stores and a common conceptual store. These stores are interconnected via weighted bidirectional links between both the L1 and L2 lexicons and between the conceptual store and each particular lexicon as well. Lexical links are stronger from L2 to L1 than from L1 to L2, a product of second-language acquisition. However, conceptual links are stronger to L1 than to L2. This model has been confirmed through a series of studies which have found that conceptual processing is stronger from L1 to L2 than from L2 to L1, while translation is faster from L2 to L1 than from L1 to L2 (i.e. translation asymmetry).

Evidence from subsequent studies has found that concreteness may mediate the presence or absence of translation or naming asymmetries (Heredia, 1996). Thus, it is not clear that a bilingual's two lexicons can be so neatly divided—a view that has received support from de Groot and colleagues (de Groot, 1994; de Groot and Nas, 1991). In addition, Heredia found that L1 and L2 are not equivalent to the more dominant and less dominant language for Spanish-English bilinguals in the United States. To account for these differences, Heredia proposed a "re-revised" hierarchical model in which dominance and not order of acquisition determines the nature of language asymmetries (see also Heredia, 1997). Studies of lexical priming have also found that dominance may not be directly related to order of acquisition. For example, Altarriba (1992) found larger priming from L2 to L1 than from L1 to L2. Thus, studies of bilingualism should consider profoundly the age at which the second language was acquired as well as the domains and frequency of use of each language, two variables that lead to different language dominance profiles. In the case of Hispanics in southern Florida and in the south-west of the United States, the second language (English) ends up being the dominant language since it is the language in which most formal education occurs. Thus, studies of semantic priming in bilinguals must consider that in certain populations the second language is the dominant language. A final criticism of the revised hierarchical model is the distinction between lexical and conceptual processing of items in a second language. In fact, many have proposed that translation equivalents may be conceptually mediated both in acquisition (Altarriba and Mathis, 1997) and in usage (de Groot et al., 1994; de Groot and Hoeks, 1995), suggesting that dominance effects need careful consideration.

While a substantial amount of work has been done with lexical priming and single-word naming, relatively little work has been done with sentence priming in bilinguals. Kroll and Borning (1987) looked at the effects of English sentences on lexical decisions to English and Spanish target words. Lexical decisions were slower to Spanish targets, but the magnitude of priming did not vary systematically with the target language. Similarly, Hernandez et al. (1996) further explored the nature of within- and between-language sentence priming in a group of Spanish-English bilinguals. The participants in the study reported Spanish to be their L1 although English, their L2, was the dominant language. Like Kroll and Borning, Hernandez et al. did not observe language asymmetries under normal viewing conditions. However, language asymmetries were found for targets which were visually degraded and for which the language was not predictable. In fact, these differences were larger in both conditions: the cross-language condition (English–Spanish priming > Spanish–English priming) and the within-language condition (English–English priming > Spanish–Spanish priming). The results from Hernandez et al. (1996) extend findings in the single-word priming literature with bilinguals by showing that sentence priming may be larger when a target is in L2 and the L2 has become the dominant language.

Most studies suggest that there are some differences between sentence and lexical priming. Altarriba et al. (1996) found that, under certain conditions, sentence context effects can produce surprising results in bilinguals. Fixation durations and naming latencies were recorded when bilinguals read sentences that contained high- and low-frequency Spanish and English words in high- and low-constraint sentences. Reaction times were faster and fixation durations were shorter for low-frequency targets in high-constraint sentences when compared to performance for these targets in low-constraint sentences across both languages. For high-frequency targets, however, an asymmetry was found. English high-frequency targets showed the same constraint effect observed for low-frequency targets, being faster in high-constraint sentences. On the other hand, Spanish high-frequency targets showed slower reaction times and longer fixation durations in high-constraint sentences. Altarriba et al. suggest that high-frequency Spanish words in high-constraint English sentences led to slower reaction times because of violations of lexical expectations. That is, there may be some lexical-level competition for a high-frequency Spanish word when the sentence provides a strong form of constraint for its English translation. The fact that this competition occurred even during first fixation durations suggests that this effect is a product of delays in word recognition.

The results obtained by Altarriba et al. are confirmed by a more recent study using Event Related Potentials (ERPs) by Moreno et al. (2002). Moreno and colleagues asked participants to listen to sentences (e.g. *Each night the campers built a …*) which had either a congruent completion (*fire*), a lexical switch (*blaze*), or a code-switch (*fuego*). Participants were also tested with idiomatic phrases (e.g. *Out of sight, out of …*) which were much more highly constrained. Lexical switches revealed greater N400 effects than congruent completions for both sentences and idiomatic phrases, suggesting that participants had more difficulty integrating these lower-constraint items into a semantic context. Code-switches, however, did not produce an increased N400. Rather, these items yielded an enhanced Late Positive Complex (LPC) which has been associated with task-relevant improbable events (Donchin and Coles, 1988; Johnson, 1986). The LPC was also modulated by proficiency in Spanish. Specifically, higher vocabulary scores in Spanish were predictive of LPCs that were smaller and peaked earlier. Given that code switches are more likely to be present in the auditory modality and are modulated by the proficiency in the language, Moreno et al. posit that the enhanced LPC is due to a physical mismatch with the stimulus. This result reveals an interesting parallel with Altarriba et al.'s results, which show slower processing of target items in the less dominant language in high-constraint sentences than in the dominant language (for similar results using a different methodology see Hernandez, 2002).

The importance of context can also be observed in a recent study by Elston-Guetler et al. (2005) in which German-English bilinguals were presented with a short film in either German or English. After the film, participants were presented with a set of sentences (i.e. *The woman gave her friend an expensive gift)* and asked to press a "yes" button when they were finished reading each item. 200 ms after pressing the button, participants were asked to make a lexical decision to a visually presented and a probe word (e.g. *poison*) or a control prime (*shell*) which remained on a computer screen for a maximum of 3000 ms.. The visual probes were "false friends": interlingual homographs which are spelt the same but have entirely different meanings (*Gift* means 'poison' in German). In order to create strong context effects that would bias against any German meaning, the sentences were all in English and the target words were all legal English words. Items were presented in separate blocks so as to assess whether the language of the film was constant across a longer session or dissipated over time. Activation of the German meaning of the homograph, for both reaction times and ERP measures, appeared, but only after the German film was viewed and only in the first two blocks. By the third block after the presentation of the German film there was no priming of the German meaning of the homographs. Finally, there was no semantic priming after presentation of the English film. One finding of particular interest was the lack of proficiency effects. The authors interpret these findings as supporting a model in which strong contexts allow L2 speakers to zoom into a particular language and essentially cut off access to another language. The use of discourse contexts has shown similar elimination of cross-language priming in certain conditions (Hernandez et al., 1996).

The results from studies which have investigated semantic processing at the sentence level strongly suggest that the bilingual's language processing mechanism relies on a single conceptual system. Priming from sentences in L1 does cross over to L2. The magnitude of these effects can vary depending on proficiency of the language or the strength of the context. However, there is little evidence from these studies that there are two separate semantic systems for each language.

22.3 **Syntactic processing**

Work on syntactic processing with bilinguals has involved two different paradigms. In some paradigms participants are asked to make explicit judgements about grammar (a practice very common in research on second language acquisition). Others, on the other hand test the nature of grammar in a more implicit manner. One paradigm that has been used in a great number of bilingual studies is the sentence interpretation paradigm developed by Bates and MacWhinney (for a review see Bates and MacWhinney, 1989). This paradigm has been used extensively to test predictions of the Competition Model of Bates and MacWhinney (1982; 1987; 1989). The Competition Model (CM) is a functionalist approach to language, in which linguistic representations are viewed not as a set of discrete and autonomous rules, but as a set of probabilistic mappings between form and meaning. The model begins with the assumption that all listeners (bilingual and monolingual) must deal with two important but occasionally conflicting tasks. On the one hand, listeners must know in advance which pieces of information in the input language carry valuable information and merit attentional priority. On the other hand, they must be sensitive to the processing costs and timing parameters of a particular language in order to deploy resources in the most efficient way. Bates and MacWhinney (1989) have referred to these two dimensions of language processing with the terms "cue validity" (the information value associated with particular linguistic forms) and "cue cost" (the processing costs involved in using those forms, including demands on perception and memory). Sentence comprehension is viewed as a process of interactive activation, a form of constraint satisfaction in which linguistic forms or cues compete and converge in order to lead to a particular interpretation, i.e. the interpretation that provides the best fit to this particular configuration of inputs.

Within this framework, languages can vary not only in terms of the presence or absence of specific form types (e.g. case-marking on nouns) but also in terms of the relative strength of form–function mappings. In other words, there are quantitative as well as qualitative differences between language types. Consider languages such as Spanish, French, Italian, German, or Russian. Compared to English, these languages offer a rich set of markings for subject–verb agreement and, as a result, subject–verb agreement is a strong cue to agent–object relations. At the same time, Spanish and Italian are pro-drop languages and therefore permit null subjects in free-standing declarative sentences like *∅ bebo agua* ('I drink water'), where the subject pronoun *yo* is omitted. Pro-drop languages are generally quite tolerant of word order variation, permitting strings which depart from the canonical subject–verb–object (SVO) word order preferred for pragmatically neutral sentences: a sentence like *María se comió una galleta* ('María ate a cookie') can also be realized with the subject NP in sentence-medial position (*Se comió María una galleta*) or sentence-final position (*Se comió una galleta María*). These languages offer a variety of other cues which can aid in identifying the thematic roles of the constituents, including clitic agreement, the accusative preposition *a* used with animate direct objects, and gender and case markings on determiners and adjectives that must agree with the nouns they modify. As a result, word order is a relatively weak and unreliable cue to semantic roles while other cues are much stronger.

English behaves quite differently. There are very few contrasts in verb morphology to agree with the subject (*I eat, you eat, they eat*), subject pronouns cannot be omitted in free-standing declarative sentences, and the canonical subject–verb–object (SVO) word order is rigidly preserved in most sentence types. Hence, in English, subject–verb agreement is a weak cue while word order is a very strong cue to agent–object roles. Note that all the languages previously described have the same basic word order as English (SVO), and all have at least some form of subject–verb agreement. The primary difference here is, then, a matter of degree: which cues to meaning should the listener trust in assigning semantic roles when processing sentences in two different languages?

The CM predicts that Spanish listeners, for instance, will rely primarily on morphological cues in sentence interpretation, ignoring word order if the two sources of information do not agree. By contrast, English listeners should rely primarily on word order cues at the expense of morphological information. Three previous studies have confirmed this prediction for Spanish and English (Hernandez et al., 1994; Wulfeck et al. 1986; Kail, 1989). Similar confirmations of cue validity and cue strength have been reported for Italian, German, French, Hungarian, Serbo-Croatian, Dutch, Hebrew, Hindi, Turkish, Warlpiri, Japanese, and Chinese (Bates et al., 1982; Bates et al., 1984; Smith and Mimica, 1984; Mimica et al., 1994; Miao, 1981; Kilborn and Ito, 1989; Bavin and Shopen, 1989; Sokolov, 1989; McDonald, 1989; Kail, 1989; MacWhinney et al., 1991; Vaid and Pandit, 1991; Vaid and Chengappa, 1988). This research employs a sentence interpretation task in which participants are presented with strings consisting of two nouns and a verb, representing various competing and converging combinations of word order, morphology, semantic information (e.g. animate vs. inanimate nouns), and pragmatic information (e.g. topicalization and/or contrastive stress). In this type of experiment, the participants' task is to choose the agent of the sentence. Results from these studies have consistently confirmed that speakers of different languages can have radically different configurations of cue strengths, in accord with predictions based on cue validity. When cues are set into competition, the strongest cues prevail, determining the assignment of agent–object roles.

A somewhat different interpretation of the range of effects just described would propose that during sentence interpretation the processing mechanisms merely perform routines that involve accessing the competence repositories—where such cues are represented, based on their validity and processing cost. Thus, the cross-linguistic differences observed in sentence interpretation tasks can be interpreted as reflecting not how actual sentence processing strategies are deployed, but instead how aspects of the grammar (in the competence repositories) are represented. One consequence of such a model is unitary and language-independent sentence processing routines, where the same sentence processor can work for any language, and cross-linguistic differences in performance are caused by language-specific grammatical representations.

Kilborn (1987; 1989) performed one of the first studies of sentence interpretation with bilinguals. Bilingual subjects listened to digitized auditory sentence stimuli in German and English, in separate sessions, administered in a counterbalanced order across participants. As a group, Kilborn's German-English bilingual subjects displayed strong patterns of forward transfer (transfer from L1 to L2) in their assignment of agent–object roles. In both languages they showed strong effects of agreement and animacy, and relatively weak effects of word order. The reaction time findings were in general in accord with these results, although Kilborn did not pursue them in detail.

Another of the earliest implementations of the sentence interpretation paradigm with bilinguals was carried out by Vaid and Pandit (1991). In this study, forty-eight Hindi-English bilinguals who used Hindi at home and English at school were asked to perform the sentence interpretation paradigm. Despite having very similar profiles of use, individuals in this group showed variable patterns of dominance: seven participants exhibited Hindi-dominant profiles in both languages, nineteen exhibited Hindi-dominant profiles in Hindi but a mixture of strategies in English (partial forward transfer), and seventeen displayed patterns of amalgamation in both languages. Only five subjects (11 percent of the total) showed patterns of differentiation between the two languages.

Hernandez et al. (1994) manipulated word order, verb agreement, and animacy in a sentence interpretation paradigm with bilingual and monolingual English and Spanish speakers. Data for percentage first noun choice and reaction times for making this choice were collected. The results revealed an amalgamated, in-between pattern of results for percentage first noun choice in the bilingual college-age group when compared to each monolingual group. Whereas monolinguals in Spanish relied almost exclusively on verb agreement, and monolinguals in English relied almost exclusively on word order, bilinguals relied on an amalgam of word order and verb agreement strategies in both languages.

So far, the work that we have reviewed has dealt with adult bilinguals who are in a relatively steady state. However, the Competition Model was proposed to account for much more dynamic and variable patterns of performance. Two particular studies have captured this dynamic aspect with adult bilinguals. The first study conducted by McDonald (McDonald, 1989) looked at late English-French bilinguals who were in their first and second year of college French. McDonald found a clear pattern of forward transfer almost from the beginning of L2 learning. By the fourth semester, bilinguals exhibited sentence interpretation profiles that were very similar to those seen in adult bilinguals in other studies. In short, even L2 learners show relatively quick developmental changes in their L2 strategies (McLaughlin et al., 2004).

A second study of interest conducted by Liu et al. (1992), investigated the nature of Chinese-English and English-Chinese bilinguals' performance when L2 is learned early or late in life. The results revealed a complex pattern related to the age of L2 acquisition and other possible factors. While late L2 learners showed the expected patterns of forward transfer, early bilinguals exposed to English between the ages of 6 and 10 showed patterns of differentiation. In addition, those who learned English before the age of 4 showed patterns of backward transfer (transfer from L2 to L1), as did individuals who had arrived in the US between 12 and 16 years of age. These results demonstrate that the direction of transfer is linked to age of L2 acquisition (perhaps instead to language dominance), and that differentiation between L1 and L2 is the least common pattern. However, that early L2 acquirers exhibited patterns of forward transfer is an interesting finding which is no doubt related to language dominance rather than age of exposure.

The results from studies using sentence interpretation tasks within the CM framework clearly lead to the important generalization that bilinguals do not function with two independent language systems. Rather, there is a considerable amount of interaction between these two systems in the form of transfer (backward and forward), as well as (in some cases) an amalgamation of strategies. This can be understood as linked to the dynamic properties of the bilingual's internalized grammars. The two grammatical components must be represented separately in the bilingual's competence repositories, but certain aspects of each might be given more prominence and are therefore more salient during the interpretation of sentences. Prominence is in part determined by the language-specific grammar which, for instance, permits or disallows word order variation. If the bilingual's grammar in either of the languages is close enough to the monolingual grammar, performance will be monolingual-like. If, instead, the internal representation of the grammar of one of the languages is not rich enough, and contains either elements from the other languages or elements that do not match either of the languages, performance will reflect transfer or amalgamation (for a similar argument see Hernandez et al., 2000).

22.4 Emergent properties of bilingual sentence processing

Early work in the framework of the Competition Model considered bilingualism to be fundamentally different from monolingual sentence processing. However, MacWhinney's Unified Model of Language Learning (UMLL) conceptualizes language learning as an emergent process (MacWhinney, 2004; 1999). In this view, L1 and L2 learning is a process in which representations are formed as language functions compete. As L2 learning progresses, increased proficiency results in sharpening of the underlying language representations. As functions become more automatized and representations are molded to the underlying linguistic input, L2 processing will experience reduced interference from L1.

Compared with monolinguals in both languages, bilinguals demonstrate an in-between pattern with regard to how they perceive and attend to different cues in each language (Hernandez et al., 1994). The ways in which bilingual development can be considered as an extension of monolingual development were examined by Reyes and Hernandez (2006). In this study, early Spanish-English bilingual children performed somewhere in between English and Spanish monolingual children in making use of word-order strategies (local cues) before subject–verb agreement. That is, bilinguals attended to subject–verb agreement cues at a later age than the typical Spanish monolingual speaker but at an earlier age than the typical English monolingual speaker. Furthermore, bilinguals' use of a second-noun strategy for interpreting NNV and VNN sentences was delayed in comparison to both English and Spanish monolinguals. Whereas English monolinguals have a defined pattern of choosing the second noun as the agent of VNN sentences by age 7, and of NNV sentences by age 9 (Von Berger et al., 1996), for Spanish monolinguals the second-noun strategy does not appear until age 11 for both VNN and NNV sentences (Reyes, 2003). However, in this study bilinguals did not show evidence of this strategy until the ages of 14–16. The effect of competing strategies also increased with age as the participants attempted to sort and integrate cues to arrive at the most efficient processing strategy. These results support the idea that bilingual language acquisition, complex though it may be, involves a process that not only resembles but also transpires within the same time-frame as monolingual first language acquisition (Paradis et al., 2003).

The UMLL also makes predictions about the role of overlap in language learning. Specifically, it predicts that functions which overlap between L1 and L2 should be easier to learn in a second language due to cross-language transfer. If ease of processing is related to less neural activity, the model would predict that neural activity should be reduced for items which overlap across languages. It is important to note that the concept of overlap differs from transfer in one important respect. Specifically, overlap exists at the level of linguistic description, whereas transfer is the process of using functions in one language to guide processing in a second language.

The importance of overlap has been noted in a number of studies. At the phonological level, there is evidence that higher similarity between a native language and English leads to better perception and production of English vowels in non-native speakers (Flege et al., 1997). At the lexical level, words that are orthographically similar across languages (*tomato–tomate*) are easier to process (Costa et al., 2000; de Groot and Nas, 1991; Gollan et al., 1997; Kotz et al., in preparation; Sanchez-Casas et al., 1992) and show fewer differences in neural activity than those which are not (de Blesser et al., 2003). Linguistic similarity also affects neural activity produced by grammatical features across languages. Li et al. (2004) asked Chinese monolinguals to perform a lexical decision task on nouns, verbs, or class-ambiguous items, and analyzed fMRI scans to identify the regions of neural activity while the participants were performing this task. Verbs in Chinese are not inflected to indicate number/person distinctions, while English inflects the third person singular (e.g. *run/runs*). In addition, the form of many Chinese verbs is identical to related nouns, while in English the few forms that exist are distinguishable by lexical stress (e.g. *conflict*). Results revealed strong overlapping regions of activity for both nouns and verbs, supporting the idea that syntactical characteristics do influence neuronal activation. Similarly, in a subsequent study by Chan et al. (2004) Chinese-English bilinguals were asked to perform lexical decisions on nouns and verbs in each language. As in the case of Chinese monolinguals, neuroimaging data from Chinese-English bilinguals during processing of Chinese items revealed large areas of overlapping activity for processing of nouns and verbs, although the processing of English terms resulted in increased activity in different brain regions.

Recent work by Tokowicz and MacWhinney (forthcoming) sheds light on the nature of transfer in late second-language learners. In that study, English-Spanish bilinguals were asked to make grammaticality judgements on sentences which varied in the extent to which syntactic functions overlapped across languages. Participants' brain activity was measured using ERPs. The first type of function involved tense marking, a feature which is similar across the two languages. The second type of function involved determiner–noun agreement (*las*[pl] *casas*[pl] vs. **la*[sg] *casas*[sg]). Like in Spanish, number in English is marked on the noun (*houses*). However, unlike in Spanish, there is no need in English for the noun to agree with the determiner (*the houses*). Participants were also asked to make decisions about sentences which manipulated gender agreement, a function which exists in Spanish but not in English (*la*[f] *casa*[f] vs. **el*[m] *casa*[f]). The results revealed increased activity for noun–verb agreement—a function which is similar across languages—as well as for determiner–noun gender agreement. In contrast, no ERP differences for gender or number agreement in Spanish were found. However, the distribution of the signal was diffuse, suggesting that it involved multiple neural generators. Taken together, these results suggest that properties of the grammar of L1 influence brain responses to L2 during early stages of learning. Furthermore, it suggests that functions which overlap across languages are easier to track in L2 than those which do not, and that the effects of overlap are present in both semantic and syntactic tasks.

Overlap is an important factor to consider in L2 acquisition. The objective of the L2 learner is to develop a representational system which contains both overlapping and functionally distinct components. The language system builds L2 by bootstrapping from L1. Hence, overlap assists by making the first steps into L2 easier. As automaticity and learning settle, the system becomes less dependent on L2.

22.5 **Parsing**

Traditional models of monolingual syntactic structure assignment to a linearly ordered string of lexical items propose that the syntactic processor, or parser, computes structure by applying minimal effort strategies (Kimball, 1973; Frazier and Fodor, 1978; see also Frazier and Clifton, 1996; Mitchell, 1994). These strategies, also referred to as routines or heuristics, are best understood as originating in the limitations imposed by human cognition: computing the simplest structure requires less computational resources and places less demands on working memory. One such strategy, Minimal Attachment, accounts for the difficulty experienced when reading the classic garden path sentence *The horse raced past the barn fell* (Bever, 1970). Here, the verb *raced*, in the reduced relative clause, is initially taken to be the matrix sentence verb, because this is the simplest structure for an input string like *The horse raced* ... This interpretation persists (the reader is led "up the garden path") until the last word in the string is reached, at which point the reader (or listener) either reanalyzes the complete string to arrive at the correct syntactic structure or deems the sentence to be ungrammatical. By another such strategy, Late Closure (see also Recency Preference; Gibson et al., 1996), the parser prefers to attach incoming material locally, to the most recently built constituent. In a sentence like *Peter said the boss will call yesterday*, the final constituent, *yesterday*, is initially attached inside the more local clause, *the boss will call*, even though the verb, *will call*, is temporally incompatible with it. The operation of these parsing routines can be observed by examining listeners' or readers' preferences with linguistic stimuli that contain local or global ambiguities. Preference is measured typically by examining the proportion of preferred interpretations in pencil-and-paper questionnaires using globally ambiguous materials, or by reaction times or eye-gaze times in reading tasks that contain materials forcing disambiguation one way or another.

If parsing strategies, like Minimal Attachment and Late Closure, are derived from the inherent properties of human cognition, there is no reason to suppose that bilinguals will parse sentences in ways that are qualitatively different from the ways monolinguals do, as argued, for example, in Fernández (2003). Studies that have compared the preferences of bilinguals and monolinguals when dealing with locally or globally ambiguous sentences find precisely this: evidence of similar parsing preferences for speakers of one or more languages. Frenck-Mestre and Pynte (1997) examined the eye movement patterns of monolinguals and bilinguals, reading sentences with local syntactic ambiguities resolved downstream in the sentence. The bilinguals were English-L1-dominant speakers of French as L2. The materials tested included sentence pairs like *Elle protège les enfants du danger/du village* ... ('She protects the children from danger/of the village'), in which attaching the prepositional phrase to the matrix sentence verb, as with *du danger*, results in a simpler structure (thus the version of the pair with prepositional phrase *du village* modifying *les enfants* is dispreferred). Also tested were sentence pairs like *Whenever the dog barked/obeyed the little girl showed her approval*, for which the simplest structure incorrectly takes the noun phrase *the little girl* to be the direct object of the verb in the subordinate clause—this is far more likely to happen with an optionally transitive verb like *obeyed* than with an intransitive verb like *barked*. Frenck-Mestre and Pynte observed that while the bilinguals had longer second-pass reading times than the monolingual participants, the patterns of preference for the resolution of the local ambiguities were identical for both types of participant: reading times were increased for the constructions that involved building more complex structure.

Frenck-Mestre (2005) examined how monolinguals and bilinguals read sentences involving the classic garden path reduced relative clause construction described earlier. The structurally equivalent sentence *The submarine destroyed during the war sank in a few seconds* might not be nearly as difficult to process as *The horse raced past the barn fell*, because the disambiguation point is reached earlier: the critical verb *destroy* is obligatorily transitive. The flexible word order of French, compared to English, and the likeness in form between the past participle and present indicative form of verbs like *détruire* permit a comparison of sentences like *Le sous-marin détruit pendant la guerre a coulé en quelques secondes*, equivalent to the English sentence above, and *Le sous-marin détruit pendant la guerre un navire de la marine royale* ('The submarine destroys during the war a ship from the royal navy'). Monolingual readers showed a preference for the structurally simpler sentences—those without a reduced relative clause—though this preference was not immediate. The bilingual readers, in contrast, exhibited difficulty throughout the prepositional phrase region and showed a preference for the more complex structure—the reduced relative clause version of the sentences. Clearly, the native language affected how the bilinguals processed these strings: the prepositional phrase following the verb *détruit* rules out, for the bilinguals, the possibility of this verb being anything other than a participle.

Evidence of forward transfer in sentence processing has been offered by a number of studies that examine how bilinguals process relative clause attachment ambiguities, as in the sentence *Peter fell in love with the sister of the psychologist who lives in California*. Here, the relative clause *who lives in California* could be interpreted as referring to *the sister* or to *the psychologist*. By a principle such as Late Closure, the relative clause should be preferably interpreted as referring to the low, more recent noun, *the psychologist*. This is indeed the preferred interpretation of the construction for speakers of English (Cuetos and Mitchell, 1988; Fernández, 2003). Yet, speakers of languages like Spanish, as well as French, Portuguese, and several others, prefer to attach the relative clause high, to the more distant noun, *the sister* (Cuetos and Mitchell, 1988; Carreiras and Clifton, 1993; 1999; Fernández, 2003). The earliest explanations of this difference in preference attributed this effect to language-specificity in the parser (e.g. Mitchell and Cuetos, 1991). Alternative accounts of this cross-linguistic difference propose that the language-specific effects are not based in the sentence-processing mechanisms, but rather driven by information outside of the parser, e.g. the default prosodic phrasing imposed by a language's phonology (Fodor, 1998) or the language-specific application of pragmatic principles (Frazier and Clifton, 1996). Whether the cross-linguistic difference is sourced in the parser or the grammar is a matter beyond the scope of this discussion; the fact that cross-linguistic differences have been widely documented in monolinguals permits examining the phenomenon with bilinguals.

Experiments comparing the relative-clause attachment preferences of speakers of two languages for which monolinguals exhibit cross-linguistic differences in preferred interpretations have demonstrated that patterns of attachment very typically match those of monolinguals of the bilingual's L1 or the bilingual's dominant language. Frenck-Mestre (1997) reports that beginner L2 learners of French (whose L1 was English) show patterns of attachment that resemble those of English monolinguals, with a preference for the low-attachment interpretation.

Similar results involving forward transfer for Portuguese-English and English-Portuguese bilinguals are reported by Maia and Maia (2005). A more complex set of findings is reported by Dussias (2001), who examined the patterns of preference for early Spanish-English bilinguals who learned both languages before age 6, and late Spanish-English bilinguals whose L2 was either Spanish or English. The late L2-Spanish bilinguals showed the same type of forward transfer pattern as in the Frenck–Mestre study, a preference for low attachment in both English and Spanish whereas the late L2-English bilinguals showed differentiation (L1 high, L2 low). Additionally, the early bilinguals exhibited no clear preference for attaching to the low or to the high noun, in either language.

A second study conducted by Dussias (2003) examined the relative clause attachment preferences of Spanish-English bilinguals who are highly proficient in both languages. Their proficiency was determined by a careful screening procedure that identified speakers with higher levels of L2 competence. In a series of experiments, both L2-Spanish and L2-English bilinguals exhibited low attachment preferences in both languages, like their English monolingual counterparts, but unlike their Spanish monolingual counterparts. Dussias contemplates an explanation for this finding that hinges on the idea that the cognitive demands placed on bilinguals might promote the use of minimal effort strategies, like Late Closure. An alternative explanation—but one that, as Dussias acknowledges, requires empirical confirmation—contends that language exposure is crucial in determining preferences: the bilinguals in this study were living in an environment where English is the majority language.

Although still empirically unconfirmed, it is plausible that the immediate linguistic environment can determine the types of preference that bilinguals have when processing the relative clause attachment construction. Yet, the factor that actually drives such preferences might not be the environment directly, but rather a variable influenced by the environment: proficiency or language dominance. Fernández (2003) examined the attachment preferences of early Spanish/English bilinguals, grouped as English- or Spanish-dominant (all were native speakers of Spanish or native speakers of both languages), and found an effect of language dominance. Spanish-dominant bilinguals had preference profiles that resembled those of Spanish monolinguals, while English-dominant bilinguals showed preferences similar to those of their English monolingual counterparts.

One final set of findings from syntactic processing in bilinguals merits our attention, though these experiments measure syntactic priming effects in production rather than perception. In these studies, participants are placed in discourse contexts where both languages must be activated, as the tasks involve moving from one language—in which a prime sentence is presented, to another—in which a target sentence is produced by the participant. The primes can be presented either auditorily or in writing, and participants are sometimes required to repeat the primes, others not. The results of these priming experiments are all quite similar: a structure provided in one language primes itself in the other.

For instance, Loebell and Bock (2003) asked participants to repeat a sentence heard in L1 (German) or L2 (English) and subsequently describe a picture in the other language. The materials included dative alternation and active/passive alternation constructions. Loebell and Bock report reliable priming effects for double object primes, prepositional object primes, and active primes. Another study conducted by Hartsuiker et al. (2004) also examined the active/passive alternation by employing a picture description task in which a confederate participant presented primes in Spanish while describing a picture, and a naïve participant described a picture in English. Hartsuiker et al. observe a reliable priming effect with both active and passive primes.

Lastly, Desmet and Declerq (2006) administered a sentence completion task to a group of Dutch-English bilinguals whose task was to complete the relative clause. The materials included primes in which a relative clause attachment was forced either high or low by the gender agreement of the relative pronoun. Prime and target items were sentence fragments presented through the relative pronoun, and fillers were sentence-completion items of different forms. In the targets, the resolution of the attachment was identified by the verb produced by the participants, which matched in number to either the high or low noun in the complex NP. Desmet and Declerq found a reliable priming effect, with relative-clause attachment primes forced to attach low.

The simplest explanation for these effects, though certainly not the only possible explanation, invokes shared representations for generating and recovering syntactic structure in both languages. A complication for priming experiments to overcome is the perhaps unavoidable fact that both languages are activated during the experimental trial, thus perhaps reducing the possibility of observing language-specific behavior.

22.6 On age of acquisition and proficiency

Although work from Tokowicz and MacWhinney (forthcoming) reveals that overlap can transfer between a bilingual's two languages, it also reveals that syntactic functions which do not overlap between languages can be learned. Hence, some syntactic information overlaps across languages whereas some does not. However semantic processing especially when it is reliant on concepts that exist in the real world (e.g. dog) is relatively language independent and thus does overlap across languages in a more consistent manner. The fact that overlap across languages is modulated by the type of function makes an interesting prediction about the difference between semantic and syntactic processing. Specifically, semantic processing should transfer more easily from one language to the other, and should be less affected by variables that are traditionally known to modulate the processing of a language in bilinguals.

Work investigating sentence processing using neuroimaging methods suggests that age of acquisition plays a more critical role than proficiency in determining the neural activity associated with grammatical processing (Wartenburger et al., 2003; Weber-Fox and Neville, 1996). A seminal study by Weber-Fox and Neville (1996) found that ERPs to syntactic anomalies differed between L1 and L2 speakers even when the latter began L2 acquisition between 1 and 3 years of age. However, differences in the electrophysiological signatures to semantic anomalies differed in individuals who learned L2 after age 11. More recently, Wartenburger et al. (2003) asked participants to detect syntactic anomalies (violations of case, gender, or number) or semantic anomalies in a set of visually presented sentences. The groups included one early high-proficiency group, one late high-proficiency group, and one late low-proficiency group. For semantic judgements, there were differences between the high- and low-proficiency late bilinguals. However, there were no differences in brain activity for semantic processing even in high-proficiency groups that differed in second-language age of acquisition (AoA). For syntactic anomalies there were significant differences between the two high-proficiency groups which differed on AoA but no differences between the two low-proficiency groups. In short, we could assert that proficiency plays a stronger role in semantic processing (Moreno and Kutas, 2005) whereas AoA plays a stronger role in syntactic processing.

The differential effects of AoA (Birdsong, 1992; 1999; Birdsong and Flege, 2001; Flege et al., 1999; Izura and Ellis, 2004) and proficiency levels in the processing of a second language (Miyake and Friedman, 1998; Moreno and Kutas, 2005; Perani et al., 1998; Snodgrass, 1993) has been the subject of a number of articles and is beyond the scope of this chapter. However, there is one interesting aspect of the debate that fits in with the notion of overlap discussed earlier. Specifically, because semantic processing relies on conceptual information, it overlaps to a great extent across languages (Kroll and de Groot, 2005; Kroll et al., 2001; Kroll et al., 2005). Syntactic and morphological information shows relatively less overlap across languages and hence transfers much less easily. Results from the studies cited above suggest that overlap can help to mitigate maturational differences that appear during language transfer. Interestingly, this is a topic that has received more attention in the bilingual imaging literature than in the psycholinguistic literature. Future studies should attempt to address this issue using traditional behavioral methods from the psycholinguistic literature.

22.7 Conclusion

Taken together, results from the bilingual sentence processing literature suggest that "bilinguals are not two monolinguals in one head." Specifically, many studies have shown that bilinguals use sentence processing strategies that are sometimes L1-like, sometimes L2-like, and sometimes in between, when processing linguistic stimuli in one or the other language. This has been shown to be true across both semantic and syntactic processing. Furthermore, we found evidence that this was also true for both explicit and implicit measures of syntactic processing. Altogether, these results support a model in which multiple constraints play a role in determining the nature of bilingual sentence processing. These constraints include the nature of a speaker's language, proficiency, and language acquisition history. In general, the more dominant language will influence the processing of the less dominant language across both semantic and syntactic processing domains. The nature of sentence processing in bilinguals is also determined by the particular characteristics of the languages being learned. For example, there is evidence that similarity in lexical forms and grammatical forms can result in increased transfer in the semantic and syntactic domains respectively. Bilinguals navigate this multidimensional landscape in order to arrive at a unique language system. Understanding the role of both speaker and language constraints on this process requires further inquiry.

Given the complexity of the task facing a bilingual, one would expect incredible amounts of interference between the languages, or an over-reliance on other cognitive systems in order to mediate between the two languages. We find evidence of neither of these. Indeed Bialystock and colleagues (2004) have recently found that bilinguals perform better on non-verbal attentional tasks than do monolinguals, implying that a lifetime of working with two competing systems leads to increased attentional control. This would suggest that the act of having to deal with competition of conflicting sources of information may have effects that go beyond the language system. Understanding how the bilingual is able to take advantage of similarities between languages at the same time as avoiding catastrophic interference is a task that should keep researchers occupied for many years to come.

References

Altarriba, J. (1991) Constraints on interlingual facilitation effects in priming in Spanish-English bilinguals. Vanderbilt University, TN.

Altarriba, J. (1992) The representation of translation equivalents in bilingual memory. In R. J. Harris (ed.), *Cognitive Processing in Bilinguals*, vol. 83: 157–74. North-Holland, Amsterdam.

Altarriba, J., Kroll, J. F., Sholl, A., and Rayner, K. (1996) The influence of lexical and conceptual constraints on reading mixed-language sentences: evidence from eye fixations and naming times. *Memory and Cognition*, 24: 477–92.

Altarriba, J., and Mathis, K. M. (1997) Conceptual and lexical development in second language acquisition. *Journal of Memory and Language*, 36: 550–68.

Bates, E., and MacWhinney, B. (1982) Functionalist approaches to grammar. In E. Wanner and L. R. Gleitman (eds), *Language Acquisition: The State of the Art*, pp. 173–218. Cambridge University Press, New York.

Bates, E., and MacWhinney, B. (1987) Competition, variation and language learning. In B. MacWhinney (ed.), *Mechanisms of Language Acquisition*, pp. 157–94. Erlbaum, Hillsdale, NJ.

Bates, E., and MacWhinney, B. (1989) *The Crosslinguistic Study of Sentence Processing*. Cambridge University Press, New York.

Bates, E., and MacWhinney, B. (1989) Functionalism and the competition model. In B. MacWhinney and E. Bates (eds), *The Crosslinguistic Study of Sentence Processing*, pp. 3–73. Cambridge University Press. New York.

Bates, E., MacWhinney, B., Caselli, C.M., Devescovi, A., Natale, F., and Venza, V. (1984) A cross-linguistic study of the development of sentence interpretation strategies. *Child Development*, 55: 341–54.

Bavin, E., and Shopen, T. (1989) Cues to sentence interpretation in Walpiri. In B. MacWhinney and E. Bates (eds), *The Crosslinguistic Study of Sentence Processing*, pp. 185–208. Cambridge University Press, New York.

Bever, T. G. (1970) The cognitive basis for linguistic structures. In J. R. Hayes (ed.), *Cognition and Language Development*, pp. 227–360. Wiley, New York.

Bialystok, E., Craik, F. I. M., Klein, R., and Viswanathan, M. (2004) Bilingualism, aging, and cognitive control: evidence from the Simon Task. *Psychology and Aging*, 19: 290–303.

Birdsong, D. (1992) Ultimate attainment in 2nd language acquisition. *Language*, 68: 706–55.

Birdsong, D. (ed.) (1999) *Second Language Acquisition and the Critical Period Hypothesis*. Erlbaum, Mahwah, NJ.

Birdsong, D., and Flege, J. E. (2001) Regular-irregular dissociations in the acquisition of English as a second language. Paper presented at the 25th Annual Boston University Conference on Language Development, Boston, MA.

Carreiras, M., and Clifton, C. (1993) Relative clause interpretation preferences in Spanish and English. *Language and Speech*, 36: 353–72.

Carreiras, M., and Clifton, C. (1999) Another word on parsing relative clauses: eyetracking evidence from Spanish and English. *Memory and Cognition*, 27(5): 826–33.

Chan, A. H. D., Li, G., Li, P., and Tan, L. H. (2004) Neural correlates of nouns and verbs in Early Bilinguals. *NeuroImage*, MO11.

Chan, A. H. D., Li, G., Li, P., and Tan, L. H. (forthcoming) Neural Correlates of Nouns and Verbs in early bilinguals. *Human Brain Mapping*.

Costa, A., Caramazza, A., and Sebastian-Galles, N. (2000) The cognate facilitation effect: implications for models of lexical access. *Journal of Experimental Psychology: Learning, Memory, and Cognition*, 26(5): 1283–96.

Cuetos, F., and Mitchell, D. C. (1988) Cross-linguistic differences in parsing: restrictions on the use of the Late Closure strategy in Spanish. *Cognition*, 30: 73–105.

Cutler, A., Mehler, J., Norris, D., and Seguí, J. (1992) The monolingual nature of speech segmentation by bilinguals. *Cognitive Psychology*, 24: 381–410.

de Blesser, R., Dupont, P., Postler, J., et al. (2003) The organisation of the bilingual lexicon: a PET study. *Journal of Neurolinguistics*, 16: 439–56.

de Groot, A. M. B. (1994) Word-type effects in bilingual processing tasks: support for a mixed-representational system. In R. Schreuder and B. Weltens (eds), *The Bilingual Lexicon*, pp. 27–51. Benjamins, Amsterdam.

de Groot, A. M. B., and Hoeks, J. C. J. (1995) The development of bilingual memory: evidence from word translation by trilinguals. *Language Learning*, 45: 683–724.

de Groot, A. M. B., and Nas, G. L. (1991) Lexical representation of cognates and noncognates in compound bilinguals. *Journal of Memory and Language*, 30: 90–123.

De Groot, A. M. B., Dannenburg, L., and Van Hell, J. G. (1994) Forward and backward word translation by bilinguals. *Journal of Memory and Language*, 33: 600–29.

Desmet, T., and Declercq, M. (2006) Cross-linguistic priming of syntactic hierarchical configuration information. *Journal of Memory and Language,* 54: 610–32.

Donchin, E., and Coles, M. G. (1988) Is the P300 component a manifestation of context updating? *Behavioral and Brain Sciences,* 11(3): 357–427.

Dussias, P. (2001) Sentence parsing in fluent Spanish-English bilinguals. In J. L. Nicol (ed.), *One Mind,Ttwo Languages: Bilingual Language Processing,* pp. 159–76. Blackwell, Oxford.

Dussias, P. (2003) Syntactic ambiguity resolution in L2 learners: some effects of bilinguality on L1 and L2 processing strategies. *Studies in Second Language Acquisition,* 25: 529–57.

Elston-Guettler, K. E., Paulmann, S., and Kotz, S. A. (2005) Who's in control? Proficiency and L1 influence on L2 processing. *Journal of Cognitive Neuroscience,* 17(10): 1593–1610.

Fernández, E. M. (2003) *Bilingual Sentence Processing: Relative Clause Attachment in English and Spanish.* Benjamins, Amsterdam.

Flege, E., Bohn, O., and Jang, S. (1997) Effects of experience on non-native speakers' production and perception of English vowels. *Journal of Phonetics,* 25: 437–70.

Flege, J. E., Yeni-Komshian, G. H., and Liu, S. (1999) Age constraints on second language acquisition. *Journal of Memory and Language,* 41: 78–104.

Fodor, J. D. (1998) Learning to parse? *Journal of Psycholinguistic Research,* 27(2): 285–319.

Frazier, L., and Clifton, C. (1996) *Construal.* MIT Press, Cambridge, MA.

Frazier, L., and Fodor, J. D. (1978) The sausage machine: a new two-stage parsing model. *Cognition,* 6: 294–325.

Frenck-Mestre, C. (1997) Examining second language reading: an on-line look. In A. Sorace, C. Heycock, and R. Shillcock (eds), *Language Acquisition, Knowledge Representation and Processing: GALA 1997,* pp. 444–8. HCRC, Edinburgh.

Frenck-Mestre, C. (2005) Ambiguities and anomalies: what can eye movements and event-related potentials reveal about second language sentence processing? In J. F. Kroll and A. M. B. de Groot (eds), *Handbook of Bilingualism: Psycholinguistic Approaches,* pp. 268–81. Oxford University Press, New York.

Frenck-Mestre, C., and Pynte, J. (1997) Syntactic ambiguity resolution while reading in second and native languages. *Quarterly Journal of Experimental Psychology,* 50A: 119–48.

Gibson, E., Pearlmutter, N., Canseco-González, E., and Hickok, G. (1996) Recency preferente in the human sentence processing mechanism. *Cognition,* 59: 23–59.

Gollan, T. H., Forster, K. I., and Frost, R. (1997) Translation priming with different scripts: masked priming with cognates and noncognates in Hebrew-English bilinguals. *Journal of Experimental Psychology: Learning, Memory, and Cognition,* 23: 1122–39.

Grainger, J., and Beauvillain, C. (1988) Associative priming in bilinguals: some limits of interlingual facilitation effects. *Canadian Journal of Psychology,* 42: 261–73.

Grosjean, F. (1992) Another view of bilingualism. In R. Harris (ed.), *Cognitive Processing in Bilinguals,* pp. 51–62. Elsevier, New York.

Hartsuiker, R. J., Pickering, M. J., and Veltkamp, E. (2004) Is syntax separate or shared between languages? *Psychological Science,* 15: 409–14.

Heredia, R. R. (1996) Bilingual memory: a re-revised version of the hierarchical model of bilingual memory. *CRL Newsletter,* 10.

Heredia, R. R. (1997) Bilingual memory and hierarchical models: a case for language dominance. *Current Directions in Psychological Science,* 6: 34–9.

Heredia, R. R., and McLaughlin, B. (1992) Bilingual memory revisited. In R. J. Harris (ed.), *Cognitive Processing in Bilinguals,* pp. 91–103. Elsevier Science, Amsterdam.

Hernandez, A. E. (2002) The effects of language asymmetries on lexical and sentential priming in Spanish-English bilinguals. In R. Heredia and J. Altarriba (eds), *Bilingual Sentence Processing,* pp. 137–64. Elsevier/Academic Press, Amsterdam.

Hernandez, A. E., Bates, E., and Avila, L. X. (1994) Sentence interpretation in Spanish-English bilinguals: what does it mean to be in-between? *Applied Psycholinguistics,* 15: 417–66.

Hernandez, A. E., Bates, E., and Avila L.X. (1996) Processing across the language boundary: a cross-modal priming study of Spanish-English bilinguals. *Journal of Experimental Psychology: Learning, Memory, and Cognition,* 22: 846–64.

Hernandez, A. E., Sierra, I., and Bates, E. (2000) Sentence interpretation in bilingual and monolingual Spanish speakers: grammatical processing in a monolingual mode. *Spanish Applied Linguistics,* 4: 179–213.

Izura, C., and Ellis, A. W. (2004) Age of acquisition effects in translation judgment tasks. *Journal of Memory* and *Language,* 50: 165.

Johnson, R. (1986) A triarchic model of P300 amplitude. *Psychophysiology,* 23(4), 367–84.

Kail, M. (1989) Cue validity, cue cost, and processing types in sentence comprehension in French and Spanish. In B. MacWhinney and E. Bates (eds), *The Crosslinguistic Study of Sentence Processing,* pp. 77–117. Cambridge University Press, New York.

Keatley, C., and de Gelder, B. (1992) The bilingual primed lexical decision task: cross-language priming disappears with speeded responses. *European Journal of Cognitive Psychology,* 4: 273–92.

Kilborn, K. (1987) Sentence processing in a second language: seeking a performance definition of fluency. PhD dissertation. University of California, San Diego.

Kilborn, K. (1989) Sentence processing in a second language: the timing of transfer. *Language and Speech,* 32: 1–23.

Kilborn, K., and Ito, T. (1989) Sentence processing strategies in adult bilinguals. In B. MacWhinney and E. Bates (eds), *The Crosslinguistic Study of Sentence Processing,* pp. 257–91. Cambridge University Press, New York.

Kimball, J. (1973) Seven principles of surface structure parsing in natural language. *Cognition,* 2: 15–47.

Kotz, S. A., Hernandez, A. E., and Friederici, A. D. (in preparation) An ERP study on L2 concreteness effects: the role of proficiency and cognate status.

Kroll, J. F. (1994) Accessing conceptual representations for words in a second language. In R. Schreuder and B. Weltens (eds), *The Bilingual Lexicon*, pp. 53–81. Benjamins, Amsterdam.

Kroll, J. F., and Borning, L. (1987) Shifting language representations in novice bilinguals: evidence from sentence priming. Paper presented at the 27th Annual Meeting of the Psychonomic Society, Seattle, WA.

Kroll, J. F., and de Groot, A. M. B. (eds) (2005) *Handbook of Bilingualism: Psycholinguistic Approaches*. Oxford University Press, New York.

Kroll, J. F., and Sholl, A. (1992) Lexical and conceptual memory in fluent and nonfluent bilinguals. In R. J. Harris (ed.), *Cognitive Processing in Bilinguals*, pp. 191–204. Elsevier, Amsterdam.

Kroll, J. F., and Stewart, E. (1994) Category inference in translation and picture naming: evidence for asymmetric connections between bilingual memory representations. *Journal of Memory and Language*, 33: 149–74.

Kroll, J. F., Tokowicz, N., Kroll, J. F., and de Groot, A. M. B. (2005) Models of bilingual representation and processing: looking back and to the future. In Kroll and de Groot (2005: 531–3). Oxford University Press, New York.

Kroll, J. F., Tokowicz, N., and Nicol, J. L. (2001) The development of conceptual representation for words in a second language. In J. Nicol (ed.), *One Mind, Two Languages: Bilingual Language Processing*, pp. 49–71. Blackwell, Cambridge, MA.

Li, P., Bates, E., Liu, H., and MacWhinney, B. (1992) Cues as functional constraints on sentence processing in Chinese. In H. C. Chen and O. Tzeng (eds), *Language Processing in Chinese*, pp. 207–234. Elsevier. Amsterdam.

Li, P., Jin, Z., and Tan, L. H. (2004) Neural representations of nouns and verbs in Chinese: an fMRI study. *Neuroimage*, 21: 1533–41.

Liu, H., Bates, E., and Li, P. (1992) Sentence interpretation in bilingual speakers of English and Chinese. *Applied Psycholinguistics*, 13: 451–84.

Loebell, H., and Bock, K. (2003) Structural priming across languages. *Linguistics*, 41: 791–824.

MacWhinney, B. (ed.) (1999) *Emergence of Language*. Erlbaum, Hillsdale, NJ.

MacWhinney, B. (2004) A unified model of language acquisition. In J. Kroll and A. M. B. Groot (eds), *Handbook of Bilingualism: Psycholinguistic Approaches*, pp. 49–67. Oxford University Press, New York.

MacWhinney, B., Osmán-Sági, J., and Slobin, D. (1991) Sentence comprehension in two clear case-marking languages. *Brain and Language*, 41: 234–49.

Maia, M., and Maia, J. M. (2005) A compreensão de orações relativas por falantes monolíngües e bilíngües de pertuguês e de inglês. In M. Maia and I. Finger (eds), *Processamento da linguagem*, pp. 163–78. Educat. Pelotas, Brazil.

McDonald, J. L. (1989) The acquisition of cue-category mappings. In B. MacWhinney and E. Bates (eds), *The Crosslinguistic Study of Sentence Processing*, pp. 375–96. Cambridge University Press. New York.

McLaughlin, J., Osterhout, L., and Kim, A. (2004) Neural correlates of second-language word learning: minimal instruction produces rapid change. *Nature Neuroscience*, 7: 703–4.

Miao, X. (1981). Word order and semantic strategies in Chinese sentence comprehension. *International Journal of Psycholinguistics*, 8: 23–33.

Mimica, I., Sullivan, M., and Smith, S. (1994) A reaction time study of sentence interpretation in native Croatian speakers. *Applied Psycholinguistics*, 15: 237–61.

Mitchell, D. C. (1994) Sentence parsing. In M. Gernsbacher (ed.), *Handbook of Psycholinguistics*, pp. 375–409. Academic Press, New York.

Mitchell, D. C., and Cuetos, F. (1991) The origins of parsing strategies. In C. Smith (ed.), *Current Issues in Natural Language Processing*, pp. 1–12. University of Texas Center for Cognitive Science, Austin.

Miyake, A., and Friedman, N. P. (1998) Individual differences in second language proficiency: working memory as language aptitude. In E. Alice, F. Healy, E. Lyle, E. Bourne Jr, et al. (eds), *Foreign Language Learning: Psycholinguistic Studies on Training and Retention*, pp. 339–64. Erlbaum, Mahwah, NJ.

Moreno, E. M., Federmeier, K. D., and Kutas, M. (2002) Switching languages, switching palabras (words): an electrophysiological study of code switching. *Brain and Language*, 80(2): 188–207.

Moreno, E. M., and Kutas, M. (2005) Processing semantic anomalies in two languages: an electrophysiological exploration in both languages of Spanish-English bilinguals. *Cognitive Brain Research*, 22: 205–220.

Paradis, M. (1987) *The Assessment of Bilingual Aphasia*. Erlbaum, Hillsdale, NJ.

Paradis, M., Johanne, Crago, M., Genesee, F., and Rice, M. (2003) French-English bilingual children with SLI: how do they compare with their monolingual peers? *Journal of Speech, Language, and Hearing Research*, 46: 113–27.

Perani, D., Paulesu, E., Galles, N. S., Dupoux, E., Dehaene, S., Bettinardi, V., et al. (1998) The bilingual brain: proficiency and age of acquisition of the second language. *Brain*, 121(10): 1841–52.

Reyes, I. (2003) A study of sentence interpretation in Spanish monolingual children. *First Language*, 23: 285–309.

Reyes, I., and Hernandez, A. E. (2006) Sentence interpretation strategies in emergent bilingual children and adults. *Bilingualism: Language and Cognition*, 9: 51–69.

Sánchez-Casas, R. M., Davis, C. W., and García-Albea, J. E. (1992) Bilingual lexical processing: exploring the cognate/noncognate distinction. *European Journal of Cognitive Psychology*, 4: 293–310.

Smith, S., and Mimica, I. (1984) Agrammatism in a case-inflected language: comprehension of agent-object relations. *Brain and Language*, 21: 274–90.

Snodgrass, J. G. (1993) Translating versus picture naming: similarities and differences. In R. Schreuder and B. Weltens (eds), *The Bilingual Lexicon*, pp. 83–114. Benjamins, Amsterdam.

Sokolov, J. (1989) Cue validity and the acquisition of Hebrew. In B. MacWhinney and E. Bates (eds), *The Crosslinguistic Study of Sentence Processing*, pp. 118–57. Cambridge University Press. New York.

Tokowicz, N., and MacWhinney, B. (forthcoming) Implicit vs. explicit measures of sensitivity to violations in L2 grammar: an Event-Related Potential investigation. *Studies in Second Language Acquisition.*

Tzelgov, J., and Eben-Ezra, S. (1992) Components of the between-language priming effect. *European Journal of Cognitive Psychology*, 4: 253–72.

Vaid, J., and Chengappa, S. (1988) Assigning linguistic roles: sentence interpretation in normal and aphasic Kannada-English bilinguals. *Journal of Neurolinguistics*, 3: 161–83.

Vaid, J., and Pandit, R. (1991) Sentence interpretation in normal and aphasic Hindi speakers. *Brain and Language*, 41: 250–74.

Von Berger, R., Wulfeck, B., and Bates, E. (1996) Developmental changes in real-time sentence processing. *First Language*, 16: 193–222.

Wartenburger, I., Heekeren, H. R., Abutalebi, J., Cappa, S. F., Villringer, A., and Perani, D. (2003) Early setting of grammatical processing in the bilingual brain. *Neuron*, 37: 159–70.

Weber-Fox, C., and Neville, H. J. (1996) Maturational constraints on functional specializations for language processing: ERP and behavioral evidence in bilingual speakers. *Journal of Cognitive Neuroscience*, 8: 231–56.

Wulfeck, B., Juarez, L., Bates, E., and Kilborn, K. (1986) Sentence interpretation strategies in healthy and aphasic bilingual adults. In J. Vaid (ed.), *Language Processing in Bilinguals: Psycholinguistic and Neuropsychological Perspectives*, pp. 199–220. Erlbaum, Hillsdale, NJ.

CHAPTER 23

Event-related brain potential (ERP) studies of sentence processing

Marta Kutas and Kara D. Federmeier

PROCESSING language is one of the major integrative acts at which the human brain excels, as it routinely orchestrates a variety of language representations and processes in real time. The intact human brain is the only known system that can interpret and respond to various visual and acoustic patterns such as *Can you open the window?* sometimes with a *No* and at other times by opening the window. Therefore, unlike researchers of other cognitive phenomena, (neuro)psycholinguists cannot avail themselves of invasive techniques in non-human animals to uncover the responsible mechanisms in the large parts of the (human) brain that have been implicated in language processing (Binder et al., 1997). Engagement of these different anatomical areas does, however, generate distinct patterns of biological activity (such as ion flow across neural membranes) that can be recorded inside and outside the heads of humans as they quickly, often seamlessly, and without much conscious reflection on the computations and linguistic regularities involved, understand spoken, written, or signed sentences.

23.1 Electrophysiology

The neural transmissions that underlie human communication involve the flow of charged particles across neural membranes. These currents generate electric potentials in the conductive media both inside and outside cells, which can be recorded as voltage differences between any two electrodes on the scalp. These measurements are especially sensitive to the currents at the receiving end of neurons, i.e. neurotransmitter-initiated voltage changes in the dendritic arbor of a neuron, which either increase the likelihood of its firing (excitatory post-synaptic potentials; EPSPs), or decrease it (inhibitory post-synaptic potentials; IPSPs). The scalp-recorded activity is the sum of the EPSPs and IPSPs from many neurons—primarily, neocortical pyramidal cells oriented in parallel—acting in concert and in like manner (Nunez 1981; Kutas and Dale 1997).

Because they involve the monitoring of groups of neurons "talking" to each other on a moment-by-moment basis at various scalp locations, electrophysiological measures are especially valuable for tracking the rapid ebb and flow of routine language processing. This involves a wide range of analytic and synthetic operations, including sensory-perceptual analyses and encoding, attentional allocation, retrieval from long-term storage, short-term storage, comparison-matching, mapping, inhibiting, organizing, and integrating different information types to create new structures—many processes that have ERP correlates in non-language tasks. These processes take place in a multi-layered system, with principles that apply to different levels of organization—sounds (phonetics and phonology), words (morphology), phrases and sentences (syntax), entire written or spoken texts (discourse and information structure), and meaning (semantics and pragmatics)—and unfold over different time-courses. All of these are temporally and spatially extended brain processes that operate on dynamic representations distributed throughout the brain and thus demand moment-to-moment monitoring. While the nature of the information representations, the timing of their availability and use, and their degree of independence and interaction are controversial, the need for a (neural) measure with a fine temporal resolution sensitive to psychological variables at intervals ranging from a few milliseconds to minutes is not.

Electrical brain activity offers a host of dependent measures in both the frequency and time domains. Until quite recently electrophysiological studies of language have been based primarily on the concept of evoked or event-related potentials, whereby some triggering event causes a change in the brain's response in a way that is relatable to its content and/or context (though see Altenmüller and Gerloff, 1998; Bastiaansen et al., 2002; Roehm et al., 2004 for alternative measures of electrical brain activity). The most common way to analyze such data is to form averages from the electroencephalogram coincident with many physically identical or conceptually similar individual trials (e.g. agreement violations), time-locked to some trigger event (generally, an external stimulus or a subject-generated movement). Random transient activity that is not synchronized to the triggering event tends to average out over many repetitions, leaving an electrical signal that presumably reflects activity causally related to the event: the event related brain potential or ERP (reviewed in Münte et al., 2000; Rösler, 2005).

Though ERPs are most often time-locked to event onsets, other critical time-points, such as word recognition points, presumed or real prosodic boundaries, moments of information delivery or ends of events can also serve as synchronizing triggers. Although most ERP analyses are based on cross-trial averages for 12-40 "similar" participants, item-based ERPs also can be created by averaging the brain's response to each single event across individuals. Müller and Kutas (1996), for example, used this approach to show differential brain processing for an individual's own name (presented only once experimentally) compared to many different individual names. Finally, though most language ERP data are scalp-recorded, one can record from neuropsychological patients using strip electrodes on the cortical surface or intracranial electrodes implanted in the brain (Halgren et al., 1994a; 1994b; Nobre et al., 1994; Fernandez et al., 2001; Halgren et al., 2002 for magnetic counterpart of ERP recordings). Such brain activity provides extremely sensitive indices of dynamic changes in brain states or operations as a function of various inputs, affording a means of tracking how and when the brain responds to events. ERPs provide an especially good link between the physical and mental world because they directly reflect brain activity whose parameters (amplitude, latency, topography) are sensitive to manipulations of psychological—for present purposes psycholinguistic—variables.

23.2 Language and the brain

Words or related items, such as meaningful pictures, sounds, or gestures, elicit characteristic patterns of electrophysiological responses reflecting the activation of perceptual, attentional, memory-related, and higher-order cognitive and neural processes that come into play as the sensory input is identified, attended, analyzed, linked to meaning, and related to larger-scale information structures (e.g. syntactic trees, situation models). Initial ERP features (sometimes called "components") to such items are especially sensitive to stimulus parameters (frequency, intensity, duration, location) and, in some cases, to the availability and allocation of attentional resources. At these early stages of processing, ERPs to language inputs are largely indistinguishable from those to non-linguistic inputs; indeed, it seems to take the brain some time to categorize a stimulus as letter-string-like (~95 ms), linguistic and/or potentially meaningful (~180 ms) (Schendan et al., 1998).

It is an oversimplification, however, to talk about "the" time course of language processing in the brain. Language stimuli are neurally complex, as they extend over space and time and contain multiple features and feature values that will typically be analyzed along multiple neural pathways that operate in parallel but with different functional characteristics and different time-courses. In this respect, psycholinguistic events (such as "lexical access," parsing, and meaning construction) are *processes* distributed over time and space, with no temporal or spatial boundary. Rather than being a momentary event, something like lexical access likely involves an accumulation of information that gradually separates word-like from non-word-like stimuli. Indeed, although lexicality-based ERP differences can first be observed around 200 ms, words and pseudo-words continue to elicit very similar ERP signatures (thus still being differentiated) well beyond 400 ms (Bentin et al., 1999). Similarly, psycholinguistic variables like word frequency affect processing in qualitatively different ways at multiple times. In the visual modality, frequency first affects the amplitude of a positivity around 150 ms (P150; Proverbio et al., 2004), a component presumed to reflect a visual processing stage sensitive to orthographic regularity. Frequency next impacts the latency of a negativity peaking from 240 to 400 ms post-stimulus-onset, with more frequent words eliciting an earlier peak than less frequent ones (Osterhout et al., 1997; King and Kutas, 1998; Münte et al., 2001). Slightly later, frequency affects the amplitude of a negativity (N400) with all else held constant. Still later, around 600+ ms, high-frequency words are associated a greater positivity, though only under some task conditions (Rugg, 1990).

As illustrated for word frequency, with increasing processing time, electrophysiological responses to language stimuli depend less on physical aspects of a stimulus and more on the nature of the information (semantic, syntactic) linked to that stimulus, the context, and task demands. A number of components that are sensitive—though not necessarily specific—to linguistic manipulations or representations have been identified. These provide functionally specific indices of cognitive and neural activity that can be used under well-defined experimental conditions to test certain types of hypotheses about the nature and separability of psycholinguistic processes and representations, even if we do not yet appreciate the exact functions indexed.

In the next sections, we introduce in turn the ERP responses that have played an important role in the study of language processing. After describing each component and discussing its functional and neurophysiological bases, we examine some of the key issues that studies using that component have addressed. We begin with the N400 (section 23.3.1), an ERP response that has been closely linked to the processing of meaning, and we describe studies using this measure that have addressed context effects in meaning construction (23.3.2), hemispheric differences in sentence processing (23.3.3), and non-literal language processing (23.3.4). We next describe a set of ERP components (the left anterior negavitity (LAN), the early left anterior negativity (ELAN) and the P600) that have been linked to various aspects of syntactic processing (23.4.1) and discuss what they have revealed about parsing (23.4.2). In section 23.5 we introduce components that unfold over longer time-courses (slow potentials and the closure positive shift (CPS)), and describe their contributions to our understanding of how information is integrated across multiple words. We end with cursory mention of what ERPs have revealed about plasticity and learning in language (section 23.6).

23.3 **Processing language meaning**

23.3.1 **N400**

The N400, a relative negativity seen between 250 and 550 ms, was originally discovered in response to semantic anomalies ending sentences (e.g. *I take my coffee with cream and dog*; Kutas and Hillyard, 1980a), but is now considered to be part of the default electrophysiological response to potentially meaningful items (words, pseudowords, pictures) in any modality. Content words generally elicit larger N400s than function words (though see King and Kutas, 1995); among function words, those with richer lexical semantic content elicit larger N400s (Kluender and Kutas, 1993). N400s generally have centro-posterior maxima, though their scalp distributions vary with stimulus features (e.g. more anterior for concrete than abstract words; Kounios and Holcomb, 1994; Holcomb et al., 1999) and input modality (e.g. more central for auditory stimuli; McCallum et al., 1984; Holcomb and Anderson, 1993). Distributional differences notwithstanding, N400 amplitude is modulated by a host of factors that render particular words/concepts more accessible, e.g. word frequency, repetition, neighborhood size, sentence position, presence of lexically or semantically associated words, and predictability within a sentence or larger discourse structure. The ERP in the region of the N400 is also sensitive to orthographic, phonological, and morphological relationships (Kutas and Federmeier, 2001; Dominguez et al., 2004; Kutas et al., 2007) and unexpected case morphology (Münte and Heinze, 1994; Hopf et al., 1998). N400s typically are not observed to grammatical violations (if these do not impact meaning) or to violations of prosody (Astesano et al., 2004). N400s have typically not been observed in music (Besson and Macar, 1987) or for non-linguistic manipulations of meaningful stimuli (improbable word font changes; Kutas and Hillyard, 1980b), but are elicited by unrelated environmental sounds (Van Petten and Rheinfelder, 1995), incongruent picture story endings (West and Holcomb, 2002), and by improbable objects in video clips of daily life events (Sitnikova et al., 2003).

N400 relatedness and repetition effects are significantly attenuated by attentional selection based on space or color (McCarthy and Nobre, 1993).

Nonetheless, they are seen even when the prime or target stimuli appear so quickly as to not leave any declarable memory trace (as with masking; Stenberg et al., 2000; Hohlfeld et al., 2004; Holcomb et al., 2005; during the attentional blink; Luck et al., 1996; Rolke et al., 2001). These results suggest that the processes reflected in the N400 are neither fully automatic nor fully controlled. Overall, neuropsychological, intracranial, and magnetoencephalographic data suggest that a large portion of the temporal lobes, encompassing areas critical for access to semantic memory, are responsible for the scalp-recorded N400, with a larger contribution from the left hemisphere than the right (for review see Van Petten and Luka, 2006). Its variable topography suggests that scalp-recorded N400s may reflect a set of spatially distributed but temporally coincident neural processes involved in meaning construction, though localization inquiries to date have been limited to very basic N400 effects.

23.3.2 **Context effects in meaning processing**

Though specific neither to language nor to semantics, the extant data suggest that N400 amplitude is a general index of the ease or difficulty of retrieving stored conceptual knowledge associated with a word (or other potentially meaningful stimulus), which is dependent upon both the stored representation itself and the retrieval cues provided by the preceding context. It is thus often linked to semantic or contextual integration processes (Chwilla et al., 1995). The N400 has played an especially important role in providing insights into meaning construction — how and when meaning is gleaned from words, sentences, and discourses (note: the nogo N200 component is also used to track word processing; Schiller et al., 2003).

One key question has concerned the time-course with which word information is used to build a message level meaning. The construction of a higher-order meaning representation might proceed in spurts, with incoming word information buffered until major linguistic (phrasal, clausal, sentential) boundaries trigger integration. Alternatively, sentence processing might proceed incrementally, with higher-order representations built and updated with each incoming word. The presence of an N400 within 200 or so ms of the onset of a lexical-semantic anomaly has consistently supported the immediacy assumption for semantic analysis. Moreover, even for words which are congruous in their context, N400 amplitudes decline progressively with the eliciting word's ordinal position within the sentence, presumably reflecting the incremental build-up of contextual information as sentences unfold (Van Petten and Kutas, 1990). Critically, such a decline is *not* observed for syntactic prose or scrambled sentences that provide a continuous stream of lexical information but no opportunity to build a coherent message-level representation (Van Petten and Kutas, 1991). Moreover, contextual influences on spoken words occur before the acoustic information is sufficient to uniquely identify the words (Van Petten et al., 1999), Such findings strongly suggest that sentence interpretations are immediate and computed incrementally, though they do not inform current debates about what types of intermediate representation (semantic, grammatical, etc.) are constructed and when, if ever, each word is processed "fully" (Frazier, 1999). Studies looking at slow potentials that evolve over the course of clauses and sentences also provide support for incremental processing, pointing to a critical role for working memory (see section 23.5 below). ERP data also suggest that clausal, prosodic, and sentential boundaries may indeed constitute important points for some integrative processes (Kutas and King, 1996; Steinhauer, 2003)—perhaps (speculatively) because the representation built at each word is not always complete.

Since the discovery of the N400 difference between contextually congruent and anomalous words in sentences, ERPs have played an important role in uncovering the nature, time-course, and functional identity of the ubiquitous context effects on word processing. ERP measures are especially useful in adjudicating between different theoretical stances on whether context effects in connected discourse arise via the same mechanisms as context effects in word pairs (such as lexical priming), or via wholly distinct mechanisms (message-level constraints), or some combination thereof. Whereas behavioral data are mixed (Duffy et al., 1989; Traxler et al., 2000), ERP data unequivocally show that whether the context is a single word, a sentence fragment, or a larger discourse, context effects manifest in qualitatively similar electrophysiological responses, implicating similar neural mechanisms. Regardless of level, context modulates the N400 region of the ERP: lexically related, sententially congruent, and discourse-appropriate items are all associated with relatively less N400 activity, in a manner graded by contextual strength (reviewed in Kutas and Federmeier, 2000). Moreover, all context effects start at about the same latency (~150–200 ms), with the impact of discourse- and sentence-level contexts occasionally preceding that of a lexically associated word. Van Petten (1993) embedded pairs of associated or unassociated words in congruent or anomalous (syntactic prose) contexts, and found that both lexical and sentential constraints reduced N400 amplitudes in a similar fashion, and additively. Thus, though lexical and message-level constraints can operate in parallel, they have qualitatively similar impacts at some processing stages. However, the nature of the interaction between lexical and sentential information has been found to vary across age groups and individuals, as well as with sentence position and contextual strength (Van Petten and Kutas, 1990; Van Petten et al., 1997; Federmeier et al., 2003). Indeed, lexical effects—of word frequency (Van Petten and Kutas, 1990) or lexical association (Van Petten et al., 1997), for example—are subsumed by message-level constraints when these are sufficiently strong, indicating that lexical priming does not necessarily have temporal or functional priority over message-level processing. More generally, such patterns highlight the importance of examining language processing at multiple levels—word, sentence, discourse—as findings at one level do not necessarily generalize well to others. ERP researchers (like other psycholinguists) have only begun to appreciate and explore the availability of different sorts of contextual information (e.g. shared assumptions and common knowledge structures between familiar language partners in a rich environment) and the critical role that they must play in the processing of natural language, which is often impoverished—i.e. noisy, missing information, and with information dropped or referred to with relatively "empty" placeholders.

Given that message-level information has a role in word processing, an important question becomes how that information is used. Many language comprehension models seem to explicitly or implicitly assume that the influence of context is relatively passive, occurring fairly late in word processing, after a word's features have already been accessed, i.e. post-lexically. On such accounts, word processing including access to meaning, proceeds in a bottom-up fashion, largely, if not completely, unaffected by sentence- or discourse-level information (Forster, 1981). Context merely eases the integration between matching features in the conceptual information activated via bottom-up processes and the message-level representation built of prior context. Alternatively, context information may be used in a more top-down fashion, such that features of upcoming words or concepts are at least partially activated prior to their occurrence, thereby affecting processing even during early ("prelexical") stages of word processing. A number of recent ERP studies have provided solid evidence supporting this latter view. Federmeier and Kutas (1999a), for example, recorded ERPs as participants read pairs of sentences designed to elicit a particular noun from a particular semantic category (e.g. *Every morning John makes himself a glass of freshly squeezed juice. He keeps his refrigerator stocked with* …). Three types of sentence endings were used: the expected completion (*oranges*), an unexpected completion from the same semantic category (*apples*), and an unexpected completion from a different semantic category (*carrots*). N400 amplitudes were smaller for expected as compared with unexpected completions; however, among unexpected completions amplitudes were smaller to items from the same category than from a different category, even though these were matched for contextual fit (plausibility). Furthermore, the degree of facilitation for the within-category violations was graded by the level of participants' expectations for the most common completions. As these were not actually presented, their impact on the processing of the categorically related words suggests that comprehenders use context to actively prepare for—i.e. predict—semantic features of upcoming items (see Figure 23.1).

Wicha and her colleagues (2003a; 2003b; 2004) demonstrated that readers and listeners also develop expectations about syntactic features (grammatical gender) of a likely upcoming word in Spanish. As participants processed sentences that were predictive of a particular noun, ERP effects were observed on the preceding article when its gender disagreed with that of the contextually expected—but not yet presented—upcoming word. Van Berkum et al. (2005) likewise showed prediction-based effects (early positivity) on ERPs time-locked to suffixes of gender-marked Dutch adjectives when these mismatched the syntactic gender of the contextually expected noun in congruent, spoken sentences; critically, these effects vanished in the absence of discourse context. Finally, DeLong et al. (2005) capitalized on a phonological regularity of English—words beginning with vowel-sounds are preceded by *an*, whereas words beginning with consonant-sounds are preceded by *a*—to look for prediction of word-forms with specific phonological content (lexemes), and not just their semantic and syntactic properties. The N400 to the indefinite article was well-predicted by the probability of its occurrence and that of

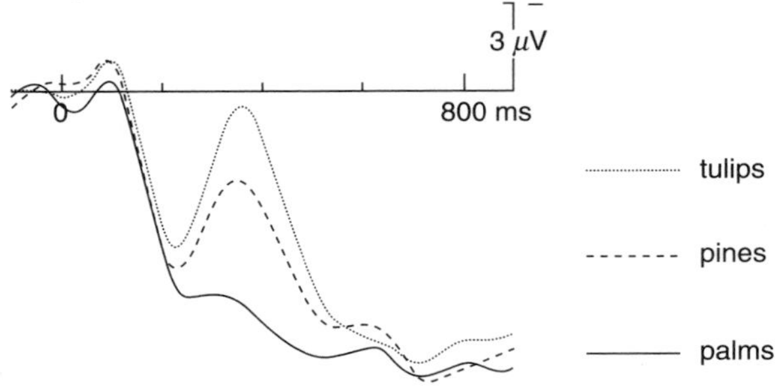

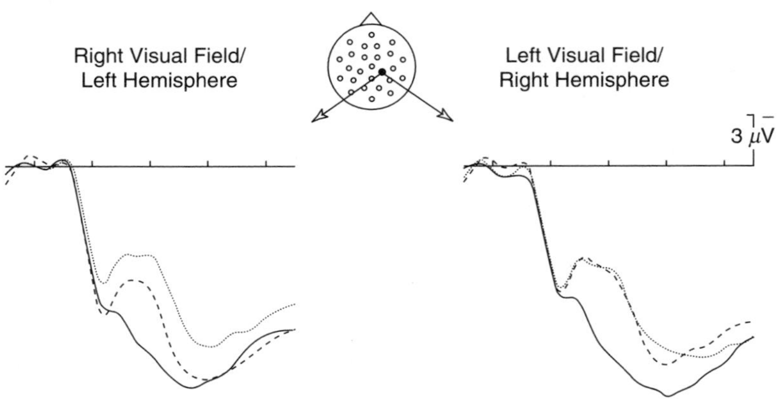

Figure 23.1 TOP: Grand average ERPs (N=18), shown at a representative right medio-central scalp site (see head icon), to the final words of sentences read for comprehension one word at a time in the center of the screen. As illustrated by the example, sentences were completed with three ending types: (1) *expected exemplars*, the highest Cloze probability completions for these contexts; (2) *within-category violations*, unexpected and implausible completions from the same semantic category as the expected exemplars; and (3) *between-category violations*, unexpected and implausible completions from a different (though related) semantic category. All unexpected items elicited increased negativity between 250 and 500 ms post-stimulus onset (N400) relative to the expected exemplars (solid line). However, despite equivalent Cloze probabilities and plausibility ratings, the N400 to the two unexpected items differed as a function of their semantic similarity to the expected completions. Within-category violations (dashed line), which shared many semantic features in common with the expected exemplars, elicited smaller N400s than did between-category violations (dotted line), which had less semantic feature overlap. The results suggest that the comprehension system anticipates and prepares to process the semantic features of likely upcoming words.

BOTTOM: Grand average ERPs (N=18) from a different group of participants who read these same sentences for comprehension in a visual half-field presentation paradigm. Sentence-context words were presented at central fixation, whereas sentence-final targets were presented with nearest edge two degrees to the left or right of fixation. Words presented to the left visual field travel initially to the right hemisphere and vice versa. The response to target words presented to the right visual field/left hemisphere (shown on the left side of the figure) yielded the same pattern as that observed with central fixation. This pattern is indicative of a "predictive" strategy, in which semantic information associated with the expected item is pre-activated in the course of processing the context. The response to targets presented to the left visual field/right hemisphere (shown on the right side of the figure) was qualitatively different: expected exemplars again elicited smaller N400s than violations, but the response to the two violation types did not differ. This pattern is more consistent with a plausibility-based integrative strategy. Taken together, the results indicate that the hemispheres differ in how they use context to access information from semantic memory during on-line sentence reading.

the upcoming—not yet seen but clearly anticipated—noun, estimated from offline Cloze procedures. These studies have in common that they find ERP influences from words never presented or not yet presented at the time of measurement—i.e. evidence of pre-activation.

23.3.3 **Hemispheric differences in sentence processing**

Though a predictive strategy may be more efficient and robust in the face of noise/ambiguity, those who have argued against it maintain that it would yield too many mistakes and/or would tax certain cognitive resources. The ideal, then, would be to use *multiple* strategies in parallel, and there is increasing evidence that the brain might do just that, by distributing processing across the two cerebral hemispheres.

Since Paul Broca's discovery (in 1861) of an association between fluent, articulate speech and the left frontal operculum, the critical role of the left hemisphere (LH) for language processing has become one of the most striking and oft-cited examples of hemispheric specialization in humans. However, recent evidence suggests that both hemispheres make critical, albeit different, contributions to aural/oral and visual/manual language comprehension. Non-invasive spatial neuroimaging data have revealed language-related activation in brain areas outside the regions classically associated with aphasia, including some in the right hemisphere (RH) (Ni et al., 2000). Moreover, some of these data, particularly those collected during the comprehension of complex narratives (St George et al., 1999; Robertson et al., 2000) or non-literal language (Bottini et al., 1994), show bilateral activation with a predominance of RH activity. One must then ask what language functions the RH supports, how these differ from LH functions, and what role they play in normal language processing.

Several studies have now combined ERP measures with visual half-field (VF) presentations traditionally used to examine hemispheric differences. This technique takes advantage of the fact that information presented in the visual periphery (more than a half degree from fixation) is initially received exclusively by the contralateral hemisphere, eliciting processing biases that persist into higher-order aspects of cognition. While such behavioral studies examine only the extent of preferential or predominant processing by one hemisphere over another, those with concurrent brain measures license decomposing the lateralized contribution of the processes underlying performance. Since these processes occur quite early—and many very quickly—the temporal resolution of ERPs (and their magnetic counterparts) gives them a unique advantage in assessing not just whether both hemispheres respond to particular types of stimulus or under particular task conditions, but whether those responses occur rapidly enough to contribute to a particular function as it unfolds.

Coulson et al. (2005) used the combined half-field ERP method to examine each hemisphere's sensitivity to lexical and message-level information. In one experiment, participants viewed associated and unassociated word pairs; primes were presented centrally and targets lateralized to the left (LVF) or right (RVF) visual fields. In a second experiment, these same word pairs were embedded in sentence contexts, wherein the targets formed plausible and implausible message-level completions. For word pairs out of context, robust effects of association, with identical onsets, were found on N400s for presentation to both VFs, though slightly bigger after RVF/LH presentation. This suggests that the LH is better equipped to make use of word-level information when that is the only context available. However, association effects for these same word-pairs within sentences were largely superseded by sentential plausibility in both VFs, suggesting that both hemispheres are sensitive to message-level information. Association exerted a very small effect on the N400s to incongruent endings for both VFs; association effects in congruent sentences, however, were only apparent for LVF/RH stimuli. Thus, when higher-level context information was available, LH processing seemed to be less affected than RH processing by the word-level cues.

Federmeier and Kutas (1999b; 2002) found that while both hemispheres use message-level context information for word processing, they do so differently. In response to lateralized presentation of the final words of the sentence pairs and ending types used to examine predictive processing, as previously described (section 23.3.2), there were equivalent-sized N400 congruency effects (difference between expected items and out-of-category violations), with similar timing in both VFs (bottom of Figure 23.1). This result suggests that RH word processing is sensitive to message-level information. However, priming for the semantically related but contextually implausible endings (within category violations) was greater following RVF/LH presentation; indeed, in the LVF/RH, responses to the two violation types were identical. In other words, only the LH showed the pattern associated with prediction; the RH's pattern, instead, was consonant with the bottom-up plausibility of the words in their sentence contexts. Since a similar pattern was obtained with lateralized line drawings, it appears to reflect something general about how each hemisphere uses sentential context rather than something specific to reading (Federmeier and Kutas, 2002).

ERP comparisons to laterally presented congruent words differing only in the extent to which they were contextually constrained suggest that predictive processing by the LH may extend to pre-semantic levels of analysis (Federmeier et al., 2005). Increased contextual constraint facilitated N400s equivalently in both VFs, providing added support for the hypothesis that the RH can build and make use of detailed message-level language information. VF-based differences in constraint effects on higher-level visual processing, however, were evident on the frontal P2, a positive potential peaking around 200 ms. P2 modulations have been linked to the detection and analysis of visual features in selective attention tasks (Hillyard and Münte, 1984; Luck and Hillyard, 1994), with larger amplitudes to stimuli containing target features. P2 responses to strongly constrained targets were enhanced only with RVF/LH presentation. These findings support the hypothesis that LH processing of sentences provides top-down information, affording more efficient visual extraction from highly expected targets. Such top-down information seems to be less available for stimuli projected initially to the RH.

In combination with behavioral studies, ERP data suggest that the right hemisphere—like the left—is able to understand words and their relationships, and to use word information to build higher-level meaning representations, albeit differently. ERPs are beginning to reveal the consequences of these differences for multiple stages of word perception and language processing. More generally, such research points to the real possibility that that there may not be a single model of language comprehension; instead, multiple mechanisms may be employed in parallel, distributed across the hemispheres. Though more perplexing for psycholinguists, such multiplicity is an effective strategy for the brain to employ, since some redundancy is useful and since it may help optimize the trade-offs engendered by choosing either a serial, bottom-up or a more interactive (bottom-up plus top-down) processing strategy. However, this also means that information from multiple processing pathways must ultimately be brought together for an understanding of hemispheric integration as well as sentence processing. These are processes we are still far from understanding, but which we assume must be highly time-dependent, since information arriving simultaneously at the same place can interact, while information that does not, cannot.

23.3.4 Non-literal language processing

The potentially different contributions of the hemispheres to language processing also have been hypothesized to be critical for figurative language processing. A long-standing distinction has been made between literal and non-literal language, which includes figurative devices such as metaphors, idioms, indirect requests, irony, and sarcasm. At issue is whether identical mechanisms can account for the comprehension of literal and figurative language, which neuropsychological data have traditionally linked to the left and right hemispheres, respectively. On the standard pragmatic view, all language is initially interpreted literally, with figurative construal pursued only after the literal construal fails (Searle, 1979). From this it follows that literal and figurative language are processed with qualitatively different neurocomputational mechanisms, with those that compute literal meaning acting first. These predictions have generally not been supported by reaction time data; substantial evidence indicates that metaphor processing is not necessarily slower nor always optional (Gildea and Glucksberg, 1983; Gibbs et al., 1997). Current processing models of metaphor comprehension thus assume that literal and non-literal language comprehension occur with similar time course, involve the same processing mechanisms, and are sensitive to the same variables (Gibbs, 1994; Wolff and Gentner, 2000).

Equivalent reaction times, however, do not necessarily mean equivalent processing (resource) demands, nor can they be unquestionably taken as evidence for identical neurocomputational mechanisms. These reasons alone would suffice to warrant electrophysiological comparisons of the processing of literal vs. metaphorical statements. If metaphorical and literal processing elicited waveforms differing in shape, and/or scalp topography, we would conclude that they do not engage identical mechanisms. Alternatively, if the only difference was in a temporal shift of some component, we might conclude that one construal precedes the other. However, across a handful of studies, ERPs elicited by words processed metaphorically are remarkably similar to those elicited by words processed literally, with only a slightly larger, though no more or less lateralized, N400 to metaphors. Context attenuates N400 amplitudes similarly in metaphorical and literal sentences (Pynte et al., 1996). These results suggest qualitatively similar processes of meaning construction—e.g. retrieving stored conceptual knowledge and contextual integration—for literal and metaphorical sentences, though with more effort for metaphors.

Further ERP evidence that literal and metaphorical interpretations can be available with similar time-courses comes from ERP recordings as participants decided whether sentences were *literally* true or false (Kazmerski et al., 2003). Both types of literally false sentence—anomalous sentences that could not be interpreted metaphorically (*The rumor was a lumberjack*) and metaphors (*The beaver is a lumberjack*)—elicited large N400s relative to literally true sentences. However, the N400s (and associated reaction times) to metaphors were smaller, at least in those with high IQs, consistent with automatic extraction of figurative meanings during the construction of literal meaning. Individuals with lower IQs, by contrast, produced slightly smaller positivities to true sentences, and same-sized N400s for metaphors and anomalies, along with good off-line metaphor comprehension. Clearly, metaphorical processing is not always obligatory or automatic, with availability of resources to meet processing demands being a critical factor.

Coulson and Van Petten (2002) reasoned that if similar mapping operations (noting correspondences between target and source domains, selecting relevant characteristics, and filtering out or actively suppressing irrelevant ones) are invoked by both literal and metaphorical sentences, but to varying degrees, it should be possible to find some literal sentences that also depend on these processes. To that end, they constructed sentences describing situations where one object was substituted, mistaken for, or used to represent another (*He used cough syrup as an intoxicant*), which required the setting up of mappings between two objects and the domains in which they commonly occur (literal mapping). These literal mapping processes were presumably intermediate to the intricate mapping used in metaphor comprehension (*He knows that power is a strong intoxicant*), and the minimal, if any, mapping used in the comprehension of literal sentences (*He knows that whiskey is a strong intoxicant*). And sentence-final words did indeed show graded N400s—smallest for literal sentences, largest for metaphors, and intermediate for the literal mapping condition. These data suggest that it is the complexity rather than uniqueness of mapping and conceptual integration processes that sometimes calls for more effort to understand metaphorical (than literal) expressions.

Essentially the same sorts of question have been asked regarding joke comprehension. Are jokes in fact neurocomputationally special? ERPs to final words of one-line jokes and non-joke straight sentences (matched on Cloze probability) do reliably differ, though the way in which they differ varies with contextual constraint, the extent to which individuals got the joke, verbal skills, handedness, and visual field of presentation (Coulson and Kutas, 2001; Coulson and Lovett, 2004; Coulson and Wu, 2005). Coulson and Williams (2005), for example, observed larger N400s to jokes relative to non-jokes only when punchlines were presented to the RVF/LH; with LVF/RH presentations, jokes and low Cloze endings elicited equivalent-sized N400s relative to high Cloze endings. ERP data, overall, indicate substantial overlap in joke and non-joke processing, with no evidence for any serial two-stage account of joke processing. Though some aspects of joke comprehension seem easier for the right hemisphere, this seems to be a matter of degree. Perhaps the most valuable lesson for all language studies is the need to keep track of whether people comprehend, and of their verbal ability, handedness, and gender, among other factors (e.g. working memory span), when assessing language comprehension.

23.4 Processing language form

23.4.1 LAN, ELAN, and P600

While the N400 has been linked to the processing of a word at the level of meaning, other ERP responses have been more closely associated with syntactic processing, honoring at least some processing, if not representational, distinctions between the two (see Figure 23.2). Syntactic anomalies are sometimes accompanied by an enhanced negativity over anterior scalp sites, of variable onset, duration, and topography (sometimes with a left hemisphere focus) called the Left Anterior Negativity (LAN). Occasionally, stretches of sentences with relatively complex hierarchical structures (e.g. embedded clauses) are accompanied by sustained frontal negativities typically

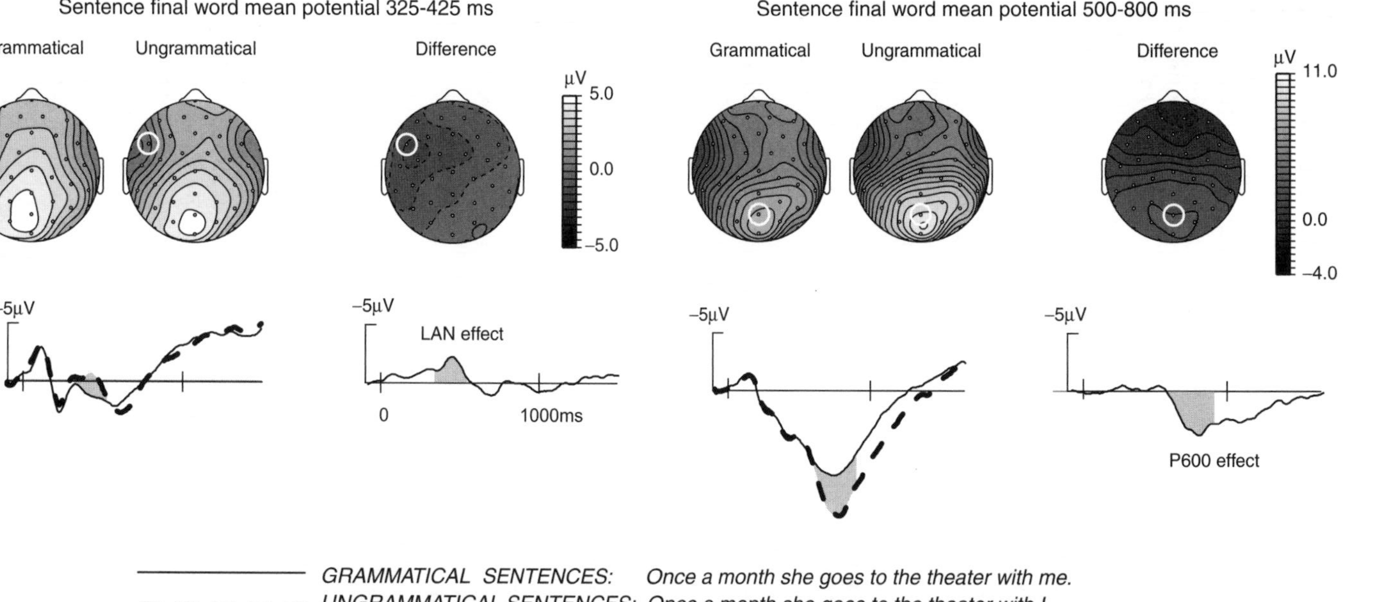

Figure 23.2 Representative data depicting a left anterior negativity (LAN) and a P600 to grammatical violations. Shown are grand average ERPs (N=16) to sentence-final words of grammatical and ungrammatical sentences which participants read one word at a time and to which they made a "sensible and grammatical" delayed response. Grammatical violations included both incorrect case markings on pronoun, as in the sample sentence, and number mismatches on verbs. Included in the stimulus set were semantically congruent and anomalous sentence endings. Spatial distribution of the mean amplitudes (shaded area) for one left frontal site between 325 and 425 ms post-final word onset and one mid-line parietal site between 300 and 500 ms (sites marked by a white circle) are shown for grammatical endings, ungrammatical endings, and the difference ERP calculated by subtracting the grammatical ERP from the ungrammatical ending ERP. (Source: unpublished data from dissertation by D. Groppe.)

spanning several words (see also section 23.4.2 below), and have typically been related to working memory processes (Fiebach et al., 2002; Felser et al., 2003); the precise relationship between the local, phasic LAN activity and these sustained slow negativities remains an open question.

Some researchers have further distinguished the phasic negativities occurring between 100-300 ms post-word onset—an early LAN, or ELAN, associated with word category errors—from those occurring between 300 and 500ms or later, associated with morphosyntactic errors (Friederici, 2002). Both this division and the functional significance of these negativities are controversial. On a domain-specific construal, LAN activity globally reflects violations of syntactic well-formedness. Alternatively, on a domain-general construal, the negativity reflects primarily working memory processes (Kluender and Kutas, 1993), perhaps with a fronto-central storage component, and a fronto-temporal retrieval component (Matzke et al., 2002), on the assumption that the extended negativity is primarily the sum of local LANs.

More precisely, some researchers identify the ELAN with an early, automatic local phrase structure-building process, during which word category information is used to assign an initial syntactic structure; its latency has been said to vary with when information about word class becomes available (Friederici et al., 1996). Consistent with this proposal, an ELAN is only seen in response to closed-class items and phrase structure violations, even in pseudo-word sentences (Hahne and Jescheniak, 2001), is insensitive to attentional manipulations, impervious to the proportion of ill-formed experimental sentences (Hahne and Friederici, 1999), does not appear until 6 years of age (Hahne et al., 2004), and is severely compromised by damage to anterior regions of the left hemisphere, as in Broca's aphasics (ter Keurs et al., 2002; Kotz and Friederici, 2003). The generality of ELAN across languages remains unknown (see Neville et al., 1991 for ELAN to phrase structure violations in English, but Hagoort and Brown, 2000 for a failure to find such evidence in Dutch).

The later LAN, while likewise elicited by phrase structure violations, also has been observed for morphosyntactic violations of various types in several languages: violations of agreement (Angrilli et al., 2002; Roehm et al., 2005), case markings (Osterhout et al., 1996; Coulson et al., 1998a; Münte, Heinze et al., 1998), and verb inflections (Gunter et al., 1997: exp. 3). These results are consistent with the proposed link between the later LAN and morphosyntactic violations and the hypothesis that it indexes a stage subsequent to initial phrase structure-building, varying in amplitude with processing difficulties in using syntactic information such as subcategorization and inflectional morphology (number, gender, case) in thematic role assignment. Morphosyntactic violations, however, appear not to be sufficient or necessary for LAN elicitation. For example, some violations of subject–verb agreement (e.g. Hagoort et al., 1993; Osterhout et al., 1996; Münte et al., 1997; Coulson et al., 1998a; Kemmer, et al., 2004) and some verb inflection violations (Gunter et al., 1997: exp. 1; Osterhout and Nicol, 1999) do not yield any LAN activity. Moreover, LAN activity has also been observed to syntactic violations that are not morphosyntactic in nature, such as argument structure violations (Friederici and Frisch, 2000: exp. 1), and to subcategorization violations (Hagoort and Brown, 2000: exp. 2), as well as in syntactically complex sentences (filler gap constructions) without violations (Kluender and Kutas, 1993). Finally, a LAN has reportedly been seen in well-formed but complex sentences, to lexical ambiguities (Hagoort and Brown 1994), and perhaps even during multiplication (Jost et al., 2004).

Syntactic violations of various sorts also elicit a relatively late, positive potential that is often largest over central and parietal sites, initially labeled the "syntactic positive shift" (SPS) but now called the "P600" (Neville et al., 1991; Osterhout and Holcomb, 1992; Friederici et al., 1993; Hagoort et al., 1993; Osterhout and Hagoort, 1999). The P600 typically occurs between 500 to 800 ms, usually as a broad peakless shift, though it can peak as early as 325 ms. P600s have been observed in response to violations of subject–verb agreement (even in syntactic prose), verb or case inflection, and phrase structure, among others. It is, however, clearly not specific to syntactic violations per se: P600s are also seen in syntactically well-formed sentences that have a non-preferred syntactic structure (e.g. at the disambiguating word following a temporary syntactic ambiguity), and in unambiguous but syntactically complex sentences (Kaan et al., 2000; Frisch et al., 2002; Felser et al., 2003).

P600s to number agreement violations are attenuated in Broca's aphasics with severe syntactic deficits (Wassenaar et al., 2004), and P600s to verb argument structure violations are severely compromised in individuals with basal ganglia damage (Kotz et al., 2003). Accordingly, the P600 is presumed to reflect some aspect of syntactic processing difficulty: e.g. a controlled process of syntactic reanalysis or repair given a mismatch between lexico-semantic and syntactic representation (Friederici, 2002); an inability of the parser to assign the preferred structure (Hagoort et al., 1993); general syntactic integration costs (Kaan et al., 2000); or structure-building, checking, and diagnosis, with a latency that depends on the time required to identify and activate elements for these operations (Phillips et al., 2005). Topographic and latency differences, however, suggest there might be a family of P600s with different distributions (frontal, parietal), latencies (early, late) and functional significances (syntactic integration, syntactic repair, and reanalysis), though the details remain controversial (Hagoort and Brown, 2000; Friederici et al., 2001; 2002; Kaan and Swaab, 2003; Carreiras et al., 2004).

Alternatively, it has been suggested that the P600 is a domain-general (not language-specific) response. This conclusion is based on observations of positivities similar to the P600 in appearance, latency, and scalp distribution but elicited by non-syntactic violations within language, such as of orthography (misspelt words; Münte, Heinze et al., 1998) and lexico-semantics post-N400, as well by various non-linguistic violations such as those in music (harmonic and melodic; Besson and Macar, 1987; Janata, 1995), geometric forms (Besson and Macar, 1987), abstract sequences (Lelekov et al., 2000), and arithmetic sequences (Nieddeggen and Rösler, 1999; Nunez-Pena and Honrubbia-Serrano, 2004). These non-linguistic P600s are also similarly modulated by the difficulty of integrating the eliciting item into context. Patel et al. (1998) thus proposed that the P600 reflects a general index of violation in any rule-governed sequence. As P600 amplitude to syntactic violations has been found to vary with the proportion of experimental sentences that are syntactically ill-formed (when well-formedness is infrequent, it is the grammatical event that elicits the P600 instead), as well as with attentional manipulations, another domain-general hypothesis equates the P600 with the P3b (Coulson et al., 1998a; 1998b). The P3b is considered a general-purpose response to low probability events often associated with categorization and/or a binary decision, which on one account reflects working memory updating (Donchin and Coles, 1988; Kok, 2001).

A definitive conclusion about the equivalence (or even non-trivial resemblance) between P600s following syntactic violations and the positivities to non-syntactic violations and/or to the P3b cannot be reached without knowledge of their neural generators. The P600 may nonetheless be useful for investigating language-processing problems that are syntactic in nature—at least under well-defined conditions, given that at present no one can predict with certainty whether a P600 (or N400) will be elicited under novel experimental conditions. There are several recent reports of P600 effects together with either a small or no N400 in response to verbs that the authors believed should elicit N400s rather than P600s; e.g. *eat* in *At breakfast, the eggs would eat every day* (Kuperberg et al., 2003) elicited a small N400 together with a moderate-sized P600; *vluchten* in *De muizen die voor de kat vluchtten renden door de kamer*/ 'The cat that *fled* from the mice ran across the room' elicited a P600 (Kolk et al., 2003; van Herten et al., 2005); *geworpen* ending the Dutch sentence *De speer heft de atleten geworpen*/ "The javelin has by the athletes *thrown*" elicited a P600 (Hoeks et al., 2004), as did *devouring* in *The meal was devouring* (Kim and Osterhout, 2005). On the basis of such results, van Herten et al. (2005) suggested that the P600 reflects monitoring for the veridicality of unexpected linguistic events, though it could also reflect the momentary call for attentional resources by a well-practiced process running largely outside the focus of attention.

An intermediate domain-specific (but non-modular) account of syntax-related ERP components can be found in the Unification Model (Hagoort, 2003a, based on Vosse and Kempen, 2000). This is a lexicalist parsing model in which all syntactic information is stored and retrieved from the mental lexicon, with the only grammatical rule being to "unite" words (each a three-tiered structure of root node, functional node, and foot node). On this model, LAN activity reflects a binding failure whenever there are no two lexical items in the unification space for which a foot node of one matches the category of a root node of another, or a category match is accompanied by an egregious mismatch in grammatical feature specifications. The P600 reflects the ongoing process of establishing unification links with an amplitude determined by the degree of competition among alternative unification options, modulated by syntactic ambiguity, syntactic complexity, and semantic/pragmatics constraints.

23.4.2 **Parsing**

As for other aspects of language processing, determining the underlying syntactic structure of a sentence (sentence parsing) is rendered difficult by ever-present ambiguities. For example, consider a sentence such as *David told the girl that*, in which the role of *that* is temporarily lexically and syntactically uncertain; it could be a complementizer signaling a complement clause continuation (*David told the girl that there would be guests for dinner*), or a relative pronoun signaling a relative clause continuation (*David told the girl that had been on the phone to hang up*). Although the parser could theoretically adopt a "wait and see" approach to such ambiguities, as previously discussed, evidence suggests instead that comprehension proceeds incrementally, with readers and listeners attempting to integrate each word into a continually evolving message-level interpretation. There may be a cost to this incremental approach: adopting the wrong analysis initially can cause processing difficulties downstream such that a comprehender is "garden-pathed," e.g. at *had*, if *that* was initially taken to be a complementizer.

A number of different types of models have been put forward to explain how the language system deals with temporary ambiguities of this kind. These models differ along a number of dimensions, including whether non-syntactic information can affect the parse and whether the parser is restricted to choosing a single analysis or considers multiple possible parses at the same time. Extensive empirical work, using both behavioral and eye tracking measures, has been dedicating to adjudicating between these different accounts (see Altmann, 1998).

Brown, Hagoort, and van Berkum (Van Berkum et al., 1999; Brown et al., 2000; Van Berkum et al., 2003), for example, examined the ERP effects of discourse-semantic constraints and lexical-syntactic (grammatical gender) constraints on each other and on on-line parsing in mini-stories that ended with a sentence containing a temporary complement/relative clause ambiguity:

> **[Two] [One]-referent discourse contexts:**
> David had told *[the boy and the girlNEU]/[the two girlsNEU]* to clean up their room before lunch time. But the boy had stayed in bed all morning, and the girl had been on the phone all the time.
>
> **Target sentence with sentential complement:**
> David vertelde het meisje *dat er* visite kwam
> David told the girlNEU *that there* would be some visitors.
>
> **Target sentence with relative clause:**
> David vertelde het meisje *dat had* zitten bellen op te hangen.
> David told the *girlNEU thatRELPR(NEU) had* been phoning to hang up.

In Dutch, where the complement clause interpretation is preferred over the relative clause interpretation in the absence of any additional information, the processing cost of being garden-pathed is evidenced in both written and spoken sentences in a P600 to *had*, which signals the less preferred, relative-clause continuation. This default complement-clause preference is overridden on-line by discourse: the availability of two potential referents for the target noun (*the girl*) biases for a relative clause reading as indexed by a P600 to *er* (*there*) introducing the sentential complement in the two-referent relative to one-referent discourse. However, the presence of a unique referent biases for a sentential complement reading, as indexed by a P600 to *had*, which disambiguates for a relative clause reading in the one-referent relative to two-referent discourse (Van Berkum et al., 1999; 2003; Brown et al., 2000). These data are clearly at odds with syntax-first theories that deny the parser any pre-parse access to discourse information (Frazier and Rayner, 1982), being more consistent with context-sensitive theories that allow the parser immediate use of discourse information (Altmann, 1998; Spivey and Tanenhaus, 1998).

In Dutch, it is only following neuter-gender nouns (such as "girl") that *dat* gives rise to a complement/relative clause ambiguity; following a common-gender noun (such as "woman") *dat* is unambiguously a complementizer (a relative clause reading would be signaled by *die*, "it"). Nonetheless, in both written and spoken sentences, a P600 is elicited by *dat* in the two-referent discourse even when the preceding noun is of common gender. Thus, even though the syntactic agreement rules of Dutch preclude a relative-pronoun reading due to the grammatical gender of the immediately preceding noun, the parser nonetheless seems to pursue a relative clause analysis. Taken together, these findings support language comprehension architectures that not only allow interaction between discourse-semantic, syntactic, and lexical levels, but wherein discourse can rapidly affect syntactic analysis (at least in the presence of structural ambiguity— though see Osterhout et al., 2004 for similar conclusions regarding unambiguous sentences).

23.5 Slow potentials and the CPS

Potentials like the P600, LAN, and N400 are observed by time-locking to the onset of a word (in an auditory stream or during word-by-word reading), and are taken to reflect processing that unfolds in response to that word (in relation to its context). However, this is only one of several critical time-scales for both neural processing and language processing, which unfold at time levels ranging from sub-milliseconds (e.g. an action potential and/or the duration between action potentials) to seconds and minutes (e.g. the unfolding of a sentence or discourse) and hours and even days and years (e.g. the consolidation of memory). Processes taking place over different time-scales differ intrinsically from one another: faster and slower processing typically underlie different types of operations, take place in different brain areas, and even possibly are carried out by different neural mechanisms. In ERP studies, for example, the response to sentences is not predictable from that to individual words; rather, responses to individual words in sentences ride on top of slower responses that develop over phrases, clauses, and sentences. For example, several studies have reported slow anterior negative potentials—for both auditory and visual sentence presentation—that often vary with working memory load, induced by syntactic, referential, or conceptual complexity and/or ambiguity (see Figure 23.3). Prolonged frontal negativities were initially described for a comparison of object vs. subject relative sentences in English, starting at *who* and spanning the course of the sentence (e.g. *The fireman who the cop speedily rescued sued the city over working conditions* vs. *The firemen who speedily rescued the cop sued the city over working conditions*); these were related to holding a displaced item in working memory pending its assignment to its usual position in a long distance (filler-gap) dependency (King and Kutas, 1995; Kutas and King, 1996; Müller et al., 1997). Similar patterns are seen with *wh*-movement in *wh*-questions (Kluender and Münte, 1998; Fiebach et al., 2001) and in response to clause-internal scrambling in German (Rösler et al., 1998). Ueno and Kluender (2003) likewise observed a prolonged frontal (bilateral) negativity in Japanese, spanning a displaced element and its canonical word position in so-called "scrambled" sentences in which word order, though legal, was non-canonical; (O–S–V) vs. canonical (S–O–V) sentences. By some accounts, "scrambling" creates a filler-gap dependency. Sentences in which events are described in reverse chronological order (*Before the psychologist submitted the article, the journal changed its policy*) also elicit a frontal negativity, beginning ~300 ms after first-word onset, that grows progressively across the sentence, compared to sentences with events described in chronological order of occurrence (*After the psychologist submitted the article, the journal*

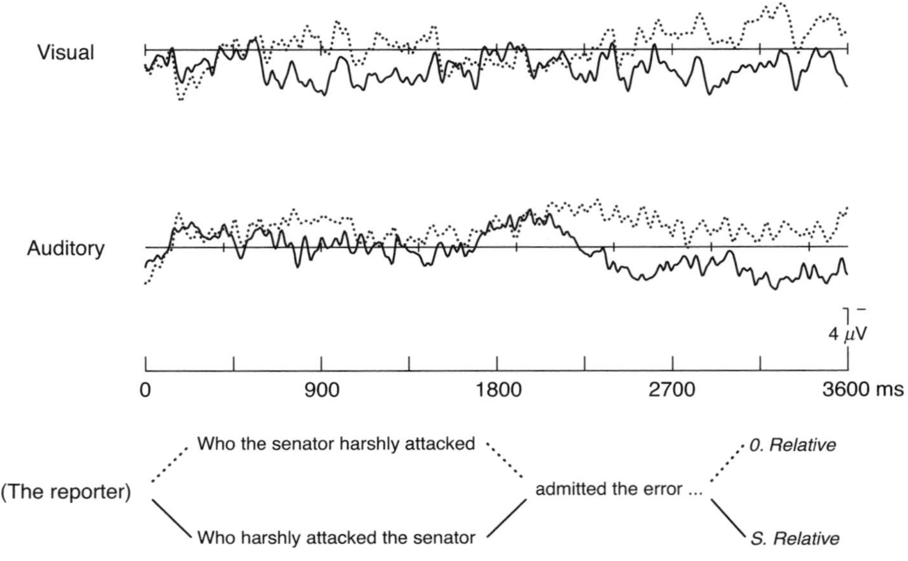

Figure 23.3 Comparison of grand average sentence-level ERPs for subject-relative vs. object-relative sentences at a site approximately over Broca's area for written sentences presented one word at a time (data from King and Kutas, 1995) and for naturally spoken sentences (data from Müller et al., 1997).

changed its policy); the amplitude of this effect is highly correlated with working memory capacity (Münte, Schilz, and Kuta, 1998). As differences in phrase structure analyses cannot be the origin of the processing problem in such sentences, Ueno and Kluender (2003) hypothesized that perhaps all processing difficulties associated with moved constituents, including filler-gap dependencies, index deviations from the preferred canonical word order, partly based on statistical frequencies of occurrence and perhaps on a general preference for canonicity in language. Finally, within the language domain, a sustained frontal negativity (just slightly longer than a typical LAN) was seen starting ~300 ms after the onset of the definite noun target in the mini-stories, described above, when the discourse had previously provided two as opposed to only one possible referent (Van Berkum et al., 1999; 2003).

Slow potentials with similar morphologies (though variable latencies and topographies as functions of type, modality, and amount of material) also have been observed in various verbal and non-verbal memory tasks accompanying information maintenance in working memory as well as episodic retrieval (Rösler et al., 1993; Donaldson and Rugg, 1999). Given their similar morphologies and sensitivities to comprehension skill or working memory load, it may be more parsimonious to associate all the slow negativities with some aspect of (working) memory processes than with linguistic processing (structural or referential) per se. Slow potentials over left frontal sites have been linked to verbal rehearsal, since in retention tasks their amplitudes co-vary with memory load, accuracy, and speech rate (Ruchkin et al., 1994; Ruchkin et al., 1999), as well as with the controlled attentional processes of maintenance, focusing, and shifting of attention (Bosch et al., 2001). Their specificity to language notwithstanding, the existence of over clause and sentence potentials that are not simple sums of their constituent transient word ERPs makes it difficult to study subprocesses in isolation with the hope of straightforwardly "scaling up" to other levels of analysis.

Modality of input is also likely to be an important factor for understanding the neural bases of language. Sentence-processing theories rarely mention whether a sentence is written or spoken, presumably because modality has little bearing on mechanisms beyond word recognition. Amplitude and timing differences across the scalp notwithstanding, many of the ERP effects discussed thus far (N400, LAN, P600, slow negativities) present with similar functional characteristics in all modalities, suggesting non-trivial similarities in neural processing. Indeed, it is in part the modality-independence of the brain response that allows the linking of components to modality-non-specific constructs. Such results have additionally been important for showing that the observed ERP patterns are not spuriously induced by the artificiality or relative slowness (on the slower end of language processing rates) of the often-used word-by-word visual presentation format.

Of course, the extent to which sentence processing is amodal in nature is an empirical question that necessitates systematic investigation for each of the hypothesized mechanisms, one by one. While evidence suggests that at least some people may "hear" words as they read them, evidence is scant on whether our "inner voices" mimic the prosodic patterns (sentence accents, intonational phrasing) of spoken language. However, a few theorists have hypothesized a phonological level of representation that impacts syntactic analysis during reading, and have suggested that punctuation (e.g. commas) might be viewed as an orthographic equivalent of prosody in speech. On this proposal, the same way that a prosodic boundary after *jogs* in (*Since Jay always jogs__a mile and a half seems like a very short distance to him*) diminishes the garden-path effect resulting from the parser's preference to interpret the ambiguous noun phrase (*a mile and a half*) as the object of the preceding verb (*jogs*) rather than the subject of the upcoming verb (seems), a comma after *jogs* would prevent the usual misleading parsing preference.

Steinhauer and Friederici (2001) reasoned that if punctuation is mediated by covert prosody, then its processing should resemble that of covert prosody. And, indeed, a centro-parietal positivity (closure positive shift, CPS) is elicited whenever a comprehender perceives a prosodic boundary, even in delexicalized speech (filtered so that only prosodic contour, and not segmental information, remains), jabberwocky, pseudowords, and hummed speech (Steinhauer et al., 1999; Pannekamp et al., 2005). Commas in written text also elicit a CPS, at least in individuals who appreciate the appropriate use of commas, suggesting that commas may covertly trigger prosodic phrase markings and determine initial parsing of sentences via the same mechanisms as speech boundaries. Prosody may also serve syntactic prediction (Isel et al., 2005).

23.6 **Plasticity and learning**

This review has focused on visual and auditory sentence processing in the average adult. We would, however, be remiss not to point out that as a direct measure of brain activity, ERPs also can inform us about both developmental and adult plasticity in language learning (see Neville and Bavelier, 1998). ERP studies with normal infants and children during language acquisition point to continual developmental changes in the configuration of language-related brain systems (including a crucial role for the right hemisphere), with differential sensitivity of different language subsystems to age and experience (Mills et al., 1997). Experience-based plasticity for language is also evident in ERP investigations in congenitally deaf adults who are native signers (compared with non-native deaf signers and normally hearing signing and non-signing adults), as well as in adults following brain damage leading to some form of aphasia, with some evidence in both for short- or longer-term recruitment of the right hemisphere (Altenmüller et al., 1997). Perhaps most surprisingly, ERP data attest to long-term plasticity in adult brains learning a second language. In one experiment, for example, ERPs to semantic and syntactic violations in sentences were examined at one month, four months, and eight months of instruction. For the fast language learners, semantic violations elicited almost native-like N400 amplitudes after only one month of instruction, whereas article–noun number agreement violations did not elicit any notable differential ERPs even after eight months, and violations of verb conjugation rules elicited an N400-like effect at one month but a P600 after eight months (reviewed in Osterhout et al., 2004), mirroring the earlier development of semantic than syntactic processing in children (Hahne et al., 2004). Tokowicz and MacWhinney (2005) found P600s only to syntactic violations similarly formed in participants' first and second language, and not for syntactic constructions specific to the second language. These results with second-language learners reinforce the obvious but often-forgotten point that it is how brains actually process stimuli, rather than the labels experimenters assign to manipulations, that determines the ERP elicited.

23.7 Conclusions

Electrophysiological researchers have described a wide array of brain processes that are sensitive to linguistic variables, though so far none is indisputably language-specific. It seems, then, that language processing in the human brain is built of the same sensory-perceptual, attentional, working and long-term memory, mapping, and integrative mechanisms, and is subject to the same principles as information processing as in other cognitive domains. Intracranial and scalp-recorded ERPs implicate many brain areas in language processing and implicate qualitatively different contributions from the two hemispheres—though how the information flow is orchestrated within, much less across the two hemispheres, remains a fascinating mystery.

In sum, the model of language processing emerging from ERP research (bolstered by studies using eye-tracking and behavioral measures) is one of a highly flexible, error-tolerant system in which lower- and higher-order representations are built moment by moment, necessitating provisional, probabilistic choices to deal with uncertainty and ambiguity along the way. These choices are influenced by information at multiple levels—lexical, sentential, discourse-referential—all potentially available at about the same time, and operating approximately parallel and with the potential for considerable interactivity (see also Hagoort, 2003a; though see Friederici, 2002 for a different conclusion). Moreover, these choices seem to entail the allocation of neural resources of various kinds to varying degrees depending upon the nature of the language input, the conceptual operations needed to construct its meaning, and the comprehender's speed of neural processing, capacity for short-term storage and processing, background knowledge-base, and developmental and learning-based experience with the language. This perhaps explains why, for example, so many different patterns of timing and relationship between syntax and semantics have been reported (Van Berkum et al., 1999; Hahne and Jescheniak, 2001; Hagoort, 2003b; Van Berkum et al., 2003; Vos and Friederici, 2003; Friederici et al., 2004; Frisch et al., 2004; van den Brink and Hagoort, 2004; Kim and Osterhout, 2005).

Finally, we think that ERPs most directly show that the accumulating information (from sensory input and semantic memory combined) seems not only to passively shape the immediate processing environment but also to provide the basis for active preparations made in anticipation of likely upcoming perceptual, grammatical, phonological, and semantic features, concepts, and words. ERPs thus afford psycho(neuro)linguists multiple glimpses into the time-course and nature of comprehenders' on-line understanding of the unfolding sentence or narrative—literal or non-literal—and the various representations and processes involved, as well as their language-processor's probabilistic guesses about the words, structures, and concepts yet to come.

Acknowledgments

This chapter has been supported by grants NICHD22614 and AG08313 to Marta Kutas. We thank Katherine DeLong, Laura Kemmer, Thomas Munte, and Thomas Urbach for their helpful comments, and Esmeralda De Ochoa for her editorial work. This report was written while Marta Kutas was a Lady Davis Fellow at Hebrew University, Jerusalem.

References

Altenmüller, E. O., and Gerloff, C. (1998) Psychophysiology and the EEG. In E. Niedermeyer and F. Lopes da Silva (eds), *Electroencephalography: Basic Principles, Clinical Applications, and Related Fields*, 4th edn, pp. 637–55. Lippincott Williams & Wilkins, New York.

Altenmüller, T. C., Marchmann, T., Kahrs, J., and Dichgans, J. (1997) Language processing in aphasia: changes in lateralization patterns during recovery reflect cerebral plasticity in adults. *Electroencephalography and Clinical Neurophysiology*, 102: 86–97.

Altmann, G. T. M. (1998) Ambiguity in sentence processing. *Trends in Cognitive Sciences*, 2: 146–52.

Angrilli, A., Penolazzi, B., Vespignani, F., De Vincenzi, M., Job, R., Ciccarelli, L., Palomba, D., and Stegagno, L., (2002) Cortical brain responses to semantic incongruity and syntactic violation in Italian language: an event-related potential study. *Neuroscience Letters*, 322: 5–8.

Astesano, C., Besson, M., and Alter, K. (2004) Brain potentials during semantic and prosodic processing in French. *Cognitive Brain Research*, 18: 172–84.

Bastiaansen, M. C. M., van der Linden, M., ter Keurs, M., Dijkstra, T., and Hagoort, P. (2002) Theta responses are involved in lexical-semantic retrieval during language processing. *Journal of Cognitive Neuroscience*, 17: 530–41.

Bentin, S., Mouchetant-Rostaing, Y., Giard, M. H., Echallier, J. F., and Pernier, J. (1999) ERP manifestations of processing printed words at different psycholinguistic levels: time course and scalp distribution. *Journal of Cognitive Neuroscience*, 11: 235–60.

Besson, M., and Macar, F. (1987) An event-related potential analysis of incongruity in music and other non-linguistic contexts. *Psychophysiology*, 24(1): 14–25.

Binder, J. R., Frost, J. A., Hammeke, T. A., Cox, R. W., Rao, S. J., and Prieto, T. (1997) Human brain language areas identified by functional magnetic resonance imaging. *Journal of Neuroscience*, 17(1): 353–62.

Bosch, V., Mecklinger, A., and Friederici, A. D. (2001) Slow cortical potentials during retention of object, spatial and verbal information. *Cognitive Brain Research*, 10(3): 219–37.

Bottini, G., Corcoran, R., Sterzi, R., Paulesu, E., Schenone, P., Scarpa, P., Frackowiak, R.S., and Frith, C.D. (1994) The role of the right hemisphere in the interpretation of figurative aspects of language: a positron emission tomography activation study. *Brain*, 117(6): 1241–53.

Brown, C. M., van Berkum, J. J. A., and Hagoort, P. (2000) Discourse before gender: an event-related brain potential study on the interplay of semantic and syntactic information during spoken language understanding. *Journal of Psycholinguistic Research*, 29(1): 53–68.

Carreiras, M., Salillas, E., and Barber, H. (2004) Event-related potentials elicited during parsing of ambiguous relative clauses in Spanish. *Cognitive Brain Research*, 20(1): 98–105.

Chwilla, D. J., Brown, C., and Hagoort, P. (1995) The N400 as a function of the level of processing. *Psychophysiology*, 32: 274–85.

Coulson, S., Federmeier, K. D., Van Petten, C., and Kutas, M. (2005) Right hemisphere sensitivity to word- and sentence-level context: evidence from event-related brain potentials. *Journal of Experimental Psychology: Learning, Memory, and Cognition*, 31: 129–47.

Coulson, S., King, J. W., and Kutas, M. (1998a) Expect the unexpected: event-related brain response to morphosyntactic violations. *Language and Cognitive Processes*, 1(1): 21–58.

Coulson, S., King, J. W., and Kutas, M. (1998b) ERPs and domain specificity: beating a straw horse. *Language and Cognitive Processes*, 13: 653–72.

Coulson, S., and Kutas, M. (2001) Getting it: human event-related brain response in good and poor comprehenders. *Neuroscience Letters*, 316: 71–4.

Coulson, S., and Lovett, C. (2004) Handedness, hemispheric asymmetries, and joke comprehension. *Cognitive Brain Research*, 19: 275–88.

Coulson, S., and Van Petten, C. (2002) Conceptual integration and metaphor: an event-related potential study. *Memory and Cognition*, 30(6): 958–68.

Coulson, S., and Williams, R. F. (2005) Hemispheric asymmetries and joke comprehension. *Neuropsychologia*, 43(1): 128–41.

Coulson, S., and Wu, Y. C. (2005) Right hemisphere activation of joke-related information: an event-related brain potential study. *Journal of Cognitive Neuroscience*, 17(3): 494–506.

DeLong, K. A., Urbach, T. P., and Kutas, M. (2005) Probabilistic word pre-activation during language comprehension inferred from electrical brain activity. *Nature Neuroscience*, 8(8): 1117–22.

Dominguez, A, de Vega, M., and Barber, H. (2004) Event-related brain potentials elicited by morphological, homographic, orthographic, and semantic priming. *Journal of Cognitive Neuroscience*, 16(4): 598–608.

Donaldson, D. I., and Rugg, M. D. (1999) Event-related potential studies of associative recognition and recall: electrophysiological evidence for context dependent retrieval processes. *Cognitive Brain Research*, 8: 1–16.

Donchin, E., and Coles, M. G. H. (1988) Is the P300 component a manifestation of context updating? *Behavioral and Brain Sciences*, 11: 357–74.

Duffy, S. A., Henderson, J. M., and Morris, R. K. (1989) Semantic facilitation of lexical access during sentence processing. *Journal of Experimental Psychology: Learning, Memory, and Cognition*, 15: 791–801.

Federmeier, K. D., and Kutas, M. (1999a) A rose by any other name: long-term memory structure and sentence processing. *Journal of Memory and Language*, 41: 469–95.

Federmeier, K. D., and Kutas, M. (1999b) Right words and left words: electrophysiological evidence for hemispheric differences in meaning processing. *Cognitive Brain Research*, 8: 373–92.

Federmeier, K. D., and Kutas, M. (2002) Picture the difference: Electrophysiological investigations of picture processing in the two cerebral hemispheres. *Neuropsychologia*, 40: 730–47.

Federmeier, K. D., Mai, H., and Kutas, M. (2005) Both sides get the point: bihemispheric sensitivity to sentential constraint. *Memory and Cognition*, 33: 871–86.

Federmeier, K. D., Van Petten, C., Schwartz, T. J., and Kutas, M. (2003) Sounds, words, sentences: age-related changes across levels of language processing. *Psychology and Aging*, 18: 858–72.

Felser, C., Clahsen, H., and Münte, T. F. (2003) Storage and integration in the processing of filler-gap dependencies: an ERP study of topicalization and *wh*-movement in German. *Brain and Language*, 87: 345–54.

Fernández, G., Heitkemper, P., Grunwald, T., Van Roost, D., Urbach, H., Pezer, N., Lehnertz, K., and Elger, C. E. (2001) Inferior temporal stream for word processing with integrated mnemonic function. *Human Brain Mapping*, 14: 251–60.

Fiebach, C. J., Schlesewsky, M., and Friederici, A. D. (2001) Syntactic working memory and the establishment of filler-gap dependencies: insights from ERPs and fMRI. *Journal of Psycholinguistic Research*, 30: 321–38.

Fiebach, C. J., Schlesewsky, M., and Friederici, A. D. (2002) Separating syntactic memory costs and syntactic integration costs during parsing: the processing of German WH-questions. *Journal of Memory and Language*, 47: 250–72.

Forster, K. I. (1981) Priming and the effects of sentence and lexical contexts on naming time: evidence for autonomous lexical processing. *Quarterly Journal of Experimental Psychology*, 33a: 465–95.

Frazier, L. (1999) *On Sentence Interpretation*. Kluwer Academic, Dordrecht.

Frazier, L., and Rayner, K. (1982) Making and correcting errors during sentence comprehension: eye movements in the analysis of structurally ambiguous sentences. *Cognitive Psychology*, 14: 178–210.

Friederici, A. D. (2002) Towards a neural basis for auditory sentence processing, *Trends in Cognitive Sciences*, 6: 78–84.

Friederici, A. D., and Frisch, S. (2000) Verb argument structure processing: the role of verb-specific and argument-specific information. *Journal of Memory and Language*, 43: 476–507.

Friederici, A. D., Gunter, T. C., Hahne, A., and Mauth, K. (2004) The relative timing of syntactic and semantic processes in sentence comprehension. *Neuroreport*, 15: 165–9.

Friederici, A. D., Hahne, A., and Mecklinger, A. (1996) Temporal structure of syntactic parsing: early and late event-related brain potential effects. *Journal of Experimental Psychology: Learning, Memory, and Cognition*, 22: 1219–48.

Friederici, A. D., Hahne, A., and Saddy, D. (2002) Distinct neurophysiological patterns reflecting aspects of syntactic complexity and syntactic repair. *Journal of Psycholinguistic Research*, 31: 45–63.

Friederici, A. D., Mecklinger, A., Spencer, K. M., Steinhauer, K., and Donchin, E. (2001) Syntactic parsing preferences and their on-line revisions: a spatio-temporal analysis of event-related brain potentials. *Cognitive Brain Research*, 11: 305–23.

Friederici, A. D., Pfeifer, E., and Hahne, A. (1993) Event-related brain potentials during natural speech processing: effects of semantic, morphological and syntactic violations. *Cognitive Brain Research*, 1: 183–92.

Frisch, S., Hahne, A., Friederici, A. D. (2004) Word category and verb–argument structure information in the dynamics of parsing. *Cognition*, 91: 191–219.

Frisch, S., Schlesewsky, M., Saddy, D., and Alpermann, A. (2002) The P600 as an indicator of syntactic ambiguity. *Cognition*, 85: B83–B92.

Gibbs, R. W. (1994) *The Poetics of mind: Figurative Thought, Language, and Understanding*. Cambridge University Press, Cambridge.

Gibbs, R. W., Bogdanovich, J. M., Sykes, J. R., and Barr, D. J. (1997) Metaphor in idiom comprehension. *Journal of Memory and Language*, 37: 141–54.

Gildea, P., and Glucksberg, S. (1983) On understanding metaphor: the role of context. *Journal of Verbal Learning and Verbal Behavior*, 22: 577–90.

Gunter, T. C., Stowe, L. A., and Mulder, G. (1997) When syntax meets semantics. *Psychophysiology*, 34: 660–76.

Hagoort, P. (2003a) How the brain solves the binding problem for language: a neurocognitive model of syntactic processing, *NeuroImage*, 20: S18–S29.

Hagoort, P. (2003b) Interplay between syntax and semantics during sentence comprehension: ERP effects of combining syntactic and semantic violations. *Journal of Cognitive Neuroscience*, 15: 883–99.

Hagoort, P., and Brown, C. (1994) Brain responses to lexical ambiguity resolution and parsing. In C. Clifton, Jr, L. Frazier, and K. Rayner (eds), *Perspectives on Sentence Processing*, pp. 45–80. Erlbaum, Hillsdale, NJ.

Hagoort, P., and Brown, C. (2000) ERP effects of listening to speech compared to reading: the P600/SPS to syntactic violations in spoken sentences and rapid serial visual presentation. *Neuropsychologia*, 38: 1531–49.

Hagoort, P., Brown, C., and Groothusen, J. (1993) The syntactic positive shift (SPS) as an ERP measure of syntactic processing. *Language and Cognitive Processes*, 8: 439–83.

Hahne, A., Eckstein, K., and Friederici, A. D. (2004) Brain signatures of syntactic and semantic processes during children's language development. *Journal of Cognitive Neuroscience*, 16: 1302–18.

Hahne, A., and Friederici, A. D. (1999) Electrophysiological evidence for two steps in syntactic analysis: early automatic and late controlled processes. *Journal of Cognitive Neuroscience*, 11: 194–205.

Hahne, A., and Jescheniak, J. D. (2001) What's left if the Jabberwock gets the semantics? An ERP investigation into semantic and syntactic processes during auditory sentence comprehension. *Cognitive Brain Research*, 11: 199–212.

Halgren, E., Baudena, P., Heit, G., Clarke, M., and Marinkovic, K. (1994a) Spatio-temporal stages in face and word processing, 1: Depth-recorded potentials in the human occipital, temporal, and parietal lobes. *Journal de Physiologie*, 88: 1–50.

Halgren, E., Baudena, P., Heit, G., Clarke, M., and Marinkovic, K. (1994b) Spatio-temporal stages in face and word processing, 2: Depth-recorded potentials in the human frontal and Rolandic cortices. *Journal de Physiologie*, 88: 51–80.

Halgren, E., Dhond, R. P., Christensen, N., Van Petten, C., Marinkovic, K., Lewine, J. D., and Dale, A. M. (2002) N400-like magnetoencephalography responses modulated by semantic context, word frequency, and lexical class in sentences. *NeuroImage*, 17: 1101–16.

Hillyard, S. A., and Münte, T. F. (1984) Selective attention to color and location: an analysis with event-related brain potentials. *Perception and Psychophysics*, 36: 185–98.

Hoeks, J. C. J., Stowe, L. A., and Doedens, G. (2004) Seeing words in context: the interaction of lexical and sentence level information during reading. *Cognitive Brain Research*, 19: 59–73.

Hohlfeld, A., Sangals, J., and Sommer, W. (2004) Effects of additional tasks on language perception: an event-related brain potential investigation. *Journal of Experimental Psychology: Learning, Memory, and Cognition*, 30: 1012–25.

Holcomb, P. J., and Anderson, J. E. (1993) Cross-modal semantic priming: a time-course analysis using event-related brain potentials. *Language and Cognitive Processes*, 8: 379–411.

Holcomb, P. J., Kounios, J., Anderson, J. E., and West, C. (1999) Dual-coding, context-availability, and concreteness effects in sentence comprehension: an electrophysiological investigation. *Journal of Experimental Psychology: Learning, Memory, and Cognition*, 25: 721–42.

Holcomb, P. J., Reder, L., Misra, M., and Grainger, J. (forthcoming) The effects of prime visibility on ERP measures of masked priming. *Cognitive Brain Research.*

Hopf, J. M., Bayer, J., Bader, M., and Meng, M. (1998) Event-related brain potentials and case information in syntactic ambiguities. *Journal of Cognitive Neuroscience*, 10: 264–80.

Isel, F., Alter, K., and Friederici, A. D. (2005) Influence of prosodic information on the processing of split particles: ERP evidence from spoken German. *Journal of Cognitive Neuroscience*, 17: 154–67.

Janata, P. (1995) ERP measures assay the degree of expectancy violation of harmonic contexts in music. *Journal of Cognitive Neuroscience*, 7(2): 153–64.

Jost, K., Beinhoff, U., Hennighausen, E., and Rösler, F. (2004) Facts, rules, and strategies in single-digit multiplication: evidence from event-related brain potentials. *Cognitive Brain Research*, 20: 183–93.

Kaan, E., Harris, T., Gibson, E., and Holcomb, P. J. (2000) The P600 as an index of syntactic integration difficulty. *Language and Cognitive Processes*, 15: 159–201.

Kaan, E., and Swaab, T. Y. (2003) Repair, revision, and complexity in syntactic analysis: an electrophysiological differentiation. *Journal of Cognitive Neuroscience*, 15: 98–110.

Kazmerski, V. A., Blasko, D. G., and Dessalegn, B. G. (2003) ERP and behavioral evidence of individual differences in metaphor comprehension. *Memory and Cognition*, 31: 673–89.

Kemmer, L., Coulson, S., De Ochoa, E., and Kutas, M. (2004) Syntactic processing with aging: an event-related potential study. *Psychophysiology*, 41: 372–84.

Kim, A., and Osterhout, L. (2005) The independence of combinatory semantic processing: evidence from event-related potentials. *Journal of Memory and Language*, 52: 205–25.

King, J. W., and Kutas, M. (1995) Who did what and when? Using word- and clause-related ERPs to monitor working memory usage in reading. *Journal of Cognitive Neuroscience*, 7: 378–97.

King, J. W., and Kutas, M. (1998) Neural plasticity in the dynamics of human visual word recognition. *Neuroscience Letters*, 244: 61–4.

Kluender, R., and Kutas, M. (1993) Subjacency as a processing phenomenon. *Language and Cognitive Processes*, 8: 573–633.

Kluender, R., and Münte, T. F. (1998) Subject/object asymmetries: ERPs to grammatical and ungrammatical *wh*-questions. Paper presented at the 11th Annual CUNY Conference on Human Sentence Processing, New Brunswick, NJ.

Kok, A. (2001) On the utility of P3 amplitude as a measure of processing capacity. *Psychophysiology*, 38: 557–77.

Kolk, H. H. J., Chwilla, D. J., van Herten, M., and Oor, P. J. W. (2003) Structure and limited capacity in verbal working memory: a study with event-related potentials. *Brain and Language*, 85: 1–36.

Kotz, S. A., and Friederici, A. D. (2003) Electrophysiology of normal and pathological language processing. *Journal of Neurolinguistics*, 16: 43–58.

Kotz, S. A., Frisch, S., von Cramon, D. Y., and Friederici, A. D. (2003) Syntactic language processing: ERP lesion data on the role of the basal ganglia. *Journal of the International Neuropsychological Society*, 9: 1053–60.

Kounios, J., and Holcomb, P. J. (1994) Concreteness effects in semantic processing: ERP evidence supporting dual-coding theory. *Journal of Experimental Psychology: Learning, Memory, and Cognition*, 20: 804–23.

Kuperberg, G. R., Sitnikova, T., Caplan, D., and Holcomb, P. J. (2003) Electrophysiological distinctions in processing conceptual relationships within simple sentences. *Cognitive Brain Research*, 17: 117–29.

Kutas, M., and Dale, A. (1997) Electrical and magnetic readings of mental functions, In M. D. Rugg (ed.), *Cognitive Neuroscience*, pp.197–237. MIT Press, Cambridge, MA.

Kutas, M., and Federmeier, K. D. (2000) Electrophysiology reveals semantic memory use in language comprehension. *Trends in Cognitive Sciences*, 4: 463–70.

Kutas, M., Federmeier, K. D., Staab, J., and Kluender, R. (2007) Language. In J. T. Cacioppo, L. G. Tassinary, and G. G. Bernston (eds), *Handbook of Psychophysiology*, 3rd edn, pp. 550–80. Cambridge University Press, New York.

Kutas, M., and Hillyard, S. A. (1980a) Reading senseless sentences: brain potentials reflect semantic incongruity. *Science*, 207: 203–5.

Kutas, M., and Hillyard, S. A. (1980b) Event-related brain potentials to semantically inappropriate and surprisingly large words. *Biological Psychology*, 11: 99–116.

Kutas, M., and King, J. W. (1996) The potentials for basic sentence processing: differentiating integrative processes. In J. L. McClelland and T. Inui (eds), *Attention and Performance 16: Information Integration in Perception and Communication*, pp.501–46. MIT Press, Cambridge, MA.

Lelekov, T., Dominey, P. F., and Garcia-Larrea, L. (2000) Dissociable ERP profiles for processing rules vs instances in a cognitive sequencing task. *NeuroReport*, 11: 1129–32.

Luck, S. J., and Hillyard, S. A. (1994) Electrophysiological correlates of feature analysis during visual search. *Psychophysiology*, 31: 291–308.

Luck, S. J., Vogel, E. K., and Shapiro, K. L. (1996) Word meanings can be accessed but not reported during the attentional blink. *Nature*, 383: 616–18.

Matzke, M., Mai, H., Nager, W., Russeler, J., and Münte, T. (2002) The costs of freedom: an ERP-study of non-canonical sentences. *Clinical Neurophysiology*, 113: 844–52.

McCallum, W. C., Farmer, S. F., and Pocock, P. V. (1984) The effects of physical and semantic incongruities on auditory event-related potentials. *Electroencephalography and Clinical Neurophysiology*, 59: 477–88.

McCarthy, G., and Nobre, A. C. (1993) Modulation of semantic processing by spatial selective attention. *Electroencephalography and Clinical Neurophysiology*, 88: 210–19.

Mills, D. L., Coffey-Corina, S. A., Neville, H. J. (1997) Language comprehension and cerebral specialization from 13 to 20 months. *Developmental Neuropsychology*, 13: 397–445.

Müller, H. M., King, J. W., and Kutas, M. (1997) Event-related potentials to relative clause processing in spoken sentences. *Cognitive Brain Research*, 5: 193–203.

Müller, H. M., and Kutas, M. (1996) What's in a name? Electrophysiological differences between spoken nouns, proper names and one's own name. *NeuroReport*, 8: 221–5.

Münte, T. F., and Heinze, H. J. (1994) ERP negativities during syntactic processing of written words. In H.-J. Heinze, T. F. Münte, and G. R. Mangun (eds), *Cognitive Electrophysiology*, pp. 211–38. Birkhäuser, Boston.

Münte, T. F., Heinze, H. J., Matzke, M., Wieringa, B. M., and Johannes, S. (1998) Brain potentials and syntactic violations revisited: no evidence for specificity of the syntactic positive shift. *Neuropsychologia*, 36: 217–26.

Münte, T. F., Schilz, K., and Kutas, M. (1998) When temporal terms belie conceptual order. *Nature*, 395: 71–3.

Münte, T. F., Szentkuti, A., Wieringa, B. M., Matzke, M., and Johannes, S. (1997) Human brain potentials to reading syntactic errors in sentences of different complexity. *Neuroscience Letters*, 235: 105–8.

Münte, T. F., Urbach, T. P., Düzel, E., and Kutas, M. (2000) Event-related brain potentials in the study of human cognition and neuropsychology. In F. Boller, J. Grafman, and G. Rizzolatti (eds), *Handbook of Neuropsychology*, vol. 1: 2nd edn, pp. 139–235. Elsevier, Amsterdam.

Münte, T. F., Wieringa, B. M., Weyerts, H., Szentkuti, A., Matzke, M., and Johannes, S. (2001) Differences in brain potentials to open and closed class words: class and frequency effects. *Neuropsychologia*, 39: 91–102.

Neville, H. J., and Bavelier, D. (1998) Neural organization and plasticity of language. *Current Opinion in Neurobiology*. 8: 254–8.

Neville, H. J., Nicol, J. L., Barss, A., Forster, K. I., and Garrett, M. F. (1991) Syntactically based sentence processing classes: evidence from event-related brain potentials. *Journal of Cognitive Neuroscience*, 3: 151–65.

Ni, W., Constable, R. T., Mencl, W. E., Pugh, K. R., Fulbright, R. K., Shaywitz, S. E., Shaywitz, B. A., Gore, J. C., and Shankweiler, D. (2000) An event-related neuroimaging study distinguishing form and content in sentence processing. *Journal of Cognitive Neuroscience*, 12: 120–33.

Niedeggen, M., and Rösler, F. (1999) N400-effects reflect activation spread during arithmetic fact retrieval. *Psychological Science*, 10: 271–6.

Nobre, A. C., Allison, T., and McCarthy, G. (1994) Word recognition in the human inferior temporal lobe. *Nature*, 372: 260–3.

Nunez, P. L. (1981) *Electric Fields of the Brain.* Oxford University Press, New York.

Nunez-Pena, M. I., and Honrubia-Serrano, M. L. (2004) P600 related to rule violation in an arithmetic task. *Cognitive Brain Research*, 18: 130–41.

Osterhout, L., Bersick, M., and McKinnon, R. (1997) Brain potentials elicited by words: word length and frequency predict the latency of an early negativity. *Biological Psychology*, 46: 143–68.

Osterhout, L., and Hagoort, P. (1999) A superficial resemblance does not necessarily mean that you are part of the family: counterarguments to Coulson, King, and Kutas (1998) in the P600/SPS-P300 debate. *Language and Cognitive Processes*, 14: 1–14.

Osterhout, L., and Holcomb, P. (1992) Event-related brain potentials elicited by syntactic anomaly. *Journal of Memory and Language*, 31: 785–806.

Osterhout, L., McKinnon, R., Bersick, M., and Corey, V. (1996) On the language specificity of the brain response to syntactic anomalies: is the syntactic positive shift a member of the P300 family? *Journal of Cognitive Neuroscience*, 8: 507–26.

Osterhout, L., McLaughlin, J., Kim, A., Greenwald, R., and Inoue, K. (2004) Sentences in the brain: event-related potentials as real-time reflections of sentence comprehension and language learning. In M. Carreiras and C. Clifton, Jr (eds), *The On-Line Study of Sentence Comprehension: Eye-tracking, ERP, and Beyond*, pp. 271–308. Psychology Press, Hove, UK.

Osterhout, L., and Nicol, J. (1999) On the distinctiveness, independence, and time course of the brain responses to syntactic and semantic anomalies. *Language and Cognitive Processes*, 14: 283–317.

Pannekamp, A., Toepel, U., Alter, K., Hahne, A., and Friederici, A. D. (2005) Prosody-driven sentence processing: an event-related brain potential study. *Journal of Cognitive Neuroscience*, 17: 407–21.

Patel, A. D., Gibson, E., Ratner, J., Besson, M., and Holcomb, P. J. (1998) Processing syntactic relations in language and music: an event-related potential study. *Journal of Cognitive Neuroscience*, 10: 717–33.

Phillips, C., Kazanina, N., Abada, S. H. (2005) ERP effects of the processing of syntactic long-distance dependencies. *Cognitive Brain Research*, 22: 407–28.

Proverbio, A. M., Vecchi, L., and Zani, A. (2004) From orthography to phonetics: ERP measures of grapheme-to-phoneme conversion mechanisms in reading. *Journal of Cognitive Neuroscience*, 16: 301–17.

Pynte, J., Besson, M., Robichon, F., and Poli, J. (1996) The time-course of metaphor comprehension: an event-related potential study. *Brain and Language*, 55: 293–316.

Robertson, D. A., Gernsbacher, M. A., Guidotti, S. J., Robertson, R. R., Irwin, W., Mock B. J., and Campana M. E. (2000) Functional neuroanatomy of the cognitive process of mapping during discourse comprehension. *Psychological Science*, 11: 255–60.

Roehm, D., Bornkessel, I., Haider, H., and Schlesewsky, M. (2005) When case meets agreement: event-related potential effects for morphology-based conflict resolution in human language comprehension. *NeuroReport*, 16: 875–78.

Roehm, D., Schlesewksy, M., Bornkessel, I., Frisch, S., and Haider, H. (2004) Fractioning language comprehension via frequency characteristics of the human EEG. *NeuroReport*, 15: 409–12.

Rolke, B., Heil, M., Streb, J., and Hennighausen, E. (2001) Missed prime words within the attentional blink evoke an N400 semantic priming effect. *Psychophysiology*, 38: 165–74.

Rösler, F. (2005) From single-channel recordings to brain-mapping devices: the impact of electroencephalography on experimental psychology. *History of Psychology*, 8: 95–117.

Rösler, F., Heil, M., and Glowalla, U. (1993) Monitoring retrieval from long-term memory by slow event-related brain potentials. *Psychophysiology*, 30: 170–82.

Rösler, F., Pechmann, T., Streb, J., Roder, B., and Hennighausen, E. (1998) Parsing of sentences in a language with varying word order: word-by-word variations of processing demands are revealed by event-related brain potentials. *Journal of Memory and Language*, 38: 150–76.

Ruchkin, D. S., Berndt, R. S., Johnson, R., Grafman, J., Ritter, W., and Canoune, H. L. (1999) Lexical contributions to retention of verbal information in working memory: event-related brain potential evidence. *Journal of Memory and Language*, 41: 345–64.

Ruchkin, D. S., Grafman, J., Krauss, G. L., Johnson, R., Canoune, H., and Ritter, W. (1994) Event-related brain potential evidence for a verbal working memory deficit in multiple sclerosis. *Brain*, 117: 289–305.

Rugg, M. D. (1990) Event-related brain potentials dissociate repetition effects of high- and low-frequency words. *Memory and Cognition*, 18: 367–79.

Schendan, H., Ganis, G., and Kutas, M. (1998) Neurophysiological evidence for visual perceptual organization of words and faces within 150 ms. *Psychophysiology*, 35: 240–51.

Schiller, N. O., Münte, T. F., Horemans, I., Jansma, B. M. (2003) The influence of semantic and phonological factors on syntactic decisions: an event-related brain potential study. *Psychophysiology*, 40: 869–77.

Searle, J. R. (1979) Expression and Meaning: Studies in the Theory of Speech Acts. Cambridge University Press, Cambridge.

Sitnikova, T., Kuperberg, G., and Holcomb, P. J. (2003) Semantic integration in videos of real-world events: an electrophysiological investigation. *Psychophysiology*, 40: 160–4.

Spivey, M. J., and Tanenhaus, M. K. (1998) Syntactic ambiguity resolution in discourse: modeling the effects of referential context and lexical frequency. *Journal of Experimental Psychology: Learning, Memory, and Cognition*, 24: 1521–43.

St George, M., Kutas, M., Martinez, A., and Sereno, M. I. (1999) Semantic integration in reading: engagement of the right hemisphere during discourse processing. *Brain*, 122: 1317–25.

Steinhauer, K. (2003) Electrophysiological correlates of prosody and punctuation. *Brain and Language*, 86: 142–64.

Steinhauer, K., Alter, K., and Friederici, A. D. (1999) Brain potentials indicate immediate use of prosodic cues in natural speech processing. *Nature Neuroscience*, 2: 191–6.

Steinhauer, K., and Friederici, A. D. (2001) Prosodic boundaries, comma rules, and brain responses: the closure positive shift in ERPs as a universal marker for prosodic phrasing in listeners and readers. *Journal of Psycholinguistic Research*, 30: 267–95.

Stenberg, G., Lindgren, M., Johansson, M., Olsson, A., and Rosén, I. (2000) Semantic processing without conscious identification: evidence from event-related potentials. *Journal of Experimental Psychology: Learning, Memory, and Cognition*, 26: 973–1004.

ter Keurs, M., Brown, C. M., and Hagoort, P. (2002) Lexical processing of vocabulary class in patients with Broca's aphasia: an event-related brain potential study on agrammatic comprehension. *Neuropsychologia*, 40: 1547–61.

Tokowicz, N., and MacWhinney, B. (2005) Implicit and explicit measures of sensitivity to violations in second language grammar: an event-related potential investigation. *Studies in Second Language Acquisition*, 27: 173–204.

Traxler, M. J., Foss, D. J., Seely, R. E., Kaup, B., and Morris, R. K. (2000) Priming in sentence processing: intralexical spreading activation, schemas, and situation models. *Journal of Psycholinguistic Research*, 29: 581–95.

Ueno, M., and Kluender, R. (2003) Event-related brain indices of Japanese scrambling. *Brain and Language*, 86: 243–71.

Van Berkum, J. J. A., Brown, C. M., and Hagoort, P. (1999) When does gender constrain parsing? Evidence from ERPs. *Journal of Psycholinguistic Research*, 28: 555–71.

Van Berkum, J. J. A., Brown, C. M., Hagoort, P., and Zwitserlood, P. (2003) Event-related brain potentials reflect discourse-referential ambiguity in spoken language comprehension. *Psychophysiology*, 40: 235–48.

Van Berkum, J. J. A., Brown, C. M., Zwitserlood, P., Kooijman, V., and Hagoort, P. (2005) Anticipating upcoming words in discourse: evidence from ERPs and reading times. *Journal of Experimental Psychology: Learning, Memory, and Cognition*, 31: 443–67.

van den Brink, D., and Hagoort, P. (2004) The influence of semantic and syntactic context constraints on lexical selection and integration in spoken-word comprehension as revealed by ERPs. *Journal of Cognitive Neuroscience*, 16: 1068–84.

van Herten, M., Kolk, H. H. J., and Chwilla, D. J. (2005) An ERP study of P600 effects elicited by semantic anomalies. *Cognitive Brain Research*, 22: 241–55.

Van Petten, C. (1993) A comparison of lexical and sentence-level context effects and their temporal parameters. *Language and Cognitive Processes*, 8: 485–532.

Van Petten, C., Coulson, S., Rubin, S., Plante, E., and Parks, M. (1999) Time course of word identification and semantic integration in spoken language. *Journal of Experimental Psychology: Learning, Memory, and Cognition*, 25: 394–417.

Van Petten, C., and Kutas, M. (1990) Interactions between sentence context and word frequency in event-related brain potentials. *Memory and Cognition*, 18: 380–93.

Van Petten, C., and Kutas, M. (1991) Influences of semantic and syntactic context on open and closed class words. *Memory and Cognition*, 19: 95–112.

Van Petten, C., and Luka, B. J. (forthcoming) Neural localization of semantic context effects in electromagnetic and hemodynamic studies. *Brain and Language*.

Van Petten, C., and Rheinfelder, H. (1995) Conceptual relationships between spoken words and environmental sounds: event-related brain potential measures. *Neuropsychologia*, 33: 485–508.

Van Petten, C., Weckerly, J., McIsaac, H. K., and Kutas, M. (1997) Working memory capacity dissociates lexical and sentential context effects. *Psychological Science*, 8: 238–42.

Vos, S. H., and Friederici, A. D. (2003) Intersentential syntactic context effects on comprehension: the role of working memory. *Cognitive Brain Research*, 16: 111–22.

Vosse, T., and Kempen, G. A. M. (2000) Syntactic structure assembly in human parsing: a computational model based on competitive inhibition and lexical grammar. *Cognition*, 75: 105–43.

Wassenaar, M., Brown, C. M., and Hagoort, P. (2004) ERP effects of subject-verb agreement violations in patients with Broca's aphasia. *Journal of Cognitive Neuroscience*, 16: 553–76.

West, W. C., and Holcomb, P. J. (2002) Event-related potentials during discourse-level semantic integration of complex pictures. *Cognitive Brain Research*, 13: 363–75.

Wicha, N. Y., Bates, E. A., Moreno, E. M., and Kutas, M. (2003) Potato not pope: human brain potentials to gender expectation and agreement in Spanish spoken sentences. *Neuroscience Letters*, 346: 165–8.

Wicha, N. Y., Moreno, E. M., and Kutas, M. (2003) Expecting gender: an event related brain potential study on the role of grammatical gender in comprehending a line drawing within a written sentence in Spanish. *Cortex*, 39: 483–508.

Wicha, N. Y. Y., Moreno, E. M., and Kutas, M. (2004) Anticipating words and their gender: an event-related brain potential study of semantic integration, gender expectancy, and gender agreement in Spanish sentence reading. *Journal of Cognitive Neuroscience*, 16: 1–17.

Wolff, P., and Gentner, D. (2000) Evidence for role-neutral initial processing of metaphors. *Journal of Experimental Psychology: Learning, Memory, and Cognition*, 26: 529–41.

CHAPTER 24

Neuroimaging studies of sentence and discourse comprehension

Ina D. Bornkessel-Schlesewsky and Angela D. Friederici

24.1 Introduction

The neural implementation of language and, by extension, the postulated existence of particular "language centers" in the brain has exerted a continuing fascination upon scientists and non-scientists alike for thousands of years. With the advent of neuroimaging methods—and particularly of functional magnetic resonance imaging (fMRI)—during the last decade of the twentieth century, the possibilities of scientific inquiry within this domain have taken on a new dimension. First, neuroimaging techniques allow for a systematic and fine-grained probing of the functional neuroanatomy of language in healthy individuals. Moreover, they provide us with new avenues of exploration with respect to classical psycholinguistic questions in sentence comprehension such as the modularity vs. interactivity debate. Neuroimaging studies of language comprehension are thus suited to providing further information not only about the neural substrate of language comprehension but also with respect to its internal organization.

The aim of this chapter is twofold. On the one hand, we adopt the classic neurolinguistic perspective and review studies that aim to examine the neural substrate of sentence and discourse processing and, thereby, to dissociate the neuroanatomical correlates of different linguistic subdomains/ subprocesses. On the other, we discuss how neuroimaging techniques may help us to adopt a new perspective on core psycholinguistic questions.

24.1.1 The networks

On the basis of the classical deficit-lesion correlations undertaken in the late nineteenth century, language comprehension was long associated primarily with "Wernicke's area", i.e. with the left posterior superior temporal gyrus (STG) and adjoining parietal regions of the cortex (see Figure 24.1). Several decades later, however, the systematic examination of comprehension abilities in aphasic patients led to the conclusion that the brain region originally thought to be responsible for language production (i.e. "Broca's area" in the posterior portion of the left inferior frontal gyrus, IFG; see Figure 24.1) also appears to be crucially involved in at least some aspects of language comprehension (e.g. Caramazza and Zurif, 1976). This observation already provides a first argument against a straightforward—and exclusive—association between different linguistic domains and distinct "language centers" in the brain. Instead, it suggests that language processing draws upon a larger network of brain regions. Different domains and information types thus manifest themselves as *modulations* of the overall network, rather than in terms of an activation of distinct brain regions for distinct sub-processes.

Nonetheless, numerous findings within the imaging literature support the idea that language processing indeed crucially engages a network of (primarily left) *fronto-temporal* brain regions in concert with a small number of other areas such as the basal ganglia (e.g. Moro et al.,

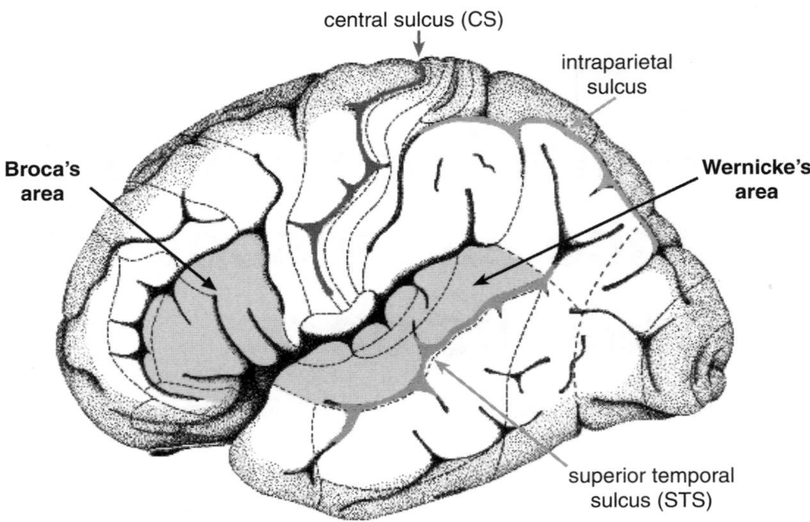

Figure 24.1 A schematic view of the left hemisphere that shows the classical language areas (Broca's area and Wernicke's area). Relevant major sulci are also marked. See Plate 2 for a color version of this figure.

2001; for a review see Friederici, 2002). An overview of the relevant cortical regions is given in Figures 24.2 and 24.3. Note that subcortical regions (e.g. the basal ganglia) are not shown in these figures. Direct comparisons between different input modalities have revealed overlapping areas (particularly in superior temporal and inferior frontal cortices), but also a number of differences. Thus, in addition to the modality-independent regions and primary visual areas in the occipital lobe, visual presentation of sentence stimuli has been shown to activate the angular and supramarginal gyri (BA39 and BA40) in the left parietal lobe and the fusiform gyrus in the left inferotemporal region. Auditory presentation, by contrast, leads to extended—and often bilateral—activation in the superior temporal gyrus including the primary auditory cortex (BA41) (see Constable et al., 2004 for a direct comparison between auditory and visual modalities).

24.1.2 The methods

Current neuroimaging methods such as positron emission tomography (PET) and fMRI provide *haemodynamic* measures of brain activity, i.e. they essentially rely on the fact that increased neural activation in a particular brain region triggers increases blood flow to that region. The most commonly used measure in fMRI is the so-called "blood oxygen-level dependent contrast" (BOLD), which reflects the ratio of oxygenated to deoxygenated blood in a given volume element (voxel). For a comprehensive introduction to the fMRI method, see Jezzard et al. (2001).

The results of functional neuroimaging studies are typically presented using *statistical parametric maps*, i.e. maps indicating statistical differences in a given *contrast* between two conditions. Contrasts follow the "subtraction logic," according to which activation of interest can be isolated by subtracting the activation in a control condition from that in a critical condition. Depending on the specificity of the question under examination, control conditions may either be rest, a low-level baseline (e.g. a string of Xs in comparison to a word as a control for activation due to the perception of a visual stimulus), or they may stem from the domain of interest itself and only differ from the critical stimulus with respect to a single feature/process (e.g. a simple control sentence in comparison to a syntactically complex sentence). Thus, this way of computing contrasts presupposes that activation for a critical condition can be parcelled into the activation engendered by the control condition and activation associated with the feature/process dissociating between the two conditions.

A final important point concerns the interpretation of functional imaging results. Thus, in contrast to deficit-lesion correlations gained

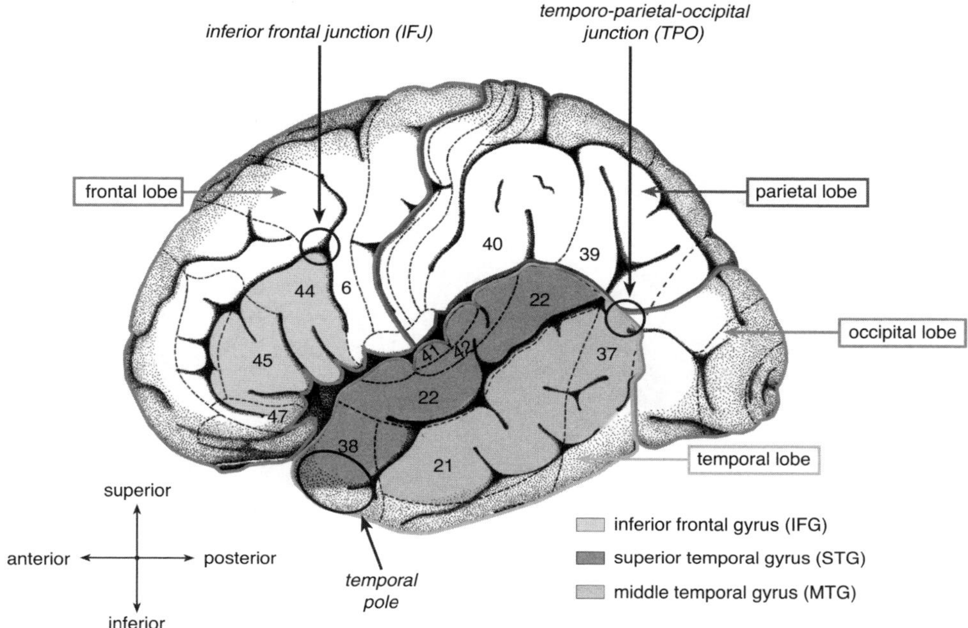

Figure 24.2 A more detailed depiction of the language-related regions in the left hemisphere, with major relevant gyri indicated by shading. The different large lobes are also marked by shaded borders. Numbers indicate language-relevant Brodmann Areas (BA), which Brodmann (1909) defined on the basis of their cytoarchitectonic characteristics. The coordinate labels superior/inferior indicate the position of a gyrus within a lobe (e.g. superior temporal gyrus) or within a BA (e.g. superior BA44). The coordinate labels anterior/posterior indicate the position within a gyrus (e.g. anterior superior temporal gyrus). See Plate 3 for a color version of this figure.

from patient studies, imaging data are purely correlative in nature. This means that they cannot be interpreted as evidence for the *necessary* involvement of a particular brain region in a specific cognitive process. A case in point concerns the role of the right hemisphere in language processing: while imaging studies consistently reveal right-hemispheric activity in response to linguistic stimuli, lesions to these regions do not show the detrimental effect on language performance that left-hemispheric lesions do. Thus, in spite of the many advantages that functional neuroimaging has to offer, patient studies still play an important role in supplementing the interpretation of their results.

24.1.3 Psycholinguistic questions and consequences

In addition to their informativity regarding the topographical representation of language in the brain, neuroimaging methods may also provide new approaches to core questions in the psycholinguistic literature on sentence comprehension. For example, they allow the debate regarding modularity vs. interactivity of comprehension to be recast in spatial rather than temporal terms. While any neuroanatomical conception of "modularity" must certainly differ conceptually from the standard psycholinguistic usage of the term, functional imaging results may nonetheless provide vital insights into the *separability* of different processes/information types. Thus, if two information types can be shown to engage distinct networks—or even distinct component parts of a shared overall network—and are thus separable in neuroanatomical terms, this would form a strong basis for the assumptions of a modular model. By contrast, a scenario in which a range of different information types (e.g. structural simplicity, verb-argument structure, and structural frequency) interacted to produce varying degrees of activation in a particular region or set of regions would be more easily

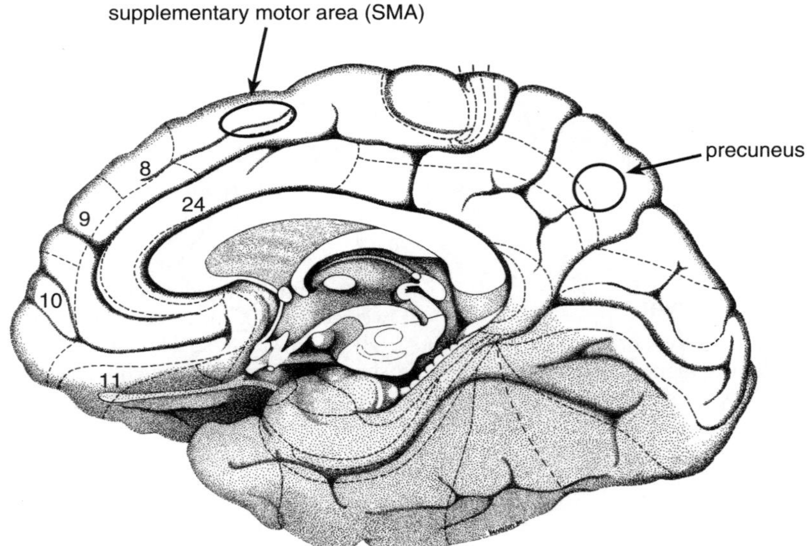

Figure 24.3 A schematic medial view of one of the hemispheres showing areas that have been implicated in language processing. Note that the cingulate gyrus, which is discussed in the text in relation to discourse processing, is BA24.

reconciled with the philosophy of an interactive architecture. In fact, as will be discussed in section 24.2.2, the truth appears to lie somewhere between these two hypothetical extremes. Nonetheless, this type of approach can provide valuable insights into which information types interact with one another (topographically) and which do not, thereby shedding further light on the fine-grained organization of the processing architecture.

Along similar lines, a method such as fMRI may be used to shed light on the classic psycholinguistic question of whether ambiguity is costly. If the comparison between ambiguous and unambiguous structures were to show increased neural activation for the former, and a possible influence of other factors (e.g. cost of disambiguation) were ruled out, this would indicate that ambiguous sentences engage more neural resources and are therefore more costly to process. Findings such as these may be taken as evidence of the serial or parallel nature of parsing.

Finally, we may use neuroimaging to ask whether reanalysis draws upon the same neural resources as initial structure building, depending on whether or not structures requiring reanalysis activate a distinct set of regions compared with those involved in high-demand initial structuring.

In this way, while the specific characteristics of neuroimaging methods—and particularly the fact that they allow us to capture similarities and differences in *space* rather than time—require key psycholinguistic questions to be considered from another perspective, we believe that precisely this new dimension may provide exciting new impulses to the quest to describe, explain, and model the internal architecture of the language comprehension system.

24.1.4 Outline of the chapter

This chapter provides an overview of current insights within the neuroimaging literature on sentence and discourse comprehension. In accordance with the two basic areas of inquiry to be addressed, it is divided into two main sections: sentence comprehension and discourse comprehension. Within each of these sections, we first provide a broad description of the functional neuroanatomy of the relevant processes (focusing, for example, on how the processing of sentences differs from that of word lists), before turning to more fine-grained differentiations within the domain under consideration. For reasons of manageability, we focus exclusively on studies at the sentence level or above, citing studies at lower levels where applicable (e.g. when we believe that these may crucially help us to understand particular subprocesses of sentence and discourse comprehension). Finally, in view of the fact that the overall neural networks subserving language comprehension have, by now, been documented in a large number of studies (for an overview, see Friederici, 2002, and section 24.1.1 above), only direct contrasts between language conditions will be considered (i.e. no baseline comparisons will be taken into account).

24.2 Sentence comprehension

24.2.1 Neuroanatomical correlates of comprehension processes at the sentence level

One of the first objectives in the examination of the brain bases of sentence comprehension was to ascertain how the neural activation observed for sentence processing differs from that elicited by linguistic stimuli not involving a sentential structure. Many studies have approached this question by comparing sentential stimuli to word lists. While contrasts of this type, of course, reveal a large number of overlapping activation sites, sentences as opposed to lists of unconnected words have been shown to engender additional activation in the anterior portion of the left superior temporal lobe (Mazoyer et al., 1993; Stowe et al., 1998; Bottini et al., 1994). This observation suggests that left anterior temporal cortex may be crucially involved in compositional operations at the sentence level. It cannot, however, shed light on the precise nature of the processes involved, for example on the question of whether the relations constructed are syntactic or semantic in nature.

More fine-grained dissociations in this regard were examined in a study by Friederici et al. (2000), in which participants listened to normal speech, jabberwocky sentences (i.e. pseudo-word sentences retaining relevant morphosyntactic information), real word lists, and pseudo-word lists. In comparison to word lists, stimuli containing a syntactic structure engendered increased activation in the planum polare (the anterior portion of the STG) bilaterally, as well as in the left posterior STG and the deep left frontal operculum (see Figure 24.4), thus suggesting a

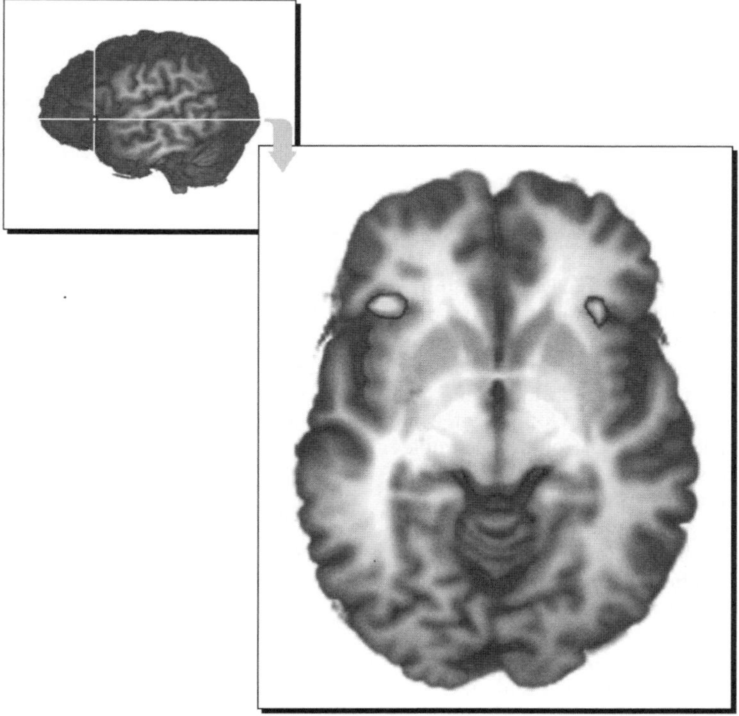

Figure 24.4 A schematic illustration of activation in the deep frontal operculum (bilaterally). The inset at the top left of the figure indicates the positioning of the axial section showing the activation. Note that activations in the anterior insula are adjacent to and partially overlapping with the activations depicted here. See Plate 4 for a color version of this figure.

specific involvement of anterior temporal and inferior frontal regions in syntactic structuring independently of meaning construction. By contrast, Vandenberghe et al. (2002) found that the activation of left anterior temporal cortex (temporal pole) is modulated by both syntactic (normal vs. scrambled sentences) and semantic (normal vs. "semantically random" sentences) factors. These authors therefore argue for a role of this cortical region in semantic composition. Interestingly, recent findings also point to a crucial role of prosody with respect to the modulation of anterior temporal activation (Humphries et al., 2005). It therefore appears either that this region performs a more general integrative function in sentence-level speech comprehension (cf. also Scott et al., 2000) or that a more fine-grained dissociation between different subregions within left anterior temporal cortex needs to be undertaken in order to allow a more precise neuroanatomical differentiation between the different information types.

Finally, it is interesting to note that the processing of regular sentence stimuli (i.e. simple sentences without violations) does not necessarily lead to increased involvement of left frontal regions, and particularly of the left IFG. Thus, in the Friederici et al. (2000) study discussed above, normal speech did not lead to frontal activation, while the three other conditions engendered increased activation of the left inferior frontal junction area (IFJ, i.e. the junction between the inferior frontal sulcus and the precentral sulcus, see Figure 24.2). As this region has been shown to play a more general role in response to increased task demands—and appears to be particularly involved in cognitive control (see Brass and von Cramon, 2004)—these findings speak in favor of a difference between more and less automatic language-related processes and/or a task-related modulation. In a similar spirit, Stowe et al. (1998) found that, while the left IFG responds more strongly to complex than to simple sentences, it also shows higher activation in response to word lists as compared to simple sentences. The authors interpreted this difference as relating to working memory demands in the different types of stimulus. Most generally, findings such as these appear to suggest that frontal (and particularly IFG) involvement in language comprehension comes into play when processing and/or strategic demands increase, but that it is not necessarily required during easy, automatic aspects of sentence comprehension.

In summary, this section has shown that sentence comprehension engages an extended network of cortical regions, some of which are common to the processing of language-related stimuli in general and some of which appear to be specific to processes applying at the sentence level. In view of the many different sub-processes and information types assumed to play a role in the overall comprehension process (see van Gompel and Pickering, Chapter 17 this volume), the question of whether the overall language network can be differentiated further and, if so, which subregions can be associated with which types of processes appears even more interesting from a psycholinguistic perspective. This issue will be addressed in the following sections.

24.2.2 Syntactic and semantic processing

A prominent line of research within the neuroimaging literature on language has been concerned with the attempt to differentiate between comprehension processes related to formal structure (syntax) and those related to sentence meaning (semantics). Several experimental approaches have been used to this purpose: violation paradigms (the comparison of syntactic and semantic violations), tasks presumably requiring different types of computation (syntactic or semantic), and the isolation of only syntactic or semantic relations in the linguistic input.

One of the earliest studies attempting to dissociate between sentence-level syntactic and semantic processes in neuroanatomical terms was reported by Dapretto and Bookheimer (1999). These authors compared syntactic and semantic computations by presenting participants with sentence pairs and requiring them to perform a "same vs. different" judgement task. The critical determinant of whether the sentence meaning was indeed the same or different depended either upon a syntactic factor (i.e. active or passive voice, 1a, b) or a lexical/semantic factor (i.e. homonymy, 1c, d).

1a. syntax same:
The policeman arrested the thief vs.
The thief was arrested by the policeman

1b. syntax different:
The teacher outsmarted the student vs. The teacher was outsmarted by the student

1c. semantics same:
The lawyer questioned the witness vs. The attorney questioned the witness

1d. semantics different:
The man was attacked by the Doberman vs.
The man was attacked by the pitbull.

The results of the study showed a differentiation within the left IFG, with the syntactic manipulation engendering increased activation in BA44 and the semantic manipulation giving rise to enhanced activation of the more anterior BA45/47. On the one hand, this differentiation within the IFG is supported by studies at the word level (cf. Bookheimer, 2002). On the other, since the fMRI methodology used in this study does not allow for a differentiation between the activation induced by the processing of the sentences themselves and the activation induced by the "sentence-matching" task, the activation observed in this study may reflect a number of different processes.

This potential difficulty was overcome in a study by Newman et al. (2003), which compared sentences with ("syntactic") subject–verb agreement violations (e.g. **The lady praises the sister and meet the artist in the night*) against sentences including an extra verb (a "thematic/semantic" violation in the terminology of the authors; e.g. **The coach watched the poet and told the visitor took in the evening*) in a grammaticality judgement task. These authors also observed increased activation in BA44 for the syntactic violation and increased activation in BA45 for the semantic violation. However, the results of this study are not quite as straightforwardly interpretable as the authors suggest, since the precise nature of the violation involving the extra verb is rather difficult to determine and may have resulted from a number of aspects of sentence processing.

In a similar spirit, Kuperberg et al. (2000) compared the processing of different types of violation in order to attempt to dissociate "syntactic" (subcategorization), "semantic" (selectional restriction), and "pragmatic" (world knowledge) processes at the sentence level. The participants' task was to judge the plausibility of each sentence.

2a. control condition:
The young man played the guitar.
2b. syntactic (subcategorization) violation:
*The young man slept the guitar
2c. semantic (selectional restriction) violation:
*The young man drank the guitar
2d. pragmatic (world knowledge) violation:
#The young man buried the guitar

In this study, all violation types showed higher activity in the left inferior temporal/fusiform cortex. With respect to the direct contrasts between the different information types, semantic vs. syntactic violations gave rise to increased activation of the right STG/middle temporal gyrus (MTG) and left insula (i.e. a region adjacent to the left deep frontal operculum shown in Figure 24.4), while pragmatic violations engendered higher activation in the left STG in comparison to both syntactic and semantic violations. Interestingly, there were no areas that showed increased activation in response to syntactic violations as opposed to the other violation types. However, this may have resulted from the particular type of violation chosen; i.e., while subcategorization is viewed as a syntactic property in certain theories of grammar, it does involve semantic aspects and certainly has in common with the selectional restriction information that it is *lexical* in nature. The particular task chosen may have also enhanced lexical-semantic processes. Thus, the main finding of this study was a general sensitivity of inferior temporal regions to linguistic anomaly, and of bilateral MTG/STG to selectional restriction and world knowledge violations.

Using a similar violation paradigm, Ni et al. (2000) compared the processing of relational syntactic information (violations of subject–verb agreement) with relational semantic processes (plausibility/selectional restriction violations). While these authors observed increased activity for semantic as opposed to syntactic violations in left IFG (BA44, 45, 47), posterior left MTG/STG, and a number of other regions, they also noted that only the syntactic condition showed a significantly more pronounced haemodynamic response in inferior frontal as opposed to temporal regions, while both cortical areas showed the same degree of activation increase for the semantic condition. The authors support this differentiation with a second experiment in which the anomalies were presented as "oddball" stimuli and participants were not required to attend to them. Here, in addition to a number of further differences, syntactic oddballs showed an activation in the left IFG not observable for the semantic oddballs, while the latter gave rise to increased activation of the posterior left STG. However, a complete dissociation between the two information types was not observed in this study either, as semantic oddballs also elicited activation in a large cluster in the IFG involving BA44, 45, and 47.

Whereas the violation studies discussed up to this point clearly implicate the involvement of temporal cortex (and especially of the left MTG/STG) in semantic processing, the results concerning inferior frontal activation for syntactic anomalies appear somewhat less consistent. The finding that areas other than the left IFG are observable for the processing of syntactic violations is thus not altogether surprising. This was the case, for example, in a comparison of syntactic and semantic violations in German (3). For these sentences, Friederici et al. (2003) observed increased activation in the left deep frontal operculum, left basal ganglia, and anterior left STG for syntactic violations, while semantic violations engendered higher mid-left STG and bilateral insular activations. In addition, both syntactic and semantic violations led to a higher activation of the posterior left STG in comparison to the correct control condition.

3a. control condition:
Das Hemd wurde gebügelt.
the shirt was ironed

3b. syntactic violation:
*Die Bluse wurde am gebügelt.
the blouse was at-the ironed

3c. semantic (selectional restriction) violation:
*Das Gewitter wurde gebügelt.
the thunderstorm was ironed

Friederici et al.'s (2003) results thus demonstrate that left inferior frontal cortex need not always be increasingly engaged when syntactic processing becomes more demanding. Rather, findings such as these suggest that increased inferior frontal involvement in the processing of syntactic information may depend upon (a) the particular *type* of syntactic information involved, and (b) the particular task employed. We shall return to the question of which types of syntactic information may be suitable to engendering activation of the left IFG—and particularly of BA44—in section 24.2.3 below.

An alternative approach to investigating the neural bases of syntax has been to compare increased syntactic processing demand with linguistic processes below the sentence level. Thus, Embick et al. (2000) observed increased activation for syntactic violations (local word order; e.g. order of preposition and determiner) in comparison to orthographic violations in the left IFG, left posterior superior temporal sulcus (STS; i.e. the sulcus between STG and MTG), and left angular and supramarginal gyri (i.e. BA39 and BA40). However, the activation difference between the two conditions was largest in the IFG. Similar results were reported by Moro et al. (2001) for syntactic (wrong ordering of determiner and noun) and morphosyntactic (gender agreement) violations in Italian in comparison to phonotactic violations. For the syntactic violation, these authors additionally observed left basal ganglia activation. Nonetheless, the conditions compared in these two studies differed substantially with respect to the level of processing necessary to accomplish the task.

Finally, Kiehl et al. (2002) examined sentence-level semantic processes independently of syntax by employing a classical N400 paradigm (see Kutas and Federmeier, Chapter 23 this volume), i.e. a comparison of sentences with semantically congruous and incongruous final words. In this study, incongruous sentences yielded increased activation of bilateral inferior frontal (BA45) and anterior temporal cortex, as well as of a number of other regions.

In summary, the studies on the neural bases of sentence-level syntactic and semantic processes discussed above show several consistent findings, but also a number of diverging results. With respect to possible consequences for psycholinguistic theories, however, the data are relatively clear in that they indicate both commonalities and differences with respect to the neural resources drawn upon by the two information types. In the context of the debate on modularity vs. interactivity, a data pattern of this type may be taken to indicate that both scenarios occur, i.e. that certain aspects of syntactic and semantic processing proceed in an autonomous fashion, while others involve an integration of the two domains. Indeed, an account along these lines fits very well with current theorizing regarding the temporal aspects of language comprehension, in which certain (temporally delimited) processing phases show autonomous and others show interactive behavior (Friederici, 2002).

24.2.3 The processing of word order variations/complex sentences

An alternative approach to the examination of syntactic processes to that described in the previous section has focused on the neuroanatomical correlates of the comprehension of complex sentences (i.e. typically sentences in which an object precedes the subject). The first finding within this line of research was that both the left IFG (BA 44/45) and left STG/STS respond to increases of syntactic complexity in English, i.e. activation in accordance with the complexity scale: object relative clauses (4c) > subject-relative clauses (4b) > conjoined active clauses (4a) (Just et al., 1996).

4a. The reporter attacked the senator and admitted the error.

4b. The reporter that attacked the senator admitted the error.

4c. The reporter that the senator attacked admitted the error.

A similar finding of increased activation of BA44 in response to object- vs. subject-relative clauses was reported by Stromswold et al. (1996) and replicated in a number of further studies

(Caplan et al., 1998: exp. 1; Caplan et al., 2000 (BA45)). While several subsequent experiments either failed to show increased inferior frontal activation for object-relative clauses (Caplan et al., 2001) or only observed this activation for particular groups of participants (Waters et al., 2003) or subsets of sentence materials (Cooke et al., 2002—albeit in BA47), the overall data pattern does speak in favor of the involvement of BA44 in the processing of complex English sentences of this type (for more recent replications see e.g. Constable et al., 2004; Keller et al., 2001).

However, even under the assumption that the data pattern itself is reliable, its interpretation has given rise to much controversy in the literature. On the one hand, several authors have used these data to argue for a crucial role of BA44 in syntactic processing (e.g. as engaging in the processing of syntactic movement operations (Grodzinsky, 2000) or of hierarchical syntactic information (Friederici, 2004)). From this perspective, the increased activation of BA44 in English object relatives is viewed as resulting from the operations somehow involved in *reconstructing* the canonical subject-before-object word order. Alternatively, it has been argued that the increased activation of BA44 in the processing of complex sentences should be attributed to higher working-memory demands (Caplan et al., 2000; Fiebach et al., 2005; Kaan and Swaab, 2002; Müller et al., 2003). These types of approach argue that the involvement of BA44 is required by the need to maintain the object in working memory until the gap position (or the subcategorizer) is encountered. Clearly, these two interpretations are very difficult to tease apart using the types of sentence discussed so far, because these invariably introduce a confound between the factors of canonicity and working memory. Moreover, non-canonical and canonical sentences of this type typically also differ with respect to a number of further dimensions, such as frequency of occurrence, acceptability, and processing difficulty in terms of standard behavioral paradigms such as self-paced reading (e.g. King and Just, 1991; Schlesewsky et al., 2000). Furthermore, object- and subject-relative clauses in English also differ in word order (relative pronoun–verb–object vs. relative pronoun–subject–verb).

A number of these potentially confounding factors have been addressed in studies examining languages other than English. In the following, we shall therefore discuss findings from Hebrew and German, before attempting to draw some conclusions with respect to the role of BA44 in the comprehension of complex sentences.

With the aim of isolating neural correlates of syntactic movement operations, Ben-Shachar et al. (2004) examined two types of word order permutation in Hebrew: topicalization (5a), in which an object is permuted to a position preceding the subject, and dative shift (5b), in which the order of the objects is reversed with respect to the (canonical) control condition.

5a. Control
John natan ['et ha-sefer ha-'adom]$_1$
[la-professor me-oxford]$_2$
John gave [ACC the-book the -red]
[to-the-professor from-Oxford]

5b. Topicalization
['et ha-sefer ha-'adom]$_1$ John natan
[la-professor me-oxford]$_2$
[ACC the-book the--red] John gave
[to-the-professor from-Oxford]

5c. Dative shift
John natan [la-professor me-oxford]$_2$
['et ha-sefer ha-'adom]$_1$
John gave [to-the-professor from-Oxford]
[ACC the-book the -red]

Ben-Shachar et al. observed increased activation of left BA44/45 (and several other regions including the left ventral precentral sulcus and posterior superior temporal sulcus (STS) bilaterally) for the topicalization condition in comparison to the control condition. By contrast, dative shift did not lead to increased inferior frontal activation, but rather modulated the activation level of the right anterior insula (an area adjacent to the right deep frontal operculum shown in Figure 24.4) and the right ventral precentral sulcus. In the spirit of Grodzinsky's (2000) movement-based approach, the authors interpret this difference between the two movement conditions as reflecting a neuroanatomical distinction between different movement types, with only A-bar movement activating BA44/45 (see Haegeman, 1994 for an introduction to different types of movement within Government and Binding Theory). They further argue that findings from a second experiment, in which both subject and object *wh-* questions led to increased left inferior frontal activation, support an account along these lines, because both question types involve A-bar movement.

However, findings from German indicate that the complete data pattern is somewhat more complex. Thus, Röder et al. (2002) showed increased activation of left BA 44/45 (as well as mid-left MTG/STG) for clause-medial word order permutations in German, a syntactic operation typically described as A-movement (e.g. Haider and Rosengren, 2003). The analysis contrasted "easy" sentences (involving 0 or 1 permutations) against "difficult" sentences (involving 2 permutations). As is apparent from the examples of the two stimulus types in (6), the German stimuli contrast with both English and Hebrew in that the relative ordering of the arguments and the verb does not change between the different conditions. Rather, only the order of the arguments themselves differs.

6a. Jetzt wird der Astronaut dem Forscher den Mond beschreiben.
now will [the astronaut]$_{NOM}$ [the scientist]$_{DAT}$ [the moon]$_{ACC}$ describe
Now the astronaut will describe the moon to the scientist.

6b. Jetzt wird dem Forscher den Mond der Astronaut beschreiben.
now will [the scientist]$_{DAT}$ [the moon]$_{ACC}$ [the astronaut]$_{NOM}$ describe
Now the astronaut will describe the moon to the scientist.

7a. Jetzt wird der Trosanaut dem Schorfer den Rond bebreuschen.

7b. Jetzt wird dem Schorfer den Rond der Trosanaut bebreuschen.

A second interesting finding by Röder et al. (2002) stems from the comparison of sentences such as (6) with analogous structures containing pseudo-words (but retaining case marking etc., as in 7). Both factors (word order and semantic content) interacted in BA44/45, thus speaking against a purely syntactic account of this region's involvement in the comprehension of the sentences under consideration.

Further findings from German show that there are interesting cross-linguistic differences with respect to the types of word order permutations that activate BA44 (45). While, as discussed in detail above, object-relative clauses engender increased activation of this region in comparison to subject-relative clauses in English, an analogous comparison in German failed to yield reliable inferior frontal activation (Fiebach et al., 2004). Rather, the study in question, which contrasted object- and subject-relative clauses that were disambiguated at different points in the sentence, revealed only a main effect of late vs. early disambiguation in the superior portion of BA44. It appears rather unlikely that this activation pattern should have resulted from the presence of an ambiguity per se, as a further experiment comparing unambiguous subject- and object-initial embedded *wh*-questions yielded the same result (Fiebach et al., 2005). As it is commonly assumed that relative clauses and *wh*-questions share the same syntactic structure (and both involve A-bar movement; cf. Haegeman, 1994), this cross-experimental replication strengthens the claim that, in German, only *clause-medial* argument order permutations (as in the Röder et al. study) but not *clause-initial* argument order permutations engender increased activation in BA44. By contrast, Fiebach et al. (2005) observed a significant activation difference within BA44 for object questions with a *long* as opposed to a short filler-gap distance, and therefore argued for a working-memory-based interpretation of their results.

Finally, the results of two recent studies from German appear well suited to shedding further light on the precise operations leading to increased activation of BA44 in the processing of word order variations. Thus, Grewe et al. (2005) and Bornkessel et al. (2005) investigated the processing of *unmarked* object-initial sentences in German, i.e. sentences in which the object-before-subject order is justified by some independent principle. Examples of such sentences are given in (8a), from Grewe et al. (2005), and (8b), from Bornkessel et al. (2005).

8a. Dann hat ihm der Lehrer den Spaten gegeben.
then has him$_{DAT}$ [the teacher]$_{NOM}$ [the spade]$_{ACC}$ given
'Then the teacher gave him the spade.'

8b. ... dass dem Jungen die Lehrer auffallen.
... that [the boy]$_{DAT}$ [the teachers]$_{NOM}$ are-striking-to
'... that the boy finds the teachers striking'

Whereas in (8a), the object-initial order is rendered highly acceptable by an independent rule on pronoun positioning in German (i.e. pronouns should precede non-pronominal arguments in the medial portion of the clause), it is justified by the particular properties of the verb in (8b) (i.e. the dative object-experiencer verb *auffallen* assigns the higher-ranked Experiencer role to the object, so that only an object-initial order allows for the thematic hierarchy to be upheld in terms of linear ordering). Neither of the two sentence types in (8) engendered increased activation of BA44 in comparison to minimally differing subject-initial controls, while this activation was observable for object-initial sentences without pronouns in the Grewe et al. study and for sentences without object-experiencer verbs in the Bornkessel et al. study. These findings show that (a) the presence or absence of BA 44 activation is independent of whether a movement operation has occurred and, thereby, (b) that it is also independent of working-memory demands which arise from the need to reconstruct to a canonical word order or an Agent-before-Patient order. Rather, Bornkessel et al. (2005) and Grewe et al. (2005) argue for an interpretation of BA44 activation in terms of the interaction of *linearization* principles, which govern how hierarchical dependencies such as subject > object, Actor > Undergoer, animate > inanimate, etc. are mapped onto linear order in individual languages. This perspective not only allows for a derivation of the interaction between formal factors (e.g. grammatical functions and argument order) with interpretive properties (e.g. thematic roles), but also provides a possible means of deriving the cross-linguistic differences discussed above. Because linearization regularities vary from language to language and differ, for example, between English and Hebrew on the one hand and German on the other in that only the latter has the verb-second property, the linearization hypothesis predicts that the cross-linguistically applicable hierarchies referred to above should interact with the structural properties of individual languages to produce the observable activation pattern in BA44 (Bornkessel et al., 2005).

24.2.4 **Syntactic ambiguity and reanalysis**

Studies examining misanalysis and subsequent recovery (reanalysis) in ambiguous sentences have been at the heart of the psycholinguistic literature on sentence comprehension for several decades. Therefore, possible neuroanatomical correlates of reanalysis—and particularly data speaking to the question of whether reanalysis engages similar or distinct brain regions to those identified for structure building and initial interpretation—are highly relevant for psycholinguistic comprehension models.

In a direct comparison of unambiguous and locally ambiguous sentences that were subsequently disambiguated towards the dispreferred analysis, Stowe et al. (2004) observed increased activation for ambiguous vs. unambiguous sentences in left BA45 and the right caudate nucleus (as part of the basal ganglia), as well as in the right posterior dorsal cerebellum and other regions. However, as no ambiguous sentences with a preferred disambiguation were included in this study, the activation patterns observed here may have resulted either from the presence of an ambiguity per se, from some aspect of the reanalysis process, or from some more general task demand (e.g. error detection).

Nonetheless, the finding of left inferior frontal activation is consistent with two further studies examining structures requiring reanalysis. As discussed in section 24.2.3, Fiebach et al. (2004) observed a main effect of the position of disambiguation (early vs. late) in subject and object relative clauses in German. In this study, the superior portion of left BA44 (BA44s) and bilateral intraparietal sulci showed increased activation for sentences with a late disambiguation. In the intraparietal sulci, this effect was independent of whether the structure was disambiguated towards a preferred or a dispreferred reading, thereby pointing to a general cost of ambiguity. Within BA44s, Fiebach et al. observed an interaction of reading span, point of disambiguation, and word order, which resulted from higher activation for object- vs. subject-relative clauses with a late disambiguation in low-span readers, but only a general effect of the point of disambiguation in high-span readers.

A similar finding of increased activation in BA44s for ambiguous vs. unambiguous German sentences involving word order variations was reported by Bornkessel et al. (2005). In contrast to the Fiebach et al. study, however, this experiment employed a clause-medial word order variation in embedded clauses (as described in section 24.2.3), and used ambiguous as well as fully unambiguous sentences. Interestingly, in addition to the main effect of ambiguity, BA44s showed the same effect of word order—and the same interaction between word order and thematic structure (see example 8)—for ambiguous and unambiguous stimuli. This finding indicates that reanalysis operations pertaining to word order draw upon similar neural resources to those supporting the initial structuring of complex sentences.

In summary, the data presently available are consistent with the claim that reanalysis mechanisms are supported by a similar network to that engaging in initial processing. More specifically, the studies discussed point to an important role of left inferior frontal cortex (particularly BA44s) both in the processing of ambiguous stimuli per se and in reanalysis. However, the involvement of this area does not appear to depend on whether it is also activated by the unambiguous sentence type corresponding to the dispreferred disambiguation. Thus, while reanalysis appears to be implemented within the "standard" language network, an association between the data and a "reanalysis as reparsing" account is also not trivial. Rather, the data pattern again supports the conception that BA44 (45) comes into play when processing demands increase, e.g. during the comprehension of (particular types of) complex sentences and in reanalysis. The role of the other regions implicated by the studies of reanalysis discussed here (e.g. the basal ganglia) clearly require further investigation. Data from patients with lesions in the basal ganglia also indicate that this structure plays a major role in reanalysis processes (Kotz et al., 2003).

24.2.5 Prosody

In comparison to the large body of neuroimaging research on linguistic sub-domains such as syntax and semantics, studies focusing specifically on the functional neuroanatomy of prosody have not become available until somewhat more recently. Therefore, despite rapidly increasing interest in this domain, only comparatively few results are currently available. Nonetheless, there is widespread agreement that, in contrast to the left-lateralized language network described above, prosodic processes appear to be associated predominantly with right-hemispheric brain circuits. In particular, as the discussion below will show, several findings point towards a predominant role of superior temporal regions of the right hemisphere in the extraction and processing of prosodic information at the sentence level.

For example, in a study seeking to isolate the brain regions engaging in the processing of sentence prosody, Meyer et al. (2002) contrasted normal sentences with pseudo-word sentences ("syntactic speech") and delexicalized speech retaining only sentence melody ("prosodic speech"). While the results for syntactic speech replicated previous findings of anterior (planum polare), mid (Heschl's gyrus), and posterior (planum temporale) aspects of the left supratemporal plane (i.e. the superior surface of the STG), prosodic speech led to a strong response of the right supratemporal plane, and particularly of the planum temporale. Moreover, both syntactic and prosodic speech led to increased activation of fronto-opercular cortices bilaterally, with a stronger response for prosodic speech. The authors attribute the right temporal activation for prosodic information to the extraction of slow-pitch information (F0) from the speech signal, while the fronto-opercular cortices appear to be somehow involved in more general processes applying to degraded or unintelligible speech.

Plante et al. (2002) also compared the processing of sentences to that of stimuli containing only prosodic information, but further included a task manipulation (passive listening vs. recognition). These authors observed bilateral superior temporal activation in response to both sentential and prosodic stimuli in the passive listening task, while the active task led to the additional recruitment of frontal regions including the inferior frontal gyrus (as well as the middle frontal gyrus and precentral sulcus). Interestingly, the lateralization of the frontal activation depended on stimulus type, with sentence stimuli leading to higher activation than prosodic stimuli in left frontal regions and vice versa in right frontal regions. This finding supports the notion that inferior frontal involvement during language comprehension may not only be task-related, but also stimulus-related.

This notion is also supported by a number of studies with patients suffering from circumscribed brain lesions, and has led to the assumption of a dynamic interplay between the left and the right hemisphere which is based on the corpus callosum, i.e. the fibre bundles interconnecting the two hemispheres (Friederici and Alter, 2004).

24.2.6 Neurocognitive models of sentence comprehension

There exist several models of the functional neuroanatomy of sentence comprehension. In accordance with the scope of this chapter, we only focus on those approaches concerned with the construction of relations at the sentence level. For a detailed account of the speech perception processes (e.g. phonological analysis) which are a prerequisite for these mechanisms, see Hickok and Poeppel (2004).

Within the *neurocognitive model of auditory sentence comprehension*, Friederici (2002) proposes that comprehension is subdivided into three processing phases. While phase 1 encompasses basic processes of constituent structuring that draw exclusively upon word category information, phase 2 involves morphosyntactic and lexical-semantic processing as well as thematic role assignment. Importantly, formal and interpretive properties are processed in parallel but independently of one another in the second phase. Finally, phase 3 is the locus of reanalysis and repair mechanisms, should these be required. In this phase, the information types processed independently of one another in phase 2 interact.

Friederici (2002) assumes that the three phases are supported by a bilateral fronto-temporal network. Word category-based structure building in phase 1 is assumed to engage the anterior portion of the left superior temporal cortex and the left frontal operculum. In accordance with the functional differentiation between the different processing streams responsible for *relational* processing in phase 2, this stage of comprehension is also associated with several brain regions. Thus, the construction of semantic relations draws upon mid left STG and MTG and BA45/47 within the left IFG, while the establishment of syntactic relations is associated with left BA44 and the frontal operculum. Friederici (2004) proposes a further distinction between these two frontal regions and their involvement in syntactic processing: while fronto-opercular cortex engages in the processing of local syntactic dependencies, the involvement of BA44 is required when higher-level hierarchical and long-distance dependencies come into play. With respect to possible neuroanatomical correlates of phase 3, Friederici et al. (2003) point to the posterior portion of left STG, a region which shows precisely the interaction between syntactic and semantic information assumed to occur within this phase (see section 24.2.2). Finally, the neurocognitive model assumes that the processing of sentence-level prosody is supported by the posterior right STG and the right frontal operculum. The interaction between the right-lateralized neural circuitry responsible for prosodic processing and the left-lateralized network supporting syntactic and semantic comprehension mechanisms is assumed to proceed via the corpus callosum (Friederici and Alter, 2004).

An entirely different conceptualization of the neural basis for language comprehension—and particularly of the interplay between syntax and semantics—has been proposed within the *declarative/procedural* model (Ullman, 2001; 2004). In accordance with the more general differentiation between declarative and procedural memory, Ullman proposes that (rule-based) syntactic knowledge should be viewed as part of the procedural system, while (lexically stored) semantic information is represented as a declarative information type. Processing within the two linguistic sub-domains is therefore expected to engage the neural networks associated with the procedural and declarative memory systems, respectively. Whereas the procedural system has been associated with a network of frontal (BA44/45, (pre-)supplementary motor area, premotor cortex), parietal (supramarginal gyrus, superior parietal lobe), cerebellar, and basal-ganglia structures, the declarative system is thought to draw primarily upon regions in the medial temporal lobe. Superior temporal regions are viewed as a possible locus for mediation between the two systems. From this perspective, inferior frontal and basal ganglia activations engendered by increased syntactic processing demands (see sections 24.2.2 and 24.2.3) are viewed as resulting from the involvement of the procedural system. Similarly, the inferior temporal activations reported by Kuperberg et al. (2000) for the processing of lexically induced violations and the observation of hippocampal and parahippocampal involvement in the processing of semantic violations (Newman et al., 2001) are interpreted as evidence for the declarative system.

A third proposal regarding the neural basis of sentence processing, the Memory, Unification, and Control (MUC) framework, was recently formulated by Hagoort (2003; 2005). Adopting the psycholinguistic assumptions of Vosse and Kempen's (2000) template-based unification model, Hagoort proposes that the storage and retrieval of templates ("syntactic frames") is supported by the posterior portion of left superior temporal cortex (the *memory* component), while template unification ("binding") is accomplished by left inferior frontal areas (the *unification* component). Furthermore, language-specific processing demands are linked to more general aspects of cognitive processing by way of the proposal that language-related mechanisms of cognitive *control* are associated with anterior cingulate cortex (see Figure 24.3) and dorsolateral prefrontal cortex (BA46/9). One of the central claims of the MUC is therefore that Broca's region can be viewed as a "unification space" for language, with increased activation of this area resulting from increased unification demands. Hagoort further assumes that different sub-regions of Broca's area engage in the unification of different types of linguistic structures: BA45 and BA47 are thought to be involved in semantic unification, BA45 and BA44 in syntactic unification, and BA44 and the inferior portion of premotor cortex (BA6) in phonological unification.

An important question for future research lies in examining how the MUC framework might be applied to the finding of Broca's area (and particularly BA44) activation for word order variations. As Vosse and Kempen state in their original paper (2000: 138), differences between object- and subject-initial verb-final structures (e.g. in German and Japanese) cannot be modeled in the same way to differences between object- (OSV) and subject-initial (SVO) sentences in English in the unification framework (i.e. via increased competition in the unification space). Nonetheless, both contrasts yield activation differences in BA44 (see section 24.2.3). As these findings have not yet been discussed in the context of the MUC framework, it will be very interesting to see how they will be approached in further developments of the model architecture.

24.3 From sentence to discourse

In comparison to the wealth of neuroimaging evidence on the comprehension of sentences, the neural mechanisms of discourse processing are somewhat less well studied. In particular, while a number of neuroimaging studies have used text passages or stories as experimental stimuli, comparatively few attempts have been undertaken to examine the neural basis of the precise mechanisms involved in comprehending linguistic units larger than the sentence. The studies that have undertaken systematic manipulations within this domain, however, attest to interesting differences between the functional neuroanatomy of sentence and discourse processing.

24.3.1 General differences between discourse and sentence processing

Studies examining the comprehension of text passages or short stories point to the involvement of a number of brain regions that are not typically observed during the processing of isolated sentences. For example, in a study comparing stories to unrelated sentences, Fletcher et al. (1995) observed additional activation for stories in bilateral temporal pole regions, left posterior STG, and in a region within posterior cingulate cortex. An additional left fronto-median region (BA8) was only activated when the stories required the attribution of a mental state, i.e. "theory of mind" (TOM)-related processes (see also Mazoyer et al., 1993 for activation of this region and the temporal pole during story comprehension, and Gallagher et al., 2000 for similar findings in a TOM task). The activation of a similar network was observed in a number of further studies examining discourse processing (e.g. Ferstl and von Cramon, 2001).

A direct comparison between processing at the word, sentence, and text levels was undertaken by Xu et al. (2005) using a carefully controlled set of stimuli. The authors selected a subset of Aesop's fables that were matched for lexical properties and complexity and presented these as coherent narratives, unconnected sentences, or random word lists. While activation in a fronto-temporal network was observed in all conditions, sentence processing led to the activation of additional left inferior frontal areas (including BA44) and bilateral temporal pole regions. In response to narratives, further activation was seen bilaterally in the precuneus, fronto-median cortex (BA8/9/10) and the temporo-parietal-occipital (TPO) junction area.

There is thus converging evidence that, in addition to the regions involved in sentence comprehension, discourse processing draws upon neural resources in bilateral anterior temporal poles, posterior cingulate cortex/precuneus, and fronto-median regions, with additional activation of the TPO junction area in the Xu et al. study.

24.3.2 Specific aspects

With respect to the specific mechanisms performed by the neural network for discourse processing and possible specializations of its different component parts, several studies have attempted to ascertain the precise role of the right hemisphere in the integration of contextual information. This line of research was inspired primarily by the "coarse coding hypothesis" (Beeman, 1998), which posits that the right hemisphere is responsible for the activation of a broad field of semantically related concepts, while the selection of specific concepts (and inhibition of alternatives) is the responsibility of the left hemisphere.

For example, St. George et al. (1999) argued in favour of coarse coding on the basis of a study comparing titled and untitled paragraphs (based on a paradigm by Bransford and Johnson, 1972). They observed increased activation in inferior frontal and temporal regions of interest in both hemispheres, as well as an interaction of the factors of hemisphere and title which was due to more right-hemispheric activation for untitled than titled paragraphs. In addition, a larger average volume was activated for untitled vs. titled paragraphs in the right middle temporal sulcus, while this pattern reversed in the left middle temporal sulcus. However, in a very similar experiment, albeit using pictures instead of titles, Maguire et al. (1999) obtained rather different results. In this study, stories with the matching picture (i.e. contextually coherent stimuli) led to increased activation in the posterior cingulate, the left temporal pole, and a ventro-medial orbital region (BA11).

Three further studies were presented as converging evidence for a crucial role of the right hemisphere in establishing coherent discourse representations. Nichelli et al. (1995) observed activation in right BA47 and right anterior STG when participants read Aesop's fables and performed a task requiring text-level inference.

Using a very different paradigm, Robertson et al. (2000) contrasted series of sentences with definite articles with the same sentences containing indefinite articles, under the assumption that the former would be regarded as more coherent. The difference between the two stimulus types correlated with increased activation of right prefrontal areas. Finally, Caplan and Dapretto (2001) contrasted two different tasks in the comprehension of a conversation. While appraisal of changes in the topic of the conversation led to a stronger right hemispheric response of the fronto-temporal network being observed (with additional cerebellar activation), a task requiring reasoning led to a stronger activation focus on left inferior frontal and posterior superior temporal regions.

The processing of text coherence was explicitly examined and contrasted against text cohesion by Ferstl and von Cramon (2001). These authors presented sentence pairs (cf. 9) that were either coherent or incoherent and cohesive or incohesive (i.e. containing a connective lexical element or not).

9a. Coherent/incohesive
Mary's exam was about to start.
The palms were sweaty.

9b. Coherent/cohesive
Mary's exam was about to start. Therefore, her palms were sweaty.

9c. Incoherent/incohesive
Laura got a lot of mail today. The palms were sweaty.

9d. Incoherent/cohesive
Laura got a lot of mail today. Therefore, her palms were sweaty.

Ferstl and von Cramon observed increased activation for coherent vs. incoherent sentence pairs in the left posterior cingulate cortex/inferior precuneus, the left fronto-median wall (BA9/10), and the left superior frontal gyrus. Cohesive vs. incohesive sentences led to a bilateral activation of the frontal eye fields which was presumably due to differences in sentence length. Both factors interacted in left BA44. On the basis of these results, the authors argue against a specific right-hemispheric involvement in the establishment of discourse coherence.

In a further study, Ferstl and von Cramon (2002) sought to disentangle the contributions of discourse coherence and TOM with respect to the fronto-median activations observed in several of the studies discussed above. This was accomplished by presenting pragmatically coherent and unrelated sentence pairs and employing an instruction that either discouraged or encouraged TOM interpretations. The authors observed an extended fronto-median activation (BA9/10/24/32 and anterior cingulate cortex) which was always present for coherent sentence pairs, but which only obtained in the incoherent sentence pairs under TOM instructions. This demonstrates that coherence and TOM aspects interact in the fronto-median wall during discourse comprehension.

Finally, Ferstl et al. (2005) report a study that dissociated between different sources of contextual (in)coherence by presenting short stories that were either consistent or included an inconsistency brought about by different information types (chronological, temporal, or related to the emotional state of the story's protagonist). Inconsistent stories always led to increased activation in right anterior temporal regions, but also showed further differences between the distinct types of inconsistency: chronological information led to activation of the left precuneus and a bilateral fronto-parietal network; emotional information engendered higher activity of the ventro-medial prefrontal cortex, the amygdala, and dorsal fronto-median cortex (BA8/9); and temporal information activated the lateral prefrontal cortex bilaterally. This differentiation indicates that a number of processes pertaining to different information types interact in the construction of a coherent discourse representation.

To summarize, studies on story/text comprehension suggest that mechanisms of discourse processing involve an extended network of neural regions in addition to those involved in sentence processing, some of which appear to provide a direct interface to more general cognitive mechanisms such as TOM-related inferencing. While several studies have suggested that the right hemisphere—and particularly right temporal areas—engage in the establishment of discourse coherence, right-hemispheric involvement does not appear to be crucially required in all cases. Moreover, as different types of information appear to engage differing neural circuits in discourse processing, a precise characterization of their interaction constitutes a very interesting and promising goal for future research, as does a closer specification of the interplay of different levels of representation within the construction of a discourse representation.

24.4 **Conclusions and outlook**

Neuroimaging studies of sentence and discourse processing have provided vital new insights into the functional neuroanatomy of language comprehension and the interaction of its component parts. Nonetheless, while there are a number of converging findings, the studies discussed in this chapter also attest to many apparent inconsistencies. These are likely to be at least partially attributable to varying experimental designs, methodologies, and, in particular, subtly differing types of linguistic manipulation (e.g. the precise type of information leading to a "syntactic" violation). Thus, future research in this domain will crucially need to employ very rigorous and tightly controlled experimental settings in order to tease apart the numerous factors which interact in the complex task of higher-level language processing. Nonetheless, the exquisite sensitivity of neuroimaging methods to these many interacting influences—to which many of the findings discussed in this chapter attest—may thereby also serve as an entirely new window on the question of which comprehension processes are similar and which differ from one another. Neuroimaging findings should therefore enable us to draw conclusions with respect to the internal organization of language comprehension that would otherwise remain hidden.

References

Beeman, M. (1998) Coarse semantic coding and discourse comprehension. In M. Beeman and C. Chiarello (eds), *Right Hemisphere Language Comprehension: Perspectives from Cognitive Neuroscience*, pp. 255–84. Erlbaum, Mahwah, NJ.

Ben-Shachar, M., Palti, D., and Grodzinsky, Y. (2004) Neural correlates of syntactic movement: converging evidence from two fMRI experiments. *NeuroImage*, 21: 1320–36.

Bookheimer, S. (2002) Functional MRI of language: new approaches to understanding the cortical organisation of semantic processing. *Annual Review of Neuroscience*, 25: 151–88.

Bornkessel, I., Zysset, S., Friederici, A. D., Von Cramon, D. Y., and Schlesewsky, M. (2005) Who did what to whom? The neural basis of argument hierarchies during language comprehension. *NeuroImage*, 26: 221–33.

Bottini, G., Corcoran, R., Sterzi, R., Paulescu, E., Schenone, P., Scarpa, P., et al. (1994) The role of the right hemisphere in the interpretation of figurative aspects of language: a positron emission tomography study. *Brain*, 117: 1241–53.

Bransford, J. D. and Johnson, M. K. (1972) Contextual prerequisites for understanding: some investigations of comprehension and recall. *Journal of Verbal Learning and Verbal Behavior*, 11: 717–26.

Brass, M., and Von Cramon, D. Y. (2004) Decomposing components of task preparation with functional magnetic resonance imaging. *Journal of Cognitive Neuroscience*, 16: 609–20.

Brodmann, K. (1909) Vergleichende Lokalisationslehre der Groflhirnrinde. Barth, Leipzig.

Caplan, D., Alpert, N., and Waters, G. (1998) Effects of syntactic structure and propositional number on patterns of regional cerebral blood flow. *Journal of Cognitive Neuroscience*, 10: 541–2.

Caplan, D., Alpert, N., Waters, G., and Olivieri, A. (2000) Activation of Broca's area by syntactic processing under conditions of concurrent articulation. *Human Brain Mapping*, 9: 65–71.

Caplan, D., Vijayan, S., Kuperberg, G. R., West, C., Waters, G., Greve, D., et al. (2001) Vascular responses to syntactic processing: event-related fMRI study of relative clauses. *Human Brain Mapping*, 15: 26–38.

Caplan, R. C. A. and Dapretto, M. (2001) Making sense during conversation: an fMRI study. *NeuroReport*, 12: 3625–32.

Caramazza, A. and Zurif, E. (1976) Dissociation of algorithmic and heuristic processes in language comprehension: evidence from aphasia. *Brain and Language*, 3: 572–82.

Constable, R. T., Pugh, K. R., Berroya, E., Mencl, W. E., Westerveld, M., Ni, W., et al. (2004) Sentence complexity and input modality effecs in sentence comprehension: an fMRI study. *NeuroImage*, 22: 11–21.

Cooke, A., Zurif, E. B., Devita, C., Alsop, D., Koenig, P., Detre, J., et al. (2002) Neural basis for sentence comprehension: grammatical and short-term memory components. *Human Brain Mapping*, 15: 80–94.

Dapretto, M., and Bookheimer, S. (1999) Dissociating syntax and semantics in sentence comprehension. *Neuron*, 24: 427–32.

Embick, D., Marantz, A., Miyashita, Y., O'neil, W., and Sakai, K. L. (2000) A syntactic specialization for Broca's area. *Proceedings of the National Academy of Sciences USA*, 97: 6150–4.

Ferstl, E. C., and Von Cramon, D. Y. (2001) The role of coherence and cohesion in text comprehension: an event-related fMRI study. *Cognitive Brain Research*, 11: 325–40.

Ferstl, E. C. and Von Cramon, D. Y. (2002) What does the fronto-medial cortex contribute to language processing: coherence of Theory of Mind? *NeuroImage*, 17: 1599–1612.

Ferstl, E. C., Rinck, M., and Von Cramon, D. Y. (2005) Emotional and temporal aspects of situation model procesisng during text comprehension: an event-related fMRI study. *Journal of Cognitive Neuroscience*, 17: 724–39.

Fiebach, C. J., Schlesewsky, M., Lohmann, G., Von Cramon, D. Y., and Friederici, A. D. (2005) Revisiting the role of Broca's area in sentence processing: Syntactic integration versus syntactic working memory. *Human Brain Mapping*, 24: 79–91.

Fiebach, C. J., Vos, S. H., and Friederici, A. D. (2004) Neural correlates of syntactic ambiguity in sentence comprehension for low and high span readers. *Journal of Cognitive Neuroscience*, 16: 1562–75.

Fletcher, P. C., Happe, F., Frith, U., Baker, S. C., Dolan, R. J., Frackowiak, R. S. J., et al. (1995) Other minds in the brain: a functional imaging study of 'theory of mind' in story comprehension. *Cognition*, 57: 109–28.

Friederici, A. D. (2002) Towards a neural basis of auditory sentence processing. *Trends in Cognitive Sciences*, 6: 78–84.

Friederici, A. D. (2004) Processing local transitions versus long-distance syntactic hierarchies. *Trends in Cognitive Sciences*, 8: 245–7.

Friederici, A. D. and Alter, K. (2004) Lateralization of auditory language functions: a dynamic dual pathway model. *Brain and Language*, 89: 267–76.

Friederici, A. D., Meyer, M., and Von Cramon, D. Y. (2000) Auditory language comprehension: an event-related fMRI study on the processing of syntactic and lexical information. *Brain and Language*, 75: 465–77.

Friederici, A. D., Rüschemeyer, S.-A., Fiebach, C. J., and Hahne, A. (2003) The role of left inferior frontal and superior temporal cortex in sentence comprehension: localizing syntactic and semantic processes. *Cerebral Cortex*, 13: 1047–3211.

Gallagher, H. L., Happé, F., Brunswick, N., Fletcher, P. C., Frith, U., and Frith, C. D. (2000) Reading the mind in cartoons and stories: an fMRI study of 'theory of mind' in verbal and nonverbal tasks. *Neuropsychologia*, 38: 11–21.

Grewe, T., Bornkessel, I., Zysset, S., Wiese, R., Von Cramon, D. Y., and Schlesewsky, M. (2005) The emergence of the unmarked: a new perspective on the language-specific function of Broca's area. *Human Brain Mapping*, 26: 178–90.

Grodzinsky, Y. (2000) The neurology of syntax: language use without Broca's area. *Behavioral and Brain Sciences*, 23: 1–71.

Haegeman, L. (1994) Introduction to Government and Binding Theory. Oxford, Blackwell.

Hagoort, P. (2003) How the brain solves the binding problem for language: a neurocomputational model of syntactic processing. *NeuroImage*, 20: S18–S29.

Hagoort, P. (2005) On Broca, brain, and binding: a new framework. *Trends in Cognitive Sciences*, 9: 416–423.

Haider, H., and Rosengren, I. (2003) Scrambling: nontriggered chain formation in OV languages. *Journal of Germanic Linguistics*, 15: 203–67.

Hickok, G. and Poeppel, D. (2004) Dorsal and ventral streams: a framework for understanding aspects of the functional neuroanatomy of language. *Cognition*, 92: 67–99.

Humphries, C., Love, T., Swinney, D., and Hickok, G. (2005) Response of anterior temporal cortex to syntactic and prosodic manipulations during sentence processing. *Human Brain Mapping*, 26: 128–38.

Jezzard, P., Matthews, P. M., and Smith, S. M. (2001) *Functional Magnetic Resonance Imaging: An Introduction to the Methods*. Oxford University Press, Oxford.

Just, M. A., Carpenter, P. A., Keller, T. A., Eddy, W. F., and Thulborn, K. R. (1996) Brain activation modulated by sentence comprehension. *Science*, 274: 114–16.

Kaan, E., and Swaab, T. Y. (2002) The brain circuitry of syntactic comprehension. *Trends in Cognitive Sciences*, 6: 350–6.

Keller, T. A., Carpenter, P. A., and Just, M. A. (2001) The neural bases of sentence comprehension: a fMRI examination of syntactic and lexical processing. *Cerebral Cortex*, 11: 223–37.

Kiehl, K. A., Laurens, K. R., and Liddle, P. F. (2002) Reading anomalous sentences: an event-related fMRI study of semantic processing. *NeuroImage*, 17: 842–50.

King, J. W., and Just, M. A. (1991) Individual differences in syntactic processing: the role of working memory. *Journal of Memory and Language*, 30: 580–602.

Kotz, S. A., Frisch, S., Von Cramon, D. Y., and Friederici, A. D. (2003) Syntactic language processing: ERP lesion data on the role of the basal ganglia. *Journal of the International Neuropsychological Society*, 9: 1053–60.

Kuperberg, G. R., Mcguire, P. K., Bullmore, E. T., Brammer, M. J., Rabe-Hesketh, S., Wright, I. C., et al. (2000) Common and distinct neural substrates for pragmatic, semantic, and syntactic processing of spoken sentences: an fMRI study. *Journal of Cognitive Neuroscience*, 12: 321–41.

Maguire, E. A., Frith, C. D., and Morris, R. G. M. (1999) The functional neuroanatomy of comprehension and memory: the importance of prior knowledge. *Brain*, 122: 1839–50.

Mazoyer, B. M., Tzourio, N., Frak, V., Syrota, A., Murayama, N., Levrier, O., et al. (1993) The cortical representation of speech. *Journal of Cognitive Neuroscience*, 5: 467–79.

Meyer, M., Alter, K., Friederici, A. D., Lohmann, G., and Von Cramon, D. Y. (2002) Functional MRI reveals brain regions mediating slow prosodic modulations in spoken sentences. *Human Brain Mapping*, 17: 73–88.

Moro, A., Tettamanti, M., Perani, D., Donati, C., Cappa, S. F., and Fazio, F. (2001) Syntax and the brain: disentangling grammar by selective anomalies. *NeuroImage*, 13: 110–18.

Müller, R.-A., Kleinhans, N., and Courchesne, E. (2003) Linguistic theory and neuroimaging evidence: an fMRI study of Broca's area in lexical semantics. *Neuropsychologia*, 41: 1199–207.

Newman, A. J., Pancheva, R., Ozawa, K., Neville, H. J., and Ullman, M. T. (2001) An event-related fMRI study of syntactic and semantic violations. *Journal of Psycholinguistic Research*, 30: 339–64.

Newman, S. D., Just, M. A., Keller, T. A., Roth, J., and Carpenter, P. A. (2003) Differential effects of syntactic and semantic processing on the subregions of Broca's area. *Cognitive Brain Research*, 16: 297–307.

Ni, W., Constable, R. T., Mencl, W. E., Pugh, K. R., Fulbright, R. K., Shaywitz, S. E., et al. (2000) An event-related neuroimaging study distinguishing form and content in sentence processing. *Journal of Cognitive Neuroscience*, 12: 120–33.

Nichelli, P., Grafmann, J., Pietrini, P., Clark, K., Lee, K. Y., and Miletich, R. (1995) Where the brain appreciates the moral of a story. *NeuroReport*, 6: 2309–13.

Plante, E., Creusere, M., and Sabin, C. (2002) Dissociating sentential prosody from sentence processing: activation interacts with task demands. NeuroImage, 17: 401–10.

Robertson, D. A., Gernsbacher, M. A., Guidotti, S. J., Robertson, R. R. W., Irwin, W., Mock, B. J., and Campana, M. E. (2000) Functional neuroanatomy of the cognitive process of mapping during discourse comprehension. *Psychological Review*, 11: 255–60.

Röder, B., Stock, O., Neville, H., Bien, S., and Rösler, F. (2002) Brain activation modulated by the comprehension of normal and pseudo-word sentences of different processing demands: A functional magnetic resonance imaging study. *NeuroImage*, 15: 1003–14.

Schlesewsky, M., Fanselow, G., Kliegl, R., and Krems, J. (2000) The subject preference in the processing of locally ambiguous wh-questions in German. In B. Hemforth and L. Konieczny (eds), *German Sentence Processing*, pp. 65–93. Kluwer, Dordrecht.

Scott, S., Blank, C., Rosen, S., and Wise, R. (2000) Identification of a pathway for intellgible speech in the left temporal lobe. *Brain*, 123: 2400–06.

St. George, M., Kutas, M., Martinez, A., and Sereno, M. I. (1999) Semantic integration in reading: engagement of the right hemisphere during discourse processing. *Brain*, 122: 1317–25.

Stowe, L. A., Broere, C., Paans, A., Wijers, A., Mulder, G., Vaalburg, W., et al. (1998) Localising components of a complex task: sentence processing and working memory. *NeuroReport*, 9: 2995–9.

Stowe, L. A., Paans, A. M. J., Wijers, A. A., and Zwarts, F. (2004) Activations of 'motor' and other non-language structures during sentence comprehension. *Brain and Language*, 89.

Stromswold, K., Caplan, D., Alpert, N., and Rauch, S. (1996) Localization of syntactic comprehension by positron emission tomography. *Brain and Language*, 52: 452–73.

Ullman, M. T. (2001) A neurocognitive perspective on language: the declarative/procedural model. *Nature Reviews Neuroscience*, 2: 717–26.

Ullman, M. T. (2004) Contributions of memory circuits to language: the declarative/procedural model. *Cognition*, 92: 231–70.

Vandenberghe, R., Nobre, A. C., and Price, C. J. (2002) The response of left temporal cortex to sentences. *Journal of Cognitive Neuroscience*, 14: 550–60.

Vosse, T., and Kempen, G. A. M. (2000) Syntactic assembly in human parsing: A computational model based on competitive inhibition and lexicalist grammar. *Cognition*, 75: 105–43.

Waters, G., Caplan, D., Alpert, N., and Stanczak, L. (2003) Individual differences in rCBF correlates of syntactic processing in sentence comprehension: effects of working memory and speed of processing. *NeuroImage*, 19: 101–12.

Xu, J., Kemeny, S., Park, G., Frattali, C., and Braun, A. (2005) Language in context: emergent features of word, sentence, and narrative comprehension. *NeuroImage*, 25: 1002–15.

CHAPTER 25

Sentence-level deficits in aphasia

Randi C. Martin, Loan C. Vuong, and Jason E. Crowther

25.1 Introduction

Studies in the 1970s and early 1980s demonstrated impaired sentence comprehension in conjunction with good single word comprehension in some aphasic patients (e.g. Caramazza and Zurif, 1976; Schwartz et al., 1980; von Stockert and Bader, 1976). These findings generated a good deal of excitement among aphasiologists and psycholinguists because they seemed to provide strong evidence for an independent syntactic processing module (see e.g. Caramazza and Berndt, 1978; Jackendoff, 1993: Ch. 11). That is, the results appeared to provide support for linguistic theories that hypothesized a system of rules for specifying grammatical well-formedness that was independent of semantics. A number of findings quickly followed these initial findings which caused problems for interpreting the patient data in terms of a deficit to an independent syntactic processing module. The complications that surfaced have given rise to heated debates concerning the proper interpretation of sentence comprehension deficits—mirroring to some extent the debates in linguistics on generative vs. non-generative grammar and in psycholinguistics on syntax-first vs. constraint-based sentence processing theories. An additional issue in the study of patient deficits, not unrelated to the debate on theoretical interpretation, is a debate on the appropriate methodology for studying patient deficits—specifically, the debate on group vs. case study approaches. For reasons outlined below, the focus of this review will be on the results from case studies in drawing theoretical conclusions, though the results of group studies will be discussed, particularly in domains in which few case studies are available. The emphasis will be on the implications of the findings from language deficits for psycholinguistic theory, rather than with the implications for the organization of language function in the brain.

The hypothesis of a specific impairment in a syntactic processing module was formulated in order to account for sentence production and comprehension patterns demonstrated by Broca's aphasics. We will begin with a brief review of the original findings from the 1970s and 1980s taken to support this hypothesis, and the findings that undermined that claim. We will also review the evidence regarding the complementary claim that syntactic comprehension deficits in patients without obvious syntactic difficulties in production could be attributed to a short-term memory deficit. We will then consider more recent versions of the syntactic deficit hypothesis for Broca's aphasia. As all these claims are problematic, given the heterogeneity of deficits in patients classified as Broca's aphasics, we will then turn to some case study evidence regarding the independence of semantic and syntactic knowledge. Although evidence for independence of these knowledge structures exists, we will show that during sentence processing, semantic, lexical, and syntactic factors interact to determine patient comprehension. We conclude with a discussion of revised versions of the short-term memory hypothesis, in which deficits in working-memory capacity (which is thought to encompass both processing and storage capacity) are posited as the source of patient sentence comprehension deficits.

25.2 **Syntactic deficit hypothesis and related short-term memory deficit hypothesis**

25.2.1 **Syntactic deficit hypothesis and early challenges to this hypothesis**

The speech of Broca's aphasics, which is slow and labored, is often "agrammatic," i.e. marked by simplified grammatical structure and the omission of function words and inflections (Goodglass and Kaplan, 1972). On clinical exam, these patients' comprehension appears to be well preserved. Thus, Broca's aphasics were traditionally thought to demonstrate a dissociation between production and comprehension. Indeed, the term "expressive aphasia" is sometimes used interchangeably with "Broca's aphasia." However, studies from the 1970s and 1980s revealed a sentence comprehension deficit for Broca's aphasics when comprehension depended on understanding the syntactic structure of the sentence. In a study that employed a sentence–picture matching task, Caramazza and Zurif (1976) reported that the errors that Broca's aphasics made on complex center-embedded object relative sentences (e.g. *The lion that the tiger chased was yellow*) were almost exclusively reversal errors (e.g. choosing a picture depicting a lion chasing a tiger). Wernicke's aphasics were just as likely to make a lexical error (i.e. choosing a picture with a lexical distracter, such as a different noun or verb) as a reversal error. Schwartz et al. (1980) demonstrated that such reversal errors for Broca's aphasics could be obtained on even simple active and passive sentences. These co-occurring production and comprehension difficulties for Broca's aphasics led Berndt and Caramazza (1980) to hypothesize a syntactic deficit as the defining feature the syndrome. This syntactic module, which was utilized during both production and comprehension, was presumably located in Broca's area in the left inferior frontal cortex. The large majority of studies on sentence comprehension since the original findings of Caramazza and Zurif (1976) have focused on patterns demonstrated by Broca's aphasics.

While the syntactic deficit hypothesis appeared to present an elegant account of the production and comprehension problems of Broca's aphasics, even the original findings of Caramazza and Zurif (1976) were problematic for this hypothesis. In their study, conduction aphasics, who have a specific difficulty in reproducing spoken utterances and do not have agrammatic speech, demonstrated comprehension performance indistinguishable from that of the Broca's aphasics. Other studies of conduction aphasics reported reduced verbal short-term memory spans; thus, it was subsequently claimed that the comprehension deficits of the conduction aphasics arose from their short-term memory deficits (Caramazza et al., 1981; Friedrich et al., 1985). It should be noted that Broca's aphasics also have reduced short-term memory capacity (Martin, 1987).

Additional problems developed for the syntactic deficit hypothesis shortly after its proposal (see Berndt, 1991; 1998; Martin, 2000, for overviews of this literature). Large-scale groups studies of comprehension revealed that all aphasic groups (i.e. Broca's, conduction, transcortical, Wernicke's) demonstrated similar rank orderings of the comprehension of different syntactic structures, with differences mainly being due to the overall level of impairment (Caplan and Hildebrandt, 1988; Naeser et al., 1987). The conclusion that all patient groups had similar comprehension deficits varying only in severity may be criticized, as more complex structures typically contain more elements overall, and thus it could be that different sources of impairment would result in similar patterns of performance. For instance, more complex sentences typically contain more words, so problems in processing such sentences could be due to difficulties in perceiving, comprehending, or retaining the words in the sentences. However, it should be noted that a case study of a mild Wernicke's aphasic revealed poor comprehension of simple passive sentences, even though the patient did not have deficits in noun comprehension or in verbal short-term memory (Martin and Blossom-Stach, 1986).

The coexistence of syntactic comprehension deficits without agrammatic speech was mirrored by the opposite dissociation of patients with agrammatic speech who did not have syntactic comprehension deficits (Kolk et al., 1985; Miceli et al., 1983; Nespoulous et al., 1988). Kolk and Van Grunsven (1985) reported the performance of eleven agrammatic patients on a sentence-picture matching task of reversible active and passive sentences. As shown in Figure 25.1, the patients varied on a continuum between chance performance on both structures to 100 percent correct on both. Thus, the patients did not demonstrate all-or-none deficits in syntactic processing. A study of four patients with

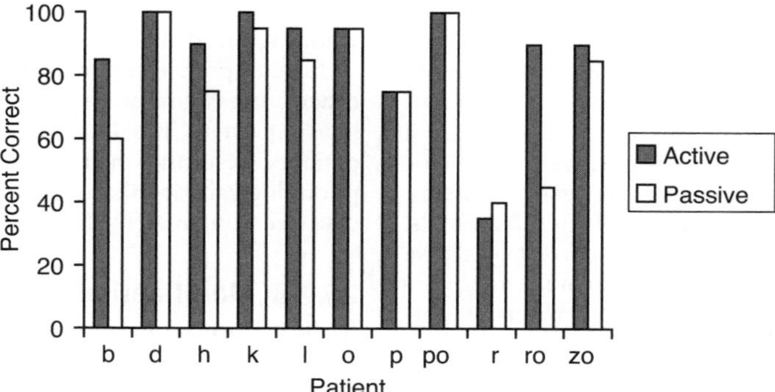

Figure 25.1 Percentage correct on sentence–picture matching for active and passive sentence for eleven agrammatic patients. Data are from Kolk and Van Grunsven (1985).

some degree of agrammatic speech found no match between degree of production deficit and degree of syntactic comprehension deficit (Martin et al., 1989), which contradicted the idea that the comprehension and production deficits were related to one another.

Another serious challenge to the syntactic deficit hypothesis came from studies of grammaticality judgements in Broca's aphasics. It was found that some patients who scored at chance in sentence–picture matching of simple active or passive sentences nevertheless performed remarkably well on grammaticality judgements (Linebarger et al., 1983; Lu et al., 2000; Lukatela et al., 1988). These studies have been criticized because they are of off-line metalinguistic tasks, and thus may require processes different from natural language comprehension (Zurif and Grodzinsky, 1983); however, studies using online grammaticality judgement techniques have also shown preserved performance (Shankweiler et al., 1989; Wulfeck, 1988). In order to account for the dissociation between comprehension and grammaticality judgements, Saffran and colleagues put forth the "mapping deficit hypothesis" (Linebarger, 1990; Saffran and Schwartz, 1988), which proposes that such patients are able to parse a sentence (e.g. analyze its syntactic structure), but are unable to assign thematic roles (e.g. agent, patient) based on the grammatical roles (e.g. subject, object) of the syntactic structure. Their findings thus implicate a separation between the processes used to determine hierarchical structure and those used to determine thematic roles based on that structure.

25.2.2 Short-term memory deficits as source of syntactic comprehension deficits

As discussed earlier, the syntactic comprehension difficulties of conduction aphasics were attributed to short-term memory deficits, and several early studies seemed consistent with that claim (Caramazza et al., 1981; Friedrich et al., 1985; Saffran and Marin, 1975). As discussed by Martin (1987), however, the theoretical account of the connection between phonological storage and syntactic processing was not clearly laid out. Caramazza et al. (1981) proposed that a limited phonological capacity would cause comprehension difficulties by narrowing the number of words that could be considered simultaneously. It is not obvious, though, how a patient with restricted phonological capacity would fail to understand a simple passive sentence such as *The boy was chased by the dog*, if the patient could comprehend *the boy* followed by comprehension of *was chased*. Presumably, once the lexical information is accessed and integrated into a syntactic frame, the original phonological code becomes irrelevant. Further, Martin (1987) found that patient EA, who had a memory span of about 1.5 words, scored 100 percent correct in comprehending the main clause of sentences such as *The boy that carried the girl had red hair*, when, according to Caramazza et al. (1981), it would be expected that she would erroneously associate *red hair* with *the girl*.

A number of more recent case studies have documented preserved syntactic processing for patients with very reduced short-term memory capacities (Butterworth et al., 1986; Friedmann and Gvion, 2003; Hanten and Martin, 2001; Martin et al., 1995;[1] Waters et al., 1991). A particularly striking case, patient BO, was presented by Waters et al. Even though BO had a span of about two words, she was able to understand a range of syntactically complex sentences. For example, on a task in which she heard a sentence and acted out the action using stuffed animals, she scored ninety-two percent correct on dative passives (e.g. *The bear was given to the donkey by the goat*) and ninety-two percent correct on center-embedded object relative sentences (e.g. *The bear that the donkey kissed patted the goat*).

A large body of data indicates the importance of the maintenance of phonological codes for digit and word span (Baddeley, 1986). For many of the patient studies described above, documenting a dissociation between reduced span and preserved syntactic processing, evidence was provided that the patient's deficit was specifically in the maintenance of phonological codes (Butterworth et al., 1986; Hanten and Martin, 2001; Waters et al., 1991).[2] Consequently, these studies indicate that the maintenance of phonology is not critical for the processes needed to integrate syntactic and semantic information across words in a sentence. The findings suggest that patients with reduced phonological capacity can access the semantic and syntactic features of each word as they hear it and construct and maintain the syntactic analysis and semantic interpretation of the sentence. Such a claim is consistent with a great deal of evidence from healthy subjects indicating immediacy of processing during sentence comprehension (Marslen-Wilson and Tyler, 1980; Altmann and Steedman, 1988). Even when the comprehender must presumably re-access a word earlier in a sentence (e.g. in a center-embedded object relative construction), they can apparently do so on the basis of the maintenance of non-phonological representations of that word. For the patients in whom reduced span was associated with a syntactic comprehension deficit, it is likely that other processes important to sentence comprehension were impaired or slowed in these patients, resulting in a greater reliance on a phonological code than would normally be the case (see Romani, 1994 for discussion).

25.2.3 Modifications of the syntactic deficit hypothesis

Despite the evidence against the syntactic deficit hypothesis and against the corollary of a short-term memory deficit as the source of syntactic comprehension deficits in non-agrammatic speakers, research on the link between agrammatism and syntactic deficits has persisted. Some have argued for a deficit in agrammatic Broca's aphasics' processing mechanisms such as slowed syntactic parsing (Haarmann and Kolk, 1991). Others hypothesized a deficit in some type of linguistic knowledge such as a deficit in structures involving double dependency (Mauner et al., 1993) or a deficit in structures involving moved elements, termed the Trace Deletion Hypothesis (TDH) (Grodzinsky, 1990; 1995; 2000; Grodzinsky and Finkel, 1998). We will focus on the TDH because it has had considerable currency in the literature, even in the face of inconsistent evidence and questions about the legitimacy of the methodology used to gather support for it.

Briefly, the latest version of the TDH (Grodzinsky, 2000) claims that agrammatic Broca's aphasics have a selective deficit in the representation of moved constituents (see examples in 1).

1a. [The boy]$_i$ [$_{VP}$ $\boldsymbol{t}_i$ kissed [the girl]].
1b. [The boy]$_i$ was [$_{VP}$ $\boldsymbol{t}'_i$ kissed $\boldsymbol{t}_i$] by [the girl].

According to a number of linguistic theories (e.g. Chomsky, 1981), a moved constituent leaves in its original position a phonologically empty but psychologically real marker, called a "trace." The TDH assumes that traces are involved in both canonical structures (e.g. English actives (as in (1a)), subject relatives, and subject clefts) and non-canonical structures (e.g. English passives (as in (1b)), object relatives, and object clefts). The verb assigns thematic role directly to the trace in the original position (e.g. Agent role to the ***t*** in (1a), Theme role to the ***t*** in (1b)), which is then transmitted to elements ***t*** is co-indexed with (e.g. the Agent role to *the boy* in (1a), the Theme role to ***t'*** in (1b), which in turn passes the Theme role to *the boy*). The TDH makes two

[1] The patient MP reported by Martin et al. (1995) had a normal auditory span, but reduced visual span. Nonetheless, his reading comprehension for syntactically complex sentences was excellent even for sentences presented in a word-by-word fashion with a rapid presentation rate.

[2] Waters et al. attributed BO's short-term memory deficit to a rehearsal deficit, which was consistent with her articulatory difficulties. However, BO failed to show a phonological similarity effect on word span even with auditory presentation. Given that the phonological similarity effect persists in normal subjects for auditory presentation under articulatory suppression (Longoni et al., 1993), the failure to observe this effect with BO suggests that she had difficulty with phonological storage in addition to whatever rehearsal deficit she might have had.

main assumptions: (1) traces are deleted from agrammatic Broca's aphasics' representation; and (2) these patients use a nonlinguistic, linear default strategy that assigns an Agent role to clause-initial subject NPs (e.g. *the boy* in 1 receives the Agent role). For canonical structures, role assignment based on this strategy and syntactic processing matches. For non-canonical structures, the strategy assigns the Agent role to the subject NP while syntax assigns the same role to the other NP argument of a transitive verb (e.g. the NP in the by-phrase *the girl* in 1b). The TDH suggests that the patients determine the filler of the Agent role by randomly choosing between the two NPs. It, therefore, predicts above-chance performance on the canonical structures and at-chance performance on the non-canonical structures.

Many studies have tested the TDH and, as mentioned above, have presented evidence refuting it (e.g. Badecker et al., 1991; Berndt et al., 1996; Druks and Marshall, 1991; 1995; Martin, 1987; Wilson and Saygin, 2004). None of these studies found a single comprehension pattern of above-chance performance on the canonical sentences and at-chance performance on the non-canonical sentences as predicted by the TDH. For example, in a review of sixty-four data sets from forty-two patients from studies that had assessed Broca's aphasics' comprehension of semantically reversible actives and passives, Berndt et al. (1996) showed that approximately one-third of the patients did well on both structures, about one third scored at chance on both structures, and the other third showed above-chance performance on actives and at-chance performance on passives. More recently, Wilson and Saygin (2004) showed that the Broca's aphasics in their study were not more impaired on grammaticality judgements of sentences with traces than of those without traces when the level of syntactic difficulty was controlled for. Specifically, they found that the patients had the most difficulty with trace/hard sentences (e.g. **Which woman did John think that saw Tony?*), the least difficulty with trace/easy sentences (e.g. **Me the dog which bit was black*), and in-between levels of difficulty with other/hard (e.g. **She donated the library the books*) and other/easy sentences (e.g. **Have they could left the city?*), respectively. Even when the patients were divided into those who showed the sentence comprehension pattern predicted by the TDH and those who did not, no difference in performance on the grammaticality judgements was found. Results from these studies are clearly at odds with the TDH.

Advocates of the TDH have rejected the disconfirming findings. Noticeably, most of those findings have been provided by studies using the case study approach. The supportive evidence for the TDH, on the other hand, has been supplied by studies using the group study approach. The appropriateness of the methodology used to test the TDH has thus been the focus of sharp exchanges between researchers from each side (e.g. Berndt and Caramazza, 1999; Caplan, 2001; Caramazza et al., 2001; Drai and Grodzinsky, 1999; Drai et al., 2001; Druks and Marshall, 1995; 2000; Grodzinsky et al., 1999; Zurif, 1996; 2001; Zurif and Pinango, 1999). The disagreement provides a clear illustration of the debate in the field over the case study vs. group study approach that we alluded to at the beginning of the chapter. As an example, Grodzinsky et al. (1999) argued that their data on the active/passive contrast had to be analyzed at the group level rather than at the single-subject level. However, this is clearly untenable if the claim is that all agrammatic Broca's aphasics show a certain pattern of sentence comprehension. Their approach is rather like arguing that one can support the claim that *all* Norwegians have an IQ of 100 by showing that the group mean for a sample does not deviate from 100. One may rebut this, as Grodzinsky et al. (1999) did, by arguing that the data had to be analyzed as a group so as to detect chance performance. The reasoning is that, if the patients randomly choose between two alternatives, then "guessing behavior, which results in chance performance, cannot, and should not, be 50 percent correct per subject" (p. 137). As Caramazza et al. (2001) pointed out, Grodzinsky et al. appeared to have confused the number of subjects with the number of trials. The argument advanced by Grodzinsky et al. holds only for cases in which a particular patient is tested on a small number of trials. Given a score of 80 percent correct, one can in fact have a reliable degree of confidence ($p < .0001$) in drawing implications from a single patient's data if the patient is tested on forty or more items (see Caramazza et al., 2001 for more detail).

Another account of the syntactic processing deficits in aphasia comes from Ullman and colleagues. Ullman et al. (1997) tested patients on a sentence completion task requiring production of a past-tense verb. They found that their Alzheimer's patients and posterior aphasic patients as groups were more impaired in the production of irregular past tenses, whereas their Parkinson's group and one anterior aphasic patient were more impaired in the production of regular past-tense verbs. They argued that this dissociation was due to general properties of posterior vs. frontal systems in which posterior regions support declarative, memory-based representations, whereas frontal/basal ganglia regions support procedural or rule-based knowledge, including grammatical knowledge that is drawn on in computing past tenses for regular verbs. Ullman et al.'s (1997) conclusions have been called into question by a number of researchers. Some have argued that a single-mechanism connectionist system supports retrieval of the past tense for both regular and irregular forms (Rumelhart and McClelland, 1986). Joanisse and Seidenberg (1999) and Patterson et al. (2001) have provided computational and empirical evidence for a single-system approach, arguing that the observed double dissociation derives from other factors, specifically semantic deficits in patients with posterior deficits and phonological deficits in patients with frontal deficits (but see Tyler et al., 2002).

The empirical facts supporting the dissociation reported by Ullman et al. have also been questioned, as numerous studies have documented cases of agrammatic patients who perform better on regular than irregular morphological transformations (de Diego Balaguer et al., 2004; Faroqi-Shah and Thompson, 2003; Laiacona and Caramazza, 2004; Marslen-Wilson and Tyler, 1997; 1998; Penke et al., 1999; Shapiro and Caramazza, 2003). It is beyond the scope of this chapter to delve into the fine points of the different positions, as the claims have to do mainly with language production rather than comprehension. It should be noted, however, that the plausibility of the claim that frontal brain regions support rule-based grammatical processing hinges in part on evidence that anterior aphasics have difficulty with such processes in comprehension as well as in production. The findings from grammaticality judgements discussed earlier provide strong evidence against such a generalization.

25.3 The independence of syntactic and semantic knowledge and the interactions of lexical, semantic, and syntactic factors in comprehension

The original findings of Caramazza and Zurif (1976) generated a great deal of excitement because they appeared to demonstrate the independence of syntactic and semantic knowledge by showing that syntactic knowledge could be selectively disrupted. As indicated above, a focus on agrammatic Broca's aphasia as a clinical syndrome did not provide the hoped-for evidence of such a dissociation, particularly when one considered the evidence from grammaticality judgements. Clearer evidence for the independence in the representation of semantic and syntactic abilities has instead been provided by case studies. Despite this representational independence, several studies show that syntactic, semantic, and lexical factors interact during processing. We will next turn to these findings.

Two single case studies provide clear dissociations between syntax and semantics. Patient JG, who had a left temporo-parietal lesion, showed impaired performance in syntactic tasks and unimpaired performance in tasks tapping lexical-semantic processing (Ostrin and Tyler, 1995). He exhibited an asyntactic comprehension pattern when tested in a sentence-picture matching task. That is, his performance was poor on semantically unconstrained sentences (e.g. *The cow bit the horse*) and was better on semantically constrained sentences (e.g. *The boy threw the ball*). In a word-monitoring experiment and a grammaticality judgement experiment, he also showed an insensitivity to a variety of grammatical violations—violations of subcategorization frame, violations of inflectional and derivational morphology, and, in a previous study, violations of word order (Tyler, 1992). However, like normal subjects, he showed semantic priming in a lexical decision task, both at the single-word level and at the sentence level. In contrast to JG, patient DM, a semantic dementia patient, performed at a high level (95 percent correct—within normal range) on a grammaticality test tapping a wide range of grammatical structures during a time period in which performance on semantic tasks declined dramatically (Breedin and Saffran, 1999). DM also showed a preserved ability to assign thematic roles based on sentence structure when tested in a sentence-enactment matching task using test animals that he had difficulty recognizing by name. He carried out the matching by consistently relying on syntactically based role assignments to the animal subjects. For example, when asked to identify the animal object "tiger" after hearing the sentence *The tiger is carrying the lion (the tiger* thus received the Agent role here) and seeing the demonstration of a lion carrying a tiger, DM pointed to the agentive object in the demonstration (which was, in fact, the lion). This pattern of performance remained even when syntactically more complex sentences, such as passives, cleft subjects, and cleft objects, were used.

The doubly dissociated patterns of disruptions and preservations of syntax and semantics exhibited by patient DM (Ostrin and Tyler, 1995) and patient JG (Breedin and Saffran, 1999) argue strongly that syntactic knowledge is represented autonomously from semantic knowledge. Studies on normal subjects suggest that constraints from these knowledge systems simultaneously interact with each other and with other sources of linguistic information, including lexical and discourse information, to determine sentence interpretation (e.g. Spivey and Tanenhaus, 1998; Trueswell et al., 1994). It is thus possible for brain damage to affect the syntactic knowledge system such that all of the outputs from the system are weakened and consequently play a lesser (but not nonexistent) role than other constraints in sentence interpretation. A study by Saffran et al. (1998) gave evidence for this interactive effect on aphasic sentence comprehension. Broca's and non-Broca's aphasics, who had shown syntactic comprehension deficits on sentence–picture matching tasks, were asked to make plausibility judgements to spoken active, passive, subject-cleft, and object-cleft sentences. Semantic constraints converged with syntactically based role assignment in plausible sentences (e.g. *The dog barked at the kitten*). In implausible sentences (e.g. *#The cheese ate the mouse*, *#The worm swallowed the bird*), the two sources of information conflicted. Results for the implausible sentences showed that when semantic constraints were strong, i.e. when one NP could plausibly fill only one of the two argument positions of a transitive verb (as in *The cheese ate the mouse*), the patients made many errors that were consistent with a semantically based thematic role assignment, even for simple active sentences. More interestingly, when semantic constraints were weaker, i.e. when both NPs were possible fillers of both thematic roles of a transitive verb (as in *The worm swallowed the bird*) and only our knowledge of the world tells us which NP is likely to be the Agent and which the Theme (e.g. it is more likely that a bird swallows a worm than vice versa), the patients made substantially fewer errors. (This pattern was shown both by Broca's and by non-Broca's aphasic patients.) The interpretation of this result is that when semantic constraints were weaker the patients were able to utilize their residual syntactic ability to assign thematic roles, thus making more correct responses.

The findings from Saffran et al. (1998) are consistent with models of sentence comprehension that suggest parallel semantic and syntactic processes (e.g. Boland, 1997; Ferreira and Stacey, 2005). In the dual-route model proposed by Ferreira and Stacey, for example, sentence input immediately activates both syntactic and semantic processes, and their output determine thematic roles assigned to participants in the sentence. The syntactic process, called theta-transmission, assigns thematic roles grammatically. The other process, called schema-transmission, assigns thematic roles based on schemas (i.e. stereotypical knowledge of events and states) that are activated from long-term memory. For example, as the sentence *The dog was bitten by the man* is processed, the concepts DOG, MAN, and BITE may activate a dog-biting schema, leading to an assignment of an Agent role to *the dog* and a Patient role to *the man*. If theta-transmission does not yield a secure set of thematic role assignment (e.g. due to increased difficulty with non-canonical sentence structures such as passive sentences or to an impairment in the system as in brain-damaged patients), then role assignment by schema-transmission will have a larger influence, causing a misinterpretation of the sentence as the dog biting the man. In the Saffran et al. study, the implausible sentence set that had stronger semantic constraints also consisted of a number of items that could potentially lead to schema activations (e.g. CAT, PUPPY, BARK; CHEESE, MOUSE, EAT; DEER, HUNTER, SHOOT). Because the patients had impaired syntactic abilities, their increased error rates in judging the plausibility of these items might have been due to the interference from schema-based role assignment.

As discussed above, recent models of sentence comprehension also allow for interactions between lexical factors and sentence structures in processing. A number of studies in neuropsychology have suggested an important role for verb processing deficits in patients' sentence comprehension impairments (e.g. Berndt et al., 1997; Breedin and Martin, 1996). More recently, Berndt et al. (2004) showed that features of verb representation interacted with sentence syntax to cause differential levels of difficulty in the processing of semantically reversible passives. The authors used a sentence–picture matching task to test a group of control subjects and two groups of aphasic patients, the "good comprehenders" who had no impairment on reversible sentences and the "poor comprehenders" who were impaired on those sentences. Verb sets were chosen such that their agents and patients varied in the amount of role prototypicality. A "proto-agent" of an action verb is one that is actively moving, while a "proto-patient" is stationary and caused to change state by agents (as in verbs like *bury*, *wash*, *kick*, *shoot*, *slap*, *spray*). Results showed that the good comprehenders were least accurate on passive sentences whose agents and patients of the verbs were not prototypical (e.g. *pull*, *push*, *chase*, *follow*, *guide*, *lead*, in which thematic agents and patients were moving and both participated in the action). They were also slower to respond when the verbs contained non-prototypical agents and patients than when the verbs contained prototypical agents and patients. These patterns of performance were in accord with the control subjects' performance patterns. Although the poor comprehenders' data were contaminated by response biases, they also showed lower response accuracy for active sentences containing non-prototypical agents and patients. Along with the results from Saffran et al. (1998), these results demonstrate that the assignment of thematic roles to noun arguments depends on a confluence of lexical, syntactic, and semantic constraints.

While processing difficulty of a sentence structure may be exacerbated by verb-specific attributes (Berndt et al., 2004), it can conversely be mitigated when verb-specific biases are matched with sentence structures (Gahl, 2002; Gahl et al., 2003). Using a sentence anomaly task, Gahl (2002) manipulated whether the structure of a sentence matched the transitive or intransitive bias of a verb (i.e. the relative frequency with which the verb appears in either form). For example, the verb *crumble* has an intransitive bias, so the intransitive sentence *The crackers crumbled in our hands* would match the verb's bias, while the transitive sentence *The children crumbled the crackers* would have a mismatch between bias and structure. Gahl found that a mixed group of aphasic patients performed at a higher level when the structure of the sentence matched the verb's bias for being either transitive or intransitive. Gahl et al. (2003) further showed for a mixed group of aphasic patients that comprehension of the passive was significantly better for passive-bias verbs (e.g. *elect*) than for active-bias verbs (e.g. *disturb*). No evident difference was found between the pattern for the Broca's aphasics and that for the fluent patients.

Together, findings from the studies reviewed above suggest representational independence of syntactic and semantic abilities and an interaction between them and lexical factors in sentence processing. These findings can be accounted for by sentence-processing models like those of Boland (1997) or Ferreira and Stacey (2005), which assume that syntactic and semantic processes occur in parallel. If we assume that the strength of all syntactic representations have been reduced for the patients, then when semantic constraints on the assignment of nouns to thematic roles about the verb are strong, they override the relatively weak outputs of the syntactic system. When semantic constraints are nil or weak, the results of syntactic processing can play a larger role. Similarly, Gahl et al.'s (2003) results showing better comprehension of passives for passive-bias verbs could be explained on the grounds that a greater weight is given to a passive interpretation for a passive-bias verb than for an active-bias verb. Although early theorizing on syntactic processing and representation may have led to the prediction of all-or-none loss, the assumption of a decrease in the strength syntactic weights would allow for continuous variation in the degree of impairment, such as that reported by Kolk and Van Grunsven (1985).

25.3.1 Varieties of working memory deficits and their relation to sentence comprehension

Some researchers take the fact that patient deficits are not all-or-none as evidence that these deficits should not be attributed to a loss of syntactic knowledge but instead to some type of working-memory deficit (e.g. Miyake et al., 1994). As mentioned above, however, the application of approaches like that of Boland (1997) to patient data allows for continuous variation in the strength of syntactic representations. One might question whether it is still necessary to posit working memory deficits as the source of some comprehension deficits. Certainly some structures would seem to require some type of working memory capacity—for example when a noun that appears early in a sentence needs to be integrated with a verb that appears later, as in center-embedded object relatives like *The boy that the girl carried had red hair*. Boland's (1997) model does not provide explicit descriptions of how such connections are made. Some recent approaches to syntactic processing give an important role to working memory requirements in predicting the difficulty of different syntactic structures (Gibson, 2000; Gordon et al., 2001; Van Dyke and Lewis, 2003). Consequently, there still seems to be a need to posit working-memory involvement, and to consider the potential negative consequences of working-memory limitations. In this section, we will consider recent neuropsychological evidence on the relation between syntactic processing and working memory.

As reviewed earlier, phonological short-term memory, as measured by traditional span measures, appears unrelated to syntactic processing ability. However, some researchers have argued that other measures of capacity that tap both processing and storage do relate to syntactic comprehension (Just and Carpenter, 1992). One such measure is reading span, in which subjects are asked to read a set of sentences aloud and recall the sentence-final words from each sentence at the end of the set. Caplan and Waters (1999) reviewed the evidence from normal and brain damaged populations on the relation between short-term memory, working memory, and sentence processing. As discussed by Caplan and Waters (1999), a number of studies of neurally intact individuals relating sentence processing to either working-memory capacity (as far from reading span) or the effect of an external load have found additive rather than interactive effects of these variables and the effect of syntactic complexity and memory capacity or load. According to additive-factors logic (Sternberg, 1998), the additive effects imply that different capacities are involved in working memory span and syntactic processing. Patient studies have provided converging results. For instance, Caplan and Waters discussed evidence that patients with dementia of the Alzheimer's type (DAT) and Parkinson's disease (PD) do not have deficits in phonological storage and rehearsal, but do have deficits in the executive function component of working memory, and have very reduced sentence spans. However, these patients did not show greater effects of syntactic complexity than did controls on sentence–picture matching, even when maintaining a concurrent digit load (e.g. see Waters et al., 1995). The DAT patients did, however, show a greater than normal effect of the number of propositions in a sentence. Caplan and Waters attribute the effect of number of propositions to non-syntactic sources. Although some previous studies have reported greater effects of syntactic complexity for DAT or PD patients than for controls (e.g. Emery, 1988; Natsopoulos et al., 1991), Caplan and Waters suggested that these deficits may have resulted from non-syntactic demands of the tasks employed (e.g. having to choose from a large number of picture choices in sentence-picture matching).

The findings from healthy and brain-damaged participants led Caplan and Waters (1999) to postulate that there is a working-memory capacity specific to the initial phases of sentence processing that is independent of the capacities tapped by short-term and working-memory tasks. They divide the procedures involved in sentence processing into interpretive and post-interpretive processes. Interpretive processes include all online syntactic and semantic processes, including those involved in semantic interpretation based on the ongoing discourse. Post-interpretive processes involve using the products of interpretive processing to carry out some task, such as sentence–picture matching or enactment of the action in the sentence. Caplan and Waters argue that interpretive processing draws on a capacity specific to sentence processing, whereas post-interpretive processing draws on the capacity tapped by standard span tasks or working-memory tasks. One problematic finding for this conclusion is that working-memory capacity and an extraneous load interact with number of propositions in a sentence in determining comprehension performance for patients and controls. It is unclear why an influence of number of propositions should be relegated to "post-interpretive" processing. (See Ferreira, 1999 for related discussion.)

Martin and colleagues (Hanten and Martin, 2000; Martin and He, 2004; Martin and Romani, 1994; Martin et al., 1994) have provided a different view on the relation between the capacities involved in span tasks and sentence processing. Specifically, they argue that span tasks tap both phonological and semantic retention (see also N. Martin and Saffran, 1997). The phonological component of span tasks is independent of the capacity involved in sentence processing. On the other hand, the semantic component does play a role in sentence comprehension in the maintenance of word meanings prior to their integration with other word meanings (Martin and He, 2004). Supporting this contention were results from patients with a semantic retention deficit who had difficulty detecting the semantic anomaly in sentences with two or three adjectives preceding a noun (e.g. *The rusty old red swimsuit*) or with two or three nouns preceding a verb (e.g. *Rocks, trees, and shrubs grew in the back yard*). These patients (AB and ML) did better when there was only one adjective before the noun or one noun before the verb, and when the adjectives followed the noun (e.g. *The swimsuit was old, red and rusty*) or the nouns followed the verb (e.g. *The gardener grew shrubs, trees and rocks in the backyard*) (Hanten and Martin, 2000; Martin and He, 2004; Martin and Romani, 1994). A patient with a phonological short-term memory deficit (EA) did not show this pattern. Although she showed worse performance overall than controls, the effect of number of adjectives or nouns and of the before/after manipulation were within the range of controls. Figure 25.2 presents the data from patients ML and AB (with semantic short-term memory deficits) and from EA (with a phonological short-term memory deficit). The results are averaged across the adjective–noun and noun–verb sentences in terms of the difference in percentage errors when there were two or three adjectives vs. one adjective (or two or three nouns vs. one noun) in the before and after conditions. Martin and colleagues argued that when the adjectives preceded the noun, they had to be maintained as individual word meanings until the noun was processed, whereas when the adjectives followed the noun, they could be integrated with the noun as each was heard. Similarly, when the conjoined nouns preceded the verb, the role of the nouns with respect to the verb could not be determined until the verb was processed, whereas when the nouns followed the verb, their role with respect to the verb could be determined as each was heard. The patients' better performance in the "after" than in the "before" conditions indicate that the patients were better able to maintain integrated semantic representations than individual word meanings. (See Haarmann et al., 2003 for related results from normal subjects.) Martin and colleagues agree with Caplan and Waters (1999) to some extent, as both groups assume that the retention of specifically syntactic structural information is independent of both phonological and semantic capacities (Martin and Romani, 1994).

MacDonald and colleagues (MacDonald et al., 2001; MacDonald and Christiansen, 2002) have offered yet another way to conceptualize the relation between working memory and sentence processing. Whereas Caplan and Waters (1999) and Martin and colleagues (e.g. Martin and Romani, 1994) assume the existence of temporary spaces devoted to the storage and processing of linguistic information in online operations, MacDonald and colleagues postulate a language system in which storage of linguistic knowledge, locus of linguistic processing and working memory resources used in processing are functionally and neuroanatomically intertwined. In this framework, a linguistic working memory task and a comprehension task are assumed to measure the same language-processing skills if they share common task demands.

MacDonald et al. (2001) used data from Alzheimer's disease (AD) patients to support their proposal. The AD patients' working memory capacities were tested in a digit-ordering task, in which participants were asked to reorder a random list of digits to a numerically increasing list.

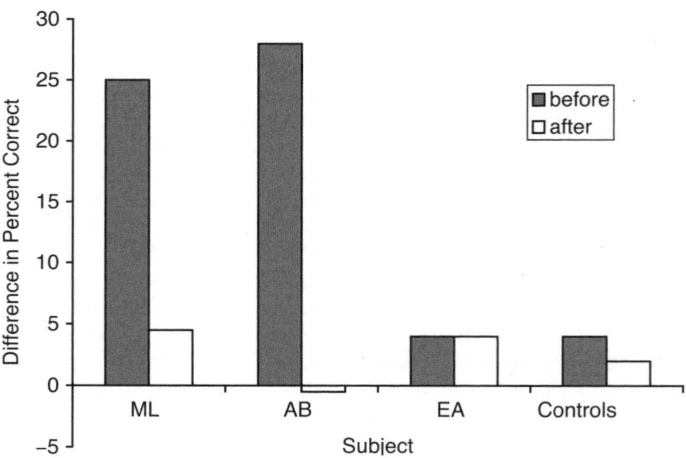

Figure 25.2 Difference in percentage errors on sentence anomaly judgements for the mean of two and three adjectives or nouns vs. one adjective or noun in the before and after conditions. Patients ML and AB showed evidence of a semantic short-term memory deficit, whereas EA had a phonological STM deficit. Data are from Martin and Romani (1994) and Martin and He (2004).

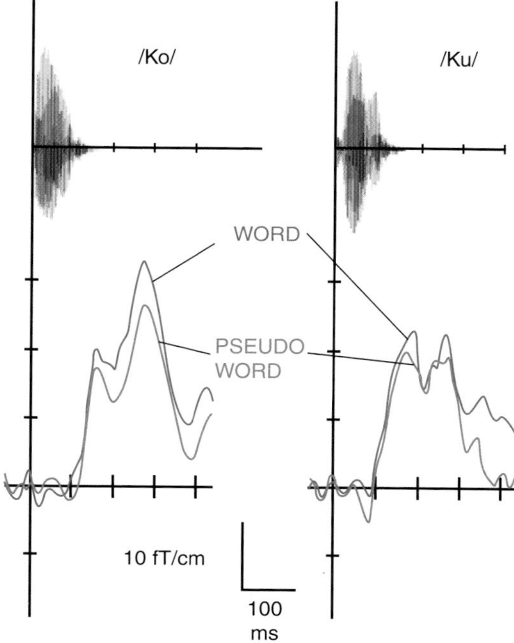

Plate 1 The Mismatch negativity (MMN) elicited by the same syllables presented in contexts where they completed a meaningful word of Finnish or a meaningless pseudo-word. The syllable-elicited MMN was larger in word context than in pseudo-word context (after Pulvermüller et al., 2001). This figure relates to Chapter 8.

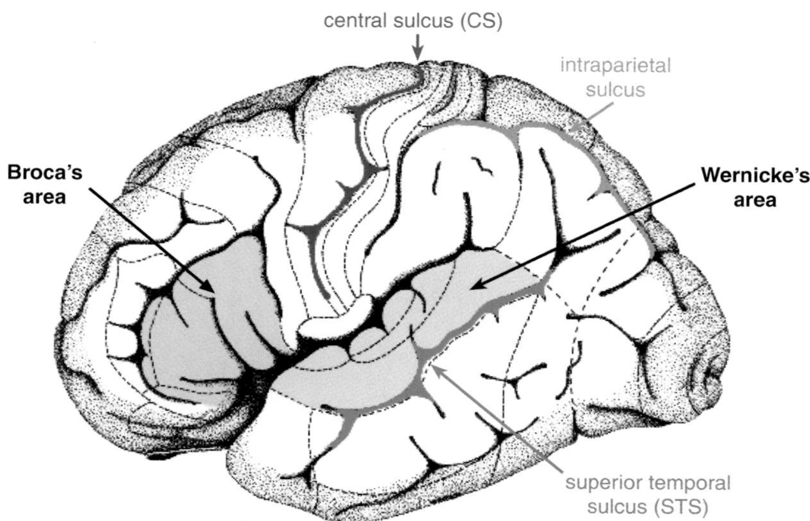

Plate 2 A schematic view of the left hemisphere and shows the classical language areas (Broca's area and Wernicke's area). Relevant major sulci are also marked. This figure relates to Chapter 24.

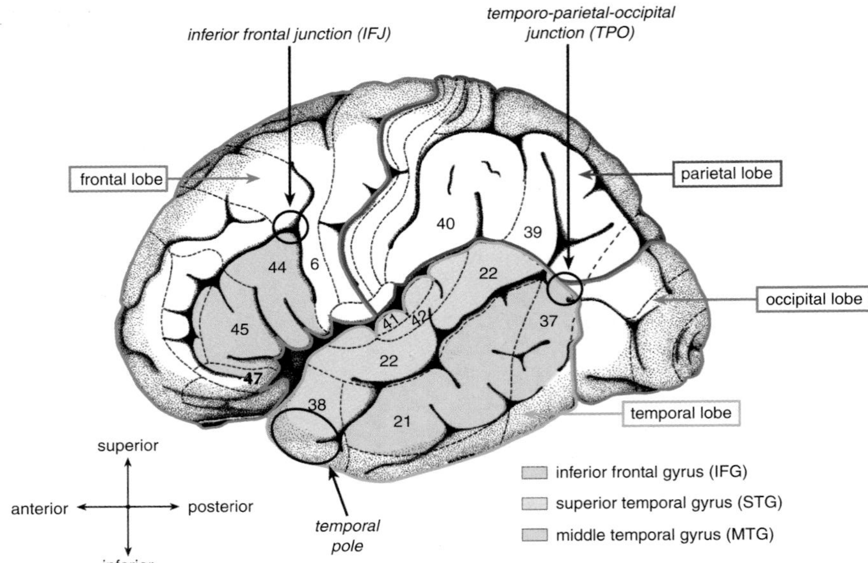

Plate 3 A more detailed depiction of the language-related regions in the left hemisphere, with major relevant gyri indicated by color-coding. The different large lobes are also marked by color-coded borders. Numbers indicate language-relevant Brodmann Areas (BA), which Brodmann (1909) defined on the basis of their cytoarchitectonic characteristics. The coordinate labels superior/inferior indicate the position of a gyrus within a lobe (e.g. superior temporal gyrus) or within a BA (e.g. superior BA44). The coordinate labels anterior/posterior indicate the position within a gyrus (e.g. anterior superior temporal gyrus). This figure relates to Chapter 24.

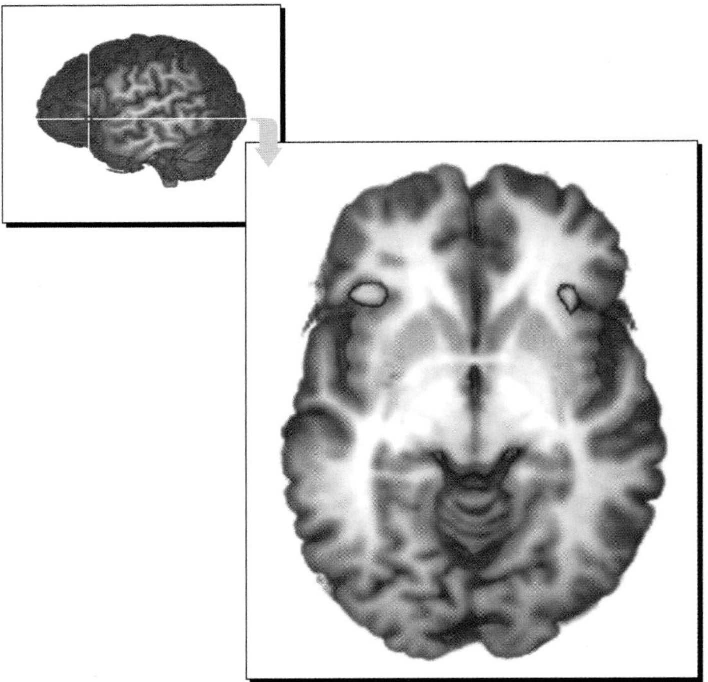

Plate 4 A schematic illustration of activation in the deep frontal operculum (bilaterally). The inset at the top left of the figure indicates the positioning of the axial section showing the activation. Note that activations in the anterior insula are adjacent to and partially overlapping with the activations depicted here. This figure relates to Chapter 24.

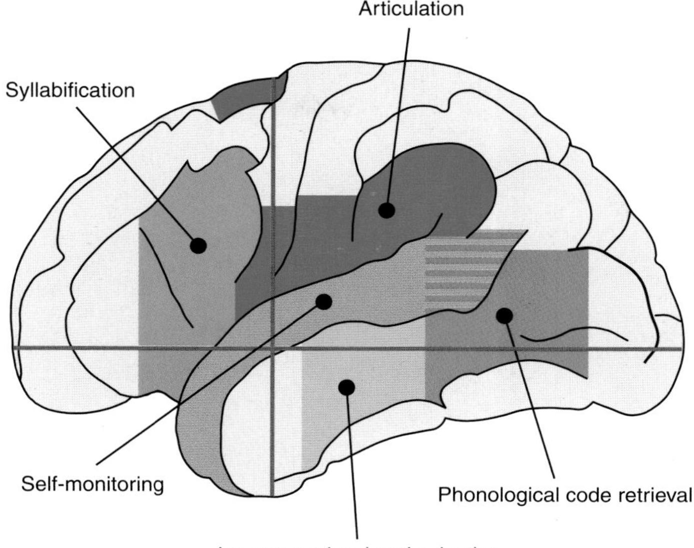

Plate 5 Left hemisphere areas involved in single word production. The labels reflect tentative assignments of processing functions. Additional areas reliably involved in word production are the left anterior insula, the left thalamus, the left fusiform gyrus, the right mid superior temporal gyrus, and the cerebellum. This figure relates to Chapter 33.

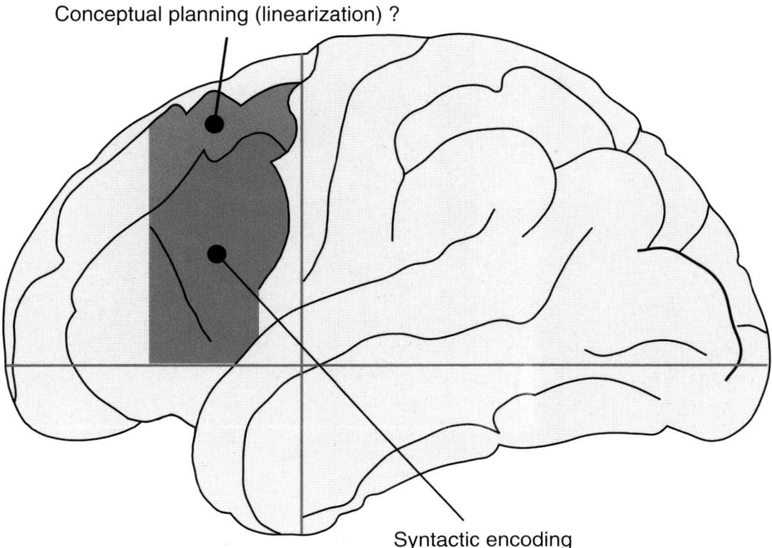

Plate 6 Left hemisphere areas involved in the production of continuous speech above the word level. The labels reflect tentative assignments of processing functions. This figure relates to Chapter 33.

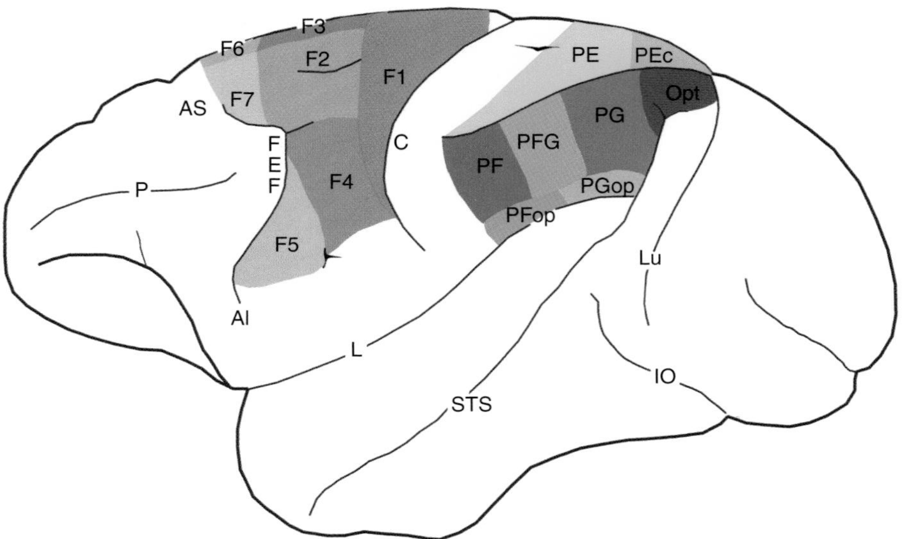

Plate 7 Lateral view of the monkey cerebral cortex. The motor areas (F1–F7) are classified according to Rizzolatti et al. (1998), while the parietal areas are named according to the nomenclature of Von Economo (1929). Mirror neurons have been described in area F5 and in the rostral part of the inferior parietal lobule (areas PF and PFG). Abbreviations: AI, inferior arcuate sulcus; AS, superior arcuate sulcus; C, central sulcus. (From Rizzolatti and Craighero, 2004.) Reprinted, with permission, from the Annual Review of Neuroscience, Volume 27 © 2004 by Annual Reviews www.annualreviews.org. This figure relates to Chapter 47.

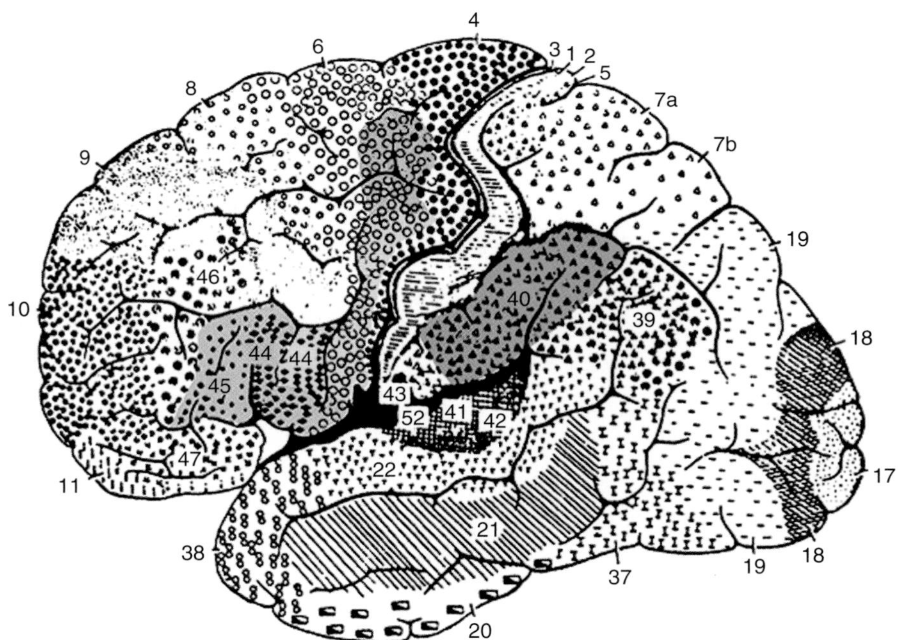

Plate 8 Lateral view of human cerebral cortex. The parietal and frontal lobe regions that are consistently activated during the observation of actions by others are shown in red and yellow, respectively. They form the core of the mirror neuron system. The areas shown in blue (area 45 and dorsal area 6) have been reported to be active during the observation of others' action in some studies. It is likely that they also contain mirror neurons. This figure relates to Chapter 47.

The patients showed impaired performance in the digit-ordering task, which was found to correlate significantly with (1) their impairment in offline grammaticality judgement of sentences containing violations of subject–verb number agreement and verb transitivity, and (2) their impairment in an online cross-modal priming task tapping processing of pronoun anaphors. As the digit-ordering performance correlated with both offline and online performance (the latter of which presumably eliminated extraneous working memory requirements), MacDonald and colleagues concluded that the digit-ordering task did not measure any independent working-memory capacity. Rather, it was argued to be just another measure of language- processing skills (as would be the case for traditional working-memory tasks such as the reading span task). However, although the task assessing pronoun reference required participants only to name a written pronoun, the latency effect for controls on naming the pronoun depended on the match between the pronoun and material presented two sentences back that could serve as the referent of the pronoun. Waters and Caplan (1996) argued the determination of pronoun reference across several sentences does not depend on syntactic factors, but instead depends on reasoning processes, which would be part of their post-interpretive processes. Consequently, the correlation between digit-ordering and pronoun resolution performance would be predicted according to the Caplan and Waters (1999) view. Moreover, it is unclear how the approach of MacDonald et al. could account for the many failures to find an interaction between working memory and syntactic complexity reported by Caplan and Waters if both draw on the same representations and processes.

25.4 **Concluding comments**

This chapter began with a discussion of claims of the independence of syntactic and semantic information. Although basing that claim on evidence from the clinical syndrome of Broca's aphasia proved to be a mistake, there nonetheless appears to be striking evidence from case studies demonstrating their independence (Breedin and Saffran, 1999; Tyler, 1992). Along with data supporting representational independence, however, data from patients have also been reported that show an interaction between lexical, semantic, and syntactic influences during sentence processing (Berndt et al., 2004; Gahl, 2002; Saffran et al., 1998). In one such study, patients were been shown to have a sensitivity to grammatical structure when semantic influences were weak, but a relative insensitivity to grammatical structure when semantic influences were strong (Saffran et al., 1998). Some might take these findings to be cautionary, as evidence of syntactic processing deficits might be undermined if patients were tested on materials with fewer semantic or other constraints. However, if one abandons the notion that syntactic deficits have to be all-or-none, but can be a matter of degree, such findings are entirely consistent with a syntactic disruption.

Important findings from neuropsychological deficits have also been reported regarding the role of short-term and working memory in sentence comprehension. Substantial evidence indicates that the retention of phonological codes does not play a critical role in syntactic processing. Even the more complex working-memory measures that tap both processing and storage do not appear to predict syntactic processing abilities, as patients with very reduced reading spans do not show a greater than normal effect of syntactic complexity on comprehension. Span measures do relate to some aspects of sentence comprehension, and the interpretive vs. post-interpretive distinction suggested by Caplan and Waters (1999) may go some way towards accounting for what is or is not related to span. However, some findings, such as the relation between effect of number of propositions and working-memory capacity and the relation between a semantic STM deficit and difficulty maintaining unintegrated semantic representations (e.g. Martin and He, 2004), seem difficult to account for in terms of demands on post-interpretive processes.

Although some progress has been made in understanding sentence processing deficits and their implications for theories of normal sentence comprehension, it is clear that much work remains to be done. Despite the abundant research on sentence processing in normal subjects, much of it has focused on a narrow range of topics specifically having to do with the questions of the autonomy of syntax or its interaction with other factors. There is a great deal of underspecification with regard to any number of issues: the means by which hierarchical structure is computed, the processing of long-distance dependencies in different constructions, the means by which thematic role mapping is carried out, the nature of lexical constraints on the generation of syntactic structure. Clearly, theoretical developments along any of these lines would be an aid in guiding research on neuropsychological cases. Conversely, findings from neuropsychology could play an important role in the future in helping to address these issues.

Author Note

Preparation of this manuscript was supported in part by NIH grant DC-00218 to Rice University. Address correspondence to: Randi C. Martin, Psychology Dept., Rice University, P.O. Box 1892, Houston, Texas 77251, e-mail: rmartin@rice.edu

References

Altmann, G., and Steedman, M. G. (1988) Interactions with context during human sentence processing. *Cognition*, 30: 191–238.

Baddeley, A.D. (1986) *Working Memory*. Oxford University Press, Oxford.

Badecker, W., Nathan, P., and Caramazza, A. (1991) Varieties of sentence comprehension deficits: a case study. *Cortex*, 27: 311–21.

Berndt, R. S. (1991) Sentence processing in aphasia. In M. T. Sarno (ed.), *Acquired Aphasia*, 2nd edn, pp. 223–70. Academic Press, San Diego, CA.

Berndt, R. S. (1998) Sentence processing in aphasia. In M. T. Sarno (ed.), *Acquired Aphasia*, 3rd edn, pp. 229–67. Academic Press, San Diego, CA.

Berndt, R. S., and Caramazza, A. (1980) A redefinition of the syndrome of Broca's aphasia: implications for a neuropsychological model of language. *Applied Psycholinguistics*, 1: 225–78.

Berndt, R.S., and Caramazza, A. (1999) How "regular" is sentence comprehension in Broca's aphasia? It depends on how you select the patients. *Brain and Language*, 67: 242–7.

Berndt, R. A., Haendiges, A., Mitchum, C., and Sandson, J. (1997) Verb retrieval in aphasia, 2: Relationship to sentence processing. *Brain and Language*, 56: 107–37.

Berndt, R.S., Mitchum, C., Burton, M., and Haendiges, A. (2004) Comprehension of reversible sentences in aphasia: the effects of verb meaning. *Cognitive Neuropsychology*, 21: 229–45.

Berndt, R. S., Mitchum, C., and Haendiges, A. (1996) Comprehension of reversible sentences in "agrammatism": a meta-analysis. *Cognition*, 58: 289–308.

Boland, J. (1997) The relationship between syntactic and semantic processes in sentence comprehension. *Language and Cognitive Processes*, 12: 423–84.

Breedin, S., and Martin, R. (1996) Patterns of verb deficits in aphasia: an analysis of four cases. *Cognitive Neuropsychology*, 13: 51–91.

Breedin, S., and Saffran, E. (1999) Sentence processing in the face of semantic loss: a case study. *Journal of Experimental Psychology: General*, 128: 547–62.

Butterworth, B., Campbell, R., and Howard, D. (1986) The uses of short-term memory: a case study. *Quarterly Journal of Experimental Psychology*, 38A: 705–37.

Caplan, D. (2001) The measurement of chance performance in aphasia, with specific reference to the comprehension of semantically reversible passive sentences: a note on issues raised by Caramazza, Capitani, Rey, and Berndt (2001) and Drai, Grodzinsky, and Zurif (2001). *Brain and Language*, 76: 193–201.

Caplan, D., and Hildebrandt, N. (1988) *Disorders of Syntactic Comprehension*. MIT Press, Cambridge, MA.

Caplan, D., and Waters, G. S. (1999) Verbal working memory and sentence comprehension. *Behavioral and Brain Sciences*, 22: 77–126.

Caramazza, A., Basili, A. G., Koller, J., and Berndt, R. S. (1981) An investigation of repetition and language processing in a case of conduction aphasia. *Brain and Language*, 14: 235–71.

Caramazza, A., and Berndt, R. S. (1978) Semantic and syntactic processes in aphasia: a review of the literature. *Psychological Bulletin*, 85: 898–918.

Caramazza, A., Capitani, E., Rey, A., and Berndt, R. S. (2001) Agrammatic Broca's aphasia is not associated with a single pattern of comprehension performance. *Brain and Language*, 76: 158–84.

Caramazza, A., and Zurif, E. (1976) Dissociation of algorithmic and heuristic processes in language comprehension: evidence from aphasia. *Brain and Language*, 3: 572–82.

Chomsky, N. (1981) *Lectures on Government and Binding*. Foris, Dordrecht.

de Diego Balaguer, R., Costa, A., Sebastián-Gallés, N., Juncadella, M., and Caramazza, A. (2004) Regular and irregular morphology and its relationship with agrammatism: evidence from two Spanish-Catalan bilinguals. *Brain and Language*, 91: 212–22.

Drai, D., and Grodzinsky, Y. (1999) Syntactic regularity in Broca's aphasia: there's more of it than you ever imagined. *Brain and Language*, 70: 139–43.

Drai, D., Grodzinsky, Y., and Zurif, E. (2001) Broca's aphasia is associated with a single pattern of comprehension performance. *Brain and Language*, 76: 185–92.

Druks, J., and Marshall, J. C. (1991) Agrammatism: an analysis and critique, with new evidence from four Hebrew-speaking aphasic patients. *Cognitive Neuropsychology*, 8: 415–33.

Druks, J., and Marshall, J. C. (1995) When passives are easier than actives: two case studies in aphasic comprehension. *Cognition*, 55: 311–31.

Druks, J., and Marshall, J. C. (2000) Kicking over the traces: a note in response to Zurif and Pinango (1999). *Brain and Language*, 75: 461–4.

Emery, O. B. (1988) The deficit of thought in senile dementia Alzheimer's type. *Psychiatric Journal of the University of Ottawa*, 13: 3–8.

Faroqi-Shah, Y., and Thompson, C. K. (2003) Regular and irregular verb inflections in agrammatism: dissociation or association? *Brain and Language*, 87: 9–10.

Ferreira, F. (1999) Distinguishing interpretive and post-interpretive processes. *Behavioral and Brain Sciences*, 22: 98–9.

Ferreira, F., and Stacey, J. (2005) The misinterpretation of passive sentences. MS.

Friedmann, N., and Gvion, A. (2003) Sentence comprehension and working memory limitation in aphasia: a dissociation between semantic-syntactic and phonological reactivation. *Brain and Language*, 86: 23–39.

Friedrich, F., Martin, R. C., and Kemper, S. (1985) Consequences of a phonological coding deficit on sentence processing. *Cognitive Neuropsychology*, 2: 385–412.

Gahl, S. (2002) Lexical biases in aphasic sentence comprehension: an experimental and corpus linguistic study. *Aphasiology*, 16: 1173–98.

Gahl, S., Menn, L., Ramsberger, G., Jurafsky, D. S., Elder, E., Rewega, M., and Audrey, L. H. (2003) Syntactic frame and verb bias in aphasia: plausibility judgements of undergoer-subject sentences. *Brain and Cognition*, 53: 223–8.

Gibson, E. (2000) The dependency locality theory: A distance-based theory of linguistic complexity. In A. Marantz, Y. Miyashita, and W. O'Neill (eds), *Image, Language and Brain*, pp. 95–126 MIT Press, Cambridge, MA.

Goodglass, H., and Kaplan, E. (1972) *The assessment of aphasia and related disorders*. Lea and Febiger, Philadelphia, PA.

Gordon, P. C., Hendrick, R., and Johnson, M. (2001) Memory interference during language processing. *Journal of Experimental Psychology: Learning, Memory, and Cognition*, 27: 1411–23.

Grodzinsky, Y. (1990) *Theoretical Perspectives on Language Deficits*. MIT Press, Cambridge, MA.

Grodzinsky, Y. (1995) A restrictive theory of agrammatic comprehension. *Brain and Language*, 50: 27–51.

Grodzinsky, Y. (2000) The neurology of syntax: language use without Broca's area. *Behavioral and Brain Science*, 23: 1–71.

Grodzinsky, Y., and Finkel, L. (1998) The neurology of empty categories: aphasics' failure to detect ungrammaticality. *Journal of Cognitive Neuroscience*, 10: 281–92.

Grodzinsky, Y., Pinango, M. M., Zurif, E., and Drai, D. (1999) The critical role of group studies in neuropsychology: comprehension regularities in Broca's aphasia. *Brain and Language*, 67: 134–47.

Haarmann, H. J., Davelaar, E. J., and Usher, M. (2003) Individual differences in semantic short-term memory capacity and reading comprehension. *Journal of Memory and Language*, 48: 320–45.

Haarmann, H., and Kolk, H. (1991) Syntactic priming in Broca's aphasia: evidence for slow activation. *Aphasiology*, 5: 247–63.

Hanten, G., and Martin, R. (2000) Contributions of phonological and semantic short-term memory to sentence processing: evidence from two cases of closed head injury in children. *Journal of Memory and Language*, 43: 335–61.

Hanten, G., and Martin, R. (2001) A developmental phonological short-term memory deficit: a case study. *Brain and Cognition*, 45: 164–88.

Jackendoff, R. (1993) *Patterns in the Mind: Language and Human Nature*. Harvester Wheatsheaf, New York.

Joanisse, M. F., and Seidenberg, M. S. (1999) Impairments in verb morphology after brain injury: a connectionist model. *Proceedings of the National Academy of Sciences of the United States of America*, 96: 7592–7.

Just, M. A., and Carpenter, P. A. (1992) A capacity theory of comprehension: individual differences in working memory. *Psychological Review*, 99: 122–49.

Kolk, H., and Van Grunsven, M. (1985) Agrammatism as a variable phenomenon. *Cognitive Neuropsychology*, 2: 347–84.

Kolk, H., Van Grunsven, M., and Keyser, A. (1985) On parallelism between production and comprehension in agrammatism. In M. L. Kean (ed.), *Agrammatism*, pp. 165–206. Academic Press, New York.

Laiacona, M., and Caramazza, A. (2004) The noun/verb dissociation in language production: varieties of causes. *Cognitive Neuropsychology*, 21: 103–23.

Linebarger, M. (1990) Neuropsychology of sentence parsing. In A. Caramazza (ed.), *Cognitive Neuropsychology and Neurolinguistics: Advances in Models of Cognitive Function and Impairment*, pp. 55–122. Erlbaum, Hillsdale NJ.

Linebarger, M., Schwartz, M., and Saffran, E. (1983) Sensitivity to grammatical structure in so-called agrammatic aphasics. *Cognition*, 13: 361–92.

Longoni, A. M., Richardson, J. T. E., and Aiello, A. (1993) Articulatory rehearsal and phonological storage in working memory. *Memory and Cognition*, 21: 11–22.

Lu, C.-C., Bates, E., Li, P., Tzeng, O., Hung, D., Tsai, C. H., Lee, S. E., and Chung, Y.M. (2000) Judgements of grammaticality in aphasia: the special case of Chinese. *Aphasiology*, 14: 1021–54.

Lukatela, K., Crain, S., and Shankweiler, D. (1988) Sensitivity to inflectional morphology in agrammatism: investigation of a highly inflected language. *Brain and Language*, 33: 1–15.

MacDonald, M., Almor, A., Henderson, V., Kempler, D., and Andersen, E. (2001) Assessing working memory and language comprehension in Alzheimer's Disease. *Brain and Language*, 78: 17–42.

MacDonald, M. C., and Christiansen, M. H. (2002) Reassessing working memory: comment on Just and Carpenter and Waters and Caplan. *Psychological Review*, 109: 35–54.

Marslen-Wilson, W. D., and Tyler, L. K. (1980) The temporal structure of spoken language comprehension. *Cognition*, 8: 1–71.

Marslen-Wilson, W. D., and Tyler, L. K. (1997) Dissociating types of mental computation. *Nature*, 387: 592–4.

Marslen-Wilson, W. D., and Tyler, L. K. (1998) Rules, representations, and the English past tense. *Trends in Cognitive Science*, 2: 428–35.

Martin, N., and Saffran, E. M. (1997) Language and auditory-verbal short-term memory impairments: evidence for common underlying processes. *Cognitive Neuropsychology*, 14: 641–82.

Martin, R. C. (1987) Articulatory and phonological deficits in short-term memory and their relation to syntactic processing. *Brain and Language*, 32: 159–92.

Martin, R. (2000) Sentence comprehension deficits. In B. Rapp (ed.), *Handbook of Cognitive Neuropsychology*, pp. 349–74. Psychology Press, Philadelphia, PA.

Martin, R., and Blossom-Stach, C. (1986) Evidence for syntactic deficits in a fluent aphasic. *Brain and Language*, 28: 196–234.

Martin, R. C., Blossom-Stach, C., Yaffee, L. S., and Wetzel, W. F. (1995) Consequences of a motor programming deficit for rehearsal and written sentence comprehension. *Quarterly Journal of Experimental Psychology: Human Experimental Psychology*, 48A: 536–72.

Martin, R. C., and He, T. (2004) Semantic short-term memory and its role in sentence processing: a replication. *Brain and Language*, 89: 76–82.

Martin, R.C., and Romani, C. (1994) Verbal working memory and sentence processing: A multiple components view. *Neuropsychology*, 8: 506–23.

Martin, R. C., Shelton, J. R., and Yaffee, L. S. (1994) Language processing and working memory: neuropsychological evidence for separate phonological and semantic capacities. *Journal of Memory and Language*, 33: 83–111.

Martin, R. C., Wetzel, F., Blossom-Stach, C., and Feher, E. (1989) Syntactic loss versus processing deficit: an assessment of two theories of agrammatism and syntactic comprehension deficits. *Cognition*, 32: 157–91.

Mauner, G., Fromkin, V. A., and Gorell, T. L. (1993) Comprehension and acceptability judgements in agrammatism: disruptions in the syntax of referential dependency. *Brain and Language*, 45: 340–70.

Miceli, G., Mazzucchi, A., Menn, L., and Goodglass, H. (1983) Contrasting cases of Italian agrammatic aphasia without comprehension disorder. *Brain and Language*, 19: 65–97.

Miyake, A., Just, M., and Carpenter, P. (1994) A capacity approach to syntactic comprehension disorder: making normal adults perform like aphasic patients. *Cognitive Neuropsychology*, 11: 671–717.

Naeser, M., Mazurski, P., Goodglass, H., Peraino, M., Laughlin, S., and Leaper, W. C. (1987) Auditory syntactic comprehension in nine aphasia groups (with CT scans) and children: differences in degree but not order of difficulty observed. *Cortex*, 23: 359–80.

Natsopoulos, D., Katsarou, Z., Bostantzopoulou, S., Grouios, G., Mentenopoulos, G., and Logothetis, J. (1991) Strategies for comprehension of relative clauses by parkinsonian patients. *Cortex*, 27: 255–68.

Nespoulous, J. L., Dordain, M., Perron, C., Ska, B., Bub, D., Caplan, D., Mekler, J., and Lecours, A. R. (1988) Agrammatism in sentence production without comprehension deficits: reduced availability of syntactic structures or grammatical morphemes? A case study. *Brain and Language*, 33: 273–95.

Ostrin, R., and Tyler, L. (1995) Dissociations of lexical function: semantics, syntax, and morphology. *Cognitive Neuropsychology*, 12: 345–89.

Patterson, K., Lambon Ralph., M. A., Hodges, J. R., and McClelland, J. L. (2001) Deficits in irregular past-tense verb morphology associated with degraded semantic knowledge. *Neuropsychologia*, 39: 709–24.

Penke, M., Janssen, U., and Kraus, M. (1999) The representation of inflectional morphology: evidence from Broca's aphasia. *Brain and Language*, 68: 225–32.

Romani, C. (1994) The role of phonological short-term memory in syntactic parsing: a case study. *Language and Cognitive Processes*, 9: 29–67.

Rumelhart, D. E., and McClelland, J. L. (1986) On the learning the past tenses of English verbs. In J. L. McClelland and D. E. Rumelhart (eds), *Parallel Distributed Processing: Explorations in the Microstructure of Cognition*, vol. 2: *Psychological and Biological Models*, pp. 216–71. MIT Press, Cambridge, MA.

Saffran, E. M., and Marin, O. S. (1975) Immediate memory for word lists and sentences in a patient with deficient auditory short-term memory. *Brain and Language*, 2: 420–33.

Saffran, E., and Schwartz, M. (1988) "Agrammatic" comprehension it's not: alternatives and implications. *Aphasiology*, 2: 389–94.

Saffran, E., Schwartz, M., and Linebarger, M. (1998) Semantic influences on thematic role assignments: evidence from normals and aphasics. *Brain and Language*, 62: 255–97.

Schwartz, M., Saffran, E., and Marin, O. S. M. (1980) The word order problem in agrammatism, I: Comprehension. *Brain and Language*, 10: 249–62.

Shankweiler, D., Crain, S., Gorrell, P., and Tuller, B. (1989) Reception of language in Broca's aphasia. *Language and Cognitive Processes*, 4: 1–33.

Shapiro, K., and Caramazza, A. (2003) Grammatical processing of nouns and verbs in left frontal cortex? *Neuropsychologia*, 41: 1189–98.

Spivey, M., and Tanenhaus, M. (1998) Syntactic ambiguity resolution in discourse: modeling the effects of referential context and lexical frequency. *Journal of Experimental Psychology: Learning, Memory, and Cognition*, 24: 1521–43.

Sternberg, S. (1998) Discovering mental processing stages: the method of additive factors. In D. Scarborough and S. Sternberg (eds), *Invitation to Cognitive Science*, vol. 4: *Methods, Models, and Conceptual Issues*, pp. 703–863. MIT Press, Cambridge, MA.

Trueswell, J., Tanenhaus, M., and Garnsey, S. (1994) Semantic influences on parsing: use of thematic role information in syntactic ambiguity resolution. *Journal of Memory and Language*, 33: 285–318.

Tyler, L. (1992) *Spoken Language Comprehension: An Experimental Approach to Disordered and Normal Processing*. MIT Press, Cambridge, MA.

Tyler, L. K., Randall, B., and Marslen-Wilson, W. D. (2002) Phonology and neuropsychology of the English past tense. *Neuropsychologia*, 40: 1154–66.

Ullman, M. T., Corkin, S., Coppola, M., Hickok, G., Growdeon, J. H., Koroshetz, W. J., and Pinker, S. (1997) A neural dissociation within language: evidence that the mental dictionary is part of declarative memory, and that grammatical rules are processed by the procedural system. *Journal of Cognitive Neuroscience*, 9: 266–76.

Van Dyke, J. A., and Lewis, R. L. (2003) Distinguishing effects of structure and decay on attachment and repair: a cue-based parsing account of recovery from misanalyzed ambiguities. *Journal of Memory and Language*, 49: 285–316.

von Stockert, T. R., and Bader, L. (1976) Some relations of grammar and lexicon in aphasia. *Cortex*, 12: 49–60.

Waters, G., and Caplan, D. (1996) The capacity theory of sentence comprehension: critique of Just and Carpenter (1992). *Psychological Review*, 103: 761–72.

Waters, G., Caplan, D., and Hildebrandt, N. (1991) On the structure of verbal short-term memory and its functional role in sentence comprehension: evidence from neuropsychology. *Cognitive Neuropsychology*, 8: 81–126.

Waters, G., Caplan, D., and Rochon, E. (1995) Processing capacity and sentence comprehension in patients with Alzheimer's disease. *Cognitive Neuropsychology*, 12: 1–30.

Wilson, S. M., and Saygin, A. P. (2004) Grammaticality judgements in aphasia: deficits are not specific to syntactic structures, aphasic syndromes, or lesion sites. *Journal of Cognitive Neuroscience*, 16: 238–52.

Wulfeck, B. (1988) Grammaticality judgements and sentence comprehension in agrammatic aphasia. *Journal of Speech and Hearing Research*, 31: 72–81.

Zurif, E. (1996) Grammatical theory and study of sentence comprehension in aphasia: Comments on Druks and Marshall (1995). *Cognition*, 58: 271–9.

Zurif, E. (2001) More on sentence comprehension in Broca's aphasia: A response to Caplan. *Brain and Language*, 79: 321–328. *Cognition*, 79: 321–8.

Zurif, E., and Grodzinsky, Y. (1983) Sensitivity to grammatical structure in agrammatic aphasics: A reply to Linebarger, Schwartz, and Saffran. *Cognition*, 15: 207–13.

Zurif, E., and Pinango, M. (1999) The existence of comprehension patterns in Broca's aphasia. *Brain and Language*, 70: 133–8.

SECTION IV

Language production

CHAPTER 26

Alignment in dialogue

Simon Garrod and Martin J. Pickering

26.1 Introduction

Almost without exception the other chapters in this handbook address the study of monologue, involving isolated language production or comprehension. Such work implicitly or explicitly adopts a perspective in which researchers attempt to understand the processes that occur when the speaker converts meaning into sound and the listener converts sound into meaning. But is such a perspective sufficient to explain dialogue?

In this chapter, we argue that psycholinguists need to think in a different way to understand processing in dialogue. According to this view, interlocutors do not use language to encode and decode messages, but rather as a means by which they can align their mental states, so that they come to have the same ideas about the topic under discussion (Pickering and Garrod, 2004). It would in principle be possible to decompose this task into discrete acts of comprehension and production, but in practice real dialogue involves constant overlaying of production and comprehension (as when the addressee provides feedback such as *yes*, *mm*, or a gesture during the speaker's contribution). It is much better to understand dialogue as a joint activity, like ballroom dancing or using a two-handed saw (Clark, 1996), and to assume that alignment follows from this inherently interactive process.

We simply assume that interlocutors seek to align their mental states, just as we assume that isolated speakers and listeners seek to encode and decode messages. This may sound overly optimistic, as people clearly do not always seek to agree with each other. But even in the most irreconcilable argument, interlocutors align on the topic that is being discussed, the referents of expressions, and so on. And of course people do misunderstand each other, but isolated speakers also sometimes make speech errors, and isolated listeners sometimes fail to understand what they hear. Full alignment (in which interlocutors have identical mental states) may never occur, but interlocutors attempt to align just as isolated speakers and listeners attempt to encode and decode. So, on the assumption that the goal of dialogue is alignment, this chapter discusses ways in which interlocutors come to achieve this state.

Just like other complex cognitive processes, alignment in dialogue involves both automatic and strategic components. However, current theories of dialogue emphasize them to different extents. Clark (1996) argued that interlocutors use various strategies to accumulate what he terms "common ground," which refers to all the information that both interlocutors believe to be shared by themselves and their conversational partner. This is actually a stricter notion than alignment, which merely refers to the information that happens to be shared. Brown and Dell (1987) made the point that information accessible to the speaker will often tend to be accessible to the listener at that point as well. This notion of shared accessibility underlies Pickering and Garrod's (2004) implicit common ground (i.e. information that is automatically made accessible to both interlocutors as a result of the interaction). To the extent that interlocutors share common ground or implicit common ground, their mental states are aligned.

In contrast to Clark's (1996) account, other accounts assume that alignment is principally the result of automatic mechanisms such as priming between interlocutors (Pickering and Garrod, 2004) or associative processes underlying memory access (Horton and Gerrig, 2005a; 2005b). In this chapter, we assess various ways in which interlocutors may become aligned, and consider whether the underlying mechanisms are largely strategic or automatic. In turn, we discuss alignment via beliefs about one's interlocutor, imitation, agreement between interlocutors, feedback, and physical co-presence.

26.2 Sources of alignment

26.2.1 Alignment via beliefs about one's interlocutor

Clark (1996) argued that common ground is partly determined on the basis of what the speakers already know or can reasonably infer about each other before the conversation begins (based on inferences about community membership or shared knowledge from previous conversations). For example, Isaacs and Clark (1987) had speakers describe pictures of New York landmarks either to other New Yorkers or to "out-of-towners," and found that they quickly established whether their listener was a New Yorker and modified the descriptions accordingly (e.g. referring to buildings by name for New Yorkers or in relation to their appearance for "out-of-towners"). Speakers similarly adjust their speech to adults versus children (e.g. Shatz and Gelman, 1973) and native vs. non-native speakers (Bortfeld and Brennan, 1997). This suggests that interlocutors explicitly infer the extent of common ground and modify their utterances accordingly.

No doubt speakers make some reasoned decisions about how to produce descriptions on the basis of what they believe their audience to know. But their choices may also reflect automatic resonance processes, of the kind exemplified in models by Logan (1988) and Hintzman (1986). Resonance could arise from the prior association of particular types of addressee with particular expressions, the activation of such types of addressee as a result of the interaction, and the subsequent activation of those expressions (Horton and Gerrig, 2005a). For example, if I know Bob is a psychologist, then I may automatically activate psychological terms when meeting Bob, and therefore circumvent the problem of deciding whether Bob is likely to understand every technical expression I use. Furthermore, Horton and Gerrig point out that information that is accessible to the speaker will also tend to be accessible to the listener because of resonance. When person A interacts with person B, information A associates with B will automatically become more accessible to A and information B associates with A will automatically become more accessible to B. The net effect is to promote the accessibility of information that they have in common (e.g. from past encounters between A and B).

Horton and Gerrig (2005a) use examples of first mentions of characters during telephone conversations to show that speakers sometimes over- or under-estimate what their interlocutor knows about the character, but argue that interlocutors are often able to repair any misunderstandings easily. In experimental studies, language users do not always take common ground into account in producing or interpreting references. For example, Horton and Keysar (1996) found that speakers under time pressure did not produce descriptions that took advantage of what they knew about the listener's view of the relevant scene. In other words, the descriptions were formulated with respect to the speaker's current knowledge of the scene rather than with respect to common ground. Keysar et al. (1998) found that listeners initially considered objects to be potential referents for expressions even when they knew that the speaker was not attending to those objects, and Keysar et al. (2000) found that listeners initially looked at objects that they knew the speaker was not aware of.

In contrast, Hanna et al. (2003) reported a similar eye-tracking experiment in which they did find evidence that listeners preferred to look at referents that they knew to be shared with the speaker. In their experiment, however, the shared information not only was visually available to speaker and listener but also had already been established as such during prior conversation. For example, at the beginning of the experiment the instruction-follower might have a red triangle that only he could see and then be asked to put another red triangle onto the board that was visible to both participants. Subsequently he would be instructed: "Now put the blue triangle on the red one," referring to the recently mentioned and visually shared red triangle. At this point the instruction-follower was more likely to gaze first at the shared triangle, thus suggesting sensitivity to information in common ground. So addressees may make reference to common ground when the discrepancy between their knowledge and that of the speaker is made especially salient. However, Hanna et al.'s immediate effects of common ground on eye movements could be due to resonance rather than strategic inference (Horton and Gerrig, 2005a).

To represent common ground, the interlocutor needs to maintain a very complex situation model that reflects both his own knowledge and the knowledge he assumes to be shared with his partner. To do this, he has to keep track of the knowledge state of his partner in a way which is separate from his own knowledge state. This is a very stringent requirement for routine communication, in part because he has to make sure that this model is constantly updated appropriately (Halpern and Moses, 1990). For example, each interlocutor would have to flag every piece of information as being in or out of common ground. Indeed, it is even more complicated when interlocutors need to differentiate common ground, their own personal knowledge, and knowledge they believe to be exclusive to their partner (e.g. in a spying scenario). Nevertheless, under certain circumstances interlocutors do engage in strategic inference relating to common ground, at least under conditions where the discrepancy between interlocutors' knowledge is very salient. Horton and Keysar (1996) found that speakers who were not under time pressure often take account of common ground in formulating their utterances. Keysar et al. (1998, 2000) argued that listeners eventually take account of common ground in comprehension, though they proposed that this occurs at a later monitoring stage, in a process that they called "perspective adjustment."

26.2.2 Alignment via imitation

People use beliefs about their interlocutors to start the process of alignment. However, we would expect the alignment process to continue after both interlocutors have made contributions, because these contributions provide valuable new information. The most straightforward way in which interlocutors could take advantage of these contributions would be to imitate aspects of them, with alignment of mental states following from the imitation of each others' behavior. Assuming there is a relatively regular relationship between behavior and mental states, people who behave in the same way will tend to develop similar mental states. In fact, there is a great deal of evidence for the ubiquity of imitation (for a review, see Hurley and Chater, 2005), and for the repetitive nature of all aspects of dialogue (e.g. Aijmer, 1996; Gries, 2005; Schenkein, 1980; Tannen, 1989).

Perhaps the clearest evidence comes from alignment of situation models themselves. Garrod and Anderson (1987) had pairs of participants play a cooperative maze game, in which they took turns to describe their positions to each other. There are many different ways to describe one's position, but participants tended to align on the same description scheme. For example, if one player said *I'm two along, four up*, her partner tended to say *I'm one along, five up*; whereas if she said *I'm at B4*, her partner tended to say *I'm at A5*. These players aligned on a "path" or a "coordinate" description scheme, rather than specific words. They also aligned on the interpretation of these descriptions, for example treating the starting point as the bottom left corner of the maze. Schober (1993) had interlocutors describe the position of objects situated between them, so that *left* and *right* had opposite meanings, and found that they tended to align on the use of their interlocutor's perspective (though cf. Schober, 1995). Watson et al. (2004) found that participants were likely to align reference frames, which presumably constitute part of the situation model. A speaker can describe a picture of a dot to the side of a chair that is itself on its side as *the dot to the left of the chair* or *the dot above the chair*. The former involves a relative reference frame (i.e. from an observer's point of view), whereas the latter involves an intrinsic reference frame (i.e. from the chair's point of view). Watson et al. found that participants tended to use a description employing the same reference frame as their confederate interlocutor, and ruled out explanations in terms of lexical priming.

Interlocutors also tend to repeat each other in terms of their grammatical choices. Levelt and Kelter (1982) telephoned (Dutch) shopkeepers and found that they tended to say *At five o'clock* in response to *At what time do you close?*, but tended to say *five o'clock* in response to *What time do you close?* This demonstrates repetition of either syntax or function words. Branigan et al. (2000) had participants take turns to describe and match picture cards, and found that they tended to use the form of utterance just used by their interlocutor. For example, they tended to use a "prepositional object" form like *the pirate giving the book to the swimmer* following another prepositional object sentence, but a "double object" form like *the pirate giving the swimmer the book* following another double object sentence. Such repetition of grammatical form is similar to the syntactic priming that takes place during isolated production (Bock, 1986; Pickering and Branigan, 1998). Similar alignment also occurs with other constructions (Cleland and Pickering, 2003; Haywood et al., 2005), and even between languages in bilinguals (Hartsuiker et al., 2004).

There is also a great deal of evidence for alignment in word choice (sometimes called *lexical entrainment*). For example, Garrod and Anderson (1987) found that interlocutors used the same expressions and, moreover, that they tended to interpret words in the same way (e.g. *line* to mean horizontal row of nodes in the maze) (see also Garrod and Clark, 1993). Brennan and Clark (1996) had directors describe a set of cards depicting common objects to matchers so that they could reconstruct the directors' array. One set of trials contained multiple objects from the same category. Directors and matchers settled on subordinate terms to refer to the objects (e.g. *penny loafer*), because basic-level terms (e.g. *shoe*) would not discriminate between these objects. A subsequent set of trials included one object from each category, so basic-level terms would now be sufficient. However, participants often continued to use the subordinate terms. Results such as these can be interpreted in terms of imitation, though they assume an explanation based on tacit agreement (see below).

Interlocutors also tend to align on such dimensions as accent and speech rate (e.g. Giles et al., 1992). There is also good evidence for "contagion" effects, whereby people tend to imitate each other's facial expressions (e.g. Bavelas et al., 1986) and other indicators of their emotional states (e.g. Hatfield et al., 1994). Not surprisingly, these external indications of alignment lead to alignment of mental states. These data are also compatible with behavioral mimicry (the chameleon effect), whereby people imitate each other's behaviors (Chartrand and Bargh, 1999).

Such imitation appears to be largely automatic, with interlocutors being almost entirely unaware that it has taken place (Pickering and Garrod, 2004). At phonological and acoustic levels it can occur very rapidly and seems largely resource-free (Fowler et al., 2003), with listeners activating appropriate muscles in the tongue while listening to speech but not during non-speech (Fadiga et al., 2002; see also Watkins and Paus, 2004). Additionally, speakers who shadow spoken words produce more faithful imitations of the original when they speak more rapidly (Goldinger, 1998).

Another interesting point is that alignment at one level can lead to greater alignment at other levels. Thus, if interlocutors start referring to entities using the same term, they are likely to accept the implications of that term and therefore conceptualize the entity in the same way. For example, Danet (1980) examined lawyers' use of terms like *foetus* vs. *unborn child* to refer to the same entity in an abortion trial. In this case, opposing lawyers were careful not to align, presumably because using the opposition's term would at least give the impression of accepting their conceptualization. Clearer evidence comes from experimental studies in which lexical repetition or semantic similarity enhances syntactic repetition between interlocutors. Thus, Branigan et al. (2000) found that such repetition was much stronger (occurring almost eighty percent of the time in their experiment) when prime and target utterances used the same verb, and Cleland and Pickering (2003) found similar results when prime and target used semantically related nouns. Pickering and Garrod (2004) suggest that such interactions between levels explain why alignment at different levels leads to alignment of mental states.

26.2.3 **Alignment via agreements between interlocutors**

There is something of a tension between the two previous sections, with the former emphasizing decisions to mold one's contributions so that they accord with beliefs about one's interlocutor, and the latter emphasizing automatic processes of imitation. We have already suggested one response: that some apparently strategic decisions may in fact reflect automatic resonance processes (Horton and Gerrig, 2005a; 2005b). However, it is also possible that some apparent imitation is in fact due to tacit agreements between interlocutors about how to refer to entities. Although explicit negotiation about reference (e.g. "Shall we call this X for the purposes of this discussion?") is very rare in most interactions (e.g. Garrod and Anderson, 1987), some researchers argue that interlocutors routinely make so-called "conceptual pacts" when they align on referring expressions (Brennan and Clark, 1996; Metzing and Brennan, 2003).

As we have noted, Brennan and Clark (1996) found that interlocutors aligned on descriptions of cards depicting objects, even when this required use of a more specific term than was necessary for discrimination. But rather than appeal to imitation, they argued that such interlocutors enter into a conceptual pact in which they (tacitly) agree to keep referring to the same object in the same way. The pact comes about because certain "conversational moves" indicate acceptance of the pact. For instance, if A refers to a shoe as a *penny loafer* and B does not query this use but rather responds to A's instruction, then both A and B assume (1) that B has accepted this term, and (2) that both know (1). (In contrast, if B queried A's expression, then the pact would not be formed.) On this account, this aspect of alignment is therefore the result of a process of negotiation (grounding) which is specialized to dialogue and involves inference.

Brennan and Clark (1996) used partner-specificity effects to support the conceptual pact explanation of lexical entrainment. They reasoned that conceptual pacts only hold for their originators, so changing the interlocutor should lead speakers to change their descriptions. This did occur to some extent. However, it is important to note that their speakers often first employed the previous term to a new interlocutor, and altered it when the new interlocutor provided explicit feedback to indicate that they had not understood the original description (p. 1491). So it is possible that partner-specificity effects at least partly reflect tendencies for speakers to use the term that they employed with their previous partner first, and only to use a different term when their new partner displays lack of understanding. Since then there have been two major studies on partner-specificity effects which come to rather different conclusions.

Barr and Keysar (2002) recorded eye movements to objects in a display as listeners interpreted repeated references to those objects. Listeners fixated objects more quickly when they were referred to repeatedly, but it did not matter whether the repetition came from the same speaker or a new speaker (who was not present during the initial reference). They concluded that partner-specific effects did not occur, and that only the improved availability of the repeated reference facilitated comprehension. However, Metzing and Brennan (2003) recorded listeners' eye movements in a similar task, but crucially included novel descriptions of previously mentioned objects. For example, an object was repeatedly called *the silver pipe* but then called *the shiny cylinder*. When the new expression was used by the original speaker, addressees searched for a long time before fixating the original object; but when it was used by a new speaker, addressees were not disrupted. They argued that these partner-specific effects were the result of conceptual pacts between interlocutors.

There are therefore empirical issues about the extent to which interlocutors respect partner-specificity in production and comprehension of expressions. But in addition, partner-specificity can be explained without appealing to conceptual pacts. In Horton and Gerrig's (2005b) terms, people may associate particular expressions with particular interlocutors (or types of interlocutor), so that they are more likely to use those terms when subsequently interacting with them again. For example, Pickering and Garrod (2004; 2005) argue that repeated references to the same objects with the same expressions become routinized and represented as such in memory. It is quite possible that such routines become associated with the person with whom they were established, and that this leads to partner-specificity effects during comprehension and production.

26.2.4 Alignment via feedback

Apart from repetition, there are other aspects of interlocutors' contributions that lead to alignment. Addressees are constantly providing feedback to the speakers that indicate understanding, disagreement, emotional reactions, and so on. When discussing Brennan and Clark's (1996) findings on how speakers changed their references following a change of partner, we pointed out that this was facilitated by explicit feedback from the new partner. This raises the question of whether feedback promotes alignment. Kraut et al. (1982) controlled the amount of feedback that listeners could give to a speaker describing a complicated movie plot. They found a range of evidence to indicate that feedback increases alignment. For example, listeners free to give any form of verbal feedback ("active" listeners) were more likely subsequently to provide descriptions of the movie characters that were similar to those of the speaker than were listeners allowed to give only limited or no verbal feedback ("restricted" listeners). Active listeners' subsequent summaries of the movie plot also showed better understanding of the movie than did those from the restricted listeners. Similarly, Bavelas et al. (2000) found that narrators who received normal feedback from their addressees told better stories than narrators who received highly reduced feedback. Presumably this meant that narrator and addressee ended up with more aligned understanding of the story in the normal feedback condition than in the reduced feedback condition. Using a tangram description task, Schober and Clark (1989) showed that listeners who actively participated in the task by being able to give feedback were better at identifying the tangrams than those who could only overhear the conversation. Presumably the speakers were tailoring their contributions to the specific listener on the basis of the feedback provided by that listener. Again, this points to the role of feedback in promoting alignment between conversational partners.

Such studies show the effectiveness of feedback, but provide little evidence about how it works, and whether different forms of feedback differ in their effects. For this we need to turn to theoretical analyses of fragments of conversation. According to Clark (1996), addressees respond to contributions by providing signals that the contribution has been grounded; in other words, that the contribution has become part of common ground (well enough for current purpose). Such signals are often (though need not be) feedback, such as *yeah*, *OK*, or a nod, which tend to indicate acceptance and understanding, or *mm*, which may merely indicate understanding. Beyond the prior establishment of common ground, Clark (1996) proposed a specific mechanism that increases the common ground as a consequence of the history of the interaction. According to Clark, the grounding mechanism works by establishing closure on dialogue contributions. In Clark and Schaefer's (1987) terms, a contribution consists of a presentation phase, in which the speaker produces an utterance directed at the addressee, and an acceptance phase, in which the addressee signals whether he has understood the utterance. Acceptance may be signalled through assertions of understanding (*uh-huh*, *I see*, etc.), presupposition of understanding (e.g. making an appropriate next turn), or by display or exemplification (e.g. giving an appropriate answer to a question or offering a paraphrase of what was said in the presentation phase). Crucially in Clark's account, closure and hence updating of common ground requires positive evidence from the interlocutor in the acceptance phase. So, the grounding account contrasts with the interactive alignment account discussed earlier, in which there is no requirement for positive evidence of acceptance.

In an alternative analysis consistent with Pickering and Garrod (2004), feedback such as *yeah*, *OK*, or a nod occurs when the addressee believes he has made a coherent update to his mental state. So long as the speaker has conveyed her message appropriately, such feedback will occur when the interlocutors are aligned, without any need for the addressee to represent the fact that they are aligned. On this account, such feedback serves to promote implicit common ground rather than full common ground (i.e. an explicit model of what is jointly available to the interlocutors). Similarly, feedback such as *eh?* or *pardon?*, or clarification requests such as repetition of part of the speaker's utterance (Ginzberg, 2004), occurs when the addressee believes he has not made a coherent update to his mental state. This feedback will therefore tend to occur when the interlocutors are not aligned, but again without the addressee needing to represent that they are not aligned. At this point, the speaker can seek to clarify her utterance using interactive repair. The speaker's first attempt to repair can employ a simple strategy of being more explicit about the part of her utterance that the addressee has queried. Although this may require some decision about whether the query refers to the last constituent or the whole utterance (for instance), there is no need to model what she believes the addressee does not know. Finally, the addressee can provide corrective feedback (e.g. replacing one of the speaker's words) when he realizes some aspect of the utterance is incompatible with his background knowledge, and the speaker can incorporate this correction, again without modeling the interlocutor.

26.2.5 Alignment via physical co-presence

A final source of alignment comes from interlocutors' shared physical environment. Schiffer (1972) argued that communicators establish mutual knowledge (similar to common ground) on the basis of physical co-presence, with something which is manifestly present to both interlocutors forming part of mutual knowledge. Clark and Marshall (1981) treated physical co-presence as one of the three sources of common ground (along with community membership and linguistic co-presence). When interlocutors are discussing an aspect of their immediate environment (e.g. objects in view or clearly audible sounds), the environment itself can assist alignment. It can clearly have direct consequences for their shared mental states (e.g. both interlocutors focus on an object that suddenly appears). But it can also serve as an additional communicative resource during dialogue, because interlocutors can combine linguistic expressions with gestures and demonstrations to align their focus of attention.

Bangerter (2004) found that interlocutors substitute pointing gestures (together with deictics such as *this*) for verbal descriptions when referents are visible to both parties and close at hand. He argued that pointing forms part of a composite signal combining gesture with speech to focus joint attention (and hence alignment). Clark and Krych (2004) manipulated whether a director could see a builder's workspace (and hence whether the space was shared) during a

Lego construction task. When the workspace was visible, the director used many deictic expressions (e.g. *here, there, this, that, like this*) and timed speech to fit in with the builder's sequence of actions. She also provided many demonstrations (deliberately positioning objects in ways to elicit responses from the builder). It appeared that the builder's actions were treated as continuous feedback by the director, and directly affected both the content and timing of the speech. Not surprisingly, having access to the shared workspace led to substantially better performance in the collaborative task (see also Kraut et al., 2003). Hence physical co-presence supported alignment.

Again, one can question the extent to which using these devices requires interlocutors to construct models of each other's mental states. On one account interlocutors may reason: If my partner is pointing at something, I can assume that he is attending to it; and if he sees me looking at the object, he knows that I am also attending to it; so it is in common ground. However, the situation may be much simpler than this, because there is evidence that viewers automatically attend to where another is looking or pointing (e.g. Langton and Bruce, 2000), and this directly increases spatial acuity in that region (Schuller and Rossion, 2001). This means that, even if interlocutors take an egocentric perspective, their attention will tend to be aligned with respect to the source of the pointing.

26.3 Discussion

We have argued that dialogue involves the alignment of mental states, so that a particular interaction is successful to the extent that such alignment occurs. Most psychological research on dialogue can be interpreted as investigating the different ways in which such alignment comes about, and we identified five different strands within this research. Throughout this review, we have emphasized that alignment can be due to strategic or automatic factors, with particular pieces of research drawing attention to one or other of these.

Some accounts focus on strategic factors, in which interlocutors construct their contributions and interpret their partners' contributions on the basis of extensive modeling of their partners' mental states and decisions about what contributions would be most useful for them. This is very much the perspective taken by Clark (1992; 1996), and his proposals can be taken as representative of this approach. On this account, speakers largely construct their utterances for the benefit of their addressees. Most aspects of their speech are intentional (e.g. even disfluencies are seen as deliberate signals that the speaker is having problems; Clark and Fox Tree, 2002). Conceptual pacts are a good example.

By contrast, other accounts treat interlocutors as largely egocentric but operating in a processing environment "designed" to promote alignment. For example, Pickering and Garrod (2004) argue that interactive alignment automatically promotes an implicit common ground. As we have seen in this chapter, there are many potential sources for extending implicit common ground, such as interactive alignment through imitation, resonance, and joint attention through physical co-presence. We suspect that dialogue processing involves a balance between dependence on implicit common ground and dependence on full common ground. To the extent that alignment through imitation and physical co-presence is automatic, relying on implicit common ground is relatively cost-free. More strategic processes of alignment that require the speaker to take the perspective of the addressee would only be used when circumstances allow. Teasing apart the contributions of implicit common ground and full common ground to alignment seems to be a major goal for future research in dialogue.

Finally, we note that our discussion has been largely limited to two-person (dyadic) exchanges considered as isolated events. However, much real dialogue is multi-party, with different people playing different roles (e.g. addressee, side-participant, overhearer) and with the roles often changing throughout the conversation. These different roles greatly affect alignment, for example with addressees aligning with the speaker better than overhearers (Schober and Clark, 1989). Similarly, alignment proceeds differently in small groups than large groups, with interlocutors aligning more with the previous speaker in small groups but with the dominant speaker in large groups (Fay et al., 2000). Additionally, dialogue has long-term effects on a community, with dyads who form part of a community (in that they have previously interacted with the same people) aligning better than dyads who do not form part of a community (Garrod and Doherty, 1994). Alignment between dyads appears to lead to the establishment of community conventions in both experimental studies (Garrod and Doherty, 1994) and simulations (Barr, 2004), and may form part of the explanation for diachronic patterns of language change.

References

Aijmer, K. (1996) *Conversational Routines in English: Convention and Creativity*. Longman, London.

Bangerter, A. (2004) Using pointing and describing to achieve joint focus of attention in dialogue. *Psychological Science*, 15: 415–19.

Barr, D. J. (2004) Establishing conventional communication systems: is common knowledge necessary? *Cognitive Science*, 28: 937–62.

Barr, D. J., and Keysar, B. (2002) Anchoring comprehension in linguistic precedents. *Journal of Memory and Language*, 46: 391–418.

Bavelas, J. B., Black, A., Lemery, C. R., and Mullett, J. (1986) "I *show* how you feel": motor mimicry as a communicative act. *Journal of Personality and Social Psychology*, 50: 322–9.

Bavelas, J.B., Coates, L., and Johnson, T. (2000) Listeners as co-narrators. *Journal of Personality and Social Psychology*, 79: 941–52.

Bock, J. K. (1986) Syntactic persistence in language production. *Cognitive Psychology*, 18: 355–87.

Bortfeld, J. K., and Brennan, S. E. (1997) Use and acquisition of idiomatic expressions in referring by native and non-native speakers. *Discourse Processes*, 23: 119–47.

Branigan, H. P., Pickering, M. J., and Cleland, A. A. (2000) Syntactic coordination in dialogue. *Cognition*, 75: B13–B25.

Brennan, S. E., and Clark, H. H. (1996) Conceptual pacts and lexical choice in conversation. *Journal of Experimental Psychology: Learning, Memory, and Cognition*, 22: 1482–93.

Brown, P. M., and Dell, G. S. (1987) Adapting production to comprehension: the explicit mention of instruments. *Cognitive Psychology*, 19: 441–72.

Chartrand, T. L., and Bargh, J. A. (1999) The chameleon effect: the perception-behavior link and social interaction. *Journal of Personality and Social Psychology*, 76: 893–910.

Clark, H.H. (1992) *Arenas of Language Use*. University of Chicago Press, Chicago.

Clark, H. H. (1996) *Using language*. Cambridge University Press, Cambridge.

Clark, H. H., and Fox Tree, J.E. (2002) Using *uh* and *um* in spontaneous speaking. *Cognition*, 84: 73–111.

Clark, H. H., and Krych, M. A. (2004) Speaking while monitoring addressees for understanding. *Journal of Memory and Language*, 50: 62–81.

Clark, H. H., and Marshall, C. R. (1981) Definite reference and mutual knowledge. In A. K. Joshi, I. A. Sag, and B. L. Webber (eds), *Elements of Discourse Understanding*, pp. 10–63. Cambridge University Press, Cambridge.

Clark, H. H., and Schaefer, E. F. (1987) Collaborating on contributions to conversations. *Language and Cognitive Processes*, 2: 19–41.

Cleland, S., and Pickering, M. J. (2003) The use of lexical and syntactic information in language production: evidence from the priming of noun-phrase structure. *Journal of Memory and Language*, 49: 214–30.

Danet, B. (1980) "Baby" or "foetus"? Language and the construction of reality in a manslaughter trial. *Semiotica*, 32: 187–219.

Fadiga, L., Craighero, L., Buccino, G., and Rizzolati, G. (2002) Speech listening specifically modultes the excitability of tongue muscles: a TMS study. *European Journal of Neuroscience*, 15: 399–402.

Fay, N., Garrod, S., and Carletta, J. (2000) Group discussion as interactive dialogue or as serial monologue: the influence of group size. *Psychological Science*, 11: 481–86.

Fowler, C. A., Brown, J. M., Sabadini, L., and Weihing, J. (2003) Rapid access to speech gestures in perception: evidence from choice and simple response time tasks. *Journal of Memory and Language*, 49: 396–413.

Garrod, S., and Anderson, A. (1987) Saying what you mean in dialogue: a study in conceptual and semantic co-ordination. *Cognition*, 27: 181–218.

Garrod, S., and Clark, A. (1993) The development of dialogue coordination skills in school children. *Language and Cognitive Processes*, 8: 101–126.

Garrod, S., and Doherty, G. (1994) Conversation, co-ordination and convention: an empirical investigation of how groups establish linguistic conventions. *Cognition*, 53: 181–215.

Giles, H., Coupland, N., and Coupland, J. (1992) Accommodation theory: communication, context and consequences. In H. Giles, J. Coupland, and N. Coupland (eds), *Contexts of Accommodation*, pp. 1–68. Cambridge University Press, Cambridge.

Ginzburg, J. (2004) Intrinsic misalignment in dialogue: why there is no unique context in a conversation. (Commentary on Pickering and Garrod's *Toward a Mechanistic Psychology of Dialogue*). *Behavioral and Brain Sciences*, 27: 197–9.

Glucksberg, S., Krauss, R. M., and Weisberg, R. (1966) Referential communication in nursery school children: method and some preliminary findings. *Journal of Experimental Child Psychology*, 3: 333–42.

Goldinger, S. D. (1998) Echoes of echoes? An episodic theory of lexical access. *Psychological Review*, 105: 251–79.

Gries, S. T. (2005) Syntactic priming: a corpus-based approach. *Journal of Psycholinguistic Research*, 34: 365–99.

Halpern, Y., and Moses, Y. (1990) Knowledge and common knowledge in a distributed environment. *Journal of the ACM*, 37: 549–87.

Hanna, J. E., Tanenhaus, M. K., and Trueswell, J. C. (2003) The effects of common ground and perspective on domains of referential interpretation. *Journal of Memory and Language*, 49: 43–61.

Hartsuiker, R.J., Pickering, M.J., and Veltkamp, E. (2004) Is syntax separate or shared between languages? Cross-linguistic syntactic priming in Spanish-English bilinguals. *Psychological Science*, 15: 409–14.

Hatfield, E., Cacioppo, J., and Rapson, R.L. (1994) *Emotional Contagion*. Cambridge University Press, New York.

Haywood, S. L., Pickering, M. J., and Branigan, H. P. (2005) Do speakers avoid ambiguities during dialogue? *Psychological Science*, 16: 362–6.

Hintzman, D. C. (1986) Schema abstraction in a multiple-trace memory model. *Psychological Review*, 93: 411–28.

Horton, W. S., and Gerrig, R. J. (2005a) Conversational common ground and memory processes in language production. *Discourse Processes*, 40: 1–35.

Horton, W. S., and Gerrig, R. J. (2005b) The impact of memory demands on audience design during language production. *Cognition*, 96: 127–42.

Horton, W. S., and Keysar, B. (1996) When do speakers take into account common ground? *Cognition*, 59: 91–117.

Hurley, S., and Chater, N. (eds) (2005) *Perspectives on Imitation*. MIT Press, Cambridge, MA.

Isaacs, E. A., and Clark, H. H. (1987) References in conversation between experts and novices. *Journal of Experimental Psychology: General*, 116: 26–37.

Keysar, B., Barr, D. J., Balin, J. A., and Brauner, J. S. (2000) Taking perspectives in conversation: the role of mutual knowledge in comprehension. *Psychological Science*, 11: 32–7.

Keysar, B., Barr, D. J., Balin, J. A., and Paek, T. S. (1998) Definite reference and mutual knowledge: process models of common ground in comprehension. *Journal of Memory and Language*, 39: 1–20.

Kraut, R. E., Fussel, S. R., and Siegel, J. (2003) Visual information as a conversational resource in collaborative physical tasks. *Human–Computer Interaction*, 18: 13–49.

Kraut, R. E., Lewis, S. H., and Swezey, L. W. (1982) Listener responsiveness and the coordination of conversations. *Journal of Personality and Social Psychology*, 43: 718–31.

Langton, S.R., and Bruce, V. (2000) You must see the point: automatic processing of cues to the direction of social attention. *Journal of Experimental Psychology: Human Perception and Performance*, 26: 747–57.

Levelt, W. J. M., and Kelter, S. (1982) Surface form and memory in question answering. *Cognitive Psychology*, 14: 78–106.

Logan, G. D. (1988) Toward an instance theory of automatization. *Psychological Review*, 95: 492–527.

Metzing, C., and Brennan, S. E. (2003) When conceptual pacts are broken: partner-specific effects on the comprehension of referring expressions. *Journal of Memory and Language*, 49: 201–13.

Pickering, M. J., and Branigan, H. P. (1998) The representation of verbs: evidence from syntactic priming in language production. *Journal of Memory and Language*, 39: 633–51.

Pickering, M. J., and Garrod, S. (2004) Toward a mechanistic psychology of dialogue. *Behavioral and Brain Sciences*, 27: 169–225.

Pickering, M. J., and Garrod, S. (2005) Establishing and using routines during dialogue: Implications for psychology and linguistics. In A.Cutler (ed.), *Twenty-First Century Psycholinguistics: Four Cornerstones*, pp. 85–102. Erlbaum, Mahwah, NJ.

Schenkein, J. (1980) A taxonomy for repeating action sequences in natural conversation. In B. Butterworth (ed.), *Language Production*, vol. 1: pp. 21–47. Academic Press, London.

Schiffer, S. R. (1972) *Meaning*. Oxford University Press, Oxford.

Schober, M. F. (1993) Spatial perspective-taking in conversation. *Cognition*, 47: 1–24.

Schober, M. F., and Brennan, S. E. (2003) Processes of interactive spoken discourse: the role of the partner. In A. C. Graesser, M. A. Gernsbacher, and S. R. Goldman (eds), *Handbook of Discourse Processes*, pp. 123–64. Erlbaum, Hillsdale, NJ.

Schober, M. F., and Clark, H. H. (1989) Understanding by addressees and over-hearers. *Cognitive Psychology*, 21: 211–32.

Schuller, A. M., and Rossion, B. (2001) Spatial attention triggered by eye gaze increases and speeds up early visual acuity. *NeuroReport*, 12: 381–86.

Shatz, M., and Gelman, R. (1973) The development of communication skills: modifications in the speech of young children as a function of listener. Monographs of the Society for Research in Child Development, 38.

Tannen, D. (1989) *Talking Voices: Repetition, Dialogue, and Imagery in Conversational Discourse*. Cambridge University Press, Cambridge.

Watkins, K., and Paus, T. (2004) Modulation of motor excitability during speech perception: the role of Broca's area. *Journal of Cognitive Neuroscience*, 16: 978–87.

Watson, M., Pickering, M. J., and Branigan, H. P. (2004) Alignment of reference frames in dialogue. *Proceedings of the 26th Annual Conference of the Cognitive Science Society.* Erlbaum, Mahwah, NJ.

CHAPTER 27

Grammatical encoding

Victor S. Ferreira and L. Robert Slevc

AT the heart of the faculty of language are the processes of grammatical encoding. Grammatical encoding has the task of selecting and retrieving the syntactic and lexical forms that can convey non-linguistic thoughts (Garrod and Pickering, Chapter 26 this volume), and then determining the morphological forms and their constituent ordering in preparation for their phonological spell-out (Meyer and Belke, Chapter 28 this volume) and eventual externalization by the oral (Fowler, Chapter 29 this volume) or manual (Emmorey, Chapter 43 this volume) articulators. As such, grammatical encoding processes most directly determine the gross characteristics of our individual utterances. Therefore, it is only a minor indulgence to claim that to understand why and how grammatical encoding carries out its duties is to understand a significant part of the why and how of language itself.

In this chapter, we describe the state of the field since the most recent prominent reviews of grammatical encoding were published about a dozen years ago (Bock, 1995b; Bock and Levelt, 1994). Following the lead of Bock (1995b), we do this primarily by describing the major debates that current research on grammatical encoding addresses. To situate these debates, section 27.1 broadly describes a consensus view of the general architecture of grammatical encoding (illustrated in Figure 27.1). This consensus holds that grammatical encoding consists of two component sets of sub-processes, one that deals with content and the other that deals with structure. Each set of sub-processes proceeds through two phases or stages, the first involving selection and the second involving retrieval. Section 27.2 then describes ongoing debates that operate within (or question aspects of) this consensus view, beginning with debates over this content-and-structure and selection-then-retrieval character of grammatical encoding. Next, section 27.3 describes two debates that have maintained a relatively high level of visibility, attesting to their fundamental status in the grammatical encoding literature: The first concerns the "incrementality" or "scope" of grammatical encoding (how far do we plan ahead in an utterance before beginning it?), and the second concerns the factors that influence syntactic choice (given an idea to express, why do we say what we say?). In section 27.4, we look forward to emerging debates in the field that are likely to receive increased attention in the coming years, largely due to the confluence of their central questions with other prominent and topical issues in cognitive science. These debates concern the relationship between grammatical encoding and eye movements, working memory, language disorders, and dialogue. With all this discussion of debate, it is easy to lose sight of the insights that the field has made and how our knowledge of the way grammatical encoding works has accumulated, and so section 27.5 closes on a constructive note, by highlighting two fundamental insights which we have gained along the way.

27.1 Grammatical encoding: a consensus model

Producing linguistic expressions involves encoding non-linguistic meanings, termed "preverbal messages" (Levelt, 1989) or "interfacing representations" (Bock, 1982), into a set of linguistic features that can ultimately be phonologically encoded. Though it is not part of the mandate of this chapter to detail the nature of preverbal messages, it is necessary to describe what theories of grammatical encoding generally require preverbal messages to represent.

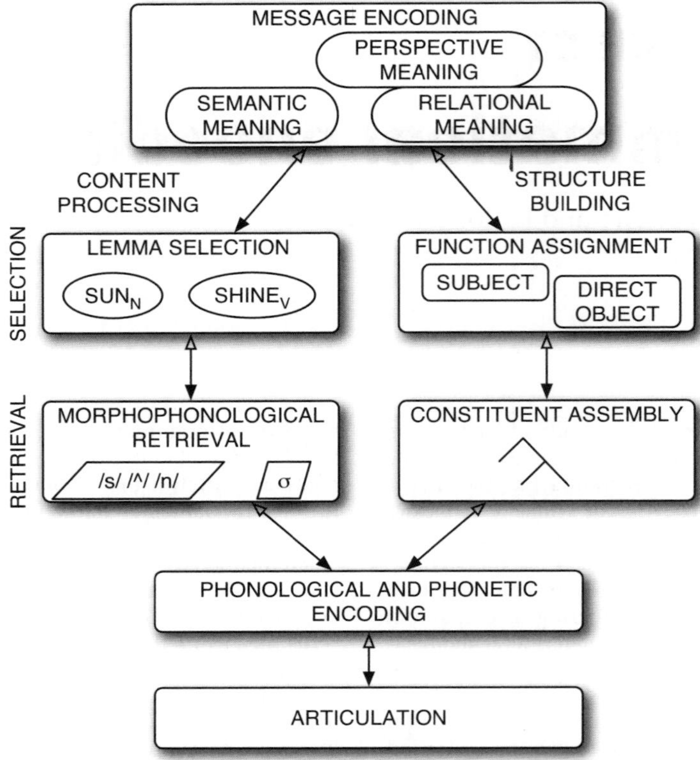

Figure 27.1 Schematic of consensus model of grammatical encoding. Filled arrowheads mark direction of primary information flow; open arrowheads mark possible feedback information flow.

27.1.1 **Message encoding**

Preverbal messages encode the meanings that speakers aim to express with their linguistic utterances. Preverbal messages are formulated by processes sometimes termed "message encoding" processes or the "message component" (Bock, 1995b; V. S. Ferreira, 2007), "conceptualization" processes (Levelt, 1989), or "referential arena processes" (Bock, 1982). The first step of message encoding is to specify the goal to be achieved by producing an utterance—whether to request something, provide information, guide action, and so forth. Any such "speech act" can only be carried out by expressing a meaning, and so the next step is to encode this meaning into the preverbal message. Meanings are encoded into what are here termed "events," which represent the "who did what to whom" that is to be expressed by linguistic utterances. Events include three specific aspects of meaning. "Semantic meaning" represents the *who*, *what*, and *whom* themselves—the semantic features of the expressed entities, states, and actions. "Relational meaning" represents how the who, what, and whom in the event relate to one another—who/what is performing which action or is in which state, who/what is having which action performed on it, and so forth. "Perspective meaning" represents which semantic or relational aspects of the event are more or less important—for example, which aspects are foreground or background, which are topic or comment, and which aspects have meaning added to them and which aspects are the added meaning.

For example, take the utterance *In San Diego, it's always sunny*. Someone might express this utterance to inform his or her interlocutor of a relevant observation (say, if they were discussing cities in southern California). This observation corresponds to an event in which the semantic meaning includes a representation of a geographical location that has the proper name *San Diego* and a state that is a weather condition brought on by unobstructed exposure to the sun. The relational meaning in the event involves attributing the state corresponding to the weather condition to the geographical location. The perspective meaning encodes that it is the geographical location that is the topic and the weather-state that is the added information (compared to, say, the meaning expressed by *It's always sunny in San Diego*).

27.1.2 **Grammatical encoding**

Once semantic, relational, and perspective meanings are encoded into at least part of a preverbal message, grammatical encoding can begin. Grammatical encoding consists of separable sub-processes that deal with formulating the content and specifying the structure of the eventual utterance. In turn, the content and structure sub-processes each proceed through two phases or stages (sometimes termed "functional" and "positional" processing; Bock, 1995b; Garrett, 1975; 1982; 1988), where linguistic features are selected from a candidate set, and then the properties of those selected linguistic features are retrieved.

27.1.2.1 Content sub-processes

Though this is possibly an oversimplification, the function of the content sub-processes of grammatical encoding is to select and then retrieve the details of the meaning-carrying or "content" words in an utterance. The first step of content processing is "lexical selection" (Bock, 1995b)—picking a set of words that "covers" (i.e. conveys a sufficient extent of) the semantic meaning represented in the preverbal message. This involves selecting lexical representations sometimes termed "lemmas" (Kempen and Huijbers, 1983; Levelt, 1989; Levelt et al., 1999) or "lexical entries" (Bock, 1995b) that attest to the existence of the appropriate meaning-covering words, and that act as pointers to the knowledge required for further processing of those words. Lemmas point to two sorts of knowledge. One is the grammatical knowledge necessary for the structure sub-processes to be discussed next, especially the form class of a word (noun, verb, etc.). The other is the knowledge necessary for the morphological, segmental, and metrical spell-out of the word. The retrieval of this morphophonological knowledge forms the second step of content processing, "lexical retrieval" (Bock, 1995b). Most theories of grammatical encoding claim that access to this metrical and phonological knowledge is mediated by distinct full lexical representations sometimes termed "lexemes" (Kempen and Huijbers, 1983; Levelt, 1989; Levelt et al., 1999) or "word forms" (see also Garrett, 1975).

For example, take the utterance *The sun shines.* Content sub-processes select and then retrieve the syntactic, morphological, and phonological details of the words *sun* and *shine*, but not the word *the* nor the suffix *-s* (which are not primary meaning-carrying words and so are termed "function" words). Lexical selection must determine the word that expresses the semantic meaning of the large gaseous body that warms the earth, and thereby select the lemma for *sun* (and not, say, *moon*), which in turn informs structure sub-processes that it is a noun. As the lemma for *sun* is accessed, lexical retrieval retrieves the singular count-noun morpheme for *sun* as well as its segmental content (/s/, /ʌ/, and /n/) and metrical specification (a single stressed syllable). A similar lexical-selection-then-lexical-retrieval process occurs for the word *shine*.

27.1.2.2 Structure sub-processes

While content sub-processes select and retrieve content words that convey semantic meaning, structure sub-processes select and retrieve the syntactic representations necessary to convey relational and perspective meaning. Like content processing, this occurs through two stages, first selecting "grammatical functions" (Garrett, 1975) and then retrieving "positional" (Garrett, 1975) or "constituent" (Bock, 1995b) structures necessary to realize those grammatical functions. For ease of description, we focus on the expression of relational meaning, returning to the role of perspective meaning below.

The first step in structure building has been termed "function assignment" (Bock, 1995b). It involves selecting grammatical functions—representations that relate one aspect of a linguistically encoded event to another—in accordance with the relational meaning represented in the preverbal message. For example, the "subject," "direct object," and "indirect object" grammatical functions relate entities in events expressed by nouns to actions or states in events expressed by verbs. Different "modifier" functions might relate a simple property in an event expressed by an adjective or a complex property expressed by a full clause to an entity expressed by a noun. Thus, function assignment involves consulting the relational meaning in a preverbal message, and determining which grammatical functions must be selected to cover that relational meaning.

Once selected, grammatical functions proceed through the second step of structure building, which has been termed "constituent assembly" (Bock, 1995b). This involves the retrieval of constituent structures that can express the grammatical functions selected at function assignment. In fixed word-order languages like English, this primarily involves arriving at a sequential ordering of words that convey the represented relational meanings. For example, in most English sentences, one of the nouns before a verb is the subject of that verb, and so a constituent structure must be assembled that specifies that sequential ordering. That is, to communicate *The sun shines*, constituent-assembly processes must make sure *sun* is mentioned before *shines*. This can be complicated because most sentences simultaneously express several aspects of relational meaning. For example, in *The bright sun that warms the earth shines*, both *bright* and *warms the earth* bear a relational meaning to *sun*, which in turn bears a relational meaning to *shines* (not to mention the relational meanings encoded in *that warms the earth*). In order for these multiple relations to be conveyed by a single sequence, constituent-assembly structures must appeal to hierarchical principles that determine how simultaneously expressed relational meanings can be embedded in one another so that an addressee can recover relational meaning from the resulting linear sequence. Free word-order languages like Japanese place less burden on sequential ordering, instead relying more heavily on affixes or "case markers" that use phonological content to convey relational meaning (e.g. the suffix *-o* applied to a noun indicates that it is the object of a verb, relatively independently of the positions of that noun and verb). The role of such affixes in structure building implies that function words and affixes (e.g. *the* and *-s* from *The sun shines*) are included as parts of constituent frames, rather than retrieved by content sub-processes (e.g. most especially Garrett, 1975). In short, relational meaning is expressed by an appropriate set of grammatical functions in an appropriate affixed sequence, as selected in the function assignment and constituent assembly stages of structure building, respectively.

This description of structure building has so far considered exclusively relational meaning; but perspective meaning also influences structure building in important ways that are often described as the "information structure" of an utterance (e.g. Lambrecht, 1994). This can be seen from the fact that a given relational meaning can be expressed with more than one combination of function assignments and constituent structures. Consider *In San Diego, it's always sunny* vs. *It's always sunny in San Diego*. Though these sentences express the same relational meaning, the different sequential orderings convey different perspective meanings, in that the first sentence is about San Diego and the second sentence is about always being sunny. Thus, perspective differences influence structure-building mechanisms by affecting both function assignment and constituent assembly processes. An example of perspective meaning primarily affecting function assignment is the difference between a sentence in the active and passive voice (which respectively assign the performer or "performee" of an action to the subject function), whereas an example of perspective meaning primarily affecting constituent assembly is the difference between the examples above (*In San Diego, it's always sunny* and *It's always sunny in San Diego*). Of course, perspective meaning could influence both stages of structure building, resulting in the production of complex perspective-communicating structures (e.g. clefts like *It is San Diego that is always sunny*).

27.1.3 On dividing and uniting

Together, the operations of the content and structure sub-processes of grammatical encoding, proceeding through their respective selection and retrieval stages, determine the gross-level characteristics of speakers' linguistic utterances. But the assumption that sentences are produced by independent content and structure sub-processes raises two thorny issues. First, why process content and structure separately? Second, if content and structure are processed separately, how are they brought together again?

The answer to the first question has to do with the sheer expressive power of language, in that we can describe with language almost any thought we can conceive, at least at some level of coarseness. This implies that the devices which create linguistic expressions must be systematic—they must be able to cover a comprehensive range of possible meanings—and they must be productive—they must be able to create, in principle, an infinity of possible linguistic expressions. This systematicity and productivity of language derives directly from the separation of content and structure. That is, because a linguistic expression is a combination of two relatively independent devices (content and structure), each of which expresses relatively independent aspects of meaning (semantic and relational/perspective meaning), these devices can be freely combined to express any semantic meaning arranged in any relational or perspective manner. If structure and content were not independent, then even if the separate semantic, relational, and perspective properties of an event were known, any previously unexperienced combination of those properties would not necessarily have a linguistic device for its expression. In short, it is the independent combination of content and structure that allows two bounded systems to express boundless meanings (for a similar argument with respect to thought processes, see Fodor and Pylyshyn, 1988).

But, if structure and content are processed separately, they must be brought together again if speakers are to produce a single utterance that combines content and structure. And, of course, the combination of content and structure has to be the *right* combination—the word that is used to express the subject of the verb better express the semantic features of the subject rather than say, the object (a process that sometimes goes awry in speech errors; for seminal observations, see Garrett, 1975). This has been dubbed the "coordination problem" (Bock, 1987a), and is a version of the more general "binding problem" in information science. (Another well-known example of the binding problem is that, because the identity and location of visually perceived objects are processed separately (e.g. Ungerleider and Haxby, 1994), perception processes must somehow keep track of which location corresponds to which identity.) At the moment, no complete solution to the coordination problem exists. Grammatical category labels (noun, verb, etc.) are likely to be critical, as are something akin to event- or thematic-role representations (agents, themes, goals, etc.). A different solution is to avoid the coordination problem altogether by claiming that content and structure are *not* represented separately, a point of view approaching that expressed by lexically based theories of syntax (e.g. F. Ferreira, 2000; Levelt, 1989; see section 27.2.2 below for further discussion on this debate). Progress on this issue awaits not only further research but also, probably, revolutionary insights into the way that cognitive mechanisms work.

27.2 **Fundamental debates: on stages and structures**

"Consensus" should not be confused with "unanimous." This section describes some of the challenges to the view just characterized that make it a consensus view and not a unanimous one. Along the way, we hope to show that, with some flexibility, enough semblance of the consensus framework can be maintained that its spirit survives (which has directed and structured research on grammatical encoding for over thirty years). Both major divisions in the consensus model have been questioned. We first discuss challenges to the idea that grammatical encoding consists of two separable stages (both with regard to content and to structure subprocesses), and then discuss challenges to the idea that content and structure are processed relatively separately.

27.2.1 **Does grammatical encoding proceed through two stages?**

The debate over the extent to which grammatical encoding can be characterized as involving staged mechanisms has played out mostly separately with respect to content and structure subprocesses, and so each is discussed in turn.

27.2.1.1 Content processing

The original modern-day view of lexical production (Garrett, 1975) and views that followed up on it (Levelt, 1989; Levelt et al., 1999) claimed that word production consults two stages of lexical representation. The first stage includes lexically specific representations that are critically syntactic in nature (i.e. one representation per word in the language, defined especially with respect to its form-class membership). This became the lemma level in current theoretical discourse. The second stage includes full word-form representations whose critical characteristic is a morphophonological nature. That this level was at least partly phonological in nature led to the claim that these representations are sound-form specific (e.g. *sun* and *son*, in all their meanings, share one of these representations), so that they became the *lexeme* level in current theoretical discourse. The syntactic-vs.-phonological distinction between these levels naturally leads to the view that the lemma level is modality-general (so that the same level is consulted in speaking or writing, hearing or reading), whereas the lexeme level is modality-specific.

A long-standing debate about these lexical representations concerns a detail of processing: is access to these stages *discrete* (Levelt, 1989; Levelt et al., 1999), in that lemmas must be fully selected before lexemes begin to be accessed? Or is access *interactive*, so that lexemes begin to be accessed even before a lemma is fully selected ("cascading"), possibly even allowing activated lexemes to influence lemma selection ("feedback"; Cutting and Ferreira, 1999; Dell, 1986; Dell et al., 1997b; Rapp and Goldrick, 2000)? This debate has maintained prominence due to its association with the modularity debate (Fodor, 1983) in psycholinguistics and cognitive science generally. It is worth noting, however, that even if processing is interactive, this leaves intact a fundamentally staged character to lexical production that Dell and O'Seaghdha (1991) termed "globally modular but locally interactive": processing still proceeds through stages of lexical selection and lexical retrieval; the debate simply concerns whether the dynamics of retrieval are influenced by the intermediate products of selection (cascading), and whether the dynamics of retrieval influence the timing or nature of selection (feedback).

A more recent challenge to the original view suggests that only one lexical stage operates during lexical production (for initial volleys, see Caramazza, 1997; Roelofs et al., 1998). Some previous models have assumed only one lexical level, either for reasons of substance or convenience (see e.g. Dell, Schwartz et al., 1997); however, these models typically assumed the sole level to be the lemma level. The new challenge suggests that the sole level of lexical representation has properties that cross-cut the distinction between lemma and lexeme. On the one hand, like lemmas, the representations are lexically specific (so *sun* and *son* have different lexical representations), but on the other hand, like lexemes, they are modality-specific (with different representations for speaking, writing, hearing, or reading). Implications of this different organization has led to tests of alternative predictions, leading to the current disagreement (Caramazza et al., 2004; Caramazza et al., 2001; Jescheniak et al., 2003).

It is important, however, to view this debate for what it is and what it is not. This challenge does not hold that production has anything other than a selection-then-retrieval character. Indeed, the one-level view is compatible with the claim that processing is discrete rather than interactive, and so in some ways is *more* staged than some versions of the two-lexical-level view. The entire debate can be summarized with the question of whether lemmas are modality specific—an important question that does not undermine the fundamental character of the consensus model described above.

This does raise the question of what kind of architecture *would* undermine the fundamental character of the consensus model. Two aspects of the consensus view are central to its selection-then-retrieval character. One is that it involves lexically specific representations—symbols of the content words in a speaker's vocabulary. The second is that these lexically specific representations mediate meaning and form. As long as lexical production requires moving through lexically specific representations to access phonological and eventually articulatory knowledge, then a selection-then-retrieval character is preserved (for a challenge to these kinds of assumptions in the domain of word reading, see Plaut et al., 1996; Seidenberg and McClelland, 1989).

27.2.1.2 Structure building

Beginning two decades ago, the discreteness-vs.-interactivity debate flared with respect to structure building, just as it had with lexical production. The question was whether function assignment could be influenced by the dynamics of constituent assembly. Some evidence suggested not (Bock, 1986a; Bock and Warren, 1985), whereas other evidence suggested so, at least indirectly (Bock, 1987b; Levelt and Maassen, 1981). Like the corresponding debate in lexical production, however, this question concerns an important processing detail of the consensus model that is relevant to its staged character, but not a fundamental challenge to that staged character.

A more recent challenge to this staged characterization comes from evidence gleaned from an especially powerful methodology for investigating structure building, namely "syntactic persistence" (which has also been termed "syntactic priming," "structural persistence," or "structural priming"—a neat 2 × 2 nomenclature design). Briefly, speakers tend to persist in the use of previously processed structures. This is typically investigated by assessing the effect of the structure of a *prime* sentence upon the subsequent production of a *target* sentence. For example, speakers who hear or say passive prime structures are likely to describe a subsequent picture with passive target descriptions, relative to whether they had heard or said active target descriptions (for a recent review, see V. S. Ferreira and Bock, 2006).

One research thread assessing syntactic persistence has explored whether constituent assembly has its own staged nature. That is, after the functional structure of an impending utterance is specified, do speakers first determine dominance relations in a constituent structure, and only afterwards *linearize* that structure into a specific word order? Evidence for this possibility is that mere word order appears to exhibit syntactic persistence (e.g. the difference in Dutch sentences like those meaning "On the table is a ball" and "A ball is on the table"; Hartsuiker et al., 1999; Hartsuiker and Westenberg, 2000; see also Vigliocco and Nicol, 1998). Alternatively, constituent structure may be undifferentiated, specifying dominance relations and linear order with a single integrated process. Evidence for this is that dominance relations by themselves do not exhibit persistence (e.g. structures like *The driver showed to the mechanic the overalls* does not cause the persistence of structures like *The patient showed the injury to the doctor*; Pickering et al., 2002).

A more fundamental challenge to the staged nature of structure building comes from recent modeling work by Chang (Chang, 2002; Chang et al., 2006; Chang et al., 2000), demonstrating that much of the evidence from syntactic persistence can be simulated by architecturally complex computational models which learn to generate sequences of words. These architectures do not work through a straightforward sequence of function assignment followed by constituent assembly. Instead, they work by developing sequencing representations akin to syntactic constructions which are triggered by a combination of lexical and event-semantic knowledge (as well as previous learning, leading to persistence). To the extent that these models can describe grammatical encoding successfully, they represent a different way of construing the structure-building process.

27.2.2 Where is the line between content and structure?

In cognitive science broadly, it is not uncontroversial to claim that structure and content are separately processed (see Fodor and Pylyshyn, 1988; Rumelhart and McClelland, 1986). Interestingly, this distinction is more firmly established within the sub-field of language production. Instead, the controversy with respect to theories of grammatical encoding has concerned the nature of the content and structure systems' representations.

The consensus model described above proposes a very neat line between content and structure: content sub-processes select and retrieve content words, structure sub-processes assign functions and build constituent structures. This view is often termed "frame-based," because it assumes structures which are strictly independent of content-word content (although structure building must be influenced by selected content words; for an initial proposal, see Garrett, 1975). A recurring challenge to this neat division comes from *lexically based* models of grammatical encoding (see especially Levelt, 1989), which claim that content words belong in the structure system, indeed forming the fundamental basis of the process of structure building.

A recent explicitly developed lexically based account of structure building comes from F. Ferreira (2000). This approach grounds structure building in a linguistic formalism called "lexicalized tree-adjoining grammar" (Joshi et al., 1975; Schabes et al., 1988). In a nutshell, the approach argues that grammatical encoding builds structure by retrieving content words that include elementary trees—component bits of syntactic structure that are unified by operations including "substitution," "adjoining," and, more recently, "overlay" (F. Ferreira et al., 2004). This kind of approach has the obvious advantage that it can straightforwardly account for how structure-building processes operate so that only certain grammatical options are used with certain content words. In a frame-based view, such lexical dependencies must either derive from distinctions represented in the preverbal message (which is not ideal, given that many such dependencies have little or no basis in meaning), or they must arise during the coordination process described above. On the other hand, lexically based accounts require additional processing machinery to explain lexically independent structure-building effects, most especially evidence that syntactic persistence occurs completely independently of lexical content (e.g. Pickering and Branigan, 1998).

A different view of the content/structure distinction comes from Pickering and Branigan (1998). This approach represents structure with "combinatorial nodes" that specify how content words can combine into constituent structures. Such nodes are viewed as similar to the traditional lemma nodes that are selected by content sub-processes; in fact, combinatorial nodes and lemma nodes form a kind of seamless network of grammar-encoding knowledge. Thus, this approach allows for the representation of the just-described lexical dependencies as well as the independence of constituent structure that is implied by patterns of syntactic persistence. From the perspective of the distinction between structure and content, this approach is mixed. Unlike the consensus view presented above, structure and content freely intermingle, but unlike lexically based approaches, structure knowledge (as represented by combinatorial nodes) and content knowledge (as represented by traditional lemmas) are fully distinct. (For a yet more integrated view of structure and content, see the superlemma approach of Sprenger et al., 2006.) In any case, the combinatorial-node-based approach is in principle compatible with a view of structure building that separates function assignment and constituent assembly, so long as function assignment can influence baseline activations of combinatorial nodes directly and constituent assembly is informed by the grammatical knowledge embodied by combinatorial nodes.

27.3 **Perennial debates: incrementality and syntactic choice**

Two particularly persistent debates in the literature on grammatical encoding concern the scope of grammatical planning and the factors influencing syntactic choice.

27.3.1 **Incrementality and the scope of planning**

Production is at least to some extent incremental (a property termed "Wundt's principle" by Levelt, 1989). This implies that grammatical encoding has two critical characteristics: it creates structure piecemeal and it does so unidirectionally. Basic evidence for incrementality is the influence of *accessibility* on grammatical encoding. Specifically, grammatical encoding processes tend to build sentence structures such that more accessible content words (e.g. ones that have been semantically primed; Bock, 1986a) are mentioned earlier than less accessible content words (more on this below). Given that more accessible words can be processed sooner, it makes sense that they would be mentioned earlier under two assumptions. First, grammatical encoding must create structures piecemeal, otherwise grammatical encoding processes would have to wait for all parts of the sentence to become accessible anyway. Second, grammatical encoding must operate unidirectionally, otherwise an accessible content word could be processed sooner even by assigning it to a later sentence position.

Whereas no clear evidence disputes the unidirectional nature of grammatical encoding, evidence for the piecemeal nature of grammatical encoding is less coherent. This is closely tied to the question of the *scope* of grammatical encoding: with respect to the eventually spoken utterance, how far ahead does the grammatical encoding process specify structure before production begins? The answer to this question is complicated by two factors. First, the scope of grammatical encoding probably varies by level of encoding, so that as production proceeds from "higher" levels (e.g. message encoding) to "lower" ones (e.g. phonological encoding), the scope of encoding narrows (for an elegant demonstration, see Dell, 1986). This can be seen in Garrett's (1975) original model, where the scope of planning at function assignment is a full clause and at constituent assembly is more phrase-like. Additional evidence supporting the idea that the highest levels of grammatical encoding involve a clause-sized scope of planning include patterns of elicited errors of subject–verb agreement (Bock and Cutting, 1992) and of pauses and hesitation during speech (Ford, 1982; Ford and Holmes, 1978). Other evidence shows that speakers can detect upcoming difficulty in a sentence surprisingly early, again suggesting substantial advanced planning (F. Ferreira and Swets, 2005). There is also evidence that the scope of planning narrows at later stages of encoding. For example, Meyer (1996) showed that when speakers produce short sentences, semantic distractors related to either subject or object nouns affected initiation times, suggesting that both nouns were semantically planned to some extent. However, phonological distractors only affected initiation times when related to subject nouns, suggesting that only the subject noun was phonologically planned (see also Wheeldon and Lahiri, 1997).

All of that said, other evidence suggests that the scope of planning at early levels of grammatical encoding can sometimes be narrower than the clause. In a pictures-description task, Smith and Wheeldon (1999) showed that speakers began utterances more slowly when the subject noun phrase was complex and the object noun phrase simple rather than vice versa. This suggests that more planning occurs for the subject noun phrase than for the object noun phrase before utterance onset. Similarly, Griffin (2001) measured speech-onset times and eye-movement patterns during a pictures-description task, and showed that lemma-level properties of names produced in direct object phrases did not affect performance; this suggests that those lemmas were not accessed prior to speech onset. These different degrees of planning scope, especially for earlier stages of grammatical encoding, probably occur because the degree to which speakers produce sentences incrementally appears to be strategically sensitive. This is illustrated directly by evidence from F. Ferreira and Swets (2002), who showed that speakers produced sentences more incrementally when under a production deadline.

27.3.2 Syntactic choice

The way that language works requires sentences which differ in meaning to also differ in form (setting aside ambiguity). Interestingly, the opposite claim is not so — sentences that differ in form do not always differ in meaning, at least not obviously. For example, the sentences *I know that San Diego is always sunny* and *I know San Diego is always sunny* differ, yet the difference in meaning between the two is extremely difficult to discover (as illustrated by the fact that papers appear every few years purporting to have done so; see e.g. Bolinger, 1972; Dor, 2005; Thompson and Mulac, 1991; Yaguchi, 2001). This raises an important question about grammatical encoding: When meaning does not guide speakers to produce one sentence form vs. another, what does?

The answer is that many factors seem to affect grammatical encoding relatively independently of meaning. Based on current research, we restrict the present analysis to just three. The first is syntactic persistence. Given a choice between two roughly meaning-equal syntactic structures, speakers tend to produce structures they have just experienced. Syntactic persistence is evident both in laboratory settings (Bock, 1986b) and in naturalistic production (Szmrecsanyi, 2004), in spoken as well as in written production (Pickering and Branigan, 1998), in isolated production as well as in dialogue (Branigan et al., 2000; Levelt and Kelter, 1982), in English, Dutch (Hartsuiker and Kolk, 1998), and German (Scheepers, 2003), and even from one language to another (Hartsuiker et al., 2004; Loebell and Bock, 2003). The reason why speakers persist in their production of syntactic structure is a matter of active debate (see V. S. Ferreira and Bock, 2006), but is probably motivated by reasons of efficiency (Bock and Loebell, 1990; Smith and Wheeldon, 2001), communication (see below; Pickering and Garrod, 2004), or learning (Chang et al., forthcoming).

The second set of factors relate to accessibility effects. Given a choice between two roughly meaning-equal structures, speakers tend to produce the one that allows for the earlier mention of more accessible sentence material. The range of factors which condition accessibility effects is impressively broad, including semantic priming (Bock, 1986a), semantic interference (V. S. Ferreira and Firato, 2002), phonological interference (Bock, 1987b), imageability (Bock and Warren, 1985; James et al., 1973), prototypicality (Kelly et al., 1986), co-reference (V. S. Ferreira and Dell, 2000), and salience or prominence (Prat-Sala and Branigan, 2000). (For additional review, see Bock, 1982; McDonald et al., 1993.)

One explanation for accessibility effects is that they make grammatical encoding proceed more efficiently. The idea is that if grammatical encoding is incremental, then producing accessible content sooner allows speakers to dispatch it sooner. This presumably circumvents the need to buffer that accessible content and buys time to access the remaining less accessible content. V. S. Ferreira (1996) provided evidence consistent with this possibility, by showing that speakers produced sentences more efficiently when grammatical encoding had more structural options available.

Under this explanation, accessibility effects might infringe on the influence of perspective meaning on grammatical encoding. Recall that speakers will produce different structures depending on what perspective they take on a situation, as represented by the perspective meaning represented in their preverbal message (*San Diego is always sunny* vs. *It is always sunny in San Diego*). At least some of such effects might be due to raw accessibility rather than to perspective meaning per se. An illustration of this distinction comes from Cowles and Ferreira (under revision), who suggested that when speakers mentioned one kind of argument earlier in sentences ("given" arguments), it was because of accessibility, whereas when they mentioned another kind of argument earlier in sentences ("topic" arguments), it was independent of accessibility.

A third set of factors which can influence grammatical encoding relatively independently of meaning are "audience-design" factors. Here, given a choice between two roughly meaning-equal structures, speakers might choose the one that would be easier for their addressee to understand (for review, see V. S. Ferreira and Dell, 2000). The most heavily investigated factor in this set has been ambiguity: all things equal, does grammatical encoding select a less ambiguous rather than a more ambiguous syntactic form?

Evidence concerning the effect of ambiguity on grammatical encoding has been mixed. Some evidence has shown that grammatical encoding processes do not preferentially select unambiguous structures, neither in spoken (V. S. Ferreira and Dell, 2000) nor written (Elsness, 1984) production, nor in dialogue (Kraljic and Brennan, 2005), nor with different kinds of structure (Arnold et al., 2004), nor with prosody (Allbritton et al., 1996; Schafer et al., 2000). Other evidence suggests that grammatical encoding might select unambiguous structures in highly interactive dialogue (Haywood et al., 2005), or in written form (Temperley, 2003), or with prosody (Snedeker and Trueswell, 2003). Keys to sorting out these mixed results probably include taking into account the effects of ambiguity-independent factors on syntactic choice (see V. S. Ferreira and Dell, 2000), and separating non-linguistic-ambiguity avoidance and linguistic-ambiguity avoidance (V. S. Ferreira et al., 2005).

27.4 **Emerging debates: relationships to input, storage, disorders, and dialogue**

Within grammatical encoding, certain current research threads have special promise for progress, due largely to their tight relationships to areas of active investigation in psycholinguistics or cognitive science. This includes work investigating eye movements, working memory, language disorders, and dialogue.

27.4.1 **Eye movements**

Research on language comprehension has benefited profoundly from the use of techniques for measuring eye movements (for a recent review and model, see Reichle et al., 1998), including a recent explosion in work on spoken-language comprehension (for seminal work, see Tanenhaus et al., 1995). The focus on comprehension was due partly to the natural fit between the functions of eye movements (to intake information) and comprehension (to understand linguistic expressions), and partly to the focus on comprehension research in psycholinguistics generally. This focus was also partly due to technological requirements of early eye movement apparatus—in particular, that they typically required the use of bite bars that interfered with spoken production. Recent technological advances, such as the development of free-viewing eye trackers, and the increasing prominence of language production research has begun to redress this imbalance.

Work investigating grammatical encoding with eye movement measures has addressed three related sets of questions. (1) What can eye movement techniques reveal about the processing stages of language production (see especially Griffin, 2001; Meyer et al., 1998; Meyer and van der Meulen, 2000)? (2) Why do speakers look where they look when describing scenes (see especially Griffin, 2004b; Griffin and Bock, 2000)? (3) How do the attentional and cognitive forces that drive eye movements influence syntactic choice (see Bock et al., 2003; Griffin and Bock, 2000) and the (in)accuracy of grammatical encoding (Griffin, 2004a)? As the use of eye movement measures continues to flourish, these investigations promise unprecedented insights into the workings of grammatical encoding.

A surprising result which has emerged from work investigating the first of the above questions is that speakers seem to fixate objects in displays well into the name-retrieval process. Most striking is evidence from Meyer and van der Meulen (2000) showing that priming the *phonological* characteristics of to-be-named objects influences fixation times to those objects, suggesting that speakers fixate objects until the sounds of their names are retrieved. Meyer (2004) considers two explanations for this effect. One is that the information uptake from the continuously fixated object may assist name retrieval. Another is that maintaining fixation avoids interference that might come from fixating other objects instead. However, a third explanation (see Griffin, 2004b) raises a kind of uncertainty problem with respect to eye movement techniques: it may be that when speakers describe displays that are in front of them (as opposed to what happens most of the time when people talk), aspects of the grammatical encoding processes non-trivially rely on the external display, which in turn influences speakers' eye movements. In particular, note that the primary task of constituent-ordering mechanisms is to correctly order the elements of linguistic representations, keeping track of which arguments have already been encoded and which arguments are yet to be encoded. An external display that places arguments in distinct spatial locations may act as a kind of mnemonic to help with this bookkeeping task (for a fleshing out of this analogy, see Bock, 1987a), and directing the eyes to those spatial locations may partially reflect the use of that mnemonic. Consequently, speakers may fixate pictures well into the name-retrieval process because doing so can help ensure the use of the right name at the right point in the sentence. An important upside to this possibility is that it may allow the use of external scenes and eye-tracking techniques to be a powerful tool for manipulating and measuring aspects of constituent assembly in a manner not yet seen in research on grammatical encoding.

27.4.2 **Storage**

The study of short-term or working memory has always held a prominent place in cognitive psychology (see Baddeley, 1986). Even so, recent years have seen increasing attention to working-memory research, presumably because the constructs of working memory are highly relevant to important and topical areas of investigation, including research on development, individual differences, aging, brain imaging, and cognitive control, among others (for review, see Miyake and Shah, 1999). The past fifteen years have also witnessed considerable research exploring the relationship between working memory and language comprehension (e.g. Caplan and Waters, 1999; Gibson, 1998; Just and Carpenter, 1992). Curiously, work on working-memory influences on language production has not seen comparable progress, despite the fact that, like comprehension, sentence production requires maintenance of linguistic and non-linguistic representations presumably in a working-memory-like store.

Still, some important work investigating the relationship between working memory and grammatical encoding has been reported. Kellogg (2004) explored the relationship between components of working-memory storage and written production using a dual-task technique, revealing that aspects of the grammatical-encoding process itself may be sensitive to the verbal-storage function of working memory. Martin and colleagues (Freedman et al., 2004; Martin and Freedman, 2001) tested patients with different kinds of short-term memory impairment, and found that patients with impaired lexical-semantic storage, but not patients with impaired input phonological storage, have trouble producing complex phrases (e.g. adjective–noun combinations; note the relationship to issues of planning scope, described above). Hartsuiker and Barkhuysen (2006) investigated the influence of working memory on the more syntactic process of subject–verb agreement, revealing that speakers with lower memory spans made more errors with increased memory load. Results like these provide clear evidence that working-memory performance is highly relevant to a variety of processes involved in grammatical encoding.

Future avenues of research that should prove especially informative and synthetic might aim to explore the role of working memory in the above-described factors that influence syntactic choice. In particular, both syntactic persistence effects and accessibility effects might involve retrieval processes that depend on working-memory functioning. Determining how those retrieval processes are affected by manipulations of, or individual differences in, working-memory processing should reveal important insights both about grammatical encoding specifically and about working memory more generally.

27.4.3 **Language disorders**

Theories of grammatical encoding and research on language-disordered populations have long enjoyed theoretical interaction (for seminal work, see Garrett, 1982). A recent and especially forward-looking research line has brought together work on language production, computational modeling, and disordered language production (Dell, Burger, and Svec, 1997; Dell, Schwartz et al., 1997; Foygel and Dell, 2000; Gordon and Dell, 2003). This work has aimed to simulate the nature of normal language production, impaired language production, and even the trajectory of language recovery. Two threads can be found within this research line. One (Dell, Schwartz et al., 1997; Foygel and Dell, 2000) considers word production and so is situated squarely within the domain of content processing described above. This work involved taking a selection-then-retrieval model of lexical access, configuring it so that it yields a language-unimpaired pattern of word-naming accuracy, and then simulating language impairment either through damage to activation-spreading and decay parameters (Dell, Schwartz et al., 1997) or to semantic or phonological parameters (Foygel and Dell, 2000). The resulting "lesioned" models, each fit to individual patients' patterns of word-naming accuracy, were used to predict performance in novel tasks (e.g. word repetition) and across the course of language recovery. This research has served to reinforce and extend the theoretical development in lexical access that has been gained in the last thirty years.

The other research thread is potentially more challenging to the consensus approach described above. Specifically, Gordon and Dell (2003) used implemented computational models to explore the possibility that certain patterns of language impairment might be due to a "division of labor" between semantic and syntactic factors with regard to the retrieval of the lexical content of utterances. The idea is that "light" verbs—ones with relatively little semantic content and whose use is thus more syntactically guided (e.g. *go*)—come to rely heavily on factors that influence structure building, whereas "heavy" verbs—ones with relatively more semantic content and whose use is thus more semantically guided (e.g. *fly*)—come to rely less on factors which influence structure building and more on content processes which retrieve lexical items. Such a trade-off between content processing and structure building does not form as fundamental a challenge to the distinction between these two classes of processes as has been seen in other domains (e.g. Dell et al., 1993; Plaut et al., 1996; Seidenberg and McClelland, 1989), but it nonetheless obliges the consensus view to explain how such interactions might arise. The lexically based approaches to structure building described above may be able to account for such interactions more easily than the frame-based approaches, because lexically based approaches can naturally account for content-structure dependencies whereas frame-based ones must ascribe such effects to the (not well-understood) coordination or binding that occurs between the products of content processing and structure building.

27.4.4 Dialogue

For decades, two lines of work in psycholinguistics have proceeded mostly separately. One, in which the consensus view is situated, views psycholinguistic theorizing as a branch of cognitive psychology, where the nature of general mechanisms is inferred from summary measures of performance during highly controlled tasks. The other line views psycholinguistic performance as language use (Clark, 1996)—as a set of tools that people use to accomplish goals in socially coordinated fashion. This work relies more on the logic and techniques used in the philosophy of language and linguistic pragmatics, observing and cataloguing performance to analyze language as a system of strategies. Study within this line focuses on *dialogue* contexts in which more than one interlocutor interact, usually in the performance of some game or task. The separation between these lines emerged partly from the heavy emphasis in the 1970s and 1980s on the study of reading—a socially impoverished setting for language use, to say the least. But valuably, in the last decade, the increasing prominence of research on language production and on spoken-language comprehension has encouraged a synthesis of these hitherto more independent lines.

Research on grammatical encoding has figured prominently in this synthesis. One relevant angle is the debate described above concerning the effects of audience design on syntactic choice (see also Brennan and Clark, 1996; Horton and Keysar, 1996; Schober and Brennan, 2003). Another angle that has become relevant to controlled research using dialogue is syntactic persistence. Branigan et al. (2000) reported robust syntactic persistence in a laboratory-based dialogue task, and the numerical size of these persistence effects was larger than that observed in previous, monologue-based demonstrations (e.g. Bock, 1986b). Pickering and Garrod (2004) brought this dialogue-based persistence effect together with research on similar semantic coordination effects (Garrod and Anderson, 1987) to propose a broad view of language use as "alignment-driven." The idea is that, in dialogue, interlocutors aim to coordinate their use of linguistic devices at all possible levels, so they use corresponding pronunciations, locutions (e.g. Clark and Wilkes-Gibbs, 1986), framing (Garrod and Anderson, 1987), and, most groundbreakingly, syntactic structures (Branigan et al., 2000) during conversation. The function of such alignment is to ultimately achieve corresponding "situation models," which can be considered analogous to preverbal messages in production theories, thereby achieving successful communication. In turn, this alignment approach to linguistic performance has come together with work in cognitive science more broadly on imitation (e.g. Iacoboni et al., 1999), embodiment (where cognitive representation is seen as critically "external" in nature; e.g. Barsalou, 1999), and "mirror-neuron" systems (whereby perception and action involve the same neural substrates; e.g. Rizzolatti et al., 1996) to form a distinct but prominent subfield within psycholinguistics. The resulting promise for cross-disciplinary interaction and unification is an extremely valuable strength of this view. Nonetheless, evidence that syntactic persistence confers the same communicative benefits as other forms of coordination during dialogue has not yet accumulated, and this is an important prerequisite for the full integration of syntactic persistence into this broader alignment framework.

27.5 Fundamental insights

Like any area of active inquiry, research on grammatical encoding is more easily characterized in terms of debate and disagreement than in terms of consensus and agreement. Nonetheless, the field has come a long way in the thirty (or so) years of its current incarnation. Below, we briefly mention two specific points on which little debate exists in mainstream theories of grammatical encoding, but on which there was at least uncertainty (if not outright rancor) in other areas or in times past.

27.5.1 Linguistic knowledge and non-linguistic knowledge are different

Every current approach to grammatical encoding postulates distinct non-linguistic and linguistic representational systems. Indeed, this separation was vital for the initial growth of the field, so that theories of grammatical encoding could develop without the burden of accounting for the nature of thought more generally. The assumption of linguistic/non-linguistic separation is not trivial. For language production, even Fodor (1983) rejected it. In other areas, there have been a number of well-known incursions on this assumption which have not managed to get a foothold in accounts of grammatical encoding. For example, the popularity of the Whorf–Sapir hypothesis has ebbed and flowed in the broader study of language over the twentieth century (see Boroditsky, 2001; Lucy, 1992; Whorf, 1956). According to this class of views, the nature of the linguistic devices offered by a language critically determines the thought patterns of those who use that language. Yet approaches to grammatical encoding have generally found it useful to postulate distinct representational systems for conceptual constructs vs. linguistic constructs (although a valuable middle ground comes from Slobin's (1996) "thinking-for-speaking" approach and related work). Similarly, views of psychological performance deriving from the behaviorist perspective (Skinner, 1957) aimed to reduce grammatical patterns to patterns of instrumental responses ingrained by reinforcement and punishment contingencies. Some connectionist and parallel-distributed-processing frameworks (Rumelhart and McClelland, 1986) could be viewed as neo-behaviorist in nature; yet it is notable that connectionist accounts of grammatical encoding of any comprehensiveness (e.g. Chang, 2002; Chang et al., 2006; Chang et al., 2000; Dell, 1986) involve a much richer and structured cognitive architecture than comparably comprehensive accounts of, say, reading (Plaut et al., 1996; Seidenberg and McClelland, 1989). Finally, the above-mentioned embodied approaches to cognition (e.g. Barsalou, 1999) promise a different way to blur the distinction between language and thought, namely by driving at least the perceptual characteristics of language into thought. Nonetheless, the account of grammatical encoding that is most embodied in nature (Pickering and Garrod, 2004) still includes independent and distinct representational systems for thought and for language. In short, among students of grammatical encoding, it is almost universally held that thinking and talking are different, and so are based on distinct systems of representation.

27.5.2 **Syntax is in there somewhere**

A constant tension in approaches to language acquisition and language comprehension is the status of syntactic representations. Some approaches (e.g. Frazier, 1988; Pinker, 1989) view syntactic knowledge as the irreducible basis of our grammatical knowledge. Others (e.g. MacDonald et al., 1994; Tomasello, 2000) view syntactic knowledge as derived from or reducible to other forms of knowledge, including conceptual and perceptual knowledge.

Among approaches to grammatical encoding, this tension is far less prominent, largely because some form of syntactic knowledge is seen as fundamental to how grammatical encoding works (as represented by the above described consensus model). Three lines of empirical work have led to this standpoint. The first comes from the speech-error observations that pioneered research on language production (Fromkin, 1971; 1973; Garrett, 1975). Specifically, it is notable that most speech-error investigations explore the fact that errant productions maintain their syntactic integrity, even when semantic integrity is compromised (see Bock, 1990). For example, because about 85 percent of word-exchange errors involve exchanging words that belong to the same grammatical categories (Garrett, 1975; Stemberger, 1985), the syntactic structures of errant utterances will conform to speakers' intentions (and will be well formed) even when their meanings do not (e.g. *That <u>log</u> could use another <u>fire</u>*, V. S. Ferreira and Humphreys, 2001; *She <u>sings</u> everything she <u>writes</u>*, Garrett, 1975). The second line is syntactic persistence. Most early work on syntactic persistence (see esp. Bock, 1986b; 1989; Bock and Loebell, 1990; Bock et al., 1992) determined that syntactic contributions to persistence are separate from conceptual, semantic, lexical, or phonological contributions. Twenty years later, the research landscape suggests that non-syntactic factors seem to influence syntactic persistence either independently of syntactic factors (e.g. Bock et al., 1992; Pickering and Branigan, 1998) or only when syntactic factors are neutralized (see esp. Chang, 2002; Griffin and Weinstein-Tull, 2003). The third line is work on the production of agreement (e.g. in English, verbs agree with the grammatical number of their subject). Specifically, patterns of agreement errors show that performance is heavily influenced by grammatical features (see Bock, 1995a) and hierarchical representation (e.g. Franck et al., 2002), with nonsyntactic influences (see Haskell and MacDonald, 2003; Thornton and MacDonald, 2003) of limited scope (Eberhard et al., 2005). Together, observations like these suggest that syntactic structures form the foundation of spoken utterances, in accordance with the approach described above.

27.6 Summary

How and why do speakers say what they say? The consensus model that opened this chapter provides a sketch of how: independent but mutually influential component systems which process structure and content proceed through stages of selecting linguistic features and then retrieving their details. How staged these processes are and where the line should be drawn between structure and content are subjects of active debate. The remaining debates outlined in this chapter provide a sketch of why speakers say what they say. In addition to the expression of meaning, speakers' utterances are influenced by incrementality of processing, the accessibility or persistence of linguistic features, audience design, working-memory demands, impairments due to brain damage, and influences during dialogue. Ongoing research will play out these debates, resolving some and generating others. This research trajectory is providing fundamental insights into the way that language works.

References

Allbritton, D. W., McKoon, G., and Ratcliff, R. (1996) Reliability of prosodic cues for resolving syntactic ambiguity. *Journal of Experimental Psychology: Learning, Memory, and Cognition*, 22: 714–35.

Arnold, J. E., Wasow, T., Asudeh, A., and Alrenga, P. (2004) Avoiding attachment ambiguities: the role of constituent ordering. *Journal of Memory and Language*, 51: 55–70.

Baddeley, A. D. (1986) *Working Memory*. Clarendon Press, Oxford.

Barsalou, L. W. (1999) Perceptual symbol systems. *Behavioral and Brain Sciences*, 22: 577–660.

Bock, J. K. (1982) Toward a cognitive psychology of syntax: information processing contributions to sentence formulation. *Psychological Review*, 89: 1–47.

Bock, J. K. (1986a) Meaning, sound, and syntax: lexical priming in sentence production. *Journal of Experimental Psychology: Learning, Memory, and Cognition*, 12: 575–86.

Bock, J. K. (1986b) Syntactic persistence in language production. *Cognitive Psychology*, 18: 355–87.

Bock, J. K. (1987a) Coordinating words and syntax in speech plans. In A. Ellis (ed.), *Progress in the Psychology of Language*, vol. 3, pp. 337–90. Erlbaum, London.

Bock, J. K. (1987b) An effect of the accessibility of word forms on sentence structures. *Journal of Memory and Language*, 26: 119–37.

Bock, J. K. (1989) Closed-class immanence in sentence production. *Cognition*, 31: 163–86.

Bock, J. K. (1990) Structure in language: creating form in talk. *American Psychologist*, 45: 1221–36.

Bock, J. K. (1995a) Producing agreement. *Current Directions in Psychological Science*, 8: 56–61.

Bock, J. K. (1995b) Sentence production: from mind to mouth. In J. L. Miller and P. D. Eimas (eds), *Handbook of Perception and Cognition*, vol. 11: *Speech, Language, and Communication*, pp. 181–216. Academic Press, Orlando, FL.

Bock, J. K., and Cutting, J. C. (1992) Regulating mental energy: Performance units in language production. *Journal of Memory and Language*, 31: 99–127.

Bock, J. K., Irwin, D. E., Davidson, D. J., and Levelt, W. J. M. (2003) Minding the clock. *Journal of Memory and Language*, 48: 653–85.

Bock, J. K., and Levelt, W. J. M. (1994) Language production: grammatical encoding. In M. A. Gernsbacher (ed.), *Handbook of Psycholinguistics*, pp. 945–84. Academic Press, San Diego, CA.

Bock, J. K., and Loebell, H. (1990) Framing sentences. *Cognition*, 35: 1–39.

Bock, J. K., Loebell, H., and Morey, R. (1992) From conceptual roles to structural relations: bridging the syntactic cleft. *Psychological Review*, 99: 150–71.

Bock, J. K., and Warren, R. K. (1985) Conceptual accessibility and syntactic structure in sentence formulation. *Cognition*, 21: 47–67.

Bolinger, D. (1972) *That's That*. Mouton, The Hague.

Boroditsky, L. (2001) Does language shape thought? Mandarin and English speakers' conceptions of time. *Cognitive Psychology*, 43: 1–22.

Branigan, H. P., Pickering, M. J., and Cleland, A. A. (2000) Syntactic co-ordination in dialogue. *Cognition*, 75: B13–B25.

Brennan, S. E., and Clark, H. H. (1996) Conceptual pacts and lexical choice in conversation. *Journal of Experimental Psychology: Learning, Memory, and Cognition*, 22: 1482–93.

Caplan, D., and Waters, G. S. (1999) Verbal working memory and sentence comprehension. *Behavioral and Brain Sciences*, 22: 77–126.

Caramazza, A. (1997) How many levels of processing are there in lexical access? *Cognitive Neuropsychology*, 14: 177–208.

Caramazza, A., Bi, Y. C., Costa, A., and Miozzo, M. (2004) What determines the speed of lexical access: homophone or specific-word frequency? A reply to Jescheniak et al. (2003). *Journal of Experimental Psychology: Learning Memory and Cognition*, 30: 278–82.

Caramazza, A., Costa, A., Miozzo, M., and Bi, Y. (2001) The specific-word frequency effect: implications for the representation of homophones in speech production. *Journal of Experimental Psychology: Learning, Memory, and Cognition*, 27: 1430–50.

Chang, F. (2002) Symbolically speaking: a connectionist model of sentence production. *Cognitive Science*, 26: 609–51.

Chang, F., Dell, G. S., and Bock, J. K. (2006) Becoming syntactic. *Psychological Review*, 113: 243–72.

Chang, F., Dell, G. S., Bock, J. K., and Griffin, Z. M. (2000) Structural priming as implicit learning: a comparison of models of sentence production. *Journal of Psycholinguistic Research*, 29: 217–29.

Clark, H. H. (1996) *Using Language*. Cambridge University Press, Cambridge.

Clark, H. H., and Wilkes-Gibbs, D. (1986) Referring as a collaborative process. *Cognition*, 22: 1–39.

Cowles, H. W., and Ferreira, V. S. (under revision) *The influence of information structure on sentence production*. MS.

Cutting, J. C., and Ferreira, V. S. (1999) Semantic and phonological information flow in the production lexicon. *Journal of Experimental Psychology: Learning, Memory, and Cognition*, 25: 318–44.

Dell, G. S. (1986) A spreading-activation theory of retrieval in sentence production. *Psychological Review*, 93: 283–321.

Dell, G. S., Burger, L. K., and Svec, W. R. (1997) Language production and serial order: a functional analysis and a model. *Psychological Review*, 104: 123–47.

Dell, G. S., Juliano, C., and Govindjee, A. (1993) Structure and content in language production: a theory of frame constraints in phonological speech errors. *Cognitive Science*, 17: 149–95.

Dell, G. S., and O'Seaghdha, P. G. (1991) Mediated and convergent lexical priming in language production: a comment on Levelt et al. *Psychological Review*, 98: 604–14.

Dell, G. S., Schwartz, M. F., Martin, N., Saffran, E. M., and Gagnon, D. A. (1997) Lexical access in aphasic and nonaphasic speakers. *Psychological Review*, 104: 801–38.

Dor, D. (2005) Toward a semantic account of *that*-deletion in English. *Linguistics*, 43: 345–82.

Eberhard, K. M., Cutting, J. C., and Bock, K. (2005) Making syntax of sense: number agreement in sentence production. *Psychological Review*, 112: 531–59.

Elsness, J. (1984) *That* or zero? A look at the choice of object clause connective in a corpus of American English. *English Studies*, 65: 519–33.

Ferreira, F. (2000) Syntax in language production: an approach using tree-adjoining grammars. In L. Wheeldon (ed.), *Aspects of Language Production*, pp. 291–330. Psychology Press/Taylor & Francis, Philadelphia, PA.

Ferreira, F., Lau, E., and Bailey, K. (2004) A model of disfluency processing based on tree-adjoining grammar. Paper presented at the Seventeenth Annual CUNY Conference on Human Sentence Processing, College Park, MD.

Ferreira, F., and Swets, B. (2002) How incremental is language production? Evidence from the production of utterances requiring the computation of arithmetic sums. *Journal of Memory And Language*, 46: 57–84.

Ferreira, F., and Swets, B. (2005) The production and comprehension of resumptive pronouns in relative clause 'island' contexts. In A. Cutler (ed.), *Twenty-First Century Psycholinguistics: Four Cornerstones*, pp. 263–78. Erlbaum, Mahwah, NJ.

Ferreira, V. S. (1996) Is it better to give than to donate? Syntactic flexibility in language production. *Journal of Memory and Language*, 35: 724–55.

Ferreira, V. S. (2007) How are speakers' linguistic choices affected by ambiguity? In A. S. Meyer, A. Krott, and L. R. Wheeldon (eds), *Language Processes and Executive Function*, pp. 63–92. Psychology Press, Hove, UK.

Ferreira, V. S., and Bock, J. K. (2006) The functions of structural priming. *Language and Cognitive Processes*, 21: 1011–29.

Ferreira, V. S., and Dell, G. S. (2000) Effect of ambiguity and lexical availability on syntactic and lexical production. *Cognitive Psychology*, 40: 296–340.

Ferreira, V. S., and Firato, C. E. (2002) Proactive interference effects on sentence production. *Psychonomic Bulletin and Review*, 9: 795–800.

Ferreira, V. S., and Humphreys, K. R. (2001) Syntactic influences on lexical and morphological processing in language production. *Journal of Memory and Language*, 44: 52–80.

Ferreira, V. S., Slevc, L. R., and Rogers, E. S. (2005) How do speakers avoid ambiguous linguistic expressions? *Cognition*, 96: 263–84.

Fodor, J. A. (1983) *The Modularity of Mind*. MIT Press, Cambridge, MA.

Fodor, J. A., and Pylyshyn, Z. W. (1988) Connectionism and cognitive architecture: a critical analysis. *Cognition*, 28: 3–71.

Ford, M. (1982) Sentence planning units: implications for the speaker's representation of meaningful relations underlying sentences. In J. Bresnan (ed.), *The Mental Representation of Grammatical Relations*, pp. 797–827. MIT Press, Cambridge, MA.

Ford, M., and Holmes, V. M. (1978) Planning units and syntax in sentence production. *Cognition*, 6: 35–53.

Foygel, D., and Dell, G. S. (2000) Models of impaired lexical access in speech production. *Journal of Memory and Language*, 43: 182–216.

Franck, J., Vigliocco, G., and Nicol, J. (2002) Subject–verb agreement errors in French and English: the role of syntactic hierarchy. *Language and Cognitive Processes*, 17: 371–404.

Frazier, L. (1988) Grammar and language processing. In F. J. Newmeyer (ed.), *Linguistics: The Cambridge Survey*, vol. 3: *Linguistic Theory: Extensions and Implications*, pp. 15–34. Cambridge University Press, Cambridge.

Freedman, M. L., Martin, R. C., and Biegler, K. (2004) Semantic relatedness effects in conjoined noun phrase production: implications for the role of short-term memory. *Cognitive Neuropsychology*, 21: 245–65.

Fromkin, V. A. (1971) The non-anomalous nature of anomalous utterances. *Language*, 47: 27–52.

Fromkin, V. A. (ed.) (1973) *Speech Errors as Linguistic Evidence*. Mouton, The Hague.

Garrett, M. F. (1975) The analysis of sentence production. In G. H. Bower (ed.), *The Psychology of Learning and Motivation*, vol. 9, pp. 133–77. Academic Press, New York.

Garrett, M. F. (1982) Production of speech: observations from normal and pathological language use. In A. Ellis (ed.), *Normality and Pathology in Cognitive Functions*, pp. 19–76. Academic Press, London.

Garrett, M. F. (1988) Processes in language production. In F. J. Newmeyer (ed.), *Linguistics: The Cambridge Survey*, vol. 3: *Language: Psychological and Biological Aspects*, pp. 69–96. Cambridge University Press, Cambridge.

Garrod, S., and Anderson, A. (1987) Saying what you mean in dialogue: a study in a conceptual and semantic co-ordination. *Cognition*, 27: 181–218.

Gibson, E. (1998) Linguistic complexity: locality of syntactic dependencies. *Cognition*, 68: 1–76.

Gordon, J. K., and Dell, G. S. (2003) Learning to divide the labor: an account of deficits in light and heavy verb production. *Cognitive Science*, 27: 1–40.

Griffin, Z. M. (2001) Gaze durations during speech reflect word selection and phonological encoding. *Cognition*, 82: B1–B14.

Griffin, Z. M. (2004a) The eyes are right when the mouth is wrong. *Psychological Science*, 15: 814–21.

Griffin, Z. M. (2004b) Why look? Reasons for eye movements related to language production. In J. M. Henderson and F. Ferreira (eds), *The Interface of Language, Vision, and Action: Eye Movements and the Visual World*, pp. 213–48. Psychology Press, New York.

Griffin, Z. M., and Bock, K. (2000) What the eyes say about speaking. *Psychological Science*, 11: 274–79.

Griffin, Z. M., and Weinstein-Tull, J. (2003) Conceptual structure modulates structural priming in the production of complex sentences. *Journal of Memory and Language*, 49: 537–55.

Hartsuiker, R. J., and Barkhuysen, P. N. (2006) Language production and working memory: the case of subject–verb agreement. *Language and Cognitive Processes*, 21: 181–204.

Hartsuiker, R. J., and Kolk, H. H. J. (1998) Syntactic persistence in Dutch. *Language and Speech*, 41: 143–84.

Hartsuiker, R. J., Kolk, H. H. J., and Huiskamp, P. (1999) Priming word order in sentence production. *Quarterly Journal of Experimental Psychology: Human Experimental Psychology*, 52: 129–47.

Hartsuiker, R. J., Pickering, M. J., and Veltkamp, E. (2004) Is syntax separate or shared between languages? Crosslinguistic syntactic priming in Spanish-English bilinguals. *Psychological Science*, 15: 409–14.

Hartsuiker, R. J., and Westenberg, C. (2000) Word order priming in written and spoken sentence production. *Cognition*, 75: B27–B39.

Haskell, T. R., and MacDonald, M. C. (2003) Conflicting cues and competition in subject–verb agreement. *Journal Of Memory And Language*, 48: 760–78.

Haywood, S. L., Pickering, M. J., and Branigan, H. P. (2005) Do speakers avoid ambiguity during dialogue? *Psychological Science*, 16: 362–6.

Horton, W. S., and Keysar, B. (1996) When do speakers take into account common ground? *Cognition*, 59: 91–117.

Iacoboni, M., Woods, R. P., Brass, M., Bekkering, H., Mazziotta, J. C., and Rizzolatti, G. (1999) Cortical mechanisms of human imitation. *Science*, 286: 2526–8.

James, C. T., Thompson, J. G., and Baldwin, J. M. (1973) The reconstructive process in sentence memory. *Journal of Verbal Learning and Verbal Behavior*, 12: 51–63.

Jescheniak, J. D., Meyer, A. S., and Levelt, W. J. M. (2003) Specific-word frequency is not all that counts in speech production: comments on Caramazza, Costa et al. (2001) and new experimental data. *Journal of Experimental Psychology: Learning Memory and Cognition*, 29: 432–8.

Joshi, A. K., Levy, L., and Takahashi, M. (1975) Tree adjunct grammars. *Journal of the Computer and System Sciences*, 10: 136–63.

Just, M. A., and Carpenter, P. A. (1992) A capacity theory of comprehension: individual differences in working memory. *Psychological Review*, 99: 122–49.

Kellogg, R. T. (2004) Working memory components in written sentence generation. *American Journal of Psychology*, 117: 341–61.

Kelly, M. H., Bock, J. K., and Keil, F. C. (1986) Prototypicality in a linguistic context: effects on sentence structure. *Journal of Memory and Language*, 25: 59–74.

Kempen, G., and Huijbers, P. (1983) The lexicalization process in sentence production and naming: indirect election of words. *Cognition*, 14: 185–209.

Kraljic, T., and Brennan, S. E. (2005) Prosodic disambiguation of syntactic structure: for the speaker or for the addressee? *Cognitive Psychology*, 50: 194–231.

Lambrecht, K. (1994) *Information Structure and Sentence Form*. Cambridge University Press, Cambridge.

Levelt, W. J. M. (1989) *Speaking: From Intention to Articulation*. MIT Press, Cambridge, MA.

Levelt, W. J. M., and Kelter, S. (1982) Surface form and memory in question answering. *Cognitive Psychology*, 14: 78–106.

Levelt, W. J. M., and Maassen, B. (1981) Lexical search and order of mention in sentence production. In W. Klein and W. Levelt (eds), *Crossing the Boundaries in Linguistics*, pp. 221–52. Reidel, Dordrecht.

Levelt, W. J. M., Roelofs, A., and Meyer, A. S. (1999) A theory of lexical access in speech production. *Behavioral and Brain Sciences*, 22: 1–75.

Loebell, H., and Bock, K. (2003) Structural priming across languages. *Linguistics*, 41: 791–824.

Lucy, J. A. (1992) *Grammatical Categories and Cognition: A Case Study of the Linguistic Relativity Hypothesis*. Cambridge University Press, Cambridge.

MacDonald, M. C., Pearlmutter, N. J., and Seidenberg, M. S. (1994) The lexical nature of syntactic ambiguity resolution. *Psychological Review*, 101: 676–703.

Martin, R. C., and Freedman, M. L. (2001) Short-term retention of lexical-semantic representations: implications for speech production. *Memory*, 9: 261–80.

McDonald, J. L., Bock, J. K., and Kelly, M. H. (1993) Word and world order: semantic, phonological, and metrical determinants of serial position. *Cognitive Psychology*, 25: 188–230.

Meyer, A. S. (1996) Lexical access in phrase and sentence production: results from picture–word interference experiments. *Journal of Memory and Language*, 35: 477–96.

Meyer, A. S. (2004) The use of eye tracking in studies of sentence generation. In J. M. Henderson and F. Ferreira (eds), *The Interface of Language, Vision, and Action: Eye Movements and the Visual World*, pp. 191–212. Psychology Press, New York.

Meyer, A. S., Sleiderink, A. M., and Levelt, W. J. M. (1998) Viewing and naming objects: eye movements during noun phrase production. *Cognition*, 66: B25–B33.

Meyer, A. S., and van der Meulen, F. F. (2000) Phonological priming effects on speech onset latencies and viewing times in object naming. *Psychonomic Bulletin and Review*, 7: 314–19.

Miyake, A., and Shah, P. (eds) (1999) *Models of Working memory: Mechanisms of Active Maintenance and Executive Control*. Cambridge University Press, Cambridge.

Pickering, M. J., and Branigan, H. P. (1998) The representation of verbs: evidence from syntactic priming in language production. *Journal of Memory and Language*, 39: 633–51.

Pickering, M. J., Branigan, H. P., and McLean, J. F. (2002) Constituent structure is formulated in one stage. *Journal of Memory and Language*, 46: 586–605.

Pickering, M. J., and Garrod, S. (2004) Toward a mechanistic psychology of dialogue. *Behavioral and Brain Sciences*, 27: 169–226.

Pinker, S. (1989) *Learnability and Cognition: The Acquisition of Argument structure*. MIT Press, Cambridge, MA.

Plaut, D. C., McClelland, J. L., Seidenberg, M. S., and Patterson, K. (1996) Understanding normal and impaired word reading: computational principles in quasi-regular domains. *Psychological Review*, 103: 56–115.

Prat-Sala, M., and Branigan, H. P. (2000) Discourse constraints on syntactic processing in language production: a crosslinguistic study in English and Spanish. *Journal of Memory and Language*, 42: 168–82.

Rapp, B., and Goldrick, M. (2000) Discreteness and interactivity in spoken word production. *Psychological Review*, 107: 460–99.

Reichle, E. D., Pollatsek, A., Fisher, D. L., and Rayner, K. (1998) Toward a model of eye movement control in reading. *Psychological Review*, 105: 125–57.

Rizzolatti, G., Fadiga, L., Gallese, V., and Fogassi, L. (1996) Premotor cortex and the recognition of motor actions. *Cognitive Brain Research*, 3: 131–41.

Roelofs, A., Meyer, A. S., and Levelt, W. J. M. (1998) A case for the lemma/lexeme distinction in models of speaking: comment on Caramazza and Miozzo (1997). *Cognition*, 69: 219–30.

Rumelhart, D. E., and McClelland, J. L. (1986) On learning the past tenses of English verbs. In J. L. McClelland and D. E. Rumelhart (eds), *Parallel Distributed Processing*, vol. 2: *Psychological and Biological Models*, pp. 216–71. MIT Press, Cambridge, MA.

Schabes, Y., Abeille, A., and Joshi, A. K. (1988) New parsing strategies for tree adjoining grammars. Paper presented at the 12th International Conference on Computational Linguistics, Budapest.

Schafer, A. J., Speer, S. R., Warren, P., and White, S. D. (2000) Intonational disambiguation in sentence production and comprehension. *Journal of Psycholinguistic Research*, 29: 169–82.

Scheepers, C. (2003) Syntactic priming of relative clause attachments: persistence of structural configuration in sentence production. *Cognition*, 89: 179–205.

Schober, M. F., and Brennan, S. E. (2003) Processes of interactive spoken discourse: the role of the partner. In A. C. Graesser and M. A. Gernsbacher (eds), *Handbook of Discourse Processes*, pp. 123–64. Erlbaum, Mahwah, NJ.

Seidenberg, M. S., and McClelland, J. L. (1989) A distributed, developmental model of word recognition and naming. *Psychological Review*, 96: 523–568.

Skinner, B. F. (1957) *Verbal Behavior*. McGraw-Hill, New York.

Slobin, D. I. (1996) From 'thought and language' to 'thinking for speaking'. In J. Gumperz and S. C. Levinson (eds), *Rethinking Linguistic Relativity*, pp. 70–96. Cambridge University Press, Cambridge.

Smith, M., and Wheeldon, L. (1999) High level processing scope in spoken sentence production. *Cognition*, 73: 205–46.

Smith, M., and Wheeldon, L. (2001) Syntactic priming in spoken sentence production: an online study. *Cognition*, 78: 123–64.

Snedeker, J., and Trueswell, J. (2003) Using prosody to avoid ambiguity: effects of speaker awareness and referential context. *Journal of Memory and Language*, 48: 103–30.

Sprenger, S. A., Levelt, W. J. M., and Kempen, G. (2006) Lexical access during the production of idomatic phrases. *Journal of Memory and Language*, 54: 161–84.

Stemberger, J. P. (1985) An interactive activation model of language production. In A. Ellis (ed.), *Progress in the Psychology of Language*, vol. 1, pp. 143–86. Erlbaum, London.

Szmrecsanyi, B. (2004) Persistence phenomena in the grammar of spoken English. Ph.D. dissertation, Albert-Ludwigs-Universität Freiburg, Germany.

Tanenhaus, M. K., Spivey-Knowlton, M. J., Eberhard, K. M., and Sedivy, J. C. (1995) Integration of visual and linguistic information in spoken language comprehension. *Science*, 268: 1632–4.

Temperley, D. (2003) Ambiguity avoidance in English relative clauses. *Language*, 79: 464–84.

Thompson, S. A., and Mulac, A. (1991) The discourse conditions for the use of the complementizer *that* in conversational English. *Journal of Pragmatics*, 15: 237–51.

Thornton, R., and MacDonald, M. C. (2003) Plausibility and grammatical agreement. *Journal of Memory and Language*, 48: 740–59.

Tomasello, M. (2000) Do young children have adult syntactic competence? *Cognition*, 74: 209–53.

Ungerleider, L. G., and Haxby, J. V. (1994) 'What' and 'where' in the human brain. *Current Opinion in Neurobiology*, 4: 157–65.

Vigliocco, G., and Nicol, J. (1998) Separating hierarchical relations and word order in language production: is proximity concord syntactic or linear? *Cognition*, 68: B13–B29.

Wheeldon, L., and Lahiri, A. (1997) Prosodic units in speech production. *Journal of Memory and Language*, 37: 356–81.

Whorf, B. L. (1956) The relation of habitual thought and behavior to language. In J. B. Carroll (ed.), *Language, Thought, and Reality: Selected Writings of Benjamin Lee Whorf*. MIT Press, Cambridge, MA.

Yaguchi, M. (2001) The function of the non-deictic that in English. *Journal of Pragmatics*, 33: 1125–55.

CHAPTER 28

Word form retrieval in language production

Antje S. Meyer and Eva Belke

MODELS of word production often distinguish between processes concerning the selection of a single word unit from the mental lexicon and the retrieval of the associated word form (e.g. Butterworth, 1980; Garrett, 1980; Levelt, 1989). In the present chapter we will first explain the motivation for this distinction and then discuss the retrieval of word forms in more detail.

28.1 Lexical selection and word form retrieval

Evidence supporting the distinction between lexical selection and word form retrieval comes from a variety of sources. First, contextual speech errors that involve entire words differ in important respects from errors involving individual segments. The interacting words in whole-word errors, such as *threw the window through the clock* (Fromkin 1973),[1] typically appear in different phrases and are members of the same syntactic category. By contrast, the words involved in sound errors (*caught torses* instead of *taught courses*) tend to belong to the same phrase, often appear adjacent to each other, and often differ in syntactic category (Dell, 1986; Garrett, 1975; 1980; see also Meyer, 1992). Based on this and related evidence Garrett (1975; 1980) proposed that speakers first generated a representation capturing the content of the utterance, where the planning units corresponded roughly to clauses, and then generated the syntactic surface structure of the utterance and its morphological and phonological form using phrases as planning units (see also Bock and Levelt, 1994; Levelt, 1989). Experimental studies support the view that speakers use different planning spans at different planning levels, and specifically that the planning span is wider at the semantic-syntactic level than at the phonological level (e.g. F. Ferreira and Swets, 2002; Jescheniak, Schriefers, and Hantsch, 2003; Meyer, 1996; Smith and Wheeldon, 1999).

Second, speakers sometimes experience "tip of the tongue" (TOT) states, i.e. they have a strong feeling of knowing a word, have access to its meaning and syntactic properties (e.g. its grammatical gender), but cannot retrieve the complete phonological form (e.g. Brown and McNeill, 1966; Vigliocco et al., 1997). Sometimes, information about the length of the word, its stress pattern, or some of its phonemes is available. TOT states demonstrate that the lexical representations of words consist of several components, which must be retrieved in separate processing steps. This view is supported by neuropsychological evidence: There are case studies of brain-damaged patients who are considerably more impaired in accessing the semantic properties of words than the phonological properties, and of patients who show the opposite pattern. These dissociations constitute strong evidence for the assumption of separate semantic and phonological representations of words (e.g. Cuetos et al., 2000; Caramazza et al., 2000; see also Caramazza and Miozzo, 1997; Dell, Schwartz et al., 1997).

Finally, there is a substantial body of experimental evidence concerning the time course of lexical access, demonstrating that information about the semantic and syntactic properties of words becomes available slightly before their

[1] All speech errors, except for those marked otherwise, stem from Fromkin (1973).

phonological forms (e.g. Indefrey and Levelt, 2004; Jescheniak et al., 2002; Schmitt et al., 2000; Schriefers et al., 1990; van Turennout et al., 1998).

While models of lexical retrieval generally agree on the broad distinction between semantic-syntactic and word form retrieval processes, they differ with regard to the precise architecture of the system. Important issues that are currently under debate are, first, the relationship between semantic, syntactic, and morphophonological units and, second, the time-course of the activation of these units. In the family of models proposed by Dell and collaborators (e.g. Dell 1986; 1988; Dell, Burger, and Svec, 1997) and by Levelt and collaborators (e.g. Levelt 1989; 1992; Levelt et al., 1991; 1999), access to morphophonological units is syntactically mediated. For instance, in Levelt's model, speakers first select a syntactic word unit (a lemma) and then the associated morphological and phonological units. Similarly, in Dell's model, activation spreads from conceptual to syntactic to morphophonological units. By contrast, the Independent Network model of language production proposed by Caramazza and colleagues (Caramazza, 1997; Caramazza and Miozzo, 1997) consists of three networks for lexical-semantic, phonological and syntactic information, respectively. Lexical-semantic representations directly and in parallel activate syntactic representations and phonological representations; i.e. word form activation is not syntactically mediated. Neuropsychological evidence supporting this view comes from studies of patients who are unable to access the grammatical representations of certain types of words but can access their phonological properties (e.g. Caramazza and Miozzo, 1997). Experimental evidence from healthy speakers concerns the representation of homophones, such as *buoy/boy* or *bat* (animal/baseball bat). According to models assuming syntactic mediation, these word pairs have distinct semantic and syntactic representations but a *shared* morphophonological representation. Given that word frequency is commonly assumed to affect the speed of word form retrieval, these models predict that a low-frequency member of a homophonous pair, such as *buoy*, should be produced as fast as its high-frequency sibling (*boy* in the example). By contrast, in the Independent Network model, the members of homophonous word pairs have distinct lexical-semantic representations, which are linked to distinct word form representations. Therefore, a low-frequency word with a high-frequency homophonous sibling should be produced as slowly as an equally low-frequency word without such a sibling. In the empirical studies both patterns of results have been observed (Caramazza et al., 2001; 2004; Jescheniak and Levelt, 1994; Jescheniak, Meyer, and Levelt. 2003; Miozzo et al., 2004; see also Shatzman and Schiller, 2004).

With respect to their assumptions about the time course of the retrieval of different types of information, models can be broadly classified as serial stage vs. cascaded models. According to serial stage models (e.g. Bloem and La Heij, 2003; Levelt, 1989; Levelt et al., 1999; Roelofs, 1992; 1997a; 1997b; see also Levelt, 1999), word planning consists of a set of discrete stages that are completed in a specific temporal order. This view entails that information about the morphophonological form of a word only becomes available after a superordinate representation (a concept in Bloem and La Heij's (2003) model and a lemma in the models proposed by Levelt et al. (1999) and by Roelofs, 1992; 1997a; 1997b) has been selected to be part of the utterance. By contrast, according to cascaded models, word planning consists of processing steps that are temporally ordered but may overlap in time (e.g. Caramazza, 1997; Dell 1986; Dell, Burger, and Svec, 1997; Humphreys et al., 1988; MacKay, 1987; Stemberger, 1985). On this view, conceptual activation suffices for word form information to become activated. The selection of concepts or lemmas is not a necessary condition for word form retrieval. Some cascaded models of lexical access (e.g. Dell, 1986; Dell, Schwartz et al., 1997; MacKay, 1987; Rapp and Goldrick, 2000; Stemberger, 1985) assume feedback from lower to higher levels of processing, such that, for instance, the ease of retrieving the forms of words can affect which words speakers might choose. Researchers have used a variety of techniques to decide between these views (e.g. Bloem and La Heij, 2003; Costa et al., 2000; Costa et al., 1999; Cutting and Ferreira, 1999; V. S. Ferreira and Griffin, 2003; Jescheniak, Hahne, and Schriefers et al., 2003; Jescheniak and Schriefers, 1998; Levelt et al., 1991; Peterson and Savoy, 1998; Rahman et al., 2003; Rapp and Goldrick, 2000). In our view, the bulk of the evidence suggests cascaded processing, possibly with some feedback between adjacent processing levels (see also Dell and O'Seaghdha 1991; 1992; Dell, Burger, and Svec, 1997; Harley, 1984; Rapp and Goldrick, 2000).

In sum, in all current models of word production the processes and representations involved in word form retrieval are distinguished from those involved in accessing the semantic and syntactic properties of words. Current controversies concern the relationships between these different types of representations and processes.

Below, word form retrieval will be considered in more detail. Following the distinctions in linguistic theory, it is usually divided into three components, morphological, phonological, and phonetic encoding, which we will discuss in turn.

28.2 Morphological encoding

Many words (e.g. *spoon*, *umbrella*) consist of a single morpheme. Other words consist of two or more morphemes (which are discrete units contributing to the word meaning; see Spencer, 1991), for instance a modifier and a head noun (*pancake*), a verb stem and a suffix (*eating*) or a prefix, a stem, and a suffix (*disrespectful*). There is abundant informal evidence that speakers have access to morphological knowledge. For instance, speakers can produce and understand novel compounds (*banana guard*, *e-shopping*) and inflect them according to the rules of the language (*e-shopper's nightmare*). In addition, the way speakers syllabify and stress words reflects their morphological structure. For example, we say *dis.ad.van.tage* (but *di.saster*) rather than *di.sad.van.tage*, preserving the integrity of the affix *dis-*. Finally, speakers sometimes commit errors such as *a hole full of floors* (V. S. Ferreira and K. R. Humphreys, 2001), in which noun stems exchange leaving an affix behind, or errors such as *his dependment—his dependence on the government* (MacKay, 1979), in which bound morphemes are attached to incorrect stems (see also Cutler,1980; Pillon, 1998). These errors demonstrate that stems and affixes are retrieved independently of each other (see also Marslen-Wilson, Chapter 11 this volume).

Levelt et al. (1999) distinguished three ways in which complex forms could be called upon in word production: by a single concept, linked to a lemma and a diacritic (e.g. *boy* + plural), by a single concept linked to two lemmas (as in semantically opaque compounds, such as *butterfly* or *parachute*), and by multiple concepts mapping onto multiple lemmas (as in semantically transparent compounds, such as *woodwork* or *pancake*). In their model, all complex forms are composed from their constituent morphemes.

Roelofs (1996; 1998) studied the production of Dutch compounds and verb–particle combinations (such as *look up*, *shut down*) using a method called "implicit priming." Participants first learned to associate pairs of words (such as *highway–bypass*, *passenger–bystander*, *rule–bylaw*). On each of the following test trials, the first member of a pair (e.g. *highway*) was presented and the participants produced the second member (*bypass*) as quickly as possible. Each word pair was tested several times in random order. The crucial feature of the paradigm is that items are combined in such a way that the responses in a block of trials are either related (as in the example, where all response words begin with *by-*) or unrelated. A robust finding is that participants produce the response words faster when they share one or more word-initial segments than when they are unrelated (Meyer 1990; 1991). The most important result of Roelofs's experiments was that the implicit priming effect was stronger when the responses shared a complete morpheme (as in the above example) than when they merely shared a syllable including the same number of segments (as in *bible*, *biker*, *biceps*). Thus, there was a specific morphological priming effect. Roelofs and Baayen (2002) showed that the size of this priming effect was the same for transparent compounds (such as *sunshine*) as for opaque compounds (such as *butterfly*), demonstrating that the effect did not have a semantic basis. A morphological priming effect was found when the responses shared a word-initial morpheme but not when they shared a word-final morpheme (Roelofs 1996; 1998). This demonstrates that speakers build compounds and verb–participle combinations by selecting the component morphemes and concatenating them, beginning with the word-initial morpheme.

Using a similar paradigm, Janssen et al. (2002; 2004) investigated how Dutch speakers generate inflected verb forms. In line with the results of the speech error research, they concluded that speakers built these forms by inserting stems and affixes into independently generated morphological frames (see also V. S. Ferreira and K. R. Humphreys, 2001).

The implicit priming experiments carried out by Roelofs and collaborators demonstrate the autonomy of a morphological planning level from a semantic and phonological level. Further evidence for the autonomy of morphological representations stems from studies by Zwitserlood and collaborators, who used short-lag and long-lag priming paradigms (Dohmes et al., 2004; Zwitserlood et al., 2000; 2002). In these experiments the morphological priming effects were distinct from semantic and phonological priming effects in both their magnitude and their longevity. Corroborating Roelofs and Baayen's (2002) findings, Zwitserlood et al. (2002) also found morphological priming effects of approximately equal strength for semantically transparent and opaque compounds. This argues against models of the mental lexicon that do not include morphological representations but view similarity effects as arising from semantic and phonological overlap because such models would predict stronger effects for transparent than opaque compounds (see Plaut and Gonnerman, 2000 for further discussion).

A much-discussed issue in the current literature on morphological processing in language production concerns the generation of derived verb forms, in particular English past tense forms. Irregular forms, such as *went* and *was*, must obviously be stored in the mental lexicon. Stemberger (2002; 2004a) and Stemberger and Middleton (2003) carried out extensive analyses of speech errors involving complex verb forms (over-tensing errors, such as *I didn't broke it*, and over-regularization errors, such as *I singed*), and concluded that irregular verb forms were stored as part of the same phonological network as simple forms (*break*, *sing*) and that during the retrieval of an irregular form, the phonological representation of the base form became activated and competed with the correct irregular form.

Regular verb forms could, in principle, be derived in two ways: They could be retrieved from the mental lexicon as units, with their internal structure being represented, or they could be generated by rule. We know of no experimental studies involving healthy English speakers addressing this issue. However, there are case studies demonstrating that the ability to process regular forms or the ability to process irregular forms can be selectively impaired in brain-damaged patients. This double dissociation can be viewed as evidence for the involvement of separate processing mechanisms in the generation of regular and irregular forms. However, Lambon Ralph and colleagues (Bird et al., 2003; Braber et al., 2005; Lambon Ralph et al., 2005) proposed that the patients' profiles in the generation of regular and irregular forms might be linked to their semantic or phonological processing deficits. For instance, the production of irregular forms relies strongly on semantic knowledge because there is often little phonological overlap between the base and the past tense form (e.g. *go–went*, *be –was*). Hence one might expect patients with semantic deficits to be more impaired in the generation of these forms than in the generation of regular forms. By contrast, many English regular forms are phonologically more complex than the most common irregular forms, and therefore patients with a phonological deficit should be more impaired in the production of regular than irregular forms. Lambon Ralph and colleagues (e.g. Braber et al., 2005) argued that the patient data largely confirm these predictions. However, Miozzo (2003), Tyler et al. (2004), and Ullman et al. (2005) argued that the patients' performance could not be fully explained by reference to their semantic and phonological deficits, and therefore postulated separate mechanisms for processing regular and irregular forms.

28.3 Representation of phonological knowledge

According to all models of word production, speakers generate the phonological forms of words out of sublexical components rather than retrieving them as units from the mental lexicon. Phonological decomposition must be postulated because the pronunciation of words in connected speech often differs from their citation forms. Connected speech consists of phonological words, which can encompass one or more morphemes, for instance two morphemes of a compound or, in English, a head morpheme and an unstressed function word (e.g. Levelt, 1992; Wheeldon and Lahiri, 1997; 2002). Importantly, phonological words are the domain for stress assignment and syllabification, and segments can assume different positions from the position taken in the citation forms. For example, the phrases *demand it* or *got to* can be produced as single phonological words and would be syllabified as *de.man.dit* and *go.to*, respectively. In some contexts, phonological segments are deleted (as in *go.to*) or assimilated (as in *handbag* pronounced as *ham.bag*; Inkelas and Zec, 1990; Nespor and Vogel, 1986; Selkirk, 1986). Clearly, speakers can only generate these connected speech forms if at some point during the course of utterance planning individual sounds are available as planning units.

Another argument for the assumption of phonological decomposition is that speakers often make speech errors that involve a single segment (*some kunny kind*) or a cluster of two or three segments that do not correspond to a complete morpheme (*stedal peel guitar*). Such sound errors are far more frequent than word errors (Boomer and Laver, 1968; Fromkin, 1971; Shattuck-Hufnagel, 1979; 1983). For a number of reasons, most sound errors cannot be viewed as articulatory errors. For instance, the errors are usually phonotactically well-formed, i.e. they result in sound sequences that are permissible in the speaker's language (Boomer and Laver, 1968; Dell et al., 2000; Fromkin, 1971; Wells, 1951; but see Mowrey and MacKay, 1990 for evidence that some errors yield phonetically and phonotactically ill-formed sequences); and sometimes the left context is altered to accommodate the error

(e.g. *a m*... *arathon* instead of *an eating*
mara... shows that the errors must arise
d... ing rather than the articulation

...esearch effort has been directed
...h sublexical processing units are
...ogical encoding. Most sound
... percent of the errors in dif-
...Meyer, 1992) involve single
...ly ten percent of the sub-
...consonant clusters (e.g.
...word onsets, which are
...ce a single segment.
...s in which clusters
...*ction*), which sug-
...ters, as units and
...rg, 1989; 1991;
...emberger and

...gical features
...t the segments
...to share more
...e expected on
...omkin, 1971;
...975; Shattuck-
... 1991b). Thus,
...do not func-
...ndependently
...ding, but they
...sses (see also
...ery few errors
...herefore, sylla-
...obably do not
...dently selected
... Meyer, 1992).
...elow, syllables
...f the metrical
...uring phonetic

...g that speakers
...s of words by
...ts comes from
...se studies used
...scribed above,
...produce sets of
...r (1990; 1991)
...esponse words
... more word-
...were unrelated.
...ffect increased
...nents. Roelofs
...esponse words
...with segments
...ogical features
...ports the view
...cal forms out
...es.

Other studies have used versions of the picture–word interference paradigm, where speakers name target pictures which are accompanied by related or unrelated spoken or written distractor words (e.g. Damian and Martin, 1999; Jerger et al., 2002; Meyer and Schriefers, 1991; Starreveld and La Heij, 1996). For instance, a speaker might see a picture of a dog and simultaneously hear the word *doll*, which is phonologically similar to the picture name, or the unrelated word *chair*. In these experiments, distractors that share word-initial or word-final segments with the target facilitate target-naming relative to unrelated distractors. In experiments with Dutch and English speakers Schiller (1998; 2000) used masked primes and found that phonologically related primes facilitated the naming of target pictures relative to unrelated ones. The size of this facilitatory effect depended on the number of segments shared by prime and target, but it did not depend on whether or not the set of shared segments corresponded to a full syllable of the target (but see Ferrand et al., 1996, who obtained an effect of syllabic structure in French).[2] This suggests that phonological facilitation arises because the prime preactivates some of the processing units that need to be selected to produce the target. The processing units appear to be segments, not syllables.

In addition to retrieving the words' segments, speakers must generate or retrieve their metrical structure. Levelt (1992; Levelt et al., 1999) argued that the syllable structure of words does not have to be stored in the mental lexicon because it can always be derived on the basis of universal and language-specific syllabification rules. The basic rule is to assign each vowel to a different syllable and to treat the intervening consonants as syllable onsets unless that violates universal or language-specific phonotactic constraints. Therefore, Levelt and colleagues postulated an on-line syllabification process, which assigns segments to syllables. In addition, even languages with relatively varied stress patterns tend to have a default pattern that applies to most words, or to most words within a syntactic class. For instance, in most English words, stress falls on the first syllable that includes a full vowel (e.g. Cutler and Norris, 1988). Levelt et al. (1999; see also Roelofs, 1997b) therefore proposed that the lexical entries for words following the default stress pattern does not include any metrical information. For the remaining words, they postulated

[2] Ferrand et al. (1997) reported a syllable-structure effect for English, but they used word naming and lexical decision, not picture-naming tasks.

lean metrical representations, specifying the number of syllables and the stress pattern.

In other models the metrical structure is lexically specified for all words. Most commonly, hierarchical metrical structures are postulated consisting of syllables and syllable constituents (e.g. Dell, 1986; Shattuck-Hufnagel, 1987; 1992; Stemberger, 1985). In many models, metrical frames not only serve as a means of representing prosodic structure but also support the ordering of segments, as will be explained below. Syllable frames with specified syllable constituents have been invoked to explain important properties of segmental ordering errors, in particular the observation that misplaced segments typically move from their correct position to the corresponding position in a new syllable. For instance, a segment stemming from a syllable onset will typically assume a new onset position (as in *some kunny kind* instead of *some funny kind*) rather than a coda position. However, this syllable position constraint can also largely be explained as resulting from the tendency of sound errors to involve word onsets, rather than word-internal segments, and from the tendency to involve phonologically similar rather than dissimilar segments (e.g. Dell et al., 2000; Shattuck-Hufnagel 1987).

In addition, there is experimental evidence from paradigms using repetition tasks and primed picture-naming tasks suggesting that the parsing of words into consonantal and vocalic elements (the CV structure) is explicitly represented in a structural frame (e.g. Costa and Sebastián-Gallés, 1998; Sevald et al., 1995; but see Meijer, 1996). This view is supported by speech error analyses showing that segmental ordering errors tend to involve syllables with the same rather than different CV structures (Stemberger, 1990; Vousden et al., 2000; see also Hartsuiker, 2002). However, in a priming study with Dutch speakers, Roelofs and Meyer (1998) did not obtain any evidence for the representation of CV structure; and they argued that the effects of CV structure seen in other studies might arise during the syllabification process rather than demonstrating the existence of stored CV representations.

28.4 Building phonological representations

The results of speech error analyses and the experimental evidence reviewed above demonstrate that speakers generate phonological forms by retrieving individual segments and assigning them to positions in metrical structures. In the following section, we discuss how these tasks are accomplished in different models of word form retrieval.

28.4.1 Segmental retrieval

According to all current models of word form retrieval, activation spreads from a word or morpheme to the corresponding phonological segments, which are eventually selected to be part of the phonological representation. The models differ in their assumptions about the time-course of the segmental activation and selection processes and in whether or not they assume feedback between the segmental and the morpheme level.

In Dell's (1986) model, all segments of a syllable are activated and selected in parallel. The segments are marked with respect to the syllable positions they are to take, and they are ordered when they are associated to the correspondingly labeled positions in syllable frames. The segments of successive syllables of a morpheme are activated in sequence. Thus, in this and related models (e.g. MacKay, 1987), segmental ordering is achieved through two mechanisms: through the association of segments to the positions of frames and through the timing of the activation of the segments.

An alternative view is that all segments of a word are activated simultaneously but are selected in sequence (e.g. O'Seaghdha and Marin, 2000; Sullivan and Riffel, 1999; Wilshire and Saffran, 2005). A third proposal, by Levelt et al. (1999) and Roelofs (1997a; 1997b), is that all segments of a word are activated and selected in parallel, but that the subsequent syllabification process is sequential, proceeding from the onset to the end of the phonological word. The order of the segments within each morpheme is specified in labeled links between the segments and the morpheme.[3] Finally, there are models in which the segments of a word are activated and selected in sequence (e.g. Dell et al., 1993; Hartley and Houghton, 1996; Sevald and Dell, 1994; Vousden et al., 2000).

Most of the empirical evidence about the time-course of segmental activation and selection comes from priming and interference experiments. Several studies have compared the effects of primes or distractors that shared word-initial or word-final segments with the targets (for a recent review see Wilshire and Saffran, 2005). As mentioned, phonologically related distractor words facilitate the naming of target pictures

[3] In the implemented version of the model (Roelofs 1992; 1997a) activation spreads in parallel from a morpheme to its segments. When the activation of a segment exceeds a threshold, a verification mechanism is triggered that checks whether the selection of the segment is licensed, i.e. whether it is appropriately linked to the target morpheme, and selects the segment when this is the case.

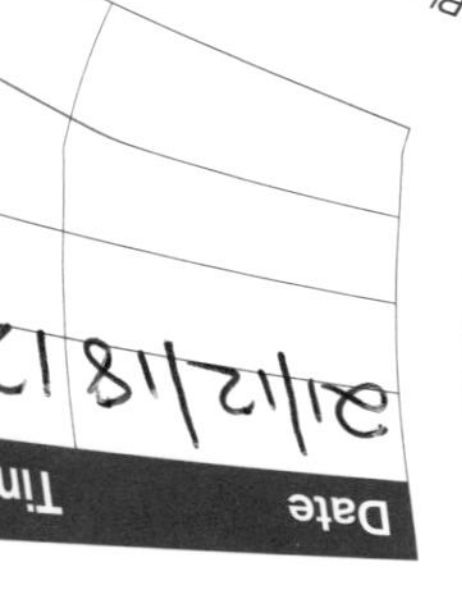

r and
its are
ones,
mag-
word-
One
t to see maximal facilitatory
g- and end-related distractors
us onset asynchronies relative
e target picture; a beginning-
might need to be presented
an an end-related one to be
ve. Some studies found such
Meyer and Schriefers, 1991;
994; Sullivan and Riffel, 1999;
n, 2003), but others failed to
ins and Ellis, 1992; O'Seaghdha
ee Wilshire and Saffran, 2005).
nce for the assumption that
oding encompasses a sequen-
omes from studies in which
tedly produce phonologically
ed words. For instance, in the
aradigm described above, par-
to produce sets of words that
e word-initial segments than
words. No difference is seen
words that share word-final
nrelated (Meyer 1990; 1991).
owed that the implicit priming
ct of an additional phonologi-
nrelated distracter were addi-
d that these effects had different
ether, the results of the prim-
st that phonological encoding
parallel component, the activa-
ical segments, and a following
nent, which is likely to be the
ification of the segments.
s of word form retrieval differ
ns about the information flow
phological and the segmental
del proposed by Levelt et al.
on spreads from a morpheme
cal segments, but not in the
. Many other models (e.g. Dell,
Burger, and Svec, 1997; Dell,
97) assume feedback between
g levels. A number of findings
he latter assumption. Most of
properties of speech errors
y and brain-damaged speakers.
lapropisms (replacements of
honologically related ones, as
notion instead of *proposal*, or
re instead of *deep phrase struc-*
ey a syntactic category con-
correct word tends to belong

to the same syntactic category as the target (e.g. Harley and MacAndrew, 2001); semantic errors tend to be more similar in their phonological form than expected on the basis of chance estimates (e.g. Dell 1986; 1990; Dell and Reich, 1981), and sound errors tend to result in existing words rather than non-words (e.g. Baars et al., 1975). These effects can readily be explained if bidirectional links between phonemes and morphemes are assumed. However, they can also be seen as demonstrating the operation of an efficient output monitor that has access to the phonological form of the planned utterance and is sensitive to syntactic and lexical constraints, as proposed by Levelt et al.

Other evidence, which represents a more serious challenge to the view that the morpheme-to-segment links are unidirectional, concerns the effects of the phonological neighborhood on word production: Words from dense neighborhoods (i.e. words that are phonologically similar to many other words) are produced faster and more accurately than words from sparser neighborhood (Stemberger, 2004b; Vitevitch, 2002; Vitevitch and Sommers, 2003; but see Vitevitch and Stamer, 2006). Based on the experimental evidence and results of computer simulations, Dell and Gordon (2003; see also Gordon, 2002; Gordon and Dell, 2001) concluded that effects of neighborhood density had a lexical-semantic and a phonological component. In other words, form-related neighbors facilitate the selection of a target word unit as well as the selection of its phonological segments. As Dell and Gordon (2003) point out, these findings challenge non-interactive accounts of word production. In such models, form-related neighbors of a target become activated through the monitoring system. For instance, when a speaker prepares to say *cap*, the related morphemes *cat* and *map* become activated because the phonological representation of *cap* is processed by the speech comprehension system in the same way as a word spoken by a different speaker would be processed (e.g. Levelt, 1989; Postma, 2000). Therefore the neighbors of the target may become available as likely error outcomes, but there is, in non-interactive models, no mechanism through which this would facilitate the correct selection of the target word or of its segments (see also Vitevitch et al., 2004; Goldrick, Chapter 31 this volume).

28.4.2 Retrieval of metrical information

Most models of phonological encoding represent metrical information lexically in frames, which are retrieved in parallel with the words' segments. An exception is the model proposed by Levelt et al. (1999), where metrical information is only stored for words with irregular stress pattern but is generated by rule for words that are stressed according to the default rule of the language.

Very few experimental studies have investigated how stress patterns are generated or retrieved. Roelofs and Meyer (1998) used the implicit priming paradigm to study the retrieval of metrical frames for words with irregular stress patterns. They obtained an implicit priming effect when the response words shared initial segments as well as the metrical structure, i.e. when they had the same number of syllables and the same stress pattern. No implicit priming effect was seen when the words shared initial segments but differed in stress or length, or when they only had the same metrical structure, but did not share the word-initial segments. As Roelofs and Meyer (1998) argued, this pattern suggests that the metrical frame for irregularly stressed words is retrieved in parallel with the set of segments, and that both must be known for an implicit priming effect to arise (see also Schiller et al., 2004).

28.4.3 Combining metrical and segmental information

In most models, the combination of metrical and segmental information is viewed as a process of inserting segments into the positions of independently retrieved metrical frames. In Dell's (1986) model, the phonological form of a word is generated in the following way. Encoding begins when the word is granted current node status, which means that it receives an extra boost of activation. The next word in the utterance is activated to a lesser degree. Activation spreads from the current node via morpheme and syllable nodes to nodes representing syllable constituents (onset, nucleus, coda), and, in the case of complex constituents (e.g. /st/, /pr/), to segments within constituents, and finally to phonological features. If the word includes several morphemes, the first morpheme is assigned current node status first. At the syllable level, the first syllable is initially the current node and receives extra activation, which is passed on to the subordinate units. Thus, all segments of a syllable become activated at the same time, but the segments of successive syllables reach their activation maxima in succession, according to their order in the utterance. Each activated unit sends a proportion of its activation back to the associated superordinate node. The phonological segments are marked with respect to the syllable all utterances or different frames for words differing in length and CV structure; (3) the processing mechanisms, for instance in whether there are unidirectional feedforward links or bidirectional links between units; or whether they assume only activation and passive decay or lateral inhibition between units as well (see Dell, Burger, and Svec, 1997 for further discussion).

As mentioned, metrical frames are invoked in many models as ordering devices for simultaneously activated segments. This is not the case for the model proposed by Levelt et al. (1999) and Roelofs (1997b), where metrical frames are stipulated only for those words that deviate from the main stress pattern of the language. As explained above, segmental ordering is achieved through the labeled links between morphemes and segments. The segments of a word are activated in parallel, and segments are selected if they are appropriately linked to the superordinate node. As in the other models mentioned above, segments are combined into syllables, but this is not achieved by assigning them to positions within syllable frames, but through a rule-based sequential syllabification process. Where possible, stress is assigned by rule. This approach allows for a straightforward treatment of resyllabification processes. As explained earlier, the syllabification of words in context is often different from the syllabification of the citations forms. Models in which segments are marked lexically with respect to the syllable positions they assume in each word need to invoke additional post-lexical processes to explain how segments are assigned to new syllable positions in connected speech. By contrast, in the model proposed by Roelofs and by Levelt et al., the affiliation of segments to syllables is determined on-line. In connected speech, the segments of morphemes which are part of the same phonological word are syllabified together and are assigned directly to the appropriate syllables (see Roelofs, 1997b for further discussion).

There are models of serial ordering in speech production that represent frames in a more implicit, distributed fashion (Vousden et al., 2000; for further discussion see Goldrick, Chapter 31 this volume) or do not assume structural frames at all. A model of the latter type is the parallel distributed processing (PDP) model proposed by Dell et al. (1993). PDP models learn to map input strings onto output strings. They commonly consist of at least three layers—an input layer, a layer of hidden units, and an output layer. Rule-like knowledge is an emergent property of the network's growing ability to map input signals onto output signals. This knowledge is encoded in the links that mediate the mapping from input to output. The PDP model of phonological encoding proposed by Dell et al. maps from lexical units via a hidden layer to output representations (phonological features) in a simple recurrent network. The network virtually pronounces words by generating a series of phoneme representations. Dell et al. augmented the basic feedforward architecture outlined above by two layers of "state units." On a given processing cycle, these layers make copies of the state of activation in the hidden unit layer and in the output layer, respectively. The state units feed back their copies to the hidden layer on the next processing cycle. This provides the network with a form of memory for preceding processing cycles, which is crucial for the generation of an ordered sequence of segments (Elman, 1990). Dell et al. showed that their model accounted well for important properties of speech errors, such as the observation that they usually result in phonotactically well-formed strings, that vowels tend to interact with vowels and consonants with consonants, and that syllable onsets are affected more often than codas. However, other findings remain unaccounted for. For instance, the model cannot explain segmental exchanges, such as *Yew Nork*, because each part of the error (the anticipation of one segment and the perseveration of the other) are treated as a separate incidents (see also Goldrick, Chapter 31 below) for a discussion of PDP models).

28.5 **Generating the phonetic code of words**

The word form representation generated during phonological encoding is generally considered to be fairly abstract in that it consists of discrete and context-independent segments. By contrast, articulatory gestures overlap in time, and how a segment is realized depends on which segments precede and follow it (e.g. Browman and Goldstein, 1992). Therefore, the phonological representation must be transformed into a phonetic representation that determines the movements of the articulators to be carried out for each word.

How speakers generate the phonetic codes of words has not been widely studied within psycholinguistics (but see Fowler, Chapter 29 this volume, and Port, Chapter 30), and most models of word form retrieval do not include phonetic encoding. Crompton (1982) and Levelt (1992) suggested that speakers had access to a syllabary, a store of pre-assembled gestural scores for frequent syllables. Low-frequency syllables are assembled out of the scores corresponding to individual segments. The syllable-sized motor programs are still fairly abstract representations of the speech movements; they do not, for instance, capture any intersyllabic coarticulatory influences or any effects of loudness, pitch, or speech rate on the way syllables are produced. Therefore, further fine-tuning of the gestures must occur during motor planning.

Access to a mental syllabary would dramatically reduce the planning effort for phonetic encoding, in particular in languages where a large proportion of all frequently occurring words is composed of a relatively small number of frequent syllables. For instance, Schiller et al. (1996) estimated that the 500 most frequent syllable types of Dutch (which has approximately 12,000 different syllable types) suffice to produce eighty percent of all word tokens.

In the model proposed by Levelt et al. (1999) and by Roelofs (1997b), phonetic encoding involves the selection of syllable units. As soon as the first phonological syllable has been generated, phonetic encoding can begin. Activation spreads from the phonological segments to all syllables that include the segments. An activated syllable is selected if its links to the segments match the syllable positions computed during syllabification. Exactly when a syllable node is selected depends on its level of activation relative to the activation levels of all other syllable nodes that are activated at the same time. Metrical information is used to set parameters for the loudness, pitch, and duration of the syllables.

Experimental support for a mental syllabary was first obtained by Levelt and Wheeldon (1994). They used a symbol-association task to elicit words that were selected to vary orthogonally in word frequency and in the frequency of their constituent syllables. For instance, speakers were trained to produce *koning* ('king') upon presentation of the string "//////", to say *advies* ('advice') upon presentation of the string of "<<<<<<", and so on. Levelt and Wheeldon found that the participants were faster to produce high-frequency than low-frequency words and, importantly, that they were faster to produce words consisting of high-frequency than of low-frequency syllables. The syllable frequency effect was carried primarily by the frequency of the second syllable of the words. This suggests that the retrieval of the second syllable was initiated slightly later than that of the first syllable, and that the participants initiated the responses only after they had retrieved both syllables. In Levelt and Wheeldon's experiment, syllable and segmental frequency could not be separated. However, Cholin et al. (2006; see also Cholin, 2004) also obtained a small but significant syllable frequency effect when Dutch speakers produced pseudo-words consisting of high- or low-frequency syllables which were carefully matched for segmental frequency. In this study, only the frequency of the first syllable of disyllabic pseudo-words affected the speech onset latencies, implying that the participants began to speak as soon as the first syllable had been fully planned (see also Meyer et al., 2003). A number of other studies have also reported syllable frequency effects in word production tasks carried out by healthy speakers and speakers with aphasia or apraxia of speech (e.g. Aichert and Ziegler, 2004; Laganaro, 2005; Perea and Carreiras, 1998; but see Wilshire and Nespoulous, 2003). However, the interpretation of these results is complicated by the fact that word and non-word reading or repetition tasks, rather than picture naming or association tasks, were used.

In a recent study, Cholin et al. (2004) found a stronger implicit priming effect when the segments shared by the response words within a set corresponded to a complete syllable in all words (as in *beacon, beadle, beaker*) than when this was not the case (as in *beacon, beadle, beatnik*, where the third item is the odd man out). This finding contrasts with the finding of picture–word interference and priming studies mentioned above that the size of facilitatory effects from phonologically related distracters and primes does not depend on whether or not the primed segments correspond to a syllable in the target. Cholin et al. concluded that the syllable-match effect in their implicit priming experiments arose because the participants aimed to prepare for the words not only on the phonological but also, where possible, on the phonetic level. They could only select a syllable program when the first syllable was the same for all words. Thus, the results support the view that syllables are planning units at the phonetic level.

28.6 **A model of word form retrieval**

We have discussed the tasks to be carried out during morphological, phonological and phonetic encoding, we have reviewed key empirical findings, and we have discussed how these can be accounted for within various theoretical frameworks. In this section, we describe, by way of summary, how word forms are retrieved in one specific model, the model proposed by Levelt et al. (1999; see also Roelofs, 1997a). We chose this model because it is, in our view, the most comprehensive model of word form retrieval presently available, though some of its assumptions are probably incorrect. Most importantly, the model is likely to be too serial: as explained above, there is now good evidence for cascading of information between levels of processing and for limited feedback between processing levels. However, the components of the model are well specified, and it captures the main steps of word planning from the selection of a lemma to the generation of the articulatory code. A unique feature of the model is its on-line syllabification process, which allows for the generation of connected speech forms of words. Finally, though this has not been shown in detail in this chapter, the implemented version of the model (WEAVER and WEAVER++; e.g. Roelofs, 1992; 1996; 1997a; 1997b; 1998; 1999; 2002; 2003; 2004) offers an accurate account of a large number of key experimental findings from a variety of paradigms.

Word form retrieval begins when a morpheme receives activation from a lemma (see Figure 28.1). Activation spreads through the network in feedforward direction only. There is also decay of activation. In WEAVER, the form encoder follows simple selection rules, which are implemented in a parallel distributed manner. Attached to each node are production rules (condition–action pairs) which select nodes if they are appropriately connected to the superordinate target node. The verification and selection process is triggered when the activation level of the node reaches a threshold.

The morphological encoder selects one or more morphemes, depending on which lemma, or lemmas, and diacritics have been selected. All morphologically complex forms are composed out of their constituent morphemes. Activation spreads in parallel from a morpheme to the associated segments. The order of the segments is captured in the links between segments and morphemes. Segments are selected if they are appropriately linked to the morpheme. For words with irregular stress pattern a simple metrical frame, encoding the number of syllables and the position of the stressed syllable, is selected as well. The string of selected segments constitutes

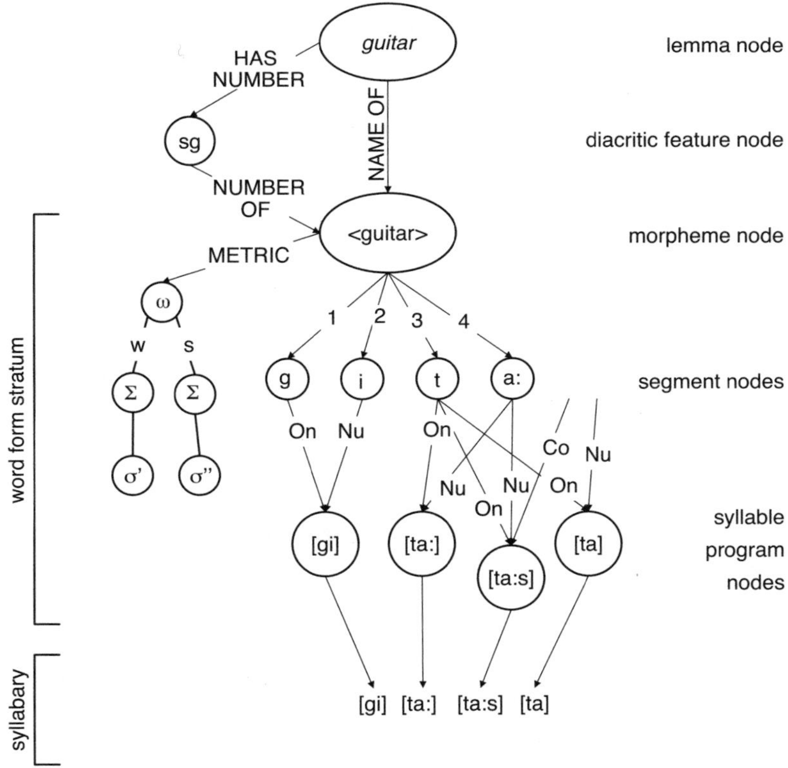

Figure 28.1 Memory representation of the word form of *guitar* (see Roelofs, 1997a).

the input to a sequential syllabification process which groups them into syllables and either links them to the retrieved metrical structure or assigns stress by rule. In morphologically complex words and in connected speech, the segments of adjacent morphemes may be syllabified together, which allows for the assignment of segments to syllable positions that do not correspond to the positions in the citation forms. The syllabified phonological representation is the input to the phonetic encoding processes. During phonetic encoding, syllable program nodes are selected based on the types and order of the segments in the phonological syllables, and metrical information is used to set the parameters for loudness, pitch contour, and word durations.

28.7 Concluding remarks

Current models of word form retrieval converge on central assumptions. They all distinguish between morphological, phonological, and phonetic representations and processes; they all assume morphological and phonological decomposition, and agree on the main processing units at these levels. In addition, they all postulate the same basic retrieval mechanisms: activation and selection of units. One might summarize the state of the art by saying that word form retrieval in language production is reasonably well understood.

What remains to be done? Most of the psycholinguistic research on word form retrieval has concerned the development of functional models of single word retrieval in speakers of Germanic languages. It is high time to extend the area of investigation in several directions. First, there is a need for systematic crosslinguistic investigations of word form retrieval. The core assumptions endorsed by current models of word form retrieval—for instance that there are several planning levels, that there is decomposition into units smaller than words, and that processing can be described in terms of the activation and selection of units—should hold for speakers of other languages as well. However, the precise nature and relative difficulty of the tasks speakers carry out during word form retrieval must depend on properties of their language. For instance, for speakers of Germanic languages, the main processing units at the phonological level appear to be phonological segments, not syllables. Chen et al. (2002; see also Chen, 2000) showed that the reverse holds for speakers of Mandarin Chinese. As they explain, this difference is likely to be related to the fact that Mandarin Chinese has fewer syllables than the Germanic languages, clear syllable boundaries, and no resyllabification, i.e. the syllable positions of segments are not altered in connected speech relative to the citation forms. Thus, syllables would appear to be far more useful phonological processing units in Mandarin Chinese than in English or Dutch, and this seems to be reflected in the units speakers use. Systematic crosslinguistic research is required to understand which processing principles are common to speakers of all languages and how speakers adapt to language-specific requirements (see also Costa et al., Chapter 32 this volume). Second, there is a need to consider how speakers generate word forms in context. There is some empirical work on the generation of phonological words (e.g. Wheeldon and Lahiri, 1997; 2002) and on the time-course of segmental retrieval in short phrases, such as *the blue kite* (e.g. Costa and Caramazza, 2002; Schriefers and Teruel, 1999); but within psycholinguistics, there is hardly any empirical research on the generation of larger prosodic units, such as phonological and intonational phrases (but see F. Ferreira, 1993; Levelt, 1989; Meyer, 1994; Watson and Gibson, 2004; see also Port, Chapter 30 below). We know that speakers generate these units (see also Kraljic and Brennan, 2005; Schafer et al., 2000) but we do not know much about *how* they do this—for instance about how and when pragmatic and syntactic variables affect phonological and phonetic planning.

Finally, an exciting and rapidly expanding new area of research is the investigation of the neurological basis of language production through neurophysiological and imaging techniques (e.g. Hickok and Poeppel, 2004; Indefrey and Levelt, 2004; Indefrey, Chapter 33 below). The challenge is to determine exactly where in the brain the processes postulated in functional models happen, how the areas involved in word production are related, and exactly when during the process of speech planning each of them becomes activated.

References

Aichert, I., and Ziegler, W. (2004) Syllable frequency and syllable structure in apraxia of speech. *Brain and Language*, 88: 148–59.

Baars, B., Motley, M., and MacKay, D. G. (1975) Output editing for lexical status in artificially elicited slips of the tongue. *Journal of Verbal Learning and Verbal Behavior*, 14: 382–91.

Berg, T. (1989) Intersegmental cohesiveness. *Folia Linguistica*, 23: 245–80.

Berg, T.(1991) Phonological processing in a syllable-timed language with pre-final stress: evidence from Spanish speech error data. *Language and Cognitive Processes*, 6: 265–301.

Bird, H., Lambon Ralph, M. A., Seidenberg, M. S., McClelland, J. L., and Patterson, K. (2003) Deficits in phonology and past-tense morphology: what's the connection? *Journal of Memory and Language*, 48: 502–26.

Bloem, I., and La Heij, W. (2003) Semantic facilitation and semantic interference in word translation: implications for models of lexical access in language production. *Journal of Memory and Language*, 48: 468–88.

Bock, K., and Levelt, W. (1994) Language production: grammatical encoding. In M. A. Gernsbacher (ed.), *Handbook of Psycholinguistics*, pp. 945–84. Academic Press, San Diego, CA.

Boomer, D. S., and Laver, J. D. M. (1968) Slips of the tongue. *British Journal of Disorders of Communication*, 3: 1–12.

Braber, N., Patterson, K., Ellis, K., and Lambon Ralph, M. A. (2005) The relationship between phonological and morphological deficits in Broca's aphasia: further evidence from errors in verb inflection. *Brain and Language*, 92: 278–87.

Browman, C. P., and Goldstein, L. (1992) Articulatory phonology: an overview. *Phonetica*, 49: 155–180.

Brown, R., and McNeill, D. (1966) The "tip-of-the-tongue" phenomenon. *Journal of Verbal Learning and Verbal Behavior*, 5: 325–37.

Butterworth, B. (1980). Some constraints on models of language production. In B. Butterworth (ed.), *Language Production*, vol. 1: *Speech and Talk*, pp. 423–59. Academic Press, London.

Caramazza, A. (1997) How many levels of processing are there in lexical access? *Cognitive Neuropsychology*, 14: 177–208.

Caramazza, A., Bi, Y. C., Costa, A., and Miozzo, M. (2004) What determines the speed of lexical access: homophone or specific-word frequency? A reply to Jescheniak et al. (2003) [Jescheniak, Meyer, and Levelt, 2003]. *Journal of Experimental Psychology: Learning, Memory, and Cognition*, 30: 278–82.

Caramazza, A., Costa, A., Miozzo, M., and Bi, Y. (2001) The specific-word frequency effect: implications for the representation of homophones in speech production. *Journal of Experimental Psychology: Learning, Memory, and Cognition*, 27: 1430–50.

Caramazza, A., and Miozzo, M. (1997) The relation between syntactic and phonological knowledge in lexical access: evidence for the "tip-of-the-tongue" phenomenon. *Cognition*, 64: 309–43.

Caramazza, A., Papagno, C., and Ruml, W. (2000) The selective impairment of phonological processing in speech production. *Brain and Language*, 75: 428–50.

Chen, J. T. (2000) Syllable errors from naturalistic slips of the tongue in Madarin Chinese. *Psychologia*, 43: 15–26.

Chen, J. T., Chen, T. M., and Dell, G. S. (2002) Word-form encoding in Mandarin Chinese as assessed by the implicit priming task. *Journal of Memory and Language*, 46: 751–81.

Cholin, J. (2004) *Syllables in Speech Production: Effects of Syllable Preparation and Syllable Frequency*. Nijmegen, Max Planck Institute, The Netherlands.

Cholin, J., Levelt, W. J. M., and Schiller, N. O. (2006) Effects of syllable frequency in speech production. *Cognition*, 99: 205–350.

Cholin, J., Schiller, N. O., and Levelt, W. J. M. (2004) The preparation of syllables in speech production. *Journal of Memory and Language*, 50: 47–61.

Collins, A. F., and Ellis, A. W. (1992) Phonological priming of lexical retrieval in speech production. *British Journal of Psychology*, 83: 375–88.

Costa, A., and Caramazza, A. (2002) The production of noun phrases in English and Spanish: implications for the scope of phonological encoding in speech production. *Journal of Memory and Language*, 46: 178–98.

Costa, A., Caramazza, A., and Sebastián-Gallés, N. (2000) The cognate facilitation effect: implications for models of lexical access. *Journal of Experimental Psychology: Learning, Memory, and Cognition*, 26: 1283–96.

Costa, A., Miozzo, M., and Caramazza, A. (1999) Lexical selection in bilinguals: do words in the bilingual's two lexicons compete for selection? *Journal of Memory and Language*, 41: 365–97.

Costa, A., and Sebastián-Gallés, N. (1998) Abstract phonological structure in language production: evidence from Spanish. *Journal of Experimental Psychology: Learning, Memory, and Cognition*, 24: 886–903.

Crompton, A. (1982) Syllables and segments in speech production. In A. Cutler (ed.), *Slips of the Tongue and Language Production*, pp.109–62. Mouton, Berlin.

Cuetos, F., Aguado, G., and Caramazza, A. (2000) Dissociation of semantic and phonological errors in naming. *Brain and Language*, 75: 451–460.

Cutler, A. (1980) Errors of stress and intonation. In V. Fromkin (ed.), *Errors of Linguistic Performance: Slips of the Tongue, Ear, Pen, and Hand*, pp. 67–80. Academic Press, New York.

Cutler, A., and Norris, D. (1988) The role of strong syllables in segmentation for lexical access. *Journal of Experimental Psychology: Human Perception and Performance*, 14: 113–21.

Cutting, J. C., and Ferreira, V. S. (1999) Semantic and phonological information flow in the production lexicon. *Journal of Experimental Psychology: Learning, Memory, and Cognition*, 25: 318–44.

Damian, M. F., and Martin, R. C. (1999) Semantic and phonological codes interact in single word production. *Journal of Experimental Psychology: Learning, Memory, and Cognition*, 25: 345–61.

Dell, G. S. (1986) A spreading-activation theory of retrieval in sentence production. *Psychological Review*, 93: 283–321.

Dell, G. S. (1988) The retrieval of phonological forms in production: tests of predictions from a connectionist model. *Journal of Memory and Language*, 27: 124–42.

Dell, G. S. (1990) Effects of frequency and vocabulary type on phonological speech errors. *Language and Cognitive Processes*, 5: 313–49.

Dell, G. S., Burger, L. K., and Svec, W. R. (1997) Language production and serial order: a functional analysis and a model. *Psychological Review*, 104: 123–47.

Dell, G. S., and Gordon, J. K. (2003) Neighbors in the lexicon: friends or foes? In N. O. Schiller and A. S. Meyer (eds), *Phonetics and Phonology in Language Comprehension and Production*, pp. 9–37. Mouton de Gruyter, Berlin.

Dell, G. S., Juliano, C., and Govindjee, J. (1993) Structure and content in language production: a theory of frames constraints in phonological speech errors. *Cognitive Science*, 17: 149–95.

Dell, G. S., and O'Seaghdha, P. G. (1991) Mediated and convergent lexical priming in language production: comment. *Psychological Review*, 98: 604–14.

Dell, G. S., and O'Seaghdha, P. G. (1992) Stages of lexical access in language production. *Cognition*, 42: 287–314.

Dell, G. S., Reed, K. D., Adams, D. R., and Meyer, A. S. (2000) Speech errors, phonotactic constaints, and implicit learning: a study of the role of experience in language production. *Journal of Experimental Psychology: Learning, Memory, and Cognition*, 26: 1355–67.

Dell, G. S., and Reich, P. A. (1981) Stages in sentence production: an analysis of speech error data. *Journal of Verbal Learning and Verbal Behaviour*, 20: 611–29.

Dell, G. S., Schwartz, M. F., Martin, N., Saffran, E. M., and Gagnon, D. A. (1997) Lexical access in aphasic and nonaphasic speakers. *Psychological Review*, 104: 801–38.

Dohmes, P., Zwitserlood, P., and Bölte, J. (2004) The impact of semantic transparency of morphologically complex words on picture naming. *Brain and Language*, 90: 203–12.

Eikmeyer, H. J., and Schade, U. (1991) Sequentialization in connectionist language production models. *Cognitive Systems*, 3: 128–38.

Elman, J. L. (1990) Finding structure in time. *Cognitive Science*, 14: 213–52.

Ferrand, L., Seguí, J., and Grainger, J. (1996) Masked priming of word and picture naming: the role of syllabic units. *Journal of Memory and Language*, 35: 708–23.

Ferrand, L., Seguí, J., and Humphreys, G. W. (1997) The syllable's role in word naming. *Memory and Cognition*, 25: 458–70.

Ferreira, F. (1993) Creation of prosody during sentence production. *Psychological Review*, 100: 233–53.

Ferreira, F., and Swets, B. (2002) How incremental is language production? Evidence from the production of utterances requiring the computation of arithmetic sums. *Journal of Memory and Language*, 46: 57–84.

Ferreira, V. S., and Griffin, Z. M. (2003) Phonological influences on lexical (mis)selection. *Psychological Science*, 14: 86–90.

Ferreira, V. S., and Humphreys, K. R. (2001) Syntactic influences on lexical and morphological processing in language production. *Journal of Memory and Language*, 44: 52–80.

Fromkin, V. A. (1971) The non-anomalous nature of anomalous utterances. *Language*, 47: 27–52.

Fromkin, V. A. (1973) *Speech Errors as Linguistic Evidence.* Mouton, The Hague.

García-Albea, J. E., del Viso, S., and Igoa, J. M. (1989) Movement errors and levels of processing in sentence production. *Journal of Psycholinguistic Research*, 18: 145–61.

Garrett, M. F. (1975) The analysis of sentence production. In G. H. Bower (ed.), *The Psychology of Learning and Motivation*, vol. 9: pp. 133–77. Academic Press, New York.

Garrett, M. F. (1980) Levels of processing in sentence production. In B. Butterworth (ed.), *Language Production*, vol. 1: *Speech and Talk*, pp. 177–220. Academic Press, New York.

Goldrick, M. (2004) Phonological features and phonotactic constraints in speech production. *Journal of Memory and Language*, 51: 586–603.

Gordon, J. K. (2002) Phonological neighborhood effects in aphasic speech errors: spontaneous and structured contexts. *Brain and Language*, 82: 113–45.

Gordon, J. K., and Dell, G. S. (2001) Phonological neighborhood effects: evidence from aphasia and connectionist modeling. *Brain and Language*, 79: 21–3.

Harley, T. A. (1984) A critique of top-down independent levels models of speech production: evidence from non-plan-internal speech errors. *Cognitive Science*, 8: 191–219.

Harley, T., and MacAndrew, S. B. G. (2001) Constraints upon word substitution speech errors. *Journal of Psycholinguistic Research*, 30: 395–418.

Hartley, T. A., and Houghton, G. (1996) A linguistically constrained model of short-term memory for nonwords. *Journal of Memory and Language*, 35: 1–31.

Hartsuiker, R. (2002) The addition bias in Dutch and Spanish phonological speech errors: the role of structural context. *Language and Cognitive Processes*, 17: 61–96.

Hickock, G., and Poeppel, D. (2004) Dorsal and ventral streams: a framework for understanding aspecits of the functional anatomy of language. *Cognition*, 92: 67–99.

Humphreys, G. W., Riddoch, M. J., and Quinlan, P. T. (1988) Cascade processes in picture identification. *Cognitive Neuropsychology*, 5: 67–103.

Indefrey, P., and Levelt, W. J. M. (2004) The spatial and temporal signatures of word production components. *Cognition*, 92: 101–44.

Inkelas, S., and Zec, D. (1990) *The Phonology–Syntax Connection.* University of Chicago Press, Chicago.

Janssen, D. P., Roelofs, A. R., and Levelt, W. J. M. (2002) Inflectional frames in language production. *Language and Cognitive Processes*, 17: 209–344.

Janssen, D. A., Roelofs, A., and Levelt, W. J. M. (2004) Stem complexity and inflectional encoding in language production. *Journal of Psycholinguistic Research*, 33: 365–81.

Jerger, S., Martin, R. C., and Damian, M. F. (2002) Semantic and phonological influences on picture naming by children and teenagers. *Journal of Memory and Language*, 47: 229–49.

Jescheniak, J. D., Hahne, A., and Schriefers, H. (2003) Information flow in the mental lexicon during speech planning: evidence from event-related brain potentials. *Cognitive Brain Research*, 15: 261–76.

Jescheniak, J. D., and Levelt, W. J. M. (1994) Word frequency effects in speech production: retrieval of syntactic information and of phonological form. *Journal of Experimental Psychology: Learning, Memory, and Cognition*, 20: 824–43.

Jescheniak, J. D., Meyer, A. S., and Levelt, W. J. M. (2003) Specific-word frequency is not all that counts in speech production: comments on Caramazza, Costa et al., and new experimental data. *Journal of Experimental Psychology*, 29: 432–38.

Jescheniak, J. D. and Schriefers, H. (1998) Discrete serial versus cascaded processing in lexical access in speech production: further evidence from the coactivation of near-synonyms. *Journal of Experimental Psychology: Learning, Memory, and Cognition*, 24: 1256–73.

Jescheniak, J. D., Schriefers, H., Garrett, M. F., and Friederici, A. D. (2002) Exploring the activation of semantic and phonological codes during speech planning with event-related potentials. *Journal of Cognitive Neuroscience*, 14: 951–64.

Jescheniak, J. D., Schriefers, H., and Hantsch, A. (2003) Utterance format affects phonological priming in the picture-word task: implications for models of phonological encoding in speech production. *Journal of Experimental Psychology: Human Perception and Performance*, 29: 441–54.

Kralijc, T., and Brennan, S. E. (2005) Prosodic disambiguation of syntactic structure: for the speaker or for the addressee? *Cognitive Psychology*, 50: 194–231.

Laganaro, M. (2005) Syllable frequency effect in speech production: evidence from aphasia. *Journal of Neurolinguistics*, 18: 221–35.

Lambon Ralph, M. A., Braber, N., McClelland, J. L., and Patterson, K. (2005) What underlies the neuropsychological pattern of irregular > regular past tense verb production? *Brain and Language*, 93: 106–19.

Levelt, W. J. M. (1989) *Speaking: From Intention to Articulation*. MIT Press, Cambridge, Mass.

Levelt, W. J. M. (1992) Accessing words in speech production: stages, processes and representations. *Cognition*, 42: 1–22.

Levelt, W. J. M. (1999) Models of word production. *Trends in Cognitive Sciences*, 3: 223–32.

Levelt, W. J. M., Roelofs, A., and Meyer, A. S. (1999) A theory of lexical access in language production. *Behavioural and Brain Sciences*, 22: 1–38.

Levelt, W. J. M., Schriefers, H., Vorberg, D., Meyer, A. S., Pechmann, T., and Havinga, J. (1991) The time course of lexical access in speech production: a study of picture naming. *Psychological Review*, 98: 122–42.

Levelt, W. J. M., and Wheeldon, L. (1994) Do speakers have access to a mental syllabary? *Cognition*, 50: 239–269.

MacKay, D. G. (1979) Lexical insertion, inflection, and derivation: creative processes in word production. *Journal of Psycholinguistic Research*, 8: 477–98.

MacKay, D. G. (1982) The problems of flexibility, fluency, and speed–accuracy trade-off in skilled behaviour. *Psychological Review*, 89: 483–506.

MacKay, D. G. (1987) *The Organization of Perception and Action: A Theory for Language and Other Cognitive Skills*. Springer, New York.

Meijer, P. J. A. (1996) Suprasegmental structures in phonological encoding: the CV structure. *Journal of Memory and Language*, 35: 840–53.

Meyer, A. S. (1990) The time course of phonological encoding in language production: the encoding of successive syllables. *Journal of Memory and Language*, 29: 524–45.

Meyer, A. S. (1991) The time course of phonological encoding in language production: phonological encoding inside a syllable. *Journal of Memory and Language*, 30: 69–89.

Meyer, A. S. (1992) Investigation of phonological encoding through speech error analyses: achievements, limitations, and alternatives. *Cognition*, 42: 181–211.

Meyer, A. S. (1994) Timing in sentence production. *Journal of Memory and Language*, 33: 471–92.

Meyer, A. S. (1996) Lexical access in phrase and sentence production: results from picture-word interference experiments. *Journal of Memory and Language*, 35: 477–96.

Meyer, A. S., Roelofs, A., and Levelt, W. J. M. (2003) Word length effects in object naming: the role of a response criterion. *Journal of Memory and Language*, 48: 131–47.

Meyer, A. S., and Schriefers, H. (1991) Phonological facilitation in picture-word interference experiments: effects of stimulus onset asynchrony and types of interfering stimuli. *Journal of Experimental Psychology: Learning, Memory, and Cognition*, 17: 1146–60.

Miozzo, M. (2003) On the processing of regular and irregular forms of verbs and nouns: evidence from neuropsychology. *Cognition*, 87: 101–27.

Miozzo, M., Jacobs, M. L., and Singer, N. J. W. (2004) The representation of homophones: evidence from anomia. *Cognitive Neuropsychology*, 21: 840–66.

Mowrey, R. A., and MacKay, I. R. A. (1990) Phonological primitives: electromyographic speech error evidence. *Journal of the Acoustical Society of America*, 88: 1299–1312.

Nespor, M., and Vogel, I. (1986) *Prosodic Phonology*. Foris, Dordrecht, The Netherlands.

O'Seaghdha, P., and Marin, J. W. (2000) Phonological competition and cooperation in form-related priming: sequential and nonsequential processes in word production. *Journal of Experimental Psychology: Human Perception and Performance*, 26: 57–73.

Perea, M., and Carreiras, M. (1998) Effects of syllable frequency and syllable neighborhood frequency in visual word recognition. *Journal of Experimental Psychology: Human Perception and Performance*, 24: 134–44.

Peterson, R. R., and Savoy, P. (1998) Lexical selection and phonological encoding during language production: evidence for cascaded processing. *Journal of Experimental Psychology: Learning, Memory, and Cognition*, 24: 539–57.

Pillon, A. (1998) Morpheme units in speech production: evidence from laboratory-induced verbal slips. *Language and Cognitive Processes*, 13: 465–98.

Plaut, D. C., and Gonnerman, L. M. (2000) Are non-semantic morphological effects incompatible with a distributed connectionist approach to lexical processing? *Language and Cognitive Processing*, 15: 445–85.

Postma, A. (2000) The detection of errors during speech production: a review of speech monitoring models. *Cognition*, 77: 97–131.

Rahman, R. A., van Turenout, M., and Levelt, W. J. M. (2003) Phonological encoding is not contingent on semantic feature retrieval: an electrophysiological study. *Journal of Experimental Psychology: Learning, Memory, and Cognition*, 29: 850–60.

Rapp, B., and Goldrick, M. (2000) Discreteness and interactivity in spoken word production. *Psychological Review*, 107: 460–99.

Roelofs, A. (1992) A spreading-activation theory of lemma retrieval in speaking. *Cognition*, 42: 107–42.

Roelofs, A. (1996) Serial order in planning the production of successive morphemes of a word. *Journal of Memory and Language*, 35: 854–76.

Roelofs, A. (1997a) The WEAVER model of word-form encoding in speech production. *Cognition*, 64: 249–84.

Roelofs, A. (1997b) Syllabification in speech production: evaluation of WEAVER. *Language and Cognitive Processes*, 12: 657–93.

Roelofs, A. (1998) Rightward incrementality in encoding simple phrasal forms in speech production: verb–particle combinations. *Journal of Experimental Psychology: Learning, Memory, and Cognition*, 24: 904–19.

Roelofs, A. (1999) Phonological segments and features as planning units in speech production. *Language and Cognitive Processes*, 14: 173–200.

Roelofs, A. (2002) Spoken language planning and the initiation of articulation. *Quarterly Journal of Experimental Psychology: Section A*, 55: 465–83.

Roelofs, A. (2003) Goal-referenced selection of verbal action: modeling attentional control in the Stroop task. *Psychological Review*, 110: 88–125.

Roelofs, A. (2004) Seriality of phonological encoding in naming objects and reading their names. *Memory and Cognition*, 32: 212–22.

Roelofs, A., and Baayen, H. (2002) Morphology by itself in planning the production of spoken words. *Psychonomic Bulletin and Review*, 9: 132–8.

Roelofs, A., and Meyer, A. S. (1998) Metrical structure in planning the production of spoken words. *Journal of Experimental Psychology: Learning, Memory, and Cognition*, 24: 922–39.

Schafer, A. J., Speer, S. R., Warren, P., and White, S. D. (2000) Intentional disambiguation in sentence production and comprehension. *Journal of Psycholinguistic Research*, 29: 169–82.

Schiller, N. O. (1998) The effect of visually masked syllable primes on the naming latencies of words and pictures. *Journal of Memory and Language*, 39: 484–507.

Schiller, N. O. (2000) Single word production in English: The role of subsyllabic units during phonological encoding. *Journal of Experimental Psychology: Learning, Memory, and Cognition*, 26: 512–28.

Schiller, N. O., Fikkert, P., and Levelt, C. C. (2004) Stress priming in picture naming: an SOA study. *Brain and Language*, 90: 231–40.

Schiller, N. O., Meyer, A. S., Baayen, H., and Levelt, W. J. M. (1996) Comparison of lexeme and speech syllables in Dutch. *Journal of Quantitative Linguistics*, 3: 8–28.

Schmitt, B. M., Münte, T. F., and Kutas, M. (2000) Electrophysiological estimates of the time course of semantic and phonological encoding during implicit picture naming. *Psychophysiology*, 37: 473–84.

Schriefers, H., Meyer, A. S., and Levelt, W. J. M. (1990) Exploring the time course of lexical access in language production: picture–word interference studies. *Journal of Memory and Language*, 29: 86–102.

Schriefers, H., and Teruel, E. (1999) Phonological facilitation in the production of two-word utterances. *European Journal of Cognitive Psychology*, 11: 17–50.

Selkirk, E. O. (1986) On derived domains in sentence phonology. *Phonology Yearbook*, 371–405.

Sevald, C. A., and Dell, G. S. (1994) The sequential cuing effect in speech production. *Cognition*, 53: 91–127.

Sevald, C. A., Dell, G. S., and Cole, J. (1995) Syllable structure in speech production: are syllables chunks or schemas? *Journal of Memory and Language*, 34: 807–820.

Shattuck-Hufnagel, S. (1979) Speech errors as evidence for a serial-ordering mechanism in sentence production. In W. E. Cooper and E. C. T. Walker (eds), *Sentence Processing: Psycholinguistic Studies presented to Merrill Garrett*, pp. 295–342. Springer, New York.

Shattuck-Hufnagel, S. (1983) Sublexical units and suprasegmental structure in speech production planning. In P. F. MacNeilage (ed.), *The Production of Speech*, pp. 109–36. Springer, New York.

Shattuck-Hufnagel, S. (1987) The role of word-onset consonants in speech-production planning: new evidence from speech error patterns. In S. Keller and M. Gopnick (eds), *Motor and Sensory Processes of Language*, pp. 17–51. Erlbaum, Hillsdale, NJ.

Shattuck-Hufnagel, S. (1992) The role of word structure in segmental serial ordering. *Cognition*, 42: 213–58.

Shatzman, K. B., and Schiller, N. O. (2004) The word frequency effect in picture naming: contrasting two hypotheses using homonym pictures. *Brain and Language*, 90: 160–9.

Smith, M., and Wheeldon, L. (1999) High level processing scope in spoken sentence production. *Cognition*, 73: 205–46.

Spencer, A. (1991) *Morphological Theory*. Blackwell, Cambridge, MA.

Starreveld, P. A., and La Heij, W. (1996) Time-course analysis of semantic and orthographic context effects in picture naming. *Journal of Experimental Psychology: Learning, Memory, and Cognition*, 22: 896–918.

Stemberger, J. P. (1983) The nature of /r/ and /l/ in English: evidence from speech errors. *Journal of Phonetics*, 11: 139–47.

Stemberger, J. P. (1985) An interactive activation model of language production. In A. W. Ellis (ed.), *Progress in the Psychology of Language*, vol.1: pp. 143–86. Erlbaum, Hillsdale, NJ.

Stemberger, J. P. (1990) Wordshape errors in language production. *Cognition*, 35: 123–57.

Stemberger, J. P. (1991a) Radical underspecification in language production. *Phonology*, 8: 73–112.

Stemberger, J. P. (1991b) Apparent anti-frequency effects in language production: the addition bias and phonological underspecification. *Journal of Memory and Language*, 30: 161–85.

Stemberger, J. P. (2002) Overtensing and the effect of regularity. *Cognitive Science*, 26: 737–66.

Stemberger, J. P. (2004a) Phonological priming and irregular past. *Journal of Memory and Language*, 50: 82–95.

Stemberger, J. P. (2004b) Neighborhood effects on error rates in speech production. *Brain and Language*, 90: 413–22.

Stemberger, J. P., and Middleton, C. S. (2003) Vowel dominance and morphological processing. *Language and Cognitive Processes*, 18: 369–404.

Stemberger, J. P., and Treiman, R. (1986) The internal structure of word-initial consonant clusters. *Journal of Memory and Language*, 25: 163–80.

Sullivan, M. P., and Riffel, B. (1999) The nature of phonological encoding during spoken word retrieval. *Language and Cognitive Processes*, 14: 15–45.

Tyler, L. K., Stamatakis, E. A., Bright, P. et al., (2004) Processing objects at different levels of specificity. *Journal of Cognitive Neuroscience*, 16: 351–62.

Ullman, M. T., Pancheva, R., Love, T., Yee, E., Swinney, D., and Hickok, G. (2005) Neural correlates of lexicon and grammar: evidence from the production, reading, and judgement of inflection in aphasia. *Brain and Language*, 93: 185–238.

van Turennout, M., Hagoort, P., and Brown, C. M. (1998) Brain activity during speaking: from syntax to phonology in 40 milliseconds. *Science*, 280: 572–4.

Vigliocco, G., Antonini, T., and Garrett, M. F. (1997) Grammatical gender is on the tip of Italian tongues. *Psychological Science*, 8: 314–17.

Vitevitch, M. S. (2002) The influence of phonological similarity neighborhoods on speech production. *Journal of Experimental Psychology: Learning, Memory, and Cognition*, 28: 735–47.

Vitevitch, M. S., Armbrüster, J., and Chu, S. (2004) Sublexical and lexical representations in speech production: effects of phonotactic probablility and onset density. *Journal of Experimental Psychology: Learning, Memory, and Cognition*, 30: 514–29.

Vitevitch, M. S., and Sommers, M. S. (2003) The facilitative influence of phonological similarity and neighborhood frequency in speech production in younger and older adults. *Memory and Cognition*, 31: 491–504.

Vitevitch, M. S., and Stamer, M. K. (2006) The curious case of competition in Spanish speech production. *Language and Cognitive Processes*, 21: 760–70.

Vousden, J. I., Brown, G. D. A., and Harley, T. A. (2000) Serial control of phonology in speech production: a hierarchical model. *Cognitive Psychology*, 41: 101–75.

Watson, D., and Gibson, E. (2004) The relationship between intonational phrasing and syntactic structure in language production. *Language and Cognitive Processes*, 19: 713–55.

Wells, R. (1951) Predicting slips of the tongue. *Yale Scientific Magazine*, 3: 9–30.

Wheeldon, L. R. (2003) Inhibitory form priming of spoken word production. *Language and Cognitive Processes*, 18: 81–109.

Wheeldon, L. R., and Lahiri, A. (1997) Prosodic units in speech production. *Journal of Memory and Language*, 37: 356–81.

Wheeldon, L. R., and Lahiri, A. (2002) The minimal unit of phonological encoding: prosodic or lexical word. *Cognition*, 85: B31–B41.

Wilshire, C. E., and Nespoulous, J. L. (2003) Syllables as units in speech production: data from aphasia. *Brain and Language*, 84: 424–47.

Wilshire, C. E., and Saffran, E. M. (2005) Contrasting effects of phonological priming in aphasic word production. *Cognition*, 95: 31–71.

Zwitserlood, P., Bölte, J., and Dohmes, P. (2000) Morphological effects on speech production: evidence from picture naming. *Language and Cognitive Processes*, 15: 563–91.

Zwitserlood, P., Bölte, J., and Dohmes, P. (2002) Where and how morphologically complex words interplay with naming pictures. *Brain and Language*, 81: 358–67.

CHAPTER 29

Speech production

Carol A. Fowler

LANGUAGE forms provide the means by which language users can make an intended linguistic message available to other members of the language community. Necessarily, then, they have two distinct characteristics. On the one hand, they are linguistic entities, morphemes and phonological segments, that encode the talker's linguistic message. On the other hand, they either have physical properties themselves (e.g. Browman and Goldstein, 1986) or, by other accounts, they serve as an interface between the linguistic and physical domains of language use.

A theory of speech production provides an account of the means by which a planned sequence of language forms is implemented as vocal tract activity that gives rise to an audible, intelligible acoustic speech signal.[1] Such an account must address several issues. Two central issues are discussed here.

One issue concerns the nature of language forms that ostensibly compose plans for utterances. Because of their role in making linguistic messages public, a straightforward idea is that language forms are themselves the public behaviors in which members of a language community engage when talking. By most accounts, however, the relation of phonological segments to actions of the vocal tract is not one of identity. Rather, phonological segments are mental categories with featural attributes. We will consider reasons for this stance, relevant evidence, and an alternative theoretical perspective.

[1] By this definition, I intend to contrast the more comprehensive theories of language production from theories of speech production. A theory of language production (e.g. Levelt et al., 1999) offers an account of planning for and implementation of meaningful utterances. A theory of speech production concerns itself only with planning for and implementation of language forms.

Another issue concerns what, at various levels of description, the talker aims to achieve (e.g. Levelt et al., 1999). In my discussion of this issue, I focus here on the lowest level of description—that is, on what talkers aim to make publicly available to listeners. A fundamental theoretical divide here concerns whether the aims are acoustic or articulatory. On the one hand, it is the acoustic signal that stimulates the listener's ears, and so one might expect talkers to aim for acoustic targets that point listeners toward the language forms that compose the talker's intended message. On the other hand, acoustic speech signals are produced by vocal tract actions. The speaker has to get the actions right to get the acoustic signal right.

Readers may wonder whether this is a "tempest in a teapot." That is, why not suppose that talkers plan and control articulations that will get the signal right, so that in a sense both articulation and acoustics are controlled? Readers will see, however, that there are reasons why theorists typically choose one account or the other.

These issues are considered in turn in the following two sections.

29.1 Language forms and plans for speaking

By most accounts, as already noted, neither articulation nor the acoustic signal is presumed to implement phonological language forms transparently. Language forms are conceived of as abstract mental categories about which acoustic speech signals provide cues.

There are two quite different reasons for this point of view. One is that language forms are cognitive entities (e.g. Pierrehumbert, 1990). In particular, word forms are associated, presumably in the lexical memory of a language user, with word meanings. As such they constitute an important part of what a language user knows that permits him or her to produce and understand language. Moreover, word forms in the lexicons of languages exhibit systematic properties which can be captured by formal rules. There is some evidence that language users know these rules. For example, in English, voiceless stop consonants are aspirated in stressed syllable-initial position. That systematic property can be captured by a rule (Kenstowicz and Kisseberth, 1979).

Evidence that such a rule is part of a language user's competence is provided, for example, by foreign accents. When native English speakers produce words in a Romance language such as French, which has unaspirated stops where English has aspirated stops, they tend to aspirate the stops. Accordingly, the word *pas*, [pa][2] in French is pronounced [p^ha] as if the English speaker is applying the English rule to French words. A second source of evidence comes from spontaneous errors of speech production. Kenstowicz and Kisseberth (1979) report an error in which a speaker intended to produce *tail spin*, but instead said *pail stin*. In the intended utterance, /t/ in *tail* is aspirated; /p/ in *spin* is unaspirated. The authors report, however, that, in the error, appropriately for their new locations, /p/ was pronounced [p^h]; /t/ was pronounced [t]. One account of this "accommodation" (but not the only one possible) is that the exchange of /t/ and /p/ occurred before the aspiration rule had been applied by the talker. When the aspiration rule was applied, /p/ was accommodated to its new context.[3]

A second reason to suppose that language forms exist only in the mind is coarticulation. Speakers temporally overlap the articulatory movements for successive consonants and vowels. This makes the movements associated with a given phonetic segment context-sensitive and lacking an obvious discrete segmental structure. Likewise, the acoustic signal which the movements produce is context-sensitive. Despite researchers' best efforts (e.g. Stevens and Blumstein, 1981) they have not uncovered invariant acoustic information for individual consonants and vowels. In addition, the acoustic signal, like the movements that produce it, lacks a phone-sized segmental structure.

This evidence notwithstanding, there are reasons to resist the idea that language forms reside only in the minds of language users. They are, as noted, the means that languages provide to make linguistic messages public. Successful recognition of language forms would seem more secure were the forms themselves public things.

Browman and Goldstein (e.g. 1986; 1992) have proposed that phonological language forms are gestures achieved by vocal tract synergies that create and release constrictions. They are both the actions of the vocal tract (properly described) that occur during speech and at the same time units of linguistic contrast. ("Contrast" means that a change in a gesture or gestural parameter can change the identity of a word. For example, the word *hot* can become *tot* by addition of a tongue tip constriction gesture; *tot* can become *sot* by a change in the tongue tip's constriction degree.)

From this perspective, phonetic gestures *are* cognitive in nature. That is, they are components of a language users' language competence, and, as noted, they serve as units of contrast in the language. However, cognitive entities need not be covert (see e.g. Ryle, 1949). They can be psychologically meaningful actions, in this case of a language user. As for coarticulation, although it creates context sensitivity in articulatory movements, it does not make gestures context-sensitive. For example, lip closure for /b/, /p/, and /m/ occurs despite coarticulatory encroachment from vowels that affects jaw and lip motion.

There is some skepticism about whether Browman and Goldstein's "articulatory phonology" as just described goes far enough beyond articulatory phonetics.[4] This is in part because it does not yet provide an account of many of the phonological systematicities (e.g. vowel harmony in Hungarian, Turkish, and many other languages; but see Gafos and Benus, 2003) which exist across the lexicon of languages and that other theories of phonology capture by means of rules (e.g. Kenstowicz and Kisseberth, 1979) or constraints (Archangeli,1997). However, the theory is well worth considering, because it is unique in proposing that language forms are public events.

[2] Slashes (e.g. /p/) indicate phonological segments; square brackets (e.g. [p]) signify phonetic segments. The difference is one of abstractness. For example, the phonological segment /p/ is said to occur in two varieties—the aspirated phonetic segment [p^h] and the unaspirated [p].

[3] An alternative account, which does not implicate rule use, is that *pail stin* reflects a single feature or gesture error. From a featural standpoint, place of articulation features of /p/ and /t/ exchange, stranding the aspiration feature.

[4] See articles in the 1992 special issue of the journal *Phonetica* devoted to a critical analysis of articulatory phonology.

Spontaneous errors of speech production have proved important sources of evidence about language planning units. These errors, produced by people who are capable of producing error-free tokens, appear to provide evidence both about the units of language that speakers plan to produce and about the domain over which they plan. Happily, the units which participate in errors have appeared to converge with units that linguistic analysis has identified as real units of the language. For example, words participate in errors as anticipations (e.g. *sky is in the sky* for intended *sun is in the sky*; this and other errors from Dell, 1986), perseverations (*class will be about discussing the class* for intended *class will be about discussing the test*), exchanges (*writing a mother to my letter* for *writing a letter to my mother*), and non-contextual substitutions (*pass the salt* for *pass the pepper*). Consonants and vowels participate in the same kinds of error. Syllables do so only rarely; however, they serve as frames that constrain how consonants and vowels participate in errors. Onset consonants interact only with onset consonants; vowels interact with vowels; and, albeit rarely, coda consonants interact with coda consonants. Interacting segments tend to be featurally similar to one another. Moreover, when segments move, they tend to move to contexts which are featurally similar to the contexts in which they were planned to occur. Segments are anticipated over shorter distances than words (Garrett, 1980), suggesting that the planning domains for words and phonological segments are different.

Historically, most error corpora were collected by individuals who transcribed the errors that they heard. As noted, the errors tended to converge with linguists' view of language forms as cognitive, not physical entities (e.g. Pierrehumbert, 1990). As researchers moved error collection into the laboratory, however, it became clear that errors occur that are inaudible. Moreover, these errors violate constraints on errors that collectors had identified.

One constraint was that errors are categorical in nature. If, in production of *Bob flew by Bligh Bay*, the /l/ of *Bligh* were perseverated into the onset of *Bay*, producing *Blay*, the /l/ would be a fully audible production. However, electromyographic evidence revealed to Mowrey and MacKay (1990) that errors are gradient. Some produce an audible token of /l/; others do not, yet show activity of a lingual muscle indicating the occurrence of a small lingual (tongue) gesture for /l/.

A second constraint is that errors result in phonologically well-formed utterances. Not only do vowels interact only with other vowels in errors, and onsets with onsets and codas with codas, but also sequences of consonants in onsets and codas tend to be permissible in the speaker's language. Or so investigators thought before articulatory data were collected in the laboratory. Pouplier (2003a; 2003b) used a midsagittal electromagnetometer to collect articulator movement data as participants produced repetitions of pairs of words such as *cop–top* or *sop–shop*. Like Mowrey and MacKay (1990), she found errorful articulations (for example, intrusive tongue tip movement toward a /t/ articulation during *cop*) in utterances that sounded error-free. In addition, however, she found that characteristically intrusions were not accompanied by reductions of the intended gesture. This meant that, in the foregoing example, constriction gestures for both /t/ and /k/ occurred in the onset of a syllable, a phonotactically impermissible cluster for her English speakers.

What do these findings imply for theories of speech production? For Pouplier and colleagues (Pouplier, 2003b; Goldstein et al., forthcoming), planning units are intended sequences of vocal-tract gestures that are coordinated in the manner of coupled oscillators. In the literature on limb movements, it has been found that two modes of coordination are stable. Limbs (or hands or fingers) may be oscillated in phase or 180 degrees out of phase (so that extension of one limb occurs when the other limb is flexing). In tasks in which, for example (Kelso, 1984; see also Yamanishi et al., 1980), hands are oscillated about the wrist at increasing rates, in-phase movements remain stable; however, out-of-phase movements become unstable. Participants attempting to maintain out-of-phase movements slip into phase. Pouplier and colleagues suggest that findings of intrusive tongue tip gestures in the onset of *cop* and of intrusive tongue body gestures in *top* constitute a similar shift from a less to a more stable oscillation mode. When *top–cop* is repeated, syllable onsets /t/ and /k/ each occur once for each pair of rime (/ap/) productions giving a 1:2 coordination mode. When intrusive /t/ and /k/ gestures occur, the new coordination mode is 1:1; that is, the new onset is produced once for each one production of the syllable rime. A 1:1 coordination mode is more stable than a 1:2 mode.

A question is what the findings of gradient, phonotactically impermissible errors imply about the interpretability of error analyses based on transcribed, rather than articulatory, corpora. Certainly these errors occur, and certainly they were missed in transcription corpora.

However, does it mean that categorical consonant and vowel errors do not occur, that planning units should be considered to be intended phonetic gestures (Pouplier) or even commands to muscles (Mowrey and MacKay), not the consonants and vowels of traditional phonetic analysis?

There are clearly categorical errors that occur at the level of whole words (recall *writing a mother to my letter*). It does not seem implausible, therefore, that categorical phonetic errors also occur. It may be appropriate (as in the model of Levelt et al., 1999) to imagine levels of speech planning, with consonants and vowels of traditional analyses serving as elements of plans at one level, giving way to planned gestures at another.

Findings that error corpora in some ways misrepresent the nature of spontaneous errors of speech production, however, have had the positive consequence that researchers have sought converging (or, as appropriate, diverging) evidence from experiments that elicit error-free speech. For example, Meyer (1991) found evidence for syllable constituents serving as "encoding" units in language production planning. Participants memorized sets of word pairs consisting of a prompt word produced by the experimenter and a response word produced as quickly as possible by the participant. Response words in a set were "homogeneous" if they shared one or more phonological segments; otherwise they were "heterogeneous." Meyer found faster responses to words in homogeneous compared to heterogeneous sets if response words shared their initial consonant or initial syllable, but not if they shared the syllable rime (that is, the vowel and any following consonants). There was no further advantage over responses to heterogeneous words when the CV of a CVC syllable was shared in homogeneous sets as compared to when just the initial C was shared. There was an advantage over responses to words sharing the initial consonant of responses to words sharing the whole first syllable. These findings suggest, as errors do, that syllable constituents are among the planning units. They also suggest that encoding for production is a sequential "left-to-right" process.

Sevald et al. (1995) obtained converging evidence with errors data suggesting that syllables serve as planning frames. They asked participants to repeat pairs of non-words (e.g. KIL KILPER or KIL KILPNER) in which the initial monosyllable either did or did not match the initial syllable of the disyllable. The task was to repeat the pair as many times as possible in four seconds. Mean syllable production time was less when the syllable structure matched. Remarkably, the advantage of matching syllable structure was no less when only syllable structure, but not syllable content, matched (e.g. KEM TILFER vs. KEM TILFNER). In the foregoing examples, it looks as if the advantage could be due to the fact that there were fewer phonetic segments to produce in the matching condition. However, there were other items in which the length advantage was reversed.

29.2 Speakers' goals as acoustic targets or vocal tract gestures

A next issue is how intended sequences of phonetic entities are planned to be implemented as actions or their consequences that are available to a listener. In principle, this issue is orthogonal to the one just considered about the nature of planned language forms. As just discussed, these forms are variously held to be covert, cognitive representations or public, albeit still cognitive, entities. Either view is compatible with proposals that, at the lowest level of description, talkers aim to achieve either acoustic or gestural targets. In the discussion below, therefore, the issue of whether language forms are covert or public in nature is set aside. It may be obvious, however, that, in fact, acoustic target theorists at least implicitly hold the former view and gesture theorists the latter.

Guenther et al. (1998) argue against gestural targets on several grounds and argue for acoustic targets. One ground for rejecting gestural targets, such as constriction location and degree, concerns the feedback information that speakers would need to implement the targets sufficiently accurately. To know whether or not a particular constriction has been achieved requires perceptual information. If, for example, an intended constriction is by the lips (as for /b/, /p/, or /m/), talkers can verify that the lips are closed from proprioceptive information for lip contact. However, Guenther et al. argue that, in particular for vowels, constrictions do not always involve contact by articulators, and therefore intended constrictions cannot be verified. In addition, they argue, to propose that talkers intend to achieve particular constrictions implies that talkers should not be able to compensate for experimental perturbations that prevent those constrictions from being achieved. However, some evidence suggests that they can. For example, Savariaux et al. (1995) had talkers produce vowels with a tube between their lips that prevented normal lip rounding for the vowel /u/. The acoustic effects of the lip tube could be compensated for by lowering the larynx (thereby enlarging the oral cavity by another means than rounding). Of the eleven participants, one compensated fully for the lip tube. Six others showed limited evidence of compensation.

A third argument for acoustic targets is provided by American English /r/. According to Guenther et al., /r/ is produced in very different ways by different speakers or even by the same speaker in different contexts. The different means of producing /r/ are acoustically very similar. One account for the articulatory variability, then, is that it is tolerated if the different means of production produce inaudibly different acoustic signals, the talker's production aim. Finally, Guenther et al. argue that ostensible evidence for constriction targets—that, for example, invariant constriction gestures occur for /b/ and other segments—need not be seen as evidence uniquely favoring gestural targets. Their model "DIVA" (originally "directions in orosensory space onto velocities of articulators"; described below) learns to achieve acoustic-perceptual targets, but nonetheless shows constriction invariance. However, there is also evidence favoring the alternative idea that talkers' goals are articulatory not acoustic. Moreover, the arguments of Guenther et al. favoring acoustic targets can be challenged.

Tremblay et al. (2003) applied mechanical perturbations to the jaw of talkers producing the word sequence *see–at*. The perturbation altered the motion path of the jaw, but had small and inaudible acoustic effects. Even though acoustic effects were inaudible, over repetitions, talkers compensated for the perturbations and showed after-effects when the perturbation was removed. Compensation also occurred in a silent speech condition, but not in a non-speech jaw movement condition. These results appear inconsistent with a hypothesis that speech targets are acoustic.

There is also a more natural speech example of preservation of inaudible articulations. In an investigation of an X-ray microbeam database, Browman and Goldstein (1991) found examples of utterances such as *perfect memory* in which transcription suggested deletion of the final /t/ of *perfect*. However, examination of the tongue tip gesture for the /t/ revealed its presence. Because of overlap from the bilabial gesture of /m/, however, acoustic consequences of the /t/ constriction gesture were absent or inaudible. As for the suggestion that constriction goals should be unverifiable by feedback when constricting articulators are not in contact with another structure, to my knowledge this is untested speculation.

As for the compensation found by Savariaux et al (1995; see also Perkell et al., 1993), Guenther et al. do not remark that the compensation is markedly different from that associated with certain other perturbations in being, for most participants, either partial or absent. Compensations for a bite block (which prevents jaw movement) are immediate and nearly complete in production of vowels (e.g. Lindblom et al., 1979). Compensations for jaw and lip perturbations during speech (e.g. tugging the jaw down as it raises to close the lips for a /b/) are very short in latency, immediate, and nearly complete (e.g. Kelso et al., 1984). These different patterns of compensation are not distinct in the DIVA model. However, they are in speakers. The difference may be understood as relating to the extent to which they mimic perturbations which occur naturally in speech production. When a speaker produces, say, /ba/ versus /bi/, coarticulation by the following low (/a/) or high (/i/) vowel will tug the jaw and lower lip down or up. Speakers have to compensate for that to get the lips shut for bilabial /b/. That routine compensation for coarticulation may underlie fast and functional compensations which occur in the laboratory (Fowler and Saltzman, 1993). However, it is a rare perturbation outside the laboratory that prevents lip rounding. Accordingly, talkers may have no routines in place to compensate for the lip tube, and have to learn them. In a gestural theory, they have to learn to create a mirage—that is, an acoustic signal that mimics consequences of lip rounding.

As for /r/, ironically, it has turned out to be a poster child for both acoustic and articulatory theorists. Delattre and Freeman (1968), whom Guenther et al. cite as showing considerable variability in American English articulation of /r/, in fact remark that in every variant they observed there were two constrictions, one by the back of the tongue in the pharyngeal region and one by the tongue tip against the hard palate. (Delattre and Freeman were only looking at the tongue, and so did not remark on a third shared constriction, rounding by the lips.) Accordingly, whether one sees variability or invariance in /r/ articulations may depend on the level of description of the vocal tract configuration deemed relevant to talkers and listeners. In Browman and Goldstein's articulatory phonology (e.g. 1986; 1995), the relevant level is that of constriction locations and degrees, and those are invariant across the /r/ variants.

Focus on constrictions permits an understanding of a source of dialect variation in American English /r/ that is not illuminated by a proposal that acoustic targets are talkers' aims. Among consonants involving more than one constriction—for example, the nasal consonants (constrictions by lips, tongue tip or tongue body, and by the velum), the liquids, /l/ (tongue tip and body) and /r/ (tongue body, tip, and lips), and the approximant /w/ (tongue body and lips)—a generalization holds regarding the phasing of the constriction gestures. Prevocalically, the gestures are achieved nearly simultaneously; postvocalically, the gesture with the more open (vowel-like) constriction degree leads (see research by Sproat and Fujimora, 1993; Krakow, 1989; 1993; Gick, 1999). This is consistent with the general tendency in syllables for the more sonorant (roughly more vowel-like) consonants to be positioned closest to the vowel. (For example, the ordering in English is /tr/ before the vowel as in *tray*, but /rt/ after the vowel as in *art.*) Goldstein (pers. comm., 15 Aug. 2005) points out that, in two dialects of American English, one spoken in Brooklyn and one in New Orleans, talkers produce postvocalic consonants in such a way that, for example, *bird* sounds to listeners somewhat like *boyd*. This is understandable if talkers exaggerate the tendency for the open lip and tongue body constrictions to lead the tip constriction. Together, the lip and tongue body configurations create a vowel sound like /ɔ/ (in *saw*); by itself, the tip gesture is like /i/ (in *see*). Together, the set of gestures yield something resembling the diphthong /ɔ^{i}/ as in *boy*.

In short, there are arguments and there is evidence favoring both theoretical perspectives—that targets of speech production planning are acoustic or else are gestural. Deciding between the perspectives will require further research.

29.2.1 Theories of speech production

As noted, theories of speech production differ in their answer to the question of what talkers aim to achieve, and a fundamental difference is whether intended targets are acoustic or articulatory. Within acoustic theories, accounts can differ in the nature of acoustic targets; within articulatory theories, accounts can be that muscle lengths or muscle contractions are targets, that articulatory movements are targets, or that coordinated articulatory gestures are targets. I will review one acoustic and one articulatory account. I chose these accounts because they are the most fully developed theories within the acoustic and articulatory domains.

29.3 The DIVA theory of speech production

In this account (e.g. Guenther et al., 1998), targets of speaking are normalized acoustic signals reflecting resonances of the vocal tract ("formants"). The normalization transformations create formant values that are the same for men, women, and children even though acoustic reflections of formants are higher in frequency for women than for men and for young children than for women. Because formants characterize vowels and sonorant consonants but not (for example) stop or fricative consonants, the model is restricted to explanation of just those classes of phones.

Between approximately six and eight months of age, infants engage in vocal behavior called babbling in which they produce what sounds like sequences of CV syllables. In this way, in DIVA, the young model learns a mapping from articulator positions to normalized acoustic signals. Over learning, this mapping is inverted so that acoustic-perceptual targets can underlie control of articulatory movements. In the model, the perceived acoustic signal has three degrees of freedom (one per normalized formant). In contrast, the articulatory system has the seven degrees of freedom of Maeda's (1990) articulatory model. This difference in degrees of freedom mean that the inverted mapping is one to many. Accordingly, a constraint is required to make the mapping determinate. Guenther et al. use a "postural relaxation" constraint whereby the articulators remain as close as possible to the centers of their ranges of motion. This constraint underlies the model's tendency to show near-invariance of constrictions despite having acoustic-perceptual rather than articulatory targets.

In addition to that characteristic, the model compensates for perturbations—not, however, distinguishing those that humans do well and poorly.

29.4 The task dynamic model

Substantially influenced by the theorizing of Bernstein (1967), Turvey (1977) introduced a theory of action in which he proposed that the minimal meaningful units of action were produced by synergies or coordinative structures (Easton, 1972). These are transiently established coordinative relations among articulators—those of the vocal tract for speech—which achieve action goals. An example in speech is the organized relation among the jaw and the two lips that achieves bilabial constriction for English /b/, /p/, or /m/. That coordinative relation is not in place when speakers produce a constriction which does not include lip closure (e.g. Kelso et al., 1984). The coordinative relation underlies the ability of speakers to compensate for jaw or lip perturbations in the laboratory, and presumably to compensate for coarticulatory demands on articulators shared by temporally overlapping phones outside the laboratory.

Saltzman and colleagues (e.g. Saltsman and Kelso, 1987; Saltzman and Munhall, 1989; see also Turvey, 1990) proposed that synergies are usefully modeled as dynamical systems. Specifically, they suggested that speech gestures can be modeled as mass-spring systems with point attractor dynamics. In turn those systems are characterized by equations that reflect how the systems' states undergo change over time. Each vocal tract gesture is defined in terms of "tract variables." Variables include lip protrusion (a constriction location) and lip aperture (constriction degree). Appropriately parameterized, the variables achieve gestural goals. The tract variables have associated articulators (e.g. the jaw and the two lips) that constitute the synergy that achieves that gestural goal. In one version of the theory, a word is specified by a "gestural score" (Browman and Goldstein, 1986) which provides parameters for the relevant tract variables and the interval of time over which they should be active. In a more recent version (Saltzman et al., 2000) gestural scores are replaced by a central "clock" that regulates the timing of gesture activation. The clock's average "tick" rate determines the average rate of speaking. As we will see later, local clock slowing can mark the edges of prosodic domains.

These systems show the equifinality characteristic of real speakers which underlies their ability to compensate for perturbations. That is, although the parameters of the dynamical system for a gesture have context independent values, gestural goals are achieved in a context-dependent manner so that, for example, as in the research by Kelso et al.(1984), lip closure for /b/ is achieved by different contributions from the lips and jaw on perturbed and unperturbed trials. The model compensates for perturbations which speakers handle without learning, but not for those such as in the study by Savariaux et al., which speakers require learning to handle, if they handle them at all.

29.5 Coarticulation

A hallmark of speech production is coarticulation. Speakers talk very quickly, and talking involves rapid sequencing of the particulate atoms (Studdert-Kennedy, 1998) which constitute language forms. Although the atoms are discrete, their articulation is not. Much research on speech production has been conducted with an aim to understand coarticulation. Coarticulation is characterized either as context-sensitivity of production of language forms or as temporally overlapping production. It occurs in both an anticipatory and a carryover direction. In the word *stew*, for example, lip rounding from the vowel /u/ begins near the beginning of the /s/. In *use*, it carries over during /s/.

Thirty years ago, there were two classes of accounts of coarticulation. In one point of view (e.g. Daniloff and Hammarberg, 1973) coarticulation was seen as "feature spreading." Consonants and vowels can be characterized by their featural attributes. For example, consonants can be described as being voiced or unvoiced, as having a particular place of articulation (e.g. bilabial for /b/, /p/, and /m/) and a particular manner of articulation (e.g. /b/ and /p/ are stops; /f/ is a fricative). Vowels are front, mid, or back; high, mid, or low, and rounded or unrounded. Many features which characterize consonants and vowels are contrastive, in that changing a feature value changes the identity of a consonant or vowel and the identity of a word that they, in part, compose. For example, changing the feature of a consonant from voiced to unvoiced can change a consonant from /b/ to /p/ and a word from *bat* to *pat*. However, some features are not contrastive. Adding rounding to a consonant does not change its identity in English; adding nasalization to a vowel in English likewise does not change its identity.

In feature spreading accounts of coarticulation, non-contrastive features were proposed to spread in an anticipatory direction to any phone unspecified for the feature (i.e. for which the feature was non-contrastive). Accordingly, lip rounding should spread through any consonant preceding a rounded vowel; nasalization should spread through any vowel preceding a nasal consonant. Carryover coarticulation was seen as inertial. Articulators cannot stop on a dime. Accordingly lip rounding might continue during a segment following a rounded vowel. There was some supportive evidence for the feature spreading view of anticipatory coarticulation (Daniloff and Moll, 1968).

However, there was also disconfirming evidence. One was a persistent finding (e.g. Benguerel and Cowan, 1974) that indications of coarticulation did not neatly begin at phonetic segment edges, as they should if a feature had spread from one phone to another. A second kind of evidence consisted of reports of "troughs" (e.g. Gay, 1978; Boyce, 1990). These were findings that, for example, during a consonant string between two rounded vowels, the lips would reduce their rounding and lip muscle activity would reduce, inconsistent with an idea that a rounding feature had spread to consonants in the string.

A different general point of view was that coarticulation was "coproduction" (e.g. Fowler, 1977)—i.e. temporal overlap in the production of two or more phones. In this point of view, for example, rounding need not begin at the beginning of a consonant string preceding a rounded vowel, and a trough during a consonant string between two rounded vowels would be expected as the rounding gesture for the first vowel wound down and before rounding for the second vowel began. Bell-Berti and Harris (1981) proposed a specific account of coproduction, known as "frame" theory, in which anticipatory coarticulation began a fixed interval before the acoustically defined onset of a rounded vowel or nasalized consonant.

For a while (Bladon and Al-Bamerni, 1982; Perkell and Chiang, 1986), there was the congenial suggestion that both theories might be right. Investigators found evidence sometimes that there was a start of a rounding or nasalization gesture at the beginning of a consonant (for rounding) or vowel string preceding a rounded vowel or nasalized consonant. Then, at an invariant interval before the rounded or nasalized phone, there was a rapid increase in rounding or nasalization as predicted by frame theory. However, that evidence was contaminated by a confounding (Perkell and Matthies, 1992). Bell-Berti and colleagues (e.g. Boyce et al., 1990); Gelfer et al., 1989) pointed out that some consonants are associated with lip rounding (e.g. /s/). Similarly, vowels are associated with lower positions of the velum compared to oral obstruents. Accordingly, to assess when anticipatory coarticulation of lip rounding or nasalization begins requires appropriate control utterances, to enable a distinction to be made between lip rounding or velum lowering due to coarticulation and that due to characteristics of phonetic segments in the coarticulatory domain. For lip rounding, for example, rounding during an utterance such as *stew* requires comparision with rounding during a control utterance such as *stee* in which the rounded vowel is replaced by an unrounded vowel. Any lip rounding during the latter utterance indicates rounding associated with the consonant string, and needs to be subtracted from lip activity during *stew*. Likewise, velum movement during a CV_nN sequence (that is, a sequence consisting of an oral consonant followed by *n* vowels preceding a nasal consonant) needs to be compared to velum movement during a CV_nC sequence. When those comparisons are made, evidence for feature spreading evaporates.

Recently, two different coproduction theories have been distinguished (Lindblom et al., 2002). In the account proposed by Ohman (1966), vowels are produced continuously. In a VCV utterance, according to the account, speakers produce a diphthongal movement from the first to the second vowel. The consonant was superimposed on that diphthongal trajectory. In the alternative account (e.g. Fowler and Saltzman, 1993), gestures for consonants and vowels overlap temporally. Any vowel-to-vowel overlap is temporal overlap, not production of a diphthongal gesture.

Evidence favoring the view of Fowler and Saltzman is the same kind of evidence that disconfirmed feature spreading theory. As noted earlier, speakers show troughs in lip gestures in sequences of consonants that intervene between rounded vowels. They should not if vowels are produced as diphthongal tongue gestures, but they are expected to if vowels are produced as separate gestures that overlap temporally with consonantal gestures.

29.5.1 Coarticulation resistance

Coarticulation has been variously characterized as a source of distortion (e.g. Ohala, 1981)—i.e. as a means by which articulation does not transparently implement essential phonological properties of consonants and vowels—or even as destructive of those properties (e.g. Hockett, 1955).

However, these characterizations overlook the finding of "coarticulation resistance"—an observation first made by Bladon and Al-Bamerni (1976), but developed largely by Recasens (e.g. 1984a; 1984b; 1985; 198); see also Farnetani, 1990). This is the observation that phones resist coarticulatory overlap by neighbors to the extent that the neighbors would interfere with achievement of the phones' gestural goals. For example,

Recasens (1984a) found decreasing vowel-to-vowel coarticulation in Catalan VCV sequences when the intervening consonant was one of the set: /ʝ/ (a dorso-palatal approximant), /ɲ/ (an alveolo-palatal nasal), /ʎ/ (an alveolo-palatal lateral), /n/ (an alveolar nasal). In the set, the consonants decreasingly use the tongue body to achieve their place of articulation. The tongue body is a major articulator in the production of vowels. Accordingly, it is likely that the decrease in vowel-to-vowel coarticulation in the consonant series occurs to prevent the vowels from interfering with achievement of the consonants' constriction location and degree. Recasens (1984b) found increasing vowel-to-consonant coarticulation in the same consonant series.

Compatible data from English can be seen in Figure 29.1. Figure 1a shows tongue body fronting

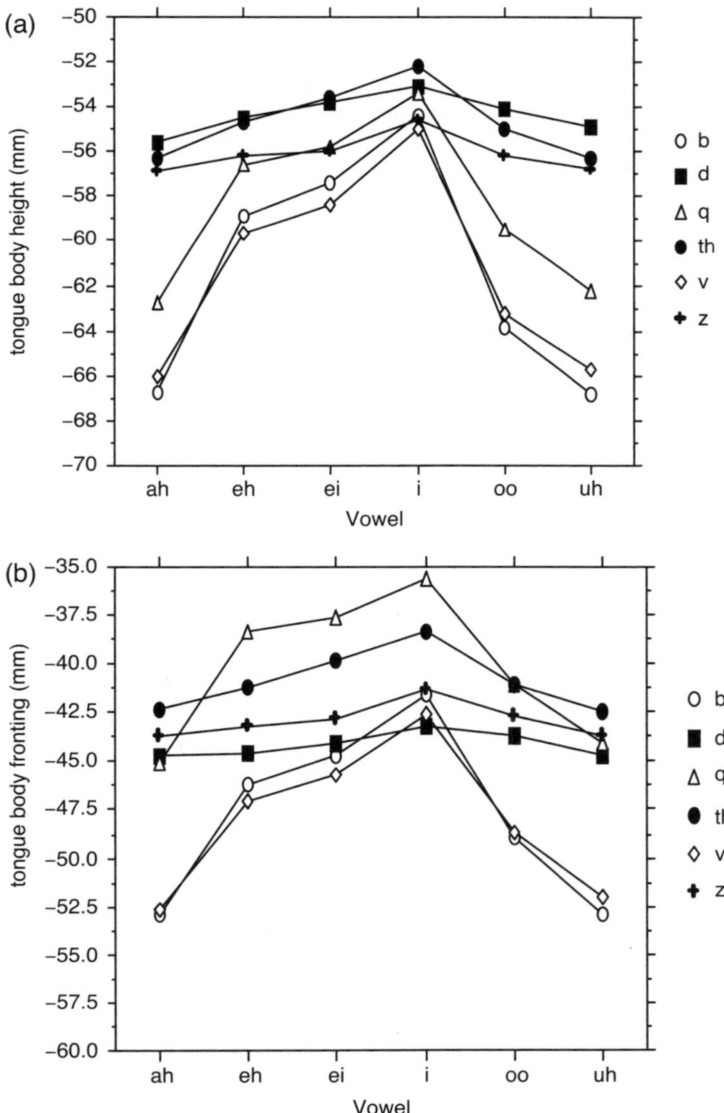

Figure 29.1 Tongue body height (a) and fronting (b) during production of three high and three low coarticulation resistant consonants produced in the context of six following stressed vowels. Measures taken in mid consonant closure.

data from a speaker of American English producing each of six consonants in the context of six following vowels (Fowler, 2005). During closure of three consonants (/b/, /v/, and /g/), there is a substantial shift in the tongue body height depending on the following vowel. During closure of the other three consonants (/d/, /z/, and /ð/, there is considerably less. Figure 1b shows similar results for tongue dorsum fronting. /b/, /v/, and, perhaps surprisingly, /g/ show less resistance to coarticulation for this speaker of American English than do /d/, /z/ and /ð/. The results for /b/ and /v/ most likely reflect the fact that they are labial consonants. They do not use the tongue, and so coproduction by vowels does not interfere with achievement of their gestural goals. The results for /g/, the fronting results at least, may reflect the fact that there is no stop in American English that is close in place of articulation with /g/ that might be confused with it were /g/'s place of articulation to shift due to coarticulation by the vowels.

29.5.2 Other factors affecting coarticulation

Frame theory (Bell-Berti and Harris, 1981) suggests a fixed extent of anticipatory coarticulation, modulated perhaps by speaking rate. However, the picture is more complicated. Browman and Goldstein (1988) reported a difference in respect to how consonants are phased to a tautosyllabic vowel depending on whether the consonants were in the syllable onset or in the coda. Consonants in the onset of American English syllables are phased so that the gestural midpoint of the consonants aligns with the vowel. In contrast, in the coda, the first consonant is phased invariantly with respect to the vowel regardless of the number of consonants in the coda.

For multi-gesture consonants, such as /l/ (Sproat and Fujimura, 1993), /r/, /w/ (Gick, 1999), and the nasal consonants (Krakow, 1989), the gestures are phased differently in the onset and coda. Whereas they are nearly simultaneous in the onset, the more open (more vowel-like) gestures precede in the coda. This latter phasing appears to respect the "sonority hierarchy" such that more vowel-like phones are closest to the vowel.

29.6 Prosody

There is more to producing speech than sequencing consonants and vowels. Speech has prosodic properties including an intonation contour, various temporal properties, and variations in articulatory "strength."

Theorists (see Shattuck-Hufnagel and Turk, 1996 for a review) identify hierarchical prosodic domains, each marked in some way phonologically. Domains include intonational phrases, which constitute the domain of complete intonational contours, intermediate phrases marked by a major ("nuclear") pitch accent and a tone at the phrase boundary, prosodic words (lexical words or a content word followed by a function word as in "call up"), feet (a strong syllable followed by zero or one weak syllables), and syllables. Larger prosodic domains often, but not always, set off syntactic phrases or clauses.

Intonation contours are patterns of variation in fundamental frequency consisting of high and low pitch accents, or accents that combine a high and low (or low and high) pitch excursions, and boundary tones at intonational and intermediate phrase boundaries. Pitch accents in the contours serve to accent information that the speaker wants to focus attention on, perhaps because it is new information in the utterance or because the speaker wants to contrast that information with other information. A whole intonation contour expresses some kind of meaning. For example, intonation contours can distinguish yes/no questions from statements (e.g. *So you are staying home this weekend ?*) Other contours can express surprise, disbelief or other expressions.

Because intonation contours reflect variation in fundamental frequency (f0), their production involves laryngeal control. This laryngeal control is coarticulated with other uses of the larynx, for example, to implement voicing or devoicing, intrinsic f0 (higher f0 for higher vowels), and tonal accompaniments of obstruent devoicing (a high tone on a vowel following an unvoiced obstruent).

Prosody is marked by other indications of phrasing. Prosodic domains from intonational phrases to prosodic words tend to be marked by final lengthening, pausing, and initial and final "strengthening." These effects generally increase in magnitude with the "strength" of the prosodic boundary (where "strength" increases with height of a phrase in the prosodic hierarchy). Final lengthening is an increase in the duration of articulatory gestures and their acoustic consequences before a phrase boundary. Strengthening is a quite local increase in the magnitude of gestures at phrase edges (e.g. Fougeron and Keating, 1997). Less coarticulation occurs across stronger phrase boundaries, and accented vowels resist vowel-to-vowel coarticulation (Cho, 2004).

These marks of prosodic structure serve to demarcate informational units in an utterance. However, we need to ask: why these marks? Final lengthening and pausing are, perhaps, intuitive. Physical systems cannot stop on a dime, and if the larger prosodic domains involve articulatory stoppings and restartings, then we should expect to see slowing to a stop and, sometimes, pausing before restarting. However, why strengthening? Byrd and Saltzman (2003) provide an account of final lengthening and pausing that may also provide some insight into at least some of the occurrences of strengthening. They have extended the task dynamic model, described earlier, to produce the timing variation that characterizes phrasing in prosody. They do so by slowing the rate of time flow of the model's central clock at phrase boundaries. Clock slowing gives rise to longer and less overlapped gestures at phrase edges. The magnitude of slowing reflects the strength of a phrase boundary. Byrd and Saltzman conceive of the slowing as a gesture (a "π gesture") that consists of an activation wave applied to any segmental gesture with which it overlaps temporally. π gestures span phrase boundaries, and therefore have effects at both edges of a phrase. Because clock slowing has as one effect, less overlap of gestures, a consequence may be less truncation of gestures due to overlap and so larger gestures.

Acknowledgments

Preparation of the manuscript was supported by NICHD grant HD-01994 and NIDCD grant DC-03782 to Haskins Laboratories.

References

Archangeli, D. (1997) Optimality theory: an introduction to linguistics in the 1990s. In D. Archangeli and D. T. Langendoen (eds), *Optimality Theory: An Overview*, pp. 1–32. Blackwell, Malden, MA.

Bell-Berti, F., and Harris, K. S. (1981) A temporal model of speech production. *Phonetica*, 38: 9–20.

Benguerel, A., and Cowan, H. (1974) Coarticulation of upper lip protrusion in French. *Phonetica*, 30: 41–55.

Bernstein, N. (1967) *The Coordination and Regulation of Movement*. Pergamon, London.

Bladon, A., and Al-Bamerni, A. (1982) One-stage and two-stage temporal patterns of coarticulation. *Journal of the Acoustical Society of America*, 72: S104.

Bladon, A., and Al-Bamerni, A. (1976). Coarticulation resistance in English /l/. *Journal of Phonetics*, 4: 137–50.

Boyce, S. (1990) Coarticulatory organization for lip rounding in Turkish and in English. *Journal of the Acoustical Society of America*, 8: 2584–95.

Boyce, S., Krakow, R., Bell-Berti, F., and Gelfer, C. (1990) Converging sources of evidence for dissecting articulatory movements into gestures. *Journal of Phonetics*, 18: 173–88.

Browman, C., and Goldstein, L. (1986) Towards an articulatory phonology. *Phonology Yearbook*, 3: 219–52.

Browman, C., and Goldstein, L. (1988) Some notes on syllable structure in articulatory phonology. *Phonetica*, 45: 140–55.

Browman, C., and Goldstein, L. (1991) Tiers in articulatory phonology, with some implications for casual speech. In J. Kingston and M. Beckman (eds), *Papers in Laboratory Phonology*, vol. 1: *Between the Grammar and the Physics of Speech*, pp. 341–76. Cambridge University Press, Cambridge.

Browman, C., and Goldstein, L. (1992) Articulatory phonology: an overview. *Phonetica*, 49: 155–80.

Browman, C., and Goldstein, L. (1995) Dynamics and articulatory phonology. In R. Port and T. van Gelder (eds), *Mind as Motion: Explorations in the Dynamics of Cognition*, pp. 175–93. MIT Press, Cambridge, MA.

Byrd, D., and Saltzman, E. (2003) The elastic phrase: modeling the dynamics of boundary-adjacent lengthening. *Journal of Phonetics*, 31: 149–80.

Cho, T. (2004) Prosodically conditioned strengthening and vowel-to-vowel coarticulation in English. *Journal of Phonetics*, 32: 141–76.

Daniloff, R., and Hammarberg, R. (1973) On defining coarticulation. *Journal of Phonetics*, 1: 239–48.

Daniloff, R., and Moll, K. (1968) Coarticulation of lip rounding. *Journal of Speech and Hearing Research*, 11: 707–21.

Delattre, P., and Freeman, D. (1968) A dialect study of American r's by x-ray motion picture. *Linguistics*, 44: 29–68.

Dell, G. (1986) A spreading-activation theory of retrieval in speech production. *Psychological Review*, 93: 283–321.

Easton, T. (1972) On the normal use of reflexes. *American Scientist*, 60: 591–9.

Farnetani, E. (1990) V-C-V lingual coarticulation and its spatiotemporal domain. In W. J. Hardcastle and A. Marchal (eds), *Speech Production and Speech Modeling*, pp. 93–130. Kluwer, The Netherlands.

Fougeron, C., and Keating, P. (1997) Articulatory strengthening at edges of prosodic domains. *Journal of the Acoustical Society of America*, 101: 3728–40.

Fowler, C. A. (1977) *Timing Control in Speech Production*. Indiana University Linguistics Club, Bloomington.

Fowler, C. A. (2005) Parsing coarticulated speech: effects of coarticulation resistance. *Journal of Phonetics*, 33: 195–213.

Fowler, C. A., and Saltzman, E. (1993) Coordination and coarticulation in speech production. *Language and Speech*, 36: 171–95.

Gafos, A., and Benus, S. (2003) On neutral vowels in Hungarian. Paper presented at the 15th International Congress of Phonetic Sciences, Barcelona.

Garrett, M. (1980) Levels of processing in speech production. In B. Butterworth (ed.), *Language Production*, vol. 1: *Speech and Talk*, pp. 177–220. Academic Press, London.

Gay, T. (1978) Articulatory units: segments or syllables? In A. Bell and J. B. Hooper (eds), *Syllables and Segments*, pp. 121–31. North-Holland, Amsterdam.

Gelfer, C., Bell-Berti, F., and Harris, K. (1989) Determining the extent of coarticulation: effects of experimental design. *Journal of the Acoustical Society of America*, 86: 2443–5.

Gick, B. (1999) The articulatory basis of syllable structure: a study of English glides and liquids. Ph.D. dissertation, Yale University.

Goldstein, L., Pouplier, M., Chen, L. Saltzman, E., and Byrd, D. (forthcoming) Action units slip in speech production errors. *Cognition.*

Guenther, F., Hampson, M., and Johnson, D. (1998) A theoretical investigation of reference frames for the planning of speech. *Psychological Review*, 105: 611–633.

Hockett, C. (1955) *A Manual of Phonetics*. Indiana University Press, Bloomington.

Kelso, J. A. S. (1984) Phase transitions and critical behavior in human bimanual coordination. *American Journal of Physiology*, 246: 1000–1004.

Kelso, J. A. S., Tuller, B., Vatikiotis-Bateson, E., and Fowler, C. A. (1984) Functionally-specific articulatory cooperation following jaw perturbation during speech: evidence for coordinative structures. *Journal of Experimental Psychology: Human Perception and Performance*, 10: 812–32.

Kenstowicz, M., and Kisseberth, C. (1979) *Generative Phonology*. Academic Press, New York.

Krakow, R. (1989) The articulatory organization of syllables: a kinematic analysis of labial and velar gestures. Ph.D. dissertation, Yale University.

Krakow, R. (1993) Nonsegmental influences on velum movement patterns: syllables, segments, stress and speaking rate. In M. Huffman, and R. Krakow (eds), *Phonetics and Phonology*, vol. 5: *Nasals, Nasalization and the Velum*, pp. 87–116. Academic Press, New York.

Levelt, W., Roelofs, A., and Meyer, A. (1999) A theory of lexical access in speech production. *Behavioral and Brain Sciences*, 22: 1–38.

Lindblom, B., Lubker, J., and Gay, T. (1979) Formant frequencies of some fixed mandible vowels and a model of speech motor programming by predictive simulation. *Journal of Phonetics*, 7: 147–61.

Lindblom, B., Sussman, H., Modaressi, G., and Burlingame, E. (2002) The trough effect in speech production: implications for speech motor programming. *Phonetica*, 59: 245–62.

Maeda, S. (1990) Compensatory articulation during speech: evidence from the analysis and synthesis of vocal tract shapes using an articulatory model. In W. Hardcastle and A. Marchal (eds), *Speech Production and Speech Modeling*, pp. 131–49. Kluwer Academic, Boston, MA.

Meyer, A. (1991) The time course of phonological encoding in language production: phonological encoding inside a syllable. *Journal of Memory and Language*, 30: 69–89.

Mowrey, R. and MacKay, I. (1990) Phonological primitives: electromyographic speech error evidence. *Journal of the Acoustical Society of America*, 88: 1299–1312.

Ohala, J. (1981) The listener as a source of sound change. In C. Masek, R. Hendrick, R. Miller, and M. Mille (eds), *Papers from the Parasession on Language and Behavior*, pp. 178–03. Chicago Linguistics Society, Chicago.

Ohman, S. (1966) Coarticulation in VCV utterances: spectrographic measurements. *Journal of the Acoustical Society of America*, 39: 151–68.

Perkell, J. and Chiang, C. (1986) Preliminary support for a 'hybrid model' of anticipatory coarticulation. In *Proceedings of the 12th International Congress of Acoustic*, pp. A3–A6.

Perkell, J. and Matthies, M. (1992) Temporal measures of labial coarticulation for the vowel /u/. *Journal of the Acoustical Society of America*, 91: 2911–25.

Perkell, J., Matthies, M., Svirsky, M., and Jordan, M. (1993) Trading relations between tongue-body raising and lip rounding in production of the vowel /u/: a pilot 'motor equivalence' study. *Journal of the Acoustical Society of America*, 93: 2948–61.

Pierrehumbert, J. (1990) Phonological and phonetic representations. *Journal of Phonetics*, 18: 375–94.

Pouplier, M. (2003a) The dynamics of error. Paper presented at the 15th International Congress of Phonetic Sciences, Barcelona.

Pouplier, M. (2003b) Units of phonological encoding: empirical evidence. Ph.D. dissertation, Yale University.

Recasens, D. (1984a) Vowel-to-vowel coarticulation in Catalan VCV sequences. *Journal of the Acoustical Society of America*, 76: 1624–35.

Recasens, D. (1984b) V-to-C coarticulation in Catalan VCV sequences: an articulatory and acoustical study. *Journal of Phonetics*, 12: 61–73.

Recasens, D. (1985) Coarticulatory patterns and degrees of coarticulation resistance in catalan cv sequences. *Language and Speech*, 28: 97–114.

Recasens, D. (1987) An acoustic analysis of v-to-c and v-to-v coarticulatory effects in Catalan and Spanish VCV sequences. *Journal of Phonetics*, 15: 299–312.

Ryle, G. (1949) *The Concept of Mind*. Barnes & Noble, New York.

Saltzman, E., and Kelso, J. A. S. (1987) Skilled action: a task-dynamic approach. *Psychological Review*, 94: 84–106.

Saltzman, E., Lofqvist, A., and Mitra, S. (2000) 'Clocks' and 'glue': global timing and intergestural cohesion. In M. B. Broe and J. Pierrehumbert (eds), *Papers in Laboratory Phonology*, vol. 5: *Acquisition and the Lexicon*, pp. 88–101. Cambridge University Press, Cambridge.

Saltzman, E., and Munhall, K. (1989) A dynamical approach to gestural patterning in speech production. *Ecological Psychology*, 1: 333–82.

Savariaux, C., Perrier, P., and Orliaguet, J. P. (1995) Compensation strategies for the perturbation of the rounded vowel [u] using a lip tube: a study of the control space in speech production. *Journal of the Acoustical Society of America*, 98: 2428–42.

Sevald, C. A., Dell, G., and Cole, J. (1995) Syllable structure in speech production: are syllables chunks or schemas? *Journal of Memory and Language*, 34: 807–20.

Shattuck-Hufnagel, S., and Turk, A. E. (1996) A prosody tutorial for investigators of auditory sentence processing. *Journal of Psycholinguistic Research,* 25: 193–247.

Sproat, R., and Fujimura, O. (1993) Allophonic variation in English /l/ and its implications for phonetic implementation. *Journal of Phonetics,* 21: 291–311.

Stevens, K., and Blumstein, S. (1981) The search for invariant correlates of phonetic features. In P Eimas and J Miller (eds), *Perspectives on the Study of Speech,* pp. 1–38. Erlbaum, Hillsdale, NJ.

Studdert-Kennedy, M. (1998) The particulate origins of language generativity: from syllable to gesture. In J. Hurford, M. Studdert-Kennedy, and C. Knight (eds), *Approaches to the Evolution of Language,* pp. 202–21. Cambridge University Press, Cambridge.

Tremblay, S., Shiller, D., and Ostry, D. (2003) Somatosensory basis of speech production. *Nature,* 423: 866–9.

Turvey, M. T. (1977) Preliminaries to a theory of action with reference to vision. In R. Shaw and J. Bransford (eds), *Perceiving, Acting and Knowing: Toward an Ecological Psychology*, pp. 211–66. Erlbaum, Hillsdale, NJ.

Turvey, M. T. (1990) Coordination. *American Psychologist,* 45: 938–53.

Yamanishi, J. Kawato, M., and Suzuki, R. (1980) Two coupled oscillators as a model for the coordinated finger tapping by both hands. *Biological Cybernetics,* 37: 219–25.

CHAPTER 30

The problem of speech patterns in time

Robert F. Port

One of the ways in which spoken languages differ from each other is in the temporal patterning of speech (e.g. Joos, 1948; Abramson and Lisker, 1964; Klatt, 1976; Ramus, 2002). These temporal patterns can be examined on several time scales, from very local (subsegmental and segmental) to global. The more global patterns—those lasting from a quarter second to a second or so—are most noticeable when we listen to speech in any language but our own. We may also become aware of rhythmic patterns in our own language when we hear it spoken by someone whose native language is something else. Along with other errors in foreign-accented speech, foreigners often seem to mangle the timing of our own language. Presumably there is some kind of pattern in the timing of speech gestures that accounts for our perception of rhythmic differences between languages. How might it be characterized? Human speech presents an extremely complex signal structured by many factors including the physiology of the vocal tract and constraints from the human perceptual system as well as patterns characteristic of the particular language (Fant, 1960; 1973). Which regions or time points are most relevant to rhythm perception? And, given some salient events, what kinds of durational measure between these events are most important for defining the temporal pattern itself? Whatever the answers are, these patterns in time create a sense that, for example, English, Spanish, and Chinese differ in their "speech rhythm." But what can be said objectively to justify even the use of the term "rhythm" in this context? Understanding linguistic rhythm is likely to be important, for example, for understanding how typical human linguistic fluency is achieved. Despite many attempts, however, a consistent and comprehensive framework for understanding speech timing has proven a challenge to researchers.

It seems likely that the problem of what the temporal patterns in a language really are will turn out to be partly a conceptual problem. Direct measurement of absolute time in seconds (treated as rational numbers in the computer) provides the raw empirical measures of time intervals, of course, but this is not at issue. The problem arises when we need to describe a pattern that is distributed over time.

30.1 Two conceptual frames for temporal patterns in speech

The conceptual tools we bring to any problem tend to shape our thinking along certain paths, even though the nature of this shaping may be difficult for us to see. Clarifying the conceptual tools we rely on may be a helpful step toward developing a broader, more flexible framework for description of temporal patterns. There seem to be two important a priori descriptive frames for describing speech patterns distributed over time: "symbol strings," using discrete, letter-like symbol tokens (such as the phonetic alphabet and orthographic words) whose patterns in time (i.e. transcriptions using an alphabet or orthography) serve as models for speech events, and "cycles," i.e. uniform motions around a circle, for measuring periodic time intervals. The data of speech research can be displayed graphically and measured in milliseconds, but a conceptual framework is needed to interpret the displays and measurements as linguistic or cognitive patterns over time. It seems that the two basic descriptive schemes above present a choice of conceptual tool.

30.1.1 Symbol strings

The first and most important framework uses letter symbols as a model for the continuous gestures and sounds of phonetics and phonology. Phonetic and phonological transcriptions employ discrete, serially ordered (and thus non-overlapping) consonants and vowels as the uniform units of human speech. Thus English speakers produce sound patterns that we identify with the orthographic word *laugh* and can transcribe as the letter sequence [læf]. A transcription having these properties is assumed to be used by speakers to say the word, and used by hearers to recognize that the word has been spoken. Clearly, phonetic and phonological segments are intuitive and vivid for us, since they have most of the properties of the orthographic letters that were learned in childhood by those receiving an alphabet-based education (Ziegler and Goswami, 2005). Phonetic segments are like letters in being discrete and serial ordered, but differ from letters primarily in that they are not graphical but are hypothesized to be psychological. Thus, it is widely assumed that the nervous system needs to represent speech to itself symbolically, i.e. using some efficient, speaker-invariant way. It is the serially ordered phonological segments that play this role, just as we use the technology of writing on paper to represent and store utterances in a language. Letter-like, speaker-independent, and rate-independent symbols constitute the primary conceptual framework that has been used by most working linguists and psychologists for at least the past century (Saussure, 1916; Bloomfield, 1933; Jones, 1950; Jakobson et al., 1952; Chomsky and Halle, 1968; Liberman et al., 1968; Ladefoged, 1965; 1972; IPA, 1999). The continua of temporally overlapping speech gestures and speech acoustics are taken to be describable by an ordered sequence of discrete segmental symbols which are static (within each symbol) and whose only temporal relationships are definable in terms of the serial order of symbols (basically the relationships of "before" vs. "after" and, in the case of phonetic features, "simultaneous" vs. "non-simultaneous"). This model may be intuitively natural for us and thus attractive, but it has long been known that ordered letter-like symbols cannot provide rich enough specification of linguistic time patterns to successfully account for speech perception (Joos, 1948; Liberman et al., 1968; Dorman et al., 1979; Lisker and Abramson, 1971).

Of course, many important temporal properties of speech can be distinguished fairly well using letter-size symbols. Phonetic segments can differentiate [tæn] vs. [ænt] vs. [næt] by reordering the symbols, and much more. They can also be used to differentiate some more explicitly temporal patterns; for example, letters are useful to describe temporal patterns found in Japanese where there are several contrasts between lexical classes with the same sequence of phonetic segmental states. The phonetic alphabet can differentiate them by simply using one vs. two segmental symbols. For example, Figure 30.1a shows pronunciations of the words

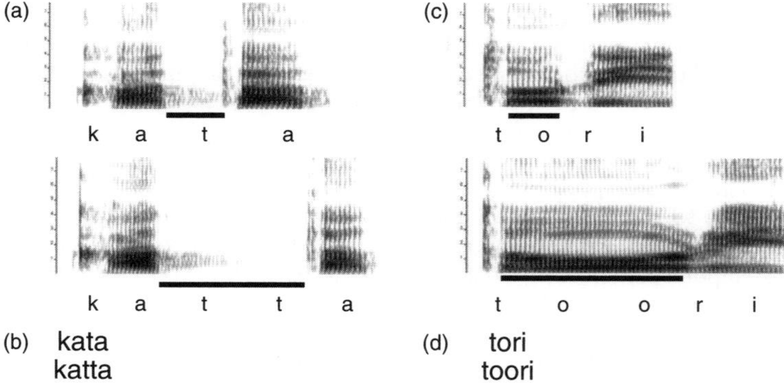

Figure 30.1 Spectrograms of Japanese minimal pairs, *kata* (shoulder) vs. *katta* (won) and *tori* (take) vs. *toori* (street) with the /t/ durations and /o/ durations marked with a black bar. The *x* axis is frequency (filtered into roughly 300 Hz bands) and *y* is time. It can be seen that both the stop and vowel segments are more than twice the duration when long as when they are short. Thanks to Kenji Yoshida for assistance with this figure.

kata and *katta* (excised from a neutral carrier sentence). The most obvious difference between the spectrograms of the two words is the duration of the [t] stop in the middle of the word (as marked by the horizontal black bar) (Dorman et al., 1979). This is normally modeled in linguistic descriptions (Vance, 1986; Tsujimura, 1995) by using one vs. two segments, as in Figure 30.1b. A similar difference between long and short vowels as in *tori* and *toori* is shown in Figure 30.1c (where the vowel is marked with black bars) and segmentally in Figure 30.1d. These segmental descriptions provide sufficient specificity for a speaker of Japanese to produce the intended words correctly. In fact, however, although the notation suggests a durational ratio between the two stops and two vowels of 2:1, the actual durational ratio tends to be closer to 3:1 in both cases (Hirata and Whiton, 2005; Hirata, 2004). But transcription using one instead of two symbols still does a reasonable job of representing these differences in duration. Later, an alternative description not depending on letters will be provided that will show why the durational ratios are about 1:3.

Many linguists and psychologists assume that everything of linguistic relevance about speech patterns in time can be captured using segment strings (e.g. Saussure, 1916; Bloomfield, 1933; Chomsky and Halle, 1968). Indeed, the observational data serving as input for most of linguistics is the phonetic transcription, a serially ordered list of symbol tokens. This seems to be the form in which speech is presented to our consciousness (Ladefoged, 1980; IPA, 1999; Bloomfield, 1933). Some linguists further assume that this list of tokens makes up a closed set and that all tokens of this set are perceptually distinct from each other (Chomsky and Halle, 1968; McCarthy, 2002), although others have disputed such a claim (Hockett, 1968; Sampson, 1977; Port and Leary, 2005). On the traditional view in linguistics, the natural and fundamental time scale of language is discrete, like letters and the integers, and not continuous in time.

A few linguists have criticized this view as reflecting a bias toward use of an alphabet (e.g. Firth, 1948; Linell, 2005), and have suggested that our segmental intuitions may result from lifelong training using letters to represent speech (Faber, 1992; Öhman, 2000; Port and Leary, 2005; Port, 2006). Phoneticians and linguists have struggled to reconcile the lack of fit between the physically observable continuous audio signals for speech and the intuitive symbol strings (Liberman et al., 1968; Fant, 1973; Ladefoged, 1984; Keating, 1984; Port, 1981). For example, the notion of phonetic segments has motivated experiments on unexpected timing cues such as those for the English voicing feature (Lisker and Abramson, 1964; Lisker, 1984) and motivated measurement by phoneticians of the durations of various segmental intervals (e.g. Klatt, 1976; Port, 1981; Ramus, Nespor and Mehler, 1999). But phoneticians generally understand that the phonetic segments of auditory phonetic transcription cannot be assigned to any specific acoustic features (see Pisoni and Levi, Chapter 1 this volume). This implies that there remains a mystery about how a consonant or vowel-like segments are related to the physical acoustic or motor forms of speech (Ladefoged, 1980; Browman and Goldstein, 1992).

An important reason for the appeal of segmental descriptions of speech is the rate invariance of this representation: a change in speaking rate need not result in a change in the phonetic or phonological transcription. This follows since strings of symbols have only serial order to encode time (although, of course, segmental symbols can be given labels like "long" and "short" or "20 ms in duration", but this is not the same as actually representing time; Lisker, 1984). Thus, distances between adjacent segments (like distances between adjacent letters) have no meaning. So the difficulty which arises is that serial order provides such a crude characterization of speech events in time that many aspects of speech timing that are critical for word specification, as well as for distinguishing between different languages, simply cannot be captured using segments alone (Port, 1986; Keating, 1985). This led to proposals for "temporal implementation rules" (Chomsky and Halle, 1968; Klatt, 1976; van Santen, 1996) which would employ durational labels like "inherent duration = 80 ms" and some arithmetic to compute "output duration targets" for each segment. But these target durations are still just symbols that need to be somehow interpreted.

The segmental model has inspired many studies of the characteristic timing patterns associated with the consonants and vowels of various languages. One product of decades of research on segmental aspects of speech is a number of generalizations about speech timing across languages (Lisker and Abramson, 1964; 1971; for reviews see Lehiste, 1970 and Klatt, 1976). For example, it seems to be generally the case that time intervals corresponding to low vowels like [a] are longer in the same context than the same intervals for high vowels like [i] and [u] (Elert, 1964; Peterson and Lehiste, 1960). It also seems to be usually the case that the constrictions for voiceless stops and fricatives, like [t, p, s, f], are longer than the corresponding voiced consonant constrictions, like [d, b, z, v] (Elert, 1964; Lisker, 1984). Of course, there are also many temporal patterns which are unique characteristics of one language (or group of close relatives) but have not been found in other languages. Some examples include mora timing in Japanese (Port et al., 1987; Han, 1994), vowel lengthening after voiced obstruents in Arabic (Port et al., 1980), and complementary vowel and obstruent durations in Germanic languages (Elert, 1964; Lehiste, 1970; Lisker, 1984; Port and Crawford, 1989).

The important thing about most of these universal and language-specific timing patterns is that segmental models simply do not provide the conceptual tools to capture most of the temporal patterns. To use segments to describe speech, one must discard everything about time except the serial order of articulatory states. And once discarded, the information is no longer available for further analysis. But how could one retain more information about temporal patterns? One might try to measure out a time unit (e.g. a cycle) relative to which phonetic events can be located.

30.1.2 Circles in time

The second conceptual tool is the "circle in time," an isochronous cycle used as a scale for describing temporal patterns. If a temporal cycle is run at a slow rate, fractions of a time circle can be used for the specification of temporal patterns. By nesting a faster circular motion within a slower one, the slower one can be cut into halves or thirds (with frequencies twice or three times or more the frequency of the largest cycle). The European tradition of musical notation is a good illustration of this concept. Musical time is measured relative to a periodic pulse (frequently a foot tap) using nested fractions (half-notes, quarter-notes, etc.). "Meter" is the term for a pattern of nested cycles which pick out particular locations in time relative to the basic (or tactus) pulse (Handel, 1989). Repeated faster cycles (usually two or three) provide clock ticks or phase zeros within a slower cycle (Handel, 1989; Port, 2003). The standard music notation system generalizes the notion of meter to create a general method of periodic pattern notation.

Of course, because the intervals are measured relative to a regular pulse, they always represent temporal ratios, and the notated patterns are thus invariant under changes in the rate of the pulses. Any piece of music can be played with some variation in rate without changing the identity of the music. So, in music, temporal locations are in effect labeled as particular phase angles relative to nested periodic cycles. The most salient temporal targets for these locations tend to be harmonic fractions of the larger cycle. Of course, only in the notation will one find perfect nesting and cycles of ideal constant durations; actual performances will normally deviate from the formal ideal (Honing, 2002). Thus, musical notation divides the musical "measure" hierarchically into smaller integer fractions. It presumes one basic cycle, either the measure or the beat, to which the other cycles are time-locked. Most music in most cultural traditions can be approximated reasonably well using such a formal notational system for rhythm, since music traditions are usually based on some preferred metrical patterns (Seeger, 1958; Lehrdal and Jackendoff, 1983; Arom, 1991).

From mathematics, there is an alternative terminology for meter using phase angles where a single complete cycle can be described equivalently as 2π radians, 360°, or the interval {0, 1} (see Abraham and Shaw, 1983; Winfree, 2001). The cycle can then be divided into integer fractions just as in musical notation. Using a {0, 1} cycle, the onsets of a series of four quarter-notes in a four-beat musical measure would be located at phase angles of 0, 0.25, 0.50, and 0.75.

The cyclic framework for thinking about time has the important property of invariance under changes in speaking rate. Still this framework has only rarely been used to describe speech (a few cases where it has been used are Martin, 1972; Abercrombie, 1967: 97–8; Pike, 1946: 35) primarily because of the high temporal variability of speech. The problem is that the circle for measuring time obviously can have only a fixed rate of angular rotation of the cycle—just like the clock on the wall. So if some cycle-like behavior has a fixed rate, then the model applies nicely, but if the behavior exhibits moment-to-moment wobble in rate, then the framework of music notation seems inappropriate. This greatly limits its utility for describing speech.

So it seems that these two descriptive models, (1) serially ordered symbol strings and (2) phase angles of repeating cycles, provide scientists of language with our primary conceptual tools for understanding speech events in time. Both offer practical descriptive terms for certain phenomena distributed over time. But the phenomena they describe are very different. Despite the overwhelming reliance on segmental description for the past century, this representation ignores too much temporal detail that is known to be important for speech production and perception, and offers no tools for description of rhythmically produced speech (Port and Leary, 2005). Period-based descriptions have been applied in a variety of ways over the years. The remainder of this chapter will survey a number of domains where the cycle framework has been applied, and will also describe some mechanisms that might explain the behavior of the nested cycles.

30.2 **Global timing constraints: "stress-timed" vs. "syllable-timed" languages**

Classical phonetic theory had little or nothing to say about possible temporal patterns in speech since it relied on letter-like segments to capture the serial order of gestures. Nevertheless, Pike (1946) boldly suggested that languages may come in two basic rhythmic styles, one based on periodic spacing of syllables and the other on periodic spacing of stressed syllables (so that unstressed syllables are constrained to fit). Abercrombie (1967) endorsed the suggestion and introduced the terms "stress-timed" (as English, German, Russian, and Arabic supposedly are) as opposed to "syllable-timed" (like French, Spanish, Telugu, and Yoruba). In the first type, some syllables are "stressed" (or emphasized) and others are not, while in the other type all syllables are equally weighted (Martin et al., 1972). This hypothesis makes predictions about the timing of various intervals that can be investigated experimentally.

Another point raised about this hypothesis is that the specific languages that were characterized as stress-timed and syllable-timed tend to differ in their constraints on the segmental structure of syllables (Dauer, 1983). Stress-timed languages, like English, tend to have some syllables that are complex, with initial and final consonant clusters and complex vowel nuclei (which tend to be the "stressed" syllables). Other syllables, the unstressed ones, tend to be much simpler, most often employing a single vowel. In contrast, typical syllable-timed languages, such as French and Spanish, tend to have much more uniform syllable types permitting few or no clusters and no complex vowel nuclei. Thus the timing regularities observed might be a consequence of mere segmental serial order patterns (Dauer, 1983; 1987).[1]

These observations have led to a great deal of research over the past few decades which has generally failed to support the predictions of isochrony (in stress-timed languages, Roach, 1982; Dauer, 1983, in syllable-timed languages, Wenk and Wioland, 1982). But, of course, perfect isochrony is only a prediction based on the notation system assuming constant-rate cycles. Another implicit assumption of the opposition of stress-timing vs. syllable-timing is that the notion of a syllable has some universal definition. In fact, no such cross-linguistic definition exists, and it is very difficult to define the notion of syllable in a universal way (Ramus, 2002).

As rigid methods of description were not supportive, attempts at statistical characterization of these speech timing types have been explored (Low and Grabe, 1995; Low et al., 2000; Ramus et al., 1999; Ramus et al., 2003). The more successful tests of the hypotheses about the typology of rhythm types have employed measures of the average variation in consonant duration (noted as ΔC in Figure 30.2) and the percentage of the total duration that was occupied by vocalic intervals (noted as %V). By this means, typical examples of stress-timed languages (English and Dutch) and syllable-timed languages (Spanish, French, Italian, and Catalan) could be separated, as shown in Figure 30.2 (from Ramus et al., 1999). The percentage of text duration that is vocalic was measured for rather small speech samples (five three-second speech samples by four speakers each) for eight languages. The results are suggestive, but have not been expanded. It is interesting that the only known example of a "mora-timed" language, Japanese, was separated nicely from both syllable-timed and stress-timed languages.

30.3 **Regular "mora timing" in Japanese**

Traditional teaching in the Japanese educational system has taught that each *kana* symbol (often

[1] Of course, if there were independent evidence of the two timing types, one could just as well argue that the syllable-structure constraints are a consequence of the characteristic timing type. If stress is alternated, then it would make sense for a language to invest in more complex syllables where the most attention is being paid. (Large and Jones, 1999).

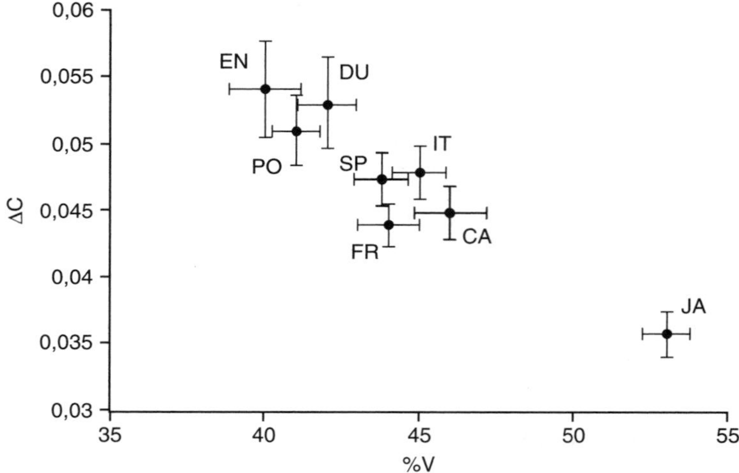

Figure 30.2 Means and standard deviations of consonant intervals in seconds plotted against the percent of overall duration that is vocalic for English (EN), Dutch (DU), Polish (PO), Spanish (SP), Italian (IT), French (FR), Catalan (CA), and Japanese (JA). Crossbars show ±1 SD across sample means. (Reproduced with permission from Ramus et. al. 1999.)

described as a syllabic writing system) takes the same amount of time to say (Homma, 1981; Beckman, 1982). This implies that word durations should come in integer-based durational ratios. Indeed, the duration of a word should be predictable from the number of moras (given a speaking rate). The speech fragment represented by a single kana symbol is called a "mora." Words can be written in this roughly syllabic writing system using an integer number of kana. But a mora is quite different from a syllable in English. Thus a consonant-vowel syllable, like *da* or *to*, is one mora, but a syllable like *hon* ("book, origin") requires two kana for its spelling and thus counts as two moras, whereas in English it is still a single syllable. Japanese has syllables with long vowels, as in *Tookyoo,* so this word counts as four moras (and requires four kana) while *Kyooto* counts as three moras (and three kana). There are also long consonants, as in *chotto* ("a little bit") (three moras, three kana) and *katta* ("won") (three moras and three kana).

Controversy arose as to whether the traditional claim is correct: are moras equal in duration? Of course, Japanese segments exhibit similar durational properties to other languages. That is, voiceless obstruents are longer than the corresponding voiced ones, low vowels are longer than high vowels, [s] is longer than the other fricatives, flaps are much shorter than other consonants, and so forth (Port et al., 1980; Beckman, 1982). This would lead one to expect that mora durations could not be constant. How could *ri* be the same duration as *sa* if the segments exhibit universal trends? In fact, they are not the same (Beckman, 1982; Port et al., 1987; Warner and Arai, 2001). Nevertheless, some researchers have continued to insist that the traditional claim is partly correct by showing that there are compensatory adjustments of neighboring moras when a mora is too long or too short (Port et al., 1987; Han, 1994). Supporters of "mora timing" point to evidence which looks at a series of neighboring moras. They note that, at least for certain styles of speech, word duration is tightly correlated with the number of moras, and that segments adjacent to a short mora (such as the long stop or vowel in Figure 30.1) are typically lengthened, which brings word duration closer to that expected for the number of moras.

Still the regularity of mora duration has remained controversial for several reasons. One is that as speaking rate is increased in Japanese, the regularity of mora timing gets much weaker (Warner and Arai, 2001). A second reason is that many phenomena about mora timing might be attributed to segmental constraints, although this account cannot explain the observed compensatory lengthening and shortening effects. Whatever the degree to which Japanese speakers may constrain their speech timing to regularize moras, it will be seen in the next section that humans everywhere engage in *some* styles of speech that involve entrainment to periodic patterns.

30.4 Deliberate metrical production

There are a number of contexts in which speakers of most languages talk in a way that exhibits periodicity. The first is when reciting a list. When a person produces a familiar list of items (e.g. the numbers, the alphabet, the days of the week), the fluent pattern is to space the stressed syllables roughly equally in time (Quené and Port, 2005). Repetitive speech that is chanted by a single speaker (e.g. a commercial chant, a tour guide's text) or by a group of speakers (e.g. communal prayer, chanting at a political rally) also seem to be invariably periodic.

Poetry presents a somewhat confusing case. In literate communities, poetry seems to be more strongly associated with the written culture, and has metrical structures that need not be defined in continuous time at all but in terms of serially ordered patterns of various kinds (Boomsliter and Creel, 1977). But some poetry styles, such as so-called doggerel verse (i.e. humorous verse such as the limerick), are normally performed aloud using meter based on periodic temporal intervals, although little research has been done on such performances. Apparently all humans are able to constrain their speech to fit some externally specified periodicities. It seems that almost all human communities have traditions of periodic speaking styles (Merriam, 1964; List, 1963). These styles and their characteristic rhythm patterns seem to be easily picked up by children by 3 or 4 years of age, and are evidently entertaining to perform and listen to throughout life. Typically, there is periodic repetition of some pulse in the speech (sometimes reinforced by coupled periodic motions of the hands, feet or trunk), and prominent events in the speech are approximately aligned in time with these pulses (Port, 2003).

30.4.1 Perceptual centers

These periodic speech patterns raise an important question whose answer is not obvious: If many patterns are periodic and can be modeled with an oscillator, what region in a continuous speech event counts as phase zero? Where exactly is the beat? What serves as the origin of the cycle or the place where a person would locate, say, a tap (Allen, 1972a; 1972b)? To take a concrete example, if a speaker regularizes the spacing of a pair of alternated monosyllables, as in *ba, spa, ba, spa*, etc., will the [b]-release and [s]-onset be equally spaced (since they are the first sound emitted for each syllable), or will the onsets of the two [a]s, or something else? One can imagine a variety of possibilities. It might be the loudness maximum of the vowel, the location of a pitch maximum, the onset of a motor gesture, or even a gesture velocity peak. It is not known if the answer is uniform across languages, but with English-speaking subjects the answer seems to be approximately the onset of the vowel (Morton et al., 1976; Patel et al., 1999). The so-called "perceptual center" or "P-center" of a stressed syllable is close to the onset of the vowel [a] for both syllables. Thus, for *ba*, the beat occurs right at the onset of the vowel, and for *spa*, the beat moves slightly to the "left" of the vowel onset showing that the [s] in *spa* has some influence on the effective location of phase zero. This notion of a perceptual center can be approximated automatically by bandpass filtering the speech signal to include energy between roughly 100 Hz and 800 Hz (the F1 region), smoothing this energy envelope in time (integrated by about a 30 ms window) and then locating a peak in the first derivative (Scott, 1993). The reason that the first formant frequency region is most important is presumably because the first formant is where most of the acoustic energy is concentrated (Fant, 1960), and the onset is most important because the auditory nerve responds most strongly to onsets of energy (Delgutte, 1997; Kato et al., 1998).

30.5 Harmonic timing effect

As noted above, there are many situations where speakers talk as if in time to a metronome, placing stressed syllable onsets at roughly equal intervals. Rhythmic production of speech is certainly not the normal way to speak, but it is something every speaker performs for short periods from time to time. In addition, if English speakers are asked to repeat a short piece of text over and over, there is a strong tendency to divide the repetition cycle into equal-interval fractions, i.e. to nest several shorter cycles within the longer cycle. Thus the onsets of stressable syllables tend to migrate toward integer fractions of the whole cycle of repeated speech (Cummins and Port, 1998; Tajima and Port, 2003). For example, if a speaker repeats aloud a phrase like *Two thirty-five* at least five times, there is a strong tendency to locate the vowel onset of each instance of *five* at one of only three locations relative to the vowel onsets of each successive repetition beginning with *Two*, as suggested by example (1). In the speaker's first or second reading of each pattern, irregular timings may result (where the beat for *five* may occur at many positions in the *Two-Two* cycle), but if the speaker continues to repeat the phrase, very quickly one of the three patterns, as in example (1a), (1b), or (1c), will become stable (Cummins and Port, 1998).

1. Three stable ways to repeat the phrase *Two thirty-five*, using boldface to suggest stress.

1a. ***Two*** *thirty-**five***, ***Two*** *thirty-**five***, ... (2 beats)

1b. ***Two thir****-ty* ***five***, ***Two thir****-ty* ***five***, ... (3 beats fast)

1c. ***Two*** *thir-ty-**five*** [rest], ***Two*** *thir-ty-**five*** [rest], ... (3 beats slow)

This has been termed the "harmonic timing effect" (Cummins and Port, 1998). To see the degree of the preference for these three patterns by English speakers, see Figure 30.3. In this experiment, participants were given a short piece of text to repeat, similar to *Two thirty-five* above. A two-toned metronomic auditory signal was presented, a high tone followed by a low tone. They were instructed to produce the first syllable (like *Two*) in time with the high tone and to produce the last syllable (like *five*) in time with the low tone. The phase lag between the high and low tones (relative to the high-high interval) was randomly varied from 0.20 to 0.70, producing a flat distribution of phase-lagged stimuli. Each metronome pattern was repeated for eight to ten cycles per trial (fewer at the slower rates) and subjects tried to hit the target pattern for each cycle. However, the frequency histogram of almost 8,000 measured phase lags in Figure 30.3 shows a strong bias toward one of the three rhythm patterns shown above in example (1). These results suggest the three formal rhythm patterns of the two- and three-beat measures shown in Figure 30.4. But the important question is: what mechanisms could cause speakers to show such strong biases toward these particular temporal patterns?

The data suggest that the formal, simple time locations illustrated in Figure 30.4 are really attractor basins in time. In fact, the attractor basins probably look much like Figure 30.3 turned upside down. These attractors encourage production of temporal patterns that are sufficiently optimal, in some sense, that speakers

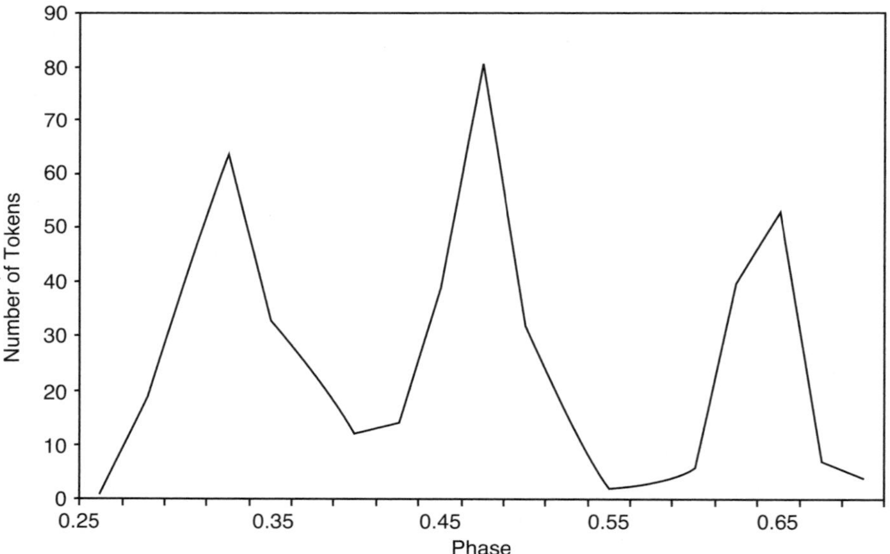

Figure 30.3 Participants were instructed to align the first syllable in a short phrase (*Two thirty-five* or *Beg for a dime*, etc.) with the first metronome pulse and the last syllable with the second pulse. The uniformly distributed target phases (as indicated by auditory pulses) could only be imitated by the participants with a bias showing three strong modes near 0.33, 0.5, and 0.66. Some lags they found very difficult to perform, such as the regions near 0.4 and 0.55. See Cummins and Port (1998) for more details. (Figure reproduced with permission from Port and Leary, 2005.)

Figure 30.4 The three peaks in Figure 30.3 suggest the three musical notation patterns shown here (using the phrase *Beg for a dime* rather than *Two thirty-five*). When the final syllable occurs near one-third, there is a rest on the third of three beats. When it occurs near one-half, there are two beats to the cycle. And when it occurs near two-thirds, the syllable *for* finds itself on the second of three beats and begins to sound somewhat stressed. (Figure reproduced with permission from Cummins and Port, 1998.)

cannot help gravitating toward these particular phase relationships. This notion of attraction shows why a dynamical model, based on limit cycles, is an improvement over the rigid circle model discussed above. A dynamical model only claims that speakers will exhibit attractors at certain phase angles; and attractors can be demonstrated in a number of ways, such as the inability to accurately imitate a pattern containing a target away from an attractor but a fairly good ability to target the attractor itself.

But is this kind of timing at the phrase level really a linguistic phenomenon? One reason for such a conclusion is that speakers of different languages entrain speech to metronomes in different ways (cf. Zawaydeh et al., 2002; Tajima and Port, 2003). Some prefer for linguistics to deal only with phenomena that can be described with serially ordered symbols (Chomsky and Halle, 1968), implying that linguistics is defined by the familiar conceptual model of letters. To insist on this is to allow our conceptual tools to restrict our domain of study.

30.6 **Modeling rhythm with dynamical systems**

Further conceptual frameworks, beyond segments and circles in time, can be developed employing additional mathematics. Models using relaxation oscillators already exist which can produce attractors at the preferred phase angles. It is known how to construct simple dynamical models that behave periodically in ways that exhibit meter-like patterns by producing attractors at harmonic fractions. These mathematical models of rhythmic behavior can also be interpreted as models of the behavior of some structures of the central nervous system (e.g. Abraham and Shaw, 1983; Kelso, 1995; Saltzman and Munhall, 1989; Guenther, 1995). One kind of mechanism that has been proposed to account for the patterns in example (1) and Figure 30.3 would employ two coupled oscillator cycles, one of which tracks the cycle of the phrase as a whole and the other cycles either two or three times faster. Phase zero of each oscillator is an attractor for syllable onsets (i.e. for energy onsets), thereby providing target times for stressed syllable beats within the phrase cycle (Port, 2003). The faster oscillators are themselves attracted to the phase zero of the slow oscillator (thus keeping them at constant phase relative to each other), and also provide targets within the long cycle for stressed syllable onsets. The faster oscillators provide target phase angles at either one-half or at one-third and two-thirds of the longer cycle. Coupling between the oscillators means that the equation for the instantaneous phase of each includes the instantaneous phase of the other oscillator as a parameter (Abraham and Shaw, 1983; Large and Jones, 1999; Port, 2003). This would prevent their relative phase from shifting very much, and thus provide a periodic target time for location of each of the stressed syllable beats. Given equations for coupled oscillators, the phase zeros of both these oscillators become attractors that draw the auditory beats of the stressed syllables toward them (Large and Jones, 1999; Port, 2003). The only strong attractors (for English speakers, at least) were, as shown in example (1), at one-third, one-half, and two-thirds of the phase cycle (Cummins and Port, 1998), although other languages may find additional stable divisions (Zawaydeh et al., 2002; Tajima and Port, 2003). This implies that 2:1 and 3:1 oscillators are easy (or familiar) to English speakers, while other ratios (such as 5:1, 7:1, etc.) are much more difficult (and less familiar). It is possible that further model development along these lines will be productive.

30.7 **Phrase edge timing phenomena**

Another prominent durational effect is associated, most noticeably, with larger edges in speech: phrases, paragraphs, and so on. It was noted early on that the vowels in the last syllable of a phrase (whether the phrase is a whole sentence or just a one-syllable word) are lengthened. Recent research suggests that this effect is much more general, and occurs in the middle of utterances such that the degree of slowing down is roughly proportional to the strength of the boundary (Byrd et al., 2000; Byrd and Saltzman, 2003). Thus the word boundary after *boys* in *Look at the boys on the field* will exhibit less slowing down than *If you see the boys, tell them to come home* and much less than *Hello boys, come on home*. This stretching or slowing appears to be achieved by decelerating all aspects of speech articulation at such boundaries. Thus consonants are also lengthened near (and especially before) a phrasal boundary (Byrd and Saltzman, 2003). The work by Byrd and Saltzman is formulated in terms of dynamical models of speech that are compatible with the dynamical models of speech rhythm discussed above.

30.8 Conclusion

The segment model for speech has dominated the thinking of phoneticians, psychologists, and phonologists for a century. But it has long been known to be inadequate to account for speech timing. These inadequacies have been ignored by many linguists because it was considered that intuitive descriptions of speech were of central relevance to linguistics. Phoneticians have turned in recent years to dynamical models of speech production and perception in order to address these inadequacies. Dynamical models for motor and perceptual cycles account for much, although we still do not know how to describe the audible rhythmic patterns of most speech in most languages. But at least some new conceptual tools are available that offer greater flexibility.

Acknowledgments

The author is grateful to Ken de Jong, Mark van Dam, and Kenji Yoshida for contributions to this essay.

References

Abercrombie, D. (1967) *Elements of General Phonetics*. Aldine, Chicago.

Abraham, R., and Shaw, C. (1983) *Dynamics: The Geometry of Behavior*, part 1. Aerial Press, Santa Cruz, CA.

Allen, G. (1972a) The location of rhythmic stress beats in English: an experimental study, I. *Language and Speech*, 15: 72–100.

Allen, G. (1972b) The location of rhythmic stress beats in English: an experimental study, II. *Language and Speech*, 15: 179–95.

Arom, S. (1991) *African Polyphony and Polyrhythm: Musical Structure and Methodology*, MIT Press, Cambridge, MA.

Beckman, M. (1982) Segment duration and the 'mora' in Japanese. *Phonetica*, 39: 113–135.

Bloomfield, L. (1933) *Language*, Holt, Rinehart & Winston, New York.

Boomsliter, P., and Creel, W. (1977) The secret springs: Housman's outline on metrical rhythm and language. *Language and Style*, 10: 296–323.

Browman, C., and Goldstein, L. (1992) Articulatory phonology: an overview. *Phonetica*, 49: 155–80.

Byrd, D., Kaun, A., Narayanan, S., and Saltzman, E. (2000) Phrasal signatures in articulation. In M. Broe and J. Pierrehumbert (eds), *Papers in Laboratory Phonology V*. Cambridge, Cambridge University Press, 70–87.

Byrd, D., and Saltzman, E. (2003) The elastic phrase: modeling the dynamics of boundary-adjacent lengthening. *Journal of Phonetics*, 31: 149–80.

Chomsky, N., and Halle, M. (1968) *The Sound Pattern of English*. Harper & Row, New York.

Cummins, F., and Port, R. (1998) Rhythmic constraints on stress timing in English. *Journal of Phonetics*, 26: 145–71.

Dauer, R. (1983) Stress-timing and syllable-timing reanalyzed. *Journal of Phonetics*, 11: 51–62.

Dauer, R. (1987) Phonetic and phonological components of language rhythm. Paper presented at the 11th International Congress of Phonetic Sciences, Tallinn, Estonia.

Delgutte, B. (1997) Auditory neural processing of speech. In W. J. Hardcastle and J. Laver (eds), *The Handbook of Phonetic Sciences*. Oxford, Blackwell, 507–38.

Dorman, M., Raphael, L., and Liberman, A. (1979) Some experiments on the sound of silence in phonetic perception. *Journal of the Acoustical Society*, 65: 1518–32.

Elert, C.-C. (1964) *Phonological Studies of Quantity in Swedish*. Stockholm, Almqvist & Wiksell.

Faber, A. (1992) Phonemic segmentation as epiphenomenon: evidence from the history of alphabetic writing. In P. Downing, S. Lima, and M. Noonan (eds), *The Linguistics of Literacy*, pp. 111–34. Amsterdam, Benjamins.

Fant, G. (1960) *The Acoustical Theory of Speech Production*. The Hague, Mouton.

Fant, G. (1973) *Speech Sounds and Features*. MIT Press, Cambridge, MA.

Firth, J. R. (1948) Sounds and prosodies. *Transactions of the Philological Society*, 127–52.

Guenther, F. (1995) Speech sound acquisition, coarticulation and rate effects in a neural network model of speech production. *Psychological Review*, 102: 594–621.

Han, M. (1994) Acoustic manifestations of mora timing in Japanese. *Journal of the Acoustical Society of America*, 96: 73–82.

Handel, S. (1989) *Listening: An Introduction to the Perception of Auditory Events*, MIT Press, Cambridge, MA.

Hirata, Y. (2004) Effects of speaking rate on the vowel length distinction in Japanese. *Journal of Phonetics*, 32: 565–89.

Hirata, Y. and Whiton, J. (2005) Effects of speaking rate on the single/geminate stop distinction in Japanese. *Journal of the Acoustical Society of America*, 118: 1647–60.

Hockett, C. (1968) *The State of the Art*. The Hague, Mouton.

Homma, Y. (1981) Durational relationship between Japanese stops and vowels. *Journal of Phonetics*, 9: 273–81.

Honing, H. (2002) Structure and interpretation of rhythm and timing. *Tijdschrift voor Muziektheorie*, 7: 227–32.

IPA (1999) *Handbook of the International Phonetic Association: A Guide to the Use of the International Phonetic Alphabet*. Cambridge University Press, Cambridge, MA.

Jakobson, R., Fant, G., and Halle, M. (1952) *Preliminaries to Speech Analysis: The Distinctive Features*, MIT Press, Cambridge, MA.

Jones, D. (1950) *The Phoneme: Its Nature and Use*. Cambridge University Press, Cambridge.

Joos, M. (1948) Acoustic phonetics. *Language Monograph*, Linguistic Society of America, 23.

Kato, H., Tsuzaki, M., and Sagisaka, Y. (1998) Acceptibility for temporal modification of single vowel segments in isolated words. *Journal of the Acoustical Society of America*, 104: 540–9.

Keating, P. (1984) Phonetic and phonological representation of stop consonant voicing. *Language*, 60: 286–319.

Keating, P. (1985) Universal phonetics and the organization of grammars. In V. Fromkin (ed.), *Phonetic Linguistics: Essays in Honor of Peter Ladefoged*, pp. 115–32. Academic Press, New York.

Kelso, J. A. S. (1995) *Dynamic Patterns: The Self-Organization of Brain and Behavior.* MIT Press, Cambridge, MA.

Klatt, D. H. (1976) Linguistic uses of segmental duration in English: acoustic and perceptual evidence. *Journal of the the Acoustical Society of America*, 59: 1208–21.

Ladefoged, P. (1965) The nature of general phonetic theories. *Georgetown University Monograph 18, Language and Linguistics*, 27–42.

Ladefoged, P. (1972) *A Course in Phonetics*. Orlando, FL, Harcourt Brace Jovanovich.

Ladefoged, P. (1980) What are linguistic sounds made of? *Language*, 56: 485–502.

Ladefoged, P. (1984) 'Out of chaos comes order': physiological, biological and structural patterns in phonetics. In M. P. R. V. D. Broeke and A. Cohen (eds), *Proceedings of the Tenth International Congress of Phonetic Sciences*, 83–95. Dordrecht, Foris.

Large, E. W., and Jones, M. R. (1999) The dynamics of attending: how we track time-varying events. *Psychological Review*, 106: 119–159.

Lehiste, I. (1970) *Suprasegmentals*. MIT Press, Cambridge, MA.

Lehrdahl, F., and Jackendoff, R. (1983) *A Generative Theory of Tonal Music*. MIT Press, Cambridge, MA.

Liberman, A. M., Delattre, P., Gerstman, L., and Cooper, F. (1968) Perception of the speech code. *Psychological Review*, 74: 431–61.

Linell, P. (2005) *The Written Language Bias in Linguistics*. Oxford, Routledge.

Lisker, L. (1984) 'Voicing' in English: a catalogue of acoustic features signalling /b/ vs. /p/ in trochees. *Language and Speech*, 29: 3–11.

Lisker, L., and Abramson, A. (1964) A cross-language study of voicing in initial stops: acoustical measurements. *Word*, 20: 384–422.

Lisker, L., and Abramson, A. (1971) Distinctive features and laryngeal control. *Language*, 47: 767–85.

List, G. (1963) The boundaries of speech and song. *Ethnomusicology*, 7: 1–16.

Low, E., and Grabe, E. (1995) Prosodic patterns in Singapore English. In *Proceedings of the XIIIth* International Congress of Phonetic Sciences, Stockholm, Vol 3: 636–9.

Low, E., Grabe, E., and Nolan, F. (2000) Quantitative characterizations of speech rhythm: syllable-timing in Singapore English *Language and Speech*, 43: 377–401.

Martin, J. (1972) Rhythmic (hierarchical) versus serial structure in speech and other behavior. *Psychological Review*, 79: 487–509.

McCarthy, J. (2002) *A Thematic Guide to Optimality Theory*, Cambridge University Press, Cambridge.

Merriam, A. (1964) *The Anthropology of Music*, Northwestern University Press, Chicago.

Morton, J., Marcus, S., and Frankish, C. (1976) Perceptual centers (P-centers). *Psychological Review*, 83: 405–8.

Öhman, S. E. G. (2000) Expression and content in linguistic theory. In M. Gustafsson and L. Hertzberg (eds), *The Practice of Language*. Dordrecht, Kluwer Academic.

Patel, A., Lofquist, A., and Naito, W. (1999) The acoustics and kinematics of regularly timed speech: a database and method for the study of the P-center problem. Paper presented at the 14th International Congress of Phonetic Sciences, San Francisco, Vol 1: 405–8.

Peterson, G. E., and Lehiste, I. (1960) Duration of syllable nuclei in English. *Journal of the Acoustical Society of America*, 32: 693–703.

Pike, K. (1946) *The Intonation of American English*. University of Michigan Press, Ann Arbor, MI.

Port, R. (1981) Linguistic timing factors in combination. *Journal of the Acoustical Society of America*, 69: 262–74.

Port, R. (1986) Invariants in phonetics. In D. Klatt and J. Perkell (eds), *Invariance and Variability in the Speech Processes*, pp. 540–58. Erlbaum, Hillsdale, NJ.

Port, R. (2003) Meter and speech. *Journal of Phonetics*, 31: 599–611.

Port, R. (2006) The graphical basis of phones and phonemes. In Ocke-Schwen Bohn and Murray J. Munro M. (eds), *Language Experience in Second Language Speech Learning: In honor of James Emil Flege*.Amsterdam, Benjamins 349–65.

Port, R. F., Al-Ani, S., and Maeda, S. (1980) Temporal compensation and universal phonetics. *Phonetica*, 37: 235–52.

Port, R. and Crawford, P. (1989) Pragmatic effects on neutralization rules. *Journal of Phonetics*, 16: 257–82.

Port, R., Dalby, J., and O'dell, M. (1987) Evidence for mora timing in Japanese. *Journal of Acoustical Society*, 81: 1574–85.

Port, R. F., and Leary, A. (2005) Against formal phonology. *Language*, 81: 927–64.

Quené, H., and Port, R. (2005) Effects of timing regularity and metrical expectancy on spoken word perception. *Phonetica*, 62: 1–13.

Ramus, F. (2002) Acoustic correlates of linguistic rhythm: perspectives. Paper presented at Speech Prosody 2002, Aix-en-Provence.

Ramus, F., Dupoux, E., and Mehler, J. (2003) The psychological reality of rhythm classes: perceptual studies. Paper presented at International Congress of Phonetic Sciences, "Speech Prosody". Barcelona.

Ramus, F., Nespor, M., and Mehler, J. (1999) Correlates of linguistic rhythm in the speech signal. *Cognition*, 73: 265–92.

Roach, P. (1982) On the distinction between 'stress-timed' and 'syllable-timed' languages. In D. Crystal (ed.), *Linguistic Controversies*, pp. 73–9. Arnold, London.

Saltzman, E., and Munhall, K. (1989) A dynamical approach to gestural patterning in speech production. *Ecological Psychology*, 1: 333–82.

Sampson, G. (1977) Is there a universal phonetic alphabet? *Language*, 50: 236–59.

Saussure, F. D. (1916) *A Course in General Linguistics*. Philosophical Library, New York.

Scott, S. K. (1993) *P-centers in Speech: An Acoustic Analysis*. Unpublished doctoral thesis, University College, London.

Seeger, C. (1958) Descriptive and prescriptive music writing. *The Musical Quaterly*, Vol 44: 184–95.

Tajima, K., and Port, R. (2003) Speech rhythm in English and Japanese. In J. Local, J., Ogden, R., and Temple, R. (eds), *Phonetic Interpretation: Papers in Laboratory Phonology*, pp. 317–34. Cambridge University Press, Cambridge.

Tsujimura, N. (1995) *An Introduction to Japanese Linguistics*. Blackwell, Oxford.

van Santen, J. P. H. (1996) Segmental duration and speech timing. In Y. Sagisaka, N. Campbell, and N. H-iguchi (eds), *Computing Prosody: Computational Models for Processing Spontaneous Speech*. Springer, New York.

Vance, T. (1986) *An Introduction to the Phonology of Japanese*. State University of New York Press, Albany, New York.

Warner, N., and Arai, T. (2001) Japanese mora timing: a review. *Phonetica*, 58: 53–87.

Wenk, B. J., and Wioland, F. (1982) Is French really syllable-timed? *Journal of Phonetics*, 10: 193–216.

Winfree, A. (2001) *The Geometry of Biological Time*. Springer, New York.

Zawaydeh, B., Tajima, K., and Kitahara, M. (2002) Discovering Arabic rhythm through a speech cycling task. In D. Parkinson and E. Benmamoun (eds), *Perspectives on Arabic Linguistics*, pp. 39–58. Amsterdam, Benjamins.

Ziegler, J., and Goswami, U. (2005) Reading acquisition, developmental dyslexia and skilled reading across languages: A psycholinguistic grain size theory. *Psychological Bulletin*, 131: 3–29.

CHAPTER 31

Connectionist principles in theories of speech production

Matthew Goldrick

31.1 Introduction

In psycholinguistics, speech production refers broadly to the processes mapping a message the speaker intends to communicate onto its form. If a speaker wishes to tell someone 'The picture I'm looking at is an animal—a feline pet,' these processes allow the speaker to generate the spoken form *cat*. Psycholinguistic theories have focused on "formulation processes"—the construction/retrieval of a plan to produce an utterance. This plan specifies the phonological structure of the utterance (e.g. an accented syllable composed of three segments, /k/ /ae/ /t/). Subsequent articulatory/motoric processes execute this plan, producing the actual movements of the speech organs. Theories of these post-formulation processes are not reviewed here (see Byrd and Saltzmann, 2003 for discussion).

Since the mid-1980s (e.g. Dell, 1986; MacKay, 1987; Stemberger, 1985) connectionist architectures have served as the dominant paradigm for characterizing theories of formulation processes. Section 31.2 below examines how two connectionist principles (localist representations and spreading activation) have influenced the development of speech production theories. The use of these principles in framing theories of speech production is discussed, followed by an illustration of how the principles have been used to account for three sets of empirical observations. Although this work has been quite successful in explaining a variety of empirical phenomena, it has failed to incorporate two principles that are central to connectionist research in many other domains: learning and distributed representations. Section 31.3 reviews two examples of more recent work which incorporate these principles into theories of speech production.

31.2 Spreading activation between localist representations

31.2.1 Localist connectionist principles

Two general connectionist processing principles (after Smolensky, 2000) have guided the bulk of connectionist research in speech production:

1. Representations are activation patterns. Mental representations are patterns of numerical activity.
2. Processing is spreading activation. Mental processes are transformations of activity patterns by patterns of numerical connections.

To instantiate the first principle, many connectionist speech production theories have assumed that different types of linguistic information are encoded using localist representations (see Page, 2000 for a detailed discussion of the use of such representational structures in connectionist networks). The two basic types of representations are illustrated in Figure 31.1. The first representational type, shown at the top of Figure 31.1, is strictly local; each linguistic

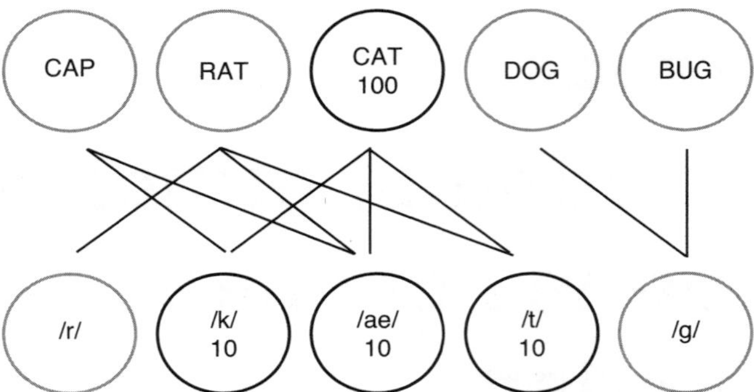

Figure 31.1 Illustration of spreading activation between strictly local (top layer) and featural (bottom layer) representations in speech production theories. Lines denote connections between units (here, all connection weights are set to 0.1). Numbers within units denote activation (units without numbers have zero activation).

object is represented by a single processing unit (e.g. each word has an independent unit such as <CAT>). The second representational type is feature-based (or "semi-local"). In such representations, a small, discrete group of processing units represents each linguistic object (e.g. each word is encoded by a small set of discrete phonemes such as /k/ /ae/ /t/).

To instantiate the second principle, the most basic element of processing in connectionist systems (localist as well as non-localist) is spreading activation. Suppose a numerical pattern of activity is imposed on some set of representational units (e.g. in Figure 31.1, the word unit <CAT>'s activation is set to 100; all other word units are inactive). This activation can then be spread to other units via a set of weighted connections (e.g. in Figure 31.1, <CAT> is linked to the phoneme units /k/ /ae/ /t/ by connections with weights of 0.1). The amount of activation a unit transmits to other units is simply the product of its activation and the weight on the connection between the units (e.g. 100 * 0.1). The activation of the target units is the sum of this incoming activation (e.g. 100 * 0.1 = 10 for each phoneme unit connected to <CAT>).

31.2.2 A generic localist connectionist framework

Following Rapp and Goldrick (2000), Figure 31.2 provides a generic representational and processing framework to illustrate how these two connectionist principles are instantiated within theories of single-word production. First, three broad levels of linguistic structure are represented by numerical patterns of activity over localist representational units. At the top of the figure are semantic representations, specifying the meaning of lexical items in a particular language. Here, a set of semantic features represents each lexical concept (e.g. {animal, feline, pet} for lexical concept {CAT}). These representations provide an interface between more general (non-linguistic) conceptual processing and those processes that specify the linguistic form of an intended message. The bottom of the figure depicts phonological representations—stored, sub-lexical representations of the spoken form of lexical items. Here, a set of phonemes represents each word's form (e.g. /k/ /ae/ /t/ for the lexical item <CAT>). The relationship between these two representations is mediated by a lexical representation; here, a unitary word-size node (e.g. <CAT>).

Most current theories of speech production (Garrett, 1980; Levelt, 1992) assume that formulation processes are implemented via two stages of activation spreading between these localist representations. The first stage begins with activation of a set of semantic feature units; activation spreads from these units, and the stage ends with the selection of the most strongly activated lexical unit (discussed in more detail below). This corresponds to selecting a lexical item to express the intended message. The second stage begins with the selection of a lexical unit, which spreads activation throughout the production network. This stage ends with the selection of the most strongly activated phoneme units. This corresponds to the construction of an utterance plan for the selected lexical item. It is important to note that these two stages may not be strictly separated; they may interact and overlap in time (e.g. Dell, 1986; see below for discussion of interactive mechanisms).

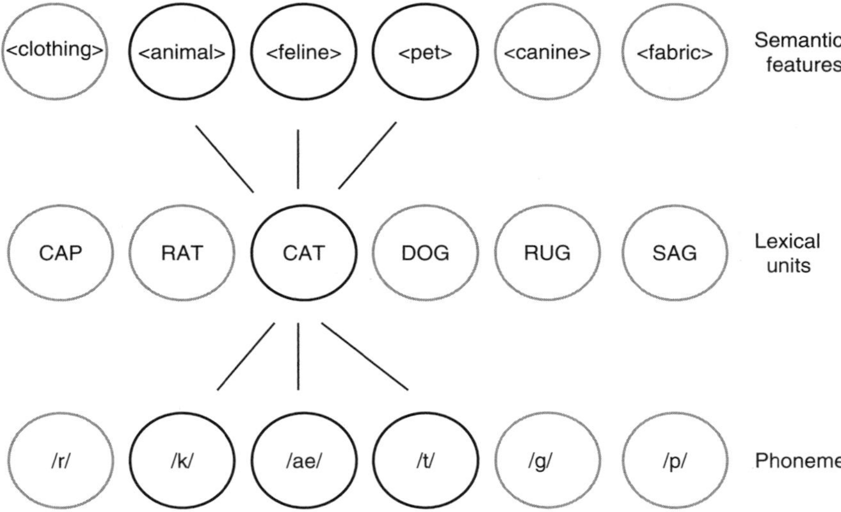

Figure 31.2 A generic representational framework for speech production. The top layer represents word meaning; the middle, mediating lexical representations; and the bottom, sub-lexical representations of form. Lines show connections between the representational units for target *cat*.

As shown by the description above, processing in localist connectionist architectures involves not only the simple spreading of activation between connected units, but also the *selection* of units at particular points in processing. This refers to processes that enhance the activation of units corresponding to one representation relative to that of other units (e.g. enhancement of a single lexical unit; enhancement of a set of phoneme units). By increasing the relative amount of activation that a unit (or group of units) can send on to other representational levels, this enhancement process allows the selected unit(s) to dominate subsequent processing. A variety of spreading activation mechanisms have been used to enhance selected representations. First, some theories propose that the selected representation's activation is simply boosted by adding extra activation to it (e.g. Dell, 1986; Dell, Schwartz, et al., 1997; Rapp and Goldrick, 2000). For example, in Dell's (1986) theory, at selection points the most highly activated node (or nodes) has its activation boosted to a pre-set high level. The node is then much more active than its competitors, allowing it to dominate processing. The second selection mechanism involves inhibiting the activation of competitors (see Dell and O'Seaghdha, 1994 for a review). This is most often realized computationally via lateral inhibitory connections among units of a similar representational type (e.g. Harley, 1995). With the activation of competitors greatly reduced, the target is able to dominate subsequent processing. A final prominent proposal for enhancing relative activation involves "gating" activation flow. In such systems, representations are not allowed to spread activation to other processing stages until they meet some activation-based response criterion (e.g. a threshold of activation: Laine et al., 1998; or a relative activation level sufficiently greater than that of competitors: Levelt et al., 1999). Since only selected representations are allowed to influence subsequent processes, they completely dominate processing at these levels.

These selection mechanisms detail how a representation comes to dominate processing. But how does the production system determine which representation to select? Generally, it is assumed that selection processes target a representation that is structurally appropriate. At the lexical level, words must be able to fit into the syntactic structure of the sentence being produced. When producing the head of a noun phrase, it is crucial that a noun (not a verb) be selected. At the phonological level, the selected segments must fit into the appropriate metrical structure. When producing the first segment of <CAT>, it is crucial that an onset consonant (not a vowel, nor a coda consonant such as /ng/) be selected. These structural influences are commonly incorporated into localist connectionist architectures by postulating distinct planning representations. One approach uses structural frames with categorically specified slots to guide selection (see Dell, Burger, and Svec, 1997, for a review). Each frame activates its slots in the appropriate sequence. When a slot is active, it enhances the activation of all units within the specified category. This activation boost ensures that structurally appropriate units are selected. For example, at the lexical level, a structural frame for noun phrases would first activate a determiner slot, enhancing the activation of all determiners. Once the determiner has been selected, the frame would activate a noun slot, enhancing the activation of all noun units. This activation support insures that the most highly activated noun (and not a verb) is selected during production.

It should be noted that the detailed structure of this generic architecture differs from that of many prominent localist connectionist theories. Although these details do not affect the account of the empirical results discussed below, they are briefly reviewed here due to their important implications for other aspects of speech production. First, note that this framework omits any representation of the grammatical properties of lexical items (e.g. grammatical category, number, gender) which play an important role in speech production (see Ferreira and Slevc, Chapter 27 this volume, for further discussion). Second, many theories assume the existence of different numbers and types of localist representations in the production system. With respect to semantic representations, some proposals make use of unitary semantic concept nodes, not sets of features (e.g. {CAT}, instead of {animal, feline, pet}; see Levelt et al., 1999; Roelofs, 1992 for discussion). With respect to phonological representations, many theories assume that, in addition to phoneme identity, multiple dimensions of phonological structure are represented (e.g. features, such as [−voice] for /k/; consonant/vowel structure, such as CVC for *cat*, and metrical structure such as location of stress; see e.g. Dell, 1988; Levelt et al., 1999). Finally, some theories assume that multiple levels of lexical representation are present (e.g. Dell, 1986; 1990; Levelt et al., 1999). A related debate concerns modality specificity: whether a given level of lexical representation is specific to the spoken modality (e.g. Caramazza, 1997) or shared across writing and speaking (e.g. Dell, Schwartz, et al., 1997). Theories with two levels of lexical representations generally assume a distinction between modality independent lexical representations (typically referred to as "lemmas," which link to grammatical information) and modality-dependent representations (typically referred to as "lexemes," which link to form information). Those with a single level either assume a single, amodal lexical representation (linking to both grammatical and form information), or distinct lexical representations for spoken and written production (which link to shared grammatical information but distinct form information). (For detailed discussions of the pros and cons of particular proposals for lexical representation(s), see Caramazza, 1997; Caramazza and Miozzo, 1997; 1998; Caramazza et al., 2004; Caramazza et al., 2001; Jescheniak et al., 2003; Levelt et al., 1999; Rapp and Caramazza, 2002; Roelofs et al., 1998.)

In spite of differences in the detailed structure of the system, this generic processing framework reflects two core assumptions shared by most speech production theories. First, it makes use of three processing levels that are shared across all current theories (conceptual, lexical, and phonological). Second, it adopts the general assumption (discussed above) that formulation involves two stages of processing. These core assumptions are sufficient to frame the discussion of the empirical results discussed below.

31.2.3 **Applying localist connectionist principles to empirical data**

Localist representations and spreading activation mechanisms have been used to account for a wide variety of empirical phenomena. The discussion in this section uses three specific sets of observations to illustrate the influence of these principles on speech production theories. Table 31.1 provides an overview. First, accounts of the contrasting influence of semantic and phonological similarity in picture naming illustrate how connectionist representational principles have influenced production theories (section 31.2.3.1). Section 31.2.3.2 discusses how connectionist processing principles play a crucial role in the explanation of mixed error biases. Section 31.2.3.3 examines how neurobiologically inspired connectionist principles have been used to understand the consequences of neurological damage.

31.2.3.1 Semantic interference vs. phonological facilitation in picture naming

An important technique for studying speech production processes has been the picture–word interference task (for a historical overview of this research, and discussion of the importance of this paradigm in the development of theoretical accounts, see Levelt, 1999; Levelt et al., 1999). In this paradigm, participants are presented with pictures (typically, black-and-white line drawings) depicting common objects and asked to name them. At some point in time close to

Table 31.1 Three sets of empirical observations that have been explained using connectionist principles in theories of speech production.

Empirical phenomenon	Connectionist account
Semantic interference vs. phonological facilitation in picture naming	**Effect of spreading activation depends on representational structure.**
In picture–word interference experiments, words in the same semantic category as the target interfere with picture naming more than unrelated controls. In contrast, words phonologically related to the target facilitate naming relative to controls.	Spreading activation from semantic representations leads to competition between strictly local lexical representations. Spreading activation from lexical representations converges on overlapping feature-based phonological representations.
Mixed-error effect	**Spreading activation allows processes at distinct representational levels to interact.**
Word errors that overlap with the target in both meaning and form (e.g. *cat* → *rat*) are more likely to occur than predicted based on the rates of purely semantic (e.g. *cat* → *dog*) and purely phonological (e.g. *cat* → *cab*) errors.	Cascading activation allows semantic neighbors to activate their phonological representations, making mixed errors more likely than purely phonological errors at the phoneme level. Feedback allows phonological representations to influence the activation of lexical representations, making mixed errors more likely than purely semantic errors at the lexical level.
Disruptions to speech production	**Spreading activation between and/or within specific representational levels is disrupted by brain damage.**
Following brain damage, individuals produce varying distributions of error types in speech production.	Disrupting spreading activation lowers activation levels, allowing noise to overwhelm the target representation. Local damage provides a superior account of error patterns compared to global disruptions of processing.

the presentation of the picture, an interfering stimulus is presented. Either a written word is superimposed on the picture, or an auditory stimulus is presented while participants look at the picture. Although participants are instructed to ignore the interfering stimulus, it can influence the time it takes them to initiate production of the picture's name. In particular, two distinct effects on naming latency are observed depending on the linguistic relationship between the interfering stimulus and the target. (Latencies are also influenced by the time difference between picture and word onset; these effects are not discussed here.)

First, semantic category relationships produce interference. In the seminal study of Schriefers et al. (1990), auditory distractor words from the same semantic category as the picture name slowed response times. If the word *dog* was presented prior to the presentation of a picture of a cat, the time to initiate the response *cat* was significantly slower (compared to trials where an unrelated word such as *mop* was presented). In contrast to interference from semantically related items, Schriefers et al. found that phonological relationships facilitate picture naming. If the word *cap* was presented at the same time or following presentation of target picture "cat," the response time was significantly faster compared to unrelated trials. Many studies have replicated the basic pattern of inhibition from semantic category members (see Roelofs, 1992 for a review; see Costa et al., 2003; Costa et al., 2005 for discussion of effects from semantically related words at different levels of categorization) and facilitation from similar-sounding words (see Starrreveld, 2000 for a review).

Many connectionist theories of speech production have used localist representational principles to account for these effects. Specifically,

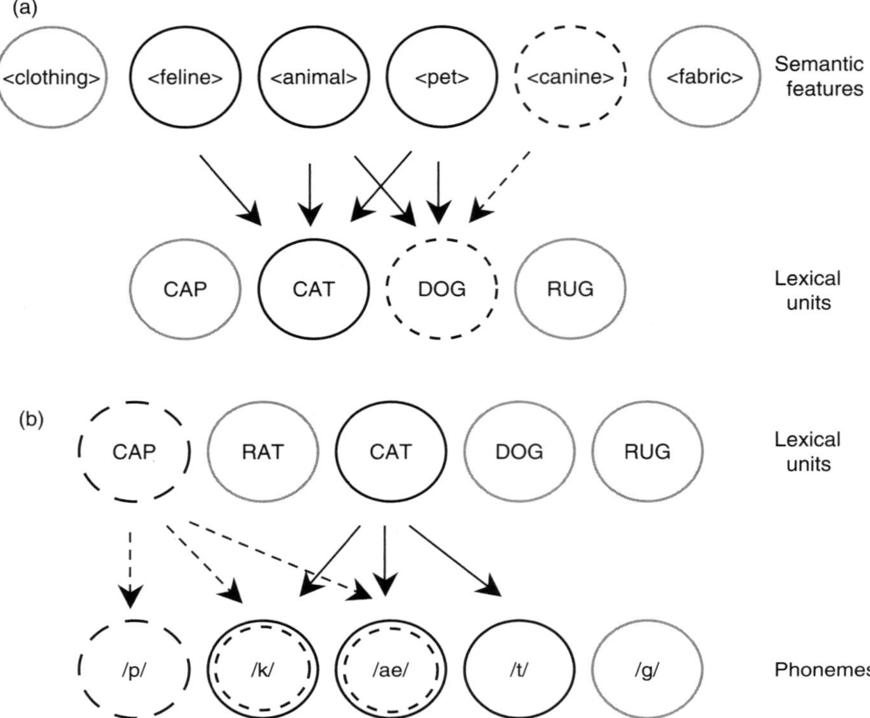

Figure 31.3 Semantic interference and phonological facilitation in the picture–word interference task reflect the structure of localist representations. Dashed lines denote activation from the distractor word. (a) Semantic interference stems from competition between coactive unitary lexical representations. (b) Phonological facilitation arises due to the activation of overlapping feature-based phonological representations.

these theories attribute contrasting effects of semantic and phonological distractors to differences in the structure of lexical and phonological representations (see e.g. Levelt et al., 1999; Roelofs, 1992). Figure 31.1 illustrates the general properties of this account. As shown in Figure 31.3a, when a semantic distractor is presented, spreading activation from the target and competitor's semantic features diverge onto two distinct lexical representations (e.g. <CAT> and <DOG>). Because lexical representations are strictly local, this spreading activation increases the activation of competitor representations, slowing the selection of the target. As shown in Figure 31.3b, a different situation occurs for phonological distractors. Spreading activation from the target and competitor's lexical representations[1] converge onto the common phonemes that they share. This enhances the target's representation, speeding selection of its phonological structure. By assuming that the localist representation of linguistic structure varies across levels, connectionist theories can account for the distinct patterns of semantic and phonological distractors.

31.2.3.2 The mixed-error effect

Errors in speech production are often classified in terms of their linguistic relationship to the target. Purely semantic errors (e.g. *cat* → *dog*) are similar in meaning, but not form; purely phonological errors (e.g. *cat* → *cap*) share form but not meaning. The term "mixed error" is generally used to refer to errors that overlap along both of these dimensions (e.g. *cat* → *rat*). Many studies

[1] An additional source of activation from word distractors is via sub-lexical conversion procedures that directly activate phonological representations from orthographic or acoustic input (e.g. Roelofs et al., 1996). In fact, Costa et al. (1999) argue that these sub-lexical processes drive the phonological facilitation effect. Regardless of the source of the activation, the presence of facilitation (as opposed to inhibition) derives from the use of feature-based localist representations (such that target and distractor overlap in structure).

have observed that mixed errors occur more often than would be predicted by the simple sum of the rates of purely semantic (e.g. *cat* → *dog*) and purely phonological (e.g. *cat* → *cap*) errors. This has been observed in studies of spontaneous speech errors (e.g. Harley and MacAndrew, 2001), experimentally induced speech errors (e.g. Brédart and Valentine, 1992), and the production errors of many aphasic individuals (e.g. Rapp and Goldrick, 2000).

This result is unexpected under a discrete version of the two-stage framework of speech production discussed above. If we assume that the two stages have a strictly serial relationship, mixed errors should simply be the sum of (independently occurring) semantic and phonological errors. During the first stage, a lexical representation is selected solely based on the intended message. Both mixed and purely semantic competitors should therefore be equally active (e.g. for target *cat*, <DOG> should be just as active as <RAT>). If processing is serial and discrete, during the second stage only the phonemes of the selected lexical item are activated. Both mixed and purely phonological competitors should therefore be equally active (e.g. /k/ /ae/ /p/ should be just as active as /r/ /ae/ /t/). Since at neither level of processing are mixed errors more likely than "pure" semantic or phonological errors, this discrete theory cannot account for the mixed-error effect.

To produce the mixed-error effect, many theories have relied on the connectionist principle of spreading activation. Specifically, the discrete architecture is enhanced by adding two spreading activation mechanisms (e.g. Dell, 1986). These are illustrated in Figure 31.4. The first is cascading activation (Figure 31.4a). Cascade allows non-selected lexical representations to exert an influence on processing at the phonological level. For example, semantic neighbors (activated via spreading activation from semantic features) are allowed to activate their phonemes (e.g. <RAT> activates /r/). This activation boost makes mixed errors more likely than purely phonological errors (e.g. /r/ is more active than /p/, meaning that *rat* is more active than *cap*).

The second mechanism is feedback (Figure 31.4b). Feedback systems allow activation from phonological representations to spread back to lexical representations (e.g. /ae/ /t/ activate <RAT>). This can combine with top-down activation from shared semantic features, boosting the activation of mixed competitors relative to that of purely semantic competitors (e.g. because it shares phonemes with the target, <RAT> is more active than <DOG>). By influencing the first stage of processing (i.e. the selection of a lexical item), feedback makes mixed-error outcomes more likely to occur than purely semantic errors.

The relative contributions and strength of cascading activation and feedback within the speech production system is a matter of some debate (see Rapp and Goldrick, 2000; Goldrick, 2006, for discussion). Furthermore, some theories have attributed the mixed-error effect not to spreading activation within the production system but to the influence of perceptual monitoring systems. These monitoring mechanisms can halt speech prior to articulation, preventing some of the errors arising during formulation processes from being overtly produced. According to such accounts, since mixed errors are both phonologically and semantically similar to the target, they are less likely to be detected by the perceptual monitor than corresponding "pure" error types. Mixed errors are therefore more likely to be overtly produced, producing the mixed-error effect (for discussion, see Levelt et al., 1999; Roelofs, 2004).

31.2.3.3 Connectionist accounts of speech production impairments

As a consequence of brain damage, many individuals suffer from impaired speech production abilities (see e.g. Berndt, Chapter 34 this volume). Given that connectionist principles reflect (in part) neurobiological processing principles, connectionism may provide a very useful framework for understanding these impairments. Most commonly, researchers have conceptualized impaired speech production performance as reflecting the distortion of the spread of activation within the production network. Theories of damage can be broadly divided into two types: those that involve global alteration of spreading activation, and those that involve alterations which are specific to particular representational levels.

Global damage mechanisms In a series of papers, Dell, Martin, Saffran, Schwartz, and colleagues (Dell, Schwartz, et al., 1997; Martin et al., 1994; Martin and Saffran, 1992; Martin et al., 1996; Schwartz and Brecher, 2000) proposed that global alterations to activation spreading could account for the range of patterns of impairment to speech production processes. They proposed two specific damage mechanisms. The first was a reduction of the ability of different representational layers in the network to spread activation to one another (the "connection weight" parameter of Dell, Schwartz, et al., 1997). If this type of activation spreading is reduced, less activation

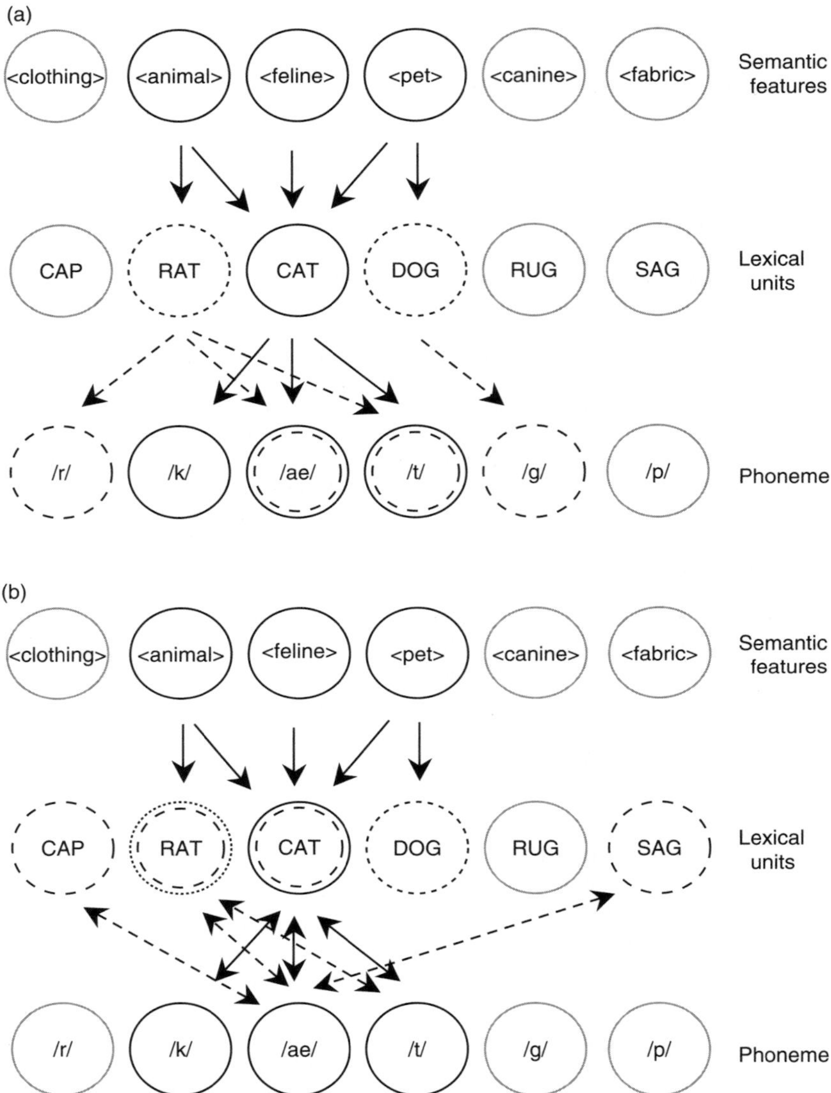

Figure 31.4 Interaction between levels of processing in speech production produces the mixed-error effect. (a) Overlapping semantic features activate semantic neighbors of the target (shown by dotted lines). Cascade allows these lexical units to activate their phonological representations (shown by dashed lines), producing an advantage for mixed errors. (b) Feedback allows phonological representations to activate lexical representations. Illustrated here is the first step of feedback: the target's phonological representation reactivates the target as well as its lexical neighbors (shown by dashed lines). (Note that these lexical representations could then, in turn, activate their non-target phonological representations; e.g. SAG could activate /g/.) Feedback from the phonology of the target combines with activation of the target's semantic neighbors (shown by dotted lines), producing an advantage for mixed errors.

flows between representational levels. Owing to lower levels of activation, noise on processing units can then overwhelm the representation of the correct response, leading to errors. The second mechanism involved a reduction of the ability of units to retain activation over time ("decay" in Dell, Schwartz, et al., 1997). Typically, the activation of a unit at a given time step is determined not just by the activation flowing into it from other representational levels but also by its activation at previous time steps. (Note that this can be conceived of as a unit spreading activation back onto itself.) Increasing decay—i.e. decreasing the amount of activation that units retain over time—can therefore serve to lower levels of activation, allowing random noise to disrupt the target and produce errors (for further discussion of the potential influence of decay on impairments to speech production, see Harley and MacAndrew, 1992; Wright and Ahmad, 1997).

To test the ability of these two mechanisms of global damage to account for aphasic naming patterns, Dell, Schwartz, et al. (1997) constructed a simulation of the formulation processes of English speakers. For twenty-one individuals with aphasia, the connection strength and decay parameters of this simulation were globally adjusted to see if the simulation could reproduce their error patterns. Specifically, for each of the twenty-one patients, the simulation's parameters were globally altered so that it matched (as closely as possible) the patient's relative proportion of: correct responses; phonologically related (e.g. *cat* → *rat*) and unrelated (e.g. *cat* → *dog*) semantic errors; phonologically related (e.g. *cat* → *cap*) and unrelated (e.g. *cat* → *rug*) word errors; and non-word errors (e.g. *cat* → *zat*). The results of this parameter-fitting procedure provided some quantitative support for the global damage theory. The simulation was able to fairly closely approximate the individual error distributions (but see Ruml and Caramazza, 2000 for a criticism of the simulation's fit to the data, and Dell et al., 2000, for a response to these criticisms).

Not only was the global damage simulation able to reproduce the patients' error patterns; the parameter fits used to account for the error distributions were able to derive novel predictions about patient performance. As discussed above, the presence of a mixed-error effect requires the presence of spreading activation between phonological and lexical representations (either lexical-to-phonological cascade or phonological-to-lexical feedback). If an individual's error pattern was fit by reducing connection strength, the spreading activation theory of mixed errors predicts that that individual's responses should show a reduced mixed-error effect. Consistent with this prediction, Dell, Schwartz, et al. (1997) found that as a group individuals whose pattern was fit by high connection weights showed a significant mixed-error effect, while individuals whose pattern was fit by low connection weights did not.

Local damage mechanisms In contrast to Dell, Schwartz, et al. (1997), many theoretical accounts of neurologically impaired speech production have proposed that deficit patterns result from distinct disruptions to specific processes (see e.g. Ruml et al., 2005, for discussion). Connectionist theories have realized this claim in a number of different ways. Foygel and Dell (2000) accounted for production impairments by independently weakening the strength of connections between semantic and lexical vs. lexical and phonological levels (see also Harley and MacAndrew, 1992). As discussed above, weakening connection strength produces errors by lowering activation levels (allowing noise to overwhelm the activation of the target). Other proposals have simulated neurological damage by increasing the strength of noise at particular representational levels (Laine et al., 1998; Rapp and Goldrick, 2000). Increased noise can overwhelm the target's activation at a particular processing level, producing errors. A final mechanism used in local connectionist architectures is disruption to lexical selection processes (e.g. reducing the amount by which the activation of the selected representation is enhanced: Harley and MacAndrew, 1992; Goldrick and Rapp, 2002; Rapp and Goldrick, 2000; or manipulations of the threshold for lexical selection: Dell et al., 2004; Laine et al., 1998). Disrupting selection interferes with the normal flow of activation in the production system, leading to errors at both the lexical and phonological levels.

A number of papers have shown that theories incorporating local-damage mechanisms provide a far superior account of the empirical data than the global-damage mechanisms proposed by Dell, Schwartz, et al. (1997). First, extensive studies (cited below) have shown that local-damage assumptions permit a much closer quantitative fit to error distributions than allowed by global damage. Second, the novel predictions made by the parameter fits of Dell, Schwartz, et al. (1997) can also be accounted for localized damage mechanisms (Foygel and Dell, 2000). Finally, and perhaps most problematic for global-damage proposals, local damage can account for empirically observed error patterns that simply cannot be produced by global damage.

Rapp and Goldrick (2000) reviewed the performance of two individuals with deficits to formulation processes (i.e. their comprehension and articulation was intact; their deficits were in mapping messages onto form). They produced only semantic errors in picture naming. As shown by a number of studies (cited below), this pattern of only semantic errors cannot be produced by simulations incorporating global damage. Similarly, Caramazza et al. (2000) review cases where individuals with formulation deficits produce only phonologically related errors. Global-damage simulations also fail to produce this pattern of performance. Global damage predicts that "pure" error patterns should not occur—damage always results in the production of a mixture of error types (e.g. not just semantic errors, but phonologically related word and nonword errors as well). In contrast, simulations with local damage can account for these patterns of errors (so long as there is an appropriate degree of interaction between representational levels; see Rapp and Goldrick, 2000; Goldrick and Rapp, 2002). For more detailed qualitative and quantitative critiques of global damage theories, see Caramazza et al. (2000), Cuetos et al. (2000), Foygel and Dell (2000), Hanley et al. (2004), Rapp and Goldrick (2000), Ruml et al. (2005), Ruml et al. (2000). This large body of work leads to the conclusion that impairments to speech production processes are the consequence of local, not global disruptions to processing.

31.3 Distributed representations: learning and processing

31.3.1 Connectionist principles outside the traditional localist framework

As noted in the introduction, the work reviewed in the previous section differs in two ways from the bulk of connectionist research in other domains. First, these localist networks assume that connection weights (specifying how activation spreads in the production system) are largely fixed to values set by the simulation designer. In contrast, learning has played a crucial role in other domains of connectionist research (e.g. Elman et al., 1996). The process of learning is in fact seen as a third general principle of connectionist theories (after Smolensky, 2000).

3. Learning is innately guided modification of spreading activation by experience.

Knowledge acquisition results from the interaction of:

- innate learning rules;
- innate architectural features;
- modification of connection strengths with experience.

A second divergence is that the research reviewed in the previous section makes use of localist representations, whereas most connectionist research assumes that mental representations are highly distributed patterns of activity (as evidenced by the title of the seminal connectionist work *Parallel Distributed Processing*, Rumelhart, McClelland, et al., 1986). In such approaches, the first principle of connectionist processing can be reformulated as:

1′. Representations are *distributed* activation patterns. Mental representations are highly distributed patterns of numerical activity.

In fact, learning and distributed representations are often closely connected in connectionist architectures. Many connectionist networks learn using error correction algorithms. In these simulations, the designer specifies the structure of input and output representations and a learning algorithm. The network is then trained using a set of examples pairing input and output patterns (e.g. the network is taught to map the pattern <animal, feline, pet> to /k/ /ae/ /t/). To allow networks to learn complex input–output mappings, many connectionist theories assume the presence of additional internal representations. These are realized using "hidden" units which mediate the relationship between the input and output units (much like the lexical level in Figure 31.2). The structure of these representations is not pre-specified in the simulation design. Instead, the representations (i.e. the response patterns of the hidden units) develop over the course of learning the mapping between input and output representations (most prominently via the method of backpropagation of error; see Rumelhart et al., 1996; Rumelhart et al., 1986 for overviews). Of particular relevance here is that these learned internal representations are often highly distributed (see e.g. Plaut et al., 1996). Rather than a single unit or a small discrete set of units responding to input patterns, inputs to these trained networks evoke a highly distributed pattern of activity over the hidden units. In this way, learning and distributed representations are often intertwined in connectionist theories.

These two principles, so crucial to connectionist accounts in other domains, were not incorporated into the localist architectures discussed in section 31.2. The remainder of this chapter considers new work that has attempted to bridge this gap. The application of connectionist learning mechanisms to problems in sentence production is reviewed first, followed by a discussion of the application of distributed representations to the processing of structure at the phonological level.

31.3.2 Learning and syntactic priming

The term "syntactic priming" is used here to refer to the observation that speakers repeat the same syntactic structures in successive utterances (this is also referred to as "structural priming" in the sentence production literature). A typical experimental paradigm for inducing this effect has participants repeat a prime sentence aloud and then describe (on a subsequent trial) a picture depicting an event. Several studies have found that participants' picture descriptions tend to reflect the structure of the prime sentence. For example, if participants repeat a passive prime sentence (e.g. *The building manager was mugged by a gang of teenagers*), they would be more likely to describe subsequent pictures using passive constructions (e.g. *The man was stung by a bee*) compared to active constructions (e.g. *The bee stung the man*). This priming is syntactic in that it does not appear to rely on the prime and target sentences overlapping in other aspects of linguistic structure such as lexical semantics, argument structure, or prosody (see Bock and Griffin, 2000 for a review of the paradigm and basic results).

What processing mechanism gives rise to this effect? As noted above, many connectionist theories assume that some activation persists on representational units over time (e.g. Dell, Schwartz, et al.'s (1997) decay parameter). Syntactic priming has been viewed as an influence of this persistence; representational units (such as slots in a structural frame) are preactivated by previous productions, allowing them to be more quickly and easily retrieved (e.g. Branigan et al., 1999). However, since units retain only a fraction of their activation, smaller and smaller amounts of activation persist across time steps. The influence of this mechanism is therefore necessarily limited in time. In contradiction to this prediction, Bock and Griffin (2000) found that syntactic priming effects can persist across extremely long lags (e.g. 10 intervening sentences; but see Branigan et al., 1999 for evidence of decay). They interpreted this as supporting an alternative account of syntactic priming based on implicit learning. According to this view, syntactic priming is a consequence of learning processes which make longer-term adjustments to the sentence production system. This has a natural interpretation within connectionist architectures. In the third connectionist principle detailed above, learning is seen as the adjustment of connection weights. Instead of relying solely on persistent activation, the system can rely on experience-driven changes to the way in which activation flows.[2]

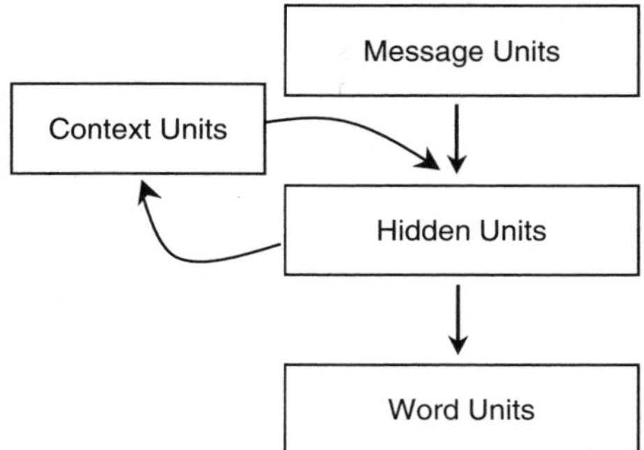

Figure 31.5 Simple recurrent network architecture of Chang et al. (2000). Message units represent the intended meaning of the sentence, and word units represent the words that make up the sentence the network produces (the network is trained to activate sequences of word units). A set of hidden units is used to mediate the mapping between these representations. To allow for the production of word sequences, a set of context units (containing a copy of the hidden unit activations from the previous time step) are allowed to influence the activation of the hidden units.

This hypothesis has been examined in simulation experiments by Chang et al. (2000). They utilized the simple recurrent network architecture (Elman, 1990; Jordan, 1986). The basic version of Chang et al.'s network is depicted in Figure 31.5. During processing, the activation of the message units is fixed to a pattern representing the meaning of a sentence. At each time step, the activation of the hidden units (the learned

[2] Note that this account is also capable of using persistent activation effects to account for other priming effects that occur only over short lags. However, it does not currently specify why different effects have different priming lags (e.g. in single-word production, why repetition priming is found over long lags while semantic priming is not; Barry et al., 2001).

internal representations discussed above) is influenced not only by this message representation but also by the context units. The context units are a copy of the hidden units' activation pattern from the previous time step. This recurrence of hidden unit activation patterns allows previous states of the network to influence processing—in effect, providing the network with "memory." Since these internal representations are sensitive to previous states, these network can be trained to produce sequences of outputs (see Elman, 1990; Jordan, 1986 for further discussion). In this case, the network learns to activate, in sequence, the word units corresponding to the intended sentence (e.g. first activating <THE>, then <CAT>, then <WALKS>).

Chang et al. (2000) trained the simulation (using the backpropogation algorithm mentioned above) to produce a set of sentences. To simulate the syntactic priming paradigm, the simulation then received further training corresponding to prime sentences. The internal connections of the network were updated based on each prime sentence, altering the flow of activation within the network. Following this additional training, the simulation was tested using new message inputs. In response to these inputs, the stimulation tended to produce the same structure as the prime sentence, replicating the syntactic priming effect. Furthermore, this influence extended across long intervening lags (e.g. 10 sentences), showing that the learning-based theory can account for Bock and Griffin's (2000) results. Subsequent work (e.g. Chang, 2002; Chang et al., 2006; Rohde, 2002) has shown that similar effects can be realized within more elaborate connectionist theories of sentence production which address some of the shortcomings of the Chang et al. (2000) simulations. These results, across varying connectionist architectures, illustrate how the third principle of connectionist architectures (experience-driven modification of connection weights) can serve as the basis for a theoretical account for speech production behavior.

It is important to note that although Chang et al. (2000) made use of distributed representations, the implicit-learning account of long-term syntactic priming is also compatible with localist representations. Both localist and distributed frameworks rely on spreading activation; theoretically, accounts based on modifications of this processing mechanism can be generalized across both representational frameworks. However, as noted above, current localist proposals have not generally considered the influence of learning on speech production.

31.3.3 Distributed representations of structure

As noted in the first section, localist connectionist architectures commonly incorporate categorically specified planning representations that guide selection of content units (e.g. a noun phrase frame guides selection of a lexical unit representing a determiner <THE>, followed by and a unit representing a noun <CAT>). Theories making use of learned internal representations (such as the simple recurrent network above) often eschew such explicit planning representations (for "frame"-less approaches to phonological processing, see Dell et al., 1993; Gupta and Dell, 1999). An alternative approach explored in recent work does not eliminate distinct planning representations, but utilizes more distributed representations of structure than localist approaches (Harris, 2002; Hartley and Houghton, 1996; Vousden et al., 2000).

Vousden et al. (2000) focused on the selection of sub-lexical phonological structure (e.g. selecting onset /k/, vowel /ae/, and coda /t/ for target <CAT>). They posit that selection is controlled by a distributed representation of syllable structure, generated by a set of oscillators (based on a more general theory of serial order proposed by Brown et al., 2000). A set of repeating oscillators sweep through the same series of values during each syllable, just as on a clock a minute hand sweeps through the same digits every hour (e.g. in every syllable, 15 minutes past represents "onset," 30 minutes past represents "vowel," 45 minutes past represents "coda"). This repeating component represents structural similarity across syllables. "Non-repeating" oscillators (i.e. oscillators with extremely long periods) take on distinct values for each syllable, allowing their system to represent the distinction between syllables. This is similar to the hour hand on a clock, which allows one to distinguish 3.30 from 4.30.

This distributed representation of structure is then used to control selection of phonological content. The time-varying oscillator states (both repeating and non-repeating) are combined to generate a dynamic control signal. The system learns a set of weights[3] on connections associating control signal states to phonological structures (following the clock analogy above, this means learning that 3.15 corresponds to /k/,

[3] See Harris (2002) for discussion of the limitations of Vousden et al.'s (2000) method and a distributed associative memory proposal for more efficiently storing the relationship between control signals and phonological structure.

3.30 to /ae/, etc.). During retrieval, the appropriate control signal is provided to the system; the oscillators then automatically generate the sequence of control signal states which cue retrieval of the stored phonological sequence.

It is important to note that this proposal shares many properties with localist connectionist planning frames. Both frameworks assume a division between structure and content. In both cases, structural representations are unlearned and categorically specified (e.g. the repeating oscillator states are pre-defined to be the same across all syllables). This property allows both frameworks to account for structural similarity effects on speech errors. A number of studies have shown that segments in similar positions are more likely to interact than those in dissimilar positions (e.g. onset consonants are more likely to interact with onset consonants as compared to those in coda; Vousden et al., 2000). By assuming categorically specified structural representations, this effect can be explained as a consequence of representational overlap between segments in similar positions. For example, in virtue of their shared structural representations, onset /k/ will be more similar to onset /g/ than coda /g/. This similarity leads to a greater likelihood of segments interacting in errors.

In spite of the properties shared by the two frameworks, there are important distinctions. As noted by Vousden et al. (2000), the oscillator mechanism provides an explicit account of how successive states of the planning representation are generated—oscillators will cycle through their states automatically, just like a clock which has been wound up will automatically cycle through the minutes of each hour. In contrast, many localist frame-based theories have failed to provide detailed sequencing mechanisms (but see Dell, Burger, and Svec, 1997). A second difference stems specifically from properties of distributed representations. As shown by Vousden et al. (2000), speech errors are influenced by distance: all else being equal, closer segments are more likely to interact with one another than more distant segments. This property is a natural consequence of the use of distributed representations. Vousden et al.'s control signal specifies slots in the planning representation using a time-varying signal. The time-dependence of this signal entails that slots which are temporally close will also have a similar structure. For example, consider a three-syllable word such as *subjective* using the clock-face analogy above. Each of the three syllables will be associated with a distinct state of the hour hand on the clock (e.g. *sub* will be 4, *jec* will be 5, and *tive* will be 6), while their internal segments are associated with distinct states of the minute hand (e.g. *s* will be 4.15, *u* will be 4.30, etc.). Because these states are generated by time-varying oscillators, the temporally close first and second syllables will be associated with closer values on the hour hand (e.g. 4, 5) than the temporally more distant first and third syllables (4, 6). Owing to the greater representational overlap, errors will be more likely to occur between the first and second syllables than between the first and third. In contrast, localist frame units do not typically represent similarity in time. In many of these theories, slots in planning representations are specified by discrete, atomic units. All slots are therefore equally similar or dissimilar. This allows the system to represent the distinction between the onsets of the first, second, and third syllables, but does not encode the fact that the first and second are closer than the first and third. (Note that localist proposals could be elaborated to include such information, but unlike the oscillator framework it is clearly not a necessary component of the representations.)

In principle, then, control signal theories incorporate the positive aspects of frame-based representations (i.e. categorically specified slots, accounting for positional similarity effects) while increasing their empirical coverage (i.e. accounting for distance effects in errors). This increased empirical coverage can be directly attributed to a connectionist processing principle: the use of distributed representations.

31.4 **Conclusions: connectionist principles in speech production theories**

Connectionist principles have had a profound impact on speech production research. For two decades, production theories have framed their discussion of behavioral data using two assumptions: mental representations are numerical patterns of activity; and processing is spreading activation between these representations. This not only has allowed specific accounts of a variety of empirical phenomena (as illustrated above) but has also supported the development of unified theories of single word production (e.g. WEAVER++; Levelt et al., 1999). As documented in the second section, more recent work has examined how speech production phenomena can be accounted for by using connectionist principles which are quite prominent in other empirical domains (learning and distributed representations). Importantly, much of this new research is cumulative in that it attempts to build on the insights of previous localist approaches. For example, in both syntax (Chang, 2002; Chang et al., 2006) and phonology (Harris, 2002; Vousden et al., 2000), many distributed, learning-based theories have incorporated the localist theories' distinction between mechanisms that control sequencing (e.g. structural frames) and mechanisms specifying representational content. In fact, as shown by Chang (2002; see also Chang et al., 2006), distributed architectures which lack this distinction can have great difficulty accounting for the empirical data. The challenge for future work will be to determine the crucial features of localist connectionist theories of production and how best to incorporate them within a learning-based, distributed representational framework.

Acknowledgement

Thanks to Robert Daland and Meredith Larson for helpful comments on the manuscript.

References

Barry, C., Hirsch, K. W., Johnston, R. A., and Williams, C. L. (2001) Age of acquisition, word frequency, and the locus of repetition priming of picture naming. *Journal of Memory and Language*, 44: 350–75.

Bock, K., and Griffin, Z. M. (2000) The persistence of structural priming: transient activation or implicit learning? *Journal of Experimental Psychology: General*, 129: 177–92.

Branigan, H. P., Pickering, M. J., and Cleland, A. A. (1999) Syntactic priming in written production: evidence for rapid decay. *Psychonomic Bulletin and Review*, 6: 635–40.

Brédart, S., and Valentine, T. (1992) From Monroe to Moreau: an analysis of face naming errors. *Cognition*, 45: 187–223.

Brown, G. D. A., Preece, T., and Hulme, C. (2000) Oscillator-based memory for serial order. *Psychological Review*, 107: 127–81.

Byrd, D., and Saltzmann, E. (2003) Speech production. In M. Arbib (ed.), *The Handbook of Brain Theory and Neural Networks*, 2nd edn, pp. 1072–6. MIT Press, Cambridge, MA.

Caramazza, A. (1997) How many levels of processing are there in lexical access? *Cognitive Neuropsychology*, 14: 177–208.

Caramazza, A., Bi, Y. Costa, A., Miozzo, M. (2004) What determines the speed of lexical access: homophone or specific-word frequency? A reply to Jescheniak et al. (2003) *Journal of Experimental Psychology: Learning, Memory, and Cognition*, 30: 278–82.

Caramazza, A., Costa, A., Miozzo, M., and Bi, Y. (2001) The specific-word frequency effect: implications for the representation of homophones in speech production. *Journal of Experimental Psychology: Learning, Memory, and Cognition*, 27: 1430–50.

Caramazza, A., and Miozzo, M. (1997) The relation between syntactic and phonological knowledge in lexical access: Evidence from the "tip-of-the-tongue" phenomenon. *Cognition*, 64: 309–43.

Caramazza, A., and Miozzo, M. (1998) More is not always better: a response to Roelofs, Meyer, and Levelt. *Cognition*, 69: 231–41.

Caramazza, A., Papagno, C., and Ruml, W. (2000) The selective impairment of phonological processing in speech production. *Brain and Language*, 75: 428–50.

Chang, F. (2002) Symbolically speaking: a connectionist model of sentence production. *Cognitive Science*, 26: 609–51.

Chang, F., Dell, G. S., and Bock, K. (2006) Becoming syntactic. *Psychological Review*, 113: 234–72.

Chang, F., Dell, G. S., Bock, K., and Griffin, Z. M. (2000) Structural priming as implicit learning: a comparison of models of sentence production. *Journal of Psycholinguistic Research*, 29: 217–29.

Costa, A., Alario, F.-X., and Caramazza, A. (2005) On the categorical nature of the semantic interference effect in the picture–word interference paradigm. *Psychonomic Bulletin and Review*, 12: 125–31.

Costa, A., Mahon, B., Savova, V., and Caramazza, A. (2003) Levels of categorization effect: a novel effect in the picture-word interference paradigm. *Language and Cognitive Processes*, 18: 205–33.

Costa, A., Miozzo, M., and Caramazza, A. (1999) Lexical selection in bilinguals: do words in the bilingual's two lexicons compete for selection? *Journal of Memory and Language*, 41: 365–97.

Cuetos, F. Aguado, G., and Caramazza, A. (2000) Dissociation of semantic and phonological errors in naming. *Brain and Language*, 75: 451–60.

Dell, G. S. (1986) A spreading activation theory of retrieval in sentence production. *Psychological Review*, 93: 283–321.

Dell, G. S. (1988) The retrieval of phonological forms in production: tests of predictions from a connectionist model. *Journal of Memory and Language*, 27: 124–42.

Dell, G. S. (1990) Effects of frequency and vocabulary type on phonological speech errors. *Language and Cognitive Processes*, 4: 313–49.

Dell, G. S., Burger, L. K., and Svec, W. R. (1997) Language production and serial order: a functional analysis and a model. *Psychological Review*, 104: 123–47.

Dell, G. S., Juliano, C., and Govindjee, A. (1993) Structure and content in language production: a theory of frame constraints in phonological speech errors. *Cognitive Science*, 17: 149–95.

Dell, G. S., Lawler, E. N., Harris, H. D., and Gordon, J. K. (2004) Models of errors of omission in aphasic naming. *Cognitive Neuropsychology*, 21: 125–45.

Dell, G. S., and O'Seaghdha, P. G. (1994) Inhibition in interactive activation models of linguistic selection and sequencing. In D. Dagenbach and T. H. Carr (ed.), *Inhibitory Processes in Attention, Memory, and Language*, pp. 409–53. Academic Press, San Diego, Calif.

Dell, G. S., Schwartz, M. F., Martin, N., Saffran, E. M., and Gagnon, D. A. (1997) Lexical access in aphasic and nonaphasic speakers. *Psychological Review*, 104: 801–38.

Dell, G. S., Schwartz, M. F., Martin, N., Saffran, E. M., and Gagnon, D. A. (2000) The role of computational models in neuropsychological investigations of language: reply to Ruml and Caramazza (2000) *Psychological Review*, 107: 635–45.

Elman, J. L. (1990) Finding structure in time. *Cognitive Science*, 14: 179–211.

Elman, J. L., Bates, E. A., Johnson, M. H., Karmiloff-Smith, A., Parisi, D., and Plunkett, K. (1996) *Rethinking Innateness*. MIT Press, Cambridge, MA.

Foygel, D., and Dell, G. S. (2000) Models of impaired lexical access in speech production. *Journal of Memory and Language*, 43: 182–216.

Garrett, M. F. (1980) Levels of processing in sentence production. In B. Butterworth (ed.), *Language Production: Speech and Talk*, vol. 1, pp. 177–220. Academic Press, New York.

Goldrick, M. (2005) Limited interaction in speech production: chronometric, speech error, and neuropsychological evidence. *Language and Cognitive Processes*, 121: 817–55.

Goldrick, M., and Rapp, B. (2002) A restricted interaction account (RIA) of spoken word production: the best of both worlds. *Aphasiology*, 16: 20–55.

Gupta, P., and Dell, G. S. (1999) The emergence of language from serial order and procedural memory. In B. MacWhinney (ed.), *Emergentist Approaches to Languages*, pp. 447–81. Erlbaum, Mahwah, NJ.

Hanley, J. R., Dell, G. S., Kay, J., and Baron, R. (2004) Evidence for the involvement of a nonlexical route in the repetition of familiar words: a comparison of single and dual route models of auditory repetition. *Cognitive Neuropsychology*, 21: 147–58.

Harley, T. A., (1995) Connectionist models of anomia: a comment on Nickels. *Language and Cognitive Processes*, 10: 47–58.

Harley, T. A., and MacAndrew, S. B. G. (1992) Modelling paraphasias in normal and aphasic speech. In *Proceedings of the 14th annual meeting of the Cognitive Science Society*, pp. 378–83. Erlbaum, Hillsdale, NJ.

Harley, T. A., and MacAndrew, S. B. G. (2001) Constraints upon word substitution speech errors. *Journal of Psycholinguistic Research*, 30: 395–417.

Harris, H. D. (2002) Holographic reduced representations for oscillator recall: a model of phonological production. In W. D. Gray and C. D. Schunn (eds), *Proceedings of the 24th Annual Meeting of the Cognitive Science Society*, pp. 423–8. Erlbaum, Hillsdale, NJ.

Hartley, T., and Houghton, G. (1996) A linguistically constrained model of short-term memory for nonwords. *Journal of Memory and Language*, 35: 1–31.

Jescheniak, J. D., Meyer, A. S., and Levelt, W. J. M. (2003) Specific-word frequency is not all that counts in speech production: comments on Caramazza, Costa, et al. (2001) and new experimental data. *Journal of Experimental Psychology: Learning, Memory, and Cognition*, 29: 432–38.

Jordan, M. I. (1986) *Serial order: a parallel distributed processing approach*. Institute for Cognitive Science Report 8604. University of California, San Diego. Repr. in J. W. Donahoe and V. P. Dorsel (eds), *Neural-Network Models of Cognition: Biobehavioral Foundations*, pp. 221–77. Elsevier Science, Amsterdam, 1997.

Laine, M., Tikkala, A., and Juhola, M. (1998) Modelling anomia by the discrete two-stage word production architecture. *Journal of Neurolinguistics*, 11: 275–94.

Levelt, W. J. M. (1992) Accessing words in speech production: stages, processes, and representations. *Cognition*, 42: 1–22.

Levelt, W. J. M. (1999) Models of word production. *Trends in Cognitive Sciences*, 3: 223–32.

Levelt, W. J. M., Roelofs, A., and Meyer, A. S. (1999) A theory of lexical access in speech production. *Behavioral and Brain Sciences*, 22: 1–75.

MacKay, D. G. (1987) *The Organization of Perception and Action: A Theory for Language and Other Cognitive Skills*. Springer, New York.

Martin, N., Dell, G. S., Saffran, E. M., and Schwartz, M. F. (1994) Origins of paraphasias in deep dysphasia: testing the consequences of a decay impairment to an interactive spreading activation model of lexical retrieval. *Brain and Language*, 47: 609–60.

Martin, N., and Saffran, E. M. (1992) A computational study of deep dysphasia: evidence from a single case study. *Brain and Language*, 43: 240–74.

Martin, N., Saffran, E. M., and Dell, G. S. (1996) Recovery in deep dysphasia: evidence for a relation between auditory-verbal STM capacity and lexical errors in repetition. *Brain and Language*, 52: 83–113.

Page, M. (2000) Connectionist modeling in psychology: a localist manifesto. *Behavioral and Brain Sciences*, 23: 443–512.

Plaut, D. C., McClelland, J. L., Seidenberg, M. S., and Patterson, K. (1996) Understanding normal and impaired word reading: computational principles in quasi-regular domains. *Psychological Review*, 103: 56–115.

Rapp, B., and Caramazza, A. (2002) Selective difficulties with spoken nouns and written verbs: a single case study. *Journal of Neurolinguistics*, 15: 373–402.

Rapp, B., and Goldrick, M. (2000) Discreteness and interactivity in spoken word production. *Psychological Review*, 107: 460–99.

Roelofs, A. (1992) A spreading-activation theory of lemma retrieval in speaking. *Cognition*, 42: 107–42.

Roelofs, A. (2004) Error biases in spoken word planning and monitoring by aphasic and nonaphasic speakers: comment on Rapp and Goldrick (2000) *Psychological Review*, 111: 561–72.

Roelofs, A., Meyer, A. S., and Levelt, W. J. M. (1996) Interaction between semantic and orthographic factors in conceptually driven naming: comment on Starreveld and La Heij (1995). *Journal of Experimental Psychology: Learning, Memory, and Cognition*, 22: 246–51.

Roelofs, A., Meyer, A. S., and Levelt, W. J. M. (1998) A case for the lemma–lexeme distinction in models of speaking: comment on Caramazza and Miozzo (1997) *Cognition*, 69: 219–30.

Rohde, D. L. T. (2002) A connectionist model of sentence comprehension and production. Ph.D. thesis, School of Computer Science, Carnegie Mellon University, Pittsburgh, PA.

Rumelhart, D. E., Durbin, R., Golden, R., and Chauvin, Y. (1996) Backpropagation: the basic theory. In P. Smolensky, M. C. Mozer, and D. E. Rumelhart (eds), *Mathematical Perspectives on Neural Networks*, pp. 533–66. Erlbaum, Mahwah, NJ.

Rumelhart, D. E., Hinton, G. E., and Williams, R. J. (1986) Learning internal representations by error propagation. In Rumelhart, McClelland, et al. (1986: 318–62).

Rumelhart, D. E., McClelland, J. L., and the PDP Research Group (1986) *Parallel distributed processing: Explorations in the microstructure of cognition: Vol. 1, Foundations*. MIT Press, Cambridge, MA.

Ruml, W., and Caramazza, A. (2000) An evaluation of a computational model of lexical access: Comment on Dell et al. (1997) *Psychological Review*, 107: 609–34.

Ruml, W., Caramazza, A., Capasso, R., and Miceli, G. (2005) Interactivity and continuity in normal and aphasic language production. *Cognitive Neuropsychology*, 22: 131–68.

Ruml, W., Caramazza, A., Shelon, J. R., and Chialant, D. (2000) Testing assumptions in computational theories of aphasia. *Journal of Memory and Language*, 43: 217–48.

Schriefers, H., Meyer, A. S., and Levelt, W. J. M. (1990) Exploring the time course of lexical access in language production: picture–word interference studies. *Journal of Memory and Language*, 29: 86–102.

Schwartz, M. F., and Brecher, A. (2000) A model-driven analysis of severity, response characteristics, and partial recovery in aphasics' picture naming. *Brain and Language*, 73: 62–91.

Smolensky, P. (2000) Grammar-based connectionist approaches to language. *Cognitive Science*, 23: 589–613.

Starreveld, P. (2000) On the interpretation of phonological context effects in word production. *Journal of Memory and Language*, 42: 497–525.

Stemberger, J. P. (1985) An interactive activation model of language production. In A. W. Ellis (ed.), *Progress in the Psychology of Language*, vol. 1, pp. 143–86. Erlbaum, Hillsdale, NJ.

Vousden, J. I., Brown, G. D. A., and Harley, T. A. (2000) Serial control of phonology in speech production: a hierarchical model. *Cognitive Psychology*, 41: 101–75.

Wright, J. F., and Ahmad, K. (1997) The connectionist simulation of aphasic naming. *Brain and Language*, 59: 367–89.

CHAPTER 32

Cross-linguistic research on language production

Albert Costa, F.-Xavier Alario, and Núria Sebastián-Gallés

32.1 Introduction

There is consensus that many aspects of the language faculty are universal. Psychologists have tried to uncover the general cognitive mechanisms underlying this universal faculty. Such an approach has been extremely fruitful and has provided the backbone of psycholinguistic research. However, languages of the world differ in many important aspects. Thus, a complementary approach is to investigate how these language specific properties may modulate the cognitive mechanisms and representations involved in language processing. For example, research in the field of language perception (reading, auditory word processing, etc.) has shown how a number of critical cross-linguistic differences can affect language processing (Paulesu et al., 2000; Cutler et al., 1983). These effects indicate that some characteristics of the cognitive system are fine-tuned to language specific properties. The lesson to learn from these observations is that a full description of the language faculty requires uncovering both the universal characteristics of the language system *and* the modulations imposed by language specific properties. This second requirement can only be achieved by conducting cross-linguistic research.

The use of different languages to inform theories of language processing has taken three different forms.

First, researchers have asked general questions about the speech production system by investigating properties that are thought to be shared across all languages. This is an important enterprise; it helps to determine the extent to which derived theoretical implications can be considered independent of the specific languages tested. In other words, this approach can help us decide which properties of the language production system are general and shared by all languages and which properties seem to have a more language-specific origin.

Secondly, researchers have asked general questions about the speech production system by making use of the specific linguistic properties that are present in certain languages. Languages which differ in some of their linguistic properties provide different contexts to explore general principles of speech production. For example, the general mechanism of agreement can be studied by investigating grammatical gender agreement (in those languages in which this feature is present, e.g. Romance languages). Alternatively, it can be studied by investigating number, person, or tense agreement in those languages where those features are present. Just as the first type of research, this approach seeks to describe general organizing principles of the language production system.

Finally, the third path refers to those studies that have assessed the extent to which contrastive linguistic properties across languages may affect the processes and representations used by the corresponding speakers.

Language production is a relatively young field of investigation. In fact, research on the processes and representations involved in language production has increased dramatically in the last decade. Between 1990 and 1994, 96 articles published in journals indexed by the database Psycinfo® included the term "language production" in their abstract. Between 2000 and 2004, this number more than doubled (214). Perhaps because of the contrastive effects observed in language perception across languages, cross-linguistic studies have started to be conducted to investigate language production as well. The growth in the number of published articles has been accompanied by an increase in the number of languages in which research in language production has been conducted.

A brief outline of a language production model (see below for more details) would distinguish between:

(a) the processes involved in establishing the message to be communicated;
(b) the processes responsible for lexicalization (i.e. "putting the message into words") and sentence construction;
(c) the processes of surface form construction involving phonological, phonetic, orthographic, as well as other representations;
(d) the processes of motor execution: via articulators in the case of speaking, via the hand in the case of writing, etc.

It is important to identify which of these levels could be tuned to language-specific properties, since it is likely that they are not all equally sensitive to cross-linguistic differences. For example, the message level, where the thoughts and message to be expressed are constructed, is generally thought to be largely language-independent (see Levelt, 1989: 103; Slobin, 1996). Also, given the shared anatomy across humans, the motor execution stage will probably show little differences across languages. Thus the most likely candidates to show cross-linguistic differences are those processes involved in lexical access, sentence construction, and phonological encoding. As we will see below, differences such as the various rules of agreement or the phonological structure of the words in a given language may produce important cross-linguistic processing differences.

In this chapter we review some of the recent research conducted in the field of language production that bears on cross-linguistic issues, as defined above. Most of the research providing relevant data for models of speech production comes from two sources:

(a) psycholinguistic experiments in which chronometric and/or accuracy performance is registered in normal speakers; and
(b) analyses of the production performance of brain damaged individuals.

Here, we will focus on the first of these two kinds of evidence. Also, as it will become clear in this review, most of the studies that we discuss were conducted in a rather limited number of languages belonging either to the Germanic family (English, Dutch, and German) or to the Romance family (Spanish, Catalan, Italian, and French). This is indicative of the fact that, although the number of languages in which research in speech production is conducted is increasing, we still lack experimental evidence from many language families.

The chapter is divided into six sections, organized according to the levels of processing postulated in language production models. In section 32.2, we review several studies that have addressed the processes involved in the retrieval from the lexicon of open-class words (i.e. lexical categories such as nouns, verbs, adjectives, certain adverbs, etc.). In section 32.3, we turn to the question of how closed-class words are retrieved from the lexicon (closed-class words are grammatical words such as determiners, prepositions, and conjunctions). The distinction between open- and closed-class words followed here was originally motivated by the contrastive effects found for open- and closed-class words in errors by aphasic and healthy speakers. Such distinction has been pervasive in language production models since the early work of Garrett (1988; 1984; 1975; see also Bock and Levelt, 1994; Levelt, 1989).

In section 32.4, we present some studies that have addressed how speakers compute agreement during speech production. Section 32.5 is devoted to the processes involved in the construction of syntactic structures during speech planning. Section 32.6 presents some research addressing the structure of the phonological and phonetic representations. Finally, in section 32.7 we review some of the research addressing the issue of phonological planning in speech production.

32.2 **Retrieving open-class words from the lexicon**

One of the central stages of language production is that of retrieving words from the lexicon. It is well accepted that lexical access proceeds in two major stages: the retrieval of words' semantic-syntactic information and the retrieval of words' phonological information (e.g. Caramazza, 1997; Dell, 1986; Garrett, 1975; Levelt et al., 1999). The processes involved in these two steps are referred to as grammatical encoding and phonological encoding, respectively. In this context, researchers have paid special attention to two main questions:

(a) What are the processing principles governing access to these two kinds of information?

(b) What is the time-course of these two processes?

A very influential framework regarding these two issues has been put forward by Levelt and collaborators (e.g. Levelt, 1989; Levelt et al., 1999). This framework has been primarily tested by exploring contextual effects in the picture–word interference paradigm. In this paradigm, participants are required to name a picture while ignoring the presentation of a distractor word. By manipulating the relationship between the target picture and the distractor, and also by manipulating the timing between the presentations of the two stimuli, different effects have been observed. For example, when the distractor word (e.g. *truck*) is semantically related to the target picture (CAR), naming latencies are slower than when both stimuli are unrelated. Conversely, when both stimuli are phonologically related (*cap*–CAR), naming latencies are faster in comparison to unrelated distractors. Although these two effects were known already in the seventies (Lupker, 1979; Rayner and Springer, 1986; Rosinski, 1977), they began to play a crucial role for theories of language production when they were interpreted as revealing different stages of word production. The first effect, the so-called "semantic interference effect," is assumed to reveal the processes involved in the translation of semantic information into lexical items (Roelofs, 1992; for converging evidence see Damian and Bowers, 2003b; but see Costa et al., 2005; Miozzo and Caramazza, 2003 for different views). This is one of the crucial processes of grammatical encoding called "lexical selection." The second effect, the so-called "phonological facilitation effect," is thought to reveal the processes involved in retrieving the morphophonological composition of the lexical items. From a cross-linguistic perspective, it is relevant to assess whether these two effects and their corresponding time-courses are present across languages.

After a series of experiments conducted in Dutch (Schriefers et al., 1990), many studies tried to replicate the semantic interference and the phonological facilitation effects in several languages including English (e.g. Vitkovitch and Tyrrell, 1999; Damian and Martin, 1999), Dutch (Starreveld and La Heij, 1995), Spanish (Costa et al., 1999), French (Alario et al., 2000), Italian (Miozzo and Caramazza, 1999), and German (Glaser and Düngelhoff, 1984). The most reliable effects observed in these studies are the following:

(a) Semantic interference effects are observed whenever the distractor word and the target picture belong to the same semantic category and participants have to name the picture using a basic-level term.

(b) Semantic facilitation effects are observed whenever the distractor-word and the target picture belong to the same semantic category and participants have to provide the category name of the target picture (e.g. animal).

(c) Phonological facilitation effects are observed whenever the distractor word and the target picture share some segmental information.[1]

(d) Semantic effects tend to be present when the distractor is presented before the picture or at the same time, while phonological effects tend to be present when the distractor is presented at the same time or after the target picture (e.g. see review and discussion in Starreveld, 2000).

Interestingly, these results are quite consistent across languages, leaving little room to postulate cross-linguistic differences in the lexical selection and phonological encoding processes revealed by these two effects. Notice that this does not imply that there is consensus about the precise origin of the semantic interference (e.g. Caramazza and Costa, 2000; Caramazza and Costa, 2001; Costa, Mahon, et al., 2003; Costa et al., 2005; Roelofs, 2001; 1992) and of the phonological facilitation effects (e.g. Starreveld and La Heij, 1996; Roelofs et al., 1996; Starreveld, 2000; 2004), nor on the relationship (strictly serial or interactive) that these two processes entertain over the time course of lexical access.

The studies we have reviewed in this section focused on the processes involved in the production of open-class words (mostly nouns), which appear to be largely shared among the languages investigated up to now. As we will see, cross-linguistic differences emerge when the processes in charge of selecting closed-class words are investigated.

32.3 **Retrieving closed-class words from the lexicon**

Research on the selection of closed-class words, in particular determiners, has been marked by strong cross-linguistic differences. This is so, in part, because the information needed to select these words varies across languages. For example, in languages such as English, the retrieval of the

[1] There are some indications of potential cross-linguistic variability on the presence of phonological facilitation effects. This evidence is reviewed below in section 32.7.

definite article (*the*) depends entirely on semantic information (definiteness). However, in Germanic, Slavic, and Romance languages, the retrieval of the determiners (and other closed-class words, such as pronouns) also depends on a grammatical property of nouns called "grammatical gender." For instance, in Dutch, nouns belong either to the so-called "neuter" gender or to the "common" gender. The definite determiners accompanying the nouns belonging to the two sets are respectively *het* (e.g. *het huis*, "the house") and *de* (e.g. *de appel*, "the apple"). Thus, the processes involved in the production of the phrase *the house* or *het huis* are necessarily different in English and in Dutch, since only in the former case is access to the grammatical properties of the noun needed to retrieve the correct determiner form.

The first study which experimentally explored the processes in charge of retrieving determiners and more concretely, the process of gender selection was conducted in Dutch using the picture–word interference paradigm (Schriefers, 1993). In this study, participants were asked to produce noun phrases of the type gender-marked determiner + adjective + noun (e.g. *het groene huis*, "the green house" or *de groene appel*, "the green apple") while ignoring distractor words that could have the same gender or a different gender than the picture name. Naming latencies were faster when the distractor word had the same gender as the picture's name. This so-called "gender congruency effect" has been replicated in several languages including Dutch (van Berkum, 1997; La Heij et al., 1998), German (Schriefers and Teruel, 2000; Schiller and Caramazza, 2002), and Croatian (Costa, Kovacic, et al., 2003). Furthermore, the gender congruency effect has been extended to the retrieval of other closed-class gender marked words such as pronouns (Costa, Kovacic, et al., 2003).

Additional studies on the origin of this gender congruency effect revealed an interesting cross-linguistic phenomenon. The gender congruency effect is absent in all Romance languages tested up to now: Italian (Miozzo and Caramazza, 1999), French (Alario and Caramazza, 2002), Catalan and Spanish (Costa et al., 1999; Miozzo et al., 2002). This cross-linguistic variability has been attributed to the different kinds of information needed to retrieve closed-class words in these two language families. While in Germanic languages the specific phonological context in which the determiner appears is irrelevant for its selection (e.g. in Dutch, neuter nouns take *het* and common nouns take *de*, irrespective of phonological context), this is not the case in Romance languages. Consider the case of singular definite determiner forms in Italian. The singular definite determiner form for feminine nouns is *la*, while the singular definite determiner form for masculine nouns can be *il* or *lo*. The selection of one of these two determiners depends on the phonological properties of the following word in the noun phrase. If the following word begins with a vowel, a consonant cluster of the form *s* + consonant, *gn*, or an affricate, then the proper masculine determiner is lo (e.g. *lo sgabello*, "the stool"; *lo gnomo*, 'the gnome'). In all other cases, the correct determiner is *il*. For example, the determiner accompanying the noun *treno* is *il* in the case of *il treno strano* (lit. "the train strange") but *lo* in the case of *lo strano treno* (lit. "the strange train"). According to some researchers (Caramazza et al., 2001), this difference in the types of information needed to select the determiner form is at the basis of the presence or absence of the gender congruency effect. This interpretation leads to a clear cross-linguistic hypothesis: for those languages in which the determiner form can be selected on the basis of only semantic and grammatical information (so-called "early selection languages"), the gender congruency effect will be present, while for those languages in which the selection of the determiner form needs to wait until the contextual phonological information is retrieved (so-called "late selection languages"), the effect will be absent (Caramazza et al., 2001; Miozzo and Caramazza, 1999, see Figure 32.1). This hypothesis reflects how the specific properties of different languages may affect the processes involved in language production, and how a better understanding of the mechanisms involved in the selection of closed-class words requires a cross-linguistic approach. Notice, however, that these cross-linguistic differences do not imply that closed-class word retrieval is governed by completely different principles in Germanic and in Romance languages. Although the *selection criteria* appear to be different for these two groups of languages, the *activation* of determiner forms seems to follow similar principles in the two language families. This conclusion comes from studies exploring the processes by which individual features (e.g. grammatical gender, number, phonological value) activate determiner forms (Alario and Caramazza, 2002; Janssen and Caramazza, 2003).

The experiments in Alario and Caramazza (2002) took advantage of the fact that, just as in Italian (see examples above), gender agreement in French is sometimes modulated by the phonological context. For example, when the

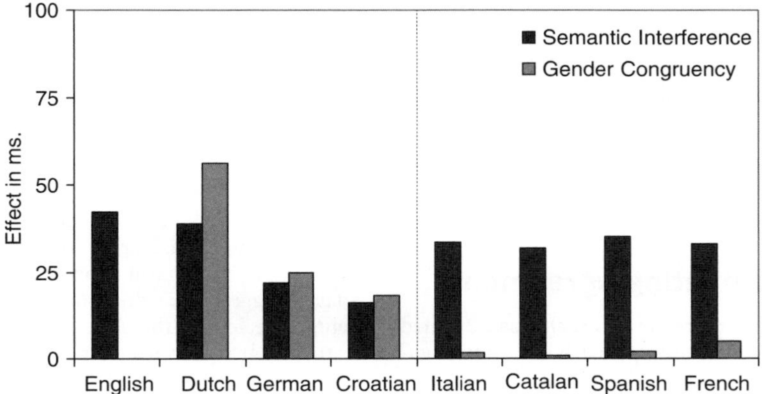

Figure 32.1 Semantic interference and gender congruency effects in various languages. Semantic interference is calculated by substracting naming latencies in the related (e.g. desk–TABLE) and in the unrelated (e.g. fork–TABLE) conditions. Gender congruency is calculated by substracting naming latencies in the gender incongruent (e.g. $\text{huis}_{\text{neuter}}$-$\text{TAFEL}_{\text{common}}$) and in the gender congruent (e.g. $\text{appel}_{\text{common}}$-$\text{TAFEL}_{\text{common}}$) conditions. The semantic interference effect is present in all languages. The gender congruency effect is observed in Germanic languages but not in Romance languages.

English: Damian and Martin (1999); Dutch: Schriefers (1993); German: Schriefers and Teruel (2000); Croatian: Costa, Kovacic et al. (2003); Italian: Miozzo and Caramazza (1999); Catalan and Spanish: Costa et al. (1999) and Costa and Caramazza (1999); French: Alario et al. (2000) and Alario and Caramazza (2002).

word following the noun begins with a consonant, the masculine form of the possessive "my" is *mon* and its feminine form is *ma* (e.g. *mon bureau*$_{masculine}$, "my desk"; *ma table*$_{feminine}$, "my table"). By contrast, if the word following the possessive begins with a vowel, then the determiner is *mon* irrespective of gender (e.g. *mon arbre*$_{masculine}$, "my tree"; *mon étoile*$_{feminine}$, "my star"). This property of French allows testing the role of the features "gender" and "phonological onset" on the activation of determiner forms. To do so, Alario and Caramazza (2002) compared the production of noun phrases where the determiner form and the noun were gender-consistent (the so-called "standard condition," e.g. *mon arbre*$_{masculine}$, "my tree") with the production of noun phrases where the determiner and the noun were not gender-congruent (the so-called "non-standard condition," e.g. *mon étoile*$_{feminine}$, "my star").[2] The results showed that noun phrase production latencies were shorter in the standard than in the non-standard condition. This result was taken as evidence that grammatical gender activates determiner forms irrespective of the other features involved in the process (e.g. independently of the phonological onset value VOWEL). More specifically, during the production of non-standard responses, the feature gender is thought to activate the inappropriate feminine form (*ma*), which results in a delay in the activation/selection of the appropriate form (*mon*). Such activation/selection delay is not present in the standard condition, where the grammatical gender and the phonological value conspire for the selection of the same determiner form (see Alario and Caramazza, 2002).

In short, this type of experiment provides evidence for a process of determiner activation that is driven by the individual features which define the determiner form to be selected. Importantly for us, similar findings have been observed when other features with similar combinatorial properties have been used in Dutch (features gender, number and diminutive; see Janssen and Caramazza, 2003) and in German (features gender, and number; see Schriefers et al., 2002; 2005). The parallel observations and interpretations in Romance and Germanic languages suggest that the process of determiner *activation* could be shared across language families. This is despite the fact that, as discussed above, the

[2] Notice that the non-standard condition is grammatical, and is indeed the only grammatical option for producing the possessive.

process of determiner *selection* seems to vary across languages.

In short, then, determiner retrieval, an interesting test case for closed-class word retrieval, appears to be governed by a combination of language-independent and language-specific principles. The language-specific principles are constrained by the phonological properties of the languages investigated.

32.4 Computing agreement

Another topic of research which has benefited from a cross-linguistic approach is the investigation of the properties that affect the syntactic agreement between different elements in an utterance. As discussed in the previous section, words in sentences hold intrinsic syntactic dependencies (e.g. determiners agree with the gender of the head noun). A central question in language production relates to how these dependencies (agreement) are computed, and the variables that affect this computation during sentence production.

One such dependency, present in most languages, is that between the number of the subject and the number of the verb in a sentence. The issue of how this agreement is computed has been experimentally explored by means of a paradigm in which participants have to complete sentence fragments. In the seminal study conducted by Bock and Miller (1991), participants were asked to complete fragments of the type (*the road to the lake*; see Figure 32.2) with a verb plus an argument. Importantly, the number of the local noun was manipulated. It could either be consistent or inconsistent with the number of the head noun (e.g. $road_{singular}$ combined with $lake_{singular}$ or with $lakes_{plural}$). Participants made more agreement errors (they produced the wrong verb form) when the local noun and the head noun had a different number value than when they did not. This effect, referred to as "attraction," has been replicated in several languages (Spanish: Vigliocco et al., 1996; French: Largy et al., 1996; Italian: Vigliocco et al., 1995). Although the precise origin of the effect is still debated, the fact that it is present in many languages suggests that the syntactic mechanisms being revealed by the effect (e.g. grammatical feature migration, verb form selection) are similar across languages.

Following a similar experimental strategy, several studies have looked at whether the process of syntactic agreement (e.g. between subject and verb) is independent of conceptual and morphophonological factors. The issue is to determine whether the syntactic process of agreement is "blind" to the conceptual and morphophonological properties of the specific words included in the utterance.

Regarding the first issue, one of the best-studied phenomena is the effect of the so-called "distributed interpretation" of noun phrases in the agreement process. In the study by Bock and Miller (1991), participants were asked to complete preambles of the sort *the picture on the postcards* or *the road to the lakes*. Crucially, in order to properly complete these two noun phrases the verb needs to be inflected in the singular, since the head of the noun phrase is a singular noun (*picture* and *road*, respectively). However, the preferred conceptual interpretation

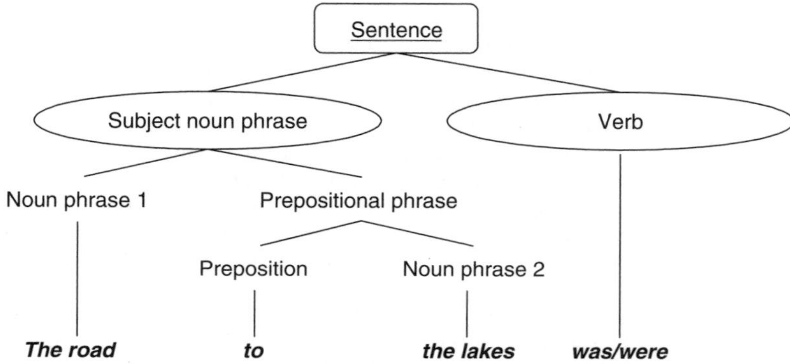

Figure 32.2 An example of the sentence preambles (without the verb) used to elicit agreement errors in speech language tasks. The properties (e.g. singular or plural number) of the head noun (*road*), of the "local" noun (*lakes*), and of the meaning of the subject noun phrase are manipulated and modulate error rates. Attraction is said to occur when the produced verb agrees with the local noun rather than with the head noun.

of the first noun phrase is that of several "tokens" (or a distributed interpretation: several pictures), while in the second noun phrase the interpretation is that of a single token (one road). The original results in English revealed an equal number of agreement errors for both preambles, suggesting that the processes of subject–verb agreement are not affected by this conceptual information (Bock and Miller, 1991). However, further studies in Italian, French, Spanish, and Dutch showed a different scenario (Vigliocco et al., 1995; Vigliocco, Butterworth, and Garrett, 1996; Vigliocco, Hartsuiker, et al., 1996; Vigliocco and Franck, 2001). In these languages, participants made more agreement errors when the preferred conceptual interpretation was that of several tokens (*the picture on the postcards*) than when such an interpretation was of a singular token (*the road to the lakes*). This cross-linguistic variation led researchers to hypothesize that languages may vary in the extent to which the selection of the verb and the corresponding agreement process is affected by conceptual properties (Vigliocco, Butterworth, and Garrett, 1996; Vigliocco, Hartsuiker, et al. 1996). Contrary to this hypothesis, however, more recent results have revealed that agreement in English seems also to be affected by the preferred conceptual interpretation of the noun phrase (Eberhard, 1999; see also Nicol and Greth, 2003 for a study with bilingual English-Spanish speakers showing the effect in the two languages). Convergent evidence for this claim comes also from a the study conducted by Thornton and MacDonald (2003) in English. By varying the conceptual property "animateness," these authors manipulated the degree to which the head or local noun could be a plausible subject for the sentence. Attraction errors on number agreement were reduced whenever the local noun was not a plausible subject (e.g. because it was inanimate) as opposed to when the local noun was animate. In other words, the conceptual feature "inanimate" of the local noun reduces the likelihood that its plural feature is used (incorrectly) to compute subject–verb agreement.

Further evidence on the effects of conceptual information in syntactic agreement comes from a series of experiments which exploit the gender agreement process in Romance languages. As discussed in the previous section, in many Romance languages some words such as determiners and adjectives agree with the grammatical gender of the noun (e.g. in Italian *il ragazzo*, "the$_{\text{masculine}}$ boy"; *la ragazza*, "the$_{\text{feminine}}$ girl"). Furthermore, for some nouns there is a correlation between the grammatical gender and the so-called "conceptual gender"; male entities (e.g. *ragazzo*, "boy"; *uomo*, "man") usually correspond to nouns with masculine grammatical gender, and female entities (e.g. *ragazza*, "girl"; *donna*, "woman") to nouns with feminine grammatical gender. However, irrespective of this regularity, gender agreement is determined by the grammatical feature of a noun and not by its semantic features. For example, the feminine noun *vittima* ("victim") calls for feminine agreement (*la vittima*) irrespective of whether the victim is a man or a woman.

This linguistic property provides the right conditions to assess the extent to which a noun's semantic information affects gender agreement, a process that is supposed to be purely grammatical. This issue has been assessed experimentally by asking participants to complete preambles with a gender-marked adjective. Crucially, the noun with which the adjective had to agree could have a conceptual gender (sex) or not. For example, the head noun *ragazza* ("girl") in the preamble *la ragazza nel parco è rossa* ("the girl in the park is red-haired") has both grammatical gender (feminine) and a conceptual gender (female), while the head noun *panchina* ("bench") in *la panchina nel parco è rossa* ("the bench in the park is red") has only grammatical gender (feminine). If gender agreement is computed only by considering grammatical information, agreement errors when inflecting the adjective (*rosso*, "red") should not differ between the two pre-ambles. However, if conceptual information of the noun is used, to some extent, during gender agreement, then errors should be less common when the noun has both grammatical and conceptual genders. The results observed in French and Italian were consistent with the second hypothesis, suggesting that conceptual information is used during gender agreement (Vigliocco and Franck, 1999; 2001).

At present, there is consensus that syntactic agreement is, to some extent, affected by conceptual information. This effect seems to be found across languages. Note however that conceptual information might not affect homogeneously all types of agreement (see Bock et al., 2004, for experimental evidence and discussion of possible differences between verb and pronoun agreement). Importantly from a cross-linguistic point of view, the opportunities given by the different linguistic properties of different languages have allowed the extension of these conceptual effects on agreement to several contexts (subject–verb agreement, gender agreement, etc.).

Cross-linguistic research has also been useful when assessing the effects of morphophonological properties on syntactic agreement. The issue at stake here is similar to the one discussed just above: to what extent do the morphophonological properties of words affect an agreement process that is supposed to be governed by purely grammatical features? Bock and Eberhard (1993) asked English native speakers to complete preambles of the sort *the ship for the crew* .... The crucial manipulation in this study involved the phonological properties of the local noun (*crew*). As in previous studies, the number of the local noun was congruent or incongruent with the number of the head noun. However, in one condition the local noun was a singular noun (*cruise*) that was a homophone of a plural word (*crews*). Despite the fact that in sentences such as *the ship for the cruise* the local noun was a "phonological pseudoplural" (ending in /z/ and, in this respect, inconsistent with the singular head noun *ship*), participants did not make more agreement errors than in sentences in which such an inconsistency was not present (*the ship of the crew*). This result suggests that the phonological properties of the local noun seem irrelevant for the process of attraction that is present when computing subject–verb agreement.

However, other studies have found positive evidence for the effects of morphophonological properties on agreement. This evidence comes mostly from manipulations of the properties of the *head* noun, rather than of the *local* noun of the preambles. For example, Vigliocco et al. (1995) took advantage of one particularity of Italian number system to assess this issue. In Italian most nouns are inflected for number (e.g. *la* $_{singular}$ *panchina* $_{singular}$, "the $_{\text{singular}}$ bench"; *le* $_{plural}$ *panchine* $_{plural}$, "the $_{\text{plural}}$ benches"). However, a subset of nouns does not carry any number inflection. These nouns are invariant with respect to number (e.g. *la città* $_{singular}$, "the $_{\text{singular}}$ city"; *le città* $_{plural}$, "the $_{\text{plural}}$ cities"). The authors compared whether agreement errors were present more often when completing preambles which contained a number-variant noun (*panchine* $_{singular}$ – *panchine* $_{plural}$) than when completing those which contained a number-invariant noun (*città* $_{singular}$ – *città* $_{plural}$). The results revealed that participants produced the wrong verb number more often when the subject (the head noun) of the sentence was ambiguous than when it was unambiguous, suggesting that the morphophonological properties of the head noun affect number agreement. Convergent evidence for such a claim comes from other languages (Dutch and German), other experimental contexts (pronoun retrieval), and other manipulations (e.g. case marking: Hartsuiker et al., 2003).

The results of these studies reveal that in various languages and contexts both semantic and morphophonological information seem to influence agreement processes. Beyond the theoretical conclusions that can be drawn from the studies revised in this section, what is important for our purposes here is to see how the different properties offered by different languages can be used to assess general issues in speech production, such as how agreement is computed.

32.5 **Accessing syntactic structures**

Perhaps one of the most relevant observations for our understanding of how grammatical encoding proceeds is the phenomenon called "syntactic priming." This phenomenon refers to the tendency of speakers to mimic syntactic structures that they have recently encountered. Interestingly, syntactic priming is present not only when the source of the repetition is the speaker's own production but also when it is the speech of others (see Garrod and Pickering, 2004; Pickering and Garrod, 2004 for a discussion of how this phenomenon relates to dialogue).

This phenomenon was first reported in English by (Bock, 1986; see also Pickering and Branigan, 1999). Other studies, also conducted in English, revealed that the effect had a clear syntactic component, in the sense that it is not explainable in terms of the closed-class words that provide the syntactic structure (Bock, 1989; V. S. Ferreira, 2003), the open-class words that compose the sentence (Pickering and Branigan, 1998), or the thematic role of the components of the sentence (Bock and Loebell, 1990). Subsequent work conducted in other languages revealed other important aspects of syntactic priming. Experiments in Dutch established that syntactic priming occurs in the same structures as in English (Hartsuiker and Kolk, 1998) and that mere word-order variations also show priming (Hartsuiker and Westenberg, 2000; Hartsuiker et al., 1999). Experiments conducted in German established that different relative-clause attachments exhibit priming (Scheepers, 2003). Interestingly, recent research has shown that syntactic priming can also be observed across languages (Meijer and Fox Tree, 2003; Hartsuiker et al., 2004; Loebell and Bock, 2003). The main observation of these studies is that processing a structure in one of the bilingual's languages can prime the analogous structures in their other language. As a first approximation, "analogous" refers to structures which are descriptively similar in syntactic terms across the two languages. This suggests that, when possible, bilingual speakers have a common representational vocabulary for the syntactic structures of their languages. Furthermore, although the number of studies is somewhat limited, syntactic priming seems to be present regardless of the directionality of the prime target (L1–L2 or L2–L1) and the level of proficiency of the bilinguals tested.

This evidence consistently points to the existence of syntactic priming in several languages (Pickering and Branigan, 1999), which leaves little room for cross-linguistic differences. Furthermore, this priming can be observed from one language to another, suggesting a great degree of commonality between the processes of syntactic encoding for production in different languages. Notice, however, that the syntactic properties of the few languages tested share a great number of relevant properties. Whether syntactic priming can be found similarly for languages with rather different syntactic properties remains an open question. Clarifying this issue in the case of languages which have diverging syntactic properties will certainly require a fine-grained description of the similarities and differences between the relevant structures across languages.

32.6 The structure of phonological and phonetic representations

The models which describe how the forms of words are retrieved and encoded generally assume a distinction between phonological and phonetic levels. During processing at the phonological level, the speaker has access to two types of information that need to be combined later on (see Figure 32.3):

(a) the specific segmental information corresponding to the word to be produced;

(b) an abstract phonological frame containing the slots to which the segmental content will be assigned during phonological encoding (e.g. Dell, 1986; 1988; Roelofs, 1997; Shattuck-Hufnagel, 1992; Levelt and Wheeldon, 1994).

Processing at the phonetic level involves the retrieval of representations that will drive the process of articulation. One prominent hypothesis in this context is that syllable programs are retrieved form a mental "syllabary" during phonetic encoding. Among the various questions which have been addressed in this context, three have generated some cross-linguistic research: the organization of segment retrieval, the role of the CV structure (the consonant-vowel sequences of words), and the role of syllabic information. We discuss these three issues in turn.

The first aspect of form encoding to have received considerable cross-linguistic attention concerns the role of syllabic representations during speech production. In section 32.2, we discussed the phonological facilitation effect observed across languages in the picture–word interference paradigm. The general finding is that when a distractor shares phonological

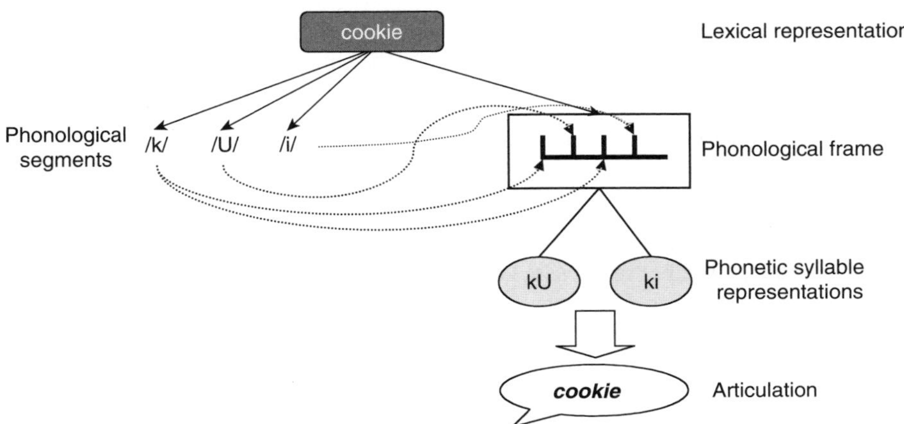

Figure 32.3 A schematic representation of the phonological encoding process. On the basis of the selected lexical item, phonological segments and a phonological frame are retrieved. Segments are then inserted in the frame in the appropriate order. The investigation of the frame has lead to seemingly different conclusions across languages (see text). Not all authors agree with all the hypotheses that are implicit in the schema. Morphological units have not been represented.

information with a target word, performance is faster and more accurate than when the distractor is unrelated. Some studies have made use of this paradigm and its variants to explore issues related to the structure of the phonological representations used across languages. For example, Ferrand et al. (1996) used a variant of the picture–word interference paradigm in which distractor word fragments (instead of words) are presented very briefly and masked. In experiments conducted in French, they observed that the fragment primes facilitated responses more when they corresponded to the whole first syllable of the picture target name than when they did not. That is, the fragment PAL facilitated the naming of the target PAL.MIER more than the naming of the target PA.LACE. A similar effect was reported in English for words with clear syllabic boundaries and no ambisyllabicity (Ferrand et al., 1997; in this study, the target pictures were replaced by target words to be read). However, these observations have been difficult to replicate in both languages (for French see Brand et al., 2003; for English see Schiller, 2000). The syllable priming effect was also absent in Spanish (Schiller et al., 2002). According to these latest studies, it would appear that, across languages, phonological priming is sensitive to the number of shared segments between prime and target rather than to the shared syllabic structure. This suggests that the segment-retrieval process is shared across languages.

The second (related) aspect of form encoding which has been investigated cross-linguistically is the nature of the phonological frame that is retrieved to encode the segments. This frame is supposed to be independent of the specific segmental content of the target word, and serves as a guide for the syllabification process during phonological encoding. In this context, the issue arises of what the structure of such a phonological frame is. An influential proposal is that this frame contains the sequence of consonant and vowels of a given word—the so-called CV structure (Clements and Keyser, 1983; Dell, 1986; Halle and Vergnaud, 1980; but see Levelt et al., 1999, for a different view).

One of the first chronometric studies to explore the role of the CV structure in speech production was conducted in English by Sevald et al. (1995). In their experiments, participants were asked to repeat two items as fast as possible during a given period of time. In some conditions, the CV structure of the first item and that of the first syllable of the second item was the same (KEM (CVC) – TIL.FER (CVC.CVC)) while in others it was different (KEM (CVC) – TILF.NER (CVCC.CVC). The number of syllables produced per second was larger in the first than in the second condition. Furthermore, this effect was independent of whether or not the two items shared precisely the same segmental content. This result was interpreted as revealing priming in the retrieval of the word's CV structure.

Along the same lines, results reported in Spanish and French (Ferrand and Seguí, 1998; Costa and Sebastián-Gallés, 1998) suggest that reusing the same CV structure of words accelerates naming latencies. In these two studies, participants were asked to read sequences of words which served as primes and, in the last trial of the sequence, to name a picture that served as target. Picture-naming latencies were faster when primes and pictures shared their CV structure (but not their segmental content) than when they did not. Convergent evidence, although somewhat less robust, for the existence of a CV structure in language production was also reported in Dutch by Meijer (1996).

However, contrasting results leading to contrasting conclusions are also present in the literature. Roelofs and Meyer (1998) ran a series of experiments in Dutch using the implicit priming paradigm (Meyer, 1990). In this paradigm, participants produce words in two different types of blocks. In the homogeneous blocks all target words share some phonological properties, while in the heterogeneous blocks they do not. The standard result in this paradigm is that when the words of a homogeneous set share their initial segments, naming latencies are faster than when they do not. Roelofs and Meyer (1998) found that this priming effect was only present when the words in the homogeneous block had also the same number of syllables and stress pattern. In contrast, whether or not the words in the homogeneous set had the same number of consonant and vowels (e.g. the same CV structure) was irrelevant for observing the priming effect. It was argued that the abstract phonological frame retrieved during phonological encoding specifies only the number of syllables and the stress pattern, but not the CV structure (for a discussion see Santiago et al., 2000).

Thus, the present cross-linguistic evidence suggests that the CV structure seems to be a relevant phonological structure in English, French, and Spanish. The results in Dutch are less clear, and more research needs to be conducted to assess whether this inconsistency actually reveals the different role of this structure in different languages, or whether it can be traced down to methodological differences across studies (see Hartsuiker, 2002 for a cross-linguistic hypothesis about the role of CV structure in Spanish and Dutch).

Converging evidence for cross-linguistic variability in the role of syllabic structure during phonological encoding also comes from an investigation in Mandarin Chinese, which led to one of the most explicit cross-linguistic hypotheses in this context (Chen et al., 2002). In their study, these authors used the implicit priming paradigm (see above) to explore the processes involved in phonological encoding in Mandarin Chinese. Priming effects were observed when the words shared the whole first syllable. However, contrary to what has been observed in Dutch and in English, there was no priming effect when the words of a given block shared their first segment only. The specific orthographic properties of Mandarin Chinese cannot account for this pattern; in fact the contrasting effects of segmental priming in Mandarin Chinese and in Dutch and English (Roelofs, 1999; Damian and Bowers, 2003a; Chen et al., 2002) were interpreted as revealing differences in the properties of these languages. The proposal is that the syllable may be a more important unit during phonological encoding in Chinese than in the other two languages, leading Chinese speakers to use the syllable as a major unit guiding form retrieval. According to these authors, the relative importance of the syllable in these languages may depend, among other things, on the number of syllable types, their complexity, and their ambisyllabic status in these languages

Finally, despite the controversial role of syllabic units in phonological encoding, and the potential cross-linguistic variations of this role, a third line of research shows that syllables play an important role in the subsequent level of processing referred to as "phonetic encoding." Following the original idea of Crompton (1981), Levelt and Wheeldon (1994) hypothesized the existence of a syllabary which contains the syllabic motor programs of the most frequently used syllables. One way to test such a hypothesis is to explore the syllable frequency effect. The agreement across studies and languages here is large. Syllables which are more frequent are produced faster than syllables that are less frequent in Dutch (Levelt and Wheeldon, 1994; Cholin et al., forthcoming), Spanish (Carreiras and Perea, 2004), German (Hutzler et al., 2005), and French (Laganaro and Alario, 2006). The syllabary containing this syllable representations is hypothesized to be located at the level of phonetic encoding, and there is some direct evidence to corroborate this hypothesis (see Laganaro and Alario, 2006, for details). Thus it appears that, at least at the level of phonetic encoding, syllables are an important unit regardless of the phonological properties of the language.

In summary, investigations on the structure of the phonological representations involved in language production provide evidence that such representations may vary cross-linguistically. However, much more research is needed, especially in unexplored languages with distinctive phonological properties, to determine which representations are universally shared and which are language-specific. Studies regarding the phonetic representations involved in speech production are more consistent across languages. This may reveal the constraints imposed by the articulatory system on the types of representations that can be produced.

32.7 Planning phonological information

There is wide agreement on the assumption that the language production system works in an incremental fashion. This means that, at some point in time, the speaker may be concurrently planning some parts of the utterance at the grammatical level and other parts at the phonological level. Accordingly, speakers do not need to finish computing an utterance at one level of processing before information starts to be processed at the next level of representation (Bock and Levelt, 1994). Although, the extent to which speakers produce language incrementally may be under strategic control (F. Ferreira and Swets, 2002), it is nevertheless relevant to explore the minimal unit of linguistic encoding that needs to be processed at one level of representation before its product can be passed on to the next level of processing.

Regarding phonological encoding, the issue of incrementality has been intensively investigated by assessing how much phonological material needs to be processed before articulation starts. In this context, it has been hypothesized that the minimal or preferred phonological unit that needs to be completed before articulation is released is the phonological word (Nespor and Vogel, 1986). The phonological word is assumed to involve a content word plus any clitic words that attach to it (e.g. the noun phrase *the red car* has two phonological words, *the red* and *car*).

Wheeldon and Lahiri (1997) provided clear evidence that the phonological word is indeed a fundamental unit of phonological encoding in a language like Dutch. These authors asked participants to perform a delayed naming task in which participants had to prepare an utterance and start articulating it when a cue appeared about 4 seconds. afterwards. Initiation times depended, among other things, on the number of phonological words composing the utterance irrespective of the number of lexical words, suggesting a critical role of the phonological word unit during phonological encoding.

Evidence suggesting that the first phonological word is enough for speakers to start their articulation comes from the study conducted in Dutch by Meyer (1996). She made use of the phonological facilitation effect in the picture–word interference paradigm to explore the scope of phonological planning. In this study, participants were presented with two target pictures and were asked to produce conjoined Noun Phrases (e.g. *de pijl en de tas*, "the arrow and the bag") while ignoring distractor words which were phonologically related to the first noun (e.g. *pijp*, 'pipe') or to the second noun (e.g. *tand*, 'tooth') of the NP. Crucially, the first noun of the NP was located in the first phonological word and the second in the second phonological word. A phonological facilitation effect (faster naming latencies for the related distractor in comparison to an unrelated distractor word) was observed for the first noun of the NP but not for the second. These results suggest that:

(a) the first phonological word needs to be computed before articulation starts; and

(b) the retrieval of the phonological properties of the second phonological word does not need to be completed before articulation proceeds.

However, subsequent research (also in Dutch) revealed a more complex scenario. Roelofs (1998) ran a series of experiments in Dutch using the implicit priming paradigm (see above). Interestingly, he observed a preparation effect when the segmental content shared by the target words was placed in the second phonological word, suggesting that the scope of phonological planning extends to the second phonological word before articulation starts. Similar results using a different paradigm and a different language (English) have been observed by Smith and Wheeldon (1999); (see also van der Meulen et al., 2001, for evidence with the eye-movement technique).

Perhaps the clearest example of using a cross-linguistic approach to the issue of the scope of phonological planning was the study of Costa and Caramazza (2002). In this study Spanish and English native speakers were asked to produce noun phrases of the type "determiner + noun + color adjective" in Spanish (e.g. *el coche rojo*, lit. "the car red") and of the type "determiner + color adjective + noun" in English (e.g. *the red car*), while ignoring distractor words that were phonologically related to the noun or the adjective of the NP. Crucially, word order in these noun phrases varies in the two languages (post-nominal adjective in Spanish, pre-nominal adjective in English). Thus, the words located in the first phonological word are different in the two languages, including the head of the NP in Spanish (determiner + noun) but not in English (determiner + adjective). This different word order offers the opportunity to assess whether the syntactic status of the element located in the first phonological word (head or complement of the NP) affects the amount of phonological material computed before articulation starts. In this study, distractor words phonologically related to the first content word of the NP facilitated naming latencies in both languages. That is, the phonological facilitation effect was present for the words located in the first phonological word (the noun in Spanish and the adjective in English). More importantly, phonologically related distractors to the second content word also speeded naming latencies in both languages. That is, the phonological facilitation effect was also present for words located in the second phonological word (the adjective in Spanish and the noun in English) regardless of their syntactic role in the NP (see also Alario et al. (2002) for converging evidence using simple picture naming). This latter observation reveals that the scope of phonological planning extends to at least two phonological words. Furthermore, this cross-linguistic comparison allows the conclusion that (at least in the specific context used in these experiments) the syntactic role of the words located in the phonological frame does not affect the scope of phonological planning.

Research in Italian with a different paradigm has led to similar conclusions. Miozzo and Caramazza (1999) took advantage of one property of determiner production in Italian: determiners depend, among other things, on the phonological properties of the following word (see discussion of this issue in section 32.3). Thus, these authors could create a context in which the phonological properties of the word following the determiner required a given determiner form, while the phonological properties of the head of the noun phrase required another determiner form (e.g. *il grande scoiattolo*, "the big squirrel", where *grande* requires the determiner *il* and *scoiattolo* calls for the determiner *lo*). Naming latencies were affected negatively by this mismatch: if the pre-nominal adjective and the noun required different determiner forms, naming latencies were longer than if they required the same determiner form. This suggests that the phonological properties of the second phonological word (*scoiattolo*) are activated when the determiner form is being retrieved, and hence before articulation. This result was replicated in French by Alario and Caramazza (2002), indicating similarly that in this other Romance language, the phonological properties of the second phonological word affect the onset of articulation.

The results observed in several languages (Dutch, German, Italian, French, and English) suggest that usually the scope of phonological encoding encompasses more than one phonological word, irrespective of the specific type of utterance produced by the speaker.[3] This is an interesting observation, given that the prosodic properties of the languages being tested are somewhat different. The extent to which this general observation can be extrapolated to more complex utterance types, and to other languages with more distant prosodic properties, is an open question.

32.8 Conclusions

In this chapter we have reviewed those topics in language production which have generated more cross-linguistic research. Some of the studies presented here have led to results that are quite homogeneous across languages (see e.g. section 32.2), while others have revealed cross-linguistic differences which potentially shape the processes involved in language production (see e.g. section 32.3). On yet other occasions, the specific linguistic properties of different languages have provided researchers with the appropriated conditions to test hypotheses about language production (see e.g. section 32.4).

Cross-linguistic research is critical for teasing apart which processes and representations are shared across languages (universal properties of the language faculty) and which ones are language-specific. In the last decade we have advanced in our knowledge of the general cognitive mechanisms and representations involved in speech production. However, this advance has largely neglected the potential influence of language differences. As a consequence, the cross-linguistic approach to language production has been rather limited, in terms both of the languages investigated and of the language-specific properties that have been considered. Moreover, the relatively great similarity between the languages tested may have prevented the appearance of cross-linguistic differences.

We think that it is time for us to assess more deeply how cross-linguistic differences (e.g. vowel harmony, ergative constructions, agglutinative morphology) may shape current models of language production. Hopefully, when the time comes for the next *Handbook of Psycholinguistics* to be written, our understanding of the language production system will be based on a larger number of languages.

[3] This evidence is consistent with the observation that phonological contextual errors (e.g. sound exchanges) quite often involve phonological elements corresponding to words located in different phonological words (Garrett, 1975). However, the contribution of strategic factors to the size of the phonological units used in speech production is still an open question.

Acknowledgements

This research was supported by two grants from the Spanish Government (BSO2001-3492-C04-01; BFF2002-10379-E), and by the McDonnell grant "Bridging Mind Brain and Behavior." Albert Costa was supported by the research program "Ramon y Cajal" from the Spanish government. F.-Xavier Alario was supported by a grant from the "Programa de Movilidad" (ref. SB2003-0322) from the Spanish government.

We thank Merrill Garrett, Gareth Gaskell, Victor Ferreira, Iva Ivanona, Alissa Melinger, and Scott Sinnett for their comments on previous versions of this chapter.

References

Alario, F.-X., and Caramazza, A. (2002) The production of determiners: evidence from French. *Cognition*, 82: 179–223.

Alario, F.-X., Costa, A., and Caramazza, A. (2002) Frequency effects in noun phrase production: implications for models of lexical access. *Language and Cognitive Processes*, 17: 299–319.

Alario, F.-X., Segui, J., and Ferrand, L. (2000) Semantic and associative priming in picture naming. *Quarterly Journal of Experimental Psychology Section A: Human Experimental Psychology*, 53: 741–64.

Bock, K. (1986) Syntactic persistence in language production. *Cognitive Psychology*, 18: 355–87.

Bock, K. (1989) Closed-class immanence in sentence production. *Cognition*, 31: 163–86.

Bock, K., and Eberhard, K. M. (1993) Meaning, sound and syntax in English number agreement. *Language and Cognitive Processes*, 8: 57–99.

Bock, K., Eberhard, K. M., and Cutting, J. C. (2004) Producing number agreement: how pronouns equal verbs. *Journal of Memory and Language*, 51: 251–78.

Bock, K., and Levelt, W. J. M. (1994) Language production: grammatical encoding. In M. A. Gernsbacher (ed.), *Handbook of Psycholinguistics*, pp. 945–84. Academic Press, San Diego, CA.

Bock, K., and Loebell, H. (1990) Framing sentences. *Cognition*, 35: 1–39.

Bock, K., and Miller, C. A. (1991) Broken agreement. *Cognitive Psychology*, 23: 45–93.

Brand, M., Rey, A., and Peereman, R. (2003) Where is the syllable priming effect in visual word recognition? *Journal of Memory and Language*, 48: 435–43.

Caramazza, A. (1997) How many levels of processing are there in lexical access? *Cognitive Neuropsychology*, 14: 177–208.

Caramazza, A., and Costa, A. (2000) The semantic interference effect in the picture–word interference paradigm: does the response set matter? *Cognition*, 75: B51–B64.

Caramazza, A., and Costa, A. (2001) Set size and repetition in the picture–word interference paradigm: implications for models of naming. *Cognition*, 80: 291–8.

Caramazza, A., Miozzo, M., Costa, A., Schiller, N., and Alario, F. X. (2001) A crosslinguistic investigation of determiner production. In E. Dupoux (ed.), *Language, Brain, and Cognitive Development: Essays in honor of Jacques Mehler*, pp. 209–26. MIT Press, Cambridge, MA.

Carreiras, M., and Perea, M. (2004) Naming pseudowords in Spanish: effects of syllable frequency. *Brain and Language*, 90: 393–400.

Chen, J.-Y., Chen, T.-M., and Dell, G. S. (2002) Word-form encoding in Mandarin Chinese as assessed by the implicit priming task. *Journal of Memory and Language*, 46: 751–81.

Cholin, J., Schiller, N. O., and Levelt, W. J. M. (forthcoming) Effects of syllable frequency in speech production. *Cognition*.

Clements, G., and Keyser, S. J. (1983) *CV Phonology: A Generative Theory of the Syllable*, vol. 9. MIT Press, Cambridge, MA.

Costa, A., and Caramazza, A. (1999). Is lexical selection in bilingual speech production language-specific? Further evidence from Spanish-English and English-Spanish bilinguals. *Bilingualism: Language and Cognition*, 2: 231–44.

Costa, A., Alario, F.-X., and Caramazza, A. (2005) On the categorical nature of the semantic interference effect in the picture-word interference paradigm. *Psychonomic Bulletin and Review*, 12: 125–31.

Costa, A., and Caramazza, A. (2002) The production of noun phrases in English and Spanish: implications for the scope of phonological encoding in speech production. *Journal of Memory and Language*, 46: 178–98.

Costa, A., Kovacic, D., Fedorenko, E., and Caramazza, A. (2003) The gender congruency effect and the selection of freestanding and bound morphemes: evidence from Croatian. *Journal of Experimental Psychology: Learning, Memory, and Cognition*, 29: 1270–82.

Costa, A., Mahon, B., Savova, V., and Caramazza, A. (2003) Level of categorization effect: a novel effect in the picture-word interference paradigm. *Language and Cognitive Processes*, 18: 205–33.

Costa, A., Miozzo, M., and Caramazza, A. (1999) Lexical selection in bilinguals: do words in the bilingual's two lexicons compete for selection? *Journal of Memory and Language*, 41: 365–97.

Costa, A., and Sebastián-Gallés, N. (1998) Abstract phonological structure in language production: evidence from Spanish. *Journal of Experimental Psychology: Learning, Memory, and Cognition*, 24: 886–903.

Costa, A., Sebastián-Gallés, N., Miozzo, M., and Caramazza, A. (1999) The gender congruity effect: evidence from Spanish and Catalan. *Language and Cognitive Processes*, 14: 381–91.

Crompton, A. (1981) Syllables and segments in speech production. *Linguistics*, 19: 663–716.

Cutler, A., Mehler, J., Norris, D., and Segui, J. (1983) A language-specific comprehension strategy. *Nature*, 304: 159–60.

Damian, M. F., and Bowers, J. S. (2003a) Effects of orthography on speech production in a form-preparation paradigm. *Journal of Memory and Language*, 49: 119–32.

Damian, M. F., and Bowers, J. S. (2003b) Locus of semantic interference in picture-word interference tasks. *Psychonomic Bulletin and Review*, 10: 111–17.

Damian, M. F., and Martin, R. C. (1999) Semantic and phonological codes interact in single word production. *Journal of Experimental Psychology: Learning, Memory, and Cognition*, 25: 345–61.

Dell, G. S. (1986) A spreading-activation theory of retrieval in sentence production. *Psychological Review*, 93: 283–321.

Dell, G. S. (1988) The retrieval of phonological forms in production: tests of predictions from a connectionist model. *Journal of Memory and Language*, 27: 124–42.

Eberhard, K. M. (1999) The accessibility of conceptual number to the processes of subject–verb agreement in English. *Journal of Memory and Language*, 41: 560–78.

Ferrand, L., and Seguí, J. (1998) The syllable's role in speech production: are syllables chunks, schemas, or both? *Psychonomic Bulletin and Review*, 5: 253–8.

Ferrand, L., Seguí, J., and Grainger, J. (1996) Masked priming of word and picture naming: the role of syllabic units. *Journal of Memory and Language*, 35: 708–23.

Ferrand, L., Seguí, J., and Humphreys, G. W. (1997) The syllable's role in word naming. *Memory and Cognition*, 25: 458–70.

Ferreira, F., and Swets, B. (2002) How incremental is language production? Evidence from the production of utterances requiring the computation of arithmetic sums. *Journal of Memory and Language*, 46: 57–84.

Ferreira, V. S. (2003) The persistence of optional complementizer production: why saying "that" is not saying "that" at all. *Journal of Memory and Language*, 48: 379–98.

Garrett, M. F. (1975) The analysis of sentence production. In G. Bower (ed.), *Psychology of Learning and Motivation*, vol. 9, pp. 505–29. Academic Press, New York.

Garrett, M. F. (1984) The organization of processing structure for language production: applications to aphasic speech. In D. Caplan, A. R. Lecours, and A. Smith (eds), *Biological Perspectives on Language*, pp. 172–93. MIT Press, Cambridge, MA.

Garrett, M. F. (1988) Processes in language production. In F. J. Newmeyer (ed.), *Linguistics: The Cambridge Survey*, vol. 3: *Language: Psychological and Biological Aspects*, pp. 69–96. Cambridge University Press, Cambridge.

Garrod, S., and Pickering, M. J. (2004) Why is conversation so easy? *Trends in Cognitive Sciences*, 8: 8–11.

Glaser, W. R., and Düngelhoff, F.-J. (1984) The time course of picture–word interference. *Journal of Experimental Psychology: Human Perception and Performance*, 10(5), 640–54.

Halle, M., and Vergnaud, J. R. (1980) Three-pimensional Phonology. *Journal of Linguistic Research*, 1: 83–105.

Hartsuiker, R. J. (2002) The addition bias in Dutch and Spanish phonological speech errors: the role of structural context. *Language and Cognitive Processes*, 17: 61–96.

Hartsuiker, R. J., and Kolk, H. H. J. (1998) Syntactic persistence in Dutch. *Language and Speech*, 41: 143–84.

Hartsuiker, R. J., Kolk, H. H. J., and Huiskamp, P. (1999) Priming word order in sentence production. *Quarterly Journal of Experimental Psychology: Human Experimental Psychology*, 52: 129–47.

Hartsuiker, R. J., Pickering, M. J., and Veltkamp, E. (2004) Is syntax separate or shared between languages? Cross-linguistic syntactic priming in Spanish-English bilinguals. *Psychological Science*, 15: 409–14.

Hartsuiker, R. J., Schriefers, H., Bock, K., and Kikstra, G. M. (2003) Morphophonological influences on the construction of subject–verb agreement. *Memory and Cognition*, 31: 1316–26.

Hartsuiker, R. J., and Westenberg, C. (2000) Word order priming in written and spoken sentence production. *Cognition*, 75: B27–B39.

Hutzler, F., Conrad, M., and Jacobs, A. M. (2005) Effects of syllable-frequency in lexical decision and naming: an eye-movement study. *Brain and Language*, 92: 138–52.

Janssen, N., and Caramazza, A. (2003) The selection of closed-class words in noun phrase production: the case of Dutch determiners. *Journal of Memory and Language*, 48: 635–52.

La Heij, W., Mak, P., Sander, J., and Willeboordse, E. (1998) The gender-congruency effect in picture-word tasks. *Psychological Research/Psychologische Forschung*, 61: 209–19.

Laganaro, M., and Alario, F.-X. (2006) On the locus of the syllable frequency effect in speech production. *Journal of Memory and Language*, ss: 178–96.

Largy, P., Fayol, M., and Lemaire, P. (1996) The homophone effect in written French: The case of verb–noun inflection errors. *Language and Cognitive Processes*, 11: 217–55.

Levelt, W. J. M. (1989) *Speaking: From Intention to Articulation*. MIT Press, Cambridge, MA.

Levelt, W. J. M., Roelofs, A., and Meyer, A. S. (1999) A theory of lexical access in speech production. *Behavioral and Brain Sciences*, 22: 1–75.

Levelt, W. J. M., and Wheeldon, L. (1994) Do speakers have access to a mental syllabary? *Cognition*, 50: 239–69.

Loebell, H., and Bock, K. (2003) Structural priming across languages. *Linguistics*, 41: 791–824.

Lupker, S. J. (1979) The semantic nature of response competition in the picture–word interference task. *Memory and Cognition*, 7: 485–95.

Meijer, P. J. A. (1996) Suprasegmental structures in phonological encoding: the CV structure. *Journal of Memory and Language*, 35: 840–53.

Meijer, P. J. A., and Fox Tree, J. A. (2003) Building syntactic structures in speaking: a bilingual exploration. *Experimental Psychology*, 50: 184–95.

Meyer, A. S. (1990) The time course of phonological encoding in panguage Production: the encoding of successive syllables of a word. *Journal of Memory and Language*, 29: 524–45.

Meyer, A. S. (1996) Lexical access in phrase and sentence production: results from picture-word interference experiments. *Journal of Memory and Language*, 35(4): 477–96.

Miozzo, M., and Caramazza, A. (1999) The selection of determiners in noun phrase production. *Journal of Experimental Psychology: Learning, Memory, and Cognition*, 25: 907–22.

Miozzo, M., and Caramazza, A. (2003) When more is less: a counterintuitive effect of distractor frequency in the picture–word interference paradigm. *Journal of Experimental Psychology: General*, 132: 228–52.

Miozzo, M., Costa, A., and Caramazza, A. (2002) The absence of a gender congruency effect in romance languages: a matter of stimulus onset asynchrony? *Journal of Experimental Psychology: Learning, Memory, and Cognition*, 28: 388–91.

Nespor, M., and Vogel, I. (1986) *Prosodic Phonology*. Dordrecht, Foris.

Nicol, J. N., and Greth, D. (2003) Production of subject–verb agreement in Spanish as a second language. *Experimental Psychology*, 50: 196–203.

Paulesu, E., McCrory, E., Fazio, F., Menoncello, L., Brunswick, N., Cappa, S. F., et al. (2000) A cultural effect on brain function. *Nature Neuroscience*, 3: 91–6.

Pickering, M. J., and Branigan, H. P. (1998) The representation of verbs: evidence from syntactic priming in language production. *Journal of Memory and Language*, 39: 633–51.

Pickering, M. J., and Branigan, H. P. (1999) Syntactic priming in language production. *Trends in Cognitive Sciences*, 3: 136–41.

Pickering, M. J., and Garrod, S. (2004) Toward a mechanistic psychology of dialogue. *Behavioral and Brain Sciences*, 27: 169–226.

Rayner, K., and Springer, C. J. (1986) Graphemic and semantic similarity effects in the picture-word interference task. *British Journal of Psychology*, 77: 207–22.

Roelofs, A. (1992) A spreading-activation theory of lemma retrieval in speaking. *Cognition*, 42: 107–42.

Roelofs, A. (1997) The WEAVER model of word-form encoding in speech production. *Cognition*, 64: 249–84.

Roelofs, A. (1998) Rightward incrementality in encoding simple phrasal forms in speech production: verb–particle combinations. *Journal of Experimental Psychology: Learning, Memory, and Cognition*, 24: 904–21.

Roelofs, A. (1999) Phonological segments and features as planning units in speech production. *Language and Cognitive Processes*, 14: 173–200.

Roelofs, A. (2001) Set size and repetition matter: comment on Caramazza and Costa (2000). *Cognition*, 80: 283–90.

Roelofs, A., and Meyer, A. S. (1998) Metrical structure in planning the production of spoken words. *Journal of Experimental Psychology: Learning, Memory, and Cognition*, 24: 922–39.

Roelofs, A., Meyer, A. S., and Levelt, W. J. M. (1996) Interaction between semantic and orthographic factors in conceptually driven naming: comment on Starreveld and La Heij (1995). *Journal of Experimental Psychology: Learning, Memory, and Cognition*, 22: 246–50.

Rosinski, R. R. (1977) Picture–word interference is semantically based. *Child Development*, 48: 643–7.

Santiago, J., MacKay, D. G., Palma, A., and Rho, C. (2000) Sequential activation processes in producing words and syllables: evidence from picture naming. *Language and Cognitive Processes*, 15: 1–44.

Scheepers, C. (2003) Syntactic priming of relative clause attachments: persistence of structural configuration in sentence production. *Cognition*, 89: 179–205.

Schiller, N. O. (2000) Single word production in English: the role of subsyllabic units during phonological encoding. *Journal of Experimental Psychology: Learning, Memory, and Cognition*, 26: 512–28.

Schiller, N. O., and Caramazza, A. (2002) The selection of grammatical features in word production: the case of plural nouns in German. *Brain and Language*, 81: 342–57.

Schiller, N. O., Costa, A., and Colome, A. (2002) Phonological encoding of single words: in search of the lost syllable. In C. Gussenhoven and N.Warner (eds), *Papers in Laboratory Phonology*, vol. 7, pp. 35–59. Mouton de Gruyter, Berlin.

Schriefers, H. (1993) Syntactic processes in the production of noun phrases. *Journal of Experimental Psychology: Learning, Memory, and Cognition*, 19: 841–50.

Schriefers, H., Jescheniak, J. D., and Hantsch, A. (2002) Determiner selection in noun phrase production. *Journal of Experimental Psychology: Learning, Memory, and Cognition*, 28: 941–50.

Schriefers, H., Jescheniak, J. D., and Hantsch, A. (2005) Selection of gender-marked morphemes in speech production. *Journal of Experimental Psychology: Learning, Memory, and Cognition*, 31: 159–68.

Schriefers, H., Meyer, A. S., and Levelt, W. J. M. (1990) Exploring the time course of lexical access in language production: picture–word interference studies. *Journal of Memory and Language*, 29: 86–102.

Schriefers, H., and Teruel, E. (2000) Grammatical gender in noun phrase production: the gender interference effect in German. *Journal of Experimental Psychology: Learning, Memory, and Cognition*, 26: 1368–77.

Sevald, C. A., Dell, G. S., and Cole, J. S. (1995) Syllable structure in speech production: are syllables chunks or schemas? *Journal of Memory and Language*, 34: 807–20.

Shattuck-Hufnagel, S. (1992) The role of word structure in segmental serial ordering. *Cognition*, 42: 213–59.

Slobin, D. I. (1996) From "thought and language" to "thinking for speaking." In J. J. Gumperz and S. C. Levinson (eds), *Rethinking Linguistic Relativity*, pp. 70–96. Cambridge University Press, New York.

Smith, M., and Wheeldon, L. (1999) High level processing scope in spoken sentence production. *Cognition*, 73: 205–46.

Starreveld, P. A. (2000) On the interpretation of onsets of auditory context effects in word production. *Journal of Memory and Language*, 42: 497–525.

Starreveld, P. A. (2004) Phonological facilitation of grammatical gender retrieval. *Language and Cognitive Processes*, 19: 677–711.

Starreveld, P. A., and La Heij, W. (1995) Semantic interference, orthographic facilitation, and their interaction in naming tasks. *Journal of Experimental Psychology: Learning, Memory, and Cognition*, 21: 686–98.

Starreveld, P. A., and La Heij, W. (1996) The locus of orthographic-phonological facilitation: reply to Roelofs, Meyer, and Levelt (1996). *Journal of Experimental Psychology: Learning, Memory, and Cognition*, 22: 252–5.

Thornton, R., and MacDonald, M. C. (2003) Plausibility and grammatical agreement. *Journal of Memory and Language*, 48: 740–59.

van Berkum, J. J. A. (1997) Syntactic processes in speech production: the retrieval of grammatical gender. *Cognition*, 64: 115–52.

van der Meulen, F., Meyer, A. S., and Levelt, W. J. M. (2001) Eye movements during the production of nouns and pronouns. *Memory and Cognition*, 29: 512–21.

Vigliocco, G., Butterworth, B., and Garrett, M. F. (1996) Subject–verb agreement in Spanish and English: differences in the role of conceptual constraints. *Cognition*, 61: 261–98.

Vigliocco, G., Butterworth, B., and Semenza, C. (1995) Constructing subject–verb agreement in speech: The role of semantic and morphological factors. *Journal of Memory and Language*, 34: 186–215.

Vigliocco, G., and Franck, J. (1999) When sex and syntax go hand in hand: gender agreement in language production. *Journal of Memory and Language*, 40: 455–78.

Vigliocco, G., and Franck, J. (2001) When sex affects syntax: contextual influences in sentence production. *Journal of Memory and Language*, 45: 368–90.

Vigliocco, G., Hartsuiker, R. J., Jarema, G., and Kolk, H. H. J. (1996) One or more labels on the bottles? Notional concord in Dutch and French. *Language and Cognitive Processes*, 11: 407–42.

Vitkovitch, M., and Tyrrell, L. (1999) The effects of distractor words on naming pictures at the subordinate level. *Quarterly Journal of Experimental Psychology: Human Experimental Psychology*, 52: 905–26.

Wheeldon, L., and Lahiri, A. (1997) Prosodic units in speech production. *Journal of Memory and Language*, 37: 356–81.

CHAPTER 33

Brain-imaging studies of language production

Peter Indefrey

33.1 The processing components of speaking

To our introspection, speaking seems to be a homogeneous and largely effortless activity. We normally do not perceive this activity as consisting of separate processing components unless something goes wrong. Problems may be transient or restricted to special circumstances. Examples are the difficulty "to find the right words" for something we would like to express, the tip-of-the-tongue experience of "knowing" the right word, but not being able to come up with it, or a slip of the tongue changing an intended *tool cart* into *cool tart*. Problems may also be long-lasting and severely interfering with our ability to communicate with others as in stuttering or agrammatism in aphasic patients. Obviously, the things that can go wrong affect different aspects of language production, suggesting the existence of components of the speaking process that can be disturbed in isolation or in different combinations. Speaking seems to be at least separable into a conceptual or meaning component ("What do I want to say?"), different form components ("I mean something, I know I have a word for it, but I cannot come up with it" or "I wanted to say something else, but somehow the sounds of the words ended up in the wrong places"), and an articulation component ("I have difficulties to pronounce words that start with a 'v'").

Models of language production (Garrett, 1980; Stemberger, 1985; Dell, 1986; Butterworth, 1989; Levelt, 1989; Dell et al., 1997; Caramazza, 1997; Levelt et al., 1999) indeed agree that there are processing levels of meaning, form, and articulation. Two comprehensive meta-analyses on brain imaging studies of word production (Indefrey and Levelt, 2000; 2004) have been based on the theoretical framework of Levelt et al. (1999), and I will adopt the production model of Levelt (1999; see Figure 33.1 below) for the discussion of brain imaging studies of continuous speech. The results of this paper do not hinge very much on this particular choice of theory. Conclusions about the involvement of brain regions in processes of language production will mainly be drawn on the basis of the presence or absence of processing components of speaking in certain experimental tasks. Such conclusions are largely theory-independent, because differences between current models do not concern the assumed processing levels but the exact nature of the information flow between them. In a second step, I will test some of these conclusions by comparing the few available data on activation time courses of brain regions and independent evidence on the timing of processes in language production. Theoretical assumptions about the information flow between processing levels do, of course, affect the validity of considerations based on the timing of certain processes. Note, however, that the time windows suggested at the end of this section for the different processing components of speaking are not theoretical postulates but—at least as far as the onsets of processes are concerned—based on experimental evidence.

Speaking normally starts by preparing a preverbal conceptual representation (message). To describe a football game, the sports commentator must, for example, conceptualize events (*Ronaldo was injured. So the coach replaced him*, *The coach replaced Ronaldo after he was injured*)

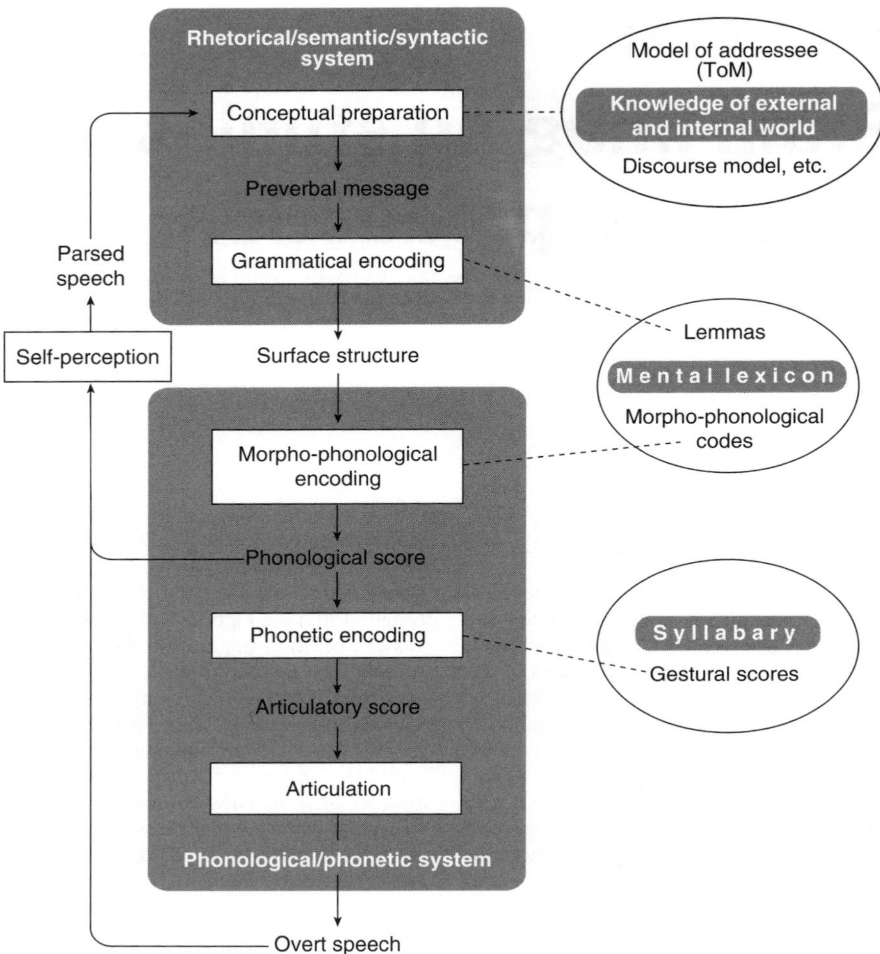

Figure 33.1 The functional architecture of language production (adapted with permission from Levelt 1999).

and spatial configurations (*Ronaldo is standing in front of the defender*, *The defender is standing behind Ronaldo*) in a particular order. These planning processes are called "linearization" and "perspective taking" (Levelt, 1989). The speaker must also take into account the audience's knowledge of the world and whether or not Ronaldo was mentioned before when referring to him (*Ronaldo*, *he*, *the Brazilian*). RONALDO and BRAZILIAN are both lexical concepts, that is concepts for which there are words. Assuming that the speaker has decided that the concept BRAZILIAN is the appropriate one, the corresponding word *Brazilian* must be selected. It is known that at this stage semantically related lexical entries such as *South American* or *Argentinian* are also activated, and compete with *Brazilian*. Occasionally one of them will be erroneously selected, which a listener may notice as a speech error (*Argentinian*) or not (*South American*). Levelt et al. (1999) assume this selection process to take place in a part of the mental lexicon (lemma level) which contains information about the grammatical properties of words. It is only after selection of a lemma that its corresponding sound properties ("morphophonological code," a sequence of phonemes) are retrieved at the word form level and fed into a morphophonological encoding process. In the case of single-word utterances, this process mainly combines the retrieved phonemes into syllables. In the case of continuous speech, morphophonological encoding has a second source of input, namely a surface structure. This structure has been created in the process of grammatical encoding on the basis of the grammatical features of the retrieved lemmas and the order and semantic relations of their corresponding concepts in the preverbal message. The fact that the coach is the actor of the replacement action, for example, will be reflected syntactically in the surface structure. Exactly how it is reflected depends on the language. Common means are case markers, position in the sentence, or number/gender agreement with the verb.

The output of morphophonological encoding is an abstract phonological representation (phonological score) containing syllables and prosodic information at different levels (phonological words and phrases, intonational phrases). In the process of phonetic encoding this representation is translated into an abstract articulatory representation, the articulatory score. For frequent syllables, articulatory representations may be retrieved from a store (syllabary) rather than created *de novo*. Finally, the abstract articulatory representation is realized during articulation by coordinating and executing the activation of the speech musculature.

Indefrey and Levelt (2004) provide the following estimates for the duration of the different processing components in the picture naming task:

conceptual preparation from picture onset to selection of target concept	175 ms
lemma retrieval	75 ms
phonological code retrieval	80 ms
syllabification (25 ms per phoneme)	125 ms
phonetic encoding till initiation of articulation	145 ms
total	600 ms

The estimates are based on the comparison of chronometric data from reaction time studies (Jescheniak and Levelt, 1994; Wheeldon and Levelt, 1995; Levelt et al., 1998, Damian et al., 2001), modeling data (Roelofs, 1992), and electrophysiological (ERP) studies (Thorpe et al., 1996; van Turennout et al., 1997; 1998; Schmitt et al., 2000; 2001). We will use these time windows of the processing components of word production throughout the next section as independent evidence to evaluate suggested assignments of processing stages to brain regions.

33.2 Brain areas involved in word production

Brain activation studies on language production have mainly focused on the single-word level, using a limited set of tasks, namely picture naming, word generation, and word or pseudo-word reading. These tasks differ with respect to the cognitive processes preceding word production as such, which have been termed "lead-in processes" by Indefrey and Levelt (2000). Picture naming, but not the other tasks, for example, involves visual object recognition. Reading tasks involve visual word recognition through grapheme-to-phoneme recoding or accessing a visual input lexicon. The lead-in processes of word generation are the least understood. The most frequent variants of this task are verb generation and word fluency. In verb generation, subjects are asked to produce one or more appropriate verbs for given noun stimuli (e.g. APPLE: *eat*, *peel*, etc.). In word fluency, subjects are typically asked to produce nouns from a given semantic category (ANIMAL: *dog*, *horse*, etc.). Next to recognition of the stimulus words, the search for response words may involve various cognitive processes from association to visual imagery, even the retrieval of whole episodes from long-term memory (see below). A more detailed discussion of the lead-in processes in word production tasks can be found in Indefrey and Levelt (2000; 2004).

Word production tasks also differ with respect to the point at which they enter the cascade of the core processes of word production. While in picture naming and word generation the result of the lead-in processes is a concept for which the appropriate lemma is then retrieved, this is not the case for the reading tasks. In word reading, the entering point depends on word properties such as their regularity and frequency. Words with irregular spelling (e.g. *colonel*) can only be pronounced on the basis of a lexical word form entry, whereas regular words can be pronounced on the basis of grapheme-to-phoneme conversion. Of course, regular words have lexical entries as well, so that the retrieval of a lexically specified word form is also an option. It depends, among other factors, on the frequency of a word and the overall orthographic regularity of a language, as to which of the two options readers prefer. Most single-word reading studies have used mixtures of regular and irregular words, so that it can be assumed that covert or overt pronunciation of at least some words began with the lexical word form. Clearly, when reading for meaning, readers activate lemma and conceptual representations as well. Strictly speaking, however, these activations are part of word recognition rather than production, so that the flow of activation is reversed compared to tasks which start out from a conceptual representation. The pronunciation of written pseudowords, finally, is a production task that enters the cascade of word production processes after the lexical stages. For lack of a lexical entry, a phonemic representation of a written pseudo-word is created by grapheme-to-phoneme conversion. This phonemic representation can then be fed into the syllabification process and the subsequent phonetic and articulatory stages.

Figure 33.2 summarizes the lead-in processes of the different word production tasks (left column), as well as the stages at which they enter the cascade of word production processes (right column).

Taken together, the properties of the tasks which have been used to study word production are such that (due to the lead-in processes) no single task allows for the identification of neural correlates of all and only the core word production components that have been psycholinguistically identified. Core word production components are, on the other hand, shared between tasks, so that their neural correlates may be identified as common activation areas across tasks. The latter consideration has served as the guiding principle for a comprehensive meta-analysis of word production experiments. Indefrey and Levelt (2004) entered the brain areas found in 82 word production experiments into a common anatomical reference space consisting of 110 regions that covered the whole brain. In a second step, they applied a binomial threshold to identify areas that were reliably replicated across studies. This threshold simply tested how probable it was that a number of studies had found the same region by chance, i.e. under the assumption that all reported areas were randomly distributed over the 110 regions. Only regions for which the chance probability was below 10 percent were considered as reliably replicated. This procedure resulted in a set of regions for each of the four tasks described above (picture naming, word generation, word reading, and pseudo-word reading). In the next step, Indefrey and Levelt identified sets of regions that were possibly related to one or more processing components of word production by analyzing which reliable areas were shared by tasks that shared certain processing components. Recall that picture naming and word generation differ in their lead-in processes but share the whole cascade of word production components from lemma retrieval onwards. The set of regions that were reliably reported for both tasks consisted of the left posterior inferior frontal gyrus (IFG), the left precentral gyrus, the supplementary motor area (SMA), the left mid and posterior parts of the superior (STG) and middle (MTG) temporal gyri, the right mid STG, the left fusiform gyrus, the left anterior insula, the left thalamus, and the cerebellum (see Figure 33.3 and Table 33.1 below). According to Indefrey and Levelt (2004), these regions can be assumed to support the core components of word production. A possible concern with respect to Indefrey and Levelt's procedure might be that the spatial resolution of a region-based meta-analysis is too low, and potentially overestimates the degree of activation overlap between studies. Reassuring evidence in this respect comes from two meta-analyses based on much smaller spatial units (so-called "voxels"). If we compare the results of Price et al. (2005) for picture naming (compared to control conditions that did not involve word production) and Poline et al. (1996) for verb generation, overlap between the two tasks is found in the same set of areas (except for the left posterior STG, which was not found by Price et al., 2005).

The strategy of across-task comparisons can be taken even further to identify neural correlates of single processing components. Indefrey and Levelt exploited the fact that reading tasks only recruit subsets of the core processes of word production. Hence core regions that are also reliably found for reading tasks should be related to the subset of shared processing components rather than to the components that are not shared. On the basis of such comparisons, they suggested candidate areas for different processing stages, from lemma retrieval to phonetic encoding and articulation. We will now discuss their tentative assignment of regions to these processing stages, to see whether they are compatible with independent evidence from timing studies and some hemodynamic studies that were designed to target specific processing components.

33.2.1 Conceptually driven lexical (lemma) selection

According to Indefrey and Levelt (2000; 2004), word-reading studies have reliably reported all core regions except for the mid section of the left middle temporal gyrus. This area was also not found in a voxel-based meta-analysis by Turkeltaub et al. (2002) analyzing eleven PET studies on word reading (see also Fiez and Petersen, 1998). Considering that word reading involves all core processing components from phonological code retrieval onwards (at least for irregular and frequent regular words), core regions other than the mid left MTG should be related to this remaining set of processes. This leaves only the mid left MTG as a possible substrate for lexical selection in word production.

Lexical selection in word production was targeted in an MEG study on picture naming (Maess

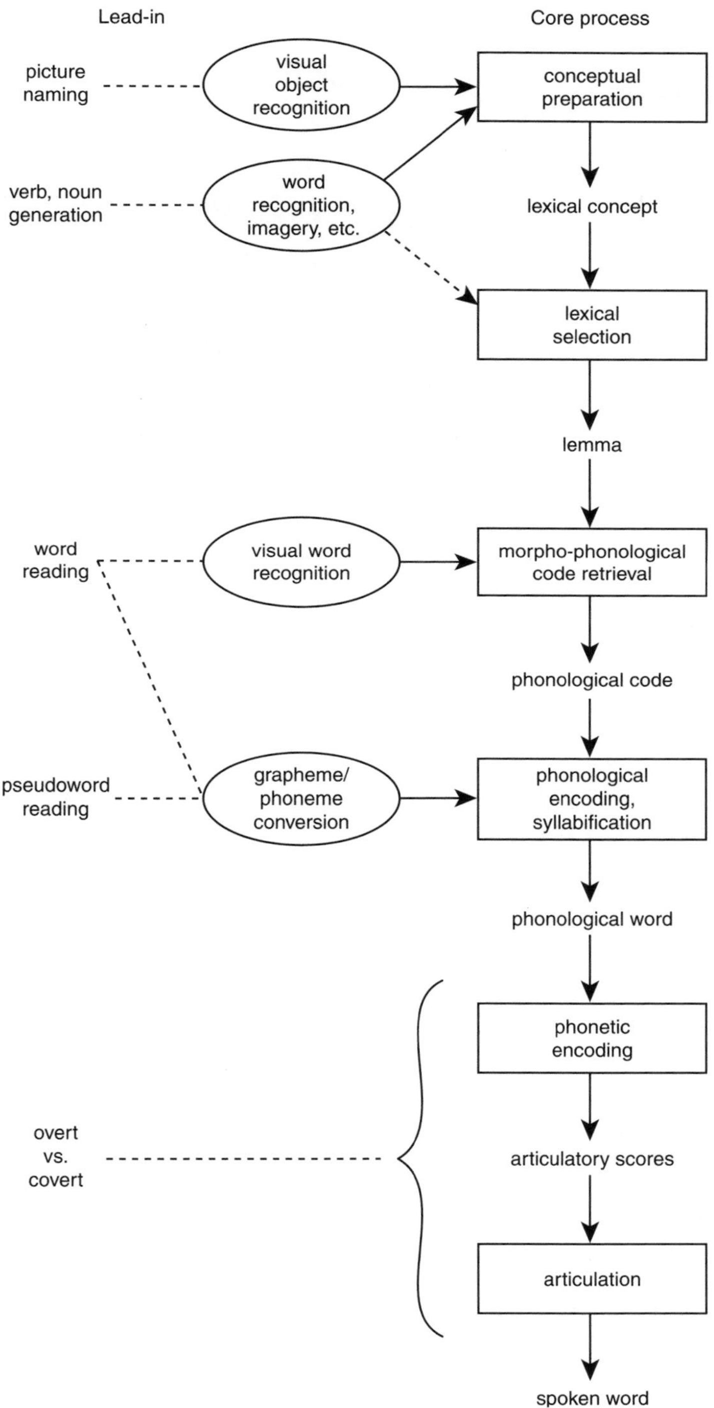

Figure 33.2 Analysis of production task components. Left column: experimental tasks and their "lead-in" processes. Middle column: core processes of word production and their characteristic output.

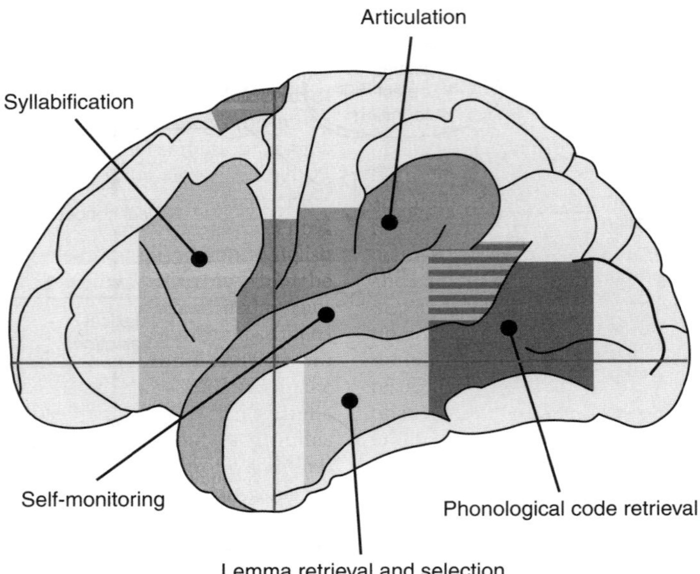

Figure 33.3 Left hemisphere areas involved in single word production. The labels reflect tentative assignments of processing functions. Additional areas reliably involved in word production are the left anterior insula, the left thalamus, the left fusiform gyrus, the right mid superior temporal gyrus, and the cerebellum. See Plate 5 for a color version of this figure.

et al., 2002) by use of the semantic category interference paradigm. In this paradigm, the naming of objects in blocks comprising other objects of the same semantic category is slowed down compared to the naming of objects in semantically heterogeneous blocks. This effect is due to competition between similar lexical entries. For subjects showing the behavioral effect, Maess et al. found significant activation differences between the same-category and the different-category conditions in the mid section of the left middle temporal lobe in the time-window of 150–225 ms post-stimulus. Since the available chronometric data on picture naming suggest a time-window between 175 and 250 ms for lemma selection (see above), these data support a role of the left mid MTG in this process not only anatomically but also with respect to timing.

An fMRI study which directly investigated the neural correlates of lemma selection was conducted by de Zubicaray et al. (2001) using a related paradigm, semantic picture–word interference. In this paradigm, competition at the lemma level is induced by presenting semantically related distractors during picture naming, for example the word *pear* when the picture shows an apple. De Zubicaray et al. found stronger left mid MTG activation for semantic distractors compared to neutral distractors (rows of X's), confirming the predicted role of this area. Interestingly, de Zubicaray et al. also found stronger left posterior superior STG activation, which they interpreted as evidence for additional competition at the word-form level. Such a finding would constitute a serious challenge for a sequential model such as Levelt et al. (1999), which assumes word form activation to take place after lemma selection, i.e. after the competition at the lemma level has been resolved. Note, however, that the control condition of this fMRI study did not involve distractor words but a nonlexical distractor, so that the additional posterior superior temporal activation may reflect word reading rather than semantic competition.

33.2.2 **Phonological code (word form) retrieval**

A core word production area that is reliably found activated, not in pseudo-word reading, but in the three other word production tasks is the left posterior superior temporal lobe. A recent study by Binder et al. (2005) suggests that this area and the adjacent angular gyrus can even be deactivated for pseudo-word reading compared to a fixation condition. Applying the

Table 33.1 Meta-analysis results for brain regions involved in language production. The number of experiments that found a region to be involved in a task ("found") is given in relation to the number of experiments that acquired data from this region ("tested") Reliably replicated brain regions are shaded in grey (see Indefrey and Levelt, 2004, for details of the reliability estimate). Experiments on picture naming, word generation, and narrative production measured cerebral blood flow increases relative to control conditions that did not involve language production. Experiments on second-language picture naming and sentence production measured cerebral blood flow increases relative to higher-level control conditions. Lesion data show brain areas where electrical stimulation interfered with picture naming. The abbreviations of gyri and subcortical structures follow Talairach and Tournoux (1988) except for SMA = Supplementary Motor Area. (Ga = angular gyrus; GF = fusiform gyrus; GFd = medial frontal gyrus; GFm,GFi = middle, and inferior frontal gyrus; GPoC = postcentral gyrus; GPrC = precentral gyrus; Gsm = supramarginal gyrus; GTs, GTm, GTi = superior, middle, and inferior temporal gyrus; LPi = inferior parietal lobule. The anatomical structures are depicted in Figures 24.1–24.4 of Bornkessel-Schlesewsky and Friederici, Chapter 24 this volume).

Task				word generation		picture naming		picture naming lesion data		L2 picture naming vs. L1 picture naming		sentence production vs. word production		narrative production	
No. experiments				25		24		7		5		4		4	
				found	tested	found	tested	found	tested	found	tested	found	tested	found	tested
Frontal	L	anterior	GFd	3	23	0	11			0	4	0	4	2	3
		posterior	GFm	12	23	2	14	1	2	0	5	0	4	3	3
			GFi	23	24	11	17	4	4	2	5	4	4	4	4
		motor	ventGPrc	7	24	8	15	1	2	0	4	1	4	0	3
			SMA	13	24	3	12			0	4	0	3	2	3
Temporal	R	mid	GTs	8	23	4	12			0	5	0	4	0	3
	L	anterior	GTs	3	22	5	19	2	5	0	4	0	4	0	3
		mid	GTs	6	22	9	20	5	6	0	5	0	4	1	4
			GTm	12	22	7	20	5	6	0	4	0	4	2	3
		posterior	GTs	10	22	9	19	5	5	0	5	0	4	3	4
			GTm	14	22	7	19	4	5	0	4	0	4	2	3
			GF	7	24	10	16	2	2	0	4	0	4	1	3
			GTi	2	21	7	19	3	6	0	4	0	4	0	3
Parietal	L	sensory	ventGPoc	0	23	3	15	2	3	0	4	0	4	0	3
		anterior	LPi	0	23	3	15	2	3	0	4	0	4	0	3
		posterior	Gsm	1	23	3	14	3	3	0	5	1	4	0	3
			Ga	1	23	1	13	0	2	0	4	0	4	2	3
			PCu	0	23	0	11			0	4	0	4	2	3
Insula	R	anterior		10	23	2	12			0	4	2	4	0	3
	L	anterior		10	23	6	13			0	4	1	4	2	3
Thalamus	L			11	24	5	11			0	4	1	4	1	3
Cerebellum	R	medial		8	19	6	9			0	4	0	3	0	3
		lateral		8	18	3	9			0	4	0	3	1	3
	L	medial		8	19	5	9			0	4	0	3	1	3

same reasoning as for lemma selection, Indefrey and Levelt (2000; 2004) suggested that this area was related to the processing component which is not involved in pseudo-word reading but in the other tasks, i.e. lexical phonological code (word form) retrieval. Timing data from MEG studies of Salmelin et al. (1994), reporting posterior middle temporal gyrus activation from 200 to 400 ms, and Levelt et al. (1998), reporting posterior superior temporal gyrus activation in the time-window between 275 and 400 ms, are in good accordance with the time-window between 250 and 330 ms assumed for word form retrieval in picture naming.

In another fMRI study using the picture–word interference paradigm, de Zubicaray et al. (2002) targeted lexical word form retrieval. This time, distractor words were phonologically related to the picture names. Such distractor words facilitate naming responses compared to phonologically and semantically unrelated distractor words. De Zubicaray et al. found reduced activation in the left superior temporal gyrus, suggesting that related distractors primed a phonological representation of the target picture names. Given that not only phonologically related word distractors but also pseudo-word distractors show a facilitation effect, this finding does not necessarily support a *lexical* phonological representation in the posterior superior STG, but it is certainly compatible with it.

If the left posterior temporal lobe subserves lexical phonological representations, these should be built up in the course of the acquisition of new words. This seems indeed to be the case. Van Turennout et al. (2005) trained subjects intensively in the pronunciation of pseudo-words consisting of two pseudo-syllables. Compared to novel stimuli, the trained items showed increasingly stronger left posterior MTG/STG and angular gyrus activation over a month of learning. Since the pseudo-words were not associated with any semantic content, the most likely interpretation is a phonological lexicalization effect.

A role of the bilateral posterior superior temporal lobes in the storage of phonological word forms ("sound-based representations of speech") accessed in speech comprehension has been proposed by Hickok and Poeppel (2000; 2004) on the basis of aphasic comprehension deficits. Wernicke's area may thus serve as a common store of lexical word form representations for word production and perception.

33.2.3 Phonological encoding

All production tasks involve the cascade of word production processes from phonological encoding (syllabification) onwards. Comparisons across tasks, therefore, can no longer provide evidence with respect to possible core areas supporting syllabification. Indefrey and Levelt (2000; 2004) reasoned that a comparison between experiments using overt articulation and experiments using covert responses might yield a distinction between syllabification and later processing stages. Syllabification is conceived of as operating on an abstract segmental representation, and should be independent of overt articulation, whereas in the subsequent stages of phonetic encoding and articulation, motor representations are built up and executed. These processes might be more recruited in overt responses. Corresponding areas might show stronger blood flow increases and therefore might be more easily detected and reported. The left posterior inferior frontal gyrus (Broca's area) was the only remaining core area which was not more often reported in experiments using overt responses (see also Wise et al. 1999; Murphy et al. 1997; Huang et al. 2001; and Ackermann and Riecker 2004 for the absence of Broca's area activation in direct comparisons of overt and covert responses). The somewhat indirect conclusion that Broca's area is the most likely candidate area for syllabification is corroborated by independent timing evidence. The chronometric data suggest a time-window between 330 and 455 ms for syllabification in picture naming. MEG data from Salmelin et al. (1994) and Sörös et al. (2003) are compatible with this time-window. The two studies agree on activation of Broca's area between 400 and 600 ms. Sörös et al. (2003) found earlier activation (before 400 ms) in one subject.

33.2.4 Phonetic encoding and articulation

Of the remaining core areas, the left precentral gyrus, the left thalamus, and the cerebellum are much more frequently found in overt-response paradigms and are most likely to be involved in articulation. The bilateral mid STG (auditory cortex) is also much more frequently found in overt-response paradigms, but this is probably due to self-monitoring of the overt speech response (see below). The exact functional roles of the supplementary motor area (SMA) and the left anterior insula in phonetic encoding or articulation are not so clear. In the meta-analyses of Indefrey and Levelt (2000; 2004) both areas are reliably found in covert-response studies and only moderately more often in overt articulation studies. With respect to the insula, this pattern of reports is better compatible with a role in articulatory planning as suggested by Dronkers

(1996) than with a role in articulatory execution. By contrast, Ackermann and Riecker (2004) and Riecker et al. (2000) directly compared overt and covert responses and found insular activation only for overt responses. In another study, insular activation increased linearly with syllable repetition rate (Riecker et al., 2005). These authors suggest an articulatory coordination function for the insula. Murphy et al. (1997), by contrast, did not find articulation-related responses in the insula. In a recent study, Shuster and Lemieux (2005) compared the overt production of multisyllabic words to the production of monosyllabic words. Both suggested functions, articulatory planning and coordination, would predict stronger responses for multisyllabic words, but Shuster and Lemieux did not find any activation difference in the left insula. Clearly, such contradictory findings point to the need for further research in order to identify the experimental conditions under which insular activation is or is not observed.

An articulation area which the meta-analyses of Indefrey and Levelt (2000, 2004) did not identify as reliably activated in word production, but which is reliably found in lesion studies (see below), is the left inferior parietal cortex anterior and close to Wernicke's area. The area may correspond to an auditory–motor interface area at the temporo-parietal junction (Wise et al., 2001; Buchsbaum et al., 2001; Hickok and Poeppel, 2000; 2004).

33.2.5 Self-monitoring

Self-monitoring involves an internal loop and an external loop. The internal loop takes as input the phonological score (the phonological word in the case of single words), i.e. the output of morphophonological encoding. The external loop takes as input the acoustic speech signal of the speaker's own voice (see Figure 33.1). An involvement of the bilateral superior temporal gyri in the external loop of self-monitoring is supported by data from McGuire, Silbersweig, and Frith (1996) and Hirano et al. (1997), who were able to induce additional bilateral superior temporal activations by distorting the subjects' feedback of their own voice or presenting the subjects with alien feedback while they spoke.

Evidence that the superior temporal gyri are also involved in the internal loop of self-monitoring comes from a study by Shergill et al. (2002), who manipulated the rate of inner speech generation. The mid parts of both superior temporal gyri (reaching more anteriorly on the left) responded more strongly to faster rates. It seems thus that the internal monitoring loop enters the pathway that is used for external monitoring and speech perception. If one accepts the premise that auditory hallucinations are based on some alteration of normal internal self-monitoring (McGuire et al., 1995; David and Busatto, 1999), evidence from this rather different line of research may be taken into account, too. Mid and posterior superior temporal areas have been found activated during auditory hallucinations (Dierks et al., 1999; Lennox et al., 2000; Shergill et al., 2000).

33.2.6 Are the hemodynamic core areas necessary for word production?

Most of the data discussed above stem from PET and fMRI studies of word production. Both techniques measure local cerebral blood flow increases that accompany a cognitive activity, such as speaking. These increases allow the conclusion that certain brain areas are active. Being active during some cognitive activity, however, does not mean the same as being necessary. Brain areas may serve supporting functions, and there may also be more then one brain area capable of supporting a particular cognitive process (degeneracy). In the case of degeneracy, a brain area may show a hemodynamic response, but its lesion would not result in a loss of function. A special case of degeneracy would be redundant activation, such that two areas are active, but either one of them would suffice for the cognitive process at hand (Friston and Price, 2003).

It is known that lesions encompassing the whole set of perisylvian core areas for word production result in a total inability to speak (global aphasia). Thus, generally speaking, the ensemble of core areas is necessary for language production. If the core areas are functionally specialized for processing stages of word production and every stage is necessary, then every single of the associated areas should also be necessary. Table 33.1 (third column) shows the cortical regions in which transient lesions induced by electrocortical or TMS stimulation reliably interfered with picture naming across seven studies (Ojemann, 1983; Ojemann et al., 1989; Schäffler et al., 1993; Haglund et al., 1994; Malow et al., 1996; Hamberger et al., 2001; Stewart et al., 2001). Comparing these regions to the common areas of picture naming and word generation experiments (first and second column) shows that all of the core areas (except possibly the left motor cortex) seem to be necessary for word production. (Of course, the results of transient lesion studies do not rule out the possibility of functional and structural reorganization after permanent lesions.) This finding supports the idea of functional specialization within the perisylvian language areas. Unfortunately, transient lesion studies have so far only recorded whether or not picture naming was impaired. It would be highly interesting to see whether the exact kinds of impairment differ between stimulation sites.

Somewhat surprisingly, there seem to be additional necessary areas in the inferior parietal cortex that are only rarely reported in hemodynamic studies. It is not clear why this is so. A possible explanation might be that inferior parietal activation areas overlapped with stronger superior temporal activation areas whose activation maxima were reported.

Figure 33.3 summarizes the tentative assignments of word production processing components to core word production areas.

33.3 Brain areas involved in the production of continuous speech

The relatively small number of studies which have looked at speech production beyond the word level fall into two groups. Some researchers did not attempt to isolate particular processing components, but simply asked their participants to speak by instructing them, for example, to recount an event of the previous day. I will refer to such paradigms as "narrative production paradigms." All of the studies analyzed here used baseline conditions without language production, so that the resulting activation patterns probably reflect the complete cascade of language production processes, starting from conceptual planning. A different set of more recent studies were aimed at sentence-level specific processes, more specifically syntactic encoding. These studies used control conditions involving word-level production, and they controlled for conceptual planning to varying degrees. Insofar as the latter studies succeeded in isolating neuronal responses to syntactic encoding, the regions showing such responses should be a subset of the regions found in the narrative production studies. We will look first at the sentence production studies and then at the narrative production studies.

33.3.1 Syntactic encoding

To identify the neural correlates of syntactic encoding, Indefrey et al. (2001) used a scene description paradigm, in which participants described the actions of colored geometrical figures either in full sentences (*The red square is pushing the green triangle away*) or in ordered lists of syntactically unrelated words (*square, red, triangle, green, push away*). In a third, intermediate condition, only local, noun-phrase internal syntactic relations but not sentence-level syntactic relations had to be encoded in the description (*red square, green triangle, push away*). The experiment was conducted in German, in which the adjective is marked for agreement with the syntactic gender of the noun. To keep the visual and conceptual processing of the scenes constant across conditions, participants were instructed to always name the "agent" of an action first. This instruction forced them to take thematic roles (Who does what to whom?) into account in all conditions, not only in the sentence condition, where syntactic functions, such as subject and object are assigned on the basis of the thematic roles. Finally, the authors varied the rate of visual scene presentation, such that the increase in syllables or words per minute between the faster rate and the slower rate corresponded to the difference between the sentence and the word list conditions, which was due to the additional grammatical morphemes and function words in the sentences. Indefrey et al. (2001) found the posterior part of Broca's area (BA 44) and posteriorly adjacent cortex (BA 6) to be more strongly activated in the sentence condition (and to a lesser extent also in the noun phrase condition) compared to the word list condition. This region was not affected by the rate manipulation, suggesting that its hemodynamic response was indeed due to the increased demand on syntactic encoding rather than to changes in the number of syllables or words per minute. This finding was replicated with a different group of subjects in Indefrey et al. (2004). In two recent studies by other groups, subjects were presented with single verbs (Kemeny et al., 2005) or word triplets (Haller et al., 2005), from which they generated sentences. Both studies reported enhanced blood flow in Broca's area (BA 44 and 45) for sentence production compared to syllable or word production control conditions. The posterior part of Broca's area, BA 44, which has been found in all four studies must be considered the cortical area that most likely has a role in syntactic encoding. Haller et al. (2005) and Kemeny et al. (2005) also found BA 45 and the right anterior insula in their sentence production conditions. Neither study fully controlled for differences at other processing levels (conceptual, lexical phonological), so a role of these two areas in syntactic encoding is possible but other processing functions cannot be excluded. No other brain region has been replicated in this set of studies. While the syntactic structures of the produced sentences were of limited variability and tightly controlled in the studies by Indefrey et al. (2001; 2004) and Haller et al. (2005), this was not the case in Kemeny et al. (2005), suggesting that the involvement of BA 44 is not restricted to a small set of syntactic structures. This conclusion is, furthermore, supported by the findings obtained in narrative production studies, to which we now turn.

33.3.2 **Conceptual planning in discourse**

As laid out above, narrative production, which to date has always been used with low-level control conditions, is certainly the most comprehensive language production paradigm. At the same time it is, by itself, the least informative with respect to the neural correlates of specific cognitive and linguistic processing components involved in speaking. In most studies using this paradigm, the aim was to investigate language production in special populations (e.g. stutterers, bilingual speakers) rather than to identify processing components. In this section we will only take into account the data that have been obtained during narrative production in healthy native language speakers in five studies (Tamas et al., 1993; Kim et al., 1997; Braun et al., 1997; 2001; Kircher et al., 2004). Looking at these data may be interesting for two reasons. First, they provide an interesting test case for the regions which have been identified so far as being related to particular component processes of language production. Narrative production as an almost natural speaking situation comprises all these processes, and the resulting activation patterns should include the corresponding regions, if they do not only show up in somewhat artificial single word or sentence production experiments. Second, we may be able to identify brain regions involved in the complex conceptual planning and discourse representations necessary to tell a cohesive story. Candidate areas would be those which are reliably found in narrative production but not in single word or sentence production. The rightmost column of Table 33.1 shows the areas which have been reliably found in narrative production. This set of areas indeed comprises the core areas of word production, i.e. those areas that picture naming and word generation tasks activate in common (left posterior inferior frontal gyrus, left posterior superior temporal gyrus, left mid and posterior middle temporal gyri, SMA), except for some areas which are involved in articulation and self-monitoring (motor cortex, cerebellum, bilateral primary auditory cortices). Absence of the latter areas is not surprising, given that covert narrative production was used in one study (Kim et al., 1997), and the two studies by Braun et al. (1997; 2001) used an oro-laryngeal motor control task which involved the production of non-linguistic sounds.

The activation of the left posterior inferior frontal gyrus during narrative production seems to comprise both Broca's area proper (BA 44/45) and the more ventral BA 47. This is similar to what has been found for single word production (Poline et al., 1996; Price et al., 2005). As discussed in the previous section, activation of BA 44/45 but not of BA 47 has also been reliably found for syntactic encoding, so that Broca's area activation during narrative production probably supports two different functions—syntactic encoding at the sentence level and phonological encoding at the word level. Both are highly automatized procedures combining smaller linguistic elements (words or phonemes) into a larger structure (sentence or syllable). It is, therefore, quite plausible that one cortical area (or distinct neuronal populations within one area) should subserve both processes. The more ventral part of the left posterior IFG (BA 47) has been linked to semantic processing in comprehension (see Fiez, 1997; Price et al., 1999; Bookheimer, 2002 for overviews). Since this region is not reliably found in sentence production tasks when semantic processing is controlled for, as shown in the previous section, a similar role in language production is conceivable.

Four regions are reliably activated in narrative production but do not belong to the common areas of word production tasks and do not seem to be involved in syntactic processing (left middle frontal gyrus, left angular gyrus, left anterior medial frontal gyrus, precuneus). One or more of these regions, therefore, might be involved in some aspect of conceptual planning beyond the sentence level. Narrative production requires linearization (Levelt, 1989: 138), the planning of the temporal order in which events will be recounted. This planning, in turn, is tightly linked to a representation of the logical and temporal order of events and actions, a so-called "script" (Schank and Abelson, 1977). There is evidence for a role of the posterior middle frontal gyrus and the left angular gyrus in script processing. Crozier et al. (1999) found both regions to be activated during the detection of errors in the order of events (*get dressed take a shower*) but not, or less so, during the detection of grammatical word order violations (*the message twice/announced was*). For the middle frontal gyrus, there are also production data suggesting a role in script processing. Sirigu et al. (1996; 1998) examined two patient groups with either lesions in Broca's area or prefrontal lesions. While patients with lesions in Broca's area were impaired in putting words in a grammatical order, patients with prefrontal lesions were impaired in ordering words according to the script actions they denoted. Note, however, that the latter patients are also frequently impaired in *performing* action sequences, so that the prefrontal cortex is certainly not specifically involved in the linearization of events for the purpose of speaking. An apparent contradiction to a role of the left middle frontal gyrus in discourse-level processing seems to be the observation that the left middle frontal gyrus is also reliably found in a single-word production task, namely verb generation (Poline et al., 1996). Indefrey and Levelt (2004) suggested that the area might be supporting a lead-in process of this type of task. A closer look at the verbs that subjects typically produce in response to a given noun shows that extracting verbs from imagined (and possibly internally verbalized) event sequences is indeed one of the strategies subject employ in such tasks (e.g. PENCIL: *sharpen, break, put away*; Indefrey, 1997).

In sum, narrative production paradigms comprise all word- and sentence-level processes. The activation patterns found with these paradigms include the areas that have been identified as being related to these processes in the previous sections. At least one additional area, the left middle frontal gyrus, seems to be involved in the planning and understanding of event sequences, and thus might at least indirectly play a role in the conceptual planning of narrative production.

Figure 33.4 summarizes the tentative assignments of brain areas to processing components that are specific to continous speech production.

33.4 Bilingual language production

So far, we have been looking at the neural correlates of speaking in the native language (L1). Probably many of the participants in the "monolingual" studies spoke one or other foreign language; and this raises the question what the activation patterns would have looked like if the participants had performed the language production tasks in their second language (L2). Common sense tells us that this would depend on their L2 proficiency. Since we know that task performance affects hemodynamic activation patterns and that low proficiency is likely to result in low performance, L2-specific activation patterns can only be interpreted in an unambiguous way, when the tasks and the proficiency

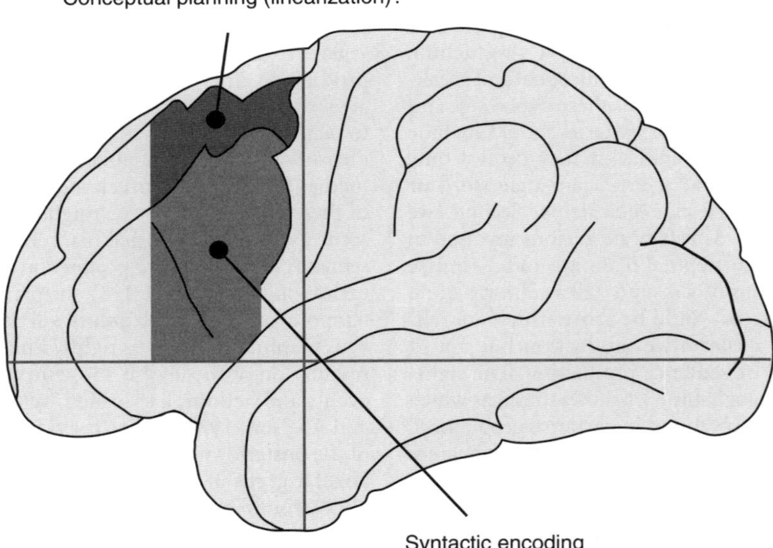

Figure 33.4 Left hemisphere areas involved in the production of continuous speech above the word level. The labels reflect tentative assignments of processing functions. See Plate 6 for a color version of this figure.

levels have been chosen such that L2 and L1 task performance are on the same level. This is indeed what most of the studies reviewed below have attempted, although not all studies report performance in sufficient detail to rule it out as a confounding factor.

33.4.1 Word level

Word generation and picture-naming tasks have been frequently used not only to study word production in the native language but also to compare first and second language production. Five experiments on picture naming (Hernandez et al., 2000; 2001; De Bleser et al., 2003; Vingerhoets et al., 2003; Rodriguez-Fornells et al., 2005; see Table 33.1 above, fourth column) used control conditions without word production components. In two word-generation studies (Klein et al., 1999; Pu et al., 2001) subjects generated verbs from stimulus nouns; in one study (Klein et al., 1995) they generated synonyms for stimulus words; and in two studies (Perani et al., 2003; Vingerhoets et al., 2003) they generated words based on a given initial letter. Note that the latter task can be performed by accessing either graphemic or phonological word representations and, in contrast to the other generation tasks, does not necessarily require lemma access from a conceptual representation. Three of the word-generation experiments used control conditions such as word repetition or counting which might have obscured some or all core components of word production.

Across word-production experiments no area was replicated as showing stronger activation when the task was performed in the native language as compared to a second language. While for the word-generation studies this finding might be attributed to the heterogeneity of task variants, the same does not hold for the picture-naming studies which had a comparable design. The populations studied with the picture-naming task varied with respect to the onset of their second language. It can be concluded that in proficient L2 speakers with both early or late L2 onset there are no L1-specific regions, i.e. regions that are only or more strongly recruited for word production in the first language.

Stronger activation for L2 word production was found bilaterally in the posterior inferior frontal gyri (BA 47) in the two studies using letter fluency. Stronger L2 activation of the left posterior inferior frontal gyrus (BA 44, 47) was also found in two picture-naming studies (De Bleser et al., 2003; Vingerhoets et al., 2003). Both had participants with late L2 onset and variable L2 exposure. By contrast, participants in the three studies reporting no differences between L2 and L1 picture naming (Hernandez et al., 2000; 2001; Rodriguez-Fornells et al., 2005) had early L2 onset and lived in L2-dominant environments. Compared to the three other studies, the L2 proficiency was also lower in De Bleser et al. (2003) and Vingerhoets et al. (2003), so that all three factors—L2 onset, proficiency, and exposure—may be influential with respect to the recruitment of the left IFG in word production. De Bleser et al. (2003) tested for a within-subject effect of proficiency by using pictures whose names were cognates in the two languages and therefore easier to retrieve ("high proficiency") and pictures with non-cognate L2 names ("low proficiency"). The L2 vs. L1 difference in the left inferior frontal cortex was only found in the low-proficiency condition. Note, however, that there was a strong performance difference between "high-proficiency" and "low-proficiency" items. Within-subject proficiency differences in word production were also investigated by Briellmann et al. (2004), who compared verb generation in quadrilingual subjects and also found increased activation for less fluent languages in the left inferior frontal gyrus (among other areas which are reliably found in L1 word generation). In sum, L1 and L2 word production seem to engage the same cortical areas. L2 speakers with late L2 onset or lower proficiency may recruit at least the left inferior frontal cortex more strongly.

Lucas et al. (2004) provide complementary data on areas that are necessary for L2 word production. In their study, twenty-five mostly fluent bilingual epilepsy patients underwent language mapping with electrical stimulation of the cortex prior to surgery. While the patients performed an object-naming task in either their first or their second language, different cortical sites were electrically stimulated and it was recorded whether the stimulation interfered with object naming or not. For every individual the procedure resulted in a map of sites that were necessary for L1 picture naming, L2 picture naming, or both. Shared sites were found in all left perisylvian regions. L1-specific sites were also found in both posterior frontal and temporal regions but more so in the frontal cortex. L2-specific sites were exclusively found in mid to posterior temporal cortex and adjacent inferior parietal sites. These data are very important for the interpretation of the two main findings from the hemodynamic studies. First, they show that although there may not be any regions that are exclusively recruited or exclusively necessary for L1 or L2 word production *across* individuals, there seem to be cortical sites in many individuals which are only necessary for word production in one of the languages. Secondly, the only region that to date has been reliably found to be more strongly activated for L2 word production, left inferior frontal cortex, does not contain any sites that are necessary for L2 but not for L1 word production. The region does contain sites that are necessary for L1 but not L2 word production. These findings suggest that L2 word production does not in all individuals share all processes that are involved in L1 word production. A consistent interpretation of both the hemodynamic data and the cortical stimulation data requires an answer to the question of why speakers activate a region (left posterior IFG) more strongly for L2 word production which seems to be at least in part specialized for L1 word production. A possible interpretation might be that L2 speakers attempt to make use of a process that is tailored to L1 word production and, therefore, less efficient for the second language. Such a process might be post-lexical syllabification, which is subject to language-specific phonotactic constraints and, as we have seen above (see section 33.2.3), seems to engage Broca's area.

33.4.2 Continuous speech

Two of the narrative-production studies reviewed above (Kim et al., 1997; Braun et al., 2001) asked their subjects not only to recount events in one language, but also to do the same in another language, which they acquired either simultaneously in early infancy or as a second language after puberty. Not surprisingly, there were no differences in the activation patterns between two early acquired (i.e. two native) languages. Note, however, that the participants in the study of Braun et al. (2001) were hearing children of deaf parents and one of their two languages was American Sign Language (ASL), which uses a different effector system. The authors used different motor control conditions for the two languages, so that effector-related activation was subtracted out in the comparison of the two languages.

In terms of activated regions and strength of activation within regions, there was also no difference between the first language and a late-acquired second language in Kim et al. (1997). However, the authors report that the exact anatomical location of the activation within Broca's area was shifted by up to about a centimeter. Such a shift was not observed in the posterior superior temporal gyrus (Wernicke's area). Unfortunately, the subjects produced the narratives covertly, so that the finding in Broca's area might be due to all kinds of linguistic differences in the narratives that were produced. Still the results fit in the general pattern we observed across single-word production studies: that differences between the activation patterns observed during first- and second-language production are more likely to be found in the posterior inferior frontal cortex than in the temporal cortex. A tentative interpretation might be based on a distinction between lexical and compositional processes. While temporal lobe areas mainly support lexical processes, the left posterior inferior frontal gyrus seems to support non-lexical compositional processes (post-lexical syllabification in word production, syntactic processing in sentence comprehension), which are subject to language-specific rules or constraints. The neuronal organization of the IFG may, therefore, be in some way optimized for the native language, and thus less efficient for later learned languages (Indefrey, forthcoming).

33.5 Conclusion

Neurocognitive studies of language production have provided sufficient evidence on both the spatial and the temporal patterns of brain activation to allow tentative—and in some cases not so tentative—conclusions about function–structure relationships. In this chapter we have identified reliable (i.e. replicated above chance) activation areas for a range of word, sentence, and narrative production tasks both in the native language and in a second language. On the basis of a theoretically motivated analysis of word production tasks, we have been able to specify relationships between brain areas and functional processing components of language production that could not have been derived from the data provided by any single task.

To date, brain-imaging studies of language production have largely been brain-mapping studies. As such, they have provided new information about the cognitive processes involved in speaking: where, when, and for how long they occur in the human brain. To extract these types of information from brain-mapping experiments presupposes the knowledge about cognitive processes provided by psycholinguistic experimentation and theory. However, brain mapping is only a necessary first step. Once brain regions subserving certain processing components are known (and this chapter shows that we are approaching this stage), their activation under certain experimental conditions can be used to answer further questions, for example with respect to competing functional models. The experiments of de Zubicaray et al. (2001; 2002) described earlier are examples of this approach. In these experiments, associations of the left mid MTG with lemma retrieval and the left posterior STG with word form retrieval are presupposed. What is tested are predictions about changes in the activation levels of the two areas that are derived from a functional model of word production (Levelt et al., 1999). This modular feedforward model assumes that a semantically related competitor should affect lemma selection but not word form retrieval (because only the word form of the eventually selected lemma will be retrieved). Hence the activation level of the left mid MTG but not the posterior STG should be altered under conditions of semantic competition. The model, furthermore, assumes that phonological facilitation which affects later processing stages of word production should not feed back to the earlier stage of lemma selection. Hence the activation level of the left posterior STG but not the mid MTG should be altered under conditions of phonological facilitation. What is crucial here is not so much the outcome of these experiments (see sections 33.2.1 and 33.2.2) as the fact that hemodynamic activation of certain brain regions is not considered interesting by itself but as a new type of dependent variable in an otherwise classic psycholinguistic experiment designed to increase our understanding of the functional rather than brain-related properties of the word production system. It is to be expected that the proportion of this type of hypothesis-testing brain-imaging studies will increase, and that the evidence they provide for psycholinguistic theory will eventually be treated on a par with classic experimental techniques.

References

Ackermann, H., and Riecker, A., (2004) The contribution of the insula to motor aspects of speech production: a review and a hypothesis. *Brain and Language*, 89: 320–8.

Binder, J. R., Medler, D.A., Desai, R., Conant, L. L., and Liebenthal, E. (2005) Some neurophysiological constraints on models of word naming. *Neuroimage*, 27: 677–93.

Bookheimer, S. (2002) Functional MRI of language: new approaches to understanding the cortical organization of semantic processing. *Annual Review of Neuroscience*, 25: 151–88.

Bookheimer, S. Y., Zeffiro, T. A., Blaxton, T, A., Gaillard W., and Theodore, W. H. (2000) Activation of language cortex with automatic speech tasks. *Neurology*, 55: 1151–7.

Braun, A. R., Guillemin, A., Hosey, L., and Varga, M. (2001) The neural organization of discourse: an (H2O)-O-15-PET study of narrative production in English and American sign language. *Brain*, 124: 2028–44.

Braun, A. R., Varga, M., Stager, S., et al. (1997) Altered patterns of cerebral activity during speech and language production in developmental stuttering: an H-2 O-15 positron emission tomography study. *Brain*, 120: 761–84.

Briellmann, R. S., Saling, M. M., Connell, A. B., Waites, A. B., Abbott, D. F., and Jackson, G. D. (2004) A high-field functional MRI study of quadri-lingual subjects. *Brain and Language*, 89: 531–42.

Brunswick, N., McCrory, E., Price, C. J., Frith, C. D., and Frith, U., (1999) Explicit and implicit processing of words and pseudo-words by adult developmental dyslexics: a search for Wernicke's Wortschatz? *Brain*, 122: 1901–17.

Buchsbaum, B. R., Hickok, G., and Humphries, C. (2001) Role of left posterior superior temporal gyrus in phonological processing for speech perception and production. *Cognitive Science*, 25: 663–78.

Butterworth, B. (1989) Lexical access in speech production. In W. Marslen-Wilson (ed.), *Lexical Representation and Process*, pp. 108–35. MIT Press, Cambridge, MA.

Caplan, D. (2001) Functional neuroimaging studies of syntactic processing. *Journal of Psycholinguistic Research*, 30: 297–320.

Caramazza, A. (1997) How many levels of processing are there in lexical access? *Cognitive Neuropsychology*, 14: 177–208.

Crozier, S., Sirigu, A., Lehericy, S., et al. (1999) Distinct prefrontal activations in processing sequence at the sentence and script level: an fMRI study. *Neuropsychologia*, 37: 1469–76.

Damian, M. F., Vigliocco, G. and Levelt, W. J. M. (2001) Effects of semantic context in the naming of pictures and words. *Cognition*, 81: B77–B86.

David, A. S., and Busatto, G. (1999) The hallucination: a disorder of brain and mind. *Nervenheilkunde*, 18: 104–15.

De Bleser, R., Dupont, P., Postler, J., et al. (2003) The organisation of the bilingual lexicon: a PET study. *Journal of Neurolinguistics*, 16: 439–56.

de Zubicaray, G. I., McMahon, K. L., Eastburn, M. M., and Wilson, S. J. (2002) Orthographic/phonological facilitation of naming responses in the picture-word task: an event-related fMRI study using overt vocal responding. *Neuroimage*, 16: 1084–93.

de Zubicaray, G. I., Wilson, S. J., McMahon, K. L., and Muthiah, S. (2001) The semantic interference effect in the picture–word paradigm: an event-related fMRI study employing overt responses. *Human Brain Mapping*, 14: 218–27.

Dell, G. S. (1986) A spreading-activation theory of retrieval in sentence Ppoduction. *Psychological Review*, 93: 283–321.

Dell, G. S., Burger, L. K., and Svec, W. R. (1997) Language production and serial order: A functional analysis and a model. *Psychological Review*, 104: 123–47.

Dierks, T., Linden, D. E. J., Jandl, M., et al. (1999) Activation of Heschl's Gyrus during auditory hallucinations. *Neuron*, 22: 615–21.

Dronkers, N. F. (1996) A new brain region for coordinating speech articulation. *Nature*, 384: 159–61.

Fiez, J. A. (1997) Phonology, semantics, and the role of the left inferior prefrontal cortex. *Human Brain Mapping*, 5: 79–83.

Fiez, J. A., and Petersen, S. E. (1998) Neuroimaging studies of word reading. *Proceedings of the National Academy of Sciences of the United States of America*, 95: 914–21.

Frenck-Mestre, C., Anton, J. L., Roth, M., Vaid, J. and Viallet, F. (2005) Articulation in early and late bilinguals' two languages: evidence from functional magnetic resonance imaging. *Neuroreport*, 16: 761–5.

Friston, K. J., and Price, C. J. (2003) Degeneracy and redundancy in cognitive anatomy. *Trends in Cognitive Sciences*, 7: 151–2.

Garrett, M. F. (1980) Levels of processing in sentence production. In B. Butterworth (ed.), *Speech and Talk*, pp. 177–220. Academic Press, New York.

Haglund, M. M., Berger, M. S., Shamseldin, M., Lettich, E., and Ojemann, G. A. (1994) Cortical localization of temporal-lobe language sites in patients with Gliomas. *Neurosurgery*, 34: 567–76.

Haller, S., Radue, E. W., Erb, M., Grodd, W., and Kircher, T. (2005) Overt sentence production in event-related fMRI. *Neuropsychologia*, 43: 807–14.

Hamberger, M. J., Goodman, R. R., Perrine, K., and Tamny, T. (2001) Anatomic dissociation of auditory and visual naming in the lateral temporal cortex. *Neurology*, 56: 56–61.

Hernandez, A. E., Dapretto, M., Mazziotta, J., and Bookheimer, S. (2001) Language switching and language representation in Spanish-English bilinguals: an fMRI study. *Neuroimage*, 14: 510–20.

Hernandez, A. E., Martinez, A., and Kohnert, K. (2000) In search of the language switch: an fMRI study of picture naming in Spanish-English bilinguals. *Brain and Language*, 73: 421–31.

Hickok, G., and Poeppel, D. (2000) Towards a functional neuroanatomy of speech perception. *Trends in Cognitive Sciences*, 4: 131–8.

Hickok, G., and Poeppel, D. (2004) Dorsal and ventral streams: a framework for understanding aspects of the functional anatomy of language. *Cognition*, 92: 67–99.

Hirano, S., Kojima, H., Naito, Y., et al. (1997) Cortical processing mechanism for vocalization with auditory verbal feedback. *Neuroreport*, 8: 2379–82.

Huang, J., Carr, T. H., and Cao, Y. (2001) Comparing cortical activations for silent and overt speech using event-related fMRI. *Human Brain Mapping*, 15: 39–53.

Indefrey, P. (1997) PET research in language production. In W. Hulstijn, H. Peters, and P. Van Lieshout (eds), *Speech Production: Motor Control, Brain Research and Fluency Disorders*, pp. 269–78. Elsevier, Amsterdam.

Indefrey, P. (2006) A meta-analysis of hemodynamic studies on first and second language processing: which suggested differences can we trust and what do they mean? *Language Learning*, 56(1): 279–304.

Indefrey, P., Brown, C. M., Hellwig, F. et al. (2001) A neural correlate of syntactic encoding during speech production. *Proceedings of the National Academy of Sciences of the United States of America*, 98: 5933–6.

Indefrey, P., Hellwig, F., Herzog, H., Seitz, R. J., and Hagoort, P. (2004) Neural responses to the production and comprehension of syntax in identical utterances. *Brain and Language*, 89: 312–19.

Indefrey, P., and Levelt, W. J. M. (2000) The neural correlates of language production. In M. S. Gazzaniga (ed.), *The New Cognitive Neurosciences*, pp. 845–65. MIT Press, Cambridge, MA.

Indefrey, P., and Levelt, W. J. M. (2004) The spatial and temporal signatures of word production components. *Cognition*, 92: 101–44.

Jescheniak, J. D., and Levelt, W. J. M. (1994) Word-frequency effects in speech production: retrieval of syntactic information and of phonological form. *Journal of Experimental Psychology: Learning Memory and Cognition*, 20: 824–43.

Kemeny, S., Ye, F. Q., Birn, R., and Braun, A. R. (2005) Comparison of continuous overt speech fMRI using BOLD and arterial spin labeling. *Human Brain Mapping*, 24: 173–83.

Kim, K. H. S., Relkin, N. R., Lee, K. M., and Hirsch, J. (1997) Distinct cortical areas associated with native and second languages. *Nature*, 388: 171–4.

Kircher, T. T. J., Brammer, M. J., Levelt, W. J. M., Bartels, M., and McGuire, P. K. (2004) Pausing for thought: engagement of left temporal cortex during pauses in speech. *Neuroimage*, 21: 84–90.

Kircher, T. T. J., Brammer, M. J., Williams, S. C. R., and McGuire, P. K. (2000) Lexical retrieval during fluent speech production: an fMRI study. *Neuroreport*, 11: 4093–6.

Klein, D., Milner, B., Zatorre, R. J., Meyer, E., and Evans, A. C. (1995) The neural substrates underlying word generation: a bilingual iunctional-Imaging study. *Proceedings of the National Academy of Sciences of the United States of America*, 92: 2899–903.

Klein, D., Milner, B., Zatorre, R. J., Zhao, V., and Nikelski, J. (1999) Cerebral organization in bilinguals: a PET study of Chinese-English verb generation. *Neuroreport*, 10: 2841–6.

Lennox, B. R., Park, S. B. G., Medley, I., Morris, P. G., and Jones, P. B. (2000) The functional anatomy of auditory hallucinations in schizophrenia. *Psychiatry Research-Neuroimaging*, 100: 13–20.

Levelt, W. J. M. (1989) *Speaking: From Intention to Articulation*. MIT Press, Cambridge, MA.

Levelt, W. J. M. (1996) Perspective taking and ellipsis in spatial development. In P. Bloom, M. A. Peterson, L. Nadel, and M. Garrett (eds), *Language and Space*, pp. 77–108. MIT Press, Cambridge, MA.

Levelt, W. J. M. (1999) Producing spoken language: a blueprint of the speaker. In C. M. Brown and P. Hagoort (eds), *The Neurocognition of Language*, pp. 83–122. Oxford University Press, Oxford.

Levelt, W. J. M., Praamstra, P., Meyer, A. S., Helenius, P. I., and Salmelin, R. (1998) An MEG study of picture naming. *Journal of Cognitive Neuroscience*, 10: 553–67.

Levelt, W. J. M., Roelofs, A., and Meyer, A. S. (1999) A theory of lexical access in speech production. *Behavioral and Brain Sciences*, 22: 1–38.

Levelt, W. J. M., Schriefers, H., Vorberg, D., Meyer, A. S., Pechmann, T., and Havinga, J. (1991) The time course of lexical access in speechpProduction: a study of picture naming. *Psychological Review*, 98: 122–42.

Lucas II, T. H., McKhann II, G. M., and Ojemann, G. A. (2004) Functional separation of languages in the bilingual brain: a comparison of electrical stimulation language mapping in 25 bilingual patients and 117 monolingual control patients. *Journal of Neurosurgery*, 101: 449–57.

Maess, B., Friederici, A. D., Damian, M., Meyer, A. S., and Levelt, W. J. M. (2002) Semantic category interference in overt picture naming: sharpening current density localization by PCA. *Journal of Cognitive Neuroscience*, 14: 455–62.

Malow, B. A., Blaxton, T. A., Sato, S. et al. (1996) Cortical stimulation elicits regional distinctions in auditory and visual naming. *Epilepsia*, 37: 245–52.

McGuire, P. K., Silbersweig, D. A., and Frith, C. D. (1996) Functional neuroanatomy of verbal self-monitoring. *Brain*, 119: 907–17.

McGuire, P. K., Silbersweig, D. A., Wright, I., et al. (1995) Abnormal monitoring of inner speech: a physiological basis for auditory hallucinations. *Lancet*, 346: 596–600.

Murphy, K., Corfield, D. R., Guz, A., et al. (1997) Cerebral areas associated with motor control of speech in humans. *Journal of Applied Physiology*, 83: 1438–47.

Ojemann, G. A. (1983) Brain organization for language from the perspective of electrical-stimulation mapping. *Behavioral and Brain Sciences*, 6: 189–206.

Ojemann, G. A., Ojemann, J., Lettich, E., and Berger, M. (1989) Cortical language localization in left, dominant hemisphere: an electrical-stimulation mapping investigation in 117 patients. *Journal of Neurosurgery*, 71: 316–26.

Perani, D., Abutalebi, J., Paulesu, E. et al. (2003) The role of age of acquisition and language usage in early, high-proficient bilinguals: an fMRI study during verbal fluency. *Human Brain Mapping*, 19: 170–82.

Poline, J. B., Vandenberghe, R., Holmes, A. P., Friston, K. J., and Frackowiak, R. S. J. (1996) Reproducibility of PET activation studies: lessons from a multi-center European experiment: EU concerted action on functional imaging. *Neuroimage*, 4: 34–54.

Price, C., Indefrey, P., and van Turennout, M. (1999) The neural architecture underlying the processing of written and spoken word forms. In C. M. Brown and P. Hagoort (eds), *The Neurocognition of Language*, pp. 211–40. Oxford University Press, Oxford.

Price, C. J., Devlin, J. T., Moore, C. J., Morton, C., and Laird, A. R. (2005) Meta-analyses of object naming: effect of baseline. *Human Brain Mapping*, 25: 70–82.

Pu, Y. L., Liu, H. L., Spinks, J. A., et al. (2001) Cerebral hemodynamic response in Chinese (first) and English (second) language processing revealed by event-related functional MRI. *Magnetic Resonance Imaging*, 19: 643–7.

Riecker, A., Ackermann, H., Wildgruber, D., et al. (2000) Articulatory/phonetic sequencing at the level of the anterior perisylvian cortex: a functional magnetic resonance imaging (fMRI) study. *Brain and Language*, 75: 259–76.

Riecker, A., Mathiak, K., Wildgruber, D. et al. (2005) fMRI reveals two distinct cerebral networks subserving speech motor control. *Neurology*, 64: 700–6.

Rodriguez-Fornells, A., van der Lugt, A., Rotte, M., Britti, B., Heinze, H. J., and Munte, T. F. (2005) Second language interferes with word production in fluent bilinguals: brain potential and functional imaging evidence. *Journal of Cognitive Neuroscience*, 17: 422–33.

Roelofs, A. (1992) A spreading-activation theory of lemma retrieval in speaking. *Cognition*, 42: 107–42.

Salmelin, R., Hari, R., Lounasmaa, O. V., and Sams, M, (1994) Dynamics of brain activation during picture naming. *Nature*, 368: 463–5.

Salmelin, R., Service, E., Kiesilä, P., Uutela, K., and Salonen, O. (1996) Impaired visual word processing in dyslexia revealed with magnetoencephalography. *Annals of Neurology*, 40: 157–62.

Schäffler, L., Lüders, H. O., Dinner, D. S., Lesser, R. P., and Chelune, G. J. (1993) Comprehension deficits elicited by electrical stimulation of Broca Area. *Brain*, 116: 695–715.

Schank, R. C., and Abelson, R. P. (1977) *Scripts, Plans, Goals and Understanding: An Inquiry into Human Knowledge Structures*. Erlbaum, Hillsdale, NJ.

Schmitt, B. M., Münte, T. F., and Kutas, M. (2000) Electrophysiological estimates of the time course of semantic and phonological encoding during implicit picture naming. *Psychophysiology*, 37: 473–84.

Schmitt, B. M., Schiltz, K., Zaake, W., Kutas, M., and Münte, T. F. (2001) An electrophysiological analysis of the time course of conceptual and syntactic encoding during tacit picture naming. *Journal of Cognitive Neuroscience*, 13: 510–22.

Shergill, S. S., Brammer, M. J., Fukuda, R. et al. (2002) Modulation of activity in temporal cortex during generation of inner speech. *Human Brain Mapping*, 16: 219–27.

Shergill, S. S., Brammer, M. J., Williams, S. C. R., Murray, R. M., and McGuire, P. K. (2000) Mapping auditory hallucinations in schizophrenia using functional magnetic resonance imaging. *Archives of General Psychiatry*, 57: 1033–8.

Shuster, L. I., and Lemieux, S. K. (2005) An fMRI investigation of covertly and overtly produced mono- and multisyllabic words. *Brain and Language*, 93: 20–31.

Sirigu, A., Cohen, L., Zalla, T., et al. (1998) Distinct frontal regions for processing sentence syntax and story grammar. *Cortex*, 34: 771–8.

Sirigu, A., Zalla, T., Pillon, B., Grafman, J., Agid, Y., and Dubois, B. (1996) Encoding of sequence and boundaries of scripts following prefrontal lesions. *Cortex*, 32: 297–310.

Sörös, P., Cornelissen, K., Laine, M., and Salmelin, R. (2003) Naming actions and objects: cortical dynamics in healthy adults and in an anomic patient with a dissociation in action/object naming. *Neuroimage*, 19: 1787–801.

Stemberger, J. P. (1985) An interactive activation model of language production. In A. W. Ellis (ed.), *Progress in the Psychology of Language*, pp. 143–86. Erlbaum, London.

Stewart, L., Meyer, B. U., Frith, U., and Rothwell, J. (2001) Left posterior BA37 is involved in object recognition: a TMS study. *Neuropsychologia*, 39: 1–6.

Tamas, L. B., Shibasaki, T., Horikoshi, S., and Ohye, C. (1993) General activation of cerebral metabolism with speech: a PET study. *International Journal of Psychophysiology*, 14: 199–208.

Thorpe, S., Fize, D. and Marlot, C. (1996) Speed of processing in the human visual system. *Nature*, 381: 520–22.

Turkeltaub, P. E., Eden, G. F., Jones, K. M., and Zeffiro, T. A. (2002) Meta-analysis of the functional neuroanatomy of single-word reading: method and validation. *Neuroimage*, 16: 765–80.

van Turennout, M., Hagoort, P., and Brown, C. M. (1997) Electrophysiological evidence on the time course of semantic and phonological processes in speech production. *Journal of Experimental Psychology: Learning Memory and Cognition*, 23: 787–806.

van Turennout, M., Hagoort, P., and Brown, C. M. (1998) Brain activity during speaking: from syntax to phonology in 40 milliseconds. *Science*, 280: 572–4.

van Turennout, M., Wagensveld, B., and Zwitserlood, P. (2005) Experience-dependent representation of phonological codes during speaking: an FMRI study. *Journal of Cognitive Neuroscience Supplement*: 230.

Vingerhoets, G., Van Borsel, J., Tesink, C. et al. (2003) Multilingualism: an fMRI study. *Neuroimage*, 20: 2181–96.

Wheeldon, L. R., and Levelt, W. J. M. (1995) Monitoring the time-course of phonological encoding. *Journal of Memory and Language*, 34: 311–34.

Wise, R. J. S., Greene, J., Büchel, C., and Scott, S. K. (1999) Brain regions involved in articulation. *Lancet*, 353: 1057–61.

Wise, R. J. S., Scott, S. K., Blank, S. C., Mummery, C. J., Murphy, K., and Warburton, E. A. (2001) Separate neural subsystems within 'Wernicke's area'. *Brain*, 124: 83–95.

CHAPTER 34

Language production in aphasia

Rita Sloan Berndt

34.1 Introduction

The act of producing language is a peculiarly human ability that typically proceeds quickly (2–3 words/second) and without apparent effort. Despite this speed and efficiency, language production is usually highly accurate. Bock (1991) reports an approximate rate of normal speech errors as one in one thousand words. In reality, of course, language production requires the precise and timely coordination of a number of distinct processes before thoughts can be realized as speech.

Aphasia is a condition in which previously normal and literate users of a language suffer a disruption in the operation of language processes, including language production, as the result of a focal brain lesion. Aphasic language production, which can differ from normal speech in a variety of different ways, highlights the number and complexity of the elements that constitute normal language. Aphasic speakers may exhibit marked reductions in fluency, may have enormous difficulty producing words to express meaning, may produce fragmented utterances interrupted by numerous pauses, and may produce words that do not express what they intended to say. These disparate symptoms may appear in different combinations with differing degrees of severity in individual patients, and may be resistant to change with the passage of time. This chapter will describe the many forms that aphasic language production can take and will attempt to interpret them within the context of psycholinguistic models of normal language production.

34.2 Language components subject to disruption in aphasia

34.2.1 Fluency

One striking aspect of aphasic speech which is immediately evident to the listener involves disruptions that occur to speech fluency. This characteristic has been used to organize different types of aphasic impairments into the fluent types (Wernicke's, conduction, anomic, and transcortical sensory aphasia) and the non-fluent types (Broca's and transcortical motor ("dynamic") aphasia). The primary empirical component of fluency is argued to be the number of words typically uttered in an uninterrupted string, with patterns in which "short string" (3–4 words maximum) and "long string" (>5 words) are dominant, describing a bimodal distribution (Goodglass et al., 1964). However, many distinct problems can contribute to dysfluency, including articulation difficulty, word-finding blocks, and gross structural impairments. It seems clear that these types of contributing problem may be selectively affected in dysfluent patients, and there have been few attempts to distinguish among or to measure them systematically (Feyereisen et al., 1991). Although psycholinguistic models of language production do not explicitly consider the effects of dysfluency on the ultimate product, interruptions in the timing of sentence processing, from whatever cause, would be quite likely to result in considerable disruption of other operations. This issue will be discussed below.

34.2.2 Sentence structure

One aspect of aphasic language that has undergone intense analysis is the set of symptoms that appear to be problems with the realization of syntactic structure. On the "short string" end of the fluency continuum, patients with agrammatic Broca's aphasia produce structurally simple and often fragmented utterances characterized by occasional omissions of bound and free grammatical morphemes. The following is a transcription of a classic Broca's aphasic speaker telling the story of Cinderella (two minute segment):

> long ago uh (2 sec) one time uh many years ago (2 sec) uh step (2 sec) two sisters and one (2 sec) god mothers yeah uh (6 sec) Cinderella is uh washing uh clothes and uh (2 sec) mop floor (4 sec) one day Cinderella big party in the castle (5 sec) two uh girls (13 sec) dresses is beautiful (2 sec) Cinderella is poor.

At the other end of the fluency continuum, patients with Wenicke's aphasia may produce relatively intact sentence structures that may be relatively empty of interpretable content. These structures are sometimes characterized by apparently misapplied (substituted) grammatical morphemes (paragrammatism). The following is a two-minute segment from a transcription of a Wernicke's speaker telling the Cinderella story (pauses < 2 sec marked with …):

> this is uh something for that and it starts out and um there is /praetihds/ and he has things to do and … but anyway … uh stuff is going along and then they think something and they think okay so he goes now he goes …. This goes on and takes all that and we see that we have things for that … it's a thing and other things … and then we /djuz/ all that and he sees that /erawl/ that well he happens to get up and goes things and he's that's good and see so good …

Although these production patterns look (and certainly sound) distinct, there is evidence that when sentence production patterns are systematically analyzed, there is considerable overlap of omissions and substitutions of grammatical morphemes across the two patient types (Bird and Franklin, 1996; Butterworth and Howard, 1987). Most attention has been directed at the structural problems of agrammatic Broca's aphasia, and many studies have indicated that structural aspects of language may be disrupted in a variety of different ways (Berndt, 1987; Saffran et al., 1989). As can be seen in the sample above, Broca's aphasics do not always omit grammatical markers, even while producing fragmentary language with little sentence structure.

34.2.3 Word retrieval

All aphasic speakers have some type of difficulty with word retrieval (anomia), but such difficulty can take a number of different forms. Overt word retrieval errors are referred to as "paraphasias"—an apparently unintended word or sound choice. Phonemic paraphasias involve production of an unintended sound in an otherwise recognizable word (*paper*/payker/), with totally unrecognizable utterances referred to as neologisms. Some paraphasias involve the production of an unintended word (a verbal paraphasia), which may be semantically related to the intended word (*globe/atlas*; a semantic paraphasia). These distinctive error types have been used to support arguments concerning the underlying source of the patient's anomia.

Word retrieval impairments can also differ across patients in the types of word that seem most difficult for them to produce. Of most importance to this discussion of sentence-level production are word retrieval deficits that appear to be greater for specific grammatical categories. In addition to the marked differences across Broca's and Wernicke's patients in the ability to produce grammatical words vs. content words, there are now many reports of patients whose verb production is significantly worse than noun production, or vice versa, even when the items to be produced are matched for frequency and length. As reviewed below, there have been numerous attempts to determine the ways in which these selective word retrieval impairments might disrupt other aspects of language production.

34.2.4 Conceptual elements and formulation of a "message"

It is widely assumed that aphasia is a relatively pure language deficit, distinct from other cognitive disorders that might be associated with cerebral injury (Goodglass and Kaplan, 1983). However, it seems clear that patients' language use critically depends on the cognitive resources that allow the formulation of a message to be conveyed, as well as the planning and coordination of elements of that message. These sorts of issue have not attracted much attention in studies of aphasic language production (but see discussion below), although there has been more interest in the memory resources required to support different aspects of production (R. Martin and Freedman, 2001; N. Martin and Saffran, 1997).

34.3 **Clinical classification of the aphasias**

The primary aphasia classification scheme in current use is based on a "classical" model of language function/brain structure that dates to the late nineteenth century (see Goodglass, 1993 for review and discussion of other classification systems). The classical model sketched in Figure 34.1, updated and expanded by Geschwind (1965), distinguishes between disorders which appear to involve motor systems (non-fluent aphasias) and those that appear to involve sensory (auditory) systems (the fluent aphasias, characterized by comprehension disturbance). The neuro-anatomical model that underlies this classification identifies a brain area necessary for speech production (Broca's area) in the left inferior frontal lobe, and another area (adjacent to primary auditory cortex) required for language comprehension (Wernicke's area) in the left superior temporal lobe. The primary contrast when these areas are affected involves Broca's aphasia (characterized by dysfluency and good comprehension) and Wernicke's aphasia (with fluent speech and poor comprehension).

The neuro-anatomical model also identifies a set of subcortical fiber tracts (the arcuate fasciculus), linking Broca's and Wernicke's areas, which allow communication between the primary language centers. These tracts are said to be necessary to support the production of heard words (repetition), as information processed in Wernicke's area must be made available to generate speech in Broca's area. Aphasia types that are distinguished by their performance on repetition tasks include Conduction aphasia, in which repetition is impaired but speech production is fluent and comprehension is intact, and the Transcortical aphasias, in which repetition is spared despite poor spontaneous speech production (Transcortical Motor Aphasia) or poor comprehension (Transcortical Sensory Aphasia). According to the model, the emergence of these patterns depends on the integrity of the arcuate fasciculus, i.e. conduction aphasia is caused by a lesion to these connective tracts that spares Broca's and Wernicke's areas, while the transcortical aphasias are caused by lesions that spare these tracts. The classical model also provides a neuro-anatomical basis for disorders of reading and writing, but these functions will not be discussed in this chapter.

Clinical aphasia tests include assessments of "spontaneous" speech (for evaluating fluency, grammatical well-formedness, and content) as well as word and sentence comprehension, word and sentence repetition, and picture naming. Classification is based on relative performance

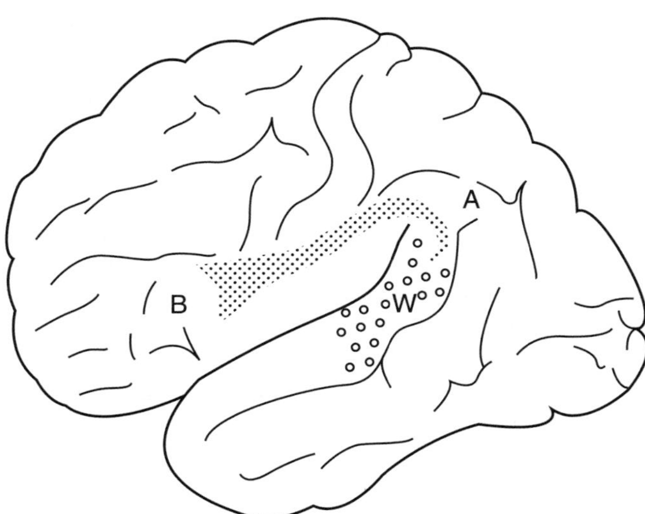

Figure 34.1 Lateral surface of the left hemisphere. B, Broca's area, lies anterior to the lower end of the motor cortex; W, Wernicke's area, lies adjacent to primary auditory cortex; stippled areas indicate the arcuate fasciculus, subcortical connection between Wernicke's and Broca's areas. (Reprinted with permission from N. Geschwind, *Science* 170: 940-44, 1965. Copyright 1965 AAAS.)

on these subtests (e.g. Goodglass and Kaplan, 1983). Although the information collected through aphasia testing may be important to some research endeavors, it is not universally agreed that knowledge of clinical classification is very useful for conducting psycholinguistic research.

As noted above in the discussion of structural disorders, the distinctions among the aphasia types are not always clear. The classification instruments quite often yield a so-called "mixed" pattern, suggesting that the patient is not classifiable (Spreen and Risser, 1998). Even within the classifiable groups, performance may be very heterogeneous in ways that are germane to the research effort. Moreover, modern imaging techniques have raised questions about the neuroanatomical generality of the classical model (Dronkers et al., 2004). For these and other reasons, many researchers have called for abandoning the classification system for purposes of research (Caramazza, 1984; Damasio, 1998). Nonetheless, much research on language production in aphasia has focused on patients with Broca's aphasia and the symptom of agrammatism, and this work will be included here.

34.4 **A model of sentence production**

Models of normal sentence production describe the hypothetical levels of representation that must be computed to generate a sentence. The model that has been most widely applied to the analysis of aphasic sentence production was developed from systematic patterns that occur in normal speech errors (Garrett, 1975). According to this model, the production of a sentence requires the generation of the following distinct levels of representation prior to actual articulation:

- The "message" level represents pre-linguistically the idea or event to be communicated. This level may call upon a variety of resources, including internal emotional or cognitive states, elements in a discourse, or external objects, or events in the environment.
- The "functional" level represents the conceptual/semantic information in the message as abstract lexical/syntactic items, specified for the thematic structure that will be conveyed.
- The "positional" level represents the abstract lexical elements of the previous level as phonologically-specified words inserted into an ordered grammatical frame that is generated through syntactic processes.
- The "phonetic" level specifies the phonetic details of the emerging representation in a manner that can provide input to the speech motor system.

This basic framework has been elaborated and expanded, especially with regard to the "two-stage" requirements of lexical encoding (Bock and Levelt, 1994; Levelt et al., 1999). The Garrett model is highlighted here because it has served as the basis for numerous attempts to understand the sources of aphasic sentence production disorders (Garrett, 1982; Schwartz, 1987; see Berndt, 2001 for review). Many of these attempts have focused on the symptoms of agrammatic Broca's aphasia, and have identified the generation of the Positional Level as the source of patients' difficulties with grammatical morphology (e.g. Caramazza and Hillis, 1989). Studies that focused on other symptoms of Broca's aphasia have located the impairment at the earlier, Functional Level (e.g. Bastiaanse and VanZonneveld, 2004). There are two primary reasons that aphasic impairments are open to multiple interpretations within the model.

First, an impairment in the construction of a specific level of the model could be realized in a number of different ways. For example, difficulty constructing a positional-level representation could result in different symptoms involving grammatical morphemes; i.e. they might be omitted from the structure or used incorrectly. Further, as noted above, patients of the same general type may manifest different sets of symptoms, even though these symptoms may be attributed to failure at a specific level of the model. Each level of the model is hypothesized to require the successful completion of a number of different processes, any one of which could potentially be a source of disruption. For example, the model holds that the construction of a positional level representation requires both the retrieval of a phonological specification of the abstract "words" available at the previous level and the assignment of those phonological elements to positions in a phrasal frame. As Garrett (1984) has pointed out, disruption of the first of these operations with sparing of the second might lead to the production of phonemic errors, but should not lead to structural difficulties. Identification of the level of the model that is affected is therefore not sufficient to account for specific symptoms.

A second problem with applying the model to the study of aphasia is that the model does not establish the temporal requirements involved in computing and integrating the elements that are necessary at each level. Because of the centrality of speech fluency disorders in aphasia, this is an important issue. But even for normal speakers, timing and coordination of different aspects of sentences are critical, as noted by Garrett (1982: 23):

> The structure of what we have said and what we are planning to say must be rapidly brought to bear on what we are currently saying, or else we will be forced to pause, or perhaps find ourselves trying to say the syntactically unsayable.

Such coordination may be particularly problematic for aphasic speakers, as fluency disruptions and word-finding blocks may interfere with the coordination of multiple elements during production.

34.5 **Resource limitations in aphasic sentence production**

One general approach to explaining language production symptoms invokes perturbations of the temporal coordination and maintenance of the different representations produced at each of these levels. These types of disruption can be viewed as performance limitations, or limitations on the cognitive resources required for language production, rather than a loss of specific linguistic elements. Some support for this position comes from results of studies of aphasic production using computer-aided sentence production systems, which arguably reduce memory requirements as well as phonological and morphological processing demands. Such studies have demonstrated, for example, that patients with very little sentence structure in their spontaneous verbal production retain considerable syntactic knowledge (Weinrich et al., 1991). Several different approaches to performance limitation accounts have been developed.

34.5.1 **The temporal window hypothesis**

One influential hypothesis about the symptoms of agrammatic Broca's aphasia explicitly invokes problems with the temporal coordination of sentence elements (Kolk and Van Grunsven, 1985; Kolk, 2005). Two types of difficulty can occur: abnormally fast *decay* of information, and abnormally long *delay* in the retrieval of other information. These two types of impairment together reduce the size of the "temporal window" within which sentence production is carried out. Support for this processing account comes from a variety of phenomena. For example, the complexity of the message to be produced affects the extent of the disruption. More complex messages (e.g. with more elements in each constituent), should place greater stress on the speaker's residual capacity for temporal integration and thus be more subject to errors. Moreover, the severity and form of aphasic symptoms can vary markedly within a patient as a function of the task; symptoms of agrammatism such as omission of grammatical morphemes may not be evident in (arguably) simpler tasks such as sentence completion.

Experimental evidence suggests that there are other ways to mitigate patients' resource limitations. Hartsuiker and Kolk (1998) used a syntactic priming task to improve the production of passive voice and other structures in twelve Dutch-speaking agrammatic Broca's aphasics. This paradigm requires speakers to repeat a sentence (e.g. in passive voice) and then to describe a picture with two actors. Normal subjects show a small but significant tendency to use the structure of the repeated sentence when describing the picture (Bock, 1986). The agrammatic speakers showed normal to above-normal priming effects, producing sentence types that were rarely produced at baseline. The results are interpreted as support for the temporal window hypothesis on the assumption that the prime sentence activates the structural elements required for the picture description sentence, thereby decreasing the time required to compute that structure (see also Saffran and Martin, 1997).

The resource limitations postulated to underlie agrammatism are not hypothesized to be directly related to its symptoms. Rather, the dysfluency, structural simplification, and grammatical morpheme omissions are argued to reflect different ways in which patients adapt to their resource limitation. Patients can resort to two types of simplification to prevent computational overload. They can attempt to produce only simple, unelaborated sentences, resulting in the marked reduction of the variety of structural forms that is characteristic of agrammatism. However, they can also attempt something more complex but omit inessential elements, resulting in grammatical morpheme omissions. This form of adaptation is argued to employ an elliptical speech register that is used in normal speech. In experimental situations that are designed to discourage ellipsis (e.g. sentence completion), grammatical morphemes may be produced relatively normally (Kolk, 2005).

Additional support for the temporal window hypothesis comes from results of treatment studies using a "processing prosthesis," a computerized production system in which patients can record (in their own voice) and save fragments of emerging sentences, replaying and rearranging them until satisfied with the result. Not only do patients produce longer and better-formed utterances while using the system (Linebarger et al., 2000), but some patients show similar structural improvements, after substantial practice with the system, even in their unaided speech (Linebarger et al., 2004; Linebarger et al., 2007). Since these improvements have occurred without any explicit structural or lexical instruction, the argument is that the system reduces processing demands because production may proceed in smaller chunks, and memory may be refreshed repeatedly by allowing the replaying of previously recorded material.

34.5.2 **Other interpretations of resource limitations**

Kolk's temporal window hypothesis was developed to account for the "classic" symptoms of agrammatic Broca's aphasia—fragmented sentences and omissions of grammatical markers. Clearly, reduction of processing resources, if severe enough, could also lead to other types of aphasic symptom. R. Martin has developed a memory-based account of another symptom that is characteristic of many types of aphasic patients—the failure to elaborate noun phrases with other content words. For example, many patients have difficulty integrating adjectives into noun phrases in languages that place the adjective prior to the noun; there is considerably less difficulty in languages that place the nouns first (Menn and Obler, 1990; Ahlsen et al., 1996). A relative scarcity of adjectival noun phrases has been reported for both non-fluent (Saffran et al., 1989) and fluent patients (Bird and Franklin, 1996), even though both types of patient produce adjectives quite normally outside the context of a noun phrase, i.e. in copular constructions such as *The moon is blue*. Adjective–noun phrases are not considered to be syntactically complex, so it is not clear that they should be subject to the "simplification" strategies described by Kolk.

R. Martin has proposed that the lexical representations computed at the Functional and Positional Levels of the model described above require different types of memory buffer to maintain information during sentence production (R. Martin and Freedman, 2001). Martin has identified two distinct types of memory impairment: to semantic and to phonological retention. When the limitation is primary for the retention of semantic information, patients have difficulty holding in memory the lexical/conceptual items at the Functional Level that will need to be assembled at the next level. Critically, Martin hypothesizes that processing at the Functional Level operates across phrases, and that less complex phrases are more easily integrated into the emerging sentence structure than more complex phrases (R. Martin et al., 2004). Noun phrases in which content words appear before the head noun are more difficult to retain when there is evidence of a semantic short-term memory impairment. In a number of studies, Martin and colleagues have shown that patients with semantic short-term memory impairment (defined on independent grounds) have difficulty producing complex phrases—both adjective–noun phrases (R. Martin and Freedman 2001) and conjoined noun phrases with semantically related nouns (Freedman et al., 2004). It is important to note that another patient with even shorter memory span, whose impairment involved retention of phonological rather than semantic information, did not show any deficits when producing complex noun phrases.

Several other patients have been described who have difficulty producing multiple content words when they are semantically related, despite good production of the individual words. Wilshire and McCarthy (2002) discussed a patient with non-fluent speech but good picture-naming that deteriorated when items were semantically blocked and presented at a fast rate. This patient was not tested on the tasks used to diagnose semantic short-term memory deficit, and his deficit was attributed to difficulty modulating activation within a lexical network (see also McCarthy and Kartsounis, 2000). Nonetheless, this type of performance would also be a likely result of semantic short-term memory limitation.

These studies focusing on the production of content words in complex phrases and in conditions of semantic competition have expanded investigations of language production impairments to those that involve structural elaboration that is not dependent on difficulty with grammatical morphemes. These efforts are aided by computational models of production that maintain the "two-stage" structure of the Garrett model but challenge its assumption of strictly serial, feedforward information flow (Dell, 1986; Roelofs, 1992). The assumption of seriality means, for example, that the selection of lexical elements at the Functional Level is controlled by information at the Message Level, and is not influenced by feedback from phonological elements as they become available at the next level. Evidence in favor of at least a limited amount of interactivity in these computational models has come from experiments with normal subjects

(N. Martin et al., 1989) and from aphasic patients (Rapp and Goldrick, 2002). The question of bidirectional influences is an important one for interpreting aphasic impairments, in which it is possible that difficulties at late stages of production (e.g. with phonological encoding) might disrupt processing at earlier stages.

Computational models force explicit consideration of the processing details of semantic/ phonological information transmission, and provide a means for evaluating the effects of perturbations in the timing of lexical activation and decay on performance. They provide a potential means of defining "resource limitations" more clearly, and to simulate different patterns of semantic/phonological impairments that occur in aphasia (e.g. Dell et al., 1997; N. Martin et al., 1994; Schwartz et al., 2006). Although these simulations have exclusively modeled single word production tasks such as word repetition and picture naming, their findings have clear implications for Functional/Positional Level interactions in sentence production.

34.6 **Effects of poor verb retrieval on sentence production**

Many aphasic speakers have more difficulty producing verbs than nouns, even when the two word classes are carefully matched on variables such as length and frequency (Miceli et al., 1984; Zingeser and Berndt, 1990). It is important to note that these studies also found patients with the opposite impairment, i.e. nouns worse than verbs, indicating that the verb deficit does not occur simply because verbs are more complex. Although difficulty producing verbs has long been thought of as a symptom limited to agrammatic Broca's aphasics (e.g. Myerson and Goodglass, 1972), other types of patient may also have more difficulty producing verbs than nouns in picture naming (Berndt and Haendiges, 2000; Berndt et al., 1997). Because of the frequent co-occurrence of selective verb production deficits with agrammatism, there have been attempts to identify a causal link between the two symptoms (Saffran et al., 1980), and this issue has generated a considerable research effort.

The effects of verb retrieval impairment on sentence production is likely to depend on the level within the model at which the verb deficit arises. It should be the case that the earlier the disruption, the more effect a verb deficit would have on other aspects of sentence production. For example, failure to select a lexical/syntactic verb representation during construction of the Functional Level representation should be quite disruptive to sentence production, since the verb representation at this level is argued to encode the argument structure that will motivate the selection of nouns (Kim and Thompson, 2000; Thompson, 2003). If verb retrieval fails at this level, the patient will be unable to generate a structural frame at the Positional Level. However, if verb retrieval fails later, at the Positional Level, the patient may be able to produce some sort of structure, although perhaps lacking a lexical verb.

Marshall and colleagues have argued that some verb impairments may arise at a very early point in production, as conceptual information in the message is transmitted to the next level to support lexical section (Marshall et al., 1993). These investigators carried out an extensive investigation with an aphasic speaker who showed severely impaired sentence production, virtually devoid of verbs. In the course of working with this patient, Marshall and colleagues noted that a major problem contributing to poor production was at the level of conceptualizing the event to be described. Using videotaped activities and action pictures, and requiring no verbal production, the authors demonstrated that the patient could not consistently identify the roles of the actors depicted (agent, etc.), and could not successfully identify which two of three pictures illustrated the same action in different contexts. The investigators carried out an experimental treatment focused on identification of the lexicalizable elements of an event, which resulted in some modest improvements in the patient's expression of verbs and their arguments.

Other studies investigating the production of verbs have focused on the complexity of verbs' argument structures as a determinant of verb-retrieval failure. In a series of papers, Thompson and colleagues have found that the production of verbs may be influenced by the number of verb arguments required by the elicitation materials, as well as by the number of argument structure arrangements that are possible for each verb (Kim and Thompson, 2000; Thompson, 2003; Thompson et al., 1997). These influences were found even outside the context of sentence production, i.e. in picture naming. Since verb argument structures should be available at the Functional Level, Kim and Thompson argue that that level is the source of verb breakdown in these patients (see also Bastiaanse and Van Zonneveld, 2004).

Still other studies have located the source of verb retrieval impairments at the Positional Level, where the phonological specification of verbs becomes available. Some support for this argument is provided by the modality-specific verb retrieval impairments that have been described (Rapp and Caramazza, 2002; Berndt and Haendiges, 2000; Hillis and Caramazza, 1995) wherein verb/noun retrieval differences occur for one modality of production (e.g. speech) but not for another (e.g. writing). Although the model described above does not explicitly consider the writing or spelling of words, the assumption is that a second Positional Level, providing orthographic rather than phonological information, would have to be postulated for writing. Since both speaking and writing words could be generated from the same (modality neutral) Functional Level representation, a deficit at that level should not allow modality differences.

Another type of argument favoring a Positional Level locus of grammatical class difficulties for some patients involves the realization of the grammatical morphemes that are hypothesized to become available at that level. Some patients with relative noun or verb production impairment in naming also demonstrate selective difficulty producing the inflections required for the affected grammatical class (Laiacona and Caramazza, 2004; Shapiro and Caramazza, 2003a). The co-occurrence of grammatical class and morphological production deficits has been taken as support for the argument that grammatical class information is represented at the level that encodes bound morphemes, i.e. at the Positional Level.

However, not all patients with significant noun/verb differences in production demonstrate co-occurring morphological impairments (e.g. Shapiro and Caramazza, 2003b), indicating that grammatical class differences (e.g. in picture-naming tasks) do not all arise from the same impairment. This position is supported by conflicting results of experimental treatment studies designed to improve verb production and then assess the impact of that improvement on sentence production. Simply providing a (spoken) verb for patients to use in a sentence, or carrying out a treatment to improve the production of a limited set of verbs, has in some cases resulted in improvement of sentence production (Marshall et al., 1998). In other studies, providing an uninflected verb to use in a sentence did not produce improvement in the structure of sentences using the target verb, but an *inflected* verb cue did improve the structure of even notoriously difficult passive voice sentences (Berndt et al., 1997; Faroqi-Shah and Thompson, 2003). Similarly, treatments that succeeded in improving retrieval of a limited set of verbs did not result in improved sentence production with those same verbs, unless the training involved the entire verb phrase including auxiliary verbs and inflections (Mitchum and Berndt, 1994; Reichman-Novak and Rochon, 1997).

These conflicting results support the idea that there are different types of verb impairment, associated with other, perhaps related, impairments, and that these have different implications for sentence production. Clearly, the relationship between verb retrieval deficits and sentence production is complex and still not understood. However, because an understanding of this relationship has considerable clinical as well as theoretical importance, further research is warranted.

34.7 **The fluent aphasias**

This review has focused primarily on the non-fluent aphasias, particularly agrammatic Broca's aphasia, simply because so much research has been devoted to understanding that production pattern. Other aphasic production disorders have generated less interest, perhaps because many fluent patients have poor language comprehension and are therefore difficult to test. However, interesting patterns of production can be found among these patients that involve both the structure and lexical content of sentences.

As noted previously, patients with Wernicke's aphasia may produce many paraphasic word production errors in their fluent speech, some of which are uninterpretable neologisms. These errors are made almost exclusively on what appear in context to be content words; function words may be produced well, and neologisms may carry legitimate inflections. This pattern thus presents a contrast to the pattern sometimes seen in Broca's aphasia, wherein the content words are produced much better than grammatical function words and inflections. This contrast has led to claims that the two deficits represent relative impairment and sparing of syntactic or semantic processing, and as support for the distinction between closed- and open-class vocabularies. This interpretation has been challenged by Ellis and colleagues (Ellis et al., 1983), who studied a patient with severe Wernicke's aphasia and neologistic jargon. These authors argued that the primary factor influencing which words would be retained was lexical frequency rather than grammatical class. They argue that more frequent words, such as function words, enjoy a higher level of resting activation within the lexical system, and are somewhat resistant to disruption for that reason. Lower-frequency words, without this advantage, are more subject to phonological disruption. Presumably, the opposite pattern of poor production of (high-frequency) function words arises from some impairment that is not sensitive to lexical frequency.

One unresolved issue in discussions of the neologistic "jargonaphasia" pattern is the contribution of patients' comprehension impairment to their output pattern. Because many of these patients appear largely unaware that they are incomprehensible, it has been argued that their comprehension impairment prevents them from monitoring their speech (e.g. Butterworth, 1979). However, it appears that the production of neologistic speech and the ability to self-monitor are dissociable. Some jargon speakers have been reported with good comprehension (Joanette et al., 1980; Butterworth and Howard, 1987), and a patient with very poor comprehension ("pure word deafness") showed clear but frustrated attempts to monitor her production—behavior quite different from the lack of awareness demonstrated by many jargonaphasics (Marshall, Robson, et al., 1998). Such contrasts lend support to the idea that there may be separate monitoring systems, only one of which relies on the auditory comprehension system. This proposal was made by Levelt (1989) in describing normal sentence production. Monitoring by an "external" route checks produced speech and results in overt corrections or repairs; an "internal" route does not require auditory input, and may result in "prepairs" signaled by pauses in speech. Marshall and colleagues (Marshall, Robson, et al., 1998) carried out a number of experiments with four patients with jargonaphasia, with different levels of comprehension ability, and argued that internal monitoring breaks down as phonological information is activated from semantics, leading to an inability to compare actual to planned output.

Other studies of patients with fluent speech have focused on the symptom of paragrammatism (aberrant sentence structure) rather than on the source of phonological errors. Many patients with Wernicke's aphasia are considerably more comprehensible than those with the jargonaphasia pattern, and so aspects of their sentence production can be investigated. Despite considerably better production of grammatical morphology, Wernicke's patients often show structural difficulties that are similar to those found in Broca's aphasia. For example, they are sensitive to sentence complexity, and have difficulty producing passive voice sentences in structured elicitation tasks (Caplan and Hanna, 1998). Like Broca's aphasics, their passive production does not improve when cued by a relevant uninflected verb, but does improve when the full passive form of the verb phrase is provided by the cue (Faroqi-Shah and Thompson, 2003). When producing semantically reversible sentences, both patient types produced a substantial number of thematic role reversal errors in passive-voice sentences, but these were manifested differently. Broca patients had great difficulty producing the grammatical morphemes for a passive structure, and even when cued with the passive form of the verb they often failed to produce the complete passive structure. Wernicke's patients, in contrast, had little difficulty with the morphology once they were cued, but seemed not to understand the mapping rule that assigns nouns to structural positions in passive voice sentences. These types of result suggest that the structural difficulties of the Wernicke's patients may arise from an early disruption in the sentence production process, as conceptual structures at the Message Level yield to abstract lexical entities that encode thematic structure at the Functional Level. The impairment in Broca's aphasia, in contrast, may involve later operations, as correctly selected Functional Level representations are inserted into a sentence frame at the Positional Level.

Butterworth and Howard (1987) have identified another type of structure common among patients with paragrammatic speech (which they label sentence "blends") that may indicate a Functional Level problem. For example, the utterance *isn't look very dear, is it?* is interpreted as a blend of *isn't very dear, is it?* and *doesn't look very dear, does it?* Blends are said to occur when two verbs are active simultaneously during sentence production. Garrett (1982) has proposed that different clause groups, headed by different verbs, may be active simultaneously at the Functional Level in the normal case; blends occur when neither of the verbs (nor its clause) becomes active enough to overcome the interference of its competitor. Although these types of production are difficult to interpret, a more complete understanding of their sources could contribute to elaboration of the processing requirements at the Functional Level.

34.8 **Conclusions**

The study of aphasic language production is challenging, and it has proven helpful to use a psycholinguistic framework as a guide in attempting to interpret the myriad symptoms that can occur. As should be clear from this review, however, there is great need to augment that model with more information about the processes required to move between levels—i.e. about the temporal requirements for successful operation of the system, about the limitations on direction of information flow during the generation of the sentence, and about the nature and capacity of the memory buffers that are needed. As summarized here, many different methods have been used to address these issues, including experiments based on psycholinguistic models, systematic analyses of aspects of elicited speech, computational modeling, and studies of the effects of treatment. These and other (perhaps yet to be developed) methods could provide converging data that will further illuminate our understanding of aphasic language production.

Acknowledgements

The preparation of this chapter, and a substantial fraction of the work reviewed here, was supported by a grant from the National Institute on Deafness and other Communication Disorders (R01DC00262) to the University of Maryland School of Medicine.

References

Ahlsen, E., Nespoulous, J.-L., Dordain, M., et al. (1996) Noun phrase production in agrammatic patients: a cross-linguistic approach. *Aphasiology*, 10: 543–59.

Bastiaanse, R., and Van Zonneveld, R. (2004) Broca's aphasia, verbs and the mental lexicon. *Brain and Language*, 90: 198–202.

Berndt, R. S. (1987) Symptom co-occurrence and dissociation in the interpretation of agrammatism. In R. Job (ed.), *The Cognitive Neuropsychology of Language*, pp. 221–33. Erlbaum, Mahwah, NJ.

Berndt, R. S. (2001) More than just words: sentence production in aphasia. In R. Berndt (ed.), *Handbook of Neuropsychology*, 2nd edn, pp. 173–87. Elsevier, Amsterdam.

Berndt, R. S., and Haendiges, A. (2000) Grammatical class in word and sentence production: evidence from an aphasic patient. *Journal of Memory and Language*, 43: 249–73.

Berndt, R. S., Haendiges, A., Mitchum, C. C., and Sandson, J. (1997) Verb retrieval in aphasia. 2. Relationship to sentence processing. *Brain and Language*, 56: 107–37.

Berndt, R. S., Mitchum, C. C., Haendiges, A., and Sandson, J. (1997) Verb retrieval in aphasia, 1: Characterizing single word impairments. *Brain and Language*, 56: 68–106.

Bird, H., and Franklin, S. (1996) Cinderella revisited: a comparison of fluent and non-fluent aphasic speech. *Journal of Neurolinguistics*, 9: 187–206.

Bock, J. K. (1986) Syntactic persistence in language production. *Cognitive Psychology*, 18: 355–87.

Bock, J. K. (1991) A sketchbook of production problems. *Journal of Psycholinguistic Research*, 20: 141–69.

Bock, J. K., and Levelt, W. J. M. (1994) Language production: grammatical encoding. In M. Gernsbacher (ed.), *Handbook of Psycholinguistics*, pp. 945–84. Academic Press, San Diego, CA.

Butterworth, B. (1979) Hesitation and the production of verbal paraphasias and neologisms in jargon aphasia. *Brain and Language*, 8: 133–61.

Butterworth, B., and Howard, D. (1987) Paragrammatisms. *Cognition*, 26: 1–37.

Caplan, D., and Hanna, J. (1998) Sentence production by aphasic patients in a constrained task. *Brain and Language*, 63: 184–218.

Caramazza, A. (1984) The logic of neuropsychological research and the problem of patient classification in aphasia. *Brain and Language*, 21: 9–20.

Caramazza, A., and Hillis, A. (1989) The disruption of sentence production: some dissociations. *Brain and Language*, 36: 625–50.

Damasio, A. (1998) Signs of aphasia. In M. Sarno (ed.), *Acquired Aphasia*, 3rd edn, pp. 25–41. Academic Press, San Diego, CA.

Dell, G. S. (1986) A spreading activation theory of retrieval in sentence production. *Psychological Review*, 93: 283–321.

Dell, G. S., Schwartz, M. F., Martin, N., Saffran, E. M., and Gagnon, D. A. (1997) Lexical access in aphasic and non-aphasic speakers. *Psychological Review*, 104: 801–38.

Dronkers, N. F., Wilkins, D. P., Vanvalin, R. D., Redfern, B. B., and Jaeger, J. J. (2004) Lesion analysis of the brain areas involved in language comprehension. *Cognition*, 92: 145–77.

Ellis, A., Miller, D., and Sin, G. (1983) Wernicke's aphasia and normal language processing: a case study in cognitive neuropsychology. *Cognition*, 15: 111–14.

Faroqi-Shah, Y., and Thompson, C. K. (2003) Effect of lexical cues on the production of active and passive sentences in Broca's and Wernicke's aphasia. *Brain and Language*, 85: 409–26.

Feyereisen, P., Pillon, A., and Departz, M. P. (1991) On the measures of fluency in the assessment of spontaneous speech production by aphasic subjects. *Aphasiology*, 5: 1–21.

Freedman, M. L., Martin, R. C., and Biegler, K. (2004) Semantic relatedness effects in conjoined noun phrase production: implications for the role of short-term memory. *Cognitive Neuropsychology*, 21: 245–65.

Garrett, M. F. (1975) The analysis of sentence production. In G. Bower (ed.), *The Psychology of Learning and Motivation*, pp. 133–77. Academic Press, London.

Garrett, M. F. (1982) Production of speech: observations from normal and pathological language use. In A. Ellis (ed.), *Normality and Pathology in Cognitive Functions*, pp. 19–76. Academic Press, London.

Garrett, M. F. (1984) The organization of processing structure for language production: application to aphasic speech. In A. Smith (ed.), *Biological Perspectives on Language*, pp. 172–93. MIT Press, Cambridge, MA.

Geschwind, N. (1965) The organization of language and the brain. *Science*, 170: 940–4.

Goodglass, H. (1993) *Understanding Aphasia,* Academic Press, San Diego, CA.

Goodglass, H., and Kaplan, E. (1983) *The Assessment of Aphasia and Related Disorders.* Philadelphia, Lea & Febiger.

Goodglass, H., Quadfasel, F., and Timberlake, W. (1964) Phrase length and the type and severity of aphasia. *Cortex,* 1: 133–53.

Hartsuiker, R. J., and Kolk, H. (1998) Syntactic facilitation in agrammatic sentence production. *Brain and Language,* 62: 221–54.

Hillis, A., and Caramazza, A. (1995) The representation of grammatical categories of words in the brain. *Journal of Cognitive Neuroscience,* 7: 396–407.

Joanette, Y., Keller, E., and Lecours, R. (1980) Sequences of phonemic approximation in aphasia. *Brain and Language,* 11: 30–44.

Kim, M., and Thompson, C. K. (2000) Patterns of comprehension and production of nouns and verbs in agrammatism: implications for lexical organization. *Brain and Language,* 74: 1–25.

Kolk, H. (2005) How language adapts to the brain: an analysis of agrammatic aphasia. In L. Progovac (ed.), *The Syntax of Nonsententials: Multi-disciplinary Perspectives,* pp. 229–58. Benjamins, London.

Kolk, H., and Van Grunsven, M. F. (1985) Agrammatism as a variable phenomenon. *Cognitive Neuropsychology,* 2: 347–84.

Laiacona, M., and Caramazza, A. (2004) The noun/verb dissociation in language production: varieties of causes. *Cognitive Neuropsychology,* 21: 103–23.

Levelt, W. J. M. (1989) *Speaking: From Intention to Articulation.* MIT Press, Cambridge, MA.

Levelt, W. J. M., Roelofs, A., and Meyer, A. S. (1999) A theory of lexical access in speech production. *Behavioral and Brain Sciences,* 22: 1–75.

Linebarger, M., McCall, D., and Berndt, R. S. (2004) The role of processing support in the remediation of aphasic language production disorders. *Cognitive Neuropsychology,* 21: 267–82.

Linebarger, M., McCall, D., Virata, T., and Berndt, R. (2007) Widening the temporal window: processing support in the treatment of aphasic language production. *Brain and Language,* 100: 53–68.

Linebarger, M., Schwartz, M. F., Romania, J. F., Kohn, S. E., and Stephens, D. L. (2000) Grammatical encoding in aphasia: evidence from a "processing prosthesis." *Brain and Language,* 75: 416–27.

Marshall, J., Pring, T., and Chiat, S. (1993) Sentence processing therapy: working at the level of the event. *Aphasiology,* 7: 177–99.

Marshall, J., Pring, T., and Chiat, S. (1998) Verb retrieval and sentence production in aphasia. *Brain and Language,* 63: 159–83.

Marshall, J., Robson, J., Pring, T., and Chiat, S. (1998) Why does monitoring fail in jargon aphasia? Comprehension, judgment and therapy evidence. *Brain and Language,* 63: 79–107.

Martin, N., Dell, G. S., Saffran, E. M., and Schwartz, M. F. (1994) Origins of paraphasias in deep dysphasia: testing the consequences of a decay impairment to an interactive spreading activation model of lexical retrieval. *Brain and Language,* 47: 609–60.

Martin, N., and Saffran, E. M. (1997) Language and auditory-verbal short-term memory impairments: evidence for common underlying processes. *Cognitive Neuropsychology,* 14: 641–82.

Martin, N., Weisberg, R. W., and Saffran, E. M. (1989) Variables influencing the occurrence of naming errors: implications for models of lexical retrieval. *Journal of Memory and Language,* 65: 462–85.

Martin, R. C., and Freedman, M. L. (2001) Short-term retention of lexical-semantic representations: implications for speech production. *Memory,* 9: 261–80.

Martin, R. C., Miller, M., and Vu, H. (2004) Lexical-semantic retention and speech production: further evidence from normal and brain-damaged participants for a phrasal scope of planning. *Cognitive Neuropsychology,* 21: 625–44.

McCarthy, R. A., and Kartsounis, L. D. (2000) Wobbly words: refractory anomia with preserved semantics. *Neurocase,* 6: 487–97.

Menn, L., and Obler, L. (1990) Cross-language data and theories of agrammatism. In L. Obler (ed.), *Agrammatic Aphasia,* pp. 1369–89. Benjamins, Amsterdam.

Miceli, G., Silveri, M. C., Villa, G., and Caramazza, A. (1984) On the basis for the agrammatics' difficulty in producing main verbs. *Cortex,* 20: 207–20.

Mitchum, C. C., and Berndt, R. S. (1994) Verb retrieval and sentence construction: effects of targeted intervention. In J. Riddoch (ed.), *Cognitive Neuropsychology and Cognitive Rehabilitation,* pp. 317–48. Erlbaum, London.

Myerson, R., and Goodglass, H. (1972) Transformational grammar of three agrammatic patients. *Language and Speech,* 15: 40–50.

Rapp, B., and Caramazza, A. (2002) Selective difficulties with spoken nouns and written verbs: a single case study. *Journal of Neurolinguistics,* 15: 373–402.

Rapp, B., and Goldrick, M. (2002) Discreteness and interactivity in spoken word production. *Psychological Review,* 107: 460–99.

Reichman-Novak, S., and Rochon, E. (1997) Treatment to improve sentence production: a case study. *Brain and Language,* 60: 102–5.

Roelofs, A. (1992) A spreading activation theory of lemma retrieval in speaking. *Cognition,* 42: 107–42.

Saffran, E. M., Berndt, R. S., and Schwartz, M. F. (1989) The quantitative analysis of agrammatic production: procedure and data. *Brain and Language,* 37: 440–79.

Saffran, E. M., and Martin, N. (1997) Effects of structural priming on sentence production in aphasia. *Language and Cognitive Processes,* 12: 877–88.

Saffran, E. M., Schwartz, M. F., and Marin, O. S. M. (1980) The word order problem in agrammatism, II: Production. *Brain and Language,* 10: 263–80.

Schwartz, M. F. (1987) Patterns of speech production deficit within and across aphasia syndromes: application of a psycholinguistic model. In M. Coltheart, G. Sartori, and R. Job (eds), *The Cognitive Neuropsychology of Language,* pp. 163–99. Erlbaum, Mahwah, NJ.

Schwartz, M. F., Dell, G. S., Martin, N., Gahl, S., and Sobel, P. (2006) A case-series test of the interactive two-step model of lexical access: evidence from picture naming. *Journal of Memory and Language,* 54: 228–64.

Shapiro, K., and Caramazza, A. (2003a) Grammatical processing of nouns and verbs in left frontal cortex? *Neuropsychologia*, 41: 1189–98.

Shapiro, K., and Caramazza, A. (2003b) Looming a loom: evidence for independent access to grammatical and phonological properties in verb retrieval. *Journal of Neurolinguistics*, 16: 85–112.

Spreen, O., and Risser, A. (1998) Assessment of aphasia. In M. Sarno (ed.), *Acquired Aphasia*, 3rd edn, pp. 71–156. Academic Press, San Diego, CA.

Thompson, C. K. (2003) Unaccusative verb production in agrammatic aphasia: the argument structure complexity hypothesis. *Journal of Neurolinguistics*, 16: 151–67.

Thompson, C. K., Lange, K. L., Schneider, S. L., and Shapiro, L. P. (1997) Agrammatic and non-brain-damaged subjects' verb and verb argument structure production. *Aphasiology*, 11: 473–90.

Weinrich, M., Boser, K., Mccall, D., and Bishop, V. (1991) Training agrammatic subjects on passive sentences: implications for syntactic theories. *Brain and Language*, 76: 45–61.

Wilshire, C. E., and Mccarthy, R. A. (2002) Evidence for a context-sensitive word retrieval disorder in a case of nonfluent aphasia. *Cognitive Neuropsychology*, 19: 165–86.

Zingeser, L., and Berndt, R. S. (1990) Retrieval of nouns and verbs by agrammatic and anomic aphasics. *Brain and Language*, 39: 14–32.

SECTION V

Language development

CHAPTER 35

The perceptual foundations of phonological development

Suzanne Curtin and Janet F. Werker

35.1 Introduction

Phonological development involves learning the organization of the individual sound units, the syllable structure, the rhythm, and the phonotactics of the native language, and utilizing these in both productive and receptive language. The initial work in phonological development focused exclusively on production, with detailed description of the onset of babbling and first words. With the advent of new methodologies, investigations broadened to include studies of infant speech perception. The early infant speech perception work sought to identify initial categories that could support phonological development. In the thirty-five years since publication of the first infant speech perception study, it has been revealed that infants are sensitive to a great deal more in speech perception than just phonetic categories. Infant speech perception provides the basis for not only the sound categories but also the syllable structure, rhythmicity, and the acceptable sound sequences of the native language—all of which are necessary for segmenting and storing words. In this chapter we will focus on how infant speech perception provides a foundation for acquiring the phonological system, and then discuss how production data and perception studies together can provide more a complete picture of the course of phonological development.

The chapter will begin with a review of key empirical findings that show how speech perception provides the foundation for phonological development. Section 35.2, on perception, begins with a review of language-general speech perception capabilities as evident in infants from birth through the first few months of life. This is followed by a review of the ways in which the ambient language modifies infant speech perception. We then discuss (section 35.3) phonological and phonetic factors in recognizing and segmenting word forms from the speech stream, and then examine the role of phonology in early lexical comprehension (section 35.4). Key empirical work from the production literature is then reviewed (section 35.5), beginning with infant babbling and continuing through the production of first words. The final section, 35.6, will review theories and models of phonological development.

35.2 Perceiving language

35.2.1 Language-general speech perception

Infants during the first year of life, and even earlier, are preparing for language. Research has shown that prenatal experience influences infants' speech perception. Neonates will change their sucking pattern in order to hear stories that were recited by their mothers in the last six weeks of pregnancy more than they will in response to novel passages. (DeCasper and Spence, 1986). At birth, infants prefer their mother's voice to the voices of other females (DeCasper and Fifer, 1980), and newborns show a preference for infant-directed speech (Cooper and Aslin, 1990). Attending to this type of speech can help to facilitate discrimination of contrasts. Acoustic analyses reveal that both voicing contrasts (Ratner and Luberoff 1984) and vowel distinctiveness (Kuhl et al., 1997; Ratner, 1984) are exaggerated in infant-directed speech. Karzon (1985) demonstrated that infants are better able to discriminate the middle syllable in *marana* vs. *malana* if it is emphasized with infant-directed prosody. Infant-directed speech also facilitates infant discrimination of non-native phonetic contrasts, as does the use of a female rather than a male voice (Panneton and Ostroff, 2003). Together, these studies demonstrate the range of information that infants are sensitive to and just how young infants are when they begin the process of language learning.

A necessary starting point for language learning is to discriminate speech sounds from non-speech sounds. Infants as young as four months show a preference for listening to speech over white noise (Colombo and Bundy, 1981), or music (Glenn et al., 1981). To account for the "special" status of speech, it has been proposed that infants possess a bias for listening to speech over other types of sound (Jusczyk, 1997). And indeed, infants as young as two months (Vouloumanos and Werker, 2004), and even newborns (Vouloumanos and Werker, 2007) listen longer to speech than to non-speech sounds that are matched in complexity and spectral frequency. This predisposition to speech might enable the infant to tune in to certain properties of the speech signal, thus guiding their acquisition process.

Optical Imaging studies reveal greater activity in the left hemisphere than the right when neonates are presented with normal forward speech but not when they are given backward speech (Peña et al., 2003), and fMRI studies reveal distinct pattern of activation to the two types of speech (Dehaene-Lambertz, Dehaene, and Hertz-Pannier, 2002). This suggests that exposure to speech at these very early stages activates specialized areas of the brain (see also Dahaene-Lambertz and Peña, 2001). Thus, typically developing infants possess some of the basic psychoacoustic and cognitive capacities essential for perceiving speech at or just before birth. This bias is shared by non-human primates (Ramus et al., 2000; Tincoff et al., 2005), indicating that this aspect of speech processing is deeply embedded in our evolutionary history.

Studies of phonetic perception with adults have demonstrated categorical perception across a number of consonant dimensions and contrasts, but also more graded, within-category discrimination (see Diehl et al., 2004 for a review). One of the classic studies demonstrated that young infants can discriminate stimuli from two sides of an adult phonemic category boundary (e.g. /ba/ from /pa/), but not two equally distant stimuli from within the /ba/ or within the /pa/ categories (Aslin et al., 1981; Eimas et al., 1971). Newborns discriminate stop consonants as evidenced by heart-rate deceleration, (Lecanuet et al., 1995), and they perceive consonant differences categorically, as indicated by high-amplitude sucking (Bertoncini et al., 1987) and by event-related potential records from the scalp (Dehaene-Lambertz and Gliga, 2004),. They are especially good at discrimination if the consonants are in well-formed syllables (Bertoncini and Mehler, 1981). Current research has further elaborated this finding by illustrating that 3–6-month-old infants show graded, within-category perception of VOT under appropriate testing conditions (McMurray and Aslin, 2005; Miller and Eimas, 1996). These findings suggest that although categorical perception may be the most easily revealed, gradient perception is also possible.

Infants discriminate consonant contrasts present in their native language as well as contrasts found in other languages (see Saffran et al., 2006 for a review). For example, Kikuyu-learning infants of 4 months are able to discriminate an English voiced/voiceless contrast (ba *vs* pa) even though this contrast is not used in the Kikuyu language (Streeter, 1976). Even more surprisingly, when tested on the voicing distinction in both English and Spanish (Spanish has a different voicing distinction from English (Lisker and Abramson, 1967), Guatemalan infants aged between 4.5 and 6 months were able to discriminate the English contrast but not the Spanish one (Lasky et al., 1975). This result could suggest that infants are not sensitive to fine-grained details in the signal. However, if this were the case, then Spanish-learning infants would not be able to acquire the language's voicing distinction. One explanation is that the English contrast, which is readily discriminated, is aligned with a language-general voicing boundary (Jusczyk, 1997), and the infants learning the Spanish voicing distinction require resetting or shifting of their perceptual categories (Aslin and Pisoni, 1980). Another explanation is that the boundary which is discriminated depends on the way the stimuli were made, and the resulting salience of some cues vs. others. In support, Burns et al. (forthcoming) found that with one set of stimuli, 6–8-month-old English and bilingual French-English infants better discriminate the French boundary than the English. Yet another explanation is that while infants show many phonetic distinctions at birth, in some cases listening experience is required to further bifurcate initial categories (see Narayan, 2005 for such evidence with nasals).

Infants also discriminate across a range of vowel categories within the first few months of life. They can discriminate vowels that are not phonemically distinguished in the native language (Swoboda et al., 1976; Trehub, 1976) and can discriminate at least some vowels that are acoustically quite similar (Marean et al., 1992). In discrimination tasks, newborns use the most extreme "point" vowels in the vowel space (e.g. /i/ and /u/) as reference anchors, showing greater generalization, and hence reduced discrimination, to close vowels when the point vowel is the standard than when the comparison vowel is the standard (Polka and Bohn, 2003). Young infants can also detect vowel pattern differences across syllable sequences (Jusczyk and Derrah, 1987).

Studies examining processing of polysyllabic utterances demonstrate that infants can perceive some phonetic contrasts in the context of polysyllabic strings (Jusczyk and Thompson, 1978). Infants are also sensitive to a number of prosodic cues within these longer sequences, such as vowel duration (Eilers et al., 1984) and pitch peaks (Bull et al., 1984). Most remarkable is infant sensitivity to rhythmic information. Newborn infants discriminate languages from different rhythmical classes (Mehler et al., 1988; Mehler and Christophe, 1995; Nazzi et al., 1998) even when the speech is low-pass filtered to remove all the segmental information. By 2–4 months infants can discriminate languages from within a single rhythmical class, and shortly after this begin to discriminate even two dialects from within the same language (for a review, see Nazzi and Ramus, 2003).

35.2.2 **Language-specific perception**

Across the first year of life, infant speech perception changes to increasingly match the phonetic distinctions used to distinguish meaning in the native language. As is the case for most other aspects of development, listening experience across the first several months of life leads to improvement in infant discrimination performance for difficult native phonetic distinctions (Kuhl et al., 2006; Polka et al., 2001).

The more surprising pattern seen in infant phonetic perception, and one that is now widely attested, is a developmental pattern which is primarily characterized by a decline in performance on non-native distinctions. Like adults, who often have difficulty discriminating acoustically similar non-native minimal pairs (e.g. Pisoni and Lively, 1995), older infants have more difficulty in making some non-native minimal-pair phonetic distinctions than do younger infants, showing that listening experience serves to winnow initial broad-based sensitivities.

In an early example of experience-based winnowing, Werker and Tees (1984) compared English and Hindi adult listeners to English- and Hindi-learning infants aged six to twelve months of age, on their ability to discriminate two Hindi distinctions which are not used in English (the Hindi retroflex-dental, /da/–/Da/ place distinction, and the Hindi voiceless aspirated vs. breathy voiced, voicing distinction /t^ha/–/d^ha/). Hindi adults performed significantly better than the English adults, particularly on the retroflex/dental place distinction. English infants of six to eight months, like the Hindi adults, discriminated both contrasts, revealing more sensitivity than adult speakers of English. In a follow-up study using both the Hindi place distinction and a Nthlakampx glottalized velar vs. uvular distinction, it was shown that the decline in performance on non-native phonetic contrasts can be seen by 10–12 months of age (Werker and Tees, 1984; Werker, 1989). This pattern of decline in performance as a function of listening experience has been found for a number of other contrasts using the same Conditioned Head Turn task as used in the initial cross-linguistic work (e.g. Anderson et al., 2003; Pegg and Werker, 1997; Werker and Lalonde, 1988), using a Visual Habituation discrimination task (Best et al., 1995), and in tasks recording event-related brain potentials (Cheour et al., 1998; Kuhl and Coffey-Corrina, 2001; Rivera-Gaxiola et al., 2003) (see Figure 35.1).

The change from language-general to language-specific perception has been described as a functional reorganization, rather than a loss (Werker, 1995), as sensitivity can be revealed under other testing conditions. When the task enables listening outside of a linguistic mode

(a)

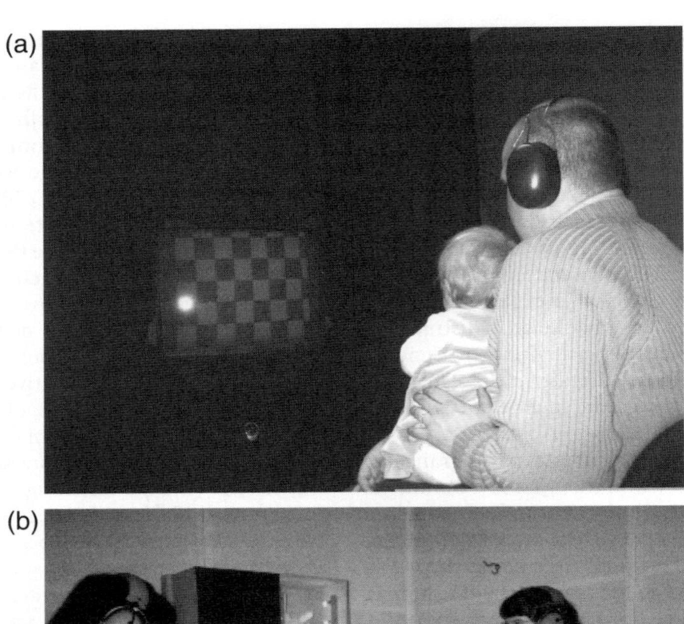

(b)

Figure 35.1 (a) The conditioned head turn procedure. The baby is reinforced with an activated toy animal and praise from the experimenter when they correctly turn their head to a change in the speech sound category. (b)The habituation/dishabituation discrimination task. Sounds are presented contingent on the baby looking toward a flashing light. Looking time to a display (e.g. checkerboard) is then scored. Trials continue until the baby reaches a criterion decline in looking time. Test trials contain both change and control trials. If the baby can discriminate the change, longer looking toward the change trials is expected.

(e.g. shortened ISI or presenting the critical acoustic cues outside a syllabic context), latent sensitivity to difficult non-native phonetic contrasts is maintained, even among adults (see Pisoni and Lively, 1995; Werker, 1995, for reviews). ERP studies have clarified this further, showing that although the ERP signature to non-native distinctions is often different from that to native phonetic distinctions, there is nonetheless ERP evidence of discrimination even of the non-native distinctions either at different electrode sites, or at the same electrode sites but at different latencies (Dehaene-Lambertz, Dupoux, and Gout, 2002; Rivera-Gaxiola et al., 2005).

Infants growing up in bilingual environments appear to show unique developmental trajectories when tuning to the properties of the native languages. Bosch and Sebastián-Gallés (2003) tested Catalan, Spanish, and Catalan-Spanish bilingual infants' discrimination of the vowel distinction /e/–/E/ (as in /dethi/ and /dEthi/), which is used in Catalan but not in Spanish. At four months, all three groups discriminated the /e/–/E/ contrast. By eight months, the Spanish monolingual infants had stopped discriminating it whereas discrimination was maintained in the Catalan monolingual group. Interestingly, however, at 8 months the bilingual infants failed, but succeeded again at 12 months, demonstrating a U-shaped developmental pattern for discrimination. This shows that it is not just listening experience that leads to maintenance of phonetic distinctions, but something more, as the bilingual infants continued to hear the /e/–/E/ contrast in one of their languages throughout this period.

In a study with French- and English-learning infants, Burns et al. (forthcoming) reported two distinct patterns of performance for bilingual infants. Here infants were tested on their ability to discriminate both the French phonemic voice/voiceless contrast (/ba/–/pa/) and the English phonemic voice/voiceless contrast (/ba/–/pa/, but phonetically [pa]–[p^ha]). By ten to twelve months French infants better discriminated the French than the English boundary, and the English infants better discriminated the English. Of interest, the bilingual English-French infants discriminated both the French and the English boundaries. This suggests an advantage that is adaptive for the bilingual environment. Similar findings have recently been reported in perception of the visual aspects of speech. When habituated to silent talking faces delivering sentences in either English or French, monolingual English infants of 4- and 6-months were able to discriminate a change to the new language. However, by 8 months, only infants being raised bilingual succeeded (Weikum et al., forthcoming).

It is now known that the age at which phonetic perception becomes language-specific is not the same for all contrasts. Frequency plays a role: infants stop discriminating two non-native phones that are variants of a single highly frequent native phone at a younger age than they do variants of a less frequent native phone (Anderson et al., 2003). Salience of the contrast in question likely plays a role, with vowel perception becoming language-specific a few months earlier than consonant perception (Kuhl et al., 1992; Polka and Werker, 1994). Indeed, acoustically quite distinct contrasts, particularly those that lie outside the phonological space of the native language (e.g. click contrasts), may remain discriminable even without listening experience (Best et al., 1988).

Various models or frameworks have been proposed to account for these types of finding. Burnham has made a distinction between "fragile" and "robust" contrasts (see Burnham et al., 2002). Fragile contrasts are those that are uncommon across the world's languages, involve phones that are acoustically quite similar, and are likely to be very vulnerable to reorganization if the specific phones are not present in the input. Robust contrasts are common across and within languages, involve more distinct features, and are more likely to remain discriminable, at least for a longer period of time, even without supportive linguistic input.

Best's PAM (Perceptual Assimilation Model: Best, 1994; Best and McRoberts, 2003) and Kuhl's NLM theory (Native Language Magnet: Kuhl, 1993) offer explanations of when and how speech perception abilities become language-specific, both based on similarity metrics. PAM relies on a gestural view of speech perception, and assumes that infants (and adults) perceive unfamiliar phones in terms of their overlap with native categories (as defined by gestural scores). Non-native contrasts that are assimilated to a single category in the native language are the least discriminable, whereas non-native phones that fall completely outside the phonological space of the first language, and are thus "non-assimilable," remain discriminable even without listening experience. Contrasts which differ in "category goodness" and/or are assimilated to two categories in the native language are intermediate in difficulty. In its most recent formulation, age of reorganization is determined not only by the degree of assimilability to the native language, but also by the number of articulatory organs involved in the distinct gesture(s) (see Best and McRoberts, 2003). The NLM theory involves three steps. It is assumed that there is some initial organization to the perceptual space, with some (acoustically defined) phonetic differences particularly stable and discriminable from one another. These "hot spots," as Kuhl calls them, serve as attractors or magnets to other phones, drawing them in and creating categories. Linguistic input "warps" the initial space. Frequently heard instances emerge as new prototypes of categories, serving to redefine or even collapse initial categories (Kuhl, 1993; 2004; but see Lively and Pisoni, 1997).

But what are the learning mechanisms that underlie the above described changes? Although stochastic processes and similarity metrics have frequently been proposed, until recently they had not been empirically tested. An artificial language learning study by Maye et al. (2002) provided the first empirical evidence that statistical learning may indeed play a role in phonetic category reorganization. In this work, two groups of infants were familiarized to different distributions of eight tokens of /da/ spanning a continuum from an initial position [da] to the unaspirated, voiceless [ta]. All infants heard all eight tokens, but one group heard more instances of stimuli 2 and 7, corresponding to a bimodal distribution of input, whereas the other group heard more instances of stimuli 4 and 5, corresponding to a unimodal distribution of input. Following familiarization, infants in the bimodal group were better able to discriminate the endpoint stimuli, 1 and 8, than were infants in the unimodal group, even though both groups of infants had heard an equal number of repetitions of stimuli 1 and 8 in the familiarization phase (Maye et al., 2002). Similar findings have recently been reported by Maye, Weiss, and Aslin (forthcoming) using a slightly different testing procedure and set of stimuli. Recent research confirms that the statistical information is available in infant directed speech to support this type of distributional learning (Werker et al., 2007).

Across the first year of life, infants also become increasingly sensitive to many other phonological properties of the native language. By 9–10 months of age monolingual learning infants show a preference for listening to lists of words that correspond to native language stress patterns (Jusczyk, Cutler, and Redanz 1993) and phonotactics (Jusczyk, Friederici, et al., 1993). Bilingual learning infants show a preference by this age for the phonotactic patterns of the language which is most dominant in their input (Bosch and Sebastián-Gallés, 2001). Just as in the case of phonetic perception (Maye et al., 2002), artificial language-learning studies have shown that infants can use distributional statistics to learn about the phonotactics of the native language (Chambers et al., 2003; Saffran and Thiessen, 2003).

35.3 **Word segmentation and word form recognition**

35.3.1 **Word segmentation**

In a classic study on word segmentation, Jusczyk and Aslin (1995) familiarized 7.5-month-old infants to two CVC words, and then presented them with passages containing the familiar words (*cup*) and passages that contained minimally differing foils (*tup*). Infants demonstrated a listening preference for the familiar passages, suggesting they extracted these words from the speech stream. Using recognizable forms also aids in speech segmentation. For example, having a highly frequent form such as *mommy* preceding another unfamiliar word vs. two unknown adjacent words aids in the segmentation of the unknown word (Bortfeld et al., 2005). Similarly, infants are better able to segment and remember novel words when they are preceded by a highly frequent function word such as *the* (Shi et al., 2006).

Being able to use familiar word information facilitates the segmentation of the speech stream. However, the number of words infants are familiar with by the time they begin segmenting is not known, and is likely highly variable across infants. Thus, researchers have studied other types of information in speech that may help infants discover word boundaries. A number of potential cues to word boundaries, such as prosodic, rhythmic, and segmental information, transitional probabilities, phonotactics, and stress have all been shown to aid in segmentation (Jusczyk et al., 1993; Turk et al., 1995; Morgan and Saffran, 1995; Saffran, Aslin, and Newport, 1996; Saffran, Newport, and Aslin, 1996; Jusczyk, 1997; McQueen, 1998). These types of cue are part of the distributional properties of the linguistic input. For example, phonotactic information includes information about the co-occurrence of particular sounds in various positions. Statistical information available about the co-occurrence of syllables has been shown to aid infants in segmenting the speech stream (Saffran, Aslin, and Newport, 1996; see Gómez, Chapter 36 this volume, for a review). Syllables themselves carry other information, such as phonotactic and prominence information. Probabilistic information in the form of phonotactics (segmental co-occurrences) is used in segmentation by nine months of age. Evidence for this comes from studies where infants are presented with CCVC sequences in a highly probable word boundary context (CCVC) and a low-probability one (CCVC). Infants are better able to segment the CVC sequence from the word boundary context. This is the case for phonotactic cues (e.g. CC sequences) regardless of whether the cluster occurs at the beginning or the end of the sequence (Mattys and Jusczyk, 2001).

The alternation of strong and weak syllables is a particularly salient property, and infants are sensitive to this information at a very young age (Gerken, 2004; Mehler et al., 1988; Mehler and Christophe, 1995; Nazzi et al., 1998). English infants prefer novel trochaic distractors to familiar trochaic (Strong–weak (Sw)) ones, but do not prefer novel iambic (weak–Strong (wS)) distractors to familiar iambic ones (Echols et al., 1997). Indeed, language-specific rhythmic patterns guide segmentation (Jusczyk, Houston, and Newsome, 1999; Polka et al., 2002). Infants exposed to Canadian French, a predominantly iambic language, segment only wS words (Polka et al., 2002), while English infants mis-parse iambic wS patterns. In this case, English babies treat the S syllable as word initial. In a word like *guiTAR*, they segment *TAR* as an initial syllable. If *TAR* is consistently followed by an unstressed word (e.g. *is*), infants treat "TAR is" as a single unit (Jusczyk et al., 1999). If two strong syllable words are next to each other, as in *COLD ICE* or *PACK ASH*, infants this age do not mis-segment (Mattys and Jusczyk, 2001). By eleven months, English-learning infants no longer mis-segment wS words. In an artificial language learning task, Curtin et al. (2005) found that both 9- and 7-month-old infants can successfully parse the stream, and during the test phase they prefer sequences that correspond to an initially stressed syllable from the familiarization phase. This was the case even though all of the test sequences had equally emphasized syllables. These results taken together confirm the hypothesis that stress is a salient cue which can be used by the infant to parse the continuous stream of speech (Jusczyk et al., 1999).

As the above review illustrates, there are a number of potential cues in the speech input which the infant can use to segment the speech stream. One question that researchers have been addressing is their relative importance in segmentation. Johnson and Jusczyk (2001) pitted coarticulation and stress against transitional probabilities to see if either one could override the statistical information. Their results for 8-month-old infants show that both coarticulatory and stress information override transitional probabilities. Recent work by Thiessen and Saffran (2003) suggests that the interplay between stress and statistical information changes over development. They found that infants around six months of age paid more attention to transitional probabilities than to stress when they were pitted against one another. It is possible that the nature of cue weighting changes over time. However, as discussed in Curtin et al. (2005), an alternative explanation could be that computation of transitional probabilities includes consideration of stress information.

35.3.2 Word form recognition

Infants as young as 4.5 months are able to recognize the sound patterns of their names (Mandel et al., 1995). By six months, they recognize their names in ongoing speech (Mandel et al., 1995; Mandel-Emer, 1997). In a study with French 11 month olds, Hallé and Boysson-Bardies (1996) presented infants with frequent familiar words and rare words without any contextual or prosodic cues. Without training on the familiar words, infants demonstrated recognition of the familiar known words. This was replicated with 11-month-old English babies (Vihman et al., 2004), but not with nine-month-olds. ERP studies show a word recognition response in infants as young as 11 months for familiar word forms, not necessarily tied to meaning (Thierry et al., 2003).

The long-term ability to remember words, even in the absence of meaning, is robust in infancy. By nine months, infants are able to retain the sound patterns of frequently presented words for two weeks (Jusczyk and Hoyne, 1997). Indeed, even newborn infants can remember a simple word form for over 24 hours (Swain et al., 1993).

Recognition of word forms requires similarity between the stored item and target, but the degree of similarity required for recognition seems to change as a function of infant age and perhaps testing conditions. At seven months infants seem to remember word forms in great detail; a change in the initial consonant of the exposure words (*cup* to *tup*) results in a lack of recognition (Jusczyk and Aslin, 1995; see also Stager and Werker, 1997). Similarly, Curtin et al. (2005) found that when 7-month-old infants segment trochaic sequences from the speech stream they demonstrate a listening preference for identical items (*DObita*, *DObita*) over ones that were segmentally the same but had stress shifted to an adjacent syllable (*DObita*, *doBIta*). By nine months infants demonstrate familiarity with segmental patterns; but when segmental information is pitted against prosodic information, infants pay attention to the prosodic cues over the segmental ones (Mattys et al., 1999).

Lower-level cues also affect word recognition. After exposure to an artificial speech stream, 7-month-old infants recognize the words they have segmented only if they agree in coarticulation information (information concerning the effect of an adjacent sound on the production of a speech sound) (Curtin et al., 2001). At 7.5 months, infants demonstrate reduced recognition of a word if it is produced by a speaker with a very different voice (male to female) from the one who originally produced it (Houston and Jusczyk, 2000). It is not only gender differences, but the overall degree of differences along a number of dimensions that cause diminished recognition (Houston and Jusczyk, 2003). Word recognition improves when all aspects, including speaker affect, focused vs. non-focused stress, speech rate, and pitch, match the original form in exposure (Singh et al., 2004).

At the same age that they are paying so much attention to stress cues, affect, etc., infants pay less attention to segmental information. At eleven months, if the onset consonant in an unstressed syllable is changed (e.g. *canárd* to *ganárd* 'duck') infants treat both words as familiar (Hallé and Boysson-Bardies, 1996). Yet, if the phonetic detail is in a stressed syllable, infants tend to treat the mispronounced word as unfamiliar (Vihman et al., 2004). Changing the stress pattern of familiar words does not affect word recognition with 11-month-old infants (Vihman et al., 2004), but shifting the stress to another syllable in segmentally equivalent word forms diminishes word recognition for 7-month-infants (Curtin et al., 2005).

By eleven months of age, infants seem to begin to weigh segmental phonetic information more heavily than suprasegmental and indexical cues, at least in tasks measuring memory for familiar words. By this age, infants recognize a word even when affect, gender, and other such cues are varied (Singh et al., 2004). This may represent an important step in how changing weightings of information in word form representations helps build a phonology (Werker and Curtin, 2005).

In summary, during the first several months of life, infants are attending to a number of cues in the speech stream, and they are using this information to begin to pull out word and sound sequences. Moreover, they are able to remember and recognize familiar word forms. This ability to parse word forms from the continuous stream of speech and to remember them are critical steps in meaningful word learning. Learning the linkage between sound patterns and meaning is not an easy task, but with stored word forms, the infant can look for meaning and/or referents to map the words on to (Jusczyk, 1997).

35.4 **Word understanding**

35.4.1 **Recognizing word-referent mappings**

Across the second half of the first year of life, infants are beginning to understand the meaning of a few very frequent word forms. A number of studies examining parent reports of children from eight to sixteen months of age attribute 8-month-old infants with comprehension of an average of 36 words (Bates et al., 1995). While, as Bates et al. point out, parents might infer comprehension from a positive response from the child, laboratory studies provide evidence for only limited word understanding in these early months. Indeed, there are only a few experimental studies providing unequivocal evidence of infants' ability to look correctly toward a referent in the presence of a label (Tincoff and Jusczyk 1999), and most of these studies indicate only partial success at best prior to 1 year (see Woodward and Markman 1998, for a review). By twelve to thirteen months, however, infants seem to show recognition comprehension of an increasing number of words.

Word recognition tasks using familiar objects and familiar words reveal that infants use phonetic detail when recognizing meaningful words (see Figure 35.2a). For example, when presented with a display of two known objects, along with the correct label for one word and a mispronounced version of the second word, infants of fourteen to twenty four months will look more rapidly and longer toward the correct object (Swingley et al., 2000; 2002). Although there is some suggestion that perhaps overall word familiarity influences recognition, the effect is seen for both well-known and recently acquired words (Bailey and Plunkett, 2002). There may, however, be an effect of neighborhood density. When required to learn a new word (e.g. *gall*) that is similar to a well-known word (*ball*), infants as old as twenty months have difficulty (Swingley and Aslin, 2002), even though in a word recognition study they can easily detect the difference.

Several studies have begun to explore the time course in word recognition, and whether or not the entire word form is necessary for recognition. Using eye tracking as a measure of comprehension, Fernald et al. (1998) found that infants aged fifteen to twenty four months are faster and more accurate in identifying familiar words and looking to the appropriate picture. Twenty-four-month-olds respond more quickly when distinguishing words that differ in all segments (*dog* vs. *tree*) than to ones that overlap (*dog* vs. *doll*), suggesting that they are attending to word-initial information (Swingley et al., 1999). Indeed, even when presented with partial words, infants of eighteen to twenty months look as quickly and reliably to the appropriate object as they do when presented with whole words (e.g. *baby* [bey] and [beybi]; Fernald et al., 2001). These studies suggest that infants monitor the speech stream continuously and incrementally.

The Preferential Looking Word Recognition Task

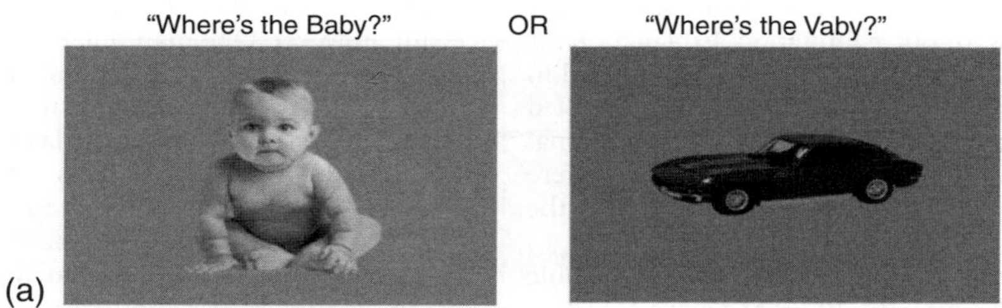

The Switch Task:

Sequential presentation of one word/object at a time

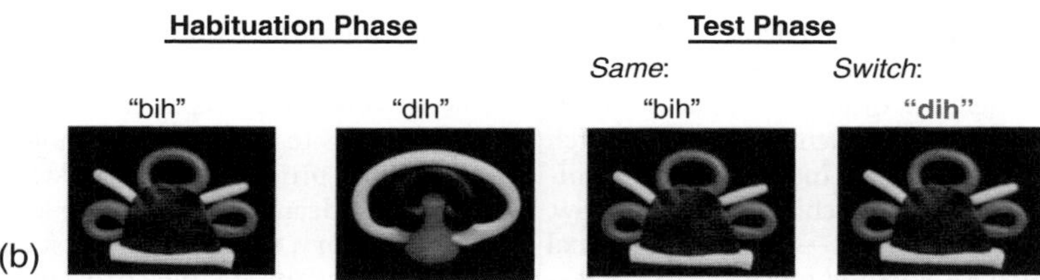

Figure 35.2 Looking tasks used in testing word recognition (a) and word learning (b) in infancy.

35.4.2 Learning new word–object associations

In naturalistic word learning contexts, early word learning (e.g. Baldwin 1995; Tomasello 1995), even early associative word learning (Hollich et al., 2000; Tomasello, 2003), is facilitated by a number of contextual and intentional cues. By thirteen to fifteen months, infants are reliably able to learn to link a heard word to an object if the two are presented together (Woodward and Markman, 1998).

A critical question in phonological development is whether infants use the phonetic knowledge built up during the first year of life to guide word learning. To investigate this question, it is necessary to use laboratory designs which carefully control the word learning situation. Empirical research on laboratory-based word learning indicates the youngest age at which infants can reliably link new words with new objects without contextual and intentional support to be around twelve to fifteen months of age (Hollich et al., 2000; Plunkett and Schafer, 1999).

In 1998, Werker, Cohen, and colleagues published a detailed article outlining an associative word-learning task, the Switch task (Figure 35.2b), which can be used to investigate the phonetic detail infants use to direct word learning. Infants are presented with two word–object pairings. On half the trials they see Object A paired with the spoken Word A, and on the other half of the trials, Object B paired with Word B. Infants are shown these pairings until their looking time declines to a criterial amount, i.e. they have "habituated." Following habituation they are shown two types of test trial. "Same" trials include a familiar word and familiar object in a familiar pairing. "Switch" trials contain a familiar word and a familiar object, but with the familiar pairing violated (e.g. Object A with Word B). If the infant has learned not only the word and the object but also the link between the two, they should be surprised at the violation and look longer on the Switch than on the Same trial. If they have learned only the words and objects and not their links, looking time should be equivalent on the Same and Switch trials. Infants of 14, but not 8, 10, or twelve months, can learn words in this procedure as long as the objects are moving (Werker et al., 1998).

Stager and Werker (1997) used the Switch task to examine the phonetic detail in newly learned words. It was found that although infants of fourteen months can learn to link phonetically dissimilar words such as [lIf] and [nim] to two different objects, they fail when the words are phonetically similar, such as [bI]–[dI], even though they can discriminate these syllables in a simple discrimination task. Stager and Werker proposed a "resource limitation" explanation for these results. Infants of fourteen months fail in this task because they are not yet accomplished word learners. Thus, the computational demands of linking words and objects interfere with their ability to attend to and access the phonetic detail in the words.

By seventeen months of age, infants are able learn the minimally different words [bI] and [dI] in the Switch task. Infants of fourteen months with particularly large vocabularies, who are presumably also more accomplished word learners, also succeed (Werker et al., 2002; Werker and Fennell, 2004). Further elaboration of the resource limitation hypothesis was provided by Fennell and others in a series of studies. If the computational demands of the Switch task are lightened by testing infants on minimally different words which they already know, e.g. *ball* [bal] vs. *doll* [dal]—which are minimal pairs in many North American dialects—infants of fourteen months succeed (Fennell and Werker, 2003). And, when the task is made easier by providing infants with pictures of both referents simultaneously, infants of fourteen months may be able to succeed even when learning two new words (Ballem and Plunkett, 2005). Indeed, even when the processing load is reduced by increasing object familiarity with no label (simply exposing the infant to an object over a period of weeks without it being given a label before bringing the infant into the lab), infants of fourteen months are able to learn minimally different words (Fennell, 2004; Fennell, p.c., June 2005).

Another way in which the word-learning task can be made easier is to present infants with very distinct forms which differ on multiple dimensions. Curtin and Werker (2004) presented 12-month-old infants with novel objects paired with trisyllabic words that differed in segmental and stress information (*BEdoka* and *tiPEgu*). Infants at this age were able to notice a switch in a mapping as demonstrated by longer looking times to the Switch trial. When the same-aged infants were habituated to a single trisyllabic string, and then presented with a switch in the stress information but with the segmental information intact, they looked longer to the Switch than to the Same trial. At the same time, infants were also presented with a switch item that differed in segmental information, but held the stress pattern constant; in this case they also looked longer to the Switch than to the Same trial.

Not all manipulations which make the task easier, or increase the acoustic salience, are successful, however. One manipulation that could make the task easier is to present the [b]–[d] contrast in a more typical word form than the atypical, and marked, consonant-lax vowel form of [bI]–[dI]. However, infants of fourteen months continue to fail in the Switch task even when tested on the more standard/canonical word forms, [bIn] vs [dIn]. Indeed, they also fail on the potentially less confusable voicing distinction [bIn]–p^hIn], and on a voicing + place distinction, [p^hIn]–[dIn] (Pater et al., 2004). In another recent report, infants of eighteen months failed to learn minimally different words which differ only in their word-medial vowel, even when acoustically quite distinct vowels were used (Nazzi, 2005). Thus, as the infant begins to establish a phonology, acoustic salience and processing factors likely play a continuing but decreasing role at the lexical level.

In summary, when infants first start linking words to meaning, they can sometimes fail to use phonetic detail. Although this difficulty has often been accounted for by claims of an underspecified representation, we offer instead a processing account. We suggest that at the initial stages of word learning, all the information about both the word form and the object is picked up. Because the task of linking words to objects is difficult, and because no abstract phonological categories are yet in place to establish weightings, the infant can make mistakes (Werker and Curtin, 2005). When the task is sufficiently simplified, however, access to and use of the phonetic detail is evident.

35.5 Producing speech

35.5.1 Babbling development

While productions of infants less than six months of age are limited to crying, vegetative sounds (sucking noises, grunts), some vocal play, cooing, and laughter (Oller 1980), during the period of roughly six to twelve months, when speech perception is becoming increasingly language-specific, infants show a number of important advances in babbling. At around six months, infants first begin to show canonical babbling, repeating CV syllables in strings. By eight months variegated babbling emerges, with the C or V changing from one syllable to the next (Oller, 1980; Stark, 1980).

Since the early suggestion by Weir (1966) that it is possible to ascertain, from listening to the babbling, what language environment infants are being raised in, researchers have looked for what Brown (1958) labeled the "babbling drift" in infant babbling. Although most early research failed to support this hypothesis (for a review, see Locke, 1983), recent evidence has provided support (for a review, see Vihman and Boysson-Bardies, 2001). Following the Weir procedure, Boysson-Bardies and colleagues (1984) played selections of babbling by 6-month-old French- and Arabic-learning infants to a group of phoneticians, who correctly identified the language of origin of the infants. Using procedures from experimental phonetics, deBoysson-Bardies and her colleagues later showed the formant values of both vowels and voicing to be like that of the native language by ten months of age (Boysson-Bardies et al., 1989; Boysson-Bardies et al., 1984). In perhaps their most convincing demonstration, they showed that by ten months, the proportionate distribution of manner classes in infant babbling had come to reflect the proportions in the adult language (Boysson-Bardies et al., 1992). Similarly, by this age, intonation differences in babbling have begun to diverge, and more closely reflect those of the native language (in this case French and English; Whalen et al., 1991).

Although it is not clear that there is native language-specificity, constraints on the phonotactic sequences infants produce are clearly seen in the canonical and variegated babbling stages. Davis and MacNeilage (2002) explain these in terms of articulatory ease, with adjacent articulators more likely to be activated in sequence than non-adjacent ones.

From this brief review, it appears that at the same ages that speech perception is becoming language-specific, so too is infant babbling. According to the Articulatory Filter Hypothesis (Vihman, 1991; 1993), babbling changes first, and acts as a filter for modifying perceptual categories. At least two other possible causal relations can be posited. In one, perception and production are each independently influenced by the ambient language. The theoretical viability of this type of relation has recently been demonstrated in a computational model (Westerman and Miranda, 2004). It is also possible that perception changes first and the reorganized perceptual categories guide production.

35.5.2 First words

In his famous book, Jakobson (1968/1941) claimed that babbling and speech were distinct. Indeed, he suggested that most children go through a period of silence after babbling and prior to the onset of speech. This proved to be incorrect, however. It is now known that babbling and speech overlap, with children continuing to vocalize both nonsense strings and meaningful words at initial entry into speech. Just as there is a continuity, albeit with some limitations, between changes in speech perception and word learning, there is now increasing data suggesting that there is a similar continuity in babbling. Segments mastered in babbling are among the first to appear in speech (Locke, 1983). And, early words adhere to the CV form first mastered in babbling, with coda Cs only emerging at a later date (Demuth 1996).

The phonological shape of early words is quite varied, although there are quite clear patterns that emerge from cross-linguistic data (see Vihman, 1996). In children's early productions, we often encounter forms which deviate from the adult target. In illustration, some children harmonize consonants (*duck* → *guck*; Smith, 1973; Goad, 1997; Pater, 1997; Bernhardt and Stemberger, 1998), some children reduce clusters (*snow* → *so*; Smith, 1973; Gnanadesiken, 2004; Barlow and Gierut, 1999), and some children substitute sounds (*rabbit* → *wabbit*; Ingram, 1981) in their productions. There are a number of potential reasons for deviations from the adult form: size of the lexicon, the perceptual system, an immature vocal tract, speech motor planning and control, and the extent to which the child's phonology has matured.

Children's productions are analyzed through a mature adult perceptual filter that may result in a disparity between child speech and adult comprehension. A study by Kornfeld and Goehl (1974) examining children's substitution of /w/ for /r/ found that some children are able to perceptually differentiate their intended /r/ productions which are realized as [w] from their intended /w/ productions, suggesting that these children acoustically mark these realizations. Thus, children's productions may manipulate sub-phonemic cues which are masked by the adult perceptual system (Macken and Barton, 1980; Hoffman et al., 1983; Scobbie, 1998). Scobbie (1998) argues that the child's expressive speech might not reveal the nature of the developing phonological system. In other words, what is deemed to be an immature system, whereby a contrast appears to be neutralized or modified in production, may be a covert contrast (Hewlett, 1988).

Whether or not children's productions are covert, clear patterns of phonological acquisition suggest that young children are sensitive to statistical information about the language input, such as sound segment frequency, and that this is reflected in their production patterns—low-frequency sounds in a language tend to be produced later and high-frequency sounds are produced sooner (Macken, 1995). Other empirically attested patterns seen in early word production include restricted consonants by position (Zamuner et al., 2005) and restricted consonants by frequency (Beckman and Edwards, 2000).

While frequency can help to explain segmental acquisition, saliency (or lack thereof) can help to explain prosodic development. Prosodic development is often described as a stage-like progression from language-general (unmarked) to language-specific (marked) patterns (Fikkert, 1994; Demuth and Fee, 1995; Demuth, 1997; Curtin, 2002). In the early stages, production of polysyllabic forms results in syllable omissions (*elephant* > [fant]). Children demonstrate this pattern when learning a number of different languages: Dutch (Fikkert, 1994), Polish (Roney, 1981), Spanish (Hochberg, 1986) and English (Smith, 1973; Pater and Paradis, 1996). Initially, the child truncates polysyllabic words to a single syllable. The child then produces disyllabic forms until finally he or she is no longer truncating words.

Traditionally, truncation patterns have been defined as the deletion of weak syllables (Allen and Hawkins, 1980; Demuth, 1995; 1997; Demuth and Fee, 1995; Gerken, 1991; 1996; Gleitman and Wanner, 1982). This analysis assumes that the full representation of the word is the child's lexicon. An alternative account of truncations argues that children's perceptual systems detect the salient properties of the signal (i.e. stressed and final syllables) (Echols and Newport 1992), suggesting that only these salient syllables are stored. Curtin (2002) argued that children have exemplar representations of words which include all of the relevant perceptual saliencies of stressed and final syllables. When children attempt to produce polysyllabic words, phonological constraints that require salient information to be included in production determine which syllables are realized (see Pater and Paradis, 1996 for a similar approach). It has also been argued that the position of the weak syllable in relation to the stressed syllable will have an effect on its rate of omission (Carter and Gerken, 1998), supporting an analysis which argues that more is involved than the deletion of weak syllables.

35.6 Perception-based approaches to phonological development

Standard theories of phonological development focus primarily on production, often beginning with the child's first productions as their starting point. However, many current and emerging models of phonological development include a role for perception as well (see Fikkert, 2007; Menn and Vihman, 2003, for reviews of theories of phonological development).

One of the guiding questions in phonological development is whether there is one lexicon that includes both production and perceptual representations, or whether there are two. Although two-lexicon models have been dominant in the past (e.g. Menn and Matthei, 1992), single-lexicon models are currently driving more theorizing and empirical research. The "one-lexicon" models being proposed are nonetheless quite diverse, from models based on Optimality Theory (e.g. Pater, 2004) to those based on Articulatory Phonology (e.g. Goldstein and Fowler, 2003).

Many models adopting an Optimality Theory (Prince and Smolensky, 1993) approach posit both a perception grammar or pathway and a production one, both of which feed into a single lexicon (Boersma, 1998; Pater, 2004). Within these models, assumptions about the initial state are varied. Hayes (2004) assumes inherent auditory boundaries, while Boersma et al. (2003) assume the preset ranking of category and perception constraints are part of the initial state. Peperkamp and Dupoux (2002) assume innate knowledge of two levels of phonological representation, distinctive features as primitives of phonological representations, feature structure of segments, types of rules that may operate on segments, and hierarchical organization of phonological constituents above the segmental level. In his theory, Pater allows for partial integration of phonetic knowledge when the rankings in the phonological system are first being set (Pater et al., 2004). The constraints and/or rankings of other theories emerge as frequency-driven generalizations from the lexicon (Beckman and Edwards, 2000; Pierrehumbert, 2003), or even specifically across the child's own lexicon (Fikkert and Levelt, forthcoming). The goal of these approaches is to converge on a phonological grammar that accounts for the patterns observed in children's productions, and early speech perception helps to determine the child's underlying representation, the initial constraint ranking, and the tools available to the child to figure out phonological patterns.

Articulatory phonology offers a different approach. Here it is assumed that the primitive units are the articulatory gestures, or vocal tract actions. These gestural units are combined and coordinated in different ways in speech production to yield different output, and are directly recovered from the acoustic signal in speech perception (Goldstein and Fowler, 2003). Phonological development entails the gradual differentiation of vocal gestures to map onto those experienced in the infant's linguistic environment (Best and McRoberts, 2003). It is further hypothesized that those native combinations that involve two gestures of the same vocal organ (i.e. the tongue vs. the tongue and the lips) will be the most difficult for infants to acquire, and perhaps the most vulnerable to loss if not in the input of the native language.

One of the most interesting and perplexing aspects of studying phonological development in children is that there is considerable variability in children across age, and across tasks. In part to account for this variability, Werker and Curtin (2005) proposed an integrated framework for understanding the link between prelexical and early lexical processing. PRIMIR (Processing Rich Information from Multidimensional Interactive Representations) argues that there is rich information available in the speech input, and that infants can pick this up and organize it along a number of multidimensional interactive planes (Figure 35.3). The earliest representations are richly detailed, encoding both phonetic and indexical information. It is only over time, and with the establishment of an adequate vocabulary containing multiple phonological contrasts, that more abstract phonemic representations emerge. It may be that some abstract representations are not solidified until the child learns to read.

PRIMIR accounts for the combination of exemplar-like and emergent phonological representations by positing multiple planes. The term "plane" is used to convey the concept that these representations are not hierarchical, but rather are dynamic and richly interactive with one another. At birth, both phonetic and indexical information are organized in a "General Perceptual" plane, with natural clusterings that become reweighted and reorganized as a function of listening experience and perceptual learning using general principles of statistical learning. This results in language-specific phonetic and indexical categories and preference for frequent phonotactic sequences and stress patterns, and ultimately results in the infants being able to appropriately segment meaningless "word forms" from continuous speech input. At this point in development, a "Word Form" plane emerges.

In the PRIMIR approach, the information in the "General Perceptual" (including reorganized categories) and the "Word Form" planes is then available, but may or may not be used depending upon the particular speech processing task. Access to the information depends on the joint activity of three dynamic filters: initial biases, the developmental level of the child, and requirements of the specific language task the child is facing (see Figure 35.3). These filters work together to differentially direct attention to one (or more) plane. This allows, for example, for access to language-specific phonetic categories in some tasks and language-general phonetic differences in others (as in Pisoni and Tash, 1974), or attention to the indexical information in a word at seven months, but attention to the segmental detail, particularly in stressed syllables, by eleven months.

Developmental change entails advancement, but this is not always obvious from the infant's performance in each and every task. PRIMIR also accounts for the observation that when infants first begin to link words to objects, they seem unable to utilize phonetic detail. PRIMIR builds on the resource limitation hypothesis

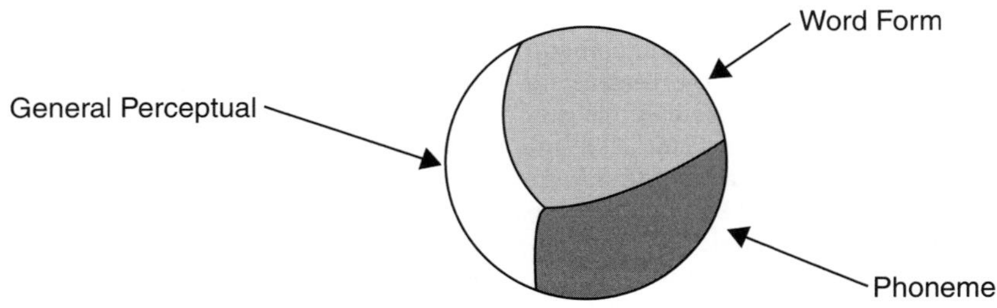

Figure 35.3 PRIMIR's three multidimensional planes.

(e.g. Fennell and Werker, 2003), by suggesting that for the novice word learner, the task of linking a word with an object interferes with utilization of the available phonetic detail. As reviewed above, when the task is made easier, access to segmental detail is available, even for the novice word learner. This is accounted for in PRIMIR by the filter of Task Demands. To account for the successful performance of older infants across even difficult tasks, PRIMIR (Werker and Curtin, 2005) proposes that after infants have established a criterial number of word–object linkages entailing any particular phonetic contrast, a "Phoneme Plane" will emerge. This Phoneme Plane includes all the information represented at the "Word Form" Plane, but with contrastive information highlighted. Once in place, the Phoneme Plane is available to drive information pick-up, enabling minimal-pair word learning.

The role of speech production is not well developed within PRIMIR in its present form. Nor is PRIMIR's relation to other phonological theories fully articulated. A critical feature of our thinking is the important role developmental changes in speech perception play in "bootstrapping" the emergence of a phonological system (Werker and Yeung, 2005). The "bootstrapping" approach is compatible with an approach that considers that either regularities in production development (even at the level of the individual child, as in Fikkert and Levelt, forthcoming) or the establishment of rankings in OT (e.g. Pater et al., 2004; Boersma et al., 2003) might contribute to the order in which General Perceptual and Word Form regularities are integrated into the Phoneme Plane in PRIMIR. It is important to note, however, that while PRIMIR includes perceptual level detail as part and parcel of the phonological representation, most other current theories of phonological development based in perception (with the exception of Articulatory Phonology) view the emerging phonological system as operating on phonological representations which are underspecified (stripped of all information that is non-contrastive with respect to phoneme categorization) (Fikkert and Levelt, forthcoming; Pater, 2004). Whether or not the underlying phonological representation is grounded in perception and phonetics (Hayes, 2004) or not (Hale and Reiss, 2000) is still a topic of debate, but the idea that children eventually develop abstract underlying phonological representations is still widely accepted in linguistic theory.

Recently, the claim that exemplar representations are available in phonological theory has begun to emerge (Pierrehumbert, 2001). According to Exemplar Theory (Goldinger 1996; 1998), every experience leaves a unique memory trace. Linguistic information is stored along with the immediate context in which it occurred, resulting in a complex representation (Lindblom, 2000). Exemplar models rely on the fact that while there is great variability in speech, it is also very systematic. As a consequence of data accumulation, systematic relationships among various dimensions appear. The resulting language categories are an emergent product of phonetic experience over time (Lindblom, 2000). Pierrehumbert (2001) proposes an exemplar model that implicitly defines word-specific probability distributions over acoustic phonetic features. It diverges from traditional phonological theory both in the use of very high-dimensional representations and in its dependence on probability theory.

PRIMIR argues for exemplar-type representations at the word-form level, but is compatible with the possibility that phonemes may not be fully specified when they begin to emerge. Once the Phoneme Plane has emerged, access to the word-form, exemplar-level detail remains possible. Hence, all the information need not be specified at the Phoneme Plane, and what information is accessed depends on how much the task engages the Phoneme vs. Word-Form Planes. In other words, phonemes may not be fully defined, or adult-like, in the beginning. However, experience with morphological alternations, word learning, and orthography will likely help to solidify these abstractions. How the developing lexicon and the phonological system evolve and/or interact is still under investigation. A goal of further theoretical development is to consider and develop these links.

35.7 Conclusion

In this chapter we have reviewed a number of key empirical findings which demonstrate the role of perception in phonological development. We illustrated the language-general speech perception capabilities evident in infants from birth through the first few months of life, demonstrated how and when the input language modifies infants' speech perception abilities, presented phonological and phonetic factors utilized in recognizing and segmenting word forms from the speech stream, and examined the role of phonology in early lexical comprehension. We then reviewed some of the empirical work from the production literature, beginning with infant babbling and continuing through the production of first words. Finally we presented current approaches to phonological development that are based in perception, with a specific focus on PRIMIR (Werker and Curtin, 2005).

While there is increasing agreement that perception lays the foundation for phonological development, a number of questions and controversies remain. The nature of the link between perception, the form of representations, and the relation between perception and production are particularly challenging questions. The increasing attempts by both psychologists and linguists to acknowledge these questions—and, more importantly, to share evidence and theorizing—positions us to make significant advances in explaining phonological development.

References

Allen, G., and Hawkins, S. (1980) Phonological rhythm: definition and development. In G. H. Yeni-Komshian, J. Kavanagh, and C. Ferguson (eds), *Child Phonology*, vol: 1: *Production*, pp. 227–56. Academic Press, New York.

Anderson, J. L., Morgan, L., and White, K. S. (2003) A statistical basis for speech sound discrimination. *Language and Speech*, 46: 155–82.

Aslin, R. N., and Pisoni, D. B. (1980) Some developmental processes in speech perception. In G. H Yeni-Komshian, J. F. Kavanagh and C. A. Ferguson (eds), *Child Phonology*, vol. 2: *Perception*, pp. 67–96. Academic Press, New York.

Aslin, R. N., Pisoni, D. B., Hennessy, B. L., and Perey, A. J. (1981) Discrimination of voice onset time by human infants: new findings and implications for the effects of early experience. *Child Development*, 52: 1135–45.

Bailey, T. M., and Plunkett, K. (2002) Phonological specificity in early words. *Cognitive Development*, 17: 1265–82.

Baldwin, D. A. (1995) Understanding the link between joint attention and language. In C. Moore and P. Dunham (eds), *Joint Attention: Its Origins and Role in Development*, pp. 131–58. Erlbaum, Hillsdale, NJ.

Ballem, K. D., and Plunkett K (2005) Phonological specificity in children at 1–2. *Journal of Child Language*, 32: 159–73.

Barlow, J. A., and Gierut, J. A. (1999) Optimality theory in phonological acquisition. *Journal of Speech, Language and Hearing Research*, 42: 1482–98.

Bates, E., Dale, P. S., and Thal, D. (1995) Individual differences and their implications for theories of language development. In P. Fletcher and B. MacWhinney (eds), *Handbook of Child Language*, pp. 96–151. Blackwell, Oxford.

Beckman, M. E., and Edwards, J. (2000) The ontogeny of phonological categories and the primacy of lexical learning in linguistic development. *Child Development*, 71: 240–9.

Bernhardt, B., and Stemberger, J. P. (1998) *Handbook of Phonological Development: From the Perspective of Constraint-Based Nonlinear Phonology.* Academic Press, San Diego, CA.

Bertoncini, J., Bijeljac-Babic, R., Blumstein, S., and Mehler, J. (1987) Discrimination of very short CV syllables by neonates. *Journal of the Acoustical Society of America*, 82: 31–7.

Bertoncini, J., and Mehler, J. (1981) Syllables as units in infant speech perception. *Infant Behavior and Development*, 4: 247–60.

Best, C. T. (1994) The emergence of native-language phonological influences in infants: a perceptual assimilation model. In J. C. Goodman and H. C. Nusbaum (eds), *The Development of Speech Perception: The Transition from Speech Sounds to Spoken Words*, pp. 167–224. MIT Press, Cambridge, MA.

Best, C. T., and McRoberts, G. W. (2003) Infant perception of nonnative contrasts that adults assimilate in different ways. *Language and Speech*, 46: 183–216.

Best, C. T., McRoberts, G. W., LaFleur, R., and Silver-Isenstadt, J. (1995) Divergent developmental patterns for infants' perception of two nonnative consonant contrasts. *Infant Behavior and Development*, 18: 339–50.

Best, C. T., McRoberts, G. W., and Sithole, N. M. (1988) Examination of perceptual reorganization for nonnative speech contrasts: Zulu click discrimination by English-speaking adults and infants. *Journal of Experimental Psychology: Human Perception and Performance*, 14: 345–60.

Bijeljac Babic, R., Bertoncini, J., and Mehler, J. (1993) How do 4-day-old infants categorize multisyllabic utterances? *Developmental Psychology*, 29: 711–21.

Boersma, P. (1998) *Functional Phonology.* Holland Academic Graphics, The Hague.

Boersma, P., Escudero, P., and Hayes, R. (2003) Learning abstract phonological from auditory phonetic categories: an integrated model for the acquisition of language-specific sound categories. *Proceedings of the 15th International Congress of Phonetic Sciences*, Barcelona, 3–9 August, pp. 1013–16.

Bortfeld, H., Rathbun, K., Morgan, J., and Golinkoff, R. (2005) Mommy and me. *Psychological Science*, 16: 298–304.

Bosch, L., and Sebastián-Gallés, N. (1997) Native language recognition abilities in 4-month-old infants from monolingual and bilingual environments. *Cognition*, 65: 33–97.

Bosch, L., and Sebastián-Gallés, N. (2001) Evidence of early language discrimination abilities in infants from bilingual environments. *Infancy*, 2: 29–49.

Bosch, L., and Sebastián-Gallés, N. (2003) Simultaneous bilingualism and the perception of a language-specific vowel contrast in the first year of life. *Language and Speech* 46: 217–43.

Boysson-Bardies, B. de (1999): *How Language Comes to Children.* MIT Press, Cambridge, MA.

Boysson-Bardies, B. de, Halle, P., Sagart, L., and Durand, C. (1989) A crosslinguistic investigation of vowel formants in babbling. *Journal of Child Language*, 16: 1–18.

Boysson-Bardies, B. de, Sagart, L., and Durand, C. (1984) Discernible differences in the babbling of infants according to target language. *Journal of Child Language*, 11: 1–15.

Boysson-Bardies, B. de, Vihman, M. M., Roug-Hellichius, L., Durand, C., Landberg, I., and Arao, F. (1992) Material evidence of infant selection from the target language: a cross-linguistic phonetic study. In C. Ferguson, L. Menn, and C. Stoel-Gammon (eds), *Phonological Development: Models, Research, Implications*, pp. 369–91.York Press, Timonium, Md.

Brown, R. (1958) *Words and Things*. Free Press, Glencoe, Ill.

Bull, D., Eilers, R. E., and Oller, D. K. (1984) Infants' discrimination of intensity variation in multisyllabic stimuli. *Journal of the Acoustical Society of America*, 76: 13–17.

Burnham, D., Tyler, M., and Horlyck, S. (2002) Periods of speech perception development and their vestiges in adulthood. In P. Burmeister, T. Piske, and A. Rohde (eds), *An Integrated View of Language Development: Papers in honor of Henning Wode*, pp. 281–300. Wissenschaftlicher Verlag Trier, Trier.

Burns, T. C., Yoshida, K. A., Hill, K., and Werker, J. F. (forthcoming) Bilingual and monolingual infant phonetic development. *Applied Psycholinguistics.*

Carter, A., and Gerken, L. (1998) Evidence for adult representations in weak syllable omissions of young children. In *Proceedings of Annual Child Language Research Forum*, 29: 101–10.

Chambers, K. E., Onishi, K. H., and Fisher, C. (2003) Infants learn phonotactic regularities from brief auditory experiences. *Cognition*, 87: B69–B77.

Cheour, M., Ceponiene, R., and Lehtokoski, A., et al. (1998) Development of language-specific phoneme representations in the infant brain. *Nature Neuroscience*, 1: 351–3.

Christophe, A., Mehler J., and Sebastián-Gallés, N. (2001) Perception of prosodic boundary correlates by newborn infants. *Infancy*, 2: 385–94.

Colombo, J. A., and Bundy, R. S. (1981) A method for the measurement of infant auditory selectivity. *Infant Behavior and Development*, 4: 219–23.

Cooper, R. P., and Aslin, R. (1990) Preference for infant-directed speech in the first month after birth. *Child Development*, 61: 1584–95.

Curtin, S. (2002) Representational richness in phonological development. Doctoral dissertation, University of Southern California.

Curtin, S., Mintz, T. H., and Byrd, D. (2001) Coarticulatory cues enhance infants' recognition of syllable sequences in speech. In A. H. J. Do, L. Dominguez, and A. Johansen (eds), *Proceedings of the 25th Annual Boston University Conference on Language Development*, pp. 190–201. Cascadilla Press, Somerville, MA.

Curtin, S., Mintz, T. H., and Christiansen, M. H. (2005) Stress changes the representational landscape: evidence from word segmentation. *Cognition*, 96: 233–62.

Curtin, S., and Werker, J. F. (2004) Patterns of new word object associations. In L. Micciulla and C. E. Smith (eds), *Proceedings of the 28th Annual Boston University Conference on Language Development*, pp. 120–28. Cascadilla Press, Sommerville, MA.

Davis, B. L., and MacNeilage, P. F. (2002) The internal structure of the syllable: an ontogenetic perspective on origins. In T. Givón and B. F. Malle (eds), *The Evolution of Language out of Pre-Language*, pp. 135–53. Benjamins, Amsterdam.

DeCasper, A. J., and Fifer, W. P. (1980) Of human bonding: newborns prefer their mothers' voices. *Science*, 208: 1174–6.

DeCasper, A. J., and Spence, M. J. (1986) Prenatal maternal speech influences newborns' perception of speech sounds. *Infant Behavior and Development*, 9: 133–50.

Dehaene-Lambertz, G., Dehaene, S., and Hertz-Pannier, L. (2002) Functional neuroimaging of speech perception in infants. *Science*, 298: 2013–15.

Dehaene-Lambertz, G., Dupoux, E., and Gout, A. (2002) Electrophysiological correlates of phonological processing: a cross-linguistic study. *Journal of Cognitive Neuroscience*, 12: 635–47.

Dehaene-Lambertz, G., and Gliga, T. (2004) Common neural basis for phoneme processing in infants and adults. *Journal of Cognitive Neuroscience*, 16: 1375–87.

Dehaene-Lambertz, G., and Peña, M. (2001) Electrophysiological evidence for automatic phonetic processing in neonates. *Neuroreport*, 12: 3155–8.

Demuth, K. (1995) Markedness and the development of prosodic structure. In J. Beckman (ed.), *Proceedings of NELS 25*, pp. 13–25. GLSA, Amherst, MA.

Demuth, K. (1996) The prosodic structure of early words. In J. Morgan and K. Demuth (eds), *Signal to Syntax: Bootstrapping from Speech to Grammar in Early Acquisition*, pp. 171–84. Erlbaum, Mahwah, NJ.

Demuth, K. (1997). Variation in acquisition: an optimal approach. In S. Davis (ed.), *Optimality Viewpoints*, pp. 77–88. Bloomington: Indiana University Linguistics Club.

Demuth, K., and Fee, E. J. (1995) Minimal words in early phonological development. MS, Brown University and Dalhousie University.

Diehl, R. L., Lotto, A. J., and Holt, L. L. (2004) Speech perception. *Annual Review of Psychology*, 55: 149–79.

Echols, C. H., Crowhurst, M. J., and Childers, J. (1997) The perception of rhythmic snits in speech by infants and adults. *Journal of Memory and Language*, 36: 202–25.

Echols, C., and Newport, E. (1992) The role of stress and position in determining first words. *Language and Acquisition*, 2: 189–220.

Eilers, R. E., Bull, D. H., Oller, D. K., and Lewis, D. C. (1984) The discrimination of vowel duration by infants. *Journal of the Acoustical Society of America*, 75: 1213–18.

Eimas, P. D., Siqueland, E. R., Jusczyk, P., and Vigorito, J. (1971) Speech perception in infants. *Science*, 171: 303–6.

Fennell, C. T. (2004) Infant attention to phonetic detail in word forms: knowledge and familiarity effects. Doctoral dissertation, University of British Columbia.

Fennell, C. T., and Werker, J. F. (2003) Early word learners' ability to access phonetic detail in well-known words. *Language and Speech*, 46: 245–64.

Fernald, A., Pinto, J. P., Swingley, D., Weinberg, A., and McRoberts, G. (1998) Rapid gains in speed of verbal processing by infants in the second year. *Psychological Science*, 9: 228–231. Reprinted in M. Tomasello and E. Bates (eds), *Language Development: The Essential Readings*. Blackwell, Oxford, 2001.

Fernald, A., Swingley, D., and Pinto, J. P. (2001) When half a word is enough: infants can recognize spoken words using partial phonetic information. *Child Development*, 72: 1003–15.

Fikkert, P. (1994) *On the Acquisition of Prosodic Structure*. Leiden: Holland Institute of Generative Linguistics.

Fikkert, P. (2007) Acquiring phonology. In P. de Lacy (ed.), *Handbook of Phonological Theory*. Cambridge University Press, New York.

Fikkert, P., and Levelt, C. (forthcoming) How does place fall into place? The lexicon and emerging constraints in children's developing phonological grammar. In B. Elan Dresher and K. Rice (eds), *Contrast in Phonology: Perception and Acquisition*. Mouton de Gruyter, Berlin.

Gerken, L. (1991) The metrical basis for children's subjectless sentences. *Journal of Memory and Language*, 30: 431–51.

Gerken, L. (1996) Prosodic structure in young children's language production. *Language*, 72: 683–712.

Gerken, L. A. (2004) Nine-month-olds extract structural principles required for natural language. *Cognition*, 3: B89–B96.

Gleitman, L. R., and Wanner, E. (1982) Language acquisition: the state of the state of the art. In E Wanner and LR Gleitman (eds), *Language Acquisition: The State of the Art*, pp. 3–48. Cambridge University Press, New York.

Glenn, S. M., Cunningham, C. C., and Joyce, P. F. (1981) A study of auditory preferences in nonhandicapped infants and infants with Down's syndrome. *Child Development*, 52: 1303–7.

Gnanadesikan, A. (2004) Markedness and faithfulness constraints in child phonology. In R Kager, J Pater, and W Zonneveld (eds), *Constraints in Phonological Acquisition*, pp. 73–108. Cambridge University Press, New York.

Goad, H. (1997) Consonant harmony in child language. In SJ Hannahs and M Young-Scholten (eds), *Focus on Phonological Acquisition*, pp. 113–42. Benjamins, Amsterdam.

Goldinger, S. D. (1996) Words and voices: episodic traces in spoken word identification and recognition memory. *Journal of Experimental Psychology: Learning, Memory, and Cognition*, 22: 1166–83.

Goldinger, S. D. (1998) Echoes of echoes? An episodic theory of lexical access. *Psychological Review*, 105: 251–79.

Goldstein, L., and Fowler, C. A. (2003) Articulatory phonology: a phonology for public language use. In N. O. Schiler and A. S. Meyer (eds), *Phonetics and Phonology in Language Comprehension and Production*, pp. 159–207. Mouton de Gruyter, Berlin.

Hale, M., and Reiss, C. (2000) Substance abuse and dysfunctionalism: current trends in phonology. *Linguistic Inquiry*, 31: 157–69.

Halle, P. A., and Boysson-Bardies, B. de (1996) The format of representation of recognized words in infants' early receptive lexicon. *Infant Behavior and Development*, 19: 463–81.

Hayes, B. (2004) Phonological acquisition in Optimality Theory: the early stages. In R. Kager, J. Pater, and W. Zonneveld (eds), *Constraints in Phonological Acquisition*, pp. 158–203. Cambridge University Press, New York.

Hewlett, N. (1988) Acoustic properties of /k/ and/t/ in normal and phonologically disordered speech. *Clinical Linguistics and Phonetics*, 2: 29–45.

Hochberg, J. (1986) The acquisition of word stress rules in Spanish. Doctoral dissertation, Stanford University.

Hoffman, P. R., Stager, S., and Daniloff, R. G. (1983) Perception and production of misarticulated /r/. *Journal of Speech and Hearing Disorders*, 48: 210–15.

Hollich, G., Hirsh-Pasek, K., and Golinkoff, R. (2000) Breaking the language barrier: an emergentist coalition model of word learning. *Monographs of the Society for Research in Child Development*, 65 (3, Serial No. 262).

Houston, D. M., and Jusczyk, P. W. (2000) The role of talker-specific information in word segmentation by infants. *Journal of Experimental Psychology: Human Perception and Performance*, 26: 1570–82.

Houston, D. M., and Jusczyk, P. W. (2003) Infants' long-term memory for the sound patterns of words and voices. *Journal of Experimental Psychology: Human Perception and Performance*, 29: 1143–54.

Ingram, D. (1981) *Procedures for the Phonological Analysis of Children's Language*. University Park Press, Baltimore, MD.

Jakobson, R. 1968. *Child Language, Aphasia, and Phonologic Universals*. Mouton, The Hague. (*Kindersprache, Aphasie und allgemeine Lautgesetze*, Uppsala: Almqvist & Wiksell, 1941).

Johnson, E. K., and Jusczyk, P. W. (2001) Word segmentation by 8-month-olds: when speech cues count more than statistics. *Journal of Memory and Language*, 44: 548–67.

Jusczyk, P. W. (1997) *The Discovery of Spoken Language*. MIT Press, Cambridge, MA.

Jusczyk, P., and Aslin, R. (1995) Infants' detection of the sound patterns of words in fluent speech. *Cognitive Psychology*, 29: 1–23.

Jusczyk, P. W., Cutler, A., and Redanz, N. J. (1993) Infants' preference for the predominant stress patterns of English words. *Child Development*, 64: 675–87.

Jusczyk. P. W., and Derrah, C. (1987) Representation of speech sounds by young infants. *Developmental Psychology*, 23: 648–54.

Jusczyk, P. W., Friederici, A. D., Wessels, J., Svenkerud, V. Y., and Jusczyk, A. M. (1993). Infants' sensitivity to the sound patterns of native language words. *Journal of Memory and Language*, 32: 402–20.

Jusczyk, P. W., and Hohne, E. A. (1997) Infants' memory for spoken words. *Science*, 277: 1984–6.

Jusczyk, P. W., Hohne, E. A., and Bauman, A. (1999) Infants' sensitivity to allophonic cues to word segmentation. *Perception and Psychophysics*, 61: 1465–76.

Jusczyk, P. W., Houston, D. M., and Newsome, M. (1999) The beginnings of word segmentation in English-learning infants. *Cognitive Psychology*, 39: 159–207.

Jusczyk, P. W., and Thompson, E. J. (1978) Perception of a phonetic contrast in multisyllabic utterances by two month-old infants. *Perception and Psychophysics*, 23: 105–9.

Karzon, R. G. (1985) Discrimination of polysyllabic sequences by one-to-four-month-old infants. *Journal of Experimental Child Psychology*, 39: 326–42.

Kornfeld, J. R., and Goehl, H. (1974) A new twist to an old observation: kids know more than they say. In *Papers from the Tenth Annual Meeting of the Chicago Linguistic Society, Parasession on Natural Phonology*, pp. 210–19. Chicago Linguistic Society, Chicago.

Kuhl, P. K. (1987) The special-mechanisms debate in speech research: categorization tests on animals and infants. In S. Harnad (ed.), *Categorical Perception: The Groundwork of Cognition*, pp. 355–86. Cambridge University Press, New York.

Kuhl, P. K. (1993) Innate predispositions and the effects of experience in speech perception: the native language magnet theory. In B. de Boysson-Bardies, S. de Schonen, P. Jusczyk, P. McNeilage, and J. Morton (eds), *Developmental Neurocognition: Speech and Face Processing in the First year of Life*, pp. 259–74. Kluwer Academic, Dordrecht, Netherlands.

Kuhl, P. K. (2004) Early language acquisition: cracking the speech code. *Nature Reviews Neuroscience*, 5: 831–43.

Kuhl, P. K., Andruski, J. E., Chistovich, I. A., et al. (1997) Cross-language analysis of phonetic units in language addressed to infants. *Science*, 277: 684–6.

Kuhl, P. K., and Coffey-Corina, S. (2001) Language and the developing brain: changes in ERPs as a function of linguistic experience. Paper presented at the meeting of the Cognitive Neuroscience Society, New York, November.

Kuhl, P. K., Stevens, E., Hiyashi, A., Deguchi, T., Kiritani, S., and Iverson, P. (2006) Infants show a facilitation effect for native language perception between 6 and twelve months. *Developmental Science*, 9: F1–F9.

Kuhl, P. K., Williams, K. A., Lacerda, F., Stevens, K. N., and Lindblom, B. (1992) Linguistic experience alters phonetic perception in infants by six months of age. *Science*, 255: 606–8.

Lasky, R. E., Syrdal-Lasky, A., and Klein, R. E. (1975) VOT discrimination by four- to six-and-a-half-month-old infants from Spanish environments. *Journal of Experimental Child Psychology*, 20: 215–25.

Lecanuet, J. P., Granier-Deferre, C., and Busnel, M. C. (1995) Human fetal auditory perception. In J.-P. Lecanuet and W. P. Fifer (eds), *Fetal Development: A Psychobiological Perspective*, pp. 239–62. Erlbaum, Hillsdale, NJ.

Lindblom, B. (2000) Developmental origins of adult phonology: the interplay between phonetic emergents and the evolutionary adaptations of sound patterns. *Phonetica*, 57: 297–314.

Lisker, L., and Abramson, A. S. (1967) Some effects of context on voice onset time in English stops. *Language and Speech*, 10: 1–28.

Lively, S. E., and Pisoni, D. B. (1997) On prototypes and phonetic categories: a critical assessment of the perceptual magnet effect in speech perception. *Journal of Experimental Psychology: Human Perception and Performance*, 23: 1665–79.

Locke, J. L. 1983. *Phonological Acquisition and Change*. Academic Press, New York.

Macken, M. A. (1995) Phonological acquisition. In J. Goldsmith (ed.), *The Handbook of Phonological Theory*, pp. 671–96. Blackwell, Cambridge, MA.

Macken, M. A., and Barton, D. (1980) The acquisition of the voicing contrast in English: a and study of voice onset time in word-initial stop consonants. *Journal of Child Language*, 7: 41–74.

Mandel, D. R., Jusczyk, P. W., and Pisoni, D. B. (1995) Infants' recognition of the sound patterns of their own names. *Psychological Science*, 6: 315–18.

Mandel-Emer, D. (1997) Names as early lexical candidates: helpful in language processing? Doctoral dissertation, State University of New York, Buffalo.

Marean, G. C., Werner, L. A., and Kuhl, P. K. (1992) Vowel categorization by very young infants. *American Psychological Association*, 28: 396–405.

Mattys, S. L., and Jusczyk, P. W. (2001) Do infants segment words or continuous recurring patterns? *Journal of Experimental Psychology: Human Perception and Performance*, 27: 644–55.

Mattys, S. L., Jusczyk, P. W., Luce, P. A., and Morgan, J. L. (1999) Phonotactic and prosodic effects on word segmentation in infants. *Cognitive Psychology*, 38: 465–94.

Maye, J., Weiss, D., and Aslin R. N. (forthcoming) Statistical phonetic learning in infants: facilitation and feature generation. *Developmental Science*.

Maye, J., Werker, J. F., and Gerken, L. A. (2002) Infant sensitivity to distributional information can affect phonetic discrimination. *Cognition*, 82: B101–B111.

McMurray, B., and Aslin, R. N. (2005) Infants are sensitive to within-category variation in speech perception. *Cognition*, 95: B15–B26.

McQueen, J. M. (1998) Segmentation of continuous speech using phonotactics. *Journal of Memory and Language*, 39: 21–46.

Mehler, J., and Christophe, A. (1995) Maturation and learning of language in the first year of life. In M. S. Gazzaniga (ed.), *The Cognitive Neurosciences: A Handbook for the Field*, pp. 943–54. MIT Press, Cambridge, MA.

Mehler, J., Jusczyk, P., Lambertz, G., Halsted, N., Bertoncini, J., and Amiel-Tison, C. (1988) A precursor of language acquisition in young infants. *Cognition*, 29: 143–78.

Menn, L., and Matthei, E. (1992) The two-lexicon model of child phonology: looking back, looking ahead. In C. Ferguson, L. Menn, and C. Stoel-Gammon (eds), *Phonological Development: Models, Research, Implications*, pp. 211–47. York Press, Timonium, MD.

Menn, L., and Vihman, M. M. (2003) Acquisition of phonology. In W. Frawley (ed.), *Oxford International Encyclopedia of Linguistics*, 2nd edn. Oxford University Press, Oxford.

Miller, J. L., and Eimas, P. D. (1996) Internal structure of voicing categories in early infancy. *Perception and Psychophysics*, 58: 1157–1167.

Mills, D. L., Prat, C., Zangl, R., Stager, C. L., Neville, H. J., and Werker, J. F. (2004) Language experience and the organization of brain activity to phonetically similar words: ERP evidence from 14- and 20-month-olds. *Journal of Cognitive Neuroscience*, 16: 1–13.

Morgan, J. L., and Saffran, J. R. (1995) Emerging integration of sequential and suprasegmental information in preverbal speech segmentation. *Child Development*, 66: 911–36.

Narayan, C. (2005) Follow your nose: non-native nasal consonant discrimination in infancy. Boston University Conference on Child Language Development, November.

Nazzi, T. (2005). Use of phonetic specificity during the acquisition of new words: differences between consonants and vowels. *Cognition*, 98: 13–30.

Nazzi, T., Bertoncini, J., and Mehler, J. (1998) Language discrimination by newborns: toward an understanding of the role of rhythm. *Journal of Experimental Psychology: Human Perception and Performance*, 24: 756–66.

Nazzi, T., and Ramus, F. (2003) Perception and acquisition of linguistic rhythm by infants. *Speech Communication*, 41, 233–43.

Oller, K. D. (1980) The emergence of the sounds of speech in infancy. In G. Yeni- Komshian, J. Kavanaugh, and C. Ferguson (eds), *Child Phonology*, pp. 93–112. Academic Press, New York.

Oller, D. K. (1986) Metaphonology and infant vocalizations. In B. Lindblom and R. Zetterstrom (eds), *Precursors of Early Speech*, pp. 21–35. Stockton Press, New York.

Panneton, C. R., and Ostroff, W. (2003, May) Task-specific influences on attention to infant-directed speech and non-native speech during infancy. Paper presented at the University of Melbourne, Australia.

Pater, J. (1997) Minimal violation and phonological development. *Language Acquisition*, 6: 201–53.

Pater, J. (2004) Bridging the gap between perception and production with minimally violable constraints. In R. Kager, J. Pater, and W. Zonneveld (eds), *Constraints in Phonological Acquisition*, pp. 219–44. Cambridge University Press, New York.

Pater, J., and Paradis, J. (1996) Truncation without templates in child phonology. In *Proceedings of the 20th Annual Boston University Conference on Language Development*, pp. 540–51. Cascadilla Press, Somerville, MA.

Pater, J., Stager, C. L., and Werker, J. F. (2004) The lexical acquisition of phonological contrasts. *Language*, 80: 361–79.

Pegg, J. E., and Werker, J. F. (1997) Adult and infant perception of two English phones. *Journal of the Acoustical Society of America*, 102: 3742–53.

Peña, M., Maki, A., Kovacic, D., et al. (2003) Sounds and silence: an optical topography study of language recognition at birth. *Proceedings of the National Academy of Sciences*, 100: 11702–5.

Peperkamp, S., and Dupoux, E. (2002) Coping with phonological variation in early lexical acquisition. In I. Lasser (ed.), *The Process of Language Acquisition*, pp. 359–85. Lang, Frankfurt.

Pierrehumbert, J. B. (2001) Exemplar dynamics: word frequency, lenition and contrast. In J. Bybee and P. Hopper (eds), *Frequency Effects and Emergent Grammar*, pp. 137–57. Benjamins, Amsterdam.

Pierrehumbert, J. (2003) Probabilistic phonology: discrimation and robustness. In R. Bod, J. Hay, and S. Jannedy (eds), *Probability Theory in Linguistics*, pp. 177–228. MIT Press, Cambridge, MA.

Pisoni, D. B., and Lively, S. E. (1995) Variability and invariance in speech perception: a new look at some old problems in perceptual learning. In W. Strange (ed.), *Speech Perception and Linguistic Experience*, pp. 433–59. York Press, Timonium, MD.

Pisoni, D. B., and Tash, J. (1974) Reaction times to comparisons within and across phonetic categories. *Perception and Psychophysics*, 15: 285–90.

Plunkett, K., and Schafer, G. (1999) Early speech perception and word learning. In M. Barrett (ed.), *The Development of Language*, pp. 51–71. Psychology Press, London.

Polka, L., and Bohn, O. S. (1996) A cross-language comparison of vowel perception in English-learning and German-learning infants. *Journal of the Acoustical Society of America*, 100: 577–92.

Polka, L., and Bohn, O. S. (2003) Asymmetries in vowel perception. *Speech Communication*, 41: 221–31.

Polka, L., Colantonio, C., and Sundara, M. (2001) A cross-language comparison of /d/–/th/perception: evidence for a new developmental pattern. *Journal of the Acoustical Society of America*, 109: 2190–2201.

Polka, L., Sundara, M., and Blue, S. (2002, June) The role of language experience in word segmentation: a comparison of English, French, and bilingual infants. Paper presented at the 143rd meeting of the Acoustical Society of America: special session in memory of Peter Jusczyk, Pittsburgh, PA.

Polka, L., and Werker, J. F. (1994) Developmental changes in perception of nonnative vowel contrasts. *Journal of Experimental Psychology: Human Perception and Performance*, 20: 421–35.

Prince, A., and Smolensky, P. (1993) Optimality Theory: constraint interaction in generative grammar. MS, Rutgers University and University of Colorado, Boulder.

Ramus, F., Hauser, M. D., Miller, C., Morris, D., and Mehler, J. (2000) Language discrimination by human newborns and by cotton-top tamarin monkeys. *Science*, 288: 349–51.

Ratner, N. B. (1984) Patterns of vowel modification in mother–child speech. *Journal of Child Language*, 11: 557–78.

Ratner, N. B., and Luberoff, A. (1984) Cues to post-vocalic voicing in mother-child speech. *Journal of Phonetics*, 12: 285–9.

Rivera-Gaxiola, M., Silva-Pereyra, J., Garcia-Sierra, A., Klarman, L., and Kuhl, P. K. (2003) Event-related potentials to native and non-native speech contrasts in 7 and 11 month old American infants. Paper presented at the 10th annual meeting of the Cognitive Neuroscience Society, New York.

Rivera-Gaxiola, M., Silva-Pereyra, J., and Kuhl, P. K. (2005) Brain potentials to native and non-native speech contrasts in seven- and eleven-month-old American infants. *Developmental Science*, 8: 162–72.

Roney, D. W. (1981) Syllable elision: aspects of the acquisition of polish phonology by the native speaker. Doctoral dissertation, Ohio State University.

Saffran, J. R., Aslin. R. N., and Newport, E. L. (1996) Statistical learning by 8-month-old infants. *Science*, 274: 1926–8.

Saffran, J. R., Newport, E. L., and Aslin, R. N. (1996) Word segmentation: the role of distributional cues. *Journal of Memory and Language*, 35: 606–21.

Saffran, J. R., and Thiessen, E. D. (2003) Pattern induction by infant language learners. *Developmental Psychology*, 39: 484–94.

Saffran, J. R., Werker, J. F., and Werner, L. (2006) The infant's auditory world: hearing, speech, and the beginnings of language. In D. Kuhn and R. Siegler (eds), *Handbook of Child Psychology*, 6th edn, vol. 2: *Cognition, Perception, and Language*, pp.58–108. Wiley, New York.

Scobbie, J. M. (1998) Interactions between the acquisition of phonetics and phonology. In M. C. Gruber, D. Higgins, K. Olson, and T. Wysocki (eds), *Papers from the 34th Annual Regional Meeting of the Chicago Linguistic Society*, vol. 2: *The Panels*, pp. 343–58. Chicago Linguistics Society, Chicago.

Shi, R., Cutler, A., and Werker, J. (2006) Form and frequency as determinants of functor sensitivity in English-acquiring infants. *Journal of the Acoustical Society of America*, 119: EL61–EL67.

Singh, L., Morgan, J., and White, K. (2004) Preference and processing: the role of speech affect in early speech spoken word recognition. *Journal of Memory and Language*, 51: 173–89.

Smith, N. (1973) *The Acquisition of Phonology: A Case Study*. Cambridge University Press, Cambridge.

Stager, C. L., and Werker, J. F. (1997) Infants listen for more phonetic detail in speech perception than in word learning tasks. *Nature*, 388: 381–2.

Stark, R. E. (1980) Prespeech segmental feature development. In G. Yeni-Komshian, J. Kavanaugh, and C. Ferguson (eds), *Child Phonology*, pp. 73–92. Academic Press, New York.

Streeter, L. A. (1976) Language perception in 2-month-old infants shows effects of both innate mechanisms and experience. *Nature*, 259: 39–41.

Swain, I. U., Zelazo, P. R., and Clifton, R. K. (1993) Newborn infants' memory for speech sounds retained over 24 hours. *Developmental Psychology*, 29: 312–23.

Swingley, D., and Aslin, R. N. (2000) Spoken word recognition and lexical representation in very young children. *Cognition*, 76: 147–66.

Swingley, D., and Aslin, R. N. (2002) Lexical neighborhoods and the word-form representations of 14-month-olds. *Psychological Science*, 13: 480–4.

Swingley, D., Pinto, J. P., and Fernald, A. (1999) Continuous processing in word recognition at twenty four months. *Cognition*, 71: 73–108.

Swoboda, P. J., Morse, P. A., and Leavitt, L. A. (1976) Continuous vowel discrimination in normal and at risk infants. *Child Development*, 47: 459–65.

Thierry, G., Vihman, M., and Roberts, M. (2003) Familiar words capture the attention of 11-month-olds in less than 250 msec. *Neuroreport*, 14: 2307–10.

Thiessen, E. D., and Saffran, J. R. (2003) When cues collide: use of stress and statistical cues to word boundaries by 7- to 9-month-old infants. *Developmental Psychology*, 39: 706–16.

Thomas, D. C., Campos, J., Shucard, D. W., Ramsey, D., and Shucard, J. (1981)Semantic comprehension in infancy: a signal detection analysis. *Child Development*, 52: 798–803.

Tincoff, R., Hauser, M., Tsao, F., Spaepen, G., Ramus, F., and Mehler, J. (2005) The role of speech rhythm in language discrimination: further tests with a nonhuman primate. *Developmental Science*, 8: 26–35.

Tincoff, R., and Jusczyk, P. W. (1999) Some beginnings of word comprehension in 6-month-olds. *Psychological Science*, 10: 172–5.

Tomasello, M. (1995) Pragmatic contexts for early verb learning. In M. Tomasello and W. E. Merriman (eds), *Beyond Names for Things: Young Children's Acquisition of Verbs*, pp. 115–46. Erlbaum, Hillsdale, NJ.

Tomasello, M. (2003) *Constructing a Language: A Usage-Based Theory of Language Acquisition*. Harvard University Press, Cambridge, MA.

Trehub, S. E. (1976) The discrimination of foreign speech contrasts by infants and adults. *Child Development*, 47: 466–72.

Turk, A., Jusczyk, P. W., and Gerken, L. (1995) Do English-learning infants use syllable weight to determine stress? *Language and Speech*, 38: 143–58.

Vihman, M. M. (1985) Language differentiation by the bilingual child. *Journal of Child Language*, 12: 297–324.

Vihman, M. M. (1991) Ontogeny of phonetic gestures: speech production. In I. G. Mattingly and M. Studdert-Kennedy (eds), *Modularity and the Motor Theory of Speech Perception: Proceedings of a Conference to Honor Alvin M. Liberman*, pp. 69–84. Erlbaum, Hillsdale, NJ.

Vihman, M. M. (1993) The construction of a phonological system. In C. A. Ferguson, L. Menn, and C. Stoel-Gammon (eds), *Phonological Development: Models, Research, Implications,* pp. 411–19. York Press, Timonium, MD.

Vihman, M. M. (1996) *Phonological Development: The Origins of Language in the Child.* Blackwell, Oxford.

Vihman, M. M., and Boysson-Bardies, B. de (2001) Adaptation to language: evidence from babbling and first words in four languages. *Language*, 67: 297–319.

Vihman, M. M., dePaolis, R., Nakai, S., and Hallé, P. (2004) The role of accentual pattern in early lexical representation. *Journal of Memory and Language*, 50: 336–53.

Vouloumanos, A., Kiehl, K., Werker, J. F., and Liddle, P. (2001) Detection of sounds in the auditory stream: event-related fMRI evidence for differential activation to speech and nonspeech. *Journal of Cognitive Neuroscience*, 13: 994–1005.

Vouloumanos, A., and Werker, J. F. (2004) Tuned to the signal: the privileged status of speech for young infants. *Developmental Science*, 7: 270.

Vouloumanos, A., and Werker, J. F. (2007) Listening to language at birth: evidence for a bias for speech in neonates. *Developmental Science*, 10: 159–64.

Weikum, W., Vouloumanos, A., Navarro, J., Soto-Faraco, S., Sebastián-Gallés, N., and Werker, J. F. (forthcoming) Visual language discrimination in infancy. *Science*.

Weir, R. W. (1966) *Language in the Crib*. Mouton, The Hague.

Werker, J. F. (1989) Becoming a native listener: a developmental perspective on human speech perception. *American Scientist*, 77: 54–59.

Werker, J. F. (1995) Exploring developmental changes in cross-language speech perception. In L. R. Gleitman and M. Liberman (eds), *Language: An Invitation to Cognitive Science*, 2nd edn, vol. 1, pp. 87–106. MIT Press, Cambridge, MA.

Werker, J. F., Cohen, L. B., Lloyd, V., Stager, C. L., and Cassasola, M. (1998) Acquisition of word-object associations by 14-month-old infants. *Developmental Psychology*, 34: 1289–309.

Werker, J. F., Corcoran, K., Fennell, C. T., and Stager, C. L. (2002) Infants' ability to learn phonetically similar words: effects of age and vocabulary size. *Infancy*, 3: 1–30.

Werker, J. F., and Curtin, S. (2005) PRIMIR: A developmental framework of infant speech processing. *Language Learning and Development*, 1: 197–234.

Werker, J. F., and Fennell, C. T. (2004) From listening to sounds to listening to words: earlysteps in word learning. In G. Hall and S. Waxman (eds), *Weaving a Lexicon*, pp. 79–109. MIT Press, Cambridge, MA.

Werker, J. F., and Lalonde, C. E. (1988) Cross-language speech perception: initial capabilities and developmental change. *Developmental Psychology*, 24: 672–83.

Werker, J. F., Pons, F. G., Dietrich, C., Kajikawa, S., Fais, L., and Amano, S. (2007) Infant-directed speech supports phonetic category learning in English and Japanese. *Cognition*, 103: 147–620.

Werker, J. F., and Tees, R. C. (1984) Cross-language speech perception: evidence for perceptual reorganization during the first year of life. *Infant Behavior and Development*, 7: 49–63.

Werker, J. F., and Yeung, H. H. (2005) Infant speech perception bootstraps word learning. *Trends in Cognitive Science*, 9: 519–27.

Westerman, G., and Miranda, E. R. (2004) A new model of sensorimotor coupling in the development of speech. *Brain and Language*, 2: 393–400.

Whalen, D. H., Levitt, A. G., and Wang, Q. 1991. Intonational differences between the reduplicative babbling of French- and English-learning infants. *Journal of Child Language*, 18: 501–16.

Woodward, A. L., and Markman, E. M. (1998) Early word learning. In W. Damon, D. Kuhn, and R. Siegler (eds), *Handbook of Child Psychology*, vol. 2: *Cognition, Perception and Language*, pp. 371–420. Wiley, New York.

Zamuner, T. S., Gerken, L. A., and Hammond, M. (2005) The acquisition of phonology based on input: a closer look at the relation of cross-linguistic and child language data. *Lingua*, 10: 1403–26.

CHAPTER 36

Statistical learning in infant language development

Rebecca Gómez

36.1 Introduction

Children learn language over such a short span of time with such seeming ease that many have assumed they must master language by means of a language-specific device (Chomsky, 1965; Wexler and Culicover, 1980). Such a device is thought to narrow down the search space of possible languages by limiting the parameters children will detect in language (Hyams, 1986; Manzini and Wexler, 1987; Roeper and Williams, 1987). Earlier in the twentieth century the idea that children might learn by means of associative principles was widespread (Skinner, 1957), but this was discounted because learning mechanisms were thought to be inadequate for acquiring the complex structure of human language (Chomsky, 1959). At that time, prosodic and distributional variations in language were not recognized as useful cues to linguistic structure, and thus it was assumed that language input could provide little useful information for learning (cf. Bates and Elman, 1996). However, learning approaches are gaining in credibility, spurred by the successes of neural network models (Elman et al., 1996), but also by discoveries with infant humans, suggesting a greater role for learning in language development than was previously assumed, and raising questions about the nature and extent of learning. The present chapter documents the infant language learning literature to date.

An approach to learning, taken for many years with adults but only in the past decade with infants, is to familiarize them with artificial languages. Although natural language stimuli are indispensable for investigating many questions in language development, they have drawbacks for assessing learning. For one, natural language is too familiar. Exposure to natural language is extensive and ongoing, making it impossible to know when and how infants learn about some particular linguistic structure. With novel stimuli, scientists can establish the point in developmental time when infants are able to detect a particular structure (e.g. Thiessen and Saffran, 2003). They can determine how much exposure is necessary for learning and what form exposure should take. And, they can ascertain how one learning experience affects another (e.g. Lany et al., 2005). Second, natural language is rich in correlated cues making it difficult to isolate the cause of learning. Is one particular cue sufficient for learning or are multiple cues needed (Billman, 1989)? If so, are some cues more powerful than others (Thiessen et al., 2005)? Artificial languages provide a useful tool for controlling prior learning and for manipulating specific variables of interest. This approach has resulted in a wealth of findings regarding the learning capabilities of children. Such capabilities enable infants to tune into the predominant auditory patterns in their native language and reflect learning across a range of linguistic tasks, including the acquisition of phoneme categories (Maye et al., 2002; Maye et al., 2005) and phonotactic dependencies (Chambers et al., 2003), phonological inference

(Gerken, 2004), segmentation of words (Saffran et al., 1996; Saffran, 2001), and acquisition of finite-state grammars (Gómez and Gerken, 1999; Saffran and Wilson, 2003; Saffran, Hauser, et al., 2005). Infant learners are also able abstract higher-order relations necessary for acquiring syntax-like structure (Gerken et al., 2005; Gómez and Lakusta, 2004).

Artificial language learning typically involves a two- to three-minute familiarization phase followed by a test. Most studies employ a two-language design so that half of the infants are exposed to Language A and half to Language B. At test, infants are exposed to strings from both languages so that what is grammatical for one group is ungrammatical for the other (Language A strings violate the constraints of Language B and vice versa). This ensures that the structure of the languages, instead of something idiosyncratic about the sound tokens used in one language or the other, is responsible for learning. Infants are tested for the amount of time they attend to different stimulus types. If learning has occurred, a group of infants will listen differentially to strings that conform to their training language vs. strings that do not (see Kemler Nelson et al., 1995). Adult learners can be used to obtain detailed information that cannot easily be gotten from infants. And comparisons between infants and adults are useful for exploring developmental differences in learning. Adults provide judgements about legal and illegal strings or are tested on their ability to produce legal sentences.

36.2 **Statistical learning**

Infant artificial language learning has become synonymous with statistical learning because of the emphasis in much of the work on learning statistical regularities. However, not all cases of artificial language learning entail learning statistical structure. For instance, some learning requires generalization of relational patterns (Gerken, 2004; Gerken et al., 2005; Gómez and Gerken, 1999; Gómez and Lakusta, 2004; Lany et al. 2005; Marcus et al., 1999).

To clarify, statistical structure abounds in the flow of information in the sensory world. Whether auditory, visual, or tactile, stimulation is rich in frequent associations and patterns over basic units. Statistical learning is thought to involve computations based on basic units. In the case of auditory stimulation, for instance, the basic units of computation are various linguistic or acoustic sounds. Statistical structure can take many forms, including the frequency of individual units of sound, frequency of co-occurrence, or the transitional probability of one unit given another. Co-occurrence frequency is defined as the frequency of two units occurring together. Transitional probability is the probability of the occurrence of one unit given another (the probability of Event B given Event A is the joint probability of Event A and Event B divided by the probability of Event A). There are other forms of statistical structure, but common to all forms is the requirement that units occur with some regularity that lends itself to mathematical description (and also presumably computation).

In a seminal paper, Saffran et al. (1996; see also Aslin et al., 1998) showed that eight-month-old humans can track transitional probabilities in sequences of syllables to discover word boundaries. They tested this by exposing infants to continuous streams of four randomly ordered three-syllable words (e.g. *tupiro*, *golatu*) such that individual syllables occurred with identical frequency. The only cues to word boundaries were the lower transitional probabilities occurring for syllables spanning words compared to the higher probabilities of syllables within words. Take a phrase like *naughty puppy*. The syllable transition in *naugh-ty* has a higher transitional probability than the transition *ty-pu* because *naugh* in the word *naughty*, is more likely to predict *ty* than *ty* is to predict *pu*. Infants in the Saffran et al. studies were able to use the differences in transitional probabilities within- vs. between-words to identify word boundaries in running speech.

This research was important for showing that very young infants can track complex sequential structure. It also raised more general questions about the role of learning in language acquisition, such as whether learning was limited to word segmentation or whether it applied to other kinds of language structure. A flurry of studies followed; and although much work remains to be done, learning appears to extend into in a range of linguistic domains.

Learning is key in the formation of speech categories (Maye et al., 2002; 2005), the ability to track phonotactic sequential structure (Chambers et al., 2003), the abstraction of phonological rules (Gerken, 2004), and the identification of word-like units in speech (Saffran, 2001). Infants are also able to acquire rudimentary syntactic structure in the form of adjacent and remote sequential dependencies (Gómez and Gerken, 1999; Gómez, 2002; Gómez and Maye, 2005; Saffran and Wilson,

2003), abstraction of sequential patterns (Gerken, 2006; Gómez and Gerken, 1999; Marcus et al., 1999), and learning of morphosyntactic category relations (Gerken et al., 2005; Gómez and Lakusta, 2004). The research also shows how learners capitalize on probabilistic input (Gómez and Lakusta, 2004; Hudson et al., 2005a; 2005b) and how they use prior experience to bootstrap learning of difficult patterns from simpler ones (Lany et al., 2005; Lany and Gómez, forthcoming). These and other findings are detailed below.

36.3 Phonological learning

36.3.1 Discrimination of speech sounds

By 8–10 months of age infants have begun to narrow the inventory of sounds that count as speech in their native language (Werker and Tees, 1984). This finding is widely recognized as experience-dependent. What is the process of change? One theory is that change is dependent on growing perceptual sensitivity to words (e.g. Mackain, 1982; Werker and Pegg, 1992). However, a puzzle is presented by the fact that infants are unable to distinguish minimal word pairs in an experimental setting before seventeen-months (Swingley and Aslin, 2000; Werker et al., 2002), even though they distinguish the speech sounds themselves much earlier (Stager and Werker, 1997). A possible solution is that infants use statistical information to home in on phoneme categories (Maye et al., 2002). Although tokens in phonetic space may vary acoustically along a dimension, such variation is not random. Rather, it patterns bimodally such that tokens of one category are closer to one another along a dimension than tokens from another category. In contrast, within-category tokens organize according to a unimodal distribution. Maye et al. asked how distributions with these different characteristics might influence infants' ability to distinguish speech contrasts.

They familiarized six-month-old infants with one of two distributions of eight speech sounds on a /da/–/ta/ continuum (the voiced unaspirated /d/ in day and the voiceless unaspirated /t/ in stay). Infants have been shown to make this discrimination (Pegg and Werker, 1997); but if perception of speech sounds is malleable then exposure to a unimodal distribution should interfere with discrimination, whereas exposure to a bimodal distribution should preserve it. This pattern of findings would support the proposal that sensitivity to the frequency distributions of speech sounds is instrumental in learning. Infants in both unimodal and bimodal conditions heard the same eight tokens along the continuum. Those in the bimodal distribution condition heard tokens near the end (2 and 7) most frequently, whereas infants in the unimodal distribution condition heard middle tokens 4 and 5 most often. After familiarization, infants were tested on their ability to discriminate alternating tokens (the endpoints 1 and 8) from non-alternating ones (repeats of tokens 3 or 6). Only infants in the bimodal condition discriminated alternating from non-alternating tokens. Familiarization with the bimodal distribution apparently led infants to retain two categories of speech sounds, whereas exposure to the unimodal distribution resulted in the formation of one. In a subsequent study with eight-month olds, Maye et al. (2005) found that exposure to a bimodal frequency distribution could enable detection of an initially undetectable contrast. Thus, it appears that the frequency characteristics of speech sounds can both blur distinctions between previously known categories and enable the formation of new ones. Is statistical learning instrumental in the more basic task of learning phonotactic structure?

36.3.2 Learning phonotactic regularities

Phonotactic regularities are the allowable positions of speech segments relative to each other in words. For instance, English words can end with an /ng/ sequence (such as in the word *sing*), but such a sequence cannot begin words. Such regularities differ from language to language and thus must be learned. This is a non-trivial task requiring infants to remember the positions of individual speech segments across innumerable syllables and words (Chambers, 2004). We know infants distinguish frequent from infrequent phonotactic patterns in their native language by nine months of age (Friederici and Wessels, 1993; Jusczyk et al., 1993; Jusczyk et al., 1994), but until recently we have not known how rapidly new phonotactic regularities are acquired or whether learning will generalize.

Chambers et al. (2003) found that sixteen-month-old infants rapidly learn consonant position regularities involving syllable onsets and codas. Infants had to learn that CVC[1] words began with one set of five consonants, but

[1] C = consonant, V = vowel.

ended with another set of five. Infants were exposed to twenty-five words in a familiarization phase less than two minutes long. At test, they discriminated novel words with the familiar pattern from ones with an unfamiliar one (constraints were reversed such that illegal items began with final consonants and ended with initial ones). In another experiment, Chambers (2004) found that the same-age infants could extend newly learned phonotactic regularities to syllables with a different vowel, suggesting that they are able to form rule-like generalizations such as "/b/ is an onset." Chambers (2004) has also found that rapid learning extends beyond the first-order onsets of syllables: sixteen month olds were able to learn second-order dependencies in which the position of a consonant, whether first or last in a syllable, depended on an adjacent vowel.

Such experiments provide insights into the kinds of phonotactic regularity infants can learn, and may shed light on the formation of phonological units. Yang (2004) has pointed out that to apply statistical operations, learners must know what kinds of unit are relevant (whether syllables or some other kind of structure). These studies raise the intriguing possibility that some aspects of syllable structure could be acquired with the same principles that are instrumental in phonotactic learning. Although the infant learners were beyond the age at which children begin showing knowledge of syllable structure, Chambers (2004) has begun testing learning of phonotactic structure in younger infants.

36.3.3 Phonological generalization

An interesting question arises as to whether learning is limited to previously encountered syllables and segments or whether learners are sensitive to higher-level abstract patterns. For instance, languages vary in the range of syllable structures they allow. English permits a range from V, CV, and CVC to complex combinations such as CCCVCCC, whereas other languages allow less variation. Presumably such variations are learned. How malleable is such learning? Saffran and Thiessen (2003) investigated whether they could change infant preferences for phonological patterns in their linguistic input by exposing nine month olds to words conforming only to CVCV or CVCCVC patterns (both of which occur regularly in English). Infants discriminated novel words exhibiting the familiarization pattern from words exhibiting the other pattern after a brief exposure, showing that their preferences for common syllable patterns are easily altered.

In another study, Saffran and Thiessen (2003) exposed the same-age infants to words with CVC syllables with onsets and codas of +Voicing/–Voicing (*dakdot*) vs.–Voicing/+V voicing (*todkad*). As in the previous study, infants discriminated words with the familiar pattern from words with the other pattern, even though both patterns can occur in English. A third study suggested that infants had abstracted the pattern at the level of features (e.g. +Voicing/–Voicing) rather than at the level of having learned only the positions of specific segments. This is an important indication that learning extends to higher-level phonological relations.

Maye et al. (forthcoming) have also asked whether infants are encoding information at the level of abstract features (e.g. voiced vs. voiceless). To address this, Maye et al. familiarized eight month olds with a bimodal phonetic distribution emphasizing a contrast at one place of articulation (/g/ versus /k/) and tested them on discrimination of a contrast at another place of articulation (/d/ versus /t/). Both the /g/–/k/ and the /d/–/t/ distributions varied along a continuum of voicing. Infants were able to make the discrimination, showing that by 8 months they are encoding speech sounds according to the abstract feature of voicing. This suggests that infants are not merely learning individual phonetic contrasts but are generalizing patterns at a higher level.

In a yet more demanding demonstration of phonological generalization, Gerken (2004) investigated nine-month-old infants' ability to learn words generated by principles of metrical stress. Principles of stress assignment, applied to words of three to five syllables in length, were ordered along a hierarchy of constraints. For instance, Constraint A states that two stressed syllables can not occur in sequence, whereas Constraint B states that heavy syllables (such as those with a consonant ending) should be stressed. Because A outranks B, the word *TON ton do RE mi* does not stress the second syllable, even though Constraint B calls for stress. Infants were familiarized with words reflecting a system of four constraints (A–D). Importantly, they were never exposed to a word requiring the transitive inference that A outranks D, but they were familiarized with words for which B outranked C and C outranked D. At test they generalized to novel words requiring the transitive inference that A outranks D. One interpretation of the findings is that infants are abstracting a system of symbolic propositions and making a transitive inference; however, Shultz and

Gerken (2005) showed that a feedforward encoder network[2] was capable of the same generalization, demonstrating that learning can be achieved by a fundamentally associative system. Importantly, the stress assignment rules were obtained from natural language, demonstrating that infants can learn a complex system of relationships found in languages of the world. This is an important demonstration because of questions regarding the relevance of artificial language studies to natural language.

The literature reviewed to this point shows rapid learning at the level of segments and their relations (Chambers, 2004; Chambers et al., 2003) and for phoneme discrimination (Maye et al., 2002). Learning is also complex, occurring across a range of generalizations (Chambers, 2004; Gerken, 2004; Maye et al., forthcoming; Saffran and Thiessen, 2003) and despite competing stress cues (Gerken, 2004). All these studies have looked at learning of individual cues such as frequency or stress; but what happens when learning is taken to another level of difficulty such as when cues of different types compete?

36.4 Word segmentation[3]

36.4.1 Competition of distributional cues

A problem faced by all children is identification of words in running speech. This is made difficult by the fact that words are not consistently demarcated by pauses (Liberman et al., 1967). Segmentation is aided by a variety of cues, including transitional probabilities of syllables (Saffran et al., 1996), word-boundary phonetics (Mattys and Juszcyk, 2001), word stress (Johnson and Jusczyk, 2001; Jusczyk et al., 1999), co-articulation (Johnson and Jusczyk, 2001), and highly familiar words (Bortfeld et al., 2005; Jusczyk, 1997), but studies have only begun to investigate the interplay of such cues. How does statistical information interact with phonological cues? Does sensitivity to a prominent cue such as stress precede sensitivity to transitional probabilities, or is the reverse the case?

Infants are sensitive to stress cues early on. By 7.5 months, infants more easily detect words in running speech that adhere to the predominant trochaic strong–weak stress pattern of English than words with an iambic weak–strong pattern (Jusczyk et al., 1999). Indeed, when presented with passages containing an iambic word such as *guitar* followed by an unstressed syllable such as *is* infants prefer to listen to *taris* over *guitar*, suggesting they are using a strong–weak segmentation strategy to identify words (Cutler and Norris, 1988; Jusczyk et al., 1999).

To use such a strategy, infants need to identify the predominant stress pattern of their native language (whether trochaic or iambic), but this is itself dependent on knowing some words (Thiessen and Saffran, 2003). One way out of this problem is if infants can use statistical information to segment words before they become sensitive to stress (Thiessen and Saffran, 2003). Infants might only segment a subset of words in their native language, but if they then form a generalization for the predominant stress pattern, they will have an additional cue for finding words in running speech. Interestingly, when stress and transitional probabilities are pitted against each other, eight month olds rely on stress (Johnson and Juszyk, 2001). What was not known, until recently, is whether infants would favor transitional probabilities over stress at an earlier age.

Thiessen and Saffran investigated this question by exposing six and nine month olds to a continuous stream of disyllabic words with trochaic or iambic stress. Infants of both ages were then tested to see if they would discriminate words from part-words. Infants are known to segment words based on trochaic, but not iambic, stress by 7.5 months of age, and do not appear to rely on iambic stress for word segmentation until 10.5 months (Juszcyk et al., 1999). Words consisted of syllables that were uniquely paired and thus had high transitional probabilities. Part-words consisted of syllables that co-occurred as frequently as the syllables in words, but contained syllables crossing word boundaries. Thus, the transitional probability of one syllable following another was lower in part-words than in words. Thiessen and Saffran reasoned that if infants favor statistical information over stress they should discriminate words and part-words the same, regardless of whether they were in the trochaic or iambic condition; but if they are already sensitive to trochaic stress they should show different patterns of discrimination.

[2] The learning algorithm involved sibling-descendant cascade-correlation. Cascade-correlation networks which recruit hidden units as needed have been useful for simulating various developmental phenomena, as compared to back-propagation learning algorithms that adjust weights in static network architectures (Schultz, 2003).

[3] See Curtin and Werker (Ch. 35 this volume) on phonological development for an extensive review of the literature on infant word segmentation.

Nine-month-olds listened longer to words than to part-words in the trochaic condition, but showed the reverse pattern in the condition with iambic stress. The latter result is consistent with having segmented words on the basis of trochaic stress. For these infants (in the iambic condition), trochaically segmented words began with the second stressed syllable of a word (as defined by high transitional probability) and ended with the first syllable of the next word, and thus consisted of part-words (two syllables spanning words). Apparently, the lower transitional probabilities of such combinations were overwritten by the powerful cue of trochaic stress, leading infants to prefer these. Six month olds were oblivious to the stress manipulation regardless of whether they were in the trochaic or iambic stress condition, demonstrating that when both cues are present younger infants will favor statistical information. This study is important for suggesting how infants might bootstrap one kind of information (knowledge of stress patterns) from another (transitional probabilities).

36.4.2 Using information obtained in one linguistic task as input to another level of learning

We have seen how learning of one kind of structure (transitional probabilities) interacts with learning of another kind (stress) at different points in development, suggesting that what learners acquire at one point in developmental time can impact later learning. How do infants fare when required to learn at multiple levels? Saffran and Wilson (2003) examined this question by asking whether twelve month olds would use the output of one process (word segmentation) as the input to another (learning the sequential ordering of words). Linguistic input is not organized such that children are first taught words, then syntax. Rather, children experience language holistically. As such, they must segment words, based on patterns of syllables or sublexical units, as a precursor to learning their sequential ordering. Saffran and Wilson exposed infants to strings such as *datopidubutobadudipa* where *dato*, *pidu*, *buto*, *badu*, and *dipa* were words arranged with constraints on their sequential ordering in strings. Infants were then tested on novel legal and illegal strings. Transitional probabilities between syllables were identical in the two sentence types (1.0 within words and 0.25 between words). Thus, in order to discriminate the sentence types, infants must have segmented words. An optional first syllable was included to prevent detection of grammatical strings based on absolute position of syllables in strings. Infants discriminated legal and illegal strings, suggesting that they were applying what they had learned as input at one level to a subsequent learning process. A question, however, is whether discrimination reflected sensitivity to the ordering of segmented words or to runs of four or more syllables.

36.5 Rudiments of syntax

36.5.1 Learning sequential word ordering

The studies reviewed thus far show that infants rapidly detect statistical structure at the level of segments and syllables, and can form generalizations from this information. The next step is to ask whether infants can track words in strings. Although syntax acquisition ultimately involves the ability to track categories in phrases (e.g. Determiner, Noun) and the hierarchical organization of phrases in strings, it is informative as a first step to investigate learning of sequential structure. Such investigations yield insights into the kinds of sequential dependencies infants can acquire (Gómez, 2002; Gómez and Gerken, 1999; Gómez and Maye, 2005; Saffran, Hauser, et al., 2005).

In one of the earliest investigations of infants' ability to track the orderings of words in sentences, Gómez and Gerken (1999) exposed twelve month olds to a subset of strings produced by one of two finite-state languages (see also Mintz, 1996). Although word order was constrained by these languages, there was still considerable variability in the orderings of words in strings. For instance, note how the position of the word *pel* varies in the strings *pel-tam-rud*, *vot-pel-jic-rud-tam*, and *vot-pel-pel-jic*. Both languages began and ended with the same words and contained the same vocabulary, but differed in the ordering of word pairs. For instance, the transition *tam-jic* found in Language 1 never occurred in Language 2. After brief exposure to a subset of strings in their training language, infants were given a five-minute play break, and then were tested. Infants listened longer to new strings from their training language than to strings from the other language, regardless of which language they heard during training. Although the constraints placed on word ordering were the same during training and test, infants were never tested on the exact strings

Table 36.1 Depiction of the two languages used in Saffran, Hauser, et al. (2005)

Predictive language	Non-predictive language
S → AP + BP + (CP)[a]	S → AP + BP
AP → A + (D)	AP → {(A) + (D)}[b]
BP → CP + F	BP → CP + F
CP → C + (G)	CP → {C + (G)}[b]

[a] Elements in parenthesis are optional.
[b] Must contain at least one category, but if both are present they must occur in left–right order.

encountered during training—demonstrating that learning was not confined to memory for particular strings, but rather generalized to novel strings with familiar co-occurrence patterns.

Saffran, Hauser, et al. (2005) have recently tested twelve month olds on yet more complex sequential structure. Saffran et al. were interested in knowing whether infants this age could track hierarchical structure, such as that found in phrases with predictive dependencies between words and phrases. To do this, they contrasted learning of a language with predictive dependencies between words in phrases with learning of one in which the relationships were non-predictive (see Table 36.1). As an example, sentences in the predictive language contained an A phrase (AP) followed by a B phrase (BP) and an optional C phrase (CP). Phrases themselves consisted of categories A–G with two to four elements each. Within-phrase dependencies differed critically in the predictive and the non-predictive language. Whereas the A phrase in the predictive language consisted of a required A-word and an optional D, both A- and D-words were optional in the non-predictive language (the same was true for the C phrase). Therefore, in the predictive language the presence of a D-word guarantees the presence of a particular A-word,whereas the relationship in the non-predictive language is highly variable. These variations in the predictability of words within phrases led to differences in learning such that infants were able to discriminate legal and illegal strings after exposure to the predictive language, but not after exposure to the nonpredictive one.

It is unclear whether infants in this study learned hierarchical phrase structure or an extremely complex finite-state grammar. A phrase structure involves knowledge of abstract word classes. Although there were multiple words in each of the A–G categories, the word classes were very small, and thus the language can be characterized as a finite-state grammar with transitions between words instead of word classes (Altmann et al., 1995). An important control was that legal and illegal test items were equated in terms of co-occurrence statistics; thus learning could not have stemmed solely from bigram statistics between pairs of words. Rather, the coherence in the predictive language appeared to lead to stronger perceptual grouping of words in phrases. But, perceptual grouping does not imply knowledge of abstract word classes. Additionally Gómez and Gerken have been unable to find evidence of tweleve month olds being able to learn syntactic categories in a much simpler paradigm (unpublished research). Thus, the likelihood that infants this age are using syntactic categories (required for a phrase structure grammar) is low. Regardless of whether infants learned a finite-state grammar or phrase structure, the learning required was challenging. Infants were exposed to fifty different strings in a twenty three-minute familiarization period requiring them to track dependent relationships between sixteen unique words. Thus, the findings show that infants are capable of tracking complex sequential structure.

36.5.2 **Generalization of sequential word order**

Researchers have also investigated how infants might generalize sequential structure. Gómez and Gerken (1999) tested this by familiarizing 12-month-olds with a finite-state grammar in one vocabulary and testing them on strings in entirely new vocabulary (infants heard strings like *fim-sog-fim-fim-tup* and were tested on *vot-pel-pel-jic*).[4] Thus, although constraints on word ordering remained the same between training and test, vocabulary did not. Because test strings were instantiated in new vocabulary, learners could not distinguish the two grammars based on transitional probabilities between remembered word pairs. Infants made the discrimination, suggesting that they had abstracted something about grammatical structure above and beyond pairs of specific words.

[4] The strings in this example do not have identical repetition structure because infants were exposed not only to different vocabulary between training and test, but also to different strings. Although different, the strings retained regularities dictated by the artificial language.

Marcus et al. (1999) reported similar findings for younger seven-month-olds exposed to simple ABA versus ABB (*wi-di-wi* vs. *wi-di-di*) patterns. As in Gómez and Gerken (1999), the vocabulary was different between training and test. Infants discriminated strings with the training pattern from those with a different pattern despite the change in vocabulary (e.g *ba-po-ba* vs. *ba-po-po*). Marcus et al. further interpreted these findings as evidence that infants are acquiring algebra-like rules involving the substitution of arbitrary elements in abstract variables. They argued that systems which learn from statistical regularities, such as connectionist architectures, are in principle incapable of such generalization (see also Marcus, 2001). However, generalization based on associative learning has been demonstrated in a number of models (Altmann, 2002a; Altmann and Dienes, 1999; Christiansen and Curtin, 1999; Gassar and Colunga, 1999; Seidenberg and Elman, 1999; Shastri, 1999; Shultz and Bale, 2001).

One can also ask to what degree such findings extend into problems of language acquisition. The infant abstraction abilities documented by Marcus et al. (1999) and Gómez and Gerken (1999) are dependent on learning patterns of repeating and alternating elements, e.g. ABB, ABA, ABCA (Gómez et al., 2000). While repeating elements occur in natural language in the form of reduplication, the patterns in these studies occur over physical stimuli in sequence. For example, recognizing *ba-po-ba* and *ko-ga-ko* as instances of the pattern ABA entails noting that the first and last syllables in sequence are physically identical. But most generalizations in syntax involve operations over variables that are not perceptually bound. Compare the pattern-based representation ABA to the category-based representation Noun Verb Noun. Abstracting ABA from *ba-po-ba* involves noting that the first and third elements in a sequence are physically identical, and thus recognition is perceptually bound. In contrast, the Noun Verb Noun relation holds over abstract categories that do not rely on perceptual identity. *Dogs eat bones* and *John loves running* share the same category-based structure, despite the obvious physical dissimilarities between category members such as *John* and *running*. Given this observation, how might we begin to examine learning involving abstract variables?

36.5.3 Category-based abstraction

The ability to perceive category relationships among words in strings is essential to linguistic productivity. An English speaker must be able to generalize from a novel string like *The pleg mooped* to *Is the pleg mooping?*. Such generalization is tremendously powerful: once a novel word is categorized, children can automatically apply syntactic constraints associated with other words in its category. How do children achieve such generalization?

The role of semantics is thought to feature importantly in linguistic category acquisition (Grimshaw, 1981; Pinker, 1984). Children first identify members of semantic categories based on referential information, and then link these to innate knowledge of syntactic categories and functions. But some have proposed that distributional information, in the form of phonological regularities within words of a class, and co-occurrence relations between classes, might also factor into such learning (Braine, 1987; Gleitman and Wanner, 1982; Morgan and Demuth, 1996; Morgan and Newport, 1981; Redington et al., 1998). These two views may not be wholly incompatible. An infant who uses distributional cues to parse categories in speech eventually has to link these categories with semantic referents. Thus, identification of relevant categories in speech could provide a leg-up for the ultimate task of mapping meaning and form (Gómez and Gerken, 2000; Naigles, 2002).

Category-based abstraction has been studied fairly extensively with older learners, and has focused on how learners acquire relations between grammatical classes (Braine, 1987; Frigo and McDonald, 1998; Mintz, 2002; Smith, 1969; Wilson, 2002). Grammatical classes are given arbitrary labels such as a, X, b, and Y. Words from these classes then combine to form legal phrases. For instance, aX and bY might be legal in a language whereas aY and bX are not. Learners are exposed to most, but not all, aX and bY phrases and then are tested to see if they will discriminate new legal phrases from illegal ones. To give an example, imagine that a-elements correspond to *a* and *the* and b-elements to *will* and *can*. Learners will only be successful at discriminating a new legal phrase (e.g. *a cat*) from an illegal one (*a eat*) if they have learned that a-elements go with nouns (the Xs), but not with verbs (the Ys). As in natural language, the functor-like a and b categories have fewer members than lexical-like Xs and Ys.

Gómez and Lakusta (2004) explored such generalization by asking whether twelve month olds would learn the relationship between specific a and b words and X and Y categories. During training infants were exposed to one of two training languages. One language consisted of aX and bY pairings, the other of aY and bX pairs. Xs were instantiated as disyllabic words and Ys were monosyllabic. Syllable number was used as a cue for distinguishing X and Y categories. This feature was chosen to mimic similar cues found in natural language. In English, for instance, nouns tend to have more syllables than verbs and also tend to receive first syllable stress (Kelly, 1992). Infants were tested on new phrases from their training language vs. phrases from the other language. In order to assess generalization, all X and Y words were novel at test. Infants discriminated between legal and illegal sentences after a short familiarization period, suggesting that they had become sensitive to the relationships between the a and b elements and the abstract feature differentiating X and Y words (syllable number). Similar learning may occur in natural language, where children exposed to English may pick up on distributional regularities distinguishing nouns and verbs and link these to specific function words.

Identifying a relationship between function words and distributional cues differentiating word classes is only the first step (Braine, 1987; Frigo and McDonald, 1998). After learners have associated a and b words with X/Y cues, they can then categorize individual a or b elements (such as *a* and *the*) on the basis of their joint association with these cues. Once function-word categories are formed, learners can rely on memory for a phrase they have heard (e.g. *the cat*) and the fact that *the* and *a* are in the same category to make an inference about a phrase they have not heard (e.g. *a cat*), regardless of whether the word has an X or Y cue.

How can this hypothesis be tested in an artificial language? We can do this by incorporating some X and Y elements into the language that do not have distinguishing cues. Learners may initially rely on X and Y cues to group function words into separate categories, but once the a and b categories are formed, learners should be able to predict a Y word, given a preceding b, regardless of whether or not distinguishing X/Y cues are present (Braine, 1987).

Gerken et al. (2005) investigated such learning with seventeen-month-old infants. They created a set of stimuli in which six feminine lexical stems appeared with the case endings *-oj* and *-u* and six masculine stems appeared with the case endings *-ya* and *-em*. Case endings in these experiments were equivalent to a and b elements. Additionally, cues distinguishing Xs and Ys were present for a subset of category members. For instance, three of six of the X words contained the derivational suffix *-k* (e.g. *polkoj*, *polku*) whereas three of the Y words contained the suffix *-tel* (e.g. *zhitelya*, *zhitelyem*). Infants were first familiarized with a subset of stimuli and were then tested to see if they would attend differentially to novel aX and bY stimuli vs. ungrammatical aY and bX ones even when the distinguishing suffix was absent (e.g. generalizing to *vannoj* and *pisarem* after hearing *vannu* and *pisarya*). The infants were able to do this; thus by seventeen months infants have gone beyond the first step of associating particular case endings with cues distinguishing X and Y category members (particular derivational suffixes) to the second one of categorizing the case endings. Having heard *vannu* they were able to treat *vannoj* equivalently. This finding is important for showing that by seventeen months, infants can form categories and dependencies between them from distributional cues in speech.

The ability to abstract categories from sequential information is a significant milestone in cognitive and language development, not only for what it implies about early abstraction abilities but because of its potentially important contribution to syntactic development. It will be important to investigate the next step of how infants link categories parsed in speech with syntactic categories on the basis of referential information.

36.5.4 **Tracking long-distance relationships in strings**

Another milestone for language learners is learning to track remote dependencies. Research thus far shows that infants are adept learners of adjacent sequential structure. However, many dependencies in language are connected by longer-distance dependencies. Some examples are phonemic segments in words, morphosyntactic dependencies between auxiliaries and inflectional morphemes (e.g. *is quickly running*), and dependencies between nouns and verbs in number and tense agreement (*The boys in the tree are laughing*). How easily do learners track remote dependencies in sequential structure?

Newport and Aslin (2004) investigated this question in the context of a word segmentation task. Adult learners had to track non-adjacent syllables in words in a continuous stream of speech. Words consisted of three syllables (e.g. *ba-du-te*, *ba-to-te*, *pi-to-ra*) with predictable relationships between the first and last CVs. There were four possible middle CVs in the word set and five non-adjacent CV pairs, with each of the medial CVs occurring in each of the five pairs. The transitional probability between the first and third CV in a word was 1.0, but the other transitions (adjacent CVs or CVs spanning word boundaries) ranged from .20 to .25. Learning was impossible. Learners tested across a series of experiments were unable to track non-adjacent structure (even after ten days of exposure).

Tracking non-adjacent dependencies in a continuous stream of syllables is an exceedingly difficult task, requiring learners to monitor information over different syllables in variable positions in the sound stream. Noting this, Newport and Aslin suggested that perhaps non-adjacent regularities of the type occurring in natural language would be easier to track. Although words do not have dependencies between non-adjacent syllables, such dependencies do occur between phonemic segments (in Hebrew and Arabic, for instance). When the structure of words was changed so that dependencies occurred between non-adjacent consonant segments, (e.g. *p_ g_ t_*) or non-adjacent vowels, (e.g. *a _ u _ e _*), learners segmented the words, demonstrating they had learned the non-adjacent dependencies.

Given the difficulty of tracking non-adjacent dependencies in continuous speech, how do learners fare at tracking non-adjacent dependencies in segmented speech? Research with natural language shows that by eighteen months infants track non-adjacent dependencies over as many as three intervening morphemes (Santelmann and Juszcyk, 1998), discriminating phrases like *is running* from *can running*. Gómez (2002) replicated the Santelmann and Jusczyk findings with 18-month-olds in an artificial language paradigm, investigating conditions that might be necessary for learning. Infants were exposed to one of two artificial languages. Language 1 sentences followed the patterns aXb or cXd (e.g. *pel-wadim-jic*, *vot-kicey-rud*, *vot-wadim-rud*). In Language 2 the relationship between the first and third elements was reversed such that *pel* sentences ended with *rud*, and *vot* sentences ended with *jic* (*pel-wadim-rud*, *vot-kicey-jic*, *vot-wadim-jic*). In both languages a and c elements were restricted to initial position, b and d elements to final position, and X elements occurred medially. Additionally, adjacent dependencies were identical in both languages (aX occurred in both languages as did Xd: e.g. compare Language 1: aXb and cXd to Language 2: aXd and cXb). Because the two languages were identical with respect to absolute position of elements and adjacent dependencies, they could only be distinguished by noting the relationship between the non-adjacent first and third words.

Gómez manipulated the size of the pool from which she drew the middle element (set size = 3, 12, or 24) while holding frequency of exposure to particular non-adjacent dependencies constant. This manipulation was meant to explore structure found in natural language, where function morphemes come from small sets and lexical morphemes come from much larger ones. She asked whether high variability in the middle element would lead to better perception of non-adjacent dependencies even though the non-adjacent dependencies were equally frequent in all set-size conditions. Eighteen-month-olds were able to acquire the non-adjacent dependency when the intervening element came from a set of 24 possible words, but not when intervening set size was smaller (2 or 12). This finding was replicated in younger fifteen month olds (Gómez and Maye, 2005) and in adult participants using a slightly more complex grammar (Gómez, 2002). At first glance, it seems paradoxical that variability can aid learning. Indeed, one might assume that high variability would add noise and impede learning. However, high variability in the large set-size condition appears to increase the perceptual salience of the non-adjacent words compared to the middle word, and thus facilitates learning.

Non-adjacent dependency learning is important for its potential role in syntactic category abstraction. Evidence comes from Mintz (2003), who isolated the most frequent non-adjacent dependencies in corpora of child-directed speech (Mintz refers to these as "frequent frames"). The words embedded in frequent non-adjacent dependencies tended to be from the same categories (e.g. noun, verb, preposition, adjective, adverb), raising the possibility that the statistical properties of non-adjacent dependencies might lead learners to form categories of elements occurring in particular non-adjacent frames. Mintz has shown that adults and children categorize words in artificial languages as a function of their co-occurrence patterns within frequent frames, lending support to this hypothesis (Mintz, 2002; 2004).

One question is: what kind of mechanism is necessary for such learning? Will a fundamentally associative mechanism suffice, or is one that is specialized for long-distance dependencies required? Onnis et al. (2005) and Elman (pers. commun.) have shown that a simple recurrent network can detect non-adjacent sequential dependencies under the same conditions as humans. The network develops graded representations in hidden units which maintain differences between non-adjacent structures when the middle element is highly variable.

Another question is why learners in the Gómez studies succeeded in acquiring non-adjacent dependencies when those in Experiment 1 of Newport and Aslin (2004) failed. A key difference is that learners in Newport and Aslin faced the added difficulty of segmenting words from continuous streams, whereas the Gómez strings were already segmented. This alone makes the requirements of learning very different. However, putting segmentation aside, the structure tested by Newport and Aslin was similar to the low-variability condition tested by Gómez (2002). Newport and Aslin subsequently found learning when they replaced syllables with segments of the same type (e.g. vowels) separated by elements of a different type (e.g. consonants). This made non-adjacent dependencies more perceptible because learners naturally differentiate these types. Learners in the Gómez studies had no a priori reason to group remotely connected elements. Instead, high variability made the non-adjacent relations perceptible. High variability of a middle element may also facilitate word segmentation (see Monaghan et al., forthcoming). Thus, while similarity of type may promote learning between non-adjacent elements in words, any process making the non-adjacent dependency more detectable may also promote learning.

The non-adjacency learning demonstrated by Gómez reflects only some dependencies in syntactic structure, raising challenges for future research. Although the remote dependency in The boy<u>s</u> in the tree <u>are</u> laughing is overtly signaled by -s and are, such dependencies are not always explicit. In The boy in the tree <u>is</u> laughing, children must track the relationship between the abstract number of the word boy and the verb are. In order to make a more plausible link to natural language, researchers will need to begin investigating learning of abstract dependencies in sequential structure.

36.5.5 **Learning probabilistic structure**

Children are exposed to various kinds of inconsistency in language input—in their own ungrammatical utterances and in the ungrammatical utterances of others. Additionally, structures vary in their regularity—e.g. in English the degree to which verbs take the regular -ed ending for the past tense and in Spanish the extent to which feminine nouns end in -a. There are other instances of inconsistency, such as when deaf children are exposed to non-native signs (Newport, 1999; Ross and Newport, 1996; Singleton and Newport, 2004) or when normal hearing children are exposed to pidgin languages. In all these instances, children must distinguish more probable from less probable structure. They must also generalize beyond the data to which they are exposed. A criticism of learning approaches is that the mechanisms are too rudimentary to detect the most appropriate structures in language, that myriad possibilities are available, and that unless the correct structures are detected, learners face a combinatorial explosion of possibilities. The studies reviewed to date suggest that infants can detect structure occurring with perfect probability (when transitional probabilities are 1.0); but what happens when probabilities are lower? Will probabilities be encoded accurately or will they be changed in some way?

Hudson Kam and Newport (2005a) tested adults and six year olds on an artificial language with probabilistic determiners to see whether there would be differences in how learners of different ages encode such input. They hypothesized that children might be more likely than adults to systematize determiner use, given more limited short-term and working memory resources. Adults were exposed to a complex language containing transitive, intransitive, and negative structures, with frequency of occurrence of determiners varying in different conditions (45 percent, 60 percent, 75 percent, and 100 percent). At test, the adults produced determiners at the same rate at which they had occurred during training. A second experiment contrasted adult and child learners. Determiners occurred 60 percent or 100 percent of the time. Adults again matched the probabilistic structure in their language, whereas children diverged. Approximately 14 percent of children in the "60 percent consistent input" condition developed a systematic rule to always use a determiner. None of the adults adopted this rule. Although the percentage of children showing this pattern was small, learning is necessarily limited in artificial language studies. Real-world examples of children exposed to probabilistic language input show a similar pattern of increased systematic rule use (Singleton and Newport, 2004; Ross and Newport, 1996).

The results raise intriguing questions about the role played by children in the transition from pidgin to creole languages. Why is it that children of pidgin speakers produce more systematic versions of their input language than their parents? One proposal is that children systematize input based on access to universal language rules (e.g. Bickerton, 1981). In contrast, Hudson Kam and Newport propose that the tendency to systematize may stem from children's cognitive limitations (see also Newport, 1990). When adults were put under conditions of increasing cognitive complexity they too showed systematization. Adults who were exposed to a language with one predominant determiner and several non-predominant ones were more likely to over-regularize use of the predominant determiner (Hudson Kam and Newport, 2005b).

How well do infants learn on exposure to probabilistic structure? Gómez and Lakusta (2004) exposed twelve month olds to artificial languages with varying degrees of probabilistic structure. In Condition 100/0 all of the training strings were from the infants' "predominant" training language. In Condition 83/17, approximately 83 percent of the training strings were from the predominant language (the remaining 17 percent of the strings were from the other language). In Condition 67/33, the split between the predominant and non-predominant training languages was 67 percent and 33 percent. Infants in the 100/0 and 83/17 conditions learned equally well, whereas learning diminished in the 67/33 condition, suggesting that infants are able to track regularities in probabilistic input even when the regularities did not occur with perfect probability (as was the case in the 83/17 condition). Learning does need to be based on some minimum degree of regularity, as demonstrated by the fact that infants in the 67/33 condition failed to learn.

36.5.6 Bootstrapping from prior learning

A final question has to do with how learning at one point in time impacts learning at another point, and how one experience builds on another. Lany et al. (2005) investigated this question in the context of learning categories in sequential structure. Adult learners were familiarized with aX and bY strings where X and Y elements were distinguished by different morphological endings (e.g. -ee or -oo). There were two each of the a and b words and six each of the X and Y words; thus a's and b's acted as functor-like elements. Pilot testing showed that generalization to unheard cases occurred after extensive exposure to the language, but not after brief exposure. In the experimental manipulation, learners were given extensive exposure in one vocabulary, followed by brief exposure to strings in new vocabulary. All aspects of vocabulary were new (even the morphological endings), requiring learners to transfer a system of underlying relationships. Learners with prior exposure transferred to the new vocabulary after brief familiarization (in contrast with learners who did not have prior exposure), showing that they were able to generalize the structural relationships from experience. Such learning is relevant for structures in language that are more consistently cued than others. For instance, the morphosyntactic dependencies between determiners and noun endings (diminutives and plurals) are more prevalent than for auxiliaries and inflectional verb endings (Lany et al., 2005). Learners could use a process like that studied by Lany et al. to transfer knowledge of morphosyntax relations from noun phrases to similar structure found in verb phrases.

Experience can also be used to bootstrap more complex learning. After exposure to a language involving a key syntactic relationship (the aX/bY language detailed above), adult learners in Lany et al. were able to detect relationships in a more complex language involving acX and bcY structure. This language was particularly challenging because the intervening c-element required learners to track non-adjacent dependencies between a-and-X and b-and-Y elements. Additionally, the more complex language was instantiated in novel vocabulary, forcing learners to draw on their knowledge of the abstract structural relationships of the aX/bY language. Learners with prior experience were able to generalize to the non-adjacent structure. Language learners who did not receive prior exposure to the more simple language did not generalize. This finding is important for showing how learners might scaffold learning of complex structure from learning of more simple forms. Studies in progress show that twelve-month-olds too are capable of generalizing knowledge of simple adjacent dependencies to more complex non-adjacent structure (Lany and Gómez, forthcoming), despite the fact that infants this age have previously been unable to track non-adjacent structure (Gómez and Maye, 2005).

36.6 Summary

Research on infant learning has yielded a wealth of findings and has raised intriguing questions besides. Infants are able to track sequential information in a number of linguistic domains, including phonotactics, phonology, word segmentation, and remote dependency learning. Infants are also able to perform phonological and morphosyntactic generalizations, suggesting that learning may contribute to linguistic productivity. In particular, infant learners appear to be highly malleable. They show change after as little as two to three minutes of exposure, even for structure occurring frequently in their native language (Saffran and Thiessen, 2003), suggesting that the influence of linguistic input on learning is pervasive and ongoing.

While the findings are promising, they are preliminary. Work on phonotactics (Chambers et al., 2003), phonemic categorization (Maye et al., 2002), and segmentation (Saffran et al., 1996) tap fundamentally into problems in these domains, yet frequency and transitional probabilities cannot explain all of learning (Yang, 2004). Gambell and Yang (2003) tested the efficacy of transitional probabilities for segmenting a corpus of child-directed speech. Transitional probabilities alone achieved very low levels of segmentation (the hit rate for correctly identifying words was only 23.3 percent). Analyses like this are useful for assessing the success of various forms of learning, particularly with respect to scaling learning performance up to the levels required for real-life language tasks. Interestingly, the low levels reported by Yang may still be enough provide an initial wedge into the problem of word segmentation. Of the 23 percent of words correctly extracted, a high proportion of these must have had trochaic stress. If infants use the subset of words they initially segment to learn the predominant stress pattern of their native language (Thiessen and Saffran, 2003), they would then have an additional cue (in the form of a trochaic template) for raising segmentation performance.

Yet another challenge is determining the primitive units of learning. Although sensitivity to phonotactic regularities could conceivably be instrumental in learning some of the syllable structures in one's native language, most would agree that some subset of syllables must be basic. Identifying primitive units is important for placing a lower bound on statistical learning (Yang, 2004) and valuable insights should arise from investigating the dynamic between the primitive structures of language and learning.

Although work on generalization and learning of long-distance dependencies has been informative, it is still limited in its implications for learning syntax. A question is whether such learning is more akin to that required for acquisition of phonological patterns. Research is needed to investigate learning of abstract long-distance relations like those involved in inflectional agreement and binding, and also to investigate how learners form hierarchical relations over categories. Although current research has uncovered rudiments of syntax-like learning, it will be a challenge to bridge the gap to real-life syntax acquisition.

Finally, there is still a great deal to discover regarding cognitive processes in learning. Although statistical learning occurs in non-linguistic domains (Fiser and Aslin, 2002a, b; Kirkham et al., 2002; Saffran et al., 1999; Saffran, Reeck, et al., 2005), we still know little about the cognitive processes involved. Is some structure more easily learned than others? Is memory retention better for certain types of structure? How lasting are the effects of learning, and how easily is memory for one form of structure overwritten by another form? Answers to these questions may provide information about the precedence of learning cues in terms of how likely they are to be recruited—an issue relevant for how learners choose among multiple types of structure (Gómez, 2002; 2005). Another question is how infants coordinate statistical information in auditory and visual domains—an issue with implications for how learners link meaning and form (Altmann, 2002b). A final question has to do with whether infants are performing computations—an assumption broadly held in the literature. In the case of word segmentation, infants are thought to compute transitional probabilities over adjacent syllables (Aslin et al., 1998; Saffran, 2003). Infants are also thought to perform computations over non-adjacent structure (Newport and Aslin, 2004). Are infants performing computations, or is discrimination the result of a simpler process? One proposal is that learners engage in the natural process of chunking on encountering sequential information (Perruchet and Vintner, 1998). Such chunks are initially randomly formed, but if they match subsequent sequences of syllables they are strengthened in memory. Otherwise, the brain's responsiveness to them fades away. The chunks encountered most frequently win out and constitute the words that are ultimately segmented, as shown in a model successfully reproducing performance levels of human subjects (Perruchet and Vintner, 1998). This account has the benefit of explaining how infants might segment words without imposing the computational demands of tracking every possible bigram. Additional work will be needed to determine the extent to which the account will hold up; but this demonstration raises a crucial question about whether learners must perform computations over linguistic input.

In summary, although a great deal of work is needed, it is no longer realistic to doubt the extent of the contribution of learning to language development. Important questions revolve around determining the basic operations and sensitivities that factor into language acquisition (whether these arise from general analytic processes or take the form of language-specific rules), the contributions of learning from regularities in input, and the interaction of the two.

Acknowledgements

Writing of this chapter was supported by an NSF CAREER award to R. Gómez (BCS-0238584) and NIH R01 HD42170 to LouAnn Gerken, R. Gómez, and E. Plante. Suzanne Curtin, L. A.. Gerken, and Gareth Gaskell provided helpful comments and suggestions.

References

Altmann, G. (2002a) Learning and development in neural networks: the importance of prior experience. *Cognition*, 85: B43–B50.

Altmann, G. (2002b) Statistical learning in infants. *Proceedings of the National Academy of Sciences*, 99: 15250–1.

Altmann, G., and Dienes, Z. (1999) Rule learning by seven-month-old infants and neural networks. *Science*, 284: 875a.

Altmann, G., Dienes, Z., and Goode, A. (1995) Modality independence of implicitly learned grammatical knowledge. *Journal of Experimental Psychology: Learning, Memory, and Cognition*, 21: 899–912.

Aslin, R., Saffran, J., and Newport, E. (1998) Computation of conditional probability statistics by 8-month-olds infants. *Psychological Science*, 9: 321–24.

Bates, E., and Elman, J. (1996) Learning rediscovered. *Science*, 274: 1849–50.

Bickerton, D. (1981) *Roots of Language*. Karoma Press, Ann Arbor, MI.

Billman, D. (1989) Systems of correlations in rule and category learning: use of structured input in learning syntactic categories. *Language and Cognitive Processes*, 4: 127–55.

Bortfeld, H., Morgan, J., Golinkoff, R., and Rathbun, K. (2005) *Mommy* and me: familiar names help launch babies into speech-stream segmentation. *Psychological Science*, 16: 298–304.

Braine, M. (1987) What is learned in acquiring words classes: a step toward acquisition theory. In B MacWhinney (ed.), *Mechanisms of language acquisition*, pp. 65–87. Erlbaum, Hillsdale, NJ.

Chambers, K. (2004) Phonological development: mechanisms and representations. Ph.D. dissertation, University of Illinois.

Chambers, K., Onishi, K., and Fisher, C. (2003) Infants learn phonotactic regularities from brief auditory experience. *Cognition*, 87: B69–B77.

Chomsky, N. (1959) A review of B. F. Skinner's *Verbal Behavior*. *Language*, 35: 26–58.

Chomsky, N. (1965) *Aspects of the Theory of Syntax*. MIT Pres, Cambridge, MA.

Chomsky, N. (1981) *Lectures on Government and Binding*. Foris, Dordrecht.

Christiansen, M., and Curtin, S. (1999) The power of statistical learning: no need for algebraic rules. *Proceedings of the Twenty-First Annual Conference of the Cognitive Science Society*, pp. 114–19. Erlbaum, Mahwah, NJ.

Cutler, A., and Norris, D. (1988) The role of strong syllables in segmentation for lexical access. *Journal of Experimental Psychology: Human Perception and Performance*, 14: 113–21.

Elman, J., Bates, E., Johnson, M., Karmiloff-Smith, A., Parisi, D., and Plunkett, K. (1996) *Rethinking Innateness: A Connectionist Perspective on Development*. MIT Press, Cambridge, MA.

Fiser, J., and Aslin, R. (2002a) Statistical learning of new visual feature combinations by infants. *Proceedings of the National Academy of Sciences*, 99: 15822–6.

Fiser, J., and Aslin, N. (2002b) Statistical learning of higher-order temporal structure from visual shape sequences. *Journal of Experimental Psychology: Learning, Memory, and Cognition*, 28: 458–67.

Friederici, A., and Wessels, J. (1993) Phonotactic knowledge of word boundaries and its use in infant speech perception. *Perception and Psychophysics*, 54: 287–95.

Frigo, L., and McDonald, J. (1998) Properties of phonological markers that affect the acquisition of gender-like subclasses. *Journal of Memory and Language*, 39: 218–45.

Gambell, T., and Yang, C. (2003) Scope and limits of statistical learning in word segmentation. In *Proceedings of the thirty fourth Northeastern Linguistic Society Meeting (NELS)*, pp. 29–30. Stony Brook University, New York.

Gassar, M., and Colunga, E. (1999) Babies, variables, and connectionist models. In M. Hahn and S. Stone (eds), *Proceedings of the Twenty-First Annual Conference of the Cognitive Science Society*, p. 794. Erlbaum, Mahwah, NJ.

Gerken, L. A. (2004) Nine-month-olds extract structural principles required for natural language. *Cognition*, 93: B89–B96.

Gerken, L. A. (2006) Decisions, decisions: infant language learning when multiple generalizations are possible. *Cognition*, 98: B67–B74.

Gerken, L. A., Wilson, R., and Lewis, W. (2005) 17-month-olds can use distributional cues to form syntactic categories. *Journal of Child Language*, 32: 249–68.

Gleitman, L., and Wanner, E. (1982) The state of the state of the art. In E. Wanner and L. Gleitman (eds), *Language Acquisition: The State of the Art*, pp. 3–48. Cambridge University Press, Cambridge.

Gómez, R. (2002) Variability and detection of invariant structure. *Psychological Science*, 13: 431–36.

Gómez, R. (2005) Dynamically guided learning. In Y. Munakata and M. Johnson (eds), *Attention and Performance XXI: Processes of Change in Brain and Cognitive Development*, pp.87–110. Oxford University Press, Oxford.

Gómez, R., and Gerken, L. A. (2000) Infant artificial language learning and language acquisition. *Trends in Cognitive Sciences*, 4: 178–86.

Gómez, R., and Gerken, L. A. (1999) Artificial grammar learning by one-year-olds leads to specific and abstract knowledge. *Cognition*, 70: 109–35.

Gómez, R., Gerken, L. A., and Schvaneveldt, R. (2000) The basis of transfer in artificial grammar learning. *Memory and Cognition*, 28: 253–63.

Gómez, R., and Lakusta, L. (2004) A first step in form-based category abstraction by 12-month-old infants. *Developmental Science*, 7: 567–80.

Gómez, R., and Maye, J. (2005) The developmental trajectory of non-adjacent dependency learning. *Infancy*, 7: 183–206.

Grimshaw, J. (1981) Form, function, and the language acquisition device. In C. Baker and J. McCarthy (eds), *The Logical Problem of Language Acquisition*, pp. 165–82. MIT Press, Cambridge, MA.

Hudson Kam, C., and Newport, E. (2005a) Regularizing unpredictable variation: the roles of adult and child learners in language formation and change. *Language Learning and Development*, 1: 151–95.

Hudson Kam, C., and Newport, E. (2005b) Getting it right by getting it wrong: When learners change languages. MS, submitted for publication.

Hyams, N. (1986) *Language Acquisition and the Theory of Parameters*. Reidel, Dordrecht.

Johnson, E., and Jusczyk, P. (2001) Word segmentation by 8-month-olds: when speech cues count more than statistics. *Journal of Memory and Language*, 44: 548–67.

Jusczyk, P. (1997) *The Discovery of Spoken Language*. MIT Press, Cambridge, MA.

Jusczyk, P., Friederici, A., Wessels, J., Svenkerud, V., and Jusczyk, A. M. (1993) Infants' sensitivity to the sound patterns of native language words. *Journal of Memory and Language*, 32: 402–20.

Jusczyk, P., Houston, D., and Newsome, M. (1999) The beginnings of word segmentation in English-learning infants. *Cognitive Psychology*, 39: 159–207.

Jusczyk, P., Luce, P., and Charles-Luce, J. (1994) Infants' sensitivity to phonotactic patterns in the native language. *Journal of Memory and Language*, 33: 630–45.

Kelly, M. (1992) Using sound to solve syntactic problems: the role of phonology in grammatical category assignments. *Psychological Review*, 99: 349–64.

Kemler Nelson, D., Jusczyk, P., Mandel, D., Myers, J., Turk, A., and Gerken, L. A. (1995) The Head-turn Preference Procedure for testing auditory perception. *Infant Behavior and Development*, 18: 111–16.

Kirkham, N., Slemmer, J., and Johnson, S. (2002) Visual statistical learning in infancy: evidence for a domain general learning mechanism. *Cognition*, 83: B35–B42.

Lany, J., Gómez, R., and Gerken, L. A. (2005) The role of prior experience in language acquisition. MS, submitted for publication.

Lany, J., and Gómez, R. (forthcoming) Infants use prior experience to bootstrap from simple to more complex structure. MS in preparation.

Liberman, A., Cooper, F., Shankweiler, D., and Studdert-Kennedy, M. (1967) Perception of speech code. *Psychological Review*, 74: 431–61.

Mackain, K. (1982) Assessing the role of experience on infants' speech discrimination. *Journal of Child Language*, 9: 527–42.

Manzini, R., and Wexler, K. (1987) Parameters, Binding Theory and learnability. *Linguistic Inquiry*, 18: 413–44.

Marcus, G. (2001) *The Algebraic Mind*. MIT Press, Cambridge, MA.

Marcus, G., Vijayan, S., Bandi Rao, S., and Vishton, P. (1999) Rule learning by seven-month-old infants. *Science*, 283: 77–80.

Mattys, S., and Juszcyk, P. (2001) Do infants segment words or recurring contiguous patterns? *Journal of Experimental Psychology: Human Perception and Performance*, 27: 644–55.

Maye, J., Werker, J., and Gerken, L. A. (2002) Infant sensitivity to distributional information can affect phonetic discrimination. *Cognition*, 82: B101–11.

Maye, J., Weiss, D., and Aslin, R. (forthcoming) Statistical phonetic learning in infants: facilitation and feature generalization. *Developmental Science*.

Mintz, T. (1996) The roles of linguistic input and innate mechanisms in children's acquisition of grammatical categories. Ph.D. dissertation, University of Rochester.

Mintz, T. (2002) Category induction from distributional cues in an artificial language. *Memory and Cognition*, 30: 678–86.

Mintz, T. (2003) Frequent frames as a cue for grammatical categories in child directed speech. *Cognition*, 90: 91–117.

Mintz, T. (2004) Twelve-month-olds categorize novel words using distributional information. Poster presented at the fourteenth Biennial International Conference on Infant Studies, Chicago, May.

Monaghan, P., Onnis, L., Christiansen, M., and Chater, N. (forthcoming) The importance of being variable: learning non-adjacent dependencies in speech processing. MS under review.

Morgan, J., and Demuth, K. (eds) (1996) *Signal to Syntax*. Erlbaum, Mahwah, NJ.

Morgan, J., and Newport, E. (1981) The role of constituent structure in the induction of an artificial language. *Journal of Verbal Learning and Verbal Behavior*, 20: 67–85.

Naigles, L. (2002) Form is easy, meaning is hard: resolving a paradox in early child language. *Cognition*, 86: 157–99.

Newport, E. L. (1990) Maturational constraints on language learning. *Cognitive Science*, 14: 11–28.

Newport, E. (1999) Reduced input in the acquisition of signed languages: contributions to the study of creolization. In M. DeGraff (ed.), *Language Creation and Language Change*, pp. 161–78. MIT Press, Cambridge, MA.

Newport, E., and Aslin, R. (2004) Learning at a distance, I: Statistical learning of non-adjacent dependencies. *Cognitive Psychology*, 48: 127–62.

Onnis, L., Destrebecqz, A., Christiansen, M., Chater, N., and Cleeremans, A. (2005) Processing non-adjacent dependencies: a graded, associative account. MS, submitted for publication.

Pegg, J., and Werker, J. (1997) Adult and infant perception of two English phones. *Journal of the Acoustical Society of America*, 102: 3742–53.

Perruchet, P., and Vintner, A. (1998) PARSER: a model for word segmentation. *Journal of Memory and Language*, 39: 246–63.

Pinker, S. (1984) *Language Learnability and Language Levelopment.* Harvard University Press, Cambridge, MA.

Redington, M., Chater, N., and Finch, S. (1998) Distributional information: a powerful cue for acquiring syntactic categories. *Cognitive Science*, 22: 425–69.

Roeper, T., and Williams, E. (1987) *Parameter Setting.* Reidel, Dordrecht.

Ross, D., and Newport, E. (1996) The development of language from non-native linguistic input. In A. Stringfellow, D. Cahana-Amitay, E. Hughs, and A. Zukowski (eds), *Proceedings of the twenteeth Annual Boston University Conference on Language Development*, pp. 634–5. Cascadilla Press, Boston, MA.

Saffran, J. (2001) Words in a sea of sounds: the output of statistical learning. *Cognition*, 81: 149–69.

Saffran, J. (2003) Statistical language learning: mechanisms and constraints. *Current Directions in Psychological Science*, 12: 110–14.

Saffran, J., Aslin, R., and Newport, E. (1996) Statistical learning by eight-month-old infants. *Science*, 274: 1926–28.

Saffran, J., Hauser, M., Seibel, R., Kapfhamer, J., Fritz, T., and Cushman, F. (2005) Cross-species differences in the capacity to acquire language: Grammatical pattern learning by human infants and monkeys. MS, submitted for publication.

Saffran, J., Johnson, E., Aslin, R., and Newport, E. (1999) Statistical learning of tonal structure by adults and infants. *Cognition*, 70: 27–52.

Saffran, J., Reeck, K., Niehbur, A., and Wilson, D. (2005) Changing the tune: absolute and relative pitch processing by adults and infants. *Developmental Science*, 8: 1–7.

Saffran, J., and Thiessen, E. (2003) Pattern induction by infant language learners. *Developmental Psychology*, 39: 484–94.

Saffran, J., and Wilson, D. (2003) From syllables to syntax: multi-level statistical learning by twelve-month-old infants. *Infancy*, 4: 273–84.

Santelmann, L., and Jusczyk, P. (1998) Sensitivity to discontinuous dependencies in language learners: evidence for limitations in processing space. *Cognition*, 69: 105–34.

Seidenberg, M., and Elman, J. (1999) Do infants learn grammar with algebra or statistics? (letter) *Science*, 284: 434–35.

Shastri, L. (1999) Infants learning algebraic rules. *Science*, 285: 1673–74.

Shultz, T. (2003) *Computational Developmental Psychology.* MIT Press, Cambridge, MA.

Shultz, T., and Bale, A. (2001) Neural network simulation of infant familiarization to artificial sentences: rule-like behavior without explicit rules and variables. *Infancy*, 2: 501–36.

Shultz, T., and Gerken, L. A. (2005) A model of infant learning of word stress. In *Proceedings of the Twenty-seventh Annual Conference of the Cognitive Science Society*, pp. 2015–20. Erlbaum, Mahwah, NJ.

Singleton, J., and Newport, E. (2004) When learners surpass their models: the acquisition of American Sign Language from inconsistent input. *Cognitive Psychology*, 49: 370–407.

Skinner, B. F. (1957) *Verbal Behavior.* Appleton-Century-Crofts, New York.

Smith, K. (1969) Learning co-occurrence restrictions: rule learning or rote learning? *Journal of Verbal Behavior*, 8: 319–21.

Stager, C., and Werker, J. (1997) Infants listen for more phonetic detail in speech perception than in word-learning tasks. *Nature*, 388: 381–2.

Swingley, D., and Aslin, R. (2000) Spoken word recognition and lexical representation in very young children. *Cognition*, 76: 147–66.

Thiessen, E., Hill, E., and Saffran, J. (2005) Infant-directed speech facilitates word segmentation. *Infancy*, 7: 53–71.

Thiessen, E., and Saffran, J. (2003) When cues collide: use of stress and statistical cues to word boundaries by 7- to nine-month-old infants. *Developmental Psychology*, 39: 706–16.

Werker, J., Fennell, C., Corcoran, K., and Stager, C. (2002) Infants' ability to learn phonetically similar words: effects of age and vocabulary size. *Infancy*, 3: 1–30.

Werker, J., and Pegg, J. (1992) Infant speech perception and phonological acquisition. In C. Ferguson, L. Menn, and C. Stoel-Gammon (eds), *Phonological Development: Models, Research, Implications*, pp. 285–311. York Press, Timonium, MD.

Werker, J., and Tees, R. (1984) Developmental changes across childhood in the perception of nonnative speech sounds. *Canadian Journal of Psychology*, 37: 278–86.

Wexler, K., and Culicover, P. (1980) *Formal Principles of Language Acquisition.* MIT Press, Cambridge, MA.

Wilson, R. (2002) Category induction in second language learning: what artificial grammars can tell us. Ph.D. dissertation, University of Arizona.

Yang, C. (2004) Universal grammar, statistics or both? *TRENDS in Cognitive Science*, 8: 451–6.

CHAPTER 37

Word learning

Melissa A. Koenig and Amanda Woodward

37.1 Introduction

What is a word? Is it a particular sequence of sounds, something that we can produce in a single breath? Is it a piece of sound or writing that picks out some particular object, person or event, or perhaps a concept? Some words fit this description, but others such as function words (e.g. *the, a, of*) do not. Is it a concept that acquires meaning due to its role in the grammatical structure of a sentence? Words certainly may play such roles, but it may not be necessary. Single words have meaning for young children well before they can string them together into phrases. Is it a sound sequence that is produced by a speaker with clear referential intentions? Children pay special attention to people's intentional cues when learning new words, however, it is possible to learn and recognize words in the absence of such cues (Werker et al., 1998).

In this chapter, we will argue that theories of word learning must account for all such aspects of a word. Word learning constitutes a "special" problem precisely because words constitute complex collections of properties. A word is a symbol. It is a linguistic unit with syntactic, morphological, and phonological properties. A word is a social convention. It is a type of intentional action that refers to a meaningful concept. Thus, children's learning of words, even simple names such as *dog, water*, and *Mommy*, requires a set of mental capacities that interact in powerful ways.

The multi-faceted nature of words creates a challenge in development, but it is also a guide to further development. Once children have begun to piece out the critical components of words, this knowledge then constrains and facilitates future learning. As Hirsh-Pasek, Golinkoff, Hollich, and their colleagues have noted, word learning requires a "coalition" of systems that become integrated during development (Hirsh-Pasek et al., 2000; Hollich et al., 2000). By 3 to 5 years of age, children have a multi-faceted arsenal of word knowledge at their disposal. This arsenal includes knowledge that is specific to the language system, as well as more general knowledge, for example, understanding others' intentions (Bloom, 2000; Woodward and Markman, 1998). Even the incomplete knowledge that infants bring to the task of word learning provides important guidance. For example, if the infant knows nothing else, knowing that a word reflects a speaker's intentions will help them to avoid learning spurious word–object links in virtue of temporal contiguity alone, and increase the likelihood of recovering the intended meaning (Baldwin and Moses, 2001).

Below, we survey children's acquisition of the essential properties of words, focusing both on the challenge of acquisition and on the generative effects of acquisition for further learning. Recent work has begun to explore the earliest roots of word knowledge, and revealed that even at the dawn of word learning, young children bring to bear their knowledge not only of speaker's intentions but also their knowledge of the conventional and contrastive nature of linguistic symbols, the link between names and conceptual categories, and the probabilistic correspondences between syntax and semantics.

37.2 Word as symbol

One essential characteristic of words is their symbolic function. Language, or the linguistic symbol, is the form of mediation that has preoccupied psychologists of both past (Piaget and Inhelder, 1969; Vygotsky, 1962) and present (Bates, 1979; Tomasello, 1999). However, no artifact or action is intrinsically or necessarily a symbol—in fact, there is no limit to the list of things that can represent other things. So how do children figure out what entities function as symbols? Interestingly, recent research demonstrates that young children begin the word-learning process with a general openness to the kinds of sign that they are willing to adopt as object labels. For example, Namy (2001) introduced eighteen-month-old infants to a range of different symbolic media, including words, gestures, non-verbal sounds, and pictograms, all of which were arbitrarily linked to their referents. Infants mapped each of these forms to the appropriate object categories, interpreting all four symbol types as object names. In fact, infants between thirteen and eighteen months of age appear to learn non-verbal "names" for objects just as readily as verbal labels (Campbell and Namy, 2003; Namy and Waxman, 1998; Woodward and Hoyne, 1999). This early flexibility or openness changes in development as slightly older children demonstrate more conservative judgment in the types of symbolic form that they will accept. Starting at around twenty months, a preference for the verbal modality emerges, grows increasingly stronger (Namy and Waxman, 1998; Woodward and Hoyne, 1999), and by twenty-six months interferes with children's ability to learn arbitrary gestures (Namy et al., 2004). It may be that as children develop a more sophisticated understanding of the conventions that govern their language, their initial amodal orientation gradually becomes focused on the dominant symbolic medium.

Symbols refer to objects, ideas, and properties; they allow us to represent things. Most importantly, symbols are not mere associates of their referents. Instead, understanding the symbolic nature of a sign requires understanding that the word is qualitatively distinct from its referent. An interesting and important issue in the study of early symbolic development is when young word learners appreciate this fact. Preissler and Carey (2004) investigated this issue by repeatedly presenting eighteen- and twenty-four-month-old children with an unfamiliar word (e.g. *whisk*) paired with a drawing of a whisk. Children were then asked for the *whisk* when given a choice between the original picture that had been paired with the whisk and a real whisk. In response, children almost always chose the real object or both the picture and the object, indicating that they assumed that the word referred to the object, not just to the picture that it had been previously associated with. In fact, children never selected the pictured whisk alone. Children's selection of the real object, either alone or with its picture, indicates that they interpreted the picture and the word symbolically—as representations of real-world objects.

It is important to note that the demonstration of early symbolic competence as discussed above involves presenting symbols in a social-referential naming routine. This signals another essential characteristic of early symbolic understanding. As stated by DeLoache (2004), "a person's intention that one entity represent another is both necessary and sufficient to establish a symbolic relation." No particular entities are intrinsic symbols. Instead, symbols are interpreted as such because we understand that they were designed to be interpreted in that way, or are very likely to be interpreted that way (Deacon, 1997). Indeed, work by Baldwin and colleagues (1991; 1993; 1996) and Tomasello and colleagues (Akhtar and Tomasello, 2002; Tomasello, 1999), summarized below, provides a wealth of convergent evidence for the conclusion that, for children, the mapping between words and objects is an intentional, symbolic relation.

37.3 **Word as type of intentional action**

The problem of induction serves to clarify the challenge that faces any word learner (Quine, 1960). In a discussion of this classic problem in philosophy of mind and language, Quine asked that we imagine a linguist who travels to a foreign land to learn the language of a newly discovered human population. A native shouts *gavagai* as a rabbit runs by. The linguist's first reasonable intuition is that *gavagai* means 'rabbit'; and although this is a reasonable first guess, there are indefinitely many ways in which the word could be interpreted. Thus, the challenge for the word learner is not to consider an infinite list of possible interpretations for a new word but to restrict the range of possible hypotheses. Despite the many possible meanings a word might have, one-year-olds often can identify a new word's meaning from fewer than ten exposures to it (Woodward et al., 1994). Furthermore, two- and three-year-old children can often approximate the correct meaning after a single exposure (Carey, 1978; Heibeck and Markman, 1987).

One critical source of information for children which helps them to restrict this list of possibilities is their knowledge of how speakers communicate. To build upon our discussion of symbolic understanding above, imagine that the young child understands both that words are likely to bear some relation to external objects and that speakers typically offer cues signaling the target of their referential intent—cues that help to clarify the relevant external object. When a new word is heard, children could then initiate a search for a candidate external object to link to that word, and they could consult cues from the speaker to help guide that search. Given that speakers typically supply a rich and redundant set of intentional cues in speech to young children, just one exposure to a new word might be sufficient for infants to register considerable information about the reference and meaning of the new term.

The pioneering research of Baldwin, Tomasello, and colleagues (e.g. Akhtar and Tomasello, 2002; Akhtar et al., 1996; Baldwin, 1991; Baldwin et al., 1996; Baldwin and Moses, 2001; Tomasello and Barton, 1994) has documented that cues to referential intent influence infants interpretations of new words by eighteen months. For example, eighteen month olds will learn the link between a new word and a novel object when the person who utters the word looks toward the toy and points to it, but will not do so when such cues are absent or indicate a contrasting object (e.g. Baldwin, 1991; Baldwin et al., 1996). Similarly, Tomasello and Barton (1994) found that twenty-four-month-old children use intentional cues when learning verbs. An experimenter introduced a novel verb (e.g. *Let's dax Mickey Mouse*) before producing either an accidental or purposeful action. Regardless of what particular action was demonstrated, infants interpreted the verb as the name for the purposeful, not the accidental, action. Children used multiple cues to infer the intentions of the speaker, took them to apply to the act done on purpose, and extended verb meaning accordingly.

Does knowledge about speaker intent play a role at the start of word learning, for example, at twelve months of age? After all, infants at this age begin to show a number of social behaviors such as gaze-following, pointing, imitation of actions on objects, social referencing, and so forth (Tomasello, 1995). One issue is whether such behaviors reflect a genuine understanding of the experiential lives of other people or whether they simply reflect sensitivity to external social contingencies (as argued e.g. by Moore, 1998). Recent evidence indicates that registering external contingencies alone is unlikely to explain infants' use of communicative cues in word learning. To start, by twelve months of age infants do more than simply respond to others' shifts in gaze; they also represent the relation between a person and the object of her attention (Phillips et al., 2002; Sodian and Thoermer, 2004; Woodward, 2004; Woodward and Guajardo, 2002). Although this relation is invisible for infants, as for adults, it is a salient feature of others' actions.

This understanding of attention informs infants' interpretation of others' communicative behavior. For example, Tomasello and Haberl (2003) found that twelve-month-old infants are able to keep track of what a person has and hasn't seen, and use this information to interpret her subsequent utterances. Specifically, infants assumed that an adult's expressions of surprise and excitement must refer to an object that the adult had not previously seen. Furthermore, several studies have shown that infants as young as 12–14 months interpret new words (and emotional expressions) based on information about the speaker's attention and apparent intention (Baldwin and Moses, 2001; Campbell and Namy, 2003; Moses et al., 2001; Woodward, 2004). In one study, Woodward (2004) reported that thirteen-month-old infants readily accepted a novel word as the name for an object when the speaker indicated the object with gaze and pointing. However, when the speaker's attention was directed elsewhere they did not accept the new label, even though they experienced strong contiguity between hearing the label and seeing the object.

This is not to say that infants possess adult-like pragmatic knowledge, or that important developments in social understanding do not occur in the first and second years of life. There is probably prolonged development in the flexibility of infants' use of attentional actions to infer referential intent. For example, in a study by Moore, Angelopoulos, and Bennet (1999), eighteen-month-olds used a speaker's line of regard to determine to which of two objects she was referring. However, when one of the objects was made extremely salient (i.e. by moving and making noise), it was not until twenty four months of age that infants assumed that the speaker was referring to the salient object. Eighteen month olds, in contrast, seemed to require some kind of explicit cue from the speaker that clarified to what they were referring.

37.4 **Word as social convention**

Among students of language, there is near-universal agreement that conventional understanding is a central element of linguistic competence. A fully competent user of language appreciates, on some level, that words convey information by virtue of shared knowledge about their relations to things external. Understanding this fact about the conventionality of language provides a foundation for putting words to use in communication. Thus, one key component of conventional knowledge is the understanding that all speakers (in a community) use the same word to convey a given meaning. Clark (1993: 67) proposed that word learning is guided by a number of pragmatic principles, including a principle of conventionality, which states: "For certain meanings, there is a form that speakers expect to be used in the language community." Thus, having learned that a person uses the word *cat* to refer to cats, learners should readily generalize this knowledge to other speakers of English.

Another key component of conventional knowledge is the understanding that linguistic forms constitute a system in which different forms convey different meanings. Therefore, if a person uses a word other than the conventionally appropriate one in a given situation, he or she must mean to convey something other than the meaning conveyed by the conventional form. This principle, termed the "principle of contrast" (Clark, 1993; for related formulations see Golinkoff et al., 1992; Markman, 1989), has been shown to contribute to children's learning of novel terms, and their correcting of initially over-general word meanings. Across many experiments, young children have been shown to use the principle of contrast to interpret new words (see Bloom, 2000; Woodward and Markman, 1998 for reviews). For example, in a preferential looking procedure, seventeen-month-old infants made use of the contrastive nature of words to interpret new words (Halberda, 2003; see Markman et al., 2003 for a related finding).

Most of the experiments which have tested children's use of contrast ask children to interpret the word use of a single speaker. However, recent findings suggest that preschoolers also expect forms to contrast in meanings across speakers. For example, Diesendruck and Markson (2001) presented three-year-old children with two novel objects, one of which the experimenter picked up and labeled, *This is a zev*. Afterward, a sleepy, secluded puppet emerged from his house and asked the child, *Can you give me the jop?*. Children typically responded by giving the puppet the object that had not been labeled *zev* by the experimenter, suggestive evidence that children attributed knowledge of *zev* to the puppet even when the puppet was not present when the naming took place (see also Au and Glusman, 1990). These findings indicate that three year olds assume that individuals would share knowledge of the novel label even if they had not been provided with explicit evidence that this was the case. Interestingly, in a control condition which replaced words with facts about objects such as *the one my uncle gave me* or *the one that goes inside a fish tank*, children did not attribute shared knowledge to the secluded puppet. These results indicate that preschool-age children know about the first two properties of conventions mentioned above, and also that they differentiate between words and other kinds of socially given information in applying these properties.

Recent research by Henderson and Graham (2005) suggests that even two year olds understand that word knowledge is shared. Children were taught a novel word while playing a finding game with the experimenter, and were later asked to select the target item from an array of objects and to generalize the new word beyond the initial exemplar to another member of the category. One group of children were taught the initial word–object mapping by one person and tested by a different person. As a result, children successfully learned the original word–object link and extended the novel label to another member of the same category. It is important to note that, in a second study, when presented with cues that signaled the experimenter's preference for a particular object, children did not assume that such information generalized to a second speaker. This ability to generalize novel labels, but not preferences, to a second speaker who was absent during the initial training suggests that infants may possess an understanding that word knowledge is uniquely conventional. Recent evidence suggests that this understanding is in place as early as nineteen months of age (Graham et al., 2006).

Important questions regarding the development of conventional understanding remain. According to Bates et al. (1979), the period between nine to thirteen months of age sees both the discovery that things have names and the onset of communicative intentions and conventional signals. According to Clark (1993), the fact that infants happily use idiosyncratic names for objects demonstrates that the principle of conventionality is not present at the start of word learning. For Hirsh-Pasek et al. (2000), infants' initial grasp of the principle of reference—that consistent phonological forms map to external entities—later evolves into the principle of conventionality in the second year of life. These views hold in common the idea that understanding "conventionality" fundamentally reflects an appreciation of the fact that word forms are used consistently across contexts. While an appropriate first gloss, it is likely that conventionality involves more than this. In addition to understanding that all speakers (within a community) use the same form–meaning pairings, children need to appreciate that these pairings form a contrastive system, that not all knowledge is shared, and that conventional systems can, in principle, vary across speakers. While each of these components has been examined in naturalistic settings, systematic experimental evidence concerning the origins of this knowledge is limited.

37.5 Word as conceptual

Words derive their expressive power from their relation to rich conceptual knowledge. The range of possible word meanings is vast. Words can name individuals, objects of a kind, relations, movements, states, properties, and so on. Across this range, meanings are organized by conceptual structure. For example, common nouns extend to members of a kind (e.g. dogs or chairs or brothers), and these kinds reflect important shared structure, at an abstract as well as perceptual level (Markman, 1989; Waxman, 2002). Other classes of word meanings are similarly dependent on conceptual structure. As examples, understanding proper names depends on conceptions of individual identity (Hall, 1998; Woodward and Markman, 1998), and understanding verbs depends on conceptions of actions and events (Hirsh-Pasek and Golinkoff, forthcoming; Huttenlocher et al., 1983).

Early in the study of language acquisition, theorists proposed that the relation between words and concepts was a relatively late achievement in development. Words were assumed to function as unconstrained associates of whole situations for babies. For example, the word *shoe* might be extended equally to shoes, socks, feet, and the routine of getting dressed. In pioneering work, Huttenlocher and her colleagues tested this long-held assumption and found it to be false (Huttenlocher and Smiley, 1987). Having analyzed the spontaneous speech of one year olds, they found that in almost all cases, nouns were used to name members of the appropriate taxonomic category. In the minority of cases in which nouns were used in the presence of thematic associates there was evidence that children were not intending to label the associate, but rather were commenting on the thematic relation or describing a prior event. Thus, even children's earliest words name members of well-organized categories.

Subsequent experiments have reinforced this conclusion, and shown the power of the connection between words and concepts from very early in life. For example, Waxman and her colleagues have found that hearing different items given the same name leads children and infants to seek out commonalities between them. That is, words function as "invitations" to form categories (Balaban and Waxman, 1997; Waxman and Markow, 1995) and as invitations to attend to regularities that are diagnostic of kind membership (Booth et al., 2005). Furthermore, Graham et al. (2004) found that labels support inductive inferences in thirteen-month-old infants: when babies observed disparate objects being given the same name, they were more likely to assume that they shared a non-visible property (such as making a noise when shaken) than when no names were given or when the objects were given different names. Similarly, Waxman and Markow (1995) have shown that a novel label applied to members of the same superordinate category can facilitate the formation of a superordinate category in twelve month olds. Thus, even very for young infants who are just beginning to produce their first words there is a tight relation between names and conceptual categories, and they can use language to categorize objects in nonobvious ways.

An issue of current debate concerns the developmental origin of this relation. On the one hand, bottom-up associative learning must play a strong role. As children hear words paired with referents, they build a store of associations that tunes their attention in subsequent learning contexts, and thereby leads to learning that generalizes to the appropriate range of referents. Smith and her colleagues have posited that this kind of attentional shaping accounts for children's tendency to extend novel common nouns to items of like shape (Landau et al., 1988; Samuelson and Smith, 2000; Smith, 1999), as well as for infants' attention to referential behaviors in word learning (Samuelson and Smith, 1998; see also Hollich et al., 2000). Consistent with the first of these suggestions, Smith and colleagues have shown that artificially boosting shape learning experiences in one year olds leads to the more rapid acquisition of count nouns outside of the laboratory (Smith et al., 2002). Thus, associative learning can yield well-tuned expectations about word–referent relations.

Others have argued that associative learning alone cannot account for the conceptual basis for word meanings. For one, many conceptual categories are organized by abstract theory-like knowledge structures and beliefs about essential and non-visible inner structure as a basis for kind membership. Our understanding of the word *cat*, for example, depends not just on our history of associations between the word and its referents: we also believe that there is complex inner structure that is essential to being a cat, even though we may know little of the specific nature of this structure and have never directly observed it. This kind of knowledge is robustly evident in young children's language use and learning (see Gelman, 2003 for a review), and may even be traceable into infancy (Mandler and McDonough, 1996; Booth et al., 2005).

Another issue of current debate concerns the extent to which the development of concepts and word meanings varies across languages and cultures. In principle there is no limit on the range of meanings words can ultimately convey. But how constrained are the very first steps in building a vocabulary? Languages vary in terms of how information is "packaged" into word meanings, and children are adept at acquiring these varied meanings. For example, languages vary widely in the lexicalization of spatial relations (Bowerman and Choi, 2003). Consider two instances that would be described using the same term, *in*, in English: an apple placed inside a bowl and a video cassette placed inside its case. In Korean, these would be described using distinct verbs to mark the tightness vs. looseness of the fit. Children acquire these two systems equally early: their production and comprehension of spatial terms reflects the language specific patterns as early as 14–18 months age (see Bowerman and Choi, 2003 for a review). Findings such as these indicate that infants are able to entertain a range of possible word meanings.

Nevertheless, it has been posited that some conceptual packages are more readily available than others to learners across languages. In particular, human perceptual and cognitive systems readily parse the world into discrete whole objects, and, because of this, it has been proposed that terms naming whole objects are privileged in development (Gentner, 1982; Gentner and Boroditsky, 2001; Markman, 1989). Consistent with this hypothesis, English-acquiring children have a bias to interpret novel words as naming whole objects rather than as names for parts or properties (Golinkoff et al., 1994; Markman, 1989). There has been debate about whether this is true for children acquiring languages in which object names are less syntactically and pragmatically salient than they are in English (Tardif et al., 1999; Choi and Gopnik, 1995; see Woodward and Markman, 1998 and Gentner and Boroditsky, 2001 for reviews). Words naming objects are less prevalent in both parents' and children's vocabularies in these languages than they are in English. However, it is not yet known whether this difference in prevalence reflects a fundamental difference in the conceptual salience of whole objects. Gentner and her colleagues (Imai and Gentner, 1997; Gentner and Boroditsky, 2001) have suggested that there is a conceptual continuum reflecting the extent to which an item is individuable. This continuum is anchored at one end by complex solid (and perhaps animate) objects. Children across language groups seem to find these highly individuable items to be compelling as possible referents. Children's interpretations vary for less individuable items (e.g. piles of a substance) based on the extent to which object labels are highlighted in their language.

37.6 **Word as grammatical unit**

In addition to being intentionally produced, meaning-bearing units in a conventional system, words can also be defined with respect to their role in larger linguistic structures—that is, they are the components combined to yield sentences. As such, words have syntactic as well as semantic properties. Though theoretically independent, there is a rough correlation between some aspects of syntax and some aspects of meaning in everyday language use. Studies of parental speech across different languages have found that syntactic cues to verb meaning exist in the sentences that children hear (Fisher et al., 1991; Lee and Naigles, 2005; Naigles and Hoff-Ginsberg, 1995). Children exploit these correlations in word learning from very early on.

One of the first examples of this was identified by Brown (1958), who found that children's interpretation of a novel word, *sib*, varied as function of the syntactic form class in which it appeared. Children identified *a sib* as a discrete object, *some sib* as a quantity of non-solid substance, and *sibbing* as the name for an action being carried out on these items. Researchers have since documented children's use of form class as a cue to word meaning as early as eighteen months of age and across form class categories including proper vs. common nouns (Hall, 1994; Hall and Belanger, 2005; Katz et al., 1974; Macnamara, 1982), nouns vs. adjectives (Taylor and Gelman, 1988; Waxman and Booth, 2001), and nouns vs. prepositions (Landau and Stecker, 1990).

While Brown argued that syntax can facilitate the acquisition of nominal meanings, others have made the stronger claim that syntax is essential for the acquisition of at least some word meanings, especially verbs. Fisher et al. (1994) presented preschool-age children with videos that depicted familiar events such as feeding and eating and described them using sentences that contained novel verbs (e.g. *The bunny is nading the elephant* vs. *The elephant is daking*). When children were asked what these verbs meant, they tended to give the appropriate paraphrases. In fact, regardless of whether children responded with innovative phrasal descriptions or simple English equivalents, their responses were sensitive to the syntax of the original sentence. Thus, children's interpretation of verb meaning appeared to be guided by syntactic cues. Similar conclusions are supported by more recent research by Fisher (1996; 2005) which presented children with novel events paired with sentences differing in the number of arguments (e.g. *She's gepping* vs. *She's gepping her*). Children by 2.5 years of age, responded to these syntactic manipulations and identified the agent of a novel verb (Fisher, 2005).

Naigles (1990) used a different methodology in her work with two year olds. She showed twenty-five-month-old children scenes that simultaneously depicted two events—a causal event involving two individuals (e.g. a duck putting a bunny in a bent position) and a non-causal event involving a single participant (e.g. same duck and bunny with free arms waving). Children either heard a novel verb in a transitive context (*The duck is gorping the bunny*) or an intransitive context (*The duck and bunny are gorping*). When children were presented with these two events on separate video screens, one that showed only the causal event and one that showed only the non-causal event and heard, *Find gorping*, two-year-olds who heard the transitive frame looked longer at the causal event and those who heard the intransitive frame looked longer at the non-causal event. More recently, it has been demonstrated that children between twenty-four and thirty months are sensitive to stable aspects of verb meaning across different syntactic contexts: after being taught a novel verb meaning in a transitive frame, children later recognized that verb when it was presented in an intransitive frame (Naigles et al., 2005). Thus, very young children use syntax, and do so flexibly, to learn a new verb.

Early in language development, learners seem to appreciate the relationship between syntactic and semantic categories and are able to use this relationship both to infer certain aspects of word meanings and to bootstrap their way into the syntax of their native language (Grimshaw, 1981; Pinker, 1994). Is syntax necessary for word learning? It depends. Although children and adults can learn the meanings of certain kinds of word such as object names, proper nouns, and substance names without the help of syntax, verbs may be different. Gleitman and Gleitman (1997) suggest that verbs may be harder to learn ostensively because of the poor temporal correspondence between verbs and what they refer to. A second reason that verbs may be harder to learn is that great flexibility exists both within and across languages as to how verbs "package" events. Events are ambiguous in a way that objects are not, making it difficult for learners to extract verb meanings simply by observing events (Fisher et al., 1994).

The evidence considered above, in combination with the strong correlation between vocabulary growth and the early development of syntactic knowledge (Fenson et al., 1994), offers strong support for the idea that syntax plays an important role in early word learning. However, it would be a mistake to overestimate the role of syntax over and above the other sources of information that are available in any given sentence. For example, part of what distinguishes the meaning of *giving* from *receiving* is the perspective (i.e. the intentions and beliefs) of the speaker on the event (Gleitman 1990). Thus, in thinking about the role of syntax in any full account of word learning, it is important to treat syntax as one important source of information, one that works in concert with information obtained from other sources of the kind discussed previously in this chapter. The child's task is to integrate these different sources of information and use them to infer the best candidate for a word's meaning.

37.7 **Conclusions**

Recently, there has been debate about whether word learning is "special" (Bloom, 2000; Markson and Bloom, 1997; Waxman and Booth, 2000). On the one hand, many of the constituent abilities that give rise to word learning are not specifically linguistic in scope. Children draw on knowledge about symbols, intentions, conventions, and categories to make sense of words. On the other hand, however, the product of this learning is quintessentially linguistic. It yields a system of symbols, grounded in conceptual structure, and bound to syntactic categories.

The research reviewed above provides compelling evidence that children's words have this multifaceted nature from very early in life. As soon as word learning can be measured in the laboratory, experiments show that it is informed by knowledge of the symbolic, intentional, and conceptual properties of words. Within a year or less of the first words, their contrastive, conventional, and syntactic properties emerge. Current inquiry focuses on the kinds of innate abilities and learning mechanisms that permit the rapid emergence of words in development.

References

Akhtar, N., Carpenter, M., and Tomasello, M. (1996) The role of discourse novelty in early word learning. *Child Development*, 67: 635–45.

Akhtar, N., and Tomasello, M. (2002) The social nature of words and word learning. In R. Golinkoff, K. Hirsh-Pasek, L. Bloom, G. Hollich, L. Smith, A. L. Woodward, N. Akhtar, M. Tomasello, and G. Hollich (eds), *Becoming a Word Learner: A Debate on Lexical Acquisition*, pp. 115–35. Oxford University Press, Oxford.

Au, T. K., and Glusman, M. (1990) The principle of mutual exclusivity in word learning: to honor or not to honor? *Child Development*, 61: 1474–90.

Balaban, M. T., and Waxman, S. R. (1997) Do words facilitate object categorization in 9-month-old infants? *Journal of Experimental Child Psychology*, 64: 3–26.

Baldwin, D. A. (1991) Infants' contribution to the achievement of joint reference. *Child Development*, 62: 875–890.

Baldwin, D. A. (1993). Early referential understanding: Infants' ability to recognize referential acts for what they are. *Developmental Psychology*, 29: 832–43.

Baldwin, D. A., Markman, E. M., Bill, B., Desjardins, R. N., Irwin, J. M., and Tidball, G. (1996) Infants' reliance on a social criterion for establishing word–object relations. *Child Development*, 67: 3135–53.

Baldwin, D. A., and Moses, L. M. (1996) The ontogeny of social information gathering. *Child Development*, 67: 1915–39.

Baldwin, D. A., and Moses, J. A. (2001) Links between social understanding and early word learning: challenges to current accounts. *Social Development*, 10: 311–29.

Bates, E. (1979) *The Emergence of Symbols: Cognition and Communication in Infancy.* Academic Press, New York.

Bates, E., Benigni, L., Bretherton, I., Camaioni, L., and Volterra, V. (1979). *The Emergence of Symbols: Cognition and Communication in Infancy.* Academic Press, London.

Bloom, P. (2000) *How Children Learn the Meaning of Words.* MIT Press, Cambridge, MA.

Booth, A., Waxman, S. R., and Huang, Y. (2005) Conceptual information permeates word learning in infancy. *Developmental Psychology*, 41: 491–505.

Bowerman, M., and Choi, S. (2003) Space under construction: language-specific spatial categorization in first language acquisition. In D. Gentner and S. Goldin-Meadow (eds), *Language in Mind: Advances in the Study of Language and Thought*, pp. 387–427. MIT Press, Cambridge, MA.

Brown, R. (1958) How shall a thing be called? *Psychological Review*, 65: 14–21.

Campbell, A. L., and Namy, L. L. (2003) The role of social-referential context in verbal and nonverbal symbol learning. *Child Development*, 74: 549–63.

Carey, S. (1978) The child as word-learner. In M. Halle, J. Bresnan, and G. A. Miller (eds), *Linguistic theory and psychological reality.* MIT Press, Cambridge, MA.

Choi, S., and Gopnik, A. (1995) Early acquisition of verbs in Korean: A cross-linguistic study. *Journal of Child Language*, 22: 497–529.

Clark, E. V. (1993) *The lexicon in acquisition*. Cambridge University Press.

Deacon, T. W. (1997) *The Symbolic Species: The Co-Evolution of Language and the Brain.* Norton and Co, New York, NY.

DeLoache, J. S. (2004) Becoming symbol-minded. *Trends in Cognitive Sciences*, 8: 66–70.

Diesendruck, G., and Markson, L. (2001) Children's Avoidance of Lexical Overlap: A Pragmatic Account. *Developmental Psychology*, 37: 630–41.

Fenson, L., Dale, P. S., Reznick, J. S., Bates, E., Thal, D., and Pethick, S. J. (1994) Variability in early communicative development. *Monographs of the Society for Research in Child Development*, 59 (5), no. 242, v–173.

Fisher, C. (1996) Structural limits on verb mapping: The role of analogy in children's interpretations of sentences. *Cognitive Psychology*, 31: 41–81.

Fisher, C. (2005) Structural limits on verb mapping: the role of abstract structure in 2.5-year-olds' interpretations of novel verbs. *Developmental Science*, 5: pp. 55–64.

Fisher, C., Gleitman H., and Gleitman, LR (1991) On the semantic content of subcategorization frames. *Cognitive Psychology*, 23: 331–392.

Fisher, C., Hall, D. G., Rakowitz, S., and Gleitman, L. (1994) Why it is better to receive than to give: Syntactic and conceptual constraints on vocabulary growth. *Lingua*, 92: 333–75.

Gelman, S. (2003) *The essential child.* Oxford University Press, Oxford.

Gentner, D. (1982) Why nouns are learned before verbs: Linguistic relativity versus natural partitioning. In SA Kucjaz ed., *Language development: Vol. 2. Language, thought and culture*, pp. 301–34. Lawrence Erlbaum Associates, Hillside, NJ.

Gentner, D., and Boroditsky, L. (2001) Individuation, relativity and early word learning. In M Bowerman and S Levinson (eds), *Language Acquisition and Conceptual Development*, pp. 215–56. Cambridge University Press, New York.

Gleitman, L. R. (1990) The structural sources of verb meanings. *Language Acquisition*, 1: 3–55.

Gleitman, L. R. and Gleitman, H. (1997) What is language made out of? *Lingua*, 100: 29–55.

Golinkoff, R. M., Hirsh-Pasek, K., Bailey, L. M., and Wenger, N. R. (1992) Young children and adults use lexical principles to learn new nouns. *Developmental Psychology*, 28: 99–108.

Golinkoff, R. M., Mervis, C. B., and Hirsh-Pasek, K. (1994) Early object labels: the case for a developmental lexical principles framework. *Journal of Child Language*, 21: 125–55.

Graham, S. A., Kilbreath, C. S., and Welder, A. N. (2004) Thirteen-month-olds rely on shared labels and shape similarity for inductive inferences. *Child Development*, 75: 409–27.

Graham, S. A., Stock, H., and Henderson, A. M. E. (2006) Nineteen-month-olds' understanding of the conventionality of object labels versus desires. *Infancy*, 9: 341–50.

Grimshaw, J. (1981) Form, function and the language acquisition device. In C. L. Baker and J. J. McCarthy (eds), *The Logical Problem of Language Acquisition*, pp. 165–82. MIT Press, Cambridge, MA.

Halberda, J. (2003) The development of a word-learning strategy. *Cognition*, 87: B23–B34.

Hall, D. G. (1994) Semantic constraints on word learning: proper names and adjectives. *Child Development*, 65: 1299–1317.

Hall, D. G. (1998) Continuity and the persistence of objects: when the whole is greater than the sum of the parts. *Cognitive Psychology*, 37: 28–59.

Hall, D. G., and Belanger, J. (2005) Young children's use of range-of-reference information in word learning. *Developmental Science*, 8: 8–15.

Hall, D. G., Waxman, S. R., and Hurwitz, W. M. (1993) How two- and four-year-old children interpret adjectives and count nouns. *Child Development*, 64: 1651–64.

Heibeck, T.H., and Markman, E. M. (1987) Word learning in children: an examination of fast mapping. *Child Development*, 58: 1021–34.

Henderson, A. M., and Graham, S. A. (2005) Two-year-olds' appreciation of the shared nature of object labels. *Journal of Cognition and Development*, 6: 381–402.

Hirsh-Pasek, K., and Golinkoff, R. M. (eds) (forthcoming) *Action Meets Words.* Oxford University Press, Oxford.

Hirsh-Pasek, K., Golinkoff, R. M., and Hollich, G. (2000) An emergentist coalition model for word learning: mapping words to objects is a product of the interaction of multiple cues. In *Becoming a Word Learner: A Debate on Lexical Acquisition*, pp. 136–64. Oxford University Press, Oxford.

Hollich, G. J., Hirsh-Pasek, K., Golinkoff, R. M., Brand, R. J., Brown, E., Chung, H.L., Hennon, E., and Rocroi, C. (2000) Breaking the language barrier: An emergentist coalition model for the origins of word learning. *Monographs of the Society for Research in Child Development*, 65(3), v–123.

Huttenlocher, J., and Smiley, P. (1987) Early word meanings: the case of object names. *Cognitive Psychology*, 19: 63–89.

Huttenlocher, J., Smiley, P., and Charney, R. (1983) Emergence of action categories in the child: evidence from verb meanings. *Psychological Review*, 90: 72–93.

Imai, M., and Gentner, G. (1997) A crosslinguistic study of early word meaning: universal ontology and linguistic influence. *Cognition*, 62: 169–200.

Katz, N., Baker, E., and Macnamara, J. (1974) What's in a name? A study of how children learn common and proper names. *Child Development*, 45: 469–73.

Landau, B., Smith, L., and Jones, S. (1988) The importance of shape in early lexical learning. *Cognitive Development*, 3: 299–321.

Landau, B., and Stecker, D. (1990) Objects and places: syntactic and geometric representations in early lexical learning. *Cognitive Development*, 5: 287–312.

Lee, J., and Naigles, L. (2005) The input to verbal learning in Mandarin Chinese: a role for syntactic bootstrapping. *Developmental Psychology*, 41: 529–40.

Macnamara, J. (1982) *Names for Things: A Study of Human Learning.* MIT Press, Cambridge, MA.

Mandler, J., and McDonough, L. (1996) Drinking and driving don't mix: inductive generalization in infancy. *Cognition*, 59: 307–35.

Markman, E. (1989) *Categorization and Naming in Children: Problems of Induction.* MIT Press: Cambridge, MA.

Markman, E., Wasow, J., and Hansen, M. (2003) Use of the mutual exclusivity assumption by young word learners. *Cognitive Psychology*, 47: 241–75.

Markson, L., and Bloom, P. (1997) Evidence against a dedicated system for word learning in children. *Nature*, 385: 813–15.

Moore, C. (1998) Social cognition in infancy: commentary on Carpenter, M., Nagell, K., and Tomasello, M. "Social cognition, joint attention and communicative competence from 9 to 15 months of age." *Monographs of the Society for Research in Child Development*, 63 (Serial No. 255).

Moore, C., Angelopoulos, M., and Bennett, P. (1999) Word learning in the context of referential and salience cues. *Developmental Psychology*, 35: 60–8.

Moses, L., Baldwin, D., Rosicky, J., and Tidball, G. (2001) Evidence for referential understanding in the emotions domain at 12 and 18 months. *Child Development*, 72: 718–35.

Naigles, L. (1990) Children use syntax to learn verb meanings. *Journal of Child Language*, 17: 357–74.

Naigles, L., Bavin, E., and Smith, M. (2005) Toddlers recognize verbs in novel situations and sentences. *Developmental Science*, 8: 424–31.

Naigles, L., and Hoff-Ginsberg, E. (1995) Input to verb learning: evidence for the plausibility of syntactic bootstrapping. *Developmental Psychology*, 31: 827–37.

Namy, L. (2001) What's in a name when it isn't a word? 17-month-olds mapping of nonverbal symbols to object categories. *Infancy*, 2: 73–86.

Namy, L., Campbell, A., and Tomasello, M. (2004) The changing role of iconicity in non-verbal symbol learning: a U-shaped trajectory in the acquisition of arbitrary gestures. *Journal of Cognition and Development*, 5: 37–57.

Namy, L., and Waxman, S. (1998) Words and gestures: infants' interpretations of different forms of symbolic reference. *Child Development*, 69: 295–308.

Phillips, A., Wellman, H., and Spelke, E. (2002) Infants' ability to connect gaze and emotional expression to intentional action. *Cognition*, 85: 53–78.

Piaget, J., and Inhelder, B. (1969) *The Psychology of the Child.* Basic Books, New York.

Pinker, S. (1994). *The Language Instinct.* Morrow, New York.

Preissler, M. A., and Carey, S. (2004) Do both pictures and words function as symbols for 18- and 24-month-old children? *Journal of Cognition and Development*, 5: 185–212.

Quine, W. V. O. (1960) *Word and Object.* MIT Press, Cambridge, MA.

Samuelson, L., and Smith, L. (1998) Memory and attention make smart word learning: an alternative account of Akhtar, Carpenter, and Tomasello. *Child Development*, 69: 94–104.

Samuelson, L., and Smith, L. (2000) Children's attention to rigid and deformable shape in naming and non-naming tasks. *Child Development*, 71: 1555–70.

Smith, L. (1999) Children's noun learning: how general learning processes make specialized learning mechanisms. In B. MacWhinney (ed.), *The Emergence of Language*, pp. 277–303. Erlbaum, Mahwah, NJ.

Smith, L., Jones, S., Landau, B., Gershkoff-Stowe, L., and Samuelson, L. (2002) Object name learning provides on-the-job training for attention. *Psychological Science*, 13: 13–19.

Sodian, B., and Thoermer, C. (2004) Infants' understanding of looking, pointing, and reaching as cues to goal-directed action. *Journal of Cognition and Development*, 5: 289–316.

Tardif, T., Gelman, S., and Xu, F. (1999) Putting the "noun bias" in context: a comparison of Mandarin and English. *Child Development*, 70: 620–35.

Taylor, M., and Gelman, S. (1988) Adjectives and nouns: children's strategies for learning new words. *Child Development*, 59: 411–19.

Tomasello, M. (1995) Joint attention as social cognition. In C. Moore and P. J. Dunham (eds), *Joint Attention: Its Origin and Role in Development*, pp. 103–30. Erlbaum, Hillsdale, NJ.

Tomasello, M. (1999) *The Cultural Origins of Human Cognition*. Harvard University Press, Cambridge, Mass.

Tomasello, M., and Barton, M. (1994) Learning words in non-ostensive contexts. *Developmental Psychology*, 30: 639–50.

Tomasello, M., and Haberl, K. (2003) Understanding attention: 12- and 18-month-olds know what is new for other persons. *Developmental Psychology*, 39: 906–12.

Vygotsky, L. (1962) *Thought and Language*. MIT Press, Cambridge, MA.

Waxman, S. (2002) Early word-learning and conceptual development: everything had a name, and each name gave birth to a new thought. In U. Goswami (ed.), *Blackwell Handbook of Childhood Cognitive Development*, pp. 102–26. Blackwell, Malden, MA.

Waxman, S., and Booth, A. (2000) Principles that are invoked in the acquisition of words, but not facts. *Cognition*, 77: B33–B43.

Waxman, S., and Booth, A. (2001) Seeing pink elephants: fourteen-month-olds' interpretations of novel nouns and adjectives. *Cognitive Psychology*, 43: 217–42.

Waxman, S., and Markow, D. (1995) Words as invitations to form categories: evidence from 12- to 13-month-old infants. *Cognitive Psychology*, 29: 257–302.

Werker, J., Cohen, L., Lloyd, L., Casasola, M., and Stager, C. (1998) Acquisition of word-object associations by 14-month-olds. *Developmental Psychology*, 34: 1289–1309.

Woodward, A. (2004) Infants' use of action knowledge to get a grasp on words. In S. R. Waxman (ed.), *Weaving a Lexicon*. MIT Press, Cambridge, MA.

Woodward, A., and Guajardo, J. (2002) Infants' understanding of the point gesture as an object-directed action. *Cognitive Development*, 17: 1061–84.

Woodward, A., and Hoyne, K. (1999) Infants' learning about words and sounds in relation to objects. *Child Development*, 70: 65–77.

Woodward, A., and Markman, E. (1998) Early word learning. In D. Kuhn and R. Siegler (eds), *Handbook of Child Psychology*, vol. 2: *Cognition, Perception and Language*, 5th edn, pp. 371–420. Wiley, New York.

Woodward, A., Markman, E., and Fitzsimmons, C. (1994) Rapid word learning in 13- and 18-month-olds. *Developmental Psychology*, 30: 553–66.

CHAPTER 38

Concept formation and language development: count nouns and object kinds

Fei Xu

38.1 Introduction

The relationship between language and conceptual development is an old question that has intrigued psycholinguists, philosophers, and psychologists for decades. Recent years have witnessed a surge of interest in this area (see Bowerman and Levinson, 2001; Clark, 2004; Gentner and Goldin-Meadow, 2003 for reviews). Many domains of conceptual representations and the corresponding linguistic representations have been investigated. At the syntactic level, researchers have explored the role of morphsyntax in spatial representations (e.g. Hermer-Vazquez et al., 1999; Hermer-Vasquez, 2001; Shusterman and Spelke, 2005), and the understanding of false belief (e.g. de Villiers and de Villiers, 2003). At the lexical level, researchers have explored how words of various grammatical classes may impact on spatial category formation (e.g. Bowerman and Choi, 2003; Pederson et al., 1998), number representations (e.g. Carey, 2004; Spelke, 2003), and representations of objects and substances (e.g. Imai and Gentner, 1997; Lucy and Gaskins, 2003; Yoshida and Smith, 2003). Some researchers have argued that language is crucial for humans' ability to represent genuinely new concepts that go beyond our initial, evolutionally given representational capacities, while others have endorsed much weaker versions of such hypotheses by suggesting that linguistic categories may allow learners to shape categories that are formed without the help of language.

Much of the work on conceptual and language development addresses the issue of how cross-linguistic variations may change the pace of conceptual development. Here we focus on a universal aspect of language: representations of count nouns which refer to object kinds. Although not all languages make the count/mass distinction syntactically, it is well accepted that even in the absence of these syntactic markers, learners make the conceptual distinction between kinds of object (or kinds of individual) and kinds of substance (or kinds of non-individuated entity) (see Bloom, 2000 for a review).

The topic of this chapter—the relationship between count nouns and object kind representations—has received considerable attention in the last few years. It raises the question of how learning count nouns that refer to object kinds may fundamentally change the child's ontology. Several researchers have suggested that infants expect words (most of them count nouns at the beginning of language development) to refer to kinds, and as such learning count nouns has important consequences for the child's conception of the world. Specifically, learning count nouns may change how children categorize objects, how they individuate objects and track them over time, and how they make inductive inferences about novel objects they have never seen before (e.g. Balaban and Waxman, 1997; Welder and Graham, 2001; Xu, 2002; 2005). This is a case where we observe the impact of language on concept formation very early in development. The question of when language effects are found is not only an important empirical and descriptive question but also one of theoretical importance. When language effects are found later in development, it may be the case that children have learned certain correlations between aspects of language and aspects of cognition without language being a causal factor in conceptual development. But if the language effects are found very early in development, one might argue that language in fact guides the formation of certain concepts. Given that children start language learning by acquiring single words towards the end of the first year and most of these words refer to object categories, the relationship between words and categories seems a promising candidate for such an investigation. In addition, other researchers have proposed alternative interpretations of the findings and suggested a rather different view on why words (count nouns) may exert influences on category formation, object individuation, and inductive inference in infancy—a word, presented as a count noun, is just another feature of the object, albeit a heavily weighted one (e.g. Sloutsky, 2003). What is the state of the evidence in this controversy?

38.2 **Count nouns and categorization**

Waxman and her colleagues have developed an elegant research program in the last ten years addressing the issue of how early noun learning impacts categorization in infants. One of their first studies investigated how presenting a common label across a set of visual displays facilitated categorization in nine-month-old infants (Balaban and Waxman, 1997). Infants were familiarized with pairs of displays depicting members of a category, e.g. rabbits. In the word condition, infants heard a count noun for the familiarization displays, *A rabbit*. In the tone condition, infants saw the same displays as in the word condition but they heard a tone instead of a count noun. On the test trials, the infants were presented with two displays: a new exemplar of the familiar category (i.e. another rabbit) and an exemplar from a new category (e.g. a pig). The proportion of the time the infants spent looking at each of the two displays was recorded. The rationale was that if infants had categorized all the exemplars from the familiarization trials, say the rabbits, as members of the same category, they should spend more time looking at the exemplar from a new category, i.e. the pig, on the test trials. Balaban and Waxman (1997) found that nine-month-old infants looked more at the pig than at the new rabbit when they had heard a count noun during familiarization, but not when they had heard a tone during familiarization. In another experiment in the same series, they found that content-filtered words, which sounded like speech although the identity of the words was obscured, behaved like count nouns in facilitating categorization. One conclusion drawn from these experiments was that the presence of a count noun invited the infants to look for commonalities across exemplars, thus speeding up the categorization process (see also Fulkerson and Haaf, 2003). In the absence of a count noun, categorization at the basic level does occur but at a much slower speed (e.g. Quinn et al., 1993).

For superordinate categories, there is little evidence that infants can form these categories without the help of language. Using manipulation time as the dependent measure, Waxman and Markow (1995) presented twelve-month-old infants with sets of objects (e.g. four different animals) during familiarization. Then on the test trials, the infants were allowed to play either with another animal or with an object from a novel superordinate category, e.g. a piece of fruit such as an apple. Three conditions were included: a noun condition, in which the infants heard a novel word, *See, a fauna?*, during familiarization; an adjective condition, in which infants heard *See the faun-ish one?*, and a no-word condition, in which infants heard *See here?* On the test trials, all infants heard the identical phrase, *See what I have?* Results showed that the infants did not show a novelty preference for the object from a new superordinate category in the no-word condition, whereas they showed such a preference in both the novel noun and novel adjective conditions. These findings suggest that infants encode category-based commonalities early on and that, before they can syntactically distinguish nouns and adjectives, both form classes encourage them to form categories, especially at the superordinate level.

To further specify the role of count nouns in category formation, Waxman and Braun (2005) showed that only consistent naming (i.e. the same count noun for all four animals presented during familiarization) facilitated categorization in an object manipulation task with twelve-month-old infants. If the infants had heard different count nouns applied to the objects during familiarization, no categorization behavior was observed during the test phase of the experiment.

At around thirteen months, there is also some evidence that infants begin to differentiate count nouns from adjectives. Waxman (1999) and Waxman and Booth (2001) found that when presented a count noun, infants formed shape-based categories, and when presented with an adjective, infants used color or texture as the basis for categorization. This is an important finding, since in the mature lexicon, count nouns refer to kinds, which are a subset of all categories that are initially mostly based on shape and with rich inductive potential (see Bloom, 2000; Gelman, 2003; and Xu, 2005 for discussions).

These studies provide strong evidence that, from around nine months, infants are able to use language input in the form of count nouns to guide the categorization process. The presence of a count noun allows them to look for commonalities across exemplars and form categories, at both the basic level and the superordinate level. One question that remains open is whether language in the form of count noun labels would exert even more powerful influences on shaping the formation of these concepts and categories. For example, would labeling change category boundaries? A study by Landau and Shipley (2001) addressed this issue with older children. Two- and three-year-old children and adults were shown two pictures of objects (animal-like or artifact-like), and either both objects were labeled with the same count noun (*a blicket*) or two different count nouns (*a sted* and *a blicket*). A set of objects that were intermediate from these two standards (by applying morphing software) was presented to the children and the adults. The question was whether the initial labeling (no word vs. one count noun vs. two count nouns) would change the generalization pattern for the intermediate objects. In this case, since the two objects looked quite different from each other, adults and children assumed that they should have two different names, i.e. there was no difference between the no-word condition and the two-word condition: in each case a category boundary was imposed somewhere in the middle of the continuum. However, when the two standards were labeled with the same count noun, all intermediate objects were accepted as members of the category, with the two standards as the two extreme ends. Data from younger children are lacking at the moment. It would be very informative to know if infants who are at the beginning of language development would also be influenced by the naming pattern in forming their categories.

38.3 **Count nouns and individuation**

Another line of research has suggested that in addition to supporting categorization, count nouns also support individuation—establishing the number of distinct objects in an event via the representation of object kinds/categories. Although all words provide criteria for categorization (e.g. a verb such as *walk* is applied to all instances of walking; an adjective such as *red* is used to refer to all instances of redness), only count nouns provide criteria for individuation (Hirsch, 1982; Macnamara, 1986; Wiggins, 1980). The concepts that underpin count nouns are what cognitive psychologists have called "kinds" and what philosophers have dubbed "sortals" or "sortal concepts." Several studies have shown that towards the end of the first year, infants begin to use representations of kinds or sortals to establish how many distinct objects are in an event (see Xu, 2005 for a review and the suggestion that "sortal kind" may be a more accurate term). For example, if a toy duck repeatedly emerges from behind an occluder then returns behind it, followed by a ball repeatedly emerging from behind the same occluder then returning behind it, twelve-month-old infants but not ten-month-old infants would expect two distinct objects (a duck and a ball) to be behind the occluder. When the occluder is removed to reveal the objects, twelve-month-olds would look longer at the unexpected outcome of one object (the duck *or* the ball) than the expected outcome of two objects (the duck *and* the ball), but the ten month olds would not do so. Furthermore, at twelve months, it is only the kind contrasts (duck vs. ball; bottle vs. cup) that lead the infants to expect two objects behind the occluder. If shown a red ball vs. a green ball, or a large cup vs. a small cup, the infants fail to establish a representation of two distinct objects in the event. Xu and her colleagues have argued that towards the end of the first year, infants begin to represent object kind/sortal concepts and these concepts provide criteria for object individuation (Xu, 1997; Xu and Baker, 2005; Xu and Carey, 1996; Xu et al., 2004; Van de Walle et al., 2000; see Bonatti, et al., 2002; Wilcox and Baillargeon, 1998; Xu, 2005; and Xu and Baker, 2005 for discussions of other relevant data and some of the controversy surrounding this line of research). Once the developmental progression has been established, an immediate question arises: what is the mechanism that drives these developmental changes? It is perhaps no accident that infants also begin to comprehend words for object categories towards the end of the first year (e.g. Huttenlocher and Smiley, 1987; Oviatt, 1980). It was hypothesized that learning count nouns may play a role in the acquisition of kind concepts. What is the empirical evidence for this claim?

Several studies have shown that infants are able to use naming as a means by which to establish how many distinct objects there are in an event. Xu (2002) conducted a series of experiments in which labeling information was provided on-line during an object individuation task as described above. Nine-month-old infants were randomly assigned to one of two conditions: a two-word condition and a one-word condition. In the two-word condition, when an object, say a toy duck, emerged from behind an occluder, the experimenter labeled the object, *Look*, [baby's name], *a duck!* in infant-directed speech. Then the duck was returned behind the occluder. Next a ball emerged from the other side, *Look, a ball!* This was repeated several times, and sometimes the object was left stationary on the stage for the infant to look at. In the one-word condition, as each object emerged from behind the occluder, the infant heard *Look, a toy!* each time. The question was whether infants could use the presence of the two distinct count nouns to establish a representation of two objects behind the occluder. On the test trials, the occluder was removed to reveal two objects (the expected outcome) or one of the two objects (the unexpected outcome). Looking times were recorded. Results showed that in the two-word condition, the infants looked longer at the unexpected outcome of one object, but they did not do so in the one-word condition. Once it has been established that infants can use two words to facilitate object individuation, the question arises of whether such effects are language-specific. In the next three experiments, Xu (2002) replicated these results with other objects and nonsense words (e.g. *a blicket* vs. *a tupa*) in the two word condition. But instead of using one word as a contrasting case, the infants heard two tones, or two very different complex sounds, or two emotional expressions (i.e. *Ah* vs. *Eww*). None of these stimuli helped infants determine the number of objects behind the occluder. Xu (2002) suggested that count nouns, by virtue of being symbolic and referring to kinds, played an important role in the process of acquiring kind concepts and establishing distinct objects in this task. Count nouns are "essence-placeholders" (Xu, 2005).

So far, however, the exact role of words remains unclear. Two important questions remain open. First, it may be argued that words simply play the role of a very efficient and useful mnemonic. Perhaps the presence of the words allowed the infants to remember the objects better in the object individuation task. That is, maybe words do not play a causal role in this process, but they facilitate the process by aiding memory of the young infants. Second, these studies have only shown that the presence of two words leads the infants to expect two distinct objects, but there is no evidence that infants expect count nouns to refer to kinds of objects. Several further studies addressed both of these questions.

In a series of experiments, twelve-month-old infants were seated in front of a table, and the experimenter showed them a box with a front slit whose content was invisible. The experimenter pulled open the front of the box, looked in, and announced, *Look, a fep!* followed by *Look, a wug!* Or sometimes she looked in and announced: *Look, a blicket!* twice. The question was whether infants would use the number of count nouns to predict how many objects should be inside the box, even though they have not been shown any objects in the labeling phase of the study. The box was then pushed towards the infant so that she could reach in to retrieve the objects. On both the one-word and the two-word trials, infants retrieved one object out of the box. After a few seconds, the object was taken away and the infant sat in front of the box empty-handed. Then the critical part of the experiment began. Since the infant had nothing else to do, she was expected to reach into the box again on all trials. However, the box was empty. What would the infant do then? On the one-word trials, infants were expected to search cursorily then give up once she found the box empty. On the two-word trials, however, infants were expected to search more persistently for a second object if they had used the two count nouns to establish a representation of two objects inside the box. Indeed, twelve-month-old infants searched longer on the two-word trials than on the one-word trials, suggesting that they had used the number of count nouns to decide how many objects should be in the box. Since no object was shown during the labeling phase, it was not possible to interpret these results as infants using words as mnemonics to help them remember the number of objects in a particular location. Furthermore, using two emotional expressions did not lead the infants to search longer for a second object. Again, the effect may be language-specific.

With nine-month-old infants, a series of studies using the object individuation task was conducted to address the issue of whether words were just mnemonics. A 2 × 2 design was employed, in which the number of objects (one vs. two distinct objects) was crossed with the number of labels (one vs. two count nouns). In two of these conditions, the one-word-one-object and the two-word-two-object conditions, the linguistic information was consistent with the perceptual information. In the other two conditions, the one-word-two-object and the two-word-one-object conditions, the linguistic information was inconsistent with the perceptual information. The question was whether infants would weigh one type of information more heavily than the other. All four labeling conditions were also compared with two no-word conditions (one with one object, the other with two objects). The results showed that when infants were given perceptual information alone without labeling, their judgement was ambiguous between one or two objects. When infants were given one label (regardless of one or two objects), they had established a representation of one object behind the occluder. When infants were given two labels (regardless of one or two objects), they had established a representation of two objects behind the occluder. It appears to be the case that the number of labels was the deciding factor in how infants had perceived the events. The linguistic information was powerful enough to override perceptual information. Since in some of the conditions only a single object was shown, the fact that infants had expected to see two objects upon hearing two distinct labels supports the idea that words were not just mnemonics that help infants remember the number of objects. Instead, the very presence of two distinct labels was the basis for positing two numerically distinct objects in the event (Xu, 2006).

In a third series of experiments, Dewar and Xu (forthcoming) asked whether these early words refer to kinds (types) or just individual objects (tokens). The studies addressed this question by asking what characteristics the infants expect the objects to have upon hearing two distinct count nouns applied to them. A looking-time method was used. In Experiment 1, nine-month-old infants watched the events presented on a puppet stage. During familiarization trials, the front of a large box was opened to reveal pairs of objects inside: either two identical objects or two objects that differed in shape, color, and texture. The test trials followed the same procedure to show the outcomes, and used the same pairs of objects as in the familiarization trials. But before the box was opened, the experimenter looked into the top of the box that had a slit and described its contents with either two labels (*I see a wug!* and *I see a dak!*) or the same label *twice* (*I see a fep!*). For an adult, hearing the content of the box being labeled with two different words would lead to the expectation of seeing two different kinds of object, and hearing the same label twice would lead to the expectation of one kind of object. The results showed that infants shared adults' intuition. Upon hearing two different labels, infants looked longer at two identical objects inside the box (the unexpected outcome) than at two different objects (the expected outcome). This pattern was reversed when infants heard a single label repeated twice: they looked longer at two different objects than two identical objects. In Experiment 2, using the same procedure, infants were presented with either pairs of identical objects or pairs of objects which differed only in shape. The results showed that when they heard two distinct labels, infants looked longer at two identical objects than at two objects differing in shape. In contrast, when they heard one label twice, the infants looked longer at two objects differing in shape than at two identical objects. In Experiment 3, infants were presented either with pairs of identical objects or with pairs of objects that differed only in color. This time the infants did not find the linguistic information informative. They looked longer at two different-colored objects irrespective of the number of labels.

These findings suggest that infants at the beginning of word learning may expect distinct labels to refer to distinct kinds of objects. The property of shape is a salient cue to kind membership (e.g. Diesendruck and Bloom, 2003; Landau et al., 1988), and nine-month-old infants expect that objects which differ in shape should have different labels. These studies present the first evidence that nine-month-old infants hold certain expectations regarding the referents of novel count nouns.

These studies provide evidence that one characteristic that is unique to count nouns—their role in individuation—may play a causal role in the acquisition of kind concepts in infancy. The very process of acquiring count nouns for objects may be an important part of the process of constructing representations of kinds.

38.4 **Count nouns and inductive inference**

A third line of research suggests that count nouns also promote inductive inference of non-obvious object properties in infancy. Baldwin et al. (1993) first investigated whether infants between nine and eighteen months are able to use perceptual similarity to make guesses about which objects are likely to have certain non-obvious sound properties (e.g. goes "moo" when turned over). The experimenter first demonstrated a non-obvious property to the infant and then handed the object over for the infant to imitate the action. Most infants happily did so, since the sounds themselves were pleasant and reinforcing. Then a set of test objects were given to the infant, some very similar to the demonstration object and some not. Importantly, some of the test objects were broken such that they could not produce the sound property. The idea was that if the infant had expected an object to have the non-obvious property but she couldn't get the object to work, she would persist in producing the relevant action. Thus the dependent measure was the number of times the infant attempted the relevant action in order to produce the sound on a non-functional object. Baldwin et al. found that infants used perceptual similarity as their guide: the more similar an object was to the demonstration object, the more likely the infant would persist in performing the relevant action to produce the sound property. Taking this research a step further, Welder and Graham (2001) replicated the main findings of Baldwin et al. and asked if providing a common label would change the generalization pattern with eighteen-month-old infants. They found that overall infants produced more actions on the objects when the demonstration object and the test object were labeled with the same count noun, *See, a blicket!* However, their results were ambiguous as to whether the presence of the count noun provided any information to override perceptual similarity. Perhaps the presence of a label simply increased the attention of the infant. Using objects that were members of real artifact kinds (e.g. a toy accordion set, or desk bells), Joshi and Xu (2006) found that in the absence of a count noun label, eighteen-month-old infants used similarity as a guide to make inferences about object properties, but the presence of a count noun allowed the infants to override perceptual similarity and produce many more target actions on low-similarity objects. In addition, they found that the language effects were only true of count nouns but not of adjectives. With younger infants, Graham et al. (2004) found that at thirteen months, consistent naming but not variable naming facilitated inductive inference. However, the overall response rate was rather low, making it more difficult to interpret the results. Perhaps a different methodology is called for with young infants who may not yet have the requisite motor skills.

38.5 An alternative view: a word is just another feature of the object

In the last few years, Sloutsky and colleagues have suggested an alternative view on the role of labeling/count nouns in early conceptual development (e.g. Sloutsky, 2003). In particular, Sloutsky has suggested that there is nothing special about words as far as facilitating categorization, individuation, and inductive inference is concerned. Instead, he advocates a view which explains the various findings reviewed above in terms of how auditory processing interacts with visual processing. The basic idea is that when infants look at objects and they hear some auditory input at the same time, there is an attention bottleneck—the infants have to choose between attending to the visual input or the auditory input. If the auditory input is familiar (e.g. words or speech sounds in general), it is relatively easy to process both visual and auditory inputs simultaneously. If the auditory input is unfamiliar (e.g. tones or other sounds), it is difficult for infants to process everything simultaneously. Instead, the infants selectively attend to the auditory stimuli at the expense of the processing of the visual stimuli. This is the source of why words appear to be special in shaping the various aspects of early conceptual development. In other words, if the infants had been familiarized with the novel tones or sounds before a categorization or individuation task, they would use the extra auditory information as much as they do word. After all, a word is just another feature of the object; surely a sound can also be another feature of an object. Any additional feature can help with the categorization and individuation process. This view is in sharp contrast with the view that suggests that words refer to kinds and that that is the basis of the observed effects of language. Appealing as Sloutsky's view may be to some, there is also evidence in the existing literature that argues against it. In categorization research, the fact that using a consistent label (the same count noun applying to all the objects) facilitated categorization but using variable labels (a different count noun for each object) did not is evidence that it is not simply a matter of being familiar with the auditory input (Waxman and Braun, 2005). This finding supports the view that using the same count noun invites infants to look for commonalities across objects, and that this is a critical part of the process of categorization. In the case of object individuation, several studies included manipulations that are relevant for the alternative view. Xu (2002) found that count nouns—whether familiar (e.g. *duck, ball*) or unfamiliar (e.g. *blicket, tupa*) helped infants individuate objects, and emotional expressions, which are highly familiar, did not. This, again, argues against the view that the crucial factor is the familiarity of the auditory input. In the Xu et al. (2005) studies, infants were not shown any objects during familiarization. They simply looked on as the experimenter opened the front box and announced the content of the box: *I see a fep! I see a wug!* Infants were able to use the linguistic information to determine how many objects were inside the box. In addition, two contrastive emotional expressions did not lead the infants to posit two objects inside the box under identical circumstances. These results support the view that count nouns are informative because they are symbols that refer. Count nouns are not attached to objects as one of their features. Lastly, Graham et al. (2004) reported a finding that was parallel to that of Waxman and Braun (2005), only consistent labels, not variable ones, promoted inductive inference in thirteen-month-old infants. In addition, Joshi and Xu (2005) found that only count nouns, but not adjectives, facilitated inductive inference and allowed infants to override perceptual similarity. In these studies, novel words (e.g. blicket, tupa) were used. Again, these results provide evidence against the view that the observed effects were due to auditory processing competing with visual processing, and the familiarity of the auditory input was the crucial factor that predicted successes or failures.

38.6 Conclusions

What is the role of language in concept formation in infancy? More specifically, does learning count nouns play a causal role in infants' acquisition of object kind concepts? The state of the evidence reviewed above suggests an affirmative answer. Pre-linguistic infants have some ability to categorize and individuate the objects around them, and they can use perceptual similarity to make guesses about non-obvious object properties. When a count noun is used to refer to an object, the infant assumes that the count noun refers to a kind of object. At least three consequences follow: if another object is referred to with the same count noun, it is a member of the same kind (for now, we leave open the interesting case of homonyms); if another object is referred to with a different count noun, it belongs to a different kind and it cannot be the same object as the first object; if another object is referred to with the same count noun, it is likely to have the same internal, non-obvious properties. To quote Lewis Carroll (1895), "When I make a word do a lot of work like that, I always pay it extra."

References

Balaban, M., and Waxman, S. (1997) Words may facilitate categorization in 9-month-old infants. *Journal of Experimental Child Psychology*, 64: 3–26.

Baldwin, D. A. (1991) Infants' contribution to the achievement of joint reference. *Child Development*, 63: 875–90.

Baldwin, D. A. (1993) Infants' ability to consult the speaker for clues to word reference. *Journal of Child Language*, 20: 395–418.

Baldwin, D. A., Markman, E. M., and Melartin, R. L. (1993). Infants' ability to draw inferences about nonobvious object properties: evidence from exploratory play. *Child Development*, 64: 711–28.

Bloom, P. (2000) *How Children Learn the Meanings of Words.* MIT Press, Cambridge, MA.

Bonatti, L., Frot, E., Zangl, R., and Mehler, J. (2002) The human first hypothesis: identification of conspecifics and individuation of objects in the young infant. *Cognitive Psychology*, 44: 388–426.

Bowerman, M., and Choi, S. (2003) Space under construction: language-specific spatial categorization in first language acquisition. In D. Gentner and S. Goldin-Meadow (eds), *Language in Mind*, pp. 388–427. MIT Press, Cambridge, MA.

Bowerman, M., and Levinson, S. S. (2001) *Language Acquisition and Conceptual Development.* Cambridge University Press, Cambridge.

Carroll, Lewis (1895) *Alice in Wonderland.* London.

Clark, E.V. (1983) Meanings and concepts. In J. H. Flavell and E. M. Markman (eds), *Handbook of Child Psychology*, vol. 3: *Cognitive Development*, pp. 787–840. Wiley, New York.

Clark, E.V. (2004) How language acquisition builds on cognitive development. *Trends in Cognitive Sciences*, 8: 472–8.

De Villiers, J. G., and de Villiers, P. A. (2003) Language for thought: coming to understand false beliefs. In Gentner and Goldin-Meadow (2003: 335–84).

Dewar, K., and Xu, F. (forthcoming) Do 9-month-old infants expect distinct words to refer to kinds? *Developmental Psychology*.

Diesendruck, G., and Bloom, P. (2003) How specific is the shape bias? *Child Development*, 74: 168–78.

Diesendruck, G., and Markson, L. (2001) Children's avoidance of lexical overlap: a pragmatic account. *Developmental Psychology*, 37: 630–41.

Fulkerson, A. L., and Haaf, R. A. (2003) The influence of labels, non-labeling sounds, and source of auditory input on 9- and 15-month-olds' object categorization. Infancy, 4: 349–69.

Gelman, S. A. (2003) *The Essential Child.* Oxford University Press, Oxford.

Gentner, D., and Goldin-Meadow, S. (eds) (2003) *Language in Mind.* MIT Press, Cambridge, MA.

Graham, S. A., Kilbreath, C. S., and Welder, A. N. (2004) 13-month-olds rely on shared labels and shape similarity for inductive inferences. *Child Development,* 75: 409–27.

Hermer-Vazquez, L., Moffet, A., and Munkholm, P. (2001) Language, space, and the development of cognitive flexibility in humans: the case of two spatial memory tasks. *Cognition,* 79: 263–99.

Hermer-Vazquez, L., Spelke, E. S., and Katsnelson, A.S. (1999) Sources of flexibility in human cognition: dual-task studies of space and language. *Cognitive Psychology,* 39: 3–36.

Hirsch, E. (1982) *The Concept of Identity.* Oxford University Press, Oxford.

Huttenlocher, J., and Smiley, P. (1987) Early word meanings: the case of object names. *Cognitive Psychology,* 19: 63–89.

Imai, M., and Gentner, D. (1997) A cross-linguistic study of early word meaning: universal ontology and linguistic influence. *Cognition,* 62: 169–200.

Joshi, A., and Xu, F. (2006) Inductive inference, artifact kind concepts, and language. MS under review.

Landau, B., Smith, L. B., and Jones, S. S. (1988) The importance of shape in early lexical learning. *Cognitive Development,* 3: 299–321.

Landau, B., and Shipley, E. (2001) Labelling patterns and object naming. *Developmental Science,* 4: 109–18.

Lucy, J. A., and Gaskins, S. (2003) Interaction of language type and referent type in the development of nonverbal classification preferences. In D. Gentner and S. Goldin-Meadow (eds), *Language in Mind,* pp. 465–92. MIT Press, Cambridge, MA.

Macnamara, J. (1986) *A Border Dispute: The Place of Logic in Psychology.* MIT Press, Cambridge, MA.

Oviatt, S.L. (1980). The emerging ability to comprehend language: an experimental approach. *Child Development,* 51: 97–106.

Pederson, E., Danziger, E., Wilkins, D., Levinson, S. C., Kita, S., and Senft, G. (1998) Semantic typology and spatial conceptualization. *Language,* 74: 557–89.

Quinn, P., Eimas, P., and Rosenkrantz, S. L. (1993) Evidence for representations of perceptually similar natural categories by three- and four-month-old infants. *Perception,* 22: 463–75.

Shusterman, A., and Spelke, E. S. (2005) Language and the development of spatial reasoning. In P. Carruthers, S. Laurence, and S. Stich (eds), *The Innate Mind,* pp. 89–106. Oxford University Press, Oxford.

Sloutsky, V. M. (2003) The role of similarity in categorization. *Trends in Cognitive Sciences,* 7: 246–51.

Spelke, E.S. (2003) What makes us smart? Core knowledge and natural language. In D. Gentner and S. Goldin-Meadow (eds), *Language in Mind,* pp. 278–311. MIT Press, Cambridge, MA.

Tomasello, M., Strosberg, R., and Akhtar, N. (1996) Eighteen-month-old children learn words in non-ostensive contexts. *Journal of Child Language,* 23: 157–76.

Van de Walle, G. A., Carey, S., and. Prevor, M. (2000) Bases for object individuation in infancy: evidence from manual search. *Journal of Cognition and Development,* 1: 249–80.

Waxman, S. R. (1999) Specifying the scope of 13-month-olds' expectations for novel words. *Cognition,* 70: B35–B50.

Waxman, S. R., and Booth, A. E. (2001) Seeing pink elephants: fourteen-month-olds' interpretations of novel nouns and adjectives. *Cognitive Psychology,* 43: 217–42.

Waxman, S. R., and Braun, I. (2005) Consistent (but not variable) names as invitations to form object categories: new evidence from 12-month-old infants. *Cognition,* 95: B59–B68.

Waxman, S. R., and Markow, D. R. (1995) Words as invitations to form categories: evidence from 12- to 13-month-old infants. *Cognitive Psychology,* 29: 257–302.

Welder, A. N., and Graham, S. A. (2001) The influence of shape similarity and shared labels on infants' inductive inferences about non obvious object properties. *Child Development,* 72: 1653–73.

Wiggins, D. (1980) *Sameness and Substance.* Blackwell, Oxford.

Wilcox, T., and Baillargeon, R. (1998) Object individuation in infancy: the use of featural information in reasoning about occlusion events. *Cognitive Psychology,* 37: 97–155.

Xu, F. (1997) From Lot's wife to a pillar of salt: evidence that physical object is a sortal concept. *Mind and Language,* 12: 365–92.

Xu, F. (2002) The role of language in acquiring kind concepts in infancy. *Cognition,* 85: 223–50.

Xu, F. (2005) Categories, kinds, and object individuation in infancy. In L. Gershkoff-Stowe and D. Rakison (eds), *Building Object Categories in Developmental Time,* pp. 63–89. Erlbaum, Mahwah, NJ.

Xu, F. (2006) Language and perception: object individuation in 9-month-old infants. Manuscript under review.

Xu, F., and Baker, A. (2005) Object individuation in 10-month-old infants using a simplified manual search method. *Journal of Cognition and Development,* 6: 307–23.

Xu, F., and Carey, S. (1996) Infants' metaphysics: the case of numerical identity. *Cognitive Psychology,* 30: 111–53.

Xu, F., Carey, S., and Quint, N. (2004) The emergence of kind-based object individuation in infancy. *Cognitive Psychology,* 49: 155–90.

Xu, F., Cote, M., and Baker, A. (2005) Labeling guides object individuation in 12-month-old infants. *Psychological Science,* 16: 372–7.

Yoshida, H., and Smith, L. B. (2003) Shifting ontological boundaries: how Japanese- and English-speaking children generalize names for animals and artifacts. *Developmental Science,* 6: 1–17.

CHAPTER 39

Learning to parse and its implications for language acquisition

John C. Trueswell and Lila R. Gleitman

39.1 Introduction

A primary purpose of language is to permit individuals to communicate their perceptions and conceptions of the world. The linguistic system that underlies this communication must therefore be designed for intricate interactions with the human perceptual and conceptual machinery. The study of adult sentence comprehension abilities shows quite clearly that this is the case (see Van Gompel and Pickering, Chapter 17, and Tanenhaus, Chapter 18 this volume). For instance, it has been found that the recognition of a word includes accessing detailed linguistic information about how that word is likely to combine syntactically and semantically with the current representation of the sentence. In addition, the referential implications of these analyses are computed in real-time and appear to exert a simultaneous influence on the ongoing structural analyses, allowing the listener to pursue referentially plausible parses and exclude implausible ones. This rapid computational dance between syntactic, semantic, and referential factors over the course of interpreting a sentence leads to the conclusion that recognition of a component word exerts immediate effects on multiple tiers of linguistic and non-linguistic representation—phonological, syntactic, semantic, and referential. These representational systems, though distinct, mutually constrain each other in a dynamic fashion (e.g. Jackendoff, 2002; MacDonald et al., 1994; Trueswell and Tanenhaus, 1994).

In this chapter we discuss how this sentence processing machinery develops in children. By way of introduction, we first sketch what is known about the adult end-state, namely that the adult listener recovers the syntactic structure of an utterance in real-time via interactive probabilistic parsing procedures (Section 1.1). We follow this review with evidence indicating that similar mechanisms are at work quite early during language learning, such that infants and toddlers attempt to parse the speech stream probabilistically. In the case of learning, though, the parsing is in aid of discovering relevant lower level linguistic formatives such as syllables and words (section 39.1.2; see also Gómez, Chapter 36 this volume). The observation that the language learner is parsing to learn while simultaneously learning to parse suggests a rather surprising picture of processing continuity over developmental time, and allows us to make predictions about the developmental time-course of sentence-level *syntactic* parsing through the preschool years and beyond (section 39.1.3).

As we review in section 39.2, experimental observations about child sentence processing abilities are still quite sparse, owing in large part to the difficulty in applying adult experimental procedures to child participants; Reaction time, reading, and linguistic judgement methods have all have been attempted with children. Though informative, the procedures have been difficult to implement experimentally, and often produce data that are difficult to interpret. However, a renewed interest in the study of sentence processing development has occurred with the introduction of new methods for recording children's eye gaze patterns while they are listening to spoken utterances in the presence of a relevant reference world (section 39.3). These data, which provide a moment-by-moment window into the interpretation process, indicate that the sentence-processing system is incremental and interactive at a relatively early stage in child development, showing sensitivity to a variety of constraints on computing sentential meaning.

At the same time there are systematic changes over developmental time in the child's reliance on certain sources of linguistic and non-linguistic evidence. By hypothesis, the sequence of such changes depends materially on the validity and reliability of evidence in the learner's past experience (rather than, or more importantly than, on changes—which surely also occur—in the child's mentality during this period of life). The dynamic abilities of the processing system itself are also found to change and mature over time. This interface system, like many others, is subject to development in information processing control, especially changes in selectional and attentional abilities. Sections 39.4 and 39.5 offer future research directions and closing remarks.

39.1.1 **Real-time sentence processing in adults**

Given the way natural languages work, listeners must recover much or all of the intended syntactic structure of an utterance. This is because the structural characteristics of an utterance, when combined with the semantics of verbs and other lexical items, convey the role assignments that are essential to propositional thought: who is doing what to whom. Additionally, the structure of an utterance simultaneously conveys intended discourse operations. For example, grammatical choices made by a speaker (whether to use the passive, include a modifier, sentence connective, etc.) reflect discourse considerations and are designed to communicate what the speaker is referring to. In short, listeners require syntactic information to infer the meaning of the sentence and the ways that it refers to the world. To discover and extract this information, listeners must look for evidence in the linguistic input about the syntactic operations that gave rise to the utterance.

Exactly how syntactic and semantic structure is recovered by a listener/reader has been a topic of some disagreement (see Van Gompel and Pickering, Chapter 17 this volume, who review the range of theoretical perspectives). Here we will assume without debate that during the comprehension of a sentence, listeners are engaged in the recovery of phonological, syntactic, and semantic characterizations of the input; and that each such characterization is maintained within partially independent representational systems ("representational modularity"). These representational systems dynamically constrain each other over time as the sentence unfolds ("dynamic interactive processing"). We assume that the computation of these representations is accomplished in real-time via probabilistic mechanisms operating on a dynamically changing input. The process of recognizing a word within a sentence activates probable phonological, syntactic, and semantic structures in parallel, including if necessary multiple alternatives within each subsystem. In turn, interface mechanisms act in real-time as the sentence is unfolding to converge on the most consistent and probable solution across these domains (see Trueswell and Tanenhaus, 1994; Kim et al., 2002).

It follows from this account that the degree of accessibility of structural alternatives will play an important role in a comprehender's ability to converge on the intended meaning of an utterance. Perhaps the best evidence for this claim comes from adult studies of ambiguity resolution during reading and listening. For instance, the most likely parse (structural description) of the sentence:

1. The gibbon hit the lemur with the stick.

is (roughly) that shown in Figure 39.1a. In minimally presuppositional circumstances, listeners will more often than not interpret *with the stick* as linking to the verb *hit* and thus as an instrument. This is so despite the fact that an alternative interpretation is available, grammatical, and seemingly just as reasonable (after all, wouldn't you hit a lemur if you saw him holding a stick?). However, the preferred parse changes radically in the following sentence:

2. The gibbon noticed the lemur with a stick.

This sentence is likely to be represented differently, as in Figure 39.1b. It is not just one word (*noticed*) that has changed, but also global aspects of the inferred sentence organization. As these examples begin to imply, features of the parse are influenced not only by general architectural principles of the language's grammar (in typical English sentences there is bound to be a subject, then a verb, then an object) but also by lexical choices: *hit* has somehow coerced *with a stick* to serve as a part of a discontinuous verb–complement relation describing the manner

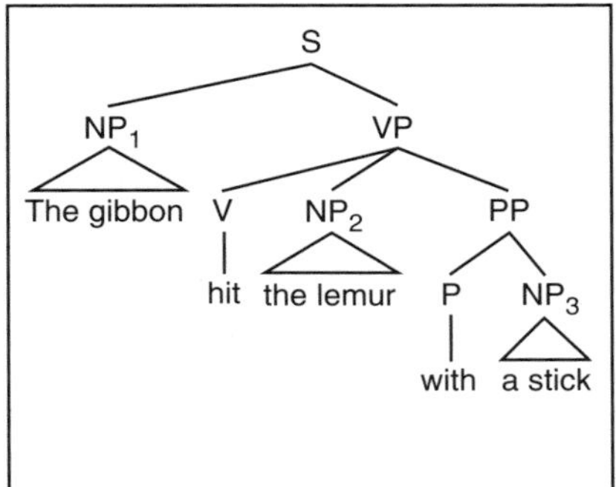

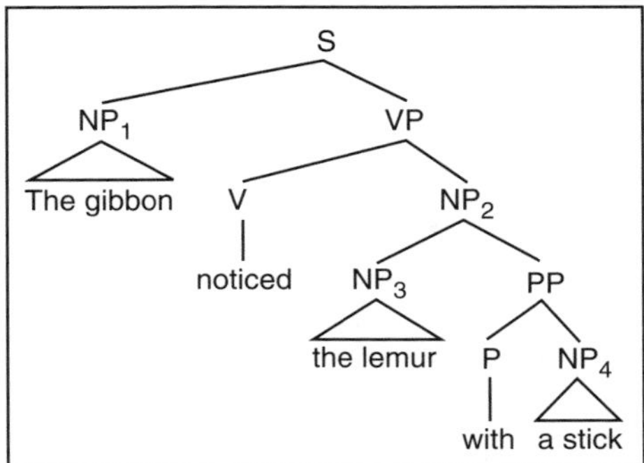

Figure 39.1 Example parse-trees of (a) VP-attachment / instrument relationship and (b) NP-attachment/modifier relationship.

by which hitting is accomplished (*hit ... with a stick*), whereas *notice* influences the same three words to be represented as embedded in the object noun phrase, one in which the general notion of lemur is restricted or modified (*lemur with a stick*).

A wealth of experimental findings document that the structural and semantic analyses that comprehenders assign *at the point of ambiguity, mid-sentence*, are determined by these lexical factors, including the probability that a given verb takes particular complements, as well as the semantic fit of constituents into the intended roles assigned by the verb (e.g. Britt, 1994; Garnsey et al., 1997; Trueswell et al., 1993; Trueswell et al., 1994). This suggests that word recognition processes are often the engine that drives parsing (see especially Novick et al., 2003; Trueswell and Kim, 1998).

The probabilistic recovery of structure is sensitive to other contingencies as well. In particular, the referential implications of these representations are computed in real-time and serve as an important top-down constraint. Consider for example the interpretation of sentence (1) in the referential settings depicted in Figure 39.2. The scenario in Figure 39.2a supports the more probable interpretation of the sentence. But the effect of the picture in Figure 39.2b—much as it was when substituting the verb *notice* for *hit*—is to shift the interpretation of *with the stick* into the noun phrase (*the lemur with the stick*). This is because the definite noun phrase *the lemur* isn't enough to determine a specific referent (Which lemur?). This interpretive requirement supports the interpretation of the PP as a modifier of the noun phrase rather than as an instrument of the verb phrase (Crain, 1981; Crain and Steedman, 1985).

Several studies indicate that adults deploy and use this referential information in real-time as well (e.g. Altmann and Steedman, 1988; Berkum et al., 1999; Tanenhaus et al., 1995). Importantly, however, studies also indicate that the effectiveness

Figure 39.2 *The gibbon hit the lemur with the stick.* (a) Referential scene that supports instrument interpretation of *with the stick.* (b) Referential scene that supports modifier interpretation of *with the stick.*

of the contextual factor depends on the availability of the structural options at issue. For instance, the effectiveness of the two-lemur scene in supporting a modifier interpretation depends on the kind of verb that is used in the sentence: verbs that prefer an Instrument role (like *hit*) show delayed and reduced referential effects (Britt, 1994; Spivey-Knowlton and Sedivy, 1995; Snedeker and Trueswell, 2004).

In a similar interactive fashion, prosodic evidence is also weighed by the listener in real-time (e.g. Beach, 1991; Kjelgaard and Speer, 1999; Marslen-Wilson et al., 1992; Snedeker and Trueswell, 2003). For instance, uttering sentence (1) with a major prosodic break after the verb (*[The gibbon hit] [the lemur with the stick]*) increases the likelihood that listeners will interpret *with the stick* as modifier; uttering it with a break after the direct object supports the instrument interpretation (*[The gibbon hit the lemur] [with the stick]*) (Snedeker and Trueswell, 2003). Importantly, like referential constraints, the effectiveness of prosodic constraints interacts with verb biases (e.g. Beach, 1991; Blodgett, 2004).

The picture emerging from these data is one in which the recognition of the word within a sentence automatically triggers linguistic representations at multiple levels. This triggering is probabilistic in nature: Using all evidence in hand, a listener is engaged in a kind of guessing game in which the linguistic procedures that gave rise to the utterance are recovered. Referential implications are also computed and, when possible, used to constrain the listener's syntactic hypotheses. Finally, local ambiguity is *the norm* in real-time language comprehension. It is close to impossible to find an utterance of even ten words in length, and of modest conceptual content, that cannot be interpreted in more than one way at some point during its hearing.[1] Computational linguists recognized this as soon as they started to implement parsers designed to handle natural text (e.g. M. Marcus et al., 1993). It has even been claimed that local ambiguity of the sort found in highly lexicalized formalisms provides a processing advantage because it permits greater flexibility in recovering structure and meaning (Steedman, 2000; Srinivas and Joshi, 1999; Kim et al., 2002). Within psycholinguistics, this view has been expressed in the Constraint-Based Lexicalist (CBL) theory of sentence processing (MacDonald et al., 1994; Trueswell and Tanenhaus, 1994).

The overall implication is that, as a constant matter in the course of understanding, the listener must rapidly evaluate competing analyses at one or more levels of representation, choosing among them as they arise, in response to differences in interpretive accessibility at each such level. As we will try to document, the same picture is likely true of learners in two ways: Accessibility constraints account for their parsing preferences, just as they do for adults. But also the construction of the parsing mechanism itself, over developmental time, is influenced by related issues of the differential accessibility of information.

39.1.2 **Learning to parse and parsing to learn: first principles.**

The dynamic sentence-processing abilities just reviewed develop incrementally in the infant and young child. Infants exhibit only fragile abilities, for example to recognize a brief phonological segment that recurs in heard speech (e.g. Jusczyk et al., 1995). But the remarkable finding is not that speech-pattern recognition starts out slowly but rather that it develops uncannily fast during the first year of life. Notice that even at the outset learners face what appear to be two ticklish and exceedingly complex problems. Apparently unlike adults, who in general have acquired the linguistically functioning formatives at the level of sound, syllable, and word, the infant must discover what these are. To take a simple example, the learner must come to realize that the two-syllable sequence /rab-it/ is a single formative at the level of the word, whereas the two-syllable sequence /read-it/ is two words (and the two-syllable sequence /rock-it/ may be either one or two words, depending on the surrounding context). But as we will try to show throughout this discussion, the adult/child tasks in deciphering the sound waves of speech are much more alike than might appear from this example. A critical similarity is that the child's discovery procedures for word-finding closely resemble the incremental, probabilistic, information-handling manipulations that characterize the adult's incremental, probabilistic procedures for mapping the sound wave of heard speech onto a linguistic representation. That is,

[1] Try e.g. *Mary had a little lamb; The missionaries are ready to eat*; or unfortunate (but genuine) headlines such as *Ohio bodies are missing New Hampshire children.*

learning to parse and parsing to learn seem to embody many of the same kinds of information processing principles. We can express this similarity as the following two organizing principles:

(i) Real-time processing continuity: from the outset, a language learner/listener is attempting real-time, incremental processing of the input speech stream.

(ii) Probabilistic processing continuity: from the outset, the detection from the speech stream of already acquired linguistic elements (including syntactic and phrasal elements) is achieved via probabilistic pattern-recognition and pattern-completion processes.

Experimental results from Aslin, Newport, and Saffran provide important illustration of these principles (e.g. Aslin et al., 1998; Saffran, 2001; 2002; Saffran et al., 1996). These studies indicate that 8- to 12-month-olds, much like adults, are sensitive to the distributional properties of syllables. This supports a learning procedure that allows infants to discover likely lexical/morphological candidates from running speech. In simplest terms, both adults and infants faced with a continuous stream of syllables will distinguish between syllable sequences which occur contiguously very often (and thus might be words) from those which co-occur rarely (and therefore are probably not words). Returning to our earlier example, *rabbit* is an early and correct lexical acquisition, but no child we know of comes to think that *labbit* or *nabbit* are words, because sequences of these component syllables are infrequent in the input. As a corollary of the probabilistic distributional learning procedure, in between cases like *read-it* and *carryoo* show up as interim lexicalizations by babies, as witnessed by such utterances as *Readit a book, Mommie* and *Carryoo, Mommie* (where the child clearly wants to be carried rather than to carry). This is in part because of the frequency of their contiguous appearance in maternal speech (*Do you want to read it? Do you want me to carry you?*) and with the characteristic strong–weak syllable pattern that characterizes English (e.g. Jusczyk et al., 1993). Such findings demonstrate the multiple constraint probabilistic nature of the 8–12-month-old learning procedure (Swingley, 2005).

Less than six months later, infants have mapped a number of these potential lexical candidates onto pre-existing conceptual representations, displaying their first understanding of words in the exposure language. In fact, so many word–meaning pairs have formed that 18-month-olds are faced with temporary ambiguity and deal with it in an adult-like manner, i.e. in real-time, as the speech unfolds. For instance, the pioneering eye gaze research of Fernald, Swingley, and colleagues shows that 18- to 24-month-olds process phonological word cohorts (*dog/doll, tree/truck*) in much the same way as adults, with the major difference being that adults know more words (Swingley et al., 1999; Allopenna et al., 1998). Upon hearing *doll* in a sentence like *Look at the doll*, 18- to 24-month-olds will temporarily consider cohort referents, such as a picture of a dog, but not non-cohort referents such as a picture of a mouse. The similarity between adult and child word recognition suggests considerable continuity over development in real-time processing abilities.

Does this processing continuity across developmental time hold above the level of the syllable and the word? That is, does it extend to the far more complex issues of sentence understanding as well? The major burden of this chapter is to document that indeed it does: that child and adult sentence processors are in principle much alike, correcting for gaps in the gradually accruing database of language knowledge.

As an initial step in defending this view, we point to evidence that very young language learners are sophisticated (and quick) at extracting abstract grammatical properties of utterances, albeit from quite simplified artificial grammars (G. Marcus et al., 1999; Gómez and Gerken, 1999). These studies showed that 7- to 12-month-olds make generalizations about the sequencing of syllables that abstract away from the particular sounds present in these syllables (see Gómez, Chapter 36 this volume). The young child's discovery of a particular grammar from the input is certainly the joint product of unlearned principles both of language design and of statistical learning procedures (see G. Marcus, 2000; Newport and Aslin, 2004; Newport et al., 2004). One useful illustration of a statistical component of grammar learning comes from Gerken (2006), who provided infants (9-month-olds) with an artificial language in which at least two alternative generalizations of the input were possible. For instance, when exposed to syllable sequences like *leledi, wiwidi, jijidi, dededi*, infants might infer that the sequences were generated by an AAB grammar, or they might infer that sequences must end in *di* (AA*di*). The results from this and other important control variants showed infants behaving probabilistically in a Bayesian manner, preferring whichever generalization was more likely given the input.

Such data suggest that children are neither unsystematic nor loosely pragmatics-driven in their attempts to parse and understand the utterances of their caregivers. Rather, they closely resemble adults in following a mechanistic multiple-constraint schema from sound to structure. The big leap for language learning must be acquiring the skills for mapping potential sentence parses onto their meanings and onto a model of the world. To understand these accomplishments requires three further framing principles (in addition to the continuity principles listed earlier) which organize language processing as much (sometimes more!) for infants and toddlers as for adults.

(iii) Representational modularity. The language processing system is innately predisposed to organize linguistic input into three quasi-independent representational domains: phonological, syntactic, and semantic.

(iv) Representational interfacing. The language learner expects systematic correspondences between these representational systems. For instance, the number and type of phrasal constituents present in an utterance will have a systematic mapping onto the number and type of participants denoted in the conceptual representation of an event.

(v) Assumption of reference. The language learner is innately predisposed to assume that communicative acts refer to the world. Hence the referential implications of interim linguistic characterizations of speech input are attempted from the outset.

Assumptions (iv) and (v) assert that a language learner must expect some systematic correspondence between the organization of the world and the organization of utterances; there is substantial logical and experimental support for this view (e.g. Baldwin, 1991; Chomsky, 1981; Fisher, 1996; Gleitman, 1990; Gleitman et al., 2005; Jackendoff, 1997; 2002). Assumption (iii), which pertains to the existence of distinct but interactive linguistic systems early in development, has been less extensively explored (though see Gleitman et al., 1973; Silva-Pereyra et al., 2005, for some evidence that even toddlers respond differentially to syntactic and semantic violations).

These five assumptions allow us to derive predictions about how child listeners ought to resolve temporary syntactic ambiguity during sentence comprehension. First, like the adult system, the child sentence comprehension system is engaged in the recovery of known syntactic and phrasal categories from the input, which is accomplished via pattern recognition processes. These higher-order syntactic and phrasal elements are likely to be discovered via distributional/statistical mechanisms similar to those proposed for lexical and grammar discovery by Newport, Gerken, and colleagues (i.e. Mintz et al., 2002; Gerken, 2002; Gómez, 2002; Gómez and Gerken, 2000; cf. Harris, 1957). At the same time, particular categories are preferred over others by the linguistic processing system and are assumed to map onto semantic and conceptual representations in systematic ways (assumptions (iv) and (v) above).

Once a repertory of syntactic representations has been acquired, we would expect a processing situation somewhat similar to the one characterized in early lexical processing (and documented by Swingley and colleagues): the child parsing system must also deal with syntactic ambiguities and must resolve these ambiguities in real-time. To the extent that the adult syntactic parsing system is a probabilistic device that weighs multiple contingencies, it follows that the child processing system, though organized and operating in the same way, must *gradually discover and learn these contingencies.*

The most valid and reliable of these contingencies ought to come online first developmentally, provided that the evidential sources supporting these contingencies have already been built by the child (e.g. in order for discourse contingencies on structure to be learned, the child needs first to understand how conversations tend to be organized). So, given the possible constraints on parsing and syntactic ambiguity resolution identified in the adult literature, we ask now which are going to be the more valid predictors of semantic/syntactic choice, and hence dominate child parsing and interpretation processes. If the infant grammar-learning *and* the adult sentence-parsing literature are any guide, we would expect the child sentence parser to grow from the bottom up in this regard, first relying disproportionately on phrasal-ordering (word-order) predictors to structure and lexically specific predictors of structure. Strong manipulations of prosodic grouping (such as imposing major prosodic breaks) should also influence early child parsing. Less reliable semantic and referential predictors of sentence structure ought to be somewhat delayed, given the irregularities and complexities of these evidential sources (see below, and Trueswell and Gleitman, 2004).

The following review of the experimental evidence of child sentence processing (sections 39.2 and 39.3) lends support to this general picture: the validity and reliability of evidential sources has a major influence on parsing development; Moreover, much as for the word recognition procedures described by Fernald, Swingley, and colleagues, newly learned lexical and phrasal constraints are used in real-time to resolve temporary ambiguity and assign structure to the input.

39.2 **Experimental exploration of child sentence processing**

39.2.1 **Methodological preliminaries and initial experimental forays**

From the start of modern psycholinguistic research in the 1960s, there has been a small cadre of investigators interested in understanding language acquisition from a sentence processing perspective. In his seminal work on the issue, Bever (1970a) explored young children's interpretation preferences for both plausible and implausible active and passive sentences. From this he concluded that English-speaking 3-year-old children employ a semantic plausibility strategy to assign roles to verb constituents, whereas children aged 4-years and older use word order strategies.[2] Somewhat ironically, this developmental paper is best known for its contribution to the adult sentence processing literature; Bever's suggestion was that word order strategies (particularly the NVN → SVO strategy) were also employed by adults, especially when interpreting temporarily ambiguous sentences (such as his infamous equestrian example *The horse raced past the barn fell*). (See also Bever, 1970b; Garrett, 1970; MacKay, 1970.) This observation in many ways launched the ambiguity resolution era in adult sentence processing, i.e. using temporarily ambiguous sentences to examine parsing preferences. But more to our present point, Bever's child work also launched a separate sub-field within language acquisition, examining in more detail the cues children use to determine role assignment (in English and other languages, e.g. Chapman and Kohn, 1978; Hakuta, 1982; Sinclair and Bronckart, 1972; Slobin and Bever, 1982). For instance, in a study of Turkish, Slobin and Bever (1982) found that children of 2–3 years relied heavily on case-marking information to perform role assignment rather than the semantic and word-order cues English children used, suggesting that children begin first to assign structure using the most reliable linguistic predictors present in their language. Indeed, Turkish has highly flexible word order but a fairly consistent case-marking system for nominative (Subject) and accusative (Object) case.

The most comprehensive cross-linguistic examination of children's use of linguistic evidence to perform role assignment was begun in the 1980s by Bates, MacWhinney, and colleagues (e.g. Bates et al., 1984). These studies used a range of tasks, including a "whodunnit" task, in which participants reported or selected the picture of the character that was the actor/agent of the event described in the utterance. Unlike most prior work, Bates, MacWhinney, and colleagues employed experimental designs that offered children and adults a full range of word order possibilities (SVO, OVS, OSV, etc.), even if these orders were ungrammatical or semi-grammatical in their native language. This work led to the development of the Competition Model of language development, which, consistent with the general claims of Slobin and Bever (1982), asserted that the age at which children begin to use particular linguistic cues to structure is determined by the cue's validity (Bates and MacWhinney, 1987; MacWhinney, 1978; MacWhinney et al., 1984).

Interestingly, this line of developmental research had limited contact with, or influence on, the then burgeoning field of adult sentence processing. Most early child studies of the sort described above provided only off-line measures of sentence comprehension (act-out tasks, picture selection, whodunnit), all of which offered insight into the ultimate interpretation that the child assigned to a sentence but little information about the moment-by-moment construction of this interpretation. Indeed, numerous researchers raised concerns about these studies for this very reason: because these studies often provided ungrammatical and anomalous material to participants, results could arguably reflect developmental and cross-cultural differences in task-specific strategies unrelated to day-to-day language use (e.g. Bridges, 1980; Gibson, 1992; Gleitman and Wanner, 1982). In retrospect, the use of globally ungrammatical and globally anomalous sentences was most

[2] One of Bever's early conjectures (1970a has not survived further experimental scrutiny: that semantic plausibility strategies developmentally precede word-order strategies in English. The highly reliable SVO order of English is detected and used by children as young as 2-years even for implausible interpretations (Bates et al., 1984).

likely the product of not having adequate real-time measures for use with children. As we will discuss in detail, measures that track the child listener's comprehension online in the presence of temporary anomalies and ambiguities have replaced the use of globally anomalous sentences in child language research.

In many ways, the Constraint-Based Lexicalist (CBL) sentence processing framework (e.g. MacDonald et al., 1994; Trueswell and Tanenhaus, 1994) is continuous with the Competition Model of Bates and colleagues. Both theories assume constraint-satisfaction mechanisms for language discovery and use, and therefore emphasize information reliability when accounting for developmental patterns. A crucial difference between these theories, however, is that the CBL assumes a central role for detailed linguistic representations in language use, along multiple partially independent dimensions (phonology, morphology, syntax, semantics), and thus more closely resembles computational, statistical NLP approaches and the general processing framework sketched by Jackendoff (2002). Representational modularity in the presence of interactive processing, a key assumption of CBL, is crucial for accounting for a broader range of phenomena found in adult sentence processing (Trueswell and Tanenhaus, 1994) and developmentally (Trueswell and Gleitman, 2004).

39.2.2 Real-time methods for use with children

Until quite recently, only heroic (perhaps we should say foolhardy) investigators attempted real-time methods with child participants (Holcomb et al., 1992; McKee et al., 1993; Swinney and Prather, 1989; Tyler, 1983; Trueswell et al., 1999; Tyler and Marslen-Wilson, 1981). Holcomb et al. (1992) examined ERPs of children, showing that children as young as 5-years showed the N400 response typical of adults when they hear semantically anomalous sentences. Tyler and colleagues (Tyler, 1983; Tyler and Marslen-Wilson, 1981) employed a word-monitoring task to study children's reference abilities, revealing online and contextual facilitation patterns consistent with the Holcomb et al. (1992) interpretation.

Swinney and Prather (1989) developed an ingenious though difficult-to-use method for studying activation of word meanings; Participants (4 years and older) heard sentences containing a lexically ambiguous word (e.g. *The boy picked up the bat and…*) and had to answer comprehension questions about these sentences. Participants also saw a picture while hearing an ambiguous word and had to make an animacy judgement about the visual depiction (*Can this eat things*?). The picture was related to one of the meanings of the ambiguous word, and priming (as compared to controls) was measured. Needless to say, this task requires considerable training, and has high drop-out rates among younger children (McKee et al., 1993). Nevertheless obtained results showed that younger children accessed only the dominant (more frequent) meaning of the ambiguous word, regardless of the sentence context, whereas older children and adults showed contextual sensitivity.

McKee et al. (1993) employed the Swinney and Prather (1989) cross-modal priming method to study antecedent activation of referential expressions, such as reflexives. This study focused primarily on acquisition issues related to children's discovery of syntactic constraints on co-reference (Principles A and B; Chomsky, 1981). In comparisons of offline and online measures, it was concluded that acquisition of this grammatical knowledge coincided with an immediate ability to use this knowledge online to activate syntactically appropriate antecedents. These findings are an important contribution to the position that the grammar is the parser (and the parser is the grammar); for an early statement of this view, see also Wanner and Maratsos (1978). To the extent that such a position is accepted, it becomes crucial to adopt a sentence-processing perspective of grammar acquisition. This is quite a different perspective from that taken when considering a "competence grammar" with universal cross-linguistic design properties that may be masked by processing ("performance") factors. (See Phillips and Wagers, Chapter 45 this volume, for a discussion of this issue.)

39.2.3 Eye movements during listening and the kindergarten-path effect

The last several years of research have seen the introduction of a new method for studying child sentence processing, in which children's direction of gaze is recorded during spoken language comprehension. This method provides a window into children's moment-by-moment shifts in visual attention as they hear expressions that are intended to refer to the objects around them. This "visual world paradigm" was developed by Tanenhaus and colleagues to study language processing abilities in adults (e.g. Tanenhaus et al., 1995; Sedivy, Tanenhaus, et al., 1999; cf. Cooper, 1974). As discussed by Tanenhaus (Chapter 18 this

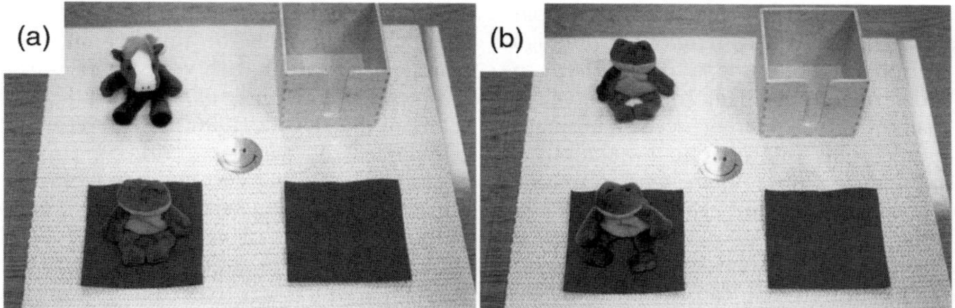

Figure 39.3 Referential settings used in Trueswell, Sekerina, Hill and Logrip (1999) (a) 1-Referent Scene; (b) 2-Referent Scene.

volume), the basic premise behind this paradigm is that by measuring how visual-attentional states line up in time with the successive arrival of words and phrases, researchers can gain insight into the real-time processes by which listeners organize utterances structurally and semantically, and how they map these representations onto the events and objects that they denote. To accept this link between data and interpretation, one need only believe that, to a useful approximation, the mind is going where the eye is going.[3]

Trueswell et al. (1999) studied 5- and 8-year-olds' eye movements in a listening paradigm modeled after adult experiments by Tanenhaus et al. (1995). The children acted upon spoken instructions to move objects in an array (see Figure 39.3). On critical trials these sentences contained a temporary Prepositional Phrase (PP) attachment ambiguity, as in:

3. Put the frog on the napkin in the box.

Notice that upon hearing the phrase *on the napkin*, a listener could (just as with sentence 1) link it to the verb *put* as a Goal, indicating where to put a frog, or link it to the Noun Phrase (NP) *the frog* as a Modifier (as in sentence 2), specifying a property of a particular frog. However, this ambiguity is "temporary" and is resolved to the Modifier interpretation by the presence of a second Goal phrase (*in the box*).

The striking finding for such sentences was that 5-year-olds showed a strong preference to interpret *on the napkin* as the Goal of *put*, even when the referential scene supported a Modifier interpretation (e.g. two frogs, one on a napkin; see Figure 39.3b). Upon hearing *on the napkin*, 5-year-olds typically looked over to a potential Goal in the scene, the empty napkin, regardless of whether there were two frogs present (pragmatically supporting a Modifier interpretation) or one frog present (supporting a Goal interpretation). In fact, 5-year-olds' preference for VP-attachment was so strong that they showed little sign of revising it: Upon hearing *napkin* children would look to the empty napkin as a potential Goal, and then frequently move a frog to that location. In two-referent cases, children were even at chance when selecting which frog to move, suggesting they never considered a Modifier interpretation. So strong are these tendencies, or—here equivalently—so unrevisable ("ballistic") is the processing machinery in young children, that the children usually stuck with the interim interpretation despite the later PP (*in the box*) which renders the original parse ungrammatical. This is particularly transparent in cases where they moved a frog to the unoccupied napkin, and then "hopped" the frog into the box.

Importantly, this child parsing behavior was localized to the ambiguity rather than the syntactic complexity of the sentence. This is shown by the fact that their eye movements and actions became adult-like when the temporary ambiguity was removed, as in the unambiguous Modifier form:

4. Put the frog that's on the napkin in the box.

The near-perfect performance on unambiguous forms rules out a more mundane explanation of these results, namely that long complicated sentences flummox young children.

[3] Such an assumption seems even less radical and more familiar when we reconsider the often unspoken assumptions behind such measures as reaction time, as assessed by the stroke of a finger on a key or lever. Nevertheless, neither psycholinguistics nor any other research field can rely too securely on a single experimental technique. The linking assumptions of this new measure certainly need to be more carefully stated and tested.

In contrast to 5-year-olds, control adult participants' responses to the temporarily ambiguous stimuli were found to depend on the referential scene provided. In particular, the presence of a two-referent scene eliminated measurable signs of syntactic misanalysis of the ambiguous phrase: there were few looks to the potential Goal and even fewer incorrect actions as compared to one-referent scenes. These results accord with the adult sentence reading literature: that top-down referential considerations contribute to parsing decisions in concert with lexico-syntactic likelihoods.[4] That is, the Gricean stricture to say "just enough" held for Trueswell et al.'s adult (but not child) participants, just as for the adults studied by Tanenhaus et al (1995).

A plausible interpretation of the children's parsing behavior is that their insensitivity to the referential elements in the scenes caused them to rely on a remaining source of evidence which could help resolve the temporary ambiguity, i.e. the grammatical preferences of the verb.[5] The verb for all test stimuli in this experiment was *put*. Sentences containing this verb almost always express a Goal, typically as a prepositional phrase. Hence a child relying on this lexical-syntactic contingency alone should interpret *on the napkin* as a Goal phrase in all cases. However, because Trueswell et al. (1999) did not manipulate the types of verbs used in the study, it was possible that the findings reflected a general structural preference on the part of children (e.g. to select the simplest syntactic structure; Frazier and Fodor, 1978).

One should however expect lexical constraints on structural analyses to play an early and potent role developmentally. Adults track subcategorization and thematic preferences to such a great extent that they immediately constrain parsing options. If children build such databases as they learn words, it follows that this information will appear as an early determinant of child parsing. Indeed, there is good evidence that children track the number and type of phrases that occur with verbs *so as to assist in recovering the meaning of these verbs* (e.g. Fisher et al., 1994; Fisher, 1996; Gillette et al., 1999; Gleitman, 1990; Naigles, 1990).

To put it another way, children from an early age track subcategorization and argument-taking properties of verbs as they map them onto their interpretations. This probabilistic evidence, which was tracked and developed so as to discover verb interpretations, does *not* behave analogously to a scaffold, which is simply discarded after its role in supporting the construction of the system is complete. Quite the contrary. Such learning-relevant properties of observed verb usage (subcategorization and selectional facts, and referential and syntactic preferences) are stored at the verb's entry in the mental lexicon, to be used to recognize the intended structure of an utterance every time that particular verb is encountered again. Children, like adults, deploy this knowledge of probabilities on the fly as a sentence unfolds in time.

The implication here may be that ambiguity resolution for known words (like *on*, *with*) is to a great extent an extension of the same mechanisms used for learning new words (Gleitman et al., 2005). Evidence is weighed pertaining to the element in question, and used to converge on a likely hypothesis regarding the best semantic and syntactic representation of that element. Use of particular sources of evidence are driven by reliability but also by whether or not the child has built up the appropriate databases relevant to the linguistic choice (Gillette et al., 1999). Indeed, under conditions in which visual world information is not informative for learning a word (e.g. for abstract words, such as most verbs) the same counterintuitive prediction has been made, and confirmed—namely that bottom-up structural predictors to word meaning,

[4] We do not conclude that referential pragmatics *determine* parsing decisions in adults, but rather they *contribute* to parsing decisions—lexical evidence exerts a simultaneous influence. One reason for this conclusion is that although Tanenhaus et al. (1995) found no signs of difficulty in two-referent scenes, Trueswell et al. (1999) did find a handful of adult action errors even in two-referent scenes. Moreover, follow-up adult studies by Novick et al. (forthcoming) reveal some real-time processing difficulty (in the form of eye movements) even in two-referent contexts, which went undetected in prior studies. Crucially, in all three studies (Novick et al., forthcoming; Trueswell et al., 1999; and Tanenhaus et al., 1995), one-referent scenes increased signs of a goal interpretation in real-time measures (as compared to two-referent scenes), thereby demonstrating a simultaneous referential *contribution* to real-time parsing abilities.

[5] While we restrict the present discussion to the major case (in English) of lexical verbs, the same or closely related generalizations apply for other argument-taking items and structures, e.g. predicate adjectives and factive nominals. For many languages other than English, for that matter, lexical verbs may not even be the major (most frequent, least marked) such realization of these functions.

such as the local syntactic environment of the word, trump possible contextual evidence (Snedeker and Gleitman, 2004; Papafragou et al., forthcoming). These effects of syntax on word learning, otherwise known as "syntactic bootstrapping" effects, suggest that the computation of sentence meaning relies on what is reliable and makes similar predictions about the development of sentence parsing abilities.

39.3 **How children parse**

Since the publication of Trueswell et al. (1999), a number of researchers have begun to use eye movement techniques to study child language comprehension processes (e.g. Arnold et al., forthcoming; Choi and Trueswell, in preparation; Epley et al., 2004; Huang and Snedeker, 2006; Hurewitz, 2001; Kidd, 2003; Nadig and Sedivy, 2002; Snedeker and Trueswell, 2004; Snedeker and Yuan, submitted; Sekerina et al., 2004; Song and Fisher, 2005; Weighall and Thompson, 2005).

39.3.1 **Verb biases in syntactic ambiguity resolution**

Snedeker et al. (2001) and Snedeker and Trueswell (2004) explored in detail Trueswell et al.'s (1999) claim that children's parsing preferences are driven almost solely by their verb-specific syntactic and semantic knowledge, with little online influence from the pertinent features of the reference world. To do so, they designed an experiment in which the effects of verb-bias were examined within two different referential contexts. The participants were again five-year-olds and adults. Target constructions contained a PP-attachment ambiguity (e.g. *Feel the frog with the feather*) in both two-referent and one-referent contexts. These contexts, or "reference worlds," showed both a frog holding a small feather and another, larger feather (see Figure 39.4). Based on the results of an earlier sentence completion study that was conducted on a separate group of adults, three different types of verbs were selected and compared: ones that typically take an instrument phrase (*hit*), ones that rarely do so (*choose*), and equi-biased verbs (*feel*). The semantic fit of the instrument noun was controlled across conditions via normative ratings: all nouns, e.g. *fan, feather*, and *stick*, were rated as being approximately equally good or poor instruments for their respective verbs.

The results were systematic and striking. Five-year-olds' eye movements and actions showed a sole reliance on the verb preferences. As shown in Figure 39.5, the proportion of looks to the potential instrument upon hearing *with the x* systematically decreased across Instrument-biased, Equi-biased, and Modifier-biased conditions. Additionally, no sensitivity to the referential scene was observed, even for equi-biased verbs. In contrast, adults' initial eye movements and actions revealed their simultaneous sensitivity to both verb-bias manipulations and referential context in the expected directions: Two-referent scenes and Modifier-biased verbs both reduced looks to, and use of, a potential instrument (e.g. a large feather), resulting in reliable effects of both the Verb-type and Referential factors.

These results and the results of Trueswell et al. (1999) have both been replicated recently using eye gaze methods (Hurewitz et al., 2001; Kidd, 2003; Weighall and Thompson, 2005) and offline methods (Kidd and Bavin, 2005). Moreover, Traxler (2002) reports a set of self-paced reading studies with older children (8–10 years) which also show reliance on lexical cues to parsing and difficulty revising. Thus, the finding that children rely on lexical evidence over and above other cues is a robust one, and not limited to the spoken domain.

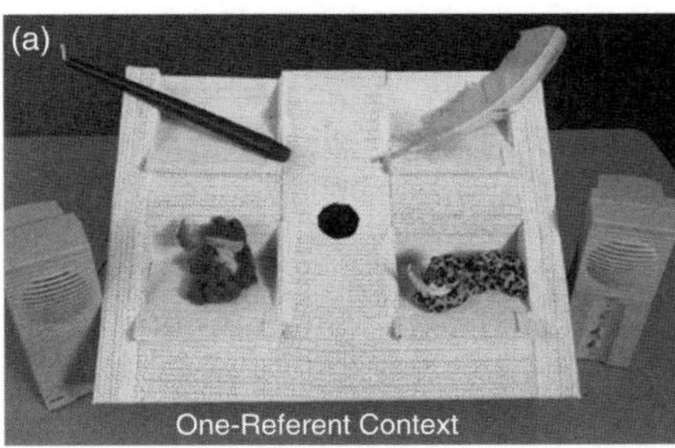

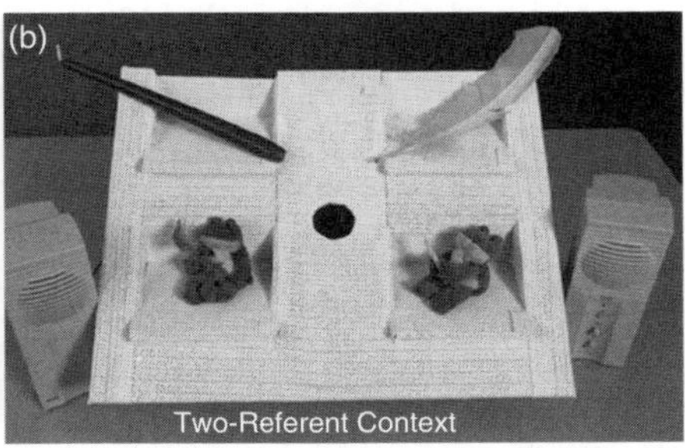

Figure 39.4 Referential settings used in Snedeker and Trueswell (2004). (a) 1-Referent Scene; (b) 2-Referent Scene.

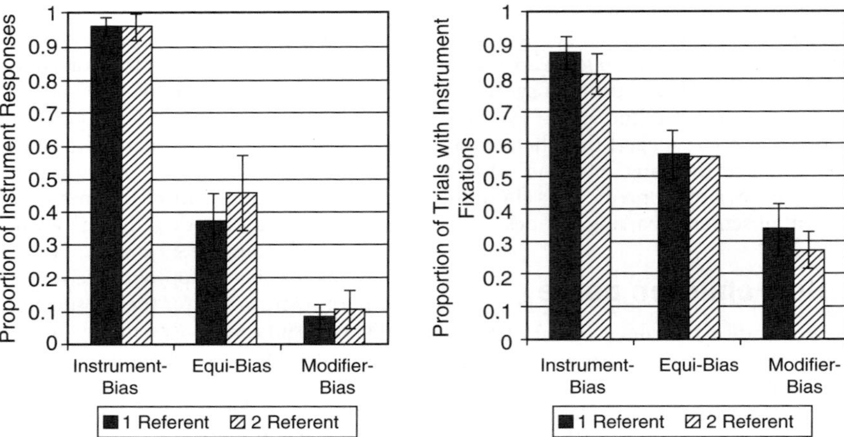

Figure 39.5 Results from Snedeker and Trueswell (2004): (a) Proportion of looks to the instrument; (b) Proportion of actions involving the use of the instrument.

The experimental work just reviewed shows a near-exclusive role of lexical evidence for informing children's parsing decisions. One possible explanation of this finding is that the child's evolving parser is "encapsulated" in the sense that it bans all information other than lexical-grammatical information in decoding word strings into their meanings. Another proposal (one we endorsed in advance in introductory remarks in this chapter) is that the parser is a multiple-constraint device from the beginning, but one that starts out limited in its database. According to this latter account, parsing is a probabilistic multiple-constraint comprehension process from the onset of learning, with the ordering of evidence use over development reflecting changes in relative availability and reliability. As various evidential databases are built and discovered to be informative, they come into use in the comprehension process.[6] Under this account, the child parsing system shows an earlier reliance on lexical sources (above and beyond other relevant information sources such as referential sources) not because it is limited in principle to this evidentiary source, but because of the high degree of reliability of lexical evidence for syntactic structuring.

Three general questions have been explored in the recent literature to probe these alternative interpretations. First, are children's parsing preferences exclusively limited to lexical evidence, as a modular view would propose, or would other reliable evidence (such as prosodic evidence) play a simultaneous role? Second, is there really any difficulty in the inference process from world to disambiguation that is pertinent in these two-referent/one-referent cases? If the child's problem is really the difficulty of using this particular referential evidence (rather than its principled "ban" on this evidential source), then it should be possible to show that young children will use referential constraints when the relevant referential domain is made more transparent. Third, are current ideas about the acquisition of parsing skewed or misguided because the information comes almost solely from English? In particular, the findings thus far have been interpreted to support the view that parsing is strongly lexicon-driven and incremental; but the findings in fact have been narrower than this: so far the evidence points to the *verb* as the locus of parsing decisions. But the verb in English, and especially in imperative sentences, reaches the ear very early during the hearing of sentences. So perhaps it is "verbness" rather than "firstness" that is leading the parsing parade. We turn now to each of these issues.

[6] This means that some inherent ordering to evidence use is imposed even on a constraint-based system, since the building of certain linguistic representations (i.e. evidential sources) serves as a prerequisite to building other, often higher-level linguistic representations (see Fisher and Gleitman, 2002; Gleitman et al., 2005).

39.3.2 Multiple constraints: prosody and lexical biases in child parsing

Snedeker and Yuan (submitted) have recently explored the extent to which non-lexical constraints on structure, in particular prosodic evidence, contributes to child parsing. The study was in all regards identical to the one-referent cases of Snedeker and Trueswell (2004), including the manipulation of lexical bias (Modifier-bias, Equi-bias, and Instrument-bias verbs). The effect of these three levels of lexical bias was examined within two different prosodic profiles, designed to support either a Modifier or Instrument interpretation. Specifically, utterances with instrument prosody had a major prosodic break after the first noun phrase (*[Now I'd like you to tap the frog] [with the feather]*). Modifier prosody placed the break after the verb (*[Now I'd like you to tap] [the frog with the feather]*). These prosodic boundaries modeled utterances produced by mothers to children in a referential communication task also reported in the paper.

As in Snedeker and Trueswell (2004), reliable effects of lexical bias were found in both eye movements and actions involving the potential instrument. Interestingly, a similar main effect of prosody was observed. Indeed, statistical modeling of the data showed independent and additive effects of both factors. Thus, it appears that multiple factors contribute to child parsing, just as in adults; children appear to have yet to acquire the less predictable referential constraints on structure.

39.3.3 What are the inferences involved in reference?

In the pragmatics literature that has followed from Grice's seminal work and the ambiguity investigations from Crain (1981) and Altmann and Steedman (1988), the absence/presence of more than one referential entity appears to be so obvious, reliable, and overwhelming as to form the first basis for interpretation of syntactic ambiguity (see again Figure 39.1). Yet the child findings just reported do not seem to fit well into this picture. The fault is not with the theory, however, but in interpreting the notion of "what is present" at too surface a level. To the investigators just cited, "what is present" means what is *conversationally present* or, if you will, *conversationally relevant*. And it is this that underlies the interpretation of named entities against the world (e.g. Lyons, 1980; Stone and Webber, 1998). Often, then, the individual or group of individuals so focused is not visible at all except by background knowledge or prior discourse information, both of which can guide the choice between definite and indefinite reference (here *the* vs. *a*) and restrictive modification.[7] Visual co-presence is often a good heuristic in deciding these matters, but like most heuristics it can be misleading.

This point was driven home in a recent adult-to-adult referential communication study by Brown-Schmidt et al. (2002). In this setting, two participants had to direct each other to pick up and move objects of different sizes and colors from their locations on a grid. The investigators observed that adults do not, in fact, utter restrictive modifiers every time there is more than one potential referent in view, or even in the large majority of such instances. Nearly half of all definite NPs uttered (48 percent) did not have a unique referent in the scene. For example, *Okay, pick up the square* might be uttered naturally as an action directive in the presence of multiple visible squares. Conversants' eye movements, actions and vocal responses all showed that they routinely achieved referential success under these conditions. This is not magic. Brown-Schmidt et al. (2002) showed that the shape of the discourse and the goals of the task had narrowed the field of possible referents down to one among those in view. For instance, a particular square might have been selected as the one to focus on by prior discussion (*Look at the right side of the display* or *Notice the green items*) so that any subsequent reference to squares had become *the* conversationally salient square rather than *a* square. Definite NPs containing restrictive modifiers were uttered only when more than one potential referent were currently in conversational focus (i.e. within the referential domain).

Thus a great deal of inferential machinery must be in place for a listener to understand the degree of specificity and modification a speaker is likely to provide when referring to visually co-present objects. Thus it is perhaps not surprising that developmental studies of definite reference have found that young children (3–6 years) tend to behave egocentrically when making referential decisions of this sort, both in their own productions but also in comprehension (Maratsos, 1976; Karmiloff-Smith, 1979). In the absence of conversational information that

[7] For instance the phrase *a wife of Henry VIII* is natural in historical narrative environments whereas *a wife of George III* would be puzzling.

might guide the child to characterize the visual referent world in the same way as the adult speaker, the child listener instead assumes that what he/she is thinking about is also what the speaker is thinking about. More concretely, when hearing *the frog*, it is the frog that the child is currently attending to that we should expect the child to think is the referent. Indeed, as Trueswell et al. (1999) noted, children's eye fixation patterns show this egocentricity: the frog they looked to first upon hearing *the frog* is a fairly good predictor of which frog they return to, and act upon, in their action of *putting*.[8]

So far, the eye-movement results (e.g. Trueswell et al., 1999; Snedeker and Trueswell, 2004) are consistent with the idea that child parsers do not systematically map between referential cues (one frog, two frogs) and linguistic expression (*the frog*, or *the frog on a napkin*). But, as just discussed, it is possible that the available referential evidence (mere visual presence of one vs. multiple frogs) was simply not sufficient to bring out some such pragmatic/linguistic knowledge in young children. Accordingly, Hurewitz and colleagues (Hurewitz, 2001; see also Trueswell and Gleitman, 2004) investigated the degree to which preceding discourse, in the form of two conversing puppets, might allow young children to characterize the visual referent world in the same way as the adult. The idea was to create a situation in which goals of the target utterance and the relevant referential domain were more transparent to the child participants than in the prior experimental situations. Space limitations preclude us from giving a fuller description of the study (see Trueswell and Gleitman, 2004), but suffice it to say the data suggest that discourse factors can influence child parsing decisions in two-referent contexts. Hearing an ambiguous phrase like *The turtle tickled the cat on the barn* is more likely to be interpreted as a modifier phrase when preceded by a question like *Which cat did the turtle tickle?* than by a generic non-focusing question like *Can you tell me something about the story?*. Nonetheless, Hurewitz et al. found that children still rely more heavily on lexical biases in these question–answer contexts than do adults in the identical setting. Taken together, these data suggest a general progression toward overcoming local lexical biases when these are in conflict with strong discourse requirements.

39.3.4 **Putting first things last: parsing development in a head-final language**

We now return to a general question that was raised at the start of this section: Is the child's mental parser tailored to specific facts about the language being learned, or is there a language-independent "universal parser" that persists throughout life? In this regard, consider again the findings of Snedeker and Trueswell (2004) demonstrating that English-speaking children exhibit a strong reliance on verb biases when making parsing decisions. What causes this special reliance on the verb? It might simply be a reflection of the well-accepted view that verbs project their arguments (e.g. Chomsky, 1981) and hence that the verb is the most reliable source for proposing structure. This would be consistent with a strict head-driven parsing theory, such as that proposed for adult parsing by Pritchett (1992). But as we have already seen, principles of grammar and the syntax–lexicon interface may sometimes cross-cut parsing properties, owing to the real-time constraints on sentence understanding. These latter constraints may instantiate the real estate agent's adage "location, location, location." Verbs appear early in most utterances, and even sentence-initially in imperatives. Perhaps children rely most on whatever information they get first. Indeed, the finding that children exhibit a general inability to revise initial commitments (Trueswell et al., 1999) suggests a disproportionate reliance on early-arising cues to structure. So verbs may play their special role in English-speaking child parsing largely because this category happens to occupy the prime real estate in most sentences.

A recent study (Choi and Trueswell, forthcoming) explores these issues by examining child parsing in Korean, a head-final language in which the distribution of morphological/lexical constraints is roughly opposite of English. For instance, in spoken Korean, sentences like

[8] This egocentric behavior was *not* observed for syntactically unambiguous materials. That is, when hearing *Put the frog that's on the napkin in the box*, the place where the child was initially looking did not predict referent choice. Here children chose the correct referent (the frog on the napkin) almost all the time. That is, when children heard clear linguistic evidence for modification, they interpreted it as such. Moreover, this linguistic evidence need not come in the form of a *that's*. As Snedeker and Trueswell (2004) showed, *Choose the frog with the stick* behaves like an unambiguous modifier because the verb is strongly biasing—reliable probabilistic lexical evidence will do.

Put the frog on the napkin and *Pick up the frog on the napkin* translate most naturally as:

5. Naypkhin-ey kaykwuli-lul nohu-sey-yo / cipu-sey-yo.
   Napkin-[e] frog-ACCUSATIVE put / pick up
   (Put / Pick up the frog on the napkin.)

The Korean sentence (5) contains a temporary ambiguity because '-[e]' is ambiguous between the genitive and locative case-marker. Thus, 'napkin-[e]' can be a modifier of 'frog-ACC' or a goal of the upcoming verb. Crucially for these items, morphosyntactic constraints (the syntax/semantics associated with the case marker) become available earlier than other constraints including referential or prosodic information, with verb information arriving last. Thus, case marker information has a temporal advantage over verb information in most Korean sentences.

Corpus analysis shows that the locative use of the Korean -[e] marker is much more common than its genitive use (about 3 to 1). Thus, the temporal priority account predicts a strong preference for a locative interpretation upon hearing 'napkin-[e]'. On this hypothesis, Korean listeners should initially consider the Goal interpretation and anticipate verbs like 'put' and not verbs like 'pick up.' Consequently, hearing 'pick up' at the end of the sentence should require a revision of 'napkin-[e]' as an NP modifier rather than a goal. Korean children may in fact fail to revise this initial commitment and perform goal-related actions even for 'pick up.'

Thus the parsing preferences of children who speak these two languages presents an opportunity to test two quite different proposed architectures for these languages. On the one theory, because in both languages verbs project their arguments, this category will essentially control the parsing procedure too: regardless of surface ordering facts, verb-lexical choice will control the interpretation of noun phrases with which it is in construction. On the other theory, verbs will more heavily influence interpretation in English than in Korean, especially for young children, who do not easily revise when led down a linguistic garden path.

Using two-frog scenes like those in Figure 39.3, Choi and Trueswell compared Korean children's and adult's responses to simple 'put' and 'pick up' sentences. With 'put'-instructions, children and adults were alike in their action and eye fixation pattern: everyone performed goal actions. However, with 'pick up'-instructions, children made a considerable number of errors, carrying out goal-related actions such as moving either of the frogs onto the empty napkin 57 percent of the time out of all Goal and Modifier actions (as compared to 0 percent goal actions for adults). That is, they interpreted 'napkin-[e]' as a goal and could not revise this initial analysis on the basis of the late-arriving verb information. This preference was also reflected in their eye data: children and adults initially looked to the empty napkin upon hearing 'napkin-[e]' but only adults blocked further consideration of the empty napkin at 'pick up'; children returned to the empty napkin upon hearing 'pick up.'

Taken together with the results from English, it appears that children rely most on the earliest-arriving potent cues to structure (verb biases in English and case-marker biases in Korean). Furthermore, the results support the idea that the parsers are underlyingly universal, in that they reflect a developing constraint-satisfaction system. Failure to revise may in fact be a general developmental phenomenon, not related to the particulars of any language (see Novick et al., 2005). Late-arriving linguistic material, if it conflicts with the current analysis of the input, is of little use, because it cannot be used to recharacterize the input in some other way.

39.3.5 The constraint-based lexicalist learner: a summary of findings

The results of several experiments support the CBL approach to language comprehension by children during the period when they are constructing the automatic mechanisms for rapid and efficient language understanding, in the age range from 4 to 6 years. All these studies took advantage of the fact, well-documented in the adult parsing literature, that the resolution of lexicosyntactic ambiguities can shed light on the internal workings of the comprehension system. An act of comprehension, followed along its course with real-time measures such as eye gaze, gives evidence about how features of the input (e.g. an ambiguous word, a complex visual scene, the preceding discourse) influence the construction of an interpretation, and when in this process they are having their effects.

The bulk of these findings show that children's comprehension is already highly nuanced and efficient early in life. Much like adults, children can make use of intricate statistical facts about verbs' individual complementation preferences and the details of the discourse-scene contingencies to converge on an interpretive choice under conditions of ambiguity. First, studies comparing child parsing in head-first vs.

head-final languages suggest that the parsing machinery manifests quite general properties of human information handling in the sense of being incremental and immediate. What differs from language to language, making parsing look quite different on its surface, is the cross-linguistic variability in overt information (e.g. presence or absence of case-marking particles) and the temporal sequence in which each morsel of this information is likely to arrive at the ear.

At the same time, these same studies reveal important differences between children and adults. The younger language users have yet to discover the full range of evidence pertaining to particular linguistic choices. They must build up relevant linguistic databases, several of which vary cross-linguistically. Minimally, learners must construct a library of English (or French, Hindi, etc.) word forms and the sentential contexts (of other words and phrase types) in which each such word occurs, as well as a picture of the language-specific phrasal types and organization (e.g. that in English, PPs serially follow their dominating head NPs). This being so, and learning being what it is, it follows that the more frequent and reliable in the input is an observable property of the system being learned, the sooner a learner will exploit this property in making parsing decisions. In particular, the literature has shown that implicit and statistically unreliable cues to discourse intention (the mere visual presence of referents in the scene observed) are not potent determinants of parsing in very young children, but occupy an important position among factors that determine the adult parse.

39.4 Future directions

This chapter has focused particularly on results from a single method: the recording of children's eye movements during spoken language comprehension. The reason for this emphasis is that this method offers a fairly direct, real-time indication of the child's attentional state during spoken language comprehension. Under most natural circumstances, one can assume that where the child is looking reflects what he or she views as relevant to the task and to the ongoing comprehension process. Moreover, the eye-tracking method allows for a moment-by-moment record of these processes.

It is likely that for the foreseeable future the visual world eye-tracking method will play a prominent role in the study of sentence processing development. Although the present discussion has focused on syntactic aspects of sentence comprehension using this method, there are already studies probing the development of referential processes, particularly pronominal reference (Arnold et al., forthcoming; Sekerina et al., 2004; Song and Fisher, 2005), and the use of common ground to interpret other referential expressions (Nadig and Sedivy, 2002; Epley et al., 2004). Moreover, topics traditionally situated in the acquisition literature, such as the acquisition of scalar quantifiers and the understanding of scalar implicatures, are now being studied from a processing perspective using the visual world paradigm (Huang and Snedeker, 2006).

However, even today eye-tracking is far from the only procedure being used to probe the child's early parsing procedures. For instance, self-paced listening (SPL) is now being used by some researchers (e.g. Felser et al., 2003), though it is in some ways limited. First, the SPL method requires speech to be spliced into unnatural units; second, the reaction-time measure that this method provides is often difficult to interpret as a direct reflection of processing load (see Tanenhaus and Trueswell, 2005 for some discussion). Perhaps more promisingly, several researchers are turning once more to the use of event-related brain potentials (ERPs) during spoken sentence comprehension (e.g. Hahne et al., 2004; Silva-Pereyra et al., 2005). This class of work is likely to make significant contributions, especially given that the method is appropriate for quite young children. For instance, Silva-Pereyra et al. (2005) report that even 30-month-old children exhibit characteristic (and differentiated) adult-like ERP responses to semantic and syntactic violations. These findings are quite exciting, because they set the stage for future research that uses the N400 and P600 effects as a metric for studying ongoing parsing processes. Within the adult sentence-processing literature N400 and P600 effects have been used to measure garden-path effects (e.g. Osterhout and Holcomb, 1993) and even the computation of long-distance (filler-gap) dependencies (e.g. Garnsey et al., 1989; Kluender and Kutas, 1993). Similar studies carried out with young children (using appropriately modified materials) are likely to provide insight into children's ongoing parsing decisions as well as a better understanding of the sorts of evidence (linguistic and non-linguistic) employed to carry out these decisions.

39.5 The place of comprehension in a theory of language acquisition

This chapter has focused on the means that children use to understand novel sentences on the fly, as these are uttered. To describe this processing machinery, we have emphasized real-time techniques (mainly, at the present state of the art, eye-tracking) which arguably track the mind's reconstruction of propositional meaning from ephemeral, probabilistic, and often highly inferential information. As for materials, we have emphasized temporarily and globally ambiguous sentences which inform investigators of the directions that the comprehension process is likely to take in case there is more than one licensed option. Present findings suggest that several sources of evidence, including scene, syntactic, and lexical distributional evidence, are brought to bear on this procedure even by children at the tender ages of 2- and 3-years; but moreover that the reliance on one or another of these evidentiary sources differs both as a function of the type of item being analyzed (e.g. noun vs. verb, abstract vs. concrete word) and as a function of the user's stage of experience with the language. These information factors themselves vary in two relevant dimensions from the point of view of learning. Some information sources are more informative than others (either for a specific language or for any language). Nevertheless, this potential for informativity only matters if the information required for using it is available. Thus adults heavily overweight discourse and referential information in resolving ambiguities just because these are informationally richest. But children cannot do the same unless these properties are made especially salient, because the requisite databases aren't available for fluent use.

It is of some interest that the computational and informational problems confronting the child parser closely resemble those facing children who are trying to learn the meanings of new words. Multiple sources of evidence—the observed reference world, the distribution of syntactic structures it can reside in, and its discourse setting—are in this case also potentially available. However, depending on the actual meaning of a new word, only some of these evidentiary sources are likely to be informative. For instance, it is easier to see that somebody is *jumping* than to see that he is *thinking*, and so the observed scene is more informative for acquiring the first of these words than it is for the second. Moreover, some potentially informative sources of evidence require time and experience to construct. For instance, the syntactic environment of *think* is highly predictive of aspects of its meaning. This word, like many verbs whose semantic content pertains to mental acts and states, occurs with tensed sentence complements (compare *Henny-Penny thinks that the sky is falling* with the non-occurring *Henny-Penny jumps that the sky is falling*). Yet the youngest learners cannot exploit this evidentiary source because they have not yet acquired the requisite syntactic knowledge of the exposure language (Gillette et al., 1999; Fisher and Gleitman, 2002; Gleitman et al., 2005).[9]

As emphasized throughout this chapter, parsing procedures diverge in their organization from abstract grammatical representation to the extent that the former is a real-time, incremental process. The need for rapid, on-the-fly decision-making also, perhaps, accounts for the reliance of parsing on non-determinative probabilistic evidence. Grammars, which must allow us to say anything we can think about at all, by their nature cannot be as heavily hemmed in by considerations of plausibility and frequency. Nevertheless, properties of parsing and of grammatical representation are likely to be closely correlated if not the same thing (see Wanner and Maratsos, 1978; Phillips and Wagers, Chapter 45 this volume). It is no accident that the grammatical formalisms most compatible with this psycholinguistic account have been independently developed within computational circles, especially among those interested in formalisms for natural language parsing. Here, many have noted the computational advantages of lexicalized/localized structure (CCG, Steedman, 2000; LTAG, Joshi et al., 1991;

[9] Both the problem of parsing acquisition and the problem of word-meaning acquisition are—almost needless to say—also influenced by the conceptual status of the learner. So the late appearance of words like *think* in child vocabularies are likely to be a function of the abstractness of the ideas these express (e.g. Huttenlocher and Smiley, 1987) as well as of the abstractness of evidentiary resources which can be brought to bear on their identification. Indeed, these may be two sides of the same coin. That is, the complexity of propositional attitudes and the complexity of the sentence-complement structures used to express them are not altogether disconnected.

HPSG, Pollard and Sag, 1987; LFG, Bresnan and Kaplan, 1982) and the need for and success of statistical mechanisms in parsing (Srinivas and Joshi, 1999; Collins and Brooks, 1995; M. Marcus, 1995; Kim et al., 2002). This consistency of theory suggests that linguistic and psycholinguistic formalisms are causally related to an extent not appreciated a decade or two ago. And, as has been detailed in the present chapter, these lexicalist tendencies are also apparent in how learners construct their means of understanding what they hear.

Acknowledgement

This work was supported by NIH Grant 1-R01-HD37507.

References

Allopenna, P. D., Magnuson, J. S., and Tanenhaus, M. K. (1998) Tracking the time course of spoken word recognition: evidence for continuous mapping models. *Journal of Memory and Language*, 38: 419–39.

Altmann, G., and Steedman, M. (1988) Interaction with context during human sentence processing. *Cognition*, 30: 191–238.

Arnold, J., Brown-Schmidt, S., and Trueswell, J.C. (forthcoming) Children's use of gender and order-of-mention during pronoun comprehension. *Language and Cognitive Processes*.

Aslin, R. N., Saffran, J. R., and Newport, E. L. (1998) Computation of conditional probability statistics by 8-month old infants. *Psychological Science*, 9: 321–24.

Baldwin, D. A. (1991) Infant contribution to the achievement of joint reference. *Child Development*, 62: 875–90.

Bates, E., and MacWhinney, B. (1987) Competition, variation, and language learning. In B. MacWhinney (ed.), *Mechanisms of Language Acquisition*, pp. 157–93. Erlbaum, Hillsdale, NJ.

Bates, E., MacWhinney, B., Caselli, C., Devescovi, A., Natale F., and Venza, V. (1984) A cross-linguistic study of the development of sentence interpretation strategies. *Child Development*, 55: 341–54.

Beach, C. M. (1991) The interpretation of prosodic patterns at points of syntactic structure ambiguity: evidence for cue trading relations. *Journal of Memory and Language*, 30: 644–63.

Bever, T. G. (1970a) The cognitive basis for linguistic structures. In J. R. Hayes (ed.), *Cognition and the Development of Language*, pp. 277–360.Wiley, New York.

Bever, T.G. (1970b) The influence of speech performance on linguistic structure. In G. B. Flores d'Arcais and W. J. M. Levelt (eds), *Advances in Psycholinguistics*, pp. 4–30. Elsevier, New York.

Blodgett, A. (2004) The interaction of prosodic phrasing, verb bias, and plausibility during spoken sentence comprehension. Doctoral dissertation, Ohio State University.

Bresnan, J., and Kaplan, R. (1982) Lexical functional grammar: a formal system of grammatical representation. In J. Bresnan (ed.), *Mental Representation of Grammatical Relations*, pp. 173–281. MIT Press, Cambridge, MA.

Bridges, A. (1980) SVO comprehension strategies reconsidered: the evidence of individual patterns of response. *Journal of Child Language*, 7: 89–104.

Britt, M. A. (1994) The interaction of referential ambiguity and argument structure in the parsing of prepositional phrases. *Journal of Memory and Language*, 33: 251–83.

Brown-Schmidt, S., Campana, E., and Tanenhaus, M. K. (2002) Reference resolution in the wild: on-line circumscription of referential domains in a natural, interactive problem-solving task. In *Proceedings of the 24th Annual Conference of the Cognitive Science Society*, pp. 148–53. Lawrence Erlbaum, Hillsdale, NJ.

Chapman, R. S., and Kohn, L. L. (1978) Comprehension strategies in two- and three-year-olds: animate agents or probable events? *Journal of Speech and Hearing Research*, 21: 746–61.

Choi, Y., and Trueswell, J.C. (forthcoming) Putting first things last: the Korean kindergarten-path effect.

Chomsky, N. (1981) Knowledge of language: its elements and origins. *Philosophical Transactions of the Royal Society of London*, 295 (1077, series B), 223–34.

Clark, H. H. (1993) *Arenas of Language Use*. University of Chicago Press, Chicago.

Collins, M., and Brooks, J. (1995) Prepositional phrase attachment through a backed-off model. *Proceedings of the Third Workshop on Very Large Corpora*, 27–38.

Cooper, R.M. (1974) The control of eye fixation by the meaning of spoken language. *Cognitive Psychology*, 6: 84–107.

Crain, S. (1981) Contextual constraints on sentence comprehension. Ph.D. Dissertation. University of California, Irvine.

Crain, S., and Steedman, M. (1985) On not being led up the garden path: the use of context by the psychological parser. In D. Dowty, L. Karrattunen, and A. Zwicky (eds), *Natural Language Parsing: Psychological, Computational, and Theoretical Perspectives*. Cambridge University Press, Cambridge.

Epley, N., Morewedge, C. K., and Keysar, B. (2004) Perspective taking in children and adults: equivalent egocentrism but differential correction. *Journal of Experimental Social Psychology*, 40(6): 760–8.

Felser, C., Marinis, T., and Clahsen, H. (2003) Children's processing of ambiguous sentences: a study of relative clause attachment. *Language Acquisition: A Journal of Developmental Linguistics*, 11(3): 127–63.

Fernald, A. (2001) How two-year-olds look as they listen: the search for the object begins at the verb. Talk presented at the 14th Annual CUNY Conference on Human Sentence Processing, 15–17 March, Philadelphia, PA.

Fisher, C. (1996) Structural limits on verb mapping: the role of analogy in children's interpretation of sentences. *Cognitive Psychology*, 31: 41–81.

Fisher, C., and Gleitman, L. R. (2002) Breaking the linguistic code: current issues in early language Learning. In C. R. Gallistel (ed.), *Steven's Handbook of Experimental*

Psychology, vol. 2: *Learning, Motivation and Emotion*. Wiley, New York.

Fisher, C., Hall, G., Rakowitz, S., and Gleitman, L. (1994) When it is better to receive than to give. *Lingua*, 92: 333–75.

Frazier, L. and Fodor, J. D. (1978) The sausage machine: a new two-stage parsing model. *Cognition*, 6: 291–325.

Garnsey, S. M., Pearlmutter, N. J., Myers, E. and Lotocky, M. A. (1997) The contributions of verb bias and plausibility to the comprehension of temporarily ambiguous sentences. *Journal of Memory and Language*, 37: 58–93.

Garnsey, S. M., Tanenhaus, M. K., and Chapman, R. M. (1989) Evoked potentials and the study of sentence comprehension. *Journal of Psycholinguistic Research*, Special Issue: *Sentence Processing*, 18: 51–60.

Garrett, M.F. (1970) Does ambiguity complicate the perception of sentences? In G. B. Flores d'Arcais and W. J. M. Levelt (eds), *Advances in Psycholinguistics*, pp. 48–60. Elsevier, New York.

Gerken, L. (2002) Early sensitivity to linguistic form. *Annual Review of Language Acquisition*, 2: 1–36.

Gerken, L. (2006) Decisions, decisions: infant language learning when multiple generalizations are possible. *Cognition*, 98: 3, B67–B74.

Gibson, E. (1992) On the adequacy of the competition model (review of the crosslinguistic study of sentence processing). *Language* 68: 812–30.

Gillette, J., Gleitman, L. R., Gleitman, H., and Lederer, A. (1999) Human simulations of vocabulary learning. *Cognition*, 73: 153–90.

Gleitman, L. R. (1990) The structural sources of verb learning. *Language Acquisition*, 1: 3–35.

Gleitman, L. R., Cassidy, K., Papafragou, A., Nappa, R., and Trueswell, J. C. (2005) Hard words. *Language Learning and Development*, 1(1): 23–64.

Gleitman, L. R., Gleitman, H., and Shipley, E. (1973), The emergence of the child as grammarian, *Cognition*, 1: 137–164.

Gleitman, L. R. and Wanner, E. (1982) The state of the state of the art. In E. Wanner and L. Gleitman (eds), *Language Acquisition: The State of the Art*, pp. 3–48. Cambridge University Press, Cambridge.

Gómez, R. L. (2002) Variability and detection of invariant structure. *Psychological Science*, 13: 431–6.

Gómez, R. L., and Gerken, L. A. (1999) Artificial grammar learning by one-year-olds leads to specific and abstract knowledge. *Cognition*, 70: 109–35.

Gómez, R. L., and Gerken, L.A. (2000) Infant artificial language learning and language acquisition. *Trends in Cognitive Sciences*, 4: 178–86.

Hahne, A., Eckstein, K., and Friederici, A. D. (2004) Brain signatures of syntactic and semantic processes during children's language development. *Journal of Cognitive Neuroscience*, 16(7): 1302–18.

Hakuta, K. (1982) Interaction between particles and word order in the comprehension of simple sentences in Japanese children. *Developmental Psychology*, 18: 62–76.

Harris, Z. (1957) Co-Occurrence and transformation in linguistic structure. *Language* 33: 283–340.

Holcomb, P. J., Coffey, S., and Neville, H. (1992) The effects of context on visual and auditory sentence processing: a developmental analysis using event-related brain potentials. *Developmental Neuropsychology*, 8: 203–41.

Huang, Y. and Snedeker, J. (2006) Online Interpretation of scalar quantifiers: insight into the semantics-pragmatics interface. In *Proceedings of the Twenty-Eighth Annual Conference of the Cognitive Science Society*. Hillsdale, NJ: Erlbaum.

Hurewitz, F. (2001). Developing the ability to resolve syntactic ambiguity. Ph.D. thesis, University of Pennsylvania, Philadelphia.

Hurewitz, F., Brown-Schmidt, S., Thorpe, K., Gleitman, L. R. and Trueswell, J. C. (2001) One frog, two frog, red frog, blue frog: factors affecting children's syntactic choices in production and comprehension. *Journal of Psycholinguistic Research*, 29(6): 597–626.

Hurewitz, F., Brown-Schmidt, S., Trueswell, J. C., and Gleitman, L. R. (in progress) The contribution of conversation goals and verb-preferences to children's syntactic decisions.

Huttenlocher, J., and Smiley, P. (1987) Early word meanings: the case of object names. *Cognitive Psychology*, 19: 63–89.

Jackendoff, R. (1997) The architecture of the language faculty. MIT Press, Cambridge MA.

Jackendoff, R. (2002) *Foundations of Language*. Oxford University Press, Oxford.

Joshi, A., Vijay-Shanker, K., and Weir, D. (1991) The convergence of mildly context sensitive formalisms. In P. Sells, S. Shieber, and T. Wasow (eds), *The Processing of Linguistic Structure*, pp. 31–91. MIT Press, Cambridge, MA.

Jusczyk, P. W., Cutler, A., and Redanz, N. J. (1993) Infants' preference for the predominant stress patterns of English words. *Child Development*, 64(3): 675–87.

Jusczyk, P. W., Jusczyk, A. M., Kennedy, L. J., Schomberg, T., and Koenig, N. (1995) Young infants' retention of information about bisyllabic utterances. *Journal of Experimental Psychology: Human Perception and Performance*, 21: 822–36.

Karmiloff-Smith, A. (1979) *A Functional Approach to Child Language: A Study of Determiners and Reference*. Cambridge University Press, New York.

Kidd, E. (2003) An investigation of children's sentence processing: a developmental perspective. Ph.D. thesis, La Trobe University.

Kidd, E., and Bavin, E. L. (2005). Lexical and referential cues to sentence interpretation: an investigation of children's interpretations of ambiguous sentences. *Journal of Child Language*, 32: 855–76.

Kim, A., Srinivas, B., and Trueswell, J. C. (2002) The convergence of lexicalist perspectives in psycholinguistics and computational linguistics. In P. Merlo and S. Stevenson (eds), *Sentence Processing and the Lexicon: Formal, Computational and Experimental Perspectives*, pp. 109–35. Benjamins, Philadelphia, PA.

Kjelgaard, M. M., and Speer, S. R. (1999) Prosodic facilitation and interference in the resolution of temporary syntactic closure ambiguity. *Journal of Memory and Language*, 40: 153–94.

Kluender, R., and Kutas, M. (1993) Bridging the gap: evidence from ERPs on the processing of unbounded dependencies. *Journal of Cognitive Neuroscience*, 5: 196–214.

Landau, B., and Jackendoff, R. (1993) What and where in spatial language and spatial cognition. *Behavioral and Brain Sciences*, 16: 217–65.

Lyons, C. G. (1980) The meaning of the English definite article. In J. Van der Auwer (ed.), *The Semantics of Determiners*, pp. 81–96. Croom Helm, London.

MacDonald, M. C., Pearlmutter, N. J. and Seidenberg, M. S. (1994) The lexical nature of syntactic ambiguity resolution. *Psychological Review*, 101: 676–703.

MacKay, D. G. (1970) Mental diplopia: towards a model of speech perception at the semantic level. In G. B. Flores d'Arcais and W. J.M. Levelt (eds), *Advances in Psycholinguistics*, pp. 76–100. Elsevier, New York.

MacWhinney, B. (1978) The acquisition of morphophonology. *Monographs of the Society for Research in Child Development*, 43(1–2), Serial No. 174.

MacWhinney, B., Bates, E., and Kliegl, R. (1984) Cue validity and sentence interpretation in English, German, and Italian. *Journal of Verbal Learning and Verbal Behavior*, 23: 127–50.

Maratsos, M. P. (1976) *The Use of Definite and Indefinite Reference in Young Children: An Experimental Study of Semantic Acquisition*. Cambridge University Press, New York.

Marcus, G. F. (2000) *Pa bi ku* and *ga ti ga*: Two mechanisms children could use to learn about language and the world. *Current Directions in Psychological Science*. 9: 145–7.

Marcus, G. F., Vijayan, S., Bandi Rao, S., and Vishton, P. M. (1999) Rule-learning in seven-month-old infants. *Science*, 283: 77–80.

Marcus, M. (1995) New trends in natural language processing: statistical natural language processing. *Proceedings of the National Academy of Science*, 92: 10052–9.

Marcus, M., Santorini, B., and Marcinkiewicz, M. A. (1993) Building a large annotated corpus of English: the Penn Treebank. *Computational Linguistics*, 19: 313–30.

Marslen-Wilson, W. D., Tyler, L. K., Warren, P., Grenier, P., and Lee, C. S. (1992) Prosodic effects in minimal attachment. *Quarterly Journal of Experimental Psychology*, 45A: 73–87.

McKee, C., Nicol, J., and McDaniel, D. (1993) Children's application of binding during sentence processing. *Language and Cognitive Processes*, 8(3): 265–90.

Mintz, T. H., Newport, E. L., and Bever, T. G. (2002) The distributional structure of grammatical categories in speech to young children. *Cognitive Science*, 26: 393–424.

Nadig, A. S. and Sedivy, J. C. (2002) Evidence of perspective-taking constraints in children's online reference resolution. *Psychological Science*, 13(4): 329–36.

Naigles, L. (1990) Children use syntax to learn verb meanings. *Journal of Child Language*, 17: 357–74.

Newport, E.L., and Aslin, R.N. (2004) Learning at a distance, I: Statistical learning of non-adjacent dependencies. *Cognitive Psychology*, 48: 127–62.

Newport, E. L., Hauser, M. D., Spaepen, G., and Aslin, R. N. (2004) Learning at a distance, II: Statistical learning of non-adjacent dependencies in a non-human primate. *Cognitive Psychology*, 49: 85–117.

Novick, J. M., Kim, A. and Trueswell, J. C. (2003) Studying the grammatical aspects of word recognition: lexical priming, parsing and syntactic ambiguity resolution. *Journal of Psycholinguistic Research*, 32(1): 57–75.

Novick, J. M., Thompson-Schill, S. L., and Trueswell, J. C. (in preparation) Information integration and garden-path recovery in the visual-world paradigm.

Novick, J. M., Trueswell, J. C., and Thompson-Schill, S. L. (2005) Cognitive control and parsing: reexamining the role of Broca's area in sentence comprehension. *Cognitive, Affective and Behavioral Neuroscience*, 5(3): 263–81.

Osterhout, L., and Holcomb, P. J. (1993) Event-related potentials and syntactic anomaly: evidence of anomaly detection during the perception of continuous speech. *Language and Cognitive Processes*, Special Issue: *Event-Related Brain Potentials in the Study of Language*, 8(4): 413–37.

Papafragou, A., Cassidy, K., and Gleitman, L. (forthcoming) When we think about thinking: the acquisition of belief verbs. *Cognition*.

Pollard, C., and Sag, I. (1987) Information-Based Syntax and Semantics. CSLI Lecture Notes.

Pritchett, B. L. (1992) *Grammatical Competence and Parsing Performance*. Chicago, University of Chicago Press.

Saffran, J. R. (2001) Words in a sea of sounds: the output of statistical learning. *Cognition*, 81: 149–69.

Saffran, J. R. (2002) Constraints on statistical language learning. *Journal of Memory and Language*, 47: 172–96.

Saffran, J. R., Aslin, R. N., and Newport, E. L. (1996) Statistical learning by 8-month-old infants. *Science*, 274(5294): 1926–8.

Sedivy, J., Tanenhaus, M., Chambers, C., and Carlson, G. (1999) Achieving incremental semantic interpretation through contextual representation. *Cognition*, 71: 109–47.

Sekerina, I. A., Stromswald, K., and Hestvik, A. (2004) How do adults and children process referentially ambiguous pronouns? *Journal of Child Language*, 31: 123–52.

Silva-Pereyra, J. F., Klarman, L., Lin, L. J., and Kuhl, P. K. (2005) Sentence processing in 30-month-old children: an event-related potential study. *Neuroreport*, 16(6): 645–8.

Sinclair H., and Bronckart, J. (1972) SVO: A linguistic universal? A study in developmental psycholinguistics. *Journal of Experimental Child Psychology*, 14: 329–48.

Slobin, D., and Bever, T. (1982) A cross-linguistic study of sentence comprehension. *Cognition*, 12: 229–65.

Snedeker, J., and Gleitman, L. (2004) Why it is hard to label our concepts. In D. G. Hall and S. R. Waxman (eds), *Weaving a Lexicon*, pp. 255–93. MIT Press, Cambridge, MA.

Snedeker, J., Thorpe, K., and Trueswell, J. C. (2001) On choosing the parse with the scene: the role of visual context and verb bias in ambiguity resolution. In *Proceedings of the 22nd Annual Conference of the Cognitive Science Society*, Edinburgh.

Snedeker, J., and Trueswell, J. C. (2003) Using prosody to avoid ambiguity: effects of speaker awareness and referential context. *Journal of Memory and Language*, 48: 103–30.

Snedeker, J., and Trueswell, J. C. (2004) The developing constraints on parsing decisions: the role of lexical-biases and referential scenes in child and adult sentence processing. *Cognitive Psychology*, 49(3): 238–99.

Snedeker, J., and Yuan, S. (submitted) The development of interactive parsing: The role of prosody and lexical biases in children's (and adults') sentence processing.

Song, H., and Fisher, C. (2005) Who's "she"? Discourse prominence influences preschoolers' comprehension of pronouns. *Journal of Memory and Language*, 52: 29–57.

Spivey-Knowlton, M., and Sedivy, J. (1995) Resolving attachment ambiguities with multiple constraints. *Cognition*, 55: 227–67.

Srinivas, B., and Joshi, A. K. (1999) Supertagging: an approach to almost parsing. *Computational Linguistics*, 252(2): 237–65.

Steedman, M. (2000) *The Syntactic Process*. MIT Press/Bradford Books, Cambridge, MA.

Stone, M., and Webber, B. (1998) Textual economy through close coupling of syntax and semantics. In *Proceedings of International Natural Language Generation Conference*, Ontario, 5–7 August.

Swingley, D. (2005) Statistical clustering and the contents of the infant vocabulary. *Cognitive Psychology*, 50: 86–132.

Swingley, D., Pinto, J. P., and Fernald, A. (1999) Continuous processing in word recognition at 24 months. *Cognition*, 71: 73–108.

Swinney, D., and Prather, P. (1989) On the comprehension of lexical ambiguity by young children: investigations into the development of mental modularity. In D. Gorfein (ed.), *Resolving Semantic Ambiguity*, Springer-Verlag, New York.

Tanenhaus, M. K., Spivey-Knowlton, M. J., Eberhard, K. M. and Sedivy, J. C. (1995) Integration of visual and linguistic information in spoken language comprehension. *Science*, 268: 1632–4.

Tanenhaus, M. K., and Trueswell, J. C. (1995) Sentence comprehension. In J. L. Miller and P. D. Eimas (eds), *Handbook of Perception and Cognition*, 2nd edn, vol. 11: *Speech, Language, and Communication*, pp. 217–62. San Diego, Academic Press, CA.

Traxler M. J. (2002) Plausibility and subcategorization preference in children's processing of temporarily ambiguous sentences: evidence from self-paced reading. *Quarterly Journal Of Experimental Psychology*, 55: 75–96.

Trueswell, J. C., and Gleitman, L. (2004) Children's eye movements during listening: developmental evidence for a constraint-based theory of sentence processing. In J. M. Henderson and F. Ferreira (eds), *The Interface of Language, Vision, and Action: Eye Movements and the Visual World*, pp. 319–46. Psychology Press, New York.

Trueswell, J. C., and Kim, A. E. (1998) How to prune a garden-path by nipping it in the bud: fast-priming of verb argument structures. *Journal of Memory and Language*, 39: 102–23.

Trueswell, J. C., Sekerina, I., Hill, N. M. and Logrip, M. L. (1999) The kindergarten-path effect: studying online sentence processing in young children. *Cognition*, 73: 89–134.

Trueswell, J. C. and Tanenhaus, M. K. (1994) Toward a lexicalist framework for constraint-based syntactic ambiguity resolution. In C. Clifton, K. Rayner, and L. Frazier (eds), *Perspectives on Sentence Processing*, pp. 155–80. Erlbaum, Hillsdale, NJ.

Trueswell, J. C. and Tanenhaus, M. K. (eds) (2005) *Processing World-Situated Language: Bridging the Language-as-Action and Language-as Product Traditions*. MIT Press, Cambridge, MA.

Trueswell, J. C., Tanenhaus, M. K. and Garnsey, S. (1994) Semantic influences on parsing: use of thematic role information in syntactic ambiguity resolution. *Journal of Memory and Language*, 33: 285–318.

Trueswell, J. C., Tanenhaus, M. K., and Kello, C. (1993) Verb-specific constraints in sentence processing: separating effects of lexical preference from garden-paths. *Journal of Experimental Psychology: Learning, Memory and Cognition*, 19(3): 528–53.

Tyler, L. K. (1983) The development of discourse mapping processes: the online interpretation of anaphoric expressions. *Cognition*, 13: 309–41.

Tyler, L. K., and Marslen-Wilson, W. (1981) Children's processing of spoken language. *Journal of Verbal Learning and Verbal Behavior*, 20: 400–16.

van Berkum, J. J. A., Brown, C. M., and Hagoort, P. (1999) Early referential context effects in sentence processing: evidence from even-related potentials. *Journal of Memory and Language*, 41: 147–82.

Wanner, E., and Maratsos, M. (1978) An ATN approach to comprehension. In M. Halle, J. Bresnan, and G. A. Miller (eds), *Linguistic Theory and Psychological Reality*, pp. 119–61. MIT Press, Cambridge, MA.

Weighall, A. R. and Thompson, M. (2005) The kindergarten-path effect revisited: children's use of context in processing structural ambiguities. Poster presented at the Architectures and Mechanisms for Language Processing Conference (AMLaP), Ghent.

CHAPTER 40

Learning to read

Rebecca Treiman and Brett Kessler

A child of 6 knows the meanings of many spoken words—10,000 by one estimate (Anglin, 1993). He or she can understand oral questions, commands, and stories. Yet if this same information is presented in written form the child is hard pressed to decipher it. How do children learn to read, and how do they reach a point at which reading seems as easy and natural as listening? In this chapter, we consider the development of reading ability, focusing on the development of single-word reading in alphabetic writing systems. We ask how children grasp the idea that writing is related to language and how they learn about the links between the letters in printed words and the sounds in the corresponding spoken words. As we will see, addressing these developmental questions requires an understanding of the nature of alphabetic writing systems and a grasp of theories of skilled reading.

40.1 Written language and spoken language

A child needs to learn many things in order to become a good reader. Written language is often more formal than spoken language, and it may use different words and different constructions. Consider the sentence *He, John Jones, is the person to whom George placed the call.* We would not be surprised to come across this sentence in a book, but we would be surprised to hear it, rather than *George called John*, when talking to a friend. To become a highly skilled reader, one must become familiar with the written language register and its conventions. For example, words like *whom* and constructions like appositional phrases are more common in written English than in spoken English. The gap between written language and spoken language is greater in languages such as Arabic than it is in English, and it can be compounded for readers of any language who speak a non-standard dialect.

Our interest here is in how children master the basics of reading in the first place. In the United States and many other countries, reading materials designed for beginners typically use words and constructions that are familiar to children in their spoken forms. What is critical, then, is that children are able to translate the printed words on the page into a speech-based representation. This may be overt speech, as when children read aloud, or an inner code that preserves certain characteristics of speech—the interior voice that children (and adults) often claim to hear when reading silently. Children who are able to translate printed language into spoken language can usually, given their extensive spoken vocabularies and their syntactic knowledge, comprehend the meaning of the print. This process of translating printed material into a speech-based form is commonly called decoding.

Decoding is made possible by the fact that writing represents language; it is glottographic (Sampson, 1985). Whether the unit of language that writing symbolizes is the phoneme (an alphabetic writing system), the syllable (a syllabic writing system), or the morpheme (a logographic writing system), writing systems assign symbols to linguistic units and present them in a conventional arrangement. Reading, then, involves recovering the linguistic units (see also Frost and Ziegler, Chapter 7 this volume). For alphabetic writing systems, which have featured in the majority of the research on reading and reading development and which are the focus of this chapter, spellings lead readers toward the phonemic representations of words. (See Hanley, 2005 for a discussion of learning to read in Chinese, a non-alphabetic writing system.) Spellings may not provide full information about words' spoken forms, however. Readers of English must fill in stress (is *present* a noun with first-syllable stress or a verb with second-syllable stress?), and readers of Swedish must fill in tone (does *anden* have a simple tone and mean "the duck" or does it have a double tone and mean "the spirit"?).

The central problem in learning to read, then, is learning to decode. Before children can begin to do this, they must understand that writing represents language and that there exists a code to be broken. We consider these early developments in the section that follows. In later sections, we go on to consider theoretical perspectives on the nature and development of decoding itself.

40.2 **Early learning about relations between writing and language**

Researchers have called the initial period of reading development—the time before children begin to decode themselves—the pre-alphabetic (Ehri, 1998) or logographic (Frith, 1985) period. The first label stresses what young children cannot do: they cannot decode alphabetic writing phoneme by phoneme. The second label implicitly proposes a hypothesis about what children do: They treat an alphabet as if it were a logography, a glottographic system in which each word or morpheme of the language is represented with its own graphic symbol. In this view, for example, young children may recognize their own name as a special, unique symbol. They do not divide the written name into components and link each component to a smaller unit of sound, but they do know that the written word represents a specific linguistic form.

The idea that writing is glottographic—that it does not record concepts directly but rather represents language, which in turn represents concepts—is an idea that needs to be learned, however. Some children who are commonly described as logographic readers do not appear to understand the basic nature of writing. Instead, they may believe that writing is semasiographic, directly encoding meaning. Anecdotal evidence for this point comes from a 3.5 year old of our acquaintance who pointed to a stop sign and told an adult that the writing on it said, "Don't cross the street." When the adult questioned her again a few minutes later about the word on the sign, the child reported that it said "Don't go." To this child, the symbol STOP represented a general meaning, one that could be expressed equally well using different words. The child did not yet seem to know that writing represents specific linguistic forms.

Several factors likely contribute to children's early belief that writing is semasiographic. Some of the symbols that are most familiar to young children, such as drawings and photographs, represent meaning in a direct way, and children may believe that writing does the same. Children can think about a cat or a table as something that can be represented symbolically, as in a picture, but it is hard for them to conceive of language, which fades quickly, as an object that can be represented. It is particularly difficult for children to conceive of phonemes as objects that can be represented, for they are difficult to access as separate units in the speech stream (see Ehri et al., 2001).

If young children believe that writing represents concepts directly, how does it do this? According to some researchers, children initially believe that writing is iconic—that it represents concepts by virtue of its physical resemblance to instances of those concepts. Supporting this view are the results of studies in which children are shown printed words such as *ballerina* and *ball* and are told that one of the words goes with a picture of a ballerina and the other goes with a picture of a ball. English-speaking pre-readers tend to use the relative sizes of the objects to solve the task. As a result, they do relatively well on pairs such as *ballerina–ball*, where the word for the bigger object is spelt with more letters, and relatively poorly on pairs such as *caterpillar–cat*, where the word for the bigger object is spelt with fewer letters (Bialystok, 1991). Similar results have been reported for Swedish-speaking (Lundberg and Tornéus, 1978) and Hebrew-speaking (Levin and Landsmann, 1989) preschoolers. Children's search for iconicity, however, is usually fruitless. Only very occasionally do words look at all like what they represent. The word *dog* can be imagined as looking like a dog, with erect ears on the *d* and a tail on the *g*, and *camel* may have two humps in the middle. But even in Chinese, where certain of the characters started off as pictures of the thing they represent, this sort of iconicity does not go very far, and the great majority of words in any language do not even represent physical objects. Children are bound to become discouraged with iconic reading strategies.

If writing does not represent meaning by virtue of iconicity, perhaps it does so by virtue of physical adjacency. This hypothesis works well for a number of the printed words that children see. For example, a child may take the word *Cheerios* on a cereal box to refer to the cereal because of the word's proximity to a photograph of a bowl of cereal and to the pieces of cereal themselves. In this case, the child's guess is correct. Experimental evidence for young children's use of adjacency comes from the moving word task. In this task, a printed word such as *girl* is placed under a picture of a girl but then is moved under a picture of a tree. Young children often report that the word now says *tree* (e.g. Bialystok, 1991).

How do children learn that writing is not necessarily related to its object by virtue of physical resemblance or adjacency? How do they learn that writing represents specific spoken words as opposed to general meanings? Children's experiences with the spellings of their names may play an important role in this learning. A child's first name is usually the first printed word that he or she can recognize and reproduce; names of family members, pets, and friends are also learned early. A child named Jane has the opportunity to observe that neither the graphic form of her name as a whole nor its individual components look at all like she does. Whether the word is near to her or her depiction or not, its interpretation is the same. That interpretation is a specific linguistic form, *Jane*. The word cannot be read as *little girl* or as *four year old*. Children's experiences with names may thus help them learn that printed words represent specific linguistic forms, and that physical similarity and contiguity do not govern interpretation. Consistent with this view, children perform better in the moving word task with proper names than with other kinds of words (Bialystok, 2000).

Young children's experiences with their names and other common words they learn by rote may cause them to believe, however, that interpretation is purely conventional: that they must memorize each word anew. Anecdotal evidence for this idea comes from Valentina, an Italian five year old, who wrote her name correctly. When asked to write the corresponding male name, *Valentino*, which differs in only the last vowel, she strung together letters that she knew in what appeared to be a random sequence (Stella and Biancardi, 1990). Apparently, Valentina did not link the letters in her name to their sounds, and so was unable to write a name that differed from hers in just one sound.

Some children may learn of the existence of systematic links between printed and spoken words only when teachers or parents start showing them how to sound out words. Other children begin to understand this on their own when they learn the names of letters and encounter words whose pronunciations are linked in an obvious way to certain of their component letters. For example, Jane can hear the full names of the letters *J* and *A* in the pronunciation of her name, and part of the name of the letter *N*. This may help her realize that the letters in her name's spelling are motivated by the word's sounds; they are not arbitrary. Experimental support for the idea that young children can use their knowledge of letter names to make sense of the relations between certain printed words and their pronunciations comes from studies in which children are taught print–speech pairs that are partly motivated by letter names (e.g. *BT* is pronounced as *beet*) and pairs that are not so motivated (e.g. *BT* is pronounced *bait*). US preschoolers learn the former kinds of pairs more easily than the latter, supporting the idea that they benefit from links between print and speech that are based on letter names (e.g. Treiman and Rodriguez, 1999). Studies of children exposed to Hebrew have led to similar conclusions (Levin et al., 2002). Letter names may thus give children a start in understanding that the spellings of printed words are systematically related to the words' pronunciations, helping children enter what has been called the partial alphabetic phase of reading development (Ehri, 1998). However, children who are limited to letter names are quite some distance from full decoding.

Once children enter school, reading instruction begins in earnest. Children are exposed to printed words and sentences and to the spoken forms to which they correspond, and they are expected to generate spoken forms on their own. Children now enter what is called the alphabetic period of reading development (Ehri, 1998; Frith, 1985), a period during which they learn about the system that links writing to speech. In the sections that follow, we consider two different theoretical perspectives on the nature of alphabetic writing systems and the nature of learning that have influenced researchers' thinking about how children learn to decode. These are the dual-route cascaded perspective and the single-route parallel connectionist perspective; or, to be brief, the dual-route and single-route perspectives.

40.3 Dual-route perspective

The dual-route perspective (see also Rastle, Chapter 5 this volume) has guided much research on reading and reading development in alphabetic writing systems. Its best-known instantiation is in the work of Coltheart and colleagues. Computer simulations of skilled readers that embody dual-route hypotheses exist for English (Coltheart et al., 2001), German (Ziegler et al., 2000), and French (e.g. Ziegler et al., 2003). Equally explicit dual-route models of reading development do not yet exist, but dual-route thinking has been influential in shaping research and theory on reading development.

The dual-route perspective states that skilled readers read words via both lexical and non-lexical routes. In the lexical route, the reader looks up a word in a mental lexicon or dictionary and, if the information has been stored there, accesses the word's pronunciation. In the non-lexical route, the reader assembles a pronunciation using rules that relate units of spelling to units of sound. Typically, both the lexical and non-lexical routes are involved in word reading. For example a reader might retrieve the full pronunciation of *fun* from his or her mental lexicon while simultaneously gaining information about the word's pronunciation by combining the pronunciations for *f*, *u*, and *n*. The non-lexical route is particularly important in allowing readers to decode words that they see for the first time.

To understand how the development of decoding is viewed from a dual-route perspective, we must consider the nature of the non-lexical route. This route, as described in current models, embodies a number of assumptions about the nature of alphabetic writing systems and the nature of learning. One set of assumptions concerns the units that are involved in spelling-to-sound translation. The dual-route view assumes that the role of letters in alphabetic writing systems is to symbolize phonemes. For example, the *b* in the English word *bit* stands for the phoneme /b/. (For an explanation of the phonetic symbols used in this chapter, see International Phonetic Association, 1999.) Any letter which does not directly symbolize a phoneme must be part of a multi-letter unit which itself stands for a phoneme. For example, the *h* of *phone* forms a unit with the *p*, and together these two letters symbolize /f/. The final *e* of *phone* forms a unit with the *o*, and these two letters symbolize /o/. Researchers who have been influenced by the dual-route view use the term grapheme to refer to the graphic symbol or group of symbols which represents a single phoneme. The assumption is that graphemes are the basic functional units of writing, and that their pronunciations are not predictable from those of their components.

The rules of the non-lexical route (see Rastle and Coltheart, 1999; Ziegler et al., 2000; and http://www.maccs.mq.edu.au/~max/DRC/FrenchDRC.doc for a list of the rules that are currently postulated for English, German, and French, respectively) link graphemes to phonemes. They capture those spelling-to-sound relations that are relatively simple and of wide utility. Each rule translates a grapheme to a phoneme. In English, for example, *oo* is pronounced as /u/, allowing *boot* to be decoded correctly. According to the dual-route perspective, then, *boot* is a regular word, one for which the non-lexical route produces the right pronunciation. *Brook* is an exception word, one that requires input from the lexical route in order to be pronounced correctly. The non-lexical route includes some rules that depend on a grapheme's position in a word. For example, English *e* is translated to /i/ at the ends of words (*he*) but as /ɛ/ in other positions (*hem*). In other cases, grapheme-to-phoneme translation depends on the surrounding letters. For example, English *c* is translated as /s/ when before *e*, *i*, or *y*, but as /k/ otherwise.

According to the dual-route view, then, skilled readers can deal with single-syllable words on two levels.[1] One level is that of whole words. Readers' knowledge of print-to-sound links at this level is captured by the lexical route. With few exceptions, each printed word corresponds to a unique spoken word, and each printed word is translated to speech in the same manner. A second level is that of graphemes and phonemes. Readers' knowledge of these links is captured by the non-lexical route, which incorporates those mappings that are most regular and predictable, closest to the one-to-one ideal.

The dual-route perspective sees learning as occurring at both the whole-word level and the level of graphemes and phonemes. Evidence for children's use of the whole-word level comes from the lexicality effect—the fact that familiar words (e.g. *home*) are pronounced more easily than otherwise similar non-words (e.g. *bome*). Evidence for use of the grapheme–phoneme level comes from the regularity effect—the fact that regular words (e.g. *road*) are pronounced more easily than exception words (e.g. *broad*). These effects have been found from an early age in children learning such languages as English (e.g. Coltheart and Leahy, 1996) and French (e.g. Sprenger-Charolles et al., 1998). The dual-route model has been influential in thinking about individual differences among typically developing children—some children may rely more heavily on the non-lexical route and others more highly on the lexical route (e.g. Eme and Golder, 2005)—and in thinking about the problems experienced by dyslexic children (e.g. Castles and Coltheart, 1993; see Snowling and Caravolas, Chapter 41 this volume for discussion of developmental dyslexia).

Although the dual-route model has played an important role in guiding studies of reading development, we believe that it is founded on

[1] Current dual-route are largely limited to single-syllable words, explaining why our discussion is limited to these types of word. Single-route models are similarly limited.

some questionable assumptions about the nature of alphabetic writing systems and the nature of learning. Alphabetic writing systems link spellings and sounds at the level of whole words and at the level of individual letters and letter groups, but these are not the only levels at which links exist. Graphic units that symbolize single phonemes—the graphemes of the dual-route view—can sometimes be broken down into smaller units. For example, application of the dual-route view to Italian would force us to treat the *ch* of *chiaroscuro* and the *gh* of *ghetto* as unitary graphemes. However, this treatment may be misleading. Italian *c* is normally pronounced as /k/ (e.g. *credenza*, *coloratura*) but as /tʃ/ before *e* or *i* (*cicerone*). The letter *h* is used after *c* in words such as *chiaroscuro* to show that the *c* has its normal /k/ pronunciation rather than the /tʃ/ that would otherwise occur before *i*. The same thing occurs in the case of *g*, as in *ghetto* (cf. *gondola*, *granita* with /g/, *gelato* with /ʤ/). If we follow the dual-route view that a letter that does not symbolize its own phoneme must form part of a grapheme with another letter, it follows that the *ch* of *chiaroscuro* and the *gh* of *ghetto* are unanalyzable entities. This is probably not the best or most psychologically realistic solution. Similar issues arise for Russian, where soft (palatalized) consonants may be spelled with a two-letter sequence, such that the first letter spells the corresponding hard consonant and the second letter is known as the soft sign. Additional evidence that digraphs can be analyzed comes from German. In this language *ah* is long /ɑː/ (*Bahn* /bɑːn/ 'path') and *a* is the corresponding short vowel /a/ (*Bann* /ban/ 'excommunication'); *h* has the same lengthening effect for other vowels as in *Mehl* /meːl/ 'flour', *Bohne* /boːnə/ 'bean', and *Führer* /fyːrɐ/ 'leader'. That the pronunciations of two-letter sequences or digraphs like *ah* and *eh* are predictable from their components would be lost by treating the digraphs as wholes. Letters with diacritical marks may be analyzable as well, as when an acute accent appears over any Irish vowel to indicate that the vowel is long. Even English shows some degree of predictability with digraphs. The various spellings of the sound /o/ in the words ***r**oll*, ***b**one*, ***b**oat*, ***b**ow*, ***s**oul*, and ***th**ough* all begin with an *o*, for example. We are not aware of any research on the degree to which learners of these and other languages benefit from the internal structure of digraphs and letters with diacritics, but we suspect that learners do benefit to some extent.

Current dual-route models, with their lists of separate rules, do not provide a way to capture generalizations that hold across a series of rules, such as that German *h* makes the preceding vowel long. The German model does not represent what is common to the digraphs *ah*, *eh*, *oh*, *uh*, *äh*, *öh*, and *üh* (they all end in *h*), and it does not represent what is common to their sounds (they are all long vowels). As Ziegler et al. (2000) noted, the number of rules that the German dual-route model must postulate would decrease considerably if such higher-level generalizations could be incorporated. Many languages have such generalizations, often more prolifically than in this German example. The dual-route model's failure to account for them is a real problem, for users of such systems may pick up these generalizations.

Another problem is that, by stressing those links between letters and sounds that are most regular and most predictable, the dual-route view downgrades patterns that are useful for relatively small subsets of words or that are less predictable. For example, the non-lexical route of the current English dual-route model translates *oo* to /u/, ignoring the fact that *oo* corresponds to /ʊ/ in some words and that it corresponds to /ʊ/ in most words where it precedes *k* (e.g. *book*, *cook*, *nook*). Another context-conditioned pattern involves the effect of a following *d* on *ea*. The likelihood of /ɛ/ pronunciations increases in this context (e.g. *head*, *dread*), although /i/ pronunciations still occur before *d* (e.g. *bead*, *mead*), as in other contexts. These kinds of pattern are fairly common in English, and they increase the degree to which pronunciation can be predicted from spelling (Kessler and Treiman, 2001). Although the English dual-route model currently includes several context-conditioned rules, it does not include the ones just mentioned, or indeed most of the other ones that Kessler and Treiman documented. Research has shown that children begin to use certain context-conditioned patterns rather early in the course of learning to read, starting as early as six or seven years for some of the patterns described above (Treiman et al., 2006). That is, children may learn not only about broad patterns like that linking *b* to /b/ but also about more specific patterns like that linking *oo* to /ʊ/ before *k*.

These observations call into question the dual-route assumption that the only links between spelling and sound that children need to learn are those highly predictive links that are found at the level of whole words and at the level of graphemes and phonemes. Patterns exist at other levels as well, not only in English but in other languages, and learning these patterns is an important part of learning to decode. Given how often children see most reasonably common words over the course of their reading experience, they need not pick up the patterns on the first or second or even hundredth exposure to a word in order for the patterns to be useful over the long run. For example, an English-speaking child who tries to read *there* for the first time may well mispronounce it as /θɪr/ because *th* is pronounced /θ/ in many words such as *think* and *ere* is often pronounced as in *here*. Indeed, the dual-route model considers *th* and *ere* as graphemes and translates them in these ways. Over time, however, the child likely notices certain regularities. *Th* spells /ð/ in other words like *this*, and *ere* spells /ɛr/ in words like *where*. The cognitive burden of learning to read *there* is not as heavy as if it had some totally unique spelling like *qgpyi*. The dual-route view sees the whole word *there* and the graphemes *th* and *ere*; it does not acknowledge these additional levels and patterns. Even if this additional information does not suffice to correctly decode a word on the first encounter, it makes the link between the printed form and the pronunciation less arbitrary and easier to remember.

Written words, in summary, are like Russian nesting dolls. Just as a smaller doll fits inside a larger one, which itself fits inside a larger one, so a spelling is a nested series of graphic units embedded in other graphic units. Each level typically adds information not explicitly present at the lower, embedded level, but at the same time that lower level is not devoid of information. Becoming a skilled user of an alphabetic writing system involves learning about all of the levels and types of information. The dual-route view of decoding, with its focus on only some of the levels, is incomplete. We turn now to the connectionist perspective, which has the potential to provide a fuller explanation.

40.4 **Single-route perspective**

Single-route connectionist models attempt to explain cognition in terms of networks of simple units. For single-word reading, these include units that represent the input (the letters in a printed word and their ordering) and those that represent the output (the sounds), as well as hidden units that mediate between these two sets of units. Learning involves modifying the connections between the units in response to exposure to a substantial number of examples. Computer programs that are meant to simulate human learners are exposed to print–speech pairs in a way that is thought to capture important aspects of a child's experience, including the fact that more common words are seen more often. The program generates a pronunciation for each presented letter string, compares it to the correct pronunciation, and adjusts the weights on its connections so as to bring the generated pronunciation closer to the correct one. Over the course of numerous exposures to words, the weights on the model's connections begin to approximate the statistical structure of the training vocabulary. For example, if a model is taught the pairs *bit*–/bɪt/, *boot*–/but/, *book*–/bʊk/, *boost*–/bust/, and *brook*–/brʊk/, the learned weights come to capture the fact that words beginning with *b* have pronunciations beginning with /b/ and that words with medial *oo* have pronunciations that contain either /u/ or /ʊ/, with the latter occurring before final *k* /k/. A model of this type was first proposed by Seidenberg and McClelland (1989) for English, and more recent models are described by Plaut et al. (1996) and Harm and Seidenberg (2004). Similar models have been implemented for other languages, such as German (Hutzler et al., 2004). These models are explicitly developmental in a sense that current dual-route models are not. The weights on the connections are initially random, to simulate a child who cannot decode, and the fully trained model is meant to simulate a skilled reader. Connectionist models of these kinds may be considered single-route models in that the same set of connections, operating in parallel, can handle both familiar words and novel words.

Our brief description of the single-route perspective helps highlight its assumptions about the nature of written language and the nature of learning. The system to be learned, an alphabetic writing system in the present case, is assumed to be structured. That structure need not be limited to one-to-one relations between letters or letter groups and phonemes, however. Indeed, connectionist models are well suited for picking up subtle patterns in a system—patterns that apply in many instances but not all. This is the kind of structure that, we have argued, characterizes English and certain other alphabetic writing systems. The models see knowledge of statistical structure as emerging gradually. A model might incorrectly translate *brook* to /bruk/ on its first exposure to this word, but with repeated exposure to this and other words the model begins to learn that *oo* is often pronounced as /ʊ/ before *k*. In our view, the assumptions made by the single-route perspective about the nature of alphabetic writing systems and the nature of learning give such models the potential to provide more realistic explanations of the development of alphabetic decoding skill than do dual-route models.

At a broad level, what is known about the development of decoding skill in children fits with the single-route connectionist perspective. These models are consistent with the lexicality effect and the regularity effect which have been observed in children and that were discussed earlier in this chapter. The models are expected to perform better on trained words than on untrained items, and better on words that conform to widespread patterns than on words that do not. However, not all words that are classified as exceptional by the dual-route view behave alike according to single-route models. For example, the vowel pronunciations of *brook* and *broad* deviate from the /u/ and /o/ that are generated by the non-lexical route of the dual-route model, and so both are exception words by that view. However, *brook* fits the pattern that *oo* is often /ʊ/ before *k*, and *broad* does not fit a broader pattern. As mentioned earlier, Treiman et al. (2006) found evidence that children, from an early age, begin to adjust their pronunciations of vowels depending on the surrounding consonants in such cases as that of *oo* before *k*. This outcome is consistent with the single-route perspective. Indeed, the non-word pronunciations produced by children at different levels of reading skill in the Treiman et al. study corresponded fairly closely to those produced by a connectionist model with different amounts of training.

Single-route models see development as occurring in a continuous rather than a stage-like manner. This contrasts with theories of reading development which divide the alphabetic phase of development into one or more earlier periods, characterized by learning of basic connections between print and speech, and a later period, characterized by learning of more complex patterns and use of larger units such as syllables and morphemes. Frith (1985), for example, refers to the alphabetic stage and the orthographic stage, and Marsh et al. (1981) distinguish between sequential decoding and hierarchical decoding. Ehri (1998) proposes the partial alphabetic phase, the full alphabetic phase, and the consolidated alphabetic phase, although she sees the distinctions among these phases as less clear-cut than do the preceding theorists. According to single-route models, children may not gain the ability to use complex context-conditioned patterns in an adult-like way until relatively late in the course of decoding development. However, this does not mean that they use qualitatively different learning mechanisms or processing procedures for complex patterns as compared with simpler patterns.

Although single-route models have promise, the existing models suffer from certain weaknesses that hinder their ability to account for the development of decoding skill in children. Some of these weaknesses concern the models' coding of spellings. The first connectionist model of single-word reading, that of Seidenberg and McClelland (1989), coded spellings as an unordered collection of three-letter substrings (trigrams) found in the word. Thus *rogue* would be coded as the set {*-ro*, *gue*, *ogu*, *rog*, *ue-*}. With this type of coding, if the model had not been trained with the word *rogue*, it would be unlikely to know that the vowel is an /o/ as opposed to an /ɑ/, because the trigrams in the word are either unique to *rogue* (*ogu*) and thus could not have been learned previously, or they don't occur in /o/ words more than in /ɑ/ words. A human reader, however, might immediately surmise that the *o* is /o/ because of the final *e*. The model of Plaut et al. (1996) includes a coding of printed words in terms of position-dependent graphemes, so that *chip* contains initial *ch*, medial *i*, and final *p*. This raises the question of how children know that certain letters in printed words are more likely to be treated as units than others; the graphemes are not built into children in the way that they are built into the model. Harm and Seidenberg (2004) used a somewhat different procedure, coding letters in terms of the position they occupy with regard to the vowel. For example, the *p* of *chip* belongs to the slot vowel + 1 and the *p* of *chimp* belongs to the slot vowel + 2. All three of these coding schemes represent a given letter differently in different positions of a word; the first scheme additionally represents a letter as different when it is in the same position but surrounded by different letters. Thus initial *b* is coded as different from final *b* in all three schemes. The *p* of *chip* is coded differently from the *p* of *chimp* in the schemes of Seidenberg and McClelland and Harm and Seidenberg, although not in that of Plaut et al. The result is that what the models learn about the pronunciation of a letter in one position will often not transfer to other positions. This lack of transfer does not fit with the nature of alphabetic writing systems. Although some letters in some writing systems are translated differently depending on their position (e.g. *e* before a single consonant vs. at the end of a word in English *hem* vs. *he*), most are not. In other words, the writing systems show a degree of generalization which is greater than expected by current single-route models. Children may show more generalization than the models too, although this issue has been little investigated. The results of Thompson et al. (1996) suggest that beginning readers learn correspondences which are to some extent tied to specific word positions, but that some generalization occurs as well.

Similar issues of generalization arise with regard to the coding of phonemes by single-route models. Syllable-initial and syllable-final phonemes are coded as different, and this causes problems for the phonological dimension like those discussed above for the spelling dimension. Also, if a model does not represent phonemes in terms of features, it will not show a preference for patterns which involve natural classes of phonemes such as hard and soft consonants (as in Russian and Irish) or short and long vowels (as in German and Irish). The model of Seidenberg and McClelland (1989) has a featural representation of phonemes, as does that of Harm and Seidenberg (2004), but Plaut et al. (1996) represent phonemes as unitary.

The hidden units of connectionist models allow them to generalize over spellings and phonemes that they code as different. In this way the models can account for higher-level generalizations in a way that dual-route models cannot. However, a model that does not account for the similarities among different spellings or the similarities among different phonemes may show less generalization than human learners. An Irish child, having seen a dozen cases in which *i* makes the preceding consonant soft, may immediately generalize to the thirteenth consonant. A model that does not capture the similarities among soft consonants would not generalize in this way. The powerful learning mechanisms that allow connectionist models to form categories and pick up patterns on the basis of exposure make it possible for them to learn generalizations that do not occur in natural writing systems and those that would be difficult for people to learn, as well as more natural generalizations.

Another weakness of single-route connectionist models, as models of human reading behavior, may lie in their assumption that humans are perfect statistical learners. Comparisons of the vowel pronunciations produced by English-language single-route models and those produced by skilled readers suggest that the models make more use of context, in certain situations, than readers do (Treiman et al., 2003). Although college students adjust their pronunciation of vowels such as *oo* depending on the following consonants, they do not adjust as much as the models. Skilled readers may have some tendency to operate with simple rules and patterns—*oo* is pronounced as /u/—even when more complex patterns could yield better prediction. These tendencies appear to be stronger in children than adults, with children taking some time to reach adult levels of context sensitivity (Treiman et al., 2006). People's tendency to use simple rules may in part reflect teaching—children are sometimes explicitly taught to pronounce *oo* as /u/—but it may go deeper. For a person, a rule that takes context into account may be intrinsically harder to learn and use than a rule that does not. For a connectionist model, there may be little difference if other factors, such as number of exposures, are equal.

Despite the problems mentioned above, we believe that single-route models fit better with what we know about the nature of alphabetic writing systems and the nature of learning than dual-route models. Given the developmental nature of connectionist models, surprisingly little research has been carried out to generate and test specific predictions for reading development in normal children. Research has tended to focus, instead, on the models' implications for children with reading disorders (e.g. Harm and Seidenberg, 1999). In the future, we hope to see more empirical research on reading development inspired by single-route models, as well as further development of the models themselves.

40.5 **Teaching of decoding**

We have addressed the development of decoding in light of the dual-route and single-route perspectives, but we have said little as yet about how children are taught or should be taught to decode. Many children are explicitly taught about the relations between certain letters and sounds in phonics instruction. In other instructional approaches, often called whole language, children are expected to figure out unknown words on the basis of context rather than decoding, and to deal with known words as wholes. We do not have the space in this chapter to say much about debates about methods of reading instruction (see Snow and Juel, 2005 for a review). However, we wish to point out that the rules taught to children in phonics instruction are in many ways like the rules of the non-lexical route of the dual-route theory. Children are taught simple patterns of wide utility, such as that *b* is pronounced as /b/ or that *oo* is pronounced as /u/. When children encounter words which do not conform to the taught rules, they are typically encouraged to memorize these exceptional items as sight words. The single-route perspective alerts us to the fact that lists of simple rules do not exhaust the regularities that exist in English and certain other alphabetic writing systems. Given the many patterns that exist, we cannot explicitly teach children every pattern that could help them. Children must learn many of the patterns themselves. Teachers can help by providing feedback on how individual words are pronounced, just as a single-route model receives feedback, so that children can adjust their spelling-to-sound knowledge. Teachers can also help by encouraging the idea that words' spellings are systematically related to their sounds. A word that does not fit a simple pattern known to a child may exemplify a more complex pattern; it does not necessarily need to be memorized by rote. For example, the pronunciation of *book* does not fit with the idea that *oo* is always pronounced as /u/, but it does fit with the idea that the pronunciation of this and other vowels may change in a systematic way with the consonantal context. Although teachers cannot teach every pattern, they can help provide the conditions under which children can learn the patterns most effectively.

40.6 **Conclusions**

Learning to read involves grasping the idea that writing represents language, and that there are systematic links between the components of printed words and the components of spoken words. In alphabetic writing systems, which have been the focus of interest in this chapter, these links are at the level of phonemes. Children need to learn these links in order to decode words and remember their spellings. Once children have this knowledge, they are in a good position to understand what they read and to learn about the special characteristics of the written language register. The development of decoding skill can be viewed from the perspective of dual-route theories of skilled decoding or from the single-route connectionist perspective. Although both views can account for some aspects of decoding development, we have argued that the single-route perspective is more promising. However, further development of the single-route models is required to realize that promise. In general, research on reading development needs to be informed by an understanding of skilled reading and an understanding of the nature of writing systems. This has not always been the case in the past, and we hope that the present chapter is a step in that direction.

Acknowledgements

We thank Gareth Gaskell and an anonymous reviewer for their comments on a draft of the chapter. Preparation of the chapter was supported, in part, by NSF grant BCS-0130763.

References

Anglin, J. M. (1993) Vocabulary development: a morphological analysis. *Monographs of the Society for Research in Child Development*, 58: 1–166.

Bialystok, E. (1991) Letters, sounds, and symbols: changes in children's understanding of written language. *Applied Psycholinguistics*, 12: 75–89.

Bialystok, E. (2000) Symbolic representation across domains in preschool children. *Journal of Experimental Child Psychology*, 76: 173–89.

Castles, A., and Coltheart, M. (1993) Varieties of developmental dyslexia. *Cognition*, 47: 149–80.

Coltheart, M., and Leahy, J. (1996) Assessment of lexical and non-lexical reading abilities in children: some normative data. *Australian Journal of Psychology*, 48: 136–40.

Coltheart, M., Rastle, K., Perry, C., Langdon, R., and Ziegler, J. (2001) DRC: A dual route cascaded model of visual word recognition and reading aloud. *Psychological Review*, 108: 204–56.

Ehri, L. C. (1998) Grapheme–phoneme knowledge is essential for learning to read words in English. In J. L. Metsala and L. C. Ehri (eds), *Word Recognition in Beginning Literacy*, pp. 3–40. Erlbaum, Mahwah, NJ.

Ehri, L. C., Nunes, S. R., Willows, D. M., Schuster, B. V., Yaghoub-Zadeh, Z., and Shanahan, T. (2001) Phonemic awareness instruction helps children learn to read: evidence from the National Reading Panel's meta-analysis. *Reading Research Quarterly*, 36: 250–87.

Eme, E., and Golder, C. (2005) Word-reading and word-spelling styles of French beginners: do all children learn to read and spell in the same way? *Reading and Writing*, 18: 157–88.

Frith, U. (1985) Beneath the surface of developmental dyslexia. In K. E. Patterson, J. C. Marshall, and M. Coltheart (eds), *Surface Dyslexia: Neuropsychological and Cognitive Studies of Phonological Reading*, pp. 301–30. Erlbaum, London.

Hanley, J. R. (2005) Learning to read in Chinese. In M. J. Snowling and C. Hulme (eds), *Science of Reading: A Handbook*, pp. 316–35. Blackwell, Oxford.

Harm, M. W., and Seidenberg, M. S. (1999) Phonology, reading acquisition, and dyslexia: insights from connectionist models. *Psychological Review*, 106: 491–528.

Harm, M. W., and Seidenberg, M. S. (2004) Computing the meanings of words in reading: cooperative division of labor between phonological and visual processes. *Psychological Review*, 111: 662–720.

Hutzler, F., Ziegler, J. C., Perry, C., Wimmer, H., and Zorzi, M. (2004) Do current connectionist learning models account for reading development in different languages? *Cognition*, 91: 273–96.

International Phonetic Association (1999) *Handbook of the International Phonetic Association: A Guide to the Use of the International Phonetic Alphabet*. Cambridge University Press, Cambridge.

Kessler, B., and Treiman, R. (2001) Relationships between sounds and letters in English monosyllables. *Journal of Memory and Language*, 44: 592–617.

Levin, I., and Landsmann, L. T. (1989) Becoming literate: referential and phonetic strategies in early reading and writing. *International Journal of Behavioural Development*, 12: 369–84.

Levin, I., Patel, S., Margalit, T., and Barad, N. (2002) Letter names: effect on letter saying, spelling, and word recognition in Hebrew. *Applied Psycholinguistics*, 23: 269–300.

Lundberg, I., and Tornéus, M. (1978) Nonreaders' awareness of the basic relationship between spoken and written words. *Journal of Experimental Child Psychology*, 25: 404–12.

Marsh, G., Friedman, M., Welch, V., and Desberg, P. (1981) A cognitive-developmental theory of reading acquisition. In G. E. MacKinnon and T. G. Waller (eds), *Reading Research: Advances in Theory and Practice*, vol. 3, pp. 199–221. Academic Press, San Diego, CA.

Plaut, D. C., McClelland, J. L., Seidenberg, M. S., and Patterson, K. E. (1996) Understanding normal and impaired word reading: computational principles in quasi-regular domains. *Psychological Review*, 103: 56–115.

Rastle, K., and Coltheart, M. (1999) Serial and strategic effects in reading aloud. *Journal of Experimental Psychology: Human Perception and Performance*, 25: 482–503.

Sampson, G. (1985) *Writing Systems: A Linguistic Introduction*. Stanford University Press, Stanford, CA.

Seidenberg, M. S., and McClelland, J. L. (1989) A distributed, developmental model of word recognition and naming. *Psychological Review*, 96: 523–68.

Snow, C. E., and Juel, C. (2005) Teaching children to read: what do we know about how to do it? In M. J. Snowling and C. Hulme (eds), *Science of Reading: A Handbook*, pp. 501–20. Blackwell, Oxford.

Sprenger-Charolles, L., Siegel, L. S., and Bonnet, P. (1998) Reading and spelling acquisition in French: the role of phonological mediation and orthographic factors. *Journal of Experimental Child Psychology*, 68: 134–65.

Stella, G., and Biancardi, A. (1990) Accesso alla lingua scritta e sistema verbale: una integrazione complessa [Oral language and the beginning of writing: A complex integration]. *Età evolutiva*, 35: 38–49.

Thompson, G. B., Cottrell, D. S., and Fletcher-Flinn, C. M. (1996) Sublexical orthographic–phonological relations early in the acquisition of reading: the knowledge sources account. *Journal of Experimental Child Psychology*, 62: 190–222.

Treiman, R., Kessler, B., and Bick, S. (2003) Influence of consonantal context on the pronunciation of vowels: a comparison of human readers and computational models. *Cognition*, 88: 49–78.

Treiman, R., Kessler, B., Zevin, J., Bick, S., and Davis, M. (2006) Influence of consonantal context on the reading of vowels: evidence from children. *Journal of Experimental Child Psychology*, 93: 1–24.

Treiman, R., and Rodriguez, K. (1999) Young children use letter names in learning to read words. *Psychological Science*, 10: 334–8.

Ziegler, J. C., Perry, C., and Coltheart, M. (2000) The DRC model of visual word recognition and reading aloud: an extension to German. *European Journal of Cognitive Psychology*, 12: 413–30.

Ziegler, J. C., Perry, C., and Coltheart, M. (2003) Speed of lexical and nonlexical processing in French: the case of the regularity effect. *Psychonomic Bulletin and Review*, 10: 947–53.

CHAPTER 41

Developmental dyslexia

Margaret J. Snowling and Markéta Caravolas

In spite of the complexities of written language systems, the majority of children learn to read easily. However, a minority have difficulty acquiring literacy skills even though they master other tasks well. These children are sometimes described as dyslexic. This chapter presents current scientific understanding of dyslexia from a developmental perspective. We begin by considering the definition of dyslexia in behavioral terms and, with the normal development of literacy as a framework, discuss how its manifestation differs according to the language in which the child is learning to read. We proceed to consider cognitive explanations of dyslexia and evidence concerning sensory, biological and environmental factors in its aetiology. We close by discussing briefly how theoretical advances in the field of dyslexia provide the rationale for effective interventions.

41.1 What is dyslexia?

The scientific study of dyslexia first came to prominence in the 1960s, when one of the main issues was whether dyslexia was different from "plain poor reading." While there was never doubt that intelligent individuals with severe reading and spelling problems exist, the use of the term "dyslexia" to describe these problems was controversial. Epidemiological studies of child populations provided data about what differentiated children with specific reading problems (dyslexia) from those who were slow in reading but for whom reading was in line with general cognitive ability (Rutter and Yule, 1975). These studies suggested there were relatively few differences in etiology; however, contrary to what might have been expected on the basis of their higher IQs, the children with specific reading difficulties made less progress in reading over two years than the generally poor readers. This finding suggested that their problems were intransigent, perhaps because of a specific cognitive deficit (cf. B. A. Shaywitz et al., 1992).

Following on from these large-scale studies, the use of the term "dyslexia" fell out of use and children were described as having specific reading difficulties (reading disorder) if there was a discrepancy between their attainment in reading as predicted by age and IQ and their actual reading attainment. However, the use of IQ as part of the definition of dyslexia has now been rejected by most authorities. First, IQ is not strongly related to reading. Second, verbal IQ may decline over time in poor readers, making it an inappropriate guide to expected achievement (Stanovich, 1986).

Aside from practical concerns, dyslexia researchers have continued using a working definition of reading disability as a significant impairment in a child or adult whose IQ is within the normal range (usually reading ability below the 25th percentile and IQ at least 90). However, studies vary in the criteria used, and this must be taken into account when interpreting findings. In a similar vein, dyslexia often co-occurs with other disorders, such as developmental coordination disorder or attention deficit hyperactivity disorder. The presence of other disorders may also affect results.

Nonetheless, an extensive body of evidence suggests that dyslexia is characterized by phonological (speech) processing impairments (Vellutino et al., 2004) and such findings have led to the reconceptualization of dyslexia as a disorder on the language continuum (Bishop and Snowling, 2004; Pennington, 2002). Importantly, phonological deficits characterize poor readers, irrespective of IQ (Swan and Goswami, 1997a) and group differences between children with specific reading disorders and those with reading problems in the context of more general learning difficulties depend on skills outside the phonological system, such as working- memory deficits (Stanovich and Siegel, 1994).

41.2 Behavioral manifestations of dyslexia

41.2.1 Dyslexia in English

In order to understand why a deficit in oral language should cause a problem for the acquisition of written language, it is important to look at the findings of studies of normal reading and spelling development (Treiman and Kessler, Chapter 40 this volume). According to Byrne (1998), learning the alphabetic principle depends on two critical foundation skills: knowledge of letter-sounds and of phoneme invariance (the concept that a phoneme as a segment of sound is invariant across acoustic contexts). At the basic level, with these skills in place, learning to read requires the child to establish mappings between the letters or letter strings of printed words and the speech sounds (phonemes) of spoken words. The mappings between orthography and phonology allow novel words to be decoded, and provide a foundation for the acquisition of later and more automatic reading skills.

The relationship between oral and written language skills has been simulated in computational models of the reading process. In the so-called Triangle model of Seidenberg, Plaut, and colleagues (Plaut et al., 1996; Seidenberg and McClelland, 1989), reading is conceptualized as the interaction of a "phonological pathway" mapping between letters and sounds and a "semantic pathway" mapping between letters and sounds via meanings. In the early stages of learning to read, children establish the phonological pathway. Later they begin to rely increasingly on word meanings to gain fluency in reading. This can be thought of as an increase in the involvement of the semantic pathway, which is particularly important for reading exception words (e.g. *yacht, pint)* that cannot be processed efficiently by the phonological pathway.

Within this model of reading development, deficits at the level of phonological representation constrain the reading development of children with dyslexia (Harm and Seidenberg, 1999; Snowling, 2000). Thus, the most common pattern of reading deficit in dyslexia is poor non-word reading in the face of better-developed word reading skills (Rack, Snowling, and Olson, 1992), which corresponds to a specific weakness in the mapping from orthography to phonology (Harm et al., 2003). In contrast, most studies which have examined regular and exception word reading in dyslexia have revealed a pattern of performance that is normal for the child's reading level (Metsala et al., 1998).

However, this profile of phonological reading impairment is not found in all poor readers. It is possible to find children who are worse at reading irregular words than non-words and who resemble adults with surface dyslexia (Castles and Coltheart, 1993; Manis et al., 1996). However, several authors have reported difficulty in isolating this *surface* subtype (Stanovich et al., 1997; Williams et al., 2003) and an alternative view is that reading behavior varies on a continuum, rather than falling into sharply delimited categories. To explain this variation, Snowling and colleagues have suggested that a child's reading profile is predicted by the severity of his or her phonological deficit, in interaction with the child's other cognitive skills (Snowling, 2000).

Spelling is often considered to be the opposite process to reading, and a common assumption is that the two skills require the same competencies. Typical spelling development in English has been described in three (Frith, 1980) to five often overlapping phases (Ehri, 1997). The phases reflect a general progression from a "precommunicative" (or "logographic") phase, when written productions bear no systematic linguistic relationship to spoken words, through the critical "semi-phonetic" and "phonetic" (or "alphabetic") phases, during which spellings become increasingly phonologically accurate, to the "transitional" and finally the "correct" (or "orthographic") phases, when orthographic conventions are increasingly applied. Most English words can not be spelt solely on the basis of sound–letter mapping rules, but also require knowledge of graphotactic or morphological rules, or simply need to be learned by rote (e.g. Cousin et al., 2002; Kemp and Bryant, 2003). It follows that spelling poses a significant challenge to children with dyslexia, and spelling difficulties among English-speakers with dyslexia tend to be serious and pervasive (Bruck, 1990; Snowling et al., 1996).

Researchers have studied spelling errors among children with dyslexia to determine whether their spelling productions are indicative of particular cognitive deficits or whether they progress through the typical phases. For example, a child with a phonological processing deficit should experience difficulties in the semi-phonetic and phonetic phases of development when phonologically accurate spelling is normally mastered. Alternatively, a child with visual perceptual problems may have problems parsing printed words and therefore fail to learn the inconsistent and irregular orthographic patterns of the system which are normally mastered during the transitional phase of spelling development. In fact, poor spellers are almost invariably found to encode phonological information less well than age-matched good spellers; indeed, as predicted by the phonological deficit hypothesis, they typically perform no better or worse than younger children of the same spelling level (Bruck and Treiman, 1990; Lennox and Siegel, 1996; Moats, 1983). Importantly, Treiman and her colleagues (Bourassa and Treiman, 2003; Treiman, 1997) have demonstrated that the majority of spelling errors, even among severely impaired English spellers, are phonologically motivated and are frequently similar to those found in younger, normally developing children.

If children with dyslexia have poor phonological skills, this may impede their learning of more complex orthographic patterns. Alternatively, several investigators (e.g. Olson et al., 1989) have explored the possibility that individuals with dyslexia compensate for their poor phonological skills by relying more strongly on their visual skills and consequently show better performance on tasks assessing knowledge of plausible orthographic patterns than on phonological tasks. In fact, there is little evidence to support this view; although children with dyslexia spell words more accurately than non-words, this advantage is of the same order of magnitude as that found for younger spelling-ability-matched control children. These findings are compatible with the view that the development of conventional orthographic knowledge is constrained by the extent to which foundation (phonological) spelling skills have been mastered (Caravolas et al., 2001), and that it is difficult for children to compensate for their phonological deficit in spelling.

41.2.2 **Dyslexia in consistent orthographies**

Thus far, we have focused on the manifestations of dyslexia in English. However, English has one of the least consistent of the alphabetic writing systems. An important question therefore is whether dyslexia has the same behavioral signature in more consistent or transparent languages.

It is well established, as noted above, that the child's ability to reflect on the sound structure of spoken words (phoneme awareness) is crucial for reading development. Initial research suggested that the role of phoneme awareness was less important in transparent orthographies (e.g. Wimmer et al., 1991) and limited to only the first year or two of literacy acquisition. However, findings from a variety of transparent languages have now shown that phoneme awareness continues to be a predictor of reading and spelling ability among children as old as the fifth grade (e.g. Hebrew: Kozminsky and Kozminsky, 1995; Dutch: Patel et al., 2004; Finnish: Müller and Brady, 2001). Caravolas et al. (2005) recently extended this finding to children in grades two–seven in a direct comparison of speakers of English and of Czech (which has a highly consistent orthography). Not only did phoneme awareness predict reading and spelling skills in both languages, but it also played an equally important predictive role.

Greater consensus exists regarding the finding that consistency of grapheme–phoneme correspondences affects the *rate* at which children acquire reading skills (e.g. Caravolas et al., 2003; Seymour, 2005). Specifically, it has been proposed that the reliable correspondence between graphemes and phonemes in transparent orthographies, in combination with phonics reading instruction (which is the standard teaching method in most European countries), helps children to learn the letter–sound correspondences of their language, which in turn enables them to quickly acquire phonological recoding skills for reading and spelling (e.g. Caravolas and Bruck, 1993; Wimmer et al., 1991).

In line with these findings from transparent languages, children with dyslexia learning to read in consistent orthographies are reported to have less serious difficulties than their English-speaking counterparts. As we have seen, English children with dyslexia generally have persistent deficits in word reading accuracy and even more severe deficits in non-word reading. Their counterparts in languages such as French (Sprenger-Charolles et al., 2003), German (Landerl et al., 1997), Dutch (de Jong and van der Leij, 2003), and Greek (Porpodas, 1999) typically attain much higher accuracy scores. For them, the primary behavioral marker of dyslexia is poor word and non-word reading fluency (e.g. Wimmer, 1993).

Cross-linguistic comparisons may be misleading, however, due to differences between the tests used in different languages. In a direct comparison of German- and English-speaking children with dyslexia, Ziegler et al. (2003) constructed word lists that were similar in form and meaning in both languages (using cognates, such as *box* and *sport*), and non-word lists that were matched for number of letters, orthographic regularity, and consistency. Although German dyslexic and control children read more quickly and accurately overall, those with dyslexia showed a non-word reading deficit of a similar order of magnitude to their

English counterparts. Moreover, both groups of children with dyslexia were sensitive to the statistical properties of orthographic patterns in words. This study demonstrated that, when similar materials are used, children with dyslexia show similar patterns and magnitudes of reading impairment regardless of the transparency of the orthography.

As in English, individuals with dyslexia experience serious and pervasive problems in learning to spell in more consistent orthographies (e.g. Alegria and Mousty, 1994; Wimmer, 1996). However, direct comparisons between languages are rare. Alegria and Mousty (1994; 1996) showed that although French individuals with dyslexia can produce spellings which plausibly represent the phonological structures of words, they have weak knowledge of the inconsistencies and irregularities of conventional spelling. On the basis of this evidence, they proposed that the spelling difficulties seen in dyslexia result from a failure to fully attend to word spellings during reading, which in turn leads to poorly specified orthographic representations. In a similar vein, Wimmer and his colleagues (e.g. Landerl and Wimmer, 2000) suggested that, although children with dyslexia may suffer phonological processing difficulties at school entry, their difficulties resolve by the end of the second grade. Their persistent difficulties in conventional spelling (and reading fluency) are attributed to a faulty timing mechanism which impedes the formation of associations between phonemes and graphemes but which is independent of the early phonological impairment. However, several other results are more compatible with a simpler, unitary phonological deficit account (French: Caravolas et al., 2003; Sprenger-Charolles et al., 2000; German: Landerl, 2001; Czech: Caravolas and Volín, 2001). These studies have shown that, like English children with dyslexia, children with dyslexia learning more transparent orthographies lag seriously behind normally developing readers in conventional spelling skills, and experience subtle but persistent phonological spelling problems.

41.2.3 Dyslexia in Chinese

We now turn to consider what is known about the literacy difficulties of Chinese-speaking children with dyslexia, and how these compare with those observed in alphabetic scripts. Chinese is often considered to be a logographic script in which each character represents a morpheme (Hanley, 2005). Because morphemes contain only one syllable, and words that contain two morphemes are written as two characters, there is a sense in which a character also represents a syllable. The majority of Chinese characters comprise a radical and a phonetic component. There are approximately 200 different radicals, which may provide a clue to word meaning, and 1,000 different phonetics, providing a clue to word sound. Chinese characters can contain up to twelve different strokes and are therefore visually complex.

A number of research groups have examined reading ability group differences in Chinese reading (e.g. Chan and Siegel, 2001). Findings have suggested that good and poor readers are sensitive to the statistical properties of the Chinese orthography, such as the regularity and consistency of the phonetics (Tzeng et al., 1995) and are similarly skilled at using the semantic component to identify familiar words, though poor readers are less able to use the radical to infer unfamiliar words (Shu and Anderson, 1997).

Ho et al. (2000) went on to investigate whether Chinese children with dyslexia experience phonological processing difficulties. Children with specific reading difficulties and a group with additional copying difficulties were individually matched with controls. As expected, all poor readers were worse than their age peers not only on regular and irregular character reading but also on phonological awareness and phonological memory tasks; on the latter tasks they were no better or worse than their reading-matched counterparts. Ho et al. concluded that a phonological deficit is a feature of dyslexia not only among readers of alphabetic orthographies but also among readers of Chinese. However, in more recent work by McBride-Chang and her colleagues (Shu et al., 2005), dyslexic and typical readers were assessed on a large battery of tests which included phonological awareness, morphological awareness and rapid naming measures. Although phonological awareness was found to account for unique variance in character reading, character writing, and reading comprehension, morphological awareness accounted for the largest amounts of unique variance in these skills. Moreover, whereas differences in morphological awareness and rapid naming performance discriminated between the groups, differences in phonological awareness did not reach statistical significance.

In summary, studies to date suggest that phonological processing skills are associated with reading difficulties in Chinese as in other writing systems. However, these findings must be interpreted with caution. The study of dyslexia in Chinese is relatively new and, as well as lacking sufficient controls, many studies have taken as their starting point dyslexia in English rather than framing the studies within studies of typically developing Chinese children (McBride-Chang, 2004). Recent findings suggest that morphological skills may be more heavily weighted in Chinese literacy, and impairments in morphological knowledge may present a more serious hindrance to literacy development than does a phonological deficit (McBride-Chang et al., 2003).

41.3 Theories of dyslexia

41.3.1 Cognitive theories

The predominant theoretical account of dyslexia views the primary cognitive cause of dyslexia as a phonological processing impairment (Ramus et al., 2003; Vellutino et al., 2004). According to this hypothesis, children with dyslexia have poorly specified phonological representations (Snowling, 2000). That is, the part of their language system that maps between word meanings to speech sounds is impaired, and it is assumed that for many lexical items that have a semantic representation, the phonological specification is global and not segmental in form (Fowler, 1991; Metsala, 1997).

Deficits in phonological representation may explain why people with dyslexia typically have difficulties with a wide range of cognitive tasks that engage phonological processes. The most consistently reported difficulties are limitations of verbal short-term memory (Brady et al., 1983) and problems with phonological awareness (Olson et al., 1989; Swan and Goswami, 1997b). There is also evidence that children with dyslexia have trouble with long-term phonological learning (Messbauer and de Jong, 2003; Vellutino et al., 1975). This problem may account for many classroom difficulties, including problems learning letter names, memorizing the days of the week or the months of the year, mastering multiplication tables, and learning a foreign language (Miles, 2006). It may also be responsible for their word finding difficulties, and the slow rates of naming of letters, digits, colors, and objects (rapid automatized naming) that are observed in some children with dyslexia (Bowers and Wolf, 1993). Taken together, the strength of the evidence pointing to phonological deficits has led to the proposal that dyslexia should be defined as a core phonological deficit (eg. Snowling, 2000). Importantly, within the "phonological core-variable difference" model of dyslexia (Stanovich and Siegel, 1994), poor phonology is related to poor reading performance, irrespective of IQ, and also language background (Goulandris, 2003).

In line with the phonological deficit model of dyslexia, persistent phoneme awareness difficulties among children with dyslexia have been documented in languages with transparent orthographies (Czech: Caravolas et al., 2005; German: Landerl et al., 1997; Dutch: de Jong and van der Leij, 2003). Verbal short-term memory deficits in individuals with dyslexia across alphabetic orthographies is also well established (French: Sprenger-Charolles et al., 2000; German: Schneider et al., 2000; Czech: Caravolas et al., 2005). A third factor that has been extensively investigated is rapid automatized naming (RAN) (de Jong and van der Leij, 1999; 2002; Wimmer, 1993; 1996). In several non-English studies, RAN has been found to be a better long-term discriminator of reading and spelling ability than phoneme awareness or verbal short-term memory (e.g. de Jong and van der Leij, 1999; Wimmer et al., 2000), and a good marker of a subtype of dyslexia in Chinese (Ho et al., 2004).

41.3.2 The automatization deficit hypothesis

An alternative to the phonological deficit hypothesis is the automatisation hypothesis (Nicolson and Fawcett, 1990). According to this theory, people with dyslexia have difficulty with the automatization of skills. The phonological deficit in dyslexia is thought to be a consequence of problems with the automatization of speech articulation which is critical for phonological development. Further, although people with dyslexia can learn to read, they have difficulty developing fluency. However, one feature that differentiates this hypothesis from the phonological hypothesis is that it places the deficit in dyslexia at a domain-general level. That is, the deficit places similar constraints on learning of all skills, including basic motor skills (Nicolson et al., 2001).

The problem of automaticity in reading fluency has also been highlighted by Lovett and colleagues, who differentiated accuracy-impaired and rate-impaired poor readers (e.g. Lovett et al., 1988). Wolf and Bowers (1999) proposed that, among children with reading disabilities, there are those with single deficits in either phonological awareness or naming speed, and a further subgroup who have the most severe problems and show double deficits. An important issue for this theory is how the relationship between rapid naming and reading is to be explained. Wolf and Bowers (1999) suggest that rapid naming speed is an index of the integrity of an orthography–phonology timing mechanism that is independent from the phonological system and that, according to Bowers and Wolf (1993), might be indicative of a specific deficit in the ability to create orthographic representations (Wimmer et al., 2000). Evidence for the theory comes from studies that show a stronger relationship between rapid naming skills and exception word reading than between phoneme awareness and exception word reading (Manis et al., 2000); Clarke et al., 2005). However, although Bowers and Wolf (1993) favor the notion of a timing deficit, others consider *RAN* deficits to be another facet of a phonological processing impairment (Wagner and Torgesen, 1987), or possibly a residual effect of poor letter naming (Bowey, 2005).

41.3.3 **Sensory and perceptual theories of dyslexia**

41.3.3.1 Visual processing deficits

Vision is clearly important for reading, and various theories have implicated deficits in visual processing in dyslexia. An influential causal hypothesis of dyslexia proposed by Lovegrove et al. (1986) suggested impairments of the visual magnocellular system—the division of the visual system that responds to rapid changes in visual stimulation and especially to moving stimuli (Stein and Talcott, 1999). There is also indirect neurological evidence for the magnocellular deficit from post-mortem findings (Livingstone et al., 1991).

Direct evidence of magnocellular impairments in dyslexia has been sought in tasks such as motion processing (e.g. Cornelissen et al., 1995; Demb et al., 1998; Witton, et al., 1998), contrast sensitivity (e.g. Ramus et al., 2003), motion coherence (Hill and Raymond, 2002), and smooth pursuit (e.g. Eden et al., 1994). However, findings are equivocal, and some studies have found no evidence of abnormal sensitivity (e.g. Hayduk et al., 1996; Williams et al., 2003), while others have suggested that group differences may be related to uncontrolled differences in IQ (Hulslander et al., 2004). Perhaps the most frequent finding is a large overlap in performance between groups with and without dyslexia, suggesting that magnocellular deficits are not specific to dyslexia (in contrast to findings regarding phonological impairments). In fact, the incidence of magnocellular deficits may be higher among normal readers than among readers with dyslexia (e.g. Skoyles and Skottun, 2004)—a finding that cannot be accommodated by a causal theory of dyslexia.

In a related body of research, a number of groups have suggested that visual attention problems may be a root cause of reading impairments, including difficulties with visual-spatial orienting (Facoetti et al., 2001), spatial localization of briefly flashed targets (Graves et al., 1999) and eye movement behavior (Biscaldi et al., 2000; Fischer and Weber, 1990). In one such study, Roach and Hogben (2004) asked adults with dyslexia and controls to detect the orientation of a line that could appear anywhere in a circular array of points either with or without a cue. Whereas normal readers derived significant benefit from the attentional cue, the people with dyslexia did not.

Another claim is that individuals with dyslexia respond less well to stimuli presented to their left than to their right visual field (Facoetti and Molteni, 2001; Hari et al., 2001), possibly reflecting a right parietal impairment. In an interesting development of the theory, Valdois et al. (2004) suggest that the visual attention deficit reduces the "attentional window" through which information is extracted from the orthographic sequence. However, as in studies of the magnocellular deficit, experimental findings have been mixed. Valdois et al. (2004) propose that phonological processing and visual attention skills are dissociable causes of dyslexia that may co-occur, although the attentional impairment may be less prevalent than the phonological. Their study of single cases, like others which have demonstrated problems of visual attention or memory in selected samples (e.g. Goulandris and Snowling, 1991; Romani et al., 1999), deserve replication not least because, although these deficits may not be a universal cause of dyslexia, they may be part of the etiology of a specific subtype or may represent problems which could aggravate the condition.

41.3.3.2 Auditory processing impairments

A related body of research has suggested that dyslexia stems from a deficit in basic auditory processing. This hypothesis, originally proposed by Tallal and colleagues (e.g. Tallal and Piercy, 1973), is appealing because it could provide a developmental account of the pervasive phonological deficits in dyslexia. Specifically, a rapid auditory processing deficit found with non-speech sounds would affect the perception of consonants distinguished by rapid changes in the speech signal; and further, poor speech perception would affect the development of phonological representations (cf. Mody, 2003).

Tallal's theory was developed from an initial series of studies of children with specific language impairment using a procedure often referred to as the Auditory Repetition Task (ART) (Tallal and

Piercy, 1973). In the ART, the child listens to two complex tones that differ in pitch. Initially the child is trained to associate different tones with different responses; they then hear a sequence of two (or more) tones and have to copy the order of the tones in the order of their responses. Temporal ordering tasks like this have been used widely as an indicator of the general efficacy of auditory processing in dyslexia, with mixed results. Tallal (1980) reported that ART performance was poor relative to that of controls for nine of the twenty reading-impaired children in her study, and that ART scores were correlated with performance on a phonological task, suggesting that impairments of reading, as well as impairments of oral language, can be the consequence of a reduced ability to process rapidly occurring auditory stimuli.

Contrasting results were obtained by Nittrouer (1999), who found that good and poor readers did not differ in performance on an ART-like task. Nor did the poor readers show impairments in the use of brief transitions to cue specific phonemic contrasts. Similarly, Marshall et al. (2001) observed that only about a quarter of children with dyslexia showed ART performance outside the normal range, and those children who were impaired also tended to take longer reaching criterion in a pre-test involving tone identification and response mapping. This observation suggests that verbal labelling skill, rather than simply efficiency in rapid auditory processing, may be important for ART performance. Indeed, the large individual differences in performance of ART-like tasks may be related to language skills, with low scores reported only for poor readers having concomitant weak language skills (Heath et al., 1999).

Investigation of auditory deficits in dyslexia has extended to tasks tapping frequency discrimination (Baldeweg et al., 1999; Hill et al., 1999), frequency modulation (Talcott et al., 2000; Witton et al., 1998), binaural processing (Dougherty et al., 1998; McAnally and Stein, 1996), backward masking (Rosen and Manganari, 2001) and more recently, amplitude onset sensitivity (Goswami et al., 2002). However, as with findings on visual impairments, the literature is replete with conflicting results (Bailey and Snowling, 2002), and an alternative suggestion is that the deficit is not a general auditory impairment but is specific to the processing of speech sounds. Consistent with this is the finding of Mody et al. (1997) that poor readers, who were impaired relative to control children in discriminating acoustically similar speech syllables, were not reliably impaired in discriminating non-speech analogues of the syllables.

41.3.3.3 Speech perception

Investigations of speech perception in dyslexia have produced some positive findings. Many studies have examined the performance of children with dyslexia on categorical perception tasks. In a typical categorization task, participants are required to listen to digitised speech versions of familiar words, synthesized to manipulate a single acoustic parameter along a continuum (e.g. *goat* to *coat* along the continuum that signals voicing). In such tasks, tokens at the ends of continua can be easily classified (in the example as *goat* or *coat*). At an intermediate point along the continuum, there is a sharp shift in the categorization of stimuli (e.g. from thinking the word is *goat* to perceiving it as *coat*). A number of studies using this paradigm have revealed subtle impairments in dyslexia (e.g. Adlard and Hazan, 1997; Masterson et al., 1995; Reed, 1989). One problem with this technique, however, is that it uses verbal labeling. As already noted above, children with dyslexia may have more problems with labeling than normal readers (e.g. Marshall, 2000), undermining their performance on these tasks.

A more precise indicator of categorical perception, specifically of how well phonemes can be assigned to distinct categories while ignoring within-category variation, is the phoneme boundary effect—the difference in discrimination between stimuli which lie across a phoneme boundary. Using this metric, Serniclaes et al. (2004) showed that the categorical perception deficit in dyslexia is not only due to reduced between-category discrimination (e.g. discriminating /k/ from /g/) but also to enhanced within-category discrimination (see also Werker and Tees, 1987). According to Serniclaes and his colleagues, such hypersensitivity to surface variation in the sounds of phonemes may pose important problems for learning to read in alphabetic systems.

In summary, there are a variety of current hypotheses concerning the role of sensory and perceptual impairments in dyslexia. The lack of consensus has highlighted some methodological issues, including problems in equating the task demands of psychophysical procedures across groups, problems of task sensitivity (Sperling et al., 2005), heterogeneity among dyslexics samples (Joanisse et al., 2000; Manis et al., 1997), and the more general challenges surrounding the search for a putative deficit that is the developmental antecedent of a disorder but now compensated (Bishop, 1997). However, another quite different explanation for the mixed findings is that sensory impairments frequently co-occur in dyslexia (they are co-morbid with the condition) but are not causally linked to it (Ramus, 2004).

Ramus et al. (2003) investigated this issue via a case series involving sixteen adults with dyslexia and controls all educated to university level. Each person participated in a battery of tests investigating phonological processing, visual processing (contrast sensitivity, motion, and speed discrimination), auditory perception (auditory masking, frequency modulation, temporal order judgements), speech perception, and tasks bearing on the automatization deficit hypothesis (balance-dual task, bead threading, finger/thumb opposition, finger tapping). As expected, the people with dyslexia showed pervasive phonological deficits, but there were no overall group differences on the perceptual or automatization tasks. Of the sixteen participants with dyslexia, ten had auditory problems, four had motor problems, and two had visual problems (these individuals also had auditory and phonological problems). It follows that neither auditory nor visual perceptual problems are necessary or sufficient to cause dyslexia. Rather, the universality of the phonological deficits in this sample corroborates evidence that the proximal cause of dyslexia is in phonological processes.

41.4 Etiology of dyslexia

41.4.1 Genetic factors

It has long been known that dyslexia runs in families; however, because families share genes as well as environments, it is important to attempt to disentangle genetic and environmental influences on reading behavior. Twin studies provide a natural experiment, allowing the comparison of two types of twin who differ in their degree of genetic relationship: identical and non-identical twins (sharing on average 100 and fifty percent of genes respectively. By comparing twin–co-twin similarity for these two twin types, it is possible to obtain an estimate of the importance of genetic variation in explaining behavioral differences.

Most twin studies of reading disability find that the proportion of variance attributable to genetic factors (heritability) is high (Pennington and Olson, 2005). However, heritability appears to be higher (and therefore the role of environmental factors lower) among more severely disabled readers (Bishop, 2001) and among those with higher IQs (Olson et al., 1999). So, genetic factors may be more important in causing some forms of reading disability than others.

The behavior-genetic method outlined above can be extended to examine whether two heritable deficits are caused by the same or different genes. Using such an approach, Gayan and Olson (2001) estimated the degree of common genetic influence across literacy and phonological awareness skills in twins selected for poor reading ability. Although phonological decoding and orthographic skills were both significantly heritable, there was only partial overlap between the genetic influences on these variables. Deficits in phonological decoding and poor phonological awareness had shared genetic origins, whereas the influences on orthographic deficits appeared to be somewhat independent of those on phonological awareness. Castles et al. (1999) went on to show that heritability was higher for poor readers who had a profile consistent with phonological dyslexia (characterized by relatively poor non-word reading) than for those with surface dyslexia (characterized by relatively poor exception word reading) who it can be assumed had less print exposure. The corollary of this—that shared environment is important in the etiology of surface dyslexia—is consistent with claims that this reading profile may be more related to teaching method and to print exposure than to constitutional factors (Stanovich et al., 1997).

A natural next step from findings of significant levels of heritability of reading disorders has been the investigation of the molecular basis of genetic influences. Various research strategies have been used (Fisher and DeFries, 2002). In linkage analysis, DNA from pairs of affected siblings is compared to find regions of the genome which show linkage. "Linkage" refers to the fact that genes which are close together on a chromosome tend to travel together across generations. Thus, correlating sequences of DNA between affected relatives can elucidate gene variations which may play a role in determining characteristics of the phenotype. In interpreting the findings from such analyses, it is important to be aware that linkage is probabilistic; complex disorders depend on the combined influence of many genes of small effect, as well as environmental influences.

To date, the strongest evidence for linkage with dyslexia is a site on the short arm of chromosome 6. Other linkages which have replicated in at least some samples are on the short arms of chromosomes two, three, and eighteen and the long arm of chromosome 15 (Grigorenko, 2005). Furthermore, progress in the search for candidate genes is well advanced. However, traditional linkage mapping has low power to detect weak associations (Fisher and De Fries, 2002).

Therefore, it is important to adopt extreme caution in interpreting current findings. What are needed are multivariate studies that ask whether there is more evidence for linkage when different reading measures are considered in combination (e.g. Marlow et al., 2003).

41.4.2 Brain bases of dyslexia

Most children with specific reading difficulties do not have any detectable neurological abnormality on gross inspection of the brain. However, evidence suggests that early neurodevelopmental abnormalities are implicated. In a now classic study involving the post-mortem brain examination of four individuals with reading disability, Galaburda et al. (1985) reported that they all had cerebral abnormalities, with the left hemisphere typically more affected than the right. Furthermore, the planum temporale, an area lying on the upper surface of the temporal lobes, showed an abnormal lack of asymmetry in these cases. However, three of the four cases had delays in oral language development and at least one continued to have marked oral language difficulties in childhood, throwing some doubt on the specificity of the reading problems in these cases. Furthermore, others have failed to replicate these findings (Rumsey et al., 1997; Preis et al., 1998).

One reason for the contradictory pattern of results may be the inclusion of different types of language and literacy problem in dyslexic samples, or the inclusion of individuals with language disorders (Leonard et al., 2001; 2002). Other symptoms that co-occur with dyslexia may also be important in defining anatomically distinct subtypes. There is, for instance, debate as to how far dyslexia can be viewed as involving cerebellar dysfunction resulting in automatization deficits (Nicolson et al., 2001; Ramus et al., 2003) and some studies have suggested that subtle motor difficulties may be part of the heritable form of the disorder (e.g. Viholainen et al., 2002). Thus, Bishop (2002) proposed that an index of motor skills may prove useful in identifying a distinct subgroup whose language or literacy problems are associated with cerebellar dysfunction.

Aside from structrual brain differences, methods such as functional magnetic resonance imaging (fMRI) and positron emission tomography (PET) have the potential to reveal functional abnormalities in the brains of people with dyslexia. Price and McCrory (2005) reviewed studies that used PET or fMRI to investigate phonological processing and reading in such people. There is striking consistency across studies despite differences in imaging procedures and test methods, and typically people with dyslexia show less activity than controls in left hemisphere temporo-parietal cortex (e.g. Paulesu et al., 1996). Furthermore, B. A. Shaywitz et al. (2002) reported that readers with dyslexia demonstrate a functional disruption in an extensive system in the posterior cerebral cortex, encompassing both visual and language regions. However, it is hard to know whether differences in brain activation are a sign of some constitutional limitation of brain processing or whether they simply reflect a person's inability to read words using a phonological approach.

Analyses that consider correlations between activation in different brain regions may help elucidate the developmental course of reading disorders. S. E. Shaywitz et al. (2003) used this approach to study three groups of young adults: people who had had reading problems since childhood (persistent poor readers), people whose childhood reading problems had resolved (compensated poor readers), and normal readers. Although persistent poor readers activated posterior reading circuits to the same extent as controls, they did not show normal connectivity between these regions and frontal language areas. In contrast, the compensated poor readers showed less activation in reading circuits in the left hemisphere and appeared to be using alternative circuits in the right hemisphere.

More recently, researchers have studied changes in the brain processes in children with dyslexia before and after remediation. Simos et al. (2002) reported one of the first studies of this kind, focusing on eight children with dyslexia who were given approximately eighty hours of one-to-one instruction. Using magnetocephalography (MEG) recording, the authors reported that in a pseudoword reading task, the children with dyslexia showed little or no activation in left temporoparietal regions before the intervention, but increased activation of the corresponding right hemisphere area. After treatment, all showed dramatic changes in regional activation profiles, with activity in the left superior temporal gyrus increasing significantly in every participant. Temple et al. (2002) have similarly reported a move towards normalisation of fMRI scans in twenty children with dyslexia after an intensive eight-week course of therapy.

41.4.3 Environmental factors in dyslexia

In addition to these biological influences, school and home environmental factors—either alone, or in combination with individual vulnerabilities—also contribute to a child's risk of developing reading problems. At the broadest level, reading disorders show social class differences that are not entirely attributable to differences in phonological skills, and poor readers often come from large families, where later-born children may face delays in language development. Direct literacy-related activities in the home are also important (Whitehurst and Lonigan, 1998; Stevenson and Fredman, 1990) and where parents themselves have literacy problems, reading-related experiences in the home may be less than optimal (Petrill et al., 2005). Outside the home, comparisons of children from the same area attending different schools have emphasized that schooling can make a substantial difference to reading achievement (Rutter and Maughan, 2002).

Importantly, genes and the environment interact; from very early in development, children differ in their interest in books, and children at risk for dyslexia may be among those who are more difficult to interest and engage. Over time, the cumulative impact of such processes leads to massive variations in children's exposure to print—a factor known to have an independent effect on reading progress (Cunningham and Stanovich 1990).

In summary, as might be expected for a complex trait, the etiology of reading disorders is varied, and depends on both genetic and environmental factors. A reasonable conclusion is that some children carry a heritable risk of reading impairment, but whether or not they are classified as dyslexic depends upon the language and school context in which they learn, and on the other skills or deficits they bring to the task of reading. In keeping with this, there is currently a move away from single-deficit models toward multi-factorial models that explain the nature and causes of dyslexia.

41.4.4 Studies of children at high risk of dyslexia

The interaction of different skills in determining the literacy outcomes of children at risk of reading failure can be seen in studies of children at family risk of dyslexia followed from the preschool years (e.g. Byrne et al., 1997; Elbro et al., 1998; Lyytinen et al., 2001; Pennington and Lefly, 2001; Scarborough, 1990). This approach is important because it can elucidate the precursors of dyslexia before formal reading instruction begins and can highlight risk and protective factors. In one such study, Snowling et al. (2003) followed fifty-six children from just before their fourth birthday until 8 years of age, who were at high risk of reading difficulties by virtue of having a first-degree relative who was dyslexic. At each testing point, the children were assessed on a broad range of oral language and cognitive measures, including tests of literacy development.

As expected, the rate of reading impairments was elevated in the at risk group. For present discussion, the critical contrast is between the high-risk children who were impaired in literacy at eight years and those who were unimpaired. The impaired children experienced delayed early language development at three years, nine months (Gallagher et al., 2000); at six years, they had persisting oral language impairments and their phonological awareness was poor. In contrast, the high-risk unimpaired group was not distinguishable from controls on oral language tests. It was noteworthy, however, that they knew fewer letters than controls before school entry, and they were as impaired as the poor outcome group in nonword reading at six years, although their phonological awareness was normal. This finding suggests that family risk of dyslexia is continuous rather than discrete, as also argued by Pennington and Lefly (2001), who found shared deficits between impaired and unimpaired children on a phoneme awareness task. Thus, it is not appropriate to think of the offspring of dyslexic parents as either dyslexic or not. Rather, many are slow in the early stages of reading, with some recovering from this slow start sufficiently to go on to be normal readers.

Within the Triangle model that we described earlier, it could be argued that the high-risk children who went on to be normal readers compensated for deficits in grapheme–phoneme knowledge by using the semantic pathway. In this light, it is interesting that the high-risk unimpaired group had better oral language skills than the impaired group. Indeed, Snowling et al. (2003) proposed that such children may use linguistic context strategically to bootstrap decoding and thereby circumvent reading problems attributable to deficits of the phonological pathway. Such strategies may be less available to similar children born into families in poor socioeconomic circumstances or where literacy was less valued.

Such studies of children at high risk of dyslexia highlight the fact that there is not a single cause of dyslexia. Rather, they point toward multi-causal theories of dyslexia in which an isolated risk factor (e.g. a phonological deficit) is less likely to lead a child to reach the diagnostic threshold for dyslexia than if the single phonological deficit coexists with another disorder, is aggravated by a sensory impairment, or is present in adverse environmental circumstances. However, when a phonological deficit is severe (Griffiths and Snowling, 2002), or when there are concomitant oral language impairments (Bishop and Snowling, 2004), compensation will be harder and, as we shall see below, interventions may not be effective (Hindson, et al., 2005).

41.5 Reading intervention

Theoretical knowledge of the relationship between phonological skills and learning to read has led to the development of effective reading intervention programs that promote phonological skills in the context of reading (National Reading Panel, 2000). In a pioneering study, Hatcher et al. (1994) compared three forms of intervention for reading difficulties: phonological awareness training, reading instruction, or combined training in reading and phonological awareness, each delivered by trained teachers. The most effective intervention for seven-year-old poor readers was the integrated program; this incorporated training in phonological awareness and letter knowledge, with the inclusion of metacognitive work making explicit the links between these foundation skills, in the context of reading from graded books and in writing activities. In subsequent work, this program was found to ameliorate the reading problems of at-risk children in mainstream schools (Hatcher et al., 2004; Hatcher et al., 2006). Findings such as these dovetail well with those of other research groups (Torgesen, 2005 for review) and have direct implications for the treatment of children with dyslexia (Vellutino et al., 2004).

An important issue, however, is the problem of "treatment resistors"—those children who, despite high-quality intervention, do not respond to teaching and continue to have reading impairments (Torgesen, 2000). These difficult-to-remediate children appear to have the most severe phonological deficits (Vellutino et al., 1996), are often socially disadvantaged, and may experience emotional and behavioral difficulties. More systematic study of these children is badly needed, because co-morbidity of dyslexia with attention deficit hyperactivity disorder is common, and some children with learning disorders are at increased risk of emotional difficulties including anxiety disorders (Snowling and Maughan, 2005).

41.6 Conclusions

There has been rapid progress in the field of dyslexia in recent years and there is now scientific evidence concerning its nature, causes and consequences. Dyslexia research has been a successful enterprise because it has built on cognitive models of how literacy skills develop in the normal population. Within this framework, we have argued that there is strong evidence that dyslexia is associated with a specific deficit in phonological processing which compromises the development of reading and spelling in English as in more regular orthographies, and possibly also in Chinese although here the evidence base is weaker. We have reviewed evidence of sensory impairments in dyslexia and suggested that these may be significant co-occurring difficulties, though not causally linked to the reading impairment.

Modern conceptions of developmental disorder view such difficulties as dimensional rather than categorical. Thus, from an educational perspective, it may no longer be relevant to ask who is dyslexic and who is not. Rather, the heritable skills underlying the acquisition of reading are continuously distributed in the population, such that some people find learning to read and write easy whereas others have extreme difficulty. We have reviewed evidence regarding both the biological bases of dyslexia and environmental factors which might affect its outcome. Within this context we would argued that whether or not a child is diagnosed "dyslexic" depends on their age and stage of development, the language in which they are learning, how they are being taught, and the criteria adopted by the educational system in which they are schooled. We anticipate that future research will be directed towards understanding how genetic variation among individuals growing up in different environments predicts their reading outcomes, and will be framed within multi-causal theories. In parallel is the need for further research examining individual differences in responsiveness to theoretically motivated interventions which prevent or ameliorate dyslexia, and the brain bases of such variation.

Acknowledgements

This chapter was prepared with support from a British Academy Research Readership to the first author.

References

Adlard, A., and Hazan, V. (1997) Speech perception in children with specific reading difficulties (dyslexia) *Quarterly Journal of Experimental Psychology*, 51: 153–77.

Alegria, J., and Mousty, P. (1994) On the development of lexical and nonlexical spelling procedures of French-speaking normal and disabled children. In G. Brown and N. Ellis (eds), *Handbook of Spelling: Theory, Process and Intervention*, pp. 211–26. Wiley, Chichester, UK.

Alegria, J., and Mousty, P. (1996) The development of spelling procedures in French-speaking, normal and reading-disabled children: effects of frequency and lexicality. *Journal of Experimental Child Psychology*, 63: 312–38.

Bailey, P. J., and Snowling, M. J. (2002) Auditory processing and the development of language and literacy. *British Medical Bulletin*, 63: 135–46.

Baldeweg, T., Richardson, A., Watkins, S., Foale, C., and Gruzelier J. (1999) Impaired auditory frequency discrimination in dyslexia detected with mismatch evoked potentials. *Annals of Neurology*, 45: 495–503.

Biscaldi, M., Fisher, B., and Hartnegg, K. (2000) Voluntary saccadic control in dyslexia. *Perception*, 29: 509–21.

Bishop, D. V. M. (1997) *Uncommon Understanding*. Psychology Press, Hove, UK.

Bishop, D. V. M. (2001) Genetic influences on language impairment and literacy problems in children: same or different? *Journal of Child Psychology and Psychiatry*, 42: 189–98.

Bishop, D. V. M. (2002) Cerebellar abnormalities in developmental dyslexia: cause, correlate or consequence? *Cortex*, 38: 491–98.

Bishop, D. V. M., and Snowling, M. J. (2004) Developmental Dyslexia and Specific Language Impairment: same or different? *Psychological Bulletin*, 130: 858–88.

Bourassa, D., and Treiman, R. (2003) Spelling in children with dyslexia: analyses from Treiman–Bourassa Early Spelling Test. *Scientific Studies of Reading*, 7: 309–33.

Bowers, P. G., and Wolf, M. (1993) Theoretical links among naming speed, precise timing mechanisms and orthographic skill in dyslexia. *Reading and Writing*, 5: 69–85.

Bowey, J. A. (2005) Predicting individual differences in learning to read. In M. J. Snowling and C. Hulme (eds), *The Science of Reading: A Handbook*, pp. 155–72. Blackwell, Oxford.

Brady, S., Shankweiler, D., and Mann, V. (1983) Speech perception and memory coding in relation to reading ability. *Journal of Experimental Child Psychology*, 35: 345–67.

Bruck, M. (1990) Word recognition skills of adults with childhood diagnoses of dyslexia. *Developmental Psychology*, 26: 439–54.

Bruck, M., and Treiman, R. (1990) Phonological awareness and spelling in normal children and dyslexics: the case of initial consonant clusters. *Journal of Experimental Child Psychology*, 50: 156–78.

Byrne, B. (1998) *The Foundation of Literacy: The Child's Acquisition of the Alphabetic Principle*. Psychology Press, Hove, UK.

Byrne, B., Fielding-Barnsley, R., Ashley, L., and Larsen, K. (1997) Assessing the child's and the environment's contribution to reading acquisition: what we know and what we don't know. In B. Blachman (ed.), *Reading Acquisition and Dyslexia: Implications for Early Intervention*, pp. 265–86. Erlbaum, Hillsdale, NJ.

Caravolas, M., and Bruck, M. (1993) The effect of oral and written language input on children's phonological awareness: a cross-linguistic study. *Journal of Experimental Child Psychology*, 55: 1–30.

Caravolas, M., Bruck, M., and Genessee, F. (2003) Similarities and differences between English and French-speaking poor spellers. In N. Goulandris (ed.), *Dyslexia in Different Languages: Cross-Linguistic Comparisons*, pp. 157–80. Whurr, London.

Caravolas, M., Hulme, C., and Snowling, M. J. (2001) The foundations of spelling ability: evidence from a 3-year longitudinal study. *Journal of Memory and Language*, 45: 751–74.

Caravolas, M., and Volín, J. (2001) Phonological spelling errors among dyslexic children learning a transparent orthography: the case of Czech. *Dyslexia*, 7: 229–45.

Caravolas, M., Volín, J., and Hulme, C. (2005) Phoneme awareness is a key component of alphabetic literacy skills in consistent and inconsistent orthographies: evidence from Czech and English children. *Journal of Experimental Child Psychology*, 92: 107–39.

Castles, A., and Coltheart, M. (1993) Varieties of developmental dyslexia. *Cognition*, 47: 149–80.

Castles, A., Datta, H., Gayan, J., and Olson, R. K. (1999) Varieties of developmental reading disorder: genetic and environmental influences. *Journal of Experimental Child Psychology*, 72: 73.

Chan, C. K. K., and Siegel, L. (2001) Phonological processing in reading Chinese among normally achieving and poor readers. *Journal of Experimental Child Psychology*, 80: 23–43.

Clarke, P., Hulme, C., and Snowling, M. J. (2005) Individual differences in RAN and reading: a timing analysis. *Journal of Reading Research*, 28: 78–86.

Cornelissen, P., Richardson, A., Mason, A., Fowler, S., and Stein, J. (1995) Contrast sensitivity and coherent motion detection measured at phototopic luminance levels in dyslexics and controls. *Vision Research*, 35: 1483–94.

Cousin, M-P., Largy, P., and Fayol, M. (2002) Sometimes, early learnt instances hinder the implementation of agreement rules: a study in written French. *Current Psychology Letters*, 8: 51–65.

Cunningham, A., and Stanovich, K. (1990) Assessing print exposure and orthographic processing skill in children: a quick measure of reading experience. *Journal of Educational Psychology*, 82: 733–40.

de Jong, P., and van der Leij, A. (1999) Specific contributions of phonological abilities to early reading acquisition: results from a Dutch latent variable longitudinal study. *Journal of Educational Psychology*, 91: 450–76.

de Jong, P., and van der Leij, A. (2002) Effects of phonological abilities and linguistic comprehension on the development of reading. *Scientific Studies of Reading*, 6: 51–77.

de Jong, P., and van der Leij, A. (2003) Developmental changes in the manifestation of a phonological deficit in dyslexic children learning to read a regular orthography. *Journal of Educational Psychology*, 95: 22–40.

Demb, J. B., Boynton, G. M., Best, M., and Heeger, D. J. (1998) Psychophysical evidence for a magnocellular pathway deficit in dyslexia. *Vision Research*, 38: 1555–9.

Dougherty, R.F., Cynader, M.S., Bjornson, B.H., Edgell, D., and Giaschi, D.E. (1998) Dichotic pitch: a new stimulus distinguishes normal and dyslexic auditory function. *Neuroreport*, 9: 3001–5.

Eden, G., Stein, J., Wood, H., and Wood, F. (1994) Differences in eye movements and reading problems in dyslexic and normal children. *Vision Research*, 34: 1345–58.

Ehri, L. C. (1997) Learning to read and learning to spell are one and the same, almost. In C. Perfetti, L. Rieben, and M. Fayol (eds), *Learning to Spell: Research, Theory and Practice*, pp. 237–69. Erlbaum, Mahwah, NJ.

Elbro, C., Borstrom, I., and Petersen, D. K. (1998) Predicting dyslexia from kindergarten: the importance of distinctness of phonological representations of lexical items. *Reading Research Quarterly*, 33: 36–60.

Facoetti, A., Lorusso, M. L., Paganoni, P., Umilta, C., and Mascetti, G. G. (2003) The role of visuospatial attention in developmental dyslexia: evidence from a rehabilitation study. *Cognitive Brain Research*, 15: 154–64.

Facoetti, A., and Molteni, M. (2001) The gradient of visual attention in developmental dyslexia. *Neuropsychologia*, 39: 352–7.

Facoetti, A., Turatto, M. L., and Mascetti, G. G. (2001) Orienting of visual attention in dyslexia: evidence for asymmetric hemispheric control of attention. *Experimental Brain Research*, 138: 46–53.

Fischer, B., and Weber, H. (1990) Saccadic reaction times of dyslexic and age-matched normal subjects. *Perception*, 19: 805–18.

Fisher, S. E., and DeFries, J. C. (2002) Developmental dyslexia: genetic dissociation of a complex trait. *Nature Neuroscience*, 3: 767–80.

Fowler, A. E. (1991) How early phonological development might set the stage for phonological awareness. In *Phonological Processes in Literacy: A Tribute to Isabell Y. Liberman*, pp. 97–117. Erlbaum, Hillsdale, NJ.

Frith, U. (1980) Unexpected spelling problems. In U. Frith (ed.), *Cognitive Processes in Spelling*. Academic Press, London.

Galaburda, A. M., Sherman, G. F., Rosen, G. D., Aboitiz, F., and Geschwind, N. (1985) Developmental dyslexia: four consecutive patients with cortical anomalies. *Annals of Neurology*, 18: 222–33.

Gallagher, A., Frith, U., and Snowling, M. J. (2000) Precursors of literacy-delay among children at genetic risk of dyslexia. *Journal of Child Psychology and Psychiatry*, 41: 203–13.

Gayan, J., and Olson, R. K. (2001) Genetic and environmental influences on orthographic and phonological skills in children with reading disabilities. *Developmental Neuropsychology*, 20(2): 483–507.

Goswami, U., Thomson, J., Richardson, U., Stainthorp, R., Hughes, D., Rosen, S., and Scott, S. K. (2002) Amplitude envelope onsets and developmental dyslexia: a new hypothesis. *Proceedings of the National Academy of Sciences*, 99: 10911–16.

Goulandris, N. (Ed) (2003) *Dyslexia in Different Languages: Cross-Linguistic Comparisons*. Whurr, London.

Goulandris, N., and Snowling, M. J. (1991) Visual memory deficits: a plausible cause of developmental dyslexia? Evidence from a single case study. *Cognitive Neuropsychology*, 8: 127–54.

Graves, R. E., Frerichs, R. J., and Cook, A. (1999) Visual localization in dyslexia. *Neuropsychology*, 13: 575–81.

Griffiths, Y. M., and Snowling, M. J. (2002) Predictors of exception word and non-word reading in dyslexic children: the severity hypothesis. *Journal of Educational Psychology*, 94: 34–43.

Grigorenko, E. L. (2005) A conservative meta-analysis of linkage and linkage-association studies of developmental dyslexia. *Scientific Studies of Reading*, 9: 285–316.

Hanley, J. R. (2005) Learning to read in Chinese. In M. J. Snowling and C. Hulme (eds), *The Science of Reading: A Handbook*, pp. 316–35. Blackwell, Oxford.

Hari, R., Renvall, H., and Tanskanen, T. (2001) Left minineglect in dyslexic adults. *Brain*, 124: 1373–80.

Harm, M. W., McCandliss, B. D., and Seidenberg, M. (2003) Modeling the successes and failures of interventions for disabled readers. *Scientific Studies of Reading*, 7(2), 155–83.

Harm, M. W., and Seidenberg, M. S. (1999) Phonology, reading acquisition and dyslexia: insights from connectionist models. *Psychological Review*, 106: 491–528.

Hatcher, P., Hulme, C., and Ellis, A. W. (1994) Ameliorating early reading failure by integrating the teaching of reading and phonological skills: the phonological linkage hypothesis. *Child Development*, 65: 41–57.

Hatcher, P. J., Hulme, C., Miles, J. N. V., Carroll, J. M., Hatcher, J., Gibbs, S., Smith, G., Bowyer-Crane, C., and Snowling, M. J. (2006) Efficacy of small group reading intervention for beginning eaders with reading-delay: a randomized controlled trial. *Journal of Child Psychology and Psychiatry*, 45: 338–58.

Hatcher, P. J., Hulme, C., and Snowling, M. J. (2004) Explicit phoneme training combined with phonic reading instruction helps young children at risk of reading failure. *Journal of Child Psychology and Psychiatry*, 45: 338–58.

Hayduk, S., Bruck, M., and Cavanagh, P. (1996) Low-level visual processing skills of adults and children with dyslexia. *Cognitive Neuropsychology*, 13: 975–1015.

Heath, S. M., Hogben, J. H., and Clark, C. D. (1999) Auditory temporal processing in disabled readers with and without oral language delay. *Journal of Child Psychology and Psychiatry*, 40: 637–47.

Hill, G. T., and Raymond, J. (2002) Deficits in motion transparency perception in adult developmental dyslexics with normal unidirectional motion sensitivity. *Vision Research*, 42: 1195–1203.

Hill, N.I., Bailey, P. J., Griffiths, Y. M., and Snowling, M. J. (1999) Frequency acuity and binaural masking release in dyslexic listeners. *Journal of the Acoustical Society of America*, 106: L53–L58.

Hindson, B., Byrne, B., Fielding-Barnsley, R., Newman, C., Hine, D. W., and Shankweiler, D. (2005) Assessment and early instruction of pre-school children at risk for reading disability. *Journal of Educational Psychology*, 97: 687–704.

Ho, C. S.-H., Chan, D., Tsang, S.-M., Lee, S.-H., and Luan, V. H. (2004) Cognitive profiling and preliminary subtyping in Chinese developmental dyslexia. *Cognition*, 91: 43–75.

Ho, C. S.-H., Law, T. P.-S., and Ng, P. M. (2000) The phonological deficit hypothesis in Chinese developmental dyslexia. *Reading and Writing*, 13: 57–79.

Hulslander, J., Talcott, J., Witton, C., DeFries, J., Pennington, B., Wadsworth, S., Willcutt, E., and Olson, R. (2004) Sensory processing, reading, IQ and attention. *Journal of Experimental Child Psychology*, 88: 274–95.

Joanisse, M. F., Manis, F. R., Keating, P., and Seidenberg, M. S. (2000) Language deficits in dyslexic children: speech perception, phonology, and morphology. *Journal of Experimental Child Psychology*, 77: 30–60.

Kemp, N., and Bryant, P. (2003) Do bees buzz? Rule-based and frequency-based knowledge in learning to spell plural -s. *Child Development*, 74(1): 63–74.

Kozminsky, L., and Kozminsky, E. (1995) The effects of early phonological awareness training on reading success. *Learning and Instruction*, 5: 187–201.

Landerl, K. (2001) Word recognition deficits in German: more evidence from a representative sample. *Dyslexia*, 7: 183–96.

Landerl, K., and Wimmer, H. (2000) Deficits in phoneme segmentation are not the core problem of dyslexia: evidence from German and English children. *Applied Psycholinguistics*, 21: 243–62.

Landerl, K., Wimmer, H., and Frith, U. (1997) The impact of orthographic consistency on dyslexia: a German–English comparison. *Cognition*, 63: 315–34.

Lennox, D., and Siegel, L. (1996) The development of phonological rules and visual strategies in average and poor spellers. *Journal of Experimental Child Psychology*, 62: 60–83.

Leonard, C. M., Eckert, M. A., Lombardino, L. J., Oakland, T., Kranzler, J., Mohr, C. M., et al. (2001) Anatomical risk factors for phonological dyslexia. *Cerebral Cortex*, 11: 148–57.

Leonard, C. M., Lombardino, L. J., Walsh, K., Eckert, M. A., Mockler, J. L., Rowe, L. A., et al. (2002) Anatomical risk factors that distinguish dyslexia from SLI predict reading skill in normal children. *Journal of Communication Disorders*, 35: 501–31.

Livingstone, M. S., Rosen, G. D., Drislane, F. W., and Galaburda, A. M. (1991) Physiological and anatomical evidence for magnocellular defect in developmental dyslexia. Paper presented to National Academy of Sciences, USA.

Lovegrove, W., Martin, F., and Slaghuis, W. (1986) The theoretical and experimental case for a visual deficit in specific reading disability. *Cognitive Neuropsychology*, 3: 225–67.

Lovett, M. W., Ransby, M. J., and Barron, R. W. (1988) Treatment, subtype and word-type effects in dyslexic children's response to remediation. *Brain and Language*, 34: 328–49.

Lyytinen, P., Poikkeus, A. M., Laakso, M. L., Eklund, K., and Lyytinen, H. (2001) Language development and symbolic play in children with and without familial risk for dyslexia. *Journal of Speech, Language, and Hearing Research*, 44: 873–85.

Manis, F.R., Doi, L.M., and Bhadha, B. (2000) Naming speed, phonological awareness, and orthographic knowledge in second graders. *Journal of Learning Disabilities*, 3: 325–33.

Manis, F. R., McBride-Chang, C., Seidenberg, M. S., Keating, P., Doi, L. M., Munson, B., et al. (1997) Are speech perception deficits associated with developmental dyslexia? *Journal of Experimental Child Psychology*, 66: 211–35.

Manis, F. R., Seidenberg, M. S., Doi, L. M., McBride-Chang, C., and Petersen, A. (1996) On the bases of two subtypes of developmental dyslexia. *Cognition*, 58: 157–95.

Marlow, A. J., Fisher, S. E., Francks, C., MacPhie, I. L., Cherny, S. S., Richardson, A. J., et al. (2003) Use of multivariate linkage analysis for dissection of a complex trait. *American Journal of Human Genetics*, 72: 561–70.

Marshall, C.M. (2000) The relation between rapid auditory processing and phonological skill in reading development and dyslexia Ph.D. thesis, University of York.

Marshall, C. M., Snowling, M. J., and Bailey, P. J. (2001) Rapid auditory processing and phonological processing in normal readers and readers with dyslexia. *Journal of Speech, Hearing and Language Research*, 44: 925–40.

Masterson, J., Hazan, V., and Wijayatilake, L. (1995) Phonemic processing problems in developmental phonological dyslexia. *Cognitive Neuropsychology*, 12(3): 233–59.

McAnally, K. I., and Stein, J. F. (1996) Auditory temporal coding in dyslexia. *Proceedings of the Royal Society, London, B*, 263: 961–5.

McBride Chang, C. (2004) *Children's Literacy Development.* Oxford University Press, Oxford.

McBride-Chang, C., Shu, H., Zhou, A., Wat, C. P., and Wagner, R. K. (2003) Morphological awareness uniquely predicts young children's Chinese character recognition. *Journal of Educational Psychology*, 92: 50–5.

Messbauer, V. C. S., and de Jong, P. F. (2003) Word, non-word, and visual paired associate learning in Dutch dyslexic children. *Journal of Experimental Child Psychology*, 84: 77–96.

Metsala, J. L. (1997) Spoken word recognition in reading disabled children. *Journal of Educational Psychology*, 89: 159–69.

Metsala, J. L., Stanovich, K. E., and Brown, G. D. A. (1998) Regularity effects and the phonological deficit model of reading disabilities: a meta-analytic review. *Journal of Experimental Psychology*, 90: 279–93.

Miles, T.R. (2006) *Fifty Years of Dyslexia Research.* Whurr, Chichester.

Moats, L. C. (1983) A comparison of the spelling errors of older dyslexic and normal second grade children. *Annals of Dyslexia*, 33: 121–40.

Mody, M. (2003) Rapid auditory processing deficits in dyslexia: a commentary on two differing views. *Journal of Phonetics*, 31: 529–39.

Mody, M., Studdert-Kennedy, M., and Brady, S. (1997) Speech perception deficits in poor readers: auditory processing or phonological coding? *Journal of Experimental Child Psychology*, 58: 112–23.

Müller, K., and Brady, S. (2001) Correlates of early reading performance in a transparent orthography. *Reading and Writing*, 14: 757–99.

National Reading Panel. (2000) *Report of the National Reading Panel: Reports of the Subgroups.* Washington, DC: National Institute of Child Health and Human Development Clearing House.

Nicolson, R. I., and Fawcett, A. J. (1990) Automaticity: a new framework for dyslexia research. *Cognition*, 35: 159–82.

Nicolson, R.I., Fawcett, A.J., and Dean, P. (2001) Developmental dyslexia: the cerebellar deficit hypothesis. *Trends in Neurosciences*, 24: 508–11.

Nittrouer, S. (1999) Do temporal processing deficits cause phonological processing problems? *Journal of Speech Language and Hearing Research*, 42: 925–42.

Olson, R. K., Datta, H. J. G., and DeFries, J. C. (1999) A behavior-genetic analysis of reading disabilities and component processes. In R. M. Klein and P. McMullen (eds), *Converging Methods for Understanding Reading and Dyslexia*, pp. 133–52. MIT Press, Cambridge, MA.

Olson, R., Wise, B., Conners, F., Rack, J., and Fulker, D. (1989) Specific deficits in component reading and language skills: genetic and environmental influences. *Journal of Learning Disabilities*, 22: 339–49.

Patel, T. K., Snowling, M. J., and de Jong, P. F. (2004) Learning to read in Dutch and English: s cross-linguistic comparison. *Journal of Educational Psychology*, 96: 785–97.

Paulesu, E., Frith, U., Snowling, M. J., Gallagher, A., Morton, J., Frackowiak, R., et al. (1996) Is developmental dyslexia a disconnection syndrome? Evidence from PET scanning. *Brain*, 119: 143–57.

Pennington, B. F. (2002) *The Development of Psychopathology: Nature and Nurture*. Guildford Press, New York.

Pennington, B. F., and Lefly, D. L. (2001) Early reading development in children at family risk for dyslexia. *Child Development*, 72: 816–33.

Pennington, B. and Olson, R. (2005) Genetics of dyslexia. In M. J. Snowling and C. Hulme (eds), *The Science of Reading: A Handbook*, pp. 453–72. Blackwell, Oxford.

Petrill, S.A., Deater-Deckard, K., Schatsneider, C., and Davis, C. (2005) Measured environmental influences on early reading: evidence from an adoption study. *Scientific Studies of Reading*, 9: 237–60.

Plaut, D. C., McClelland, J. L., Seidenberg, M. S., and Patterson, K. (1996) Understanding normal and impaired word reading: computational principles in quasi-regular domains. *Psychological Review*, 103: 56–115.

Porpodas, C. D. (1999) Patterns of phonological and memory processing in beginning readers and spellers of Greek. *Journal of Learning Disabilities*, 32: 406–16.

Preis, S., Jaencke, L., Schittler, P., Huang, Y., and Steinmetz, H. (1998) Normal intrasylvian anatomical asymmetry in children with developmental language disorder. *Neuropsychologia*, 36: 849–55.

Price, C. J., and McCrory, E. (2005) Functional brain imaging studies of skilled reading and developmental dyslexia. In M. J. Snowling and C. Hulme (eds), *The Science of Reading: A Handbook*, pp. 473–96. Oxford, Blackwell.

Rack, J. P., Snowling, M. J., and Olson, R. K. (1992) The non-word reading deficit in developmental dyslexia: a review. *Reading Research Quarterly*, 27: 29–53.

Ramus, F. (2004) Neurobiology of dyslexia: a reinterpretation of the data. *Trends in Neurosciences*, 27: 720–26.

Ramus, F., Rosen, S., Dakin, S. C., Day, B. L., Castellote, J. M., White, S. et al. (2003) Theories of developmental dyslexia: insights from a multiple case study of dyslexic adults. *Brain*, 126: 1–25.

Reed, C. (1989) Speech perception and the discrimination of brief auditory cues in reading disabled children. *Journal of Experimental Child Psychology*, 48: 270–92.

Roach, N. W., and Hogben, J. H. (2004) Attentional modulation of visual processing in adult dyslexia: a spatial cuing deficit. *Psychological Science*, 15: 650–54.

Romani, C., Ward, J., and Olson, A. (1999) Developmental Surface Dysgraphia: what is the underlying cognitive impairment? *Quarterly Journal of Experimental Psychology*, 52: 97–128.

Rosen, S., and Manganari, E. (2001) Is there a relationship between speech and nonspeech auditory processing in children with dyslexia? *Journal of Speech Language Hearing Research*, 44: 720–36.

Rumsey, J. M., Donohue, B. C., Brady, D. R., Nace, K., Giedd, J. N., and Andreason, P. (1997) A magnetic resonance imaging study of planum temporale asymmetry in men with developmental dyslexia. *Archives of Neurology*, 54: 1481–9.

Rutter, M., and Maughan, B. (2002) School effectiveness findings 1979-2002. *Journal of School Psychology*, 40: 451–75.

Rutter, M., and Yule, W. (1975) The concept of specific reading retardation. *Journal of Child Psychology and Psychiatry*, 16: 181–97.

Scarborough, H. S. (1990) Very early language deficits in dyslexic children. *Child Development*, 61: 1728–43.

Schneider, W., Roth, E., and Ennemoser, M. (2000) Training phonological skills and letter knowledge in children at risk for dyslexia: a comparison of three kindergarten intervention programs. *Journal of Educational Psychology*, 92: 284–95.

Seidenberg, M. S., and McClelland, J. (1989) A distributed, developmental model of word recognition. *Psychological Review*, 96: 523–68.

Serniclaes, W., Van Heghe, S., Mousty, P., Carré, R., and Sprenger-Charolles, L. (2004) Allophonic mode of speech perception in dyslexia. *Journal of Experimental Child Psychology*, 87 (336–61).

Seymour. P. H. K. (2005) Early reading development in European languages. In M. J. Snowling and C. Hulme (eds), *The Science of Reading: A Handbook*, pp. 296–315. Blackwell, Oxford.

Shaywitz, B. A., Shaywitz, S. E., Pugh, K. R., Mencl, W. E., Fulbright, R. K., Skudlarksi, P., et al. (2002) Disruption of posterior brain systems for reading in children with developmental dyslexia. *Biological Psychiatry*, 52: 101–10.

Shaywitz, B. A., Fletcher, J. M., Holahan, J. M., and Shaywitz, S. E. (1992) Discrepancy compared to low achievement definitions of reading disability: results from the Connecticut longitudinal study. *Journal of Learning Disabilities*, 25(10): 639–48.

Shaywitz, S. E., Bennett, B. A., Fulbright, R. K., Skudlarski, P., Mencl, E., Constable, R. T., et al. (2003) Neural systems for compensation and persistence: young adult outcome of childhood reading disability. *Biological Psychiatry*, 54: 25–33.

Shu, H., and Anderson, R. C. (1997) Role of radical awareness in the character and word acquisition of Chinese children. *Reading Research Quarterly*, 32: 78–89.

Shu, H., McBride-Chang, C., and Wu, S. (2006) Understanding Chinese developmental dyslexia: Morphological Awareness as a core cognitive construct. *Journal of Educational Psychology*, 98: 122–33.

Simos, P. G., Fletcher, J. M., Bergman, E., et al. (2002) Dyslexia-specific brain activation profile becomes normal following successful remedial training. *Neurology*, 58: 1203–13.

Skoyles, J., and Skottun, B. (2004) On the prevalence of magnocellular deficits in the visual system of non-dyslexic individuals. *Brain and Language*, 88: 79–82.

Snowling, M. J. (2000) *Dyslexia*, 2nd edn. Blackwell, Oxford.

Snowling, M. J., Gallagher, A., and Frith, U. (2003) Family risk of dyslexia is continuous: individual differences in the precursors of reading skill. *Child Development*, 74: 358–73.

Snowling, M. J., Goulandris, N., and Defty, N. (1996) A longitudinal study of reading development in dyslexic children. *Journal of Educational Psychology*, 88: 653–69.

Snowling, M. J., and Maughan, B. (2005) Reading and other learning disabilities. In C. Gillberg, R. Harrington, and H. C. Steinhausen (eds), *Clinician's Deskbook of Child and Adolescent Psychiatry*, pp. 417–46. Cambridge University Press, Cambridge.

Sperling, A., Lu, Z.-L., Manis, F., and Seidenberg, M. S. (2005) Deficits in perceptual noise exclusion in developmental dyslexia. *Nature Neurosciences* (July, online).

Sprenger-Charolles, L., Colle, P., Lacert, P., and Serniclaes, W. (2000) On subtypes of developmental dyslexia: evidence from processing time and accuracy scores. *Canadian Journal of Experimental Psychology*, 54: 87–103.

Sprenger-Charolles, L., Siegel, L., Bechennec, D., and Serniclaes, W. (2003) Development of phonological and orthogrpahic processing in reading aloud, in silent reading, and in spelling: a four-year longitudinal study. *Journal of Experiemental Child Psychology*, 84: 194–217.

Stanovich, K. E. (1986) Matthew effects in reading: some consequences of individual differences in the acquisition of literacy. *Reading Research Quarterly*, 21: 360–4.

Stanovich, K. E., and Siegel, L. S. (1994) The phenotypic performance profile of reading-disabled children: a regression-based test of the phonological-core variable-difference model. *Journal of Educational Psychology*, 86: 24–53.

Stanovich, K. E., Siegel, L. S., and Gottardo, A. (1997) Converging evidence for phonological and surface subtypes of reading disability. *Journal of Educational Psychology*, 89: 114–27.

Stein, J., and Talcott, J. (1999) Impaired neuronal timing in developmental dyslexia: the magnocellular hypothesis. *Dyslexia*, 5: 59–77.

Stevenson, J., and Fredman, G. (1990) The social environmental correlates of reading ability. *Journal of Child Psychology and Psychiatry and Allied Disciplines*, 31: 681–98.

Swan, D., and Goswami, U. (1997a) Picture naming deficits in developmental dyslexia: the phonological representations hypothesis. *Brain and Language*, 56: 334–53.

Swan, D., and Goswami, U. (1997b) Phonological awareness deficits in developmental dyslexia and the phonological representations hypothesis. *Journal of Experimental Child Psychology*, 60: 334–53.

Talcott J. B., Witton, C., McLean, M. F., et al. (2000) Dynamic sensory sensitivity and children's word decoding skills. *Proceedings of the National Academy of Sciences* (USA), 97: 2952–7.

Tallal, P. (1980) Auditory-temporal perception, phonics and reading disabilities in children. *Brain and Language*, 9: 182–98.

Tallal, P., and Piercy, M. (1973) Developmental aphasia: impaired rate of non-verbal processing as a function of sensory modality. *Neuropsychologia*, 11: 389–98.

Temple, E. (2002) Brain mechanisms in normal and dyslexic readers. *Current Opinion in Neurobiology*, 12: 178–83.

Temple, E., Poldrack, R. A., Protopapas, S., Nagarajan, T., Salz, P., Tallal, P., Merzenich, M. M., and Gabrieli, J. D. E. (2000) Disruption of the neural response to rapid acoustic stimuli in dyslexia: evidence from functional MRI. *Proceedings of the National Academy of Science, USA*, 97: 13907–12.

Torgesen, J. K. (2000) Individual differences in response to early interventions in reading: the lingering problem of treatment registers. *Learning Disabilities Research and Practice*, 15: 55–64.

Torgesen, J.K. (2005) Recent discoveries from research on remedial interventions for children with dyslexia. In M. J. Snowling and C. Hulme (eds), *The Science of Reading: A Handbook*, pp. 521–37. Oxford: Blackwell.

Treiman, R. (1997) Spelling in normal children and dyslexics. In B. Blachman (ed.), *Foundations of Reading Acquisition and Dyslexia: Implications for Early Intervention*. Erlbaum, Mahwah, NJ.

Tzeng, O., Zhong, H., Hung, D., and Lee, W. (1995) Learning to be a conspirator: a tale of becoming a good Chinese reader. In B. de Gelder and J. Morias (eds), *Speech and Reading: A Comparative Approach*, pp. 222–46. Erlbaum, Hove, UK.

Valdois, S., Bosse, M.-L., and Tainturier, M.-J. (2004) The cognitive deficits responsible for developmental dyslexia: review of evidence for a selective visual attentional disorder. *Dyslexia*, 10: 339–63.

Vellutino, F. R., Fletcher, J. M., Snowling, M. J., and Scanlon, D. M. (2004) Specific reading disability (dyslexia): what have we learnt in the past four decades? *Journal of Child Psychology and Psychiatry*, 45: 2–40.

Vellutino, F. R., Scanlon, D. M., Sipay, E., Small, S., Pratt, A., Chen, R., et al. (1996) Cognitive profiles of difficult-to-remediate and readily-remediated poor readers: early intervention as a vehicle for distinguishing between cognitive and experiential deficits as basic causes of specific reading disability. *Journal of Educational Psychology*, 88: 601–38.

Vellutino, F. R., Steger, J. A., Harding, C. J., and Spearing, D. (1975) Verbal versus non-verbal paired associate learning in poor and normal readers. *Neuropsychologica*, 13: 75–82.

Viholainen, H. T. A., Cantell, M., Lyytinen, P., and Lyytinen, H. (2002) Development of early motor skills and language in children at risk for familial dyslexia. *Developmental Medicine and Child Neurology*, 44: 761–9.

Wagner, R. K., and Torgeson, J. K. (1987) The nature of phonological processing and its causal role in the acquisition of reading skills. *Psychological Bulletin*, 101: 192–212.

Werker, J. F., and Tees, R. C. (1987) Speech perception in severely disabled and average reading children. *Canadian Journal of Psychology*, 41: 48–61.

Whitehurst, G. J., and Lonigan, C. J. (1998) Child development and emergent literacy. *Child Development*, 69: 848–72.

Williams, M. J., Stuart, G. W., Castles, A., and McAnally, K. I. (2003) Contrast sensitivity in subgroups of developmental dyslexia. *Vision Research*, 43: 467–77.

Wimmer, H. (1993) Characteristics of developmental dyslexia in a regular writing system. *Applied Psycholinguistics*, 14: 1–33.

Wimmer, H. (1996) The non-word reading deficit in developmental dyslexia: evidence from children learning to read German. *Journal of Experimental Child Psychology*, 61: 80–90.

Wimmer, H., Landerl, K., Linortner, R., and Hummer, P. (1991) The relationship of phonemic awareness to reading acquisition: more consequence than precondition but still important. *Cognition*, 40: 219–49.

Wimmer, H., Mayringer, H., and Landerl, K. (2000) The double-deficit hypothesis and difficulties in learning to read a regular orthography. *Journal of Educational Psychology*, 92: 668–80.

Witton, C., Talcott, J. B., Hansen, P. C., Richardson, A. J., Griffiths, T. D., Rees, A., et al. (1998) Sensitivity to dynamic auditory and visual stimuli predicts non-word reading ability in both dyslexic and normal readers. *Current Biology*, 8: 791–7.

Wolf, M., and Bowers, P. G. (1999) The double-deficit hypothesis for the developmental dyslexias. *Journal of Educational Psychology*, 91(3), 415–38.

Ziegler, J. C., Perry, C., Ma-Wayatt, A., Ladner, D., and Schulte-Korne, G. (2003) Developmental dyslexia in different languages: language specific or universal? *Journal of Experimental Child Psychology*, 86: 169–93.

CHAPTER 42

Genetics of language disorders: clinical conditions, phenotypes, and genes

Mabel L. Rice and Filip Smolík

The source of the human language capacity has been a topic of inquiry at least since the time of the ancient philosopher/historian, Herodotus, who lived from about 484 to 425 BC, and reported what is sometimes referred to as the "first psycholinguistic experiment" (Herodotus, 1964). He related that an Egyptian king carried out a natural experiment in which he ordered the isolation of two infants in order to see which language they would begin to speak. At two years, their first word was reported to be *becos*, the Phrygian word for bread. This lexical choice was seen as proof of the innate priority of Phrygian over Egyptian, as the more ancient language. Mercifully, such drastic experimental methods are long past. Although the issue of inherited sources of language abilities is not yet resolved, modern experimental and genetic methods have significantly enhanced our knowledge base, including glimpses of the pathways from genes to molecules to particular dimensions of language aptitude and disorders.

This chapter focuses on the genetics of language impairments of children. Modern methods of gene discovery are most effective at detecting genetic contributions to conditions in which individuals vary from the ordinary. Persons who do not acquire language in the expected ways show variation that can be linked or associated with genetic variations. Studies of children capitalize on the period when language impairments can be detected, before compensatory mechanisms are developed to obscure the individual variations or maturational mechanisms kick in to modulate the early impairments. Thus, just as in ancient times, there is great interest in young children's language abilities as a window into inherited mechanisms.

At the core of genetics inquiry is a possible link between variation in the genetic attributes of an individual with variation in target abilities or traits. The term "phenotype" refers to the behavioral manifestation of an underlying inherited trait. In the case of language impairments, there are multiple dimensions of possible phenotypes that intertwine language symptoms with more general cognitive and sensory symptoms. Contemporary collaborations of geneticists and behavioral scientists working on the issue call for precision in defining the phenotype of inherited language impairment, in order to yield precise genetic discoveries (Smith and Morris, 2005; Smith, 2004; Morris, 2004; Fisher, 2005; Tager-Flusberg, 2005). In effect, the focus on genetic variations has also brought a strong focus on the behavioral manifestations of language impairment.

Symptoms of children's language impairment are intrinsically benchmarked to the developmental trajectory of change over time as children move from the early manifestations of infant language through the full course of change to get to the adult language levels. Ultimately, phenotypes must be carefully specified in terms of the developmental arc. For example, it is important to differentiate between the possibility that the genetic contribution is in the timing mechanisms that activate the beginnings of the language system, or if the genetic contribution is focused on particular dimensions of language ability, or both.

As suggested by the crude experiment related by Herodotus, language acquisition is at the interface of environmental and genetic influences. Unlike the ancient researcher-king, we have no reason to believe there is one particular innate human language that is coded genetically as a default language. Instead, children must be exposed to their native language in order to develop the language. Modern theories, even those that posit a strong genetic component, recognize that there are learned aspects of language as well as genetically guided aspects. The genetic contributions play out in an interaction with environmental factors, including the language(s) spoken by persons in the child's family, the child's opportunities to use language in social interactions, and the child's general state of health, among others.

This chapter begins the discussion of the genetics of language disorders with two preliminary sections. Section 42.1 highlights the dimensions of language of interest and the section 42.2 provides a brief preview of the different methods used to investigate the genetics of language disorders. Section 42.3 lays out the symptoms of language impairment associated with different clinical groups of children, subdivided according to dimensions of language and related abilities. In effect, this is a survey of the landscape of possible phenotypes, and a reminder of the multidimensional attributes of language and the ways they play out in clinical comparisons. The clinical conditions vary in the extent of identified genetic etiology and identified symptomology, and no condition has a full map of genetic and language phenotypic relationships. Overall, the landscape reveals how dimensions of the language phenotype may or may not hang together, and may or may not share common genetic influences. Section 42.4 summarizes current investigations of the FOXP2 gene, as a case study of the steps involved in relating language disorders and genes, and progress toward the molecular level. Section 42.5 brings in recent investigations of the genetics of reading and speech impairments and possible overlap with language impairments. Section 42.6 describes the outcomes of twin studies, and the ways that phenotype definitions interact with genetic interpretations. The conclusions return to "the first psycholinguistic experiment" reported by Herodotus, updated to the modern scientific context.

42.1 Language as a phenotype

Although psycholinguists are well aware of the multidimensional nature of language representations, uses, and processing, these dimensions are not always carefully explicated in investigations of the genetics of language disorders and some confusions can ensue. Highlighted here are some of the dimensions and distinctions that are central to current genetic investigations.

First, it is important to differentiate speech skills from other language skills. In the literature on language impairments, limitations in speech ability are manifest as problems in producing speech sounds clearly and accurately. These problems may or may not coexist with an underlying neuromotor deficit in the oral mechanisms ("oromotor dysfunction") or a severe neurocognitive deficit that precludes meaningful communication via speech. Differentiations among the phonological, motor production, and neurocognitive requirements of speech as a symbolic system are not well sorted out. The term "speech sound disorder" (SSD) was recently coined as an overarching descriptive term for describing speech disorders from a genetic perspective (Online Mendelian Inheritance in Man, 2005). At a functional level, difficulties with speech can lead to very limited intelligibility, which in turn can confound estimates of children's other language skills, such as morphology, or related skills, such as repetition of non-words as an index of verbal memory. Measurements of speech are typically based on word production tasks, or general estimates of intelligibility of spontaneous utterances. Overall, it is important to keep in mind that co-occuring speech impairments can introduce significant complexities in the language phenotype.

Furthermore, as discussed below, new research has identified multiple gene sources of SSD (Stein et al., 2004; Smith et al., 2005), which are in turn linked to reading disability but not to language impairments. Thus, speech disorders and language disorders may not share common inherited sources (although this does not rule out the possibility that speech genetics are unrelated to language disorders, a point discussed below). For now, the possibility of inherited SSD as an unidentified complication in some studies of language impairment must be kept in mind.

The semantic, syntactic, and pragmatic dimensions of language have been studied as phenotypes. Investigations of semantics often focus on the lexicon, usually at the very earliest stages of vocabulary growth, and are often indexed by performance on standardized tests of receptive vocabulary. Syntax has multiple dimensions of interest, but the one that will be highlighted here is morphosyntax, or the interface of morphology and syntax, i.e. the ways in which certain morphemes interact with word order rules in the formulation of clauses. In English, this is evident in the use of morphemes to mark finiteness in clauses. This is a set of morphemes consisting of auxiliary and copula *BE* (as in *Patsy is working*; *Patsy is happy*), auxiliary *DO* (e.g. *Does Patsy work?*), regular and irregular past tense (e.g. *Patsy worked yesterday*; *Patsy ran home*), and third person singular present tense *-s* (e.g. *Patsy likes to work*). This set of morphemes interacts with a set of word order rules in the relationship among questions, simple clauses, and sites for finiteness marking, as in *Is she working?*; *Is she happy?*; *Does she like to work?*; *Patsy is working, isn't she?* This interface has been the focus of recent theoretical advances in models of the adult grammar (Chomsky, 1995) and child grammar (Guasti, 2002; Wexler, 1994). It has proven fruitful for the identification of areas of the grammar that can be affected or spared across different clinical conditions, and has a growing literature base of comparable findings. These interrelationships provide a rich entry point into children's grammars to evaluate the ways in which their grammars might be impaired or spared. Assessments can be drawn from analyses of samples of spontaneous utterances, performance on age-normed tests (Rice and Wexler, 2001), or experimental tasks.

Studies of pragmatics have focused on the use of language in social contexts. This area can be further subdivided into rules for discourse/conversational interactions, relating a story narrative, and sociolinguistic conventions such as politeness and code switching to correspond to characteristics of the interlocutor. Related abilities include the ability to take the perspective of others, to entertain a "theory of mind" involving assumptions about the intentions of interlocutors and other persons, and to organize a narrative structure for a story. Tasks range from structured observational assessments as in the Autism Diagnostic Observation Schedule, ADOS (Lord et al., 1999), other rating scales, standardized assessments of story narratives, and experimental tasks. Non-verbal elements, such as eye gaze, visual attention, and pointing, are included as key elements in many of the assessments.

Descriptions of the language phenotype can include all or part of these dimensions of language, in more or less specific ways to describe individual components. At the most general level, individuals are described categorically as affected or unaffected. This can be at the level of clinical assessment comprising informal observations and expert judgement, without formal behavioral documentation of language skills, although this is no longer the gold standard. A common approach is to use omnibus language assessment instruments that sample multiple dimensions, usually heavily weighted toward semantics and syntax, without clear differentiation of discrete areas such as morphosyntax. This method yields psychometrically reliable quantitative scores that describe a child's performance relative to a normative sample of children. Interpretation is general, at the level of global language ability. Tests are often further subdivided into the performance modalities of receptive versus expressive tasks. Although that distinction has considerable clinical value, it will not be pursued here because it has not been informative in the genetics studies, at least to date.

In typically developing children, growth in these dimensions of language proceeds in tandem, in a well-synchronized manner which yields characteristic profiles of children benchmarked to ages. Textbooks on language acquisition lay out the expected sequence of language skills for toddlers, preschoolers, early and late elementary years, and beyond. Because of the close synchrony, it is often assumed that there is an intrinsic linkage among the elements of the emerging language system. This assumption, however, is challenged by studies of children with language impairment, who demonstrate the ways in which the dimensions of language can be selectively weak or strong, and not well synchronized. The promise of genetic inquiry is to evaluate the extent to which the etiological factors are the same across all components of language, which in turn could help clarify the selective sparing or weakness in some linguistic dimensions relative to others.

42.1.1 Benchmarking to the developmental trajectory

The notion of "language disorder" is inherently linked to expected levels of performance. In most assessments, the comparison level is established by performance of children the same age, a conventional procedure for normative estimates.

The obtained score is compared to the performance level distribution of children of the same age, and, typically, "language disorder" is arbitrarily defined at the bottom end of the distribution—usually one standard deviation or more below the mean score, or, roughly, at the 15th percentile or below. An alternative method is to compare affected children's performance on a given dimension of language or cognitive performance to a control group of children at equivalent language levels, i.e. younger children at the same general level of language development. This approach is often used in tandem with the conventional way of establishing "language disorder" relative to age expectations. The advantage of this design is to examine the extent to which children's language disorders are characterized by a general language delay or immaturity, in which the children's language closely resembles that of younger children, vs. the extent to which particular dimensions of language fall further behind a general immaturity. In this way, it is possible to determine if affected children show selective deficits, controlling for more general language abilities. It is valuable to differentiate between language delay, which is plausibly a matter of immaturity traceable to a delayed emergence of language, and language disruption, characterized by selective deficits in particular dimensions of language (Rice et al., 1995; Rice and Wexler, 1996b; Rice, 2004; Rice and Warren, 2005). Obviously, it is important to ascertain if the etiological influences are the same for these two possibilities.

42.2 **Brief overview of genetic methods**

Multiple methods are involved in the study of the genetics of language disorders. Fisher (2006) defines a gene as "a stretch of DNA whose linear sequence of nucleotides encodes the linear sequence of amino acids in a specific protein." Conventional labels are used to describe locations, such as "7q31" to indicate a location on chromosome 7. Individuals vary in the actual nucleotide sequences. Different persons can have distinctive versions of any particular gene, known as "alleles" or "allelic variants." Modern human genetics, at the molecular level, aims to determine causal links between the genetic makeup of an individual (genotype) and phenotypic characteristics. At the phenotype level, families are identified with individuals affected with a trait of interest. An initial level of investigation can determine if affected individuals "aggregate" within families, i.e. if an affected individual is more likely to have affected relatives than an unaffected individual. At the molecular level, genotyping methods can determine the inheritance patterns of each section of chromosome with each family. Then statistical methods are used to investigate whether the inheritance of any chromosomal interval is correlated (or "linked") with the inheritance of the trait. This process is referred to as "linkage analysis." The full human genome is thought to have 30,000 genes. Linkage analyses often starts with known "markers" or locations along a chromosome. With modern means, it is possible to scan the entire genome. However, if linkage is found, it may narrow the search to a section of tens or hundreds of genes; more intensive methods are needed to identify individual genes.

Phenotyping for linkage analysis can be done in two ways. One is categorical, i.e. identification of an individual as "affected" or "unaffected." Another approach, more appropriate for complex human traits, employs quantitative data (such as test scores) for calculation of a quantitative-trait-locus (QTL). This method simultaneously searches for genetic locations that are related to the differences in a quantitative trait. Both methods have been used in genetic studies of language disorders. Classically, studies of children with-known clinical syndromes, such as Down syndrome, employ a categorical phenotype. More recently, studies have used quantitative language phenotypes based on test scores to investigate children/families who do not carry other clinical diagnoses.

At the behavioral-genetics level, twin studies are a classic method. The estimation of genetic influences is based on the comparison of monozygotic (identical) and dizygotic (fraternal) twins. While monozygotic (MZ) twins share 100 percent of their genetic material, dizygotic (DZ) twins share 50 percent, just like normal siblings. If a trait is not influenced by genetic factors, members of MZ and DZ twin pairs should be similar to the same degree, on average. In inherited traits, members of MZ twin pairs will be more similar to each other because their genes are identical. This is the base for estimating heritability of a trait, i.e. the extent to which the trait is influenced by genetic factors. Modern analytic methods allow researchers to extract substantially more information from twin data than just heritability estimates. In particular, twin studies can provide information about the extent to which multiple traits are influenced by the same genetic factors. This makes it possible to determine whether behavioral or cognitive traits, such as various aspects of language ability, share underlying biological mechanisms, and to what extent.

42.3 **Symptoms and syndromes: bottom-up and top-down**

Although it is well known that language disorders are associated with clinical syndromes of genetic causes, precise description of the nature of the language disorders is a relatively recent phenomenon. Comparisons across conditions can identify dimensions of similarity and differences in the profile of symptoms, and the extent to which language dimensions can be selectively spared or impaired, thereby revealing properties of the internal structure of the language system and the extent to which they are derived from the same biological sources (see Rice and Warren, 2004; 2005 for compilations of expert papers).

Smith and Morris (2005: 97–8) delineate two possible approaches to genetic investigation of language disorders: The top-down approach aims for "scrupulous phenotype definition to aid in identification of genes affecting specific language disorders"; the bottom-up approach consists of "characterization of the language phenotypes in known genetic syndromes as models of gene effects." The two approaches in tandem are informing current inquiries in a search for gene discoveries that clarify gene effects and possible neurological pathways involved in language disorders.

A summary of language symptoms associated with clinical conditions and the sources of genetic variation per condition are provided in Table 42.1. The symptom descriptions are cast in relatively general terms, in order to facilitate comparison across clinical conditions. It is most accurate to regard the "yes" or "no" judgements about deficit areas as comparisons to age peers, i.e. "yes" means roughly "yes, there is a deficit relative to age expectations," with a few exceptions noted below. The source literature has a wealth of detail and points of dispute around these generalizations that interested readers will

Table 42.1 Summary of clinical symptoms associated with diagnoses of language disorders.

	Specific Language Impairment	**Autism Spectrum Disorder**	**Williams syndrome**	**Fragile X**	**Down syndrome**
Speech impairment	Minimal overlap	20–50 percent non-verbal*	?	Yes	Yes
Oromotor dysfunction	No	No (if verbal)	No	Yes	Yes
Cognitive deficit	No	No (if verbal)	Yes	Yes	Yes
Vocabulary delay	Yes	Yes	Yes	Yes	Yes
Vocabulary loss	No	Yes	No	No	No
Morphosyntax disruption	Yes	Yes	No	?	Yes
Morphosyntax strength	No	No	Yes	?	No
Pragmatic deficits	mild?	Yes-diagnostic	No-?	Yes	Yes
Genetics	7q31	15q11-q13	Deletion 7q11.23 Cognition GTF21?	FMR 1/7q27.3	Trisomy Chromosome 21

*20–50% of children with this diagnosis are estimated to be non-verbal. If the children are verbal, oromotor dysfunction or cognitive deficit are unlikely.

want to pursue further (cf. Rice and Warren, 2004). A further caveat is that the comparisons across symptoms are not intended to meet formal criteria for profile analyses. See Mervis and Robinson (2005) for discussion of the rigorous empirical standards for formal profile characterizations. Finally, the genetic sources listed in the table are confirmed for the syndromic conditions and tentative for specific language impairment and autism.

42.3.1 Specific Language Impairment

The condition of Specific Language Impairment (SLI) is a non-syndromic condition identified by the presence of a language disorder in the absence of other disorders. Conventionally, it is defined by inclusionary criteria, such that language development does not meet age expectations (often defined as performance roughly in the 15th percentile range, or below), and exclusionary criteria, such that affected children do not show intellectual impairments, hearing loss, autism, or neuromotor disabilities. It is estimated that 7 percent of 5-year-old children meet the criteria for SLI, with the estimate increased to 10 percent if the non-verbal intelligence range is allowed to dip into the border of below normal/intellectually impaired (Tomblin et al., 1997). The condition is of obvious interest for possible genetic contributions, in that the variation in language ability is the major presenting symptom (although there is a long-standing debate in the literature about whether there are more subtle differences in non-verbal cognitive ability or processing, as well, cf. Leonard, 1998).

42.3.1.1 Non-overlap with speech, oromotor, or cognitive impairments

Table 42.1 reports little overlap of speech impairments with SLI: a large-scale epidemiological investigation reported an estimated overlap of speech impairment for only 2 percent of the children so diagnosed (Shriberg et al., 1999) At the same time, it is the case that children with speech impairments are much more likely to be identified for clinical services, presumably because of the obvious symptoms of limited intelligibility. This means that in much of the literature, research participants identified as SLI may have speech impairments unless they are explicitly screened and excluded, because most studies rely on clinical caseloads for recruitment. Thus, although the population estimates are of little overlap of speech and language impairments, the distribution of speech impairments in clinical caseloads can generate an impression of greater convergence. As noted above, recent findings (Stein et al., 2004; Smith et al., 2005) reveal genetic linkage for speech sound disorders, although so far these linkages do not seem to hold for SLI. Importantly, oromotor dysfunction, involving poor neurological control of the speech mechanisms, is not part of the SLI diagnosis, by exclusionary criterion. Cognitive deficit is also excluded, although the exact boundary lines are rather malleable and studies labeled as "SLI" sometimes include children at levels of non-verbal intelligence that could be considered as borderline intellectually impaired. The caveat is that although this generalization holds across most of the literature, in some studies, including genetic studies, the exclusionary criteria for non-verbal intelligence can be significantly relaxed. The risk is that if the sources of variation of non-verbal intelligence are not the same as the sources of variation of verbal abilities, this difference could introduce error into the analyses of genetic effects on language impairment.

42.3.1.2 Language delay

A delayed onset for early vocabulary acquisition, and continued delays in vocabulary acquisition, are widely recognized as characteristic of SLI. Longitudinal analyses confirm that the delay persists at least to 8 years of age, with close benchmarking to the growth trajectories of younger children in a classic delay pattern (Rice et al., 2006). Beyond 8 years of age, vocabulary acquisition is known to be tightly associated with reading development, and reading is also likely to be affected in persons with SLI (cf. Catts et al., 2002). This means that the estimates of inherited and environmental effects on vocabulary can become complicated for children beyond 8 years, given that reading abilities and habits mediate such effects. Interestingly, there are no reports of a regression or loss in vocabulary levels for children with SLI, in the sense that once words are learned they do not subsequently disappear. Instead the evidence points toward a picture of a delayed start-up, and then a growth trajectory that follows very closely the patterns expected for younger children.

The cause of delayed language onset is unknown. For some time the focus has been on the role of environmental input, with advantages attributed to children whose mothers are better educated and whose families have social and financial advantages. Although this assumption is widely held, the empirical evidence has been relatively modest. A recent study of the language of 1,766 epidemiologically ascertained 24-month-old children investigated a large number of potential predictor variables. The results clearly indicated that risk was not associated with particular strata of parental educational levels, socioeconomic resources, parental mental health, parent practices, or family functioning. Instead, the predictors were predominately endogenous and neurobiological in nature, including positive familial history of late talking, and the child's early motor development (Zubrick et al., forthcoming). In the context of current advances in animal model genetics (cf. Fitch, Chapter 48 this volume), further studies of a likely relationship between early motor development and language emergence in young children seem in order.

42.3.1.3 Morphosyntactic deficits

At another language level, the morphosyntactic domain of finiteness is interesting in several ways. In his models of the adult grammar, Chomsky (1995) has argued that morphosyntax is a discrete dimension of the grammar. Wexler (1994) proposed a model of how morphosyntax is expected to be a relatively discrete area of grammatical acquisition for children. Observations of children with SLI clearly support the assumption of discreteness. Children with SLI make mistakes very similar to those of younger children. Their mistakes are highly constrained. In contexts where finiteness morphemes are obligatory in a sentence, they tend to omit them. For example, in the following sentences the morphemes in parentheses are likely to be omitted: *Patsy (is) working, Patsy work(ed) yesterday, Patsy like(s) to work, (Is) she working?* Although errors such as *Patsy *are working* or **Do she working?* are possible, they are very unlikely. At the same time, the rate of omission is greater for the children with SLI than that of younger children at equivalent general levels of language acquisition. In this way, the sentences generated by affected children are unlike those of the younger children. Overall, it is as if this part of the grammar starts even later for affected children, and ends up out of synch with the other dimensions of language growth—a disruption that persists well into the middle years of childhood, and probably beyond. Even so, the growth patterns of finiteness acquisition follow that of younger children, although offset by a couple of years relative to the general language level. It is as if within this part of the grammar, the start-up is delayed; once the finiteness system emerges it is predisposed to follow the same path as that of unaffected children, but because it follows the same growth trajectories it does not "catch up" and instead remains relatively weak, at least into early adolescence if not beyond (Rice, Wexler and Hershberger, 1998; Rice et al., 2004). Although maturational models have been out of favor as interpretive frameworks for language acquisition (cf. Wexler, 2003), the growth evidence points strongly toward maturationally timed mechanisms of change over time that guide the development of children with SLI in a manner very like that of unaffected children (Rice, 2004).

It is possible that morphosyntax is a generally difficult linguistic property for children, and all children with language disorders could be expected to show such deficits. On the other hand, if morphosyntax can be selectively disrupted, it could also be a particular area of strength. As indicated in Table 42.1, there is reason to believe that morphosyntax is relatively spared in the condition of Williams syndrome, to be described below.

42.3.1.4 Pragmatic limitations

There are numerous reports documenting that the pragmatic competencies of children with SLI are not quite as robust as expected for their age levels, although these youngsters do not show more general social deficits in clinical range. Conversely, it is also true that SLI is more likely in groups of children identified as behaviorally/socially disordered. The picture is complicated, however, by the fact that children with limited language skill, such as children learning English as a second language, can also show subtle pragmatic deficits and fall to the margin of social acceptance by their peers, suggesting that limited language skill can contribute to limited social skills. To date, it is not possible to fully sort out whether it is a matter of social consequences of a language disorder, or social causes of a language disorder (cf. Redmond and Rice, 1998).

Some investigators have explored the possibility that the pragmatic dimension of language can be selectively impaired in the face of otherwise normal language acquisition. This is of interest because such a selective language deficit may be at the border of the diagnostic categories of SLI and autism. At present this work is at the exploratory stage (Bishop and Norbury, 2002; Adams, 2002).

42.3.1.5 Genetics of SLI

The genetics of SLI has emerged in phases. Family aggregation and twin studies have demonstrated that the condition is highly heritable (e.g. Rice, Haney and Wexler, 1998; Stromswold, 2001). Recently, a significant advance appeared with the discovery of Lai et al. (2001), who reported a gene mutation involving a minor change in one letter of DNA in chromosome 7q31 in an extended family (known as KE) with symptoms of SLI, although the family also displayed other symptoms not characteristic, such as pronounced oromotor dysfunction, significant speech impairments, and intellectual impairments. Further, the protein encoded by the gene was identified as a member of the "forkhead-box" or FOX domain, similar to over forty other human proteins. This protein was named FOXP2, because it was the second member to be discovered in the P subgroups of FOX proteins. This discovery has opened up new lines of inquiry into the molecular level of genetic influences on language, at the level of human language acquisition, to be discussed further below, and at the level of language evolution across species, discussed in the chapter by Fitch.

To continue the story of the KE family here, the possible overlap of symptoms with SLI raised the question of whether FOXP2 would be found in other samples of persons with SLI. In effect, this is a case of a gene known to cause severe symptoms that overlap at least in part with those of SLI. This gene is then a candidate for a genetic contribution to SLI, given that other mutations of the gene may cause less severe phenotypes. Newbury et al. (2002) report null findings; more recent reports find evidence for localization in the same region (O'Brien et al., 2003; SLI Consortium, 2002), but no identification of the gene(s).

42.3.2 Autism Spectrum Disorder

Autism is a developmental disorder which is diagnosed based on the presence of deficits in three areas: communication; social interaction; and repetitive and stereotyped behaviors, interests, and activities (American Psychiatric Association, 1994). More recently, the term "Autism Spectrum Disorder" (ASD) refers to the existence of substantial subgroups of individuals who share some core characteristics of autism but still differ in important ways. This includes conditions such as Asperger syndrome (primarily a social disorder), pervasive developmental disorder (mild social or communication disorder), and severe mental retardation.

Not all children with ASD are verbal, i.e. use words to communicate. Estimates of the proportion of affected children who are non-verbal range from 20 to 50 percent (Lord and Rutter, 1994; Lord et al., 2004). The children who are verbal can be characterized as unlikely to have oromotor dysfunction (i.e. without significant SSD), with a general language delay comprising vocabulary deficits, possible loss of learned vocabulary, and morphosyntactic delays. The extent to which language delays are congruent with levels of nonverbal intelligence is not clear, although it is likely to be affected by whether or not a child is verbal or non-verbal (Lord et al., 2004). Tager-Flusberg (2004) concludes that most verbal children with autism have normal non-verbal intelligence. Pragmatic deficits, on the other hand, are a defining deficit of autism and are widely regarded as the unifying feature (Lord and Paul, 1997; Tager-Flusberg, 1999). Thus, the pragmatics dimension is impaired in all people with autism, who may or may not have concomitant language problems.

Behavioral genetics studies point toward a genetic base for autism. There is a higher risk in families that have an affected child (Santangelo and Folstein, 1999), and twin studies yield higher concordance rates for MZ than DZ twins (Bailey et al. 1995). Chromosome duplication in the region of 15q11–q13 has been identified for a savant skills cluster of individuals with autism (Dykens et al., 2004). No genes have been identified for idiopathic autism, i.e. autism with no identifiable cause. Although consensus regions of interest have been identified, the challenges include phenotypic heterogeneity within and between the studied samples, and potential multiple interactive gene effects.

42.3.3 Syndromic conditions: Williams, fragile X, Down syndrome

Language impairments are associated with three syndromic conditions for which there are known genetic etiologies. Of the three, the nature of the language impairments have been most extensively studied for Down syndrome (cf. Abbeduto and Murphy, 2004) and Williams syndrome (Morris, 2004; Zukowski, 2004); investigations of fragile X are in earlier stages (Bailey, et al. 2004). As summarized in Table 42.1, the conditions differ with regard to the likelihood of oromotor dysfunction: persons with Williams syndrome are likely to be spared, but such limitations are more characteristic of persons with fragile X or Down syndrome. All three conditions are characterized by cognitive deficit and vocabulary delay, although with no indication of vocabulary loss. Morphosyntax differentiates Williams and Down syndrome, where it is relatively strong in the former and weak in the latter condition, and unknown in fragile X. Pragmatic deficits are well documented for fragile X and Down syndrome, and more controversial for Williams syndrome, where there are decided social strengths as well as more subtle social/interactive weaknesses.

The known genetic etiologies differ for the three conditions. Williams syndrome is known to be caused by a gene deletion at 7q11.23. Precise phenotyping led to the identification of genes contributing to specific aspects of the syndrome. Deletion of the elastin (ELN) gene leads to connective tissue abnormalities of heart tissue (Ewart et al., 1993); deficits in visuospatial constructive cognition are attributed to the LIM-kinase 1 (LIMK1) gene deletion (Frangiskakis et al., 1996); and cognitive impairment is thought to be due to the deletion of one copy of the GTF21 gene (Morris et al., 2003) (see Smith and Morris, 2005 for an overview). Fragile X is caused by a disruption in expression of protein from the fragile X mental retardation gene (FMR1) (Verkerk et al., 1991). The protein, known as fragile X mental retardation protein (FMRP), is associated with normal brain function (Imbert et al., 1998.) (cf. Bailey et al., 2004). Although much investigation has focused on the physical, social, and behavioral phenotypes of fragile X, the possible role of FMRP in language disorders associated with the syndrome is unknown. Most cases of Down syndrome are caused by trisomy of chromosome 21 or a critical region of it. Although the genetic basis is well known, the exact mechanisms of genetic influence on phenotypes have yet to be worked out (cf. Abbeduto and Murphy, 2004).

42.3.4 Symptoms and syndromes reprise: bottom-up, top-down

The bird's-eye view of language disorders within clinical conditions provided by Table 42.1 captures the dimensionality of the language phenotype (and a glimpse of the speech phenotype and its comorbidity across clinical conditions), and a sketch of the known genetic etiologies for the conditions. From the bottom-up perspective, if a genetic condition produces a relatively consistent pattern of language delay or disruption, it provides evidence that the functional components of the human language faculty have a counterpart in the biological makeup of an individual. For instance, morphological and syntactic abilities seem to be more impaired in Down syndrome than in Williams syndrome, while the two syndromes produce similar levels of vocabulary impairment. This suggests that morphosyntactic abilities can be impaired independently of vocabulary to a certain extent. Because different levels of impairment are produced by different genetic conditions, the impaired language components must be influenced by different biological mechanisms. This provides an important lead in determining which aspects of the language faculty are more related to each other and which are more independent, and the extent to which individual components are relatively robust or vulnerable.

Progress on the genes/phenotype interface is uneven. At the top-down level, more detail is available about the language symptoms of SLI than the other conditions, although the genetic information is at early stages. In contrast, at the bottom-up level, knowledge of the protein expression implicated in fragile X is known, but the investigation of language disorders characteristic of the syndrome is at the earliest stages. The example of Williams syndrome, where different genes affect different aspects of the syndrome, is a powerful example of how precise phenotyping can enhance genetic discovery, although the genetics of language disorders is not yet at that level. Progress on the language phenotype of fragile X and Williams syndrome could be especially informative given the more advanced understanding of the functional properties of the identified gene variants.

Among the complexities to be overcome are the likelihood of multiple gene involvement, with many-to-many mapping of genes and phenotypes. Effects of genes on phenotypes are both additive and pleiotropic (cf. Hartl and Jones, 1999). "Additivity" refers to the fact that multiple genes may (and usually do) influence a single trait, while "pleiotropy" means that a single gene may influence multiple different phenotypes or traits. More detailed consideration of the FOXP2 gene illustrates these complexities.

42.4 FOXP2 as a case study of a top-down approach

Although the extent to which FOXP2 is implicated in the broad SLI phenotype is unknown at present, the trail of discovery is highly informative. It is the first discovery of a gene mutation that causes speech and language disorders. Further, it shows the full course of gene to molecular levels of genetic influence that govern neurocortical structures likely to be involved in speech and language—the first such trail to be established. Finally, the discovery process highlights again the crucial role of phenotyping in sorting out genetic influences.

Researchers became interested in the speech and language disorders in the KE family because of their inheritance patterns (cf. Hurst et al., 1990;

Lai et al., 2001; Marcus and Fisher, 2003; Fisher, 2005). The distribution of the impairment conformed to the monogenic dominant inheritance pattern; such a pattern is produced if a single copy of the disordered version (allele) of the gene is sufficient to cause the disordered phenotype. The mode of inheritance suggested that it might be possible to identify a gene responsible for the developmental disorder present in KE family members. Researchers conducted systematic search of the impaired locus using linkage analysis. This narrowed down the possible location of a mutated gene to a region on chromosome 7 with about seventy genes. Before conducting a systematic search in this region, researchers were able to identify the particular mutated gene with the help of information from a child unrelated to the KE family. The child suffered from symptoms similar to the affected members of the KE family in the language and speech areas (Lai et al., 2000). The child was known to have a genetic condition, called translocation, consisting of exchange of two short sections of genetic material on chromosomes 7 and 5. One of the breakpoints on chromosome 7 between which the exchanged material from chromosome 5 was inserted fell into the region previously identified in the affected KE family members as the location of their genetic mutation. Using these two sources of information, researchers were able to determine the gene involved and the mutation that was causing its malfunction in the affected members of KE family.

An important aspect of the FOXP2 discovery is that the researchers not only identified the chromosomal location and the affected gene but also discovered the protein coded by the affected gene. The protein FOXP2, which was also used to name the affected gene, is a member of a broader group of proteins which play regulatory roles in the expression of other genes. Many proteins from this family are known to influence embryogenesis, having an influence on the timing sequence of the ontogenetic events during the development of tissue and organ structure. Lai et al. (2001: 522) concluded that the disruption of the FOXP2 gene, which renders the resulting protein dysfunctional and unavailable at critical stages of embryogenesis, "leads to abnormal development of neural structures that are important for speech and language." Consistent with this view, a number of imaging studies reported abnormal findings in the anatomical structures of affected family members' brains (Watkins, Vargha-Khadem, et al., 2002; Belton et al., 2003) and their functional responses (Watkins et al., 1999). The discovery of the FOXP2 gene hence demonstrates a successful course of research from a speech/language trait with a conspicuous pattern of inheritance, through the implication of an individual gene, to a plausible hypothesis about the mechanism of the gene's influence on language development. Thus, FOXP2 appears to be pleiotropic for impairment in speech and language, plausibly attributable to the fundamental neural structures affected.

The precise nature of the speech and language impairment in the KE family has been a matter of discussion since the first reports about the family. Although Gopnik (1990) and Gopnik and Crago (1991) suggested that the family members have major problems with grammatical processing, especially morphological analysis, other researchers pointed out that their language impairment is broader and affects all areas of language (Vargha-Khadem et al., 1995; Watkins, Dronkers, and Vargha-Khadem, 2002). Also, unlike most children with SLI, the KE family members suffer from severe speech problems. However, there is general agreement that the KE family members have relatively spared non-verbal cognitive abilities; although non-verbal IQ in affected family members tends to be lower than in the unaffected members, it is higher than their verbal performance and mostly within normal limits. The discrepancy between impaired language and relatively spared non-verbal cognition is also present in the unrelated child who was instrumental in discovering the exact location of the FOXP2 gene. It is important to note that the decision to study this child was made on the basis of the similarity between the symptoms, i.e. in the phenotype. The child showed severe language delay, relatively spared non-verbal cognition, and a specific pattern of speech problems. This is a clear example of how the pattern of strengths and weaknesses in the phenotype of a genetic disorder can serve as a criterion for matching people whose problems may have similar genetic base.

Research that followed the discovery of the FOXP2 gene suggested that the gene is probably not involved in the typical cases of specific language impairment (Newbury et al., 2002; Meaburn et al., 2002). That is not surprising, as the inheritance of SLI does not correspond to the autosomal dominant pattern witnessed in the KE family (see e.g. Rice, Haney, and Wexler, 1998; Tallal et al., 2001). Also, it is extremely unlikely that a complex cognitive ability like language is mediated by a single gene.

Follow-up studies have used QTL analyses in an effort to identify possible multiple gene influences. The SLI Consortium (2002) reported results of a genome-wide scan for QTL contributing to low language ability. The study identified two chromosomal locations, one on chromosome 16q and one on chromosome 19q. A subsequent study (SLI Consortium, 2004) confirmed these linkages. At the same time, another linkage study using classical categorical phenotyping methods (Bartlett et al., 2002) found linkage only at a site on chromosome 13. At this early stage of inquiry it is unclear if the different outcomes are related to differences in phenotype definitions, computational methods, or other unknown sampling differences.

42.5 **Reading, speech, and language: suggestions of genetic overlap**

Table 42.1 compared the condition of SLI, defined on the basis of language phenotype, with other clinical conditions of known genetic etiology in which language disorders are concomitant with other symptoms. This allowed for consideration of top-down versus bottom-up perspectives, as ways to examine phenotype/gene relationships. Investigations of reading and related speech/ phonological abilities are also yielding promising findings.

There are more genetic studies of reading disability than language disability, and it is quite possible that genes or chromosomal regions implicated currently in dyslexia will be found to influence language as well, given that children with language impairments are at high risk for reading impairments (Catts et al., 2002). In particular, many studies on dyslexia found linkage between particular regions and measures of phonological processing. Smith et al. (2005) reported pleiotropic linkage of regions on chromosomes 6 and 15 to measures of phonological short-term memory and to speech disorder in a sample of children with SSD. The linkage was found in regions previously implicated in reading disability (see also Stein et al., 2004 for linkage to chromosome 3). Because phonological short-term memory deficits are included in the phenotype of specific language impairment (Weismer et al., 2000; Botting and Conti-Ramsden, 2001), the finding demonstrates the complex genetic relationships between related traits. Besides reading disability, speech appears to be another domain that might lead to discovery of language-related genes. MacDermot et al. (2005) studied a group of patients suffering from speech apraxia symptoms similar to those experienced by the affected KE family members. The study detected one family with members who carried a dysfunctional copy of the FOXP2: the dysfunction was different from that in the KE family and other previously studied cases but it resulted in similar deficits, including speech and language disorder. While the rarity of this finding (about fifty families were screened) confirms that FOXP2 is probably not involved in typical cases of SLI, the study confirms that FOXP2 dysfunction consistently leads to speech and language problems, and that screening on a speech deficit may facilitate discovery of genes related to language problems.

42.6 **Twin studies: low language ability and SLI**

The primary contribution of twin studies to the research on genetic language disorders comes from the studies of populations with low language abilities. This is because the twin pairs used in twin studies usually come from the general population with no specific disorders: recruiting a sample of twins suffering from a particular disorder would be rather difficult and costly. Twin studies dealing with language impairment thus typically rely on sub-samples drawn from larger studies where one or both members of the twin pair shows low performance on various measures of language functioning. Language impairment in twin studies is thus not defined in a way directly comparable to other clinical syndromes, such as SLI. On the other hand, this approach makes it possible to evaluate similarities and differences between the low-performance population and general population in terms of genetic influences on particular aspects of language.

Stromswold (2001) provided a review and metaanalysis of numerous twin studies that addressed various questions regarding heritability of language in normal as well as impaired individuals. Here the focus is on a recent study that constitutes a good example of what questions may be asked in twin studies, and what conceptual and methodological issues arise when using twin data to study genetics of impaired language. The Twin Early Development Study (TEDS; see Trouton et al., 2002) is a large longitudinal study focusing on the development of linguistic and non-verbal cognitive abilities and their relationship during development. The data from the study were analyzed in numerous publications that give a glimpse of the complexities involved in assessment and analysis of twin data.

42.6.1 **Delay vs. disruption in the low-performing children**

The question whether typical and impaired language systems are structurally equal or different is similar to the problem of language delay vs. language disruption discussed in the first half of this chapter. The distinction between delayed and disrupted language is essential in defining the phenotype of language disorders; and, as the previous sections suggested, precise definition of disorders' phenotypes is essential for success in understanding the relationships between genetics and language.

Based largely on the data from the TEDS, Plomin and Kovas (2005) argued that impaired language is essentially the low end of a natural ability continuum. This would correspond to the view of language impairment as delayed, but essentially normal language. However, the data from TEDS do suggest some important differences between language in typically developing and low-performing children. Spinath et al. (2004) reported an analysis suggesting that children with low language ability (below the 5th percentile) show higher heritability for language skills than children with normal language. This suggests that there are genetic mechanisms responsible for the impaired language which are not present in individuals with a typical language ability level: "language disability tends to be more strongly under the influence of genetic factors than does language ability in normal range" (Spinath et al., 2004: 452). Such a finding means that the biological underpinnings of language impairment differ from genetic factors responsible for normal language variation, supporting the view that disruption in the language system is present at the low end of language abilities.

42.6.2 Level of analysis: global vs. task-specific heritability

Another perspective on the question of delay vs. disruption comes from the analyses of shared genetic influences. Twin studies allow researchers to estimate the overlap of genetic factors influencing different traits. Different disorders tend to produce different profiles of strengths and weaknesses in various domains of language, which points to the presence of relatively independent mechanisms responsible for various aspects of language knowledge. Twin studies can provide a lead here on the identity of those mechanisms. However, the degree to which language consists of independent mechanisms is a matter of discussion. Some researchers argue that the heritable aspects of language are global, influencing all areas of language performance, and that they are closely related to the non-verbal intelligence and general cognitive ability, the "g-factor" (Pedersen et al., 1994; Plomin, 1999; Price et al., 2004).

Twin studies based on the TEDS often treated language as a global trait in their analyses. For instance, Viding et al. (2003) and Colledge et al. (2002) collapsed all language measures to one overall indicator, which they then used in their analyses; this procedure created perhaps a more powerful measure of the cognitive abilities common to all language tasks, but it made it impossible to detect any pattern of relationships within the language measures. The studies found a "substantial" overlap between language and non-verbal cognition; of the genetic influences on language and non-verbal cognition, slightly more than a half were common for these two domains. While it suggests that there indeed are common genetic factors responsible for variability in verbal and non-verbal abilities, it also provides evidence that independent genetic influences on language and non-verbal cognition exist.

Other studies, such as Dale et al. (2000) and Dionne et al. (2003), analyzed measures of grammatical knowledge and vocabulary separately, and concluded that they reflect largely the same phenotypic and genetic mechanisms. These conclusions are quite similar to those of Viding et al. (2003) and Colledge et al. (2002) for the relationship between verbal and non-verbal abilities: the genetic factors influencing measures of grammar and vocabulary overlap to a significant extent but are not identical.

Price et al. (2004) studied children within the TEDS twin sample who fell under the 10th percentile on either verbal or non-verbal performance. They reported that between 2 and 4 years of age, the genetic contribution to the relationship between verbal and non-verbal measures increased dramatically. Such results are consistent with the view that the g-factor increasingly influences all aspects of cognitive performance during development. However, the study used different aggregate measures at 2, 3, and 4 years of age, and the 4-year battery was much more extensive than the previous tests. The aggregate measures summarize common components of a wide variety of tasks, which corresponds to the definition of the g-factor. It is thus not surprising that an increasingly extensive battery of tests will provide a measure that is closer to the general cognitive factor. Such a general cognitive factor, however, reflects coordination between a variety of different cognitive abilities: "The g factor is a product of individual differences in a wide variety of cognitive abilities … Because the g factor is common to all kinds of cognitive performance … [it] must essentially reflect variance in the speed and efficiency of information processing" (Jensen, 1993: 53). An important question remains: what are the cognitive abilities or tasks that are being coordinated?

One recent study based on the TEDS tested explicitly whether there is a specific pattern of strengths and weaknesses in language, or whether the impairment has a global impact on language. Bishop et al. (2006) reached substantially different conclusions from most other research using the TEDS data. Following predictions by Rice and Wexler (1996a; 1996b) that morphosyntactic abilities are likely to be inherited and to be relatively independent of other dimensions of language, Bishop et al. investigated the genetic relationships between various measures of language performance in 6-year-old language-impaired children from the TEDS pool. Among other measures, the study included measures of syntax and morphology (verb inflection subtests of the TEGI; Rice and Wexler, 2001), and the Sentence Structure subtest of CELF-R (Semel et al., 1987) and phonological short-term memory (non-word repetition task; Botting and Conti-Ramsden, 2001).

The most important finding was that syntactic and morphological measures were not influenced by the same genetic factors as were measures of phonological short-term memory. At the same time, the study suggested genetic relationships between the two syntactic-morphological measures. The results strongly suggest that language is not a uniform cognitive domain, and that genetics may influence different aspects of language performance independently.

To summarize, the twin studies are a promising source of information about the genetic influences on language and its components. However, any method is sensitive to the effects of design and data processing. Successful linkage of language impairment and related disorders usually requires rather detailed and narrowly targeted measures of performance. Twin studies may be helpful in determining genetic relationships between such targeted measures, but this is only possible when such measures are used directly in the genetic analyses, not as part of large aggregate scales.

42.7 Conclusions

To return to the "first psycholinguistic experiment" reported by Herodotus, the question of the source of the human language capacity is very timely. Yet the hubris (not to mention the questionable ethics) of the experimenter are much out of place in today's world. The overarching conclusion is that the progress to date on the genetics of language and the likely breakthroughs of the future are to be built on convergent findings moving across a broad front of scientific inquiry. Modern genetics methods and advances have generated scientific momentum, and have focused energies on the problem in unprecedented ways. At the same time, advances in theories of language acquisition and language impairments, in tandem with more precise measurement methods, play a crucial role in furthering genetics advances. The close and crucial interrelationship between phenotype definitions and genotype assessment requires close synchrony for sorting out the connection between biological underpinnings and language aptitude and disorders. Contributions of many scientists are required, and are well under way.

Although there are reasons to be cautiously optimistic about continued genetic advances (although the challenges are formidable), this does not bring the guarantee of biological cures for language impairments. Indeed, it is most likely that treatment options will continue to focus on the interface of the environment and inherited language abilities. In the broader perspective, the advances in genetics may well be applied to advances in intervention techniques that adjust the training goals to the individual's abilities, and the timing of intervention goals to times in the growth trajectory when the individual is most likely to benefit from the intervention (cf. Rice, 2004). Given the devastating consequences of language impairments in the lives of affected persons, the achievement of genetically calibrated intervention methods would be a most welcome advance.

References

Abbeduto, L., and Murphy, M. M. (2004) Language, social cognition, maladaptive behavior, and communication in Down syndrome and fragile X syndrome. In M. L. Rice and S. F. Warren (eds), *Developmental Language Disorders: From Phenotypes to Etiologies*, pp. 77–98. Erlbaum, Mahwah, NJ.

Adams, C. (2002) Practitioner review: The assessment of language pragmatics. *Journal of Child Psychology and Psychiatry*, 36: 289–306.

American Psychiatric Association (1994) *Diagnostic and Statistical Manual of Mental Disorders*, 4th edn. APA, Washington, DC.

Bailey, A., Lecouteur, A., Gottesman, I., Bolton, P., Simonoff, E., Yuzda, E., and Rutter, M. (1995) Autism as a strongly genetic disorder: evidence from a British twin study. *Psychological Medicine*, 25: 63–77.

Bailey, A., Palferman, S., Heavey, L., and LeCouteur, A. (1998) Autism: the phenotype in relatives. *Journal of Autism and Developmental Disorders*, 28: 369–92.

Bailey, D. B., Roberts, J. E., Hooper, S. R., Hatton, D. D., Mirrett, P. L., Roberts, J. E., and Schaaf, J. M. (2004) Research on fragile X syndrome and autism: implications for the study of genes, environments and developmental language disorders. In M. L. Rice and S. F. Warren (eds), *Developmental Language Disorders: From Phenotypes to Etiologies*, pp. 121–52. Erlbaum, Mahwah, NJ.

Bartlett, C. W., Flax, J. F., Logue, M. W., Vieland, V. J., Bassett, A. S., Tallal, P., et al. (2002) A major susceptibility locus for specific language impairment is located on 13q21. *American Journal of Human Genetics*, 72: 1251–60.

Belton, E., Salmond, C. H., Watkins, K. E., Vargha-Khadem, F., and Gadian, D. G. (2003) Bilateral brain abnormalities associated with dominantly inherited verbal and orofacial dyspraxia. Human Brain Mapping, 18: 194–200.

Bishop, D. V. M., Adams, C. V., and Norbury, C. F. (2006) Distinct genetic influences on grammar and phonological short-term memory deficits: evidence from 6-year-old twins. *Genes, Brain and Behavior*, 5: 158–69.

Bishop, D. V. M., and Norbury, C. F. (2002) Exploring the borderlands of autistic disorder and specific language impairment: a study using standardized diagnostic instruments. *Journal of Child Psychology and Psychiatry*, 43: 917–29.

Botting, N., and Conti-Ramsden, G. (2001) Non-word repetition and language development in children with specific language impairment. *International Journal of Language and Communication Disorders*, 36: 421–32.

Catts, H. W., Fey, M. E., Tomblin, J. B., and Zhang, X. (2002) A longitudinal investigation of reading outcomes in children with language impairments. *Journal of Speech, Language, and Hearing Research*, 45: 1142–57.

Chomsky, N. (1995) *The Minimalist Program*. MIT Press, Cambridge, MA.

Colledge, E., Bishop, D. V. M., Koeppen-Schomerus, G., Price, T. S., Happé, F. G. E., Eley, T. C., Dale, P. S., and Plomin, R. (2002) The structure of language abilities at 4 years: a twin study. *Developmental Psychology*, 38: 749–57.

Dale, P. S., Dionne, G., Eley, T. C., and Plomin, R. (2000) Lexical and grammatical development: a behavioural genetic perspective. *Journal of Child Language*, 27: 619–42.

Dionne, G., Dale, P. S., Boivin, M., and Plomin, R. (2003) Genetic evidence for bidirectional effects of early lexical and grammatical development. *Child Development*, 74: 394–412.

Dykens, E. M., Sutcliffe, J. S., and Levitt, P. (2004) Autism and 15q11-q13 disorders: behavioral, genetic, and pathophysiological issues. *Mental Retardation and Developmental Disabilities Research Review*, 10: 284–91.

Ewart, A. K., Morris, C. A., Atkinson, D., Jin, W., Sternes, K., Spallone, P., Stock, A. D., Leppert, M., and Keating, M. T. (1993) Hemizygosity at the elastin locus in a developmental disorder, Williams syndrome. *Nature Genetics*, 5: 11–16.

Fisher, S. E. (2005) Dissection of molecular mechanisms underlying speech and language disorders. *Applied Psycholinguistics*, 26: 111–28.

Fisher, S. E. (2006) Tangled webs: tracing the connections between genes and cognition. *Cognition*, 101: 270–97.

Frangiskakis, J. M., Ewart, A. K., Morris, C. A., Mervis, C. B., Bertrand, J., Robinson, B. F., Klein, B. P., Ensing, G. J., Everett, L. A., Green, E. D., Proschel, C., Gutowski, N. M., Noble, M., Atkinson, K. L., Odelberg, S. J., and Keating, M. T. (1996) LIM-kinase1 hemizygosity implicated in impaired visuospatial constructive cognition. *Cell*, 86: 59–69.

Gopnik, M. (1990, Sep) Genetic basis of grammar defect. *Nature*, 347: 26.

Gopnik, M., and Crago, M. B. (1991, Apr) Familial aggregation of a developmental language disorder. *Cognition*, 39: 1–50.

Guasti, M. T. (2002) *Language Acquisition: The Growth of Grammar*. MIT Press, Cambridge, MA.

Hartl, D. L., and Jones, E. W. (1999) *Essential Genetics*. Jones & Bartlett, Sudbury, MA.

Herodotus (1964) *Histories: Book II*, trans. G. Rawlinson. Dent, London.

Hurst, J., Baraitser, M., Auger, E., Graham, F., and Norell, S. (1990) An extended family with a dominantly inherited speech disorder. *Developmental Medicine and Child Neurology*, 32: 352–55.

Imbert, G., Feng, W., Nelson, D. L., Warren, S. T., and Mandel, J. L. (1998) FMR1 and mutations in fragile X syndrome: molecular biology, biochemistry and genetics. In R. D. Wells and S. T. Warren (eds), *Genetic Instability and Hereditary Neurobiological Diseases*, pp. 27–53. Academic Press, New York.

Jensen, A. R. (1993) Why is reaction time correlated with psychometric *g*? *Current Directions in Psychological Science*, 2: 53–6.

Lai, C. S., Fisher, S. E., Hurst, J. A., Levy, E. R., Hodgson, S., Fox, M., Jeremiah, S., Povey, S., Jamison, D. C., Green, E. D., Vargha-Khadem, F., and Monaco, A. P. (2000) The SPCH1 region on human 7q31: genomic characterization of the critical interval and localization of translocations associated with speech and language disorder. *American Journal of Human Genetics*, 67: 357–68.

Lai, C. S. L., Fisher, S. E., Hurst, J. A., Vargha-Khadem, F., and Monaco, A. P. (2001) A forkhead-domain gene is mutated in a severe speech and language disorder. *Nature*, 413: 519–23.

Leonard, L. B. (1998) *Children with Specific Language Impairments*. MIT Press, Cambridge, Mass.

Lord, C., and Paul, R. (1997) Language and communication in autism. In D. J. Cohen and F. R. Volkmar (eds), *Handbook of Autism and Pervasive Developmental Disorders*, 2nd edn. Wiley, New York.

Lord, C., Risi, S., and Pickles, A. (2004) Trajectory of language development in autistic spectrum disorders. In M. L. Rice and S. F. Warren (eds), *Developmental Language Disorders: From Phenotypes to Etiologies*, pp. 7–30. Mahwah, NJ, Erlbaum.

Lord, C., and Rutter, M. (1994) Autism and pervasive development disorders. In E. Taylor (ed.), *Child and Adolescent Psychiatry: Modern Approaches*, vol. 3, pp. 569–93. Blackwell, Oxford.

Lord, C., Rutter, M., DiLavore, P. C., and Risi, S. (1999) *Autism Diagnostic Observation Schedule*. Los Angeles, Calif.: Western Psychological Services.

MacDermot, K. D., Bonora, E., Sykes, N., Coupe, A.-M., Lai, C. S. L., Vernes, S. C., Vargha-Khadem, F., McKenzie, F., Smith, R. L., Monaco, A. P., and Fisher, S. E. (2005) Identification of FOXP2 truncation as a novel cause of developmental speech and language deficits. *American Journal of Human Genetics*, 76: 1074–80.

Marcus, G. F., and Fisher, S. E. (2003) FOXP2 in focus: what can genes tell us about speech and language? *Trends in Cognitive Sciences*, 7: 257–62.

Meaburn, E., Dale, P. S., Craig, I. W., and Plomin, R. (2002) Language-impaired children: no sign of the FOXP2 mutation. *Neuroreport*, 13: 1075–7.

Mervis, C. B., and Robinson, B. F. (2005) Designing measures for profiling and genotype/phenotype studies of individuals with genetic syndromes or developmental language disorders. *Applied Psycholinguistics*, 26: 41–64.

Morris, C. A. (2004) Genotype-phenotype correlations: lessons from Williams Syndrome Research. In M. L. Rice and S. F. Warren (eds), *Developmental Language Disorders: From Phenotypes to Etiologies*, pp. 355–72. Erlbaum, Mahwah, NJ.

Morris, C. A., Mervis, C. G., Hobart, H. H., Gregg, R. G., Bertrand, J., Ensing, G. J., Sommer, A., Moore, C. A., Hopkin, R. J., Spallone, P. A., Keating, M. T., Osborne L., Kimberley, K. W. and Stock, A. D. (2003) GTF21 hemizygosity implicated in mental retardation in Williams syndrome: genotype-phenotype analysis of five families with deletions in the Williams syndrome region. *American Journal of Medical Genetics*, 123A, 45–9.

Newbury, D. F., Bonora, E., Lamb, J. A., Fisher, S. E., La, C. S. L., Baird, G., Jannoun, L., Slonims, V., Stott, C. M., Merricks, M. J., Bolton, P. F., Bailey, A. J., Monaco, A. P., and the International Molecular Genetic Study of Autism Consortium (2002) FOXP2 is not a major susceptibility gene for autism or specific language impairment. *American Journal of Human Genetics*, 70: 1318–27.

O'Brien, E. K., Zhang, X., Nishimura, C., Tomblin, J. B., and Murray, J. C. (2003) Association of specific language impairment (SLI) to the region of 7q31. *American Journal of Human Genetics*, 72: 1536–43.

Online Mendelian Inheritance in Man (OMIM) McKusick-Nathans Institute for Genetic Medicine, Johns Hopkins University (Baltimore, Md/) and National Center for Biotechnology Information, National Library of Medicine (Bethesda, Md.) URL: http://www.ncbi.nlm.nih.gov/omim/

Pedersen, N. L., Plomin, R., and McClearn, G. E. (1994) Is there G beyond g? (Is there genetic influence on specific cognitive abilities independent of genetic influence on general cognitive ability?) *Intelligence*, 18: 133–43.

Plomin, R. (1999) Genetics and general cognitive ability. *Nature*, 402: C25–C29.

Plomin, R., and Kovas, Y. (2005) Generalist genes and learning disabilities. *Psychological Bulletin*, 131: 592–617.

Price, T. S., Dale, P. S., and Plomin, R. (2004) A longitudinal genetic analysis of low verbal and non-verbal cognitive abilities in early childhood. *Twin Research*, 7: 139–48.

Redmond, S. M., and Rice, M. L. (1998) The socioemotional behaviors of children with SLI: social adaptation or social deviance? *Journal of Speech, Language, and Hearing Research*, 41: 688–700.

Rice, M. L. (2004) Growth models of developmental language disorders. In M. L. Rice and S. F. Warren (eds), *Developmental Language Disorders: From Phenotypes to Etiologies*, pp. 207–40. Erlbaum, Mahwah, NJ

Rice, M. L., Haney, K. R., and Wexler, K. (1998) Family histories of children with SLI who show extended optional infinitives. *Journal of Speech, Language and Hearing Research*, 41: 419–32.

Rice, M. L., Redmond, S. M. and Hoffman, L. (2006) MLU in children with SLI and young control children shows concurrent validity, stable and parallel growth trajectories. *Journal of Speech, Language, and Hearing Research*, 49: 793–808.

Rice, M. L., Tomblin, J. B., Hoffman, L., Richman, W. A., and Marquis, J. (2004) Grammatical tense deficits in children with SLI and nonspecific language impairment: relationships with non-verbal IQ over time. *Journal of Speech, Language, and Hearing Research*, 47: 816–34.

Rice, M. L., and Warren, S. F. (eds) (2004) *Developmental Language Disorders: From Phenotypes to Etiologies*. Erlbaum, Mahwah, NJ.

Rice, M. L., and Warren, S. F. (2005) Moving toward a unified effort to understand the nature and causes of language disorders. *Applied Psycholinguistics*, 26: 3–6.

Rice, M. L., Warren, S. F., and Betz, S. K. (2005) Language symptoms of developmental language disorders: an overview of autism, Down syndrome, fragile X, specific language impairment, and Williams syndrome. *Applied Psycholinguistics*, 26: 7–28.

Rice, M. L. and Wexler, K. (1996a) A phenotype of specific language impairment: extended optional infinitives. In M. L. Rice (ed.), *Toward a Genetics of Language*, pp. 215–38. Erlbaum, Mahwah, NJ.

Rice, M. L., and Wexler, K. (1996b) Toward tense as a clinical marker of specific language impairment in English-speaking children. *Journal of Speech, Language and Hearing Research*, 39: 1239–57.

Rice, M. L., and Wexler, K. (2001) *Rice/Wexler Test of Early Grammatical Impairment*, Psychological Corporation, San Antonio, TX.

Rice, M. L., Wexler, K., and Cleave, P. L. (1995) Specific language impairment as a period of extended optional infinitive. *Journal of Speech, Language, and Hearing Research*, 38: 850–63.

Rice, M. L., Wexler, K., and Hershberger, S. (1998) Tense over time: the longitudinal course of tense acquisition in children with specific language impairment. *Journal of Speech, Language and Hearing Research*, 41: 1412–31.

Santangelo, S. L., and Folstein, S. E. (1999) Autism: a genetic perspective. In H. Tager-Flusberg (ed.), *Neurodevelopmental Disorders*, pp. 431–47. MIT Press, Cambridge, MA.

Semel, E. M., Wiig, E., and Secord, W. (1987) *Clinical Evaluation of Language Fundamentals Revised*. Psychological Corporation, San Antonio, TX.

Shriberg, L. D., Tomblin, J. B., and McSweeny, J. L. (1999) Prevalence of speech delay in 6-year-old children and comorbity with language impairment. *Journal of Speech, Language, and Hearing Research*, 42: 1461–81.

SLI Consortium (2002) A genomewide scan identifies two novel loci involved in specific language impairment. *American Journal of Human Genetics*, 70: 384–98.

SLI Consortium. (2004, Jun) Highly significant linkage to the SLI1 locus in an expanded sample of individuals affected by specific language impairment. *American Journal of Human Genetics* 74: 1225–38.

Smith, S. D. (2004) Localization and identification of genes affecting language and learning. In M. L. Rice and S. F. Warren (eds), *Developmental Language Disorders: From Phenotypes to Etiologies*, pp. 329–54. Mahwah, NJ: Erlbaum.

Smith, S. D., and Morris, C. A. (2005) Planning studies of etiology. *Applied Psycholinguistics*, 26: 41–64.

Smith, S. D., Pennington, B. F., Boada, R., and Shriberg, L. D. (2005) Linkage of speech sound disorder to reading disability loci. *Journal of Child Psychology and Psychiatry*, 46: 1057–66.

Spinath, F. M., Price, T. S., Dale, P. S., and Plomin, R. (2004) The genetic and environmental origins of language disability and ability. *Child Development*, 75: 445–54.

Stein, C. M., Schick, J. H., Taylor, H. G., Shriberg, L. D., Millard, C., Kundtz-Kluge, A., Russo, K., et al. (2004) Pleiotripic effects of a chromosome 3 locus on speech-sound disorder and reading. *American Journal of Human Genetics*, 74: 283–97.

Stromswold, K. (2001) The heritability of language: a review and metaanalysis of twin, adoption, and linkage studies. *Language*, 77: 647–723.

Tager-Flusberg, H. (1999) A psychological approach to understanding the social and language impairments in autism. *International Review of Psychiatry*, 11: 325–34.

Tager-Flusberg, H. (2004) Do autism and specific language impairment represent overlapping language disorders? In M. L. Rice, and S. F. Warren (eds), *Developmental Language Disorders: From Phenotypes to Etiologies*, pp. 31–52. Erlbaum, Mahwah, NJ.

Tager-Flusberg, H. (2005) Designing Studies to Investigate the relationships between genes, environments, and developmental language disorders. *Applied Psycholinguistics*, 26: 29–40.

Tallal, P., Hirsch, L. S., Realpe-Bonilla, T., Miller, S., and Brzustowicz, L. M. (2001) Familial aggregation in specific language impairment. *Journal of Speech, Language and Hearing Research*, 44: 1172–82.

Tomblin, J. B., Records, N. L., Buckwalter, P., Zhang, X., Smith, E., and O'Brien, M. (1997) The prevalence of specific language impairment in kindergarten children. *Journal of Speech and Hearing Research*, 40: 1245–60.

Trouton, A., Spinath, F. M., and Plomin, R. (2002) Twins early development study (TEDS): A multivariate, longitudinal genetic investigation of language, cognition and behavior problems in childhood. *Twin Research*, 5: 444–8.

Vargha-Khadem, F., Watkins, K., Alcock, K., Fletcher, P., and Passingham, R. (1995) Praxic and non-verbal cognitive deficits in a large family with a genetically transmitted speech and language disorder. *Proceedings of the National Academy of Sciences*, 92: 930–3.

Verkerk, A., Pieretti, M., Sutcliffe, J. S., Fu, Y., Kuhl, D., Pizzuti, A., Reiner, O., Richards, S., Victoria, M., Zhang, F., Eussen, B., van Ommen, G., Blonden, L., Riggins, G., Chastain, J., Kunst, C., Galjaard, H., Caskey, C. T., Nelson, D., Oostra, B., and Warren, S. (1991) Identification of a gene (FMR-1) containing a CGG repeat coincident with a breakpoint cluster region exhibiting length variation in fragile X syndrome. *Cell*, 65: 905–14.

Viding, E., Price, T. S., Spinath, F. M., Bishop, D. V. M., Dale, P. S., and Plomin, R. (2003) Genetic and environmental mediation of the relationship between language and non-verbal impairment in 4-year-old twins. *Journal of Speech, Language, and Hearing Research*, 46: 1271–82.

Watkins, K. E., Dronkers, N. F., and Vargha-Khadem, F. (2002) Behavioural analysis of an inherited speech and language disorder: comparison with acquired aphasia. *Brain*, 125: 452–64.

Watkins, K. E., Gadian, D. G., and Vargha-Khadem, F. (1999) Functional and structural brain abnormalities associated with a genetic disorder of speech and language. *American Journal of Human Genetics* 65: 1215–21.

Watkins, K. E., Vargha-Khadem, F., Ashburner, J., Passingham, R. E., Connelly, A., Friston, K. J., Frackowiak, R. S. J., Mishkin, M., and Gadian, D. G. (2002) MRI analysis of an inherited speech and language disorder: structural brain abnormalities. *Brain*, 125: 465–78.

Weismer, S. E., Tomblin, J. B., Zhang, X., Buckwalter, P., Chynoweth, J. G., and Jones, M. (2000) Non-word repetition performance in school-age children with and without language impairment. *Journal of Speech, Language, and Hearing Research*, 43: 865–78.

Wexler, K. (1994) Optional infinitives, head movement and the economy of derivations. In D. Lightfoot and N. Hornstein (eds), *Verb Movement*, pp. 305–50. Cambridge University Press, Cambridge.

Wexler, K. (2003) Lenneberg's dream: learning, normal language development and specific language impairment. In Y. Levy and J. Schaeffer (eds), *Language Competence Across Populations: Toward a Definition of Specific Language Impairment*, pp. 11–62. Erlbaum, Mahwah, NJ.

Zubrick, S. R., Taylor, C. L., Rice, M. L. and Slegers, D. (forthcoming) An epidemiological study of late talking 24-month-old children: prevalence and predictors. *Journal of Speech, Language and Hearing Research.*

Zukowski, A. (2004) Investigating knowledge of complex syntax: insights from experimental studies of Williams syndrome. In M. L. Rice and S. F. Warren (eds), *Developmental Language Disorders: From Phenotypes to Etiologies*, pp. 99–120. Erlbaum, Mahwah, NJ.

SECTION VI

Perspectives

CHAPTER 43

The psycholinguistics of signed and spoken languages: how biology affects processing

Karen Emmorey

Linguistic research over the last few decades has revealed substantial similarities between the structure of signed and spoken languages (for reviews see Emmorey, 2002; Sandler and Lillo-Martin, 2006). These similarities provide a strong basis for cross-modality comparisons, and also bring to light linguistic universals that hold for *all* human languages. In addition, however, biology-based distinctions between sign and speech are important, and can be exploited to discover how the input–output systems of language impact online language processing and affect the neurocognitive underpinnings of language comprehension and production. For example, do the distinct perceptual and productive systems of signed and spoken languages exert differing constraints on the nature of linguistic processing? Recent investigations have suggested that the modality in which a language is expressed can impact the psychological mechanisms required to decode and produce the linguistic signal. This chapter explores what aspects of language processing appear to be universal to all human languages and what aspects are affected by the particular characteristics of audition vs. vision, or by the differing constraints on manual versus oral articulation.

Sign language processing is appropriately compared to speech processing, rather than to reading, because unlike written text, which can be characterized as "visual language," sign language consists of dynamic and constantly changing forms rather than static symbols. Further, neither sign language nor spoken language comes pre-segmented into words and sentences for the perceiver. The production of writing, although performed by the hand, differs substantially from sign language production because writing derives its structure from a separate system (the orthography of a spoken language). In contrast to written language, sign and speech are both primary language systems, acquired during infancy and early childhood without formal instruction.

43.1 Sign perception and visual processing

Although non-signers may interpret the visual signed signal simply as a collection of rapid hand and arm motions, signers quickly extract complex meaning from the incoming visual signal. Similarly, speakers extract meaning from a rapidly changing acoustic stream, if they know the language. Listeners and viewers are able to automatically parse an incoming auditory or visual linguistic signal by virtue of stored internal representations. Speech perception involves segmentation of speech sounds into phonemic units. For signed languages, a first question is whether signs actually exhibit sublexical linguistic structure that could be used by a parser to segment visual signed input. Is it possible to have a phonology that is not based on sound?

43.1.1 Phonology in a language without sound

Several decades of linguistic research has shown that signed languages, like spoken languages, have a level of structure in which meaningless elements are combined in rule-governed ways to create meaningful forms (e.g. Stokoe, 1960; Battison, 1978; Sandler, 1986; Brentari, 1998). For spoken languages, these elements are oral gestures that create sounds. For signed languages, manual and facial gestural units are combined to create distinct signs. The discovery that sign languages exhibit phonological structure was groundbreaking because it demonstrated that signs are not holistic pantomimes lacking internal organization. Furthermore, this discovery showed that human languages universally develop a level of meaningless linguistic structure and a system that organizes this structure.

Briefly, signs are composed of three basic phonological parameters: hand configuration, location (place of articulation), and movement. Orientation of the hand/arm is another contrasting parameter, but many theories represent orientation as a sub-component of hand configuration or movement, rather than as a basic phonological element. Figure 43.1 provides illustrations of minimal pairs from LIS (*Lingua Italiana dei Segni*, Italian Sign Language). The top part of the figure illustrates two LIS signs that differ only in hand configuration. Not all sign languages share the same hand configuration inventory. For example, the "t" hand configuration in American Sign Language (the thumb is inserted between the index and middle fingers of a fist) is not found in European sign languages. Chinese Sign Language contains a hand configuration formed with an open hand with all fingers extended except for the ring finger, which is bent—this hand configuration does not occur in American Sign Language (ASL). In addition, signs can differ according to where they are made on the body or face. Figure 43.1b illustrates two LIS signs that differ only their place of articulation, and these different locations do not add meaning to the signs. Signs can also differ minimally in orientation, as illustrated in Figure 43.1c. Finally, movement is another contrasting category that distinguishes minimally between signs, as shown in Figure 43.1d.

In addition to segment-like units, syllables have also been argued to exist in signed languages (Brentari, 1998; Corina and Sandler, 1993; Wilbur, 1993). The syllable is a unit of structure that is below the level of the word but above the level of the segment, and is required to explain phonological form and patterning within a word. Although sign phonologists disagree about precisely how sign syllables should be characterized, there is general agreement that a sign syllable must contain a movement of some type. In ASL, several phonological constraints have been identified that must refer to the syllable. For example, only certain movement sequences are allowed in bisyllabic (two-movement) signs: circle + straight movements are permitted, but straight + circle movements are not (Uyechi, 1994). Although a straight + circle movement sequence is ill-formed as a single sign, it is well-formed when it occurs in a phrase. Thus, the constraint on movement sequences needs to refer to a level smaller than the word (the constraint does not hold across word boundaries), but larger than the segment. Within Sandler's (1986) Hand Tier model, signed segments consist of Movements and Locations, somewhat akin to Vowels and Consonants.

However, syllables in signed language differ from syllables in spoken language because there is little evidence for internal structure within the signed syllable. Spoken syllables can be divided into onsets (usually, the first consonant or consonant cluster) and rhymes (the vowel and final consonants). Such internal structure does not appear to be present for sign syllables, although some linguists have argued for weight distinctions, i.e. "heavy" vs. "light" syllables, based on differences in movement types. Because of the lack of internal structure, there do not appear to be processes such as resyllabification in sign languages (e.g. a segment from one syllable becomes part of another syllable). These facts are important, given the emphasis that speech production models place on syllabification as a separate processing stage (e.g. Levelt et al., 1999).

Syllabification processes and/or the use of a syllabary may be specific to phonological encoding for speech production. The syllable likely serves as an organizational unit for speech, providing a structural frame for multisegmental words. For example, MacNeilage (1998) argues that the oscillation of the mandible creates a frame around which syllable production can be organized. Meier (2000; 2002) points out that signing differs dramatically from speaking because signing does not involve a single, predominant oscillator, akin to the mandible. Rather, signs can have movement that is restricted to just about any joint of the arm. Thus, sign production

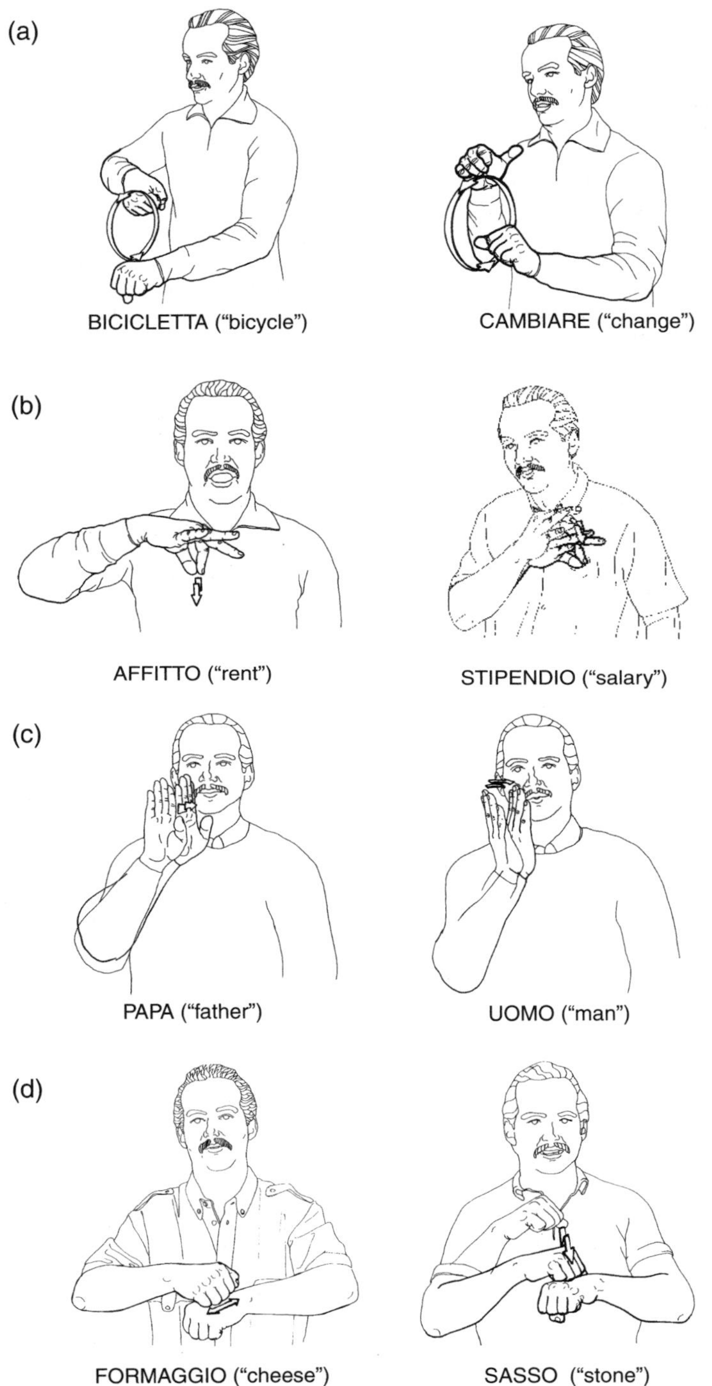

Figure 43.1 Examples of minimal pairs in Lingua Italiana dei Signi, LIS (Italian Sign Language) (a) signs that contrast in hand configuration; (b) signs that contrast in place of articulation (location); (c) signs that contrast in orientation; (d) signs that contrast in movement. Illustrations from V. Volterra (ed.), *La lingua italiana dei segni*. Bologna: Il Mulino, 1987 (new edn 2004). Copyright © Virginia Volterra and Elena Radutzky. Reprinted with permission.

may not be constrained to fit within a frame imposed by a single articulator. Further, multi-segmental signs (e.g. signs with more than three segments) are relatively rare, regardless of how signed segments are defined (see Brentari, 1998). In contrast, syllabification processes for speech production may serve a critical framing function for words, which can contain many segments.

In sum, the linguistic evidence indicates that sign languages exhibit a level of sublexical structure that is encoded during sign production and that could be used to parse an incoming visual linguistic signal. A next question is whether signers make use of such internal representations when perceiving signs. Evidence suggesting that they do comes from studies of categorical perception in American Sign Language.

43.1.2 Categorical perception in sign language

Just as hearing speakers become auditorily tuned to perceive the sound contrasts of their native language, ASL signers appear to become visually tuned to perceive manual contrasts in American Sign Language. Two studies have now found evidence of categorical perception for phonologically distinctive hand configurations in ASL (Emmorey et al., 2003; Baker et al., 2005). "Categorical perception" refers to the finding that stimuli are perceived categorically rather than continually, despite continuous variation in form. Evidence for categorical perception is found (1) when perceivers partition continuous stimuli into relatively discrete categories and (2) when discrimination performance is better across a category boundary than within a category. For these categorical perception experiments, deaf signers and hearing non-signers were presented with hand configuration continua that consisted of two handshape endpoints with nine intermediate variants. These continua were either generated via a computer morphing program (Emmorey et al., 2003) or from a live signer (Baker et al., 2005). In addition, Emmorey et al. (2003) investigated categorical perception for place of articulation continua. For all experiments, participants performed a discrimination task in which they made same/different judgements for pairs or triplets of images from a continuum, and an identification task in which each stimulus was categorized with respect to the endpoints of the continuum (the discrimination task always preceded the categorization task).

Deaf ASL signers and hearing English speakers (non-signers) demonstrated similar category boundaries for both hand configuration and place of articulation (Emmorey et al., 2003; Baker et al., 2005). This result is consistent with previous studies which found that deaf and hearing participants exhibit similar perceptual groupings and confusability matrices for hand configuration and for place of articulation (Lane et al., 1976; Poizner and Lane, 1978). Thus, these ASL categories may have a perceptual as well as a linguistic basis. However, only deaf signers exhibited evidence of categorical perception, and only for distinctive hand configurations. Only deaf signers were sensitive to hand configuration category boundaries in the discrimination task, performing significantly better across category boundaries than within a hand configuration category (Emmorey et al., 2003; Baker et al., 2005).

Interestingly, neither group exhibited categorical perception effects for place of articulation (Emmorey et al., 2003). Lack of a categorical perception effect for place of articulation may be due to more variable category boundaries. In speech, categorical perception is modulated by the nature of the articulation of speech sounds. For example, categorical perception is often weak or not present for vowels, perhaps because of the more continuous nature of their articulation compared to stop consonants (Fry et al., 1962). The same may be true for place of articulation in sign language. For example, the location of signs can be displaced within a major body region in casual signing (Brentari, 1998) or completely displaced to the side during whispering. Category boundaries for place of articulation appear to be much less stable than for hand configuration. Categorical perception may only occur when articulations are relatively discrete for both sign and speech.

The fact that only deaf signers exhibited categorical perception for ASL hand configurations indicates that linguistic experience is what drives these effects. However, categorical perception effects are weaker for sign than for speech. Deaf signers' discrimination ability within hand configuration categories was better than the near-chance discrimination ability reported within stop consonant categories for speech (e.g. Liberman et al., 1957). Nonetheless, the sign language results resemble discrimination functions observed for categorical perception in other visual domains, such as faces or facial expressions (e.g. Beale and Keil, 1995; de Gelder et al., 1997). Discrimination accuracy within visual categories tends to be relatively high; generally, participants perform with about 70–85 percent mean accuracy rates within categories. The difference in the strength of categorical perception effects between speech and sign may arise from psychophysical differences between audition and vision.

In sum, deaf signers appear to develop special abilities for perceiving aspects of sign language that are similar to the abilities that speakers develop for perceiving speech. These findings suggest that categorical perception emerges naturally as part of language processing, regardless of language modality. In addition, the results indicate that phonological information is utilized during the perception of moving nonsense signs (Baker et al., 2005) and when viewing still images of signs (Emmorey et al., 2003). Further research is needed to discover what parsing procedures might be used to identify sign boundaries, and whether categorical perception processes might play a role in segmenting the signing stream.

43.2 **Processing universals and modality effects in the mental lexicon**

Many models of spoken word recognition hypothesize that an acoustic-phonetic representation is sequentially mapped onto lexical entries, and lexical candidates which match this initial representation are activated (e.g. Marslen-Wilson, 1987; McClelland and Elman, 1986; Goldinger et al., 1989). As more of a word is heard, activation levels of lexical entries which do not match the incoming acoustic signal decrease. The sequential matching process continues until only one candidate remains which is consistent with the sensory input. At this point, word recognition can occur. This process is clearly conditioned by the serial nature of speech perception. Since signed languages are less dependent upon serial linguistic distinctions, visual lexical access and sign recognition may differ from spoken language. To investigate this possibility, Grosjean (1981) and Emmorey and Corina (1990) used a gating technique to track the process of lexical access and sign identification through time.

43.2.1 **The time course of sign vs. word recognition**

In sign language gating tasks, a sign is presented repeatedly, and the length of each presentation is increased by a constant amount (e.g. one videoframe or 33 msec). After each presentation, participants report what they think the sign is and how confident they are. Results from such studies show that ASL signers produce initial responses which share the place of articulation, orientation, and hand configuration of the target sign but differ in movement (Grosjean, 1981; Emmorey and Corina, 1990). The movement of the sign is identified last, and coincides with lexical recognition. This pattern of responses suggests that, similarly to the speech signal, the visual input for sign activates a cohort of potential lexical candidates that share some initial phonological features. This set of candidates narrows as more visual information is presented—until a single sign candidate remains. Clark and Grosjean (1982) showed further that sentential context did not affect this basic pattern of lexical recognition, although it reduced the time to identify a target sign by about 10 percent.

However, unlike spoken word recognition, sign recognition appears to involve a two- stage process of recognition in which one group of phonological features (hand configuration, orientation, and place of articulation) initially identifies a lexical cohort, and then identification of phonological movement leads directly to sign identification. Such a direct correlation between identification of a phonological element and lexical identification does not occur with English and may not occur for any spoken language. That is, there seems to be no phonological feature or structure, the identification of which leads directly to word recognition. Movement is the most temporally influenced phonological property of sign, and more time is required to resolve it. For speech, almost all phonological components have a strong temporal component, and there does not appear to be a single feature that listeners must wait to resolve in order to identify a word.

Furthermore, both Grosjean (1981) and Emmorey and Corina (1990) found that signs were identified surprisingly rapidly. Although signs tend to be much longer than words, only 35 percent of a sign had to be seen before the sign was identified (Emmorey and Corina, 1990). This is significantly faster than word recognition for English. Grosjean (1980) found that approximately 83 percent of a word had to be heard before the word could be identified. There are at least two reasons why signs may be identified earlier than spoken words. First, the nature of the visual signal for sign provides a large amount of phonological information very early and simultaneously. The early availability of this phonological information can dramatically narrow the set of lexical candidates for the incoming stimulus. Second, the phonotactics and morphotactics of a visual language such as ASL may be different from those of spoken languages. In English, many words begin with similar sequences, and listeners can be led down a garden path if a shorter word is embedded at the onset of a longer word—for example, "pan" in "pantomime." This phenomenon does not commonly occur in ASL. Furthermore, sign initial cohorts seem to be much more limited by phonotactic structure. Unlike English, in which many initial strings have large cohorts (e.g. the strings [kan], [mæn], and [skr] are all shared by thirty or more words), ASL has few signs which share an initial phonological shape (i.e. the same hand configuration and place of articulation). This phonotactic structure limits the size of the initial cohort in ASL. The more constrained phonotactics and the early and simultaneous availability of phonological information may conspire to produce faster identification times for ASL signs.

In sum, lexical access and word recognition are generally quite similar for spoken and signed languages. For both language types, lexical access involves a sequential mapping process between an incoming linguistic signal and stored lexical representations. For signed languages, this appears to be a two-stage process in which one set of phonological elements are initially accessed and then identification of movement leads to sign recognition. Finally, the phonotactics of ASL (and possibly other signed languages) leads to proportionally faster recognition times for signs than for words.

43.2.2 **The organization of a sign-based lexicon: evidence from tip-of-the-fingers**

A tip-of-the-tongue (TOT) experience refers to the state in which a speaker is temporarily unable to retrieve a word from memory, while being sure that he or she knows the word (see Brown, 1991; Schwartz, 1999 for reviews). Often, speakers are able to retrieve the first letter and sometimes the number of syllables, which provides evidence for the organization of spoken language lexicons. The existence and nature of TOTs in spoken languages suggest that independent processing stages provide access to word meanings and word forms (e.g. Dell et al., 1997; Garrett, 1975; Levelt et al., 1999). However, for signed languages, the division between semantic and phonological form has been questioned because they exhibit a high degree of iconicity. For example, Stokoe (1991) proposes a theory of "semantic phonology" in which representations of a sign's form can be derived from aspects of its semantics. Semantic phonology eliminates form/meaning distinctions and rejects duality of patterning for signed languages (Armstrong et al., 1995). Under such a model, a "tip-of-the-fingers" experience should not occur for signers because there is no clear division between semantics and phonology.

Thompson et al. (2005) investigated whether a "tip-of-the-fingers" (TOFs) experience occurs for ASL signers and whether TOFs are similar to TOTs. Thonmpson et al. (2005) conducted a small diary study and also experimentally elicited TOFs by asking signers to translate English words (e.g. what is the sign for "Moscow"?). Thompson et al. (2005) found that ASL signers reported having TOF experiences in which they could retrieve detailed semantic information, but had little or no access to the sign form. TOFs were similar to TOTs in that the majority involved proper names, and participants sometimes had partial access to phonological form (e.g. recalling the hand configuration and location of a sign, but not its movement). Although some TOF phonological parameters were iconic, there was no relationship between degree of iconicity for a particular parameter and access to it during a TOF. This separation between semantic and phonological retrieval provides evidence against semantic phonology (Stokoe, 1991), and indicates that independent processing stages provide access to lexical meanings and lexical forms for both sign and speech.

In addition, lexical access during sign production parallels access during sign perception. That is, during a TOF participants were equally likely to recall hand configuration, location, and orientation, which constitute the onset of a sign, and least likely to recall movement, which unfolds over time. These results parallel the gating studies of sign perception, indicating that phonological onsets are privileged for both signed and spoken languages.

Perhaps the most remarkable aspect of the TOFs for signs was participants' frequent recall of as many as three out of the four phonological parameters. This qualitative aspect of TOFs has further implications for models of signed language production, and distinguishes TOFs from TOTs. TOFs appear to be qualitatively quite different from TOTs with respect to the amount of phonological information that is retrieved simultaneously. However, recall of three phonological parameters did not result in more TOF resolutions compared to when fewer or no parameters were recalled. Thus, signs appear to be stored as a set of phonological attributes where retrieval of one or more attributes does not result in immediate access to the full phonological representation. TOFs therefore can occur when any one parameter is insufficiently activated.

In sum, the existence of a tip-of-the-fingers phenomenon for sign language argues for a two-stage model of lexical access and a division between semantic and phonological representations. The nature of recall for TOFs was analogous to TOTs in that partial phonological information (most frequently from word onsets) was sometimes retrieved. However, lexical TOFs differed from TOTs in the amount of information simultaneously available. The results of the Thompson et al. (2005) study suggest that the ASL mental lexicon is not organized by a single phonological parameter (e.g. hand configuration) that guides retrieval. Rather, sign production appears to parallel sign perception, such that when in a TOF, signers are least likely to retrieve the movement of the target sign. More generally, the findings argue for a language universal processing pattern in which onsets have a special status, regardless of language modality.

43.2.3 The preference for non-concatenative morphology: a processing explanation

Signed languages differ from spoken languages in the type of combinatorial processes that most often create morphologically complex words. Specifically, signed languages show a marked preference for non-concatenative (simultaneous) morphological processes, in contrast to the preference for linear affixation exhibited by spoken languages. Examples of typical simultaneous morphological processes are given in Figure 43.2 from British Sign Language (BSL). In Figure 43.2a,

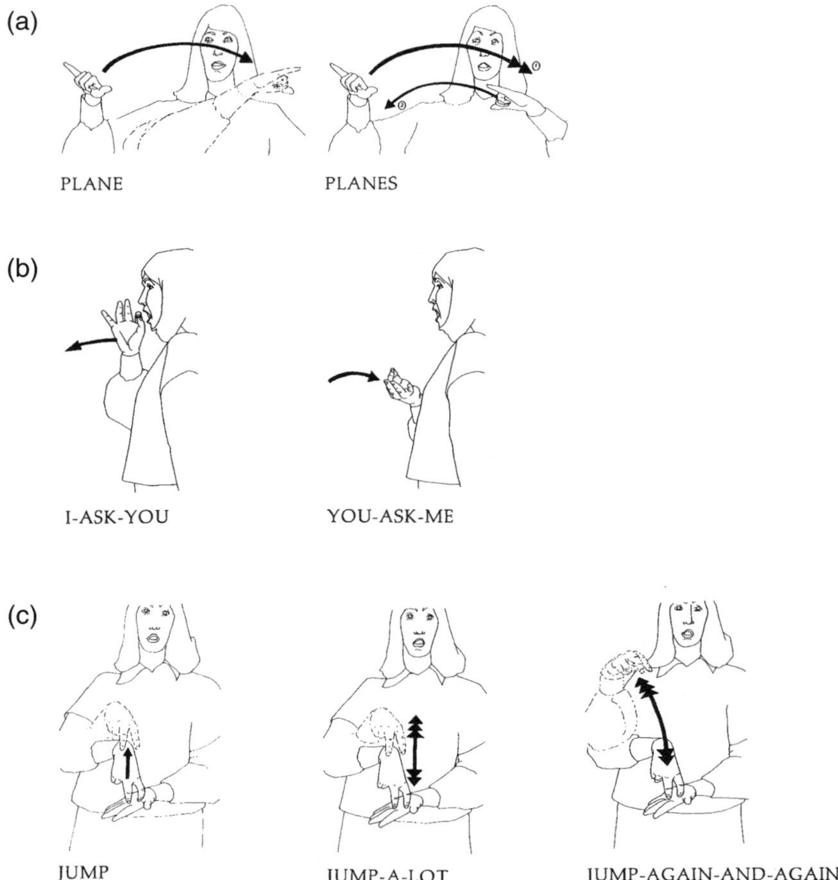

Figure 43.2 Examples of non-concatenative (simultaneous) morphology in British Sign Language (BSL) From Kyle and Woll (1985). Reprinted with permission.

a second hand is added to indicate plural. In Figure 43.2b, the direction of movement of the verb indicates subject and object arguments, and in Figure 43.2c, aspectual information is indicated by the type of the movement superimposed on the verb stem.

Linear affixation has been documented in signed languages. For example, ASL contains a few suffixes: the multiple suffix (Wilbur, 1987), the agentive suffix -ER, and a negative suffix ZERO (Aronoff et al., 2005). Aronoff et al. (2005) also describe a derivational prefix in Israeli Sign Language. However, the majority of morphological processes in signed languages appear to be simultaneous. In fact, Bergman (1982) claims that Swedish Sign Language has neither suffixation nor prefixation, but exhibits several types of reduplication and other non-concatenative morphological process. Similarly, Sutton-Spence and Woll (1999) describe only non-concatenative morphological processes for British Sign Language, with the exception of compounding. Thus far, the data from numerous signed languages indicates that linear affixation is rare and that simultaneous expression of a stem and its morphological markings is the preferred linguistic encoding.

In contrast, for spoken languages, simultaneous affixation (e.g. template morphology, infixation, reduplication) is relatively rare, and linear affixation is the preferred linguistic encoding for morphological processes. Cutler et al. (1985) argue that processing constraints underlie the rarity of morphological processes which alter the phonological integrity of the base form (e.g. infixation which inserts an affix into the middle of a word). Languages avoid processes that disrupt the structural integrity of linguistic units. Hall (1992) also argues that the rarity of non-concatenative (simultaneous) morphology is due to the processing complexity associated with discontinuous elements in general (e.g. center embedding or verbs with particles). Concatenative morphology requires much less computational complexity because of the straightforward mapping between the surface form of a word and its underlying representation (Anderson, 1992). Given these arguments, why do signed languages prefer non-concatenative morphology, and does it pose the same processing challenges that it does for spoken languages?

First, signed languages appear to favor non-concatenative morphology because the visual modality affords parallel processing. Vision can easily encode spatially distinct information in parallel (unlike audition), and as we have noted, the hand configuration, place of articulation, and orientation of signs are perceived nearly simultaneously. Second, the capacity for short-term memory is limited by articulation rate (Baddeley, 1986), and signs take longer than words to articulate (Bellugi and Fischer, 1972). Universal constraints on short-term memory capacity and a slower articulation rate may induce sign languages to disfavor linear affixation. Third, unlike the non-concatenative processes of infixation and circumfixation, the morphological processes of signed languages do not *interrupt* the base form and do not involve discontinuous affixes. As can be seen in the examples in Figure 43.2, in no case is the base form of the BSL sign actually interrupted by the morphological marking. Discontinuous circumfixation is not the correct analysis for these forms since the morphological marking is superimposed onto the verb stem. Thus, the morphological parsing difficulties that arise from non-concatenative processes in spoken languages do not arise for signed languages.

Finally, evidence for signed languages' aversion to linear affixation comes from Supalla's (1991) finding that when the linear morphology of a spoken language is transferred to the visual modality, deaf children exposed to this artificial language do not acquire the system and in fact, alter it to create simultaneous (spatial) morphological encoding. In the United States, Manually Coded English (MCE) is the cover term for sign systems developed in the 1970s to represent the morphology and syntax of English, such as Signing Exact English or SEE (Gustason et al., 1980). MCE was invented by educators (many fluent in ASL) as a means to make English accessible to deaf children. The basic vocabulary of MCE borrows heavily from the lexicon of ASL, but its inflectional morphology is strictly sequential and based on English morphology. For example, to express "He asked her," the MCE sign HE is made at the forehead with an "E" hand configuration, the ASL sign REQUEST is produced (with no spatial inflection), then the MCE suffix -ED is produced, followed by the MCE sign HER made at the chin with an "R" hand configuration (see Figure 43.3). To express "He asked her" in ASL (or in BSL), the verb ASK is directed from the location in signing space associated with the subject (the referent of "he") to the location of the object (the referent of "her") (see Figure 43.3b). Tense is not expressed morphologically in ASL. Further, pronouns in signed languages are generally directed toward locations in signing space to convey co-reference.

Supalla (1991) found that children exposed only to Manually Coded English modify the inflectional morphology of verbs and pronouns

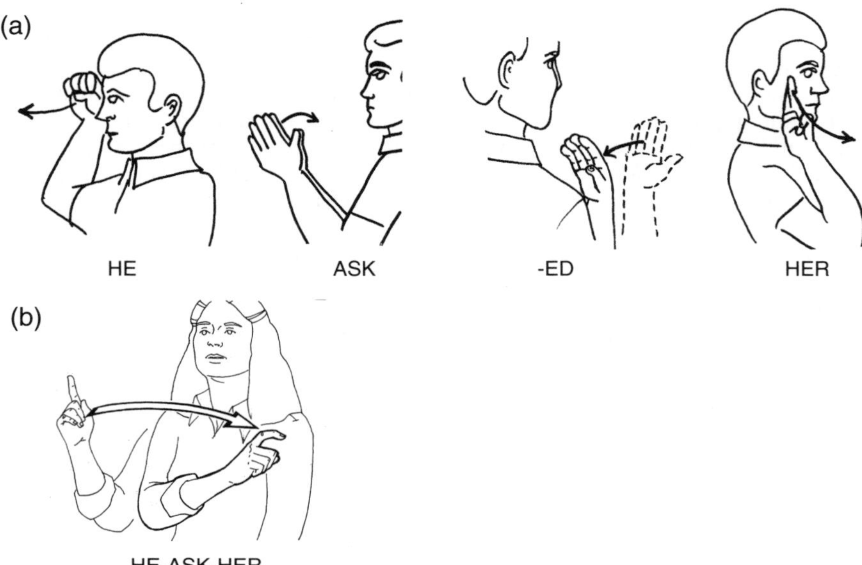

Figure 43.3 Examples of Manually Coded English (MCE) and ASL. (a) the MCE sentence 'He asked her'; (b) the equivalent sentence in ASL. The MCE signs are reprinted from Gustason et al. (1972). Reprinted with permission. ASL illustration copyright ©Ursula Bellugi, The Salk Institute.

to take advantage of the visual modality. That is, these children produce spatial non-linear modifications to base verbs in order to mark verb arguments, despite the fact that they were exposed only to linguistic input that produced these distinctions linearly. The children's spatial morphological creations were idiosyncratic, but they were systematic within a child and similar to the grammatical morphology found in signed languages of the world. Stack (1999) also found that Jamie, a young child exposed only to MCE, failed to acquire the non-spatial pronouns and linear inflections of MCE; rather, she created a pronominal system that utilized space and innovated non-linear morphology to express linguistic notions such as plurality (by reduplication), reciprocal aspect (the second hand mirrors the first), and lexical arguments (indicated by the beginning and endpoints of a verb). These results suggest that not only does the visual modality easily afford non-linear affixation, but visual processing may actually demand it.

43.3 **Comprehension and discourse: the unique role of space for signed languages**

The comprehension of sign language discourse depends upon interpreting the meaning of locations in signing space. For example, for many (if not most) signed languages, discourse referents are associated with locations in signing space, and pronominal signs and "agreeing" verbs (like ASK in Figure 43.3b) can be directed toward those locations to refer back to the associated referents. In addition, signing space is used to convey information about spatial relationships among objects. In this case, signing space serves both a topographic and a referential function (Emmorey et al., 1995). Several psycholinguistic studies have explored how ASL signers understand and maintain the associations between referents and spatial locations, and whether the same processing mechanisms hold for spoken and signed languages. These studies are briefly summarized below.

43.3.1 **Understanding spatial coreference**

To understand a sentence containing a pronoun, a perceiver must correctly assign an antecedent to the pronoun, which for languages like ASL involves interpreting the direction of the pronoun (where the pointing sign is directed) and recalling the referent associated with the targeted location. Emmorey et al. (1991) used the probe recognition methodology to investigate whether ASL pronouns re-activate their antecedents, as has been found with spoken language pronouns (e.g. Corbett and Chang, 1983; Gernsbacher, 1989). In the Emmorey et al. (1991) study, deaf participants viewed videotaped ASL sentences with and without pronouns and responded to probe signs presented after the pronoun. Participants had to decide whether the probe sign occurred in the sentence, and probe signs were either antecedent or non-antecedent nouns. Response times to antecedent nouns were faster than to non-antecedent nouns, and response times to antecedent nouns were faster when a pronoun was present in the sentence. Furthermore, Emmorey (1997) found that ASL pronouns suppress activation of non-antecedents, when the appropriate baseline condition is used. These results indicate that ASL pronouns activate their antecedents and suppress non-antecedents in memory, just as has been found for spoken languages (Gernsbacher, 1989).

In addition, ASL agreeing verbs license phonologically null pronouns. In clauses with agreeing verbs, subjects and objects appear as null elements that do not have an overt lexical form. Null pronouns are permitted to occur because of the morphological marking of agreeing verbs (see Figure 43.2b for an example of a BSL agreeing verb and Figure 43.3b for an ASL example). Using the same probe recognition methodology, Emmorey and Lillo-Martin (1995) found that null pronouns that were licensed by ASL agreeing verbs activate their antecedents to the same extent as overt pronouns. Again, these results parallel what has been found for spoken languages (e.g. Bever and McElree, 1988; Fodor, 1989) and suggest that the psycholinguistic mechanisms involved in anaphora resolution are universal and not dependent upon language modality.

Finally, Emmorey and Falgier (2004) investigated the unique case of "locus doubling," in which a single referent is associated with two distinct spatial locations (van Hoek, 1992). Emmorey and Falgier (2004) asked whether an ASL pronoun activates both its antecedent referent and the location associated with that referent. In this experiment, participants were presented with an introductory discourse that associated a referent (e.g. MOTHER) with two distinct locations (e.g. $\text{STORE}_{\text{left}}$, $\text{KITCHEN}_{\text{right}}$), and a continuation sentence followed that either contained a pronoun referring to the referent in one location or contained no anaphora (the control sentence). Deaf participants made lexical decisions to probe signs presented during the continuation sentences, and the probe signs were either the referent of the pronoun, the referent-location determined by the pronoun, or the most recently mentioned location (not referenced by the pronoun). The results indicated that response times to referent nouns were faster in the pronoun than in the no-pronoun control condition and that response times to the location signs did not differ across conditions. Thus, the spatial nature of coreference in ASL does not alter the processing mechanism underlying the online interpretation of pronouns. Pronouns activate only referent nouns, not spatial location nouns associated with the referent.

In sum, results from a series of sign language comprehension experiments indicate that the processing mechanisms used to resolve and interpret coreference relations do not differ cross-linguistically or cross-modally. Pronouns, whether spatialized pointing signs, spoken words, or null elements licensed by verb morphology, activate antecedents and suppress non-antecedents in memory, thereby improving the accessibility of coreferent nominals within the discourse (Gernsbacher, 1989). Language modality does not appear to affect co-reference resolution processes, despite great differences in the surface form of spoken and signed pronominal systems.

43.3.2 **Understanding spatial descriptions**

Most spoken languages encode spatial relations with prepositions or locative affixes. There is a grammatical element or phrase that denotes the spatial relation between a figure and ground object, e.g. the English spatial preposition *on* indicates support and contact, as in *The cup is on the table*. The prepositional phrase *on the table* defines a spatial region in terms of a ground object (the table), and the figure (the cup) is located in that region (Talmy, 2000). Spatial relations can also be expressed by compound phrases such as *to the left* or *in back of*. Both simple and compound prepositions constitute a closed class set of grammatical forms for English. In contrast, signed languages convey spatial information using classifier constructions in which spatial relations are expressed by where the hands are placed in signing space or with respect to the body (e.g. Supalla, 1982; Engberg-Pedersen, 1993). For example to indicate 'The cup is on the table,' an ASL signer would place a C classifier handshape (a curved handshape referring to the cup) on top of a B classifier handshape (a flat hand referring to the table). There is no grammatical element specifying the figure–ground relation; rather, there is a schematic and isomorphic mapping between the location of the hands in signing space and the location of the objects described (Emmorey and Herzig, 2003). This spatialized form has important ramifications for the nature of addressee vs. speaker perspective within spatial descriptions and for how these descriptions are understood.

Figure 43.4a provides a simple example of an ASL spatial description. An English translation of this example would be "I entered the room. There was a table to the left." In this type of narrative, the spatial description is from the point of view of the speaker (for simplicity and clarity, "speaker" will be used to refer to the person who is signing.) The addressee, if facing the speaker, must perform a mental transformation of signing space. For example, in Figure 43.4a, the speaker indicates that the table is to the left by articulating the appropriate classifier sign on his left in signing space. Because the addressee is facing the speaker, the location of the classifier form representing the table is actually on the right for the addressee. There is a mismatch between the location of the table in the room being described (the table is on the left as seen from the entrance) and what the addressee actually observes in signing space (the classifier handshape referring to the table is produced to the addressee's right). In this case, the addressee must perform what amounts to a 180° mental rotation to correctly comprehend the description.

Although spatial scenes are most commonly described from the speaker's point of view (as in Figure 43.4a), it is possible to indicate a different viewpoint. ASL has a marked sign that can be glossed as YOU-ENTER, which indicates that the scene should be understood as signed from the addressee's viewpoint (see Figure 43.4b). When this sign is used, the signing space in which the room is described is, in effect, rotated 180° so that the addressee is "at the entrance" of the room. In this case, the addressee does not need to mentally transform locations within signing space. However, ASL descriptions using YOU-ENTER are quite unusual and rarely found in natural discourse. Furthermore, Emmorey et al. (1998)

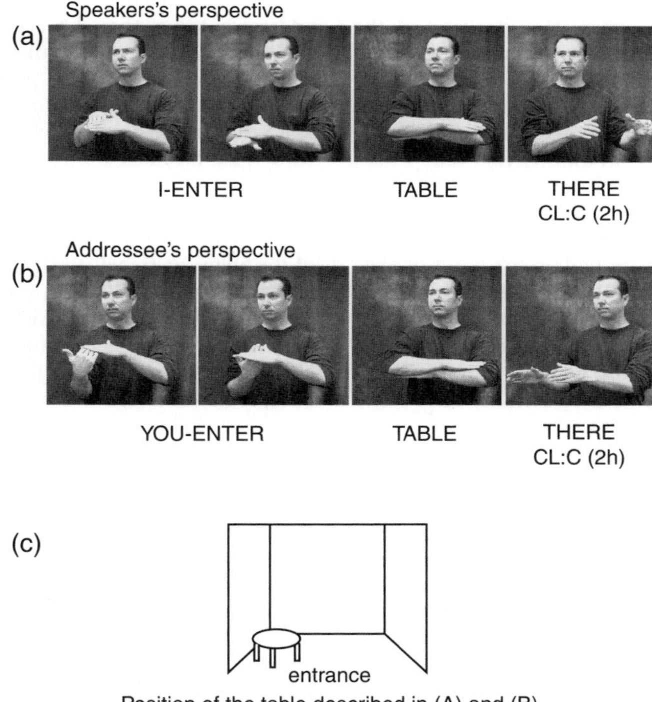

Figure 43.4 Illustration of ASL descriptions of the location of a table within a room, described from (a) the speaker's perspective or (b) the addressee's perspective. Signers exhibit better comprehension for room descriptions presented from the speaker's perspective, despite the mental transformation that this description entails. Reprinted from Emmorey (2002), with permission.

found that ASL signers comprehended spatial descriptions much better when they were produced from the speaker's point of view compared to the addressee's viewpoint. In that study, signers viewed a videotape of a room and then a signed description and were asked to judge whether the room and the description matched. When the room was described from the addressee's perspective (using YOU-ENTER), the description spatially matched the room layout shown on the videotape, but when signed from the speaker's perspective (using I-ENTER), the description was the reverse of the layout on the videotape (a simplified example is shown in Figure 43.4). Emmorey et al. (1998) found that ASL signers were more accurate when presented with descriptions from the speaker's perspective, despite the mental transformation that these descriptions entailed.

One might consider this situation analogous to that for English speakers who must understand the terms *left* and *right* with respect to the speaker's point of view (as in *on my left*). The crucial difference, however, is that these relations are encoded spatially in ASL, rather than lexically. The distinction becomes particularly clear in situations where the speaker and the addressee are both in the environment, observing the same scene. In this situation, English speakers most often adopt their addressee's point of view, for example giving directions such as, *Pick the one on your right*, or *It's in front of you*, rather than *Pick the one on my left* or *It's farthest from me* (Schober, 1993; Mainwaring et al., 1996). However, when jointly viewing an environment, ASL signers do not adopt their addressee's point of view but use "shared space" (Emmorey and Tversky, 2002). Signing space is shared in the sense that it maps to the physically observed space and to both the speaker's and addressee's view of the physical space. In such situations, there is no true speaker vs. addressee perspective and no mental transformation is required by the addressee. Furthermore, spatial descriptions of jointly viewed environments are not altered by the location of an addressee. That is, in these situations, ASL signers do not need to take into account where their addressee is located, unlike English speakers, who tend to adopt their addressee's viewpoint (Emmorey and Tversky, 2002). These differences between languages derive from the fact that signers use the actual space in front of them to represent observed physical space.

In sum, the spatialization of linguistic expression in ASL affects the nature of language comprehension by requiring an addressee to perform a mental transformation of the linguistic space under certain conditions. Specifically, for descriptions of non-present environments, an addressee must mentally transform the locations within a speaker's signing space in order to correctly understand the left/right arrangements of objects with respect to the speaker's viewpoint. For speech, spatial information is encoded in an acoustic signal, which bears no resemblance to the spatial scene described. An English speaker describing the room in Figure 43.4 might say either *You enter the room, and a table is to your left* or *I enter the room, and a table is to my left.* Neither description requires any sort of mental transformation on the part of the addressee because the relevant information is encoded in speech rather than in space. However, when English speakers and addressees discuss a jointly viewed scene, an addressee may need to perform a type of mental transformation if the speaker describes a spatial location from his or her viewpoint. Again, this situation differs for ASL signers because the speaker's signing space maps to the observed physical space and to the addressee's view of that space. Signing space is *shared*, and no mental transformation is required by the addressee. When shared space is used, speakers and addressees can refer to the same locations in signing space, regardless of the position of the addressee. Thus, the interface between language and visual perception (how we talk about what we see) has an added dimension for signers (they also see what they talk about). That is, signers see (rather than hear) spatial descriptions, and there is a schematic isomorphism between aspects of the linguistic signal (the location of the hands in signing space) and aspects of the spatial scene described (the location of objects in the described space). Signers must integrate a visually observed linguistic signal with a visually observed environment or a visual image of the described environment.

43.4 **Speaking vs. signing**

Currently, very little is known about the psycholinguistic mechanisms that translate thoughts into linguistic expression for signers, and it is unclear whether models of speech production can simply be appropriated for sign language. According to most production models, successful speech involves (1) the selection of a word that is semantically and syntactically appropriate, (2) retrieval of the word's phonological properties, (3) rapid syllabification of the word in context, and (4) articulatory preparation of the associated gestures (see Levelt, 1999 for review).

Sign production is likely to involve these components as well, although evidence for syllabification processes is weak (see above). In this section, I discuss aspects of sign production that are unique to the visual-manual modality and review some provocative parallels and contrasts between the nature of speech and sign production.

43.4.1 **Lexical selection and phonological encoding during sign production**

Evidence for the time course of lexical selection and phonological encoding for speech production comes from the picture–word interference task (Schriefers et al., 1990). In this task, subjects are presented with a picture that they must name, and a distractor name is presented either prior to, at the same time, or after the presentation of the picture. Subjects are told to ignore the distractor item, which they find difficult to do. If a semantically related word (e.g. *goat* for a picture of a sheep) is presented at the same time or slightly (100–400 msec) before the presentation of the picture, subjects are much slower to name the picture. That is, semantic inhibition occurs, and speakers are slow to produce the name of the object. In contrast, if a phonologically related word (e.g. *sheet* for a picture of a sheep) is presented at the same time or shortly (100–400 msec) after presentation of the picture, subjects are quicker to name the picture. That is, phonological facilitation occurs, and speakers are faster at producing the object name. Evidence for early phonological facilitation has been mixed (e.g. Starreveld, 2000; Schriefers et al., 1990), but the general pattern of results suggests that activation of semantic information occurs early in lexical retrieval, while phonological encoding occurs simultaneously with or subsequent to lexical selection.

Recently, Corina and Knapp (2006) investigated lexical selection processes for ASL using a picture–sign interference task. Deaf participants were asked to sign the name of a picture, and response time was measured from the time of picture presentation to when the participant's hands moved from a rest position, breaking an infrared beam. Superimposed on the picture was an image of a signer producing a sign that was either phonologically or semantically related to the picture, e.g. MATCH–cigarette (a semantically related sign–picture pair) or ORANGE–ice cream (a phonologically related sign–picture pair—the signs ORANGE and ICE-CREAM are both made with an S handshape at the mouth). Both the distractor sign and the picture were clearly visible because the overlaid image of the signer was semi-transparent (but still quite recognizable). Corina and Knapp (2006) found that, like speakers, signers exhibited semantic interference when they had to name a picture that was preceded by a semantically related sign (-130 msec "SOA"—the time between the onset of the picture and the onset of the superimposed distractor sign). Semantic interference was not found with zero or later SOAs. Thus, as for speech, sign production involves the early retrieval of lexical semantic information, and sign production can be disrupted (slowed) by the prior activation of a semantically related sign.

However, the evidence for phonological facilitation was not as clear-cut. No significant phonological effects were observed at any of the SOAs used in the experiment (-130, 0, +130 msec), and an examination of the number of shared phonological parameters also revealed no significant facilitation effects from distractor signs that shared one, two, or three phonological parameters with the target sign (the picture name). There was no evidence of increased facilitation with increased phonological overlap. However, further post hoc analyses indicated that distractor signs which shared movement and location with the target sign produced significant facilitation effects at all SOAs, while signs which shared handshape and location or handshape and movement did not.

The fact that phonological facilitation was only observed when sign pairs shared movement and location supports phonological models that treat hand configuration as an autonomous element and movement and location as segmental units that could frame sign production (e.g. Sandler, 1986; Corina, 1993). In addition, phonological facilitation based on shared movement and location for sign production is consistent with results from a perceptual similarity judgment study. Hildebrandt and Corina (2002) found that native ASL signers rated non-signs that shared movement and location as highly similar, and essentially ignored handshape similarity. It is possible that movement and location form a syllabic unit that is perceptually salient and that can be primed during sign production.

In sum, the picture–sign interference results of Corina and Knapp (2006) indicate that semantic inhibition occurs only at an early SOA (−130msec), while phonological facilitation (based on shared movement and location) occurs at both early and late SOAs. This pattern of results mirrors what has been found for spoken languages, and suggests that lexical selection precedes phonological encoding for sign, as it does for speech (note, however, that the data do not rule out cascaded activation of phonological representations during lexical selection).

43.4.2 Slips of the hand

In her well-known 1971 paper "The non-anomalous nature of anomalous utterances," Victoria Fromkin demonstrated that slips of the tongue (speech errors) were not random mistakes in speaking, but revealed something about speech planning and the nature of the mental representation of phonology. She argued that speech errors provide evidence for the underlying units of speech production: "despite the semi-continuous nature of the speech signal, there are discrete units at some level of *performance* which can be substituted, omitted, transposed, or added" (Fromkin, 1971: 217; emphasis in the original). Errors of sign production provide similar evidence for the status of the major phonological parameters as discrete units involved in sign production.

Sign error corpora collected for ASL by Newkirk et al. (1980) and for Deutsche Gebärdensprache (DGS; German Sign Language) by Hohenberger et al. (2002) document exchange, preservation, and anticipation errors which involve hand configuration, place of articulation, or movement (see also Leuniger et al., 2004). Figure 43.5 provides an example of a hand configuration anticipation error in DGS. The signer planned to sign SEINE ELTERN ('his parents'), and incorrectly produced SEINE with a Y handshape instead of a B handshape. The Y hand configuration of the sign ELTERN was anticipated and substituted for the intended B hand configuration of SEINE.

The existence of such errors suggests that these phonological parameters constitute units in the production of signed utterances. As noted above, many models of sign language phonology treat hand configuration as a separate autosegment, much as tone is represented for spoken languages. The speech error data from tone languages suggests that tones are independent units that can participate in exchange, anticipation, or perseveration errors (Gandour, 1977)—just as we find for hand configuration in sign language. Unlike tone, however, hand configuration errors are much more common than errors involving other phonological parameters (Newkirk et al., 1980; Hohenberger et al., 2002). Speech errors involving tone do not appear to be more frequent than errors involving consonants or vowels (Wen, 2000). One possible explanation for the frequency of hand configuration errors is that hand configuration is the most complex phonological parameter (Brentari, 1998; Sandler and Lillo-Martin, 2006). The feature geometry required to represent hand configuration requires several hierarchical nodes and more features than are needed to specify the movement or location of a sign. This complexity may render hand configuration more vulnerable to error during sign production.

The fact that movement exchange errors occur (Klima and Bellugi, 1979) argues for a phonological representation in which movement is represented as a separate unit, rather than deriving from articulation constraints, as was proposed by Uyechi (1995). The data also support the analysis of place of articulation as a

Figure 43.5 Illustration of the intended phrase SEINE ELTERN ('his parents') and a slip of the hand in Deutsche Gebärdensprache (German Sign Language) In the slip, the Y hand configuration of ELTERN is anticipated and substituted for the intended B hand configuration of SEINE. From Hohenberger et al. (2002). Reprinted with permission.

high-level unit within the representation of a sign, rather than as a phonetic feature(s) associated with a segment slot (as place of articulation is often represented for consonants). This argument derives from evidence indicating that phonetic features do not operate as units in speech production and rarely participate in speech errors (see Roelofs, 1999). Thus, since place of articulation in sign participates in exchange and other types of errors, it suggests that this parameter is a unit rather than a feature for the purposes of sign production.

Both the ASL and DGS error corpora contained very few sign exchange errors, e.g. LIKE, MAYBE TASTE instead of TASTE, MAYBE LIKE ('Taste it, and maybe you'll like it'; Klima and Bellugi, 1979). Word exchanges are argued to take place at a separate stage of sentence planning (Garrett, 1975; Levelt, 1989). Hohenberger et al. (2002) report that only 1 percent of errors were sign exchanges, compared to 15 percent word exchange errors found in the Frankfurt corpus of spoken German errors. In addition, Hohenberger et al. (2002) did not find evidence for morpheme stranding errors, and no stranding errors were reported by Newkirk et al. (1980). A morpheme stranding error in English would be *That's why they sell the cheaps drink* for the intended *That's why they sell the drinks cheap* (Garrett, 1988). In this example, the *-s* suffix is "stranded" or left behind when the two words exchange. The fact that stranding errors do not occur in sign languages is likely due to the rarity of sign exchange errors and to the fact that morphological processes are non-concatenative rather than affixal. Stranding errors may only occur when morphemes are arranged linearly, rather than articulated simultaneously.

Finally, Hohenberger et al. (2002) found that sign errors were repaired much faster than speech errors. The locus of repairs for speakers is most often after the word (Levelt, 1983), but for DGS signers the error was preferentially caught somewhere within the sign, i.e. before the signer finished articulating the sign containing the error. For DGS, 57 percent of repairs were made within the word; in contrast, only 27 percent of the error repairs of Dutch speakers occurred within the word (from Levelt, 1983). Hohenberger et al. hypothesize that the longer articulation time for signs allows for earlier detection of sign errors compared to speech errors. Early repair of errors also explains the lack of sign exchange errors, because the slip is detected before the second exchanged sign is produced.

In sum, data from slips of the hand provide evidence for phonological encoding during sign production. Signs are not produced as gestural wholes without internal structure. As with speech, phonological elements in sign language can be anticipated, perseverated, and exchanged during production. Sign and speech appear to differ with respect to the speed of error detection and the nature of word and morpheme level errors. The slower rate of sign articulation leads to earlier error repairs for signers and to fewer exchange errors. The linear affixation processes found in most spoken languages lead to morpheme stranding errors that are not observed for sign languages.

43.4.3 **Sign monitoring**

Levelt (1983, 1989) proposes that speakers monitor their internal speech and can intercept errors before they are overtly uttered—he terms this "prearticulatory editing." It is reasonable to hypothesize that signers also have such an internal monitor. Working-memory experiments with ASL provide evidence for a non-overt articulatory-based system of sign rehearsal that is used during short-term memory tasks (Wilson and Emmorey, 1997; 1998). This rehearsal system appears to be equivalent to subvocal rehearsal for speech, and provides evidence for a type of inner signing. Like speakers, signers may be able monitor this internal signing, catching errors before they are actually articulated. In fact, Hohenberger et al. (2002) report that a small proportion of sign errors (8 percent) are detected *prior to* articulation of the intended (target) sign. For example, an incorrect hand configuration can be produced and corrected during the movement transition to the target sign. In addition, signers produce the signed equivalent of *um* (a 5 handshape with wiggling fingers), which indicates they are having production difficulty (Emmorey, 2002). Signers also sometimes stop signing and shake their head, suggesting that they have detected an error prior to articulation. These data support the existence of an internal monitor for sign production. Whether this monitor operates on a phonological or a phonetic (articulatory) representation is currently under investigation in my laboratory.

Sometimes errors or inappropriate words do nonetheless slip through, and speakers also monitor their overt speech and can catch errors by listening to their own voice. Herein lies a potentially interesting difference between sign and speech. Speakers hear their voices, but signers do not look at their hands and cannot see their own faces. Facial expressions convey critical grammatical information for signed languages (e.g. Zeshan, 2004). When speakers are prevented from hearing their own voices (e.g. by wearing headphones emitting loud white noise) or when speakers silently mouth words, they are less likely to detect speech errors compared to when they can hear themselves speak (Lackner and Tuller, 1979; Postma and Noordanus, 1996). These results suggest that speakers rely to some extent on auditory feedback to detect errors in production. Levelt (1989) proposes that the perceptual monitor for overt speech operates via the language user's speech-understanding system. However, this cannot be the entire story for sign language monitoring, because the sign-understanding system operates on the basis of visual input, which is unavailable or distorted for self-signed input. Signers cannot see their own grammatical facial expressions, the view of their own hands falls in the far periphery of vision, and they have a "backward" view of their hands. Thus, it is problematic to simply adopt the same processing system which parses visual input when comprehending another's signing in order also to parse the visual input from one's own signing. It is possible that the nature of the perceptual loop for sign monitoring is quite different from that for speech monitoring. My colleagues and I are currently investigating this hypothesis by examining how differences in visual feedback impact sign language production.

43.5 Summary and conclusions

Psycholinguistic studies of sign language have revealed (and continue to reveal) significant insights into the nature of human language processing. Linguistic and psycholinguistic evidence has established that all human languages have a level of meaningless sublexical structure which must be assembled during language production and which is exploited during language perception. Both signers and speakers exhibit categorical perception effects for distinctive phonological categories in their language, and both combine phonological units prior to articulation, as evidenced by slips of the tongue and hand. Signs, like words, are not holistic gestures without internal structure. Furthermore, the fact that signs are generally more iconic than words does not lead to a lack of separation between the representation of meaning and the representation of form. Signers experience a tip-of-the-fingers state (analogous to the tip-of-the- tongue state) in which semantic information is retrieved, while access to the form of the sign is somehow blocked. The study of signed languages has identified universal properties of language processing and exposed aspects of language processing that are impacted by the biology of the language processing system.

Specifically, biology has an impact of the speed of linguistic articulation: the tongue is quicker than the hands. Biology also affects language perception: the auditory system is particularly adept at processing rapid, temporal sequences, while the visual system can easily process shape and location information presented simultaneously within the visual field. These biological differences exert specific effects on language processing and linguistic structure.

With respect to lexical processing, language modality affects the time course of word recognition and the nature of morphological parsing. Words take proportionally longer to recognize than signs. More of a word must be heard before it can be recognized, probably owing to the phonotactics of speech (many words share an initial cohort), the fact that words tend to contain more segments than signs, and the fact that word onsets may be less informative than sign onsets. In addition, it has been argued that spoken languages avoid non-concatenative morphological processes such as reduplication and circumfixation because such processes have a high processing cost (e.g. the stem is disrupted and difficult to identify). Thus, spoken languages prefer linear affixation. In contrast, the biology of signed languages favors non-concatenative morphology because movement "affixes" can be superimposed onto a sign stem without disrupting lexical recognition. Further, linear affixation results in processing costs for signed languages because affixes increase articulation time, thus increasing demands on working memory. In fact, when the linear affixation processes are transferred to the visual-gestural modality via Manually Coded English, children fail to acquire the linear morphology and often create simultaneous morphological processes that are not observed in their input.

The modality of signed languages affords the use of signing space to convey linguistic distinctions. Signed languages tend to use signing space for co-reference functions and to convey topographic information about spatial relationships. Despite large differences in the form of signed and spoken pronouns, psycholinguistic studies indicate that the same mechanisms underlie coreference processing, namely, activation of pronominal antecedents and suppression of non-antecedents in memory. In contrast, the use of space to convey spatial information leads to some modality-specific effects on language comprehension. For example, ASL signers make use of "shared space" when describing jointly observed scenes, which does not require a particular viewer perspective. In contrast, English speakers must adopt a spatial perspective (*It's on my left* or *It's on your right*). When comprehending descriptions of non-present spatial scenes, viewers of ASL must perform a mental transformation of signing space. English speakers are not faced with such spatial computations. Thus, although co-reference processing appears to be largely unaffected by the spatialization of linguistic form, the processing mechanisims required to comprehend and produce spatial descriptions are clearly affected by the visual-spatial modality.

In conclusion, signed languages provide a unique tool for investigating the psycholinguistic mechanisms which underlie language processing. Their study reveals both universal and biology-specific mechanisms, and clarifies the nature of constraints on spoken language processing. Future studies may reveal how the biology of language affects the nature of output monitoring, the nature of perceptual segmentation, and the interplay between language and other cognitive systems.

Acknowledgements

Preparation of this chapter was supported by grants from the National Institute on Child Health and Human Development (R01 HD13249; R01 HD047736). I thank Virginia Volterra for help with the LIS examples in Figure 43.1.

References

Anderson, S. R. (1992) *A-morphous Morphology*. Cambridge University Press, Cambridge.

Armstrong, D. F., Stokoe, W. C., and Wilcox, S. E. (1995) *Gesture and the Nature of Language*. Cambridge University Press, Cambridge.

Aronoff, M., Meir, I., and Sandler, W. (2005) The paradox of sign language morphology. *Language*, 81: 301–44.

Baddeley, A. (1986) *Working Memory*. Clarendon Press, Oxford.

Baker, S., Idsardi, W., Golinkoff, R. M., and Petitto, L. A. (2005) The perception of handshapes in American Sign Language. *Memory and Cognition*, 33: 887–904.

Battison, R. (1978) *Lexical Borrowing in American Sign Language*. Linstok Press, Silver Spring, MD.

Beale, J. M., and Keil, F. C. (1995) Categorical effects in the perception of faces. *Cognition*, 57: 217–39.

Bellugi, U., and Fischer, S. (1972) A comparison of sign language and spoken language, *Cognition*, 1: 173–200.

Bergman, B. (1982) *Forskning om Teckenspråk* [Research on sign language]. Stockholm University.

Bever, T., and McElree, B. (1988) Empty categories access their antecedents during comprehension. *Linguistic Inquiry*, 19, 35–43.

Brentari, D. (1998) *A Prosodic Model of Sign Language Phonology*. MIT Press, Cambridge, MA.

Brown, A. (1991) A review of the tip-of-the-tongue experience. *Psychological Bulletin*, 109: 204–23.

Clark, L., and Grosjean, F. (1982) Sign recognition processes in American Sign Language: the effect of context. *Language and Speech*, 25: 325–40.

Corbett, A., and Chang, F. (1983) Pronoun disambiguation: accessing potential antecedents. *Memory and Cognition*, 11: 283–94.

Corina, D. P. (1993) To branch or not to branch: underspecifications in ASL handshape contours. In G. Coulter (ed.), *Phonetics and Phonology: Current Issues in ASL Phonology*, pp. 63–96. Academic Press, New York.

Corina, D. P. and Knapp, H. (2006) Lexical retrieval in American Sign Language production. In L. M. Goldstein, D. H. Whalen, and C. T. Best (eds), *Papers in Laboratory Phonology 8: Varieties of Phonological Competence*, pp. 213–39. Mouton de Gruyter, Berlin.

Corina, D. P., and Sandler, W. (1993) On the nature of phonological structure in sign language. *Phonology*, 10: 165–207.

Cutler, A., Hawkins, J., and Gilligan, G. (1985) The suffixing preference: a processing explanation. *Linguistics, 23*: 723–58.

de Gelder, B., Teunisse, J-P., and Benson, P. J. (1997) Categorical perception of facial expressions: categories and their internal structure. *Cognition and Emotion*, 11: 1–22.

Dell, G. S., Schwartz, M. F., Martin, N., Saffran, E. M., and Gagnon, D. A. (1997) Lexical access in aphasic and nonaphasic speakers. *Psychological Review*, 104: 801–38.

Emmorey, K. (1997) Non-antecedent suppression in American Sign Language. *Language and Cognitive Processes*, 12: 103–12.

Emmorey, K. (2002) *Language, Cognition, and the Brain: Insights from Sign Language Research*. Erlbaum, Mahwah, NJ.

Emmorey, K., and Corina, D. (1990) Lexical recognition in sign language: effects of phonetic structure and morphology. *Perceptual and Motor Skills*, 71: 1227–52.

Emmorey, K., Corina, D., and Bellugi, U. (1995) Differential processing of topographic and referential functions of space. In K. Emmorey and J. Reilly (eds), *Language, Gesture, and Space*, pp. 43–62. Erlbaum, Hillsdale, NJ.

Emmorey, K., and Falgier, B. (2004) Conceptual locations and pronominal reference in American Sign Language. *Journal of Psycholinguistic Research*, 33: 321–31.

Emmorey, K., and Herzig, M. (2003) Categorical versus gradient properties of classifier constructions in ASL. In K. Emmorey (ed) *Perspectives on Classifier Constructions in Signed Languages*, pp. 222–46. Erlbaum, Mahwah, NJ.

Emmorey, K., Klima, E. S., and Hickok, G. (1998) Mental rotation within linguistic and nonlinguistic domains in users of American Sign Language. *Cognition*, 68: 221–46.

Emmorey, K. and Lillo-Martin, D. (1995) Processing spatial anaphora: referent reactivation with overt and null pronouns in American Sign Language. *Language and Cognitive Processes*, 10: 631–64.

Emmorey, K., McCullough, S., and Brentari, D. (2003) Categorical perception in American Sign Language. *Language and Cognitive Processes*, 18: 21–45.

Emmorey, K., Norman, F., and O'Grady, L. (1991) The activation of spatial antecedents from overt pronouns in American Sign Language. *Language and Cognitive Processes*, 6: 207–28.

Emmorey, K., and Tversky, B. (2002) Spatial perspective choice in ASL. *Sign Language and Linguistics*, 5: 3–25.

Engberg-Pedersen, E. (1993) *Space in Danish Sign Language: The Semantics and Morphosyntax of the Use of Space in a Visual Language.* Signum, Hamburg.

Fodor, J. (1989) Empty categories in sentence processing. *Language and Cognitive Processes*, 4: 155–209.

Fromkin, V. A. (1971) The non-anomalous nature of anomalous utterances. *Language*, 47: 27–52.

Fry, D. B., Abramson, A. S., Eimas, P. D., and Liberman, A. M. (1962) The identification and discrimination of synthetic vowels. *Language and Speech*, 5: 171–89.

Gandour, J. (1977) Counterfeit tones in the speech of southern Thai bidialectals. *Lingua*, 41: 125–43.

Garrett, M. (1975) The analysis of sentence production. In G. Bower (ed.), *Psychology of Learning and Motivation*, vol. 9, pp. 133–77. Academic Press, New York.

Garrett, M. (1988) Processes in language production. In F. J. Newmeyer (ed.), *Linguistics: The Cambridge Survey*, vol. 3: *Language: Psychological and Biological Aspects*, pp. 69–96. Cambridge University Press, Cambridge.

Gernsbacher, M. (1989) Mechanisms that improve referential access. *Cognition*, 32: 99–156.

Goldinger, S. D., Luce, P. A., and Pisoni, D. B. (1989) Priming lexical neighbors of spoken words: effects of competition and inhibition. *Journal of Memory and Language*, 28: 501–18.

Grosjean, F. (1980) Spoken word recognition processes and the gating paradigm. *Perception and Psychophysics*, 28: 267–83.

Grosjean, F. (1981) Sign and word recognition: a first comparison. *Sign Language Studies*, 32: 195–219.

Gustason, G., Pfetzing, D., and Zawolkow, E. (1980) *Signing Exact English*. Modern Signs Press, Los Alamitos, CA.

Hall, C. J. (1992) *Morphology and Mind: A Unified Approach to Explanation in Linguistics*. Routledge, London.

Hildebrandt, U., and Corina D. (2002) Phonological similarity in American Sign Language. *Language and Cognitive Processes*, 17: 593–612.

Hoek, K. van (1992) Conceptual spaces and pronominal reference in American Sign Language. *Nordic Journal of Linguistics*, 15: 183–99.

Hohenberger, A., Happ, D., and Leuniger, H. (2002) Modality-dependent aspects of sign language production: evidence from slips of the hands and their repairs in German Sign Language. In R. P. Meier, K. Cormier, and D. Quinto-Pozos (eds) *Modality and Structure in Signed and Spoken Languages*, pp. 112–42, Cambridge University Press, Cambridge.

Klima, E., and Bellugi, U. (1979) *The Signs of Language*. Harvard University Press, Cambridge, MA.

Kyle, J., and Woll, B. (1985) *Sign Language: The Study of Deaf People and Their Language*. Cambridge University Press, Cambridge.

Lackner, J. R., and Tuller, B. H. (1979) Role of efference monitoring in the detection of self-produced speech errors. In W. E. Cooper and E. C. T. Walker (eds), *Sentence Processing: Psycholinguistic Studies Presented to Merrill Garrett*, pp. 281–94. Erlbaum, Hillsdale, NJ.

Lane, H., Boyes-Braem, P., and Bellugi, U. (1976) Preliminaries to a distinctive feature analysis of American Sign Language. *Cognitive Psychology*, 8: 263–89.

Leuniger, H., Hohenberger, A., Waleschkowski, E., Menges, E., and Happ, D. (2004) The impact of modality on language production: evidence from slips of the tongue and hand. In T. Pechmann and C. Habel (eds), *Multidisciplinary Approaches to Language Production*, pp. 219–77. Mouton de Gruyter, Berlin.

Levelt, W. J. M. (1983) Monitoring and self-repair in speech. *Cognition*, 14: 41–104.

Levelt, W. J. M. (1989) *Speaking: From Intention to Articulation*. MIT Press, Cambridge, MA.

Levelt, W. J. M. (1999) Models of word production. *Trends in Cognitive Sciences*, 3: 223–32.

Levelt, W. J. M., Roelofs, A., and Meyer, A. S. (1999) A theory of lexical access in speech production. *Behavioral and Brain Sciences*, 22: 1–75.

Liberman, A. M., Harris, K. S., Hoffman, H. S., and Griffith, B. C. (1957) The discrimination of speech sounds within and across phoneme boundaries. *Journal of Experimental Psychology*, 54: 358–68.

MacNeilage, P. (1998) The frame/content theory of evolution of speech production. *Behavioral and Brain Sciences*, 21: 499–546.

Mainwaring, S., Tversky, B., and Schiano, D. (1996) Perspective choice in spatial descriptions. IRC Technical Report, 1996–06. Interval Research Corporation, Palo Alto, CA.

Marslen-Wilson, W. (1987) Functional parallelism in spoken word recognition. *Cognition*, 25: 71–102.

McClelland, J. L., and Elman, J. (1986) The TRACE model of speech perception. *Cognitive Psychology*, 18: 1–86.

Meier, R. P. (2000) Shared motoric factors in the acquisition of sign and speech. In K. Emmorey and H. Lane (eds), *The Signs of Language Revisited: An Anthology to Honor Ursula Bellugi and Edward Klima*, pp. 333–57, Erlbaum, Mahwah, NJ.

Meier, R. P. (2002) Why different, why the same? Explaining effects and non-effects of modality upon linguistic structure in sign and speech. In R. P. Meier, K. Cormier, and D. Quinto-Pozos (eds), *Modality and Structure in Signed and Spoken Languages*, pp. 1–26, Cambridge University Press, Cambridge.

Newkirk, D., Klima, E., Pedersen, C. C., and Bellugi, U. (1980) Linguistic evidence from slips of the hand. In V. Fromkin (ed.), *Errors in Linguistic Performance: Slips of the Tongue, Ear, Pen, and Hand*, pp. 165–98. Academic Press, New York.

Poizner, H., and Lane, H. (1978) Discrimination of location in American Sign Language. In P. Siple (ed.), *Understanding Language through Sign Language Research*, pp. 271–87. Academic Press, New York.

Postma, A., and Noordanus, C. (1996) Production and detection of speech errors in silent, mouthed, noise-masked, and normal auditory feedback speech. *Language and Speech*, 39: 375–92.

Roelofs, A. (1999) Phonological segments and features as planning units in speech production. *Language and Cognitive Processes*, 14: 173–200.

Sandler, W. (1986) The spreading hand autosegment of American Sign Language. *Sign Language Studies*, 50: 1–28.

Sandler, W., and Lillo-Martin, D. (2006) *Sign Language and Linguistic Universals*. Cambridge University Press, Cambridge.

Schober, M. F. (1993) Spatial perspective-taking in conversation. *Cognition*, 47: 1–24.

Schriefers, H., Meyer, A., and Levelt, W. J. M. (1990) Exploring the time course of lexical access in speech production: picture-word interference studies. *Journal of Memory and Language*, 29: 86–102.

Schwartz, B.L. (1999) Sparkling at the end of the tongue: the etiology of tip-of-the-tongue phenomenology. *Psychonomic Bulletin and Review*, 6: 379–93.

Stack, K. M. (1999) Innovation by a child acquiring Signing Exact English II. Doctoral dissertation, University of California at Los Angeles.

Starreveld, 2000) On the interpretation of onsets of auditory context effects in word production. *Journal of Memory and Language*, 42: 497–525.

Stokoe, W. (1960) Sign language structure: an outline of the visual communication systems of the American Deaf. *Studies in Linguistics, Occasional Papers 8*, available from Linstok Press, Silver Spring, MD.

Stokoe, W. (1991) Semantic phonology. *Sign Language Studies*, 71: 107–14.

Supalla, S. (1991) Manually coded English: the modality question in signed language development. In P. Siple and S. D. Fischer (eds), *Theoretical Issues in Sign Language Research*, pp. 85–109, University of Chicago Press, Chicago.

Supalla, T. (1982) Structure and acquisition of verbs of motion and location in American Sign Language. Ph.D. dissertation, University of California, San Diego.

Sutton-Spence, R., and Woll, B.(1999) *The Linguistics of British Sign Language: An Introduction*. Cambridge University Press, Cambridge.

Talmy, L. (2000) *Toward a Cognitive Semantics*, vol. 1: *Concept Structuring Systems*. MIT Press, Cambridge, MA.

Thompson, R., Emmorey, K., and Gollan, T. (2005) Tip-of-the-fingers experiences by ASL signers: insights into the organization of a sign-based lexicon. *Psychological Science*, 16: 856–60.

Uyechi, L. (1995) *The Geometry of Visual Phonology*. CSLI Publications, Stanford, CA.

Wen, I.P. (2000) Mandarin phonology: evidence from speech errors. Doctoral dissertation, State University of New York, Buffalo.

Wilbur, R. B. (1987) *American Sign Language: Linguistic and Applied Dimensions*, 2nd edn. College Hill, Boston, MA.

Wilbur, R. B. (1993) Syllables and segments: hold the movements and move the holds! In G. Coulter (ed.), *Phonetics and Phonology: Current Issues in ASL Phonology*, pp. 135–68. Academic Press, San Diego, CA.

Wilson, M., and Emmorey, K. (1997) A visual-spatial "phonological loop" in working memory: evidence from American Sign Language. *Memory and Cognition*, 25: 313–20.

Wilson, M., and Emmorey, K. (1998) A "word length effect" for sign language: further evidence on the role of language in structuring working memory. *Memory and Cognition*, 26(3), 584–90.

Zeshan, U. (2004) Head, hand, and face: negative constructions in sign languages. *Linguistic Typology*, 8: 1–57.

CHAPTER 44

Spoken language processing by machine

Roger K. Moore

44.1 Introduction

The past twenty-five years have witnessed a steady improvement in the capabilities of spoken language technology, first in the research laboratory and more recently in the commercial marketplace. Progress has reached a point where Automatic Speech Recognition (ASR) software for dictating documents onto your PC is available as an inexpensive consumer product in most computer stores, Text-to-Speech (TTS) synthesis can be heard in public places giving automated voice announcements, and Interactive Voice Response is becoming a familiar option for people paying bills or booking cinema tickets over the telephone (Holmes and Holmes, 2002).

These developments have not come about as a result of any deep insights into the way in which human beings process and generate spoken language, but largely as a consequence of the introduction of "data-driven" (machine learning) approaches to building spoken language systems coupled with the relentless increase in available computing power. Indeed, the view has been expressed that so-called knowledge about human spoken language behavior was positively harmful to progress in spoken language processing by machine (Jelinek, 1985). So, rather than being a practical instantiation of the latest theories of human spoken language behavior, a contemporary Spoken Language System captures the immense variability observed in natural spoken language by exposure to very large corpora of speech and text material. Powerful mathematical techniques are then used to estimate the parameters of the underlying models, and to search the resulting data structures for key processes such as automatic speech recognition and synthesis.

This chapter addresses these issues by presenting the main computational approaches employed in contemporary spoken language systems, and this forms the bulk of the material here. Future prospects are discussed at the end of the chapter in the context of the obvious shortcomings of current technology, and the potential for achieving a unified approach to human and machine spoken language processing is addressed briefly.

44.1.1 Spoken language systems

The structure of a typical spoken language system is illustrated in Figure 44.1. The lexical content of an incoming utterance is recognized by the ASR engine and transcribed into some form of textual representation. Due to the high risk of recognition errors (word insertions, deletions, and substitutions), the output of the ASR is not normally a single text string, but a data structure containing a number of alternative hypotheses as to what might have been said (e.g. a lattice or a rank-ordered "n-best" list) together with associated "confidence measures." The "language interpreter" sorts these alternatives (a process known as "re-scoring") and performs some form of syntactic and semantic analysis in order to derive concept fragments that are relevant to the given application. For example in a travel planning scenario, a user might say *I want to go to New York*, in which case the output of the language interpreter might consist of a formal expression such as <destination_place = "New York">. In many instances the information

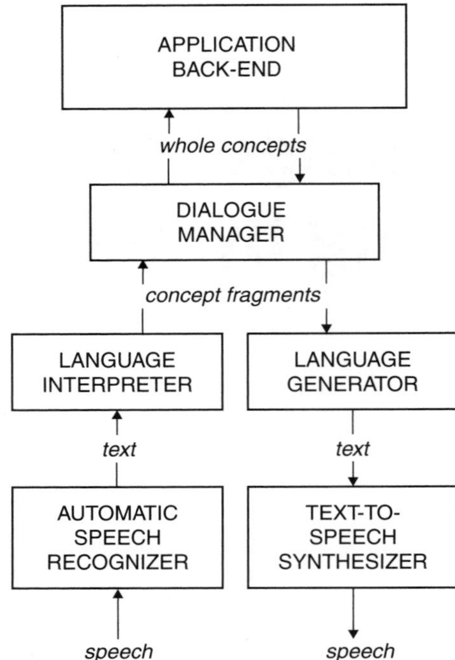

Figure 44.1 Structure of a typical spoken language system.

provided in the user's utterance may be insufficient to complete a transaction, in which case the "dialogue manager" component might generate a clarification query to the user through the "language generator" which is then spoken by the TTS engine—for example, *When would you like to travel?* Through such conversational interaction with the user, the dialogue manager accumulates information until it is able to complete the transaction through access to the "application back-end" which, in this example, would consist of a database of travel information.

Different applications demand alternative intermediate representations and different system strategies. For example, a "command and control" type spoken language system would be concerned with actions and responses, and would usually require fast processing and thus the involvement of minimal dialogue, thereby favoring speed over recognition accuracy. An example of such an application would be the hands-free operation of various functions in a moving vehicle. On the other hand, an "information" type of spoken language system (such as travel planning) would be concerned with the storage and retrieval of facts and data. Such a system would be expected to remember users' statements accurately, to provide reliable answers to users' questions, and to enter into a negotiation-style dialogue that would enable the system to iterate to a point where it has satisfied the requirements of the user. A third and more unusual type of spoken language system is in "communications" where speech can be converted into a purely data representation for transmission and resynthesis. This type of spoken language system has use in areas ranging from military applications of low data-rate voice coding to more exotic applications such as speech-to-speech language translation.

Many of the potential applications of spoken language systems are quite compelling—hence the preponderance of talking and listening machines in science fiction. Indeed, it is often said that *speech is the "natural" way to interact with your computer*. However, whilst it may be true that speech is a more intuitive and hands-free way of accessing information, controlling things, and communicating, it can hardly be said to be natural to talk to a machine. This means that application designers (and researchers) have to be aware that users behavior in voice-based applications may be quite unusual in comparison with human–human dialogue, and that there may be viable alternatives to speech-based interaction. For example, some users may find it faster to generate documents using two-fingered typing than speaking to an error-prone ASR system. As a consequence, there is considerable interest in "multi-modal dialogue" (Taylor et al. 1989; Gibbon et al., 2000) in which speech complements other input/output modalities such as pointing, gesture, clicking, and typing. In such applications, the challenge is to automate the coordination and integration of the speech-based channels with the other modes, but the potential is to offer powerful capabilities such as allowing the user to be able to say things like *Put that there*.

Another issue is that whilst spoken language processing has made great strides, it is not really usable "straight out of the box." Systems need to be optimized for each application, each different computer platform, different environments, different users and different languages—and such reconfiguration currently involves significant manual effort. Whilst there is considerable interest in creating a technology for spoken language systems that is independent of such variables, the state of the art remains quite sensitive, and much current research is directed towards techniques for adapting to new situations (Junqua and Wellekens, 2004).

In order to give a high-level impression of the relative difficulties associated with the different components of a spoken language system, it has been said that if speech synthesis is like squeezing toothpaste out of its tube, then speech recognition is like trying to get it back in again. Similarly, it has been said that interacting with a contemporary spoken language dialogue system is like trying to play pinball with most of the table obscured.

44.2 Automatic Speech Recognition (ASR)

The main components of a contemporary ASR system are illustrated in Figure 44.2. This structure may at first seem a little surprising to someone working on "human speech recognition" (HSR), in that the architecture does not explicitly reflect a hierarchical organization of processes based on a linear progression of transformations from acoustic signal through sub-lexical to lexical representations. Indeed, it is the failure of such explicit structures to recognize real speech in the 1970s that led to the development of this much more successful arrangement (Klatt, 1977).

The basic principle underlying the architecture shown in Figure 44.2 is that all of the knowledge about how speech is produced is expressed *probabilistically* in an "integrated network" of statistical models representing all possible utterances (within the constraints of the systems lexicon and syntax) (Jelinek *at al.*, 1982; Rabiner and Juang, 1993). The models are usually expressed as "stochastic finite-state automata" in a formalism known as "hidden Markov modeling" (HMM). The process of "recognition" is defined (mathematically) as a search through the network of HMM states in order to find the *most probable* explanation of the incoming signal (Jelinek 1998). The search process is conducted using an efficient algorithm known as "dynamic programming" (or "Viterbi" search), which can be guaranteed to find the best explanation (Bellman 1957; Viterbi 1967). The use of probability and statistics has been found to be the only viable method for generalizing from seen to unseen data (Jelinek 1996), and, in direct contrast to the knowledge-based approaches of the 1970s, the stochastic approach has been termed "ignorance modeling" (Makhoul and Schwartz, 1984).

The architecture shown in Figure 44.2 is essentially divided into two sections: the upper part represents the steps used to compile knowledge about speech into the integrated network of HMM states, and the lower (much simpler) part represents the recognition process itself. The speech knowledge is derived from substantial corpora of training data (which could consist of hundreds or even thousands of hours of recorded speech material together with millions of words of text) overlaid on the a-priori structure implicit in the statistical models. Powerful mathematical techniques are used to re-estimate the parameters of the models given the training data (Baum, 1972).

Therefore, in order to configure a contemporary ASR system for a given application, the first step is to obtain the largest possible corpora of speech and text data that are specific to that application. From the text corpus it is possible to define the core vocabulary/lexicon and thence to train the "language model." The speech corpus is used to train the "acoustic model" and the "noise model." A pronouncing dictionary is also required.

44.2.1 Acoustic modeling

The purpose of the "acoustic model" is to be able to assign a probability to *any possible sound sequence*, and it is typically constructed from a

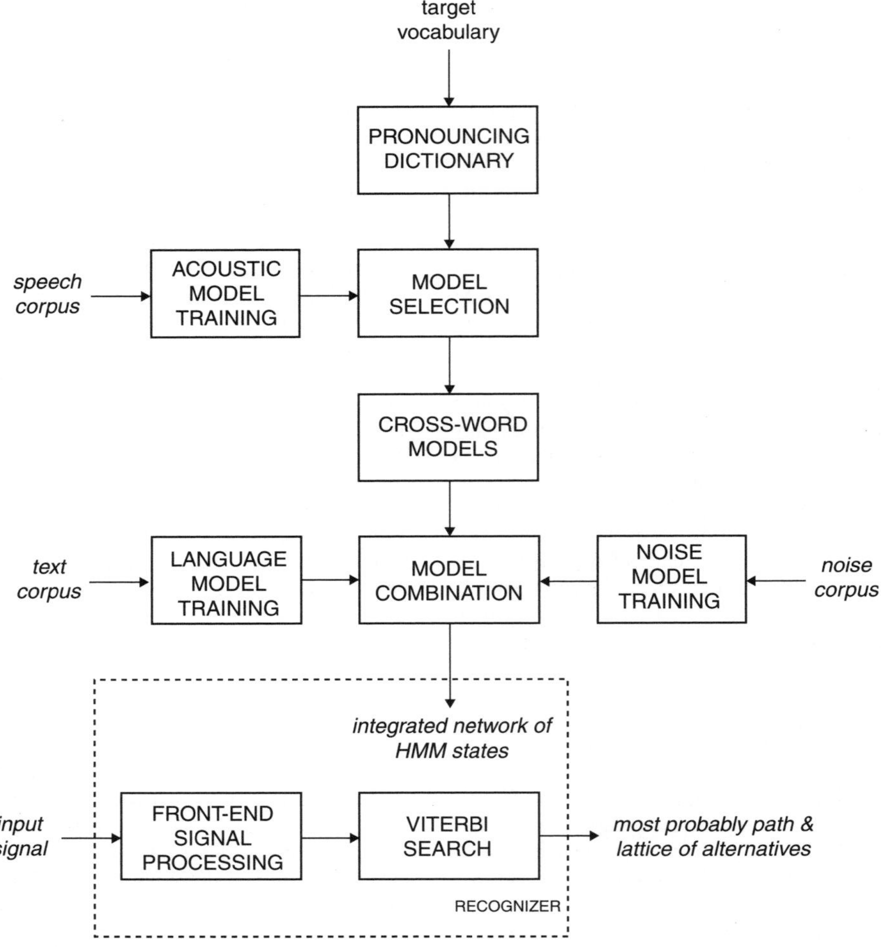

Figure 44.2 Block diagram of a contemporary automatic speech recognition (ASR) system.

set of context-dependent sub-word HMMs, where each HMM is a stochastic finite-state automaton whose parameters represent the acoustic realization of a given phone in a particular preceding and following context. If the context is limited to one phone either side—a common arrangement—then such sub-word HMMs are referred to as "triphones." An example of a triphone might be an acoustic model for the phone /t/ in the context of a preceding /s/ and a following /r/, thereby capturing the context-sensitive properties of the phone /t/ in the consonant cluster /str/. Sub-word HMMs are simple automata consisting of a small number of states—often three—with transitions between them (see Figure 44.3). Each state contains a probability density function (composed of a mixture of Gaussian distributions) that models the acoustic properties of the particular sound represented by the state. The transitions represent the probability of moving from one state to another, and they capture the time evolution of the phone.

As an aside, the reader may be interested to note that it is the probabilistic nature of the representations in each state that give rise to the "hidden" behavior in the HMM formalism. If each state were to be uniquely associated with a single acoustic pattern (rather than a distribution of sounds), then the behavior would not be hidden and the model would be a "Markov model." The power of the HMM paradigm in recognition is precisely that the underlying models are not uniquely associated with particular

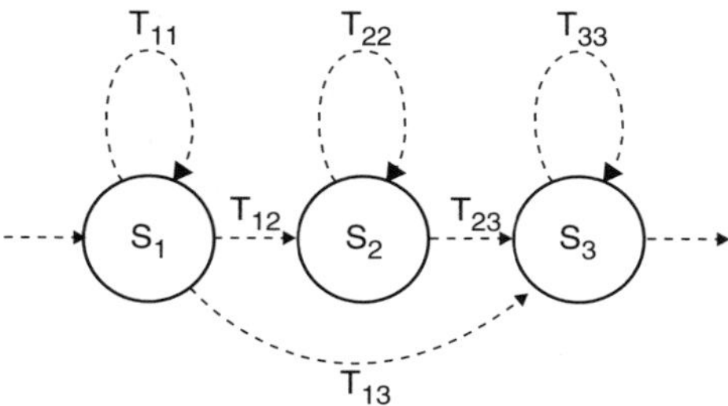

Figure 44.3 Structure of a three-state hidden Markov model (HMM).

instances of a sound, but are able to generalize (interpolate and extrapolate) over all possible sound patterns.

It is also important not to confuse the three states in a typical sub-word HMM with the three phones implicated in a triphone; the three states in a triphone HMM represent the time-varying characteristics of a single phone as influenced by the context of the immediately adjacent phones.

In order to perform word recognition, word-level HMMs are effectively constructed for each lexical entry by selecting the appropriate sub-word HMMs from the available set and concatenating them together to form the word (see Figure 44.4). However, due to the fact that the amount of available training data is finite, it may not always be possible to find a sub-word model with a matching context. In such a case it is usual to "back off" to a shorter context version, and ultimately to a "context-independent phone" (monophone)—a three-state HMM that has been trained on *all* examples of a particular phone, not just tokens in a given context. This entire process allows models to be constructed for target application words that were never spoken in the training data. Hence the application vocabulary can be considerably larger than the training vocabulary—a significant step forward from earlier word-based ASR schemes popular in the 1960s and 1970s in which the vocabularies were essentially fixed.

The acoustic model is either trained on speech from a known user, in which case it is termed "speaker-dependent," or it is trained on speech from a wide variety of speakers, in which case it is termed "speaker-independent." The latter scheme inevitably has lower recognition accuracy due to the inherent differences between speakers, but it is important for applications in which the users are unknown (such as telephone enquiry systems). Speaker-dependent systems

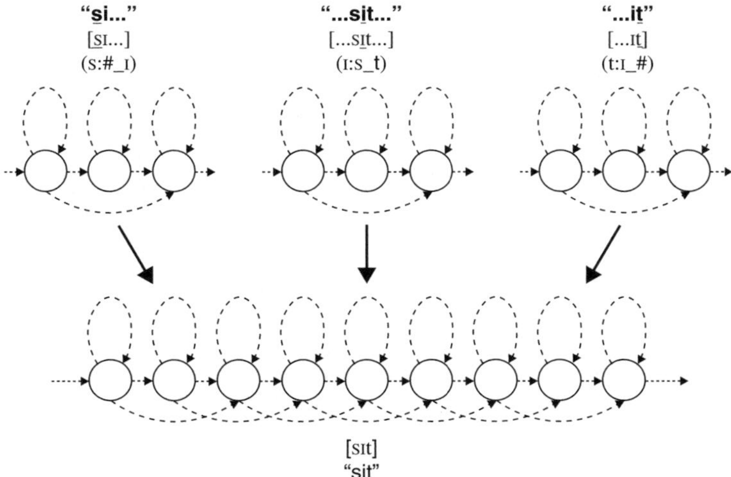

Figure 44.4 A whole-word HMM constructed from sub-word HMMs.

give the best performance, and this is what is used for desktop dictation; the only downside is that each user has to commit time to providing sufficient training data.

Many contemporary systems are "speaker-adaptive"—i.e. they are initially configured to be speaker-independent, but speech which occurs during use is treated as extra training data and the acoustic models are adapted towards the vocal characteristics of the specific user. Popular acoustic model adaptation techniques are "maximum likelihood linear regression" (Leggetter and Woodland, 1994), "vocal tract length normalization" (Lee and Rose, 1996), and "Eigen-voices" (Kuhn et al., 2000). All of these techniques tackle the basic issue of how to change the multitude of parameters in a system using only a small number of new observations by effectively deriving a low-dimensional sub-space that links all the different parameters together. In this way, the values of all of the parameters may be adapted to represent the new data in a coordinated manner. Maximum likelihood linear regression has proved to be particularly successful, but vocal tract length normalization is compelling because of its direct link with hypothesized gross physical properties of a user's vocal apparatus.

44.2.2 Language modeling

The purpose of the "language model" is to be able to assign a probability to *any possible word sequence*, and it may either be expressed as a probabilistic finite-state syntax (e.g. as a stochastic regular or context-free grammar) or, for more flexible applications, as a set of statistical "*n*-grams." In the latter case, a typical value for *n* may be three, in which case the language model would be referred to as a "trigram" language model. The language model can also be thought of as a mechanism for predicting the next word in a sequence. For example, in a sentence such as *The cat sat on the* ..., a trigram language model would estimate the probabilities of all possible next words based on the preceding two word fragment *on the*.

Although trigrams are the most common form of language model, it is clear from the above example that important longer-term dependencies are inevitably ignored by such an approach. Much research has thus been directed to higher-order *n*-grams but, even for trigrams, a finite corpus is unlikely to contain all the combinations that are permissible in language. Hence it is usual to estimate the probability of unobserved items by "backing off" to lower-order *n*-grams (and ultimately to "unigram" statistics).

Ideally, language models are trained on a text corpus that is representative of the target application, in which case the resulting ASR would be "task-dependent." Language models trained on more general material give rise to "task-independent" ASR, but just like speaker-independent systems, task-independent systems can perform poorly. Since general text corpora are easier to find than task-specific corpora, there has been significant amount of research into language model adaptation (Bellegarda, 2004). Combining the information from different corpora is posed as a statistical problem, and solutions include methods for "model interpolation" (i.e. merging the two sources of information in a balanced way) and more powerful approaches for "constraint specification" (based on the matching of extracted features). Other approaches use topic information, semantic knowledge, or syntactic structure to extract relevant data from the adaptation corpus.

Most of these methods are highly mathematical in nature; but of particular interest are techniques such as "dynamic cache," in which dynamic shifts in word usage are captured by means of a short-term memory that overrides the probabilities being generated by the long-term background model, and "trigger models," in which dependencies which have a longer range than the base n-gram are detected and exploited.

44.2.3 Noise modeling

Real-world environments contain many different sound sources, not just the speaker of interest. The speech to be recognized may have to compete with engine noise (in a vehicle), air conditioning (in an office), or other talkers (in a public place). Also, the incoming speech may have been altered by reverberation (due to room acoustics) or distorted by being passed over a communications channel (such as a mobile telephone).

A practical ASR system thus has to accommodate these effects, and for continuous sounds this is achieved using a noise model containing a running estimate of the background. Techniques such as "spectral subtraction" (Boll, 1979) and "cepstral mean normalization" (Rosenberg et al., 1994) are then used during recognition to remove the estimated background energy from each input speech frame.

For non-continuous sounds, it is usual to derive an explicit inventory of HMM "noise models" covering likely non-speech sounds (including lip smacks and other user-generated noises). These models can then be used as extra (non-speech) entries in the lexicon, or combined with the speech models using techniques such as "HMM decomposition" (Varga and Moore, 1990) or "parallel model combination" (Gales and Young, 1995). These algorithms allow for speech and structured noise to occur at the same time, and HMM decomposition can even be used to recognize multiple voices simultaneously (Varga and Moore, 1991).

More recent techniques have been explicitly inspired by the human auditory system. For example, research into "computational auditory scene analysis" (Brown, 2003) has lead to the development of "missing data theory" (Cooke et al., 2001) which is able to capture information about known and unknown sound sources and distortions within a probabilistic framework.

44.2.4 Pronunciation modeling

The purpose of the pronunciation model is to minimize the recognition errors which occur due to pronunciation variation within or between individual talkers. Information about idiolect and accent variation can be encoded in a lexicon containing both the orthographic and phonetic transcriptions for all the words in the ASR's vocabulary. Information about variant pronunciations can be obtained using either "knowledge-based" approaches (i.e. pronunciation dictionaries) or "data-driven" approaches, using either manual or automatic transcriptions to generate lists of variants (Wester and Fosler-Lussier, 2000). The use of data driven approaches means that information on variation can be incorporated into the system on the basis of actual pronunciations occurring in the training data.

44.2.5 Training an ASR system

The process of "training" an ASR system is essentially one of estimating the values of all of the parameters in the language model, acoustic model, noise model, and pronunciation model. In a contemporary system this process usually involves substantial quantities of speech and text data coupled with powerful machine learning algorithms (Everman et al., 2005). A high volume of data is normally required (hundreds of hours of speech, and millions of words of text) owing to the large number of parameters that have to be estimated. For example, in a state-of-the-art "large-vocabulary continuous speech recognition" system, the acoustic model may contain 300,000 Gaussian probability density functions.

Training a language model is relatively straightforward, since it essentially involves counting the frequencies of the relevant n-grams. Training an acoustic model is considerably more complicated because it involves a "forced alignment" of the acoustic training data with the HMMs for the corresponding transcription. This process itself uses ASR-style search (although constrained by the "correct" answer), and several iterations are required in order to allow the parameters to converge to their final values. The full training algorithm is known as "Baum–Welch" re-estimation (Baum, 1972), but many systems use "Viterbi training," which, although not strictly correct from a mathematical perspective, can give much faster training times.

44.2.6 Recognition

The process of "recognition" involves some form of front-end signal processing followed by the dynamic programming/Viterbi search.

The incoming speech waveform is usually transformed into a cepstral representation derived on a "Mel" frequency scale. The reason for doing this is to derive an independent set of features that fit with the assumptions built in to the hidden Markov models. The resulting data vectors, which may be framed every 10–30 msec, are referred to as "mel-frequency cepstral coefficients." Clearly this has to be the same data representation that is used in the training of the acoustic models.

The Viterbi search involves finding the route through the integrated network of HMM states which corresponds most closely to the sequence of incoming speech vectors (where "closeness" is measured using probability). The resulting most-probable path reveals the sequence of words that are most likely to have been spoken—even for continuous speech—and these are output by the recognizer (together with an n-best list or lattice of alternatives). If noise models are involved, then the path would also reveal the most likely non-speech events as they occur in sequence with (or simultaneous with) the target speech (Barker et al., 2005). Hence, it can be seen that the use of a "silence" model allows an ASR system to make intelligent speech/non-speech decisions based on the global context rather than using a simple local decision; i.e. it can be part of the recognition process, rather than a precursor to it. This point clearly illustrates the power and robustness of implementing recognition as an integrated search over all constraints rather than as a linear sequence of processing stages, each of which may give rise to irrecoverable errors. This process is known as "delayed decision-making."

Another very interesting property of sequential search is that it can be configured to operate *continuously*—i.e. an ASR can be inputting acoustic signal data and outputting the recognition results at the same time and without stopping. This is feasible because in a time-synchronous search, the algorithm maintains a list of alternative explanations of the input up to the current time (along with their associated probabilities). As time progresses, these hypotheses are updated and the top-ranking explanation at any given time instant may be different from that at another time instant. However, there will be an instant some time in the past where all hypotheses agree about the explanation up to that point—i.e. all the competing paths through the integrated network converge at some point in the past and no further input can change that situation. This means that the explanation of the input signal up to that point may be output. The algorithm for doing this is known as "partial traceback" (Spohrer et al., 1980), and it can be seen in operation in most desktop dictation systems.

44.2.7 Automatic lip-reading

Speech is of course not purely an acoustic signal. Human listeners are able to gain a significant advantage if they can see a speaker's lips (especially in noisy environments) (Brooke and Summerfield, 1983; Summerfield et al., 1989), and the same is true for ASR. As a consequence, a significant amount of research has been addressed towards audiovisual integration for improving the robustness of ASR since the 1980s (Petajen et al.,1988; Rubin and Vatikiotis-Bateson, 1998; Schwartz et al., 2004). As with the human listener, it has been shown that it is possible to improve the noise tolerance of both small and large vocabulary ASR by about 10 dB by combining the acoustic and the visual information (Potamianos et al., 2003).

44.3 Text-to-Speech Synthesis (TTS)

The main components of a TTS system are illustrated in Figure 44.5. Unlike ASR, a typical TTS architecture accords much more closely with traditional linguistically motivated accounts of spoken language, and reflects a more or less linear sequence of transformations from input text to output speech. However like ASR, TTS has also benefited from the introduction of the "data-driven paradigm" in which corpora of annotated speech recordings are used to estimate the parameters of the underpinning models (Dutoit, 1997). Also, some of the most recent systems even uses ASR-style dynamic programming/Viterbi search in order to optimize the output signal.

44.3.1 Markup handling

The first stage in a practical TTS system usually involves analyzing the input text and unpacking the linguistic content from the paralinguistic and non-linguistic information, and expressing the result using some form of hypertext markup language. For example, in a typical application such as reading out e-mail messages, the input to a TTS system would consist of a mixture of header information (most of which would not need to be spoken), core message content, and other relevant objects such as emoticons ("smileys"). A pre-processing stage would thus parse such data into its relevant components, mark them up using hypertext, and then output the resulting data structure for further processing.

44.3.2 Text normalization

Arbitrary text which is intended to be read aloud contains many features that require careful interpretation before the precise spoken form can be derived. As well as straightforward features such as case and punctuation, texts also contain more complex phenomena such as abbreviations and acronyms. An abbreviation such as *Mr* is relatively easy to handle, but others may be more difficult. For example, *Dr* could represent *Doctor* or *Drive*, and thus the context needs to be analyzed in order to resolve the ambiguity. Similarly, an acronym such as *IBM* would need to be decomposed so that it can be spelt out as the three separate words *I*, *B*, *M*, whereas NATO has to be left unaltered so that it can be pronounced as a single word. All such issues are resolved by the process known as "text normalization," and the necessary procedures are usually implemented as a set of manually derived transformation rules.

44.3.3 Prosodic assignment

The third stage in a typical TTS system is concerned with the assignment of stress and intonation patterns, and this is realized through

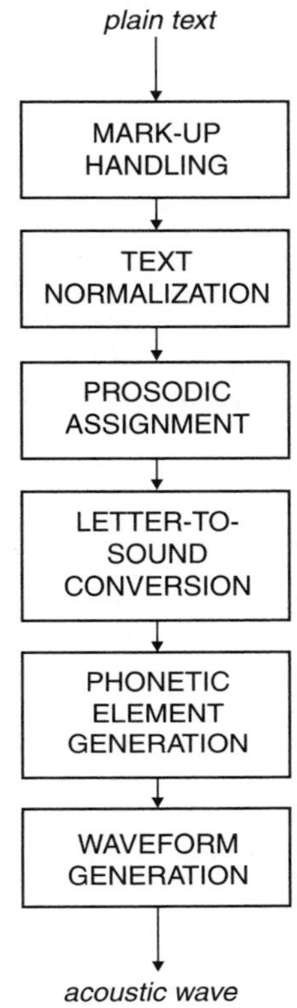

Figure 44.5 Block diagram of a contemporary text-to-speech (TTS) system.

the addition of further hypertext markup. For intonation, following some form of linguistic analysis, markers may be inserted into the text using an agreed standard for labelling prosody such as ToBI (Silverman et al., 1992). Also, phrase boundaries are marked to enable the insertion of appropriate pauses into the subsequent output. In principle, all of these assignments require some degree of "understanding" of the text, and thus can involve quite sophisticated natural language-processing algorithms.

44.3.4 Letter-to-sound conversion

The marked-up normalized input text is converted to a phonetic form representing the output pronunciation using a process known as "letter-to-sound" conversion. Such orthographic-to-phonetic conversion usually consists of a pronouncing dictionary and a mechanism for handling exceptions, i.e. items that cannot be found in the dictionary. The exceptions are converted using either explicit letter-to-sound "rules" or, more usually these days, a pattern recognition-based process that can generate likely pronunciations for unknown words after being training on a large pronouncing dictionary.

44.3.5 Phonetic element generation

The next stage in a typical TTS system is the generation of "context-dependent" phonetic elements that implement the required transitions from one sound into another. It is at this point that a number of significantly different alternative approaches become possible.

For many years, the main approach to TTS converted the phonetic specification of the output utterance into a "parametric" form that related to the control parameters of an electrical analogue of the human vocal tract. Such "formant-based" synthesizers used parameters such as formant frequencies (resonances in the vocal tract), voicing, and pitch to construct an output sound sequence from first principles. In this case, the phonetic element generation process consisted of converting the phonetic string into a continuous parallel sequence of control parameter values, usually involving fairly sophisticated interpolation between different phonetic target positions.

More recently, the majority of TTS systems have abandoned the parametric approach in favor of selecting fragments of pre-recorded utterances from a large corpus of recordings and linking them together in order to construct the target phonetic sequence. In some such systems, the fragments consist of fixed-context *units* (such as "diphones"—a segment of speech starting from the middle of one phone and ending in the middle of the next), whereas in more sophisticated systems, the units are of variable context. In the latter case, units are selected for concatenation using a sophisticated search technique (such as dynamic programming) in order to construct the highest quality sequence from the given corpus.

The advantage of the formant-based approach is that state-of-the-art systems are able to provide good intelligibility with only modest computational costs (in terms of small processing and memory requirements: < 50 MIPS and < 5 Mbytes). As a result, formant-based TTS systems have found a market in portable devices such as PDAs, mobile phones, and toys. The advantage of concatenative TTS systems is that they can provide very high-quality voices (since they are based on recordings of actual talkers) but the large corpora, coupled with the necessary search process, means that the computational requirements can be quite high (> 1,000 MIPS and > 1 Gbytes). As a consequence, unit-selection based TTS systems have found a market in centralized facilities such as telephone call centers.

44.3.6 Waveform generation

The final stage in a TTS system is the production of the audio waveform. In formant synthesis, this process involves a conversion from the parametric control parameters into an acoustic signal using a combination of digital voice/voiceless sound generators and formant filters. It is this conversion that gives such synthesizers their characteristic robotic timbre, and the resulting lack of naturalness can be a barrier to some applications. In concatenative synthesis, since the input to this stage consists of samples of real speech, all that is required is to concatenate the waveform fragments as smoothly as possible using a suitable signal processing algorithm such as PSOLA (pitch-synchronous overlap and add). It has been found that the intelligibility of unit-selection based TTS is highly dependent on the quality of the concatenation process and the rate at which the joins occur.

44.3.7 Audiovisual synthesis

As with ASR, there is considerable interest in the potential for exploiting the visual components of speech in TTS, and many researchers have investigated the synthesis of lip movements (Cohen and Massaro, 1990; Ezzat and Poggio, 1998; Beskow, 2004; Schwartz et al., 2004). The process usually involves the introduction of an inventory of suitable "visemes," and follows essentially the same production path as for the acoustic signal. Synthetic lip movements are used either to lend reality to an animated character (Theobald et al., 2004) or to aid speech perception in noise.

44.4 Spoken language dialogue systems

The two previous sections have outlined the processes involved in automatic speech recognition and text-to-speech synthesis. Whilst these are core components of a spoken language system, it is clear that turning speech into words (ASR) and turning words into speech (TTS) are not enough to construct a viable application. Words are not just arbitrary sequences of symbols; they are organized according to linguistic rules into structures that convey meanings that relate to the real world and to the specific application context in which a system is being deployed. It is only through the meanings that a user can engage with the system and its application. There are thus three key issues in a spoken language interface.

The first issue is concerned with *language coverage*: can a user remember exactly what to say? In a very simple application, there may only be a small set of available commands. In this case, a well-trained user will easily be able to operate the system using a fixed vocabulary and a telegraphic linguistic style, and the ASR could effectively be connected directly to the application back-end. However, in most real-life applications (especially those involving interaction with information), the size of vocabulary and breadth of possible linguistic expressions are such that the user could not conceivably remember what is allowed and what is not allowed. Instead, such a user would recourse to their natural language, and a "language interpreter" is required in order for the system to figure out what the user means in terms that are relevant to the application back-end. Similarly, the complexity of most applications is such that the output messages cannot be simply selected from a fixed list of stock (pre-recorded) responses. Instead, a "language generator" is required to create appropriate linguistic expressions for output by the TTS.

The second issue is concerned with *transaction complexity*. If a user is able to express his/her requirement in one utterance, then the output of the language interpreter can be sent directly to the application back-end—and this might be quite appropriate in a command-and-control type application. If, however, the application is such that a user finds it difficult (or unnatural) to provide all of the necessary information in one utterance, then multiple interactions with the user will be needed for the system to determine the missing information and to complete the transaction. Therefore, in the situation where the complexity of the transaction is high, a "dialogue manager" is required in order to mediate between the user and the application back-end.

The third issue is concerned with *application complexity*. If a user is unfamiliar with the total functionality of a given application, then some process is required, not only to figure out what the user might mean (the language interpreter) or to help the user complete the transaction (the dialogue manager), but also to provide high-level help and guidance in the use and capabilities of the system. This type of behavior would require more general *artificial intelligence* processes that are concerned with modeling users, user requirements, long-term planning, etc. Few systems have such capabilities at the current time.

The core components of a contemporary spoken language dialogue system are thus language processing and dialogue management.

44.4.1 Language processing

As has been seen, a spoken language dialogue system typically has two language processors: a spoken language *interpreter*, which converts the lexical output of an ASR into the conceptual representations relevant to the application, and a spoken language *generator*, which transforms the application-specific conceptual representations into a lexical form suitable for presentation as input to the TTS. Different applications invoke different concepts. For example, *command and control* applications involve commands and responses, *information* applications involve questions, answers, and statements, and *communication* applications usually involve some form of intermediate data representation or "inter-lingua." It is the job of the language processors to use linguistic knowledge (in the form of rules and/or probabilistic expressions) to apply syntactic and semantic constraints to aid understanding (through interpretation of the ASR output), expression (through generation of the TTS output), and orchestration (through interaction with the dialogue management process).

In principle, spoken language interpretation should involve "syntactic" analysis in order to determine the grammatical structure of an utterance, followed by "semantic" analysis in order to derive the intentions of the speaker. In reality, the linguistic structure of natural speech is so different from classical notions based on the analysis of well-formed texts that a practical spoken language dialogue system is obliged to use more pragmatic methods of linguistic analysis. For example, a common approach is "semantic grammar," in which the types of phrase structure rule that would normally be associated with syntactic analysis are used to extract meaning directly. The result is an approach that scans the output of the ASR for fragments that are meaningful in the context of the application domain (Ward, 1991), and this can be quite successful in the face of the disfluencies and ill-formedness that are prevalent in spontaneous speech.

The key processes within spoken language generation are content planning, sentence planning, surface realization, and prosody assignment (Walker and Rambow, 2002). The content planner makes decisions about what should be said in the context of the application and the state of the dialogue, and it may operate top-down (by breaking down high-level goals into single communicative acts) or bottom-up (by organizing low-level goals into a coherent high-level plan). The sentence planning, surface realization, and prosody assignment uses natural language generation techniques to convert the output of the content planner into the marked up form required by the TTS engine. In some systems, these three processes are replaced by a simple template-based mechanism in which high-level representations are mapped directly onto hand-crafted strings, with the added possibility of inserting values for application-specific variables.

Language processing can also aid ASR by interacting with the language modeling component to predict which words are more likely in a given context, and TTS by resolving linguistic issues in text normalization (e.g. *£2.50* → "two pounds and fifty pence"), part-of-speech assignment (e.g. *read* → /red/ or /ri:d/) and prosodic analysis.

44.4.2 Dialogue management

The main purpose of the "dialogue manager" in an SLDS is, through interaction with a user, to integrate sufficient fragmentary information to be able to present complete well-formed concepts to the application back-end, and at the same time piece together data returning from the application back-end into a form that can be presented to the user in a helpful and timely manner. The aim is usually to complete a successful *transaction* as efficiently as possible by maximizing task success and minimizing cost, thereby maximizing user satisfaction (Walker et al., 2000).

Dialogue managers can vary from application to application (Young and Proctor, 1989; Zue et al., 1994), but a generic research system might include components such as a discourse manager, a discourse context manager, a reference resolution manager, a behavioral agent, a plan manager, a response planner, and a world knowledge base (Allen et al., 2000). The discourse manager identifies the intended speech acts and maintains information on the current position and next steps in the application, and the context manager ensures a continuity of global topic flow and local topic salience. The reference resolution manager identifies salient referents for referring expressions such as noun phrases, and the behavioral agent interfaces with the application back-end and determines system actions. The plan manager constructs, evaluates, and executes plans, and the response planner determines the most effective communicative acts to achieve the system goals. Finally, the world knowledge base maintains a description of the current state of the world taking into account alternative hypotheses.

Practical spoken language dialogue systems often bypass many of these linguistically motivated processes and instead implement either a simple state-based mechanism or a more flexible frame-based approach to dialogue control (McTear, 2004; Delgado and Araki, 2005) using standardized scripting languages such as VoiceXML or SALT (speech application language tags). In a finite-state dialogue manager, flow is defined by a hand-crafted network in which each state represents some action to be taken (such as asking a question) and the transitions specify the order of events. In a frame-based dialogue manager, frames are data structures that are used as containers for slots into which key fragments of information must be inserted (such as a destination). In this case, flow is determined by which slots have yet to be filled. The advantage of the frame-based approach is that it gives the user some flexibility and is capable of deriving multiple pieces of information from one utterance. The disadvantage is that the user may pursue an inefficient line of interaction.

This leads on to one of the key issues for dialogue management in an SLDS: who should be in control of the dialogue flow? In a "system-led dialogue," the system interrogates the user in order to determine what they are trying to do, whereas in a "user-led dialogue," the system is entirely reactive to user actions. In a "mixed-initiative dialogue," both the user and the system may take the lead. Most contemporary spoken language dialogue systems are system-led so that the user behavior is encouraged to fall within the limited linguistic capabilities of the system. The disadvantage is that system-led dialogues restrict the users ability to ask questions or to change the topic.

Just as the ASR component may misrecognize a user's utterance, and the TTS component may mispronounce the user's name, so the dialogue manager may provide the user with erroneous information (due to a false interpretation of the user's intention). This means that error handling is an important aspect of a spoken language dialogue system (Carlson et al., 2005), and behaviors such as graceful degradation and efficient error recovery are key to a successful system implementation.

44.5 Future prospects

44.5.1 Hot topics

Apart from continually improving existing capabilities, research into spoken language systems is also extending into new areas in order to introduce additional human-like functionality and behavior. For example, there is growing interest in "Embodied Conversational Agents": speech-enabled animated characters that can act as a receptionist, a tour guide, or a personal tutor (Cassell et al., 2000; Pelachaud and Poggi, 2001). Such communicative interface agents bring together all of the features of a spoken language dialogue system into a visible form, and can be used to populate virtual-reality environments with conversationally interactive synthetic characters (Beskow et al., 2005).

A different but related area of new research in machine spoken language processing is the recognition and generation of emotion and expressive behavior (Murray and Arnott, 1993; Cowie et al., 2001). Such research is seen to be of particular relevance to applications such as interactive voice response in call centers, where it may be important to be able detect the emotional state of the user (e.g. in the course of a complaint) so that appropriate action can be taken.

44.5.2 The limits of current spoken language systems

Notwithstanding the impressive progress that has taken place in machine spoken- language processing, it is nevertheless the case that, unlike human operators, engineered solutions are quite fragile in dealing with real-user environments. State-of-the-art spoken language systems are quite poor at accepting input that is spontaneous, emotional, whispered, accented, disfluent, interrupted, contaminated, from the young/elderly/non-native, or which is rich in previously unencountered words, expressions, and behaviors. Similarly, although contemporary systems deliver output that is human-like and reasonably intelligible, they still lack expressiveness and are non-reactive to the communicative situation. Also, once trained, the behavior of current spoken language systems is essentially fixed. Minor adaptation can take place (e.g. to accommodating a change in the noise level), but spoken language systems are currently unable to learn to handle new concepts or tasks that arise in the course of an ongoing interaction.

Clearly, human spoken language processing is considerably more robust and flexible than current spoken language technology. For example, the data illustrated in Figure 44.6 shows that the accuracy of ASR is about an order of magnitude worse than that of human listeners across a range of tasks of varying difficulty from digit recognition to the transcription of conversational speech (Lippmann, 1997). Similarly, the intelligibility of TTS is significantly lower than that of natural human speech, especially for material with a low degree of linguistic redundancy such as a person's name.

These performance shortfalls have a significant impact on the usability and widespread deployment of spoken language systems, and this situation has been acknowledged by some of the leading industry practitioners:

> The industry has yet to bridge the gap between what people want and what it can deliver. Reducing the ASR error rate remains the greatest challenge. (Huang, 2002)
>
> After sixty years of concentrated research and development in speech synthesis and text-to-speech (TTS), our gadgets, gizmos, executive toys and appliances still do not speak to us intelligently. (Henton, 2002)

In fact it has been estimated that, even if the present rate of incremental progress can be sustained, it will still take another twenty to forty years (or more) before ASR reaches the level of accuracy exhibited by a human listener (Huang, 2002; Moore, 2003).

For many applications, of course, performance may not need to reach human levels for a spoken language system to have an advantage over alternative modes of human–machine

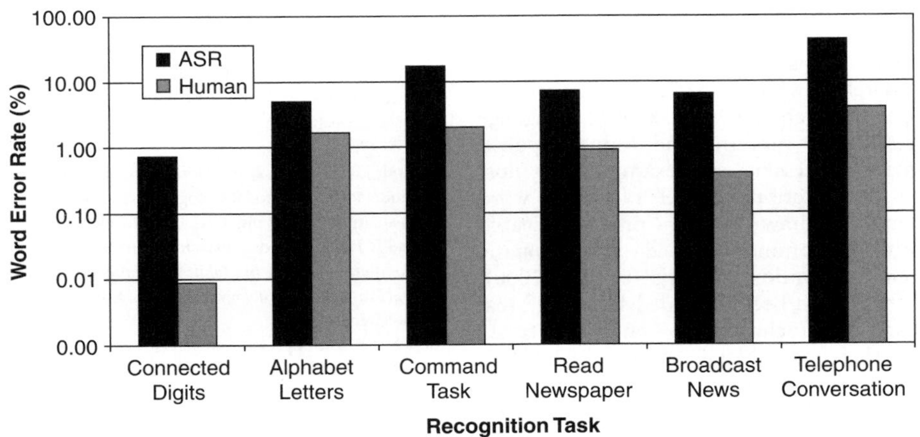

Figure 44.6 Comparison of human and automatic speech recognition.

interaction (Moore, 2004). Nevertheless, the time-scales quoted above may still be overly optimistic. For example, it has been estimated that the amount of training data needed to reach human levels of performance is of the order of 1,000,000 hours of speech (Moore, 2003). Similarly, for TTS it has been suggested that the size of database needed to capture 100 different talking styles and 10,000 different voices would be 5,000 Gbytes (Keller, 2001). These exceedingly large figures give a strong indication that the current algorithms for spoken language processing suffer from a devastating lack of "prior" knowledge about the structure and purpose of spoken language encoded in a form suitable for computational use.

44.5.3 Towards human levels of performance

There is thus a growing acceptance in the research community that current performance is asymptoting well short of desirable levels, and that in order to move on to the next generation of spoken language processing systems, a paradigm shift may be needed in the underlying algorithms and technology. Unfortunately, there is little consensus as to which particular research directions should be pursued. For example, in ASR some researchers favor extending the current statistical modeling frameworks to handle richer dynamic and segmental structures (Russell, 1993; Ostendorf et al., 1996), others are attempting to ground their models using articulatory constraints from human speech production (Gutkin and King, 2005), while others are regressing back to earlier template matching techniques that were abandoned due to lack of computer power (De Wachter et al., 2003).

There is also a small but growing community of researchers who are explicitly attempting to bridge the gap between spoken language processing by machine and human spoken language processing. For example, the most recent computational models of human word recognition draw heavily on the search algorithms commonly used in automatic speech recognition (Norris et al., 2000), and these have been extended to handle real acoustic data (Scharenborg, ten Bosch, et al., 2003; Scharenborg, McQueen, et al., 2003). This is clearly a very important step forwards, but the immediate consequence is that such models inevitably suffer from the same limitations as the automatic systems.

44.5.4 Towards a computational theory of spoken language processing

Issues concerning the differences between human and automatic spoken language processing have been discussed in the literature (Pols, 1999; Moore and Cutler, 2001), but credible proposals for achieving a unified computational theory are virtually nonexistent. Part of the problem may be that the challenges that need to be addressed extend far beyond the fields of speech technology and psycholinguistics. Future progress may depend on finding answers to fundamental questions about the architecture of the human brain, the functioning of the human mind, and the evolution and acquisition of human language. It would thus seem that the derivation of a unifying theory capable of explaining and predicting both human and machine spoken language processing behavior could form an important "grand challenge" in the newly emerging field of "Cognitive Informatics" (Wang, 2003; Moore, 2005).

References

Allen, J., Byron, D., Dzikovska, M., Ferguson, G., Galescu, L., and Stent, A. (2000) An architecture for a generic dialogue shell. *Natural Language Engineering*, 6: 213–28.

Barker, J. P., Cooke, M. P., and Ellis, D. P. W. (2005) Decoding speech in the presence of other sources. *Speech Communication*, 45: 5–25.

Baum, L. E. (1972) An inequality and associated maximization technique in statistical estimation for probabilistic functions of a Markov process, *Inequalities*, 3: 1–8.

Bellegarda, J. R. (2004) Statistical language model adaptation: review and perspectives. *Speech Communication*, 42: 93–108.

Bellman, R. E. (1957) *Dynamic Programming*. Princeton University Press, Princeton, NJ.

Beskow, J. (2004) Trainable articulatory control models for visual speech synthesis, *Journal of Speech Technology*, 7: 335–49.

Beskow, J., Edlund, J. G, and Nordstrand, M. (2005) A model for multi-modal dialogue system output applied to an animated talking head. In W. Minker, D. Bühler, and L. Dybkjaer (eds), *Spoken Multimodal Human-Computer Dialogue in Mobile Environments, Text, Speech and Language Technology*, p. 93–116. Kluwer Academic, Dordrecht.

Boll, S. (1979) Suppression of acoustic noise in speech using spectral subtraction. IEEE Trans. *Audio, Speech and Signal Processing*, 27: 113–20.

Brooke, N. M., and Summerfield, A. Q. (1983) Analysis, synthesis and perception of visible articulatory movements. *Journal of Phonetics*, 11: 63–76.

Brown, G. J. (2003) Auditory scene analysis. In M. A. Arbib (ed.), *The Handbook of Brain Theory and Neural Networks*, 2nd edn, pp. 132–5. MIT Press, Cambridge, MA.

Carlson, R., Hirschberg, J., and Swerts, M. (2005) Error handling in spoken dialogue systems. *Speech Communication*, 45: 207–09.

Cassell, J., Sullivan, J., Prevost, S., and Churchill, E. (2000) *Embodied Conversational Agents*. MIT Press, Cambridge, MA.

Cohen, M. M., and Massaro, D. W. (1990) Synthesis of visible speech. *Behavioral Research Methods and Instrumentation*, 22: 260–3.

Cole, R. A., Massaro, D. W., de Villiers, J., Rundle, B., Shobaki, K., Wouters, J., Cohen, M., Beskow, J., Stone, P., Conners, P., Tarachow, and Solcher, D. (1999) New tools for interactive speech and language training: using animated conversational agents in the classrooms of profoundly deaf children. In *Proceedings of the ESCA/Socrates MATISSE Workshop on Method and Tool Innovations for Speech Science Education*, pp. 45–52.

Cooke, M. P., Green, P. D., Josifovski, L. B., and Vizinho, A. (2001) Robust automatic speech recognition with missing and uncertain acoustic data. *Speech Communication*, 34: 267–85.

Cowie, R., Douglas-Cowie, E., Tsapatsoulis, N., Votsis, G., Kollias, S., Fellenz, W., and Taylor, J. (2001) Emotion recognition in human-computer interaction. *IEEE Signal Processing Magazine*, 18: 32–80.

Delgado, R. L. C., and Araki, M. (2005) *Spoken, Multilingual and Multimodal Dialogue Systems*. Wiley, Chichester.

De Wachter, M., Demuynck, K., van Compernolle, D., and Wambacq, P. (2003) Data driven example based continuous speech recognition. In *Proceedings of Eurospeech*, Geneva, pp.1133–6.

Dutoit, T. (1997) *An Introduction to Text-to-Speech Synthesis*. Kluwer Academic, Boston.

Everman, G., Chan, H. Y., Gales, M. J .F., Jia, B., Mrva, D., Woodland, P., and Yu, K. (2005) Training LVCSR systems on thousands of hours of data. In *Procedings of IEEE ICASSP.*

Ezzat, T., and Poggio, T. (1998) MikeTalk: a talking facial display based on morphing visemes. In *Proceedings of the Computer Animation Conference*, Philadelphia.

Gales, M. J .F., and Young, S. J. (1995) Robust speech recognition in additive and convolutional noise using parallel model combination. *Computer Speech and Language*, 9: 289–307.

Gibbon, D., Mertins, I., and Moore, K. (2000) *Handbook of Multimodal and Spoken Dialogue Systems: Resources, Terminology and Product Evaluation*. Kluwer Academic, Boston, MA.

Gutkin, A., and King, S. (2005) Detection of symbolic gestural events in articulatory data for use in structural representations of continuous speech. In *Proceedings of the IEEE International Conference on Acoustics, Speech, and Signal Processing*, pp. 885–8. IEEE Signal Processing Society Press, Philadelphia, PA.

Henton, C. G. (2002) Fiction and reality of TTS. *Speech Technology Magazine*, 7: 36–9.

Holmes, J. and Holmes W (2002) *Speech Recognition and Synthesis*. Taylor & Francis, Boston, MA.

Huang, X. D. (2002) Making Speech Mainstream. Microsoft Speech Technologies Group, http://www.microsoft.com/speech/docs/HuangSpeechArtfinal.htm

Jelinek, F. (1985) "Every time I fire a linguist, the performance of my system goes up". Public statement at the IEEE ASSPS Workshop on Frontiers of Speech Recognition.

Jelinek, F. (1996) Five speculations (and a divertimento) on the themes of H. Bourlard, H. Hermansky and N. Morgan. *Speech Communication*, 18: 242–46.

Jelinek, F., Mercer, R. L., and Bahl, L. R. (1983) Continuous speech recognition: statistical methods. In P. R. Krishniash and L. N. Kanal (eds), *Handbook of Statistics*, vol. 2, pp. 549–73, North-Holland, Amsterdam.

Jelinek, F. (1998) *Statistical Methods for Speech Recognition*. MIT Press, Cambridge, MA.

Junqua, J.-C., and Wellekens, C. (2004.) Special issue on adaptation methods for speech recognition. *Speech Communication*, 42.

Keller, E. (2001) Towards greater naturalness: future directions of research in speech synthesis. In E. Keller, G. Bailly, A. Monaghan, J. Terken, and M. A. Huckvale (eds), *Improvements in Speech Synthesis*, pp. 3–17. Wiley, Chichester, UK.

Klatt, D. H. (1977) Review of the ARPA speech understanding project. *Journal of the Acoustical Society of America*, 62: 1345–66.

Kuhn, R., Junqua, J. C., Nguyen, P., and Niedzielski, N. (2000) Rapid speaker adaptation in Eigenvoice space. *IEEE Transactions: Speech Audio Processing*, 8: 695–707.

Lee, L., and Rose, R. C. (1996) Speaker normalization using efficient frequency warping procedures. In *Proceedings, IEEE ICASSP.*

Leggetter, C. J., and Woodland, P. (1994) Speaker adaptation of continuous density HMMs using linear regression. In *Proceedings of the International Conference on Spoken Language Processing*, pp. 451–4.

Lippmann, R. (1997) Speech recognition by machines and humans. *Speech Communication*, 22: 1–16.

Makhoul, J., and Schwartz, R. (1984) Ignorance modeling. In J. Perkell and D. H. Klatt (eds), *Invariance and Variability in Speech Processes* Erlbaum, Hillsdale, NJ.

McTear, M. F. (2004) *Spoken Dialogue Technology*. Springer, London.

Moore, R. K. (2003) A comparison of the data requirements of automatic speech recognition systems and human listeners. In *Proceedings of Eurospeech*, Geneva, pp. 2582–4.

Moore, R. K. (2004) Modeling data entry rates for ASR and alternative input methods. In *Proceedings of INTERSPEECH*, Jeju, Korea.

Moore, R. K. (2005) Towards a unified theory of spoken language processing. In *Proceedings of the 4th IEEE International Conference on Cognitive Informatics*, Irvine, Calif.

Moore, R. K., and Cutler, A. (2001) Constraints on theories of human vs. machine recognition of speech. In *Proceedings of the SPRAAC Workshop on Human Speech Recognition as Pattern Classification*, Max Planck Institute for Psycholinguistics, Nijmegen.

Murray, I. R., and Arnott, J. L. (1993) Towards the simulation of emotion in synthetic speech: a review of the literature on human vocal emotion. *Journal of the Acoustical Society of America*, 93: 1097–108.

Norris, D., McQueen, J., and Cutler, A. (2000) Feedback on feedback on feedback. *Behavioral and Brain Sciences*, 23: 299–370.

Ostendorf, M., Digilakis, V., and Kimball, O. A. (1996) From HMMs to segment models: a unified view of stochastic modeling for speech recognition. *IEEE Transactions, Speech and Audio Processing*, 4: 360–78.

Pelachaud, C., and Poggi, I. (2001) Towards believable interactive embodied agents. Paper presented at Fifth International Conference on Autonomous Agents workshop on Multimodal Communication and Context in Embodied Agents, Montreal.

Petajan, E. D., Brooke, N. M., Bischoff, B., and Bodoff, D. A. (1988) Experiments in automatic visual speech recognition. In *Proceedings of the 7th Symposium of the Federation of Acoustical Societies of Europe*, Edinburgh, pp. 1163–70.

Pols, L. (1999) Flexible, robust, and efficient human speech processing versus present-day speech technology. In *Proceedings of the 14th International Congress of Phonetic Sciences (ICPhS-99)*, San Francisco, USA, pp. 9–16.

Potamianos, G., Neti, C., Gravier, G., Garg, A. and Senior, A. W. (2003) Recent advances in the automatic recognition of audio-visual speech. In *Proceedings, IEEE*, 91: 1306–26.

Rabiner, L., and Juang, B.-H. (1993) *Fundamentals of Speech Recognition*. Prentice-Hall, New York.

Rosenberg, A., Lee, C.-H., and Soong, F. (1994) Cepstral channel normalization techniques for HMM-based speaker verification. In *Proceedings, ICSLP*, pp.1835–8.

Rubin, P., and Vatikiotis-Bateson, E. (1998) *Auditory-Visual Speech Processing, Speech Communication* (special issue), 26.

Russell, M. J. (1993) A segmental HMM for speech pattern modeling. In *Proceedings of the IEEE International Conference on Acoustics, Speech and Signal Processing*, pp.640–3.

Scharenborg, O., McQueen, J., ten Bosch, L., and Norris, D. (2003) Modeling human speech recognition using automatic speech recognition paradigms in SpeM. In *Proceedings, Eurospeech,* Geneva, pp. 2097–100.

Scharenborg, O., ten Bosch, L., Boves, L., and Norris, D. (2003) Bridging automatic speech recognition and psycholinguistics: extending Shortlist to an end-to-end model of human speech recognition. *Journal of the Acoustical Society of America*, 114: 3023–35.

Schwartz, J.-l., Berthommier, F., Cathiard, M.-A., and de Mori, R. (2004) *Audio Visual Speech Processing, Speech Communication* (special issue), 44: 1–216.

Silverman, K., Beckman, M. B., Pirelli, J., Ostendorf, M., Wightman, C., Price, P., Pierrehumbert, J., and Hirschberg, J. (1992) ToBI: a standard for labeling English prosody. In *Proceedings of the 2nd International Conference on Spoken Language Processing* (ICSLP), Banff, Canada, pp. 867–70.

Spohrer, J. C., Brown, P. F., Hochschild, P. H., and Baker, J. K. (1980) Partial traceback in continuous speech recognition. In *Proceedings of the IEEE International Conference on Cybernetics and Society*, pp. 36–42.

Summerfield, A. Q., MacLoed, A., McGrath, M., and Brooke, N. M. (1989) Lips, teeth, and the benefits of lipreading. In A. W. Young and H. D. Ellis (eds), *Handbook of Research in Face Processing*, pp. 223–33. North-Holland, Amsterdam.

Taylor, M. M., Neel, F., and Bouwhuis, D. G. (1989) *The Structure of Multimodal Dialogue*. North-Holland, Amsterdam.

Theobald, B. J., Bangham, J. A., Matthews, I. A., and Cawley, G. C. (2004) Near-videorealistic synthetic talking faces: implementation and evaluation, *Speech Communication*, 44: 127–40.

Varga, A.P., and Moore, R. K. (1990) Hidden Markov model decomposition of speech and noise. In *Proceedings of the International Conference on Acoustics, Speech and Signal Processing*, pp. 845–8: IEEE.

Varga, A. P., and Moore, R. K. (1991) Simultaneous recognition of concurrent speech signals using hidden Markov model decomposition. In *Proceedings of ESCA EUROSPEECH*, Genova, Italy.

Viterbi, A. J. (1967) Error bounds for convolutional codes and an asymptotically optimum decoding algorithm. *IEEE Trans. Information Theory*, IT-13, pp. 260–9.

Walker, M. A., Kamm, C., and Liman, D. (2000) Towards developing general models of usability with PARADISE. *Natural Language Engineering*, 6: 363–77.

Walker, M. A., and Rambow, O. C. (2002) Spoken language generation. *Computer Speech and Language*, 16: 273–81.

Wang, Y. (2003) Cognitive informatics: a new transdisciplinary research field. *Brain and Mind*, 4: 115–27.

Ward, W. (1991) Understanding spontaneous speech: the Phoenix system. In *Proceedings of the International Conference on Acoustics, Speech and Signal Processing*, pp.365–7, IEEE.

Wester, M., and Fosler-Lussier, E. (2000) A comparison of data-derived and knowledge-based modeling of pronunciation variation. In *Proceedings, ICSLP*, pp. 270–3.

Young, S. J., and Proctor, C. E. (1989) The design and implementation of dialogue control in voice operated database inquiry systems. *Computer Speech and Language*, 3: 329–53.

Zue, V., Seneff, S., Polifroni, J., Phillips, M., Pao, C., Goodine, D., Goddeau, D., and Glass, J. (1994) PEGASUS: a spoken dialogue interface for on-line air travel planning. *Speech Communication*, 15: 331–40.

CHAPTER 45

Relating structure and time in linguistics and psycholinguistics

Colin Phillips and Matthew Wagers

45.1 Linguistics and psycholinguistics

The field of psycholinguistics advertises its mentalistic commitments in its name. The field of linguistics does not. Psycholinguistic research frequently involves ingenious experimental designs, fancy lab equipment such as eye-trackers or electroencephalograms (EEGs), large groups of experimental subjects, and detailed statistical analyses. Linguistic research typically requires no specialized equipment, no statistical analyses, and somewhere between zero and a handful of cooperative informants. Psycholinguistic research is most commonly conducted in a Department of Psychology. Linguistic research is not. Some of these differences may contribute to the widespread perception, well-represented among linguists and psychologists alike, that the concerns of psycholinguistics are somehow more psychological than those of linguistics, and that psycholinguistics can be looked to for psychological validation of the constructs proposed by linguists. Although this view of the relation between the two fields gives the impression of a neat division of labor, we find it misleading, and suspect that it may have led to unrealistic expectations, and consequently to disappointments and mutual frustration.

In this commentary we focus on issues in the representation of unbounded syntactic dependencies, as a case study of what psycholinguistic methods can and cannot tell us about linguistic questions, and vice versa. This is an area where a rich linguistic literature and a sizeable body of psycholinguistic research address closely related phenomena. The most widely discussed form of unbounded dependency occurs when a noun phrase (NP) such as *which voters* in (1) appears in a position that is structurally distant from the verb that it is an argument of (e.g. *bribe* in (1)). Following standard practice, we mark the canonical position of the direct object of *bribe* with an underline or *gap* in (1), but it is a matter of great controversy whether such gap positions are a part of the mental representation of sentences like (1). After reviewing some of the competing linguistic analyses of unbounded dependency constructions in section 45.2, we discuss in section 45.3 the contributions of psycholinguistics to the question of how these dependencies are represented.

1. Which voters did the prosecutor suspect that the candidate wanted his operatives to bribe ___ before the election?

The status of constraints on long-distance dependencies, such as the ban on dependencies that span relative clause boundaries, as illustrated in (2), is a major topic of linguistic research. In section 45.4 we discuss the effects of such constraints on language processing and their implications for the relation between linguistic and psycholinguistic models.

2. *Which voters did the prosecutor ask [$_{NP}$ the operative [$_{RC}$ that bribed ___]] to testify against his boss?

As far as we can tell, there is no principled difference between the psychological relevance of psycholinguistic and linguistic research. Most modern linguists have serious mentalistic commitments (and those that do not are of little concern to us here).[1] The data that linguists and psycholinguists collect and the theories that they develop based on those data are all "psychological," in the sense that they aim to explain some aspect of human cognitive abilities. There are certainly differences in the issues and methods that the two fields tend to pay closest attention to; but we are unaware of reasons to think that either discipline has more direct access to psychological evidence, and we would include in this those strains of psycholinguistics that draw on cognitive neuroscience methods, as we do in our own work. Since this is not a standard position, we will briefly attempt to substantiate this claim.

There is broad agreement that mastery of a language involves at least an (unconscious) understanding of the range of possible expressions that can be represented in the language, and also an ability to identify those expressions that cannot be represented in the language. It is also agreed that since the expressive power of human languages is too large for any individual to simply memorize the possible representations of his language, a speaker must have the ability to generate, recognize, and interpret novel expressions of the language relatively quickly in order to speak and understand. Since humans are able to learn any language for which they receive adequate exposure from an early age, it is also agreed that the ability to learn language is a key component of the human capacity for language. Understanding each of these abilities is an important part of the task of explaining how human language works, and it is perhaps an accident of history or methodology that different sub-fields have emerged that focus on each of these problems.

Linguistic theory typically focuses on characterizing the representations that a speaker of a language can entertain, often allied with the question of what is a "possible human language." Theoretical linguists have generally paid less attention to questions about how these representations might be retrieved or constructed in real-time tasks such as speaking and understanding. In contrast, questions about real-time processes have been central in adult psycholinguistics, whereas less attention has been given to the question of why certain expressions are possible and others are impossible. This focus of adult psycholinguistics upon mechanisms that are closely tied to speaking and understanding is sometimes justified by the notion that these are more directly related to common behaviors, or by the assumption that the goal of psycholinguistics is to provide "processing models." However, a look at psycholinguistic work with children casts doubt upon this rationale. Developmental psycholinguistics has devoted much attention to the question of what children can and cannot represent at different ages. Studies of children's real-time processing and detailed studies of learning have become more prominent only recently. Much work in developmental psycholinguistics asks the same questions about children that linguists ask about adults. Therefore, the question of what a speaker can and cannot represent, and the question of how the representations are constructed in time, are presumably both psychologically respectable concerns. We suspect that the disciplinary divisions have more to do with the methodological biases of the respective fields.

There are obvious differences between the data collection methods most commonly used in linguistics and psycholinguistics. The primary data of theoretical linguistics comes from native speakers' intuitive judgements about the acceptability of sentences or the availability of specific interpretations. Such data are relatively easy to come by, making it possible to establish a large number of facts about many different languages in relatively little time. Psycholinguistic data, on the other hand, typically require a good deal more effort. In order to establish reliable generalizations about reaction times, focal brain activity, or any of a number of other common dependent measures, one needs to use specialized equipment, test large numbers of experimental items on large numbers of participants, devise ingenious ways to hide one's goals from the participants, and use complex statistical analyses to interpret the results. It can take a lot of work to establish just one fact, and it can be difficult to conduct experiments on a number of different languages.

The different data collection practices of linguistics and psycholinguistics have a clear impact upon the fields. First, they affect the empirical scope of the fields. Thanks to its low-tech methods, linguistics has amassed a large body of findings from a very diverse set of languages, including languages for which only a small number of

[1] We should emphasize that we are concerned in this commentary with what we take to be the "best practices" in either field. It is not difficult to find instances of careless misrepresentation of linguistic data, uninterpretable experimental designs, unwarranted inferences from brain activation patterns, etc., of which neither field would be proud. Our interest here is more in what can be learned from carefully conducted work in either field.

speakers remain. In contrast, most psycholinguistic research has been confined to a handful of closely related western European languages. Second, differences in data collection methods affect what linguists and psycholinguists spend their time on, shape what is valued in the two fields, and also affect the safeguards that the two fields place on data reliability. In psycholinguistics data collection is sufficiently difficult that great value is placed on elegant experimental designs that make it possible to establish a single fact, and many procedural safeguards are put in place in order to ensure that results are reliable. In linguistics, on the other hand, data collection methods are relatively trivial, and receive correspondingly little attention (although there is obvious value in the use of carefully controlled test sentences). Except when dealing with speakers of scarce languages, replication and verification of the empirical facts is straightforward, and hence fewer safeguards are needed to avoid the damaging effects of bogus findings. It is therefore understandable that in linguistics little value is placed on establishing individual facts. Greater value is placed on weaving together large bodies of facts into interesting general theories. The term "theoretical" in "theoretical linguistics" is all too often taken to imply that the field is somehow less concerned with empirical facts. This is unwarranted. The term merely reflects the fact that the empirical side of the field is sufficiently easy that most time is spent worrying about what the facts all mean.[2] Similarly, psycholinguists take questions of theory seriously, although such questions take up less time on a day-to-day basis.

It is sometimes objected that the results of linguistics are less reliable or objective than those of psycholinguistics (e.g. Ferreira 2005), or that they provide less direct access to the workings of the mind or brain. Linguists are often criticized—and frequently criticize themselves—because they "do not run experiments." Aside from the mundane concern that all findings should be reported carefully and honestly, we do not see the force of this objection. Most of the linguistic literature is built upon robust acceptability judgements, and robust judgements become statistically reliable with rather small samples—unbiased agreement among half a dozen friends will do (e.g. two-tailed sign test). One can often do without the half dozen friends, too, if one is sufficiently confident about the judgement. There are, of course, examples of errors and disagreements, and notorious cases of judgements that are subtle at best, but these are the exception rather than the rule. In our own work we often run large acceptability rating studies as controls for our on-line studies. These studies cost little effort, since the materials are independently needed for the on-line studies, but the results are almost never surprising, and are generally so robust statistically as to indicate that we tested more subjects than needed. As far as we can tell, if linguists were to replace their standard informal experiments with larger-scale acceptability judgement studies, the main consequence would be to slow the discovery of new facts.[3] Furthermore, linguistic methods are typically used to support rather direct inferences from the observed data. If a sentence is judged to be unacceptable (and various obvious controls for plausibility, memory, etc. are satisfied), then it is inferred that the sentence is not a well-formed product of the speaker's language system. In psycholinguistics, on the other hand, we typically draw rather more indirect inferences. A 30-ms slowdown in the time that it takes to press a button may be used to infer the presence of a structural ambiguity or the need for parsing revision. A 2-microvolt positive deflection in an averaged scalp voltage may be used to infer that selective disruption is occurring in syntactic processing. These experimental methods are more appropriate than acceptability judgements for selectively targeting unconscious processes, and they certainly have more fine-grained temporal resolution, but they are not more direct windows into the mind.

Overall, we see little reason to view the concerns or the methods of either linguistics or psycholinguistics as more or less psychological in nature. This may seem obvious to some, and bizarre to others. However, we suspect that some of the misunderstanding and mutual frustration

[2] See Miller (1990) for an interesting related commentary. Miller argues that linguists and psychologists tend to have different notions of what constitutes a satisfying explanation, and that this is a source of misunderstanding: "Linguists tend to accept simplifications as explanations. [...] For a psychologist, on the other hand, an explanation is something phrased in terms of cause and effect, antecedent and subsequent, stimulus and response" (p. 321).

[3] There are certainly cases where the subtlety of the judgements using standard methods raises the hope that larger-scale experimentation might provide more clarity about the data. However, throwing more subjects at a task is no guarantee of success. For example, experienced linguists are good at excluding effects of garden paths from their judgements and at constructing mental models that are relevant for evaluating the (un-)availability of quantifier scope ambiguities. Untutored experimental participants normally lack these skills, and so could add as much noise as clarity to a large-scale rating study.

that one sometimes encounters derives from the unrealistic expectation that psycholinguistics will provide psychological validation of linguistic models. Any kind of theory testing requires experimental tools that are commensurate with the hypotheses being tested, and for any given linguistic hypothesis there is no guarantee that the current tools of psycholinguistics are well suited for testing that hypothesis. An example of this that features prominently in sections 45.3 and 45.4 is that the detailed timing information provided by psycholinguistic and neurolinguistic measures is most revealing when evaluating hypotheses that make clear timing predictions.

In discussions about linguistics and psycholinguistics one encounters frequent references to the search for the "psychological reality" of linguistic constructs. We suspect that the term is unhelpful, since it contributes to the notion that psycholinguistic experiments license inferences about the mind that are inherently more privileged than the conclusions of lower-tech linguistic arguments. This in turn contributes to the notion that if a linguistic hypothesis does not clearly impact the tasks of speaking and understanding studied by psycholinguists then it is not a serious psychological hypothesis, and may discourage linguists from taking the psychological implications of their theories more seriously.

Another reason for linguists' frequent reluctance to take seriously the psychological implications of their theories may be the "competence-performance distinction" (Chomsky, 1965). At a basic level this is used to draw a distinction between what formal linguists do and do not consider their primary concern to be; but it is used in so many different ways that it may have led to more confusion than clarity. It is sometimes used to describe the necessary distinction between behavior and the mechanisms that generate behavior, or to describe the logical distinction between a declarative and procedural specification of a formal system. At other times it is used to refer to the difference between what a cognitive system could achieve with unbounded resources and what it can achieve when it is subject to real-life resource limitations. Finally, it is used to refer to a hypothesized division of labor between a cognitive system that specifies possible and impossible representations—the grammar—and distinct systems that generate or recover these representations in real-time—the parser and producer (for further discussion see Berwick and Weinberg, 1984; Phillips, 1996; 2004). This final hypothesis may contribute to a common misperception among linguists that they are investigating a cognitive system that is *necessarily* distinct from what the psycholinguists are concerned with. This distinction is certainly possible, but it is an empirical hypothesis. It leaves a state of affairs where many linguists are committed mentalists, but are less certain of what their mentalistic commitments entail (e.g. what is the claim of a syntactic or phonological "derivation" a claim about?). This makes it more difficult to see where the concerns of linguists and psycholinguists are mutually relevant (see Boland, 2005, for another perspective on this issue).

The remainder of this chapter uses a case study of long-distance dependencies in linguistics and psycholinguistics to further illustrate the importance of tools that are commensurate with the hypotheses being tested.

45.2 Linguistic analyses of long-distance dependencies: a primer

45.2.1 Getting started

In this section we introduce some key properties of syntactic long-distance dependencies, and we compare different linguistic accounts of how they are encoded, emphasizing where the competing theories agree and where they disagree. The phenomena that we are concerned with here are variously known as "long-distance dependencies," "unbounded dependencies," "displacement," "extraction," or "movement." All but the last of these implies no commitment to a particular linguistic analysis. The term "movement" is generally associated with transformational grammar analyses, and we use it here only in that context. The term "long-distance dependency" often refers to a broader class of syntactic phenomena including antecedent–pronoun relations, but we primarily use it here in a sense that is interchangeable with the other terms. We will also use the standard psycholinguistic terms "filler" and "gap" to refer to the components of the dependencies (Fodor, 1978), with no commitment to a specific theoretical account intended.

In order to understand the importance of long-distance dependencies in language, it is helpful to highlight the fact that local linguistic dependencies are (i) pervasive and (ii) in competition with one another. Many relations in natural language syntax appear in highly local configurations, as the examples in (3) illustrate:

3a. THEMATIC DEPENDENCIES
Marcel$_{\text{AGENT(x)}}$ memorized$_{\text{f(x)(y)}}$ a poem$_{\text{THEME(y)}}$.

3b. CASE ASSIGNMENT
His father often rebuked$_{ACC}$ him$_{ACC}$.
3c. AGREEMENT
The critics$_{3PL}$ were$_{3PL}$ initially unkind.
3d. SCOPE
Albert wonders [$_{CP}$ who [$_{C'}$ Gilbert loves]].

Often a dependent element can participate in several relationships in one configuration—for example, a direct object can receive both its case and its thematic role in a sisterhood configuration with the verb. At other times, those relationships place competing configurational demands on elements. In such cases, one or more of the dependencies must be satisfied from a non-local position. For example, in the passive construction below, the subject *the doctor* participates in a local case/agreement relation with the auxiliary verb, while it bears the thematic role most typical of a head-complement configuration with the verb *consulted*, which we find in the corresponding active construction.

4a. PASSIVE
[*The doctor*$_{THEME}$] was frequently *consulted* by the diplomat.
4b. ACTIVE
The diplomat frequently *consulted* [*the doctor*$_{THEME}$]

We would like a theory of syntactic dependencies to explain how the thematic relationship between the predicate *consult* and its argument *the diplomat* is expressible in two different phrase structure configurations. Passive constructions reflect one class of displacement that retains a relatively local flavor: similar phenomena include Raising, Control, and Exceptional Case Marking. Other displacement phenomena establish relations between indefinitely distant elements. We refer to such dependences as "unbounded" or "long-distance" dependencies. Consider *wh*-interrogatives in English, as in (5).

5a. The teacher said that the police falsely accused the students of the crime.
5b. The teacher said that the students were falsely accused ___ of the crime.
5c. Which students did the teacher say ___ were falsely accused ___ of the crime?
5d. The teacher said which students ___ were falsely accused ___ of the crime.

The NP *the students* is an embedded direct object in (5a), where it appears in a local relation with the verb *accuse* that assigns its thematic role. The same NP is a passive subject in (5b), where it appears in a local relation with an auxiliary verb that it agrees with in number. In (5c, d) the NP *which students* still receives a thematic role from the same verb and governs agreement on the same auxiliary, but appears locally to neither. In these examples the position of the *wh*-phrase marks scope, i.e. whether the sentence is a direct or indirect question. The examples show that multiple syntactic relations *can* be satisfied locally, but an element normally appears in only one local configuration at a time. The other relations require non-local dependencies.

Long-distance dependencies with gaps are established in a number of other cases, such as relativization, topicalization, comparatives, and adjective–*though* constructions (6–9).

6. RELATIVE CLAUSES
The aristocrat hired *a young maid who* he realized ___ would become his closest confidante.
7. TOPICALIZATION
These chapters, most critics agree you can safely skip ___.
8. COMPARATIVES
The first draft was much *longer* than anyone had suspected it to be ___.
9. ADJECTIVE-"THOUGH"
Sophisticated though he thought his friends were ___, they failed to catch the obscure allusion.

These instances of syntactic action-at-a-distance are recognized in all theories of syntax; but different theories have different means of encoding these phenomena, and there has been much interest in finding linguistic and psycholinguistic evidence that might choose among the competing theories.

45.2.2 **Competing accounts of long-distance dependencies.**

Long-distance dependencies create a separation between the position where a phrase is pronounced and the verb (or other head) which determines its thematic role. Here we review several mechanisms for analyzing this separation, with an emphasis on how different theories encode long-distance dependencies, rather than on the empirical merits of their respective analyses.

We should emphasize that there is little real disagreement between theories about the notion that sentences involve multiple levels of representation. Where theories diverge is on the question of what information these different levels of representation contain, and how they are related to one another. Transformational grammar models are famous for the claim that there are multiple levels of representation that are specifically syntactic, and that they are related to one another by movement operations that convert each successive structure into the next; but other theories also adopt multiple levels of representation, which are sometimes non-syntactic in nature, and are related to one another by various mechanisms. All theories that we are aware of take advantage of different levels of representation in capturing the various phenomena associated with long-distance dependencies. For example, when a pronoun or reflexive element is contained inside a displaced NP, it generally retains the coreference possibilities that it would have if the NP were not displaced ("reconstruction" effects). In some theories this parallel between displaced and non-displaced NPs is captured in syntactic terms, in others this can be captured in terms of a semantic or argument structure level of representation.

45.2.2.1 Transformational accounts

The earliest models in transformational generative grammar (TGG; Chomsky, 1957; 1965) accounted for displacement in a purely derivational manner. The surface word order of a sentence was taken to be derived by first forming an underlying phrase structure, generated by rewriting phrase structure rules, and by then applying successive structural transformations to this initial representation. In the development of transformational grammar identified with Chomsky's *Aspects* model (Chomsky 1965), the initial structure or "deep structure" was taken to encode the thematic relations of a sentence, and was also taken to be the primary encoding of sentence meaning. Application of transformations yielded a "surface structure" representation that served as the primary interface with phonological systems. When an argument was moved by a transformational operation, its initial local relation to its thematic role assigner was not preserved. In these accounts the relationship between a filler and its gap was encoded in the underlying representation and the derivational history, but crucially not in the surface structure.

45.2.2.2 Transformations with traces

In the early TGG models the relationship between a displaced argument and its predicate was encoded in the same way as the relationship between other predicates and arguments—through local phrase structure composition in the generation of deep structure—but this configuration was not retained in surface structures. The introduction of phonologically null categories, or *traces*, into TGG models in the 1970s (Chomsky, 1973; Fiengo, 1977) effectively endowed surface structures with a record of the transformations that had taken place. Displacement operations continued to be captured by means of transformational operations, but filler-gap dependencies could now be encoded in surface structure representations, as in the example in (10). Thus, a grammar that encodes long-distance dependencies using phonologically empty categories is in no way logically dependent on a transformational system.

10. [Which letter]$_i$ did Marcel write t_i to his mother?

While traces, and empty constituents generally, have played an important role in many TGG models, like Government and Binding (GB) theory (Chomsky, 1981), Tree-Adjoining Grammar (Kroch and Joshi, 1985; Frank, 2002), and Minimalist Program models (Chomsky, 1995), they have also featured in some versions of Generalized Phrase Structure Grammar (GPSG: Gazdar et al., 1985) and Head-driven Phrase Structure Grammar (HPSG: Pollard and Sag, 1994), approaches that explicitly reject transformational derivations. Indeed, much of the work that traces accomplish in classical GB theory results from their interaction with representational well-formedness constraints, as opposed to derivational conditions on transformations. Recognition of this point has led a number of syntacticians working in the TGG tradition to propose theories that use empty categories but lack transformational derivations (e.g. Koster, 1978; Rizzi, 1986; Brody, 1995).

Some recent proposals in the context of the Minimalist Program (Chomsky 1995) have argued that traces should be replaced with a notion of unpronounced copies of the displaced phrase. However, these proposals retain the crucial feature of all transformational theories, namely that a predicate is related to a displaced argument in exactly the same way it is related to a non-displaced argument—by local phrase structure relations. It is this property that has led to a search for decisive psycholinguistic evidence.

45.2.2.3 Path marking with category labels

We have already seen that a long-distance dependency between a displaced phrase and an empty category can be encoded in a non-transformational grammar. However, a long-distance dependency of this kind cannot be directly generated in a grammar which uses standard syntactic categories and restricts itself to only context-free phrase structure rules, since there can be no rule that directly relates the filler and the (indefinitely distant) gap. However, if we distinguish a category that dominates a gap and one that does not, then we can encode the dependency using context-free phrase structure rules. Call the category dominating a verb and a gap VP_{GAP}, and its dominating category S_{GAP}. If we admit a rule that rewrites S as a WH phrase and an S_{GAP} (11), then we can create a chain of local links between a displaced constituent and a gap position. In effect, the category label encodes a GAP feature that is passed through the tree between the wh-phrase and the gap, across a potentially unbounded distance.

11. $S \rightarrow WH\ S_{GAP}$
$S_{GAP} \rightarrow NP\ VP_{GAP}$
$VP_{GAP} \rightarrow V\ GAP$

However, once the GAP-feature passing mechanism is introduced, one could take the next step and make a lexical distinction between those verbs that combine with an overt constituent and those capable of linking to a higher constituent via the GAP-feature passing mechanism (12). This long-distance linking mechanism raises the possibility of doing without gaps altogether, and relying instead on the passing of GAP-features. Current analyses in HPSG exemplify this approach (Pollard and Sag, 1994; Sag et al., 2003).

12. $VP_{GAP} \rightarrow V_{GAP}$

For concreteness, consider the two sentences in (13), the first a multi-clause declarative, the other a corresponding topicalization.

13a. The gossip columnist knew the publisher rejected the dilettante's manuscript.
13b. The dilettante's manuscript, the gossip columnist knew the publisher rejected.

Sag et al. (2003) assume that the embedded verbs in the two examples have different but related feature specifications. In both cases the verb *rejected* is specified as taking two arguments. In (13a) one of those arguments belongs to the verb's complement list, COMPS; however, in (13b), that same argument has been moved to the verb's GAP list (a lexical feature that contains information about missing arguments) and the verb's COMPS list is null. Figure 45.1 is a schematic HPSG representation of sentence (13b). The contents of the GAP feature are inherited by successive phrase structure nodes that dominate the verb until the argument listed in the GAP list can be bound to a corresponding displaced argument. In Figure 45.1 the completion of the dependency is marked by the fact that the GAP feature is empty in the top-level S node.

Hence, approaches like HPSG provide the tools to syntactically mark a path that connects structurally distant participants in a dependency, and therefore allow the encoding of non-local predicate-argument relations, reducing the need for empty categories.[4] The key difference between this approach and theories that use empty categories to represent long-distance dependencies lies in whether predicate–argument relations are syntactically encoded in a uniform fashion.

45.2.2.4 Beyond constituency

In the foregoing frameworks, the challenge is to encode non-local dependencies within the notion of constituency offered by standard phrase structure grammars. Those approaches have devised systems that relate arguments with their non-constituent predicates, either through identity with a sister of the predicate, as in trace-based theories, or through feature inheritance and matching. Alternately one might extend the notion of what counts as a constituent. Combinatory Categorial Grammar (CCG: Steedman, 2000) exemplifies this approach. CCG is a species of categorial grammar (Ajudkiewicz, 1935; Bar-Hillel, 1953), a lexicalized formalism that assigns to expressions the syntactic types either of a function or an argument. The syntactic type controls the combinatory possibilities of a given expression and it is an idiosyncratic property of individual lexical items. Predicates missing arguments in canonical positions can be established as constituents, by means of rules like Functional Composition and Type Raising. In this way CCG could be viewed as sharing the feature inheritance property of HPSG analyses, albeit in a derivational fashion. In another approach, Lexical-Functional Grammar (Bresnan, 2001) encodes dependencies via mappings between "c-structure" (constituent structure) and other levels of representation, such as "f-structure" (function structure, which represents grammatical roles like

[4]As should be clear from the discussion here, the use of sequences of local feature passing relations to encode long-distance dependencies reduces the need for empty categories, but does not exclude their use. Accordingly, one finds a number of transformational theories that exploit the equivalent of local feature passing mechanisms (e.g. Kayne, 1984; Manzini, 1992). These mechanisms have proven to be particularly useful for capturing constraints on long-distance dependencies in which the dependency is blocked by an element that intervenes between the filler and the gap.

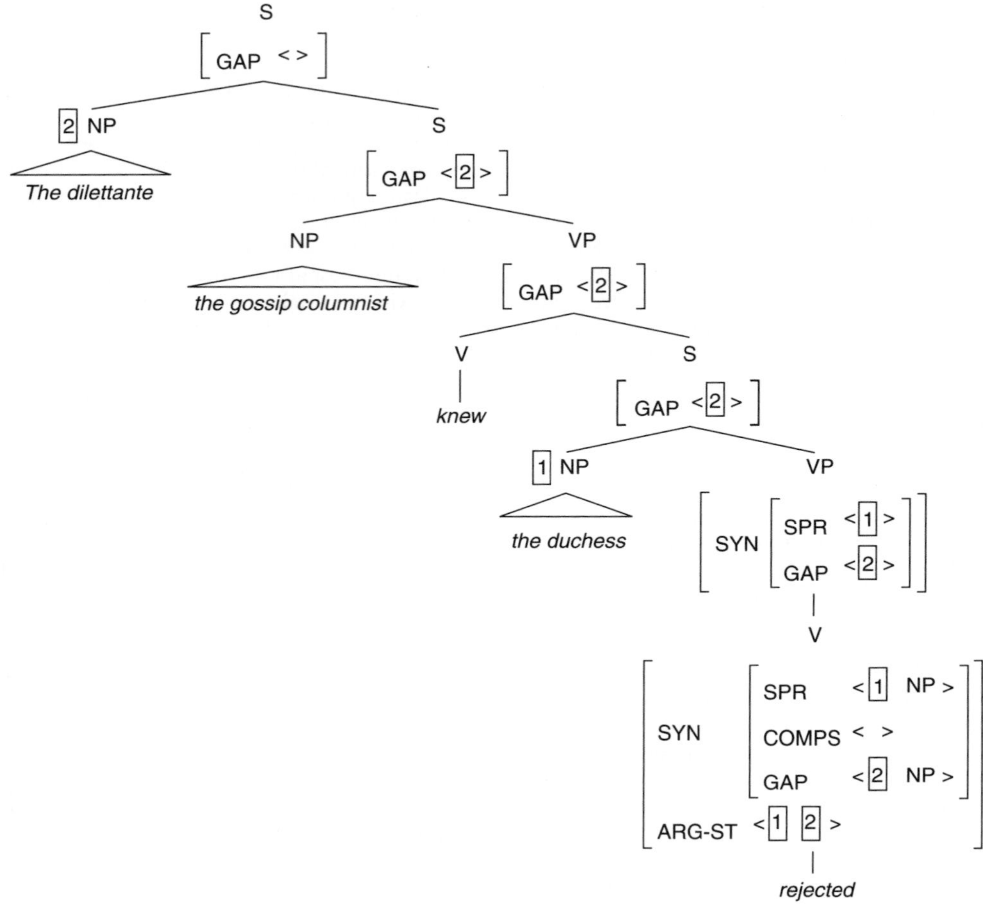

Figure 45.1 Schematized HPSG representation of sentence (13b). ARG-ST: argument structure list; COMPS: complements list (for the object arguments); SPR: specifier list (for the subject argument); GAP: gap list (for missing arguments).

Subject, Object, etc.) and "a-structure" (argument structure, which represents argument/thematic roles).

Because the experimental studies discussed in section 45.3 focus on whether or not long-distance dependencies involve traces, we do not detail the analyses of long-distance dependencies found in CCG, LFG, etc., for which there are many readable introductions (CCG: Steedman and Baldridge, 2003; LFG: Bresnan, 2001). While there are a number of different formal accounts of long-distance dependencies, it is important not to lose sight of the fact that many central insights are shared across frameworks.

45.3 **Long-distance dependencies and the status of gaps**

Although the representations posited by grammatical theories are largely motivated by distributional analyses based upon native speaker intuitions, there has been recurring interest in whether psycholinguistic evidence can be brought to bear on theoretical controversies. In the case of long-distance dependencies in particular, psycholinguistics has sometimes been viewed as a kind of appellate court that might decide in favor of one class of analyses or another. In this section and the next we discuss psycholinguistic findings relevant to the status of gaps and to constraints on long-distance dependencies, respectively, and argue that psycholinguistic arbitration has been most effective when its tools are commensurate with the linguistic hypotheses being tested.

Psycholinguistic evidence on the status of gaps has consisted principally of information about the time course of long-distance dependency construction and the timing of semantic activation of displaced phrases.[5]

It is by now relatively uncontroversial that the parser completes long-distance dependencies without waiting for unambiguous evidence for the position of the gap. Having identified a displaced filler, the parser posits a gap at the first position that might allow satisfaction of the filler's thematic requirements. This corresponds to what Fodor (1978) describes as a "filler-driven" parsing mechanism, contrasting with a "gap-driven" alternative. An important line of evidence comes from the "filled-gap effect," a temporary disruption in reading times upon encountering an NP where a gap had been expected (Crain and Fodor, 1985; Stowe, 1986). Stowe compared self-paced reading times for sentences containing a displaced *wh*-phrase like (14a) with closely matched sentences that lacked displacement (14b). She found increased reading times at the direct object NP *us* in (14a) relative to (14b) and interpreted this as a surprise effect, resulting from interpreting the *wh*-phrase as a displaced direct object as soon as the verb *bring* is reached, and before finding direct evidence for a direct object gap. This approach of forming linguistic dependencies before key bottom-up information is available is commonly referred to as "active" dependency formation.

14a. My brother wanted to know who Ruth will bring us home to at Christmas.

14b. My brother wanted to know if Ruth will bring *us* home to Mom at Christmas.

Active construction of filler-gap dependencies has been observed in many languages, including Dutch (Frazier, 1987; Frazier and Flores D'Arcais, 1989; Kaan, 1997), Russian (Sekerina, 2003), Hungarian (Radó, 1999), Italian (de Vincenzi, 1991), German (Schlesewsky et al., 2000), and Japanese (Aoshima et al., 2004). Furthermore, evidence for active dependency formation comes from a number of paradigms, include event-related potentials (ERPs: Garnsey et al., 1989; Kaan et al., 2000; Phillips et al., 2005); plausibility measures in eye-tracking or self-paced reading (Traxler and Pickering, 1996; Phillips 2006) and in the "stops making sense" task (Tanenhaus et al., 1985); cross-modal lexical priming (Nicol and Swinney, 1989; Nicol et al., 1994); and head-mounted eye-tracking (Sussman and Sedivy, 2003). We review examples from these paradigms below.

The filled gap effect provides information about the timing of long-distance dependency formation, but it is compatible with differing accounts of how long-distance dependencies are encoded. The filled gap effect in a sentence like (14a) shows only that the long-distance dependency is completed *at some time before* the overt direct object NP *us*. If we suppose that the dependency is formed at the position of the verb *bring*, then the timing evidence is compatible with a trace-based account in which an empty category is constructed as the sister of the verb *bring* as soon as the verb is reached, and is also compatible with a trace-free account in which a link is forged between the filler and the verb as soon as the verb is reached. Either account predicts a surprise effect at the following overt object NP.

Findings from other techniques provide similar evidence on the timing of dependency formation. For example, in a plausibility manipulation paradigm, Traxler and Pickering (1996) recorded eye movements while participants read sentences like (15).

[5] In this context one sometimes encounters discussion of the rise and fall of the Derivational Theory of Complexity (DTC) in the 1960s as evidence in favor of gap-less theories. We will leave aside this literature here (for contrasting accounts see Townsend and Bever, 2001; Phillips, 1996), since we see it as orthogonal to questions about the status of gaps. The DTC was the hypothesis that the "perceptual complexity" of a sentence was directly proportional to the number of steps in its transformational derivation. A common argument is that the DTC was resoundingly disconfirmed in the late 1960s and that this therefore argues against transformational theories of grammar. This argument is not relevant to our current concerns, for at least two reasons. First, DTC was a hypothesis about transformations, and as we have emphasized, empty categories and transformational rules are independent syntactic constructs. Second, what the DTC studies are purported to have shown is that it is hard to find an experimental measure that is proportional to the total number of transformational operations in the derivation of a sentence. The search for such a measure may be seen as a substitute for measures of individual parsing operations, which were hard to obtain with the tools of the 1960s. Today we still have no global measure that co-varies with the number of transformational operations in a sentence, but this point is moot, since more sensitive psycholinguistic measures have made it easier to track individual parsing operations.

15a. That's the pistol with which the heartless killer *shot* the hapless man yesterday afternoon ____.

15b. That's the garage with which the heartless killer *shot* the `apless man yesterday afternoon ____.

(15a) has a perfectly sensible, plausible interpretation, whereas (15b) is semantically anomalous, due to the predicate *shoot* taking *garage* as an instrument argument. Traxler and Pickering show that this anomaly is detected as soon as the verb is reached. This indicates that the parser has formed the dependency at least by this point. A closely related result can be found in an ERP study by Garnsey et al. (1989), who varied the plausibility of the filler-verb combination in an embedded question in sentences like (16), and observed detection of the semantic anomaly at the verb, as indexed by the N400 evoked response.

16. The businessman knew which {customer | article} the secretary called ____ at home.

A series of recent ERP studies in English provide a different index of long-distance dependency completion. Processing of the verb that allows completion of a *wh*-dependency elicits a posterior positivity relative to the same verb in a sentence without a *wh*-dependency (17a, b: Kaan et al., 2000). Kaan and colleagues use this finding to suggest that the P600 is an index of "syntactic integration difficulty" in general. Although the interpretation of this effect remains uncertain (cf. Fiebach et al., 2002; Phillips et al., 2005), its timing again shows that long-distance dependencies are formed as soon as an appropriate verb is encountered.

17a. NO WH-DEPENDENCY
Emily wondered whether the performer in the concert had *imitated* a pop star for the audience's amusement.

17b. WH-DEPENDENCY
Emily wondered which pop star the performer in the concert had *imitated* for the audience's amusement.

Pickering and Barry (1991) use the fact that filler-verb relations are constructed immediately at the verb to argue that empty categories cannot be mediating the filler-verb relation. Pickering and Barry pay particular attention to cases where the verb and the putative empty category are separated by another constituent. Their primary argument is based on examples like those in (18). The double object construction in (18a) is noticeably difficult to process, presumably because the length and complexity of the recipient argument of the verb *give* makes it harder to associate the theme argument *a prize* with the verb. However, displacement of the theme argument (18b) makes it considerably easier to process. Pickering and Barry argue that a trace-based account incorrectly predicts that (18b) should cause the same processing load as (18a), since the representation of (18b) would contain a trace in the same location as *a prize* in (18a). On the other hand, a trace-free theory could relate the displaced argument *the prize* in (18b) to the verb *give* as soon as the verb is reached, accounting for the reduced processing difficulty. A similar argument can be constructed based on Traxler and Pickering's eye-tracking study, illustrated in (15).

18a. We gave [every student capable of answering every single tricky question on the details of the new and extremely complicated theory about the causes of political instability in small nations with a history of military rulers] [*a prize*]

18b. That's *the prize* that we gave [every student capable of answering every single tricky question on the details of the new and extremely complicated theory about the causes of political instability in small nations with a history of military rulers]

The argument developed by Pickering and Barry involves mapping a representational claim onto a timing prediction. They assume that if fillers are linked to verbs through the mediation of an empty category, then the timing of this operation should coincide with the linear position of the empty category in the sequence. Their argument is therefore only as strong as the timing prediction. As pointed out in various replies (Gibson and Hickok, 1993; Gorrell, 1993; Crocker, 1994) the parser might easily construct an empty category position in advance of its linear position, such as by projecting argument positions as soon as a verb is reached. If this assumption about the parser is adopted, then the predicted timing contrast between the competing theories is neutralized.

Using related logic, one might look to the processing of head-final languages in search of decisive evidence on the status of empty categories. However, the arguments in this area have the same limitations as Pickering and Barry's argument, but in the opposite direction. In head-final languages like Japanese, all arguments canonically appear before the verb. Therefore, in a trace-based representation of filler-gap dependencies in such languages, the position of the empty category appears before the verb. In the spirit of Pickering and Barry's argument, one might suppose that a trace-based representation would allow filler-gap dependencies to be completed before the verb is reached, whereas a trace-free theory would delay completion of the dependency until the verb. And, indeed, Aoshima and colleagues have presented evidence for preverbal dependency completion using a Japanese adaptation of the filled gap effect paradigm (Aoshima et al., 2004). They show that, when a fronted dative NP is processed, a dative NP in an embedded clause engenders a reading-time slowdown (with respect to an embedded dative NP in a structure without a long-distance dependency). Based on this evidence, Aoshima and colleagues conclude that filler-gap dependencies can be formed in advance of the verb in Japanese, and also suggest that this favors a trace-based representational model. However, this argument in favor of empty categories has exactly the same weakness as Pickering and Barry's argument against empty categories. If the parser for Japanese allows the verb position to be constructed before the overt verb is reached, then direct filler-verb relations may be constructed in advance of the verb. Similar concerns apply to the timing-based argument for traces presented by Lee (2004), who demonstrates a filled gap effect in subject positions in English.

The experimental paradigms discussed so far all provide useful information about the timing of dependency completion, yet they yield few solid conclusions about what representations are being constructed. One limitation of these measures is that they often rely on semantically-based effects to draw inferences about syntactic computations. Implausibility detection measures implicate semantic representations; the filled-gap effect is ambivalent between a syntactic or semantic explanation; and the ERP P600 effects at best suggest that something syntactic happens when a verb is processed following a displaced phrase, although even this interpretation is not certain. A final potential source of evidence comes from studies of filler reactivation.

Drawing on evidence from on-line cross-modal lexical priming tasks (Nicol and Swinney 1989; Nicol et al., 1994) and off-line probe recognition scores (McElree and Bever, 1989), it has been argued that fillers are lexically reactivated at the gap site. This phenomenon might be taken as evidence that displaced constituents combine with verbs in the same way that arguments in canonical positions combine with verbs, and by extension could be presented as evidence in favor of a trace-based analysis. When these findings first appeared there was considerable interest in the possibility that they might constitute psycholinguistic confirmation of the "psychological reality" of traces (and in certain linguistic circles one still hears them discussed in such terms). However, they are subject to the now familiar limitations. First, the reactivation of a lexical code at the verb or gap site does not clearly favor one representational approach over another. Reactivation of the lexical code of the filler may reflect construction of an empty category, or may equally reflect construction of a direct link from a verb to the filler. Gap-site priming effects have also been reported in preverbal positions in head-final languages (German scrambling: Clahsen and Featherston, 1999; Japanese scrambling: Nakano et al., 2002). However, just as with the Japanese filled gap effect, such arguments depend on the questionable assumption that verb positions are constructed only when the overt verb is reached in such languages. Second, the reactivated code need not be strictly lexical, since only the contextually relevant meaning of an ambiguous filler is reactivated at the gap site (Love and Swinney, 1996). Consequently, we are ultimately left with further information on the time-course of semantic interpretation that is consistent with multiple syntactic accounts.

In the absence of theoretically decisive timing arguments, it is sometimes claimed that considerations of parsimony should favor a trace-free theory (Pickering, 1993) or that the behavioral results most directly implicate a trace-free account (Sag and Fodor, 1994). Why posit multiple levels of syntactic representation if one level will suffice? Why appeal to phonologically empty categories if we can do without them? We find such arguments to be somewhat disingenuous, for a couple of reasons. First, competing theories agree on the need for multiple levels of representation for sentences, but disagree on the issue of how many of these levels are syntactic or semantic and how the levels are related to one another. Phenomena that are explained in terms of empty categories in one theory must be accounted for using other machinery in a theory that lacks empty categories. Simplifying one's syntax often leads to complications at other levels of representation (cf. Jackendoff 2002: 144–8). Second, while we acknowledge the need for caution in proliferating the inventory of empty categories in the grammar, it strikes us as odd to claim that phonologically empty syntactic formatives are inherently objectionable. Perceptual processes, whether in language or in other domains, involve the construction of many kinds of mental object that do not correspond to a clearly defined sensory stimulus.

In speech perception we detect segments that are masked or absent in the input; in vision we perceive objects that are not present in the distal stimulus; in syntax we perceive combinatorial structure that is not encoded in the phonological form of a sentence. Taken in this context, the notion of empty categories is rather banal. This does not, of course, entail that they are needed, merely that one should continue to search for good empirical arguments rather than falling back on questionable claims of parsimony.

In sum, a constellation of findings spanning multiple experimental approaches have converged in support of the idea that long-distance dependency formation is a rapid, top-down process. Moreover, it is an active process, occurring as soon as there is sufficient information to posit a gap, often at the point of encountering the verb, and in head-final languages in advance of the verb. However, this is a timing result that does not clearly correlate with particular ways of encoding the relation between a verb and a displaced argument. In this area psycholinguistic tools have so far proven inconclusive. We see this more as a practical failure than a principled one. More ingenious methods of probing syntactic representations might yet succeed in distinguishing the competing theories.

45.4 Experimental studies of constraints on dependencies

A possible moral of the previous section is that psycholinguistic measures of timing can be used to resolve representational controversies only to the extent that the competing representational accounts yield clear predictions about timing. In this section we consider two issues that may be better suited to psycholinguistic testing, specifically because they involve clearer timing predictions. By exploring how real-time language processing is affected by constraints on long-distance dependencies, we can address whether linguistic and psycholinguistic models should be viewed as accounts of the same underlying mechanisms, and also the extent to which grammatical constraints might be reducible to constraints on language processing.

45.4.1 Island constraints

Although filler-gap dependencies may span long distances, they are also subject to a number of restrictions that have attracted substantial interest in linguistics since classic studies in the mid-1960s (Chomsky, 1964; Ross, 1967). Following terminology introduced by Ross, contexts that block filler-gap dependencies are widely known as "islands." Syntactic islands include relative clauses (19a), *wh*-clauses (19b), factive clauses (19c), subjects (19d), adjuncts (19e), and coordinate structures (19f).

19a. *What did the agency fire the official that recommended ___?
19b. *Who do you wonder whether the press secretary spoke with ___?
19c. *Why did they remember that the corrupt CEO had been aquitted ___?
19d. *What did the fact that Joan remembered ___ surprise her grandchildren?
19e. *Who did Susan watch TV while talking to ___ on the phone?
19f. *What did the Senate approve ___ and the House reject the bill?

There have been numerous attempts to capture the common property or properties that underlie these and other island constraints. For example, Chomsky's (1973) Subjacency Constraint captured the effects of a number of islands under a constraint that blocks filler-gap dependencies that cross two or more bounding nodes (NP or S) in one step. A number of good summaries of different formal accounts of islands are available (e.g. Manzini, 1992; Culicover, 1997). However, our concern here is less with adjudicating competing formal accounts, and more with how these constraints impact the relation between linguistic and psycholinguistic models.

There is widespread skepticism over the issue of whether linguistic and psycholinguistic models are concerned with the same mental phenomena. Psycholinguists are often suspicious of linguists' obsession with ephemeral constructions which rarely occur in real life situations. Meanwhile, in linguistics there is a long-standing tradition of distancing theoretical models from claims about real-time processes. In an influential statement of objectives for the field Chomsky states: "When we say that a sentence has a certain derivation with respect to a particular generative grammar, we say nothing about how the speaker or hearer might proceed, in some practical or efficient way, to construct such a derivation" (Chomsky 1965: 9). In support of this position it has been claimed that the parser initially builds coarse-grained representations that lack the detail required of the grammar (Townsend and Bever, 2001) and that language is not "readily usable" (Chomsky and Lasnik, 1993: 18). In this context, it is relevant to ask whether real-time language processes are sensitive to constraints on filler-gap dependencies and other phenomena that are central concerns of grammatical theory. To the extent that these are reflected in real-time language processing mechanisms, there is more reason to think that linguists and psycholinguists are concerned with the same mental representations.

45.4.2 The timing of island constraints

A number of studies have addressed the impact of island constraints on real-time language processing. Most published studies on this topic have concluded that island constraints do impact language processing, and in doing so have shown different ways in which island constraints may be reflected in comprehension processes.

One line of research asks whether the parser suspends its normal "active" search for gaps in positions where this would lead to an island constraint violation. Typically, the logic of these studies is to show that a manipulation that yields a measurable experimental effect when a well-formed gap is posited yields a null effect at comparable positions inside syntactic islands. For example, Stowe (1986: experiment 2) followed up on her demonstration of the filled gap effect (FGE) by showing that the FGE is not observed inside a syntactic island. The NP *Greg's* in (20a) is the object of a complement PP, and thus occupies a potential gap site for the fronted wh-phrase, as in a sentence like (22a). This NP was read more slowly in (20a) than in a control condition that lacked *wh*-fronting (20b), an FGE that suggests that the parser actively posited a gap site in the prepositional object position. In contrast, the NP *Greg's* in (21a) is embedded inside a subject NP. Subjects are typically islands for *wh*-fronting, and hence the NP *Greg's* does not occupy a potential grammatical gap site, as shown by the unacceptability of (22b). Stowe found no FGE at this NP, suggesting that the parser made no attempt to posit a gap inside the island. Similar findings about the disappearance of the FGE in island environments have been reported in French (Bourdages, 1992) and Japanese (Yoshida et al., 2004).

20a. The teacher asked what the team laughed about Greg's older brother fumbling.
20b. The teacher asked if the team laughed about Greg's older brother fumbling the ball.
21a. The teacher asked what the silly story about Greg's older brother was supposed to mean.
21b. The teacher asked if the silly story about Greg's older brother was supposed to mean anything.

22a. The teacher asked what the team laughed about ___.
22b. *The teacher asked what the silly story about ___ was supposed to mean.

Other studies have made a related argument using the plausibility manipulation paradigm introduced above. Traxler and Pickering (1996) showed that manipulation of the semantic plausibility of a filler–verb combination elicited an immediate reading-time slowdown at the verb in examples like (23), but no corresponding slowdown at the same verb when it appeared inside a relative clause (24), again suggesting immediate effects of island constraints.[6]

23. *Preamble: Waiting for a publishing contract*
The big city was a fascinating subject for the new book.

23a. We like the book that the author wrote unceasingly and with great dedication about while waiting for a contract.
23b. We like the city that the author wrote unceasingly and with great dedication about while waiting for a contract.

24a. We like the book that the author who wrote unceasingly and with great dedication saw while waiting for a contract.
24b. We like the city that the author who wrote unceasingly and with great dedication saw while waiting for a contract.

In contrast to the studies that have shown the absence of active dependency completion effects in island environments, a number of other studies have demonstrated processing disruption when the search for a gap encounters the boundary of a syntactic island. Three different ERP studies have measured the effect of encountering an island boundary while searching for a gap site for a filler. McKinnon and Osterhout (1996) compared ERP responses elicited by sentences like (25a), containing an illicit extraction from a *when*-clause, with closely matched sentences that lack an island constraint violation (25b). The P600 response characteristic of responses to syntactic anomalies was elicited at the word *when*, indicating that comprehenders are immediately sensitive to island domains while processing filler-gap dependencies. However, this effect is open to multiple interpretations: the P600 response may

[6] Wagers and Phillips (2006) demonstrate island sensitivity without relying on a null effect. They show an immediate plausibility effect in the second conjunct of a coordinate structure, indicating sensitivity to the Coordinate Structure Constraint.

reflect calculation of ill-formedness in a formal account of island constraints, or it may instead reflect disruption to the process of searching for a gap by the presence of a second *wh*-phrase. These two possible interpretations are represented in two other ERP studies of island effects that have elicited left anterior negativity (LAN) effects one word after the beginning of an island domain (Neville et al., 1991; Kluender and Kutas, 1993).

25a. *I wonder which of his staff members the candidate was annoyed *when* his son was questioned by.

25b. I wonder whether the candidate was annoyed *when* his son was questioned by his staff member.

Related effects can be found in a study by McElree and Griffith (1998) using a "speed–accuracy tradeoff" (SAT) paradigm in which participants were trained to give acceptability judgements immediately upon hearing a tone that occurs at specific intervals after the end of a test sentence. Unsurprisingly, when the tone appears very shortly after the sentence, accuracy is low, and when the tone appears after a longer delay, accuracy is higher. The interest of the SAT paradigm is that it allows the researcher to precisely track the time-course of increases in accuracy. McElree and Griffith show that sensitivity to an island violation begins to emerge almost immediately after the verb in sentences with relative clause island violations such as (26). This effect may reflect detection of the island violation at the verb position, but it more likely reflects detection of the violation at the preceding word *who* that begins the relative clause, which appeared only 250 ms earlier.

26. *It was the essay that the writer scolded the editor who admired.

If island constraints can be held responsible for the disappearance of filled gap effects and plausibility effects inside islands, and for the various effects of island-boundary detection, then we can conclude that constraints on filler-gap dependencies have a more or less immediate impact upon language comprehension processes.[7] This, and related experimental findings showing the immediate effects of other grammatical constraints (e.g. binding constraints: Nicol and Swinney, 1989; Sturt, 2003; Kazanina et al., 2007), suggest that the parser constructs the same kinds of representation that linguists are concerned with, and make it more difficult for linguists to argue that real-time processes are irrelevant to their concerns. The findings are at least consistent with the stronger position that the grammar is a real-time structure building mechanism (e.g. Phillips, 1996; 2004; Kempson et al., 2001), but it by no means entails this view.

45.4.3 The origin of island constraints

Findings about the immediacy of island constraints do not show that the constraints are "psychologically real" in the sense that they lend greater psychological respectability to the formal linguistic description of the constraint. The experimental findings indicate that the same properties that account for the unacceptability of island violations also affect real-time comprehension processes, but do not indicate whether island constraints are more appropriately viewed as formal constraints on structures or as the products of independent constraints on memory, focus, or any other factors that might affect language processing.

In contrast to formal accounts of island constraints, it has often been suggested that island constraints may ultimately derive from limitations on real-time language processing. Some accounts assume that the island constraints are grammaticized, but ultimately owe their presence in grammars to constraints on language processing (Fodor, 1978; 1983; Berwick and Weinberg, 1984; Hawkins, 1999), whereas other accounts assume that island constraints are genuine epiphenomena that are not explicitly represented in a speaker's grammar (Deane, 1991; Pritchett, 1991; Kluender and Kutas, 1993). For example, some accounts have proposed that the impossibility of extraction from a subject NP (27) may reflect the order of structure building operations in language processing.

27. *Who did [$_{NP}$ the news about ___] surprise everybody?

Pritchett (1991) suggests that the islandhood of subjects is a natural consequence of his "head-driven" parsing architecture, which allows the parser to start building a phrase only once the head of that phrase has been encountered. Since subject NPs precede the head of the phrase that they are a part of, e.g. an auxiliary or a verb, the head-driven architecture prevents subject NPs from being immediately attached into the parse tree. This, in turn, delays the completion of a filler-gap dependency into the subject NP,

[7] There is a small number of studies whose results suggest that gaps are posited inside syntactic islands in real time (Pickering et al., 1994: expt. 1; Clifton and Frazier, 1989), but these results are open to alternative explanations.

and Pritchett suggests that this is what underlies the unacceptability of subject island violations. A related mechanism is responsible for subject island effects in a study by Hawkins (1999).

Attempts to derive island constraints from constraints on real-time structure building share a simple prediction, which can be tested using psycholinguistic methods. If the unacceptability of a gap in a given location is due to the parser's difficulty or inability to construct a gap in that location, then speakers should indeed find it difficult or impossible to construct such gaps during real-time processing. Phillips (2006) describes a test of this prediction, taking advantage of the phenomenon of "parasitic gaps" (Engdahl, 1983; Culicover, 2001)—constructions in which otherwise ill-formed gaps are rendered acceptable when they appear in a sentence with an additional well-formed gap. (28a) is another illustration of the islandhood of subject NPs. In this case, the illicit gap is inside an infinitival clause that is the complement of a subject NP. When the illicit gap in (28a) is combined with the acceptable direct object gap in (28b), the result is an acceptable sentence (28c). (These judgements have been confirmed in controlled rating studies.) The first gap in (28c) is referred to as a "parasitic gap," since its well-formedness relies upon the presence of another gap.

28a. *What did the attempt to repair ___ ultimately damage the car?
28b. What did the attempt to repair the car ultimately damage ___?
28c. What did the attempt to repair $\_\_\__{pg}$ ultimately damage ___?

The phenomenon of parasitic gaps is interesting in its own right, but parasitic gap examples like (28c) are particularly interesting from the perspective of real-time processing, since the illicit gap precedes the gap that licenses it. If the parser actively posits gaps in all positions where a well-formed gap might appear, then it should be able to create a gap upon reaching the embedded verb *repair* in sentences like (28), and should then seek an additional licensing gap in order for the sentence to be well-formed. If, on the other hand, the parser more strictly avoids positing gaps inside islands, then the parser should never construct an illicit gap like the one shown in (28a). This would imply that well-formed constructions like (28c) must be parsed in a non-incremental fashion, constructing the parasitic gap only after the licensing gap has been confirmed.

Using an implausibility detection paradigm similar to Traxler and Pickering (1996), Phillips (2006) shows that active gap creation occurs in potential parasitic gap environments just as in more familiar environments. A slowdown reflecting implausibility detection occurs immediately at the underlined verb when it appears inside an island that supports parasitic gaps, as in (29), where the subject NP contains an infinitival complement clause. This suggests that speakers actively created a gap inside the subject NP, despite its islandhood. No corresponding slowdown is observed in islands that do not support parasitic gaps. The finite relative clause in (30a) creates an island for filler-gap dependencies, but unlike the examples in (28) this violation cannot be "rescued" by combination with a well-formed gap (30b, c). The lack of a plausibility effect implies that the parser failed to posit a gap in this environment, and therefore that the parser constructs gaps inside islands in precisely the environments where the grammar of parasitic gaps makes this possible.

29. The school superintendent learned {which schools/which high school students} the plan to *expand* ...
30a. *What did the reporter that criticized ___ eventually praise the war?
30b. What did the reporter that criticized the war eventually praise ___?
30c. *What did the reporter that criticized ___ eventually praise ___?

These findings are directly relevant to claims that island phenomena can be reduced to effects of difficulty in the processing of filler-gap dependencies. The unacceptability of the subject island violation in (28a) cannot be due to difficulty in real-time gap creation, since the experimental results show that speakers readily create a filler-gap dependency into the subject NP. If the unacceptability of the gap in (28a) is not reducible to processing constraints, then this lends credence to a formal account of the island constraint. Of course, this argument does not necessarily extend to other types of island, even including other types of subject island like (30a). Nevertheless, it would seem odd to claim that highly unacceptable islands, such as the extraction from a relative clause in (30a), are grammatically well-formed and are epiphenomena of constraints on processing, whereas less severe violations like (28a) are grammatically ill-formed.

In sum, the studies reviewed in this section suggest that it is possible to use psycholinguistic results to learn about the form of the grammar, even in the same domain of long-distance dependencies that proved to be more difficult to test in section 45.3. The difference is that in this section we have been considering questions about the grammar that have direct timing consequences, and hence are well-suited for psycholinguistic testing.

45.5 Conclusion

We see no principled reason why the fields of linguistics and psycholinguistics should not have an ongoing and mutually beneficial interaction. This reflects, in part, the fact that we struggle to draw a clear distinction between the two areas. Both fields have serious mentalistic commitments, and we see neither as having more privileged access to the psychological mechanisms of language. In cases where linguists are unwilling to take their mentalistic commitments sufficiently seriously, or where psycholinguists are dismissive of the complexities that linguists spend their time worrying about, we will continue to find skepticism and suspicion from both directions. The relation between the fields has sometimes been viewed in hierarchical terms, according to which linguistics should look to psycholinguistics as a court of arbitration for its disputes, but not vice versa. We find this view, and the related notion of the "psychological reality" of linguistic constructs, to be somewhat unhelpful. The hypotheses that linguists develop on the basis of distributional analyses of informant judgements are just as psychological as hypotheses developed on the basis of analyses of complex reaction time or eye-gaze data. It is conceivable that when linguists investigate acceptability judgements they are studying a cognitive system that is distinct from the processing systems with which psycholinguists are more commonly concerned; but we should stress that this distinction is an empirical hypothesis, and one that has received very little direct testing. Therefore, in the absence of good evidence to the contrary, we assume that linguists and psycholinguists are exploring the same cognitive system, albeit with different tools. We take the case study of long-distance dependencies to show that the prospects for influence from psycholinguistics to linguistics (and vice versa) are good, and are subject to merely practical limitations. One field can successfully influence the other only when its tools are commensurate with the hypotheses that are being tested. This should come as no surprise.

Acknowledgements

Preparation of this chapter was supported in part by grants to Colin Phillips from the National Science Foundation (BCS-0196004) and the Human Frontiers Science Program (RGY-0134). We are grateful to Norbert Hornstein, Nina Kazanina, and Jeff Lidz for useful discussion of many of the issues addressed here.

References

Ajdukiewicz, K. (1935) Die syntaktische Konnexität. *Studia Philosophica*, 1: 1–27. English translation in S. McCall (ed.), *Polish Logic 1920-1939*, pp. 207–31. Oxford University Press, Oxford.

Aoshima, S., Phillips, C., and Weinberg, A. S. (2004) Processing filler-gap dependencies in a head-final language. *Journal of Memory and Language*, 51: 23–54.

Bar-Hillel, Y (1953) A quasi-arithmetical notation for syntactic description. *Language*, 29: 47–58.

Berwick, R., and Weinberg, A. S. (1984) *The Grammatical Basis of Linguistic Performance*. MIT Press, Cambridge, MA.

Boland, J. E. (2005) Cognitive mechanisms and syntactic theory. In A. Cutler (ed.,), *Twenty-First Century Psycholinguistics: Four Cornerstones*, pp. 23–42. Erlbaum, Mahwah, NJ.

Bourdages, J. S. (1992) Parsing complex NPs in French. In H. Goodluck and M. S. Rochemont (eds), *Island Constraints: Theory, Acquisition and Processing*, pp. 61–87. Kluwer Academic, Dordrecht.

Bresnan, J. (1978) A realistic transformational grammar. In J. Bresnan, M. Halle, and G. Miller (eds), *Linguistic Theory and Psychological Reality*, pp. 1–59. MIT Press, Cambridge, MA.

Bresnan, J. (2001) *Lexical-Functional Syntax*. Blackwell, Oxford.

Brody, M. (1995) *Lexico-logical Form*. MIT Press, Cambridge, MA.

Chomsky, N. (1957) *Syntactic Structures*. Mouton, The Hague.

Chomsky, N. (1964) *Current Issues in Linguistic Theory*. Mouton, The Hague.

Chomsky, N. (1965) *Aspects of the Theory of Syntax*. MIT Press, Cambridge, MA.

Chomsky, N. (1973) Conditions on transformations. In S. Anderson and P. Kiparsky (eds), *A Festschrift for Morris Halle*, pp. 232–86. Holt, Rinehart & Winston, New York.

Chomsky, N. (1981) *Lectures on Government and Binding*. Foris, Dordrecht.

Chomsky, N. (1995) *The Minimalist Program*. MIT Press, Cambridge, MA.

Chomsky, N., and H. Lasnik, (1993) The theory of Principles and Parameters. In J. Jacobs, W. Sternefeld, and T. Vennemann (eds), *Syntax: An International Handbook of Contemporary Research*, pp. 506–69. Berlin: de Gruyter. Repr. in Chomsky (1995: 13–127).

Clahsen, H., and Featherstone, S. (1999) Antecedent-priming at trace positions: evidence from German scrambling. *Journal of Psycholinguistic Research*, 28: 415–37.

Clifton, C. E., Jr, and Frazier, L. (1989) Comprehending sentences with long-distance dependencies. In M. K. Tanenhaus and G. N. Carlson (eds), *Linguistic Structure in Language Processing*, pp. 273–317. Dordrecht: Kluwer Academic.

Crain, S., and Fodor, J. D. (1985) How can grammars help parsers? In D. Dowty, L. Kartunnen, and A. M. Zwicky (eds), *Natural Language Parsing: Psycholinguistic, Computational, and Theoretical Perspectives*, pp. 94–128. Cambridge University Press, Cambridge.

Crocker, M. W. (1994) On the nature of the principle-based sentence processor. In C. Clifton, Jr, L. Frazier, and K. Rayner (eds), *Perspective on Sentence Processing*, pp. 245–66. Erlbaum, Hillside, NJ.

Culicover, P. (1997) *Principles and Parameters: An Introduction to Syntactic Theory*. Oxford University Press, Oxford.

Culicover, P. (2001) Parasitic gaps: a history. In P. S. Culicover and P. Postal (eds), *Parasitic Gaps*, pp. 3–68. MIT Press, Cambridge, MA.

Deane, P. (1991) Limits to attention: a cognitive theory of island constraints. *Cognitive Linguistics*, 2: 1–63.

de Vincenzi, M. (1991) *Syntactic Parsing Strategies in Italian*. Kluwer Academic, Dordrecht.

Engdahl, E. (1983) Parasitic gaps. *Linguistics and Philosophy*, 5: 5–34.

Ferreira, F. (2005) Psycholinguistics, formal grammars, and cognitive science. *Linguistic Review*, 22: 365–80.

Fiebach, C. M., Schlesewsky, M., and Friederici, A. D. (2002) Separating syntactic memory costs and syntactic integration costs during parsing: the processing of German wh-questions. *Journal of Memory and Language*, 47: 250–72.

Fiengo, R. (1977) On trace theory. *Linguistic Inquiry*, 8: 35–62.

Fodor, J. D. (1978) Parsing strategies and constraints on transformations. *Linguistic Inquiry*, 9: 427–73.

Fodor, J. D. (1983) Phrase structure parsing and the island constraints. *Linguistics and Philosophy*, 6: 163–223.

Frank, R. (2002) *Phrase Structure Composition and Syntactic Dependencies*. MIT Press, Cambridge, MA.

Frazier, L. (1987) Syntactic processing: Evidence from Dutch. *Natural Language and Linguistic Theory*, 5: 519–60.

Frazier, L., and Flores D'Arcais, G. B. (1989) Filler-driven parsing: a study of gap filling in Dutch. *Journal of Memory of Language*, 28: 331–44.

Garnsey, S. M., Tanenhaus, M. K., and Chapman, R. M. (1989) Evoked potentials and the study of sentence comprehension. *Journal of Psycholinguistic Research*, 18: 51–60.

Gazdar, G., Klein, E., Pullum, G., and Sag, I. (1985) *Generalized Phrase Structure Grammar*. Harvard University Press, Cambridge, MA.

Gibson, E., and Hickok, G. (1993) Sentence processing with empty categories. *Language and Cognitive Processes*, 8: 147–61.

Gorrell, P. (1993) Evaluating the direct association hypothesis: a reply to Pickering and Barry (1991), *Language and Cognitive Processes*, 8: 129–46.

Hawkins, J. (1999) Processing complexity and filler-gap dependencies across languages. *Language*, 75: 224–85.

Jackendoff, R. (2002) *Foundations of Language*. Oxford University Press, New York.

Kaan, E. (1997) Processing subject–object ambiguities in Dutch. Doctoral dissertation, University of Groningen.

Kaan, E., Harris, A., Gibson, E., and Holcomb, P. (2000) The P600 as an index of syntactic integration difficulty. *Language and Cognitive Processes*, 15: 159–201.

Kamide, Y., and Mitchell, D. C. (1999) Incremental pre-head attachment in Japanese parsing. *Language and Cognitive Processes*, 14: 631–62.

Kayne, R. (1984) *Connectedness and Binary Branching*. Foris, Dordrecht.

Kazanina, N., Lau, E., Lieberman, M., Yoshida, M., and Phillips, C. (2007) Effects of syntactic constraints on the processing of backward anaphora. *Journal of Memory and Language*.

Kempson, R., Meyer-Viol, W., and Gabbay, D. (2001) *Dynamic Syntax*. Blackwell, Oxford.

Kluender, R., and Kutas, M. (1993) Subjacency as a processing phenomenon. *Language and Cognitive Processes*, 8: 573–633.

Koster, J. (1978) *Locality principles in syntax*. Foris, Dordrecht.

Kroch, A., and Joshi, A. K. (1985) The linguistic relevance of Tree Adjoining Grammar. MS-CIS-85–16: University of Pennsylvania.

Kurtzman, H. S., and Crawford, L. S. (1991) Processing parasitic gaps. In T. Sherer (ed.), *Proceedings of the 21st Annual Meeting of the North East Linguistics Society*, pp. 217–31. GLSA, Amherst, MA.

Lee, M.-W. (2004) Another look at the role of empty categories in sentence processing (and grammar) *Journal of Psycholinguistic Research*, 33: 51–73.

Love, T., and Swinney, D. (1996) Coreference processing and levels of analysis in object-relative constructions: demonstration of antecedent reactivation with the cross-modal priming paradigm. *Journal of Psycholinguistic Research*, 25: 5–24.

Manzini, M. R. (1992) *Locality*. MIT Press, Cambridge, MA.

McElree, B., and Bever, T. G. (1989) The psychological reality of linguistically defined gaps. *Journal of Psycholinguistic Research*, 18: 21–36.

McElree, B., and Griffith, T. (1998) Structural and lexical constraints on filling gaps during sentence comprehension: a time-course analysis. *Journal of Experimental Psychology: Learning, Memory, and Cognition*, 24: 432–60.

McKinnon, R., and Osterhout, L. (1996) Constraints on movement phenomena in sentence processing: Evidence from event-related potentials. *Language and Cognitive Processes*, 11: 495–523.

McKoon, G., Allbritton, D., and Ratcliff, R. (1996) Sentential context effects on lexical decisions with a cross-modal instead of all-visual procedure. *Journal of Experimental Psychology, Language, Memory and Cognition*, 22: 1494–7.

McKoon, G., and Ratcliff, R. (1994) Sentential context and on-line lexical decision tasks. *Journal of Experimental Psychology, Language, Memory and Cognition*, 20: 1239–43.

McKoon, G., Ratcliff, R., and Ward, G. (1994) Testing theories of language processing: an empirical investigation on the on-line lexical decision task. *Journal of Experimental Psychology: Learning, Memory, and Cognition*, 20: 1219–28.

Miller, G. A. (1990) Linguists, psychologists, and the cognitive sciences. *Language*, 66: 317–22.

Nakano, Y., Felser, C., and Clahsen, H. (2002) Antecedent reactivation in the processing of scrambling in Japanese. *MIT Working Papers in Linguistics*, 43: 127–42.

Neville, H. J., Nicol, J., Barss, A., Forster, K., and Garrett, M. (1991) Syntactically-based sentence processing classes: evidence from event-related brain potentials. *Journal of Cognitive Neuroscience*, 3: 151–65.

Nicol, J. L., Fodor, J. D., and Swinney, D. (1994) Using cross-modal lexical decision tasks to investigate sentence processing. *Journal of Experimental Psychology: Learning, Memory and Cognition*, 20: 1229–38.

Nicol, J. L., and Swinney, D. (1989) The role of structure in coreference assignment during sentence comprehension. *Journal of Psycholinguistic Research*, 18: 5–19.

Nicol, J., Swinney, D., Love, T., and Hald, L. A. (1997) *Examination of Sentence Processing with Continuous vs. Interrupted Presentation Paradigms*. Center for Human Information Processing Technical Report 97–3. University of California, San Diego.

Phillips, C. (1996) Order and structure. Ph. D. dissertation, MIT.

Phillips, C. (2004) Linguistics and linking problems. In M. Rice and S. Warren (eds), *Developmental Language Disorders: From Phenotypes to Etiologies*, pp. 241–87. Erlbaum, Mahwah, NJ.

Phillips, C. (2006) The real-time status of island phenomena. *Language*, 82: 795–823.

Phillips, C., Kazanina, N., and Abada, S. H. (2005) ERP effects of the processing of syntactic long-distance dependencies. *Cognitive Brain Research*, 22: 407–28.

Pickering, M. (1993) Direction association and sentence processing: a reply to Gorrell and to Gibson and Hickok. *Language and Cognitive Processes*, 8: 163–96.

Pickering, M. J., and Barry, G. D. (1991) Sentence processing without empty categories. *Language and Cognitive Processes*, 6: 229–59.

Pickering, M. J., Barton, S., and Shillcock, R. (1994) Unbounded dependencies, island constraints and processing complexity. In C. Clifton, Jr, L. Frazier, and K. Rayner (eds), *Perspectives on Sentence Processing*, pp. 199–224. Lawrence Erlbaum, London.

Pollard, C., and Sag, I. A. (1994) *Head-Driven Phrase Structure Grammar*. University of Chicago Press, Chicago.

Pritchett, B. L. (1991) Subjacency in a principle-based parser. In R. C. Berwick (ed.), *Principle-Based Parsing: Computation and Psycholinguistics*, pp. 301–45. Kluwer Academic, Dordrecht.

Radó, J. (1999) Some effects of discourse salience on gap-filling. Poster presented at the 12th Annual CUNY Conference on Human Sentence Processing.

Rizzi, L. (1986) On chain formation. In H. Borer (ed.), *The Syntax of Pronominal Clitics*, pp. 65–76, Academic Press, New York.

Ross, J. R. (1967) Constraints on variables in syntax. Ph.D. dissertation, MIT.

Sag, I. A., and Fodor, J. D. (1994) Extraction without traces. In R. Aranovich, W. Byrne, S. Preuss, and M. Senturia (eds), *Proceedings of the 13th Annual Meeting of the West Coast Conference on Formal Linguistics*, pp. 365–84. CSLI, Stanford, CA.

Sag, I. A., Wasow, T., and Bender, E. M. (2003) *Syntactic Theory: A Formal Introduction*. CSLI, Stanford, CA.

Schlesewsky, M., Fanselow, G., Kliegl, R., and Krems, J. (2000) The subject preference in the processing of locally ambiguous wh-questions in German. In B. Hemforth and L. Konieczny (eds), *German Sentence Processing*, pp. 65–93. Kluwer Academic, Dordrecht.

Sekerina, I. A. (2003) Scrambling and processing: dependencies, complexity, and constraints. In S. Karimi (ed.), *Word Order and Scrambling*, pp. 301–24. Blackwell, Malden, MA.

Steedman, M. (2000) *The Syntactic Process*. MIT Press, Cambridge, MA.

Steedman, M., and Baldridge, J. (2003) Combinatory Categorial Grammar. Unpublished tutorial paper, online: http://groups.inf.ed.ac.uk/ccg/publications.html

Stowe, L. A. (1986) Evidence for on-line gap-location. *Language and Cognitive Processes*, 1: 227–45.

Sturt, P. (2003) The time course of the application of binding constraints in reference resolution. *Journal of Memory and Language*, 48: 542–62.

Sussman, R. S., and Sedivy, J. C. (2003) The time-course of processing syntactic dependencies: evidence from eye-movements during spoken wh-questions. *Language and Cognitive Processes*, 18: 143–63.

Swinney, D., Ford, M., Frauenfelder, U., and Bresnan, J. (1988) On the temporal course of gap filling and antecedent assignment during sentence comprehension. MS.

Swinney, D. A., Onifer, W., Prather, P., and Hirshkowitz, M. (1979) Semantic facilitation across sensory modalities in the processing of individual words and sentences. *Memory and Cognition*, 7: 159–65.

Tanenhaus, M., Stowe, L., and Carlson., G. (1985) The interaction of lexical expectation and pragmatics in parsing filler-gap constructions. In *Proceedings of the Seventh Annual Cognitive Science Society Meeting*, pp. 361–5, Irvine, CA.

Townsend, D. J., and Bever, T. G. (2001) *Sentence Comprehension: The Integration of Habits and Rules*. MIT Press, Cambridge, MA.

Traxler, M. J., and Pickering, M. J. (1996) Plausibility and the processing of unbounded dependencies: an eye-tracking study. *Journal of Memory and Language*, 35: 454–75.

Wagers, M., and Phillips, C. (2006) (Re)active filling. Talk presented at the 19th Annual CUNY Conference on Human Sentence Processing, New York.

Wanner, E., and Maratsos, M. (1978) An ATN approach to comprehension. In M. Halle, J. Bresnan, and G. A. Miller (eds), *Linguistic Theory and Psychological Reality*, pp. 119–61, MIT Press, Cambridge, MA.

Yoshida, M., Aoshima, S., and Phillips, C. (2004) Relative clause prediction in Japanese. Talk presented at the 17th Annual CUNY Conference on Human Sentence Processing, College Park, MD.

CHAPTER 46

Working Memory and Language

Susan E. Gathercole

46.1 Introduction

Working memory is the capacity to store and manipulate information over brief periods of time (Baddeley and Hitch, 1974). Extensive research over the past three decades has established that working memory is not a single store, but a memory system comprising separable interacting components. Functioning in concert, these components provide a kind of flexible mental workspace that can be used to maintain and transform information in the course of demanding cognitive activities, and that acts as a temporary bridge between externally and internally generated mental representations.

The purpose of this chapter is to consider what roles, if any, working memory plays in the human capabilities to handle language. One possibility is that the comprehension of language is dependent upon working memory, as a consequence of the ephemeral nature of the speech input. The acoustic content of the language stream is transmitted at great speed, with the units that form the basis of perception—phonemes, or phonetic features—represented by transitions in the frequencies of the acoustic signal that can be complete in as little as 1/50 of a second. Comprehension of spoken language is by no means reducible to the identification of individual words: the detailed content of the message is transmitted also via the syntactic structure of the lexical sequence, signalling underlying semantic structure. The task of the listener is to extract meaning from the content of this transient acoustic record. On this basis it has been suggested that the temporary storage capacities of working memory may play a crucial role in supporting the multiple processes involved in the perception and comprehension of language inputs.

A second possibility is that the working memory system supports the learning of language rather than language processing per se. It will be argued in this chapter that in fact this is by far the most significant contribution made by working memory to the human facility with language. Individually and in concert, the subsystems of working memory play vital and highly specific roles both in language learning in particular and in learning more generally. Before discussing potential links between working memory and language in detail, though, it is necessary to specify in greater detail exactly what working memory entails.

46.2 The concept of working memory

Working memory consists of a set of processes and mechanisms that can be used to support the temporary storage and manipulation of information in the course of complex cognitive activities. The concept of a multicomponent working memory was first advanced by Baddeley and Hitch (1974), and their model, elaborated over the subsequent years, remains the most influential theoretical account in the field. The most recent version of the model consists of four components, each with a limited capacity (Baddeley, 2000). The central executive lies at the heart of the model, and is responsible for a range of high-level functions including the control of attention and action (Baddeley, 1986; Baddeley et al., 1998), the temporary activation of long-term memory (Baddeley, 1998), coordination of multiple tasks (e.g. Baddeley et al., 1991), and shifting between tasks or retrieval strategies (Baddeley, 1996). Two further components provide domain-specific storage within working memory. The phonological loop represents material in a phonological form, and consists of a short-term store subject to rapid decay, supplemented by a subvocal rehearsal process that can be used to reactivate the phonological representations in the store (Baddeley, 1986; Burgess and Hitch, 1999). The visuo-spatial sketch-pad is specialized for the maintenance of visual and spatial material (Baddeley and Lieberman, 1980; Logie, 1994). There is substantial evidence that the phonological loop and visuo-spatial sketch-pad represent dissociable systems with distinct functional and neuroanatomical underpinnings (Della Sala and Logie, 2002; Vallar and Papagno, 2002). Finally, the episodic buffer, provides the capacity to integrate representations both from the subsystems of working memory and from long-term memory in a multi-dimensional code (Baddeley, 2000).

Working memory is related to but distinguishable from short-term memory. The term working memory is used in two senses: first, to refer to the working memory system of processes involved in the temporary storage and manipulation of information (such as the Baddeley and Hitch, 1974, model outlined above), and second, as a label for tasks that require participants to store information while engaging in other cognitively demanding activities. A classic working memory task is reading span—a paradigm in which the participant is asked to make a meaning-based judgement about each of a series of visually presented sentences, and then remember the last word of each sentence in sequence (e.g. Daneman and Carpenter, 1980). Another variant of complex memory span which is widely used with younger children is counting span, in which the participant counts the number of target items in a series of successive arrays, and then attempts to recall in sequence the tallies of the arrays (Case et al., 1982).

Proponents of the Baddeley and Hitch (1974) model have suggested that the storage demands of complex memory tasks are met by the appropriate domain-specific storage system, with processing demands supported principally by the central executive (Baddeley and Logie, 1999; Cocchini et al., 2002). Thus, complex memory span such as listening and counting span are interpreted as tapping both the central executive and the phonological loop (Lobley et al., forthcoming), whereas analogous visuo-spatial complex memory tasks (Jarvis and Gathercole, 2003; Shah and Miyake, 1996) may draw upon the resources of the central executive and the visuo-spatial sketch-pad. The substantial residual domain-general component to such complex span tasks (e.g. Bayliss et al., 2003; Kane et al., 2004; Swanson and Sachse-Lee, 2001) are interpreted as reflecting central executive function.

The term "short-term memory" is conventionally reserved for tasks that tap the storage capacities of the working memory system but impose only minimal demands on processing. Verbal short-term memory tasks typically involve serial recall of words, letters, or digits (e.g. Conrad and Hull, 1964; Pickering and Gathercole, 2001), whereas visuo-spatial tasks involve the retention of either visual patterns or sequences of movements (e.g. Smyth and Scholey, 1996; Wilson et al., 1987).

Other significant accounts of working memory have also been advanced. Some theorists have conceptualized working memory as a limited resource that can be flexibly allocated to support either processing or storage (e.g. Daneman and Carpenter, 1980; Just and Carpenter, 1992). An alternative view is that working memory consists of activated long-term memory representations, and that short-term memory is the subset of working memory that falls within the focus of attention (Cowan, 2001; Engle et al., 1999). The differences between these models are significant; but for the present purposes it is sufficient to note that these models share a common distinction between domain-specific short-term storage and more general capacities related to attentional control and processing.

46.3 Language comprehension

It has been argued that the dependence of the many processes involved in the syntactic and semantic analysis of language on working memory is a logical necessity: Waters and Caplan (2005: 403) recently claimed: "Language comprehension must involve a temporary storage or working memory (WM) system." In this section, this claim is evaluated in the light of evidence from experimental, neuropsychological, and developmental studies. It will be proposed that the working memory system described in the section above is not involved in the skilled processing of language for meaning, but that representations in working memory of linguistic communications may nonetheless play a significant role in guiding behavior.

46.3.1 Sentence processing and short-term memory

In the 1980s, there was extensive interest in the possibility that verbal short-term memory provides a buffer to incoming language that is consulted in the course of normal comprehension processes. In fact, the need for buffer storage, particularly when the language structures were complex and syntactically demanding, had long been identified in theories of language comprehension (Clark and Clarke, 1977; Kintsch and van Dijk, 1978). In the emerging field of cognitive neuropsychology, the identification of adult patients with acquired left hemisphere damage which resulted in severe impairments in verbal short-term memory capacity provided the opportunity to test this hypothesis. The prediction was clear: if short-term memory plays a significant role in comprehension, the very low memory span of STM patients should lead to substantial impairments in processing the meaning of language. Independent findings from many research groups and many different patients provided little support for this prediction. Despite the severity of their short-term memory deficits, patients typically had few difficulties in processing sentences for meaning, except under conditions in which lengthy, unusual, and ambiguous syntactic structures were used, or the sentences were essentially lengthy memory lists (see Caplan and Waters, 1990; Gathercole and Baddeley, 1993; Shallice and Vallar, 1990, for reviews).

These findings led to proposals that, although under most circumstances the language processor operates on-line without recourse to information stored in verbal short-term memory, these representations may be consulted in an off-line mode to enable backtracking and possible reanalysis of spoken language under conditions where necessary (McCarthy and Warrington, 1987). Consistent with this view, there is now substantial evidence that verbal short-term memory supports the ability to remember but not to comprehend recently encountered sentences, even when syntactically complex structures that may require off-line analysis are employed. Thus, although individuals with low short-term memory spans (either children or adults) are relatively poor at repeating sentences, their comprehension of the sentences is commensurate with that of individuals with normal memory function when comprehending sentences, even when the complex syntactic structures such as embedded and relative clauses, and passive forms, are used (Hanten and Martin, 2000; McCarthy and Warrington, 1987; Willis and Gathercole, 2001). These findings indicate that although the processes involved in comprehending a sentence do not depend directly on short-term memory, it can be used to provide continued access to sentence representations when necessary, for example, in attempting to repeat a recent input.

46.3.2 Sentence processing and working memory

We now turn to the possibility that the working memory system more generally—rather than the specific verbal short-term storage capacities of the system—support the processing of language for meaning. One widely used method of assessing working memory capacity, particularly for verbal material, is provided by complex memory span tasks such as reading span (Daneman and Carpenter, 1980). In this task, the participant is required to read aloud each of a sequence of sentences, and finally to recall the terminal word or each sentence in the original sequence, thereby combining both processing (of the sentence) and storage (of the sentence-terminal words). Consistent with claims that working memory must be required to meet the demands of rapid processing of the unpredictable incoming language signal (e.g. Waters and Caplan, 1999), individual differences in complex memory span have been found to relate to several aspects of sentence processing. King and Just (1991) compared the reading times and reading comprehension of individuals with low and high reading spans on various kinds of syntactically complex sentence. Differences in comprehension accuracy between reading span groups were greatest for sentences containing the most complex embedded clauses (object-relative clauses) such as *The reporter the senator attacked admitted the error*. Low-span participants were particularly slow in reading the critical part of the sentence in which the syntactic structure had be evaluated. MacDonald et al. (1992) found that individual differences in memory span were also linked with the resolution of syntactic ambiguities: whereas high-span participants appeared to construct parallel representations of potential interpretations prior to the resolution point of a sentence, low-span individuals did not. There is also evidence that only high-span individuals have sufficient working memory capacity to use contextual information to disambiguate syntactic ambiguities (Just and Carpenter, 1992).

The processes of integration and inferencing over larger bodies of text may be constrained by working memory, too. Daneman and Carpenter (1983) investigated the role of working memory in textual integration in a study that employed passages such as: … *he went and looked among his baseball equipment. He found a bat that was very large and brown and was flying back and forth in the gloomy room.* Because of the preceding context, readers usually interpret *bat* as a baseball bat, but the subsequent information about the locomotion of the object forces the reader to reinterpret it as an animal. To do this, Daneman and Carpenter claimed that the reader must recover active representations of the original surface form of the word *bat.* Readers with low working memory capacity, they argued, would be less likely to maintain active representation of prior material as a consequence of the heavy demands placed by incoming sentences on their relatively inefficient processing operations. In other words, the low-working-memory individuals were hypothesized to have maintained the efficiency of sentence processing at the cost of failing to maintain recent working memory representations. Successful recovery from these "garden path" passages should therefore be less frequent for these individuals.

More recently, Cain et al. (2004) have made similar claims that working memory provides a temporary work space in which text comprehension processes such as integration and inferencing can take place. Their large-scale longitudinal study established that measures of working memory capacity such as reading span predict unique variance in reading comprehension tasks that tax integration and comprehension monitoring in children aged between 8 and 11 years of age, even after differences in reading skills and verbal ability have been taken into account. These findings accord well with previous reports of close associations between working memory skills and comprehension abilities in child groups (e.g. Oakhill et al., 1986; Seigneuric et al., 2000).

The involvement of working memory in language comprehension was formalized in Just and Carpenter's (1992) CC READER production system model, designed on the basis that both processing and storage are fuelled by a common resource—activation. Old elements such as the representations of previously encountered passages in a text are maintained by activation; if the activation level exceeds a threshold, it is said to be represented in working memory. If the total amount of activation available for a particular comprehension task exceeds the available activation resources, however, the activation used to maintain old elements is scaled back. Individual differences in working memory capacity are modeled by varying the total amount of activation that the system has available to support processing and storage.

The CC READER model successfully accommodated a range of findings that relate working memory to sentence processing. For example, the model uses the amount of activation available to determine whether one or two syntactic interpretations will be represented for syntactically ambiguous regions of sentences such as those employed by Daneman and Carpenter (1983). The model also simulates the processing efforts involved in reading syntactically complex sentences such as object-relative clauses in both high- and low-span readers (King and Just, 1991).

In subsequent years, however, there has been little support beyond this research group for the claim that working memory capacity plays an intrinsic role in processing at the sentence level. First, the replicability of many of the key findings have been called into question (see Caplan and Waters, 1999, for review). A further problem is the lack of support for the core prediction that increases in syntactic complexity will impose greatest demands on working memory capacity constraints. Patients with Alzheimer's dementia have poor working memory capacities, but do not experience differential levels of difficulty with syntactically complex sentences, even when combined with a concurrent memory load (Rochon et al., 1994; Waters and Caplan, 2002). Finally, working memory function declines with old age but is not accompanied by greater deficits in processing syntactically complex vs. simple sentences (Waters and Caplan, 2005).

In their theory of working memory and language comprehension, Caplan and Waters (1999) distinguish between the interpretive processing of language—involving on-line, obligatory processes such as word recognition, lexical, syntactic, and semantic activation, and the assignment of thematic roles—and post-interpretive processing which uses the meaning of sentences to perform other cognitive activities. They propose that the initial interpretive processing is supported by a specialized working memory resource that is independent of the working memory system tapped by complex memory span tasks. The detailed nature of this language-serving working memory system and its characteristics are as yet unspecified, although it is speculatively linked with the dominant perisylvian association cortex.

According to Caplan and Waters, the consciously controlled working memory system associated with complex memory span tasks can represent and use the propositional content in the service of other cognitive tasks once sentence processing is complete. An example they give is of the sentence *Please pick up four tomatoes, a pound of apricots, prune juice, shallots, six apples, and a bag of carrots on the way home* (1999: 79). The task here is not just to process the sentence for meaning, but to maintain its contents for a sufficient period to guide action appropriately, and it is at this point at which working memory may make its contribution.

Our own recent findings underscore this possible link between working memory and the ability to follow instructions. We tested 5- and 6-year-old children on two sentence processing tasks involving spoken instructions relating to manipulation of a set of objects placed in their full view (Gathercole, Darling, Evans, Jeffcock, and Stone 2007). The instructions all employed simple syntactic structures and high-frequency verbs, but varied in length from short (e.g. *Touch the white bag*) to long (e.g. *Touch the blue folder then pick up the red ball and put it in the green folder*). In one version of the task, the child was asked to repeat the sentence immediately; in the other version, the task was to carry out the instruction. In both cases, the accuracy of the response was scored. Each child was also tested on measures of verbal short-term memory, working memory, and also non-verbal reasoning ability, and the purpose of the study was to determine which if any of these cognitive abilities predicted young children's abilities to both remember and perform spoken instructions. The results were striking. Scores on a measure of working memory—backwards digit span—were very highly associated with the child's accuracy in performing the instructions ($r=.51$, $p<.001$). Accuracy of performing the instructions was not, however, related to non-verbal ability scores ($r=.27$, $p>.05$).

These results indicate that there is a highly specific link, in childhood at least, between working memory and the use of spoken instructions to guide action. Of course, performing a sequence of actions imposes very different demands on memory to the immediate repetition of an instruction. The instruction has to be retained for a sufficient period to guide action through to the final step of the action sequence, rather than for immediate recall. Remembering an instruction for the purposes of action also requires accurate place-keeping, to enable the actor to locate the next uncompleted proposition in the sequence. Indeed, in a recent study we observed that children with impairments of working memory experience particular difficulties in keeping their place in complex task structures (Gathercole et al., 2006). In the same study, it was also noted that low-memory children struggled to follow classroom instructions such as *Put your sheets on the green table, arrow cards in the packer, put your pencil away, and come and sit on the carpet* and *Now that you've finished, write your name on the sheet, find your maths book, and stick the sheet in the next clean page*. Together, these findings provide substantial support for Waters and Caplan's (1999) claim that representation of sentence structures in general working memory may be used flexibly to support cognitive activities, but do not form the basis for the process of comprehension itself.

The contributions of the working memory system identified by the methods of cognitive psychology to the processing of spoken language for the purposes of comprehension are therefore subtle rather than substantial in nature. Working memory does not appear to provide a necessary input into the routine processes involved in the syntactic and semantic processing of sentence forms across a fairly wide range of complexity. However, when the ongoing cognitive activity requires use of the sentence meaning that extends beyond simple on-line comprehension, working memory does come into play. Simple repetition of recent language inputs can be mediated by the verbal storage component of working memory, whereas either the use of an instruction to guide a series of actions or an attempt to integrate distinct propositions in a spoken or written discourse may require the fuller complement of processing and storage capacities that constitute working memory.

46.4 **Language learning**

Although the role played by working memory in the processing and comprehension of language inputs is relatively minor in both children and adults, its contribution to language learning is substantial. Here, two areas of contribution are considered: the first focuses on the involvement of verbal short-term memory in word learning, and the second summarizes the consequences for language learning of the severe impairments of working memory that accompany the developmental pathology Specific Language Impairment.

46.4.1 Vocabulary acquisition and verbal short-term memory

The ability to learn new words lies at the core of the development of language, forming the foundation for our capacities to understand the spoken and written communications of others and also to formulate and produce our own language outputs. Across the early years of life, the child rapidly acquires several thousands of words as part of an emerging competence in language, learning up to 3,000 new word forms per year during the school years (Nagy and Herman, 1987). The apparent rapidity and ease of vocabulary development has been widely observed: Carey (1978) used the term "fast mapping" to describe the child's preparedness to store a new word's phonological representation with preliminary hypotheses about its referent's physical and syntactic-semantic properties.

There is substantial evidence linking the process of storing the unfamiliar phonological structure of a new word with verbal short-term memory (see Gathercole (2006) for review). Short-term memory skills and the abilities to learn new words are closely associated during the childhood years. Generally speaking, children with relatively small vocabularies for their age perform poorly on measures of verbal short-term memory such as auditory digit span and the immediate repetition of non-words such as *woogalamic* or *loodernaypish* (Avons et al., 1998; Gathercole and Baddeley, 1989; Gathercole et al., 1992; Gathercole et al., 1997; Michas and Henry, 1994). This link between short-term memory skills and vocabulary knowledge is typically strongest for individuals during the early stages of acquiring a new language. For example, in a longitudinal study Gathercole et al. (1992) found a strong association between short-term memory and native vocabulary scores at 4 and 5 years of age that diminished to a non-significant level by 8 years (see also Gathercole, 1995; Gathercole et al., 2005). In foreign language learning, the association between short-term memory and vocabulary knowledge shows the same shift with increasing language competence. Thus, whereas verbal memory scores are highly associated with current and future knowledge of foreign vocabulary during the early years of studying a language (Masoura and Gathercole, 1999; 2005; Service, 1992; Service and Kohonen, 1995), in more advanced language learners the association is much weaker (Cheung, 1996).

The diminishing role of short-term memory in vocabulary learning with increasing language competence seems likely to result from other opportunities for supporting language learning as the individual's lexicon expends. One important change as an individual develops a larger vocabulary is that new words are more likely to overlap substantially with other existing lexical entries, providing a source of lexical support for learning the new form which may decrease dependence on the temporary phonological representation in short-term memory. Such beneficial lexical contributions to immediate memory for non-words are now well established (Gathercole et al., 1999; Roodenrys and Hinton, 2002; Thorn and Frankish, 2005; Vitevitch and Luce, 2005).

Evidence for the increasing dependence on lexical mediation during vocabulary learning was recently provided by Masoura and Gathercole (2005), who investigated a sample of Greek children who had on average three years' experience of studying English as a second language. Non-word repetition ability in this sample was highly related to knowledge of English vocabulary (r =.48, p <.001), in line with the typical developmental association between short-term memory and vocabulary learning. However, the children also completed a vocabulary learning task involving paired associate learning of familiar Greek words with their English translation equivalents. Learning of these new English words was associated not with non-word repetition scores, but with the children's existing knowledge of English. We interpret these results as indicating that by this level of English proficiency, the children's learning of the phonological forms of new words in second-language was no longer supported by verbal short-term memory, but was mediated instead by access to lexical phonological representations of close neighbors in their reasonably sized lexicons. Such lexically supported learning has the advantage of capitalizing on knowledge structures (which may be semantic, conceptual, or phonological in form) that have already been constructed, rather than depending on a fragile and limited-capacity temporary storage system.

Experimental analogs of natural vocabulary acquisition such as the paired-associate learning paradigm have provided a valuable means of exploring the theoretical underpinnings of the association between short-term memory and word learning, allowing control over the nature and frequency of exposure to the novel stimuli. Using these methods, it has been established that children with relatively weak short-term memory skills are indeed slower to learn the novel phonological forms of new words, such as the name *Sommel* for an unfamiliar toy monster (Gathercole and Baddeley, 1990a) or of the label *foltano* paired with a description of a noisy dancing fish (Gathercole et al., 1997). The link with short-term memory is, however, restricted to the phonological aspects of learning. When either the stimulus items to be learned consist of familiar rather than unfamiliar phonological forms (Gathercole and Baddeley, 1990a; Gathercole et al., 1997) or the novel phonological form is used as a cue to elicit associated semantic information rather than vice versa (Gathercole et al., 1997), rate of learning is independent of measures of short-term memory. Thus when possible, children will support their word learning by using conceptual and lexical attributes rather than verbal short-term memory. The link between vocabulary learning and short-term memory is accordingly strongest under conditions where such alternative opportunities to mediate learning are not available.

Findings from experimental studies of word learning in adult participants have substantially reinforced the conclusion that verbal short-term memory mediates the phonological learning of new words. Studies employing paired-associate paradigms have established that learning of non-word/word pairs such as *kipser/chicken* is disrupted by conditions known to impair the functioning of the phonological loop, such as articulatory suppression, phonological similarity, and increased word length (Papagno et al., 1991; Papagno and Vallar, 1992). In contrast, learning of pairs of familiar but unassociated words such as *table/lion* is unaffected by these manipulations. These results indicate that verbal short-term storage contributes specifically to learning novel phonological forms, but does not underpin the semantically-mediated learning of stimuli with existing lexical representations.

Further evidence for this position was provided by P. V., an adult neuropsychological patient with damage to the left hemisphere which resulted in a profound deficit in verbal short-term storage. Although P. V. adequately learned associations between pairs of words in a paired-associate learning task, she was quite unable to learn any non-word/word pairs across trials. Similar patterns have also been observed in other cases of acquired and developmental impairments of short-term memory (Baddeley and Wilson, 1993; Trojano and Grossi, 1995). These individuals were able to function at a normal level across a range of intellectual tasks. However, they both shared a highly specific deficit in learning verbal material that was phonologically unfamiliar, despite normal learning of pairs of familiar words. Robust associations between short-term memory and new word learning in adults have also been found in other laboratory paradigms (Atkins and Baddeley, 1998; Gupta, 2003).

Baddeley et al. (1998) argued on the basis of this evidence that one of the primary functions of the phonological loop is to support the long-term learning of the sound structure of new words. They proposed that initial encounters with the phonological forms of novel words are represented briefly in the short-term store, and that these representations form the basis for the gradual process of abstracting a stable specification of the sound structure across repeated presentations. Conditions which impair the quality of the temporary phonological representation in the phonological loop, such as a storage mechanism with a low functional capacity due to either noisy or degraded representations, will reduce the efficiency of the process of abstraction, leading to slow rates of learning. Similar claims that new word learning depends on verbal short-term storage have been advanced by Gupta, MacWhinney, and associates (Gupta and MacWhinney, 1997; see also Martin and Gupta, 2004).

Poor verbal short-term memory skills alone may not necessarily have distrastrous consequences for vocabulary learning. Recent findings from a longitudinal study of children with poor short-term memory skills between the ages of 5 and 8 years indicates that, with time, slow rates of phonological learning can be compensated by the huge redundancy of exposure to natural language and the use of other strategies for mediating learning (Gathercole, Tiffany et al., 2005). Importantly, though, these low-memory children were slow and inaccurate in their learning of unfamiliar verbal stimuli under experimental conditions that prevented non-phonological learning, indicating that the basic mechanism underlying word learning remained impaired in these individuals (Gathercole et al., 2003).

Finally, it is important to note that interpretation of the evidence linking verbal short-term memory with vocabulary learning remains the topic of vigorous debate. Many researchers have suggested that poor performance on tasks such as non-word repetition and digit span may be a consequence not of a short-term memory deficit per se, but of weaknesses in other skills that may have an impact on word learning, such as phonological sensitivity (Bowey, 1996; de Jong et al., 2000; Hu and Schuele, 2005), phonological segmentation (Masterson et al., 2005; Metsala, 1999), access to lexical representations (Snowling et al., 1991), or speech output processes (Sahlen et al., 1999).

It is certainly the case that in developmental samples in particular, this range of verbally based skills are typically highly associated, making it difficult in practice to dissociate one influence from another. It is therefore important to note that the claim that verbal short-term storages mediates phonological learning is not only dependent on individual differences studies of children, but is substantially reinforced by independent evidence both from experimental studies using validated methods of functionally this component of memory (e.g. Papagno et al., 1991; Papagno and Vallar, 1992) and from neuropsychological patient in whom deficits of verbal short-term storage are dissociated from other phonological processing abilities (e.g. Vallar and Baddeley, 1984).

46.4.2 Specific Language Impairment and working memory

The most dramatic evidence linking working memory function with language learning comes from studies of Specific Language Impairment (SLI). SLI is a relatively common developmental condition in which a child fails to develop at the typical rate despite normal general intellectual abilities, adequate exposure to language, and in the absence of hearing impairments. Affected children have greatest problems in learning word forms and the grammatical structure of language, with acquisition of semantics and pragmatics relatively spared (Bishop, 1997; Leonard, 1997).

Current interest in working memory function in SLI was sparked principally by Gathercole and Baddeley's (1990b) findings that a group of children with SLI had severe impairments in non-word repetition, a task closely linked with verbal short-term memory function (Gathercole et al., 1994). The findings were dramatic: the SLI group had a mean age of 8 years, had the language abilities of the average 6-year-old child, but performed at the level of a 4 year old in non-word repetition. The nonword repetition impairment has subsequently been established in many independent studies to be a hallmark of SLI (see Roy and Chiat, 2004, for review), and has been adopted both as a clinical indicator of SLI (Conti-Ramsden, 2003; Dollaghan and Campbell, 1998) and as a phenotypic marker of the genetic basis for SLI (Bishop et al., 1996) associated with abnormalities of chromosome 16q (SLI Consortium, 2002). The impairment is particularly significant as it captures the language-learning difficulties of individuals with SLI in a simple paradigm that mimics word learning.

The co-occurrence of severe impairments of non-word repetition and language learning in Specific Language Impairment fits well with the proposal that short-term memory plays a key role in supporting the phonological learning of language (Baddeley et al., 1998; Gathercole, forthcoming). By this account, at least one of the problems faced in learning language by a child with SLI is a severe deficit in verbal short-term storage. Further investigations are, however, required to identify the more detailed nature of this deficit. We have recently begun an experimental program designed to do this, starting by comparing the recall accuracy of spoken non-words such as *fiemoychee* with comparable syllables presented in isolation for immediate serial recall as in *fie ... moy ... chee* (Archibald and Gathercole, forthcoming). If the non-word repetition deficit in SLI reflects an underlying impairment of short-term memory, the SLI group should be impaired to an equivalent extent in both tasks. In fact, the SLI group performed less accurately than the younger language-matched controls in non-word repetition but not in serial recall—raising the interesting possibility that children with SLI have particular difficulties with features of non-word inputs, such as the rapid rate of transmission of phonological information and presence of prosodic contour.

Other studies have established that the memory deficit in SLI is not restricted to tasks requiring short-term storage only. Children with SLI also show evidence of impairments of working memory, performing poorly on verbal complex memory span tasks that require both verbal storage and processing (Ellis Weismer et al., 1999; Montgomery, 2000a; 2000b). In a recent study (Archibald and Gathercole, forthcoming, a), we compared a group of children with SLI on a range of standardized measures of short-term and working memory (population mean = 100, *SD* = 15). These children consistently performed at very low levels on the complex span measures of working memory (group mean = 74.5), although on tests of visuo-spatial working memory, their scores were appropriate for their age (Archibald and Gathercole, forthcoming b).

Further investigation has indicated that this disproportionate deficit in SLI children occurs when verbal short-term storage loads are combined with significant processing demands in either the verbal or visuo-spatial domains (Archibald and Gathercole, forthcoming d).

46.4.3 **Short-term memory, working memory, and language learning: a synthesis**

The evidence reviewed in this second part of the chapter establishes close links between the working memory system and language learning. First, verbal short-term memory appears to mediate the long-term learning of the sound patterns of new words. Second, the severe language-learning problems of children with SLI are invariably accompanied by deficits in working memory, and are found both in tasks requiring verbal short-term storage only and in tasks imposing both processing and verbal storage demands.

Some insight into the different roles placed by different components of the working memory system in the learning of language can be provided by comparing the learning abilities and achievements of children with different kinds of working memory deficit. These profiles are summarized in Table 46.1. Consider first children with deficits specific to verbal short-term memory. Our own data established that a group of children with extremely low verbal short-term memory scores between 5 and 8 years nonetheless achieved normal level of competence in the areas of vocabulary, language, literacy, and mathematics at 8 years of age (Gathercole, Tiffany et al., 2005), although they did have subtle persisting new-word learning deficits (Gathercole et al., 2003). In contrast, children with SLI have deficits both in verbal short-term memory and in more general working memory (Archibald and Gathercole, forthcoming, a; 2005a). A third relevant group are children with learning difficulties in reading and mathematics, who typically show marked deficits on measures of working memory but not on verbal short-term memory (Gathercole et al., forthcoming; Pickering and Gathercole, 2004). Notably, the language abilities of the majority of these children lie in the normal range.

What sense can be made of these mappings between working memory strengths and weakness and learning abilities? It is widely believed that measures of verbal short-term memory and verbal working memory are both supported by the verbal short-term storage capacity of working memory, but are differentiated by the additional processing and multi-task coordination requirements of complex memory span served by the attentionally based domain-general component of working memory (e.g. Bayliss et al., 2003). On this basis, the pattern of associations shown in Table 46.1 indicates that severe deficits in language learning consistently arise only when deficits in verbal short-term storage are twinned with a central executive impairment, as in SLI. Neither verbal storage nor general processing deficits alone are sufficient to significant delay and disturb the normal developmental course of language acquisition, although their conjunction has disastrous consequences for multiple aspects of language development. We do, however, know that verbal short-term storage is required for new-word learning under conditions that do not allow the use of non-phonological strategies, particularly during the early stages of acquiring a new language.

Working memory capacity also appears to be crucial for academic learning, as illustrated by the large and consistent deficits on working memory measures in children with learning difficulties (Gathercole et al., 2006). We have recently proposed that working memory acts as a bottleneck for learning in many of the

Table 46.1 Patterns of deficits i working memory and learning domains in three groups of children.

Group	Working memory		Learning domain		
	Verbal STM	Verbal WM	Language	Reading	Mathematics
STM deficit	yes	no	no	no	no
Specific Language Impairments	yes	yes	yes	yes	yes
Learning difficulties	minority	yes	minority	yes	yes

individual learning episodes required to increment the acquisition of knowledge (Gathercole, 2004; Gathercole et al., forthcoming). By this account, children with impairments of working memory struggle to meet the working memory demands of many classroom learning activities, resulting in frequent task failures and poor learning outcomes across academic domains. According to this analysis, children with SLI are in double jeopardy, possessing both impaired word-learning mechanism (in verbal short-term storage) and poor working memory support for general learning. It may be the co-occurrence of both deficits that yields the substantially deficit in language learning in this population.

46.5 Conclusions

Working memory—the set of processes and mechanisms involved in the temporary storage and manipulation of material—represents a flexible cognitive resource that can be used to support both the processing of language in skilled language users and the learning of language during development. The comprehension of sentences and longer passages of spoken and written language appears to proceed relatively independently of working memory, although it does appear to provide a representation of the products of the syntactic and semantic products of comprehension that can be flexibly used to guide behavior. Examples of such uses of working memory are repeating sentences, and also following complex instructions.

Working memory plays a more direct role in supporting language learning during development. Learning the phonological structures depends heavily on short-term verbal storage, particularly during the early period of acquisition of a language. The more general processing and storage capacity of the working memory system provides a flexible workspace to support the range of complex cognitive activities in which the child engages in the course of academic learning. Children with impairments of both verbal storage and more general working memory function typically encounter profound difficulties in language learning.

References

Archibald, L. M. D., and Gathercole, S. E. (forthcoming a) Short-term and working memory in Specific language Impairment. *International Journal of Communication Disorders.*

Archibald, L. M. D., and Gathercole, S. E. (forthcoming b) Visuospatial immediate memory in Specific Language Impairment. *Journal of Speech, Language, and Hearing Research.*

Archibald, L. M. D., and Gathercole, S. E. (forthcoming c) Nonword repetition in Specific Language Impairment: more than just a phonological short-term memory deficit. *Psychonomic Bulletin and Review.*

Archibald, L. M. D., and Gathercole, S. E. (2005b) The complexities of complex memory span: specifying storage and processing deficits in Specific Language Impairment. *Journal of Memory and Language.*

Atkins, P. W. B., and Baddeley, A. D. (1998) Working memory and distributed vocabulary learning. *Applied Psycholinguistics*, 19: 537–52.

Avons, S. E., Wragg, C. A., Cupples, L., and Lovegrove, W. J. (1998). Measure of phonological short-term memory and their relationship to vocabulary development. *Applied Psycholinguistics*, 19: 583–601.

Baddeley, A. D. (1986) *Working Memory*. Oxford University Press, Oxford.

Baddeley, A. D. (1996) Exploring the central executive. *Quarterly Journal of Experimental Psychology*, 49A: 5–28.

Baddeley, A. D. (1998) Recent developments in working memory. *Current Opinion in Neurobiology*, 8: 234–8.

Baddeley, A. D. (2000) The episodic buffer: a new component of working memory? *Trends in Cognitive Sciences*, 4: 417–23.

Baddeley, A. D., Bressi, S., Della Sala, S., Logie, R. H., and Spinnler, H. (1991) The decline of working memory in Alzheimer's Disease: a longitudinal study. *Brain*, 114: 2521–42.

Baddeley, A. D., Emslie, H., Kolodny, J., and Duncan, J. (1998) Random generation and the executive control of working memory. *Quarterly Journal of Experimental Psychology*, 51A: 819–52.

Baddeley A. D., Gathercole S. E., and Papagno C. (1998) The phonological loop as a language learning device. *Psychological Review*, 105: 158–73.

Baddeley A. D., and Hitch G. (1974) Working memory. In G. Bower (ed.), *The Psychology of Learning and Motivation*, 8, pp. 47–90, Academic Press, New York.

Baddeley, A. D. and Lieberman, K. (1980) Spatial working memory. In R. Nickerson (ed.), *Attention and Performance VIII*, pp. 521–39. Erlbaum, Hillsdale, NJ.

Baddeley, A. D., and Logie, R. H. (1999) Working memory: the multiple-component model. In A. Miyake and P. Shah (eds), *Models of Working memory: Mechanisms of Active Maintenance and Executive Control*, pp. 28–61. Cambridge University Press, New York.

Bayliss, D. M., Jarrold, C., Gunn, M. D., and Baddeley, A. D. (2003) The complexities of complex span: explaining individual differences in working memory in children and adults. *Journal of Experimental Psychology: General*, 132: 71–92.

Bishop D. V. M (1997). *Uncommon understanding: development and disorders of language comprehension in children*. Psychology Press, Hove, UK.

Bishop, D. V. M., North, T., and Donlan, C. (1996) Nonword repetition as a behavioral marker for inherited language impairment: evidence from a twin study. *Journal of Child Psychology and Psychiatry*, 37: 391–403.

Baddeley, A. D. and Wilson, B. A. (1993) A developmental deficit in short-term memory: implications for language and reading. *Memory*, 1: 65–78.

Bowey, J. A. (1996) On the association between phonological memory and receptive vocabulary in five-year-olds. *Journal of Experimental Child Psychology*, 63: 44–78.

Burgess, N., and Hitch, G. J. (1999) Memory for serial order: a network model of the phonological loop and its timing. *Psychological Review*, 106: 551–81.

Cain, K., Oakhill, J., and Bryant, P. (2004) Children's reading comprehension ability: concurrent prediction by working memory, verbal ability and component skills. *Journal of Educational Psychology*, 96: 31–42.

Caplan, D., and Waters, G. S. (1990) Short-term memory and language comprehension: a critical review of the psychological literature. In G. Vallar and T. Shallice (eds), *Neuropsychological Impairments of Short-Term Memory*, pp. 337–89. Cambridge University Press, Cambridge.

Caplan, D., and Waters, G. S. (1999) Verbal working memory and sentence comprehension. *Behavioral and Brain Sciences*, 22: 77–126.

Carey, S. (1978) The child as word learner. In M. Halle, J. Bresnan, and G. Miller (eds), *Linguistic Theory and Psychological Reality,* pp. 264–293. MIT Press, Cambridge, MA.

Case, R., Kurland, M., and Goldberg, J. (1982) Operational efficiency and the growth of short-term memory span. *Journal of Experimental Child Psychology*, 33: 386–404.

Cheung, H. (1996) Nonword span as a unique predictor of second-language vocabulary learning. *Developmental Psychology*, 32: 867–73.

Clark, H. H., and Clarke, E. V. (1977) *Psychology and language*. Harcourt Brace Jovanovitch, New York.

Cocchini, G., Logie, R. H., Della Sala, S., MacPherson, S. E., and Baddeley, A. D. (2002) Concurrent performance of two memory tasks: evidence for domain-specific working memory systems. *Memory and Cognition*, 30: 1086–95.

Conrad, R., and Hull, A. J. (1964) Information, acoustic confusion, and memory span. *British Journal of Psychology*, 55: 429–32.

Conti-Ramsden, G. (2003) Processing and linguistic markers in young children with specific language impairment. *Journal of Speech, Language and Hearing Research*, 46: 1029–37.

Cowan, N. (2001) The magical number 4 in short-term memory: a reconsideration of mental storage capacity. *Behavioral and Brain Sciences*, 24: 87.

Daneman, M., and Carpenter, P. A. (1980) Individual differences in working memory and reading. *Journal of Verbal Learning and Verbal Behavior*, 19: 450–66.

Daneman, M., and Carpenter, P. A. (1983) Individual differences in integrating information between and within sentences. *Journal of Experimental Psychology: Learning, Memory and Cognition*, 9: 561–84.

Della Sala, S., and Logie, R. H. (2002) Neuropsychological impairments of visual and spatial working memory. In A. D. Baddeley, M. D. Kopelman, and B. A. Wilson (eds), *Handbook of Memory Disorders*, 2nd edn, pp. 271–92. Wiley, Chichester, UK.

Dollaghan, C., and Campbell, T. F. (1998) Nonword repetition and child language impairment. *Journal of Speech, Language and Hearing Research*, 41: 1136–46.

Ellis Weismer, S., Evans, J., and Hesketh, L. (1999) An examination of working memory capacity in children with specific language impairment. *Journal of Speech, Language, and Hearing Research*, 42: 1249–60.

Engle, R. W., Kane, M. J., and Tuholski, S. W. (1999) Individual differences in working memory capacity and what they tell us about controlled attention, general fluid intelligence, and functions of the prefrontal cortex. In A. Miyake and P. Shah (eds), *Models of working Memory: Mechanisms of Active Maintenance and Executive Control*, pp. 102–34. Cambridge University Press, New York.

Gathercole, S. E. (1995) Is nonword repetition a test of phonological memory or long-term knowledge? It all depends on the nonwords. *Memory and Cognition*, 23: 83–94.

Gathercole, S. E. (2004) Working memory and learning during the school years. *Proceedings of the British Academy*, 125: 365–80.

Gathercole, S. E. (2006) Nonword repetition and word learning: the nature of the relationship. *Applied Psycholinguistics*, 27: 513–43.

Gathercole, S. E., Alloway, T. P., Willis, C. S., and Adams, A. M. (2006) Working memory in children with reading disabilities. *Journal of Experimental Child Psychology*, 49: 265–77.

Gathercole, S. E. and Baddeley, A. D. (1989) Evaluation of the role of phonological STM in the development of vocabulary in children: a longitudinal study. *Journal of Memory and Language*, 28: 200–13.

Gathercole, S. E. and Baddeley, A. D. (1990a) The role of phonological memory in vocabulary acquisition: a study of young children learning new names. *British Journal of Psychology*, 81: 439–54.

Gathercole, S. E., and Baddeley, A. (1990b) Phonological memory deficits in language disordered children: is there a causal connection? *Journal of Memory and Language*, 29: 336–60.

Gathercole, S. E., and Baddeley, A. D. (1993) *Working Memory and Language*. Hove, Erlbaum, UK.

Gathercole, S. E., Darling, E., Jeffcock, S., and Stone, J. (2007) Working memory abilities and children's performance in laboratory analogues of classroom activities. MS.

Gathercole, S. E., Frankish, C., Pickering, S. J., and Peaker, S. (1999) Phonotactic influences on short-term memory. *Journal of Experimental Psychology: Learning Memory and Cognition*, 25: 84–95.

Gathercole, S. E., Hitch, G. J., Service, E., and Martin, A. J. (1997) Short-term memory and new word learning in children. *Developmental Psychology*, 33: 966–79.

Gathercole, S. E., Lamont, E., and Alloway, T. P. (2006) Working memory in the classroom. In S. J. Pickering and G. Phye (eds), *Working Memory and Education*. Elsevier, New York.

Gathercole, S. E., Tiffany, C., Briscoe, J., Thorn, A. S. C., and the ALSPAC Team (2003) Episodic long-term memory in children with poor phonological loop function. MS.

Gathercole, S. E., Tiffany, C., Briscoe, J., Thorn, A. S. C., and the ALSPAC Team (2005) Developmental consequences of phonological loop deficits during early childhood: a longitudinal study. *Journal of Child Psychology and Psychiatry*. 46: 598–611.

Gathercole, S. E., Willis, C., and Baddeley, A. D. (1991) Differentiating phonological memory and awareness of rhyme: reading and vocabulary development in children. *British Journal of Psychology*, 82: 387–406.

Gathercole, S. E., Willis, C., Emslie, H., and Baddeley, A. D. (1992) Phonological memory and vocabulary development during the early school years: a longitudinal study. *Developmental Psychology*, 28: 887–98.

Gathercole, S. E., Willis, C., Emslie, H., and Baddeley, A. D. (1994) The children's test of nonword repetition: a test of phonological working memory. *Memory*, 2: 103–27.

Gupta, P. (2003) Examining the relationship between word learning, nonword repetition, and immediate serial recall in adults. *Quarterly Journal of Experimental Psychology*, 56A: 1213–36.

Gupta, P., and MacWhinney, B. (1997) Vocabulary acquisition and verbal short-term memory: computational and neural bases. *Brain and Language*, 59: 267–333.

Hanten, G., and Martin, R. C. (2000) Contributions of phonological and semantic short-term memory to sentence processing: evidence from two cases of closed head injury in children. *Journal of Memory and Language*, 43: 335–61.

Hu, C. F., and Schuele, C. M. (2005) Learning nonnative names: the effect of poor native phonological awareness. *Applied Psycholinguistics*, 26: 343–62.

Jarvis, H. L., and Gathercole, S. E. (2003) Verbal and non-verbal working memory and achievements on national curriculum tests at 11 and 14 years of age. *Educational and Child Psychology*, 20: 123–40.

Just, M. A., and Carpenter, P. A. (1992) A capacity theory of comprehension: individual differences in working memory. *Psychological Review*, 99: 122–49.

Kane, M. J., Hambrick, D. Z., Tuholski, S. W., Wilhelm, O., Payne, T. W., and Engle, R. W. (2004) The generality of working memory capacity: a latent variable approach to verbal and visuo-spatial memory span and reasoning. *Journal of Experimental Psychology: General*, 133: 189–217.

King, J., and Just, M. A. (1991) Individual differences in syntactic processing: the role of working memory. *Journal of Memory and Language*, 30: 580–602.

Kintsch, W. and van Dijk, T. A. (1978) Towards a model of text comprehension and production. *Psychological Review*, 85: 363–94.

Leonard, L. B. (1997). *Children with Specific Language Impairment*. MIT Press, Cambridge, MA.

Lobley, K., Gathercole, S. E., and Baddeley, A. D. (forthcoming) Is there a role for the phonological loop in verbal complex span? *Quarterly Journal of Experimental Psychology.*

Logie, R. H. (1994) *Visuo-Spatial Working Memory*. Erlbaum, Hove, UK.

McCarthy, R. A., and Warrington, E. K. (1987) Understanding: a function of short-term memory? *Brain*, 110: 1565–78.

MacDonald, M. C., Just, M. A., and Carpenter, P. A. (1992) Working memory constraints on the processing of sentence ambiguity. *Cognitive Psychology*, 24: 56–98.

Martin, N., and Gupta, P. (2004) Exploring the relationship between word processing and verbal short-term memory: evidence from associations and dissociations. *Cognitive Neuropsychology*, 21: 213–28.

Masoura, E., and Gathercole, S. E. (1999) Phonological short-term memory and foreign vocabulary learning. *International Journal of Psychology*, 34: 383–8.

Masoura, E. V., and Gathercole, S. E. (2005) Phonological short-term memory skills and new word learning in young Greek children. *Memory*, 13: 422–9.

Masterson, J., Laxon, V., Carnegie, E., Wrighht, S., and Horslen, J. (2005) Nonword recall and phoneme discrimination in four-to six-year old children. *Journal of research in Reading*, 28: 183–201.

Metsala, J. L. (1999) The development of phonemic awareness in reading disabled children. *Applied Psycholinguistics*, 20: 149–58.

Michas, I. C., and Henry, L. A. (1994) The link between phonological memory and vocabulary acquisition. *British Journal of Developmental Psychology*, 12: 147–64.

Montgomery, J. (2000a) Verbal working memory in sentence comprehension in children with specific language impairment. *Journal of Speech, Language, and Hearing Research*, 43: 293–308.

Montgomery, J. (2000b) Relation of working memory to off-line and real-time sentence processing in children with Specific Language Impairment. *Applied Psycholinguistics*, 21: 117–48.

Nagy, W. E., and Herman, P. A. (1987) Breadth and depth of vocabulary knowledge: implications for acquisition and instruction. In: M.G. McKeown and M. E. Curtis (eds), *The Nature of Vocabulary Acquisition*, pp. 19–35. Erlbaum, Hillsdale, NJ.

Oakhill, J. V., Yuill, N. and Parkin, A. J. (1986) On the nature of the difference between skilled and less-skilled comprehenders. *Journal of Research in Reading*, 9: 80–91.

Papagno, C., and Vallar, G. (1992) Phonological short-term memory and the learning of novel words: the effects of phonological similarity and item length. *Quarterly Journal of Experimental Psychology*, 44A: 47–67.

Papagno, C., Valentine, T., and Baddeley, A. D. (1991) Phonological short-term memory and foreign-language vocabulary learning. *Journal of Memory and Language*, 30: 331–47.

Pickering, S. J., and Gathercole, S. E. (2001) *Working Memory Test Battery for Children*. Psychological Corporation, London.

Pickering, S. J., and Gathercole, S. E. (2004) Distinctive working memory profiles in children with special educational needs *Educational Psychology*, 24: 393–408.

Rochon, E., Waters, G. S., and Caplan, D. (1994) Sentence comprehension in patients with Alzheimer's disease. *Brain and Language*, 46: 329–49.

Roodenrys, S., and Hinton, M. (2002) Sublexical or lexical effects on serial recall of nonwords. *Journal of Experimental Psychology: Language, Memory and Cognition*, 28: 29–33.

Roy, P., and Chiat, S. (2004) A prosodically controlled word and nonword reptition task for 2- to 4-year olds: evidence from typically-developing children. *Journal of Speech, Language, and Hearing Research*, 4: 223–34.

Sahlen, B., Reuterskiold-Wagner, C., Nettelbladt, U., and Radeborg, K. (1999) Non-word repetition in children with language impairment: pitfalls and possibilities. *International Journal of Language and Communication Disorders*, 34: 337–52.

Seigneuric, A., Ehrlich, M. F., Oakhill, J. V., and Yuill, N. M. (2000) Working memory resources and children's reading comprehension. *Reading and Writing*, 13: 81–103.

Service, E. (1992). Phonology, working memory, and foreign-language learning. *Quarterly Journal of Experimental Psychology*, 45A: 21–50.

Service, E., and Kohonen, V. (1995) Is the relation between phonological memory and foreign-language learning accounted for by vocabulary acquisition? *Applied Psycholinguistics*, 16: 155–72.

Shah, P., and Miyake, A. (1996) The separability of working memory resources for spatial thinking and language processing: an individual differences approach. *Journal of Experimental Psychology: General*, 125: 4–27.

Vallar G & Shallice T (1990). *Neuropsychological impairments of short-term memory*. Cambridge University Press, Cambridge.

SLI Consortium (2002) A genomewide scan identifies two novel loci involved in specific language impairment. *American Journal of Human Genetics*, 70: 384–98.

Smyth, S. S., and Scholey, K. A. (1996) The relationship between articulation time and memory performance in verbal and visuospatial tasks. *British Journal of Psychology*, 87: 179–91.

Snowling, M., Chiat, S., and Hulme, C. (1991) Words, nonwords and phonological processes: aome comments on Gathercole, Willis, Emslie and Baddeley. *Applied Psycholinguistics*, 12: 369–73.

Swanson, H. L., and Sachse-Lee, C. (2001) Mathematical problem solving and working memory in children with learning disabilities: both executive and phonological processes are important. *Journal of Experimental Child Psychology*, 79: 294–321.

Thorn, A. S. C., and Frankish, C. R. (2005) Long-term knowledge effects on serial recall of nonwords are not exclusively lexical. *Journal of Experimental Psychology: Learning, Memory and Cognition*, 31: 729–35.

Trojano, L., and Grossi, D. (1995) Phonological and lexical coding in verbal short-term memory and learning. *Brain and Cognition*, 21: 336–354.

Vallar, G., and Baddeley, A. D. (1984) Phonological short-term store, phonological processing and sentence comprehension: a neuropsychological case study. *Cognitive Neuropsychology*, 1: 121–41.

Vallar, G., and Papagno, C. (2002) Neuropsychological impairments of verbal short-term memory. In A. D. Baddeley, M. D. Kopelman, and B. A. Wilson (eds), *Handbook of Memory Disorders*, 2nd edn, pp 249–70. Wiley, Chichester, UK.

Vitevitch, M. S., and Luce, P. A. (2005) Increases in phonotactic probability facilitate spoken nonword repetition. *Journal of Memory and Language*, 52: 193–204.

Waters, G. S., and Caplan, D. (2002) Working memory and online syntactic processing in Alzheimer's disease: studies with auditory moving window presentation. *Journals of Gerontology Series B: Psychological Sciences and Social Sciences*, 57: 298–311.

Waters, G. S., and Caplan, D. (2005) The relationship between age, processing speed, working memory capacity, and language comprehension. *Memory*, 13: 403–13.

Willis, C. S., and Gathercole, S. E. (2001) Phonological short-term memory contributions to sentence processing in young children. *Memory*, 9: 349–64.

Wilson, J. T. L., Scott, J. H., and Power, K. G. (1987) Developmental differences in the span of visual memory for pattern. *British Journal of Developmental Psychology*, 5: 249–55.

CHAPTER 47

Language and mirror neurons

Giacomo Rizzolatti and Laila Craighero

47.1 Introduction

Communication is a process of exchanging information via a common system. There are many natural ways in which individuals may communicate. Besides linguistic communication, which is at the core of human communication, humans communicate using arm gestures, body postures, facial expressions, eye contact, and head and body movements.

Communication may be intentional and non-intentional. In both cases, the sender and the receiver of the messages must have a common code. The difference is that in the case of intentional communication the sender plays the leading role and imposes the communication on the receiver, while in the case of non-intentional communication, the sender sends the message without having any intention to do so. The message is just there. If sender and receiver have a common code, the message reaches the receiver, regardless of the will of the sender.

Of these two types of communication, the non-intentional one is the most basic and primitive. It is evolutionarily necessary because, in social life, individuals have to understand what others are doing, whether or not those others intend to be understood. As will be argued later, it is very plausible that intentional communication is an evolutionarily late development of non-intentional communication.

47.2 Neurophysiological basis of non-intentional communication

47.2.1 General considerations

Actions done by others are probably the most important stimuli of our lives. Most of others' actions do not convey intentional information to the observer. From them, however, we understand what others are doing and we can infer why they are doing it. This involuntary communication is fundamental for interpersonal relations, and is at the basis of social life.

What is the mechanism underlying our capacity to understand others' actions? The traditional view is that actions done by others are understood in the same way as other visual stimuli. Thus, action understanding is based on the visual analysis of the different elements that form an action. For example, when we observe a girl picking up a flower, the analyzed elements would be her hand, the flower, and the movement of the hand towards the flower. The association of these elements and inferences about their interaction enables the observer to understand the witnessed action. The discovery of neurons that code selectively biological motion has better specified the neural basis of this recognition mechanism (Perrett et al., 1989). Actions done by others are coded in a specific part of the visual system devoted to this task, which in humans includes some extrastriate visual areas and the region of the superior temporal sulcus (STS) (see Allison et al., 2000; Puce and Perrett, 2003).

It has been recently argued that visual information alone does not provide a *full* understanding of the observed action (Rizzolatti et al., 2001; Jeannerod, 2004). According to this view, a full action understanding can be achieved only when the observed action activates the corresponding motor representation in the observer. In this way, the observed action enters into the observer's motor network, and enables him or her to relate it to other similar actions and to actions that usually follow the observed one. Without the involvement of the motor system, the visual representation of the action may lead to its recognition, but critical elements for understanding what the action is about (e.g. how it refers to other actions and how to reproduce it) are lacking.

These theoretical considerations received strong support from the discovery that in the motor cortex of the macaque monkey there is a particular set of neurons that discharge both when the monkey observes a given motor act and when it does the same act. These neurons, called "mirror neurons," represent a system that directly matches observed and executed actions. Their properties will be described in the next section.

47.2.2 Mirror system in monkeys

Mirror neurons were originally discovered in the rostral part of the ventral premotor cortex (area F5, see Figure 47.1) of the macaque monkey. Like all neurons of this area, mirror neurons have motor properties. They code mostly distal hand actions such as grasping, holding, tearing, and manipulating. Their defining functional characteristic is that they become active not only when the monkey does a particular action (like grasping an object) but also when it observes another individual (monkey or human) performing a similar action. Mirror neurons do not respond to the sight of a hand mimicking an action or to meaningless intransitive movements. Similarly, they do not respond to the observation of an object alone, even when it is of interest to the monkey (Gallese et al., 1996; Rizzolatti et al., 1996a).

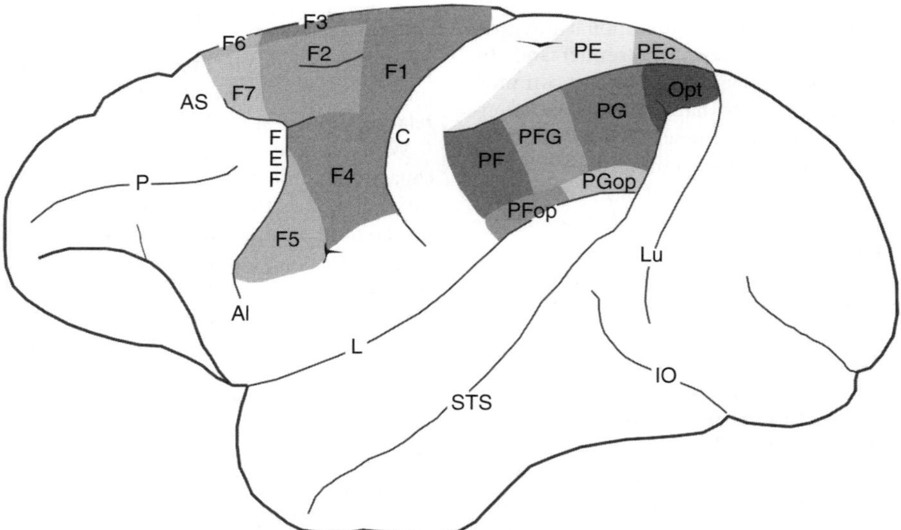

Figure 47.1 Lateral view of the monkey cerebral cortex. The motor areas (F1–F7) are classified according to Rizzolatti et al. (1998), while the parietal areas are named according to the nomenclature of Von Economo (1929). Mirror neurons have been described in area F5 and in the rostral part of the inferior parietal lobule (areas PF and PFG). Abbreviations: AI, inferior arcuate sulcus. AS, superior arcuate sulcus. C, central sulcus. (From Rizzolatti and Craighero, 2004.) Reprinted, with permission, from the Annual Review of Neuroscience, Volume 27 © 2004 by Annual Reviews www.annualreviews.org. See Plate 7 for a color version of this figure.

The vast majority of F5 mirror neurons show a marked similarity between the observed action effective in triggering them and the executed action effective in triggering them. This sensory–motor congruence is occasionally extremely strict. In these cases the effective motor action and the effective observed action coincide both in terms of goal (e.g. grasping) and in terms of how the goal is achieved (e.g. precision grip). For most mirror neurons, however, the congruence is broader and is confined to the goal of the action.

Early studies on mirror neurons examined the upper sector of F5, where hand actions are mostly represented. Recently, a study was carried out on the properties of neurons located in the lower part of F5 where neuron activity is mostly related to mouth actions (Ferrari et al., 2003). The results showed that two classes of mouth mirror neurons could be distinguished: ingestive and communicative mirror neurons. Ingestive mirror neurons, which represent the majority of mouth mirror neurons, respond to the observation of actions related to ingestive functions (e.g. grasping food with the mouth). Virtually all of them show a good correspondence between the effective observed and the effective executed action. More intriguing are the properties of the communicative mirror neurons. For them, the most effective observed action is a communicative gesture, such as lip smacking. However, most of them strongly discharge when the monkey actively performs an ingestive action (Figure 47.2, neuron 76). A few are also active during monkey communicative gestures (Figure 47.2, neuron 33).

This discrepancy between the effective visual input (communicative) and the effective active action (ingestive) is rather intriguing. There is,

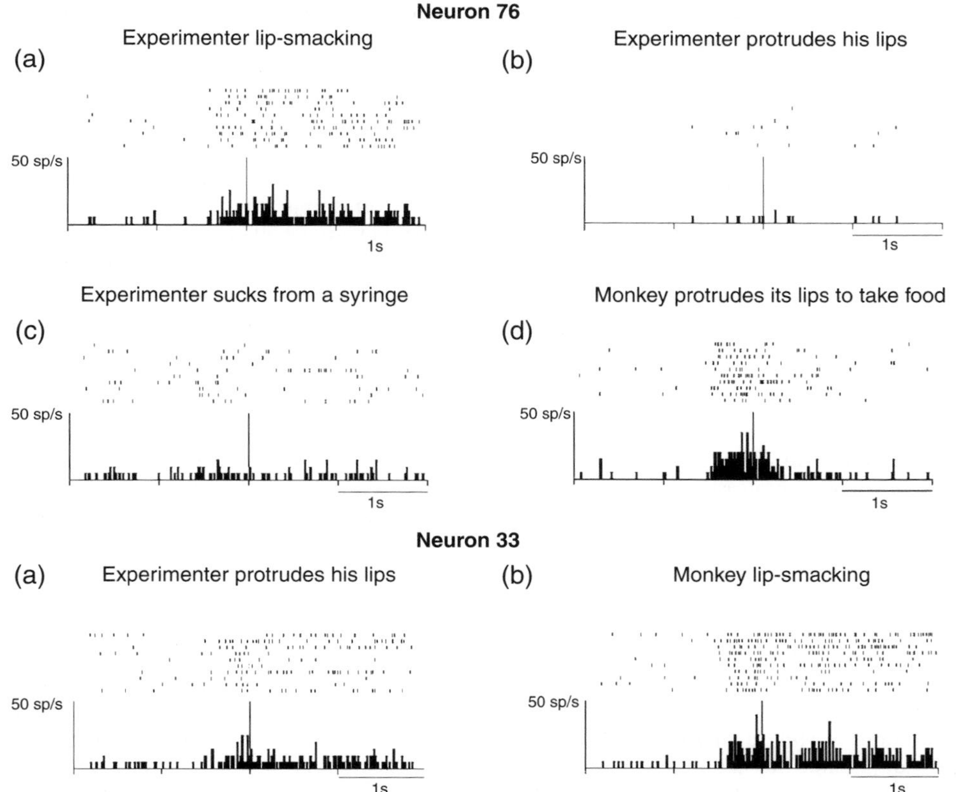

Figure 47.2 Examples of two mouth mirror neurons. Neuron 76 responds to the observation of a communicative gesture (lip smacking). Its motor activity is related, however, to monkey's food ingestion. Neuron 33 responds to the observation of a communicative gesture (lip protrusion) and discharges when the monkey does a communicative gesture (lip smacking). (Modified from Ferrari et al., 2003.)

however, evidence suggesting that in evolution, monkey communicative gestures—or at least some of them—derived from ingestive actions (see below). From this perspective, one may argue that the communicative mouth mirror neurons found in F5 reflect a process of corticalization of communicative functions not yet freed from their original ingestive basis.

An issue recently addressed was whether mirror neurons are able to recognize actions from their sound. Kohler et al. (2002) recorded F5 mirror neuron activity while the monkey was observing a "noisy" action (e.g. ripping a piece of paper), or was presented with the sound of the action without seeing it. The results showed that about 15 percent of mirror neurons responsive to presentation of actions accompanied by sounds also responded to the presentation of the sound alone. Most of them discharged specifically to the sound typical of the observed action. These neurons were dubbed "audiovisual" mirror neurons. The properties of audiovisual neurons strongly suggest that mirror-neuron system is involved in action recognition whatever the modality through which the action is presented.

47.2.3 Monkey mirror neuron system and intention recognition

The motoric coding of the actions of others has an important consequence: It enables the observer to infer future acts of the observed agent by using links among motor acts in his or her motor repertoire. The existence of such an inference mechanism was recently tested by studying the activity of neurons of the inferior parietal lobule (IPL).

As shown by Mountcastle (Mountcastle et al., 1975) and Hyvarinen (1982), many IPL neurons discharge in association with specific *motor acts*. In a recent study, single neurons were recorded from IPL and tested for their motor properties. Neurons discharging selectively in association with grasping movements were tested in two main conditions. In one, the monkey grasped a piece of food located in front of it and brought it to its mouth, while in the other, the monkey grasped the same object and then placed it into a container (Fogassi et al., 2005). The results showed that for most recorded neurons (about 75 percent), the discharge *during* grasping depended on the motor act which *followed* grasping. A series of control experiments demonstrated that this selectivity was not dependent on force, movement kinematics, or type of grasped stimulus. This selectivity of IPL grasping mirror neurons may appear, at first glance, as uneconomical. In fact, fewer neurons are needed if a single set of grasping neurons are used for all possible actions in which grasping is required. However, the cost in number of neurons is offset by the benefits of efficiency: the IPL organization just described is extremely well suited for providing fluidity in action execution. Each neuron codes a specific motor act and simultaneously, being embedded in a specific *chain* of motor acts, facilitates execution of the next act. This enables a continuous sequence of motor acts without any pause between them.

In the same experiment, a series of IPL grasping mirror neurons were tested for their visual responses in the two conditions used in the motor task. The actions were performed by one of the experimenters in front of the monkey. The first motor act was always the same—grasping—but there were cues (e.g. presence or absence of the container) that allowed the monkey to predict which action was likely to follow. The results were analogous to those found on the motor side. Namely, for the majority of IPL mirror neurons, the discharge during grasping done by the experimenter depended on whether the following act was bringing the food to the experimenter's mouth or placing it into the container.

These data suggest a simple mechanism that may mediate the capacity of individuals to read the intentions of others. When an individual starts the first motor act of an action, he or she has clear what is the goal for the entire action. Action *intention* is set before the beginning of the movements, and, as shown by IPL motor properties, is reflected immediately in the neuron discharge. Because the neurons coding motor acts in different action chains have mirror properties, their activation signals not only grasping but, more specifically, grasping-for-eating, or grasping-for-placing. Thus, by their activation, the monkey is able to predict the goal of the observed action, and in this way to "read" the intention of the acting individual.

47.2.4 Mirror system in humans: neurophysiological evidence

A large amount of data indicate that in humans, the observation of actions done by others activates cortical areas involved in motor control. Evidence for this effect comes from electroencephalographic (EEG) and magnetoencephalographic (MEG) recordings from motor areas, transcranial magnetic stimulation experiments (TMS), and brain imaging studies.

It is well known from EEG studies that active movements of the recorded individual, such as wrist opening/closure, desynchronize the EEG rhythms of the areas around the central sulcus. EEG and MEG studies showed a similar desynchronization, although less marked, during the observation of action by others (Altschuler et al., 1997; Hari et al., 1998; Cochin et al., 1998; 1999). A desynchronization of cortical rhythms during observation and execution of finger movements was recently also shown using implanted subdural electrodes, a technique that allows a better signal localization than surface EEG. Most interestingly, the desynchronization during the observation and execution of these movements was present in functionally delimited hand and *language* motor areas (Tremblay et al., 2004).

Fadiga et al. (1995) recorded motor evoked potentials (MEPs) from the right arm and hand muscles (in normal volunteers), elicited by transcranial magnetic stimulation (TMS) of the hand field of the left primary motor cortex. By using this technique, they were able to assess the motor cortex excitability in various conditions, and thus to establish whether the motor system was activated during action observation. Stimulation was performed while volunteers were observing an experimenter grasping objects (transitive hand actions) or performing meaningless arm gestures (intransitive arm movements). Detection of the dimming of a small spot of light and presentation of objects were used as control conditions. The results showed that the observation of both transitive and intransitive actions produced an increase in the MEPs. For both hand and arm movements, the increase selectively concerned those muscles that the volunteers used when producing the observed movements.

Similar results were also found by other groups (Brighina et al., 2000; Gangitano et al., 2001; Clark et al., 2004; see Fadiga et al., 2005). Among these studies, a particularly interesting one is Gangitano et al. (2001), which showed the presence of a strict temporal coupling between the changes in cortical excitability and the dynamics of the observed action. MEPs, which were recorded from hand muscles at different time intervals during passive observation of grasping, matched the time-course of the kinematics of the observed action.

The TMS results are particularly important for two reasons. First, they show that the observation of actions performed by others specifically activates the sets of neurons that are used to replicate the observed action. Second, they indicate that, unlike in the monkey, the human mirror neuron system also resonates for intransitive actions. Thus, the human mirror system appears to have the capacity, absent in monkeys, to replicate internally actions performed by others even when these actions have no apparent goal.

47.2.5 **Mirror system in humans: brain imaging studies**

Observation of actions done by others activates a complex network formed, in humans, by occipital and temporal areas and by two cortical regions whose function is predominantly or fundamentally motor (e.g. Rizzolatti et al., 1996b; Grafton et al., 1996; Grèzes et al., 1998; Iacoboni et al., 1999, 2001; Nishitani and Hari, 2000, 2002; Grèzes et al., 2001, 2003; Buccino et al., 2001; Perani et al., 2001; Decety et al., 2002; Koski et al., 2002, 2003; Manthey et al., 2003). These two regions are the rostral part of the inferior parietal lobule and the lower part of the precentral gyrus plus the posterior part of the inferior frontal gyrus (IFG) which basically corresponds to area 44. These regions form the core of the human mirror neuron system (Figure 47.3). Occasionally, other regions are also found to be active during the observation of others' actions. These regions are the dorsal premotor cortex and the sector of IFG most likely corresponding to area 45.

The areas forming the human mirror neuron system show a somatotopic organization. In an fMRI study, normal volunteers were presented with video clips showing actions done with the mouth, hand/arm and foot/leg. Action observation was contrasted with the observation of a static face, hand, and foot respectively (Buccino et al., 2001). Observations of object-related *mouth* actions determined signal increase in the lower part of the precentral gyrus and of the *pars opercularis* of IFG, bilaterally. In addition, two activation foci were found in the parietal lobe. One was located in the rostral part of the

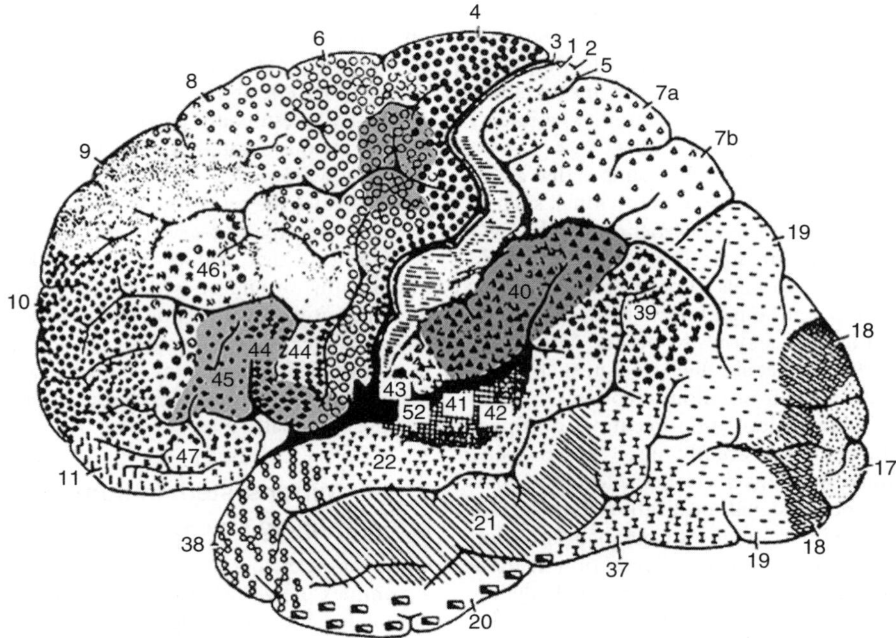

Figure 47.3 Lateral view of human cerebral cortex. The parietal and frontal lobe regions that are consistently activated during the observation of actions by others are shown in red and yellow, respectively (See Plate 8 for a color version of this figure). They form the core of the mirror neuron system. The areas shown in blue (area 45 and dorsal area 6) have been reported to be active during the observation of others' action in some studies. It is likely that they also contain mirror neurons.

inferior parietal lobule (most likely area PF), while the other was located in the posterior part of the same lobule. Observations of object-related hand/arm actions determined signal increase in two sectors of the frontal lobe, one located in the *pars opercularis* of IFG, and the other located in the precentral gyrus. The latter activation was more dorsally located than that found during the observation of mouth movements. As in the case of mouth actions, two activation foci were found in the parietal lobe. The rostral focus was in the rostral part of the inferior parietal lobule, but more posteriorly located than that observed during mouth actions, while the caudal focus was essentially in the same location as that for mouth actions. Finally, observations of object-related foot/leg actions determined an activation of a dorsal sector of the precentral gyrus and an activation of the posterior parietal lobe.

In the second part of the same experiment, volunteers were presented with a mimed version of the object-directed actions. Unlike in the monkey, in which mimed actions do not excite mirror neurons, in humans, mimed actions produced a signal increase in the frontal sector of the mirror neuron system. In contrast, no activation was found in the inferior parietal lobule. This finding is in accord with lack of inferior parietal lobule activation found also in other studies in which intransitive actions were used (e.g. finger movements; Iacoboni et al., 1999; 2001; Koski et al., 2002; 2003). Considering that visual information reaches premotor cortex through the inferior parietal lobule, it is hard to believe that the observation of intransitive actions does not produce any activation of this structure. Instead, activation may be more difficult to detect for intransitive actions compared to transitive actions for the following reason. The inferior parietal lobe receives direct information from the inferotemporal cortex, in addition to that from visual areas responsive to biological motion. Thus, it is likely that the presence of objects in transitive actions produces a source of activation in addition to that due to action observation, thereby resulting in a statically significant activation of inferior parietal lobule for the transitive actions. In mimed actions, where there is no object, the activation does not reach statistical significance.

47.2.6 Which actions activate the mirror neuron system?

Humans recognize actions done not only by humans but also by animals. Are animal actions recognized by the mirror neuron system or is the visual system alone sufficient? Recently, Buccino et al. (2004) addressed this question in an fMRI experiment. Video clips showing silent mouth actions performed by humans, monkeys, and dogs were presented to normal volunteers. Two types of action were shown: biting food, and oral communicative actions (speech reading, lip smacking, barking). As a control, static images of the same actions were presented. The results showed that the observation of biting, regardless of whether performed by a man, a monkey, or a dog, produced a signal increase in the inferior parietal lobule and in the *pars opercularis* of the IFG plus the adjacent precentral gyrus. The left parietal and the left frontal activations were virtually identical for observation of all three species, whereas the right-side foci were stronger during the observation of actions made by a human. Different results were obtained with communicative actions. Observing a human speak activated the left *pars opercularis* of IFG, whereas the observation of lip smacking—a monkey communicative gesture—activated a small focus in the right and left *pars opercularis* of IFG; finally, the observation of barking did not produce any frontal lobe activation. In this case the activation was only present in visual areas.

These results show that actions done by others can be recognized through different mechanisms. Actions belonging to the motor repertoire of the observer, regardless of whether they are done by a conspecific, are mapped onto his or her motor system. Actions that do not belong to this repertoire do not excite the motor system of the observer and are recognized on a visual basis. It is likely that these two different ways of recognizing actions have two different psychological counterparts. In the first case the motor "resonance" translates the visual experience into an internal "first person knowledge," whereas this is lacking in the second case.

Further evidence that the mirror neuron system is strongly activated when the observer sees an action that is part of his or her motor repertoire has been recently provided by Calvo-Merino et al. (2005). They used fMRI imaging to study differences in brain activation between watching an action that one has learned to do and an action that one has not. Experts in classic ballet, experts in the Brazilian martial art capoeira, and inexpert controls viewed videos showing dancers performing classical ballet or capoeira. The results showed greater bilateral activations in premotor cortex, intraparietal sulcus region, right superior parietal lobe, and left posterior STS when expert dancers viewed movements that they have been trained to perform compared to movements that they had not. These results show that the mirror system is particularly active when it integrates observed actions of others with an individual's personal motor repertoire.

The presence of activations during action observation in an area classically considered to be exclusively related to speech might be surprising. However, in recent years, clear evidence has been accumulated that human area 44 contains (as does monkey area F5, the monkey homolog of area 44) a motor representation of hand movements (Krams et al., 1998; Binkofski et al., 1999; Iacoboni et al., 1999; Gerardin et al., 2000; Ehrsson et al., 2000; Tremblay et al., 2004), in addition to that of orolaryngeal movements. It appears, therefore, that the posterior sector of IFG is involved in both non-intentional communication (i.e. recognition of object-related actions) and intentional (verbal) communication—a finding that suggests, as we will see in the next section, a link between these two forms of communication.

47.3 Mirror neurons and language

Humans mostly communicate by sounds. Sound-based languages, however, do not represent the only natural way for communicating. Languages based on gestures (signed languages) represent another form of complex, fully structured communication system. By using sign language, people express abstract concepts, learn mathematics, physics, philosophy, and even create poetry (see Corballis, 2002). Nonetheless, the fact that signed languages represent a fully structured communication system has not changed the view, which many share, that speech is the only *natural* human communication system, and that the evolutionary precursor of human speech consists of animal calls. The argument goes as follows: humans emit sound to communicate, animals emit sounds to communicate, therefore human speech evolved from animal calls.

The logic of this syllogism is rather shaky. Its weakness becomes apparent when one examines animal calls and human speech more closely. First, the anatomical structures underlying primate calls and human speech are different. Primate calls are mostly mediated by the cingulate cortex and by deep, diencephalic and brain stem structures (see Jürgens, 2002). In contrast, the circuits underlying human speech are formed by areas located around the Sylvian fissure, including the posterior part of IFG. It is hard to imagine how in primate evolution, the call system shifted from its deep position found in non-human primates to the lateral convexity of the cortex where human speech is housed.

Second, speech in humans is not, or is not necessarily, linked to emotional behavior, whereas animal calls are. Third, speech is mostly a dyadic, person-to-person communication system. In contrast, animal calls are typically emitted without a well-identified receiver. Fourth, speech is endowed with combinatorial properties that are absent in animal communication. As Chomsky (1966) rightly stressed, human language is "based on an entirely different principle" from all other forms of animal communication. Finally, humans do possess a "call" communication system like that of non-human primates and its anatomical location is similar. This system mediates the utterances that humans emit when in particular emotional states (cries, yelling, etc.). These utterances, which are preserved in patients with global aphasia, lack the referential character and the combinatorial properties that characterize human speech.

The advocates of the sound-based theory of language origin consider a strong argument in favor of this theory to be the presence of referential information in some animal calls (e.g. Pinker, 1994). The famous study of the alarm calls of vervet monkeys (Cheney and Seyfarth, 1990), as well as other studies that extended these observations to other species and other communicative contexts (social relationship, food, inter-group aggression), showed that evolution tried this pathway. The reason why this attempt did not succeed is the lack of flexibility inherent in any communicative system based on emotions. In a non-emotional communication system the same word, for example the word *fire*, which is basically an alarm message ("escape"), may assume a completely different meaning. It may indicate, for example, that the fire is ready and we can start to cook our meal ("approach message"), as well as conveying other positive messages. This flexibility cannot occur in an emotional communicative system because a referential meaning cannot indicate a behavior that is in contrast with the emotion that generated it. Thus the same utterance or call cannot convey, in different contexts, an escape and an approach message.

If not animal calls, what could be the origin of human speech? An alternative hypothesis is that the path leading to speech started with gestural communication. This hypothesis, first proposed by the French philosopher Condillac, has recently found several defenders (e.g Armstrong et al., 1995; Corballis, 2002). According to this theory, the initial communicative system in primate precursors of modern humans was based on very simple, elementary gesturing. Sounds were then associated with the gestures and became progressively the dominant way of communication.

The discovery of mirror neurons provided strong support for the gestural theory of speech origin. Mirror neurons create a direct link between the sender of a message and its receiver. Thanks to the mirror mechanism, actions done by one individual become messages that are understood by an observer without any cognitive mediation. The observation of an individual grasping an apple is immediately understood because it evokes the same motor representation in the parieto-frontal mirror system of the observer. Similarly, the observation of a facial expression of disgust is immediately understood because it evokes the same representation in the amygdala of the individual observing it (Gallese et al., 2004).

On the basis of this fundamental property of mirror neurons, and the fact that the observation of actions like hand grasping activates the caudal part of IFG (Broca's area), Rizzolatti and Arbib (1998) proposed that the mirror mechanism is the basic mechanism from which language evolved. In fact, the mirror mechanism solved, at a initial stage of language evolution, two fundamental communication problems: parity and direct comprehension. Thanks to the mirror neurons, what counted for the sender of the message also counted for the receiver. No arbitrary symbols were required. The comprehension was inherent in the neural organization of the two individuals.

A criticism of this view is based on the fact that the monkey mirror neuron system is constituted of neurons coding object-directed actions. Thus, the monkey mirror neuron system forms a closed system, which by definition does not appear to be particularly suitable for intentional communication. Yet, if this is true for the monkey, it is not the case for the human mirror system. As reviewed above, TMS and brain imaging studies have shown that activation of the human mirror system is achieved by presentation of intransitive actions (Fadiga et al., 1995; Maeda et al., 2002) as well as during pantomime observation (Buccino et al., 2001, Grèzes et al., 2003).

It is difficult to specify how the shift from a closed system of monkeys to an open, intentionally communicative system, in humans might have occurred. The view, however, that communicative actions derived from a more ancient system of non-communicative gestures is not new. Van Hoof (1967), for example, proposed that many of the most common communicative gestures of the monkey, such as lip smacking, are ritualizations of ingestive actions that monkeys use for affiliative purposes. The fact that mouth mirror neurons respond both to the observation of communicative actions and during the execution of ingestive actions appears to give a neurophysiological basis to this idea (Ferrari et al., 2003; see also above, mirror system in monkeys).

Similarly, Vygotsky (1934) suggested that intransitive actions derive in children from object-directed transitive actions. For example, when objects are located close to a child, the child grasps them. When they are located far from the child, the child extends his or her hands towards the objects. Because the mother understands this gesture, the child uses it again and again and, eventually, attempts to reach objects become communicative gestures. Thus, the transition from object-directed to intentional communicative gesture can be accommodated by the mirror neuron hypothesis of language evolution.

47.3.1 From gestures to sound

It is rather unlikely that the gestural communications, which appeared in the ancestors of Homo sapiens, reached the sophisticated complexity shown by modern sign languages. It is much more plausible, as also suggested by Arbib (2005), that gestures emitted for communicative purposes were soon accompanied by sounds, and that the speech development prevented the occurrence of a fully-fledged sign language.

The major problem in this evolutionary scenario is to understand how sounds, initially meaningless, became associated with gestures which conveyed specific meanings. Onomatopeia, that is, the similarity between the sound of a word and the noise produced by a corresponding natural event, is one of the suggested possibilities. Another possibility is represented by interjectional utterances emitted by individuals in certain conditions. The problem with both these hypotheses is that they can account for only a very limited number of words. Thus, although they explain the origin of some words, they lack the generality necessary to explain most of the links between sound and meaning.

An interesting theory attempting to explain this link was advanced many years ago by Paget (1930). This theory, called "schematopoeia", posits that human communication started with manual gestures. These gestures were accompanied by unintentional, but analogous, movements of tongue, lips, and jaw. Later, the gesticulating individuals discovered that the expiration of air through the oral cavities produced audible gestures. This was the beginning of voiced speech.

Paget gives many examples of parallelism between sound and meaning from a variety of languages. For vowels, he suggests that *a* (as in *large*) often refers to anything that is large, wide open, or spacious; *i*, especially in its narrow or thin variety (as in *mini*), often refers to something that is small or pointed; and *aw* (as in *yawn*) generally indicates a cavity. For consonants, he suggests that *m* implies a continuous closure, while *dr* or *tr* denotes running or walking. According to this explanation, the great majority of words were originally pantomimic (Paget, 1930: 159). This pantomimic origin is not readily evident in modern languages because, according to Paget, words are built by addition of separate significant elements in the manner of Chinese ideographs.

The schematopoeia theory is obviously very speculative. Its central tenet, however—that there is a basic, natural link between hand/body gestures and speech gestures—is very ingenious. It suggests a clue as to how an opaque gestural system, like the orolaryngeal system, could convey understandable messages, thanks to the close correspondence between hand/body gestures, intrinsically known to the observers, and oro/laryngeal gestures Furthermore, it has a clear neurophysiological prediction: if hand-arm and speech gestures are strictly linked, they must have a common neural substrate.

A series of recent studies support this prediction. TMS experiments have shown that *right-hand* motor excitability increases during reading and during spontaneous speech, whereas no language-related effects are found under these conditions in the left-hand motor area or in the leg representations of either hemisphere (Tokimura et al., 1996; Seyal et al., 1999; Meister et al., 2003). Meister et al. (2003) stressed that the increase of hand motor cortex excitability cannot be due to word articulation because word articulation recruits motor cortex bilaterally, but the observed activation was strictly limited to the left hemisphere. The facilitation appears, therefore, to result from a co-activation of the right hand motor area with the language network.

Similar conclusions were also reached by Gentilucci and his co-workers (2001). In a series of behavioral experiments, they showed normal volunteers one of two 3-D objects, one large and the other small, randomly presented. On the visible face of both objects, either two Xs or a series of dots could appear. The volunteers were required to grasp the objects and, regardless of the symbols written on the object, to open their mouth in all conditions. The kinematics of hand, arm, and mouth movements were recorded. The data showed that in spite of the instruction to open the mouth in the same way in all conditions, lip aperture and the peak velocity of lip aperture increased when the hand movement was directed to the large object (Figure 47.4).

In another experiment, the authors employed a similar experimental procedure, but asked the participants to pronounce a syllable (e.g. *gu* or *ga*) instead of simply opening their mouths. The syllables were written on the objects in the same locations as the symbols in the previous experiment. The results showed that lip aperture was larger when the participants grasped a larger object. Furthermore, the maximal power level

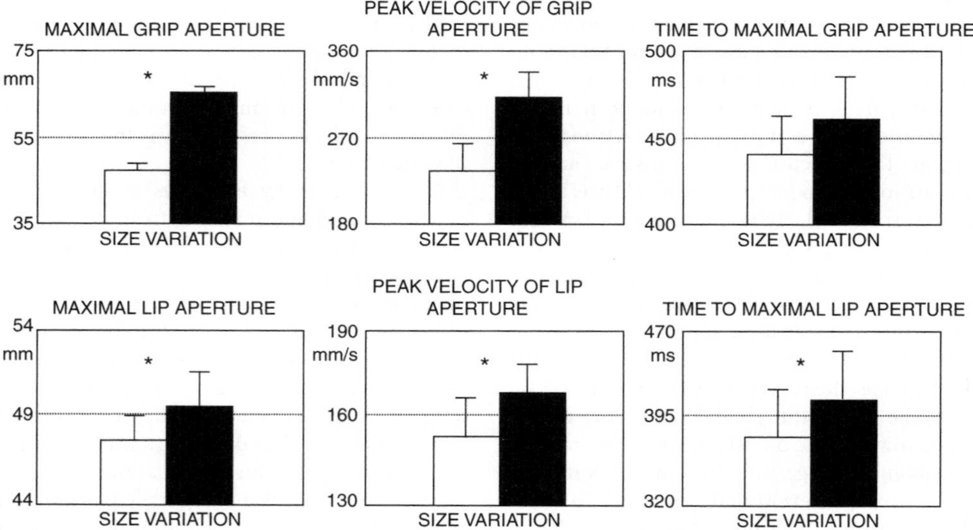

Figure 47.4 Influence of hand grasping on mouth aperture. Upper row: mean values of grasp parameters. Lower row: mean values of lip aperture parameters. Open bar: movements directed towards the small object. Black bars: movements directed to the large object. Left: maximal grip and lip aperture. Center: peak velocity. Right: time to maximal hand and mouth aperture.

Source: Modified from Gentilucci et al. (2001). Used with permission.

recorded during syllable emission was also higher when volunteers grasped the large object (Gentilucci et al., 2001).

These experiments indicate that both buccal movements and the orolaryngeal synergies necessary for syllable emission are linked to manual gestures. Most importantly, hand actions producing large movements share a neural substrate with large mouth actions, precisely as proposed by Paget's theory.

Finally, evidence for a link between gesturing and speech also comes from clinical studies. Hanlon et al. (1990) showed that, in aphasics, pointing with the right hand to a screen where objects are presented facilitates object naming. Similarly, Hadar et al. (1998) found that word retrieval is facilitated through gesturing in brain-damaged patients.

Clearly, the reviewed experiments do not prove the schematopoeia theory. Nonetheless, they indicate that the theory is not as bizarre as one may think initially: a link between hand gestures and the speech system is present in modern Homo sapiens.

47.3.2 The appearance of echo-mirror neurons

The association between specific sounds and communicative gestures has obvious advantages, such as the possibility of communicating in the dark or when hands are busy with tools or weapons. Nonetheless, to achieve effective sound communication, the sounds conveying messages previously expressed by gesture ("gesture-related sounds") ought to be clearly distinguishable and, most importantly, should maintain constant features; they must be pronounced in a precise, consistent way. This requires a sophisticated organization of the motor system related to sound production, and a rich connectivity between the cortical motor areas controlling voluntary actions and the centers controlling the orolaryngeal tract. The large expansion of the posterior part of the inferior frontal gyrus culminating in the appearance of Broca's area in the human left hemisphere is, most likely, the results of the evolutionary pressure to achieve this voluntarily control.

In parallel with these modifications occurring in the motor cortex, a system for understanding them should have evolved. We know that in monkey area F5, the homolog of human area 44, there are neurons—the so called "audiovisual neurons" (Kohler et al., 2002; see also above, mirror system in monkeys), that respond to the observation of actions done by others as well as to the sounds of those actions. This system, however, is tuned for recognition of the sound of physical events and not of sounds done by individuals. In order to understand the proto-speech sounds, a variant of the audiovisual mirror neuron system tuned to resonate in response to sounds emitted by the orolaryngeal tract should have evolved. A more sophisticated acoustic system, enabling a better discrimination of the gesture-associated sounds, has also probably evolved. Note, however, that an improvement in auditory discrimination would be of little use if the gesture-related sounds did not activate the orolaryngeal gesture representation in the brain of the listener.

47.3.3 Echo-mirror neuron system and the problem of its functional role

Is there evidence that modern humans have a mirror neuron system that responds to sounds produced by the orolaryngeal tract and that naturally accompanies gesticulation? Considering the sophistication of the speech system in our species, it is difficult to prove this point. There is clear evidence, however, that humans are endowed with a motor system that resonates selectively in response to speech sounds (the "echo mirror neuron system").

Fadiga et al. (2002) recorded MEPs from the tongue muscles in normal volunteers instructed to listen carefully to acoustically presented verbal and non-verbal stimuli. The stimuli were words, regular pseudo-words, and bitonal sounds. In the middle of words and pseudo-words there was either a double *f* or a double *r*. *F* is a labio-dental fricative consonant that, when pronounced, requires virtually no tongue movements, whereas *r* is a linguo-palatal fricative consonant that, in contrast, requires marked tongue muscle involvement to be pronounced. During the stimulus presentation, the left motor cortex of the participants was stimulated with single pulse TMS. The results showed that listening to words and pseudo-words containing the double *r* produced a significant increase of MEP amplitude recorded from tongue muscles compared to listening to bitonal sounds and words and pseudo-words containing the double *f* (Figure 47.5).

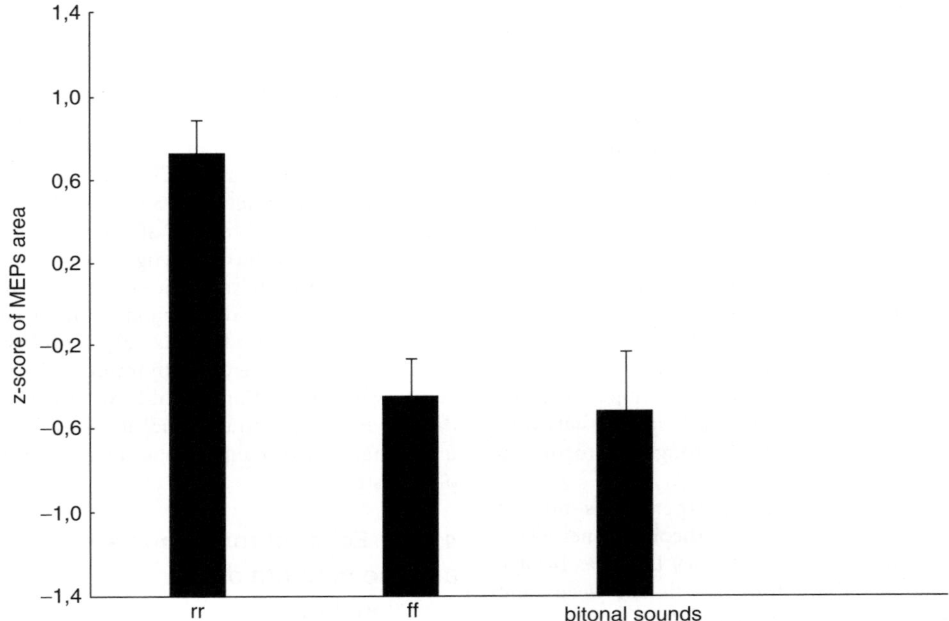

Figure 47.5 Total areas of the normalized motor evoked potentials (MEPs) recorded from tongue muscles during listening to words and bitonal sounds. "rr" and "ff" refer to verbal stimuli containing a double lingua-palatal fricative consonant "r", and a double verbal labio-dental fricative consonant "f", respectively. (Modified from Fadiga et al., 2002.)

Results congruent with those of Fadiga et al. (2002) were obtained by Watkins et al. (2003). Using the single pulse TMS technique, they recorded MEPs from a lip muscle (*orbicularis oris*) and a hand muscle (first *interosseus*) in four conditions: listening to continuous prose, viewing speech-related lip movements, listening to non-verbal sounds, and viewing eye and brow movements. Compared to viewing eye and brow movements, listening to and viewing speech enhanced the MEP amplitude recorded from the *orbicularis oris* muscle. Intriguingly, the MEPs obtained when subjects listened to non-verbal sounds also increased compared to viewing eye and brow movement. This increase was very likely due to activation of a human mirror system similar to that of the monkey audio-visual mirror neurons (Kohler et al. 2002).

All of these effects were seen only in response to stimulation of the left hemisphere. No changes of MEPs in any condition were observed following stimulation of the right hemisphere. Finally, the size of MEPs elicited in the first *interosseus* muscle did not differ in any condition.

Taken together, these data suggest that a mirror neuron system for speech sound—an echo-mirror neuron system—exists in humans: When an individual listens to verbal stimuli, there is an automatic activation of his speech-related motor centers. Did this system evolve from the hypothetical gesture-related sounds mirror system discussed in the previous section? There is no doubt that speech is not purely a system based on sounds as such. As shown by Liberman (Liberman et al., 1967; Liberman and Mattingly, 1985; Liberman and Whalen, 2000), an efficient communication system cannot be built by substituting tones or combinations of tones for speech. There is something special about speech sounds that distinguish them from other auditory material, and this is their capacity to evoke the motor representation of the heard sounds in the listener's motor cortex. Note that this property, postulated by Liberman on the basis of indirect evidence, is now demonstrated by the existence of the echo-mirror neuron system. One may argue, however, that this property is only for translating heard sounds into pronounced sounds. In other words, the basic function of mirror neurons—understanding—will be lost here and only the imitation function, developed on the top of former (see Rizzolatti and Craighero, 2004) would be present.

It is possible that an echo-mirror neuron system would evolve solely for the purpose of translating heard sounds into pronounced sounds. We are strongly inclined, however, to think that the motor link that this system provides to speech sounds has a more profound evolutionary significance. First, as discussed above there is a consistent link in humans between hand actions and orolaryngeal gestures, similar to the one present in the monkey for hand and mouth action. Thus, if these neurons acquired mirror properties, as other types of F5/Broca's area neuron did, a category of neurons evolve coding orolaryngeal tract gestures simultaneously with body-action gestures. In other words, neurons appeared which coded phonetics simultaneously with semantics. In this way, heard speech sounds produced not only a tendency to imitate the sound but also an understanding of the accompanying body-action gestures (much as audio-visual mirror neurons allow understanding of the actions that produce the sounds). Second, once a primitive sound-to-meaning linkage was established, it served as the base for the development of additional, increasingly arbitrary, links between sounds and actions—i.e. the development of words. These arbitrary links greatly extended the possibilities for rich communication while requiring a lengthy, culturally bound learning period. Finally, given the necessity of distinguishing among more speech sounds in more combinations, the links between heard speech sounds and orolaryngeal gestures became stronger (as in the modern echo-mirror system), whereas there was little pressure to further develop the link between sound and meaning given the success of the learned system of arbitrary linkages.

47.4 Conclusions

The aim of the present chapter has been to describe the functional properties of mirror neurons systems, and to show how a mechanism originally devoted to non-intentional communication becomes in evolution the mechanism at the basis of intentional communication. The reconstruction of how speech appeared in evolution can only be hypothetical. Nonetheless, evidence collected in the last few years strongly supports the hypothesis that human speech evolved from gestural communication rather than from animal calls.

We have not addressed the problem of the origin of grammar. We recognize the importance of this issue—for many scholars the most important issue—but at present there are not sufficient neurophysiological data to discuss its origin, even at a very hypothetical level. Nor have we discussed the growing behavioral and neurophysiological evidence showing that during speech processing there is activation of non-speech areas and of the motor system in particular. These findings and their implications are dealt with in detail in the excellent chapters in this volume by Glenberg (21) and Pulvermüller (8).

Acknowledgements

We are grateful to Arthur Glenberg for his comment on the manuscript. The study was supported by EU Contract IST 2001-35282, Mirrorbot; EU Contract NEST 012738, Neurocom; Cofin 2004 (GR); OMLL, EUROCORES Programme; EU Contract NEST 5010, "Learning and development of Contextual Action."

References

Allison, T., Puce, A., and McCarthy, G. (2000) Social perception from visual cues: role of the STS region. *Trends in Cognitive Science*, 4: 267–78.

Altschuler, E. L., Vankov, A., Hubbard, E. M., Roberts, E., Ramachandran, V. S., and Pineda, J. A. (2000) Mu wave blocking by observation of movement and its possible use as a tool to study theory of other minds. *Society of Neuroscience Abstract*, 68.1.

Altschuler, E. L., Vankov, A., Wang, V., Ramachandran, V. S., and Pineda, J. A. (1997) Person see, person do: human cortical electrophysiological correlates of monkey see monkey do cell. *Society of Neuroscience Abstract*, 719.17.

Arbib, M. A. (2005) From monkey-like action recognition to human language: an evolutionary framework for neurolinguistics. *Behavioral and Brain Sciences*, 28: 105–24.

Armstrong, A. C., Stokoe, W. C., and Wilcox, S. E. (1995) *Gesture and the Nature of Language*. Cambridge University Press, Cambridge.

Binkofski, F., Buccino, G., Posse, S., Seitz, R. J., Rizzolatti, G., and Freund, H. (1999) A fronto-parietal circuit for object manipulation in man: evidence from an fMRI-study. *European Journal of Neuroscience*, 11: 3276–86.

Bookheimer, S. (2002) Functional MRI of language: new approaches to understanding the cortical organization of semantic processing. *Annual Review of Neuroscience* 25: 151–88.

Brighina, F., La Bua, V., Oliveri, M., Piazza, A., and Fierro, B. (2000) Magnetic stimulation study during observation of motor tasks. *Journal of Neurological Sciences*, 174: 122–6.

Buccino, G., Binkofski, F., Fink, G. R., Fadiga, L., Fogassi, L., Gallese, V. et al. (2001) Action observation activates premotor and parietal areas in a somatotopic manner: an fMRI study. *European Journal of Neuroscience*, 13: 400–4.

Buccino, G., Lui, F., Vanessa, N., Patteri, I., Lagravinese, G., Benuzzi, F., et al. (2004) Neural circuits involved in the recognition of actions performed by nonconspecifics: an FMRI study. *Journal of Cognitive Neuroscience*, 16: 114–26.

Calvo-Merino, B., Glaser, D. E., Grezes, J., Passingham, R. E., and Haggard, P. (2005) Action observation and acquired motor skills: an FMRI study with expert dancers. *Cerebral Cortex*, 15: 1243–9.

Cheney, D. L.,and Seyfarth, R. M. (1990) *How Monkeys See The World: Inside The Mind Of Another Species*. University of Chicago Press, Chicago.

Chomsky, N. (1966) *Cartesian Linguistics*. Harper & Row, New York.

Clark, S., Tremblay, F., and Ste-Marie, D. (2004) Differential modulation of corticospinal excitability during observation, mental imagery and imitation of hand actions. *Neuropsychologia*, 42: 105–12.

Cochin, S., Barthelemy, C., Lejeune, B., Roux, S., and Martineau, J. (1998) Perception of motion and qEEG activity in human adults. *Electroencephalography and Clinical Neurophysiology*, 107: 287–95.

Cochin, S., Barthelemy, C., Roux, S., and Martineau, J. (1999) Observation and execution of movement: similarities demonstrated by quantified electroencephalograpy. *European Journal of Neuroscience*, 11: 1839–42.

Corballis, M. C. (2002) *From Hand to Mouth: The Origins of Language*. Princeton University Press, Princeton, NJ.

Decety, J., Chaminade, T., Grèzes, J., and Meltzoff, A. N. (2002) A PET exploration of the neural mechanisms involved in reciprocal imitation. *NeuroImage*, 15: 265–72.

Ehrsson, H. H., Fagergren, A., Jonsson, T., Westling, G., Johansson, R. S., and Forssberg, H. (2000) Cortical activity in precision- versus power-grip tasks: an fMRI study. *Journal of. Neurophysiology*, 83: 528–36.

Fadiga, L., Craighero, L., Buccino, G., and Rizzolatti, G. (2002) Speech listening specifically modulates the excitability of tongue muscles: a TMS study. *European Journal of Neuroscience*, 15: 399–402.

Fadiga, L., Craighero, L., and Olivier, E. (2005) Human motor cortex excitability during the perception of others' action. *Current Opinion in Neurobiology*, 15: 213–18.

Fadiga, L., Fogassi, L., Pavesi, G., and Rizzolatti, G. (1995) Motor facilitation during action observation: a magnetic stimulation study. *Journal of Neurophysiology*, 73: 2608–11.

Ferrari, P. F., Gallese, V., Rizzolatti, G., and Fogassi, L. (2003) Mirror neurons responding to the observation of ingestive and communicative mouth actions in the monkey ventral premotor cortex. *European Journal of Neuroscience*, 17: 1703–14.

Fogassi, L., Ferrari, P. F., Gesierich, B., Rozzi, S., Chersi, F., and Rizzolatti, G. (2005) Parietal lobe: from action organization to intention understanding. *Science*, 308: 662–7.

Gallese, V., Fadiga, L., Fogassi, L., and Rizzolatti, G. (1996) Action recognition in the premotor cortex. *Brain*, 119: 593–609.

Gallese, V., Keysers, C. and Rizzolatti, G. (2004) A unifying view of the basis of social cognition. *Trends in Cognitive Sciences*, 8: 396–403.

Gangitano, M., Mottaghy, F. M., and Pascual-Leone, A. (2001) Phase-specific modulation of cortical motor output during movement observation. *Neuroreport*, 12: 1489–92.

Gentilucci, M., Benuzzi, F., Gangitano, M., and Grimaldi, S. (2001) Grasp with hand and mouth: a kinematic study on healthy subjects. *Journal of Neurophysiology*, 86: 1685–99.

Gerardin, E., Sirigu, A., Lehericy, S., Poline, J. B., Gaymard, B., Marsault, C., et al. (2000) Partially overlapping neural networks for real and imagined hand movements. *Cerebral Cortex*, 10: 1093–104.

Grafton, S. T., Arbib, M. A., Fadiga, L., and Rizzolatti, G. (1996) Localization of grasp representations in humans by PET, 2: Observation compared with imagination. *Experimental Brain Research*, 112: 103–11.

Grèzes, J., Armony, J. L., Rowe, J., and Passingham, R. E. (2003) Activations related to "mirror" and "canonical" neurones in the human brain: an fMRI study. *NeuroImage*, 18: 928–37.

Grèzes, J., Costes, N., and Decety, J. (1998) Top-down effect of strategy on the perception of human biological motion: a PET investigation. *Cognitive Neuropsychology*, 15: 553–82.

Grèzes, J., Fonlupt, P., Bertenthal, B., Delon-Martin, C., Segebarth, C., and Decety, J. (2001) Does perception of biological motion rely on specific brain regions? *NeuroImage*, 13: 775–85.

Hadar, U., Wenkert-Olenik, D., Krauss, R., and Soroker, N. (1998) Gesture and the processing of speech: neuropsychological evidence. *Brain and Language*, 62: 107–26.

Hanlon, R. E., Brown, J. W., and Gerstman, L. J. (1990) Enhancement of naming in nonfluent aphasia through gesture. *Brain and Language*, 38: 298–314.

Hari, R., Forss, N., Avikainen, S., Kirveskari, S., Salenius, S., and Rizzolatti, G. (1998) Activation of human primary motor cortex during action observation: a neuromagnetic study. *Proceedings of the National Academy of Science of the United States of America*, 95: 15061–5.

Hyvarinen, J. (1982) Posterior parietal lobe of the primate brain. *Physiological Review*, 62: 1060–129.

Iacoboni, M., Koski, L. M., Brass, M., Bekkering, H., Woods, R. P., Dubeau, M. C., et al. (2001) Reafferent copies of imitated actions in the right superior temporal cortex. *Proceedings of the National Academy of Science of the United States of America*, 98: 13995–9.

Iacoboni, M., Woods, R. P., Brass, M., Bekkering, H., Mazziotta, J. C., and Rizzolatti, G. (1999) Cortical mechanisms of human imitation. *Science*, 286: 2526–8.

Jeannerod, M. (2004) Visual and action cues contribute to the self-other distinction. *Nature Neuroscience*, 7: 422–3.

Jürgens, U. (2002) Neural pathways underlying vocal control. *Neuroscience and Biobehavioral Review*, 26: 235–58.

Kohler, E., Keysers, C., Umiltà Fogassi, L., Gallese, V., and Rizzolatti, G. (2002) Hearing sounds, understanding actions: action representation in mirror neurons. *Science*, 297: 846–8.

Koski, L., Iacoboni, M., Dubeau, M. C., Woods, R. P., and Mazziotta, J. C. (2003) Modulation of cortical activity during different imitative behaviors. *Journal of Neurophysiology*, 89: 460–71.

Koski, L., Wohlschlager, A., Bekkering, H., Woods, R. P., and Dubeau, M. C. (2002) Modulation of motor and premotor activity during imitation of target-directed actions. *Cerebral Cortex*, 12: 847–55.

Krams, M., Rushworth, M. F., Deiber, M. P., Frackowiak, R. S., and Passingham, R. E. (1998) The preparation, execution and suppression of copied movements in the human brain. *Experimental Brain Research*, 120: 386–98.

Liberman, A. M., Cooper, F. S., Shankweiler, D. P., and Studdert-Kennedy, M. (1967) Perception of the speech code. *Psychological Review*, 74: 431–61.

Liberman, A. M., and Mattingly, I. G. (1985) The motor theory of speech perception revised. *Cognition*, 21: 1–36.

Liberman, A. M., and Whalen, D. H. (2000) On the relation of speech to language. *Trends in Cognitive Sciencess*, 4: 187–96.

Maeda, F., Kleiner-Fisman, G., and Pascual-Leone, A. (2002) Motor facilitation while observing hand actions: specificity of the effect and role of observer's orientation. *Journal of Neurophysiology*, 87: 1325–9.

Manthey, S., Schubotz, R. I., and von Cramon, D. Y. (2003) Premotor cortex in observing erroneous action: an fMRI study. *Brain Research. Cognitive Brain Research*, 15: 296–307.

Meister, I. G., Boroojerdi, B., Foltys, H., Sparing, R., Huber, W., and Topper, R. (2003) Motor cortex hand area and speech: implications for the development of language. *Neuropsychologia*, 41: 401–6.

Mountcastle, V. B., Lynch, J. C., Georgopoulos, A., Sakata, H., and Acuna, C. (1975) Posterior parietal association cortex of the monkey: command functions for operations within extrapersonal space. *Journal of Neurophysiology*, 38: 871–908.

Nishitani, N., and Hari, R. (2000) Temporal dynamics of cortical representation for action. *Proceedings of the National Academy of Science of the United States of America*, 97: 913–18.

Nishitani, N., and Hari, R. (2002) Viewing lip forms: cortical dynamics. *Neuron*, 36: 1211–20.

Paget, R. (1930) *Human Speech*. Harcourt Brace, New York.

Perani, D., Fazio, F., Borghese, N. A., Tettamanti, M., Ferrari, S., Decety, J., et al., (2001) Different brain correlates for watching real and virtual hand actions. *NeuroImage*, 14: 749–58.

Perrett, D. I., Harries, M. H., Bevan, R., Thomas, S., Benson, P. J., Mistlin, A. J., Chitty, A. J., Hietanen, J. K., and Ortega, J. E. (1989) Frameworks of analysis for the neural representation of animate objects and actions. *Journal of Experimental Biology*, 147: 87–113.

Pinker, S. (1994) *The Language Instinct: How the Mind Creates Language*. Morrow, New York.

Puce, A. and Perrett D.I. (2003) Electrophysiological and brain imaging of biological motion. *Philosophical Transactions of the Royal Society, London*, series B, 358: 435–45.

Rizzolatti, G., and Arbib, M. A. (1998) Language within our grasp. *Trends in Neurosciences*, 21: 188–94.

Rizzolatti, G., and Craighero, L. (2004) The mirror-neuron system. *Annual Review of Neuroscience*, 27: 169–92.

Rizzolatti, G., Fadiga, L., Fogassi, L., and Gallese, V. (1996) Premotor cortex and the recognition of motor actions. *Cognitive Brain Research*, 3: 131–41.

Rizzolatti, G., Fadiga, L., Matelli, M., Bettinardi, V., Paulesu, E., Perani, D., et al. (1996) Localization of grasp representation in humans by PET, 1: Observation versus execution. *Experimental Brain Research*, 111: 246–52.

Rizzolatti, G., Fogassi, L., and Gallese, V. (2001) Neurophysiological mechanisms underlying the understanding and imitation of action. *Nature Reviews Neuroscience*, 2: 661–70.

Rizzolatti G, Luppino G, Matelli M. (1998) The organization of the cortical motor system: new concepts. *Electroencephalography and Clinical Neurophysiology*, 106: 283–96.

Seyal, M., Mull, B., Bhullar, N., Ahmad, T., and Gage, B. (1999) Anticipation and execution of a simple reading task enhance corticospinal excitability. *Clinical Neurophysiology*, 110: 424–9.

Tokimura, H., Tokimura, Y., Oliviero, A., Asakura, T., and Rothwell, J. C. (1996) Speech-induced changes in corticospinal excitability. *Annals of Neurology*, 40: 628–34.

Tremblay, C., Robert, M., Pascual-Leone, A., Lepore, F., Nguyen, D. K., Carmant, L., et al. (2004) Action observation and execution: intracranial recordings in a human subject. *Neurology*, 63: 937–8.

Van Hoof, J. (1967) The facial displays of the catarrhine monkeys and apes. In D. Morris (ed.), *Primate Ethology*, pp. 7–68. Weidenfield & Nicolson, London.

Von Economo, C. (1929) *The Cytoarchitectonics of the Human Cerebral Cortex*. Oxford University Press, London.

Vygotsky, L. S. (1934) *Thought and Language*. MIT Press, Cambridge, MA.

Watkins, K. E., Strafella, A. P., and Paus, T. (2003) Seeing and hearing speech excites the motor system involved in speech production. *Neuropsychologia*, 41: 989–94.

CHAPTER 48

The evolution of language: a comparative perspective

W. Tecumseh Fitch

48.1 Introduction

The evolution of language is one of the most fascinating events in the history of life on earth (Maynard Smith and Szathmáry, 1995; Hauser et al., 2002; Nowak et al., 2002). Understanding how, why, and when language evolved has become the focus of a rapidly-growing interdisciplinary research effort (Christiansen and Kirby, 2003; Fitch, 2005b), sometimes termed "biolinguistics" (Jenkins, 1999; Givón, 2002). Language does not fossilize, and the fossil record relevant to language evolution is thus exceedingly sparse and provides few dependable indicators about when or why language evolved. Although I will review the relevant fossil record briefly here, I conclude that further empirical progress will require additional sources of evidence. Two promising lines of research are an increased understanding of the neural and genetic mechanisms underlying language, and rigorous application of the comparative method. Both approaches seem destined to play a central role in any future science of biolinguistics (Hauser et al., 2002; Pinker and Jackendoff, 2005). A focus on mechanisms will provide the empirical framework for delineating and understanding each subcomponent of the language capacity. "Language" as a whole is clearly far too complex to be determined by a single mechanism or gene, and a componential view that sees the language faculty in a broad sense as composed of several more specific mechanisms is a necessity for future progress (Hauser et al., 2002). By considering different components of language independently, we can focus on the details of these mechanisms, and move beyond definitional debates ("What is Language? Do animals have Language?"). Thus, a crucial and non-trivial task, shared by psycholinguistics and biolinguistics, is to delineate a well-defined, empirically accessible suite of mechanisms that together make up the language faculty.

The other key new component of biolinguistics, and the core topic of this review, is comparative biology, in particular the explicit use of a broad comparative method (Harvey and Pagel, 1991; Parker, 1996). "Language" as a whole is unique to our species, a fact that blocks comparative analysis at a gross level. By focusing exclusively on linguistic mechanisms in humans, or at best homologous mechanisms in primates, linguists and psychologists have often neglected a rich source of empirical data available for understanding our own species: the wide variety of species who have solved similar problems using independently evolved mechanisms, or who (equally enlightening) use mechanisms homologous to our linguistic mechanisms for different purposes. In many cases, however, when we address specific sub-components of language, we find that similar mechanisms have evolved in other species or cognitive realms. Discovering homologs or analogs of linguistic mechanisms will enable us to understand both the physiological, developmental, and genetic basis of the language faculty and often also to discover evolutionary constraints operating during phylogeny. Careful application of the comparative method allows us to trace phylogeny by using *homologous* characters shared with our primate or mammal relatives to reconstruct traits present in extinct ancestors. Equally important, and more often neglected, we can analyze adaptation by examining *convergent* evolution in more distantly related species. When a similar trait evolves in two distantly related species, such as vocal learning in birds, whales, and humans, we can exclude phylogenetic or developmental inertia as the causes. Detailed similarities that evolve convergently are often the strongest evidence available that the trait in question is a bona fide adaptation to the task.

This review has three parts. First, in section 48.2, I briefly review hominid evolution, integrating comparative data with the relevant fossil record. Section 48.3 discusses the biology and evolution of speech. I begin with speech both because human speech production is well understood from a mechanistic viewpoint, and because the comparative approach has recently yielded valuable insights into speech evolution (Fitch, 2000a). Anatomically, humans have an unusual vocal tract, and it has been argued for many years that this is a crucial innovation underlying our ability to communicate linguistically—some authors argue *the* crucial innovation. I will review recent work on vocal production in non-human animals that challenges this idea. Our anatomical differences from animals are less pronounced than previously thought, strongly suggesting that the importance of vocal anatomy has been overemphasized. Neural control, not vocal morphology, seems critical.

In section 48.4, I turn to language per se, providing a tentative comparative analysis of what features of human language need to be explained. I review three separate features that deserve further consideration. These are the neural bases for complex, imitative signal generation (signal), the intentional communication of complex propositional information (semantics), and a structural means of retrievably linking these two components together (syntax). Each of these three components needs to be considered, and treating any one of them as *the* single, critical basis for language is overly simplistic and unlikely to yield insight. Each feature may have a separate genetic basis and/or evolutionary history, and each provides different challenges at the mechanistic and evolutionary (functional/phylogenetic) levels.

48.2 The paleontological and comparative database

Since the late 1960s, scientists interested in language evolution have focused mainly on two sources of data: the fossil record, and comparative studies of primate communication systems. I will briefly review these two approaches, and their core findings, before turning to the application of a broader comparative approach to language that forms the heart of this review. In the 6–7 million years that humans have been evolving separately from chimpanzees, we have evolved a large suite of differences (including relative hairlessness, large brains, bipedal locomotion, major changes in reproductive physiology and behavior, and of course language). The starting point for our discussion will be the last common ancestor of humans and chimpanzees. I then briefly review the fossil data, stressing relatively uncontroversial aspects of the interpretation of the hominin fossil record.

48.2.1 The last common ancestor of humans and chimpanzees

Sometime around seven million years ago, a population of apes who represented the last common ancestors (LCAs) of humans and chimpanzees lived in the forests of equatorial Africa. Although humans have been evolving, in a broad sense, since the origin of life on earth, our independent evolutionary history starts with this LCA. Although the LCA was an ape, it was not a chimpanzee: chimpanzees have been evolving since the split, just as we have. Unfortunately, we have no fossil record for this species. Thus we must use the comparative method to reconstruct the anatomy and behavior of the LCA, using what is known about humans, chimpanzees, and other apes (Seyfarth and Cheney, 2005). Thanks to decades of concerted efforts by field and laboratory researchers, our knowledge of chimpanzee behavior is now quite rich (Goodall, 1986; Tomasello and Call, 1997; Boesch and Boesch-Achermann, 2000).

Apes ("hominoids") are relatively large-bodied primates, mostly vegetarian, currently confined to warm rainforests in the Old World. The apes are divided into two main groups. The gibbons and siamangs (or "lesser" apes) form the smaller subgroup. Gibbons live in tropical forests of Asia, are highly arboreal, and generally live in small territorial groups composed of long-term monogamous pairs and their dependent offspring.

Gibbons exhibit unusual behaviors shared with humans: long-term mating partnerships and male parental care. Thus, despite their greater phylogenetic distance, some aspects of gibbon social behavior may provide better models for these aspects of human evolution than the other "great" apes, which show little or no monogamy or paternal care. The relative neglect of the "lesser" apes in discussions of human evolution is regrettable. Gibbons advertise their presence with periodic loud, long species-typical vocalizations called "long calls," often produced as duets between the adult male and female mates, and often termed "song." Gibbon long calls are unlearned, and a gibbon raised in acoustic isolation will produce a normal song (Brockelman and Schilling, 1984; Geissmann, 1984; 2000). Thus, as for other known primate calls, learning plays at best a minor role in gibbon call acoustics. There is no evidence for tool use in gibbons.

The other branch of the ape family, the great apes, include the Asian orang-utans and the African apes: chimpanzees, gorillas, and humans. After long debate about the precise relationships within this ape clade, molecular data (Wilson and Sarich, 1969; Lovejoy, 1981; Carroll, 2003) have convinced scholars that humans and chimpanzees (including bonobos) are more closely related to each other than they are to gorillas, with orang-utans representing the most distant members of the group. Because humans are nested within the apes, we are, biologically speaking, a type of great ape. All great apes are relatively long-lived, have an unusually low reproductive rate, and normally bear a single infant that develops slowly and has a very long dependent period. These facts have interesting implications for human evolution (Lovejoy, 1981). Non-human apes are primarily vegetarian, but chimpanzees and orang-utans (like humans) enjoy meat occasionally, when they can get it.

Because chimpanzees are our nearest cousins, they are of particular interest in reconstructing the LCA. Chimpanzees are now broken into two species, the widespread "common" chimpanzee, *Pan troglodytes*, which exists across a broad swath of equatorial Africa, and the bonobo or "pygmy" chimpanzee, *Pan paniscus*, restricted to the dense rainforests of central Africa. These two chimpanzees appear to have split from each other only about 1.5 million years ago. Thus, neither species is closer phylogenetically to humans. Both forms produce loud long calls called "pant hoot" sequences, with a complex structure that is species-typical and largely innate (Goodall, 1986; de Waal, 1988; Arcadi, 1996). Chimpanzees and humans both produce a "laughing" vocalization in playful affiliative situations (Berntson et al., 1990), and also produce screams and cry vocalizations that are more widely shared among primates and mammals (Newman, 1992). Chimpanzees and bonobos both have a repertoire of grunts, hoots, and screams which play an important role in their social behavior (Goodall, 1986; de Waal, 1988). All of these vocalizations appear to have a powerful innate basis (Eibl-Eibesfeldt, 1970), and despite some recent evidence for some limited vocal learning abilities in chimpanzees, there is no evidence that chimpanzees (or any other non-human primates) can learn complex vocalizations like speech or song (Hauser, 1996; Janik and Slater, 1997; Crockford et al., 2004). Chimpanzees raised in a human home will not learn even rudiments of speech (Hayes and Hayes, 1951) and, in general, primates can be trained to control their vocalizations only with great difficulty (Larson et al., 1973). Recent evidence suggests that some chimp food calls may be "functionally referential" in that listeners can infer food type from call acoustics (Zuberbühler, 2003), but neither chimpanzees nor other apes have referential alarm calls like those of vervet monkeys (Seyfarth et al., 1980b; Seyfarth et al., 1980a). We thus infer that there were no referential alarm calls in the LCA. Finally, chimpanzees often "drum" with the hands or feet on resonant structures (Arcadi et al., 2004). Drumming is a very unusual behavior in the animal world, which, judging by its similarities with gorilla chest beating and human drumming, was probably present in the LCA (Fitch, 2006).

A striking aspect of chimpanzee behavior shared with humans is their use of tools for extractive foraging (Beck, 1980), already known to Darwin (1871). The observations of Goodall (1968; 1986) made clear the extent and complexity of this behavior. Chimpanzee populations vary in tool use (Whiten et al., 1999), but some chimpanzee populations use multi-part stone tools to crack open nuts (Boesch and Boesch-Achermann, 2000). Nut cracking is a complex task, mainly practiced by females, that is difficult for young chimps to learn. Tool use in other great apes (orang-utans and, recently, gorillas) has been documented but is more sporadic. Although the *construction* of stone tools appeared much later in human evolution (see below), the comparative data indicate that the LCA already used stone tools, setting the stage for one of the most striking human specializations.

A second interesting similarity between chimpanzees and humans is group hunting of monkeys for meat (Goodall, 1986; Boesch and Boesch-Achermann, 2000). Meat provides a rich source of nutrition for the otherwise mainly vegetarian chimpanzees (insects such as termites provide another important source of protein, which also sometimes involves tool use). Hunting behavior is seen more often in males than in females, and incorporates group strategies for corralling monkey prey. Meat is typically shared preferentially with those individuals who participated actively (Boesch and Boesch-Achermann, 2000). We tentatively conclude that the LCA used stone and other tools and hunted for meat. The data from chimpanzees suggest that tool use was primarily a female activity, and hunting a male activity. In contrast, ape call morphology and meaning is largely innate, involving poorly developed vocal control, suggesting that the LCA was similarly vocally limited. These aspects of LCA behavior set the stage for the initial branching of our own lineage, traditionally termed "hominids" or more recently, "hominins."

48.2.2 **Hominin fossil data: from *Australopithecus* to modern *Homo***

Our clade split from that of chimpanzees in the late Miocene, 6–7 million years ago (MYA). The Miocene (23–25 MYA) was the golden age of apes: many large-bodied, relatively large-brained ape species had successfully occupied a diverse set of ecosystems throughout the Old World. However, by about 8 MYA, apes had been largely replaced by monkeys, who reproduce more rapidly and have gut specializations that allow them to more efficiently digest vegetable matter (Jablonski, 1998; Cameron, 2004). By 8 MYA, the apes had been reduced to a few relict populations, taking refuge in the stability of the rainforests, where, except for humans, they remain today. This inversion of a common prejudice assuming ape superiority provides a useful corrective to simplistic *scala natura* notions of evolution. A critical question in human evolution arises: what did humans do differently that allowed us to succeed where most apes failed?

The hominin fossil record is rich compared to that of other living apes, and recent fossil finds are radically changing our view of hominin evolution. Two recent surprises include the discovery of a new fossil species, *Sahelanthropus tchadensis*, with hominin characters dated to around 6–7 MYA (Brunet et al., 2005)—very close to the time of the split between humans and chimps as estimated from molecular data, and the recent discovery of small-brained archaic hominids apparently representing a relative of *Homo erectus* living on the island of Flores only 12,000 years ago (Brown et al., 2004; Morwood et al., 2005). These and other recent discoveries generate a confusing fluidity in the current literature, including a host of new proposed genus names (many unlikely to last long; Cela-Conde and Ayala, 2003). Rather than attempting to sort through this controversy, I will focus on the main elements that have remained consistent for many years. The fossil record supports a traditional idea of three "grades" on the path between the LCA and modern *Homo sapiens*: australopithecines, *Homo erectus*, and archaic *Homo sapiens* (the last common ancestor of Neanderthals and modern humans). However, the newer fossil data shows that the "family tree" of fossil hominins is bushy, rather than progressing in a neat line to modern humans. The bushiness of this phylogenetic tree renders dubious any claim that a particular fossil specimen is directly on the line to modern humans.

48.2.2.1 Stage 1: bipedalism

The discovery of well-preserved skeletons of australopithecine hominids in the 1970s demonstrated that hominids began walking bipedally before brain size increased (Johanson and White, 1979). The first radiation of true hominins occurred in the early Pliocene around 5 MYA, and included many species that survived (in Africa) for millions of years (including gracile australopithecines like *Australopithecus afarensis* and robust australopithecines like *Paranthropus* (=*Australopithecus*) *boisei*). Members of the former lineage are considered to be ancestral to modern humans. These bipedal australopithecine fossils had brain volumes in the range of modern chimpanzees (Kappelman, 1996). They retained some adaptations for tree climbing, and probably slept in trees like chimpanzees. These early hominins moved into a variable and complex habitat: a mosaic of woodlands and grasslands. They probably used stone tools in this environment, at least to open nuts, as do modern chimpanzees, and possibly to crack open scavenged bones to extract nutrient-rich marrow. A fossil clue to behavior is that gracile australopithecines had reduced sexual dimorphism of the canine teeth (Johanson and White, 1979), which suggests the possibility of a movement towards a monogamous mating system (typically accompanied by reduced dimorphism; Lovejoy, 1981).

48.2.2.2 Stage 2: Out of Africa I: tool making and brain expansion

After several million years of small-brained bipedal australopithecines, we see major changes with the appearance of early *Homo erectus* (often termed *Homo ergaster* in Africa), including a significant increase in body and brain size (Walker and Leakey, 1993). These were the first humans to venture out of Africa into Asia, where they persisted until very recently. Body-size dimorphism, and canine dimorphism, was reduced to modern human levels (Kappelman, 1996). Some paleontologists believe that *H. erectus/ergaster* is the first hominin in the genus *Homo* (Wood and Collard, 1999). They are associated with more sophisticated tool making via flaking technology, and their symmetrical blade toolkit was to persist for an extended period. There is considerable debate about whether these hominids controlled fire (hearths in China associated with *Homo erectus* provide imperfect evidence; Weiner et al., 1998), but clearly these hominids were doing something different from their earlier forebears in Africa. The reduction in body-size dimorphism suggests that a more monogamous mating system, with male parental care, had arisen (Lovejoy, 1981). Various authors have suggested that these early members of our own genus had developed some sort of protolanguage, but there is no consensus on what the nature of that system might have been (Donald, 1991; Bickerton, 2000; Arbib, 2005).

48.2.2.3 Stage 3: Out of Africa II

The final stage of hominin evolution before the appearance of modern humans is represented by our last common ancestor with Neanderthals. *Homo neanderthalensis* is now generally agreed to be a separate species of human, large-bodied and large-brained like ourselves (Foley, 1998). Neanderthals shared a common ancestor with modern humans between 1 and 0.5 MYA, and did not contribute appreciably the modern human gene pool (Krings et al., 1997). This large-brained common ancestor is traditionally called "archaic *Homo sapiens*" but increasingly given an independent species name (e.g. *Homo heidelbergensis, Homo helmei* or *Homo antecessor*). These early humans had emerged, again, from Africa, and by 0.5 MYA were well established throughout Eurasia. They used complex stone tools and clearly controlled fire (Goren-Inbar et al., 2000; Goren-Inbar et al., 2002; Goren-Inbar et al., 2004).

Archaic *Homo sapiens* provides a clear fossil clue relevant to language: an enlargement of the thoracic canal hypothesized to reflect enhanced breathing control. Finally, a plausible skeletal indicator of speech-related capacity can be seen in the last stage of human evolution (MacLarnon and Hewitt, 1999). Although these authors provide a convincing case that thoracic canal size is associated with enhanced breathing control, such control is equally relevant to singing (Fitch, 2005b), and consistent with Darwin's proposal that protolanguage was more musical than linguistic in the modern propositional sense (Darwin, 1871; Mithen, 2005). Nonetheless, the data from the thoracic canal combine with those from FOXP2 (see section 48.4.1) to suggest that complex vocal signals appeared relatively late in hominid evolution. Other proposed fossil indicators of language shed even less light on the timing of speech and language evolution (discussed briefly below).

48.3 The evolution of speech: the comparative approach in action

Speech is the default signaling system for human language whenever the audio-vocal modality is available. However, language can be expressed equally well in the visuo-manual modality via sign (Stokoe, 2005). Thus, it is important to distinguish the evolution of speech from that of language per se: they are linked but separable components of the faculty of language, in a broad sense. Thanks to some pioneering acoustic work by Philip Lieberman and colleagues, discussed below, we know more about speech evolution than most other aspects of language. Recent progress in research on this topic offers valuable lessons for other branches of biolinguistics.

The starting point for this discussion is the age-old question of whether animals lack language because of vocal or cognitive limitations. 2,000 years ago, noting that dolphins were mammals with large brains, Aristotle suggested that their inability to speak results from their lack of lips and a "loose" tongue. The seventeenth-century discovery of apes launched an ongoing debate as to whether their lack of speech is caused by neural or peripheral differences from humans, and in 1779 Camper suggested that speech was impossible for orangutans because of their large air sacs (Camper, 1779). Since that time, various differences in peripheral anatomy have been blamed for ape speechlessness. But by 1871, Darwin, though aware of the anatomical differences, concluded that apes' (and most other animals') hindrance was mental, not morphological (Darwin, 1871). The anatomical difference he discussed was the now-famous descended larynx of humans (Bowles, 1889; Howes, 1889).

Adult humans have a larynx which lies unusually low in the throat relative to other primates and, until very recently (Fitch and Reby, 2001), this descended larynx was thought to be unique to our species (Negus, 1949; Sasaki et al., 1977; Crelin, 1987). With the development of the source-filter theory of speech production, the significance of this peculiar trait became clear (Lieberman et al., 1969). Laryngeal lowering in humans is accompanied by a descent of the hyoid bone and tongue root. This vocal tract reconfiguration creates an unusual "two-tube" vocal tract, which allows humans to make a wider variety of formant patterns than would otherwise be possible, including especially the point vowels /i, a, u/. Lieberman and colleagues did not claim that vocal-tract reconfiguration was necessary for speech in general; rather, that *modern* human speech requires the greater phonetic diversity resulting from our reconfigured vocal tract (Lieberman and Crelin, 1971; Lieberman et al., 1972). The point vowels and improved speech encoding were argued to be necessary to achieve high-speed encoding of complex meanings into speech sounds, and thus transcend the limitations of short-term auditory memory. Thus, the reconfigured vocal tract of modern humans was seen as driven by the needs of linguistic communication.

I believe that this argument is as sound today as it was when first advanced in 1969 and, despite various attacks (Boë et al., 2002), it has stood the test of time quite well (e.g. Carré et al., 1995). Considerable converging data indicate that the human two-tube vocal tract allows production of point vowels that would otherwise be difficult or impossible to produce. However, new comparative data casts doubt upon further extrapolations from these basic facts, suggesting that the descent of the larynx has been overemphasized in discussions of language evolution. The first and more basic observation is that, although most mammals have a high laryngeal position during resting breathing, when they vocalize, they generally lower their larynx. Animal vocal anatomy has traditionally been studied in post-mortem specimens, and an essentially static viewpoint on this system was assumed (Negus, 1949; Crelin, 1987). But, for vocal acoustics, the relevant anatomical issue is clearly vocal tract configuration *during vocalization*. From this viewpoint, the first X-ray video recordings of vocalizing animals were quite surprising: in all the mammals so far tested (goats, pigs, tamarins, and dogs), the larynx descends dynamically during vocalization (Fitch, 2000b). Often, as in dogs barking, the larynx descends considerably, pulling the tongue root with it, so during vocalization the vocal tract configuration nears the human 1:1 oral/pharyngeal dimensions. Based on current data, it appears that laryngeal descent during vocalization is typical of mammals, and represents a homologous trait inherited from our common ancestor (Fitch, 2002). Given dynamic vocal tract reconfiguration abilities in mammals, there is no reason to suppose that a dog's vocal tract is inherently incapable of producing a wide variety of speech sounds—if a human brain were in control. Second, it is perfectly plausible that speech in early hominids was accomplished via dynamic vocal tract reconfiguration, rather than by the permanent reconfiguration seen in modern humans.

These data left open the possibility that *permanent* descent of the larynx is a uniquely human trait. However, other comparative data indicate that the resting position of the larynx in some adult male deer species is halfway down the throat: they possess a *permanently* descended larynx comparable to our own (Fitch and Reby, 2001). Even more impressive, they pull the larynx as far down as physiologically possible during vocalization—to the inlet of the sternum. Since that time, a permanently descended larynx has been discovered in several other species, including all of the big cats in the genus *Panthera* (Weissengruber et al., 2002), the Mongolian gazelle *Procapra gutturosa* (Frey and Riede, 2003), and koalas, *Phascolarctos cinereus* (Fitch, 2002). A permanently descended larynx is thus now known to occur in at least eight non-human mammals.

The convergent evolution of permanent laryngeal descent in at least four different mammal lineages suggests that some common adaptive problem is being solved. None of these species produces complex multisyllabic utterances, or point vowels, and vocalizations are not particularly complex in any of these species. Thus something other than phonetic diversity must have driven the evolution of a permanently descended larynx in these species. The convergent evolution of a descended larynx in mammals that lack speech, *whatever* its adaptive function, proves that speech is not the only possible function underlying the evolution of this trait. Some critics have overlooked this central fact, observing that deer are not primates, and incorrectly concluding that they are irrelevant to human evolution (see e.g. Randerson, 2001). But it is precisely the phylogenetic distance between us and deer or lions that makes this adaptively relevant: the more mild laryngeal descent recently documented during chimpanzee ontogeny (Nishimura, 2005) is presumably homologous with that in humans, and thus provides weaker support for any specifically *adaptive* hypotheses. By dissolving any necessary link between laryngeal descent and speech, these data support the plausibility of a pre-adaptive account of human vocal tract configuration, where the human larynx first functioned as in lions, tigers, and deer.

I have argued that the driving force behind laryngeal descent in other species was vocal-size exaggeration, and this hypothesis has been subjected to empirical test. Formants provide acoustic cues to body size in many vertebrates, and laryngeal lowering provides a way to lower formant frequencies, and thus exaggerate the impression of size conveyed by vocalizations (see Fitch and Reby, 2001; Fitch, 2002; Fitch and Hauser, 2002, for full details). In red deer (the best-studied species so far), size exaggeration seems to be the only reasonable hypothesis left standing, with other plausible hypotheses having been empirically rejected (Reby et al., 2005). The size exaggeration hypothesis is based on quite general principles that also apply to humans, so it also provides a plausible pre-adaptive explanation for the descent of the larynx in early hominids. The fact that the larynx descends again at puberty, but only in males, is consistent with a current size exaggeration function even in humans (Ohala, 1984)—but not with any model that posits laryngeal descent functions only for phonetic diversity.

There are several take-home messages from this comparative work. First, the discoveries just discussed resulted from the isolation of a vocal mechanism peculiar to humans, the reconfigured vocal tract. Without Lieberman's hypothesis about its relevance to human speech, the descended larynx in animals remained unnoticed for centuries. Thus adaptive theories can drive empirical work and the acquisition of new knowledge—if they make testable predictions. Second, and more important, the discovery that the descended larynx is not unique should be a cause for excitement, not despair, for anyone interested in this odd human trait, especially how it develops and why it evolved. For example, an understanding of the behavioral and evolutionary significance of this trait using playback studies is already well under way in deer (Reby et al., 2005). Red deer now provide an animal model to further explore the developmental, physiological, and genetic basis for a descended larynx (Reby and McComb, 2003), and a closely related Chinese species, Père David's deer, does *not* have a permanently descended larynx. This species successfully interbreeds with red deer, and hybrids already exist, providing a basis for a quantitative genetic analysis to pinpoint the genetic basis for laryngeal descent in deer. Given the conservation of genetic and developmental programs among vertebrates, there is a good chance that the same gene(s) will be present in humans, and relevant to vocal reconfiguration in our own species. Thus, the discovery of a descended larynx in animals opens doors to empirical study that would remain shut if the trait were uniquely humans, as believed until a few years ago.

48.3.1 Implications for fossil reconstruction

These new data have sobering implications regarding fossil indicators of speech abilities in fossil hominids (Fitch, 2000a). Any attempt to reconstruct vocal anatomy from fossils (in particular the timing of human vocal tract reconfiguration) must face the fundamental problem that none of these soft tissues fossilizes, and none of the skeletal indicators so far proposed turns out to provide inter-specifically reliable cues to vocal anatomy. The most serious problem for any paleontologist attempting fossil reconstructions is provided by the recent discoveries of non-human animals with descended larynges: in none of these species are there obvious skeletal indicators of vocal tract reconfiguration.

There have been many suggestions about possible fossil indicators for speech and language, which range from reasonably plausible to quite unconvincing. Starting with the most easily refuted proposals, many authors have suggested (following DuBrul, 1958) that upright bipedalism is directly linked to the descended larynx and reconfigured vocal tract. Any direct connection between uprightness/bipedalism and laryngeal descent is rendered implausible by the fact that many organisms have independently evolved bipedalism without any vocal tract reconfiguration. For instance, all birds are bipedal, and none is known to have a permanently descended larynx. Among mammals, kangaroos and their allies, and several groups of rodents, locomote bipedally by hopping, and none of these mammals has a reconfigured vocal tract. Finally, many primates spend a large amount of time in an upright position while sitting or climbing, and no non-human primate is known to have a descended larynx. Thus, uprightness alone is insufficient to drive vocal tract reconfiguration. A more plausible version of this hypothesis is that bipedalism drove changes in skull morphology, which—perhaps in combination with other factors like brain growth—drove a descended larynx. For example, the attainment of orthograde bipedalism has been suggested to require the movement of the spinal column forward, to lie under the cranium. Combined with a retraction of the face (which causes the loss of the snout seen in most mammals), this concomitant of bipedalism could lead to a reduction of the space for the larynx and tongue, "squeezing" the larynx and tongue root down into the pharynx in order to maintain overall tongue size and shape (Wind, 1983; Aiello and Dean, 1998). The relevant aspect of skull morphology most often suggested to correlate with larynx position is basicranial angle (Lieberman and Crelin, 1971; Laitman and Reidenberg, 1988), but recent studies have shown this to be uncorrelated with vocal tract dimensions in modern humans (Lieberman and McCarthy, 1999). Comparative data from retrognathic dog and cat breeds are also inconsistent with this hypothesis.

The discovery of a well-preserved Neanderthal hyoid bone (Arensburg et al., 1989), with essentially human anatomy, led its discoverers to claim that the Neanderthal vocal-tract was modern, with a descended larynx (Arensburg et al., 1990; Arensburg, 1994) (the hyoid supports the base of the tongue, and provides a bony attachment for many vocal-tract muscles). Critics correctly observed that the morphology of the hyoid provides no reliable indication of the position of the larynx, and human hyoid anatomy shows no obvious changes as the larynx descends either in infancy or later during puberty in males (Lieberman et al., 1989). Another proposal by Kay and colleagues suggested that the size of the hypoglossal canal provides an indication of increased vocal control (Kay et al., 1998). Because the hypoglossal nerve contains most of the motor fibers that innervate the tongue and other vocal articulators, these researchers made the reasonable assumption that a large hypoglossal canal would indicate a high ratio of motor neurons to tongue muscle fibers and hence increased speech motor control. However, subsequent comparative analyses indicated great variability in canal diameter among modern humans, and substantial overlap with measurements from humans and apes (DeGusta et al., 1999). Currently, the only plausible skeletal indicator relevant to speech production is the diameter of the thoracic canal (MacLarnon and Hewitt, 1999), and, as previously mentioned, even this cannot discriminate increased control for song from that for speech (Fitch, 2005c). In summary, I suggest that the persistent attempts to deduce speech or language from fossils have been uniformly unsuccessful, and the controversial discussions in this area have shed more heat than light on language evolution.

48.3.2 Conclusions

The examples from speech production reviewed in this section show how adopting a broad comparative stance to investigate well-defined mechanisms can enrich our understanding of the evolution of a core human characteristic. In the process, we have been able to answer the age-old question about where the key limitations lie that prevent most animals from speaking: somewhere in the brain. I conclude that vocal morphology and physiology is not the primary constraint keeping animals from language. Our core focus in understanding language per se should thus be on the nervous system.

48.4 The biology and evolution of language per se

As stressed above, a componential breakdown of language is a key first step to deeper understanding. Accepting that language encompasses several key components, we still need to determine what these components are. On what aspects of brain and behavior should we focus? It would be naive to suppose that the proper breakdown will respect traditional disciplinary boundaries (e.g. between phonetics, phonology, semantics, and syntax). The difficulty and importance of this problem should not be underestimated. I will suggest a tentative breakdown of the language faculty, informed by comparative data, that reflects an emerging current consensus in this field (e.g. encompassing the diverse views expressed in Christiansen and Kirby, 2003). However, given the incompleteness of our understanding, this breakdown must be considered provisional.

I suggest at least three sub-components underlie the cognitive capacity for language, and differentiate humans from most of our animal relatives, with the nearest traditional linguistic category indicated in parentheses:

1. *Signal imitation* (phonology): a capacity for complex, structured imitation, including particularly vocal imitation, which is not present in other primates but is a prerequisite for the buildup of a large, shared lexicon of signals.
2. *Structure generation and mapping* (morphology and syntax): a combinatorial, hierarchical, rule-based system with the requisite computational power and complexity to allow arbitrarily complex meanings to be mapped onto equally complex signals (and vice versa).
3. *Semiotic drive* (semantics/pragmatics): an ability and propensity to produce and interpret signals with intentional, propositional meaning, incorporating both an *intent* to inform and a *disposition* to interpret utterance as intentionally informative.

Each of these three components appears to differentiate us from chimpanzees and other primates, and can serve as target sub-faculties in the search for the neural and genetic mechanisms underlying language. The first component—vocal learning of complex signals—has repeatedly evolved convergently in various quite distantly related species, thus offering a rich comparative database and basis for empirical study.

48.4.1 Signal imitation

It has been known for nearly a century that if you raise an infant chimpanzee in a human home, they will imitate many aspects of human behavior and learn to perceive and interpret a significant number of words (Yerkes and Yerkes, 1929). But they will not spontaneously learn to speak even a single word. Even with intensive training and reinforcement, at best a few words are mastered (Hayes, 1951; Hayes and Hayes, 1951). This finding has been replicated in at least three different instances with the same result: chimps cannot learn to speak. Research on a number of other primates (e.g. Larson et al., 1973; Owren et al., 1993) reveals only very limited ability to control and modify vocalizations, and available current data consistently indicate that a profound inability to imitate complex vocalizations characterizes non-human primates and most other mammals (Janik and Slater, 1997). But vocal imitation is not uniquely human: it has evolved convergently in birds and aquatic mammals, and the best current estimates suggest five independent evolutionary origins of complex vocal imitation.

The fact that vocal imitation has evolved in our distant relatives is excellent news for those interested in understanding this ability, and research on the brain mechanisms of vocal learning in songbirds has become one of the fastest growing fields in neuroscience (Marler and Slabbekoorn, 2004). Birdsong has become *the* model system for the neural basis of socially acquired traits, and this work has had some important implications for humans (Nottebohm, 1999). For instance, Nottebohm's discovery that neurogenesis underlies acquisition of new songs in some songbirds led to the discovery that new neurons can be born in the adult human brain. In addition to this mechanistic understanding, birdsong research has some interesting evolutionary implications (Doupe and Kuhl, 1999). Song learning in songbirds shares with human speech two peculiarities—a sensitive period for song learning and the necessity of a babbling stage—that evolved convergently and thus suggest an adaptive function. This renders plausible the hypothesis that babbling, by closing the auditory/motor loop, is a necessary stage in the ontogeny of a vertebrate which can vocally imitate (in response both to the demands of variability in the vocal apparatus of each individual and to the basic indeterminacy of vertebrate neural development). This is a strong hypothesis, since it could easily be falsified by showing a vocal learner that has no babbling stage (I know of no explicit reports of babbling in dolphins, whales, or seals).

In most vocal imitators the vocal apparatus involves a novel, newly evolved system: birds use a syrinx to make sounds, and toothed whales like dolphins and killer whales use a novel nasal bursa system. Besides humans, there is only one other group known to use the primitive tetrapod vocal apparatus—the larynx—to imitate complex sounds. These are the pinnipeds or seals, particularly the phocid or earless seals, which all appear to have complex learned vocalizations. Unfortunately, most seal "song" occurs underwater in the polar regions, and we know much less about seal vocalization than birdsong (Stirling and Thomas, 2003; Van Parijs, 2003). Most of the support for learning comes from regional or "dialectal" differences among populations, which can be difficult to separate from genetic variation (e.g. Terhune, 1994); and the clearest demonstration of complex vocal learning in seals comes from a seal who learned to imitate human speech (Ralls et al., 1985).

An orphaned harbor seal named "Hoover" was raised by Maine fisherman during infancy and then donated to the New England Aquarium in Boston. As Hoover approached sexual maturity he began producing speechlike sounds, and by the age of 6 years produced quite intelligible sentences such as *Hey Hoover, get ova' here* with a recognizable New England accent. Thus humans and seals are the only groups known who can imitate speech-like sounds with a larynx. Seals thus provide a potential model species for studying vocal learning, using a brain and vocal apparatus similar to our own.

Regarding the genetic basis of human vocal control, the gene FOXP2 provides one of the most exciting discoveries so far to come from applying the comparative approach to gene sequencing. FOXP2 is a gene involved in oral-motor control and speech production. Its role in language was discovered by studies of a large British family whose affected members share a mutated copy of the gene (Marcus and Fisher, 2003). Despite a misleading initial characterization as a "grammar gene" specific to morphosyntax (Gopnik, 1990; Pinker, 1994), more careful work has documented a suite of disabilities in these patients, focused on oral motor control, but also including some intriguing speech perceptual problems (Vargha-Khadem et al., 1995). The real cause for excitement about this gene became apparent when it was sequenced in other primates (Enard et al., 2002). FOXP2 is an ancient gene shared by most vertebrates, and it codes for a transcription factor: a protein that binds to DNA and controls the expression of other genes. The human variant of this gene differs from that of other primates in only a few relevant places, meaning that only two relevant amino acids have changed in the coded protein. Thus, very small changes in a gene sequence can have profound effects on the phenotype. This is an important, and sobering, demonstration: with some 30 million base pairs differentiating humans and chimpanzees, sifting through the human and chimpanzee genomes in search of the ones which actually make a difference for our distinctive human phenotype is like searching for a needle in a haystack. Today, FOXP2 remains the only clearly identified gene involved in language which differentiates normal humans from chimpanzees and other primates. Of course, this single gene is not alone responsible for human speech abilities. Rather, it plays an important role in the complex, cascading network of gene expression that underlies vocal control in our species.

The isolation of the human variant of FOXP2 allows us to use the full arsenal of molecular biology in understanding increased vocal control. Recently, a mouse with a genetically engineered disruption ("knockout") in the FOXP2 gene has been created (Shu et al., 2005). Homozygous knockouts have severe motor impairments and do not survive to adulthood. Heterozygous knockouts (with one normal copy of the gene) appear to have relatively normal learning and memory, delayed growth and motor development, and a significant reduction in the number of ultrasonic vocalizations they produce. Crucially, however, both types of knockout produce normally structured vocalizations, and it is only the *rate* of vocalization that is decreased. Thus, mouse knockouts provide no clear evidence that FOXP2 plays a role in mouse vocal control. Investigations of the brains of knockout mice revealed severe organizational abnormalities in the cerebellum, but (despite careful searching) no basal ganglia abnormalities. Svante Paabo's lab in Leipzig has recently produced a *knock-in* mouse possessing the human variant of the FOXP2 gene. Although no one expects these mice to talk, they offer an exciting, first-ever chance to understand the specific effects that the human-specific form of the gene has on mammalian brain development and microcircuitry. In summary, FOXP2 provides a model for understanding other gene ↔ brain mappings, and we can expect rapid and important progress.

The recent discovery of "mirror neurons" in monkeys has fueled considerable speculation about the role of gestures in early human communication systems (Corballis, 2003; Arbib, 2005). Mirror neurons are motor neurons which fire when a monkey performs reaching actions, but also when a monkey sees someone else perform the same action (Rizzolatti et al., 1996). They thus link perception and action in a way suggested to underlie the reciprocity of linguistic signs (Rizzolatti and Arbib, 1998). Similar patterns of activity in brain imaging studies support the idea that a homologous system exists in humans (Iacoboni et al., 1999). Some commentators have suggested that mirror neurons underlie gestural imitation in primates, and thus provide support for gestural origins theories of speech (Corballis, 2003)—the old idea of a gestural protolanguage (Hewes, 1973). However, the fact that monkeys do not imitate (Tomasello and Call, 1997) provides little support for this link, as does the existence of similar neurons linking actions with sounds (Kohler et al., 2002). Thus more recent discussions have stressed the potential role of mirror system as a precursor for imitation and/or theory of mind, rather than imitation per se (Arbib, 2005). It may be more insightful to see the mirror system as exemplifying a general cross-modal matching system, with multiple roles in language including signal interpretation (speech or sign) and the understanding of goals and intentions (as in theory of mind, see below) (Iacoboni et al., 2005).

48.4.2 Structure

A minimal model of language involves complex signals (of the sort that vocal learning allows), complex concepts, and, crucially, some syntactic method of mapping between the two. That these three functions are separable is demonstrated, first, by the fact that chimpanzees (and many other vertebrates) clearly have complex concepts (e.g. about their social and spatial world; Vauclair, 1996), but only simple unlearned vocalizations. Second, songbirds have complex concepts *and* complex learned vocal signals (Kroodsma and Parker, 1977; Emery and Clayton, 2004). The more complex birdsongs are roughly as complex as speech, and in principle would be capable of conveying complex concepts, but songbirds appear to lack a means of linking these two domains. The link between signal and meaning is thus a crucial missing component that keeps birdsong from being a language. This complex mapping system is a key component of syntax (or morphosyntax, or even phonomorphosyntax), and the comparative data clearly point to its being a key ingredient of language that other animals apparently lack.

Mapping arbitrary novel concepts to signals obviously involves a complex process, the focus of much of modern linguistics. Several sources of evidence lead to the conclusion that some non-linguistic thought has a tree-like hierarchical structure (e.g. data from human vision (Simon, 1962; Marr, 1982) and categorization (Holyoak and Morrison, 2005), or playback studies concerning primate social structure (Bergman et al., 2003)). To successfully convey arbitrary thoughts between individuals we need to preserve this structure during encoding and decoding. In speech, this involves hierarchically structured signals (phonology) and, crucially, a mapping between signal and meaning that can recoverably express the hierarchical structure of thought. Since cognitive representations are high-dimensional, while the output signal is low-dimensional, a recoverable mapping of arbitrarily complex cognitive representation onto the speech signal entails the cyclic application of a structure-preserving operation. "Structure-preserving" is a key qualifier, because ordinary iterative or recurrent processes flatten out structure with each cycle, rendering the original conceptual structure unrecoverable from the signal (Fitch, 2005a).

Thus, even an extremely simple model suggests that a key requirement for syntax—typically termed "recursion" in linguistics—is virtually entailed by some basic assumptions about novelty, signals, and cognition. Despite the diversity of models of grammar which exist today in linguistics, most current approaches take recursion as a basic necessity (including government and binding, minimalism, construction grammars, tree-adjoining grammars, categorial grammar, and many others; Brown and Miller, 1996; Van Valin, 2001). Thus, from a biological perspective, most models of syntax have in common the need for cyclically applied, structure-preserving mappings that has not been demonstrated in any animal communication system (Hauser et al., 2002). Several sorts of comparative data could be relevant to understanding recursive mapping. Most basically, can animals create and/or perceive hierarchical structure at the signal level (the phonological level)? Without a hierarchical signal, the question of a hierarchical mapping to meaning seems moot. An assay to test various levels of phonosyntactic ability has recently been developed (Fitch and Hauser, 2004) that is relevant to the ability to form embedded structures, and can be applied to any vertebrate. In one primate species, cotton-top tamarins, subjects fail to process signals structured at the context-free level, suggesting that complex hierarchical embedding is unavailable to this species. A rich comparative database can easily be generated using this paradigm, and testing is planned or ongoing in rhesus macaques, chimpanzees, and several bird species, as well as with human infants of various ages. Unfortunately, despite repeated suggestions, this assay is not a test for recursion. Recursion is a property of the underlying algorithm for processing the signal, not of the signal itself, and a more direct understanding of the underlying neural processes will be necessary to test for recursion. If we do find hierarchical processing in animals (with birdsong being one likely candidate), we can begin to explore its neural basis in earnest.

If humans turn out to be unusual in possessing an ability to recursively map between conceptual and phonological structures, we can begin to ask about the neural precursors for such an ability in other animals. Where might such an ability come from? Several plausible hypotheses exist: that syntactic capabilities developed from hierarchical control in the motor control domain (Lieberman, 2000), that syntactic recursion was inherited from the complex cognitive structures underlying social intelligence in primates (Seyfarth et al., 2005), spatial reasoning, or complex navigation (Hauser et al., 2002). Each of these hypotheses leads to testable predictions about the neural basis of hierarchical mapping. In each case, however, a more detailed and explicit theoretical model of the putative source domain (motor control, social cognition, etc.) will be required. This is thus an area of great relevance to biolinguistics, and will require collaboration between computational neuroscientists, cognitive neuroscientists, and linguists (both theoreticians and psycholinguists).

48.4.3 The semiotic drive: semantics

Meaning is one of the most puzzling features of language, and in its full linguistic form is a feature that apparently sets us off sharply from other animals. Although all mammals communicate, the repertoire of signals, and the concepts they convey, are strictly finite, and small in number (Smith, 1969; Wilson, 1972). The unique aspects of semantics include encoding and decoding an infinite variety of novel meanings (making "infinite use of finite means"), and entail some key aspects of pragmatics captured by Gricean maxims (Grice, 1975). Ordinary communicative use of language typically entails both representations of others' minds, and an intention to modify their contents. To obey the Gricean maxim of "informativeness" I must know what you know, and what you don't know, and then attempt to provide you with relevant information in the latter category. Although this goal is presumed by most human speech acts, virtually all evidence suggests that this maxim, with all it entails, is unattainable in other animals, including chimpanzees. While honeybees certainly inform their sisters about flower locations, and vervets inform their groupmates about approaching predators, in neither case does a model of what the hearer *knows and doesn't know* appear to enter into the signalers' behavior. A striking illustration of this absence of a "theory of mind" is provided by the demonstration that a mother macaque is no more likely to produce predator calls when her unsuspecting infant is placed in a cage with a concealed predator than when she is watching the predator alone (Cheney and Seyfarth, 1992). Despite primates' sophisticated interpretive abilities on the receiving side (Bergman et al., 2003), the notion that vocalizations should be informative, in this rich Gricean sense, seems obvious only to humans.

What possible selection pressures could drive such intentional sharing of complex, novel information? Based on both evolutionary theory and the animal communication literature, we know that "altruistic" information exchange is unlikely to evolve via sexual selection: the dual traps of Machiavellian deceit and Zahavian handicaps tend to keep sexual signal meanings simple (Fitch, 2004). A male songbird has both complex conceptual structures and a complex signal, capable in principle of informing potential mates about what a wonderful territory he has. In the mate choice context, however, there is immediate and powerful selection to exaggerate his account, leading in turn to skeptical females who evaluate the territory for themselves (Krebs and Dawkins, 1984). Thus, such a communication system will never get off the ground evolutionarily without some other forces keeping it "honest" (Zahavi, 1987; 1993). This renders suspect the common assumption that sexual selection played a critical role in the evolution of information exchange in human language. A more promising evolutionary route to low-cost honest information exchange is kin selection (Fitch, 2005b). Because sharing information with kin can improve inclusive fitness, many honest signaling systems appear to have been driven by kin communication. For example, kin selection accounts for the evolution of the honeybee dance language, because honeybees are sharing information with their closely related sisters (Wilson, 1975). The idea that language evolved to share information with kin, and particularly dependent offspring, renders somewhat understandable why more species *don't* have this capability: most species do not combine highly dependent, long-lived offspring with parents possessing a huge store of hard-earnt, environment-specific information worth conveying.

An important task is the identification of cognitive, neural, and genetic mechanisms that underlie the collaborative information sharing that typifies our species. Three separate and converging lines of research seem promising. First, a core characteristic of autism may be a reduced ability to represent the minds of other humans (Baron-Cohen, 1995; Baron-Cohen et al., 1999); potentially helpful to delineate both the neural and genetic basis of "theory of mind." Understanding the action of discovered gene candidates will require appropriate animal models, and two promising lines of research are emerging. Work on the development of shared attention and collaborative goals in human infants, combined with careful comparative study of related abilities in apes (mostly lacking) and other animals, provide a key comparative foundation (Tomasello and Call, 1997). Recent data show that chimpanzees are more sophisticated mind-readers in a competitive situation (food competition) than in the sort of collaborative situations that had previously been tested (where they repeatedly failed) (Povinelli et al., 1990; Hare et al., 2000). Surprisingly, however, domestic dogs *succeed* in such collaborative, information-sharing contexts (Hare et al., 2002); dogs may provide a better model for this crucial aspect of human behavior than our nearest primate relative. Again, it is the broad comparative approach, rather than one focused only on primates, that appears to offer greatest potential.

Other recent comparative work suggests some aspects of social cognitive ability result from selection on other factors. In a monumental survey of domesticated animals, Darwin noted that all domesticated animals tend to show certain peculiar traits in common, relative to their wild progenitors (Darwin, 1875). In addition to the critical trait of tameness, domestic animals have smaller teeth, shorter snouts, black-and-white coloration, curly tails, floppy ears, and smaller brains. Each of these traits has been thought to be a possible adaptation, in the sense of being selected by humans for practical use. For example piebald coloration was hypothesized to make animals easier for herdsman to locate visually (Belyaev, 1984). But a classic and beautiful experiment by Belyaev and colleagues revealed such hypotheses to be superfluous. On a farm in Siberia, Belyaev rigorously selected foxes for a single simple characteristic: tameness. The experiment continued over forty years, and continues today (Trut, 1999; Trut, 2001). The results were striking: almost the entire suite of correlated traits mentioned above appeared in the foxes selected only for tameness (but not in unselected controls, or in foxes selected for aggressiveness). The other traits seem to represent automatic by-products of selection for tameness, apparently either side effects of the selected genes or linked "hitchhiker" traits caused by neighboring genes. Intriguingly, like dogs, domesticated foxes also excel at a cooperative task at which wolves and chimps fail. Thus, a seemingly complex and specific cognitive mechanism underlying social cognition, known only in humans and domesticated animals (cf. Kaminski et al., 2005), may be an automatic by-product of selection for tameness or sociability.

48.5 Conclusions

The data reviewed here show that a broad comparative approach is not only an important arm of biolinguistics—logically necessary at a minimum to say what is or is not uniquely human—but offers a promising path to progress in understanding the biology and evolution of core characteristics of language. Despite the fact that no known animal species has language in the full human sense, many species have analogs or homologs of specific sub-components of language, such as vocal imitation or cooperative gaze following. Thus animal studies can help us understand the computational capacities underlying language, along with the neural and genetic basis of these abilities. Despite a tendency for students of language evolution to focus exclusively on adaptive hypotheses, such hypotheses are rarely scientifically satisfying by themselves, and their value lies in their ability to generate testable predictions. For those interested in adaptive theorizing, the comparative database provides a rich, but frequently ignored, source of constraint and inspiration. The data I have reviewed here suggest that studies of cognition and communication in birds, seals, deer, lions or dogs are likely to shed as much, if not more, light on core questions in biolinguistics as the traditional focus on primate communication systems.

Biolinguistics today stands at a crossroads where the data from ethology, linguistics, molecular biology, and neuroscience have become far too voluminous to be fully digested by any single human; and future progress will require cooperation between disciplines. Such progress requires some agreement about the problems to be solved, a shared global model of language, and agreement concerning what count as valid approaches and data. Then, individual workers can attack specific sub-problems knowing that they are contributing to a larger whole. With luck and effort, biolinguistics may provide major insights in our lifetimes. But this will require an atmosphere of mutual respect among disciplines, a goal that has been surprisingly difficult to attain in this field (Bickerton, 2003; Newmeyer, 2003). The task for linguistics is to provide a consensus view of the key characteristics of language that need to be explained, encompassing the many viewpoints that exist in the field today. If linguists do not step in to play a leading role in this field, they can anticipate the rise of linguistically uninformed models of language and language evolution. Fools will rush in where angels fear to tread.

According to Albert Einstein, "everything should be as simple as possible, but not simpler." Language is one of the most complex phenomena on our planet, and we should not be surprised when it resists our attempts to oversimplify, or proves our initial simple hypotheses incorrect. Nor should we be surprised if attempts to understand language that are ungrounded in mechanism or comparative biology repeatedly fail. Future understanding will demand breadth and sophistication. The ultimate goal of biolinguistics is a theory of language well-grounded in neuroscience, molecular genetics, and psycholinguistics; and this ultimate theory will have to be more sophisticated than any scientific theory that currently exists, not least because it must encompass a successful theory of cognitive neuroscience (how brains generate minds) and more besides. If we are to achieve this daunting goal, we must cast aside outdated metaphors, put to rest old animosities, and grapple with biological, mechanistic reality. A crucial ingredient for success will be learning to take advantage of the richness of the broad comparative database.

References

Aiello, L. C., and Dean, C. (1998) *An Introduction to Human Evolutionary Anatomy*. Academic Press, New York.

Arbib, M. A. (2005) From monkey-like action recognition to human language: An evolutionary framework for neurolinguistics. *Behavioral and Brain Sciences*, 28: 105–67.

Arcadi, A. C. (1996) Phrase structure of wild chimpanzee pant hoots: patterns of production and interpopulation variability. *American Journal of Primatology*, 39: 159–78.

Arcadi, A. C., Robert, D., and Mugurusi, F. (2004) A comparison of buttress drumming by male chimpanzees from two populations. *Primates*, 45: 135–9.

Arensburg, B. (1994) Middle Paleolithic speech capabilities: a response to Dr. Lieberman. *American Journal of Physical Anthropology*, 94: 279–80.

Arensburg, B., Schepartz, L. A., Tillier, A. M., Vandermeersch, B., and Rak, Y. (1990) A reappraisal of the anatomical basis for speech in middle Paleolithic hominids. American Journal of Physical Anthropology 83: 137–46.

Arensburg, B., Tillier, A. M., Vandermeersch, B., Duday, H., Schepartz, L. A., and Rak, Y. (1989) A middle paleolithic human hyoid bone. *Nature*, 338: 758–60.

Baron-Cohen, S. (1995) *Mindblindness*. MIT Press, Cambridge, MA.

Baron-Cohen, S., Ring, H. A., Wheelwright, S., Bullmore, E. T., Brammer, M. J., Simmons, A., and Williams, S. C. R. (1999) Social intelligence in the normal and autistic brain: an fMRI study. *European Journal of Neuroscience* 11: 1891–8.

Beck, B. B. (1980) *Animal Tool Behavior: The Use and Manufacture of Tools by Animals*. Garland STPM Press, New York.

Belyaev, D. K. (1984) "Foxes." In I. L. Mason (ed.), *Evolution of Domesticated Animals*, pp. 211–14. Longman, London.

Bergman, T. J., Beehner, J. C., Cheney, D. L., and Seyfarth, R. M. (2003) Hierarchical classification by rank and kinship in baboons. *Science*, 302: 1234–6.

Berntson, G. G., Boysen, S. T., Bauer, H. R., and Torello, M. S. (1990) Conspecific screams and laughter: cardiac and behavioral reactions of infant chimpanzees. *Developmental Psychobiology*, 22: 771–87.

Bickerton, D. (2000) "How protolanguage became language." In C. Knight, M. Studdert-Kennedy, and J. R. Hurford (eds), *The Evolutionary Emergence of Language: Social Function and the Origins of Linguistic Form*, pp. 264–84. Cambridge University Press, Cambridge.

Bickerton, D. (2003) "Symbol and structure: a comprehensive framework for language evolution." In M. Christiansen and S. Kirby (eds), *Language Evolution*, pp. 77–94. Oxford University Press, Oxford.

Boë, L.-J., Heim, J.-L., Honda, K., and Maeda, S. (2002) The potential Neandertal vowel space was as large as that of modern humans. *Journal of Phonetics* 30: 465–84.

Boesch, C., and Boesch-Achermann, H. (2000) *The chimpanzees of the Taï forest* (Oxford University Press, Oxford).

Bowles, R. L. (1889) Observations upon the mammalian pharynx, with especial reference to the epiglottis. *Journal of Anatomy and Physiology*, London, 23: 606–15.

Brockelman, W. Y., and Schilling, D. (1984) Inheritance of stereotyped gibbon calls. *Nature*, 312: 634–6.

Brown, E. K., and Miller, J. (1996) *Concise Encyclopedia of Syntactic Theories*. Pergamon, Oxford.

Brown, P., Sutikna, T., Morwood, M. J., Soejono, R. P., Jatmiko, Wayhu Saptomo, E., and Due, R. A. (2004) A new small-bodied hominin from the Late Pleistocene of Flores, Indonesia. *Nature*, 431: 1055–61.

Brunet, M., Guy, F., Pilbeam, D., Lieberman, D. E., Likius, A., Leon, M. P. D., Zollikofer, C., and Vignaud, P. (2005) New material of the earliest hominid from the Upper Miocene of Chad. *Nature*, 434: 752–5.

Cameron, D. W. (2004) *Hominid Adaptations and Extinctions*. University of New South Wales Press, Sydney.

Camper, P. (1779) Account of the Organs of Speech of the Orang Outang. In *Philosophical Transactions of the Royal Society of London*, 69: 139–59.

Carré, R., Lindblom, B., and MacNeilage, P. (1995) Acoustic factors in the evolution of the human vocal tract. Compte Rendu, Académie des Sciences, Paris, IIb 320: 471–6.

Carroll, S. B. (2003) Genetics and the making of *Homo sapiens*. *Nature*, 422: 849–57.

Cela-Conde, C. J., and Ayala, F. J. (2003) "Genera of the human lineage." In *Proceedings of the National Academy of Sciences*, USA, 100: 7684–9.

Cheney, D. L., and Seyfarth, R. M. (1992) "Meaning, reference, and intentionality in the natural vocalizations of monkeys." In T. Nishida, W. C. McGrew, P. Marler, M. Pickford, and F. d. Waal (eds), *Topics in Primatology*, vol. 1: *Human Origins*, pp. 315–30. Tokyo University Press, Tokyo.

Christiansen, M., and Kirby, S. (eds) (2003) *Language Evolution*. Oxford University Press, Oxford.

Corballis, M. C. (2003) "From hand to mouth: the gestural origins of language." In M. Christiansen, and S. Kirby (eds), *Language Evolution*, pp. 201–18. Oxford University Press, Oxford.

Crelin, E. (1987) *The Human Vocal Tract*. Vantage Press, New York.

Crockford, C., Herbinger, I., Vigilant, L., and Boesch, C. (2004) Wild chimpanzees produce group-specific calls: a case for vocal learning? *Ethology*, 110: 221–43.

Darwin, C. (1871) *The Descent of Man and Selection in Relation to Sex*. John Murray, London.

Darwin, C. (1875) *The Variation of Animals and Plants under Domestication*. John Murray, London.

de Waal, F. B. M. (1988) The communicative repertoire of captive bonobos (*Pan paniscus*), compared to that of chimpanzees. *Behaviour*, 106: 183–251.

DeGusta, D., Gilbert, W. H., and Turner, S. P. (1999) "Hypoglossal canal size and hominid speech." In *Proceedings of the National Academy of Science*, USA 96: 1800–4.

Donald, M. (1991) *Origins of the Modern Mind*. Harvard University Press, Cambridge, MA.

Doupe, A. J., and Kuhl, P. K. (1999) Birdsong and human speech: ommon themes and mechanisms. *Annual Review of Neuroscience*, 22: 567–631.

DuBrul, E. L. (1958) *Evolution of the Speech Apparatus*. Charles C. Thomas, Springfield, MA.

Eibl-Eibesfeldt, I. (1970) *Ethology: The Biology of Behavior*. Holt, Rinehart & Winston, New York.

Emery, N. J., and Clayton, N. S. (2004) The mentality of crows: convergent evolution of intelligence in corvids and apes. *Science*, 306: 1903–7.

Enard, W., Przeworski, M., Fisher, S. E., Lai, C. S. L., Wiebe, V., Kitano, T., Monaco, A. P., and Paäbo, S. (2002) Molecular evolution of FOXP2, a gene involved in speech and language. *Nature*, 418: 869–72.

Fitch, W. T. (2000a) The evolution of speech: a comparative review. *Trends in Cognitive Science*, 4: 258–67.

Fitch, W. T. (2000b) The phonetic potential of nonhuman vocal tracts: comparative cineradiographic observations of vocalizing animals. *Phonetica*, 57: 205–18.

Fitch, W. T. (2002) "Comparative vocal production and the evolution of speech: reinterpreting the descent of the larynx," In A. Wray (ed.), *The Transition to Language*, pp. 21–45. Oxford University Press, Oxford.

Fitch, W. T. (2004) "Kin selection and "Mother Tongues": a neglected component in language evolution." In D. K. Oller, and U. Griebel (eds), *Evolution of Communication Systems: A Comparative Approach*, pp. 275–96. MIT Press, Cambridge, MA.

Fitch, W. T. (2005a) "Computation and Cognition: Four distinctions and their implications." In A. Cutler (ed.), *Twenty-First Century Psycholinguistics: Four Cornerstones*, pp. 381–400. Erlbaum, Mahwah, NJ.

Fitch, W. T. (2005b) The evolution of language: a comparative review. *Biology and Philosophy*, 20: 193–230.

Fitch, W. T. (2005c) "The evolution of music in comparative perspective." In G. Avanzini, L. Lopez, S. Koelsch, and M. Majno (eds), *The Neurosciences and Music II: From Perception to Performance*, pp. 29–49. New York Academy of Sciences, New York.

Fitch, W. T. (2006) The biology and evolution of music: a comparative perspective. *Cognition* 100: 173–215.

Fitch, W. T., and Hauser, M. D. (2002) "Unpacking "honesty": vertebrate vocal production and the evolution of acoustic signals." In A. M. Simmons, R. F. Fay, and A. N. Popper (eds), *Acoustic Communication*, pp. 65–137. Springer, New York).

Fitch, W. T., and Hauser, M. D. (2004) Computational constraints on syntactic processing in a nonhuman primate. *Science*, 303: 377–380.

Fitch, W. T., and Reby, D. (2001) "The descended larynx is not uniquely human." In *Proceedings of the Royal Society*, London, B 268: 1669–75.

Foley, R. (1998) The context of human genetic evolution. *Genome Research*, 8: 339–47.

Frey, R., and Riede, T. (2003) Sexual dimorphism of the larynx of the Mongolian Gazelle (*Procapra gutturosa* Pallas, 1777) (Mammalia, Artiodactyla, Bovidae). *Zoologischer Anzeiger*, 242: 33–62.

Geissmann, T. (1984) Inheritance of song parameters in the gibbon song analyzed in 2 hybrid gibbons (*Hylobates pileatus* s *H. lar*). *Folia Primatologica*, 42: 216–25.

Geissmann, T. (2000) "Gibbon song and human music from an evolutionary perspective." In N. L. Wallin, B. Merker, and S. Brown (eds), *The Origins of Music*, pp. 103–123. MIT Press, Cambridge, MA.

Givón, T. (2002) *Bio-Linguistics: The Santa Barbara Lectures*. Benjamins, Amsterdam.

Goodall, J. (1968) The behaviour of free-living chimpanzees in the Gombe Stream Reserve, Tanzania. *Animal Behaviour Monographs*, 1: 161–311.

Goodall, J. (1986) *The Chimpanzees of Gombe: Patterns of Behavior*. Harvard University Press, Cambridge, MA.

Gopnik, M. (1990) Feature-blind grammar and dysphasia. *Nature*, 344: 715.

Goren-Inbar, N., Alperson, N., Kislev, M. E., Simchoni, O., Melamed, Y., Ben-Nun, A., and Werker, E. (2004) Evidence of hominin control of fire at Gesher Benot Ya'aqov, Israel. *Science*, 304: 725–7.

Goren-Inbar, N., Feibel, C. S., Verosub, K. L., Melamed, Y., Kislev, M. E., Tchernov, E., and Saragusti, I. (2000) Pleistocene milestones on the out-of-Africa corridor at Gesher Benot Ya'aqov, israel. *Science*, 289: 944–7.

Goren-Inbar, N., Sharon, G., Melamed, Y., and Kislev, M. (2002) "Nuts, nut cracking, and pitted stones at Gesher Benot Ya'aqov, Israel." *Proceedings of the National Academy of Sciences*, USA, 99: 2455–60.

Grice, H. P. (1975) "Logic and conversation." In D. Davidson, and G. Harman (eds), *The Logic of Grammar*, pp. 64–153 Dickenson, Encino, CA.

Hare, B., Brown, M., Williamson, C., and Tomasello, M. (2002) The domestication of social cognition in dogs. *Science*, 298: 1634–6.

Hare, B., Call, J., Agnetta, B., and Tomasello, M. (2000) Chimpanzees know what conspecifics do and do not see. *Animal Behaviour*, 59: 771–85.

Harvey, P. H., and Pagel, M. D. (1991) *The Comparative Method in Evolutionary Biology*. Oxford University Press, Oxford.

Hauser, M., Chomsky, N., and Fitch, W. T. (2002) The Language Faculty: what is it, who has it, and how did it evolve? *Science*, 298: 1569–79.

Hauser, M. D. (1996) *The eVolution of Communication*. MIT Press, Cambridge, MA.

Hayes, C. (1951) *The Ape in Our House*. Harper, New York.

Hayes, K. J., and Hayes, C. (1951) The intellectual development of a home-raised chimpanzee. *Proceedings of the American Philosophical Society*, 95: 105–9.

Hewes, G. W. (1973) Primate communication and the gestural origin of language. *Current Anthropology*, 14: 5–24.

Holyoak, K. J., and Morrison, R. G. (eds) (2005) *Cambridge Handbook of Thinking and Reasoning*. Cambridge University Press, New York.

Howes, G. B. (1889) Rabbit with an intra-narial epiglottis, with a suggestion concerning the phylogeny of the mammalian respiratory apparatus. *Journal of Anatomy and Physiology*, London, 23: 263–72, 587–97.

Iacoboni, M., Molnar-Szakacs, I., Gallese, V., Buccino, G., Mazziotta, J. C., and Rizzolatti, G. (2005) Grasping the intentions of others with one's own mirror neuron system. *PLOS Biology*, 3: e79.

Iacoboni, M., Woods, R. P., Brass, M., Bekkering, H., Mazziotta, J. C., and Rizzolatti, G. (1999) Cortical mechanisms of human imitation. *Science*, 286: 2526–8.

Jablonski, N. G. (1998) The response of catarrhine primates to Pleistocene environmental fluctuations in East Asia. *Primates*, 39: 29–37.

Janik, V. M., and Slater, P. B. (1997) Vocal learning in mammals. *Advances in the Study of Behavior*, 26: 59–99.

Jenkins, L. (1999) *Biolinguistics: Exploring the Biology of Language*. Cambridge University Press, New York.

Johanson, D. C., and White, T. D. (1979) A systematic assessment of early African hominids. *Science*, 203: 321–30.

Kaminski, J., Riedel, J., Call, J., and Tomasello, M. (2005) Domestic goats, Capra hircus, follow gaze direction and use social cues in an object choice task. *Animal Behaviour*, 69: 11–18.

Kappelman, J. (1996) The evolution of body mass and relative brain size in fossil hominids. *Journal of Human Evolution*, 30: 243–76.

Kay, R. F., Cartmill, M., and Balow, M. (1998) The hypoglossal canal and the origin of human vocal behavior. *Proceedings of the National Academy of Sciences* (USA), 95: 5417–19.

Kohler, E., Keysers, C., Umiltà, M. A., Fogassi, L., Gallese, V., and Rizzolatti, G. (2002) Hearing sounds, understanding actions: action representation in mirror neurons. *Science*, 297: 846–9.

Krebs, J. R., and Dawkins, R. (1984) "Animal signals: mind reading and manipulation." In J. R. Krebs, and N. B. Davies (eds), *Behavioural Ecology*, pp. 380–402. Sinauer, Sunderland, MA.

Krings, M., Stone, A., Schmitz, R., Krainitzki, H., Stoneking, M., and Pääbo, S. (1997) Neandertal DNA sequences and the origin of modern humans. *Cell*, 90: 19–30.

Kroodsma, D., and Parker, L. D. (1977) Vocal virtuosity in the brown thrasher. *Auk*, 94: 783–5.

Laitman, J. T., and Reidenberg, J. S. (1988) Advances in understanding the relationship between the skull base and larynx with comments on the origins of speech. *Journal of Human Evolution*, 3: 99–109.

Larson, C. R., Sutton, D., Taylor, E. M., and Lindeman, R. (1973) Sound spectral properties of conditioned vocalizations in monkeys. *Phonetica*, 27: 100–12.

Lieberman, D. E., and McCarthy, R. C. (1999) The ontogeny of cranial base angulation in humans and chimpanzees and its implications for reconstructing pharyngeal dimensions. *Journal of Human Evolution*, 36: 487–517.

Lieberman, P. (2000) *Human Language and Our Reptilian Brain: The Subcortical Bases of Speech, Syntax and Thought*. Harvard University Press, Cambridge, MA.

Lieberman, P., and Crelin, E. S. (1971) On the speech of Neanderthal man. *Linguistic Inquiry*, 2: 203–22.

Lieberman, P., Crelin, E. S., and Klatt, D. H. (1972) Phonetic ability and related anatomy of the newborn and adult human, Neanderthal man, and the chimpanzee. *American Anthropologist*, 74: 287–307.

Lieberman, P., Klatt, D. H., and Wilson, W. H. (1969) Vocal tract limitations on the vowel repertoires of rhesus monkeys and other nonhuman primates. *Science*, 164: 1185–7.

Lieberman, P., Laitman, J. T., Landahl, K., and Gannon, P. J. (1989) Folk physiology and talking hyoids *Nature*, 342: 486.

Lovejoy, C. O. (1981) The origin of man. *Science*, 211: 341–350.

MacLarnon, A., and Hewitt, G. (1999) The evolution of human speech: the role of enhanced breathing control. *American Journal of Physical Anthropology*, 109: 341–63.

Marcus, G. F., and Fisher, S. E. (2003) FOXP2 in focus: what can genes tell us about speech and language? *Trends in Cognitive Sciences*, 7: 257–62.

Marler, P., and Slabbekoorn, H. (2004) *Nature's Music: The Science of Birdsong*. Academic Press, New York.

Marr, D. (1982) *Vision: A Computational Investigation into the Human Representation and Processing of Visual Information*. Freeman, San Francisco, CA.

Maynard Smith, J., and Szathmáry, E. (1995) *The Major Transitions in Evolution*. Oxford University Press, New York.

Mithen, S. (2005) *The Singing Neanderthals: The Origins of Music, Language, Mind, and Body*. Weidenfeld & Nicolson, London.

Morwood, M. J., Brown, P., Jatmiko, Sutikna, T., Saptomo, E. W., Westaway, K. E., Due, R. A., Roberts, R., Maeda, T., Wasisto, S., and Djubiantono, T. (2005) Further evidence for small-bodied hominins from the Late Pleistocene of Flores, Indonesia. *Nature*, 437: 957–8.

Negus, V. E. (1949) *The Comparative Anatomy and Physiology of the Larynx*. Hafner, New York.

Newman, J. D. (1992) "The primate isolation call and the evolution and physiological control of human speech." In J. Wind, B. A. Chiarelli, B. Bichakjian, and A. Nocentini (eds), *Language Origins: A Multidisciplinary Approach*, pp. 301–23. Kluwer Academic, Dordrecht.

Newmeyer, F. (2003) "What can the field of linguistics tell us about the origins of language?" In M. Christiansen, and S. Kirby (eds), *Language Evolution*, pp. 58–395. Oxford University Press, Oxford.

Nishimura, T. (2005) Developmental changes in the shape of the supralaryngeal vocal tract in chimpanzees. *American Journal of Physical Anthropology*, 126: 193–204.

Nottebohm, F. (1999) "The anatomy and timing of vocal learning in birds." In M. D. Hauser and M. Konishi (eds), *The Design of Animal Communication*, pp. 63–110. MIT/Bradford, Cambridge, MA.

Nowak, M., Komarova, N. L., and Niyogi, P. (2002) Computational and evolutionary aspects of language. *Nature*, 417: 611–17.

Ohala, J. J. (1984) An ethological perspective on common cross-language utilization of Fø of voice. *Phonetica*, 41: 1–16.

Owren, M. J., Dieter, J. A., Seyfarth, R. M., and Cheney, D. L. (1993) Vocalizations of rhesus (*Macaca mulatta*) and Japanese (*M. fuscata*) macaques cross-fostered between species show evidence of only limited modification. *Developmental Psychobiology*, 26: 389–406.

Parker, S. T. (1996) "Using cladistic analysis of comparative data to reconstruct the evolution of cognitive development in hominids." In E. P. Martins (ed.), *Phylogenies and the Comparative Method in Animal Behavior*, pp. 361–98. Oxford University Press, New York.

Pinker, S. (1994) *The Language Instinct*. Morrow, New York.

Pinker, S., and Jackendoff, R. (2005) The faculty of language: what's special about it? *Cognition*, 95: 201–36.

Povinelli, D. J., Nelson, K. E., and Boysen, S. T. (1990) Inferences about guessing and knowing by chimpanzees (*Pan troglodytes*). *Journal of Comparative. Psychology*, 104: 203–10.

Ralls, K., Fiorelli, P., and Gish, S. (1985) Vocalizations and vocal mimicry in captive harbor seals, *Phoca vitulina*. *Canadian Journal of Zoology*, 63: 1050–6.

Randerson, J. (2001) Intimidation tactics may have led to speech. *New Scientist*, 29 Aug.

Reby, D., and McComb, K. (2003) Anatomical constraints generate honesty: acoustic cues to age and weight in the roars of red deer stags. *Animal Behaviour*, 65: 519–30.

Reby, D., McComb, K., Cargnelutti, B., Darwin, C., Fitch, W. T., and Clutton-Brock, T. (2005) Red deer stags use formants as assessment cues during intrasexual agonistic interactions. *Proceedings of the Royal Society, London*, B 272: 941–7.

Rizzolatti, G., and Arbib, M. A. (1998) Language within our grasp. *Trends in Neuroscience*, 21: 188–94.

Rizzolatti, G., Fadiga, L., Gallese, V., and Fogassi, L. (1996) Premotor cortex and the recognition of motor actions. *Cognitive Brain Research*, 3: 131–41.

Sasaki, C. T., Levine, P. A., Laitman, J. T., and Crelin, E. S. (1977) Postnatal descent of the epiglottis in man. *Archives of Otolaryngology*, 103: 169–71.

Seyfarth, R. M., and Cheney, D. (2005) Constraints and preadaptations in the earliest stages of language evolution. *Linguistic Review*, 22: 135–59.

Seyfarth, R. M., Cheney, D. L., and Bergman, T. J. (2005) Primate social cognition and the origins of language. *Trends in Cognitive Sciences*, 9: 264–6.

Seyfarth, R. M., Cheney, D. L., and Marler, P. (1980a) Monkey responses to three different alarm calls: evidence of predator classification and semantic communication. *Science*, 210: 801–3.

Seyfarth, R. M., Cheney, D. L., and Marler, P. (1980b) Vervet monkey alarm calls: semantic communication in a free-ranging primate. *Animal Behaviour*, 28: 1070–94.

Shu, W., Cho, J. Y., Jiang, Y., Zhang, M., Weisz, D., Elder, G. A., Schmeidler, J., De Gasperi, R., Gama Sosa, M. A., Rabidou, D., Santucci, A. C., Perl, D., Morrisey, E., and Buxbaum, J. D. (2005) "Altered ultrasonic vocalization in mice with a disruption in the *Foxp2* gene." *Proceedings of the National Academy of Sciences*, USA, 102: 9643–8.

Simon, H. A. (1962) The architecture of complexity. *Proceedings of the American Philosophical Society*, 106: 467–82.

Smith, W. S. (1969) Messages of vertebrate communication. *Science*, 165: 145–50.

Stirling, I., and Thomas, J. A. (2003) Relationships between underwater vocalizations and mating systems in phocid seals. *Aquatic Mammals*, 29: 227–46.

Stokoe, W. C. (2005) Sign language structure: an outline of the communicative sysystems of the American deaf (reprinted). *Journal of Deaf Studies and Deaf Education*, 10: 3–37.

Terhune, J. M. (1994) Geographical variation of harp seal underwater vocalizations. *Canadian Journal of Zoology*, 72: 892–7.

Tomasello, M., and Call, J. (1997) *Primate Cognition*. Oxford University Press.

Trut, L. N. (1999) Early canid domestication: the farm-fox experiment. *American Scientist*, 87: 160–8.

Trut, L. N. (2001) "Experimental studies of early canid domestication." In A. Ruvinsky, and J. Sampson (eds), *The Genetics of the Dog*, pp. 15–42. CABI Publishing, New York.

Van Parijs, S. M. (2003) Aquatic mating in pinnipeds: a review. *Aquatic Mammals*, 29: 214–26.

Van Valin, R. D. (2001) *An Introduction to Syntax*. Cambridge University Press, New York.

Vargha-Khadem, F., Watkins, K., Alcock, K., Fletcher, P., and Passingham, R. (1995) "Praxic and nonverbal cognitive deficits in a large family with a genetically-transmitted speech and language disorder." *Proceedings of the National Academy of Sciences*, USA, 92: 930–3.

Vauclair, J. (1996) *Animal Cognition: An Introduction to Modern Comparative Psychology*. Harvard University Press, London.

Walker, A., and Leakey, R. E. (eds) (1993) *The Nariokotome Homo Erectus Skeleton*. Harvard University Press, Cambridge, MA.

Weiner, S., Xu, Q., Goldberg, P., Liu, J., and Bar-Yosef, O. (1998) Evidence for the use of fire at Zhoukoudian, China. *Science*, 281: 251–3.

Weissengruber, G. E., Forstenpointner, G., Peters, G., Kübber-Heiss, A., and Fitch, W. T. (2002) Hyoid apparatus and pharynx in the lion (*Panthera leo*), jaguar (*Panthera onca*), tiger (*Panthera tigris*), cheetah (*Acinonyx jubatus*), and domestic cat (*Felis silvestris* f. *catus*). *Journal of Anatomy* (London), 201: 195–209.

Whiten, A., Goodall, J., McGrew, W. C., Nishida, T., Reynolds, V., Sugiyama, Y., Tutin, C. E. G., Wrangham, R. W., and Boesch, C. (1999) Cultures in chimpanzees. *Nature*, 399: 682–5.

Wilson, A. C., and Sarich, V. 0M. (1969) A molecular time scale for human evolution. *Proceedings of the National Academy of Sciences*, USA, 63: 1088–93.

Wilson, E. O. (1972) Animal communication. *Scientific American*, 227: 52–60.

Wilson, E. O. (1975) *Sociobiology*. Harvard University Press, Cambridge, MA.

Wind, J. (1983) "Primate evolution and the emergence of speech." In É. d. Grolier (ed.), *Glossogenetics: The Origin and Evolution of Language*,, pp. 15–35. Harwood Academic, New York.

Wood, B., and Collard, M. (1999) The human genus. *Science*, 284: 65–71.

Yerkes, R. M., and Yerkes, A. W. (1929) *The Great Apes*. Yale University Press, New Haven, CT.

Zahavi, A. (1987) "The theory of signal selection and some of its implications." In V. P. Delfino (eds), *International Symposium of Biological Evolution*,, pp. 305–27. Adriatica, Bari.

Zahavi, A. (1993) The fallacy of conventional signalling. *Proceedings of the Royal Society*, London, 340: 227–30.

Zuberbühler, K. (2003) Referential signaling in non-human primates: cognitive precursors and limitations for the evolution of language. *Advances in the Study of Behavior*, 33: 265–307.

CHAPTER 49

Thinking across the boundaries: psycholinguistic perspectives

Merrill Garrett

49.1 Introduction

Once upon a time, not so very long ago in the larger scheme of things, language was deemed just another piece of learned behavior. Famously, Skinner's book *Verbal Behavior* (1957) was intended as a reduction of language to its roots in the dominant learning theory of the time—a learning theory that tied present action exclusively to past observable contingencies of experience. Less than a decade later, there was a burgeoning experimental enterprise devoted to the study of the mental operations underlying language use, reflecting the regularities of a mental "grammar" designed to capture "potential" rather than "actual" human language behavior. Clearly, somewhere about then, ideas about language changed dramatically. Those perspectives around the mid-1960s launched contemporary psycholinguistics.

What about our perspectives now, as we stand at the beginning of the twenty-first century? How are the problems of "then" related to the problems of "now"? And is there change under way that will look as significant at the middle of this century as were the events of the 1960s for the ensuing four decades? My own conviction is that two things will bulk large in the historical scene. One is the importation of brain and biology into cognitive science in general and psycholinguistics in particular. The other is more subtle, but equally significant. It is the embedding of language in more general theories of mind.

Several things are involved in this latter shift. One is the growth in understanding of visuospatial systems and of links between our spatial sensibilities and language. Another is the elaboration of theories of human judgement and decision-making and links to the organization of executive control and memory systems. And there is the reawakening of interest in the evolutionary underpinnings of language and other characteristically human features of cognition—an interest obviously confounded with the increased emphasis on the neuroscience of language and cognition. The two have become increasingly entwined over the past decade.

Biological constraints on language theory have, of course, been present from the beginning of the modern period. But they were initially abstract—the identification of an innate language capacity with universal grammar. This lent powerful levers to the early debate, but, barring occasional appeal to language disorders, the arguments rarely reached the level of particular claims about brain. The flowering of cognitive neuroscience injected a new class of concrete claims about brain organization and mechanism for language into the mix. These in turn interacted with the elaboration of biologically based treatments of vision, memory, and executive control, fueling the urge to fit language into the matrix of other cognitive systems.

I'll trace some of these trends in my remarks. But this commentary is emphatically not a systematic "historical piece"—it is truncated and selective in its reference to specific research and research scientists (for excellent discussions that provide detailed background for the field from different vantage points, see e.g. Blumenthal, 1970; Nadel and Piattelli-Palmarini, 2003). One might roughly describe the changes in practices and attitudes toward psycholinguistic problems in terms of three periods:

(1) 1955–1970: shaking the shackles of behaviorism and establishing the field;
(2) 1970–1990: exploring the fundamental problems and finding new directions;
(3) 1990s–: building cognitive science; investing in new methods; sparring and dancing with the neuroscience side.

49.2 **Establishing a field**

Psycholinguistics did not spring full born from a bed of behaviorism in 1960. Nevertheless, a striking feature of the evolution of psycholinguistics is its link to the disengagement of psychology from behaviorist strictures. It energized research on language that focused on 'demonstrations' of the psychological effects of abstract language structure. This new investment in language processing study was launched by Chomsky's assault on behaviorist psychology in his review (Chomsky, 1959) of Skinner's book on language (1957). Chomsky's critique demonstrated the inherent limitations of behaviorist approaches to language—indeed, to the study of cognition in general. That intellectual stance, coupled with the tools of grammatical theory and the characterization of relations between grammatical theory and language processing theory as sketched by Miller and Chomsky (1963), set the tone for early psycholinguistic research. The major strands that evolved over the immediately following years focused on the processing of different classes of grammatical structure ("complexity" metrics of mental processing) and on first accounts of the emergence of language capacity in very young children.

The urge to dispel the ghosts of behaviorism was powerful. It fostered a preoccupation with demonstrating the workings of complex mental representations. Grammatical theory provided a rich class of examples of exactly that, and the impulse to validate and certify that complexity was compelling. The performance/competence distinction was a hot topic because there was a real need to establish the goals of psychological theory. New paradigms for the study of mind were implicit in the approach Chomsky, Miller, and others were taking to language. The performance/competence discussions captured the essential quality of the new objectives. The view that competence models were the appropriate target for psychological explanation led naturally to experimentation that revolved around early transformational grammars. In this context, it is easy to understand the importance attached to examining and defining the relation between formal linguistic systems and language performance systems.

Phillips and Wagers (Chapter 45 this volume) provide a useful expression of contemporary perspectives on the relations between linguistics and psycholinguistics. They observe that there is no principled difference between psycholinguistic and linguistic research vis-à-vis psychological relevance. This is a view that I would readily endorse. The basic observations that drive both fields are incontrovertibly psychological. They reflect mental states of language users. The difference arises in the data typically acquired in the two fields, and what one does with it. And that derives from differences in the goals of the research enterprise. In this context, Phillips and Wagers criticize the sometime focus on the "psychological reality of linguistic constructs." It is a misleading phrase if taken to imply that linguistic constructs have no psychological license that is not bestowed by psycholinguistic experiment.

Two observations might be made of this diagnosis. One is to recognize that the term is in part a hangover from the early period marked by skepticism in the psychological community about the relevance of "formal systems" of grammar for accounts of language use. Early experimentation expressly and aggressively asserted the psychological relevance of grammatical theory, but nevertheless attempted to confront the skepticism directly by demonstrating the "reality" of structural claims about language when real-time language use was at issue. This was a double-edged sword. It was meant both to legitimize grammatical theory in the mainstream psychological community (the 'consciousness-raising objective') and to substantively explore the implementation of grammars in processing systems that would solve (some piece of) the form-to-meaning mapping when constrained by typical temporal and human resource limitations. None of this latter has changed—though the impetus for the former has dissipated with the establishment of cognitive science as the basic scientific paradigm for psycholinguistics.

The preoccupations of those early times may still muddy the current dialog by carryover of the "psychological reality" tag (by my observation, rather rarely now). But there remain significant questions about the instantiation of grammars in mental processes. Linguists focus on judgments of well-formedness and interpretation across sentence forms—and on the virtues of the different ways to represent the regularities of these and related judgements. That focus leads to impressively comprehensive accounts of structural systems that cannot be supplanted by the fragments of psycholinguistic theory we have on hand—impressive as some of those fragments are. Occasional quixotic efforts to dispense with grammar notwithstanding, the basic engine for psycholinguistic research remains the interplay between the structure of linguistic knowledge and claims for procedural implementations of that knowledge. We can and should dispense with the "psychological reality" label, but remain committed to integrating formal treatments of language with the psycholinguistics of comprehension, production, and development.

In addition to the performance-competence issues, other important changes in perspective unfolded over the first couple of decades of research. Three introductory psycholinguistics texts written in the 1970s are instructive. What were the topics covered—and what were not? Fodor et al. (1974) had an extensive discussion of grammar, its motivations and relation to the study of language processing. A bit later, Foss and Hakes (1978) and Clark and Clark (1977) had mostly similar topic coverage but less emphasis on the justification of grammatical theory. The points of overlap in the texts have been constants in the research scene over the years. In all these works, speech processing, word recognition, parsing, and language development figure prominently. But there is little or nothing on bilingualism, computational modeling, and neuroscience (barring some references to language pathology). Only one treated production processes at length, and one discussed pragmatic processes. These omissions and exceptions have emerged as important contemporary concerns. These changes in topic coverage—from early texts to the current volume—resonate in the remainder of this discussion.

49.3 Exploring the territory and finding new directions

The psycholinguistic community was, at the outset of the periods under discussion, relatively small, and to a significant extent isolated from general psychology. Both these conditions have changed greatly. The field is now much larger, and at the same time more diffused into different areas of psychological research, as well as into linguistics proper and into computer science. The growth of the field has been accompanied by important changes and additions to the research targets noted above. In global terms, this shift toward "assimilation" of psycholinguistics into a psychology and linguistics transformed by cognitive science is the most important aspect of change in the contemporary period.

The definitive preoccupation of early psycholinguistics was parsing. These were unique questions about the complex grammatical structures assigned to sentences, but done in real-time and with the potential contributions of whatever knowledge sources might be relevant or convenient. Parsing was a "special" point of contact between linguistics and psycholinguistics—and one not represented in the psychology of the time. That condition has largely remained constant over the ensuing development of the field (though one can see parsing logic and terminology appearing in some non-language areas of psychology over the last couple of decades). Other points of contact between general psychology and psycholinguistics had a foot in both camps. These were in development, lexical processing, and speech perception research. All these areas have undergone significant changes that now—to varying but significant degrees—combine psycholinguistic and general psychological theory. Looking at the evolution of these areas leads naturally to the state of current research and some probable future directions.

49.3.1 Lexical processing

During the early stages of psycholinguistics, the focus of lexical processing was ambiguity and its interaction with various contextual constraints. Within general psychology, major interest revolved around the phenomena of semantic priming and its implications for memory systems. The relation between those interests, and others shortly to be mentioned, is too complex to easily summarize, and I am not going to try. These have become especially intertwined in the experimental approaches that focus on lexical decision and naming tasks and interaction with context (see e.g. Swinney, 1984). Suffice to say that the research scene over the years saw a kind of multi-valued melding of these research approaches as the theoretical debates over the relation between form-driven and meaning-driven lexical recognition processes bloomed and sported in both written-word and spoken-word domains. So, William Marslen-Wilson's "cohort theory" (1984) for spoken word recognition took its cues from the embedding of words in sentence environments, with emphasis on an interactive relation to contextual constraint. On the other hand, Ken Forster's proposals (1976) for visual word recognition systems pressed a modular agenda more focused on word structure and basic retrieval issues. This double agenda is united by a focus on the structure of the mental lexicon. The numbers of investigators involved in such work has steadily grown, and it is a flourishing contemporary subfield.

In contemporary psychology at large, the lexical inventory continues to serve the purposes of many investigators who use it as an entry wedge for the study of conceptual and memory systems. Linguistically motivated lexical structure remains incidental, perhaps surfacing as an awareness of the need to control some variables ignored in earlier memory research. But, some new bridges are being built that were not prominent in early stages of psycholinguistic research. So, for example, the question is seriously posed whether there is a principled difference between the linguistic lexicon and the general memory systems that record experience with words. Episodic representations of words (form-based) are distinguished from "semantic representations" of words across the board, but drawing parallel distinctions does not settle the question whether the general memory records are the same as the mental lexicon entries that provide structure for parsing and interpretation. Episodic renderings for new words are clearly necessary: we learn new words all the time. How do these records enter "language processing space"? Do they? Is there something 'special' about language learning that determines a different status for lexical elements acquired at early stages? How can we evaluate that question and its ramifications for first- and second-language learning? Those questions have become acute in several areas of contemporary psycholinguistic research. They were largely ignored or taken for granted in early psycholinguistic research. The salience of such questions is, of course, linked to the explosion of interest in second-language acquisition and phenomena of bilingualism—topics to which we will return.

49.3.2 Speech perception research

At the half-century mark, speech research was dominated by engineering approaches, and for a brief heady time, lived off the technical fallout of World War II, dreaming of voice typewriters and other marvels of machine speech processing. That research community was not much connected to the overall emerging psycholinguistic research picture. The sobering realization that speech was more complex than it first seemed triggered changes that brought basic human language processing studies and speech research into closer contact. In particular, research at Haskins Lab led by Alvin Liberman and colleagues was a major force in changing this picture. The Haskins program led to the revision of the physical cue mapping approach and fostered the "motor theory" of speech perception. That theory rationalized perceptual operations by appeal to a structural system not obviously manifest in the signal structure. It was a very special knowledge-based approach. To do the "right" sorting of the physical data, it used an abstraction based on production regularities—not motor control, but formulae for exercising motor control. In many ways this was a model for the new cognitive paradigm and a high point for the integration of psycholinguistic theory and speech research (see Mattingly and Studdert-Kennedy, 1991, for a survey of perspectives on this period).

Speech research has spun off in various directions since that time. It is, as ever, more the child of technology than are other areas of language research, and the explosive growth in computational power has relatively recently made more evident differences in agenda that arise from practical engineering objectives and research that aims at an explanation of human language capacities. That latter is rich with new findings and initiatives (see e.g. Slifka et al., 2004). But extraordinary computational power and brute force successfully applied have provided some workable versions of the commercial systems that were the mirages of the 1950s and 1960s. Accordingly, the emphasis on human models as the basis for machine models has faded somewhat from the prominence it enjoyed in the 1970s and 1980s. I suspect the tide will turn again, but that remains to be seen.

49.3.3 Developmental psycholinguistics

Two major strands of developmental investigation occupied the early and middle periods of psycholinguistics. These were, roughly labeled, syntax acquisition and infant speech perception, and for the most part they were separate in their exercise. That research has evolved to a contemporary state in which they have begun to interact. Significant currents for future research are rising from that interaction as questions about the early emergence of lexical and prosodic capacities come up against questions of phonological development. We look first at the infant speech work.

Some of the most striking work on language development in the new psycholinguistic paradigm revolved around speech perception in infancy. It was an area in which the conviction that innate capacity was a powerful determinant of performance could be experimentally exercised for age ranges not considered feasible for questions of syntax. Infant speech perception was thus a prime target for grappling with the thrust of the innateness hypothesis. It remains so today. Peter Eimas's research group at Brown demonstrated phonetic discrimination capacities in infants at a few months age (Eimas et al., 1971), launching a sweeping range of investigations into the nature and basis of that capacity. Within this arena, questions about the role of experience and its interaction with endogenous perceptual mechanisms flourished and became a major research focus. Work with neonates by Jacques Mehler and colleagues (see e.g. Mehler and Bertoncini, 1981) established significant speech processing capacities at very earliest stages of development. Several things were shortly added that enriched the problem space. So, in particular, though the early speech work revealed remarkably sophisticated capacities for discrimination of speech sounds, it was not much tuned to finding ways in which infant capacities lead to phonological competence—and to mature prosodic and lexical systems. That thrust came later in work by Peter Jusczyk and others (see Gerken and Aslin, 2005, for a retrospective overview). That work engaged questions of infant sensitivity to prosodic cues for speech stream segmentation at word and phrasal levels. It demonstrated precocious capacities for identifying structure that have evoked efforts at explanation in terms of both endogenous and experiential terms. Other work (e.g. Werker and Tees, 1984) linked the unfolding of language particular features of speech perception to lexical development. That is a hot topic now, and relates to many other facets of language processing capacity that are tied to a lexical focus (see below).

If we turn away from the speech scene, the dominant developmental focus was, and is, syntax. Generative grammar issues greatly sharpened the syntax focus from the outset of the modern psycholinguistics movement. Acquisition was, of course, a long-standing interest in psychology both American and European. The major preoccupation in first-language learning revolved around questions of what children could say and when, but the significance of what was reflected in their production took on a new cast. Studies of syntactic development were pursued largely as questions about grammatical knowledge—when does knowledge of a particular language structure emerge and what is the role of experience in the process? Though reliance on corpora of child speech remained dominant, experimental studies of comprehension began to be a major factor. Some remarkably clever experimental procedures began to reveal precocious capacities for syntax (see e.g. McDaniel et al., 1996).

Nevertheless, questions continued to be posed primarily as claims of grammatical competence rather than of processing capacity. Processing factors were occasionally appealed to, but were not a major focus of theoretical effort. That condition has changed rapidly in recent years, and the structure of research into early language acquisition has grown more intertwined with processing questions. Developmental accounts of the segmentation of continuous speech, with attendant lexical recognition and parsing issues, have become more visible (e.g. as those noted above in the speech processing areas). Moreover, the centrality of lexically driven processes in contemporary parsing theory also feeds into this, as do diverse issues of word learning and its ties to sentence syntax and semantics. Indeed, the work on word learning has tentacles that reach the heart of almost every area of psycholinguistics. Accounts of how children learn word meanings slipped their traditional descriptive moorings to become increasingly experimental (e.g. Carey and Bartlett, 1978) and explanatory (e.g. Markman, 1990). The word-learning focus brings the ingredients of language and cognition into sharp relief (Bloom, 2000). Work on syntactic bootstrapping by Lila Gleitman (1990) and semantic bootstrapping by Steve Pinker (1984) highlights differences in learning based on meaning contrasts and configurational contrasts. There really is no escaping the mutual embrace of developmental and general psycholinguistic issues.

49.3.4 Parsing

Initial-stage psycholinguistic research in the 1960s—as discussed in section 49.2 regarding performance/competence issues—dealt only in passing with real-time processing for structure. That static structural focus rapidly changed as interest grew in the specific mechanisms for assigning complex sentence structures in real time. Parsing issues became the central concern for psycholinguistics of the ensuing decades, and by far the dominant focus was on sentence comprehension. Embedded in the parsing research profile is a theoretical watershed that remains central to psycholinguistic study—though attitudes toward it have evolved in interesting ways that we will note later. This is the debate over interactive vs. modular processing.

Jerry Fodor's monograph on modularity appeared in 1983 and was an immediate focus for an already briskly simmering debate. It was a catalyst that roused not only the experimental community but also the neuropsychology community (somewhat ironically, given Fodor's avowed skepticism about the neuroscience side of cognitive research). The work crystallized a range of assumptions animating research in language—by virtue of either accepting or rejecting them as working principles. Fodor offered eight diagnostics for modular systems. I use the term "diagnostic" advisedly, since Fodor, of all people, certainly did not intend them to be used definitionally. His most immediate target was the analysis of language, but the ideas he laid out have been discussed in the context of a variety of other cognitive systems. Fodor's analysis of modularity was a formula adopted by many, and became the focus of an evolving controversy in cognitive science at large.

Incremental processing issues are paramount in the parsing game. The question of what drives on-line decision making has been the center of a rich scientific controversy. Two strands of research, one linguistically and computationally inspired and the other more experimentally inspired, ran in tandem and occasionally intertwined through that period. The experimental focus was to see how fine-grained might be the parcellation of the input string for parsing and interpretation. Answers to on-line processing puzzles were aggressively pursued, with William Marslen-Wilson and Lorraine Tyler major contributors to pressing that agenda using various reaction time measures (see e.g. Tyler and Marslen-Wilson, 1982). Over the years there has been much experimental wrestling with both lexical and structural ambiguity, and major efforts concerned with the impact of general background knowledge on ambiguity resolution, both lexical and syntactic.

Early ideas about parsing strategy from the linguistic side were crystallized by Lyn Frazier and Janet Fodor (1978). That work provided an influential platform for experimental attacks on parsing principles. Proposals for structurally driven parsing strategies revolved around analyses of temporary ambiguity—garden path phenomena—and the means and time-course for its resolution. Work from computational linguistics was a significant force in this analytic and empirical effort. The fusion of the linguistic and computational thought that began around that time spun out in a continuing stream, spawning multiple dissertations and monographs with variations on parsing ideas. Computational and experimental attacks on these problems grew in importance, and the debate over the ensuing couple of decades mixed the psycholinguistic and computational ingredients in a sometimes bewildering stew of claims and counterclaims. Intuitions about ambiguity resolution were combined with sundry experimental findings, not infrequently generated from different languages. The complexity of the problem, coupled with the intrinsic variability in human performance, made consensus very hard to come by. Nevertheless, I would count it as one of the most highly productive periods of language science.

The rough bottom line as far as experiment was concerned was that the assimilation of constraints follows the input data stream very closely—though not uniformly with regard to structural type. Lexical indeterminacy proved to be generally resolved over time-windows of a few hundreds of milliseconds, with structural indeterminacy more variable, though often only marginally greater in time frame. Lexical, discourse, and background knowledge effects on interpretation are generally available roughly within a word or two of a decision point, in some cases sooner. Efforts to grapple with these general findings invoked strategies of delay, parallelism, and backtracking (both conscious and unconscious). But the constraints on performance underdetermine the computational solutions, and theoretical options severely taxed the limitations of the available reaction time experimental techniques. Various responses to this unfolded. One was increased reliance on the developing procedures for using electrophysiology and eye movement to study language. These began to exert an increasing impact in the late 1980s and 1990s. Somewhat later, and strongly continuing in the present scene, has been the use of free-field eye-pointing measures and combinations of brain imagery with electrophysiology. These several added modes of observation, in concert with more traditional behavioral measures, widened the empirical stream without much deepening it.

What emerges from this tangle? The upshot is yet to be sorted out. But, the picture is, in my view, a tantalizing one. The evidence for distinct systems of computation for sentence form and for sentence meaning has been growing at about the same pace as evidence for rapid interaction among the systems. The evidence, both behavioral and neuroscience based, that attests to specialized subsystems in language is powerful. The evidence that the different informational sources are combined with extraordinary rapidity is powerful. We are going to have to find some common ground. It will be a multi-systems perspective which, I believe, has the charming quality of letting the field eat its cake and have it too. In particular, the debates about interactive and modular processing must assume a different cast. More anon, but first a word on the other elephant in the room.

49.3.5 Theoretical alternatives: connectionism

In this environment, there emerged a theoretical movement with strong commitment to simulation and modeling and, most particularly, to neurally inspired mechanisms of computation. Classical cognitive science is construed as based on symbolic computation. Cognition is modeled in terms of mental states that are symbolically represented. Information transformations apply to change one information representation into another, and in this way the processing that constitutes cognition is reconstructed over the sequence of operations. The brain is agreed to be ultimately involved, of course, but at this level of description, it is not a significant player in the theoretical enterprise. This is not to say that neuroscience is irrelevant to classical cognitive modeling; it is to say that it was not central to the theoretical objectives.

Connectionist models offered a different characterization in a number of respects. Computation is deemed sub-symbolic because it models cognition at the level of information-processing units that are not themselves representational—i.e. they are intended to be analogous to neurons. A network of such interacting units computes outcomes that must be interpreted with respect to cognitive values, but the elementary units and their interactions are not interpretable in the way of symbolic operations in classical cognitive systems. Parallel computation, with activation passing according to weights associated with connections between the units, provided the base for systems of pattern recognition and information retrieval in several cognitive domains. The distributed processing in such models is virtuous in terms of speed of processing and other general features of human performance (e.g. reconstruction of wholes from partial cues, graceful degradation of performance following damage to the system). PDP models as a species of connectionist architectures were the parade case in the launch of the movement in the 1980s (McClelland et al., 1986).

Initial stages of this movement in psycholinguistics, and more generally in cognitive science, were confrontational, with the modes of research based on symbolic systems and those based on connectionist assumptions construed as competing paradigms for explanation. The exchanges between Fodor and Pylyshyn (1988) and Smolensky (1988) highlighted the initial stages of the symbolic/sub-symbolic controversy. Fodor and Pylyshyn argued that connectionist models as conventionally construed could not capture core features of cognition (systematicity and compositionality). To be successful, such systems must implement symbolic systems. Smolenksy and others arguing in similar vein, maintained that the sub-symbolic paradigm captures significant features of human cognition, and doing so required sub-symbolic computation; this was essential to the explanatory force of the modeling. This argument has bounced back and forth at considerable length, with (by my observation) no real agreement on what would count as a criterion for the representational issues that divide symbolic and sub-symbolic claims. But, I am not going to approach this still smoldering fire. When push comes to shove, I'm inclined to think that few in the connectionist camp think symbolic computation can be dispensed with entirely. And, conversely, most proponents of symbolic computation see a significant role for sub-symbolic modes of processing. On those grounds, some have decided it is more productive to discuss how far the sub-symbolic camel's nose can plausibly go under the symbolic cognitive tent flap. Two prominent debates are cases in point.

Pinker and Prince's critique of the past-tense learning account offered by Rumelhart and McClelland (1986) was another landmark. Pinker and Prince (1988) detailed the respects in which the PDP simulation failed to capture essential features of the human language behavior in this specific domain. In this case, the empirical disagreements were pitched in terms that permitted evaluation of the adequacy of the modeling. That generated a continuing debate, with some exchanges based on variations of the original connectionist model and the potential for dealing with the empirical challenges posed by Pinker and Prince. Ultimately a number of proposals that combine both connectionist and rule based systems operating in concert emerged—not to everyone's satisfaction, of course. But I take this feature of the debate over modeling of the past tense as a cue here.

Another detailed and empirically constrained debate revolves around Max Coltheart's DRC model (Coltheart et al., 2001) and diverse comparisons with PDP word recognition models (Seidenberg and McClelland, 1989). Again, there is a large literature involving many contributors. The adequacy of the competing models to account for a wide range of normal and pathological performance in visual word recognition tasks has been at issue. The DRC model uses connectionist computational capabilities but without the strictures of a PDP network lacking lexical representations. The DRC model has been remarkably resilient in the face of empirical challenge. There seems to be interesting "middle ground" here.

A considerable amount of new work has appeared since the initial stages of the PDP movement which is either agnostic about the ultimate status of connectionist models in accounts of one or another facet of cognition, or avowedly integrative, treating the two kinds of approach as simultaneously at work. There are numerous ways to make a combination, ranging from the incorporation of representational elements into the network, to the physical separation of a system into rule driven and connectionist net components. The movement toward hybrid models began in earnest in the 1990s and is now well established, with a substantial range of comparisons of hybrid and non-hybrid systems (see e.g. Marcus, 1998; 2003, *re* language; see e.g. Wermter and Sun, 2000, for more general issues). The hybrid card doesn't necessarily solve the controversy, of course, since one may agree that both symbolic and non-symbolic capacities are part of cognition without agreement about how specific cognitive systems are to be modeled.

It is worth noting that considerations of symbolic and sub-symbolic processing do not exhaust the impact of connectionist modeling in psycholinguistics. The connectionist ethos for modeling has been interactive. So, issues of symbolic and sub-symbolic computation to one side, the development and implementation of modeling techniques with extensive connectivity was facilitated. Networks readily lend themselves to the implementation of models for parallel integration of information sources. Constraint satisfaction models that variously combine phonological, syntactic, semantic features in statistically driven solutions to word recognition, lexical disambiguation, parsing, reference fixing, etc., began to play a prominent role in psycholinguistic models. This feeds back into the modularity debate noted in section 49.3.4. But we will step away for the moment from theoretical matters to take note of some changes of research targets which have had great impact on the field and are now deeply involved in its future.

49.3.6 New direction: cross-linguistic emphasis

Cross-linguistic psycholinguistic research gained in prominence in the middle period of psycholinguistics. English was the primary research vehicle in the early stage, partly for the accidental effects of the influence of US-based research and partly for reason of some tacit assumptions about language processing inherited from the linguistics community. It took a while for the idea of language specific processing principles to take root and become a force in theory construction. Early work made strong, and somewhat unreflective, assumptions about the universality of processing structures. The idea of general constraints on information processing (time and memory limitations) led to an inclination to generalize findings from English across languages. But issues of language-specific structures, and the potential interactions with parsing principles, were never far from the surface, and when they began to take hold, the transformation of assumption and research investment was rapid. This change was already taking place in linguistics as the study of generative grammar was increasingly internationalized. In the midst of this, there was yet another very important ingredient: ASL. The emergence of the study of signed language was driven by pioneering work in Ursula Bellugi's lab at the Salk Institute in San Diego (Klima and Bellugi, 1979). Its significance for the evaluation of the information processing constraints imposed by modality, as well as their interaction with linguistic structure, was immediate and compelling.

The impact of these factors was combined with the rapid growth of European psycholinguistic research. In particular, a highly significant expansion of the community occurred with the establishment of the Max Planck Institute for Psycholinguistics in Nijmegen in the late 1970s. Psycholinguistic work in different languages was already beginning to produce some differences in experimental outcomes that could not be ignored. The MPI investment in psycholinguistics raised the ante, and the race was on to provide accounts of the interaction of language-specific structure with information processing constraints. Cross-language variation in processing became a prominent tool for theory building. Comparisons of processing in Germanic and Romance languages were very soon augmented by work in a number of non-European languages, consolidating a major shift in early psycholinguistic perspectives. Broadening the language base was not the only expansion of practice. The same period brought greater attention to another language performance system: language production.

49.3.7 New direction: language production

The study of production processes gained major momentum in the 1980s and 1990s. The principal impetus for the early study in production was the revival of speech error work by Vicki Fromkin (1971) in her corpus-based studies that combined linguistic theory with explicit processing claims for language generation. A number of others (e.g. Garrett, 1975; Cutler, 1982) followed her lead, and that work laid a foundation that new experimental study subsequently transformed into a more diverse scientific enterprise, as production work became a major component of the psycholinguistic research scene.

That expansion was influenced by Gary Dell's (1986) experimental exploration of error-motivated production modeling. His work also incorporated network models into production systems, and provided an important alternative theoretical focus to the emerging language production scene. The currents stirred by Dell's work were enriched by two other influences, one deriving from work by Kay Bock and colleagues and the other from work by Pim Levelt and colleagues. Bock elaborated two major ideas in research paradigms with powerful spin-offs. These were studies of structural priming (Bock, 1986) and studies of agreement mechanisms (Bock and Miller, 1991). That work transformed production study in the 1990s, and its impact has continued to grow, with related research projects under way at many sites in the US and Europe. Coincident with the emergence of Bock's research foci, the MPI production group headed by Pim Levelt was developing methods and reaching for experimental tests usable for production research. The work with word–picture interference paradigms is one aspect of this that has been very effective in the elaboration of the lexically based processing component of production models. Levelt's work has, of course, been far broader than this single prominent example. In 1989, he provided an extraordinary synthesis of theory and experimentation in his book *Speaking: From Intention to Articulation*. It encompassed a wide range of experimental and observational studies in an integrated framework for language generation. That exercise in problem-setting and hypothesis generation has been an engine for research progress that has entered a second decade without losing its relevance.

As production work has developed in the last decade, interactions between comprehension and production research have grown, and interest has expanded in building a theory that accounts for the ways in which the two major performance systems are integrated. That trend is an instance of a general movement which takes more seriously the need to explain and exploit relations among performance systems. This encompasses not only the integration of comprehension and production theory, but the projection of both into developmental theory. Theories of language pathology have long been grounds for exercising contrasts between "competence-based" and "performance-based" accounts of the compromise of function. The corresponding move in development is well under way. That agenda must pick a path for developing language capacity through emerging processors for production and comprehension as well as through a grasp of the structural properties of a specific language—or, more challenging still, two specific languages (see section 49.3.8).

49.3.8 New direction: bilingualism

The study of how different languages reflect real-time processing constraints contributes materially to evaluation of psycholinguistic theory, as noted in section 49.3.6. But what about the residence of different languages in the same mind? Bilingualism—or more generally "multilingualism"—has become increasingly important as a target for explanation. We are interested in differences between languages and the principles that account for processing across languages, but the question of how two different systems (of varying degrees of similarity) can be co-residents of the same head has moved closer to center stage. This is often rationalized in terms of the practical need to take account of the fact that more people in the world are multilingual than are monolingual. But the theoretical leverage is most striking. We are forced to confront directly the effects of learning at different developmental stages, the consequences of exercise and neglect, of inhibition and control, and, instrumental to all these, of the lexical and structural similarities and differences among languages. This has been most evident in the study of lexical systems, and there is a fascinating accumulation of experimental findings, sometimes with counterintuitive outcomes—for example, even highly fluent second-language exercise strongly continues to implicate primary-language lexical representation. Studies of lexical processes focus dominantly on phonological/semantic links, but syntactic processes will be of increasing importance. This is because notions of greater or lesser structural similarity between two languages are increasingly invoked to account for differing outcomes in studies of interference between languages during learning and use. The same is true for studies of electrophysiology and imaging which imply different patterns of neural activation for the languages of the bilingual population under investigation.

49.3.9 Neuropathologies of language and the biology of language

Lenneberg's (1967) book was a rallying point for those interested in the biology of language. That contribution fitted directly into the general ethos of the time. His summary of the case for biological effects on the emergence of language reflected in detailed ways the rising tide of grammar based thought about language. Investigations inspired by that work ramified through many areas, including the study of normal and disordered language, cognitive development, and the pedagogy of second language learning. Aphasia study was, of course, a major factor in the early biological equation. The history of aphasia research substantially predated the psycholinguistic period, but in important ways the currents of thought which animated much of that work were compatible with the emerging perspective of language as an isolable mental faculty. The clinical perspectives in the field at that time were dominated by syndrome ideas derived from earlier structural views of language, and the details were not in synchrony with the new grammatical and psycholinguistic theories. But there was a readiness to look for a fit between language pathology and new language theory. Aphasia theory is very much phenomenon-driven, and efforts to recast core phenomena of aphasia in terms of the emerging psycholinguistic theory were not long in coming. Moreover, there was a heightened interest in the application of some of the new tools for performance evaluation to patient populations. Studies by Edgar Zurif and Alfonso Caramazza (e.g. Caramazza and Zurif, 1976) contributed substantially to activating experimental modes of attack and to the integration of aphasia research into the psycholinguistic mainstream. The growth in the volume and sophistication of experimental work in aphasia was truly remarkable in the stretch from 1970 to 1990. The impact of aphasia research on psycholinguistics in many ways foreshadowed the impact of cognitive neuroscience and the explosion of interest in imaging technology. But the impulse to use brain information in an attempt to constrain cognitive theory in aphasia study was limited by uncertainties associated with lesion data.

I note that there are two agendas here. The powerful "function separation" arguments based on language pathology must be distinguished from the arguments about brain location of function X. Good evidence for behavioral dissociations is not compromised by fuzzy brain data. That fundamental contribution of aphasia study to the evidence base for language-processing architectures sometimes gets lost in the contention over uncertainties about which part of the brain is responsible for the loss of function. These arguments might be linked, given an appropriate theory of brain and behavior relations, but they are not the same. Just to be clear about this: imagine for a moment that we have incontrovertible evidence from the study of aphasic patients that language functions X and Y may be selectively lost or preserved by brain injury. We may be unable to tell at that point what the neural substrate is, but we can be sure that function X and Y are not the same. Should later investigation reveal that function X and Y implicate a common neural area in an imaging experiment, we will have a pretty puzzle that signals more our ignorance about the use of imaging data to tell how the brain does things than it signals an error about the individuation of functions X and Y.

49.4 **Building cognitive science; using new methods; sparring and dancing with neuroscience**

The current psycholinguistic scene shows a sharply different landscape from that of the initial decades of research. The major components of that changed landscape were commented on above, but several matters require re-emphasis and comment.

49.4. 1 **New techniques**

Established techniques in early psycholinguistic work relied on various efficiency and error measures, coupled with reaction times for tasks. Global measures of language processing gradually gave way to more detailed measures suitable for assessment of sentence comprehension as it unfolded in time. Dual task measures were, and still are, a prominent mode of tackling this problem. For similar reasons, self-paced reading was a major method for the study of parsing. These and related methods grew in sophistication over the first couple of decades of psycholinguistic research, and they remain central to the effective application of a number of new methods that began to contribute in major ways. These changes in psycholinguistic method began with two new methods: electrophysiology-based and eye movement-based measures.

Electrophysiology offered a different way to evaluate the type and time-course of mental events. EEG based measures of performance based on event-related potential methods blossomed following the work of Helen Kutas and Steve Hillyard (1983). They demonstrated the specific sensitivity of an ERP signal to the relative difficulty of integrating a word into the interpretation of a sentence. That set off a stampede of interest in such measures. The evolution of that technology as it became more widely available broadened the menu, and from the early 1990s to the present the range of targets expanded from its lexical semantic beginnings to encompass a range of morphological, syntactic, and prosodic issues. Roughly coincident was the development of computer-controlled studies of eye movement during reading. Keith Rayner's (1978) work was a major force in demonstrating how to get close to the temporal sequence of processing for printed text in ways that linked to different types of language structure. These two methods were somewhat later augmented by another powerful tool based on eye-pointing measures for free field gaze tracking. Michael Tanenhaus and colleagues began the exploitation of this measure around the mid-1990s, and it rapidly assumed a major role in the experimental study of language processing (the "visual world paradigm"; see Tanenhaus et al., 1995) The key to all these methods is the early detection of changes in the information-processing profile using tasks that are close to the normal exercise of language. The combination of these measures with traditional behavioral measures has enabled temporal questions of language processing to be addressed more precisely than at any prior period of the history of the field.

Against this background, the study of brain factors in cognition blossomed with new force in the 1990s. The new techniques of imaging (PET, fMRI) transformed attitudes toward brain/behavior questions that had earlier been based only on brain lesion data of problematic character—though by no means everybody's attitudes. I have observed a fair bit of grumbling about the journal space devoted to pretty pictures that show where (maybe) some mundane feature of mental life stirs the neural terrain. In caricature, the grumbling is understandable. But there are some positive things to say about the imaging wave.

For openers, we should distinguish between the stand-alone imaging approach and brain-based measures used to augment electrophysiology measures. The question of the location of generators for ERP signatures has been a vexed question—though not one that affects the basic utility of the measure for the individuation and timing of mental processes. Electrophysiology is a powerful experimental tool, so to the extent that evolving brain-imaging techniques may augment or clarify our use of that measure, they represent a win. Second, it is charitable to bear in mind that there is a shake-out time when the infrastructure for new research modes is developed. We forget the horrors of some of the early behavioral demonstration studies—in general, the excesses of initial enthusiasm when the ground rules for doing good work are still being discovered. Third, it is as clear as anything can be that the brain does "specialize" in many ways. We don't have so good a grip on that issue for higher order cognitive functions as we do for e.g. sensory and motor functions. But, properly exploited, knowledge of how the brain allocates its physical resources can contribute to our science.

The use of brain-based measures that purport to identify specific brain structures involved in the exercise of language poses a different and challenging set of issues. The important query is this: what will finding out that brain area X is active during language processing tell us about the mental systems for language use? "Little or nothing" is the presumptive answer. That may be largely true at the moment, but it is not a necessary condition. Several things that are likely to occur can get us past the analysis of futility. Here are three candidates.

First, the temporal resolving power of the imaging techniques is improving and can be applied to the problem of ordering events in mental systems. Many investigators are intensely interested in this question, and a variety of techniques under way or in development hold promise for that task (e.g. new-generation MR, MEG, TMR). As those procedures become more precise and accessible, they will contribute something new to the mix of information about mental computation (see e.g. Friederici et al., 2003). Second, we need to better understand the significance of the "background activity" in neural systems. When activation is not boosted in some area for a target task, what does that mean precisely vis-à-vis its processing role? Is it something ever so modest (the necessary work is trivial for the system)—or is it really "nothing"? A related question is this: suppose we find different activation changes in a common neural component. What interpretation should be made when a region of brain is differentially activated across tasks that decompose a complex cognitive process—like syntactic organization and pragmatic interpretation? We know the task components are distinguishable, but what if they use the same physical machine to do their work (see Kuperberg et al., 2003, for an example)? In general, we want to be able to say what demands a computation places on a neural system rather than just saying that the activation of a given area is "above threshold" vis-à-vis some control condition. Right now, we don't well understand what activation changes mean with respect to the nature of information processing operations. Finally, and in concert with the first two, the scope and detail of associations between the physical character of brain systems and mental typology must achieve some explanatory force. We are rather far from that goal, but the outlines of what it would be like to have such models can be seen. We know that the neuro-architectonic details matter, and that the functions which neural systems perform are related to their microstructure. Efforts to rationalize differences in specializations for homologous areas of the right and left hemispheres are a case in point (e.g. Gazzaniga, 2000). Given some quite foreseeable progress on these problems, genuinely informative claims about cognitive processes will be forthcoming from studies of the neuroanatomy and neurophysiology of specific areas of brain and their links to the behavioral systems they support (see Poeppel and Embick, 2006, for useful discussion of these problems).

Things are changing in many more ways—greatly interesting ways—than just the rise in our ability to peer at the brain machine that supports talking and listening. The next section skims through a couple that seem sure to be high-profile. But, as a parting shot to the imaging remarks, it is clear that the nature of the research targets discussed below is well suited to exploit the potential contribution of brain based science.

49.4.2 Some trends for the future? Brief comments on agendas for research

At the outset of this commentary, I asserted a belief in the enduring impact of two factors: the revolution in brain and biology, and the entanglement of language and cognition. The new force of these research foci and their interaction during the last decade is transforming the language sciences. So efforts to explore the links between language and other cognitive systems are increasingly visible—and increasingly diverse in character. Parade cases arise in vision and in memory systems. For example, there is a long-standing effort to connect significant aspects of language and visual cognition. Ray Jackendoff's theoretical efforts in this area have had a sustained influence (Jackendoff, 1987) in both linguistics and psychology. The nature of visual representations of objects and their embedding in space and time has many links to the conceptual frameworks within which linguistic expressions are developed. The pressure to evaluate this general idea empirically has been under way for some time, with many intriguing outcomes (e.g. Bloom et al., 1996). Interest in this set of ideas is not new, but the current context raises the profile of intersections between visual cognition and language. Moreover, the brute facts of the contact between these systems emerge continually because of the exercise of the visual world paradigm discussed in section 49.4.1. Not only representational issues, but a rationalization of real-time processing interactions between the systems will occupy a major role in coming years. Another example is the debate over the role of working memory systems in language processing (see e.g. Caplan and Waters, 1999). That controversy over specializations of memory function is a single strand and precursor of what is becoming a much broader inquiry, with focus on the connection between language and a complex of executive functions related to general planning, judgement, and decision-making (e.g. Harley et al., 2006). This will be less a debate about the utilization of common resources and more an exploration of the relation of language to the basic operations of those systems. The elaboration of planning theory and of judgement and decision-making theory has finally begun to provide the beginnings of counterpoint to the detail of language theory in several ways—some of which I will return to below.

The other key marker in the modern research themes for language is the revival of interest in the evolution of language. This has been under way for a few years and shows no signs of abating. The effort to understand how language arose in the human species is coupled with and driven by the rapidly expanding knowledge of its biological substrate. Questions of how the emergence of language relates to the emergence of other characteristically human cognitive capacities have assumed the character of potentially researchableproblems rather than speculative exercise. The unique neuroanatomical and genetic factors now available for recruitment into the debate have only begun to exert their effects. The biological data permit us to think about relations between biology and cognitive behavior at unprecedented levels of detail (see e.g. Piattelli-Palmarini and Uriagareka, 2004).

It is worth emphasizing that the contemporary work is quite different in character from the struggles over comparative behavioral work with chimpanzees set in motion by the Gardners (1969), by Premack (1971), and others more than three decades ago. That work played on a narrower stage, dominated by the initial preoccupation with claims and counterclaims for whether chimpanzee performance with artificial systems displayed a scientifically interesting overlap with human language, with little communal satisfaction as to the answer. In fact, the work was tremendously important for the collateral consequences, and most particularly David Premack's (1976) work on chimpanzee cognition. The impact on our appreciation of the significance of the study of theory of mind was profound. Claims for theory of mind and executive function in normal and impaired human development exploded in several directions. But, the beautiful irony is the intricate loops back to the communicative function of language, and to ways in which this may—or may not—account for the emergence of human language capacity when construed in the broader terms of systems for planning, social interaction, and behavioral control.

So recent efforts to embed language in the larger cognitive mix have a quite different flavor from earlier research. The focus is more sharply on the nature of cognitive systems which overlap essentials of language. Music (see e.g. Koelsch and Siebel, 2005) and number (see e.g. Carey, 2004; Gelman and Gallistel, 2004) are recent cases. The idea that recursive structural capacities are cognitive keystones that link language to these and other domains has been suggested at various times by several investigators (see, most recently and notably, Hauser et al., 2002). With that comes the preoccupation with basic mechanisms of mind and their developmental and comparative evaluation, as exemplified in various attacks on questions of sensitivity to different types of sequential dependency (e.g. Gómez, 2002; Fitch and Hauser, 2004; Newport et al., 2004). These and related ideas arise in several recent discussions of the biological antecedents for language.

There are in fact, a number of other issues that might be cited here: mirror neurons and language, statistical learning in development, some fascinating trends in computational linguistics, new studies in pragmatics, and even a renaissance in conventional linguistic relativity claims, among others. But this has gone on long enough, and I'll stop on a metatheoretical note.

Theoretical impulses driven by the confrontation of symbolic models, and sub-symbolic connectionist models are getting steadily more rational. The furore has subsided to some extent. The use of network models and the appeal to notions of activation spreading are firmly embedded in discussions of processing. And the coexistence of connectionist approaches and earlier information flow models to mental processes is a fact of the research landscape. Hybrid models that combine symbolic and sub-symbolic approaches will dominate the future theory of complex mental systems. A tunnel-vision approach that treats mental processes exclusively in terms of interactive connectionist assumptions, or exclusively symbolic and modular assumptions, was never very realistic. There have been several notable efforts that combine the two approaches, and that perspective will be the preferred mode if it is not already.

A synthesis that captures the strengths of both types of mechanism is not a weak eclecticism. It is the solution with the best empirical warrant for tackling questions we ultimately can't avoid. What does it mean to have precise metalinguistic intuitions? To entertain a proposition? To appreciate the notions of "limits" and "boundaries" for categories? To think mathematically? How can a machine composed of neurons do all those things? Where and to what extent can any of these be represented without a calculus of symbols? A network machine will do the data crunching. It must ultimately move through a sieve of symbols to capture the nature of our subjective experience and our virtuosity in the real-world application of these concepts in language, logic, music, mathematics, and the host of intricate and precise perceptual and motor acts that embed us in our physical surround. As I write these words and as you read them, neither of us is afloat willy-nilly on a sea of approximations—even though "approximations" may be a major player in the operations of the machines that support our thought. So much should be obvious. Finding the answers is somewhat less so. It is, in fact, a major puzzle to me why there has ever been the slightest temptation to downgrade the significance of the consciously available constructs of mind in favor of computational claims for their underpinning—whatever the form of those underpinnings. One may readily acknowledge the profound importance of uncovering and describing the infrastructure for conscious cognition without relinquishing the certainty that attaches to the qualitative character of that experience, and to the necessity for reconstructing it.

References

Bever, T. G. (1972) The integrated study of language behavior. In J. Morton (ed.), *Language: Biological and Social Factors*, pp. 159–206. Logos Press, London,

Bloom, P. (2000) *How Children Learn the Meaning of Words*. MIT Press, Cambridge, MA.

Bloom, P., Peterson, M., Nadel, L., and Garrett, M. (eds) (1996) *Language and Space*. MIT Press, Cambridge, MA.

Blumenthal, A. (1970). *Language and Psychology: Historical Aspects of Psycholinguistics*. Wiley, New York.

Bock, J. K. (1986) Syntactic persistence in language production. *Cognitive Psychology*, 18: 355–87.

Bock, J. K., and Miller, C. A. (1991). Broken agreement. *Cognitive Psychology*, 23: 45–93.

Caplan, D., and Waters, G. (1999) Verbal working memory and sentence comprehension. *Behavioral and Brain Sciences*, 22: 77–94.

Caramazza, A., and Zurif, E. (1976) Dissociation of algorithmic and associative processes in language comprehension: evidence from aphasia. *Brain and Language*, 3: 572–82.

Carey, S. (2004). Bootstrapping and the origins of concepts. *Daedalus*, 59–68.

Carey, S., and Bartlett, E. (1978). *Acquiring a single new word*. Proceedings of the Stanford Child Language Conference, 15: 17–29. (Republished in Papers and Reports on Child Language Development 15: 17–29.)

Chan, S., and Franklin, J. (1998) Symbolic connectionism in natural language processing. *IEEE Transactions on Neural Networks*, 9: 739–55.

Chomsky, N. (1959) A Review of B. F. Skinner's *Verbal Behavior. Language*, 35: 26–58.

Clark, E., and Clark, H. (1977) *Psychology and Language: An Introduction to Psycholinguistics*. Harcourt Brace Jovanovich, New York.

Coltheart, M., Rastle, K., Perry, C., Langdon, R., and Ziegler, J. (2001) DRC: A dual route cascaded model of visual word recognition and reading aloud. *Psychological Review*, 108: 204–56.

Cutler, A. (eds) (1982) *Slips of the Tongue*. Mouton, Amsterdam.

Dell, G. (1986) A spreading activation theory of retrieval in sentence production. *Psychological Review*, 93: 283–321.

Ejmas, P., Siqueland, E., Jusczyk, P., and Vigorito, J. (1971) Speech perception in infants. *Science*, 171: 303–6.

Fitch, W. T., and Hauser, M. D. (2004). Computational constraints on syntactic processing in nonhuman primates. *Science*, 303: 377–80.

Fodor, J. A. (1983) *The Modularity of Mind*. MIT Press, Cambridge, MA.

Fodor, J. A., Bever, T. G., and Garrett, M. F. (1974) *The Psychology of Language: An Introduction to Psycholinguistics and Generative Grammar*. McGraw-Hill, New York.

Fodor, J., and Pylyshyn, Z. (1988) Connectionism and Cognitive Architecture: A Critical Analysis. *Cognition*, 28: 3–71.

Forster, K. I. (1976) Accessing the mental lexicon. In R. Wales and E. Walker (eds), *New Approaches to Language Mechanisms*, pp. 257–87. North-Holland, Amsterdam.

Foss, D., and Hakes, D. (1978) *Psycholinguistics: An Introduction to the Psychology of Language*. Prentice-Hall, New York.

Frazier, L., and Fodor J. D. (1978) The sausage machine: a new two-stage parsing model *Cognition*, 6: 291–325.

Friederici, A., Ruchemeyer, J., Hahne, A., and Fiebach, C. (2003)The role of left inferior frontal and superior temporal cortex in sentence comprehension: localizing syntactic and semantic processes. *Cerebral Cortex*, 13: 170–7.

Fromkin, V. (1971) The non-anomalous nature of anomalous utterances. *Language*, 47: 27–52.

Gardner, A., and Gardner, B. (1969) Teaching sign language to a chimpanzee. *Science*, 165: 664–72.

Garrett, M. F. (1975) The analysis of sentence production. In G. Bower (ed.), *The Psychology of Learning and Motivation: Advances in Research and Theory*, vol. 9, pp. 133–77. Academic Press, New York.

Gazzaniga, M. (2000), Neuroscience: regional differences in cortical organization *Science*, 289: 1887–8.

Gelman, R., and Gallistel, C. R. (2004). Language and the origin of numerical cognition. *Science* 15: 306: 441–3.

Gerken, L., and Aslin, R. (2005) Thirty years of research on infant speech perception: the legacy of Peter W. Jusczyk. *Language Learning and Development*, 1: 5–21.

Gleitman, L. (1990) The structural sources of verb meanings. *Language Acquisition*, 1: 3–55.

Gómez, R. (2002) Variability and detection of invariant structure. *Psychological Science*, 13: 431–6.

Harley, T., Jessiman, L., and MacAndrew, S. (2006) The control of language: a biological, developmental and psycholinguistic model.

Hauser, M., Chomsky, N., and Fitch, W. (2002). The faculty of language: what is it, who has it, and how did it evolve? *Science* 298*:* 1569–79.

Jackendoff, R. (1987) On beyond zebra: the relation of linguistic and visual information. Cognition, 26: 89–114.

Klima, E., and Bellugi, U. (1979) *The Signs of Language.* Harvard University Press, Cambridge, MA.

Koelsch, S., and Siebel, W.A. (2005) Towards a neural basis of music perception. *Trends in Cognitive Sciences*, 9: 578–84.

Kuperberg, G., Holcomb, P., Sitnikova, T., Greve, D., Dale, A. M., Caplan, D. (2003) Distinct patterns of neural modulation during the processing of conceptual and syntactic anomalies. *Journal of Cognitive Neuroscience*, 15: 272–93.

Kutas, M., and Hillyard, S. A. (1983) Event-related brain potentials to grammatical errors and semantic anomalies. *Memory and Cognition*, 11: 539–50.

Lenneberg, E. (1967) *The Biological Foundations of Language*. Wiley, New York.

Levelt, W. J. M. (1989) *Speaking: From Intention to Articulation*. MIT Press, Cambridge, MA.

Marcus G. (2003) *The Algebraic Mind: Integrating Connectionism and Cognitive Science*. MIT Press, Cambridge, MA.

Marcus, G. (1998) Rethinking eliminative connectionism. *Cognitive Psychology*, 37: 243–82.

Markman, E. (1990) Constraints children place on word meanings. *Cognitive Science*, 14: 57–77.

Marslen-Wilson, W. (1984) Function and process in spoken word recognition. In *Attention and performance X: Control of language processes*, pp. 125–50. Erlbaum, Hillsdale, NJ.

Mattingly, I., and Studdert-Kennedy, M. (eds) (1991) *Modularity and the Motor Theory of Speech Perception: Proceedings of a Conference to Honor Alvin M. Liberman.* Erlbaum, Hillsdale, NJ.

McClelland, J., Rumelhart, D., and Hinton, G. (1986) The appeal of parallel distributed processing. In D. Rumelhart, J. McClelland, et al. (eds), *Parallel Distributed Processing*, vol. 1: *Foundations*, pp. 3–44. MIT Press, Cambridge, MA.

McDaniel, D., McKee, C., and Cairns, H. (eds), *Methods for Assessing Children's Syntax*. MIT Press, Cambridge, MA.

Mehler, J. (1981). The role of syllables in speech processing: infant and adult data. *Philosophical Transactions of the Royal Society*, *B* 295: 333–52.

Mehler, J., and Bertoncini, J. (1981). Syllables as units in infant perception. *Infant Behavior and Development*, 4, pp. 271–84.

Miller, G., and Chomsky, N. (1963) Finitary models of language users. In R. Luce, R. Bush, and E. Galanter (eds), *Handbook of Mathematics*, vol 2. Wiley, New York.

Nadel, L., and Piattelli-Palmerini, M. (eds) (2003) *Encyclopedia of Cognitive Science.* Macmillan, London.

Newport, E., Hauser, M., Spaepen, G., and Aslin, R. (2004). Learning at a distance, II: Statistical learning of non-adjacent dependencies in a nonhuman primate. *Cognitive Psychology*, 49*:* 85–117.

Piattelli-Palmarini, M., and Uriagereka, J. (2004) The immune syntax: the evolution of the language virus In L. Jenkins (ed.), *Variation and Universals in Biolinguistics*, pp. 341–77. Elsevier, Oxford.

Pinker, S. (1984) *Language Learnability and Language Development.* Harvard University Press, Cambridge, MA.

Pinker, S., and Prince, A. (1988) On language and connectionism. *Cognition*, 28: 73–195.

Poeppel, C., and Embick, D. (2006) Defining the relation between linguistics and neuroscience. In A. Cutler (ed.), *Twenty-First Century Psycholinguistics.* Erlbaum, London.

Premack, D. (1971) Language in chimpanzee? *Science* 172: 808–22.

Premack, D. (1976) *Intelligence in Ape and Man*. Erlbaum, Hillsdale, NJ.

Rayner, K. (1978) Eye movements in reading and information processing. *Psychological Bulletin*, 85: 618–60.

Rumelhart, D. E., & McClelland, J. L. (1986) On learning the past tenses of English verbs, Chapter 18. In : J. L. McClelland, D. E. Rumelhart, and the PDP research group. *Parallel distributed processing: Explorations in the microstructure of cognition. Volume II.* MIT Press, Cambridge, MA.

Seidenberg, M., and McClelland, J. (1989) A distributed developmental model of word recognition and naming. *Psychological Review*, 96: 523–68.

Skinner, B. F. (1957) *Verbal Behavior*. Appleton-Century-Crofts, New York.

Slifka, J., Manuel, S., Matthies, M. (eds) (2004) *From Sound to Sense: 50+ years of discoveries in speech communication.* Conference Proceedings, MIT. http://www.rle.mit.edu/soundtosense/conference/start here.htm

Swinney, D. (1984) Theoretical and methodological issues in cognitive science: a psycholinguistic perspective. In W. Kintsch, J. Miller, and P. Polson (eds), *Methods and Tactics in Cognitive Science*, pp. 217–32. Erlbaum, Hillsdale, NJ.

Tanenhaus, M., Spivey-Knowlton, M., Eberhard, K., and Sedivy, J. (1995) Integration of visual and linguistic information in spoken language understanding. *Science*, 268: 1630–4.

Tyler, L., and Marslen-Wilson W. (1982) The resolution of discourse anaphors: some online studies. *Journal of Semantics*,1: 297–314.

Werker, J. F., and Tees, R. C. (1984). Cross-language speech perception: evidence for perceptual reorganization during the first year of life. *Infant Behavior and Development*, 7: 49–63.

Wermter, S. and Sun, R. (eds) (2000) *Hybrid Neural Systems*. Springer, New York.

Subject index

Author index